INTELLECTUAL PROPERTY IN EUROPE

AUSTRALIA

The Law Book Company
Brisbane · Sydney · Melbourne · Perth

CANADA

Carswell
Ottawa · Toronto · Calgary · Montreal · Vancouver

AGENTS

Steimatzky's Agency Ltd., Tel Aviv
N.M. Tripathi (Private) Ltd., Bombay
Eastern Law House (Private) Ltd., Calcutta
M.P.P. House, Bangalore
Universal Book Traders, Delhi
Aditya Books, Delhi
MacMillan Shuppan KK, Tokyo
Pakistan Law House, Karachi, Lahore

INTELLECTUAL PROPERTY IN EUROPE

by

GUY TRITTON
Barrister at Law

LONDON
SWEET & MAXWELL
1996

Published in 1996 by
Sweet & Maxwell Limited of
100 Avenue Road, London NW3 3PF
Computerset by Interactive Sciences, Gloucester
Printed and bound in Great Britain by
Athenæum Press Ltd, Gateshead, Tyne & Wear

Reprinted 1997

No natural forests were destroyed to make this product:
only farmed timber was used and replanted

A CIP catalogue record for this book is available from the British Library

ISBN 0 421 54230 6

PREFACE

For professionals, intellectual property has several facets: the patent agent or trade mark agent is principally concerned with the acquisition of registered intellectual property rights; competition law departments of solicitors are principally concerned with the interaction between intellectual property and competition law; and litigation specialists are principally concerned with the enforcement of intellectual property. Because of these specialisations, books on intellectual property tend to emphasise one aspect depending on the author's specialisation. Thus, a competition law book will not tell the reader how to obtain patent or trade mark protection. The aim of this book is to provide a complete and exhaustive study of intellectual property in Europe which is as useful to a patent agent as it is to a competition lawyer or intellectual property barrister. Firstly, it concerns itself with the nature and variety of intellectual property throughout Europe and the acquisition of intellectual property in Europe. Secondly, it examines the effect of the European Community treaty and the European Economic Area Agreement on all aspects of intellectual property, but principally the interaction between the free movement of goods provisions, the anti-competition provisions and intellectual property. Finally it examines intellectual property in the context of jurisdictional issues in Europe.

Many may question the usefulness of such an approach. Will not such a book prove to be a curate's egg? It is hoped that this will not be the case. Three illustrations should prove the advantage of having a full coverage of intellectual property matters in Europe. Competition lawyers will be familiar with the *Maize Seeds* case which marked the start of a more tolerant approach from the European Court of Justice and European Commission towards exclusive licences. The case actually concerned certified seeds. Many may have not been aware of the real distinction between certified and basic seeds and the basis of protection for propagating material under the 1979 and 1991 UPOV Convention. However, that this distinction was important was demonstrated in the *Louis Erauw-Jacquerie v. La Hesbignonne* case, which concerned basic seeds. Another illustration is in the trade mark field. The Trade Mark Directive was primarily concerned with harmonising national trade mark laws. Its interrelationship with the free movement of goods provisions of the E.C. Treaty is not apparent. However, its *travaux preparatoires* suggest that its enactment into domestic law is intended to merely permit a Community-wide principle of exhaustion and not an international exhaustion right. With regard to jurisdiction issues, the jurisdiction provisions of the new Community Trade

Mark and Community Plant Variety Regulations interact intimately with the Brussels and Lugano Convention and knowledge of both Regulations and the latter conventions is necessary.

This book has been written during a period of considerable development in intellectual property in Europe. On an international level, the Madrid Protocol will soon profoundly affect and simplify applications for trade marks in Europe. The 1991 UPOV Convention has now been ratified in many European countries and will affect the nature of plant variety rights. At a Community level, many of the E.C. Commission's efforts in the intellectual property rights have come to fruition. In the trade mark area, as of April 1, 1996, one will be able to apply for a Community Trade Mark. Domestic laws of Member States have been substantially harmonised by the Trade Mark Directive. In the copyright and design field, the E.C. Commission has introduced the directive for the legal protection of computer programs; a directive on rental and lending rights and neighbouring rights; a directive harmonising the term of copyright and a directive on satellite and cable retransmissions. In the legislative pipeline is a directive for the legal protection of databases. In the design field, proposals for a Community Design and a directive harmonising design protection within the Community are well advanced. In the plant variety rights field, the Community has introduced a Community Plant Variety Right. In the patent field, the E.C. Commission has experienced mixed fortunes. The Community Patent has not progressed for some time and there is considerable doubt whether it will ever come into force. The draft Biotechnological Directive was thrown out by the European Parliament as a result of persistent lobbying by environmental groups concerned about the patenting of animals and humans. However, the Supplementary Protection Certificate which extends protection for patented pharmaceutical products has been of considerable success.

The ECJ has been busy with the perennial problems of the interrelationship of intellectual property rights with Articles 30 to 36 (the free movement of goods provisions) and Articles 85 and 86 (the anti-competition provisions). Thus, there have been recent decisions concerning Articles 30 to 36 and the assignment of trade marks (*IHT Internationale Heiztechnik GmbH* and *Ideal Standard*) and Article 86 and refusal to licence (*TV Listings*). The E.C. Commission is seeking to replace the Patent and Know How Block Exemption with the Technology Transfer Block Exemption but the Commission's proposals have met considerable resistance from industries. At the time of going to press, it has not come into force but it is anticipated that the present draft will be enacted substantially as it is.

In the jurisdictional field, Dutch courts have recently been granting pan-European injunctions against patent infringement. This practice is studied in detail.

The effect of these international and European developments have meant that differences in national intellectual property rights have considerably diminished. Most domestic intellectual property laws of Member States are now derived from international conventions or European Community legislation. Increasingly, legal advisers look at the decisions of other jurisdictions. English courts are increasingly likely to examine the laws and decisions of other states (*e.g.* see *PLG v. Ardon* (1994) (construction of scope of European patents); *Hazelgrove* [1995] (right to modify patented articles) and *Wagamama v. Rajamama* (1995) (scope of trade mark rights). In such circumstances, an atomised country by country view of intellectual property can be a rather repetitious and arid exercise. Because of the high degree of harmonisation, I felt that it was better to examine the founding treaties, conventions and legislation and emphasise any substantial differences in their implementation in contracting states.

Even though only one name may appear on the front cover, many people have helped me in the preparation of this book. I would like to thank Jo Davies of Reddie & Grose for his help with the Patents chapter; Christopher Morcom of my chambers for his help with the Trade Marks chapter; Roger Wyand of my Chambers for his help with the Copyright chapter; Alison Firth of New Court Chambers for her help with the Designs chapter; Margaret Llewellyn for her help on the Plant Variety Rights Chapter; William Richards for his help on the Enforcement and Abuse of a Dominant Position Chapter; Mark Brealey and Nicholas Green of Brick Court Chambers for their help on the Licensing and Enforcement of EEA Competition Law; Mark Abell of Field Fisher Waterhouse for his help with the Franchise Chapter and Jeremy Scoles for his help with the Jurisdiction Chapter. Many an errant comment was corrected and without their help, this book would have been the poorer. I would like to thank Sweet & Maxwell for their unstinting patience whilst they awaited over the years the behemoth that this book has become and for their help and attention at the editing stage. Finally, I would like to thank my mother for getting me started on this project in 1989.

It is intended that this book will be annually supplemented. Thus, if there are any mistakes or developments in the law, I would appreciate hearing them, care of Sweet & Maxwell.

Finally, I have attempted to state the law as it stands on October 1, 1995.

Guy Tritton
One Essex Court
Middle Temple, London

TABLE OF CONTENTS

CHAPTER THREE

TRADEMARKS IN EUROPE

CHAPTER SIX

PLANT VARIETY RIGHTS IN EUROPE

CHAPTER SEVEN

ENFORCEMENT OF INTELLECTUAL PROPERTY

CHAPTER EIGHT

LICENSING OF INTELLECTUAL PROPERTY

CHAPTER NINE

INTELLECTUAL PROPERTY AND JOINT VENTURES

CHAPTER TEN

FRANCHISING

CHAPTER ELEVEN

ABUSE OF A DOMINANT POSITION

CHAPTER TWELVE

ENFORCEMENT OF E.C. AND EEA COMPETITION LAW

CHAPTER THIRTEEN

JURISDICTION AND INTELLECTUAL PROPERTY

TABLE OF CASES

(References are to paragraph numbers)

TABLE OF STATUTES

(References are to paragraph numbers)

TABLE OF STATUTORY INSTRUMENTS

(References are to paragraph numbers)

RULES OF THE SUPREME COURT

(References are to paragraph numbers)

TABLE OF TREATIES AND CONVENTIONS

(References are to paragraph numbers)

TABLE OF E.C. DIRECTIVES

(References are to paragraph numbers)

Draft Directives

TABLE OF E.C. REGULATIONS

(References are to paragraph numbers)

CHAPTER ONE

INTRODUCTION

1. INTELLECTUAL PROPERTY IN EUROPE

1.001

> "Intellectual Property's prime aim is the recognition of the moral and economic value of intellectual creation in the cultural, social and economic development of nations."

With these words, the Director General Arpad Bogsch introduced the World Intellectual Property Organisation Conference at the Louvre, Paris on June 1–3, 1994. Few other fields of laws can claim a more noble justification. Intellectual property has one feature which distinguishes it from other areas of law; its purpose is not to regulate affairs between persons as with the laws of tangible property, tort, contract, competition, commercial and even criminal law, but to reward the creator and promote economic and technological progress. In Europe, a developed trading bloc which is moving from a basic manufacturing and industrial stage to a sophisticated manufacturing and post-industrial stage, the importance of intellectual property cannot be overemphasised. Information, ideas and innovation constitute the basic tools of post-industrial economy. With the ready availability and increased sophistication of copying devices and the profit to be made from pirate copies, such tools would be substantially valueless without the protection of intellectual property laws.

Intellectual property laws were originally developed by states to have effect only in their territories. However, it was quickly realised in the nineteenth century that international co-operation was required to ensure that works of nationals were protected internationally and that there was a mutual reciprocity of protection between states. Since the founding intellectual property convention, the 1883 Paris Convention on Intellectual Property, few other areas of laws have been subject to so much international scrutiny and international legislation. This is paradoxical because intellectual property laws are so territorial and nationalistic in their effect. The result of such an international approach has been to ensure a considerable degree of harmonisation of intellectual property laws in Europe.

This book examines and analyses the nature and extent of intellectual property protection in Europe in a "top-down" way. In other words, this book does not attempt to discuss and compare the intellectual property laws of each European country. Instead, it examines and discusses the international conventions, the European treaties and the secondary legislation which has and is responsible for the high degree of harmonisation that now exists in Europe, especially within the European Union and the European Economic Area. Many would question whether such an approach is appropriate because practitioners are only concerned with national laws and not the convention or international legislation which gave rise to the national laws. However, nowadays, much of European intellectual property law is harmonised to such a degree that an examination of national intellectual property laws in Europe would be an exercise in repetition. Furthermore, the practitioner nowadays often takes a global view as to the obtaining, protection and enforcement of intellectual property. In these circumstances, an international or regional approach is often more helpful than a country by country analysis which often fails to provide a clear and concise overview. Also, national courts are far more keen to take an international approach to the application and interpretation of intellectual property laws. This often includes looking at decisions of other jurisdictions and also at the founding conventions. Indeed, in the European Community, national courts are obliged to interpret legislation which implements a Community directive in accordance with the objectives of that directive.

1.002 In recent years, the enforcement and licensing of intellectual property in the European Community has been considerably affected by the free movement of goods and the competition provisions in the European Community Treaty which limit their enforcement within the Community. Furthermore, the enforcement of intellectual property has become considerably international in nature. Rightholders are now able in certain jurisdictions to obtain extraterritorial relief when seeking to enforce their rights. Thus, jurisdictional rules as to the appropriate forum has become increasingly important. Yet again, a country by country analysis of jurisdictional rules would fail to provide a clear and concise picture to the international forum shopper.

This book is split into three specific sections. The first section is concerned with the existence, nature and extent of intellectual property in Europe. Patents, trade marks, copyright, design rights and plant variety rights are all examined in a European context, including a full analysis of international, European and Community conventions, laws and initiatives in each area. Where there are clear differences between countries' laws, these are highlighted in each Chapter so that the reader is alerted to the differences. They are rarely substantial in nature. The second section concerns the effect of the European Community Treaty on the enforcement and licensing of intellectual property. The enforcement of intellectual property rights is affected by the free movement of goods and services and the anti-competition provisions of the E.C. Treaty. The licensing of intellectual property is only affected by its anti-competition provisions. The third section examines the issue of jurisdiction in the context of intellectual property litigation in Europe.

In the rest of this chapter, the reader is introduced to the European Community, the European Economic Area, bilateral agreements in the field of intellectual property in Europe and intellectual property conventions that affect Europe.

2. European Community

(a) History of E.C. Treaty

1.003 On March 25, 1957, France, Germany, Belgium, the Netherlands, Luxembourg and Italy signed the Treaty of Rome which gave birth to the European Economic Community (EEC). The Treaty of Rome was intended to provide for closer economic ties between Member States and the establishment of a single customs union in the Community. Although only concerned with economic co-operation, its parents were the Two World Wars, and from the outset it was envisaged that the Treaty of Rome would lead to closer union between the Member States, eliminate nationalism and thus promote peace and prosperity.

Since 1957, the United Kingdom, Eire, Denmark, Greece, Spain and Portugal have joined the European Community ("E.C.").[1] All countries which have acceded to the European Community are known as the Member States. Recently, Austria, Sweden and Finland have voted to join the E.C. Furthermore, Hungary, Cyprus, Malta and Turkey have applied for membership.

The Treaty of Rome has evolved over the years. Originally, it established the European Commission, Council, European Parliament and European Court of Justice (ECJ). In the last decade, its development has been fast. In 1986, the 12 Member States signed the Single European Act (SEA). The principal purpose of the SEA was to eliminate the remaining barriers to the single internal market within the self imposed deadline of December 31, 1992 which was to be achieved by an immense programme of harmonisation. In addition, the SEA extended the sphere of Community competence and introduced a number of procedural changes designed to accelerate the community decision-making process. In 1992, the Treaty on European Union (TEU) was signed at Maastricht. It came into force on November 1, 1993. The extent of the TEU is far wider than the original Treaty of Rome. Firstly, it made substantial amendments to the EEC Treaty which widened its scope and effect beyond its original economic field. In doing so, it renamed the EEC Treaty as the European Community (E.C.) Treaty. The most important provision was to set a goal for full economic and monetary union and the creation of a single currency by January 1, 1999.[2] It also introduced the concept of Citizenship of the Union.[3] Secondly, the TEU established the European Union

[1] The European Economic Community (EEC) is now known as the European Community (E.C.) following the Treaty on European Union.
[2] Britain and Denmark were permitted to opt out of this provision.
[3] E.C. Treaty, Art. 8.

(EU) which stands as a separate Treaty. This treaty is political in nature, seeking to establish co-operation in various fields such as foreign and security policy and defence. However, it has little relevance from a legal viewpoint because it has no legal provisions. Accordingly, when considering the effect of the law of the European Community, reference is made to the European Community Treaty (E.C.). However, in older books, reference is made to the EEC Treaty. Readers should be aware that the two are fundamentally similar especially in relation to intellectual property but copies of the EEC Treaty preceding the TEU must be considered out of date.

(b) Structure and framework of the E.C. Treaty

1.004 The E.C.'s institutions broadly reflect the division in modern democratic countries of power between the legislature, the executive and the judiciary. The Treaty of Rome originally provided for an Assembly (Parliament), a Council, a Commission and a Court of Justice.[4] A first instance court called the Court of First Instance (CFI) to take over some of the workload of the ECJ was set up in October 1988.[5]

(i) Council[6]

1.005 The Council which consists of representatives of the Member States can be considered as the legislature of the E.C. It exists to ensure co-ordination of the general economic policies of the Member States.[7] However, it is only involved in decisions which are germane to the E.C. Treaty. Although the Council is the ultimate legislative body, its powers are substantially restricted. Thus, in most cases, it can only act on the basis of a proposal from the Commission and often must consult the European Parliament. It can only amend a proposal from the Commission if it does so unanimously. Furthermore, if it wishes to override Parliament's objection to a measure, it must do so by unanimous vote.

Generally, the majority of Community legislation can be enacted by a qualified majority.[8] However, fiscal measures and measures relating to the free movement of goods require a unanimous vote.[9] The Council only meets a few times a month but much of its work is done by the Committee of Permanent Representatives (COREPER) who consist of representatives who scrutinise and sift proposals coming from the Commission prior to a final decision being made by the Council.

[4] EEC Treaty, Art. 4(1).
[5] [1989] O.J. C215/1.
[6] E.C. Treaty, Arts. 145–154.
[7] Art. 145.
[8] The required minimum vote for a qualified majority is 54 votes. Each Member State is assigned a certain number of votes with the big four states carrying 10 votes each.
[9] Furthermore, under the Luxembourg Accords (which do not have the force of law but have been followed in practice), a Member State may insist on a unanimous vote where vital national interests are at stake.

(ii) Commission[10]

1.006 The Commission, which loosely approximates to the executive body of a democracy, exists to ensure that the provisions of the Treaty and the Council's decisions are applied. It has powers to formulate non-binding recommendations and opinions. In practice, major legislation enacted by the Council will often originate from proposals from the Commission. It initiates and drafts legislation intended to put the E.C. Treaty's objectives into effect. Furthermore, it is a surveillance authority which ensures that Member States and their laws are not in breach of the E.C. Treaty.[11] It is very important in the field of competition where it plays a very large role as an investigator into anti-competitive behaviour within the Community and as an enforcer of Community competition legislation.

(iii) European Parliament[12]

1.007 Originally, the European Parliament was known as the Assembly and consisted of representatives of members of parliaments of the Member States. Its functions were advisory and supervisory. In 1979, direct elections were introduced. Under the SEA and the TEU, its influence in the legislation making process has been substantially increased. Although it is not itself a legislative body, it must now be consulted about secondary legislation. In many areas, the Council must see Parliament's opinion on draft legislation although they are not obliged to follow its opinion. In 1977, Parliament was given a second opportunity to object to draft legislation. If, at this stage it does reject it, the Council may still adopt it provided it acts unanimously.[13] Parliament also has the power of final assent in respect of admission of new members and the conclusion of association agreements with non-Member countries. In certain defined areas, Parliament plays a much closer co-operative role with the Council and may prevent draft legislation being enacted if such is rejected after the breakdown of agreement between the Council and Parliament.[14]

(iv) European Court of Justice and Court of First Instance

1.008 The European Court of Justice's task is to ensure that "in the interpretation and application of this Treaty the law is observed".[15] It is the supreme authority on all matters relating to Community law. However, it is an interpretative court and not the ultimate appellate court in relation to national disputes concerning Community law. Thus, parties may refer a matter of Community law to the ECJ for a preliminary ruling but the national court must apply the ECJ's ruling to the dispute.[16] The ECJ

[10] E.C. Treaty, Arts. 155–163.
[11] It can bring proceedings against a Member State under Art. 169.
[12] E.C. Treaty, Arts. 137–144.
[13] See Joint Declaration of the European Parliament, Council and Commission [1977] O.J. C89/1. Incorporated in the E.C. Treaty as Art. 189c.
[14] Art. 189b. This happened with the Biotechnological Directive.
[15] Art. 164.
[16] Art. 177.

consists of 13 Judges and six Advocates General. The latter's task is to assist the Court by making reasoned submissions on cases brought before the Court of Justice.[17] The ECJ may also via the preliminary ruling mechanism rule on the validity of Community legislation.[18]

The ECJ has played a very important role in the interpretation of the Treaty of Rome in relation to intellectual property. In particular, it has provided a considerable body of jurisprudence on the relationship between intellectual property and the free movement of goods.

In 1988, the Court of First Instance was established.[19] Its jurisdiction is confined to disputes between the Community and its servants, cases involving proceedings brought by the Commission in the field of E.C. competition law, proceedings brought by individuals in relation to the validity of Community legislation (save anti-dumping laws) and the failure to act of Community institutions.[20] There is a right of appeal on issues of law to the ECJ.

(c) Source of E.C. law

1.009 The primary source of E.C. law is the Treaty of Rome. This has been amended over the years principally by the Acts of Accession of acceding States and also by the Single European Act and the Treaty on European Union. If international agreements are entered into by the Community institutions pursuant to Article 228 of the Treaty of Rome, these agreements become an integral part of the Community legal order.[21] Article 5 obliges all Member States to take all appropriate measures to ensure the fulfilment of Member States' obligations under the Treaty of Rome.[22]

The E.C. Treaty expresses the principles upon which the European Community is founded. However, it provides little in terms of detail which is required for the purposes of legal certainty. This applies especially so to the United Kingdom which does not have a civil code legal system and thus is not experienced in the application of general principles to factual situations. Thus, Article 189 of the Treaty of Rome allows the Council and Commission to put those principles into practice by enacting secondary legislation. Under Article 189, there are four types of Community legislative acts:

(1) Regulations which are binding in their entirety and are directly applicable in all Member States;
(2) Directives which are binding as to the result to be achieved, upon each Member State to which it is addressed, but leave to the national authorities the choice of form and methods;

[17] Art. 166.
[18] Art. 177.
[19] [1988] O.J. C215/1.
[20] E.C. Treaty, Arts. 173, 175.
[21] Opinion of ECJ 1/91, [1991] I E.C.R. 6079; [1992] 1 C.M.L.R. 245.
[22] Thus a "dualist" country like the U.K. which does not regard international law as part of its legal system unless incorporated by an Act of Parliament passed the European Communities Act 1972 to enact the Treaty of Rome as domestic law.

(3) Decisions which are binding in their entirety upon those to whom they are addressed;[23]

(4) Recommendations and opinions which are only of persuasive effect and have no binding force.[24]

(i) Direct applicability

1.010 Once a Member State has ratified and enacted the Treaty of Rome, it and the legislation generated by it becomes legally effective in Member States without the need for further enactment. Thus, in the United Kingdom, section 2(1) of the European Communities Act 1972 provides that:

> "All such rights, powers, obligations and restrictions from time to time created or arising by or under the Treaties, and all such remedies and procedures from time to time provided for by or under the Treaties, as in accordance with the Treaties are without further enactment to be given legal effect or used in the United Kingdom shall be recognised and available in law, and be enforced, allowed and followed accordingly . . . "

Other Member States which are dualist have enacted similar legislation. Monist states (*i.e.* a state whose domestic laws recognises the force of international conventions ratified by that state) will not have required such implementing legislation. Once the Treaty of Rome has become part of a Member State's legal order, it is said to be "directly applicable".

(ii) Direct effect

1.011 Much Community legislation is addressed to Member States and does not prima facie impose any obligations or grant any rights to individuals of those states. Directives are often intended to give rights to individuals but require implementation by Member States for such rights to become domestic law. In such cases, individuals will not normally be able to rely upon them in legal proceedings. Provisions of Community law which are found to be capable of application by national courts *at the suit of individuals* are termed "directly effective".[25] Hence, an individual may if certain conditions are fulfilled rely upon a non-implemented directive in proceedings before a national court.

[23] Decisions are not always declared as being as a "decision". The test as to whether a ruling is a Decision within the meaning of Art. 189 is whether it is a "measure emanating from the competent authority intended to produce legal effects and constituting the culmination of procedure within that authority, whereby the latter gives its final ruling in a form from which its nature can be identified"—Case 54/65, *Compagnie de Forges de Chatillon, Commentry et Neuves-Maison v. High Authority*: [1966] E.C.R. 185, at 195; [1966] C.M.L.R. 525.

[24] Art. 189.

[25] The distinction between these two doctrines direct effect and direct applicability was first pointed out by Winter in "Direct Applicability and Direct Effect: two distinct and different concepts in Community law" (1972) C.M.L.Rev. 425.

(1) Requirements for Community provision to be "directly effective"

1.012 The European Court of Justice has been asked many times to adjudicate whether a Community legislative act has direct effect and what the consequences are of a provision being directly effective. Its case law, principally on the issue as to whether directives could be relied on by individuals in national courts, establishes that for a Community provision to have direct effect, it must fulfil the following three conditions:

(i) The provision must impose a clear and precise obligation on Member States
(ii) The provision must be unconditional, *i.e.* not accompanied by any reservation; if however, it is subject to certain exceptions, they must be strictly defined and limited
(iii) The Member State must not have an effective power of discretionary judgment as to the application of the rule in question.[26]

(a) Articles of Treaty of Rome

1.013 The ECJ has stated that the Treaty of Rome is more than an agreement creating mutual obligations between Member States but also imposes obligations on individuals and also confers on them legal rights.[27] Whether an Article has direct effect depends on whether it fulfils the three conditions outlined above.[28] For the purposes of this book, all the provisions on the free movement of goods and services, competition and discrimination on the grounds of sex and nationality have direct effect.

(b) Regulations

1.014 Regulations are described in Article 189 as being general in application, binding in their entirety and directly applicable in all Member States. As such, a regulation will invariably have direct effect. Occasionally, a regulation will need national implementation to create a legislative measure which is certain and clear enough to be directly effective.[29]

[26] These rules were first set out by A. G. Gand in the case of Case 57/65, *Alfons Lutticke GmbH v. Hauptzollamt Sarreloius* [1966] E.C.R. 205; [1971] C.M.L.R. 674. See also Case 9/70, *Franz Grad v. Finanzamt Traunstein* [1970] E.C.R. 825; [1971] C.M.L.R. 1, Case 41/75, *Van Duyn v. Home Office* [1974] E.C.R. 1337; [1975] 1 C.M.L.R. 1; Case 51/76, *Verbond van Nederlandse Ondernemingen v. Inspecteur der Invoerrechten en Accijnzen* [1977] E.C.R. 113; [1977] 1 C.M.L.R. 413; Case 148/78, *Pubblico Ministero v. Ratti* [1979] E.C.R. 1629; [1980] 1 C.M.L.R. 96.

[27] Case 26/72, *Van Gend en Loos v. Nederlandse Administratie der Belastingen* [1963] E.C.R. 1; [1963] C.M.L.R. 185.

[28] *e.g.* see Case 57/65, *Alfons Lutticke GmbH v. Hauptzollamt Saarlouis* [1966] E.C.R. 205; [1971] C.M.L.R. 674.

[29] See, for example, Case 78/76, *Steinike und Weinlig v. Germany* [1977] E.C.R. 595; [1977] 2 C.M.L.R. 688. Here it was held that the inclusion of rules relating to state aids (which the ECJ have held do not have direct effect) into an agricultural regulation did not make those rules "directly effective" by their mere inclusion.

(c) Directives

1.015 Directives are "binding as to the result to be achieved, upon each Member State to which it is addressed, but shall leave to the national authorities the choice of form and methods".[30] Accordingly, prima facie, the Treaty of Rome never intended that directives should be relied on by individuals in actions before national courts. Rather, it was intended that individuals rely upon the national legislation which implemented a directive. However, in many cases, a Member State fails to implement correctly or in time a directive in breach of its obligations under the directive.

In such circumstances, the Court of Justice has held that directives will be directly effective provided that they fulfil the above three conditions. Thus, a directive will not be directly effective where the time limit for its implementation has not expired.[31] A directive can be directly effective even if the relevant Member State has implemented it. Thus, where a Member State has not properly implemented a directive, an individual can rely on the direct effect of a directive.[32]

(d) Decisions

1.016 A decision is binding in its entirety upon those to whom it is addressed.[33] By their very nature, decisions only impose obligations on those to whom they are addressed. It is not thought that other persons can seek to rely upon such decisions in private actions for the same reasons as apply to directives. Decisions intended for Member States are analogous to directives and will be directly effective provided the three conditions described above are met.[34]

(e) Recommendations and Opinions

1.017 Neither recommendations nor opinions have legal effect under the Treaty of Rome and are merely persuasive.[35] However, the ECJ has said that national courts are

> "bound to take Community recommendations into consideration in deciding disputes submitted to them, in particular where they clarify the interpretation of national provisions adopted in order to implement them or where they are designed to supplement binding EEC measures".[36]

[30] Art. 189.
[31] Case 148/78, *Pubblico Ministero v. Ratti* [1979] E.C.R 1629; [1980] 1 C.M.L.R. 96.
[32] *e.g.* see Case 51/76, *VNO v. Inspecteur der Invoeerechten en Accijnzen* [1977] E.C.R 113; [1977] 1 C.M.L.R. 413.
[33] Art. 189.
[34] See *Grad v. Finanzamt Traunstein*, above.
[35] Art. 189.
[36] Case C-322/88, *Grimaldi v. Fonds des Maladies Professionelles* [1989] E.C.R. 4407; [1991] 2 C.M.L.R. 265.

(f) International agreements

1.018 The Court of Justice has held that where provisions of international agreements concluded between Community institutions and third parties confer clear rights on individuals, then such provisions are directly effective. Thus, the ECJ held that decisions of the Council of Association established by an EEC-Turkey Agreement were capable of being directly effective provided that regard was given to its wording and the purpose and nature of the agreement itself and the provision contained a clear and precise obligation which was not subject in its implementation or effects to the adoption of any subsequent measure.[37] The European Economic Area Agreement which covers the E.C. states and EFTA states and whose provisions are broadly similar to that of the E.C. Treaty is an international agreement concluded by means of the procedure laid down in Article 228 of the E.C. Treaty and thus the parallel provisions on free movement of goods and competition will be directly effective in courts of Member States.

(2) Consequences of Community provision being directly effective

1.019 If an article of the Treaty of Rome or a regulation is found to be directly effective, it can be relied upon in a national court. In particular, it can be relied upon by an individual against another individual. In this sense, such provisions are said to have horizontal effect.

The consequence of a directive being found to be directly effective is more complicated. There are two principal consequences arising out of the direct effectiveness of directives. Firstly, a Member State cannot rely upon its failure to implement a directive against an individual. Secondly, national courts are obliged to interpret national law in order to ensure that the objectives of directives are achieved.

(a) Vertical effect of "directly effective" directives

1.020 Article 189 imposes an obligation on Member States to implement directives. In *Marshall v. South West Hampshire Area Health Authority*,[38] the ECJ ruled that an individual may rely upon the direct effect of directives against the State regardless of the capacity in which the State was acting. However, it held that Article 189 meant that a directive did not of itself impose obligations on an individual and that a provision of a directive could not be relied upon against an individual in national courts.[39] The

[37] See Case C-192/89, *Sevince v. Staatssecretaris van Justitie* [1990] I E.C.R. 3461; [1992] 2 C.M.L.R. 57; Case 12/86, *Demirel v. Stadt Schwäbisch Gmmd* [1987] E.C.R. 3719; [1989] 1 C.M.L.R. 421.

[38] Case 152/84, *Marshall v. South West Hampshire Area Health Authority* [1986] 1 Q.B. 401; [1986] E.C.R. 723; [1986] 1 C.M.L.R. 688.

[39] See also Case 79/83, *Von Colson and Kamann v. Land NordRhein-Westfalen* [1984] E.C.R. 1891; [1986] 2 C.M.L.R. 430 where this principle was reaffirmed.

ECJ has subsequently said that a directive may be relied on against organisations or bodies which are subject to the authority or control of the State or which have special powers beyond those which result from normal relations between individuals.[40]

(b) Interpretation of national law in accordance with directives

1.021 In *Von Colson and Kamann v. Land NordRhein-Westfalen*,[41] the ECJ ruled that national courts must interpret national law in such a way as to ensure that the objectives of a directive are achieved. In *Marleasing SA v. La Comercial Internacional de Alimentacion SA*,[42] the plaintiff sought a declaration that certain contracts were void under Spanish law on the grounds of lack of cause. The defendants contended that Directive 68/151 which should have been in force in Spain from the date of its accession and which provided an exhaustive list of situations in which nullity could be invoked did not permit lack of cause as a ground. On reference to the ECJ, it said the national courts must *as far as possible* interpret national law in the light of the wording and purpose of the directive in order to achieve the result pursued by the directive. It added that this was regardless of whether the national provisions in question were adopted before or after the directive. Accordingly, it would seem that the rule as expressed in *Von Colson* applies regardless as to whether the legislation in question was specifically introduced to implement the directive or not. However, the obligation on national courts to interpret domestic law to comply with E.C. law is tempered by the general principles of law which form part of Community law and in particular the principles of legal certainty and non-retroactivity.[43] These principles apply where the application of the *Van Colson* principle would conflict with an individual's right to assume that domestic law is valid and subsisting.

National courts have interpreted the above two cases to mean that where there is ambiguity about the nature and extent of domestic legislation, the interpretation which is most consistent with a directly effective directive in the same field must be given. However, national courts have resisted any tendency to construe national legislation in accordance with a directive where such would clearly conflict with the wording and evi-

[40] Case C-188/89, *Foster v. British Gas plc* [1990] E.C.R. 3313; [1990] 2 C.M.L.R. 833. However, see English Court of Appeal's ruling in *Doughty v. Rolls Royce plc* [1992] IRLR 126 where it ruled that Rolls Royce, then a nationalised undertaking, did not fall within the concept of a public body such that an individual could rely on the direct effect of a directive against it.

[41] See above. n. 39.

[42] Case C-106/89, [1990] I E.C.R. 4315; [1992] 1 C.M.L.R. 305.

[43] Case 80/86, *Kolpinghuis Nijmegen* [1987] E.C.R. 3969; [1989] 2 C.M.L.R. 18.

dent intention of the national legislature.[44] Clearly, in a horizontal action between individuals, a contrary approach would give horizontal effect to directives contrary to the ECJ's ruling in *Marshall.*

Generally, in construing the meaning of a directive, it is wrong to use the minutes of Council meetings as an aid to interpretation.[44a]

(iii) Liability of Member State in damages for failure to properly implement directive

1.022 Recently, the ECJ has held that a Member State must compensate an individual for its failure to implement a directive. In *Francovich v. Italy,*[45] Italy had failed to implement a directive which was designed to guarantee the payment of arrears of wages to employees in the event of their employer's insolvency. The time limit for the directive's implementation had expired and the Court of Justice had already held in Article 169 proceedings that Italy was in breach of its Community obligations in failing to implement the directive. The ECJ held that the directive was not directly effective as it was not sufficiently clear and precise. However, it held that a Member State who failed to implement a directive was liable to compensate individuals if certain conditions were satisfied. These are:

(a) The directive involved rights conferred on individuals;
(b) The contents of those rights could be identified on the basis of the provisions of the directive;
(c) There was a causal link between the State's failure and the damage suffered by the persons affected.

It should be noted that the three conditions are not contingent on the directive being directly effective. The above test is less stringent than the test for the direct effectiveness of directives. In France, the Conseil d'Etat has awarded damages against the state for losses suffered as a result of a ministerial order in breach of an E.C. directive.[46]

[44] In England, see *Duke v. GEC Reliance Ltd* [1988] A.C. 618; *Webb v. EMO (Air Cargo) Ltd* [1992] 4 All E.R. 929, H.L.; *R. v. British Coal Corporation* [1993] 1 C.M.L.R. 721. In Germany, see *Re a Rehabilitation Centre* [1992] 2 C.M.L.R. 21. *Cf. Litster v. Forth Dry Dock & Engineering Co. Ltd* [1990] 1 A.C. 546 where the House of Lords stated that where regulations had been introduced specifically to implement an E.C. Directive, then U.K. courts must interpret domestic law to comply with the directive if necessary supplying the necessary words by implication in order to achieve a result compatible with E.C. law.

[44a] Case 310/90, *Conseil National de L'Orde Des Architectes v. Egle* [1992] I E.C.R. 177, [1992] 2 C.M.L.R. 113; Case 237/84, *Re Business Transfer Directive: E.C. Commission v. Belgium* [1986] E.C.R. 1247, [1988] 2 C.M.L.R. 865; Case C–292/89, *R. v. Immigration Appeal Tribunal, ex p. Antonissen* [1991] I E.C.R. 745, [1991] 2 C.M.L.R. 373 and Case C–306/89, *Re Transport Workers: E.C. Commission v. Greece* [1991] I E.C.R. 5880, [1994] 1 C.M.L.R. 803.

[45] Cases C-6/90 & 9/90, *Francovich v. Italy* [1991] I E.C.R. 5357; [1993] 2 C.M.L.R. 66.

[46] *Rothmans & Philip Morris* and *Arizona* [1993] 1 C.M.L.R. 93, Conseil d'Etat.

(d) Supremacy of E.C. law

1.023 The Treaty of Rome is silent on the issue of whether Community law is superior to the domestic law of a Member State. In the early days, in several cases, this issue came before national courts and the ECJ. On a national level, initially, courts viewed the EEC Treaty as an international convention which was recognised at a domestic level. If the Member State was monist, the EEC Treaty became part of domestic law from the moment of ratification. If the Member State was dualist, it required incorporation by a domestic statute before becoming law in that state. However, whether a state was monist or dualist, the real issue was whether the E.C. Treaty in effect merely became another part of domestic law or whether in fact, it had a higher authority.

The ECJ has consistently ruled that EEC law takes precedence over national law. Thus, in *Costa v. ENEL*,[47] there was a conflict between a number of Treaty provisions and a later Italian statute. It was argued on the basis of *lex posterior derogat priori*,[48] that the Italian law took priority. In *Internationale Handelgesellschaft mbH v. Einfuhr-und Vorratsstelle für Getreide und Futtermittel*,[49] a plaintiff claimed in German proceedings that an E.C. Regulation was invalid because it conflicted with provisions of the German constitution. The ECJ was unequivocal when these cases concerning conflict between EEC laws and domestic laws were referred to it under Article 177. It consistently ruled that laws derived from the Treaty of Rome must take precedence over domestic laws whether constitutional in nature or otherwise. In *Simmenthal Spa v. E.C. Commission*,[50] a later case, the Italian constitutional court had ruled that it would be prepared to declare any national law conflicting with E.C. law as invalid. However, in the case itself, where there was a conflict between E.C. and domestic law, the Italian judge was unsure as to whether he should wait for the domestic law to be declared invalid by the constitutional court or merely refuse to apply it. On reference to the ECJ, the latter held that a national court was obliged to apply EEC law and should refuse to apply any conflicting provisions of national legislation even if adopted subsequently and that it was not necessary to wait for the domestic law to be annulled. In the British case of *R. v. Secretary of State for Transport, ex p. Factortame Limited (No. 2)*,[51] the ECJ said, in the context of interlocutory proceedings, that a national court must refuse to apply a rule of national law if such would prevent it giving interim relief based upon Community law.

1.024 The courts of Member States were initially slow to recognise the supremacy of EEC law. In *Costa v. ENEL* and *Internationale Handelgesellschaft*, the Italian and German constitutional courts refused to

[47] Case 6/64 [1964] E.C.R. 585; [1964] C.M.L.R. 425.
[48] "The later law repeals the former law."
[49] Case 11/70 [1970] E.C.R. 1125; [1972] C.M.L.R. 255.
[50] Case 92/78 [1979] E.C.R. 777; [1980] 1 C.M.L.R. 25.
[51] [1990] 3 C.M.L.R. 867.

acknowledge the supremacy of E.C. law. However, there is no doubt that national courts now recognise the supremacy of EEC law. In the United Kingdom, national courts have recognised the supremacy of EEC law where it conflicts with domestic law.[52] Where the law is not directly effective, U.K. courts have been more reluctant to give Community law precedence over national laws.[53] In other Member States, courts have moved from their early stance such that E.C. law now takes precedence. Even the most chauvinist of Member States, France, now recognises the supremacy of E.C. law.[54] In Germany, the German constitutional court has reversed its position taken in *Internationale Handelgesellschaft* and now accepts the supremacy of E.C. law where it is directly effective provided that the latter respected fundamental rights.[55] In Italy, the constitutional court has reversed its earlier position in *Costa v. ENEL* and now recognises the supremacy of E.C. law.

On a final note, the surrender of sovereignty to the E.C. by Member States has been voluntary. In principle, few legal theorists doubt that such surrender is reversible and that ultimate legal and political control remains with the Member States.[56]

(e) Enforcement of Community law

1.025 As discussed earlier, the E.C. Treaty is not merely an international convention which is addressed to Member States. It affects individuals conferring rights and obligations on them. It forms part of a Member State's domestic law and provided the relevant provision is directly effective, can be relied upon in a national court. The ECJ cannot hear such proceedings but under Article 177, may rule on the interpretation and validity of Community laws. However, proceedings before national courts constitute only one method of enforcement of Community law. Often, affected persons have neither the time, resources nor inclination to enforce Community laws.

Accordingly, the E.C. Treaty provides for the enforcement of Community laws in various ways apart from private actions. Firstly, under the E.C. Treaty and its secondary legislation, the E.C. Commission is often empowered, especially in competition law, to enforce Community law against Member States and individuals. Secondly, the E.C. Treaty pro-

[52] See *Macarthys Ltd v. Smith* [1979] I.C.R. 785, C.A.; *Garland v. British Rail Engineering* [1983] 2 A.C. 751, H.L.; *Factortame Ltd v. Secretary of State for Transport* [1989] 2 All E.R. 692, H.L.; *Pickstone v. Freemans* [1989] A.C. 66, H.L.; *R. v. Sec. of State for Transport ex p. Factortame (No. 2)* [1991] 1 All E.R. 106; *McKechnie v. UBM Building Supplies (Southern) Ltd* [1991] I.C.R. 710, Employment Appeal Tribunal. In contrast, see the early case of *Felixstowe Dock & Railway Co. v. British Transport Docks Board*: [1976] 2 C.M.L.R. 655, C.A.

[53] See para. 1–021 and n. 44.

[54] *Nicolo Semoules* [1990] C.M.L.R. 173; *Boisdet*: [1991] 1 C.M.L.R. 3.

[55] *Application of Wunsche Handelgesellschaft* [1987] 3 C.M.L.R. 225; *Re Kloppenberg*: [1988] 3 C.M.L.R. 1. Where a directive is not directly effective, the Bundesgerichtshof refused to interpret domestic law against its clear meaning to comply with an E.C. Directive, see *Re a Rehabilitation Centre* [1992] 2 C.M.L.R. 21.

[56] *e.g.* see Lord Denning in *Macarthys Ltd v. Smith* [1979] I.C.R. 785 at 789.

vides for various mechanisms to ensure that Community institutions and Member States comply with their obligations under the E.C. Treaty. Thus, Article 169 enables the Commission to bring proceedings against Member States for failure to fulfil an obligation under the Treaty. Article 170 permits a Member State to bring an action against another Member State for the latter's failure to fulfil its Community obligations. Article 173 permits an individual to request the ECJ to review the legality of acts done by Community institutions on the grounds of lack of competence, infringement of an essential procedural requirement, infringement of the E.C. Treaty or of any rule of law relating to its application, or misuse of powers. Similarly, under Article 175, an individual can bring proceedings before the ECJ if a Community institution fails to act in infringement of the E.C. Treaty. Finally, under Article 178 and 215(2), the ECJ has jurisdiction to award damages in a case of non-contractual liability against a Community institution where it or its servants act in breach of the general principles common to the laws of the Member States. Below are discussed those proceedings which are relevant to individuals rather than between Member States and institutions of the Community.

(i) Preliminary rulings procedure of ECJ

1.026 Article 177 provides that:

> "The Court of Justice shall have jurisdiction to give preliminary rulings concerning:
> (a) the interpretation of this Treaty
> (b) the validity and interpretation of acts of the institutions of the Community
> (c) the interpretation of the statutes of bodies established by an act of the Council, where those statutes so provide
>
> Where such a question is raised before any court or tribunal of a member State, that court or tribunal may, if it considers that a decision on the question is necessary to enable it to give judgment, request the Court of Justice to give a ruling thereon.
>
> Where any such question is raised in a case pending before a court or tribunal of a Member State, against whose decisions there is no judicial remedy under national law, that court or tribunal shall bring the matter before the Court of Justice."

It should be noted that the ability to make a reference under Article 177 is limited. Only national courts have jurisdiction when it comes to the *application* of E.C. law to disputes between individuals. Accordingly, the ECJ will not rule on the application of Community law to a set of facts even if that is the overriding issue in a case. Instead, it will put forward an abstract interpretation of the law.[57] The ECJ will only rule in real dis-

[57] This often includes "helpful guidance" as the application of its interpretation to a particular set of facts!

putes—it will not give a ruling on hypothetical questions.[58] Also, the ECJ is not an appellate court from the court of last instance of a Member State. If a party to proceedings considers that the court of last instance has wrongly applied Community law or refused to make a reference because it considers the interpretation of Community legislation to be clear and unambiguous, the party cannot appeal to the ECJ.

Any court or tribunal may refer an issue to the ECJ provided that they have a public element. Thus, an arbitrator appointed to settle privately a dispute between parties can not make use of Article 177.[59]

Under Article 177, a distinction should be made between courts which fall within Article 177(2) and Article 177(3). The former have a discretion to refer to the ECJ when an issue as to interpretation arises whereas the latter are obliged in such circumstances to refer. Whilst it is not free from doubt, it would appear that where a decision by an inferior court is not capable of appeal, for the purposes of Article 177, such a court would fall within Article 177(3) and thus must refer to the ECJ if an issue as to the interpretation of Community law is raised.[60] Inferior courts of a Member State are free to request a ruling from the ECJ even if there exists a clear domestic precedent or ruling given by a superior domestic court.[61]

1.027 The ECJ in *CILFIT Srl v. Ministro della Sanità* has said that national courts (whether courts of last instance or not) need not refer automatically an issue to the ECJ when a question of the interpretation or validity of a Community law is raised. There is no need to refer when (a) the question of E.C. law is irrelevant (b) the Community provisions have already been interpreted by the Court of Justice even though the questions at issue are not strictly identical or (c) the correct application is so obvious as to leave no scope for reasonable doubt.[62] The last category must be assessed in the light of the specific characteristics of Community law, the particular difficulties to which its interpretation gives rise, and the risk of divergences in judicial decisions within the Community.[63]

[58] *Weinand Meilike v. Adv Orga Meyer AG*, *The Times*, October 20, 1992.

[59] Case 102/81, *Nordsee Deutsche Hochseefischerei GmbH v. Reederei Mond Hochseefischerei Nordstern AG & Co. KG* [1982] E.C.R. 1095.

[60] See *Costa v. ENEL*, above n. 47, where the ECJ said that "national courts against whose decisions as in the present case there is no judicial remedy must refer the matter to the Court of Justice". In this case, the national court was an Italian magistrate's court. In England, difficulties may arise where leave to appeal is refused, see *Magnavision NV v. General Optical Council* [1987] 2 C.M.L.R. 262 and *Chiron v. Murex Diagnostus* (No. 8) [1995] F.S.R. 309, C.A.

[61] Case 146/73, *Rheinmuhlen-Dusseldorf* [1974] E.C.R. 139; [1974] 1 C.M.L.R. 523, ECJ. *Cf.* Wood J.'s remarks to contrary in *Enderby v. Frenchay Health Authority* [1991] I.C.R. 382, E.A.T.

[62] Case 283/81, *CILFIT Srl v. Ministra dello Sanità* [1982] E.C.R. 3415; [1983] 1 C.M.L.R. 472, ECJ. Conditions (b) and (c) are analogous to the French administrative law principle of *acte claire*.

[63] For cases on "need to refer" in England, see *Bulmer v. Bollinger* [1974] Ch. 401, C.A.; *R. v. Henn* [1978] 1 W.L.R. 1031; *R. v. Inner London Education Authority, ex p. Hinde* [1985] 1 C.M.L.R. 716, H.C.

A court other than of last instance has a discretion to refer. Factors like time, cost, work load of the ECJ and the wishes of the parties should be taken into account.[64] Where the issue is raised at a court of last instance, then the issue as to whether the matter falls within the *CILFIT* criteria becomes of crucial importance. If such a court takes the view that there is no need to refer, then that is the end of the matter.[65]

Where the decision involves a ruling on the invalidity of a Community measure, the ECJ has stated that inferior national courts do not have jurisdiction to declare Community measures invalid and that if they had any doubts, a reference must be made.[66] Furthermore, if a party seeks a reference under Article 177 that a Community act is invalid, the ECJ may refuse jurisdiction if the party concerned could have brought proceedings under Article 173 for annulment of the act but failed to do so within the two month period.[67]

(ii) *Judicial review of acts of Community institutions*

1.028 Article 173 of the Treaty of Rome as amended by the TEU provides:

> "The Court of Justice shall review the legality of acts adopted jointly by the European Parliament and the Council, of acts of the Council, of the Commission and of the European Central Bank other than recommendations and opinions and of acts of the European Parliament intended to have legal effect *vis-a-vis* third parties.
>
> It shall for this purpose have jurisdiction in actions brought by a Member State, the Council or the Commission on grounds of lack of competence, infringement of an essential procedural requirement, infringement of this Treaty or any rule of law relating to its application, or misuse of powers.
>
> The Court shall have jurisdiction under the same conditions in actions brought by the European Parliament and the European Central Bank for the purpose of protecting their prerogatives.
>
> Any natural or legal person, may under the same conditions, institute proceedings against a decision addressed to that person or against a decision which, although in the form of a Regulation or a Decision addressed to another person, is of direct and individual concern to the former.

[64] See Lord Denning M.R. in *Bulmer v. Bollinger*.

[65] However, in Germany, the German Federal Constitutional Court will review decisions by courts of last instance where it is clear that the court's decision does not comply with the *CILFIT* criterion—see *Re VAT Directive* [1982] 1 C.M.L.R. 527; [1989] 1 C.M.L.R. 873; *Re Patented Feedingstuffs* [1989] 2 C.M.L.R. 902.

[66] Case 314/85, *Foto-Frost v. Hauptzollamt Lubeck-Ost* [1987] E.C.R. 4199, at 4232; [1988] 3 C.M.L.R. 57.

[67] Case C-188/92, *TWD v. Germany* [1994] I E.C.R. 833.

> The proceedings provided for in this Article shall be instituted within two months of the publication of the measure, or of its notification to the plaintiff, or, in the absence thereof, of the day on which it came to the knowledge of the latter, as the case may be."

Article 173 permits individuals to challenge the legality of Community acts. Any act which produces legal effects for the parties concerned and brings about a change in their legal position is an act capable of annulment under Article 173.[68]

For an individual to challenge an act of a Community institution, he must show that it is of direct and individual concern to him if it is not a decision addressed to him. The ECJ has given many decisions as to whether an individual has satisfied these criteria. In *Plaumann v. E.C. Commission*,[69] a German importer of clementines sought to challenge a decision by the Commission addressed to the German government whereby it refused the latter permission to reduce its customs duties on clementines. The ECJ held that in order for the applicant to avail himself of Article 173, he must show that the decision affects him because of certain characteristics which are peculiarly relevant to him, or by reason of circumstances in which he is differentiated from all other persons, and not by the mere fact that he belongs to a class of persons who are affected. This test is easier to recite than apply. It is clear that the number of persons affected by a Community measure is not relevant.[70] However, if the applicant forms part of a "closed" class of persons to whom the measure is directed such that no one else is capable of entering that class or being affected by the same measure, then the case law of the ECJ suggests that the measure is one of "direct and individual" concern to that applicant.[71] Where the Community measure was issued as a result of proceedings initiated by the applicant, the latter will normally have little difficulty in showing that the measure is of direct and individual concern to him.[72]

[68] Case 8–11/66, *Re Noordwijks Cement Accoord* [1967] E.C.R. 75; [1967] C.M.L.R. 77, ECJ (registered letter sent to companies by Commission notifying them that their immunit from fines under E.C. competition law was at an end was an act capable of review under Article 173). *Cf. Nashua Corporation v. E.C. Commission & Council* [1990] 1 E.C.R. 719; [1990] 2 C.M.L.R. 6 (preliminary measures paving way for final decision not a reviewable act).

[69] Case 25/62: [1963] E.C.R. 95; [1964] C.M.L.R. 29, ECJ.

[70] Case 1/64, *Glucoseries Reunies v. E.C. Commission* [1964] E.C.R. 413; [1964] C.M.L.R. 596.

[71] *e.g.* see Case 106/63, *Toepfer v. E.C. Commission* [1965] E.C.R. 405; [1966] C.M.L.R. 111; Case 41/70, *International Fruit Co. v. E.C. Commission* [1972] E.C.R. 1219; [1975] 2 C.M.L.R. 515; Cases 113/77, 118–121/77, *Japanese Ballbearings* [1979] E.C.R. 1185; [1979] 2 C.M.L.R. 257; *Sofrimport SARL v. E.C. Commission* [1990] I E.C.R. 2477; [1990] 3 C.M.L.R. 80. See also Greaves, "Locus Standi under Article 173 when seeking annulment of a Regulation" [1986] 11 E.L.Rev. 119.

[72] See Case 26/76, *Metro-SB-Grossmarkte v. E.C. Commission* [1977] E.C.R. 1875; [1978] 2 C.M.L.R. 1.

1.029 In several cases, the ECJ, in ruling that the applicant does not have *locus standi*, has said that the validity of Community acts is open to attack under Article 177 in national proceedings.[73] In a recent case, the ECJ has refused jurisdiction under Article 177 where a party sought a reference that a Community decision addressed to the German government was invalid because the party had been informed of the decision and of their right to challenge it and had failed to do so within the two month period provided for in Article 173.[74]

Provided the action is brought within the two month period, the Court will review the decision on the four grounds of lack of competence, infringement of an essential procedural requirement, infringement of the Treaty or any rule of law relating to its application or misuse of powers. The Court of Justice does not interpret these provisions restrictively and will often show little reluctance in reviewing the reasoning behind the act or decision almost *de novo*. If the proceedings under Article 173 are successful, the ECJ will declare the measure void under Article 174.

(iii) Failure to act by institutions of Community

1.030 Article 175 provides:

> "Should the European Parliament, the Council or the Commission, in infringement of the Treaty, fail to act, the Member States and the other institutions of the Community may bring an action before the Court of Justice to have the infringement established.
>
> The action shall be admissible only if the institution concerned has first been called upon to act. If, within two months of being so called upon, the institution concerned has not defined its position, the action may be brought within a further period of two months.
>
> Any natural or legal person may, under the conditions laid down in the preceding paragraphs, complain to the Court of Justice that an institution of the Community has failed to address to that person any act other than a recommendation or opinion.
>
> The Court of Justice shall have jurisdiction under the same conditions in actions or proceedings brought by the European Central Bank in the areas falling within the latter's field of competence and in actions or proceedings brought against the latter."

Article 173 and 175 are complementary in nature. Thus, where there is uncertainty as to which article should be invoked, it is not necessary to characterise the proceedings as being under one or the other Article since

[73] *e.g.* see Case 101/76, *Koninklijke Scholten-Honig v. E.C. Council and Commission* [1977] E.C.R. 797; [1980] 2 C.M.L.R. 669 and case 103/77, *Royal Scholten-Honig (Holdings) Ltd v. Intervention Board for Agriculture Produce* [1978] E.C.R. 2037; [1979] 1 C.M.L.R. 675 where in the first case, the ECJ held that the applicant had failed to establish *locus standi* but annulled the regulation in the later case on reference under Art. 177.

[74] Case C-188/92, *TWD v. Germany* [1994] I E.C.R. 833.

both Articles merely prescribe one and the same method of recourse.[75] The institutions called upon to act must be under a clear and definable obligation for Article 175 to be invoked.[76]

Although Article 175 is silent on the issue of who has *locus standi*, the ECJ has implied the condition under Article 173 that the failure to act is of individual and direct concern to the applicant. In effect, the applicant must fulfil two conditions. Firstly, that the act if carried out would be of direct and individual concern and secondly that the applicant is legally entitled to demand action.[77]

1.031 Once the relevant institution is called upon to act, it may execute the act requested, define its position or do nothing. Normally, the relevant institution (normally the Commission) will define its position in a letter to the applicant. Often, this merely amounts to a refusal to act in writing. In such circumstances, Article 175 is no longer relevant and the applicant is obliged to issue proceedings under Article 173 for annulment of the communication which defines the institution's position. The applicant must show that the conditions under Article 173 are fulfilled, in particular that the act requested is of direct and individual concern to him.[78] Moreover, the applicant must show in Article 173 proceedings relating to a definition of position pursuant to a request under Article 175 that the applicant is entitled to demand that action be taken.[79]

If the applicant can satisfy the above requirements, the Court will review whether the institution's failure to act constitutes an infringement of the Treaty. Often, it will rule that the institution has a discretion in the pursuit of the objectives under the Treaty and accordingly, the institution is under no obligation to act. However, often the applicant's procedural rights will have been infringed (*i.e.* the right of a complainant to a full hearing) and the Court may order that such rights are respected.

If an action is successful under Article 175 or 173 is successful, then the Court will order that the institution shall take all necessary measures to comply with the judgment of the Court of Justice.[80]

(iv) Incidental review of regulations before the ECJ

1.032 Article 184 provides that:

> "Notwithstanding the expiry of the period laid down in the third paragraph of Article 173, any party may in proceedings in which a Regulation of the Council or of the Commission is in issue, plead the

[75] *e.g.* see case 15/70, *Chevalley v. E.C. Commission* [1970] E.C.R. 975.

[76] *European Parliament v. E.C. Council* [1985] E.C.R. 1513; [1986] 1 C.M.L.R. 138.

[77] Case 15/71, *Firma MackPrang v. E.C. Commission* [1971] E.C.R. 797; [1972] C.M.L.R. 52; Case 246/81, *Bethell v. E.C. Commission* [1982] E.C.R. 2277; [1982] 3 C.M.L.R. 300; Case 247/87, *Star Fruit Company S.A. v. E.C. Commission* [1989] E.C.R. 291; [1990] 1 C.M.L.R. 733; Case 42/71, *Nordgetreide v. E.C. Commission* [1972] E.C.R. 105; [1973] C.M.L.R. 177.

[78] *Star Fruit Company SA v. E.C. Commission*, above n. 77.

[79] *e.g.* see *Bethell v. Commission*, above, n. 77.

[80] Art. 176.

grounds specified in the first paragraph of Article 173, in order to invoke before the Court of Justice the inapplicability of that Regulation."

This provision permits parties to plead that a regulation is inapplicable where such is *incidental* to the main proceedings in proceedings before the Court of Justice. In proceedings before national courts, parties are free to raise an issue as the validity of a regulation by reference to the ECJ under Article 177. Article 184 cannot be used directly to attack a regulation.[81] The Court of Justice will not permit Article 184 to be used to evade time limits under Article 173 or Article 175.[82] However, where the validity of an act is based on the validity of a regulation, then Article 184 permits a party to claim that the regulation is inapplicable and thus the act invalid. Accordingly, Article 184 is often used when allied to a claim under Article 173 where the challenged act derives its validity from a regulation which the applicant claims is invalid.[83] However, it can be used with Article 175 where a failure to act is justified by resort to an invalid regulation.[84] Although Article 184 is expressed to only apply to regulations, it is sufficient for the act challenged to produce similar effects to that of a regulation for it to be challenged under Article 184.[85]

The grounds for review are the same as in Article 173. It should be noted that Article 184 only entitles the Court of Justice to rule that the regulation is inapplicable *inter partes*. It does not result in the annulment of the regulation.

(f) E.C. and intellectual property

1.033 The Treaty of Rome never actually mentions the word "intellectual property". The nearest reference is to "industrial and commercial property" in Article 36. The conflict between a common market and industrial protection rights that interrupted the free movement of goods was recognised by lawyers immediately after the entry into force of the EEC Treaty. Initially, commentators put forward the view that industrial property was excluded from the scope of the EEC Treaty and was governed purely by national law.[86] Thus, it was thought that obstacles to the aims of the common market could be eliminated solely by means of the harmonisation of intellectual property laws. This approach contrasted with lawyers and academics who maintained that in certain circum-

[81] Case 31/62, *Milchwerke Heinz Wohrmann & Sohn v. E.C. Commission* [1962] E.C.R. 501; [1966] C.M.L.R. 152.

[82] See *Wohrmann ibid.* and *E.C. Commision v. Belgium* [1978] E.C.R. 1881.

[83] *e.g.* see case 92/78, *Simmenthal Spa v. E.C. Commission* [1979] E.C.R. 777; [1980] 1 C.M.L.R. 25, ECJ.

[84] Case 32/58, *SNUPAT v. High Authority* [1959] E.C.R. 127.

[85] See *Simmenthal*, above, n. 83.

[86] *e.g.* see Gotzen Sen, GRUR Int. 1958, referred to at p. 7 of Johannes *Industrial Property and Copyright in European Community Law* (1976) Sitjhoff. Sen's reasoning was based on Art. 36 and Art. 222 of the Treaty of Rome which discussed in the Chapter on Enforcement of Intellectual Property.

stances, industrial property and the exercise of their rights would result in anti-competitive practices and that the competition provisions of the Treaty of Rome applied as much to such practices as others.[87] This view which de-emphasised the free movement of goods provisions was soon accepted in the 1960s. However, as pointed out, this approach merely accepted that Community law and national intellectual property laws were capable of interacting with each other.[88]

Examination of the founding Member States' laws provided several solutions as to how to reconcile intellectual property with the freedom of goods and services and the competition laws of the Community. Thus, German antitrust law prohibited restrictions in licences which extended beyond the "scope of the patent". Other commentators suggested that the traditional exclusionary effects of industrial protection rights should be restricted under the EEC Treaty where parallel protection rights were held by the same person on the basis that an inventor should only have one opportunity to obtain remuneration for his invention.[89]

1.034 In the early cases of the ECJ on the interrelationship of intellectual property and the Treaty of Rome, it was clear that analogies based on national law were to be of little assistance. The ECJ clearly considered that the objectives of the Treaty of Rome, especially the objective of a common market, meant that a new approach was required. It was clear that national analogies and US analogies were of little help because in those cases, the conflict between intellectual property laws and other laws, notably anti-competition laws, was a conflict between laws of equal status. In contrast, at an early stage, the ECJ had ruled that Community law must take precedent over national laws.[90] Accordingly, Community free movement of goods provisions were to restrict the effect of national intellectual property laws. Gradually, from its first decision in the early 1960s in *Consten & Grundig v. E.C. Commission*[91] to the present day, the ECJ developed principles which delineated the relationship between Community law and national intellectual property rights. This jurisprudence means that in most factual circumstances, a legal advisor can say with a fair degree of certainty whether a rights owner is justified in exercising his rights where there is a Community dimension to such an exercise (*i.e.* an effect on trade between Member States).

Moreover, in the 1960s, the E.C. Commission was concerned about the use of intellectual property rights to prevent trade between Member States. Accordingly, it initiated a programme of harmonisation of intellectual property rights in Member States. This programme has resulted in

[87] *e.g.* see Van Themaat, GRUR Int. 1964, p. 21.
[88] Johannes, p.8.
[89] Koch and Froschmaier, "The Doctrine of Territoriality in Patent Law and the European Common Market", *IDEA, the Patent, Trademark and Copyright Journal of Research and Education*, (1965), Vol. 9, p. 343.
[90] See paras. 1.023 *et seq.*
[91] Case 56/64, *Etablissements Consten & Grundig v. E.C. Commission* [1966] E.C.R. 299; [1966] C.M.L.R. 418.

considerable harmonisation in the fields of copyright and neighbouring rights (including computer software), trade marks, semiconductor rights and to a lesser extent, patent rights. Harmonising proposals in the field of industrial design, plant variety rights, databases and patents are currently in the pipeline. Moreover, in the field of competition law, the E.C. Commission has been active in the enactment of several regulations which concern the interaction of intellectual property and Community law on competition.[92]

3. European Economic Area

(a) History to EEA

1.035 In 1960, the European Free Trade Association (EFTA) was established for those states which did not wish to join the E.C. but wished to participate in a free trade zone which was limited in scope. The founding members were Austria, Denmark, Norway, Portugal, Sweden, Switzerland and the United Kingdom. Thereafter, Iceland, Finland and Liechtenstein joined. In 1973, Denmark and the United Kingdom joined the E.C. and the rest concluded bilateral Free Trade Agreements with the Community ("the 1972 FTAs"). In 1984, the Community, its Member States and EFTA countries started to consider co-operation in areas beyond the framework of the FTAs. In particular, the parties examined areas such as standardisation, simplification of trade documentation, research and development, mobility of workers, social and consumer matters and intellectual property. As E.C. integration grew apace, EFTA countries began to look at further integration. In 1989, the President of the Commission proposed that a new form of association between E.C. and EFTA states were formed. This was to lead to the European Economic Area Agreement (EEA Agreement). The aim of this agreement was to provide for a much more systematic and thorough integration of E.C. and EFTA states without actually having to extend E.C. membership to the EFTA countries.

In August 1991, the E.C. Commission asked the ECJ under Article 228 to rule on the compatibility with the E.C. Treaty of the judicial mechanism planned in the EEA Agreement. The ECJ gave an adverse opinion stating that the EEA judicial system conflicted with the EEC Treaty.[93] The negotiations reconvened and concluded fresh texts to which the ECJ gave its approval.[94]

1.036 On May 2, 1992, the EEA Agreement was signed by the European Community, its twelve Member States and the seven States of EFTA. The ratification process progressed smoothly until Switzerland in a referendum rejected the EEA Agreement. This resulted in a Protocol to the EEA

[92] The reader is referred to the Chapters on Licensing of Intellectual Property and Abuse of a Dominant Position.
[93] Opinion 1/91 [1991] I E.C.R. 6079; [1992] 1 C.M.L.R. 245.
[94] Opinion 1/92 [1992] I E.C.R. 282; [1992] 2 C.M.L.R. 217.

Agreement to take this rejection into account. Eventually, the EEA Agreement and this Protocol was ratified by all remaining States and came into force on January 1, 1994.[95] Also on May 2, 1992, the EFTA states signed two agreements which established three new institutions—the EFTA Standing Committee (analogous to the E.C. Council and composed of representatives of the EFTA countries); an EFTA Surveillance Authority (ESA), an independent body equivalent to the E.C. Commission for ensuring that EFTA States fulfilled their EEA obligations; and the EFTA Court which was to have a parallel jurisdiction to the ECJ.[96] These separate agreements were necessary because although the E.C. had its own institutions for overseeing the proper implementation of the EEA Treaty in its Member States, there were no equivalent institutions in the EFTA states.

At present, the relevance of the EEA is in doubt. Three of the EFTA states, Finland, Sweden and Austria have voted to join the E.C. Thus, only Norway, Iceland and Liechtenstein will be members of the EEA of which the latter two are not E.C. members. Switzerland is in a special position because it is still a member of EFTA but not of the EEA. It too has applied to become an E.C. Member State but following the rejection by its electorate of the EEA, its application has been frozen. However, the relevance of the EEA is that it provides an invaluable stepping stone to membership of the E.C. Thus, it is anticipated that central and eastern Europe countries may become members of the EEA prior to becoming members of the E.C.[97]

(b) Fundamental aspects of EEA

1.037 The general objective of the EEA is to promote a continuous and balanced strengthening of trade and economic relations between the Contracting Parties with equal conditions of competition and the respect of the same rules with a view to creating a homogeneous European Economic Area.[98] The economic objective is to be attained through the extension of the E.C. common market rules to the EFTA States. The homogeneity objective is to be attained through the application of common rules and the permanent updating of these rules following the evolution of the E.C. rules. The fundamental provisions of the EEA Agreement replicate the provision of the E.C. Treaty in relation to the four freedoms of the E.C., *i.e.* free movement of goods, person, services and capital thus extending these freedoms to the EFTA countries. Also, other policies of the E.C. such as environment and social policy are included in the EEA Agreement. However, there is no enlargement of the E.C. policies in the field of agriculture, fiscal harmonisation and E.C. common policies

[95] [1994] O.J. L1.

[96] Agreement on a Standing Committee of the EFTA States and Agreement between the EFTA States on the Establishment of a Surveillance Authority and a Court of Justice.

[97] See a speech given by Mr Delors on September 10, 1993 at the annual meeting of the International Institute for Strategic Studies in Brussels.

[98] Art. 1(1) EEA.

towards third countries. As well as replication of the above provisions of the E.C. Treaty, the EEA Agreement includes much of the Community secondary legislation whether regulations, directives or decisions of the ECJ by annexing it to the EEA Agreement. This "bundle of law" is referred to as the *acquis communautaire* of the EEA Agreement. Special provisions are included as to the interpretation of this *acquis communautaire* in line with rulings of the ECJ. Also, the EEA Agreement envisages the addition of future E.C. legislation to its body of legislation.

In particular, for the purposes of this book, the EEA Agreement and its *acquis communautaire* covers *inter alia* the fields of technical barriers to trade, intellectual property and competition.

Although many of the fundamental provisions of the EEA and E.C. Treaty are identical in nature, it would be a mistake to assume that their application will be identical under the two treaties. The distinction between the EEA and the E.C. Treaty was expressed by the ECJ when giving its opinion on the compatibility of the intended judicial mechanism of an EEA Court with the Treaty of Rome. The Court stated that where the EEA provisions are identical with the provisions of the E.C. Treaty, it does not mean that they should be interpreted in the same way. In particular, the ECJ stated that the provision of the E.C. Treaty on free movement of goods and competition, far from being an end themselves must be interpreted as a means for achieving the objectives of the Treaty, namely the achievement of economic integration leading to an internal market and economic and monetary union. In contrast, there was no such objective in the EEA Treaty. Furthermore, the ECJ said that in relation to the objective of homogeneity in the EEA, that the fact that provisions in the EEA were identical to that of the E.C. Treaty did not mean that they should be interpreted identically.[99]

(c) Structure and Framework of the EEA Agreement

1.038 The EEA Agreement sets out the objectives of the EEA, non-discrimination provisions, the substantive provisions relating to the four freedoms, various other provisions relating to social policy, consumer protection, environment, statistics and company law, the institutional provisions including the decision-making procedure, measures safeguarding homogeneity, surveillance mechanism, settlement of disputes and safeguard measures whilst the final part deals with the "cohesion fund". Appended to the agreement are 49 protocols and 22 Annexes which constitutes the *acquis communautaire*.

The two freedoms relating to the free movement of goods and competition law are discussed in the relevant Chapters. The *acquis communautaire* relating to intellectual property is briefly discussed here but the reader is referred to the relevant chapter for detailed information.

The Contracting Parties to the EEA are the E.C., its Member States

[99] See Opinion 1/91 [1991] I E.C.R. 6079; [1992] C.M.L.R. 245.

and EFTA states.[1] Whilst the EEA Agreement is an agreement reached by the E.C. with EFTA states under Article 228 of the E.C. Treaty, there were certain areas, in particular intellectual property rights, where Member States retained competences. Accordingly, Member States and EFTA States need to be parties to the Agreement. The EEA Agreement applies to the territories of the E.C. and EFTA states.

Under the EEA Agreement, adopted regulations and directives do not automatically become part of the internal order of the Contracting Parties. Under Article 7, the EEA Agreement states that such provisions shall be binding upon the Contracting Parties and "be, or be made, part of their internal order" as follows:

(a) an act corresponding to an EEC Regulation shall as such be made part of the internal legal order of the Contracting Parties
(b) an act corresponding to an EEC directive shall leave to the authorities of the Contracting Parties the choice of form and method of implementation

This provision is similar to Article 189 of the Treaty of Rome but does not refer to the direct applicability of regulations. This omission which was the result of intense argument from dualist states suggests that regulations may need to be enacted in EFTA states before they form part of domestic law. With regard to the "direct effect" of directives in EFTA states, it is unclear whether Article 6 of the EEA Agreement which deems that in the case of identical provisions in the EEA and E.C. Treaties, the EEA provision should be interpreted according to ECJ case law, means that under the EEA Agreement, directives shall have direct effect.[2]

(d) *Acquis communautaire*

1.039 The EEA Agreement incorporates 1700 E.C. secondary legislative acts. This has been achieved by 22 annexes. The incorporation of such legislation has been done by a reference technique with appropriate modifications rather than by actual incorporation. Those regulations, directives and decisions which have been incorporated are binding on the Contracting Parties. Recommendations, notices, communications, guidelines, etc., are non-binding acts which the Contracting Parties must take note of.

In relation to intellectual property, Article 65(2) of the EEA Treaty provides that Protocol 28 and Annex 17 which contain specific provisions and arrangements concerning intellectual, industrial and commercial property shall unless otherwise specified apply to all products and services. The reference to "intellectual" property which is not mentioned in the E.C. Treaty is in line with the ECJ's interpretation of "industrial and commercial property" in Article 36 of the E.C. Treaty.

Protocol 28 sets out general provisions on intellectual property and is

[1] Art. 2(c).
[2] See Blanchet, Piiponen, Westman-Clement, The Agreement on the EEA, (1994), p. 21. For the meaning of "direct effect", see paras. 1.011, *et seq.*

discussed later.[3] Annex 17 refers to E.C. legislation on intellectual property which is included as *acquis communautaire*. At the cut-off date of July 31, 1991, only three E.C. legislative acts in the field of intellectual property were in force. These were the Semiconductor Directive, the Trade Mark Directive and the Software Directive. Since the cut-off date and the entry into force of the EEA, the E.C. has legislated further in the field of intellectual property. In particular, there has been the creation of a supplementary protection certificate for medicinal products, a directive on rental, lending and allied rights in the field of copyright, a regulation on the protection of geographical indications and designations of origin for agricultural products and foodstuffs, a directive harmonising the term of copyright, a regulation on a Community trade mark, a regulation on a Community Plant Variety Right, a communication on intellectual property rights and standardisation and a directive on the co-ordination of certain rules concerning copyright and rights related to copyright applicable to satellite broadcasting and cable retransmission. It is intended that the E.C. legislative acts be incorporated as an "Additional Package" into the EEA Agreement following discussion between E.C. and EFTA experts. The application of the relevant *acquis communautaire* in an E.C. and EEA context is discussed in detail in the relevant chapter.

Whether intended E.C. legislation in the field of intellectual property will be included in the EFTA depends on their adoption by the EEA Joint Committee.[4]

(e) Institutions of the EEA

1.040 The EEA is intended to act as a two pillar system with the Community and the EFTA side taking care of their own internal matters. Accordingly, the implementation, enforcement and interpretation of the EEA by the E.C. and its Member States is effected by the institutions of the E.C. On the EFTA side, new institutions have been established which parallel the institutions of the E.C. so as to ensure the effective implementation of the EEA Act in EFTA states. Also, various joint bodies are established in particular for joint decision making and dispute settlement.

(i) Common EEA institutions

1.041 The common E.C.-EFTA bodies are the EEA Council, the EEA Joint Committee, the EEA Parliamentary Committee and the EEA Consultative Committee. The EEA Council which consists of members of the E.C. Council, E.C. Commission and one member of the government of each EFTA state is responsible for the implementation of the EEA Agreement and laying down general guidelines for the work of the EEA Joint Committee. The EEA Joint Committee has the task of ensuring the effective implementation and operation of the Agreement. Its most important role

[3] See paras. 1.045 to 1.046.
[4] See below.

is that it is responsible for the introduction of new legislation into the EEA Agreement. In practice this will mean being consulted by the E.C. Commission as to proposed E.C. legislation and the scrutiny of new E.C. legal acts to see whether they should be incorporated into the EEA Agreement. Finally, there is the EEA Joint Parliamentary Committee which does not have any powers concerning EEA legislation but is merely consultative in nature.

(ii) New EFTA institutions

1.042 Under two Agreements signed at the same time as the EEA Agreement, the EFTA states undertook to set up an EFTA Surveillance Authority (ESA), analogous to the E.C. Commission, whose primary task is to ensure the fulfilment by the EFTA states of their obligations under the EEA Agreement; an EFTA court analogous to the ECJ and a Standing Committee of the EFTA states whose role is to facilitate the elaboration of decisions taken on an EEA level.

Of importance is the division of jurisdiction between the ECJ and EFTA court. It was originally proposed to have an EEA court consisting of judges from the ECJ and EFTA states. However, this was not acceptable to the ECJ which considered it incompatible with the E.C. Treaty. In its Opinion, the ECJ stated that although many provisions of the E.C. and EEA Treaty were identical, that did not mean that they could be interpreted in the same way because the E.C. Treaty's objectives were more integrative and profound than those of the EEA.[5] Accordingly, the ECJ was of the Opinion that there would be a polluting effect. The judicial mechanism was then renegotiated which resulted in a two pillar system with the ECJ having competence on the E.C. side and the EFTA Court having responsibility on the EFTA side. The ECJ approved this arrangement in its second Opinion.[6]

The EFTA Court's competence is more limited than that of the ECJ.[7] It has competence to rule on whether in ESA/EFTA state proceedings, an EFTA state has failed to fulfil its obligations under the EEA Agreement;[8] disputes between two EFTA states;[9] advisory opinions on the interpretation of the EEA Agreement;[10] proceedings brought by an EFTA state against a decision of the ESA on grounds of lack of competence, infringement of an essential requirement, infringement of the EEA Agreement or any rule of law relating to its application or misuse of powers;[11] similar proceedings brought by an individual member against a decision of ESA which is addressed to him or direct and individual concern[12] and pro-

[5] Opinion 1/91 [1991] I E.C.R. 6079; [1992] 1 C.M.L.R. 245.
[6] Opinion 1/92 [1992] I E.C.R. 282. [1992] 2 C.M.L.R. 217.
[7] In general, see Art. 108(2) of EEA Agreement for general competence of EFTA Court.
[8] Art. 31, ESA/Court Agreement.
[9] Art. 32, *ibid.*
[10] Art. 34.
[11] Art. 36, *ibid.*
[12] Art. 36, *ibid.*

ceedings brought by an EFTA state where the ESA fails to act in infringement of the EEA Agreement.[13] The above provisions have similar parallel provisions in the E.C. Treaty. However, they are not as extensive. For instance, whilst an individual can bring proceedings for the annulment of an ESA decision, he cannot bring proceedings for the annulment of other legislative acts *i.e.* regulations and directives of E.C. incorporated into the EEA by the EEA Joint Committee.

(f) Legislative procedure under EEA

1.043 It is intended under the EEA that secondary legislation will originate from the E.C. institutions. The EEA provides for a consultative, examination and adoption procedure prior to such legislation becoming part of the EEA. Firstly, the E.C. Commission is obliged to informally consult the EFTA states and if necessary, a preliminary exchange of views in the EEA Joint Committee will take place.[14] Experts of the EFTA states will participate in the preparatory stage of draft measures.[15] Once a relevant E.C. legal act has been formally adopted by the E.C. Council or E.C. Commission, the EEA Joint Committee will take a decision whether to incorporate it, subject to amendment, into the EEA.[16] The provisions then become law in each Member State subject to the constitutional requirements in each EFTA state.[17] Thus, it is anticipated that EFTA states which are dualist will have to ratify each secondary legislative act into their domestic law. This of course differs from the procedure under the E.C. Treaty where it is assumed that provisions which are "directly applicable" such as regulations become law in Member States without the need for further ratification.

(g) Uniform interpretation and surveillance of EEA and E.C. provisions

1.044 The EEA legal system is closely based on that of the E.C. system. Indeed, the intention was the former should in key respects be identical to the latter. In almost 40 years of the existence of the E.C. Treaty, the ECJ has played a vital part in interpreting the provisions of the E.C. Treaty in particular in the field of intellectual property. The drafters of the EEA Treaty were keen to ensure that there was uniform interpretation of identical provisions in both treaties. In relation to rulings of the ECJ given prior to the signing of the agreement, Article 6 of the EEA Agreement provides that:

> "Without prejudice to the future developments of case law, the provisions of this Agreement in so far as they are identical in substance

[13] Art. 37.
[14] Art. 99, EEA.
[15] Art. 100.
[16] Art. 102.
[17] Art. 103.

> to corresponding rules of the Treaty establishing the European Economic Community and the Treaty establishing the European Coal and Steel Community and the acts adopted in application of these two Treaties, shall, in the implementation and application be interpreted in conformity with the relevant rulings of the Court of Justice of the European Communities given prior to the date of signature of the Agreement."

In relation to identical provisions adopted after the signing of the Agreement, a more complex procedure had to be adopted because of the ECJ's wariness of a joint "EEA Court" approach to the E.C. and EEA Agreement. Accordingly, the EEA Treaty sets up a system of exchange of information between the ECJ, EFTA Court, CFI and courts of last instance of EFTA states.[18] Most importantly, Article 3(2) of the ESA/Court Agreement obliges the EFTA Court to "pay due account" to the principles laid down by the ECJ after the date of signature of the EEA Agreement which concern either the EEA or provisions identical in substance which appear in the E.C. Treaty. It is likely that in practice, this will mean that the EFTA Court will rarely depart from an interpretation of the ECJ on an identical provision.[19]

Also, the EEA Treaty provides for co-operation between the E.C. Commission and ESA.[20]

(h) Intellectual Property and EEA

1.045 In the process of drafting the EEA Agreement, both E.C. and EFTA experts were keen to put genuine intellectual property provisions in the EEA Agreement. It was eventually agreed that the basic intellectual property provisions would go into a protocol (Protocol 28) and the secondary law into an annex (Annex 17). Article 65(2) of the main part of the Agreement provides a reference point to the protocol and annex by stating that they both contain specific provisions and arrangements concerning intellectual, industrial and commercial property, which, unless otherwise specified, apply to all products and services. The other explicit reference in the main part of the EEA Agreement is to "industrial and commercial property" in Article 13 which replicates exactly Article 36 of the E.C. Treaty.[21]

Protocol 28 contains nine articles which address three types of issue: level of protection, commitment to participate in or adhere to different Community measures or international conventions and matters relating to third countries or to international activities.

On the question of level of protection, Article 1(2) of Protocol 28 obliges Contracting Parties to adjust their legislation on intellectual prop-

[18] Art. 106.
[19] See Blanchet Piiponen, Westman-Clement, *The Agreement on the European Economic Area* (1994), p. 37.
[20] Art. 109.
[21] Including the omission of a reference to "intellectual" property.

erty so as to make it compatible with the principles of free circulation of goods and services and with the level of protection of intellectual property attained in Community law, including the level of enforcement of those rights. Article 1(3) provides for a more specialised adjustment procedure whereby EFTA states are obliged, following a request and consultation with Contracting Parties, to adjust their legislation on intellectual property in order to reach "at least the level of protection of intellectual property prevailing in the Community upon signature of the Agreement".

Article 2 of the Protocol obliges Contracting Parties to respect the principle of exhaustion of rights developed in Community law by the ECJ.[22]

1.046 Article 3 obliges Contracting Parties to undertake to use their best endeavours to conclude within a period of three years after the entry into force of the Community Patent Agreement negotiations with a view to the participation of the EFTA states. Furthermore, Article 3 requires EFTA states to ensure that their patents laws comply with the substantive provisions of the European Patent Convention.[23] Article 4 makes certain provisions as to the extension of semiconductor protection to persons from third countries.

Article 5 obliges Contracting Parties to obtain their adherence before January 1, 1995 to the Paris Convention (Stockholm 1967 revision), the Berne Convention (Paris 1971 revisions), the Rome Convention for the Protection of Performers, Producers of Phonograms and Broadcasting Organisation; the Madrid Protocol concerning trade marks; the Nice Agreement concerning the International Classification of Goods and Services (Geneva 1977, amended 1979); the Budapest Treaty on the International Recognition of the Deposit of Microorganisms for the purposes of Patent Procedure and the Patent Co-operation Treaty. In relation to the Madrid Protocol, Finland, Ireland and Norway must adhere by January 1, 1996 and in the case of Iceland, by January 1, 1997. Additionally, Contracting Parties were required to ensure that their domestic legislation complies with their duties under the Paris, Berne and Rome Convention upon entry into force of the EEA Agreement.

Articles 6, 7 and 8 of Protocol 28 provide for a framework of co-operation between Contracting Parties in relation to future developments in intellectual property. Article 6 provides that Contracting Parties agree without prejudice to the competence of the E.C. and its Member States in relation to intellectual property, to improve the regime established by the EEA Agreement as regards intellectual property in the GATT regime. Article 7 provides for consultation between Contracting Parties in the

[22] In relation to patents, this provision takes effect at the latest one year after the entry into force of the EEA Agreement. The application of the exhaustion of rights principle in the EEA Agreement is discussed in the Chapter on the Enforcement of Intellectual Property.

[23] The EEA patent provisions are discussed in more detail in the Chapter on Patents in Europe.

field of intellectual property. Article 8 provides that Contracting Parties agree to enter into negotiations in order to enable full participation of interested EFTA states in future measures concerning intellectual property which might be adopted in Community law.

Finally, Article 9 safeguards the competence of the E.C. and its Member States in matters of intellectual property.

Intellectual property measures that have been adopted via the *acquis communautaire* route are discussed above and in the relevant chapters.[24]

4. Switzerland

1.047 Since the entry into force of the EEA, Switzerland, whose electorate voted against joining the EEA, found itself in a unique position as being the only member of EFTA who had not joined the EEA. Accordingly, the relationship between the E.C. and Switzerland is still governed by the 1972 Free Trade Agreement. With regard to intellectual property, there has been a long tradition of co-operation between the E.C. and EFTA. Switzerland has introduced new laws in the field of trade mark, neighbouring rights and semiconductor topographies to ensure compatibility with Community law. Switzerland also intends to submit a law concerning supplementary protection certificates similar to that provided for in the E.C.[25] It wishes to become a member of the Community Patent Agreement[26] and is desirous of co-operation in future Community legislation on the Community trade mark, design and plant varieties. Furthermore, it wishes to enter into negotiations with the E.C. on issues relating to the protection of geographical indications and designations of origin of agricultural products and foodstuffs. Despite these measures, at least one commentator has said that the non-ratification of the EEA Agreement could entail a step backwards as compared to the situation prevailing before the EEA.[27]

5. E.C., EFTA and Central and Eastern European Countries

1.048 The E.C. and EFTA have concluded a number of agreements with Central and Eastern European Countries ("CEECs"). The E.C. has concluded five Association Agreements with the Czech and Slovak Republics, Hungary, Bulgaria and Romania. The EFTA states have concluded five Free Trade Agreements with the same countries.

In relation to intellectual property, the E.C. agreements provide a basic general level of protection of intellectual property, a list of international

[24] See para. 1.039.
[25] See para. 2.116.
[26] Through the mechanism in Art. 8.
[27] Blanchet, Piiponen, Westman-Clement, *The Agreement on the European Economic Area*, p. 254.

conventions to be complied with and guarantees concerning the means of enforcement. The FTA Agreements contain basic provisions on the level of protection of intellectual property; a definition of the notion of intellectual property; a most favoured nation clause;[28] particular standards of protection to be provided for particular types of intellectual property, including conditions under which compulsory licences may be granted; a list of international conventions to be ratified and particular standards to be adhered to with regard to the procedure for acquiring, maintaining and enforcing intellectual property rights.

6. International and European Intellectual Property Conventions

1.049 The importance of proper intellectual property protection to the economies of European countries has meant that most are members of the fundamental intellectual property conventions, namely the Paris Convention for the Protection of Industrial Property, the Berne Convention for the Protection of Artistic and Literary Works, the Rome Convention for the Protection of Performers, Producers of Phonograms and Broadcasting Organisations, the Madrid Agreement and its Protocol concerning the International Registration of Marks, the Patent Co-operation Treaty concerning the obtaining of international patents, the European Patent Convention and the International Convention for the Protection of New Varieties of Plants. These conventions are discussed in detail in the relevant chapters.

The above conventions have meant that in many respects, intellectual property laws in European countries have been harmonised and that the obtaining of intellectual property rights has become easier and less costly. As international conventions signed by Contracting States, they rely upon such states to implement them into domestic law. The law of monist states recognise international conventions as forming part of their domestic legal order without further need for legislation. In dualist states, international conventions must be enacted by the national legislature before they form part of domestic law.

Most of the above conventions are intended either to harmonise national laws on intellectual property or to provide for an easier and simpler system of obtaining internationally protected intellectual property rights. The interpretation and enforcement of rights is left to the individual states. Even the European Patent Convention which both harmonises Contracting States' patent laws and provides for a centralised patent application system does not provide for a patent appellate court responsible for the interpretation of the convention nor provide for a central enforcement procedure of a European patent against potential infringers. In this respect, they must be considered less sophisticated than

[28] *i.e.* an obligation to ensure that a party to the FTA affords equal or better protection to the other party of the FTA as it affords to third party states.

Community measures such as the Community Trade Mark, the Community Plant Variety Right and the proposed Community Patent whereby the obtaining, enforcement and interpretation are intended to be both centralised and have effect throughout the Community.

Chapter Two

PATENTS IN EUROPE

1. Introduction

2.001 Inventors seeking patent protection in the world will invariable apply for patents in Europe. At present, Western Europe, the United States and Japan represent the developed world and the number of potential users of the patented product or process is highest in Western Europe. What distinguishes Western Europe from the other two is that it is a trading bloc which constitutes several, generally well-developed and comparatively rich countries. The applicant for patent protection now has a variety of options when seeking patent protection. He can make a series of parallel national filings in several nations, he can make use of the Patent Cooperation Treaty or he can file for a European patent under the European Patent Convention ("the Munich Convention"). Furthermore, he can make hybrid applications whereby he seeks patent protection using an amalgamation of the above routes. The situation will be even more complicated when and if the Community Patent Convention ("the Luxembourg Convention") comes into force. This convention only applies to E.C. countries.

This chapter explains the different types of routes. It sets out where applicable the procedure for obtaining a patent and the substantive law as to whether an invention is patentable. Finally, it compares the differing routes. In keeping with the "top-down" approach of this book, it focuses on the acquisition of patents via centralised means. It does not set out the national patent law of each European country. This should not deter the reader because the accession of almost all European countries to the Paris Convention, PCT and EPC has meant that there has been a high degree of harmonisation of substantive national patent law throughout Europe. National differences are noticeable in two areas: the procedure for obtaining national patents in each country and the enforcement of patents in litigious proceedings.

2. Paris Convention

2.002 The Paris Convention[1] represents the first efforts of several countries to adopt a common approach to intellectual property. It was first entered into in 1883 and has since been amended several times.[2] The most

[1] The official name is the Paris Convention for the Protection of Industrial Property.
[2] Brussels (1900), Washington (1911), The Hague (1925), London (1934), Lisbon (1958), Stockholm (1967) as amended in 1979.

recently revised Treaty called the "Stockholm Treaty" was last amended in 1979. Most countries of the world and all European countries have now acceded to the Convention. Its main principles are as follows:

a) Nationals of a country belonging to the Convention must enjoy in other countries of the Convention the same rights with regard to intellectual property as their own nationals.[3]
b) In relation to patents, the filing of a patent application in a Contracting State gives the applicant a right of priority in respect of other applications for the same invention of 12 months in any other Contracting State.[4] Thus, subsequent filings of patent applications in other Contracting States will not be rendered invalid by subsequent events such as publication, exploitation or other events that occurred in the 12 month "priority" period.[5]
c) Contracting States have the right to enact measures providing for "compulsory licences" for abuses of the patent, in particular for failure to work. Such licences are not to be applied before the expiry of four years from the date of filing of the patent application or three years from the date of the grant of the patent, whichever is the later.[6]
d) The Convention provides for periods of grace for the payment of fees and for domestic legislation to provide for restoration of patents which have lapsed due to non-payment of fees.[7]

2.003 The Paris Convention also provides for an Assembly and Executive Committee.[8] These two bodies are designed to ensure that the Convention is implemented in the Contracting States and to develop the Convention in the future. Administrative tasks are performed by the International Bureau. This collects and collates all new national intellectual property laws of Contracting States. It publishes a monthly periodical and conducts studies designed to facilitate the protection of intellectual property. These bodies play an important supervisory role and continually monitor the world intellectual property situation and seek to develop the harmonisation of intellectual property laws.

The Paris Convention has provided the framework for the Patent Co-operation Treaty, the European Patent Convention and the Community Patent Convention. Under Article 19 of the Paris Convention, Contracting States are allowed to enter into separate treaties provided that these

[3] Art. 2(1), Paris Convention.
[4] Art. 4.
[5] Art. 4(B).
[6] Art. 5. In the E.C., Community law forbids each Member State to allow compulsory licences for failure to work the patent in its own state where the patent has been worked in another state which is a member of the Common Market — see Case C – 30/40 - Case C – 235/89 *Compulsory Licences: E.C. v. Italy & United Kingdom* [1992] E.C.R. I 829; [1992] 2 C.M.L.R. 709.
[7] Art. 5, *bis*.
[8] Art. 13, 14.

agreements do not contravene the provisions of the Paris Convention. Thus, the PCT specifically states that no provision of it is to be interpreted as diminishing the rights of nationals or residents of Contracting States to the Paris Convention.[9] Similarly, both preambles to the EPC and CPC state that the respective conventions are special agreements within Article 19 of the Paris Convention.

All European countries are signatories to the Paris Convention. It thus has had the effect of harmonising patent law to a considerable degree in Europe.[10]

3. Patent Co-operation Treaty

(a) Fundamentals of PCT

2.004 The Patent Co-operation Treaty was set up in order to rationalise patent applications for member states. Its aim is to centralise, simplify and render more economical patent applications for a series of countries. In essence, it is a procedural treaty and does not concern itself with the actual grant of patents which is left to national patent offices. It is a world-wide treaty to which over 70 countries have acceded, including almost all the important industrial countries. This is however considerably less than those who are members of the Paris Convention (as amended). The treaty was signed on June 19, 1970 and came into force on June 1, 1978 and countries have been becoming members up to the present day. Almost all European countries have ratified the convention. Countries that have acceded to it are deemed to belong to the International Patent Co-operation Union.

In summary, the PCT permits an applicant to file an "International Application" at his local national patent office, called the "Receiving Office" for the countries that he wishes to have patent protection which are called the "Designated States". Upon receipt of the application, the Receiving Office will check that the application complies with certain formalities. It will then remit copies to the International Bureau of WIPO in Geneva which acts as the administrative office for the PCT. It also sends copies of the application to a patent office which is designated as the International Searching Authority ("ISA"). This office will make a search of the prior art and then send the International Search Report ("ISR") to the International Bureau at WIPO and also to the applicant. The applicant is given an opportunity, if necessary, to amend the patent application. The international patent application and the international search report are then sent to the patent offices of the Designated States ("the Designated Offices") and the international application enters the national phase. This ends the International Phase under the PCT and the

[9] Art. 1(2), PCT.

[10] The breakaway republics of Slovenia, Bosnia-Hercegovina and Croatia have recently acceded to the Paris Convention.

responsibility for further prosecution of the patent applications lies with the applicant and the Designated Offices.

An applicant who is a resident or national of a Contracting State which has acceded to Chapter II of the PCT may make a demand that the application be subject to an international preliminary examination by the appropriate International Preliminary Examining Authority ("IPEA"). This is sometimes called a PCT-II application. The ISR will be sent to the IPEA. The IPEA will draw up an opinion to which the applicant can respond with argument or amendment prior to the IPEA drawing up an International Preliminary Examination Report ("IPER") which is sent to WIPO and the applicant. Then those countries which the applicant has elected to receive the IPER (which must be countries which have acceded to Chapter II and are called "Elected States") will receive the IPER from WIPO and the international PCT phase ends. The IPER constitutes a preliminary opinion on the patentability of the invention and is not binding on the patent offices of the Elected States ("the Elected Offices").

The PCT complements the Paris Convention which is concerned with rationalising the *substantive* patent laws of countries. However, it specifically states that no provision of the Treaty is to be interpreted as diminishing the rights of any national or resident of a country which is party to the Paris Convention.[11]

The PCT procedure is now explained in more detail. The legislation for the PCT is contained in the treaty itself and the Implementing Regulations.[12] For practitioners, WIPO has published a looseleaf "PCT Applicant's Guide" which is continually updated.[13]

(b) International application

(i) Filing of international applications

2.005 International applications must be filed with the national office of the Contracting State for which the applicant is a national or resident of.[14] This office is called the Receiving Office.[15] The application must be on a printed form provided by the Receiving Office or WIPO.[16] This provides a comprehensive check-list and should be completed carefully with the assistance of the guide-notes.[17]

If the applicant wishes to make a PCT-II application, *i.e.* obtain an International Preliminary Examination Report in prosecuting his appli-

[11] Art. 1(2), PCT.

[12] The abbreviation "PCTr" is used to denote a rule in the Implementing Regulations.

[13] This is available at most national patent offices and copies can be obtained direct from WIPO, 34 Chemin des Colombettes, CH–1211 Geneva, Switzerland

[14] PCTr 19(1). Contracting States can make arrangements that nationals or those who reside in a Contracting State can file at another Contracting State's patent office. Thus, Switzerland acts as Receiving Office for Liechtenstein.

[15] Art. 10 PCT.

[16] PCTr 3. Certain Receiving Offices have telegraphic, facsimile and teleprinter facilities for filing. The reader should consult the PCT's Applicant's Guide.

[17] An example of the prescribed form can be seen in the PCT's Applicant Guide.

cation in the Elected States, then the applicant must be a resident or national of a Contracting State which is bound by Chapter II of the PCT and the Receiving Office must act for a Contracting State bound by Chapter II.[18]

The following information is required:

a) the title of the invention;
b) a petition that the application be processed according to the PCT;
c) the designation of at least one Contracting State;[19]
d) the name and state of the applicant and if applicable, his agent;[20]
e) the name of the inventor if such information is required by a law of one of the Designated States at the time of filing;[21]
f) a priority claim if applicable;[22]
g) choice of type of protection;[23]
h) an abstract, a description, a claim or claims and drawings where required;[24]
i) a signature by the applicant.[25]

(ii) Language of international application

2.006 The international application must be in a language permitted by the Receiving Office. This varies but must be one of the following languages: English, French, German, Dutch, Japanese, Russian, Danish, Finnish, Icelandic, Swedish, Spanish and Norwegian.[26] The languages that are allowed for each European Receiving Office are set out in the table at the end of this section.

If the international application is not filed in English, French, German, Japanese, Russian or Spanish, then the ISA will prepare an English translation of the international application and is entitled to charge a fee for this.[27] Accordingly, the applicant may well be advised to prepare documentation in one of the above languages if the Receiving Office permits a choice of languages for the international application.

[18] Art. 31(2)(a), PCTr 14, 18.
[19] Alternatively, the applicant can choose to designate countries via a regional patent treaty — Art 45. The EPC is a regional treaty within Art. 45 of the PCT.
[20] Whether an agent is required or not depends on each Contracting State. For European countries, see Table at 2.022.
[21] Art. 4(1)(v) PCT, PCTr 4.1(a)(v).
[22] See PCTr 4.10.
[23] If not stipulated, the application will be deemed to be for a patent.
[24] Art. 3(2), 4 and 11, PCT. Detailed rules as to the requirements of the application are given in PCTr 3, 4.
[25] PCTr 4.15.
[26] Art. 3(4), PCTr 12.
[27] PCTr 48.3(b).

(iii) Procedure upon receipt of application

2.007 The Receiving Office, after satisfying itself that the formalities have been complied will notify the applicant and WIPO. Furthermore, it will keep one copy of the application ("the home copy"), send one copy to WIPO ("the record copy") and another copy to the competent International Search Authority ("the search copy"). The record copy must be sent within 13 months of the priority date.[28] The Receiving Office will give an international filing date to the application which is deemed to be a regular national filing as defined by the Paris Convention and thus acts as the priority date.[29]

(iv) Contents of the international application

2.008 The description must disclose the invention in a manner sufficiently clear and complete for the invention to be carried out by a person skilled in the art.[30] It must specify the technical field to which the invention relates and the background art. Further it must disclose the invention as claimed and state the advantageous effects, if any, of the invention with reference to the background art. Where a Designated State requires a "best mode" for carrying out the invention, then this must be set out as well. If it is not already clear, it must be shown how the invention is capable of being exploited industrially.

The claim or claims must define the matter for which protection is sought, they must be clear and concise and must be fully supported by the description.[31] Drawings must be provided where they are necessary for an understanding of the invention.[32] General claims by reference to the description or drawings are not permitted.[33] Claims must identify those features which form part of the prior art and must contain a characterising portion stating precisely the technical features which in combination with the "prior art" features, the patent application is designed to protect.[34] Dependent claims are permissible as are dependent claims which refer to more than one other claim provided they refer to such claims in the alternative. However, multiple dependent claims cannot serve as a basis for any other multiple claim.[35]

The application must relate to only one invention.[36]

[28] PCTr 22.1.
[29] Art. 11(4) PCT.
[30] Art. 5 PCT.
[31] Art. 6 PCT.
[32] Art. 7.
[33] PCTr 6.
[34] PCTr 6.3. Generally this rule is not enforced in the International Phase.
[35] PCTr 6.4. For example, it is permissible to have a Claim 7 which is based on an inventive feature - Claims 1 to 6. However, it is not permissible to have a Claim 8 which is based on Claims 1 to 7 plus an inventive feature as Claim 7 is itself a multiple dependent claim.
[36] PCTr 13.

(v) Claiming priority

2.009 The PCT permits the claiming of priority from one or more earlier applications.[37] The substantive requirements are governed by Article 4 of the Stockholm Act of the Paris Convention. Thus, there is a grace period of 12 months during which the applicant may claim the priority of an earlier application.[38] The applicant may designate the same Contracting State from which it is claiming priority by reason of an earlier application in that state. Where in an international application, the priority of one or more national applications filed in or for a designated State is claimed or where the priority of an international application having designated only one State is claimed, the conditions for and the effect of the priority claim in that State is governed by the national law of that State.[39] A copy of the priority document must be provided within 16 months of the priority date to WIPO or the Receiving Office.[40]

(vi) Defects in the application

2.010 If the application is found by the Receiving Office not to have complied with the above formalities, then it must invite the applicant to file the required correction.[41] In most circumstances, the international filing date is then deemed to be the date of receipt of the required corrections.[42] The late payment of fees does not affect the deemed filing date although it may result in the application being deemed to have been withdrawn.[43]

(vii) Designation of contracting states

2.011 The application must designate all states where the applicant requires patent protection.[44] The applicant can make "precautionary designations" provided that at least one specific designation is made. These will then become specific designations provided that they are confirmed before the expiry of 15 months from the priority date, otherwise they will be deemed to have withdrawn.[45] This gives the applicant time to consider which states he wishes to designate, as designation fees only become payable for such states when they are confirmed.

Importantly, in Europe, one cannot designate Belgium, France, Greece, Italy or Ireland as national applications. They can only be desig-

[37] Art. 8 PCT.
[38] *ibid.*
[39] Art. 8(2)(b).
[40] PCTr 17.
[41] Art. 11(2)(a) PCT.
[42] Art. 11(2)(a), 14 PCT, PCTr 20.
[43] Art. 112, 14, PCTr 27. See para. 2.021.
[44] Art. 4 PCT.
[45] PCTr 4.9(b).

nated for a European patent via the European Patent Convention.[46] In such circumstances, one should designate the European Patent Office as the Designated Office for a European Patent in the application form.[47]

(c) International search

2.012 Each application is subject to an international search by an International Searching Authority ("ISA"). The relevant ISA is that prescribed by the Receiving Office.[48] The object of the search is to discover relevant prior art.[49] The ISA is usually a national patent office or an institution like the EPO. The ISA will not carry out a search if the international application relates to a subject-matter which it is not required to search. These categories correspond to inventions generally considered unpatentable by national laws. These include scientific and mathematical theories; plant or animal varieties; methods for treatment of the human or animal body and computer programs.[50] Furthermore, if more than one invention has been claimed for, the ISA may ask for additional fees to be paid in respect of each additional invention.

The ISA will translate the international application into English if it is not in English, French, German, Japanese, Spanish or Russian.[51] The ISA is entitled to charge a fee for this.[52]

An international search report ("ISR") will then be drawn up by the ISA within 3 months of receipt of the search copy by the ISA or 9 months from the priority date whichever is the later.[53] A copy is sent to the applicant and WIPO.[54] The report must be in the language in which the International Application is to be published.[55] Furthermore, if the report is not in English, WIPO will, free of charge, prepare an English translation.[56]

The ISA is under a duty to look at certain prior art.[57] This consists of

[46] These countries have taken advantage of Art. 45(2) PCT which allows the national law of an Elected or Designated State which belongs to a regional treaty to provide that such designation or election in an international application shall have the effect of an indication of the wish to obtain a regional patent under the regional patent treaty. It should be noted that the ultimate effect is the same as a European patent under the EPC results in the granting of national patents.

[47] See Art. 45(1). The application then becomes a Euro-PCT application. This is discussed below, at para. 2.099 *et seq.*

[48] Art. 16, PCTr 35. See table below, at para. 2.022.

[49] Art. 15, 16.

[50] PCTr 39. The ISA will search for prior art in computer programs if it is equipped to do so (see PCTr 39.1 (vi)).

[51] PCTr 48.3(b).

[52] *ibid.*

[53] Art. 18, PCTr 42.

[54] Art. 18, PCTr 45.

[55] PCTr 43.4 For language of publication, see below, at para. 2.014.

[56] PCTr 45.

[57] Art. 15(4), PCTr 34.

national and regional patent documents.[58] The Report must contain the citations of documents considered to be relevant and list the fields searched.[59] Copies of the cited documents may be sent to the applicant or the Receiving Office upon request upon payment of the costs of the ISA in preparing and mailing the documents.[60]

(d) Amendment of the claims

2.013 The applicant has one opportunity to amend the claims upon receipt of the International Search Report.[61] The amendments may not go beyond the disclosure in the international application as filed.[62] The applicant has an opportunity to file a brief statement explaining the amendments.[63] Such amendments must be made within two months of receipt of the International Search Report or 16 months from the priority date whichever time limit expires later.[64] If the applicant is to submit a demand for preliminary examination, he should file amendments with the demand.[65]

(e) Publication of the application

2.014 WIPO must publish the application in the form of a pamphlet promptly after the expiry of 18 months from the priority date of the application along with the search report and amendments.[66] If the search report or amendments of claims are not ready, this does not prevent the application being published. However, these will be published later.[67]

The application is published in the language it was filed in if such language was English, German, Japanese, Russian or Spanish. Otherwise the application is only published in English.[68] The ISA is responsible for preparing this English translation and may charge a fee for the translation.[69] If the application is published in a language other than English, the International Bureau will prepare English translations free of charge

[58] These are stipulated to include international patents and published patent applications, and national patents and published applications of France in or after 1920, Germany, the Soviet Union, Switzerland, the United Kingdom and the USA; inventors' certificates of the Soviet Union; utility certificates of France and patents and published applications in English, German, French and Spanish which have been made available to the ISA — PCTr 34.
[59] PCTr 43.
[60] Art. 20, PCTr 44.3.
[61] Art. 19.
[62] If the national law of a Designated State permits amendments to go beyond such disclosure, then failure to comply with such a requirement has no consequence in that state—Art. 19(3).
[63] Art. 19, PCTr 46.4.
[64] PCTr 46.
[65] PCTr 53, 62. If the demand has already been sent off, then he should file the amendments with the IPEA at the same time as he files the amendments with the International Bureau.
[66] Art. 21, PCTr 48.
[67] PCTr 48.2.
[68] PCTr 48.3.
[69] PCTr 48.3.

of the title, abstract and the ISR. These are published in both English and the language of filing.[70]

The applicant may ask the International Bureau to publish the application before the expiry of the 18 month period. The advantage of doing so is that WIPO must communicate to the national patent offices of Designated States promptly after publication.[71] Thus this expedites the process.

The application will not be published if it is deemed withdrawn or notice of its withdrawal is received by the International Bureau before technical preparations for publication have been completed.[72] Generally, technical preparations are completed by the 15th day before the date of publication.[73] The notice of withdrawal may state that withdrawal is to be effective only on condition that international publication can be avoided.[74]

The effect of publication is that provisional protection for the applicant in a Designated State may arise as with the national publication of un-examined national applications.[75] However, Contracting States can (and usually will) make such provisional protection run from the time that a translation of the International application into the language in which national applications are published has been published, made available to the public or transmitted to the potential infringer.[76]

(f) Communication to designated offices

2.015 The international application along with the international search report must be communicated by the International Bureau to each Designated Office (unless the latter waives such requirements).[77] This must be done promptly after publication of the international application or in any event within 19 months of the priority date.[78] The applicant is notified of the states that the international application has been sent to. The application is sent in the language in which it was published or, at the request of the Designated Office, the language in which it was filed or both.[79]

(g) Copy, translation and fee to designated offices—national phase

2.016 Not later than the expiry of 20 months from the priority date, the applicant must furnish a copy of the international application (unless already provided by WIPO) and a translation into an official language of the

[70] PCTr 48.3(c).
[71] PCTr 47.
[72] Art. 21(5). An application will be deemed to have been withdrawn if it does not comply with the requirements of the PCT and its Implementing Regulations and the applicant has failed to notify the relevant body of the corrections—see PCTr 20.7.
[73] See PCT's Applicant Guide, Vol. I, International Phase, s. 240.
[74] See PCT's Applicant Guide, Vol. I, International Phase, s. 376.
[75] Art. 29(1).
[76] Art. 29(2). See table, para. 2.022.
[77] Art. 20, PCTr 47.1.
[78] PCTr 47.1(b).
[79] PCTr 47.3.

Designated Office and the national fee to each of the Designated Offices.[80] National laws may allow for a longer period.[81] The Designated Office may also ask for translations of the request and, if there are any amendments to the claims, the claims as filed and claims as amended.[82] As stated earlier, provisional protection may not be available for the international application until such a translation has been published, made available or transmitted to a potential infringer.[83]

The international application now enters the national phase and further prosecution is between the applicant and the national patent office of each Designated State. The Designated Office will not process or examine the international application until the expiry of the period in which the translation should have been provided and the national fee paid.[84] If the applicant makes an express request that the office process or examine the application, then it may do so before the expiry of such a period.[85]

The Designated Office may review the refusal of an international filing date or a deemed withdrawal by the Receiving Office, or a deemed withdrawal by the International Bureau because the Receiving Office has failed to send a record copy to the International Bureau.[86] If the Designated Office finds that the refusal or deemed withdrawal resulted from an error or omission on behalf of the Receiving Office or International Bureau, it may treat the application as if such error or omission had not occurred.[87] Furthermore, the Designated Office itself must not reject an international application without giving the applicant the opportunity to correct the said application as if it were a national application.[88]

The applicant will usually be permitted to further amend the claims during the prosecution of the application before the national patent office.[89]

(h) International preliminary examination—chapter II PCT

2.017 An applicant who is a national or resident of a Contracting State bound by Chapter II of the PCT and who has filed an international application at a Receiving Office which acts for a Contracting State which is bound by Chapter II may request that an International Preliminary Examination ("IPE") is undertaken by an International Preliminary Examining Auth-

[80] Art. 22, PCTr 49.
[81] Art. 22(3). In the U.K. the same time limit applies but a one month extension is available — see PAr 110(3), Generally, see table, para. 2.022. Where the EPO is a Designated Office, the period allowed is 21 months.
[82] PCTr 49.5(a).
[83] Art. 29(3).
[84] Art. 23.
[85] Art. 23(2).
[86] Art. 25(1).
[87] Art. 25(2).
[88] Art. 26.
[89] Art. 28, PCTr 52.

ority ("IPEA").[90] The IPEA will compile a report on the patentability of the international application called the International Preliminary Examination Report ("IPER"). It is important to note that the IPER is not binding on the Designated States and is essentially preliminary in nature.[91] Its usefulness is thus limited as it involves the payment of fees and national patent offices are not obliged to waive their own examination fees. Thus, it may often lead to additional expenditure for the applicant. Furthermore, the applicant may only elect Contracting States where he intends to use the results of the IPER that are party to Chapter II. This excludes Greece, Spain, Switzerland and Liechtenstein, all of whom have expressly declared under Article 64(1)(a) that Chapter II of the PCT is not applicable. However, most applicants find it useful to buy time as it gives a clearer picture of both the patentability and their own commercial position prior to substantive examination in Elected States.

The IPEA will examine the international application according to international accepted criteria for patentability and it thus gives the applicant an early opportunity to evaluate the chances of obtaining patent protection in Elected States. Also, if the IPER has been compiled by the Elected Office of an Elected State, then it will stand as the national examination report in such circumstances and the Elected Office will often refund their own examination fees. This is particularly true where the EPO is an Elected Office and has acted as the IPEA.[92]

The objective of the IPE is to formulate a preliminary and non-binding opinion on the question of whether the claimed invention appears to be novel, involves an inventive step and is industrially applicable.[93] It is not to determine whether the invention is patentable according to national law.[94]

(i) Procedure

2.018 The applicant must make a demand to WIPO for its application to be examined.[95] The demand must be in the language of the international application or if different, the language of publication.[96] It must be on a printed form and contain among the Designated States at least one State bound by Chapter II.[97] The applicant may elect States after the demand although only Designated States may become Elected States.[98] The demand must be signed by the applicant. The applicant must pay a handling fee to the IPEA.[99] Furthermore, the IPEA may require a preliminary

[90] Art. 31(2)(a).
[91] Art. 33(1).
[92] See the Euro-PCT route at para. 2.102.
[93] Art. 33.
[94] Art. 35.
[95] Art. 31.
[96] PCTr 55.
[97] Art. 31, PCTr 53.2
[98] Art. 31(4), PCTr 56.
[99] PCTr 57.

examination fee.[1] If the IPEA is not the ISA, then WIPO will send a copy of the application and the International Search Report along with any amendments to the IPEA.[2]

(ii) Substantive examination by the IPEA

2.019 The IPEA shall take into consideration all the documents cited in the international search report.[3] Everything made available by the public anywhere in the world by means of written disclosure including drawings and other illustrations is considered prior art provided that such was made available before the priority date (whether the international filing date of the application or an earlier date by which it claims priority).[4] Non-written disclosure is not taken into account by the IPEA for the purposes of what is prior art but the report must call attention to such non-written disclosure.[5] Similarly, patent and patent applications which were published after the priority date of an international application but filed before such a date are not deemed part of the prior art for the purposes of both novelty and inventive step.[6] This is important as most national laws and the EPC do take into account such publications when considering novelty but not inventive step. However, the IPER must draw attention to such applications.[7] The IPEA may consider a "mosaic" of prior art provided such a combination is obvious to a person skilled in the art.[8]

The IPEA will not carry out an IPE where the subject matter of the invention comprises of the following:

(i) scientific and mathematical theories;
(ii) plant or animal varieties or essentially biological processes for the production of plants and animals other than microbiological processes and the products of such processes;
(iii) schemes, rules or methods of doing business, performing purely mental acts or playing games;
(iv) methods for treatment of the human or animal body by surgery or therapy as well as diagnostic methods;
(v) mere presentations of information;
(vi) computer programs to the extent that the IPEA is not equipped to carry out an IPE concerning such programs.[9]

The IPEA will prepare an opinion as to the patentability of the application. The applicant is given an opportunity to make written submissions and/or to amend the application if the IPEA forms the opinion

[1] PCTr 58.
[2] PCTr 62.
[3] Art. 33(6).
[4] PCTr 64.
[5] PCTr 64.
[6] PCTr 64.3, 65.2
[7] PCTr 64.2, 70.10
[8] PCTr 65.
[9] Art. 34(4)(a)(i), PCTr 67.

that the application is not novel, obvious or not capable of industrial application or is otherwise defective.[10]

An international preliminary examination report must be prepared within 28 months from the priority date or within nine months if the demand for preliminary examination was filed after the expiry of 19 months from the priority date.[11] The report states whether the criteria of novelty, inventive step and industrial applicability have been fulfilled.[12] Furthermore, it will cite relevant documents. Copies of the report are sent to the International Bureau and the applicant.[13] The IPER is prepared in the language of publication of the international application.[14] The International Bureau will then send the IPER to each Elected Office and where necessary, if the IPER is not in an official language of the Elected Office, the latter may request that it be translated into English.[15]

(iii) Translation and national fee to elected offices—national phase chapter II

2.020 Provided that the election of any Contracting State has been effected prior to the expiry of the nineteenth month from the priority date, the applicant may furnish a copy of a translation of the international application not later than the expiry of 30 months from the priority date[16] or a longer period if stipulated by national laws.[17] Generally, amendments of the international application will be permissible during examination of the application before the national patent office.[18] Furthermore, a national fee will usually be payable.

(i) Fees under the PCT

2.021 There are three fees which must be paid in connection with every international application. Firstly, there is the "transmittal fee" which is payable to the Receiving Office for its tasks.[19] Secondly, there is the search fee which is payable to the ISA.[20] Thirdly, there is the "international fee" which is payable to the International Bureau—this comprises of the basic fee and designation fees.[21] Each designation of a state requires a designation fee to be paid although the maximum amount due is 10 designation fees. However, designation fees are not required for precautionary designations until they are confirmed.[22] In such circumstances, the rule con-

[10] Art. 34(2)(b), PCTr 66.
[11] PCTr 69.
[12] Art. 35(2), PCTr 70.6.
[13] PCTr 71.1.
[14] PCTr 70.16 and see above, para. 2.014.
[15] Art. 36, PCTr 72.
[16] Art. 39.
[17] Art. 39(1)(b). See table, para. 2.022.
[18] See PCT's Applicant Guide, Vol. II, National Phase, s. 58.
[19] PCTr 14.
[20] PCTr 16.1.
[21] PCTr 15.1, 96.
[22] PCTr 4.9(c), 15.5.

cerning maximum payment of 10 designation fees does not apply and a confirmation fee is also required.

All fees must be paid to the Receiving Office within one month of receipt of the international application.[23] The exception to this rule is that designation fees are payable within one year of the date of receipt of the international application if it does not claim priority from an earlier application or if it does claim priority, then it must be paid within one year from the date of priority or one month from the date of receipt of the international application, whichever is the later.[24] Designation and confirmation fees for precautionary designations must be paid before the expiry of 15 months from the priority date.[25]

If the applicant fails to pay designation fees for specifically designated States, the International Bureau will invite the applicant to pay the amount and a late payment fee within one month of the date of the invitation.[26] If he fails to do so, then all or some of the Designations are withdrawn.[27] The International Bureau will not invite the applicant to pay designation fees for precautionary designations.

If an IPER is sought, a handling fee and preliminary examination fee will be payable.[28]

(j) Table of European Contracting States of PCT

(See Table on page 50)

4. European Patent Convention

(a) Fundamentals of EPC

2.023 The European Patent Convention came about from a political initiative for a centralised system of granting patents in Europe, with all the attendant economies of scale and the avoidance of the duplicated work of several national patent offices. Certain countries, especially France, felt the need for a system which was more complete and rigorous than the PCT which had been signed but had not come into force and thus in 1973 in Munich, the EPC was born and entered into force in October 1977. Austria, Belgium, Denmark, France, Germany, Greece, Ireland, Italy, Liechtenstein,[38] Luxembourg, Monaco, Netherlands, Portugal, Spain, Sweden, Switzerland and United Kingdom have all now ratified the EPC. Furthermore, EEA countries are obliged to accede to the EPC as part of their duties under the EEA Agreement.[39]

[23] PCTr 14, 14.4, 16.1(f).
[24] PCTr 15.4(b).
[25] PCTr 4.9(b), (c), 15.5.
[26] PCTr 16bis.1,2.
[27] *ibid.*
[28] PCTr 57.58
[38] A designation of Liechtenstein will automatically invoke a designation for Switzerland and vice versa — [1980] OJEPO 407.
[39] See Introduction Chapter.

Contracting State and whether bound by Chapter II	Language of int'l application where national patent office of C.S. is Receiving Office	Prescribed ISA where national patent office of C.S. is Receiving Office	Prescribed IPEA where national patent office of C.S. is Receiving Office	Agent required?	Expiry of time (for provision of translation when Designated State (from priority date)	Expiry of time for provision of translation when Elected State (from priority date)	Language of translation where C.S. is Designated or Elected
Austria-II	German	EPO	EPO	YES if non-resident	20 ms	30 ms	German
Belgium-II[29]	Dutch, English, French, German	EPO	EPO	NO	n/a	n/a	n/a
Bulgaria-II	English, Russian	Russian PO or EPO	Russian PO or EPO	YES if non-resident	21 ms	31 ms	Bulgarian
Czech Republic-II	English, French, German	EPO	EPO	YES	21	30	Czech or Slovak
Denmark-II	Danish, English	EPO or Swedish PO	EPO or Swedish PO	YES if non-resident	20	30	Danish
Finland-II	English, Finnish or Swedish	EPO or Swedish PO	EPO or Swedish PO	YES if non-resident	20	30	Finnish
France-II[30]	French	EPO	EPO	YES if non-resident	n/a	n/a	n/a
Germany-II	German	EPO	EPO	YES if non-resident	20	30	German
Greece[31]	English, French, German	EPO	n/a	YES if non-resident	n/a	n/a	n/a
Hungary-II	English, French, German	Austrian PO or Russian PO	Austrian PO or Russian PO	NO	21	30	Hungarian
Ireland-II[31a]	English	EPO	EPO	YES if non-resident	n/a	n/a	n/a

Contracting State and whether bound by Chapter II	Language of int'l application where national patent office of C.S. is Receiving Office	Prescribed ISA where national patent office of C.S. is Receiving Office	Prescribed IPEA where national patent office of C.S. is Receiving Office	Agent required?	Expiry of time (for provision of translation when Designated State (from priority date)	Expiry of time for provision of translation when Elected State (from priority date)	Language of translation where C.S. is Designated or Elected
ITALY-II[32]	English, French, German	EPO	EPO	NO	n/a	n/a	n/a
LUXEMBOURG-II	French, German	EPO	EPO	NO	20	30	French or German
MONACO-II	French	EPO	EPO	NO	20	30	French
NETHERLANDS-II	Dutch, English	EPO	EPO	Yes if non-resident	20	30	Dutch
NORWAY-II	English, Norwegian	EPO or Swedish PO	EPO or Swedish PO	Yes if non-resident	20	30	Norwegian
POLAND-II	English, French, German	EPO	EPO	YES if foreign national	20	30[33]	Polish
PORTUGAL-II	English, French, German	EPO	EPO	YES if non-resident	20	30	Portuguese
ROMANIA-II	English, French, German, Russian	EPO, Austrian PO or Russian PO	EPO, Austrian PO or Russian PO	YES if non-resident	20	30	Roma nian
RUSSIA-III[34]	Russian	Russian PO	Russian PO	YES is non-resident	20	30	Russian
SLOVAKIA-II	English, French, German	EPO	EPO	YES	21	31	Slovak
SLOVENIA-II	English	EPO	EPO	YES if non-resident	21	31	Slovenia

Contracting State and whether bound by Chapter II	Language of int'l application where national patent office of C.S. is Receiving Office	Prescribed ISA where national patent office of C.S. is Receiving Office	Prescribed IPEA where national patent office of C.S. is Receiving Office	Agent required?	Expiry of time (for provision of translation when Designated State (from priority date)	Expiry of time for provision of translation when Elected State (from priority date)	Language of translation where C.S. is Designated or Elected
SPAIN	Spanish	EPO	n/a	YES if non-resident	20	n/a	Spanish
SWEDEN-II	Danish, English, Finnish, Norwegian, Swedish	EPO or Swedish PO	EPO or Swedish PO	YES if non-resident	20	30	Swedish
SWITZERLAND[35]	German, French	EPO	n/a	NO	n/a	n/a	n/a
UNITED KINGDOM-II[36]	English	EPO	UK PO	NO	20	30	English
EUROPEAN PATENT CONVENTION-II[37]	English, French, German	n/a	n/a	YES	21	31	English, French or German

[29] National law treats designation or election of Belgium under PCT as application under EPC with EPO as designated and/or Elected Office.
[30] National laws treats designation or election of France under PCT as application under EPC with EPO as designated and/or Elected Office.
[31] National laws treats designation or election of Greece under PCT as application under EPC with EPO as designated and/or Elected Office.
[31a] National laws treats designation or election of Ireland under PCT as application under EPC with EPO as designated and/or Elected Office.
[32] National laws treats designation or election of Italy under PCT as application under EPC with EPO as designated and/or Elected Office.
[33] Poland has recently changed this period from 20 to 30 months. It is effective for an international application with a filing date after March 1994 or where in the case of existing applications, the priority date is no earlier than July 1, 1992.
[34] Since the breakdown of the Soviet Union, only the Russian federation has joined the PCT. The information here is based on the old Soviet Union and may be inaccurate.
[35] Receiving Office for Liechtenstein nationals or residentials. National law treats designation or election of Switzerland under PCT as application under EPC and EPO as designated and/or Elected Office.
[36] Receiving Office for residents or nationals of Isle of Man and Hong Kong.
[37] For more details on the interrelationship between the EPC and the PCT, see para. 2.099 *et seq*.

(i) Scheme of the EPC

2.024 The EPC provides for a centralised prosecution up to grant at the European Patent Office ("EPO") of patent applications in respect of Member States. Once granted, it results in the grant of national patents in those Member States which were designated by the applicant. It provides for the establishment of the European Patent Office (EPO) whose headquarters are in Munich.[40] Applicants who wish to obtain national patents in Member States (called "Designated States") can make an application under the EPC to the EPO. The EPO will process the application, conduct a search on the application, publish it, examine it and if it is found patentable under the EPC, grant national patents for the Designated States. The EPC also provides for third parties to bring opposition proceedings at the EPO to revoke the European patent *in toto* within nine months from grant.[41]

Thus the applicant obtains what is often called a "bundle" of national patents in the Designated States. Once granted, the issues of validity and infringement post-grant are matters for national law and national courts although the national laws of Member States have been harmonised to a considerable extent by the EPC.[42]

(ii) EPC and harmonisation of national patent laws

2.025 The EPC determines whether a European application is patentable.[43] Moreover, Member States of the EPC are obliged to ensure that European patents:

(i) have the same effect and are subject to the same conditions as national patents in Member States;[44]

(ii) confer on its proprietor the same rights as would be conferred by a national patent;[45]

(iii) are given the same or more protection upon publication as that of a published national patent application;[46]

(iv) can only be revoked on grounds specified in the Treaty.[47] These are that the subject-matter of the European patent is not patentable; the European patent does not disclose the invention in a manner sufficiently clear and complete for it to be carried out by a person skilled in the art; the subject matter of the European patent extends beyond the content of the application as filed or if the patent was granted on a divisional application, beyond

[40] There is also an office at The Hague which will act as Receiving Office and as the Search Division.
[41] Art. 99.
[42] Art. 64(3). See below, para. 2.025.
[43] Art. 2.
[44] Art. 2.
[45] Art. 64.
[46] Art. 67.
[47] Art. 138.

the content of the earlier application as filed; the protection of the European patent has been extended or if the proprietor of the European patent is not entitled to the patent;[48]

(v) must have the same prior right effect as a national patent application and a national patent.[49]

The effect of the above requirements has meant that Member States have been compelled to harmonise their substantive patent laws in accordance with the EPC. Thus, in the United Kingdom, the Patents Act 1977 was enacted so that the U.K. could fulfil its obligations under the EPC. However, the interpretation of the EPC as to the scope of European patents and parallel national patents by national courts varies from Member State to Member State. No appeal lies from a national patent office or a court of a Member State to the Boards of Appeal of the EPO or to any other international court. Conversely, a decision from the Boards of Appeal denying patent protection cannot be appealed to a national court. This has meant that in reality, there has been no legal co-ordination of national and EPO's approach to issues of patentability and infringement. This has meant a divergence of standards applied as to patent law issues.[50]

2.026 With regard to the question of infringement, Article 69 states that the claims of a European patent determine the extent of protection conferred by the grant of a European patent. As to how this is to be interpreted by the national courts when applying it in infringement proceedings, the Protocol on the Interpretation of Article 69 of the Convention states that:

> "Article 69 should not be interpreted in the sense that the extent of the protection conferred by a European patent is to be understood as that defined by the strict, literal meaning of the wording used for the claims, the description and drawings being employed only for the purpose of resolving an ambiguity found in the claims. Neither should it be interpreted in the sense that the claims serve only as a guideline and that the actual protection conferred may extend only to what, from a consideration of the description and drawings by a person skilled in the art, the patentee has contemplated. On the contrary, it is to be interpreted as defining a position between these extremes which combines a fair protection for the patentee with a reasonable degree of certainty for third parties."

Despite this Protocol, the extent of protection and enforcement of Euro-

[48] Art. 138.

[49] Art. 139(1).

[50] For a discussion as to differences between the EPO's approach and national patent laws, see *Criteria of Patentability: Is the EPO in step with National Laws?* by Dr Axel von Hellfeld—a speech given at a conference held by ESC on February 28/March 1, 1990 at the EPO. For a more detailed comparison of the EPO and national patent office's approach to the patentability of computer-related inventions, see "Patentability of Software/Computer Related Inventions in Europe", *Hilary Pearson, Patent World* (April 1992).

pean patents in designated countries still varies and is still influenced by that country's previous patent jurisprudence although it would seem that national courts are looking more to the EPO and decisions of other Member States when they come to consider the question of infringement.[51]

Recently, two major Member States in the EPC have adopted converging approaches to infringement of European patents. Thus German and English courts, in assessing the extent of protection of the claims of a patent, have ruled that the scope of a patent must be determined by its language and that, while the extent of protection goes beyond the literal wording of the claims so as to include functional equivalents, it only includes functional equivalents which are deducible from the wording of the claims.[52] Even in the issue of infringement of national patents, there is a high degree of convergence in Member States' approaches to infringement of a patent.[53]

(iii) Fundamental features of a European patent

2.027 The essential features of a European patent is that they provide for protection for a period of 20 years from the date of filing of the application and are granted for inventions which are new, involve an inventive step and are susceptible of industrial application.[54]

Recently, the EPC has been amended so as to allow Contracting States to extend the term of a European patent, or to grant corresponding protection following immediately after the expiry of the term of the patent, in order to take account of delay caused by the invention requiring an authorisation order before it can be put on the market in a state.[55] The amendment will not come into force until two years after the ninth Contracting State has deposited its instrument of ratification or accession or the third month following the deposit of the instrument of ratification or accession by the last Contracting State to ratify.[56]

This amendment to the EPC coincides with the European Com-

[51] See Axel von Hellfeld, Enforcement of European Patents, *Patent World*, December 91/ January 1992.

[52] *PLG v. Ardon* [1995] FSR 119. This passage represents the courts conclusions after reviewing German cases including *Improver Corp v. Remington, Heavy Metal Oxidant Catalyst, Ion Analyser* and *Handle Cord for Battery* whereupon the Court stated that such an approach appeared to be more in conformity with the Protocol to Art. 69 than previous English case law based on common law. However, see the decision of Aldous J in *Assidaman Multipack Ltd v. The Mead Corporation* [1995] F.S.R. 225 where he held that the Court of Appeal's decision was either *obiter dicta or per incuriam.*

[53] See "Claim Interpretation: Europe's Patents Claims" *Managing Intellectual Property* (October 1994) p. 28.

[54] Art. 63, 53.

[55] Act Revising Art. 63 of the Convention of the Grant of European Patents (European Patent Convention) [1992] OJEPO 1.

[56] Art. 4. It is considered that this will occur around 1997 — see "Report on Diplomatic Conference on Resolution of Article 63 EPC" [1992] I.I.C. 248. However, Spain is causing difficulties in the ratification of Art. 63.

mission's Regulation on Supplementary Protection Certificates which has introduced an equivalent measure for national patents.[57]

(iv) Legal documentation of the EPC

2.028 Besides the Treaty itself, the Articles of the EPC provide for secondary legislation called Implementing Regulations.[58] These form an integral part of the Treaty but in case of conflict, the Treaty prevails.[59] Such considerations also apply to the Protocols appended to the EPC. The EPO publishes an Official Journal (OJEPO) which contains selected decisions of the Board of Appeal and Enlarged Board of Appeal and decisions and notices of the Administrative Council and President of the EPO. The EPO publishes Guidelines for the Examination in the European Patent Office which are of considerable assistance for applicants and professional representatives.[60] These are extensive but not binding. The EPO publishes considerable informational material of which "How to Get a European Patent — Guide for Applicants" is a helpful and digestible source of information. Furthermore, the EPO keeps a register known as the Register of European Patents which contain the required particulars of published European patent applications and European patents during opposition.[61] Entries made in the Register are published weekly in the European Patent Bulletin.[62]

The EPO allows for public inspection of published European patent applications upon payment of an administrative fee.[63] Access to the register is possible via telecommunications.

(v) Administration of the EPC

2.029 The EPC is run and managed by the EPO and the Administrative Council.[64] The task of the EPO is to grant European patents as supervised by the Administrative Council. Its seat is at Munich but it has a subsidiary branch at The Hague. It has five divisions — the Receiving Section which is based at The Hague; the Search Division which is responsible for drawing up European search reports — this is based at The Hague as well; the Examining Division which is responsible for the substantive examination of the application; the Opposition Division which is responsible for the examination of oppositions against any European patent and the Legal Division which is concerned with legal questions on interpretation of the EPC the Register of European Patents and the upkeep and maintenance of the list of European Patent Attorneys.[65] Furthermore, there is a two-

[57] See 2.115.
[58] Denoted as EPCr.
[59] Art. 164.
[60] Denoted as Guid.
[61] Art. 127, EPCr 92.
[62] Art. 129(a)
[63] Art. 128(4), EPCr 94.
[64] Art. 4.
[65] Art. 15 to 20.

tiered appellate structure consisting of the Board of Appeal and the Enlarged Board of Appeal. The latter hears appeals on important points of law or to ensure uniform application of the law. Only the Board of Appeal or the President of the EPO may remit a question to the EBA. The appellant has no right himself to demand a reference to the EBA but may request that a reference is made.[66]

The Administrative Council which consists of representatives of Member States is empowered under the Treaty to carry out certain administrative duties like *inter alia* the establishment of sub-offices of the EPO, the election of the President of the EPO, the fixing of financial provisions, the criteria for professional representatives who are entitled to appear before the EPO, the recruitment of employees and the accession of European states to the EPC. Furthermore, it is competent to amend the time limits laid down in the Convention and the Implementing Regulations.[67]

The EPO essentially finances itself from fees for applications (including renewal fees for pending applications) and payments made by Contracting States in respect of renewal fees for European Patents levied in those states.[68]

(vi) Relationship of EPC to international conventions and national patents

2.030 The European Patent Convention (EPC) is a regional convention for the grant of patents in Europe.[69] It constitutes a special agreement within the Paris Convention and a regional treaty within the Patent Co-operation Treaty.[70] European patents can be granted on the basis of an international application filed in accordance with the PCT (called a Euro-PCT filing).[71] In the Euro-PCT route, the initial part of the procedure is governed in accordance with the provisions of the PCT whereas the regional phase before the EPO as a designated Office or elected Office is governed mainly by the EPC. Besides being a Designated or Elected Office, the EPO will act as a Receiving Office as well as an International Searching Authority and Preliminary Examining Authority under the PCT.

Furthermore, the EPC forms a basis for the Community Patent Convention (CPC).[72] Thus, when and if the CPC comes into force, any application for a European patent which designates any E.C. country will be treated as an application for a Community patent instead of a national patent.[73]

[66] Art. 21, 22, 112.
[67] Art. 33, 35.
[68] Article 37.
[69] Only European countries can accede to the EPC — Art. 166.
[70] See Preamble to the EPC and Art. 150–158 EPC. See "Unnamed patent application" I.P.D. 4085, September 1981 for an analysis of the relevance of the EPC being a special agreement within the meaning of Art. 19 of the Paris Convention in relation to priority rights.
[71] See Art. 150 to 158, EPCr 104, Guid. A-VII; E-XI.
[72] [1990] OJEPO 224. On CPC, see below, at para. 2.111.
[73] CPC Art. 2(1).

(b) Substantive requirements for a European patent

2.031 A European patent may be granted for an invention which is new, involves an inventive step and which is susceptible of industrial application.[74]

(i) Novelty

2.032 An invention is considered new if it does not form part of the state of the art.[75] The state of the art is held to comprise everything made available to the public by means of a written or oral description by use or in any other way before the date of filing or priority date (whichever is the earliest).[76] This is stipulated to include European patent applications filed before but published after the date of filing.[77] For the purposes of examination before the EPO, the state of the art will mainly consist of the documents listed in the search report. Examination for novelty will then amount to consideration of the prior art and general knowledge. Examiners are not entitled to use their own general knowledge unless it can be proven.[78]

2.033 *Availability to the public*—the requirement of "availability to the public" will be satisfied if it is possible for members of the public to gain knowledge of the matter and there is no obligation of confidentiality.[79] The requirement of "availability to the public" is an absolute one. Thus, it is not necessary to show that the public has actually seen the prior art provided that it is available to the public.[80] In certain circumstances, it may be unclear as to whether there has been a disclosure to the public. The TBA has held that "public" in this context means "skilled person".[81] Thus, an oral disclosure before a circle of persons who were unable to understand the technical teaching at a lecture will not constitute an enabling disclosure as they would have been unable to reproduce such information before other skilled members of the public.[82] When considering the issue of availability to the public, careful regard must be had to the circumstances of the case where such an issue arises. Thus, if a patent application lays claim to the chemical composition of a product, it is not anticipated merely because the product has existed before the filing date and been available to the public as the claim is to the chemical structure of the product and not the product itself. In such circumstances, it

[74] Art. 52(1).
[75] Art. 54(1).
[76] Art. 54(2). Art. 89.
[77] Art. 54(3). This provision only applies if there is a Designated State in common between the "prior art" and the application in issue — Art. 54(4). The EPO will permit different claims for those states affected by the rule — EPCr 87, Guid. C IV 6.3. Note that such prior applications are not to be taken into account for the purpose of inventive step — Art. 56.
[78] T–157/87, *Kubat*: [1989] EPOR 221.
[79] See Guid. C IV 5.1–2, D V 3.1–2.
[80] T–444/88 *Japan Styrene Paper*: I.P.D. 13222, December 1990.
[81] T877/90 *Hooper/T-Cell Growth factor*: [1993] EPOR 6, TBA.
[82] *ibid.*

must be shown that the chemical composition of the product can be analysed and reproduced by the skilled person.[83] If such can be ascertained, it does not matter whether or not the public should have a reason for analysing the product.[84] Thus, the likelihood of investigating the chemical structure and/or the burden involved in doing so is irrelevant.[85] In the case of "selection" patents, this analysis must be somewhat modified as the requirement of availability to the public will only be satisfied if the skilled person would have seriously contemplated making the selection from the prior art.[86]

Certain disclosures of the invention itself prior to the date of filing are treated under the EPC as not being prejudicial provided they occurred no earlier than six months before the filing of the European patent application. These are oral disclosures due to evident abuse in relation to the applicant or his legal predecessor or the display of the invention at an official or officially recognised exhibition falling within the terms of the Convention on international exhibitions signed at Paris on November 22, 1928.[87]

As mentioned above, for the purposes of novelty but not obviousness, European patent application filed before the priority date but published afterwards are treated as constituting the prior art.[88] Where a document is published during the priority interval, this will be treated as prior art to the extent that priority is not validly claimed.[89] With regard to prior national rights where there has been no disclosure prior to the priority date, these are dealt with after grant of the patent according to the national patent law of the relevant Contracting State.[90]

Where the application claims a substance for a particular purpose, a hidden or secret use may validly be claimed as novel even where the product is known.[91]

2.034 *Enabling disclosure*—with regard to chemical compounds, the Guidelines state that disclosure in prior documents, together with knowledge generally available on the effective date of the documents, must

[83] *Availability to the public: Reference by the President of the EPO*: [1993] EPOR 241, EBA. See also TBA *Prior Use/PACKARD* [1995] OJEPO VI/3/1995 where the TBA stated that for the chemical structure to be available to the public, there must be "direct and unambiguous access to such information by means of known analytical techniques which were available for use by a skilled person before the filing date".

[84] *ibid.*

[85] TBA Prior use/PACKARD [1995] OJEPO VI/3/95.] See para. 2.059 for "selection" patents.

[86] T–366/90, *Unilever/Interesterification process*: [1993] EPOR 383, TBA.

[87] Art. 55. The EPO publishes annually in the OJEPO a list of exhibitions falling within the terms of the Convention which have been registered by the International Exhibition Bureau.

[88] Art. 54(3), 56.

[89] G3/93 *Opinion* dated 16/4/94 [1995] OJEPO 18, [1994] EPOR 521 Vol. 10/XV. See also Schlich "Publish and be Damned" [1991] 7 E.I.P.R. 327 for a criticism of this decision.

[90] Art. 139(2); Guid. C–IV 6(a). See T–4/80, *BAYER/Polyether Polyols*: [1979–1985] Vol. B EPOR 260. [1982] OJEPO 149 & T–550/88, *Mobil Oil*: April 1992 IPD 15045.

[91] G02/88, *Mobil Oil III*: [1990] OJEPO 93, [1990] EPOR 73.

enable the skilled person to make the claimed invention. It is not sufficient for prior art merely to disclose the invention. It must also *enable* the person skilled in the art to make the invention in order to rebut a claim of novelty. Thus, the Guidelines incorporate a judgment from the TBA whereby they said:

> "It is the view of the Board that a document does not effectively disclose a chemical compound, even though it states the structure and the steps by which it is produced, if the skilled person is unable to find out from the document or from common general knowledge how to obtain the required starting material or intermediates. Information, which can only be obtained after a comprehensive search, is not to be regarded as part of common general knowledge."[92]

Thus if a prior document discloses the structure of a chemical substance and the method for its manufacture, this will not anticipate a claim for the chemical product if the starting and intermediate products required to manufacture the chemical substance are not available from the document or general knowledge.[93]

2.035 *"Mosaicing" prior art*—the Guidelines make it clear that in considering novelty, it is not permissible to combine items of prior art together. However, material referred to in a document is treated as being incorporated into that document.[94] Claimed subject-matter which is derived directly and unambiguously from a prior art document will not be novel but care must be taken not to treat the teaching of a document as including well-known equivalents in considering the novelty as opposed to the obviousness of a claimed invention.[95]

(ii) Inventive Step

2.036 An invention will be considered as involving an inventive step if having regard to the state of the art, it is not obvious to a person skilled in the art.[96] The prior art is not to be taken for the purposes of inventiveness as including national prior rights and earlier European patent applications which are published after the filing date of the application in question.[97]

The Guidelines state:

> "The term obviously means that which does not go beyond the normal progress of technology but merely follows plainly or logically from the prior art, *i.e.* something which does not involve the exercise of any skill or ability beyond that to be expected of the person skilled in the art. In considering inventive step, as distinct from

[92] T–206/83, *ICI*: [1987] OJEPO 5; [1986] EPOR 232.
[93] T–206/83, *ICI*: [1987] OJEPO 5; [1986] EPOR 232.
[94] Guid. C-IV 7.1. See T–153/85, *Amoco*: [1988] OJEPO 1; [1988] EPOR 116.
[95] Guid. C-IV 7.2.
[96] Art. 56.
[97] Art. 54, 56, 139(2).

novelty, it is fair to construe any published document in the light of subsequent knowledge and to have regard to all the knowledge generally available to the person skilled in the art at the priority date of the claim."[98]

The EPO has also stated that:

> "patents granted under the EPC should have an inventive step sufficient to ensure to the patentees a fair degree of certainty that if contested the validity of the patents will be upheld by national courts. This standard should therefore anyhow not be below what may be considered as average amongst the standards presently applied by the Contracting States."[99]

Such an approach is clearly important as national courts have the rights to revoke European patents. EPO examiners have little idea or experience of national courts' approach to validity of patents.

It is almost always a step in determining whether the invention as claimed has an inventive step to state the problem and the associated effect which follows from the use of the claimed invention. This requires that the nature of the problem should be determined on the basis of objective criteria and requires the assessment of the technical success *vis-à-vis* the state of the closest art.[1] The issue of obviousness is much more case-dependent than the issue of novelty. Thus, the assistance that other cases can give is limited. However, the approach of the EPO in certain areas can be ascertained from its Guidelines which gives examples of what is to be considered inventive or obvious and also from cases of the Boards of Appeal.

2.037 *Objective approach*—as in the case of novelty, inventive step is an objective concept. Thus when assessing inventive step, the case history of the invention is irrelevant. As the TBA said:

> "As in the case of novelty, inventive step is an objective concept. Objectivity in the assessment of inventive step is achieved by starting out from the objectively prevailing state of the art in the light of which the problem is determined which the invention addresses from an objective point of view . . . and consideration is given to the question or obviousness of the disclosed solution to this problem as seen by the man skilled in the art and having those capabilities which can be objectively expected of him. This also avoids the retrospective approach which inadmissibly makes use of knowledge of the invention, as feared by the applicant."[2]

[98] Guid. C-IV 9.3.
[99] *AECI Ltd.*, IPD 4120 December 1991/January 1992.
[1] T–1/80, *BAYER/Carbonless Copy Paper*: [1981] OJEPO 206, [1979–1985] Vol. B 250; T–20/81, *Shell*: [1982] OJEPO 217; [1979–1985] Vol. B EPOR 335; T–184/82, *Mobil*: [1979–1985] Vol. C EPOR 690; IPD 7091, November 1984, TBA.
[2] T–24/81 *BASF AG*: [1983] OJEPO 133; IPD 6020, April 1982.

Thus, in determining the issue of inventive step, one must consider the problem which the invention deals with and what the skilled person without knowledge of the patent application would have done. For example, where an application related to a passivating agent for passivating contaminated metals on a cracking catalyst using a combination of antimony and tin, the use of antimony and tin compounds separately as passivating agents was known. The TBA held that whilst it would appear to be obvious to try a combination of antimony and tin as a passivating agent, such was not the proper question to ask but whether the skilled person would have done so with any expectation of solving the ambitious technical problem underlying the patent in suit. The TBA held that in such a case, the skilled person would not have expected that the combination would have solved the problem. Furthermore, the combination of antimony and tin was not the first choice in view of the almost unlimited number of unexplored combinations in the catalytic field.[3]

2.038 *Man skilled in the art*—the person skilled in the art will be presumed to be an ordinary practitioner aware of what was common general knowledge in the art at the relevant date. He will be presumed to have had access to everything in the state of the art including documents cited in the search report.[4] Where it was contended that a prior art document disclosing a particular type of perfumed pack for volatile flavourants was not addressed to a skilled man considering the problem of perfuming highly reactive washing powder, the EPO held that the state of the art to be considered is absolute and not to be confined to the alleged addressee of the document.[5] However, it may not be obvious to the skilled person to use such knowledge. A man skilled in a particular art will be deemed to be conversant with neighbouring fields of technology but not more remote fields.[6] The skilled person does not have to be the same person for all aspects of obviousness. Thus, if it is obvious to a person skilled in a particular field to consult a specialist in another neighbouring field to solve a problem, then that specialist will become the man skilled in the art. Thus, in considering whether it was obvious to use glass fibre to replace components in a conveyor-belt cleaning apparatus, the skilled man was the materials specialist and not the conveyor-belt specialist.[7]

2.039 *"Mosaicing" prior art*—it may be claimed that an invention is obvious because the essential elements of it have been anticipated or obvious and thus the whole invention is obvious. The Guidelines state that the invention claimed must be considered as a whole and thus such

[3] T–274/87, *Phillips*: [1989] EPOR 207; IPD 11054, October 1988.
[4] Guid. C-IV 9.6.
[5] T–107/82, *Unilever's Application*: [1979–85] Vol. B 534, IPD 6114.
[6] See T–176/84, *Mobius*: [1986] OJEPO 50: [1986] EPOR 117; T–28/87, *Kerber*: [1989] OJEPO 383; [1989] EPOR 377.
[7] Guid. C-IV 9.6; T–32/81, *Fives-Cail Babcock SA*: [1982] OJEPO 225, [1979–1985] Vol. B EPOR 377; IPD 5086, October 1982, TBA.

an approach would not be correct unless the essential features bear no functional relationship to each other and the invention as a whole is merely a juxtaposition of such features.[8] The converse is that the EPO will permit the combining of two or more documents in order to defeat a claim of inventive step but only if such a combination would have been obvious to the person skilled in the art at the effective priority date of the claim under examination.[9] If this is the case, a person skilled in the art is deemed to be capable of distinguishing between those features in a prior art document that are relevant to the problem he is trying to solve and those features which are irrelevant.[10]

In contrast, an applicant seeking to prove inventive step can consider various documents together mosaically to demonstrate a general trend pointing away from the invention.[11] Similarly, a skilled person is unlikely to combine two documents if the methods that they teach point in different directions especially where one document refers to a technique of more than 50 years old.[12]

2.040 *Ex post facto analysis*—the EPO Guidelines warn against examiners holding that an invention is obvious with the benefit of hindsight. Thus, it says:

> "It should be remembered that an invention which at first sight appears obvious might in fact involve an inventive step. Once a new idea has been formulated it can often be shown theoretically how it might be arrived at, starting from something known, by a series of apparently easy steps. The examiner should be wary of *ex post facto* analysis of this kind. He should always bear in mind that the documents produced in the search have, of necessity, been obtained with foreknowledge of what matter constitutes the alleged invention."[13]

Thus, the TBA criticised an opponent who appealed by saying that:

> "in seeking to analyze retrospectively how a skilled person might have been able to arrive at the concept of the invention in two mental stages, the appellants are adopting a typical *ex post facto* approach which fails to do justice to the objective standards by which inventive step is to be assessed. The consistent case law of the

[8] Guid. C-IV 9.3a.
[9] Guid. C-IV 9.7 See also T–2/83, *Rider* [1984] OJEPO 265; [1979–1985] EPOR Vol. C 715.
[10] T–238/85, *Discovision*: IPD 11052, October 1988.
[11] *Mowbray* IPD 5102, December 1982/January 1983, TBA; See also T14/81, *Solvay & Cie* IPD 6083, September 1983, TBA—prejudice against using gaseous catalysts poisons in general admissible in considering inventive step of a gaseous catalytic process.
[12] T–366/89, *Corning Glass/Moulding*: [1993] EPOR 266, TBA. In contrast, see T–169/84, *Mitsuboshi/Endless power transmission*: [1987] EPOR 120 where the Examining Board combined a contemporary document with one 90 years earlier.
[13] Guid. C-IV 9.9.

Board requires that the question of obviousness be considered from the viewpoint of the existing technical problem."[14]

2.041 *Formulation of idea*—the very formulation of an idea may confer inventiveness on a new product. Thus, the Guidelines give the example of formulating the problem of indicating to the driver of a motor vehicle at night the line of the road ahead by using the light from the vehicle itself, saying that as soon as the problem is stated in this form, the technical solution, namely the provision of reflective markings along the road surface, appears simple.[15]

2.042 *Generalisation*—often, the inventive step lies in the inventor transforming the problem into a more general problem and drawing upon general prior art and applying it to the specific problem. In such cases, the TBA has warned its Examining Division against the danger of over-generalising the problem. It has said:

> " . . . it will be possible in most cases by heightening the level of generalisation to define a problem which is the same for a certain state of the art and for the invention. But to transform the actual problem as stated in the description of the application into a more general problem may be said to be one of the hallmarks of inventive step. The ordinary skilled person is not endowed with such a power of generalisation. Therefore . . . the teaching of a document may have narrower implications for persons skilled in the art and broader implications for a potential inventor who first perceives the problem which his future invention is intended to solve. The assessment of inventive step must look at the situation solely from the practical viewpoint of the skilled person."[16]

2.043 *Long-felt want*—the features of a claim may appear to be trivial and obvious in hindsight but may well be inventive if the combination of such features led to a process which fulfilled a long-felt need.[17] However, an applicant must prove, if he relies on commercial success to overcome an obviousness objection, that such success arose from the invention and not other causes like skilful advertising or lack of economic motivation to invent.[18] However, where an opponent argues that the invention merely represents the combination of techniques contained in two prior art documents, then the invention may well be non-obvious if the opponent

[14] T–2/85, *DUT Pty* IPD 9089, November 1986, TBA. See also, T–227/89, *TORAY/Flame retarding polyester composition*: [1993] EPOR 107.

[15] Guid. C-IV 9.4.

[16] T–124/82, *Union Carbide Corporation*: [1979–1985] EPOR Vol. B 586; IPD 6102, October 1983, TBA.

[17] See T–106/84, *Michaelsen/Packing Machine*: [1979–1985] EPOR Vol. C 959, [1985] OJEPO 132; T–90/89, *Frisco Findus*: IPD 14030, February 1991.

[18] See T–24/86, *BASF*. [1983] OJEPO 133; IPD 6020, TBA; T–80/86, *Maschinefabriek G.J. Nijhuis BV*: IPD 11094, January/February 1989, TBA.

himself was aware of all the prior art for some years before the priority date and yet did not think of combining the two together.[19]

2.044 *"One-way street" argument*—whilst an unexpected result is required, it does not follow that any invention with an unexpected result involves an inventive step. If the invention would have been discovered in the fullness of time on the grounds of improved suitability for the prior art, then such will be obvious notwithstanding there is a newly discovered effect in another kind of use. This is known as the "one-way street" argument. It presupposes the existence of the skilled person, free to consider obvious modifications of the known prior art, being in a "one-way street" which would inevitably lead to the invention.[20] The EPO has said that:

> "Whilst the existence of a surprising effect appears to be an essential condition for the inventive step, this may not necessarily override the conclusion of the obviousness in another respect, particularly if the skilled man had had compelling reasons to consider the same entity as an inevitable or even unique solution of that or another known problem.[21]

Thus, a patent application for a sterile compress containing dry salt was held to be inventive and novel as against compresses using moist sodium chloride as there were unexpected healing qualities and there had been no suggestion that such compresses could be improved merely by simply presenting them in a dry state rather than a wet state.[22]

2.045 *Disadvantages of prior art*—generally, it is wrong to say that the disadvantages of the prior art would have led a skilled person to the invention. The disadvantages of existing prior art are often only fully apparent by comparison with the invention itself. Thus, such disadvantages will not usually be regarded as an incentive which would lead the skilled person to the invention.[23]

(iii) Industrial application

2.046 An invention must be capable of industrial application for it to be patentable under the EPC. This condition is satisfied if it can be made or used in any kind of industry including agriculture.[24] This provision is interpreted widely. Industry is to be construed as meaning activities carried out con-

[19] T–271/84, *Air Products & Chemicals Inc*: [1987] EPOR 23; IPD 10093, November 1987, TBA.
[20] See T–10/83, *Bexford*: [1979–1985] EPOR Vol. C 726; IPD 6103, October 1983, TBA.
[21] T–102/82, *Molynycke AB*: [1979–1985] EPOR Vol. B 530, IPD 6100, October 1983, TBA. For absent decision on similar grounds, see T–699/91 *Tektronix* [1995] EPOR 389.
[22] T-102/82, *Molyuycke AB* [1979–1985] EPOR Vol. B 530, IPD 6100, October 1983, TBA.
[23] T–127/82, *Shell*: [1979–1985] EPOR Vol. B 587; IPD 7037, June 1984.
[24] Art. 57.

tinuously, independently and for financial gain.[25] Thus, use of a product in a beauty parlour has been held to constitute industrial application.[26]

Article 52(4) deems methods for treatment of the human or animal body by surgery or therapy and diagnostic methods practiced on the human or animal body as not being inventions which are susceptible of industrial application. However, this is expressed not to apply to substances or compositions for use in any of these methods. This has most relevance to pharmaceutical inventions and is discussed below.[27]

(iv) Unity of invention

2.047 The European patent application must relate to one invention only or to a group of inventions so linked as to form a single inventive concept.[28] This objection can only be raised by the EPO either by the Search Division or the Examining Division. It cannot be raised as a ground for opposition or before the national courts as a ground for revocation.[29] The applicant must file a divisional application if he is not content to limit his application to the first invention.[30]

In chemical inventions involving claims for intermediates and end-products where the intermediates were required for the preparation of the end-products, the EPO will permit the claiming of both intermediates and end-products claims as well as the preparation of the end products as such relates to a group of inventions so linked as to form a single inventive concept.[31] Where the application claims two or more claims relating to differing uses for an inventive product, then the claims fall within a single inventive concept.[32]

(v) Categories of inventions deemed unpatentable

2.048 The EPC does not define "invention" but specifically deems that the following are not inventions within the EPC:

(a) discoveries, scientific theories and mathematical methods;
(b) aesthetic creations;

[25] T–144/83, *Du Pont*: [1987] EPOR 6; IPD 9098, December 1986, TBA.
[26] T–36/83, *Roussel-Uclaf*: [1986] OJEPO 295; [1987] EPOR 1; IPD 9097, December 1986, TBA. See also T74/93 *BTG/contraceptive method* [1995] EPOR 279 where there is a rather amusing discussion as to whether contraception as practised by a prostitute is capable of industrial application.
[27] See para. 2.055 *et seq.*
[28] Art. 82.
[29] See Art. 100, 138. For where the Search Division raises the question of unity, see below at para. 2.083.
[30] See below, at para. 2.091.
[31] T–57/82, *BAYER AG*: [1979–1985] EPOR Vol. B 474; IPD 5088, October 1982, TBA.
[32] W–11/89, *X/Fibre Fleece*: [1933] EPOR 514 (decision of TBA on the meaning of the equivalent provision in the Patent Co-operation Treaty).

(c) schemes, rules and methods for performing mental acts, playing games or doing business and programs for computers;
(d) presentations of information.[33]

However, the EPC only excludes such categories from fulfilling the requirement of patentability if the alleged invention relates to the above categories "as such".[34] The examiner will disregard the form and kind of claim and concentrate on its content in order to identify the real contribution which the subject matter claimed, considered as a whole, adds to the known art.[35] The above exceptions are either abstract or non-technical. Thus, a patentable invention must be of both a concrete and technical nature.[36]

The EPO Guidelines gives examples of what it considers to be mere discoveries. Thus, if a man finds out a new property of a known material or article, that is a mere discovery but if he puts that property to practical use, that may be a patentable invention. Similarly, the finding of a substance freely occurring in nature is a mere discovery but the process of isolating and obtaining that substance from its surroundings may be patentable. If the naturally occurring substance can be properly characterised by its structure, by the process by which it is obtained or by other parameters and it is "new" in the absolute sense of having had no previous recognised existence, then the substance *per se* may be patentable. Thus, the EPO gives as an example that of a "new" substance which is discovered as being produced by a micro-organism.[37]

Where claims contain non-technical elements and known technical elements, the claim will only be allowed if the interaction of the two types produces a technical effect.[38] This criteria that the invention must have a "technical effect" is important in the field of computer-related inventions. There have been several cases on the patentability of such inventions. The reader is referred to the section on Computers.[39]

2.049 The EPC states that "methods for treatment of the human or animal body by surgery or therapy and diagnostic methods practiced on the human or animal body shall not be regarded as inventions which are susceptible or industrial application". However, this provision does not apply to products used in such methods.[40] This provision is important in the field of pharmaceutical inventions.[41]

The EPC specifically states that patents shall not be granted for (i)

[33] Art. 52(2).
[34] Art. 52(2), Guid. C-IV 2.1.
[35] Guid. C-IV, 2.2.
[36] Guid. C-IV, 1.2(ii).
[37] Guid. C-IV, 2.2 In any case, plant and animal varieties other than those produced by microbiological processes are excluded from patentability under the EPC — see below, at para. 2.051.
[38] See T–26/86, *Koch & Sterzel*: [1988] OJEPO 19; [1988] EPOR 72; T–158/88, *Beattie*: IPD 15058, May 1992.
[39] See below, at para. 2.050.
[40] Art. 52(4).
[41] See below, at para. 2.055.

inventions which would be contrary to "ordre public" or morality, or (ii) plant or animal varieties or essentially biological processes for the production of plants or animals (this provision does not apply to microbiological processes or their products)[42] In relation to the first category, the EPO says that the purpose of this is to "exclude from protection inventions likely to induce riot or public disorder, or to lead to criminal or other generally offensive behaviour" and give an example of a letter-bomb as falling within the category. They say that "a fair test to apply is to consider whether it is probable that the public in general would regard the invention as so abhorrent that the grant of patent rights would be inconceivable".[43] Recently, the E.P.O. has stated that it is not immoral to patent living organisms.[43a] This aspect and the second part are important and relevant in the area of the patentability of biotechnological inventions.

The application of these rules excluding patentability are discussed in more detail below in relation to particular categories of inventions.

(1) Computer-related inventions

2.050 Article 52 of the EPC states that computer programs along with mathematical methods, schemes, rules and methods for performing mental acts and presentations of information are not to be regarded as patentable. This is qualified by Article 52(3) which states that this exclusion of patentability only applies to the extent that the European patent relates to such excluded subject-matter or activities "as such".

The EPO guidelines elaborate on this provision and give guidance for examination in this area. They say:

> "A computer program claimed by itself or as a record on a carrier, is not patentable irrespective of its content. The situation is not normally changed when the computer program is loaded into known computer. If however, the subject matter as claimed makes a technical contribution to the known art, patentability should not be denied merely on the ground that a computer program is involved in its implementation. This means, for example, that program-controlled machines and program-controlled manufacturing and control processes should normally be regarded as patentable subject matter. It follows also that, where the claimed subject matter is concerned only with the program-controlled internal working of a known computer, the subject matter could be patentable if it provides a technical effect. As an example consider the case of a known data-processing system with a small fast-working memory and a larger but slower further memory. Suppose that the two memories are organised under program control, in such a way that a process

[42] Art. 53.
[43] Guid. C-IV 3.1.
[43a] Plant Genetic Sciences and Biogen EP 242 236 [1995] EIPR D–188.

which needs more address space than the capacity of the fast-working memory can be executed at substantially the same speed as if the process data were loaded entirely in the fast memory. The effect of the program in virtually extending the working memory is of technical character and might therefore support patentability.[44]

This emphasis on "technical effect" has been mirrored in various decisions of the Technical Board of Appeal. An invention which incorporates a mathematical method into a technical process which produces a certain change to a physical entity will be patentable even if the claim is to a method. Thus a claim to a "method of digitally processing images in the form of a two-dimensional data array" by an operator matrix and for apparatus for carrying out the method, preferably a suitably programmed conventional computer, was held to be patentable as it produced a direct technical result and because the claim related to a technical process carried out under the control of a program rather than to a computer program *as such*.[45] Furthermore, the EPO will not, when considering the novelty of the invention, be overly exacting. Thus, it will look at the novelty of the entire invention and not just consider the novelty of the parts of the claim which do not relate to computer programs.[46] The way the EPO applies the "technical effect" criteria can be seen in a series of decisions by the Technical Board of Appeal in relation to European patent applications brought by IBM for computer-related inventions.[47] The approach of the EPO would appear to be a pragmatic one which lays emphasis on a case-by-case approach.[48] It would seem that the approach of national courts to the patentability of computer-related inventions is converging with that of the EPO.[49]

(2) Biotechnological inventions

2.051 As mentioned above, Article 53(b) stipulates that patents shall not be granted for plants or animal varieties or essentially biological processes for the production of plants or animals with the proviso that this exception to patentability does not apply to microbiological processes or their products. With the rise of genetic engineering as the *wunderkind* techno-

[44] Guid. C-IV 2.2.

[45] T–208/84, *VICOM*: [1987] EPOR 74.

[46] T–208/84, *VICOM* [1987] EPOR 74; T–26/86, *Koch & Sterzel*: [1988] OJEPO 19; [1988] EPOR 72.

[47] T–115/85, *IBM/Computer Related Invention*: [1990] EPOR 107; T–22/85, *IBM/Document Abstracting and Retrieving*; T–06/83, *IBM/Data Processor Network*: [1990] EPOR 91; T–83/86, *IBM/Text Clarity Processing*: [1990] EPOR 606; T–52/85, *IBM/Semantically Related Expressions*: [1989] EPOR 454; T–95/86, *IBM/Text Processing*: [1990] EPOR 181. For a recent decision see T–40/90, *IBM Editable document form* [1995] EPOR 185.

[48] See Axel von Hellfeld, "Protection of Inventions Comprising Computer Programs by the European and German Patent Offices—A Confrontation" *Computer Law Practice*, (1986) p. 182. See also Sherman, "Patentability of Computer-Related Inventions in the UK and EPO" [1991] EIPR 85.

[49] See Pearson, "Patentability of Software/Computer Related Inventions in Europe" *Patent World*, April 1992, p. 12.

logy of the 1990s, it is inevitable that many biotechnological concerns will be interested in patenting their efforts. As genetic engineering is often concerned with the transmutation of living organisms, this area raises, in principle, many ethical questions, in particular whether living organisms should be patentable. At present, the EPO has had to take on the unenviable role as to which, if any, biotechnological inventions are patentable.

2.052 *Animal inventions*—the question as to what is meant by "animal varieties" in Article 53(b) was highlighted in the *Onco-mouse/HARVARD* European patent application.[50] In this case, oncogenic sequences had been incorporated into mice, thus producing transgenic mice. The oncogenic sequences made the mouse more susceptible to cancer and thus useful as a research subject. Thus, the relevant claims were:

> "17. A transgenic non-human mammalian animal whose germ cells and somatic cells contain an activated oncogeny sequence introduced into said animal, or an ancestor of said animal, at a stage no later than the 8-cell stage, said oncogeny optionally being further defined according to any one of Claims 3 to 10.
>
> 18. An animal as claimed in Claim which is a rodent."

The Examining Division was in some difficulty because the phrase "animal varieties" in Article 53(b) which in the German and French text was *Tierarten* and *race animale* (all of which versions are equally authentic) had differing meanings. *Tierarten* means "species" in English, whilst "animal varieties" and *races animales* denotes subcategories below the species level.[51] Thus the Division held that Article 53(b) precluded patent protection for animals in general. The Technical Board of Appeal disagreed and invoked the well-established principles that exceptions to patentability must be construed narrowly and held that the exclusion of animal varieties did not exclude animals in general. The case was remitted back to the Examining Board who held that as the claims were for non-human mammals and rodents, these were higher taxonomic units than either *Tierarten* or *races animales* and thus the invention was patentable. The Technical Board of Appeal also held that the Examining Board must consider whether the invention constitutes a microbiological process. Furthermore, it invoked Article 53(a) and said that the Divisional Board must weigh the possible suffering to animals and risks to the environment on one hand and the invention's usefulness to mankind on the other. The Examining Board held that on moral grounds, the invention was justified.[52] Thus a European patent was granted. Oppo-

[50] T–19/90, *HARVARD/Onco-Mouse*: [1990] OJEPO 476.

[51] For a more detailed analysis on the differences between these, see Volker Vossius, *Patent Protection for Animals; Onco-mouse/HARVARD*: [1990] 7 EIPR 250.

[52] For a detailed analysis of possible moral and environmental concerns in biotechnological inventions, see Michelle Paver, "All Animals are Patentable but Some are More Patentable than Others", *Patent World*, March 1992, p. 9 and Alex von Funer, "Of Mice and Morals", *Managing Intellectual Property*, July/August 1994, p. 21.

sition proceedings have been raised by 16 parties, many of them ecological parties. The grounds raised by them would appear to cover the same ground as that argued before the TBA when the application was being prosecuted and thus the success of this opposition appears rather doubtful.[53]

2.053 *Plant inventions*—before the decision in *Onco-mouse/HARVARD*,[54] the TBA had earlier considered the field of plant inventions. In *CIBA-GEIGY/Propagating Material*,[55] the TBA considered whether claims for propagating material, treated with a chemical agent for cultivated plants were patentable. The TBA said:

> "No general exclusion of inventions in the sphere of animate nature can be inferred from the European Patent Convention . . . The skilled person understands the term 'plant varieties' to mean a multiplicity of plants which are largely the same in their characteristics and remain the same within specific tolerances after every propagation cycle. This definition is reflected in the International Convention for the Protection of New Varieties of Plants of December 2, 1961, which is intended to give the breeder of a new plant variety a protective right (Article 1(1)) extending both to the reproductive or vegetative propagating material and also to the whole plant (Article 5(1)). Plant varieties in this sense are all cultivated varieties, clones, lines, strains and hybrids which can be grown in such a way that they are clearly distinguishable from other varieties, sufficiently homogeneous, and stable in their essential characteristics. The legislator did not wish to afford patent protection under the European Patent Convention to plant varieties of this kind, whether in the form of propagating material or of the plant itself.[56]

The TBA continued and said that Article 53(b) EPC prohibited only the patenting of plants or their propagating material in the genetically fixed form of the plant variety. It said that the very wording of Article 53(b) EPC before the semi-colon precluded the equation of plants and plant varieties.[57] It thus held that the innovation of the invention lay not within the sphere of plant breeding which was concerned with the genetic modification of plant but rather by means of chemical agents acting on the propagating material in order to make it resistant to agricultural chemicals. The TBA in effect held that provided the plant innovation is not protected by plant breeders' rights, then it was patentable if the general prerequisites are met.[58] It subsequently held that where the applicant had

[53] See Jaenichen/Schrell, "The 'Harvard Onco-Mouse' in the Opposition Proceedings before the EPO" [1993] 9 EIPR 345.
[54] T–19/90, *HARVARD/Onco-Mouse*: [1990] OJEPO 476.
[55] T–49/83, *CIBA-GEIGY*: [1984] OJEPO 112, [1979–1985] EPOR Vol. C 758.
[56] *ibid.*, at para. 2.
[57] *ibid.*, at para. 3 and 4.
[58] *ibid.*, at para. 4.

developed a process for rapidly developing hybrids and commercially producing hybrid seeds, a product-by-such-process claim was held not to fall within Article 53(b) because the claimed hybrid seeds or plants, considered as a whole generation population were not stable and therefore could not be considered as a "variety".[59] More recently the EPO has adopted a more restrictive approach as to whether a plant invention is not a "variety". In *Plant Genetic Sciences and Biogen*, the EPO considered the patentability of plant inventions. Firstly, they stated that under Article 53(a), it is not immoral *per se* to patent living organisms. Inventions which obviously prejudiced the environment would be contrary to "ordre public". However, plant biotechnology could not be regarded *per se* as more immoral than traditional selective breeding since both involved the introduction of novel genetic material.

On Article 53(b) they used the UPOV definition of plant variety, *i.e.* a plant grouping below a species which is distinct, uniform and stable. The EPO said a product claim which embraced "plant varieties" was not patentable. Processes for the production of plants were of two kinds: technical processes which were patentable and essentially biological processes which were not (unless they were microbiological). Thus, processes for genetic modification of plants were patentable as they were technical processes. Plant varieties produced as a result of a microbiological process were not patentable by way of exception.[60–61]

The TBA has said, in opposition proceedings for the patenting of plants that a fair test for determining whether a violation of Article 53(a) of the EPC has occurred is whether it is probable that the public in general would regard the invention as so abhorrent that the grant of a patent would be inconceivable.[62] Thus, the EPO's narrow restrictive approach to the meaning of "plant varieties" concurs with its approach to the meaning of "animal varieties" in Article 53(b).

2.054 *"Essentially biological processes"*—Article 53(b) excludes the patentability of essentially biological processes for the production of animals or plants but not for microbiological processes or their products. Such an exception will be narrowly construed.[63] The Board of Appeal in the context of plants stated that:

> "Whether or not a (non-micro-biological) process is to be considered as essentially biological within the meaning of Article 53(b) has to be judged on the basis of the essence of the invention taking into account the totality of human intervention and its impact on the result achieved. It is the opinion of the Board that the necessity for human intervention alone is not yet a sufficient criterion for its not

[59] T–320/87, *Hybrid Plants/LUBRIZOL*: [1990] OJEPO 3; [1990] EPOR 173, at para. 14.
[60–61] EP 242–256; [1995] EIPR D–188. T356/93 [1995] EPOR 357. See also para. 6.005.
[62] Opposition proceedings against Lubrizol's patent EP-B1-122 791—see Jaenichen/Schrell, "The EPO's Recent Decisions on Patenting Plants", [1993] 12 EIPR 466.
[63] T–320/87, *Hybrid Plants/LUBRIZOL*: [1990] OJEPO 3; [1990] EPOR 173, at para. 6.

> being 'essentially biological'. Human interference may only mean that the process is not a 'purely biological' process, without contributing anything beyond a trivial level. It is further not a matter simply of whether such intervention is of a quantitative or qualitative character.[64]

A product-by-process claim is nevertheless a product claim even if biological in nature and thus is not a claim for an essentially biological process for the production of plants or animals within the meaning of Article 53(b).[65]

(3) Methods and products for medical and veterinary treatment

2.055 Under the first sentence of Article 52(4), methods for the treatment of the human or animal body by surgery or therapy and diagnostic methods practiced on the human or animal body are not regarded under the EPC as inventions which are susceptible of industrial application.[66] Therapy includes treatment with chemical substances or treatment with compositions in general.[67] The EPO have held that the exception to patentability in Article 52(4) must be construed narrowly and does not apply to non-therapeutic treatments.[68] The EPO makes it clear that patents may be obtained for surgical, therapeutic and diagnostic instruments and their manufacture.[69] Claims for the use of a substance or composition for the treatment of the human or animal body by therapy will fall within this prohibition.[70] However, this restriction does not apply to a claim to particular substances or compositions for use in any such method.[71]

Consequently many inventions relate to claims to substances for use for a particular medical purpose. With regard to the patentability of such substances, it is necessary to distinguish between known and unknown substances. New therapeutic substances may be patentable even where they are naturally occurring substances.[72] What is the situation where a known substance which was not known to have any therapeutic effect is discovered to have such an effect (described as a "first medical indication

[64] T–320/87, *Hybrid Plants/LUBRIZOL*: [1990] OJEPO 3; [1990] EPOR 173. See also Jaenichen/Schrell, "The EPO's Recent Decisions on Patenting Plants", [1993] 12 EIPR 466, at 469.

[65] T–19/90, *HARVARD/Onco-Mouse*: [1990] OJEPO 476; 1990 EPOR 501, at para. 4.9.2.

[66] As to discussion as to what amounts to therapeutic treatment (*i.e.* treatment by therapy) see T–36/83, *Roussel-Uclaf*: [1987] EPOR 1; IPD 9097, December 1986 (claim to use of chemical product for skin-cleansing did not relate to medical therapy); T–81/84, *William Rorer*: [1988] EPOR 297; IPD 10054, July/August 1987 (treatment of menstrual discomfort held to be a therapeutic treatment).

[67] G05/83, *EISAI*: [1985] OJEPO 64; [1979–1985] EPOR Vol. B 241, at para. 10.

[68] T–144/83, *Du Pont*: [1987] EPOR 6; IPD 9098, December 1986, TBA.

[69] Guid. C-IV 4.2, 4.3.

[70] G05/83, *EISAI*: [1985] OJEPO 64; [1979–1985] EPOR Vol. B 241, at para. 12.

[71] Art. 52(4), 2nd sentence. See also G05/83, *EISAI*: [1985] OJEPO 64, [1979–1985] EPOR Vol. B 241, at para. 14.

[72] See above, at para. 2.048.

invention")? Also what is the situation where a substance which is known to have therapeutic effects is found to have a new and inventive therapeutic effect (described as a "second medical indication invention")?

2.056 *First medical indication inventions*—Article 54(5) of the EPC provides that a product for use in a medical or veterinary method does not lack novelty, even where the product is itself known and part of the state of the art "provided that its use for any method referred to in that paragraph is not comprised in the state of the art." This Article clearly permits patent protection for first medical indication inventions. The required novelty for the medicament which forms the subject-matter of the claim is derived from the new pharmaceutical use.[73] In a first medical indication invention, an application may contain claims in terms of a broad statement of therapeutic purpose and does not need to be limited to a specifically disclosed individual therapeutic purpose even if the description only discloses a specific therapeutic purpose.[74] The Guidelines say that a claim for a first medical indication invention should be in a form such as "substance of composition X" followed by the indication of the use, *i.e.* "for use as a medicament as an anti-bacteria or for curing disease Y".[75] It is important that such a claim is distinguished from a claim "Use of substance or composition X for the treatment of disease Y" as such will be regarded as relating to a method for treatment explicitly excluded from patentability by Article 52.[76]

2.057 *Second and Further Medical Indication Inventions*—in *Eisai*,[77] the Enlarged Board of Appeal held that Article 54(5) did not prevent the patenting of second medical indication inventions. In general, the EBA held that no intention to exclude second medical indication inventions generally from patent protection could be deduced from the terms of the EPC or the legislative history of the Articles in question. The main difficulty was that the wording of Article 54(5) suggested on the principle of *expressio unius est exclusio alterius* that one could not patent known products for second or further medical uses. However, the EBA disregarded the principle and held that a European patent could be granted with claims directed to the use of a substance or composition for the manufacture of a medicament for a specified new and inventive therapeutic application.[78]

A claim for a second or further medical use must be specifically set out in the claim and the extent of protection will be so limited as such an

[73] G05/83, *EISAI*: [1985] OJEPO 64; [1979–1985] EPOR Vol. B 241.
[74] T–128/82, *Pyrrolidine Derivaties/Hoffmann-La Roche*: [1979–1985] EPOR Vol. C 987; [1984] OJEPO 164; IPD 7050, July/August 1984, TBA. See also T–36/83, *Roussel-Uclaf* [1987] EPOR 1; IPD 9097, December 1986.
[75] Guid. C-IV 4.2.
[76] Guid. C-IV 4.2. See G05/83, *EISAI*: [1985] OJEPO 64; [1979–1985] EPOR Vol. B 241.
[77] G05/83, *EISAI*: [1985] OJEPO 64, [1979–1985] EPOR Vol. B. 241.
[78] The so-called "Swiss" claim.

invention will be considered in accordance with the principles of selection inventions.[79] Claims for second medical indication inventions must be in the form "Use of substance or composition X for the manufacture of a medicament for therapeutic application Z" in order to avoid possible objections that the invention is for a method of therapy.[80] Claims for different uses are allowable provided that they form a single general inventive concept.[81]

(4) Claims for non-medical uses of a known product

2.058 Many applications contain claims for a new and inventive use of a product. In this section, one considers such claims where the use is non-medical. In relation to a claim for a new use of a known product for a particular non-medical purpose, there has been little dispute that such is patentable.[82]

Greater dispute occurred over a claim for the known use of a known substance for a new purpose. The EBA has had to consider this point in the case of *Mobil Oil*.[83] The respondent argued that a distinction should be drawn between a claim for "a new use of an old thing for a new purpose" and a claim for "an old use of an old thing for a new purpose". It accepts the former was capable of being novel but that the latter kind of claim could never be novel because the only novel feature of the claim was a "mental novelty" devoid of technical effect.[84] The EBA held that what was important was whether the functional technical feature of the invention had been made available to the public. If the claim included a "new means of realisation" by which the new purpose could be achieved, then such was a novel technical feature.[85] In the declaratory part of its judgment, it held that a claim to the use of a known compound for a particular purpose which is based on a technical effect that is described in the patent should be interpreted as including that technical effect as a functional technical feature and accordingly was not open to objections of novelty, provided that the technical feature had not been previously made available to the public.

The EBA came to the same conclusion in *BAYER/Plant Growth*.[86] In this case, the facts were that a compound X, which was previously known and used as affecting plant growth, was found to be useful as a plant fungicide. The only possible novelty in the claimed invention lay in the use of the compound as a fungicide rather than as a growth regulator.

[79] See Paterson, "Patentability of Further Uses of Known Product under the EPC" [1991] 1 EIPR 16.
[80] This type of claim can of course be used for a first medical indication invention.
[81] Art. 82 and Guid. C-IV 4.2. See para. 2.047.
[82] G05/83, *EISAI*: [1985] OJEPO 64; [1979-1985] EPOR Vol. B 241, EBA; G02/88, *Mobil Oil III/Friction reducing additive*: [1990] OJEPO 93; [1990] EPOR 73, EBA.
[83] G02/88, *Mobil Oil III*: [1990] OJEPO 93 as corrected by 969; IPD 13029, March 1990, EBA.
[84] *ibid.* Para. 7.1.
[85] *ibid.*
[86] G06/88, *BAYER/Plant Growth*: [1990] OJEPO 114; [1990] EPOR 257.

The EBA held that the technical features of the claim and the underlying invention had not been made available to the public by the prior art and thus was novel. The Guidelines states that the examiner should take into account characteristics not explicitly stated but implied by a particular use, *i.e.* in deciding the novelty of a hook for a crane over a known fish hook of similar shape, the examiner should take into account the differences of size and strength implied by such uses.[87]

(vi) Selection inventions

2.059 The term "selection invention" is used to describe the discovery of a particular product in a known class of products which has an unexpected and surprising effect. In this field, the issues of novelty and inventive step are often inextricably intertwined. If a selection product does not contain a surprising effect, it will often be adjudicated that the particular product is anticipated by disclosure of the class of products from which it comes, even though the issue of surprise or unexpectedness goes more to the question of obviousness. Selection inventions are most common in the chemical field.

In the area of selection inventions, the Guidelines make it clear that a generic disclosure does not take away the novelty of any specific example but that a specific disclosure does take away the novelty of a generic claim.[88] Thus where a substance was known to have catalytic properties in a wide range of proportions, a patent application claiming a sub-range of that range will be novel if the sub-range is not merely an arbitrary selection of the wide range but has some added technical feature even if this feature can be produced by different proportions of the catalyst outside the sub-range.[89] Where a specification in a prior art patent discloses two classes of starting substances which are combined to give a product and that specification contains examples of individual entities in each class, then nevertheless a substance resulting from the reaction of a specific pair from the two lists can be regarded as novel.[90] In other words, the EPO will not deem the prior document to disclose every combination of the two starting classes.[91]

The selected product must have unexpected and surprising effects when viewed against the prior art. Thus where an invention was concerned with the preparation of a selected class of cardenolides for therapeutic treatment, which had a better therapeutic ratio than those described in the prior art, a patent was granted as the technical effect did not flow from the state of the art.[92]

[87] Guid. C-IV 7.6.
[88] Guid. C-IV 7.4.
[89] F198/84, *Hoechst*: [1985] OJEPO 209; [1979–1985] EPOR Vol. C 987.
[90] T–12/81, *BAYER/Diastereoisomers*: [1979–1985] EPOR Vol. B 308; [1982] OJEPO 296.
[91] T–7/86, *DRACO/Xanthenes*: [1989] EPOR 65; IPD 11043, September 1988.
[92] T–2/82, *Nativele*: IPD 7043, June 1984, TBA.

Chemical inventions: intermediates

2.060 Often, where a chemical end-product compound is patentable, the applicant will wish to claim patent protection for intermediate chemical compounds used for making the end-product. The basic criteria for a chemical intermediate to be patentable was established in *BAYER/Cyclopropane.*[93]

The applicant had claimed a patent for an insecticide consisting of substituted bromostyril-cyclopropane carbonic acid esters of a particular structural formula. This formed a sub-class of a large class of esters which constituted the prior art. The sub-class differentiated itself from the prior art in that it limited possibilities of substitution on the acid and alcohol parts of the molecule and also had a bromo-atom in a certain position. Evidence was provided that this sub-class exhibited a surprisingly better effect in comparison with structurally close compounds. The EPO held that the sub-class of acid esters was patentable.

The applicant also claimed under the same patent for the corresponding class of bromostyril-cyclopropane carbonic acids as intermediates for the production, via acid chlorides into the carbonic esters.[94] The Examining Board refused to allow patent protection of this claim stating that the intermediates themselves were not novel and inventive. It said that the inventive step of the subsequent products could only be transferred to the intermediate products if the unexpected qualities of the end-products were determined exclusively by the structure of the intermediates. The applicant appealed to the TBA which allowed the appeal.

2.061 In the context of considering whether a claim for an intermediate product was inventive where the end-product was inventive, the TBA held the following:

i) Novel intermediates must contribute partially to the structural characteristics to the patentable end-product.
ii) The claimed intermediate must itself be based on an inventive step to be patentable. In considering the novelty of the intermediate compound, one must examine the prior art close to the intermediate compounds to determine whether there was anything which would direct the skilled man towards the structures of the intermediate compound in order to prepare the end-products.
iii) Furthermore, one must consider whether the claimed intermediates can be derived in an obvious manner from prior art close to the end-product. Provided that the claimed intermediate contributes to the structural differentiation of the claimed end-product, this question will normally be answered in the negative. Thus, the TBA held that the claimed intermediate carbonic acid

[93] T–65/82, *BAYER/Cyclopropane*: [1983] OJEPO 327; [1979–1985] EPOR Vol B. 484.
[94] The combination of an organic acid with an acid chloride to give an ester is a well known reaction in organic chemistry.

was unsuitable for preparing the known prior art carbonic acid esters.

iv) If there is no suitable intermediate in the prior art for the purpose of preparing the claimed end-products, then it will usually be inventive over the close-to-the-intermediate state of the art compounds as it would not be obvious to modify such compounds for the purpose of making the claimed end-product as that would require foreknowledge of the invented claimed end-product.

v) Where there are other known intermediates which are *capable* of making the claimed end-products, then the claimed intermediates must produce a surprising comparative advantage over them in order to be patentable. This may come from an unexpected reactivity or surprisingly better yield but will not come from the mere fact that the claimed end-products could equally be well prepared from the claimed novel intermediate as opposed to the known intermediates.[95–96]

(c) Practice and procedure under the EPC

(i) The Applicant

2.062 Unlike the Patent Co-operation Treaty or the Paris Convention, a European patent application can be filed by any natural or legal person regardless of their nationality or place of residence.[97] A European patent application may be filed by joint applicants or by two or more applicants designating different Contracting States.[98] Thus applicants can allocate different Contracting States between themselves.

The right to a European patent belongs to the inventor or his successor in title.[99] If the inventor is an employee, then the entitlement to a European patent shall be determined in accordance with the law of the State in which the employee is mainly employed or if this is indeterminable, the state where the employer has his place of business to which the employee is attached.[1] The EPC includes a Protocol on Jurisdiction and the Recognition of Decisions in Respect of the Right to the Grant of a European Patent. This is discussed elsewhere in detail but basically gives the national courts of the Contracting States the power to determine who has

[95–96] These five criteria constitute a distillation of the decision. See also T–22/82, *BASF*: [1979–1985] EPOR Vol. B 414; IPD 5089, October 1982; *BAYER/Acetophenone derivatives*: [1987] EPOR 284 (structure of new intermediates led directly to an unexpected improvement in yield in patentable multi-stage chemical process).

[97] Art. 58.

[98] Art. 59.

[99] Art. 60.

[1] Art. 60(1).

the right to the European patent.[2] If a final decision finds that someone other than the applicant has the right to the European patent application, then that person may within three months of the decision being given, prosecute the application itself, file a new application or request that the application be refused.[3] If the successful claimant chooses to file a new application, the original application is deemed to be withdrawn on the date of filing of the new application.[4] The claimant should notify and provide proof to the EPO that he has begun proceedings against the applicant. The EPO will then stay proceedings provided that publication has taken place.[5]

If there are two or more persons who have independently made the invention, then the right to the European patent belongs to the patent application which has the earliest date of filing or priority date (whichever is the earlier)[6] provided the earlier patent application is subsequently published. This provision only has effect in relation to the Designated States specified in the patent application.

It should be noted that the EPC expressly provides for the assignment of a European patent application.[7]

(ii) Languages in the EPO

2.063 English, French and German are the official languages of the EPO and European patent applications must be filed in one of these languages.[8] All proceedings must then be conducted up to grant in the language chosen for the application which is called the language of the proceedings.[9]

The exceptions to the above rule are as follows:

(a) if the applicant has its residence or principal place of business in a Contracting State which has a language other than English, French or German. In such case, the applicant may file an application in an official language of that State.[10] However, a translation of the application must be filed within three months or 13 months of the priority date (whichever is the later) into one of the official languages which then becomes the language of the proceedings.[11] During prosecution of the application, other

[2] See Chapter on Jurisdiction in Europe at para. 13.058.

[3] Art. 61. If a new application is filed under Art. 61, it will be entitled to the priority date of the usurping application provided that the subject matter of the new application does not extend beyond that of the usurping application. It is not necessary for the usurping application to be pending for Art. 61 to be applicable — see G3/92, Judgment dated June 13, 1994, [1994] OJEPO.

[4] EPCr 15(1).

[5] EPCr 13(1).

[6] Art. 60(2), 87, 89.

[7] Arts. 71–74. This must be in writing, requires the signature of the parties to the contract and must be registered—Art. 72 and EPCr 20.

[8] Art. 14(1).

[9] Art. 14(3).

[10] Art. 14(2).

[11] EPCr 6.1. If not filed in time, the application is deemed to have been withdrawn.

documents may be filed in the official language of the Contracting State concerned but translations into the language of the proceedings must be filed within one month of the filing of the document.[12] If this is not done, the document is deemed not to have been received.[13]

(b) Documents for evidence may be filed in any language but the EPO may require them to be translated.[14]

(c) Oral proceedings may be conducted in any one of the official languages provided notice is given to the EPO.[15]

Publication of the application takes place in the language of the proceedings.[16]

The EPC gives a Contracting State the power to stipulate that provisional protection in its state for published European applications, where that State has been designated, is conditional on the filing of translation of the claims into the official language of the state.[17] Furthermore, a Designated State may provide that at grant, translations of the text of the application into the official language of the Designated State must be provided within a certain time limit.[18]

(iii) Designation of contracting states

2.064 Applicants may only designate countries for the grant of a European patent which have acceded to the EPC. An applicant must designate at the time of filing all the countries which it desires a patent for.[19] These may be withdrawn any time up to the grant of the European patent but any state which is not designated in the request for grant may subsequently be designated.[20] A fee for each Designated State must be paid. The actual procedure is explained below.

The general rule is that the applicant must indicate in which states he wishes to obtain protection upon filing the application and he cannot subsequently supplement that list.[21] This is analogous with international applications.[22] If no state at all is designated, then no date of filing will be recognised.[23] Because of the importance of such a rule, the EPO has established a working practice in this area.[24] An applicant may now

[12] Art. 14(4), EPCr. 6.2.
[13] Art. 14(5).
[14] EPCr 1(3).
[15] EPCr 2.
[16] Art. 14(6) and Arts. 14(7), 97(5).
[17] Art. 67(3).
[18] Art. 65. All Contracting States save Luxembourg and Monaco have taken advantage of this provision. This considerably adds to the cost of obtaining a European patent. Art. 65(1) has recently been amended by a decision of the Administrative Council dated December 13, 1994, see para. 2.088.
[19] Art. 79.
[20] See Guid. A-III, 12.2.
[21] Art. 79(1).
[22] Art. 4(1)(ii), PCTr 4.9.
[23] Art. 80(b) EPC.
[24] Legal Advice 7, [1980] OJEPO 395.

designate all states as a precautionary measure. Applicants then may consider the desired territorial effect of the application up to the expiry of the period for paying the designation fees. Normally an applicant will be notified of potential loss of rights.[25] Accordingly, an applicant may indicate of which states he wishes to be reminded, should he not have paid designation fees. This is now a standard feature of the filing form. Thus, by default, the EPO form asks for precautionary designation of all states and then asks the applicant to indicate the states that he intends to pay designation fees and would like to be notified in case of non-observance.

(iv) Priority

2.065 An applicant can claim priority for a European patent application for an earlier patent application filed in any state party to the Paris Convention within the previous 12 months.[26] If priority is validly claimed, the priority date will count as the date of filing of the European patent application in order to establish what is prior art which could be used to challenge the application.[27] The Legal Board of Appeal has held that the Paris Convention could not be interpreted as giving a right of priority for a patent application based on anything other than an earlier patent application.[28]

In order for priority to be conferred on an application, it is necessary that the later application must relate to the same invention and contain the same subject matter as the application from which priority is being drawn.[29] This does not require identical wording but the essence of the disclosures must be the same. The EPO will not concentrate on the claims but on the earlier application as a whole.[30] Where an application claims priority from an earlier filing but it is held that priority is not validly claimed in respect of certain claims, any publication of the first filing prior to the date of filing of the later application will constitute prior art to the extent that priority is not validly claimed.[31]

The EPO has stated that as a general rule, it will only examine the formal conditions for claiming the right to priority. If during examination, prior art is revealed which falls between the actual filing date and the priority date, then the EPO will check to ensure that where the two applications differ that the subject matter of the claim is derived directly and unambiguously from the disclosure of the invention in the priority document.[32]

[25] EPCr 69.
[26] Art. 87(1) EPC.
[27] Art. 89, 54(2).
[28] J–15/80, *Arenhold*: [1981] OJEPO 7 corrected at [1981] OJEPO 546.
[29] Art. 87(1), (4).
[30] T–184–84, *NGK Insulators*: [1986] EPOR 169; IPD 9113, February 1987, TBA.
[31] G3/93 Reference by President of EPO EBA [1995] OJEPO 18. For a criticism of this decision, see Schlich "Publish and be Damned" [1995] 7 EIPR 327.
[32] See Art. 88(4) and Guid. C-V, 2, Guid. C–V, 2.4. Art. 88(4) implements Art. 4H of the Paris Convention.

Failure to file within the 12 month period is incapable of remedy even where the applicant is without fault.[33]

2.066 *Procedural conditions*—the applicant claiming priority must file a declaration of priority, the State, the date of filing and the file number of the previous application and a copy of the previous application certified by the national authority along with a certificate stating the date of the filing of the previous application.[34] The failure to state the date of filing and the state will result in automatic loss of priority.[35] The EPO will call on the applicant to correct other deficiencies.[36] The priority document must be filed within 16 months after the earliest priority date and translations must be filed within 21 months after the earliest priority date.[37]

(v) Contents of the patent application

2.067 The accompanying notes with the printed form for a European patent application set out the main formalities that are required. These can be divided between the request for a European patent and the actual application itself. The request must include an indication that a European patent is sought, the designation of at least one Contracting State and information identifying the applicant.[38]

The actual application must contain a description of the invention, one or more claims, any drawings referred to in the description of the claims and an abstract.[39] Furthermore, the application must designate the inventor[40] and if the applicant is not the inventor must designate the origin of the applicant's right to the European patent.[41] These requirements are discussed in more detail.

The date of filing is deemed to be the date on which these requirements have been fulfilled.[42]

Description

2.068 The description must include the title of the invention, an indication of the technical field to which the invention relates; an account of the background art and a disclosure of the invention.[43] The disclosure of the

[33] Art. 122(5), EPCr 41(3).
[34] Art. 88, EPCr 38.
[35] EPCr 38(1), 41(2).
[36] Art. 91, EPCr 41.
[37] EPCr 38(3), (4).
[38] Art. 80.
[39] Art. 78.
[40] Art. 81 and EPCr 19. An incorrect designation of an inventor can only be rectified with the consent of the wrongly designated person. Where the application failed to designate all the inventors, the consent of the already designated inventors was not required as they were not "wrongly designated" inventors — see J8/82, *Fujitsu*: [1979–1985] EPOR Vol. A 111; IPD 7038, June 1984, LBA.
[41] EPCr 17.
[42] Art. 80.
[43] EPCr 27.

invention must be in a manner sufficiently clear and complete for it to be carried out by a person skilled in the art and must include a detailed account of at least one way of carrying out the invention claimed.[44] However, whilst the specification need not describe all ways of achieving the invention, it must disclose more than isolated examples and disclose a technical concept fit for generalisation which would enable the skilled person to achieve the invention without undue difficulty.[45] Whilst it is important that the description adequately allows a party to carry out the invention, errors can be corrected if the skilled person would have recognised the defect and remedied it without difficulty.[46]

The description forms the basis for the claims and along with the drawings is used to interpret the claims.[47] It is important that this requirement be complied with when filing the application. This is because the description cannot be amended so as to extend beyond the content of the application as filed.[48] Finally, the description must explain how the invention is capable of industrial application.[49]

Any advantageous effects of the invention *vis-à-vis* the background art should be stated but must not disparage other products or policies.[50]

Claims

2.069 The claims must define the matter for which protection is sought in terms of its technical features.[51] They must be clear and concise and supported by the description.[52] However, the EPO takes the view that it is possible to support broad claims from a narrow base. Thus, it gives the example of an application as filed describing the preparation of a novel chemical compound having particular properties. A claim which defines that compound along with certain higher homologues may well be supported by such a description if the skilled man would have no reason to doubt the soundness of such a generalisation.[53] The EPC states that wherever appropriate the claims must comprise two parts — a first ("prior art") portion and a characterising portion. The "prior art" portion must contain the designation of the subject-matter of the invention and the technical features necessary to define the invention but which in combination, are part of the prior art. The "characterising" portion designates the

[44] Art. 83, EPCr 27(1)(f). For the requirement to make microorganisms available to the public by means of deposit with a registered institution, see below. See also T–740/90, *Lesaffre*: [1993] EPOR 465.
[45] T–435/91, *Unilever*: [1994] OJEPO Vol. 10/XV.
[46] T–171/84, *Air Products*: [1986] OJEPO 95; [1986] EPOR 210; IPD 9087, November 1986, TBA.
[47] Art. 69(1).
[48] Art. 123(2).
[49] EPCr 27(1)(f).
[50] EPCr 27(1)(b), 34(1)(b).
[51] Art. 84.
[52] Art. 84. See T–2/80, *BAYER AG*: [1979–1985] EPOR Vol. B 257; IPD 4111, November 1981, TBA.
[53] T–133/85, *Xerox Corporation*: [1989] EPOR 116; IPD 11092, January/February 1989, TBA.

technical features that, when combined with the "prior art" features, it is desired to protect.[54] The mere inclusion of features in the "prior art" part of a claim will not be regarded by the EPO as a binding statement as to the lack of novelty in such features. The determination of novelty must be decided purely in the light of the objective facts of the case.[55] Thus where an applicant finds that he has wrongly attributed a claimed feature to the prior art section rather than the characterising section, he may transpose the feature accordingly.[56] Where an applicant puts in a section of "preferred features" in the specification, these are not to be treated as claims requiring claims fees.[57]

Claims to use stated for a particular purpose are proper alternatives to method claims for carrying out an activity.[58] If the subject matter of a European patent is a process, the protection conferred by the patent extends to the products directly obtained by such process.[59] However, an actual claim for a products-by-process is not admissible unless the product itself fulfills the requirement for patentability.[60]

Claims stating the essential features of an invention may be followed by one or more claims concerning particular embodiments of that invention[61] Such dependent claims must contain if possible at the beginning a reference to the independent claim, and then state the additional features it is desired to protect.[62] Dependent claims can refer to other dependent claims but if so they should be grouped together in an appropriate way.[63] References to the description or drawing should not be used unless absolutely essential.[64] Provided that there is unity of invention, a European patent application may contain independent claims in different categories, *i.e.* product and process.

Where the applicant wished to file different claims for different states because of prior national rights in certain Designated States, the applicant should not file two or more sets of claims in his application but should file broad claims and amend at the appropriate time.[65]

Disclaimers of prior art may be contained in claims. Such disclaimers will be permitted if the subject matter remaining in the claim cannot be defined more clearly and concisely by positive technical means. This is

[54] EPCr 29(1).
[55] T–6/81, *Siemens*: [1979–1985] EPOR Vol. B 294; IPD 5029, May 1982, TBA.
[56] *ibid.*
[57] G05/83, *EISAI*: [1985] OJEPO 64; [1979–1985] EPOR Vol. B 241; J–15/88, *Neo Rx:* IPD 13198, November 1990; T–490/90, *ARI*: IPD 14145, August 1991, TBA.
[58] G06/83, *Pharmuka*: [1985] OJEPO 67; T–36/83, *Roussel-Uclaf*: [1987] EPOR 1; IPD 9097, December 1986.
[59] Art. 64(2).
[60] T–150/82, *Internatinal Flavours*: [1979–1985] EPOR Vol. C 629; IPD 7092, November 1984, TBA.
[61] EPCr 29(3).
[62] EPCr 29(4).
[63] EPCr 29(4), Guid. C-III, 3.5, 3.6, 3.6a. For the position under the PCT, see para. 2.008.
[64] EPCr 29(6), (7).
[65] J–2/82, *Warner Lambert Company*: IPD 7094, November 1984, LBA.

even if the disclaimer relates to an earlier application but which had not been published at the time of examination.[66]

The EPC discourages applications with a large number of claims. In particular, it charges a claims fee for each claim over and above ten claims.[67]

Drawings

2.070 Drawings often assist the reader in understanding the specification. Where the intelligibility of technical features in claims can be increased by use of reference numerals from the drawings, then they should be included in the claims. Such reference signs will not be construed as limiting the claim.[68] However, references to drawings should not be used unless absolutely essential.[69]

Detailed provision are laid in the Rules as to the layout and structure of drawings and these should be consulted.[70]

Abstract

2.071 The abstract merely serves for use as technical information and cannot be taken into account for any other purpose. It must contain a precise summary of the disclosure as contained in the description, the claims and the drawings and the technical field to which the invention pertains. It should be so drafted as to constitute an efficient instrument for the purpose of searching in the particular technical field.[71]

Micro-organisms

2.072 Where an invention concerns a microbiological process or its product then, unless the use of the micro-organism is available to the public or can be described in the application so that it can be carried out by a person skilled in the art, then the micro-organism must be deposited with a recognised depositary institution not later than the date of filing of the application in order to comply with the requirement that the application disclose the invention in a manner sufficiently clear and complete for it to be carried out by a person skilled in the art.[72] If the invention concerns

[66] T–04/80, *BAYER/Polyether polyols*: [1979–1985] EPOR Vol. B 260; IPD 5017, April 1982, TBA.

[67] EPCr 29(5), 31(1).

[68] EPCr 29(7).

[69] EPCr 29(6), 70.

[70] EPCr 32.

[71] Art. 85, EPCr 33.

[72] Art. 83, EPCr 28. A list of the recognised depositary institutions are available from the EPO. In England, they are the National Collection of Industrial Bacteria Torry Research Station, Aberdeen (non-pathogenic bacteria (including actinomycetes) and bacteria preservable by freezing or freeze-drying (with exceptional circumstances)); Culture Centre of Algae and Protozoa, Cambridge, U.K. (algae other than large seaweeds, free-living protozoa and parastic non-pathogenic protozoa maintable *in vitro*; National Collection of Animal Cell Cultures, Porton Down, Salisbury, Wilts., U.K.; National Collection of Food Bacteria, Shindfield, Reading (bacteria, including actinomycetes, preservable without significant change by liquid nitrogen, freezing or lyophilisation, up to and including Hazard Group 2).

the derivation of a product from strains within a class of micro-organisms, it is not necessary to deposit a preferred strain of that class according to the following rules if the description of the application contains a method to discover a preferred strain which would produce the desired product.[73]

The application as filed with the EPO must contain relevant information available to the applicant on the characteristics of the micro-organism and the depositary institution as well as the file number of the culture deposit.[74] The information relating to the depositary institution and file number must be filed within the earliest of the following periods: a period of sixteen months from the filing date or priority date; by the date of submission of a request for early publication of the application or within one month after the EPO has communicated to the applicant that a right to inspection of the files has arisen as the applicant has invoked rights against a third party.[75]

A person may request on a recognised form to the EPO that the deposited culture be released to him after the date of publication of the European patent application.[76] The requester must only use the culture or any culture derived therefrom for experimental purposes only and must not make the deposited culture available to third parties until the patent is no longer in force or the application has been withdrawn.[77] The applicant can indicate to the EPO that samples only be issued to an expert nominated by the requester prior to the date that technical preparations for publication of the application are deemed to have been completed.[78] Such an expert can be either one approved by the applicant or recognised as an expert by the President of the EPO.[79] The expert will be under the same obligations as the requester would have been.[80]

(vi) Fees

2.073 The EPO provides for a series of fees to be paid within certain time limits. These fees are the filing fee, the search fee, a fee per designated state, a fee per claim over 10 claims, an examination fee and a fee for grant and printing.[81] Failure to pay within the time limits or "grace" periods results in the application being withdrawn. The EPO occasionally changes its fees and these are laid down in the Rules relating to Fees.[82] Guidance

[73] T–239/87, *Nabisco Brands Inc.* [1988] EPOR 311; IPD 11031, July–August 1988.
[74] EPCr 28(1)(b) & (c).
[75] EPCr 28(2).
[76] EPCr 28(3), (7). The requester is entitled to have the deposited culture made available prior to such a date if the applicant has invoked rights against it — Art. 128(2).
[77] EPCr 28(3). For the definition of derived culture, see EPCr 28(6).
[78] See EPCr 28(4). As for the date when this is deemed to have occurred, see para. 2.084.
[79] EPCr 28(4), (5).
[80] EPCr 28(5)(b).
[81] At the date of writing, the fees in pounds sterling were as follows: filing fee—£250; search fee—£792; fee per Designated State—£146 (for extension to Slovenia, Lithuania or Estonia—£83 per "extension"); claim fee per claim over 10 claims—£33; examination fee—£1167; grant fee—£583 and opposition fee—£500.
[82] Referred to as RFees.

concerning the amount of fees is published in each issue of the Official Journal of the EPO. Payment must be made to the EPO.[83] The consequences of failing to pay fees in time is set out in relation to each stage.

In addition to the payment of fees payable at particular stages of the prosecution of the application, renewal fees must be paid to the EPO for European patent applications in respect of the third year and subsequent years calculated from the date of filing.[84] These particular payments must be made in advance. A payment for the coming third year must be paid after two years has elapsed at the end of the month containing the anniversary of the filing date.[85] If this date is missed, payment can be validly made within six months following this date provided that an additional fee of 10 per cent of the amount of the normal fee is paid within the same period.[86] If the renewal fee and any additional fee is not paid in time, the application is deemed to have been withdrawn.[87] It is possible to apply to have the patent application restored if there has been no fault on the applicant's behalf. If such is the case, then an application must be made within six months of the expiry of the additional time limit.[88] The last renewal fee falls due for the year in which the mention of the grant of the patent is published.[89] The patent will not be granted before all renewal fees have been paid.[90]

(vii) Communication and filing with the EPO

2.074 Notifications between the EPO and the applicant or his representative is normally done by post. However, there is provision for notification by delivery inside the EPO, public notice or by technical means as determined by the President of the EPO.[91] Thus European applications may be filed by facsimile at the EPO or a competent national authority of a Contracting State which permits filing by facsimile.[92] However, written confirmation reproducing the contents of the facsimile documents must at the invitation of the Receiving Section be supplied within a non-extendable period of one month otherwise the application will be refused. If by post, it must be by registered letter and is deemed to have been delivered on the tenth day following its posting.[93] Where a representative has been appointed, notification is made to him.[94]

[83] Art. 5 RFees.
[84] Art. 86(1).
[85] EPCr 37(1).
[86] Art. 86(2), EPCr 37(2), Art. 2.5, RFees.
[87] Art. 86(3).
[88] Art. 122.
[89] Art. 86(4).
[90] Art. 97(2)(c), EPCr 51(9).
[91] EPCr 77(2), 79 (notification by delivery by hand), 80 (public notification).
[92] At present, the German, U.K., Denmark, French, Austrian, Swedish and Swiss patent offices permit filing by facsimile. See Decision of President of EPO (May 26, 1992) [1992] OJEPO 299.
[93] See EPCr 78.
[94] EPCr 81.

(viii) General provisions regarding the EPO's decision-making process

2.075 *Decisions of the EPO*—the EPO is not restricted in its examination of an application to considering the facts, evidence and arguments provided by the parties.[95] Furthermore, it may disregard facts and evidence which are not submitted in due time by the parties.[96] However, the EPO may only make its decision based upon grounds or evidence on which the parties concerned have had an opportunity to present their comments.[97] It will only consider the European application or text in the text submitted to or agreed by the applicant or the proprietor of the patent.[98]

2.076 *Observations from third parties*—the EPO may also, following the publication of the application, hear observations from third parties concerning the patentability of the invention. Such observations must be in writing and include a statement of grounds on which they are based. In such a case, the observations must be communicated to the applicant or proprietor of the patent for comment.[99] Such a third party cannot request an oral hearing as he is not deemed to be a party to the proceedings.[1]

2.077 *Oral hearings*—the EPO may have an oral hearing if it considers it to be expedient or if one of the parties to the proceedings requests so.[2] Generally speaking, the applicant will not be allowed more than one oral hearing on the same subject. However, the TBA has stressed that the right to an oral hearing is an extremely important procedural right which the EPO should take all steps to safeguard.[3] Oral proceedings before the Receiving Section, the Examining Section and the Legal Division are not public.[4] However, oral proceedings before the Boards of Appeal and the Opposition Division are public including the delivery of the decision unless there would be serious and unjustified disadvantages in doing so.[5]

2.078 *Taking of evidence*—the means of taking and giving evidence may include the hearing of parties, requests for information, the production of documents, hearing of witnesses, opinions by experts, inspection and sworn statements in writing.[6] Where the EPO considers it necessary to hear evidence orally, it will issue a summons to the person concerned to

[95] Art. 114.
[96] Art. 114(2).
[97] Art. 113(1).
[98] Art. 113(2).
[99] Art. 115.
[1] Art. 115(1), 116.
[2] Art. 116(1).
[3] T–668/89, *Ashland*: IPD 13159, September 1990.
[4] Art. 116(3).
[5] Art. 116(4).
[6] Art. 117(1).

appear before it or request that the competent court in the country of residence of the person concerned take such evidence.[7] Such a summons must give at least two months' notice to the witness.[8] A witness summoned to the EPO may request that he give his evidence at a competent court in his country of residence.[9] The taking of oral evidence may be given on oath.[10] More detailed provisions for the taking of evidence are contained in the Implementing Regulations.[11]

2.079 *Loss of rights*—if there are any loss of rights resulting from the Convention and which does not follow from the refusal of a European patent application or the grant, renovation or maintenance of the European patent, then the EPO must communicate the loss of rights to the person concerned.[12] The person concerned may within two months after the notification apply for a decision on the matter by the EPO if he considers that the finding of the EPO is inaccurate.[13]

(d) Prosecution of application before EPO

(i) The filing of the patent application

2.080 The request for grant of a European patent application must be filed on the prescribed EPO form.[14] This is provided with an explanatory note and sets out the mandatory requirements for the request form. The application must be filed either at the EPO in Munich or its branch at The Hague or Berlin or if the national law permits, in the patent office of a Contracting State.[15] However, divisional applications must be filed at the EPO.[16] Applications may be filed directly, by post or by facsimile to the EPO or in the latter case, with those countries which permit facsimile applications.[17] The request must be signed either by the applicant or his representative.[18]

2.081 *Filing fees*—a filing fee, search fee, a fee per claim over 10 claims and a fee per Designated State are payable upon filing.

The filing and search fee must be paid within one month after the filing of the application.[19] The designation fees must be paid within 12 months of the filing date or the earliest priority date. In the latter case, payment

[7] Art. 117(3).
[8] EPCr 71.
[9] Art. 17(4).
[10] Art. 117(5)–(6).
[11] EPCr 72–76.
[12] Art. 119, EPCr 69(1).
[13] EPCr 69(2).
[14] EPCr 26.
[15] Art. 75.
[16] Art. 75(3).
[17] See footnote 92. If filed by facsimile, the applicant must file hard copies within a month—[1992] OJEPO 299.
[18] EPCr 26(2)(i).
[19] Art. 78(2).

may still be made up to the expiry of one month after the date of filing if that period expires later.[20]

If the fees are not paid within these periods, they may still be validly paid within a period of grace of one month of notification of a communication pointing out the failure to observe the time limit although a surcharge becomes payable.[21] If the filing or search fee is still not paid, the application is deemed withdrawn.[22] If the designation fee is not paid in time, then the designation of that particular state is deemed to be withdrawn.[23]

Claim fees must be paid within one month of filing of the application. If this is not done, they may still be validly paid within one month of notification of a communication pointing out the failure to observe the time limit. If the fee is still not paid, then the claims concerned shall be deemed to have been abandoned.[24]

Once the final or extended time limits for paying the filing, search or designation fees have expired, then the applicant does not have the possibility of having its rights restored.[25]

(ii) Preliminary examination of application

2.082 Once an application examination is filed, the Receiving Section examines whether the application satisfies the formal requirements and accords a date of filing.[26] Furthermore, it checks to see if the filing and search fees have been paid and, if necessary whether a translation of the application in the language of the proceedings has been filed in time.[27]

(iii) Search under the EPC

2.083 A search is drawn up on the basis of the claims with due regard to the description and any drawings. In practice, few search reports are completed before publication of the patent application. If the applicant has indicated a legitimate interest in acceleration of the search process, the EPO will endeavour to speed up the search.[28] The European search report does not contain reasons and expresses no opinion whatever as to the patentability of the invention as covered by the application.

The Search Division will examine documentation held for the purposes of novelty and inventive step.[29] The Search Division only looks for

[20] Art. 79(2).
[21] EPCr 85a.
[22] Art. 90(3).
[23] Art. 91(4).
[24] EPCr 31.
[25] Art. 122(5), Guid. A-II, 4.11; A-III, 12.2; Guid. E-VIII 2.2.4.
[26] Art. 80, 90.
[27] Art. 90. For language of the proceedings, see para. 2.063.
[28] See [1989] OJEPO 523 for procedure for request for accelerated search. This has now been replaced by "PACE" [1995] 1–2 OJEPO 57. This states that where the application for a European patent is the first filing (*i.e.* it does not claim priority), the EPO Search Division will endeavour to provide a search report not later than six months from the date of filing.
[29] EPCr 44.

published prior applications and will not look for unpublished prior applications with earlier priority dates in the field of search.[30]

Once it has been drawn up, the search report is sent to the applicant along with any cited documents.[30a] The applicant then has the option of withdrawing, amending or proceeding with the application. If the Search Division considers that the unity of invention requirement is not fulfilled, it will draw up a European search report for the first invention and invite the applicant to pay further search fees for subsequent inventions contained in the application.[31] These fees are refunded if it is found by the Examining Division that there is unity of invention.[32] The Search Division will also determine the definitive content of the abstract.[33]

(iv) Publication of the application

2.084 The EPO is obliged to publish a European patent application as soon as possible after the expiry of period of eighteen months from the date of filing or the priority date.[34] This will include the search report if it is available. Otherwise the search report is published separately.[35] The publication will include any amended claims which are amended 10 weeks or more before the expiry of the 18 month period following the date of filing or, if priority is claimed, following the date of priority.[36]

Publication is important because it provides for provisional protection of the patent which cannot be less than that provided for national unexamined published applications and must give rise to at least the right to reasonable compensation in the event of infringement.[37] However, Contracting States can provide that such provisional protection is not available until such time as a translation of the claims into one of its official languages has been made available to the public or has been communicated to the person using the invention in that state.[38] Once publication has occurred, the public may on request inspect the files relating to the application.[39] Finally, publication of an application can have serious consequences because the specification then becomes part of the prior art and could thus be fatal to a subsequent application based on the same

[30] Guid. B VI 4.1; EPCr 44(3).

[30a] Art. 92(2).

[31] EPCr 46. The Search Division must given its reasons—see W–4/85, *Schick*: [1987] OJEPO 63; W–7/86, *Muckter*: [1987] OJEPO 67, [1987] EPOR 176 in relation to an application under PCT where the international search was done by EPO as International Search Authority.

[32] EPCr 46(2).

[33] EPCr 47.

[34] Art. 93.

[35] Guid. A-VI, 1.3, 1.5.

[36] EPCr 49(3), [1978] OJEPO 312.

[37] Art. 67(2), 64.

[38] Art. 67(3). All countries require translation of claims into an official language of that country before provisional protection is available. In France, Greece, Italy, Switzerland and the U.K., the patentee may claim damages, whereas the other countries only permit compensation reasonable in the circumstances. Generally, and for information concerning limitation periods, see Hellfeld, "Enforcement of European Patents" [Dec, 1991–Jan, 1992] *Patents World* 20.

[39] Art. 128.

invention. Publication of an application will not occur if the application is refused, withdrawn or deemed to have been withdrawn before the termination of the technical preparations for publication.[40] Such preparations are deemed to have been completed seven weeks before the end of the 18 month period from the filing date or the priority date (if claimed).[41]

(v) Examination of the application

2.085 *Request for examination*—the applicant must file a request for examination before the expiry of a period of six months after the date on which the European Patent Bulletin mentions the publication of the search report.[42] In practice, the request for examination forms an integral part of the request for grant of a European patent and the applicant can pay the examination fee upon filing.[43] The request will not be deemed to have been filed until after the examination fee has been paid and cannot be withdrawn.[44] Failure to make a request or pay the fee within the time period will result in a communication from the EPO pointing out the failure to observe the time limit. The applicant then has a period of grace of one month to make such a request upon payment of a surcharge fee.[45] It is important to note that if this period is not complied with, the applicant cannot apply to restore the application.[46]

If the applicant wishes to expedite the examination procedure, he is advised to make a request for examination before he receives the search report and dispense with the invitation that the EPO issues asking the applicant if he wishes to proceed with the application.[47] In such a case, the application proceeds automatically to the examination stage.

2.086 *Procedure during examination*—the Examining Division's task is to consider, in the light of the search report, whether the application complies with the requirements of the EPC and in particular whether the invention is patentable.[48] The examining process involves a constructive dialogue between an examiner allocated to the application and the applicant as to the patentability of the invention. Thus the EPO has stated that the guiding principle of the examining procedure is that a decision on

[40] EPCr 48(2).
[41] [1993] OJEPO 55. Decision of President of EPO re: completion of technical preparations for publication of European patent application. It is possible that publication will not occur if request is received four weeks before the date of due publication—see Notice [1993] OJEPO 56.
[42] Art. 94(2).
[43] This is refunded in full if the application is withdrawn—Art. 10b RFees.
[44] Art. 94(2), Guid. A-VI, 2.2. If the application is abandoned before it is passed from the Search Division to the Examination Division, the examination fee should be returned.
[45] EPCr 85b.
[46] Art. 122(5).
[47] Art. 96(1), [1995] 1–2 OJEPO 57.
[48] Art. 94(1).

whether to grant a patent or refuse the application should be reached in as few actions as possible.[49]

The applicant may put forward its own observations on the search report and any amended claims prior to receipt of any communication from the examiner allocated to his application. This will have the effect of speeding up the process.[50] Otherwise, the examiner will invite the applicant, if he has any objections of the application to file his observations and where appropriate to amend the description, claims and drawings within a certain time limit.[51] Failure to do so will result in the application being deemed withdrawn although the applicant can request further processing of the application within two months of the notification that the application has been refused or deemed to have been withdrawn.[52] Further communication may ensue and if the differences cannot be resolved by correspondence, the applicant may request oral proceedings at any time.[53]

The decision-making process of the EPO is discussed in more detail elsewhere.[54]

(vi) Grant of the patent

2.087 If the Examining Division concludes that the application fulfills the requirements of the EPC, then it will make a decision to grant a European patent provided that the applicant has:

(a) approved the text in which it is intended to grant the patent;
(b) paid the fee for grant and printing and ensure, where applicable, renewal fees and claim fees have been paid in time;
(c) filed translation of the claims in the two other official languages of the EPO in time.[55]

The procedure is that the EPO informs the applicant of the text in which it intends to grant the patent and asks him to indicate within a set period (at present four months extendible upon request by a further two months) whether he approves the text notified (this is called the "Rule 51(4)" communication). Once the applicant has notified the EPO that he approves the text, then the EPO invites the applicant to pay within a set period (currently three months) the fees for grant and printing and to provide translations of the claims (if not already done) into the two other official languages of the EPO ("this is called the 'Rule 51(6)" communication").[56] Failure to comply with the above time limits results in the application being deemed to have been withdrawn although the appli-

[49] Guide to applying for a European Patent [1990] point 160.
[50] EPCr 86(2), [1995] 1–2 OJEPO 57.
[51] Art. 96(2), EPCr 51(2), (3), 86(3).
[52] Art. 121, 96(3).
[53] Art. 116. The EPO must accede other than in exceptional circumstances to a request for an oral hearing—T–668/89, *Ashland Oil*: IPD 13159 September 1990.
[54] See above, at para. 2.075 *et seq.*
[55] Art. 97(2), EPCr 51(6).
[56] EPCr 51(4)–(6).

cant may request further processing upon receipt of the communication stating that the application has been deemed to have been withdrawn.[57]

The actual grant of a European patent takes effect on the date on which the European Patent Bulletin mentions the grant. The EPO will at the same time publish a specification of the European patent containing the description, claims and any drawings.[58] Any amendments must not contain matter which goes beyond the application as filed.[59]

(vii) Grant of European patent and transfer into national patents

2.088 The grant of a European patent results in the obtaining of a "bundle" of national patents for the states designated in the application. Contracting States can stipulate that owners of European patents must provide translations into an official language of that state and that if they fail to do so, the patent is *void ab initio* in the relevant state.[60]

At present Austria, Belgium, Denmark, France, Germany, Greece, Ireland, Italy, Netherlands, Portugal, Spain, Sweden and the United Kingdom have all enacted legislation requiring that translations of the applications into one of their official languages be provided within three months from the date on which the mention of the grant or the decision to maintain the patent as amended is published in the European Patent Bulletin. Switzerland and Liechtenstein stipulate that translations must be provided by the date of mention of the grant. Only Luxembourg does not require at present translations of the European patent specification. The Administrative Council have recently amended the Convention so that the period for supplying translations of the patent must be a minimum of three months from the date of mention of the grant of the patent.[61] This decision does not come into force until January 1, 1996 to permit Switzerland and Liechtenstein time to amend their national patent laws. As of October 7, 1992, there will be no need to prepare separate sets of claims to cover only processes and/or methods for chemical and pharmaceutical inventions in Greece and Spain.

It has been noted that the cost of translations can easily double the cost of the prosecution up to grant.[61a]

(viii) Amendments

2.089 *Procedure and Practice*—prior to receipt of the search report, the applicant is not entitled to amend the description, claims or drawings.[62] After receipt of the search report, the applicant may of his own volition

[57] EPCr 51(8), Art. 121. This applies as the time limits are fixed by the EPO and not by the Convention or its Implementing Regulations.
[58] Art. 97(4), 98, EPCr 54.
[59] See below, at para. 2.089.
[60] Art. 65.
[61] Decision dated December 13, 1994, [1995] OJEPO 91 amending Art. 65(1).
[61a] Boff, "EPC Translation", 1995 2 EIPR 319.
[62] EPCr 86(1).

amend the description, claims or drawings.[63] After receipt of the first communication from the Examining Division, the applicant may amend the description, claims and drawings only once without consent of the Examining Division.[64] Thereafter up to grant of the patent, Examining Division consent is required. In considering whether or not to give its consent, the Examining Division will balance the need for speedy grant against the commercial damage that would be inflicted upon the public by the existence of invalid patents.[65]

Once the applicant has given approval to the text pursuant to a Rule 51(4) communication, the applicant is generally bound by his approval and substantive amendments are generally no longer admissible.[66] Once the Rule 51(6) communication has been sent, the Examining Board has a restricted discretion to permit further amendments.[67]

2.090 *Substantive law*—amendments are only permissible if they do not contain subject-matter which extends beyond the content of the application as filed.[68] For this purpose, no distinction should be drawn between subject-matter in the specification or claims.[69] This rule has been likened to a "novelty test". In applying this test, the EPO must look to see if the proposed amendment adds anything novel over the description as filed.[70] If it does, then the amendment will not be allowed. It is important that it is the change in content (*i.e.* the subject-matter of the amendment) and not the amended claim *in toto* that is compared with the content of the original application.[71] An amendment to a claim without a corresponding change to the description of the application may be

[63] EPCr 86(2). As to how amendments should be made, see Guid. E-II & [1985] OJEPO 172.

[64] Art. 123, EPCr 86(3).

[65] T–675/90, *Euro-Celtique*: [1994] 1 EPOR 66, TBA.

[66] Guid. C-IV, 4.9–4.10; [1989] O.J. 43. For an example of the exercise of the discretion under EPCr 86(3), see T–375/90, *Site Microsurgical Systems/Ophthalmic microsurgical system*: [1993] EPOR 588, TBA (amendment permissible after Rule 51(4) communication because applicant was prompt and amendment sought to avoid narrow interpretation by competitor); T–182/88, *University of California*: [1989] EPOR 147, IPD 13085, June 1990 (addition of method claims specifically adapted for Austria after Rule 51(4) communication permissible as EPO's interest in speedy completion outweighed by A's interest in obtaining proper patent protection in Austria).

[67] G7/93, *Late amendment/WHITBY II* [1995] EPOR 49, which states that discretion must be exercised restrictively balancing the interests of the applicant with that of the EPO's interest in bringing proceedings to a close. *Cf.* T–675/90, *Euro-Celtique* [1994] 1 EPOR 66, TBA.

[68] Art. 123(2).

[69] T–14/83, *Swintons*: [1984] OJEPO 105; T–139/83, *USS Engineers*: [1979–1985] EPOR Vol. C 855; IPD 6111, November 1983, TBA.

[70] See T–201/83, *Shell/Lead Alloys*: [1984] OJEPO 481; [1979–1985] EPOR Vol. C 905; T–194/84, *General Motors* [1979–1985] EPOR Vol. C 855; IPD 11042, September 1988; T–133/85, *Xerox Corporation*: [1989] EPOR 116; IPD 11092, January/February 1989.

[71] Otherwise, any amendment which involves a generalisation or omission of a feature would always be permissible as an application as filed always anticipates a later, more generic amended application—see T–194/84, *General Motors*: [1989] EPOR 351; IPD 11042, September 1988, TBA.

deemed an amendment which contains subject-matter going beyond the content of the application as filed and thus inadmissible. Thus, where an applicant wished to amend their claims to include a recirculating copier in which odd-numbered sheets were copied and stored, whereas in the description as originally filed, it was the even numbered sheets that were copied and stored, the TBA held that the proposed claims contained information that went beyond the content of the application as filed and was therefore not allowable.[72]

Where the amendment seeks to replace or remove a feature from a claim, this will be permissible provided that the skilled person would directly and unambiguously recognise that the feature is not presented as essential in the disclosure, it is not indispensable for the function of the invention in the light of the technical problem it serves to solve and the replacement or removal requires no real modification of other features to compensate for the change.[73] Thus, where an applicant sought to amend an application for an invention for winding apparatus by substituting the phrase "rotatable carrier" for "rotatable disc" when the original application made no mention of rotatable disc, such an amendment was allowable because a skilled person would have understood immediately that the configuration of the carrier was of no consequence.[74] A feature which is added to the application during its examination and which merely limits protection conferred by patent does not constitute the addition of subject matter which extends beyond the application as filed.[75] Generally, a mere disclaimer out of already broadly disclosed subject matter is permissible, but not if the limitation is to be considered as producing a technical contribution to the subject matter of the claimed invention.[75a]

Amendments are possible after grant during opposition proceedings but not in such a way as to extend the protection conferred by the claims.[76] This condition is in addition to the requirement that the subject matter of the patent must not extend beyond the content of the application as filed.[77] However, where the claims are evidently inconsistent with the totality of the disclosure of the patent, the patentee will be permitted during opposition proceedings to amend the claim even if this broadens the scope of the patent. Thus, the TBA has said:

[72] See T–133/85, *Xerox* [1989] EPOR 116; IPD 11092, January/February 1989. This case discusses the relationship between Art. 84 (claims must be supported by description) and Art. 123(2) (amendment must not contain subject matter which extends beyond the contect of the application as filed).

[73] T–691/90, *Critikon/Infusion apparatus*: [1994] EPOR 51, TBA, applying T–331/87, *HOUDAILLE/Removal of feature* [1991] EPOR 194; T–260/85, *AMP/Coaxial connector*: [1989] EPOR 403.

[74] *Maschinenfabrik Rieter*: IPD 6021, April 1983, TBA.

[75] G–1/93, *Advanced Semi Conductor Products*: [1994] OJEPO 541, [1995] EPOR 97.

[75a] CIG–1/93 Advanced Semiconductor Products, *ibid* and T–526/ALEXXON/Lubricating oil additive [1995] EPOR 306.

[76] Art. 123(3).

[77] Art. 100(c) corresponding to the pre-grant Art. 123(2) provision.

> "It becomes immediately apparent, once recourse is had to the description and drawings of the patent specification, that what is defined [in the unamended claim] could not be that for which protection was sought and that the intended meaning must have been the equivalent of what was sought in respect of the amended claim. In other words, on a fair interpretation of the claim in the light of the totality of disclosure of the patent the protection conferred on but it has not in fact been extended.[78]

The effect of this rather ingenious argument will be very much diminished by the fact that a patentee is no longer permitted to bring opposition proceedings in relation to his own patents.[79]

(ix) Divisional applications

2.091 A divisional application has to be filed by the applicant if the earlier patent application does not fulfil the requirements as to unity of invention and the applicant is not happy to limit the application.[80]

The divisional application can be filed only in respect of subject-matter which does not extend beyond the content of the earlier application.[81] If it complies with this rule, it will be accorded the same date of filing and where applicable, the same priority date of the earlier application. Only states designated in the earlier application may be so designated in the divisional application.[82]

A divisional application may be filed up to the date when the applicant approves the text for grant of the patent (the Rule 51(4) communication).[83] It must be directly filed with the EPO.[84] The language of the initial application must be employed in any consequent divisional application.[85] A filing fee, search fee and designation fee must be paid in respect of each European divisional application within one month of the filing of the division application. However, payment of the designation fees may be made before the expiry of the 12 month period from the filing date of the earlier application or if priority is claimed, the priority date.[86] The applicant will be given a one month "grace period" from notification of a communication pointing out the failure to observe the above time limits for which a surcharge fee is payable.[87] The applicant

[78] T–108/91, *SEARS/Lockable Closure*: [1993] EPOR 407 at 414, TBA.
[79] See para. 2.092.
[80] See above, at para. 2.083.
[81] Art. 76(1). Guid. A-IV, 1.2; C-VI. 9.1–6.
[82] Art. 76(2).
[83] EPCr 25. See also, 910/92 Divisional Application [1995] EPOR 268.
[84] Art. 76(1).
[85] EPCr 4. If the applicant has filed an application in a Contracting State's official language which is not English, French or German (the official languages of the EPO), then he may file the divisional application in the Contracting State's original language but must file a translation within one month of such a filing (EPCr 4, 6(1)).
[86] EPCr 25, Art. 79(2). In practice, division of an application never occurs within the first 12 months.
[87] EPCr 85a, 25.

must comply with these time limits if he wishes to maintain the divisional application as he will not be able to re-establish his rights.[88]

As the divisional application is treated as having the same date of filing as the earlier application, renewal fees may be due upon the actual filing of the divisional application. If so, these and any other renewal fees which would fall due with a period of four months from filing must be paid within that period to the EPO or within six months of the due date upon payment of an additional fee.[89]

(x) Opposition proceedings

2.092 The EPC allows third parties to apply to revoke a European patent within nine months of the mention of its grant. Although, the European patent is now a "bundle" of national patents, the EPC specifically allows third parties to bring revocation proceedings before the EPO which, if successful, will result in the revocation of the European patent *in toto* in all the Designated States. Such proceedings are called opposition proceedings and are dealt with by the Opposition Division. Opposition proceedings may only be brought on the grounds that the subject matter of the patent is not patentable under the EPC[90]; the patent does not disclose the invention in a manner sufficiently clear and complete for it to be carried out by a person skilled in the art and the subject-matter of the European patent extends beyond the content of the application as filed.[91] Thus, an opponent cannot object on the basis of lack of unity of invention, that the claims are not clear and concise or supported by description or that the patentee is not entitled to the patent. A European patent owner cannot bring opposition proceedings against his own patent.[92]

The party bringing opposition proceedings ("the opponent") must file a Notice of Opposition within the nine month period from grant of the patent and pay an opposition fee.[93] The EPO recommends that parties use the pre-printed form available free of charge from the EPO. The Notice of Opposition must include a written reasoned statement of the grounds on which the opposition is based as well as an indication of the facts, evidence and arguments presented in support of these grounds.[94] The Notice of Opposition should include two copies of any documents referred to.[95]

[88] Art. 122(5).
[89] EPCr 37(3), Art. 86(2).
[90] An opponent cannot allege that a patent is invalid because of national prior rights—T–550/88, *Mobil/Admissibility* [1990] EPOR 391, TBA.
[91] Art. 100.
[92] G–9/93, *Peugeot & Citroen*: [1994] OJEPO Vol. 10/XV [1995] EPOR 260, reversing Decision G–1/84.
[93] Art. 99(1), EPCr 55, 56.
[94] ECPr 55, Art. 99(1). The written statement can be provided after filing of the Notice of Opposition but before the expiry of the nine month period—EPCr 56(1).
[95] EPCr 59.

The EPO will check that the formalities have been complied with.[96] If these have been complied with, it will notify the patent owner of the opposition proceedings, provide the owner with the written statement and invite him to file his observations and any amendments he considers necessary within a certain period (usually four months).[97]

The opposition proceedings then enters a period of substantive examination. Documents referred to by a party in opposition proceedings should be filed with the notice of opposition or written submissions. If not, they should be filed in "due time" upon invitation by the EPO, failing which the EPO may decide not to take into account any argument based on them.[98] The parties will be consulted and if request, an oral hearing can be arranged.[99] The owner of the patent may at this stage also be invited to file an amended specification and/or claims.[1]

The patent may either be maintained, revoked or maintained in an amended form.[2] Parties are given the right if the EPO intends to maintain an amended patent to submit observations within two months if they disapprove of the text in which it is intended to maintain the patent.[3] The owner of a patent amended during opposition proceedings must pay printing fees and file a translation of any amended claims in the other two official languages within three months from the expiry of the above period.[4] The EPO publishes the result of the opposition proceeding and any new specifications of amended European patents.[5] However, such amendments must not extend the protection conferred.[6]

The Opposition Division has the right to apportion costs in opposition proceedings. Such an apportionment which will take into account the renumeration of the representatives must only take into consideration the expenses necessary to assure proper protection of the rights involved.[7]

[96] EPCr 56.

[97] EPCr 57(1). The patent proprietor cannot file amendments if the opposition is found to be inadmissible—see T–550/88, *Mobil/Admissibility*: [1990] EPOR 391, TBA.

[98] Art. 14(2). If an opponent submits documents outside the nine month period, these should only be disregarded if it is clearly established that they could have been submitted earlier and reasons for disregarding such document must be given—see T–156/84, *Air Products*: [1989] EPOR 47; IPD 10103, February 1988. See also T–951/91 *DuPont/late submission* [1995] EPOR 398 at 410, where TBA refused to admit late evidence as there was no good reason for the delay. In that case, however, the TBA emphasised that the main criteria for deciding on the admissibility of a late filed document is its relevance. (See p. 409).

[99] Guide to applying for a European patent, Para. 183.

[1] EPCr 58.

[2] Art. 102.

[3] EPCr 58(4).

[4] EPCr 58(5). There is a further grace period of two months - see EPCr 58(6) but a surcharge is payable.

[5] Art. 103.

[6] Art. 122(3).

[7] EPCr 63. In practice, the amount awarded by the EPO is small, *i.e.* 100 to 500 DM is common.

There is no right of appeal on the sole issue of costs in opposition proceedings unless the amount fixed is in excess of the Rules relating to fees.[8]

(xi) Appeals

2.093 There are three appellate bodies. The Technical Board of Appeal (TBA) is responsible for appeals from decisions concerning the refusal or grant of a European patent or from decisions of an Opposition Division.[9] The Legal Board of Appeal (LBA) is responsible for the few appeals which are purely on a matter of law and contain no technical element.[10] The Enlarged Board of Appeal (EBA) is the highest appellate body in the EPO and is concerned with the uniform application of the law and where an important point of law arises.[11] Only the Board of Appeal or the President of the EPO can refer any question or point of law to it.[12] Each body has its own procedural rules.[13]

Appeals lie from the decisions of the Receiving Section, Examining Division, Opposition Division and the Legal Division and the filing of an appeal suspends the effect of such decisions.[14] Any party to proceedings adversely affected by a decision may appeal and other parties in the proceedings automatically become parties to the appeal.[15] The appeal lies from the decision and not from the grounds of the decision. Therefore, a party may raise fresh reasons even though such are unconnected with the reasons in the decision under appeal.[16]

A party may only appeal against an adverse interlocutory decision if it appeals the final decision unless the interlocutory decision allows for a separate appeal.[17] This may force a party to accept an adverse interlocutory decision which may prejudice the presentation of its case rather than wait to have the patent application refused and then appealing the decision with all the attendant risks and delay that such a course entails.

A notice of appeal must be filed in writing with the EPO within two months of notification of the adverse decision and must contain the name and address of the appellant and a statement identifying the decision and the extent to which amendment or cancellation of the decision is requested and an appeal fee must be paid.[18] Within four months after the date of notification of the decision, a written statement setting out the

[8] Art. 106(4), (5).

[9] Art. 21(3)(a), (4).

[10] Art. 21(3)(c).

[11] Decision numbers beginning with "T" are those of the TBA. Correspondingly, "J" indicates Legal Board of Appeal and "G" indicates the EBA.

[12] Art. 112.

[13] These are shorthanded to RApp for Rules of Procedure of the Board of Appeal; RLegApp for the Rules of Procedure of the Legal Board of Appeal and REnLApp for Rules of Procedure of the Enlarged Board of Appeal.

[14] Art. 106.

[15] Art. 107.

[16] T–611/90, *Mitsui/Ethylen Copolymer*: [1991] EPOR 481; IPD 14144, August 1991 TBA.

[17] Art. 106(3).

[18] Art. 108, EPCr 64.

grounds of the appeal must be filed.[19] These time limits cannot be extended.[20]

In practice the appellate stage is primarily a written procedure and thus arguments should be fully developed in writing although an oral hearing can be requested.[21] There is fundamentally little difference between the examination procedure and the appeal procedure and accordingly, new evidence will generally be admissible in appeal proceedings.[22]

If the decision is *ex parte* (*i.e.* the appellant is not opposed by another party to the proceedings) against a department, then the department concerned shall be given an opportunity to rectify its decision if it is clear that there are fundamental deficiencies in the first instance proceedings, unless special reasons present themselves for doing otherwise.[23]

The Boards of Appeal may reject or allow the appeal. If the latter, it can either exercise any power within the competence of the department which was responsible for the appealed decision or remit the case to the department for further prosecution.[24] The appeal fees may be reimbursed if the department concerned accepts its mistake or there has been a substantial procedural violation.[25]

(xii) Time limits

2.094 As with the prosecution of any patent application in any patent office, compliance with time limits is extremely important and the consequences of failure to do so can be fatal. Thus although the above sections each contain information on time limits relevant to that stage of proceedings, general information concerning time limits is set out here.

There are three kinds of time limits which are provided for in the EPC. Firstly, there are time limits laid down in the EPC or its Implementing Regulations which are computed from the date of filing or priority date.

[19] The grounds of appeal must give full reasons for their appeal otherwise they will be inadmissible—see J–22/86, *Medical Biological Sciences/Oral Prosthesis*: [1987] OJEPO 280; [1987] EPOR 87; T–220/83, *Huls*: [1986] OJEPO 249; [1987] EPOR 87 and T–145/88, *Nicolon/Statement of Grounds*: [1991] EPOR 357; IPD 14105, June 1991, TBA.

[20] Art. 108.

[21] See Point 194, "Guide to Applying for a European Patent" and Art. 116. See also RApp 11, *et seq.*

[22] T–1/80, *BAYER/Carbonless Copying Paper*: [1981] OJEPO 206; [1979–1985] Vol. B 250. However, the Appeal Board may disregard facts or evidence which were not submitted in due time—Art. 114(2).

[23] Art. 109(1), Art. 10 RApp.

[24] Art. 111(1).

[25] EPCr 67. For an example of substantial procedural violation, see T–185/82, *Patrick Posso*: [1979–1985] EPOR Vol. C 696; IPD 7049, July/August 1984 (applicant confused dates of prior art in its submissions on obviousness and EPO failed to notify applicant of error and refused application). For example of when appeal fees will not be refunded, see T–12/82, *Sciaky Bros*: [1979–1985] EPOR Vol. B 395; IPD 7042, June 1984, TBA—auxiliary claim submitted on appeal after main claim had been rejected by Examining Board—case remitted to Examining Division for consideration of the auxiliary claim but appellant not entitled to have appeal fees reimbursed; T–27/83, *Compagnie Francaise de l'Azote (COFAZ)*: IPD 6113, November 1983, TBA—rejection based on clear misunderstanding of the state of the art but no substantial procedural violation.

Secondly, there are time limits whose duration is laid down in the EPC or its Implementing Regulations, but which are computed from an event other than the date of filing or priority date. Thirdly, there are time limits set by the EPO during the proceedings to grant. With the exception of the time limits for the re-establishment of rights, the EPO will draw the attention of the applicant to each of the time limits in the second and third category.[26]

For the purposes of calculating time limits, the general principle is that time starts on the day following the day on which the relevant event occurred. For time limits which start from the date of notification, the relevant date is the receipt of the document notified.[27] For the expiry of a time period where a particular date is not stated, the Implementing Regulations should be consulted.[28] In relation to documentation sent by post to the EPO, the relevant date is the *actual* date of receipt by the EPO. The EPO does not provide for a *deemed* day of receipt being a certain number of days after posting.[29] A general interruption or dislocation of the mail delivery service will postpone the relevant date.[30] However, where an applicant cannot prove such an interruption or dislocation but merely that there has been an unusual postal delay, this will not be sufficient to postpone the relevant date.[31] Notifications sent by the EPO to the applicant will usually be done by registered letter and deemed to be delivered to the applicant on the tenth day after sending unless the letter fails to reach the addressee or has reached him at a later date. If there is any dispute, the EPO must establish that the letter has reached its destination or establish the date on which it was received.[32]

2.095 *Failure to observe time limits*—where an applicant fails to observe a time limit, the applicant may be forced to pay surcharge fees and, if he remains in default, ultimately this will result in loss of rights. No decision need be taken for this to happen but the EPO must notify applicants of any loss of rights.[33] If the applicant considers that the EPO has wrongfully removed his rights, he may apply for a decision from the EPO within two months after notification of the communication of loss of rights.[34]

[26] Annex VIII, Guide to Application for a European Patent.
[27] EPCr 83.
[28] See EPCr 83(3) to (5) and EPCr 85.
[29] T–702/89, *Allied Signal*: [1993] EPOR 580.
[30] EPCr 85(2).
[31] T–702/89, *Allied Signal*: [1993] EPOR 580, TBA (postal delay of six days).
[32] EPCr 78(3).
[33] EPCr 69. See T–26//88, *Akzo*: IPD 14065 which held (in the context of a failure by a patentee within the time limit set by Art. 102(4) to pay printing fee and file translations of amended claims during opposition proceedings pursuant to EPCr 58(5)) that the patent was automatically revoked and thus the communication under EPCr 69 notifying of loss of rights was not a "decision" that could be appealed. Thus, the patentee's remedy lay in the re-establishment of rights and not by way of appeal against the communication notifying him of loss of rights. However, see EPCr 69(2).
[34] EPCr 69(2).

Where the EPO has correctly assessed that the applicant has failed to observe a time limit, various consequences follow. Firstly, one must differentiate between time limits set by the EPC and its Implementing Regulations and those set by the EPO itself. In the latter case, the legal consequences of failure to reply within the set time limits do not ensue and are retracted if the applicant requests further processing of the application within two months of the date on which the decision refusing the application or the communication that the application is deemed to have been withdrawn was notified.[35] The omitted act must be done within this period as well and a fee for further processing must be paid.[36]

Where the time limit is set by the EPC and the Implementing Regulations, then there is no general provision for further processing or automatic extension of time limits. In some situations, the applicant may by paying a surcharge fee within a grace period maintain his application. The reader is referred to the relevant sections.

Where the period or extended period has expired, then loss of rights will ensue. However, there is a general provision for restoration of the application if the applicant or his representative were unable to observe the time limit despite all due care required by the circumstances.[37] Such an application must be filed within two months from the removal of the cause of non-compliance but in any rate within a year following the expiry of the unobserved time limit.[38] The application must state the grounds on which it is based and must set out the facts on which it relies.[39] Furthermore, a fee for the re-establishment of rights must be paid.[40]

2.096 Importantly, one cannot apply for restoration of loss of rights in the following circumstances:

(a) Failure to pay the filing, search and designation fees within the

[35] Art. 121. See strict interpretation of this rule in J–47/92, *Further processing/SILVER SYSTEM*: [1994] OJEPO Vol. 10/XV.

[36] Art. 121(2).

[37] Art. 122(1). There are many cases on what constitutes "due care", see T–301/85, *ICI*: [1986] EPOR 340; IPD 9090, November 1986, TBA (patent agent failed to file grounds of appeal because he was involved in a serious road accident and his clerk failed to make a computer entry on ICI's reminder system—application restored as all due care had been taken); T–73/89, *Xerox Corporation*: IPD 13097, July 1990 (failure to observe appeal time limits due to overwork and isolated slip did not amount to lack of fault on patent agent's behalf); T–112/89, *Borg Warner*: IPD 14029, February 1991; T–869/90, *Texaco*: IPD 14107, June 1991; T–315/90, *Baxter Traveno*: IPD 14146, August 1991; T–30/90, *Grain Processing*: IPD 14176, October 1991 (appeal outside time limit—application for restoration of rights refused); J–13/90, *Castleton*: [1994] EPOR 76 (applicant has right to be warned of impending loss of rights if such a warning is to be expected in all good faith).

[38] Art. 122(2) or in the case of failure to pay renewal fees, six months following the expiry of the additional time limit of 6 months—see para. 2.073. See J–17/89, *Lion Breweries*: IPD 13133, August 1990 on the interpretation of date of removal on non-compliance.

[39] Art. 122(3).

[40] Art. 122(3). This must be paid prior to the making of the application as Art. 122 does not permit the payment of fees to have retrospective effect—see J–15/80, *Arenhold*: [1981] OJEPO 7 corrected at [1981] OJEPO 546.

prescribed time limits (taking into account the "grace period" of one month from notification of communication pointing out the time limit has not been observed).[41]

(b) Failure to file within the priority period.[42]

(c) Failure to make a request for examination (taking into account the "grace period" of one month from notification of the communication pointing out the failure to observe the time limit).[43]

(d) Failure by a person, other than the applicant who has been adjudged to be entitled to the grant of the European patent, to prosecute the application as his own application or file a new European patent application within the prescribed time limit.[44]

(e) Failure to file a divisional application or pay fees for it.[45]

(f) Failure to make an application for restoration of loss of rights within the prescribed time limit.[46]

(xiii) Correction of errors

2.097 The Implementing Regulations permit upon request, the correction of linguistic errors, errors of transcription and mistakes in any document filed with the EPO.[47] If the request for correction concerns a description, claims or drawings then the correction must be obvious in the sense that it is immediately evident that nothing else would have been intended than what is offered as the correction.

The EPO has generously interpreted this provision where there is no damage to public interest. Thus, where an applicant's professional representatives had initially failed to claim priority from two priority dates rather than one, the LBA held, allowing the correction, that the mistake had been clearly explained, the applicants and their professional representatives had acted promptly to rectify the mistake and there was no danger to the public interest because the published specification included on its front page a warning that a request had been made under Rule 88 to claim priority from a second application.[48] However, on amendment on descriptions and claims, the EPO is very strict indeed because of the possible effect on third parties.

[41] Art. 122(5), Art. 78(2), EPCr 85a.
[42] Art. 122(5), Art. 76(1).
[43] Art. 122(5), Art. 94(2), EPCr 85b.
[44] Art. 122(5), Art. 61(3).
[45] Art. 122(5), Art. 76(3), EPCr 25.
[46] Art. 122(5).
[47] EPCr 88.
[48] J–4/82, *Yoshida Kogyo KK*: [1982] OJEPO; [1979–1985] EPOR Vol. A 102; IPD 5103, December 1982/January 1983, LBA. See also J–8/80, *RIB LOC*: [1980] OJEPO 293. *Cf.* J–13/80, *General Datacomm Industries*: OJEPO, January 1983; [1979–1985] EPOR Vol. A 129; IPD 5106, December 1982, January 1982, LBA where the LBA refused to allow an amendment under Rule 88 to include a reference to a computer program appended to a priority document that the applicant had failed to file.

(xiv) Accelerated prosecution of European patents[49]

2.098 The grant of a European patent is at present a lengthy process and can take up to five to six years. In many circumstances, the applicant needs a patent to be granted earlier.[50] In such circumstances, he may prefer to use a PCT or Euro-PCT route.[51] If however, the applicant uses the EPC route, there are several ways of accelerating the prosecution of a European patent application.

(a) An applicant with a legitimate interest in a rapid search and/or examination may simply indicate this by a reasoned statement. The EPO will then endeavour to speed up the search and/or examination.
(b) The EPO has stated that it will give priority to applicants who make their first filing at the EPO. For these applicants, it will take all necessary steps to ensure that search reports are drawn up as quickly as possible and are available to the applicant no later than nine months from the filing date.
(c) An applicant can make a request for examination without waiting for a communication from the Examining Division. This should be accompanied by a substantive response to the search report including reasoned observations and/or appropriate amendments to the claims. The applicant can further waive its right to receive a communication from the EPO under Article 96.[52] Such behaviour will often cause the EPO to make every effort to issue the first communication within seven months following receipt of the application by the Examining Division.
(d) Once the applicant has received the text for grant for his approval under Rule 51(4), the time for grant of the patent will be considerably shortened if the text is approved without delay and no requests for further amendments are made.

5. The EPC, PCT and EPO

(a) Introduction

2.099 The EPC is a regional treaty for the purposes of the PCT.[53] The PCT provides that where a State which is designated or elected under the PCT is also a party to a regional treaty, then that application may be treated as

[49] Generally, see *Notice of the EPO concerning accelerated prosecution of European patent applications* [1989] OJEPO 523. This notice has been reprinted quite often, *e.g.* see [1994] OJEPO 244. It has recently been replaced by "PACE" [1995] OJEPO 57.
[50] Although Art. 67 gives provisional protection to published European applications, the deterrent effect of a granted patent is usually much more than a published application.
[51] As to the PCT route, see above at para. 2.009 *et seq*. As to the Euro-PCT route, see below, at para. 2.099 *et seq*.
[52] This Article concerns the invitation by the EPO to the applicant as to whether he wishes the EPO to proceed with further examination of the application where the applicant has received the search report after he has made a request for examination.
[53] Preamble to EPC.

an application for a regional patent.[54] Accordingly, the EPC permits the EPO to be a Designated Office and an Elected Office under the PCT.[55] This means that if a PCT applicant is considering obtaining European patents in those countries which are signatories to the EPC, he can obtain European patents in those countries by merely requesting a European patent in his PCT application. Once publication of the international application has been completed and the application sent in English, French or German to the EPO, the EPO will process the application and, if found patentable, grant European patents for the relevant Member States. This route is called the Euro-PCT route (although it should perhaps more accurately be known as the PCT-Euro route).

Where the EPO is an Elected Office, the EPO will make use of the International Preliminary Examination Report (IPER) in the prosecution of the European application. As mentioned earlier, the IPER is a non-binding preliminary opinion on the patentability of an invention. If the IPER is done by the EPO, then it will be very persuasive. This route is called the Euro-PCT II route.

As a procedural way of obtaining national patents in many countries, the PCT and EPC are fully compatible with each other and provide an extremely useful route for applicants who wish to obtain patent protection in a number of industrialised countries besides Europe.

The EPO can also act as a Receiving Office, International Search Authority and International Preliminary Examining Authority within the PCT even when it is not a Designated Office or Elected office.[56]

The advantages and disadvantages of the Euro-PCT and Euro-PCT II route over a "pure" EPC application and national applications are discussed elsewhere.

(b) EPO as a receiving office

2.100 If the applicant is a resident or national of a State which is a signatory to both the EPC and PCT, then the EPO may act as a Receiving Office.[57] The international application must be filed in triplicate in English, French or German.[58] If the application is filed with an authority of a Contracting State for onward transmittal to the EPO as the Receiving Office, the Contracting State must ensure that the application reaches the EPO not later than two weeks before the end of the 13th month after filing, or if priority is claimed, after the date of priority.[59] The EPO will then process the matter according to the PCT and PCT guidelines.[60] A professional representative is required to act for the applicant if he does not have a resi-

[54] Art. 45(1) PCT.
[55] See Art. 150–158 EPC and EPCr 104a, 104b, 104c. For meaning of "Designated Office" and "Elected Office", see para. 2.004.
[56] For meaning of these, see above, at para. 2.004.
[57] Art. 151 EPC. For meaning of "resident or national of a Contracting State", see PCTr 18.
[58] EPCr 104.
[59] EPCr 104.
[60] See para. 2.005 *et seq*. and Guid. IX–2.

dence or principal place of business within the territory of one of the Member States to the EPC.[61]

(c) EPO as an International Searching Authority

2.101 The EPO will act as an International Searching Authority for applicants who are residents or nationals of a Contracting State to the PCT.[62] If it holds that there is no unity of invention, then it will charge an additional fee equal to the amount of the search fee for each further invention.[63] The Boards of Appeal are responsible for deciding on a protest made by an applicant against the imposition of such additional fees.[64] The EPO will not charge for copies of documents cited in the ISR but will charge for translating the application into English if it is not in an official language of the PCT.[65] Where the international application is withdrawn or is deemed withdrawn, the EPO will refund the applicant all or some of the search fee.[66] In order to assist applications in Eastern Europe, the EPO has recently announced that search fees will be reduced by 75 per cent for PCT applications which are filed in Albania, Bulgaria, Czech Republic, Estonia, Hungary, Latvia, Lithuania, Poland, Slovakia, Slovenia and states belonging to the former Soviet Union.[67]

(d) EPO as an International Preliminary Examining Authority

2.102 The EPO will act as an International Preliminary Examining Authority for applicants who are residents or nationals of a Contracting State to Chapter II of the PCT.[68] Applications must be made in English, French or German. There is a handling fee and a much larger preliminary examination fee.[69] The EPO as IPEA will charge an additional fee equal to the preliminary examination fee for each additional invention that it examines.[70] The Boards of Appeal are responsible for deciding on a protest made by an applicant against the imposition of such additional fees.[71] The EPO will refund the preliminary examination fee by 100 per cent if the demand for preliminary examination is considered as if it had not been made and 75 per cent if the application is withdrawn before the start of the international preliminary examination.[72] Where the EPO is

[61] See PCT's Applicant Guide—Vol. 1, Annex C.
[62] Art. 154 EPC.
[63] EPCr 104a. Generally, see para. 2.012.
[64] Art. 154(3).
[65] See PCTr 44.3, 48.3 and PCT's Applicant's Guide, Vol. 1, Annex D.
[66] For precise details, see PCT's Applicant Guide, Vol. 1, Annex D.
[67] Administrative Decision 15/12/194 [1995] OJEPO 1–2/1995 14.
[68] Art. 155.
[69] However, the preliminary examination fee is much less than a regular examination fee under the EPC.
[70] EPCr 104a, Art. 34(3)(a) PCT.
[71] Art. 155(3). This contrasts with an EP Application where only if the Examining Division refuses to agree to the applicant's protest will it go to appeal.
[72] See PCTr 58.3 and PCT Applicant's Guide, Vol. 1, Annex E.

also an Elected Office, then the fee for examination at the "Euro" stage by the EPO as Elected Office will be reduced by 50 per cent.[73] The EPO has recently announced that preliminary examination fees will be reduced by 75 per cent where a PCT application was filed in Albania, Bulgaria, Czech Republic, Estonia, Hungary, Latvia, Lithuania, Poland, Slovakia, Slovenia and states belonging to the former Soviet Union.[74]

(e) EPO as a Designated Office: the Euro-PCT route[75]

2.103 The EPO will act as a Designated Office for those states which are signatories to both the PCT and the EPC where the applicant requests in his international application that he wishes to obtain a European patent for that State.[76] The applicant may also wish to obtain national protection in that State as well as the European patent route. In such a case, there will be two Designated Offices being the national patent office and the EPO. However, if the application is for Belgium, France, Greece, Italy or Monaco, then the application will be treated as an application for a European patent as no national patents can be obtained in these countries via an international application under the PCT and the EPO will be the only Designated Office.[77] Only one PCT Designation Fee is required for a Euro-PCT application, although the EPO will in the "Euro" phase of the application require designation fees under the EPC for each Member State to be paid as one would for a "pure" EPC application.[78]

Where the EPO is a Designated Office, the International Bureau of WIPO will send a copy of the application along with the international search report to the EPO promptly after publication of the international report or, at the latest, by the end of the nineteenth month from the priority date.[79] The application is then governed by the EPO in accordance with its own procedural and substantive laws. The EPO will thus publish a translation of the international application into one of its official languages if necessary, make a supplementary search if necessary, examine the application to ensure that it meets the substantive patent requirements of the EPC and either grant or refuse the application. The following sections deal with the practice in the EPO which is specific to Euro-PCT applications as opposed to normal EPC applications. Time limits differ if the application is a Euro-PCT II application.

[73] See PCT Applicant's Guide, Vol. II, National Chapter, E.P.

[74] Administrative Decision 15/12/194 [1995] OJEPO 1–2/1995 14.

[75] The EPO has published a detailed guide called "Information for PCT Applicants" for where the EPO is a Designated Office—[1991] OJEPO 328–339.

[76] Art. 153 EPC.

[77] See PCT's Applicant's Guide, Vol. II, General Part, p. 3 and Art. 153 EPC, Art. 45(2) PCT.

[78] EPCr 104b.

[79] See Art. 20(1)(a) PCT and PCTr 47. The applicant does not need to send a copy of the international application to the EPO—See PCT's Applicant Guide, National Chapter, E.P. and PCTr 49.1(a).

Publication of translation—publication of the application by the International Bureau takes the place of publication by the EPO. However, if the international application is not in an official language of the EPO, the applicant must provide a translation of the application into English, French or German within 21 months of the priority date to the EPO which it will publish.[80] In such a case, the EPC provides for provisional protection to be effective from the date of publication.[81] If a translation is not provided within the time limit, the application is deemed withdrawn.[82] **2.104**

Fees—in essence, the applicant pays a "national" fee and then the fees are the same as under the EPC.[83] Thus the applicant must pay the PCT "national" fee and a designation fee for each Member State of the EPC in which the applicant desires patent protection. Furthermore, the applicant must pay a claims fee per claim over 10 claims. If a supplementary search report is required, the applicant must also pay a search fee for this.[84] All these fees must be paid within 21 months of the priority date. However, if the "national" fee, the designation fees or the search fee have not been paid in this period, payment can be made within a period of grace of one month of notification of a communication from the EPO, provided that within this period a surcharge is paid.[85] If this is not done, the application is deemed withdrawn.[86] **2.105**

Request for examination—the applicant must file a request to the EPO for examination of the application within 21 months of the priority date or six months after the publication of the International Search Report under the PCT, whichever is the later.[87] If this is not done, then it may still be filed within a period of grace of one month of notification of a communication pointing out the failure to observe the time limit provided a surcharge fee is paid.[88] The EPO will not process or examine an international application prior to expiry of the above periods unless the applicant specifically makes such a request.[89] As with EPC applications, a fee for examination is required. **2.106**

[80] Art. 22(1) PCT; EPCr 104(b).
[81] See Art. 158(3) and Art. 67 EPC.
[82] Art. 24 PCT.
[83] The national basic fee as a PCT-Euro application enters the "Euro" phase is U.K. £250 (in November 1994).
[84] EPCr 104b. The search fee is reduced by 20 per cent where the ISR has been made by the Australian Patent Office, the Japanese Patent Office, the USSR Patent Office or the US Patents and Trademark Office. No supplementary search report is required where the ISR is compiled by the Swedish or Austrian Patent Office.
[85] EPCr 85a. Note that the grace period does not apply to claims fees. These will be deemed to have been withdrawn—EPCr 104c(3).
[86] EPCr 104b, Art. 157, 158, Art. 24 PCT. Where the applicant fails to pay all designation fees but pays at least one, then the application is only deemed withdrawn in relation to that Member State—see EPCr 104c.
[87] EPCr 104b(1); Art. 94(2), 150, 157 EPC.
[88] EPCr 85b.
[89] Arts. 22, 23 PCT.

2.107 *Supplementary search report*—the EPO will prepare its own search report to supplement the ISR unless the latter was made by the EPO, the Swedish or Austrian Patent Office.[90] This will be based on the claims which are contained in the application (either original or amended) on the date the search is started. A supplementary search fee must be paid for this. The search report will then be sent to the applicant and if it arrives after the applicant has made a request for examination of the application, the EPO will invite the applicant to indicate whether it wishes to proceed further with the application. If the applicant wishes to proceed further, he must notify the EPO.

(f) EPO as an elected office: the Euro-PCT II route[91]

2.108 The EPO will act as an Elected Office if the applicant has made a demand for an IPER and has elected at least one State which is a signatory to both the PCT and the EPC and also which is bound by Chapter II of the PCT. At present, of the Member States of the EPC, only Greece, Spain, Switzerland and Liechtenstein are not bound by Chapter II of the PCT. An applicant will thus "elect" as well as "designate" the EPO if it intends to use the results of the IPER in proceedings before the EPO.[92] As previously stated, the IPER is a preliminary non-binding opinion on whether the invention is patentable and is based on the ISR, the application and any amendments.

Substantive examination of a Euro-PCT II application by the EPO at the "Euro" stage will be conducted in the same way as for applications where the EPO is a Designated Office. Where the EPO was the IPEA, the substantive examination will normally be carried out by the examiner responsible for making the IPER.[93] At the "Euro" stage, the examiner may have the benefit of the supplementary search and so the examination may not be a formality. The Guidelines for the EPO state that the IPER must be regarded as an opinion and may be departed from if new facts and evidence are produced or if there is a material difference between the substantive patentability requirements under the PCT and EPC.[94] This suggests that otherwise it is to be considered binding. Thus, examination reports drawn up by any other IPEA must be examined carefully and if the reasons put forward in the IPER are sound, they must not be disregarded.[95]

[90] Arts 157(2), 96(1) and PCT's Applicant' Guide, Vol. II, National Chapter, E.P.
[91] For a detailed analysis of the deadlines and procedural steps before the EPO as an Elected Office, see "Information for PCT applicants"—[1991] OJEPO 339–351.
[92] Art. 156 EPC.
[93] Guid. E-IX 6.4.
[94] Guid E-IX-6.4.2. The substantive requirements are virtually the same—see Arts. 33, 34(4) PCT, PCTr 64, 65, 67 and Arts. 52–57 of the EPC.
[95] Guid. E-IX-6.4.2.

2.109 *Procedure*—The EPO will be notified of its election by the International Bureau.[96] The procedural rules as to the provision of fees and translations is the same as where the EPO is only a Designated Office except that the applicable period is 31 months and not 21 months from the priority date.[97] This is so even if some of the European States designated in the application to the EPO are not members of Chapter II of the PCT and thus cannot be elected.[98]

The substantive examination will not begin before the expiry of the 31 month period from the earliest priority date unless the applicant has expressly so requested.[99] Somewhat complicated rules of the PCT apply in relation to amendment of claims before the EPO as an elected Office. In effect, where election of the EPO is effected prior to the expiry of the nineteenth month from the priority date, then the EPO's rules on amendments during the examination procedure apply provided that the applicant is allowed to amend its application before the expiry of 31 months from the priority date.[1] Where the election of the EPO has been effected after the expiry of the nineteenth month, then the EPO rules on amendment during the examination procedure will apply.[2]

Importantly, if the EPO was the IPEA, the examination fee will be reduced by 50 per cent.[3]

(g) EPO acting in a combination of roles

2.110 The EPO can act as Receiving Office, International Searching Authority, International Preliminary Examining Authority, Designated Office and Elected Office or combine any of these roles. In a Euro-PCT II application, the EPO could act as all bodies. If the applicant wishes to restrict itself to obtaining patents in States which are Member States of both the PCT and EPC, then the apparent outcome, that is of patents being granted in these countries, is the same under both routes. The merits of the various routes are discussed below.[4]

6. Community Patent Measures

(a) Community patent convention

2.111 In the 1960s, the fear that national intellectual property rights would be used to restrict trade within the EEC led the E.C. Commission and the six original Member States to seek solutions to this problem in the fields of

[96] Art. 31(7) PCT, PCTr 62.1(a).
[97] EPCr 104b, Art. 39(1)(a) PCT.
[98] See PCT's Applicant's Guide, Vol. 1, Annex B2.
[99] Art. 40 PCT.
[1] PCTr 78, Art. 41 PCT.
[2] PCTr 52.1, 78.2, Art. 41 and 28 EPC. If the communication from the International Bureau to the EPO under PCTr 47.1 is made after the expiry of the 19 month period, then the applicant may make amendments within four months from such a date.
[3] PCT's Applicant Guide, Vol. II, National Chapter, E.P.
[4] See para. 2.127 *et seq.*

patents, trade marks and designs. In 1965, a complete draft of an EEC patent law not only provided for a centralised grant procedure for unitary European patents but also a system of law governing them. In 1969, following a break of four years due to political reasons caused by the United Kingdom's request to join the EEC, it was proposed that this draft be split into two conventions. The first was intended to create a centralised European procedure for any European country regardless of whether or not it was a member of the EEC which granted European patents that would have the legal value of a bundle of national patents. By the second convention, it was intended to create a European patent for the Common Market which was of a unitary and autonomous character and governed by a common system of law. The first convention led to the Munich Convention establishing the European Patent Convention. The second convention led to the Luxembourg Convention establishing the Community Patent Convention in 1975. This provided that the Community patent was of a unitary nature which could only be granted, transferred, revoked or allowed to lapse in respect of the whole Community.[5]

Since then, the European Patent Convention entered into force on October 1, 1977. The Community Patent Convention required the ratification of the nine E.C. States that had signed it. However, Denmark and Ireland were not able to ratify the Convention for constitutional reasons. This deadlock and further difficulties over the ratification of the Convention by Spain in the 1980s led to two conferences in Luxembourg in 1985 and 1989. At the first conference, agreement was reached on the Protocol on Litigation and the Establishment of a Community Patent Appeal Court. These provisions essentially provided for national designated patents courts to adjudicate on the infringement and validity of Community patents and revoke them if necessary. However, the conferences provided for the establishment of Community Patent Appeal Court (COPAC) which is to have exclusive jurisdiction to determine issues raised on appeals concerning certain provisions of the CPC and the validity of the Community Patent.[6]

At the second conference in 1989, it was agreed that the CPC would only enter into force upon ratification by the 12 signatory E.C. states. However because of the continuing difficulties caused by Denmark, Ireland and Spain, a Protocol for the Possible Modification of the Conditions of Entry into Force of the CPC was agreed. This provided that if the CPC had not entered force by December 31, 1991, another conference would be reconvened in order for the Member States to unanimously amend the number of States which had to ratify the CPC in order for it to come into force. Unfortunately, no agreement was reached at an

[5] Art. 2(2).

[6] For a detailed analysis of the jurisdictional rules on litigation under the CPC, see David Young Q.C. and Colin Birss, "Forum Shopping under the Community Patent Convention" [1992] EIPR 361 and Foglia, "Procedural Aspects of Litigation under the Community Patent" [1990] IIC 970.

Intergovernmental Conference in Lisbon in July 1992 in relation to this Protocol.[7]

2.112 Accordingly, at present, it is not likely that the CPC will be ratified whether for all the Member States or in its amended form under the Protocol for the majority of the States. Commentators have said that it is unlikely that it will ever come into force.[8] An amendment made at the 1989 Luxembourg conference, requiring translation of the full specification into all the languages of the Community within a specified time limit, means that the cost of obtaining a Community patent especially with the likelihood of Community enlargement will be prohibitive for all but multinationals. Furthermore, there would appear to be two legal problems. Firstly, the interaction of the CPC with the Lugano Convention on jurisdiction and enforcement of judgments is problematic.[9] Secondly, the failure of the CPC to remove the ability of Member States to make a reservation that the working of the invention in Member State A did not amount to the working of the invention in Member State B and thus give rise to the grant of a compulsory licence is in conflict with the jurisprudence of the ECJ in relation to intellectual property and Articles 30 to 36.[10] Now that the original fear that national intellectual property rights would be used to partition the Community has been considerably reduced by the jurisprudence of the ECJ,[11] at present, there appears little incentive to ratify the CPC and it has been said that ratification of the 1989 Luxembourg Convention would be equivalent to "putting a dead man on the throne".[12]

Consequently, the detailed provisions of the CPC are not discussed in this edition of this book.

[7] The conference was very secret and non-governmental observers were excluded. It is thus not exactly clear what happened at the conference. See Burnside, "The Community Patent Convention; Is it Obsolete in its Present Form" [1992] EIPR 285 at 288.

[8] See van Benthem, "The European Patent System and European Integration" [1993] IIC 435 at 443.

[9] The Protocol on the Settlement of Litigation Concerning the infringement and validity of Community Patents expressly enacts that the Brussels Convention applies to proceedings concerning infringement or validity of a Community Patent. However, the CPC at present has not sought to reconcile the provisions of the Lugano Convention with it. Whilst this should not present too many technical difficulties because the Lugano Convention is virtually identical to the Brussels Convention, it means that the CPC must be amended which will require some degree of time and effort from all concerned parties—for a recognition of this problem in the context of the proposed Community Registered Design, see the Green Paper on the Legal Protection of Industrial Design, Brussels, June 1991, III/F/513/EN at para. 9.3.3.4.

[10] See Burnside, "The Community Patent Convention; Is it Obsolete in its Present Form" [1992] EIPR 285 at 287–288. Recent decisions of the ECJ have ruled that such a provision in national law is contrary to Articles 30 to 36 and accordingly, Member States have been obliged to change their national patent laws in this respect, see para. 7.078. This renders the reservations ineffective and means that the CPC is actually deficient in this regard as opposed to national laws.

[11] See van Benthem, "The European Patent System and European Integration" [1993] IIC 435 at 443 and Burnside, "The Community Patent Convention; Is it Obsolete in its Present Form" [1992] EIPR 285.

[12] Burnside, *ibid.*

(b) Biotechnological patent directive

2.113 *Introduction*—on October 20, 1988, the E.C. Commission submitted to the Council a proposal for a directive on the legal protection of biotechnological inventions. The Commission was of the opinion that the protection for such inventions in Member States varied considerably. This partly arose out of what was patentable in biotechnology, especially with the development of technology from the classical microbiology of bacteria and fungi into high life forms, *e.g.* plants and animals. Secondly, the Commission considered that such protection as was available was generally less favourable than in the USA and Japan. Consequently, the E.C. was failing to capitalise on the new wunderkind biotechnology. The aim of the directive was to increase the protection for such inventions throughout the Community and also to harmonise protection in the Member States.[13]

In 1989, as the large majority of Member States were also contracting states to the EPC, the directive had to co-exist with Article 53 of the European Patent Convention. This has been examined above in the context of European patents.[14] In summary, this Article excludes patent protection for inventions which were contrary to "ordre public" or morality and also excludes protection for "plant or animal varieties or essentially biological processes for the product of plants or animals" but such exclusion does not apply to "microbiological processes or the products thereof". This provision, which was drafted in the 1970s, is relatively coarse. However, the EPO and the Boards of Appeal have several times had to address the issue of the patentability of animal and plant inventions and a body of law has developed in this area.[15] Because of the requirements of the EPC, Contracting States are obliged to ensure that European patents "have the same effect and are subject to the same conditions" as national patents.[16] The effect of the above is that the national patent legislation of Contracting States to the EPC must closely approximate to that of the EPC. Accordingly, any directive from the Commission which imposed differing obligations on Member States to that of the EPC in the area of patent law would cause a direct conflict between those states' obligation under the Treaty of Rome and the European Patent Convention.

2.114 The Commission's proposal was subject to many amendments from the European Parliament and the Council. In this period, the 1991 UPOV Convention on Plant Variety rights was introduced so as to allow double protection for plant invention both under plant variety law and patent

[13] For a commentary on the draft directive of 1989 and its history, see Whaite and Jones, "Biotechnological Patents in Europe—the Draft Directive [1989] EIPR 145.
[14] See para. 2.051.
[15] See para. 2.012 *et seq.*
[16] Art. 2(2) EPC. See above, at para. 2.025.

law. This removed one difficulty to the proposed directive which up to then, had been obliged to consider the effect on plant variety protection if it increased patent protection.

On February 7, 1994, the Council adopted a common position on the Directive by a qualified majority with the Danish, Spanish and Luxembourg delegations voting against the Directive.[17]

On February 28, 1995, the European Parliament rejected the draft Biotechnological Directive by 240 votes to 188 despite a Common Position being adopted on the Directive on February 21, 1995. The main reason for opposition was that many Members of the European Parliament were persuaded by the environmental groups that it would remove virtually all restrictions on the patenting of life. It is unlikely that the Commission will attempt to resuscitate the directive in an amended form in the foreseeable future.[17a]

(c) Supplementary protection for patented pharmaceutical products

2.115 *Introduction*—most countries provide for a regulatory framework for the testing of pharmaceuticals prior to them being placed on the market. The Commission has introduced two directives in this field, one for the medicinal products for human use[18] and one for veterinary products.[19] Often, there will be substantial delays prior to the product coming on the market.[20] Clearly, where a pharmaceutical is the subject of a patent, this reduces the effective term of protection and often would make its exploitation uneconomic. A survey in 1988 of more than 300 pharmaceutical products showed that the effective patent life of pharmaceutical products in Europe was eight years.[21] In the 1980s, several countries including the United States, Japan, Italy and France introduced legislation which provided for the restoration of the patent term for pharmaceuticals. Such legislative measures were seen to have put many European pharmaceutical companies at a competitive disadvantage. Thus, the Commission proposed that a regulation conferring supplementary protection for pharmaceuticals should be enacted. Eventually, a regulation which

[17] See [1994] O.J. C101/65.

[17a] For a review of the death of the directive and the consequences of the rejection, see Roberts "The Former Biotech Patents Directive", *Patent World* [1995], p. 27.

[18] Dir. 65/65.

[19] Dir. 81/851.

[20] A "new" pharmaceutical (*i.e.* one which is not bioequivalent to an existing marketed product) will typically take some 12 years to reach the market—see Whaite and Jones, "Pharmaceutical Patent Term Restoration—the European Commission's Proposed Regulation" [1990] 5 EIPR 179.

[21] See Lelkes, von Uexkull and Tauchner, "Patent Term Restoration in Europe: Taking Advantage of the Supplementary Protection Certificate" *Patent World*, December 1992/January 1993, p. 14.

created a supplementary protection certificate for medicinal products was passed which came into force on July 2, 1993 in all Member States.[22]

The regulation does not extend the life of the patent as such. Instead, it provides for the grant of a *sui generis* supplementary protection certificate which is deemed broadly to have the same effect as a patent.[23] It is only available for patents relating to the active ingredients of medicinal or veterinary products used in human or animal healthcare. The calculation of the duration of the certificate is somewhat complicated but its effect is to give a limited extension of protection.

Importantly, there is a pending application by Spain to declare the regulation void as misuse of the European Treaty.[24]

The regulation is now considered in detail.

2.116 *Qualifying conditions*—a certificate will be granted if the following conditions are satisfied in the Member State in which the application is made.

(a) The product is protected by a basic patent in force.
(b) A valid authorisation to place the product on the market as a medicinal product has been granted in accordance with Directive 65/65/EEC (*medicinal products for human use*) or 81/851/EEC (*veterinary products*).
(c) The product has not already been the subject of a certificate.
(d) The authorisation referred to in (b) is the first authorisation to place the product on the market in the Community as a medicinal product.[25]
(e) The application is lodged within six months of the date of authorisation or six months from the date of grant (whichever is the latest).[26]

2.117 The reference to "product" is defined as constituting the active ingredient or combination of active ingredients of a medicinal product which itself is defined as:

[22] Council Regulation 1768/92, [1992] O.J. L182/1. For detailed commentary on this SPC Regulation, see Lelkes, von Uexkull and Tauchner, "Patent Term Restoration in Europe: Taking Advantage of the Supplementary Protection Certificate *Patent World*, December 1992/January 1993, p. 14; Whaite and Jones, "Pharmaceutical Patent Term Restoration—the European Commission's Proposed Regulation" [1990] 5 EIPR 179; Whaite and Jones "Pharmaceutical Patent Term Restoration: The European Commission's Regulation" [1992] 9 EIPR 324; Cook, "The Supplementary Protection Certificate—How is it Working in Practice" *Patent World*, February 1994, p. 29.

[23] See Adams, "SPC: Challenge to Regulation 1768/92" [1994] EIPR 323 at p. 324.

[24] Case C–350/92, *Kingdom of Spain v. Council of the European Communities*. Discussed in Adams *ibid*. The general opinion of advisors is that this application is very unlikely to succeed. If however it did, it could put in doubt the validity of many of the Community intellectual property directives and regulations as the Spanish government is claiming the procedural legislative mechanism used for the SPC regulation (which is the mechanism used for many other intellectual property directives and regulations) was *ultra vires* and a misuse of powers.

[25] Regulation 1768/92, arts. 2 and 3.

[26] Art. 7.

> "any substance or combination of substances presented for treating or preventing disease in human beings or animals and any substance or combination of substances which may be administered to human beings or animals with a view to making a medical diagnosis or to restoring, correcting or modifying physiological functions in human beings or in animals.[27]

2.118 *Subject matter and scope of protection*—the certificate confers the same rights as conferred by the basic patent and is subject to the same limitations and the same obligations.[28] Invariably, protection will be more narrow than that of the patent as it is restricted to the:

> "product covered by the authorisation order to place the corresponding medicinal product on the market and for any use of the product as a medicinal product that has been authorised before the expiry of the certificate."[29]

It has been suggested that the most appropriate interpretation of this definition is that protection will be conferred on the active ingredient however formulated and for any therapeutic use covered by a marketing authorisation granted before expiry of the certificate.[30]

Difficulty arises where the authorisation order covers products beyond those specifically mentioned in the patent. For a SPC certificate to be granted for a particular product, the product must be *inter alia* "protected by a basic patent in force". Does this mean only those products mentioned expressly in the patent description or more widely, those products which infringe the patent? In Germany, the main claim of the patent disclosed a basic antibacterial amine compound and anomers thereof whilst the patent specification disclosed the hydrochloride salt. The proprietors petitioned the German patent office for an SPC covering both the base compound and any salts thereof (*i.e.* wider than the specific disclosure in the patent). The Examiner refused the application in part by arguing that salts other than the hydrochloride salt were not contained in the original patent.[31] In the U.K., the Patent Office has taken a more liberal approach. A patentee sought to obtain an SPC for a nonapeptide in the form of its acetate salt. The claim did not refer to the salt but it had been mentioned in the specification in connection with the isolation of the peptide. The patentee argued that on a purposive construction approach, the nonpeptide acetate salt would almost certainly infringe the patent. The Patent Office accepted this and granted an SPC for the nona-

[27] Art. 1(a), (b).

[28] Art. 5. This has been interpreted in the U.K. as meaning that the SPC will be subject to any compulsory licences that the patent was subject to—*Application by Fauldings Pharmaceuticals plc*, Judgment October 6, 1994, Patents Court, Case 17138, [1994] IPD, December 1994, p. 6. [1995] EIPR D–16.

[29] Art. 4.

[30] See Whaite and Jones, "Pharmaceutical Patent Term Restoration: The European Commission's Regulation" [1992] 9 EIPR 324 at p. 325.

[31] Cited Hansen and Hill, [1994] Patents and Licensing 27

peptide acetate salt.[31a] It is submitted that the expression "covered by the patent" must include any potential infringing product regardless as to whether it is expressly mentioned in the specification.[31b] Otherwise, where a company has obtained an authorisation order for a product which is not expressly mentioned in the patent but is clearly an infringing product, it will not be able to obtain a SPC which would thus deny it protection where clearly protection existed before. This may give rise to difficulties for a national patent office illsuited to determining the protection afforded by claims. However, it is submitted that the patent office should take a liberal, broad approach. An apparent danger of this approach is that the patent office might grant SPCs to products which do not infringe the basic patent. However, the owner of an SPC cannot initiate infringement proceedings against products which would not have infringed the basic patent.[32]

There is some doubt as to how strict will be the interpretation of the phrase "product covered by the authorisation order".[33] The Council and Commission have stated that such a definition does not mean that salts or esters of the active ingredient are excluded and "does not rule out the possibility of obtaining a new certificate for a salt or an ester regarded as a new active ingredient.[34]

2.119 *Duration of protection*—the certificate takes effect at the end of the lawful term of the basic patent. The period of protection is calculated as the period which elapsed between the date on which the application for a basic patent was lodged and the date of the first authorisation to place the product on the market in the Community reduced by a period of five years.[35] However, the duration of the certificate may not exceed five years from the date on which it takes effect.[36]

It should be noted that whilst an applicant in a Member State cannot apply for a SPC until authorisation to market the product has been

[31a] In the matter of Supplementary Protection App. No. SPC/GB93/017 in the name of Takeda Chemical Industries Ltd, Patent Office MM 89 Fos. 135, 15 September, 1994.

[31b] See Adams, "Supplementary Protection Certificates", The Salt Problem [1995] 6 EIPR 277 where he discusses the approaches of several patent offices of Member States to SPCS. An argument against a wide interpretation is that as the SPC confers the same rights as conferred by the basic patent, the SPC holder may sue for infringements of its rights where the alleged infringing product is not covered by the SPC but where clearly it infringes the basic patent.

[32] Art. 4.

[33] See discussion as to scope of SPC in relation to process claims and medical indication claims in patents in Lelkes, von Uexkull and Tauchner, "Patent Term Restoration in Europe: Taking Advantage of the Supplementary Protection Certificate" *Patent World*, December 1992/January 1993, p. 14.

[34] Annex to Common Position text of the Regulation agreed at the Council Meeting on 19/12/91. See Whaite and Jones, "Pharmaceutical Patent Term Restoration: The European Commission's Regulation" [1992] 9 EIPR 324 at 324–325.

[35] Art. 13(1). For those suffering from arithmetical fatigue, examples of calculations of the relevant period are given in Whaite and Jones, "Pharmaceutical Patent Term Restoration: The European Commission's Regulation" [1992] 9 EIPR 324.

[36] Art. 13(2).

granted for that state, the calculation of the period of protection is determined by the date of the first authorisation to place the product on the market "in the Community". If there is a considerable delay between the grant of the first authorisation order in the Community and the grant of the order in the Member State in which the application is made, the duration of protection under the SPC may be seriously affected.

2.120 *Entitlement to SPC*—the holder of the basic patent or his successor in title is entitled to the grant of a supplementary protection certificate.[37] Although the regulation does not address it, the prevailing opinion is that the applicant does not need to be the proprietor of the marketing authorisation.[38] Thus, where a licensee holds the authorisation, application for the SPC could be made in the name of the patentee. Difficulties may arise when independent parties each possess novel and inventive process patents for the same active ingredient. Under the regulation, a supplementary protection certificate cannot be granted for a product if it is already the subject of a certificate. Once one party with a process patent has obtained a certificate following authorisation of the product, the other patent owner will not be able to obtain a certificate even if it is the older patent.[39]

2.121 *Procedural conditions*—these are set out in Articles 8 to 11. In summary, application must be made to the patent office which granted the basic patent or on whose behalf it was granted (*i.e.* not the EPO if an European patent) and must include a copy of the authorisation order. A fee may be payable. Publication of the grant of a certificate will take place. National patent offices of Member States may require the payment of annual fees.[40]

As a certificate can only be granted if the basic patent is in force, applicants may be advised to make parallel applications in relation to several basic patents if the validity of some of those patents are in doubt.[41]

2.122 *Licences and SPC*—the SPC Regulation does not expressly deal with the status during the SPC period of existing licences under the basic patent. It has been suggested that Article 5 which states that the certificate shall be subject to the same limitations and obligations as that of the

[37] Art. 7.
[38] Lelkes, von Uexkull and Tauchner, "Patent Term Restoration in Europe: Taking Advantage of the Supplementary Protection Certificate" *Patent World*, December 1992/January 1993, p. 14 at p. 17.
[39] See Art. 3(c), Art. 4 and analysis in Lelkes, von Uexkull and Tauchner, "Patent Term Restoration in Europe: Taking Advantage of the Supplementary Protection Certificate" *Patent World*, December 1992/January 1993, p. 14 at p. 17–18.
[40] Art. 12.
[41] See Cook, "The Supplementary Protection Certificate—How is it Working in Practice" *Patent World*, February 1994, p. 29 at 30.

basic patent means that the licence continue into the period covered by the SPC.[42] Germany has specifically legislated that this is the case.[43]

2.123 *Transitional provisions*—any product which on January 2, 1993 was protected by a basic patent and for which the first authorisation to place it on the market as a medicinal product in the Community was obtained after January 1, 1985 is entitled to the grant of a certificate.[44] In the case of Germany and Denmark, the second date is replaced by January 1, 1988 and in the case of Belgium and Italy by January 1, 1982. Applications for certificates which are covered by these transitional provisions must have been made by July 2, 1994.[45]

The regulation does not come into force until January 2, 1998 for those Member States whose national law did not on January 1, 1990 provide for the patentability of pharmaceutical product. At present, this means Spain, Portugal and Greece.

2.124 *EPC and regulation*—as mentioned earlier, Article 63 of the EPC has been amended (although the amendment is not yet in force) so as to permit Member States to extend the term of a European patent.[46] This amendment is much broader in scope than the regulation as it covers non-medical products. Furthermore, the EPC applies to certain non-E.C. states. Accordingly, once in force, states which are both members of the EPC and E.C. may extend protection beyond that stipulated in the Regulation.

7. EEA Patent Legislation

(a) Acquis communautaire

2.125 In the field of patent law, the E.C. had not issued any legislation prior to the cut-off date of July 31, 1991 (when the annexes to the EEA Agreement listing the EEA relevant *acquis communautaire* were closed.) Accordingly, no secondary legislation in the field of patent law was included as *acquis* into the EEA Agreement. Since the cut-off date, the Supplementary Protection Certificate Regulation has been adopted. This formed part of the "Additional Package" (composed of E.C. acts adopted between July 31, 1991 and the entry into force of the EEA) and is then to be adopted into the EEA Agreement with appropriate amendments.

[42] Cook, "The Supplementary Protection Certificate—How is it Working in Practice" *Patent World*, February 1994, p. 29 at 32.

[43] Lelkes, von Uexkull and Tauchner, "Patent Term Restoration in Europe: Taking Advantage of the Supplementary Protection Certificate" *Patent World*, December 1992/January 1993, p. 14.

[44] Art. 19. It has been held in U.K. Patent Office proceedings that for an application under the transitional rules to succeed, it is necessary for an authorisation order to exist in the United Kingdom and not as Article 19 might suggest merely within the E.C.—see *Yamanouchi's SPC/Fornaterol funnarate*, decision dated September 8, 1993 (SRIS 0/112/93).

[45] Art. 19(2).

[46] See para. 2.027.

EFTA states are also obliged to harmonise their patent laws with the substantive provisions of the EPC.[47] Various derogations are permitted from this rule. Finland must comply with the provisions of the EPC regarding the patentability of pharmaceutical and foodstuffs by January 1, 1995.[48] Iceland must comply with the provisions regarding the patentability of pharmaceuticals by January 1, 1997. Where patent protection is provided for in these countries for such products, rights owners of such patents in Contracting Parties may rely upon their rights even if such products have been marketed in Finland or Iceland by them or with their consent.[49]

(b) Community Patents

2.126 Article 3 of Protocol 28 to the EEA Agreement deals with the difficult issue of the accession of countries to the Community Patent Convention. Article 3(1) provides that the Contracting Parties undertake to use their best endeavours to conclude, within a period of three years after the entry into force of the Community Patent Convention, negotiations with a view to the participation of the EFTA states in the CPC. For Iceland, the relevant date is not earlier than January 1, 1998. With the accession of Austria, Finland and Sweden to the E.C., this provision has little application now as these states will be bound by the CPC which, when in force, will have effect throughout the E.C. Article 3(2) provides that specific conditions for the participation of the EFTA states in the CPC are subject to further negotiations. The obligation to join the CPC is further diluted in Article 3(3) which states that the Community undertakes after the entry into force of the CPC to invite "those EFTA States who so request to enter into negotiations" in accordance with Article 8 of the CPC Agreement. Article 8 of the CPC permits members of the EPC who have a free trade agreement with the E.C. to enter into negotiations with a view to enabling that State to "participate" in the CPC on the basis of a special agreement which determines the conditions and details of the application of the CPC to that state. Article 3(1) to (3) mean that the obligation of EFTA States to join the CPC in the near future is slight.

8. Comparison of National, PCT, EPC and Hybrid Routes

(a) Obtaining patents in Europe: comparison of routes

2.127 An inventor who wishes to obtain patents for one or more countries in Europe has a variety of routes by which he can obtain protection. Because of the ability to claim priority from an applicant for a patent in

[47] Art 3(4), Protocol 28.
[48] Art. 3(5).
[49] Art. 3(6). This provision is considered in more detail in the EEA section in the Chapter on the Enforcement of Intellectual Property.

the 12 months after first filing, there are many ways of combining the differing routes. This section reviews the commonly used routes.

(i) National routes

2.128 *Description*—the applicant makes an application or applications for patents under national patent laws in the countries where he seeks protection. He will normally claim priority from the earliest application.

2.129 *Advantages and disadvantages*—if an applicant seeks protection in only one country, then the national route is the cheapest and the fastest. Furthermore, it is very accessible to a person of limited resources. The language will be the same if he files in his country and thus translation costs will be avoided. The examination and search in a national patent office will be sensitive to the national patent law and thus the patentee will have a greater certainty as to the effectiveness of the patent in contentions proceedings. One advantage of the national route is that in many European countries, there is no real examination. Thus, in France, Belgium, Italy, Luxembourg, Monaco, Portugal and Greece, applications have a much better chance of success and will lead to grant more quickly than via an EPC route or PCT-II route.

Where the applicant is seeking protection in more than one country, the duplication of effort means that as more countries are applied for, the costs increase proportionately with no economies of scale. Furthermore, conducting parallel proceedings in several countries using local patent counsel can become very complex. A recent study has shown that the EPC approach became cheaper when applying for patents in three or more major EPC countries.[49a]

(ii) PCT-national

2.130 *Description*—the applicant uses the Patent Co-operation Treaty to make a single application covering PCT Contracting States. The PCT provides for the centralisation of the application, search and (if requested and the applicant is a resident or national of a state that has acceded to Chapter II of the PCT) preliminary examination stage. If successful, the application will be likely to be granted as national patents.

2.131 *Merits and disadvantages*—where an applicant is seeking patent protection in several countries, the PCT provides a relatively quick and cheap way of obtaining patent protection. In a positive application (*i.e.* one which is in order and clearly novel and unobvious as against the prior art), an application under Chapter II of the PCT will normally be granted within three years.[50] Search reports are normally provided

[49a] "Costs of Patenting in Europe—a study conducted by the EPO", *Patent World 1995*, p. 26.

[50] Helmut Sonn, "National Patents, EPC or PCT: Which Route to Choose?" *Patent World*, April 1991, p. 38 at p. 42.

within 18 months of the priority date.[51] This means the applicant will normally have the ability to prevent publication of the patent on request (which can be made up to 15 days before the due publication date).[52] The cost of an international application is relatively cheap being approximately DM 8,200 for Chapter I and DM 14,200 for Chapter I and II. However, this does not take into account the cost of the national phase.

The main disadvantage as against using the EPC is that a straight PCT-national filing will be expensive if the applicant requires protection in a large number of countries. If the applicant desires protection in France, Italy, Belgium, Greece or Monaco then a PCT-national route becomes a Euro-PCT application by default. In this case, it will be more expensive to use the PCT route as against the EPC route or straight national route. However, many applicants use the PCT route to buy time before deciding whether or not to go ahead.

(iii) Application under the EPC

2.132 *Description*—the applicant files an application with a national patent office or EPO for a European patent designating several countries who are members of the EPC.

2.133 *Merits and disadvantages*—the EPC provides a simplified system for obtaining patents in Western European countries. Where one designates many Member States, there are attendant economies of scale. It has proved to be a very popular route for obtaining patents in Western European countries. Where the applicant seeks protection in more than a few countries, it is cheaper to use the EPC than to file parallel national applications. Moreover, it will be cheaper than using the PCT-national route.[52a]

The disadvantages are that it will often take up to five to six years to obtain a European patent. This is considerably in excess of national PCT routes.[53] The EPC applicant will have to pay during this time annual renewal fees without obtaining any protection in the meanwhile and without any certainty as to the outcome of the application. It is rare that a search report will be available before publication and one must notify the EPO seven weeks in advance of the date of publication in order to prevent publication. This means that an applicant will often not know whether his application is likely to succeed as against the prior art and yet will be unable to prevent publication which will prejudice any later applications. Furthermore, the EPO grants claims in a style which does not take into account any specific claim interpretation of any of the relevant

[51] International Search Reports should be available at the latest sixteen months from the priority dates—see PCTr 22.1(a), 42.1.

[52] See Sonn at p. 42 International Publication takes place promptly after the expiry of 18 months from the priority date of the application.

[52a] See para. 2.129.

[53] Except in France, where an application can take up to five or six years as well.

national courts. Thus, there is uncertainty as to the width of the patent monopoly when it comes to contentious proceedings in national courts.[54]

Furthermore, the EPC is only available for countries of the EPC and is an expensive route and only economically worthwhile as against other routes if the application seeks protection in most west European countries.[54a] Moreover, where protection is desired quickly or where the application is likely to encounter problems at the examination stage, the applicant may be better advised to seek protection through the PCT-I or national route.[55]

(iv) National patent-EPC route

2.134 *Description*—the applicant files a national patent application. Within the priority period, he files for a European patent claiming priority from the national application.

2.135 *Merits and disadvantages*—this route has several advantages from a first application under the EPC. Firstly, the applicant is given a period of one year to consider his actions. The national filing is much cheaper than filing at the EPO and thus costs can be saved, especially if the application turns out to be an inappropriate one. Hopefully, a national search will have been done, or a search by the EPO as a requested "private search", within the 12 month period in order to determine whether to proceed further. Also, the EPO is generally more critical than national patent offices about attempts to alter the content of the description and claims for an application once filed.[56] Another advantage is that one can quickly obtain patent protection via the national route. This has the effect of deterring would-be infringers much better than a published European application. If the European patent is granted, the home application or patent may be dropped.

The disadvantage of this route is that the EPO has said that it will give priority to European patent applications which do not claim priority and has said that it aims to ensure that search reports are available to the applicant no later than six months from the filing date. Thus, the EPO has said that where the applicant merely wishes to consider his options and is happy to pay the extra cost of a first filing in the EPO as against a national filing, he could make a first filing in the EPO and then make a second application in the EPO, claiming priority from the first filing.[57]

[54] This was seen in dramatic effect with the litigation by Improver on its European patent against Remington in various Member States with widely varying results. See Sonn, "National Patents, EPC or PCT: Which Route to Choose?" *Patent World*, April 1991, p. 38 at p. 42.

[54a] The average cost of filing a European application, with 20 pages of description 10 claims and numbering 61,000 words, is about DM 95,000. See, "Costs of Patenting in Europe—a study conducted by the EPO" (1995) Patent World, 26 at 27.

[55] See paras. 2.128 to 2.131.

[56] See Sonn, "National Patents, EPC or PCT: Which Route to Choose?" *Patent World*, April 1991, p. 38, at p. 40.

[57] *ibid.* at p. 524.

However, this option does not overcome the problems of obtaining a search report before publication and is not as cheap as making a national first filing.

(v) Euro-PCT application (chapter I and II)

2.136 *Description*—the applicant makes an international application under the PCT for countries in Europe. An international search is done by the International Searching Authority. Where those countries belong to the EPC, he designates the EPO as a designated Office which takes over the processing of the international application for those countries. If he chooses the Chapter II route, then an International Preliminary Examination Report is compiled along with the International Search Report and the application then goes to the EPO where the EPO as an Elected Office prosecutes the application for countries which belong to the EPC. Importantly, a PCT application which designates Belgium, France, Greece, Italy or Monaco, becomes a Euro-PCT application by default.[58]

2.137 *Advantages and disadvantages*—there are many advantages to this route. The Euro-PCT route is relatively quick and will in a positive application result in a European patent being granted within three years or less from the PCT-filing date. This compares favourably to both national patent routes and much more favourably to the EPC route. Furthermore, the International Search Report is delivered prior to 18 months from the priority date which is much faster than the EPC route and compares well with the national route. As this usually arrives before technical preparations for publication have been started, it gives the applicant an opportunity to withdraw or amend the application after seeing the international search report but before publication. This contrasts with the EPC route whereby the search report is usually available after publication. Under the EPC, technical preparations for publication are deemed to have begun seven weeks before publication as opposed to 15 days under the PCT. Thus, the Euro-PCT route gives the applicant a much better chance to maintain the secrecy of an application it does not intend to pursue than under the EPO. Alternatively, it gives the applicant the chance to amend his claims before publication, taking into account the prior art that has been unearthed in the search report. There is much also to commend the Euro-PCT II route whereby the EPO prepares the International Search Report and the International Preliminary Examination Report. In this case, the EPO will not require a supplementary search report and 50 per cent of the examination fee will be refunded.

The disadvantage of this route is that it is somewhat more expensive than merely using the EPC route.[59] The Euro-PCT or Euro-PCT II route

[58] See above, at para. 2.011.
[59] In 1990, it was estimated that the extra cost using the Euro-PCT II route over the EPC route was DM 2,386—see Sonn, "National Patents, EPC or PCT: Which Route to Choose?" *Patent World*, April 1991, p. 38 at p. 42.

is better than a straightforward national-PCT route in money terms because one only pays one PCT-designation fee for countries which are members of the EPC; no supplementary search fee is charged where the EPO has acted as the ISA and in a Euro-PCT II application, 50 per cent of the EPO's examination fees will be refunded if it has acted as the IPEA. It should be remembered that where patent protection is sought for Belgium, France, Greece, Italy and Monaco, the PCT-national route is not available and any such application will be treated as Euro-PCT application with the EPO as a Designated or Elected Office. The Euro-PCT route may be rather "top-heavy" if patent protection is required only in a few countries, especially where those countries are not members of the EPC.

(vi) Recommended route

2.138 Where an applicant seeks patent protection in several European countries, the Euro-PCT II route is recommended. The applicant should make a first national filing to preserve its position. He should then examine the national search report and if encouraging, he should file an international application under the PCT using the EPO as International Searching Authority and International Preliminary Examining Authority and designate the EPO as an elected Office for the EPC- countries. The national filing should then be withdrawn just prior to grant of the European patent if it is still alive.[60] This route has the advantage that where designated States are members of the EPC, the applicant can designate that State as well under the PCT. Accordingly, there is a high degree of flexibility.[61]

In other circumstances, where protection is only sought in a few countries, a national-PCT route or straightforward national applications may be more appropriate in order to save money.

9. Table of Membership of European Countries to the Paris Convention, PCT I & II, EPC and EEC

2.139 All European countries including the breakaway Yugoslavian republics are members of the Paris Convention. The table below sets out the membership of European countries to the PCT, EPC and E.C.

[60] Most countries will not permit a national and European patent to co-exist—eg see Patents Act 1977, s. 73.

[61] This is the recommendation given in Sonn, "National Patents, EPC or PCT: Which Route to Choose?" *Patent World*, April 1990. Helmut Sonn is a very experienced Austrian patent attorney.

State	PCT (Chapter I or II)	EPC	EC
Austria	●/II	●	●
Bosnia-Hercegovina			
Bulgaria	●/II		
Croatia			
Czech Republic	●/II		
Denmark	●/II	●	●
Finland	●/II		●
France	●/II	●	●
Germany	●/II	●	●
Greece	●/I	●	●
Hungary	●/II		
Ireland	●/II	●	●
Italy	●/II	●	●
Liechtenstein	●/I	●	
Luxembourg	●/II	●	●
Monaco	●/II	●	●
Netherlands	●/II	●	●
Norway	●/II		
Poland	●/II		
Portugal	●/II	●	●
Romania	●/II	*	

Slovakia	●/II		
Slovenia	●/II	*	
Spain Sweden	●/I ●/II	● ●	● ●
United Kingdom	●/II	●	●

* A European patent can be extended to Slovenia and Romania pursuant to bilateral agreements entered into between them and the EPO. There are also extension agreements with Lithuania and one expected for Latvia. National law modelled on EPC rather than the EPC itself is applied to the patent.[62]

[62] [1994] OJEPO 75.

Chapter Three

TRADEMARKS IN EUROPE

1. Introduction

3.001 Supranational efforts to standardise trade mark law in Europe and to make the acquisition of trade marks cheaper and easier have come from two sources: the E.C. Commission and WIPO.[1] For a long period, their efforts went unrewarded. However, recently, their efforts have come to fruition and by 1996 or 1997, there should be in force both Community measures and international treaties which will largely achieve the above aims.

On the international side, WIPO has secured the adherence of all E.C. countries and most other European countries to the Madrid Agreement or its Protocol, which are treaties designed to centralise and simplify the filing for trademarks worldwide. The Madrid Agreement is in force. It is anticipated that the Protocol will come into force in 1995 or 1996 (three months after four parties have ratified it).

On the European side the Commission's efforts in the trade mark field were intended by it to remove the barrier of territoriality that trade mark rights could cause and to standardise the acquisition and enforcement of trade marks so that there was a level playing field in the Community. To this end, it has issued a harmonising trade mark directive which aims to broadly standardise trade mark law throughout the Member States of the Community and a regulation for a Community Trade Mark which is to be of unitary effect throughout the Community. At present, in 1995, the trade mark directive has been implemented by the majority of Member States. It is anticipated that the Community Trade Mark regime will become operative in early 1996.[2]

2. National Trademarks

3.002 At present, most European countries are adherents to the Paris Convention and the Madrid Agreement or its Protocol. Thus, the fundamental aspects of their trade marks laws are the same. Furthermore, the majority of Community states have brought into force the First Trade mark Harmonisation Directive. Despite the above measures, considerable diversity

[1] World Intellectual Property Organisation.

[2] See Davies, "*Are Trade Mark Owners Ready to Brave the Costa Brava*" [1994] EIPR 47 at p. 48.

remains. In particular, the directive has several optional provisions which Member States are not obliged to enact. This section seeks to compare the various different types of national trade mark laws in Europe. There are four principal areas where there is a substantial amount of diversity of national trade mark laws.

(a) First-to-file v. first-to-use

3.003 The first difference lies between those countries which give the exclusive right to use a trademark to the first to apply for the mark as opposed those countries which give the exclusive right to the first to use the mark. This difference is conveniently summarised as the first-to-file v. first-to-use distinction. It is important to emphasise that the distinction is not always clear. Many first-to-file countries give protection to a greater or lesser extent to prior users of a registered trade mark. The converse is not true. First-to-use countries do not give protection to a party which has innocently registered a trade mark as against a party seeking to enforce its prior unregistered rights.

Within the Community, implementation of the Trade Mark Directive has considerably reduced Member States' differences in this area. Under the Trade Mark Directive, Article 4(4)(b) (an optional provision) permits owners of unregistered trade marks to oppose the registration of marks subsequently applied for. Moreover, Article 6(2) permits Member States to provide a defence of local "prior use". Germany, Denmark, France, Italy, Greece and the United Kingdom have all enacted Article 4(4)(b).[3] The draft Benelux Trade Mark Law[4] only gives prior users' rights where the applicant has applied for the mark in bad faith. Portugal makes it incumbent on the user of a nonregistered mark to apply within 6 months of him first using the trade mark. Otherwise, he risks losing his rights in the mark to a later applicant.[5] With regard to Article 6(2), the draft Benelux law, Denmark, Greece, Italy, France, Germany, United Kingdom and Ireland law provide for local "prior user" rights. However, Portugal have not enacted this provision because their laws do not recognise such rights.

Outside the Community (not including recently acceded States) Austria, Hungary, Czech Republic, Slovak Republic, Romania and Poland adhere to the first-to-file system. Switzerland, Sweden, Hungary and Bulgaria adhere to the first-to-use system. In the former countries, generally, registration will either be refused on absolute grounds—*i.e.* the sign is not distinctive, comprises of heraldic symbols, etc., or on the basis of a prior registration or application. Prior unregistered users have no rights to prevent an application proceeding to registration and often will

[3] Indeed, under the Trade Mark Directive, Art. 4(2)(d) (a mandatory provision) permits the cancellation of a registration or the opposition of an application on the basis of a well-known mark in another Member State. At present, neither Ireland nor Spain has enacted the Directive.

[4] December 2, 1992 (not yet in force).

[5] *i.e.* an applicant may be prevented.

have no defence to an infringement action brought by the registered proprietor. Accordingly, in these countries, it is often the practice to apply for a trademark before using it as there is no point in building up a reputation in a mark only to lost it to another applicant for registration.

3.004 In some first-to-file countries (as well as in first-to-use countries), limited grounds for opposition or cancellation of a registration is granted in relation to the prior use of an identical or similar mark. Thus, in Austria, Hungary, Romania and Poland, it is only prior unregistered marks which are "well-known" within the meaning of Article 6bis of the Paris Convention that can be used to oppose an application or invalidate an existing registration. "Well-known" has an international meaning. Thus, it is not necessary normally to show that the mark was well-known in the state of application.

Generally, first-to-file countries give little protection to defendants in infringement proceedings who can show prior use.

In the first-to-use countries, a registered trade mark will always be in danger of being struck off if a third party can show that it used the mark earlier and there is a danger of confusion. The degree of prior use required to resist an application for a trade mark differs between countries. In the United Kingdom, Ireland and Denmark, the general test is whether use of the registered mark would have been likely to cause deception or confusion at the date of the application. In Sweden, Finland and Norway, a person engaged in commerce will acquire exclusive rights in a trade mark if he has acquired a reputation in the mark by extensive use.[6] Such prior use can be relied upon to cancel an existing registration provided that proceedings are brought within a reasonable time.

(b) Scope of exclusive right

3.005 The second area of diversity lies in the protection awarded by a registered trademark. All countries give the registered proprietor the exclusive right to use the mark in the course of trade. The differences lie in whether that merely relates to goods and services covered by the registration or is broader in scope. The Trade Mark Directive contains obligatory provisions for Community states as to the conferring of exclusive rights on the trade mark proprietor as against any identical or similar sign which is used on identical or similar goods to that covered by the registration where there exists a likelihood of confusion or association.[7] Article 5(2) of the directive also makes it an optional provision to give the proprietor rights to prevent the use of an identical or similar mark on dissimilar goods where the registered mark has a reputation in a Member State and such use would without due cause take unfair advantage of or be detrimental to the distinctive character or the repute of the mark.[8]

[6] The position in Sweden and Finland is likely to change in the near future because of their recent accession to the European Community.
[7] Art. 5(1)(b).
[8] First Trade Mark Directive, Art. 5(2). See below, at para. 3.074.

In the E.C., Denmark, France, Germany, Greece, Portugal and Italy have all enacted Article 5(2) into domestic trade mark legislation. The United Kingdom has also included Article 5(2) into the new Trade Marks Act 1994. The draft Benelux Trade Mark Law also provides protection pursuant to Article 5(2). Spain's current law does not provide this protection.

Outside the E.C., it is rare for European countries to extend the protection of registered marks to similar or dissimilar goods. Generally, protection will only extend to goods which are specified in the registration (*e.g.* Poland, Switzerland) or to goods and services supplied in the course of the proprietor's business (*e.g.* Sweden, Norway and Finland[9]).

(c) Degree of *ex officio* search and examination

3.006 The third area where differences remain is in the degree of *ex officio* search and examination by national trade mark offices. *Ex officio* examination as to whether procedural requirements have been complied with and whether there exist absolute grounds for refusing the application is carried out in all European countries. Most countries permit opposition proceedings to be lodged within certain time limits after publication of the application or registration. However, some, like Bulgaria and Switzerland, will not publish applications and make no provisions for pre-grant oppositions. Some countries like Switzerland and Denmark provide for post-grant oppositions within a limited period after publication of the registration. The greatest difference between offices is whether they conduct searches for prior registrations or applications. The Benelux Office and Austrian Office will conduct a search for conflicting marks but will not refuse the application if the search is adverse. Thus the applicant rather than the office decides whether to continue with the application. Switzerland will search and provide a confidential advice only on request and payment of a fee. The trade mark offices of Greece, Romania, Portugal, Sweden, Norway and Finland conducts searches for prior marks and examine for conflicting marks. The most extensive *ex officio* search of prior registrations and examinations are carried out in the United Kingdom and Ireland. However, even these do not search for unregistered marks. The Trade Mark Directive does not affect differences in national practices of trade mark offices of Member States.

(d) Assignment of trademarks

3.007 Until recently, there was considerable difference in European countries' laws as to whether a trade mark could be assigned without the underlying business. Because the function of a trade mark is to indicate trade origin, an assignment of a trade mark without the underlying business could

[9] Sweden, Finland and Austria's recent accession to the European Community means that they will have to enact the Trade Mark Directive.

undermine such a function. The First Trade Mark directive does not deal with the issue of assignment of a trademark. The United Kingdom, Italy, Ireland, Austria, Finland, France, Benelux countries, Norway, Sweden, Hungary, Poland, Romania and Portugal allow such an assignment, although the registry office of most countries has the ability to refuse such an assignment if the public are likely to be deceived or confused as to the trade origin of the trademarked goods or services. Germany and Switzerland have recently amended their laws to permit assignment of trade marks without the business. Bulgaria does not permit the assignment of trade marks without the business.

3. International Treaties

(a) Paris convention

3.008 The Paris Convention for the Protection of Industrial Property in 1883 constituted the result of the first international effort to standardise and simplify the protection of intellectual property rights in Member States. It has been amended several times and its last amendment was at Stockholm in 1967. European countries are Member States of the Paris Convention.[10] Its fundamental principle is that Member States are not allowed to discriminate between their nationals and nationals of other Member States.[11] Thus, nationals of Member States enjoy the same rights, advantages and protection as nationals in any other Member State of the Convention.

The Paris Convention provides that the conditions for the filing and registration of trade marks are determined by national laws.[12] It is thus primarily concerned with the harmonisation of substantive trade mark law. In relation to trade marks, the Convention makes the following provisions:

(a) Once a trade mark application has been filed in a Member State, the applicant has a period of six months in which to file corresponding applications in other Member States without losing any rights. In effect, the subsequent filings are giving a priority date of the first filing. This protects the applicant against third party rights acquired after the first filing but before subsequent convention filings.[13]

(b) An application for the registration of a mark filed by a national of a Member State may not be refused or its registration invali-

[10] See table at 3.085.
[11] Art. 2.
[12] Art. 6(1).
[13] Art. 4.

dated on the ground that filing or registration has not been effected in the country of origin.[14]

(c) Goods infringing a registered trade mark can be seized on importation.[15]

(d) A registered trade mark may only be cancelled after a reasonable period because of non-use of the mark and only if the person concerned cannot justify his inaction.[16]

(e) Use of a trade mark in a form differing in elements but which does not alter the distinctive character of the mark does not invalidate or diminish the protection granted by the mark.[17]

(f) Concurrent use of the same mark on identical or similar goods by industrial or commercial establishments considered as co-proprietors of the mark under domestic law may not prevent registration nor diminish the protection of the mark provided that such use does not result in misleading the public and is not contrary to public interest.[18]

(g) No indication of the registered mark is required on the goods.[19]

(h) "Well-known" marks are to be protected in Member States.[20]

(i) Heraldic symbols, flags, armorial bearings, State emblems, etc., are not registrable.[21]

(j) A trade mark registered in the country of origin of an applicant must be accepted for filing and registration "as is" in other Member States unless:
   (i) it infringes third party rights or
   (ii) it is devoid of distinctive character or
   (iii) it is contrary to morality or public order or is liable to deceive the public.[22]

(k) Service marks are to be protected.[23]

(l) Collective marks are to be protected.[24]

(m) Trade names are to be protected.[25]

In addition, various provisions are made in the field of unfair competition.[26]

[14] Art. 6(2). "Country of origin" is defined as the Country of the Union where the applicant has a real and effective industrial or commercial establishment, or, if he has no such establishment within the Union, the country of the Union where he has his domicile or if he has no domicile within the Union but is a national of a country of the Union, the country of which he is a national—Article $6^{quinquies}$(2).
[15] Art. 9.
[16] Art. 5(c)(1).
[17] Art. 5(c)(2).
[18] Art. 5(c)(3).
[19] Art. 5(c)(d).
[20] Art. 6bis.
[21] Art. 6ter.
[22] Art. $6^{quinquies}$.
[23] Art. 6^{sexies}.
[24] Art. 7bis.
[25] Art. 8.
[26] Art. 10bis.

The Paris Convention is merely an international convention. In most states, an international convention has no force of law in a Member State until enacted in the appropriate way into domestic legislation. Thus, whilst all European countries have acceded to the Paris Convention (as amended), this does not mean that all its requirements have been made part of each country's domestic law. For instance, under English law, ratification of an international convention has no effect until implemented by national legislation. Even in countries where an international convention forms part of domestic laws upon ratification, as in France, Italy and Germany, the interpretation of such international law will differ. What is clear is that the Paris Convention laid down the cornerstones for harmonisation of trade mark law and has played an invaluable part over the last 100 years in enabling the standardisation of trade mark law in the world and preventing discrimination between nationals of different nations.

(b) Madrid Agreement

3.009 Under Article 19 of the Paris Convention, Member States of the Paris Union are given the right to enter into treaties for the protection of intellectual property rights provided that such does not contravene provisions of the Paris Convention itself. In 1891, shortly after the Paris Convention itself, the Madrid Arrangement for the International Registration of Marks ("the Madrid Agreement") was signed and ratified by four countries. The fundamental object of this Convention was to provide an international procedure for applicants who wished to acquire registered trade marks in countries that had ratified the Madrid Agreement. As such it was essentially a procedural Convention as opposed to the Paris Convention which sought to harmonise the substantive trade mark law of Member States. Since 1891, the number of states that have ratified the Madrid Agreement has increased considerably and the Madrid Agreement itself has been revised several times, the last three revisions being the 1957 Nice Revision and the Stockholm Revisions of 1967 and 1979. All states party to the Madrid Agreement are either subject to the Nice or the Stockholm Revisions. A single set of regulations governs the text of both revisions.

Most European countries eventually ratified the Madrid Agreement. However, its provisions were unacceptable to certain countries including United Kingdom, Denmark, Ireland and Greece in Europe and, elsewhere, the United States, Australia and Japan. Accordingly, in the 1980s, and spurred on by the possibility of the Community Trade Mark becoming a serious rival to the Madrid Agreement, the governing body of the Madrid Agreement, WIPO, made efforts to draw up a Protocol (in effect, an alternative Convention) to the Madrid Agreement which made important changes to the Madrid Agreement so that the system would prove acceptable to the above countries. Their efforts culminated in a Diplomatic Conference in June 1989 which resulted in the adoption of the Protocol Relating to the Madrid Agreement Concerning the International Registration of Marks ("the Madrid Protocol"). This is discussed below.[27–28]

The Madrid Agreement is administered by the International Bureau of WIPO. The legislative governing body consists of delegates of countries who have acceded or ratified it.[29]

(i) Fundamental provisions of the Madrid (Stockholm) Agreement

3.010 As mentioned above, the Madrid Agreement provides an international procedure for applying for trade marks in several or all Member States. The fundamental provisions of the Madrid (Stockholm) Agreement are set out below. Only two European countries (Portugal and San Marino) have ratified the earlier Nice version and for the purpose of brevity, this book does not deal with the relatively minor differences.[30]

(a) Only nationals of Member States or persons domiciled or legal persons who have a real and effective industrial or commercial establishment in a Member State may apply under the Madrid Agreement.[31]

(b) A qualifying person referred to above may obtain protection in other Member States (Designated States) for a mark *already registered in his country of origin* ("home" registration) by means of an international application to the International Bureau, WIPO. "Country of origin" is defined as the Member State where the applicant has a real and effective industrial or commercial establishment, alternatively the Member State where he is domiciled or if none of these, the Member State of which he is a national.[32]

(c) Registration for the Designated states takes place upon receipt of the application for international registration.[33] National offices of designated states have at most 12 months from the date of the international registration of the mark to refuse protection in their territory based on grounds set out in the Paris Convention.[34] Otherwise registration in all designated states is automatic.

(d) If the "home" registration is struck off the registry for any

[27–28] See para. 3.019, below.

[29] Arts. 10, 11.

[30] The reader is referred to Chartered Institute of Patent Agents and the Institute of Trade Mark Agents *United Kingdom Trade Mark Handbook* for the text of the Nice Revision.

[31] Madrid Agreement, Arts. 1(2), 2; Paris Convention, Art. 3. For a detailed discussion on the meaning of these requirements, see Souter, "The Right of Nationals of Non-Madrid Union Countries to Own International Registration" [1995] 7 EIPR 333.

[32] Art. 1(2), (3). All member Countries of the Madrid Union have notified WIPO that under Art. 3ter that protection in their countries shall only be granted upon express request of the applicant.

[33] Art. 4(1).

[34] See Art. 5(1),(2).

reason within five years of the date of international registration, then all registrations in the designated countries also fall.[35] This provision is known as the "central attack" provision. Once this period has expired, the registration of the mark in each designated state becomes independent of the "home" registration.[36] Similarly, if the "home" registration is altered within the same period, such an alteration takes effect in all designated States.[37]

(e) Registration of a mark is effective for 20 years with the possibility of renewal for further 20 year periods.[38]

(f) The working language is French.[39]

(ii) Procedural steps

3.011 *International Application*—the application for international registration must be made on a prescribed form. The particulars must correspond to the particulars of the "home" registration. The application must include *inter alia*, the goods and services in respect of which protection of the mark is claimed. If colour is claimed, the application must have appended to it a colour version of the mark and the colour claimed in words. The Implementing Regulations make detailed provisions as to the form content and accompanying documentation of an international registration.[40] A "basic" fee is charged for an application for international registration which may be paid in two parts; the second part payable before the expiry of the tenth year of registration.[41]

Application is made to the national intellectual property office of the country of origin of the applicant.[42] Once the Community Trade Mark regulation is in force, applications may also be made to the Community Trade Mark Office.[43] The relevant office shall ensure and certify that the application complies with the Madrid Agreement and its Implementing Regulations.[44]

3.012 *Priority*—an applicant may claim priority under the Paris Convention from one or more earlier applications.[45] It is not necessary to comply with the formalities set out in the Paris Convention—the right of priority is automatic.[46]

[35] Art. 6(3).
[36] Art. 6(2).
[37] Art. 6(3).
[38] Art. 6(1).
[39] MAr. 7(1) (MAr.—Madrid Agreement Rules).
[40] MAr. 7, 8, 9.
[41] MAr. 10.
[42] Art. 1(2). "Country of origin" is defined as the Madrid country where the applicant has a real and effective industrial or commercial establishment. Failing this, the Madrid country where he has his domicile or failing that, the Madrid country of which he is a national—Art. 1(3).
[43] Art. 3(1).
[44] Art. 3(1).
[45] See Paris Convention, Art. 4 and MAr. 8(vi).
[46] Art. 4(2).

3.013 *Processing of international application*—upon receipt of a proper application from the relevant office, the International Bureau registers the mark in the International Register.[47] The application is given a "date of international registration".[48] This date is the date on which the International Bureau is in possession of the application. However, if the International Bureau receives the application within two months of the international application being filed at the national office, then the date of filing of the international application at the national office becomes the date of international registration.[49] Alternatively, where the national offices receives the international application before the date of recording on the national register, if the application is received within two months of the recording of the registration of the national application of the "home" registration on which the application for international registration is based, then the date of international registration is the date of the recording of the "home" registration.[50] Designated national offices are notified of the registration and the marks are published in the Official Journal (*Les Marques Internationales*).[51]

Upon payment of a fee, the International Bureau will undertake searches for prior international marks.[52]

3.014 *Refusal by national offices*—as mentioned above, national offices may refuse an international registration within 12 months of the date of international registration of the mark.[53] Such refusal must be based upon Paris Convention grounds.[54] A statement of grounds of refusal must be provided.[55] The applicant or his agent will be notified of the refusal by the International Bureau. Notification of provisional or final decisions following refusals must be in accordance with the Implementing Regulations.[56] The applicant must be afforded the opportunity to defend his rights before final refusal takes place.[57]

Similarly, where the office of the country of origin decides within five years from the date of international registration to invalidate wholly or partially the international registration resulting in a complete removal of protection in all designed States, the above procedure must be followed.[58]

[47] Art. 3(4), MAr. 14. For the information to be recorded on the Registry, see MAr. 14(2).
[48] Art. 3(4).
[49] MAr. 15(1), (2).
[50] MAr. 15(2)(ii).
[51] Art. 3(4), MAr. 30.
[52] Art. 5ter(2).
[53] Art. 5(2). If the period provided by domestic law is shorter, then it prevails. As to calculation of time limits for notification of refusal, see MAr. 17.
[54] Art. 5(1).
[55] For detailed regulations, see MAr. 16.
[56] See MAr. 16.
[57] Art. 5(6).
[58] Art. 6(4).

3.015 *Renewal of International Registration*—an applicant may upon payment of the relevant fee renew protection for further period of 20 years.[59] Six months before the expiry of the preceding 20 year period, the International Bureau will remind the owner of the date of expiry.[60] In order to renew the international registration, the applicant must pay the relevant fee any time in the year before the expiry of the preceding 20 year period.[61] Furthermore, the applicant may, upon payment of the relevant fee and a surcharge fee within six months of the expiry of the international registration, obtain renewal of the international registration.[62] Renewals are recorded on the International Register.[63]

3.016 *Fees*—an application for international registration is subject to an international fee which must be paid before registration takes place. This fee is made up of a "basic" fee, a supplementary fee for each class of the International Classification and complementary fee for each state for which protection is requested.[64] Furthermore, the Office of the country of origin may fix a national fee.[65] Fees must be paid in Swiss francs.[66]

The basic fee may be payable in two parts, the first part payable when the international application is made and the balance within the expiry of ten years from the date of registration.[67] Renewal fees are similarly calculated on the aggregate of a basic fee and supplementary and complementary fees.[68]

3.017 *Representation*—an applicant may use one representative for the purposes of applications and proceedings before the International Bureau and name the representative it on the international application.[69] Where such a representative is recorded, the latter will only address the duly authorised representative except in the case of a reminder that the initial period of 20 years is about to expire, both will be notified.[70]

3.018 *Miscellaneous*—where the specification of goods and services is too vague, the International Bureau will inform the National Office and invite that it be remedied.[71] Assignments of international registrations must be notified to and recorded by the International Bureau.[72] Assign-

[59] Art. 7.
[60] MAr. 24.
[61] MAr. 25(1), (2).
[62] MAr. 25(3).
[63] MAr. 28.
[64] Art. 8(2). If the International Bureau considers that the applicant has wrongly classified the goods and services for which protection is claimed, it may be required to pay extra supplementary fees—MAr. 12.
[65] Art. 8(1).
[66] MAr. 32.
[67] MAr. 10, 32.
[68] Art. 7(1).
[69] MAr. 2. Or later, upon payment of a fee — MAr. 2(1)(h).
[70] MAr. 2(2), 24.
[71] MAr. 13.
[72] Art. 9[bis].

ments of international registrations for part of the protected goods or services are likewise notified to and recorded by the International Bureau. Designated States are given the right to refuse recognition of the validity of the assignment if the goods or services included in the part so assigned are similar to those in respect of which the mark remains registered for the benefit of the assignor.[73] The Madrid Agreement provides for a group of countries to become in effect "one country" for its purposes.[74] Thus, Belgium, Luxembourg and the Netherlands who have a Uniform Law which provides for a single supra-national trade mark right in the three countries and a single trade mark office in The Hague represent "one country" for the purposes of the Madrid Agreement.

(c) The Madrid Protocol

3.019 The Madrid Agreement in all its revisions was never acceptable to certain countries, in particular, the common law countries. These countries and other countries which conducted thorough examination of trade mark applications had a series of objections to the Madrid Agreement. Firstly, there was the dependency of the international mark on a home registration. In countries such as France where registration was obtained by deposit, such a registration was considerably easier to obtain than in countries where a thorough examination was required before grant of the mark. This meant that nationals of those latter states would be at an unfair advantage in obtaining international registration.[75] Similarly, nationals of countries whose trade mark laws were harsher than others were disadvantaged. Thus, in the United States, where actual use of the trade mark is required before registration was possible, United States nationals were disadvantaged against nationals of Member States where there was no such requirement.[76] Secondly, countries like the U.K., where a thorough search and examination took place, considered the 12 month period from date of international registration for the refusal of protection too short to comply with. Thirdly, the possibility of "central attack" on the international registration within five years of the date of registration was unacceptable.[77] Fourthly, the only official language was French which was unacceptable to English-speaking countries. Fifthly, the distribution of international fees was considerably less than that received from domestic applications.

The non-ratification of the Madrid Agreement by important industrial and commercial countries reduced its attractiveness. International regis-

[73] Art. 9ter(1).
[74] Art. 9^{quater}.
[75] See Llewelyn, "International Registration of Trade Marks and the UK" [1986] 3 EIPR 79 at 77; Kaufman, "Madrid Agreement: Will Reform Proposals Attract More Members?" [1990] 11 EIPR 407; Davies, "Are Trade Mark Owners Ready to Brave the Costa Brava" [1994] EIPR 47.
[76] Under the Madrid Agreement, the national office of a Designated State can only refuse protection for an international registration on grounds set out in Paris Convention Art. 6^{quinquies}B. This does not include non-use.
[77] See Tatham, "'Central attack' and the Madrid Agreement" [1985] 4 EIPR 91.

trations were comparatively few. Furthermore, most international applications were based on "home" registrations from a few countries, principally E.C. countries.[78] Thus, when the E.C. began to discuss the implementation of a Community Trade Mark, valid for the whole Community, WIPO realised that such could constitute the death-knell for the Madrid Agreement. Accordingly, WIPO proposed a new treaty to run in parallel with the Madrid Agreement. Various proposals were put forward in the 1980s. Eventually a Diplomatic Conference in June 1989 resulted in the adoption of the Madrid Protocol (a treaty entitled "Protocol Relating to the Madrid Agreement Concerning the International Registration of Marks"). This was signed by most of the countries that had ratified the Madrid Agreement and also, importantly, within the Community by Denmark, United Kingdom, Ireland, and Greece. Furthermore, it is expected that Finland, Sweden and Norway will join by 1995 or 1996.[79] Moreover, the European Community is a signatory to the Convention, thus allowing the future Community Trade Mark Office to be designated as an office for the purposes of the grant of a Community Trade Mark.[80] Importantly, the accession of the United States to the Protocol is now likely and imminent.[81] It is also likely that International Trade Marks obtained on the basis of the Protocol will be available in 1995 or 1996.[82]

The Protocol generally covers the same subject matter as the Madrid (Stockholm) Agreement and adopts the wording and numbering of it *mutatis mutandis*. It differs in certain key areas which are dealt with below. At present there are draft Implementing Regulations for both the Protocol and the Madrid Agreement which closely mirror the current regulations of the Madrid Agreement.

Fundamental differences between the Madrid Agreement and the Protocol

(a) International registration based on "home" application— 3.020

Under the Madrid Agreement, there must exist a home *registration* before an application for international registration is made and international registration is granted. Under the Protocol, it is sufficient that a home *application* for a trade mark has been made.[83]

[78] See Llewelyn p. 76, cited above at n. 75.
[79] See Davies, "Are Trade Mark Owners Ready to Brave the Costa Brava" [1994] EIPR 47 at p. 48.
[80] Art. 14(1)(b) of the Madrid Protocol permits intergovernmental organisations to become party to the Protocol. NB This provision does not appear in the Madrid Agreement.
[81] Although recently the ratification of the Protocol in the United States has experienced political difficulties.
[82] See Davies, "Are Trade Mark Owners Read to Brave the Costa Brava" [1994] EIPR 47 at 48. On April 6, 1995, the U.K. ratified the Protocol and it currently awaits ratification by one other country before it becomes a reality. WIPO are confident that it will become operational in early 1996.
[83] Art. 2, Protocol.

3.021 *(b) Period of protection reduced*—The period of protection under the Protocol is only 10 years with the possibility of renewal for further 10 year periods.[84]

3.022 *(c) Extension of time limits for refusal*—The Protocol extends the time limit for national trade mark offices of designated States to refuse protection to an international application in its territory. The basic period of 12 months remains. However, due to pressure during negotiations from countries like the U.K., Denmark and Ireland where an extensive examination is undertaken, contracting parties can declare that the 12 month period is replaced by an 18 month period.[85] Also, the office can refuse protection after the 18 month period has expired if opposition proceedings have been commenced against the applicant, provided that the International Bureau has been informed of the possibility that oppositions may be filed after the expiry of the 18 month limit and notification of refusal based on the opposition is made not later than seven months from the date on which the opposition period began.[86] This is clearly designed to be an experiment as the Assembly has the right to modify this system after ten years.[87]

3.023 *(d) Fees*—Generally, the fee system is the same as under the Madrid Agreement. However, under the Protocol, the office of a designated state can charge an "individual fee" equivalent to a fee it would have charged a domestic applicant for a 10 year term. The applicant does not pay a complementary fee for each state which charges an individual fee. Also, if all the designated states in the application for international registration charge individual fees, the applicant does not pay any supplementary fees.[88]

3.024 *(e) "Central attack" period extended*—The Protocol keeps the principle of central attack as set out in the Madrid Agreement.[89] Because an international registration is based upon a "home" application, it was realised that the home application might eventually be refused after five years from the date of the international registration. Thus the Protocol permits an international registration to be centrally invalidated after this five year period provided that opposition, rejection, cancellation or revocation proceedings have begun before the expiry of the five year period.[90]

[84] Arts. 6, 7.
[85] Art. 5(2)(b).
[86] Art. 5(2)(c). If the opposition period expires before the end of seven months, than notification of refusal must be made within one month of the expiry of the opposition period—Art. 5(2)(c)(ii).
[87] Art. 5(2)(e).
[88] Art. 8 (see para. 3.016).
[89] Art. 6(3).
[90] Art. 6(3).

(f) Transformation of "centrally invalidated" international registration—Although the Protocol retains the "central attack" principle, this was an unpalatable part of the Madrid Agreement to several countries. Accordingly, the Protocol permits the transformation of a centrally invalidated international registration into national or regional applications.[91] Whilst the applicant could have always filed a fresh application in the event of a successfully and centrally attacked registration, the Protocol provides that the transformed application maintains the priority date of the failed international registration. Such an application for transformation must be done within three months from the date on which the international registration was cancelled and must not seek to extend the specified goods and services contained in the failed international registration. This provision is important under the Protocol because it may often be the case that the "home" applications never matures to registration. Under the Madrid Agreement, one cannot apply until one has a "home" registration.[92] **3.025**

(g) Protocol applies to intergovernmental organisations—Under the Protocol, any intergovernmental organisation may become a party, as well as countries, provided that at least one of the Member States of the organisation is a party to the Paris Convention and the organisation has a regional office for the purposes of registering marks.[93] This provision is not to be confused with the provisions under the Madrid Agreement and the Protocol to permit the substitution of a common office and single territory for several Contracting States.[94] This provision was provided so that the Community Trade Mark Office can be designated and the Protocol can be used to obtain a Community Trade Mark covering the Common Market. As such, an application under the Protocol is similar to an international patent application under the Patent Co-Operation Treaty, which designates the European Patent Office where the applicant wishes to obtain protection in countries that adhere to the European Patent Convention. **3.027**

(h) Interface between the Madrid (Stockholm) Agreement and the Protocol—The Madrid (Stockholm) Agreement and the Protocol are designed to work parallel but separately from each other. Thus, an application based on a "home" application in an office of a state which has ratified the Protocol can only designate states which have acceded to the Protocol. Similarly, an international application based on a "home" registration in a state which has only ratified the Madrid (Stockholm) Agreement can only designate Madrid countries. Where an application is made in a state which has ratified both, the provisions of **3.028**

[91] Art. 9^{quinquies}.
[92] See para. 3.010.
[93] Art. 14(1)(b).
[94] Art. 9^{quater} in both Agreement and Protocol. The Netherlands, Belgium and Luxembourg have availed themselves of this option.

the Protocol has no effect in designated states that have also ratified both.[95] In such circumstances, where a home application is made in a state that has ratified both the Madrid Agreement and the Protocol, a dual system will operate with the Protocol applying to Protocol-only countries and the Madrid Agreement to others. It is not clear whether the Protocol *in toto* does not apply to states that have ratified both treaties or only those aspects of the Protocol that relate to designated states. For instance, can an international registration based on a "home" application (the use of a "home" application only being permissible under the Protocol) in a state that has only ratified the Protocol designate countries that have ratified both? If the Protocol has no effect in such countries, then under the Madrid Agreement, they cannot recognise the validity of an international registration based on a "home" application.[96]

3.029 *(i) Applications may be in English or French under Protocol*—The draft regulations to the Protocol allow English as well as French to be used in the course of prosecuting a trade mark application under the Protocol.

(d) Trademark Registration Treaty

3.030 In 1973, WIPO, in its efforts to overcome the lack of popular support for the Madrid Agreement, after considerable negotiation, obtained the signatures of several nations to the Trademark Registration Treaty (TRT). The treaty merely aimed at providing a more simplified and centralised way of filing applications in various countries. Contracting States were left to decide whether a mark was registrable. Thus, the TRT merely acted as a central trade mark filing system. Despite the generally uncontroversial provisions of the TRT, the United States, who was a consistent opponent of the Madrid Agreement, never ratified it because Congress remained unpersuaded that the use requirement should be watered down in any way whatsoever. This sunk the TRT, which has now been superseded by other treaties, especially the Protocol. It must now be considered a "dead letter" and of only historical interest.[97]

4. Community Trade Mark Legislation

(a) Community Trade Mark

(i) Introduction

3.031 In the early years of the European Community, there was considerable concern that the enforcement of trade marks could and would be used as barriers to trade between Member States. Thus, in the 1960s and 1970s,

[95] Art. 9^sexies^.

[96] In general, see Kunze, "Madrid Protocol", *Managing Intellectual Property* (March 1994) p. 50, where he examines the "safeguard" provision of Art. 9^sexies^.

[97] See Llewelyn, "International Registration of Trade Marks and the UK" [1986] 3 EIPR 74.

the European Commission began work on the establishment of an E.C. trade mark. Such a trade mark was to be supranational and to provide territorial protection in all Member States of the E.C. In 1973, a Working Party was set up and in 1976, a Memorandum on the Creation of an E.C. trade mark was drawn up which laid the foundation stone for the E.C. Regulation for a Community Trade Mark.

An initial difficulty was whether the Treaty of Rome conferred competence on the Commission to draw up a Community Trade Mark system. Article 235 enables the Council, acting unanimously on a proposal from the Commission and after consulting the Assembly, to take "appropriate measures" to attain one of the objectives of the Community if the Treaty did not provide the institutions of the Community with the necessary powers. The Commission considered that Article 235 provided it with the appropriate legal mechanism for introducing the CTM on the basis that national trade mark rights impede free movement of goods and competition in the Community.[98] Later, the Commission justified the introduction of the CTM because:

> "legal conditions must be created which enable undertakings to adapt their activities to the scale of the Community, whether in manufacturing and distributing goods or in providing services."[99]

The adoption of a Community Trade Mark Regulation was delayed by two political problems. Firstly, there was a failure to agree about the location of the Community Trade Mark Office (CTMO). On October 20, 1993, Spain won this battle and the CTMO is to be situated in Alicante. Secondly, there was considerable dispute over the languages of the CTMO. This problem has now been resolved with the adoption of five official languages.[1] These problems having been resolved, the Community Trade Mark Regulation 40/94 was signed on December 20, 1993.[2] It is due to come into force in 1995 or 1996.

(ii) Fundamental principles of the Community Trade Mark

3.032 The CTM Regulation provides for a single filing for a registration covering the whole of the Community as single unitary territory. It will operate alongside Member States' national trade mark registration systems. Most of the substantive provisions mirror those in the trade mark harmonisation directive. Thus, there should be little conflict or divergence between the substantive law of the Community Trade Mark and that of the trade

[98] See Working Paper of the Commission, "The Need for a European Trade Mark System—Competence of the European Community to create one" [1979] O.J. III/D/1294 and commentary on it in Morcom, "The Legitimacy of a European Trade Mark System" [1980] EIPR 359 where he questions the legitimacy of the measure. In that article, the author expresses fears that the then draft Regulation was contrary to Art. 36 and 222 because it would take away national trade mark rights, both registered and unregistered. In fact the Regulation, as adopted, respects such rights.

[99] See Para. 1 of the Recital of the CTM Regulation.

[1] The provisions on language at the CTMO are discussed below, at para. 3.049.

[2] [1994] O.J. L11/1.

mark laws of Member States once the directive has been implemented. The CTMO will not *ex officio* refuse applications on the basis of prior conflicting rights. Thus, the onus is on the owners of prior conflicting rights to oppose the application. It is expected that because of the large number of national rights existing in the Community, this will result in about 80 per cent of applications being opposed.

The CTM will be compatible with the Madrid Agreement and its Protocol so that an application for a CTM will be able to form the basis of an international registration under the Madrid Agreement and its Protocol.

The enforcement of CTMs are the responsibility of national Community Trade Mark courts which Member States are required to designate or appoint. Appeals from the Boards of Appeal of CTMO will lie to the European Court of First Instance.

(iii) Substantive law

3.033 *Unitary Character*—A CTM has effect throughout the entire Community and cannot be dealt with in any way save in respect of the whole Community.[3]

3.034 *Types of CTM*—A CTM may consist of any signs capable of being represented graphically, particularly words, names, designs, letters, numeral, the shape of goods or their packaging provided such signs are capable of distinguishing the goods or services of one undertaking from another.[4]

3.035 *Who may own a CTM?*—Any natural or legal person who is a national of a Member State; national of a Paris Convention country; is domiciled or has his seat or real and effective industrial or commercial establishment with the above countries or is a national of a country which accords equivalent protection to Community national as it does to its own nationals may be proprietors of a CTM.[5]

3.036 *Absolute grounds for refusal*—Registration will not be granted to trade marks devoid of distinctive character; trade marks which consist exclusively of signs or indications which may serve in trade to designate the kind, quality, quantity, intended purpose, value, geographical origin or the time of production of the goods or of rendering of the service or other characteristics of the goods or service; trade marks which consist exclusively of signs of indications which have become customary in the current language or in the bona fide and established practices of the trade;[6] signs which consist exclusively of the shape which results from

[3] Art. 1.2. The exception is that licensing a CTM in part of the Community is permissable.
[4] Art. 4.
[5] Art. 5.1.
[6] For the relevance of the italicised section, see last paragraph of 3.036.

the nature of the goods or the shape of goods which is necessary to obtain a technical result or the shape which gives substantial value to the goods; trade marks which are contrary to public policy or to accepted principles of morality; trade marks which are of such a nature as to deceive the public for instance as to the nature, quality or geographical origin of the goods or service; trade marks which have not been authorised by the competent authorities and are to be refused pursuant to Article 6ter of the Paris Convention and trade marks which include badges emblems or escutcheons other than those covered by Article 6ter of the Paris Convention and which are of particular public interest, unless the consent of the appropriate authorities to their registration has been given.[7]

The above conditions apply even if the grounds of non-registrability only apply in part of the Community.[8] Furthermore, the above italicised grounds for refusal do not apply if the mark has in consequence of the use which has been made of it become distinctive in fact in relation to the goods of services applied for.[9]

3.037 *Relative grounds for refusal*—The CTMO will not *ex officio* refuse an application on the basis of prior rights. However, the proprietor of an earlier trade mark may oppose an application for the registration of a trade mark on one or more of the following grounds:

(i) It is identical with an earlier trade mark and the goods or services applied for are identical with the goods or services for which the earlier trade mark is protected.[10]

(ii) If because it is identical or similar with an earlier trade mark and/or the goods or services covered by the trade marks are identical or similar, there exists a likelihood of confusion on the part of the public in the territory of which the earlier mark is protected. The likelihood of confusion may include the likelihood of association with the earlier trade mark.[11]

(iii) It is identical or similar with an earlier trade mark and although the goods or services covered by the trade marks are dissimilar, the earlier trade mark has a reputation in the Community (if a CTM) or a reputation in the Member State concerned (if a national trade mark) and the use without due cause of the trade mark applied for would take unfair advantage or be detrimental to the distinctive character or the repute of the earlier trade mark.[12]

For these purposes, "earlier trade mark" is defined to mean a Community trade mark, a trade mark registered in a Member State or an

[7] Art. 7.
[8] Art. 7.2.
[9] Art. 7(3).
[10] Art. 8(1)(a).
[11] Art. 8(1)(b).
[12] Art. 8(5).

application for such with the relevant date being earlier than the date of the application in question. Furthermore, it includes a trade mark which is "well-known" in a Member State according to Art. 6bis of the Paris Convention.[13]

The proprietor of a non-registered mark can also oppose registration of an application provided that he acquired rights to the mark prior to the date of the application, the mark has *more than mere local significance* and the mark confers on the proprietor the right to prohibit the use of a subsequent trade mark.[14] This last provision means that one looks to the national laws of the Member State where the mark is based to see if the proprietor of the earlier non-registered mark would have the right to prevent the use of the later mark.[15]

3.038 *Rights of CTM proprietors*—The CTM gives exclusive rights to prevent third parties from using in the course of trade:

(i) signs which are identical to the CTM in relation to goods or services specified in the registration;
(ii) signs which are identical or similar to the CTM in relation to goods identical or similar to those covered in the registration where a likelihood of confusion on the part of the public exists (such to include the likelihood of association);
(iii) signs which are identical or similar to the CTM on goods which are not similar to those covered in the registration where the CTM has a reputation in the Community and the use of that sign without due cause takes unfair advantage of, or is detrimental to the distinctive character or repute of the CTM.[16]

"Use in the course of trade" includes, *inter alia* affixing the sign to the goods or to the packaging; offering the goods, marketing the goods, stocking the goods or offering or supplying services thereunder; importing or exporting goods under the sign and using the sign on business papers and in advertising.[17]

The proprietor's rights accrue from the date of publication of the *registration*. However, the proprietor is entitled to reasonable compensation for acts done after the date of publication of the *application* if such would have constituted an infringement of his trade mark rights if done

[13] Art. 8(2).
[14] Art. 8(4).
[15] However, on application for revocation of a CTM, in addition to the Art. 8(4) ground, a CTM may be struck off the register if its use "may be prohibited pursuant to the national law governing the protection of any other earlier right and in particular: a right to a name, a right of personal portrayal, a copyright and an industrial property right"—Art. 52(2). There is no requirement that this earlier right has more than mere local significance. Thus, rather enigmatically, the owner of an unregistered mark of mere local significance may not be able to oppose a CTM application but could successfully apply for revocation of an already registered CTM. See para. 3.051.
[16] Art. 9.
[17] Art. 9(2).

after the date of publication of the registration.[18] Furthermore, the proprietor is entitled to prevent his mark from being used generically in dictionaries and other reference books by demanding that the next edition of the publication carries an indication that the mark is a registered trade mark.[19]

Defences of third parties—A CTM cannot be used to prevent a third party from using in the course of trade his own name and address; to describe the characteristics of goods or services in some way or to indicate the intended purpose of a product or service in particular as accessories or spare parts provided the use is in accordance with honest practices in industrial or commercial matters.[20] **3.039**

Exhaustion of rights—A CTM cannot be used to prohibit its use in relation to goods which have been put on the market in the Community under that trade mark by the proprietor or with his consent.[21] This principle does not apply where there exist legitimate reasons for the proprietor to oppose further commercialism of the goods especially where the condition of the goods is changed or impaired after they have been put on the market.[22] **3.040**

Transfer of CTM—A CTM may be assigned separately from the underlying business in respect of some or all of the goods or services for which it is registered.[23] However, if the transfer is likely to mislead the public, the CTMO will not register the transfer unless the successor agrees to limit the registration of the CTM to goods or services in respect of those goods or services which it is not likely to mislead.[24] The assignment must be in writing and requires the signatures of the parties to the contract unless it is a result of a judgment otherwise it is void.[25] **3.041**

Licensing—A CTM may be licensed for some or all of the goods for which it is registered and for the whole or part of the Community.[26] The licence may be exclusive or non-exclusive. The owner of a CTM may bring trade mark proceedings against a licensee who contravenes any provision in his licensing contract with regard to its duration, the form covered by the registration in which the trade mark may be used, the scope of the goods or services for which the licence is granted, the territory in which the trade mark may be affixed or the quality of the goods manufactured or of the services provided by the licensee.[27] It is implicit in **3.042**

[18] Art. 9(3).
[19] Art. 11.
[20] Art. 12.
[21] Art. 13(1).
[22] Art. 13(2).
[23] Art. 17.
[24] Art. 17(4).
[25] Art. 17(3).
[26] Art. 22(1).
[27] Art. 22(2).

the above that where other terms of the licence are breached, the CTM owner's cause of action against the licensee is purely for breach of contract and products placed on the market by the defaulting licensee are not to be treated as infringing products. However, there is nothing in the Regulation which prevents the CTM owner from terminating the licence for such breaches. A licensee may only bring proceedings for infringement of a CTM if the proprietor consents. However, the holder of an exclusive licence may bring proceedings if the proprietor of the trade mark after formal notice has not brought infringement proceedings within an appropriate period.[28] Moreover, a licensee is entitled to intervene in infringement proceedings brought by the owner of a CTM for the purposes of obtaining compensation for damage suffered by him.[29]

3.043 *Collective Marks*—The CTM allows for the registration of collective marks used to distinguish the goods or services of the members of an association from those of other undertakings.[30] Collective marks can, unlike normal marks, designate the geographical origin of goods or services but do not entitle the proprietor to prohibit a third party from using in the course of trade such signs or indications provided he uses them in accordance with honest practices in industrial or commercial matters and, in particular, may not be invoked against a third party who is entitled to use a geographical name.[31]

An applicant for a collective mark must submit regulations to the CTMO specifying who is authorised to use the mark, the conditions of membership of the association and the sanctions for non-compliance.[32] An application will be refused if the mark is likely to mislead the public as regards the character and significance of the mark, in particular if it is likely to be taken to be something other than a collective mark.[33]

3.044 *Relationship between CTMs and national trade marks*—Generally, the CTM regime and national trade marks are intended to co-exist independently of each other. However, the Regulation does specifically delineate the relationship between the two regimes in several respects. Firstly, it safeguards the rights of owners of earlier national trade marks to oppose the use of a later CTM unless the owner has acquiesced in the use of the mark for five years and been aware of such use and failed to file revocation proceedings whether before the CTMO or by way of counterclaim.[34]

Secondly, the CTM Regulation gives specific protection to proprietors of earlier rights applicable only in a particular locality. Such persons may

[28] Art. 22(3).
[29] Art. 22(4).
[30] Art. 64(1).
[31] Art. 64(2).
[32] Art. 65(1).
[33] Art. 66(2).
[34] Arts. 8, 53(2), 106.

oppose the *use* of the CTM in the territory where his right is protected in so far as the law of the Member State permits.[35] If the proprietor has acquiesced for five years in the use of the CTM, being aware of such use, he may not oppose the use of the CTM but the CTM owner cannot exercise his rights against the former.[36]

(iv) Procedural law

3.045 *Application for CTM*—Applications for a CTM can be filed at the CTMO or the central industrial property office of a Member State.[37] The Application must contain a request for the registration of a CTM, information identifying the applicant, list of goods or services in respect of which the registration is requested and a representation of the mark.[38]

3.046 *Priority*—CTM applications may claim a priority date to the application if applicable under the Paris Convention.[39] Applicants claiming priority must file a declaration of priority and a copy of the previous application.[40]

In order to persuade proprietors of national marks to register their marks as CTMs, a CTM application which is identical to an earlier national mark and whose goods or services are identical with or contained within those for the earlier mark can claim the seniority of the earlier trade mark in respect of the Member State for which it is registered.[41] Seniority has the sole effect of conferring on the CTM the same rights as that granted under the earlier national trade mark if the latter is surrendered or lapses.[42] If the earlier trade mark is revoked, declared invalid or surrendered *prior* to the registration of the CTM, the seniority claimed fails.[43] The situation is more complicated if the earlier trade mark is revoked, declared invalid or surrendered after grant of the CTM. Prima facie, the removal from the register of an earlier trade mark which a CTM claims priority after registration does not affect the seniority claim. However, Article 14 of the First Trade Mark directive specifically permits a party to establish the invalidity or revocation of the earlier trade mark *a posteriori* where the seniority of the earlier mark which has been surrendered or allowed to lapse is claimed for a CTM. *A fortiori*, this suggests that revocation or a declaration of invalidity of an earlier trade mark which remains on the register would repudiate any claim of

[35] Art. 107.
[36] Art. 107(2), (3).
[37] Art. 25.
[38] Art. 26.
[39] Art. 29.
[40] Art. 30.
[41] Art. 34.
[42] Art. 34(2).
[43] Art. 34(3). The wording of this paragraph does not refer to the earlier trade mark being allowed to lapse. Art. 34(2) specifically distinguishes between surrender and lapse of a mark. Thus, it may be that non-payment of a renewal fee would merely constitute allowing the trade mark to lapse and not a surrender of the mark. If so, this should not prevent a claim of seniority if it occurs prior to registration of the CTM.

seniority that existed for an existing registered CTM. Thus, if a party can show that the earlier trade mark from which the CTM claims seniority from is invalid, then the CTM's seniority claim lapses regardless as to when the earlier trade mark came off the register. The proprietor of a CTM may claim seniority of an earlier national mark registered for identical goods or services even after registration of the CTM.[44]

3.047 *Examination*—Upon receipt of an application, the CTMO will examine it to ensure that it has complied with the procedural formalities; that the applicant is entitled to file a CTM application and that there are no absolute grounds for refusal.[45] If the trade mark contains a non-distinctive element, the CTMO may request that the applicant disclaims any exclusive right to such an element.[46] The CTMO will then compile a search report of earlier CTM or CTM applications which could be cited against the application.[47] Furthermore, the CTMO will send a copy of the application to the industrial property office of each Member State which has informed the CTMO of its decision to operate a search of its own register of trade mark for CTM applications.[48] These offices will send within three months from receipt their search report on the application. The reports will then be sent to the applicant. Earlier CTM proprietors and applicants who are cited in the search report are notified by the CTMO upon publication of the application. The CTMO will not *ex officio* refuse an application on the basis of earlier prior rights. If at this stage, the application has not been refused, the application is published not earlier than one month after the sending of the search reports to the applicant.[49]

3.048 *Opposition*—Since the CTMO will not *ex officio* reject any application on the basis of third party rights, an application for a CTM will only be rejected on relative grounds on the basis of opposition brought by third parties. Third parties are given the right to make observations and, within three months of the publication of the application, to oppose the registration.[50] Opponents must establish an earlier right under Article 8.[51] Opposition proceedings can be brought by the proprietor of the earlier trade mark and also by licensees authorised by the proprietors.[52] Opposition proceedings are then instituted. The application will then proceed to registration if it is not successfully opposed.

[44] Art. 35.
[45] Art. 36–38.
[46] Art. 38(2).
[47] Art. 39.
[48] Art. 39(2).
[49] Arts. 39(7) and 40(1).
[50] Arts. 41 and 42.
[51] Art. 8 sets outs the relative grounds for refusal — see para. 3.037.
[52] Art. 42(1)(a). Where the opposition is based on an unregistered mark pursuant to Art. 8(4) (see para. 3.037), opposition proceedings can be brought by the proprietor of the mark or persons authorised under the relevant national law to exercise those rights.

Languages—An application for a CTM must be filed in one of the official languages of the Community.[53] However, the official languages of the CTMO are only English, French, German, Italian and Spanish.[54] If an application has been filed in a Community language other than an official CTMO language, the CTMO will arrange to have the language translated into the CTMO language as indicated by the applicant.[55] Furthermore, all the applicants must indicate a second language which must be a language of the CTMO, the use of which he accepts, for the purposes of opposition, revocation or invalidity proceedings.[56] This second language can be used by the CTMO in written communications to the applicant if the application was not made in a language of the CTMO.[57] **3.049**

In opposition, revocation or invalidity proceedings, the language chosen for the notice of opposition or application for revocation or invalidity must be an official language of the CTMO and becomes the language of the proceedings if it is the language of the application or the second language indicated.[58] Otherwise, the notice or application for revocation must be translated at the opponent or applicant for revocation's expense into the language of the application or the second language.[59] Applications, entries in the Register of CTM and other information required to be published under the Regulation must be published in all the official languages of the Community.[60]

Duration and Renewal of CTM—CTM's are registered for a period of 10 years with the option to renew for successive 10 year periods.[61] A fee must be paid to renew a CTM. **3.050**

Revocation of CTM—A CTM may be revoked if it has not been the object of genuine use in the Community for a continuous five year period;[62] has become generic for the goods or services which it covers due to the acts or inactivity of the proprietor; has become misleading due to the use made of it by the proprietor; or if the proprietor no longer satisfies the requirements under the Regulation as to who may own a CTM.[63] A CTM may also be declared invalid on application to the **3.051**

[53] Art. 115(1).
[54] Art. 115(2).
[55] Art. 115(3).
[56] Art. 115(3).
[57] Art. 115(4).
[58] Art. 114(5), 114(6).
[59] Art. 114(6).
[60] Art. 116.
[61] Art. 46.
[62] If, after the expiry of the five year period but prior to the filing of the application to revoke or counterclaim, genuine use of the mark starts or resumes, then the application to revoke will fail unless the commencement or resumption of use within a period of three months preceding the filing date and preparations for this occurred only after the proprietor became aware that the application or counterclaim might be filed—Art. 50(1)(a).
[63] Art. 50. As to who may own a CTM, see para. 3.035.

CTMO or on the basis of a counterclaim if one or more of the following conditions are satisfied:

(i) The proprietor of the mark is not entitled to own a CTM;[64]
(ii) Absolute or relative grounds of refusal apply;[65]
(iii) The applicant was acting in bad faith when prosecuting the application;[66]
(iv) If national law would prohibit the use of the mark on the grounds of protection of an earlier right and in particular the right to a name, the right of personal portrayal, copyright or an industrial property right.[67]

Several particular defences to a claim for revocation exist under the following heads. Firstly, if a mark although non-distinctive has become distinctive as a consequence of the use which has been made of it, it is not to be declared invalid under Article 7(1)(b),(c) or (d).[68] Secondly, an earlier trade mark owner or other right owner cannot object to the registration of a CTM if he has consented to its registration.[69] Thirdly, the proprietor of a CTM or national trade mark right cannot object or exercise his rights against a later trade mark if he acquiesced while being aware of its use in its use for a period of five successive years in the Community or the relevant Member State.[70]

The effects of a revocation on a CTM are that it shall be deemed to have had no effect after the date of the application for revocation or that of the counterclaim.[71] A declaration that a CTM is invalid is effective *ab initio*.[72] Any retroactive effect of revocation or invalidity does not affect any decision on infringement which has been enforced prior to the revocation or invalidity decision or any contract concluded in so far as it has been performed prior to the revocation or invalidity decision.[73]

Applications to revoke are conducted in the CTMO in a similar fashion as that of opposition proceedings.[74]

3.052 *General provisions as to conduct of proceedings before the CTMO*—The CTMO can examine all relevant facts before it in *ex parte* proceedings but must restrict itself to facts, evidence and argument presented by parties in *inter partes* proceedings.[75] Oral proceedings

[64] Art. 51(1)(a). See previous footnote.
[65] Art. 51(1)(a), Art. 52.
[66] Art. 51(1)(b).
[67] Art. 52(2). Note the more restricted ground when opposing an application, see para. 3.037 and footnote 15.
[68] Art. 51(2). The provisions of Art. 7(1)(b)–(d) are set out in italics in the section on Absolute Ground for Refusal at para. 3.036.
[69] Art. 52(3).
[70] Art. 53.
[71] Art. 54(1).
[72] Art. 54(2).
[73] Art. 54(3).
[74] See Arts. 55 and 56.
[75] Art. 74.

before the CTMO are possible upon a request by a party or at the instigation of the CTMO.[76] Evidence taking can include hearing the parties, requests for information, the production of documents, hearing witnesses, opinion by experts and sworn statements.[77] An applicant who fails to comply with a CTMO time limit may apply for re-establishment of rights. Such an application must be made within two months from the removal of the cause of non-compliance.[78] Costs may be awarded against the losing party in *inter partes* proceedings.[79]

3.053 *Division of jurisdiction between CTMO and courts of Member States*—Once a CTM is granted, CTMs are to be enforced and litigated in Member States. The rules as to which Member State to bring an action for infringement of a CTM are somewhat complex. Generally speaking, the Brussels Convention prima facie applies to proceedings relating to a CTM.[80] The applicability of the Brussels Convention to national trade marks is dealt with in the chapter on Jurisdiction.[81] However, the CTM Regulation excludes most of the relevant provisions of the Convention and provides its own jurisdictional rules.[82]

CTMs must be litigated in Community trade mark courts. Member States must designate national courts as Community trade mark courts of first and second instance.[83] Such courts have exclusive jurisdiction to try infringement actions (including actions for reasonable compensation for infringing acts done between publication of the application and publication of the CTM registration); actions for declaration of non-infringement and counterclaims for revocation or declaration of invalidity.[84] Such proceedings must be brought:

(a) before the courts of the Member States in which the defendant is domiciled otherwise;
(b) in the courts of the Member State in which the defendant has an establishment otherwise;
(c) in the court of the Member State in which the plaintiff is domiciled otherwise;
(d) in the court of the Member State in which the plaintiff has an establishment otherwise;
e) in Spain.[85]

The above rules can be ousted by agreement that another Community

[76] Art. 75.
[77] Art. 76.
[78] Art. 78.
[79] Art. 81.
[80] Art. 90(1).
[81] See Chapter 13.
[82] Art. 90(2).
[83] Art. 91.
[84] Art. 92.
[85] Art. 93.

trade mark court have exclusive jurisdiction and also by the defendant submitting to the jurisdiction in another Community trade mark court.[86] If a Community trade mark court has jurisdiction under the above rules, its jurisdiction extends to all acts of infringement committed or threatened within the territory of any of the Member States.[87] Furthermore, Community trade mark courts in the Member State where the acts of infringement occurred or are threatened have concurrent jurisdiction to try infringement actions.[88] If jurisdiction is based on this rule, the court only has jurisdiction in respect of acts committed or threatened within the territory of the Member State in which the court is situated.[89]

Under the Regulation, one cannot bring an action for revocation or declaration of invalidity before a national court. This can only be done at the CTMO. However, during an infringement action, a CTM Court can entertain a counterclaim for revocation or a declaration of invalidity.[90] The Regulation appears to allow a claim for revocation in a Community trade mark court otherwise than by way of counterclaim where it is claimed that the CTM is invalid through lack of use or on account of an earlier right of the defendant.[91]

If the CTMO has already determined the application relating to the same subject matter and cause of action between the same parties then no counterclaim can be brought.[92] If a proprietor of a CTM is not a party to the proceedings, he must be joined as a party in accordance with national law.[93] If the counterclaim is successful, the court must notify the CTMO who will revoke or declare invalid the CTM.[94] A CTM court may stay proceedings on a counterclaim on application by the proprietor that the defendant submit an application for revocation or a declaration of invalidity before the CTMO within a specified time limit.[95]

[86] CTM Regulation, Art. 93(4), Brussels Convention, Arts. 17 and 18.
[87] Art. 94.
[88] Art. 93(5).
[89] Art. 94(2).
[90] Art. 95(1).
[91] Art. 95(3). However, it is not clear whether the wording of this section achieves this purpose. The subsection states that a court can revoke or declare invalid a CTM in actions for infringement (actual or threatened) [see reference in Art. 95(3) to Art. 92(a) and (c)]. However, Art. 95(3) continues by saying that a plea relating to revocation or invalidity of the CTM submitted otherwise than by way of counterclaim shall be admissible "in so far as the *defendant* claims that the rights of the proprietor of the CTM could be revoked for lack of use or that the CTM could be declared invalid on account of an earlier right of the *defendant*". The reference to defendant suggests that the party seeking to revoke or have declared invalid a CTM must be a defendant in proceedings for infringement of CTM. If such is the case, it is difficult (at any rate under English law) to see how any claim for revocation or a declaration of invalidity will be otherwise than as a counterclaim.
[92] Art. 96(2).
[93] Art. 96(3). A licensee or (exclusive licensee may bring proceedings for infringement of a CTM (Art. 22(3)) without joining the proprietor as a party to the action.
[94] Art. 96(6).
[95] Art. 96(7).

3.054 *Enforcement of CTM in Community trade mark courts*—In considering an action based on the CTM, a CTM court must apply national law, including its private international law where the Regulation makes no specific provision.[96] The court must apply the rules of procedure applicable to the same type of action relating to a national trade mark in its Member State.[97] If it finds that infringement has occurred, it must issue an order prohibiting the defendant from proceeding with the infringing acts.[98] In relation to other sanctions, it may only grant relief that is permitted under the laws (including its private international law) of the Member State where the infringement occurred.[99]

3.055 *Provisional Measures*—A Community trade mark court may grant such provisional relief in respect of a CTM as is available under its laws in respect of a national trade mark even where another court has jurisdiction as to the substance of the matter.[1] Furthermore, a CTM court whose jurisdiction is based on any ground other than being the CTM court of the Member State where the infringement took place, may grant provisional measures which, subject to any necessary procedure for recognition and enforcement under the Brussels Convention, are applicable in the territory of any Member State.[2]

3.056 *Related Actions*—Generally, the provisions in the Brussels Convention on related actions apply. Thus, where proceedings involving the same cause of action and between the same parties are brought in the courts of different Contracting States, any court other than the court first seised must decline of its own motion jurisdiction.[3] Where related actions are brought in the courts of different Contracting States, any court other than the first seised may stay its proceedings.[4] The CTM Regulation makes specific provisions that mirror the Brussels Convention. Thus a CTM court must stay proceedings where the validity of the CTM is already in issue before another CTM court or the CTMO.[5] Similarly, the CTMO must stay proceedings for revocation where the validity of the CTM is already in issue before a CTM court, unless a party to the proceedings before the CTM court requests and is granted a stay of the court proceedings.[6]

Similarly, where concurrent proceedings under an identical national

[96] Art. 97(2).
[97] Art. 97(3).
[98] Art. 98(1).
[99] Art. 98(2).
[1] Art. 99(1).
[2] Art. 99(2).
[3] Brussels Convention, Art. 21.
[4] Brussels Convention, Art. 22. Actions are deemed to be related where they are so closely connected that it is expedient to hear and determine them together to avoid the risk of irreconcilable judgments resulting from separate proceedings—Art. 22, 3rd para. See para. 13.023 *et seq.*
[5] CTM Regulation, Art. 100(1).
[6] Art. 100(2).

trade mark and CTM registered for identical goods or services are brought in the courts of different Member States, the court other than the court first seised must decline jurisdiction.[7] Where the marks are valid for similar goods or services and/or similar to each other, the court other than the first seised may stay its proceedings.[8]

3.057 *Appeals*—Appeals from the first instance Trade Mark courts lie to the second instance Community trade mark courts. Whilst the regulation makes no provision, **Article 177** of the Treaty of Rome gives the ECJ power to give preliminary rulings concerning the validity and interpretation of acts of the institutions of the Community. This is not by way of appeal and a request for a preliminary ruling must be made in the course of the proceedings.

In proceedings before the CTMO, appeals from the various divisions of the CTMO lie to the Boards of Appeal.[9] An appeal from the Board of Appeal to the Court of First Instance on the grounds of lack of competence, infringement of an essential procedural requirement, infringement of the Treaty, of the Regulation or any rule of law relating to their application or misuse of power.[10]

3.058 *Conversion of CTM registration or application into national trade mark application*—An application or proprietor can convert a CTM application or registration where it has been refused or declared invalid into a national application.[11] However, if the CTM has been revoked on the grounds of non-use, conversion may not take place unless in the Member State for which conversion is requested the CTM has been put to use which would be considered to be genuine use under the laws of that Member State.[12] A request for conversion must be made within three months from the date of communication of the refusal or revocation.[13] Such a converted application will enjoy the priority date of the refused or invalidated CTM application or registration.[14]

[7] Art. 105(1)(a). If judgment has already been given in the other court, the court must reject the action—Art. 105(2), (3).

[8] Art. 105(1)(b).

[9] Arts. 57–62.

[10] Art. 63. These grounds are identical to those laid down in Art. 173 which permits the ECJ to review the legality of acts of the Council and Commission (which includes decisions of the Commission). It might be thought that E.C. Treaty **Art. 177** permits the Boards of Appeal to ask for a preliminary ruling on the interpretation or validity of the Regulation or its rules. However Art. 177 can only be relied upon "where such a question is raised before any court or tribunal of a *Member State* . . . ". Although, the Boards of Appeal are tribunals situated in a Member State, they are not established or constituted by a Member State and accordingly, it is unlikely that Art. 177 could be relied upon in these circumstances.

[11] Art. 108(1).

[12] Art. 108(2).

[13] Art. 108(4). If revoked by a national court, the relevant date is that when the decision acquired the authority of a final decision—Art. 108(6).

[14] Art. 108(3).

(v) Entry into force of CTM Regulation

3.059 The CTM regulation enters into force on April 14, 1994.[15] However, applications for CTMs must wait until the Administrative Board of the CTMO fix a date. At present, it is anticipated that the CTMO will open on January 1, 1996 for the filing of new application and that full operation will start on 1, April 1996. Applications filed in the period January 1, to March 31, 1996 will be given a filing date of April 1, 1996.

(vi) Merits of CTM over national trade marks and International trade mark (the Madrid Agreement and its Protocol)

3.060 Doubts about the attractiveness of the CTM regime have been expressed in comparison to national trade mark applications and international applications made under the Madrid Agreement or its Protocol (once in force).[16] Firstly, there is concern about the difficulty about choosing a proposed mark for a CTM application which does not conflict with prior rights. Under the CTM regulation, a third party with an earlier registration, an applicant with an earlier application in a Member State or the proprietor of an earlier unregistered trade mark in a Member State (provided it is of more than mere local significance) may oppose an application or revoke a CTM. The sheer number of possible prior rights in the E.C. will persuade applicants to choose a national route where there will be fewer rights to be concerned about.

Secondly, there are doubts about the strength of a CTM. The CTMO only searches for prior CTMs and CTM applications. It is not yet clear which trade mark offices of Member States will conduct their own searches of national trade marks. The CTMO has no *ex officio* power to refuse an application on the basis of a prior right. The CTMO must merely inform the proprietors of earlier Community marks (but not proprietors of earlier national marks) of the CTM application. Accordingly, a registered CTM cannot be regarded as a "strong" registration. In countries where there are extensive and thorough *ex officio* examinations (*e.g.* U.K., Denmark and Ireland), many will prefer the strength of a national trade mark as against a weak Community trade mark.

Thirdly, problems may arise from the requirement that registration can only be obtained for the whole of the E.C. ("the unitary principle"). What is the position if the E.C. is expanded to incorporate other countries (and there are a number waiting to join) where third parties own conflicting rights with Community trade mark registrations or applications? Should the CTM be retrospectively invalidated or should the third party be prevented from using the mark? It is likely that provisions would be made which would allow a division of rights with the CTM

[15] Art. 143(1). Date of publication was January 14, 1994.

[16] For a useful summary of the pros and cons of the CTM v. the Madrid Agreement, see Davies, "Are Trade Mark Owners Ready to Brave the Costa Brava?" [1994] EIPR 47 at p. 49.

being confined to the original territory and the third party rights confined to its original territory.[17] However, such a concession would strike at the heart of the reason for the CTM, namely that it should never be used to prevent the free flow of trademarked goods across the internal borders of the E.C.

Fourthly, the location of the office in Alicante in Spain and the provisions as to languages and translations may mean that the applicant must incur considerable time and expense in prosecuting his application.

Fifthly, once the Madrid Protocol is ratified, it will make the obtaining of a number of national registrations much easier and simpler. The advantage the Madrid Protocol has over the CTM is that if there is a difficulty with an earlier right in a Member State, registration can be obtained in the remaining countries whereas such a right could well be fatal to an application for a CTM (although the CTM can be converted into national trade mark applications).

However, in favour of the CTM, is that it is expected to provide a much cheaper route to obtaining protection throughout the Community than obtaining separate national registrations. At present, it is not clear how it will compare financially to using the Madrid Protocol to obtain protection in the Community. It may well be that a hybrid route, *i.e.* a Madrid application which uses the CTM to obtain protection in the Community will prove the most economical. Secondly, the owner of a CTM need only use it in one Member State in order to maintain its validity whereas the owner of parallel national registrations will have to use it in all states where he has registrations.

(b) First Trade Mark Harmonisation Directive 89/104

(i) Introduction

3.061 The Trade Mark Directive results from the Commission's decision to implement a Community Trade Mark. In 1976, the Commission produced a Memorandum on the creation of an E.C. trade mark and made a comprehensive survey of the need for trade marks as facilitators of the process of identifying and choosing goods and services. In concluding that there was a need for a Community Trade Mark which covered the territory of the E.C. in order to facilitate the free movement of goods, the Commission realised that upon instituting the mechanism of a European trade mark, national trade mark laws would continue to exist. Differences in the application of such laws were perceived as being a potential obstacle to the free movement of goods. Accordingly, the Memorandum called for an approximation of national trade mark laws of Member States in order to complement the Community Trade Mark. It was intended that both should be implemented together but with the political difficulties over the CTM, especially the siting of the CTMO, the Commission pushed ahead with its harmonisation program.

[17] See Morcom, "The Legitimacy of European Trade Mark System" [1980] EIPR 359.

The Commission chose to harmonise trade mark laws by way of a directive. The first draft was published in 1980 and after a considerable degree of discussion between the Commission, the Parliament, Member States and other interest groups, the First Trade Mark Directive was adopted by the Council on December 21, 1988.[18] The directive should have been implemented in Member States by December 31, 1992.[19] By August 1994, most Member States had implemented it or were in the process of implementing the directive.[20] Because the mandatory provisions of the directive have "direct effect", the state cannot rely upon its failure to implement such provisions as against a concerned party.[21] This may be important in relation to *ex officio* objections by an intellectual property office in relation to the prosecution of trade mark applications.

(ii) Structure and contents of directive

3.062 As the name of the directive suggests, it is not intended to be an exhaustive harmonisation act. It seeks to harmonise those provisions of national trade mark law which most directly affect the functioning of the internal market.[22] In other areas, Member States are free to maintain their existing laws or legislate as they wish. Thus, the directive states that it does not deprive the Member States of the right to continue to protect trade marks acquired through use and that Member States "remain free" to fix procedural provisions concerning: registration, revocation and invalidity; the effects of invalidity or revocation; the application to trade marks of law of the Member States other than trade mark law such as the provisions relating to unfair competition, civil liability or consumer protection; eligibility for the grant of a trade mark; renewal of trade marks, fees and effect of non-compliance with procedural rules.[23] However, where there are approximating provisions in the directive, such provisions are exhaustive.[24] These provisions concern the main areas of trade mark law, in particular registrability of a mark, the effect of prior rights and rights given by registration. Accordingly, a Member State may not enact provisions in these areas which are incompatible or not mentioned in the directive. The substantive provisions are generally in the same terms as the corresponding provisions of the CTM Regulation.

The directive distinguishes between mandatory and optional provisions. Member States must enact the former and may enact the latter. At the end of this chapter is a table setting out whether each Member

[18] For more detail on the background to harmonisation and the drafting history of the directive, see Gielen, "Harmonisation of Trade Mark Law in Europe: The First Trade Mark Harmonisation Directive of the European Council" [1992] EIPR 262.

[19] See Art. 16. The Council has deferred the implementation date to December 31, 1992 pursuant to Art. 16(2). [1992] O.J. L6/35 of January 11, 1992.

[20] See table at end of para. 3.085.

[21] See Introduction Chapter as to meaning of "direct effect".

[22] See Recital 1 and 10 of the Dir.

[23] See Recital 4–7.

[24] *e.g.* see Recital 7.

State has implemented the directive and which optional provisions they have implemented.

(iii) Signs of which a trade mark may consist

3.063 The Directive states that:

> "a trade mark may consist of any sign capable of being represented graphically, particularly words, including personal names, designs, letters, numerals, the shape of goods or of their packaging, provided that such signs are capable of distinguishing the goods or services of one undertaking from those of other undertakings."[25]

This is a very wide definition and is the same as in the CTM Regulation. All that is required is that the mark is distinctive and capable of being represented graphically.

(iv) Grounds for refusal or invalidity

(1) Absolute grounds for refusal

Mandatory grounds

3.064 Article 3 of the Directive gives a list of grounds which will cause a mark to be unregistrable or liable to be removed from the register. These are:

(a) Signs which cannot constitute a trade mark. It is assumed that this means symbols which do not fall within the definition of a trade mark in the directive, *i.e.* a symbol which is incapable of being represented graphically and inherently incapable of distinguishing goods from different undertakings.[26]

(b) Trade marks which are devoid of distinctive character; consist exclusively of signs or indications which may serve, in trade, to designate the kind, quality, quantity, intended purpose, value, geographical origin or the time or production of the goods or of rendering of the service or other characteristics of the goods or service; trade marks which consist exclusively of signs or indications which have become customary in the current language or in the *bona fide* and established practices of the trade.[27]

3.065 *Secondary meaning*—The above provisions are derived from Article 6^{quinquies} of the Paris Convention. However, if any mark which falls into these categories has become factually distinctive by use in the market place prior to the date of application for registration, then it must not be refused registration.[28] The Directive also provides an optional provision allowing Member States to enact that an application shall not be refused

[25] Art. 2.
[26] Art. 3(1).
[27] Art. 3(1)(b)–(d).
[28] Art. 3(3).

or a registration revoked if the distinctive character was obtained after the date of application for registration or after the date of registration.[29]

Other mandatory absolute refusal provisions are:

(c) signs which consist exclusively of the shape which results from the nature of the goods themselves, or the shape of goods which is necessary to obtain a technical result or the shape which gives substantial value to the goods;[30]
(d) trade marks which are contrary to public policy or to accepted principles of morality;[31]
(e) trade marks which are of such a nature as to deceive the public, for instance as to the nature, quality or geographical origin of the goods or service;[32]
(f) trade marks which consist of heraldic symbols, flags etc.[33]

Optional provisions[34]

3.066 Member States may enact that a trade mark shall not be registered or if registered declared invalid where:

(a) the use of the trade mark may be prohibited pursuant to provisions of law other than trade mark law of the Member State concerned or of the Community;[35]
(b) The trade mark covers a sign of high symbolic value, especially a religious symbol;[36]
(c) The trade mark is for badges, emblems other than covered by Article 6ter of the Paris Convention;[37]
(d) The application for the trade mark is made in bad faith;[38]
(e) In the case of collective marks, guarantee marks or certification marks, where the "function of those marks so requires".[39]

Most of these provisions already form part of national trade mark laws. As mentioned already, the directive accepts that prima facie non-distinctive marks which have become factually distinctive by use are registrable. However, this does not apply to trade marks which are likely

[29] Art. 3(3), 2nd sentence.
[30] Art. 3(1)(e).
[31] Art. 3(1)(f).
[32] Art. 3(1)(g). Art. 15(2) permits Member States to derogate from this provision and provides that signs or indications which serve in trade to designate the geographical origin of goods or services, *e.g.* Champagne, may constitute collective guarantee or certification marks, but if so, there must be a defence of honest practices in industrial or commercial matters available to an otherwise infringer.
[33] Art. 3(1)(h). The reader is referred to Art. 6ter of the Paris Convention from whence the Article is derived.
[34] Art. 3(2)(a)–(d).
[35] Art. 3(2)(a).
[36] Art. 3(2)(b).
[37] Art. 3(2)(c).
[38] Art. 3(2)(d).
[39] Art. 15(1). The meaning of this rather cryptic phrase is unclear.

to deceive the public.[40] For instance, national offices will need to consider whether the trade mark is misleading as to geographical origin (a ground of refusal for which there is no provision in the directive that evidence of distinctiveness can overcome). Thus, if a haulage company uses the mark "YORK" and is established in York, this will suffice. However, if a haulage company used the mark "STORNOWAY" and comes from Littlehampton, even if it is distinctive of the haulage company, the mark may be misleading. Similar analysis will apply to marks prima facie indicative of quality and the nature of goods and services.

The provision on shapes alters certain Member State's trademark laws. The grounds on which registration of a shape can be refused are designed to prevent concurrent protection in other areas of intellectual property, *e.g.* patent and design and also to prevent the monopolisation of certain shapes to the detriment of competitors.[41]

(2) Relative grounds for refusal

Mandatory grounds

3.067 An application will be refused registration or if registered, declared invalid, if it conflicts with an earlier trade mark. A conflict will occur:

(a) if it is identical with an earlier trade mark in both form and the goods and the services covered by the respective applications or registrations;

(b) if it is similar to an earlier trade mark in respect of both the mark and the goods and the services covered by the application and there is a likelihood of confusion on the part of the public which includes a likelihood of association with the earlier mark;

(c) if the mark itself is identical or similar to an earlier Community trade mark but the goods or services it has applied for are dissimilar to those covered by the earlier Community trade mark, where the latter has a reputation in the Community and where the use of the later trade mark without due cause would take unfair advantage of, or be detrimental to, the distinctive character or the repute of the earlier Community trade mark.[42]

"Earlier trade marks" are defined as Community trade marks, marks registered in a Member State or at the Benelux Trade Mark Office and international registered marks which have effect in the relevant Member State where the date of application is earlier than the date of application for registration, taking into account any priorities claimed.[43] Community Trade Marks which can claim seniority from an earlier national mark are

[40] Art. 3(3) only applies to Art. 3(1)(b)–(d) and does not apply to Art. 3(1)(g).
[41] See Gielen, at p. 265, cited at n. 18 *supra* and E.C. Supplement Bulletin 5/1980.
[42] Arts. 4(1)(a), (b) and 4(3).
[43] Art. 4(2)(a).

also defined as an earlier trade mark.[44] "Earlier trade mark" also includes applications for trade marks subject to their registration and marks which are well known in a Member State as set out in Article 6bis of the Paris Convention at the date of application or priority date of the application.[45]

Optional grounds

3.068 Seven optical grounds for refusal or invalidity are mentioned in Article 4(4). These are:

(a) if the mark itself is identical or similar to an earlier trade mark but the goods or services it has applied for are dissimilar to those covered by the earlier trade mark and the earlier trade mark has a reputation in the Member State and where the use of the later trade mark without due cause would take unfair advantage of, or be detrimental to, the distinctive character or the repute of the earlier trade mark;[46]

(b) where there is an earlier non-registered trade mark and the owner has the right to prohibit the use of a subsequent trade mark;[47]

(c) where a third party has an earlier non-trade mark right such as a right to a name; a right of personal portrayal, copyright or other industrial property rights.

(d)-(f) where the trade mark is identical or similar to:

- (i) an earlier collective trade mark which expired within three years of the date of application;
- (ii) an earlier guarantee or certification mark which expired within a term of years to be fixed by Member States or;
- (iii) an earlier trade mark which expired within two years preceding the date of application.

(g) where the trade mark is liable to be confused with a mark which was in use abroad on the filing date of the application and which is still in use there provided that at the date of the application, the applicant was acting in bad faith.

These provisions, in particular those concerning an earlier trade mark covering dissimilar goods, are derived from Benelux law which has developed considerable case law in this field. The provisions permitting the refusal of registration based on earlier unregistered rights was at the insistence of those countries like the United Kingdom, Denmark and Ireland where such rights are recognised. The proprietor of the non-registered mark must possess the right to prohibit the use of a subsequent

[44] Art. 4(2)(b).

[45] Art. 4(2)(d).

[46] Compare this to the mandatory ground where the earlier Community trade mark has a Community reputation.

[47] *i.e.*in England, the owner of the non-registered mark could succeed in an action for passing off against use of the applied for mark.

trade mark—thus in the United Kingdom, he must be able to bring a successful action for passing-off against the applicant if the applicant used the mark. This will involve a national office or court hypothetically considering the use of the mark applied for on the goods or services claimed for and determining whether for all or some of them, an action for passing-off would lie.

(v) Rights conferred by a trade mark

Mandatory provisions

3.069 *Rights*—Article 5(1) of the Directive confers on the proprietor exclusive rights to prevent all third parties not having consent of the owner from using in the course of trade:

(a) any sign which is identical with the trade mark in relation to goods or services which are identical for those which the trade mark is registered;
(b) any sign where because, of its identity with, or similarity to, the trade mark and the identity or similarity of the goods or services covered by the trade mark and the sign, there exists a likelihood of confusion on the part of the public, which includes the likelihood of association between the sign and the trade mark.

3.070 *Defences*—Article 6 provides that it shall be a defence to any infringement action that a third party is using his own name or address or indications concerning the characteristics of goods or services, *e.g.* the quality, intended purposes, geographical origin, etc. Furthermore, a third party may actually refer to the registered trade mark when "it is necessary to indicate the intended purpose of a product or service, in particular as accessories or spare parts".[48] However, these defences are only available where the potential infringer uses them in accordance with honest practices in industrial or commercial matters. Furthermore, Article 6(2) permits a defence against infringement of a registered trade mark to owners of earlier rights in particular localities if such a right is recognised by the Member State in question.

The directive provides for a defence based on exhaustion of rights.[49] Article 9(1) also makes it a defence to an action for infringement of trade mark in a Member State where the defendant trades under a later registered mark if the plaintiff has acquiesced for a period of five successive years in the use of the later trade mark registered in the same Member State, unless registration of the later mark was obtained in bad faith.

[48] Art. 6(1)(c).
[49] See para. 3.075.

Optional provisions

Rights—Article 5(2) provides that Member States may enact that use in the course of trade of any sign which is identical with, or similar to, the trade mark in relation to goods or services which are not similar to those for which the trade mark is registered is an act of infringement where the latter has a reputation in the Member State and where use of that sign without due cause takes unfair advantage of, or is detrimental to, the distinctive character or the repute of the trade mark. **3.071**

Under the optional provision, Member States may expressly include as acts of infringement affixing the sign to goods or their packaging, offering the goods or putting them on the market or stocking them for these purposes under the sign, or offering or supplying services under the sign; importing or exporting the goods under the sign or using the sign on business papers and in advertising.[50]

Defences—Article 9(2) permits Member States to enact that no action can be brought by the proprietor of an earlier right or trade mark as set out in Article 4(4)(a)–(c) as set out above if the proprietor has acquiesced for five years in the use of a later mark registered in that Member State while being aware of such use in respect of the goods or services for which the later mark was registered unless such registration was obtained *mala fides*. **3.072**

Comment—The final text of this part of the Directive was again inspired by Benelux law. Article 5(1)(a) is clear and will not burden the proprietor of the registered trade mark with the necessity of gathering evidence of likelihood of confusion. Article 5(1)(b) will give rise to three main issues to a court—whether the third party's mark is similar to the registered mark; whether the goods or services provided under the third party's mark are similar to those covered in the registration and whether *because of such similarity*, there is a likelihood of confusion. This test suggests that the concept of similarity is independent of the concept of confusion. A court must first decide whether the marks are similar and/or the goods or services are similar and if the answer is yes, then decide whether in the circumstances there is a danger of confusion. It may be that Member States' courts will look to Benelux law where the Benelux Court of Justice held that there is similarity between a mark and a sign when taking into account the particular circumstances of the case, such as whether the distinctive power of the mark and the sign, each looked at as a whole and in correlation, show such a resemblance aurally, visually or conceptually that by this resemblance alone associations between the **3.073**

[50] Art. 5(3). It should be noted that the mandatory provision Art. 5(1) (see para. 3.069) uses the phrase "use in the course of trade". It is difficult to say that any of the provisions in Art. 5(3) do not relate to "use in the course of trade". Accordingly, whilst Member States may enact that the conditions in Art. 5(3) are expressly forbidden, it would be unwarranted derogation from Art. 5(1) to expressly *exclude* those provisions in Art. 5(3) or any of them from constituting acts of infringement.

sign and the mark are evoked.[51] This approach should be distinguished from, *e.g.* the old trade mark law in the United Kingdom where the similarity of a potential infringing mark was determined by the degree and risk of confusion.[52] The Court should be wary of adopting too arbitrary an approach to the issue of similarity as such an approach may fall within Article 36(2) of the Treaty of Rome if the decision would affect trade between Member States.[53]

In determining the likelihood of confusion, are the courts of Member States free to apply their old national case law criteria? National courts are required to interpret the directive so as to give effect to the objectives of the directive.[54] In the Recitals of the Directive, the Directive makes specific reference to factors which should be taken into account when considering the likelihood of confusion, namely the recognition of the trade mark on the market, the association which can be made with the registered sign and the degree of similarity between the marks and the goods. The Recital continues that the ways in which likelihood of confusion is established and in particular the onus of proof are matters for national *procedural* rules. This suggests strongly that the way a court applies the *substantive* test of confusion is intended to be a matter of Community law and if necessary, the court should make a reference under Article 177 to the ECJ for clarification of the manner of application of the test of confusion.[55]

It should be noted that the definition of infringement does not include a requirement that the offending sign be used as a trade mark. Under previous United Kingdom law, use of a sign only infringed a registered trade mark if such use was "likely to be taken as being use as a trade mark".[56] Where a registered mark is somewhat descriptive, a defence that the sign is not being used as a trade mark but to describe the nature or character of the goods or service has often proved to be an invaluable defence. Under the directive, this defence is expressly limited to the protection provided to a third party[57] by Article 6.

What is meant by "likelihood of association"? The Council and the Commission have noted in the minutes of the meeting of the Council at which the Directive was adopted that the concept of "likelihood of association" is a concept which in particular has been developed by Bene-

[51] Case A/25, *Union v. Union Soleure* (20583) and Gielen, at p. 266, cited, n. 18 above.
[52] See Trade Marks Act 1938, s. 4.
[53] See *Ideal Standard*, Decision of ECJ of June 26, 1994.
[54] *e.g.* see Case 14/83, *Von Colson v. Land Nordrhein-Westfalen* [1984] E.C.R. 1891; [1986] 2 C.M.L.R. 430 ECJ and Introduction Chapter at para. 1.021.
[55] See contrasting approach of ECJ for period prior to entry in force of Trade Mark Directive in Case C-317/91, *Deutsche Renault v. Audi* [1993] I.E.C.R 6277.
[56] Trade Marks Act 1938, s. 4(1)(a).
[57] *i.e.* where the mark is used to indicate the defendant's name or address, describe the quality of the goods, etc. See para. 3.070. Art. 6 is widely expressed and it is probable that where a defendant claims that he is not using the sign as a trade mark, he will be able to avail himself of Art. 6.

lux case law.[58] Thus, it is likely that courts unfamiliar with such a concept will be persuaded to look to such case law in interpreting it. Gielen gives an example of "Nissan Tercel" under Benelux law being held to be associated by the public with "Toyota Tercel" where the registered mark is "Tercel" but where no risk of confusion on the public as far as origin exists.[59] In another Benelux case, the Court of Appeal of Brussels rejected a submission by the Defendant, that in the light of the Directive, infringement proceedings ought to be limited to circumstances in which there is a risk of confusion about the origin of the product.[60] However, the fact that the directive deems that the likelihood of *association* to be included in the phrase "likelihood of confusion" requires further examination and suggests that association is a subset of confusion. Against this interpretation is that as A. 5(2) provides for infringement, where mere confusion does not occur, *a fortiori* A. 5(1)(b) must do as well otherwise there would be greater protection in relation to dissimilar goods than similar goods. The courts will have to determine whether the concept of "likelihood of association" is one to be considered *in vacuo* or whether it refers to the danger of association by the public in relation to the trade origin, quality of goods, character, etc., of the goods used in the course of trade under the respective marks.

Recently, the United Kingdom High Court has rejected a Benelux approach to the meaning of "likelihood of association". In a detailed judgment, the Court concluded that it was not obliged to follow the Benelux approach; that the minutes of Council Meetings which referred to A. 5(1)(b) as being a concept which had been developed by Benelux case law were confidential and could not be relied upon for the purposes of interpretation; that the primary function of a trade mark was to identify the trade mark origin of the goods or services to which it was applied and that accordingly, the meaning of "likelihood of association" had to be subsumed in this the classic confusion as to trade origin. This "likelihood of association" meant associated in the sense that one mark is an extension of the other or otherwise derived from the same source.[60a]

[58] The status of these Minutes is uncertain. They are said to be confidental and unpublished. It is unlikely, however, that they can be relied upon—see para. 1.021.

[59] Gielen p. 266, cited at n. 18. He also refers to a decision of the Benelux Court of Justice where it held that famous trade mark "Monopoly" was infringed by "Anti-Monopoly" (which related to a game which was similar to Monopoly but totally anticapitalistic) by reason of likelihood of association. Note that under the 1938 Act, such would constitute an infringement as well because it is not an answer that by adding something outside the registered mark, the defendant has distinguished his goods from those of the plaintiff, *i.e.* by adding his own name—see *Lever Bros. v. Sunniwite* [1949] 66 RPC 84 at 89; *Saville v. June Perfect* [1941] 58 RPC 161, C.A.

[60] See Gielen, p. 266, cited at n. 19 *supra*. *Regina v. Procter & Gamble* Court of Appeal of Brussels 27/51993 (1993) 1 E.R. 112. The appellant's packaging was held to infringe on the basis of likelihood of association. See Kauperman Sauder, "Questions about the 1994 UK Trade Marks Act" [1994] 2 E.I.P.R. 67 at 69, 70.

[60a] *Wagamama Ltd v. City Restaurants plc* English High Ct. (Judgment 31/7/95 unreported). Interestingly, Gielen was an expert witness in this case but the judge did not accept his evidence that Article 5(1)(b) did not change existing Benelux law.

3.074 In relation to the optional Article 5(2), the court of a Member State which enacts such a provision will have to determine: (a) whether the mark is similar to the registered mark; (b) whether the latter has a reputation in the Member State and; (c) whether use of that sign without due cause takes unfair advantage of, or is detrimental to, the distinctive character or the repute of the trade mark. In relation to the question of reputation, is this more than merely *de minimis* or does the reputation need to be substantial? Under the English law of passing-off where the requirement of reputation has been considered at length, the important consideration is whether the plaintiff has built up a goodwill to the point where substantial damage will be caused to it by the acts he complains of. Gielen suggests that reputation need certainly not be established among the public at large—30–40 per cent of a relevant sector would suffice.[61] In relation to (c), Gielen refers to a case concerning two marks, *Claeryn* for a Dutch gin and *Klarein* for a liquid cleaning agent.[61a] In Dutch, both had identical pronunciation. The Benelux Court held that one of the advantages of a trade mark is the capacity to stimulate the desire to buy the kind of goods for which the mark is registered and that this capacity can be adversely affected by the use of the mark or a similar sign for non-similar goods. This would be the case when by the loss of exclusivity the mark is no longer capable of arousing immediate association with the goods for which it is registered and used or that the goods for which the infringing mark is used appeal to the public senses in such a way that the attractive power of the mark is affected.[62] Article 5(2) protects the registered trade mark against dilution. There is no requirement that there be confusion. As such, it emphasises the trade mark's owner's private interest in preventing damage to goodwill or lost sales as a result of such damage.[62a]

The Article 9(2) optional defence has some interesting ramifications. For instance, a Member State could provide that the owner of a copyright in a trade mark is not allowed to sue for *copyright* infringement against use of such a design on the goods covered by the registration if the former has acquiesced for five successive years in such use and there is no element of bad faith.

(vi) Exhaustion of the rights conferred by a trade mark

3.075 Article 7 seeks to incorporate the principe of exhaustion of rights established by the ECJ in relation to Articles 30 to 36 and the enforcement of trademarks. It provides that a trade mark shall not entitle the proprietor to prohibit its use in relation to goods which have been put on the market

[61] See Gielen, p. 267, cited at n. 18 *supra*. See also Sanders *op. cit.* at p. 72 where he discussed in detail the concept of reputation within the meaning of Article 5(2).
[61a] Colgate Palmolive BV–NV Koninklijke Distleerderijen Gruen Lucas Bols, BCJ; March 1, 1975. See Sanders *ibid.* at p. 71, n. 41.
[62] See *ibid.*, for further examples of what the Benelux court held constituted infringement under the equivalent provision of Benelux law.
[62a] Sauder, *op. cit.*, [1995] 2 E.I.P.R. 67 at 70.

in the Community under that trade mark by the proprietor or with his consent. There is one exception provided by Article 7(2) which provides that where:

> "there exists legitimate reasons for the proprietor to oppose further commercialisation of the goods especially where the condition of the goods is changed or impaired after they have been put on the market."

This Article only applies to trade marked goods placed *in the Community* by the owner or with his consent.[63] In general, the ECJ has rejected as part of Community law, an international exhaustion of rights principle.[64] However, with the codification of an E.C.-wide exhaustion of rights principle, it has been questioned as to whether a more liberal domestic law principle, that says a trade mark proprietor exhausts his rights in a trade-marked product once it is placed anywhere in the world by him or with his consent, is incompatible with the Community Directive.[65] Indeed the preparatory works to the directive and the CTM Regulation demonstrate that the Commission and the Economic and Social Committee deliberately chose not to include an international exhaustion of rights principle on the basis that it would result in discrimination of the industry in the Community in so far as third countries did not acknowledge the principle of international exhaustion.[66] Following these observations, the Commission amended its original proposal to include marketing "in the Community". In its Explanatory Memorandum to its amended proposal for the CTM Regulation, the Commission commented on this amendment to what was then Article 11:

> "Paragraphs 1 and 2 of this Article correspond to Parliament's opinion. On the question of international exhaustion of the rights conferred by a Community trade mark, the Commission has formed the opinion that the Community legislator should refrain from introducing this principle and make do with the rule of Community-wide exhaustion. The Community must however be empowered to conclude at some future time with important trading partners, bilateral or multilateral agreements, whereby international exhaustion is introduced by the contracting parties. The restriction to Com-

[63] Actually, the EEA Agreement has extended this principle to cover the placing of goods in any EEA country—see para. 7.118 *et seq.*

[64] *e.g.* see Case 51/75; *EMI Records Ltd. v. C.B.S.*: [1976] E.C.R. 811; [1976] 2 C.M.L.R. 235.

[65] See Chapter on Enforcement of Intellectual Property at para. 7.029 *et seq.* All E.C. Member States' laws provide for an international exhaustion of rights doctrine in relation trade marks—in the U.K., see Trade Marks Act 1938, s.4(3)(a), and *Revlon v. Cripps* [1980] FSR 85; *Colgate Palmolive v. Markwell Finance* [1990] RPC 197; *Castrol Ltd v. Automotive Oil Supplies Ltd* [1983] RPC 315.

[66] See proposal by Economic and Social Committee to amend Art. 6(1) (and Art. 11(1) of the Regulation) to limit exhaustion of rights to marketing within the Community and its reasoning thereto—Document 1-611/83, August 1, 1983 at 63. Generally, see Rasmussen, "Exhaustion of Trade Mark Rights Pursuant to Directive 89/104" [1995] 4 EIPR 174.

munity-wide exhaustion, however, does not prevent the national courts from extending this principle, in cases of a special nature, in particular, where even in the absence of a formal agreement, *reciprocity is guaranteed.*"[67]

In the light of this, the Commission amended the proposed directive as well. Accordingly, it has been commented on that the inescapable conclusion of the directive and regulation is that there is no room for a conflicting or supplementary domestic international exhaustion of rights principle.[68] However, the Commission's observations suggests that national courts may apply an international principle of exhaustion where there is "guaranteed reciprocity". One awaits a preliminary ruling on this point from the ECJ.

Article 7(2) further mirrors ECJ jurisprudence relating to parallel import cases involving trade-marked goods where the packaging, mark itself and the condition of the underlying goods have been changed.[69] In such cases, the ECJ has developed particular rules on whether a trade mark proprietor can enforce his rights[70] and it is submitted that national courts should have recourse to the case law of the ECJ in this area in deciding whether a proprietor can take advantage of Article 7(2). However, at present, courts of Denmark have asked for preliminary rulings from the ECJ on whether a national court should only consider national law in conjunction with Article 7(1) and (2) in relation to repackaging cases or whether the free movement of goods provisions in particular Article 36(1) and (2) of the Treaty of Rome should be also considered.[71]

(vii) Licensing

3.076 Article 8(1) stipulates that a trade mark may be licensed for some or all of the goods or services for which it is registered and for the whole or part of the Member State concerned and may be exclusive or non-exclusive. Article 8(2) also permits a proprietor of a trade mark to sue his own licensee for trade mark infringement if he contravenes any provision in the licence with regard to: the duration; the form of the trade mark; the scope of goods or services for which the licence is granted; the territory in

[67] COM (84) 470, Explanatory Memorandum at VI.

[68] See Rasmussen "Exhaustion of Trade Mark Rights Pursuant to Directive 89/104" [1994] 4 EIPR 174.

[69] See Case 102/77 *Hoffmann La Roche v. Centrafarm*: [1978] E.C.R. 461; Case 3/78 *American Home Products Corporation v. Centrafarm*: [1978] E.C.R. 1823, [1979] 1 C.M.LR. 326; Case 1/81, *Pfizer Inc v. Eurim-Pharm GmbH*: [1981] E.C.R. 2913; [1982] 1 C.M.L.R. 406.

[70] This is discussed in the Chapter on Enforcement of Intellectual Property Rights at para. 7.062.

[71] *Bayer v. Paranova A/S*. Referred to the ECJ by the Danish Supreme Court. It should be noted that once Community secondary legislation has a complete and exhaustive legislative measures designed to guarantee protection of a specific interest set out in Art. 36, recourse to Art. 36 is not permitted. See in para. 7.032 in Chapter on Enforcement of Intellectual Property.

which the trade mark may be affixed or the quality of the goods manufactured or the services provided by the licensee.

The ability of a trade mark owner to invoke his rights against goods or services which do not comply with the provisions of a licence merely reflect the concept of a licence—that the proprietor agrees not to sue the licensee for trade mark infringement on those goods which comply with the licence. Thus, if a trade-marked good of inferior quality is sold, the proprietor can obtain an injunction against the sale of such goods by the licensee and, more importantly, third parties to whom the goods have been sold. The proprietor can also repudiate the licence but that only gives the proprietor a right in damages for trade-marked goods already sold which do not comply with the licence. This provision enables the proprietor to prevent the distribution of improperly trade-marked goods in the Community.

As commented on by Gielen, it is not clear whether Article 8(2) is mandatory or optional. Can Member States provide for fewer grounds for trade mark infringement by the licensee than those mentioned in the Directive? The Recitals are silent on this aspect of licensing. It would seem that the absence of any reference to "any Member State may" in the Article means that the provision is mandatory and that all grounds must be included.

(viii) Non-use of registered trade marks

3.077 The Directive provides that registered trade marks which are not used for a period of five years from the date of completion of the registration procedure or a subsequent period of five years are liable to revocation and a reduction in the rights of the proprietor.[71a] This provision is designed to ensure that non-used trade marks do not clutter national registries and prevent the registration of genuinely used trade marks. Accordingly, Article 10 provides that if a registered trade mark has not been put to genuine use by the proprietor or by another party with his consent within a continuous period of five years since the completion of the registration procedure in the Member State concerned, in relation to the protected goods or services, its powers are greatly diminished. The trade mark is deemed to be used if it has been used in a form differing in elements which do not alter the distinctive character of the mark or has been affixed to goods solely for export purposes.[72]

Article 11 makes it a mandatory provision that a registered trade mark which has not been used according to Article 10 cannot be used to have a later trade mark declared invalid. Furthermore, the Directive gives two other optional provisions, namely that such a non-used mark cannot be relied upon to oppose a trade mark application and cannot be invoked in infringement proceedings where a counterclaim for revocation would have been successful on the basis of non-use.

[71a] Arts. 10–13.

[72] Art. 10(2). Transitional provisions governing non-use are provided for in Art. 10(4).

Article 12 entitles a person to bring revocation proceedings for such unused registered trade marks. However, if after the expiry of five years, genuine use commences prior to the date of the application for filing of revocation, then no person may bring such proceedings save that use in the three month period prior to the date of application is disregarded where preparations for the commencement of resumption of use occurred only after the proprietor became aware that the application for revocation might be filed.

(ix) Grounds for revocation/invalidity

3.078 The Directive permits revocation on three distinct grounds. These are mandatory. The first of these is on the basis of non-use for five successive years as mentioned above.[73] The second ground is if the trade mark has become a common name in respect of a good or service for which it is registered as a consequence of the action or otherwise of the proprietor.[74] The third ground if, in consequence of the use made of the mark by the proprietor or with his consent, the trade mark is liable to mislead the public, in particular as to the nature, quality or geographical origin of the goods or services for which the trade mark is registered.[75] This last ground will always be a danger for a mark which is prima facie indicative of some characteristic of the traded good or service but which is factually distinctive. If the protected good or service is changed so that the descriptive mark fails to accurately describe a particular characteristic, it is liable to mislead. Thus, if a firm operating out of London who are the proprietors of a mark "LONDON" for haulage trailers suddenly move their operations to Paris, this might mislead the public and render the mark liable to be revoked.

It should be noted that marks are also liable to be declared invalid under Article 3 or Article 4. The directive specifically leaves Member States free to determine the effects of revocation or invalidity.[76] This should be contrasted with the CTM Regulation which deems revoked CTMs to have no effect from the date of the application for revocation and invalid CTMs to be void *ab initio*.[77]

Where grounds exist for the refusal of registration, revocation or invalidity of a trade mark in respect of only some of the goods or services for which that trade mark has been applied for or registered, refusal of registration or revocation or invalidity may be allowed but only covering those goods or services.[78] Provided the goods or services covered by the registration are of similar kind, this should not cause undue hardship to the proprietor of the mark because of his ability to oppose registration

[73] Art. 12(1).
[74] Art. 12(2)(a).
[75] Art. 12(2)(b).
[76] Recital 5.
[77] CTM Regulation, Art. 54.
[78] Art. 13.

and bring infringement proceedings for goods or services of a similar kind to those specified in the registration.

(x) Collective marks, guarantee marks and certification marks

3.079 The Directive does not harmonise protection for collective marks or guarantee or certification marks.[79] At present, the existence of protection for such marks differs under Member States' trade mark laws. Where Member States do provide such protection, the Directive permits an additional ground of objecting to the registration of such marks where the function of those marks so requires.[80] The Directive expressly empowers Member States in relation to certification marks to derogate from Article 3(1)(c) and permit the registration of signs or indications which may serve in trade to designate the geographical origin of the goods or services.[81]

(c) Regulation on the Protection of Geographical Indications and Designations of Origin for Agricultural Products and Foodstuffs

3.080 The E.C. has issued several regulations which regulate the nomenclature used for foodstuffs and beverages. In particular, the E.C. Commission has been keen to legislate in the field of geographical designations to prevent traders adopting misleading geographical names. Historically, its approach has been piecemeal legislation covering particular areas.[82] Such regulations have importance for trade mark practitioners because they reserve certain words indicative of products to a particular class of products. Moreover, where there exists exhaustive legislation in a field, a party cannot have resort to Article 36 under the E.C. Treaty to justify exercising trade mark rights to prevent movement in the Community.[83]

Recently, the E.C. Council has issued a regulation on the protection of geographical indications and designations of origin for agricultural products and foodstuffs[84] and a regulation on certificates of specific character for agricultural products and foodstuffs.[85] The object of these

[79] *e.g.* see Art. 15(1).

[80] Art. 15(1). This provision is somewhat obscure. In the United Kingdom, s.5, Sched. 2 to the Trade Marks Act 1994 provides for a ground of objection that the certification mark that the mark must not mislead as to character or significance.

[81] Art. 15(2). It is a defence to claim usage of the mark accords with honest practices in industrial or commercial matters or that the defendant is entitled to use a geographical name.

[82] For example, Reg. 823/87, dated March 16, 187 which lays down special provisions relating to quality wines produced in specified regions. Art. 15 of the Reg. (as amended by Art. 13 of Reg 2032/89) reserves particular names such as Champagne as coming from specific regions. This reg. was relied upon in *Taittinger SA v. Allbev Ltd "Elderflower Champagne"* [1993] FSR 641, C.A., where the word "champagne" was used in relation to a beverage which did not originate from the Champagne region of France.

[83] See Chapter on Enforcement of Intellectual Property at para. 7.032.

[84] Council Reg. 2081/92.

[85] Council Reg. 2082/92.

regulations are to regulate the use of names which are indicative of geographical origin or particular characteristics of agricultural products and foodstuffs. In essence, they provide for a registration system whereby the registration name is reserved for products coming from within a particular region or which have particular characteristics.[85a]

3.081 *Regulation 2081/92*—this regulation lays down rules on the protection of designations of origin and geographical indications of agricultural products intended for human consumption which are referred to in Annex II of the E.C. Treaty. The following foodstuffs are also covered: beer, natural mineral waters and spring waters, beverages made from plant extracts, bread, pastry and other bakers' wares and natural gums and resins and agricultural products consisting of hay and essential oils.[86] However, the regulation does not apply to wine products or to spirit drinks. This is because the E.C. has already legislated substantially in this area. The list of foodstuffs protected under the regulation can be increased.[87]

The regulation defines "designations of origin" as being the name of a region or country used to describe an agricultural product or foodstuff which originates in that region or country and where the product foodstuff's quality is essentially due to a particular geographical environment with its "inherent natural and human factors, and the production, processing and preparation of which take place in the defined geographical area".[88] "Geographical indication" is defined slightly differently as meaning the name of a region or country used to describe an agricultural product or foodstuff emanating from a particular region which "possesses a particular quality, reputation or other characteristics attributable to that geographical origin and the production and/or processing and/or preparation of which take place in the defined geographical area".[89] Provided that the "mark" falls within either of these categories, a group of producers of such products can apply for registration under the regulation of the name in relation to such products.[90] The application must set out all the details relating to the name of the product or foodstuff, a des-

[85a] For commentary on this Regulation, see Schwab, "The Protection of Geographical Indications in the EEC" [1995] 5 EIPR 242.

[86] Art. 1.

[87] Art. 1(1).

[88] Art. 2(2)(a).

[89] Art. 2(2)(b).

[90] Art. 5. Applications may be made by a natural or legal person (as opposed to a group) in exceptional circumstances where the person concerned is the only producer in the geographical area defined at the time the application is submitted and where that person engages in authentic and unvarying local methods and the geographical area possesses characteristics which differ appreciably from those of neighbouring areas and/or the characteristics of the product are different—Arts. 1 and 2 Reg. 2037/93 laying down detailed rules of application of Council Reg. No 2081/92 on the protection of geographical indications and designations or origin for agricultural products and foodstuffs.

cription of it, the definition of the geographical area, evidence that the product or foodstuff comes from that area, a description of the product process, the importance of the geographical environment or origin to that product, detail of inspection structures and specific labelling details.[91] The application is sent to the Member State where the region is located who forward it to the Commission. The Commission then investigates the application. If successful, the name enters on the register.[92] Once a name is registered, it is protected against any direct or indirect commercial use, any misuse, imitation or evocation or misleading indications.[93]

3.082 Importantly, the regulation provides that once a designation of origin or geographical indication is registered, an application for registration of a trade mark which is essentially and confusingly similar to the reserved name and which relates to the same type of product must be refused if submitted after the date of the publication of registration.[94] Where trade marks have been registered in breach of this condition, they must be declared invalid. Even where the application for the trade mark was lodged before the date of publication of the name, registration must be refused if publication of the "name" occurred before the trade mark was registered.[95] The regulation further provides that use of a trade mark confusingly similar to a registered geographical indication or designation of origin, which was registered in good faith before the date on which the application for registration was lodged, may continue notwithstanding the registration of the geographical indication or designation of origin where there are no grounds for invalidity or revocation of the trade mark as provided by Article 3(1)(c), (g) and Article 12(2)(b) of the Trade Mark Harmonisation Directive.[96] These Articles respectively refer to situations where the trade mark consists of a sign or indication of the nature, quality or geographical origin; in circumstances where the use of the mark is likely to mislead the public as to the nature, quality or geographical origin of the product.[97] Finally, a designation of origin or geographical indication will not be registered where in the light of a trade mark's reputation and renown and the length of time it has been used, registration is liable to mislead the consumer as to the true identity of the product.[98]

[91] Art. 4(2).
[92] Art. 6.
[93] Art. 13(1). Generally, where a plaintiff proves a breach of the Regulation, it is entitled to damages and an injunction—*e.g.* see *Taittinger SA v. Allbe Ltd "Elderflower Champagne"* [1993] F.S.R. 64, C.A. at 673.
[94] Art. 13(1).
[95] Art. 13(1).
[96] Art. 14(2).
[97] Art. 14(2) of the Reg. is silent on whether the registration *itself* (as opposed to use of the mark) may continue where its conditions are fulfilled. As Art. 14(1) provides for situations where the mark is to be declared invalid, it would seem that the registration *itself* should also be permitted to remain.
[98] Art. 14(3).

Regulation 2082/92[99]

3.083 In a similar way to Regulation 2081/92, Regulation 2082/92, which provides for certificates of specific character for agricultural products and particular foodstuffs, lays down rules for the registration of names of agricultural products and foodstuffs of specific character.[1] "Specific character" is defined as the feature or set of features which distinguishes an agricultural product or a foodstuff clearly from other similar products or foodstuffs belonging to the same category.[2] The product or foodstuff must be made using traditional raw materials or be characterised using traditional raw materials or be characterised by a traditional composition or a mode of production and/or processing reflecting a traditional type of product and/or processing.[3] The name must be specific in itself or express the specific character of the agricultural product or the foodstuff.[4] A name may not be registered if it merely refers to claims of a general nature used for a set of agricultural products or foodstuffs or to those provided for specific Community legislation or is misleading.[5]

Upon registration, the name may only be used by producers complying with the registered product specification unless the group who has applied for the name has requested that only they be allowed to use the name and that use of the name would not be lawful, recognised and economically significant for similar agricultural products or foodstuffs.[6] Importantly, Regulation 2082/92 does not make any specific provision for conflicts between registered trade marks and their applications and such reserved names.

5. EEA Legislation

3.084 The only *acquis communautaire* in the field of trade marks which is incorporated into the EEA Agreement is the Trade Mark Directive.[7] Thus, the Trade Mark Directive now applies to EFTA countries as well as E.C. states. The Directive is incorporated into the EEA Agreement by the normal method of referencing. Material amendments are that the provisions concerning the Community Trade Mark in the Trade Mark Directive do not apply to EFTA states unless the Community Trade

[99] [1992] O.J. L208/9. See also its implementing Reg. 1848/93 laying down detailed rules for its application.
[1] The particular foodstuffs eligible for protection are beer, chocolate preparations, confectionary, bread and other baker's wares, pasta, pre-cooked meals, prepared condiment sauces, soups or broths, beverages made from plant extracts and ice cream and sorbets—Annex to Reg.
[2] Art. 2(1).
[3] Art. 4(1).
[4] Art. 5.
[5] Art. 5(2).
[6] Arts. 13(2) and 15.
[7] Annex XVII.4, EEA Agreement.

Mark extends to them.[8] Thus, EFTA trade mark laws do not need to take account of, for the purpose of registration, conflicts with earlier CTMs until the CTM Regulation is effective in the EFTA country.

Another important point is that the provision in the Trade Mark Directive which incorporates the ECJ's exhaustion of rights principle into domestic trade mark is changed into an EEA exhaustion of rights principle.[9] Thus, where a trade marked good is marketed in a Contracting State (*i.e.* an E.C. or EFTA state) by the proprietor or with his consent, the proprietor cannot exercise his trade mark rights to prevent further movement in the good.[10]

The Community Trade Mark Regulation which was adopted by the E.C. Council after the cut-off date of July 31, 1991 forms part of the "Additional Package" of E.C. acts, acts adopted between this date and the entry into force of the EEA. Its applications to EFTA states is under discussion between E.C. and EFTA experts.

The Regulation on the Protection of Geographical Indications and Designations of Origin for agricultural products and foodstuffs and its accompanying regulations also forms part of the "Additional Package". Its inclusion into Annex XVII of the EEA is not at all certain due to some divergences of opinion between the Parties.[11]

(6) Tables

TABLE A—Table of trade mark protection in European countries

3.085

Country	Paris Convention	Madrid Agreement[12]	Protocol to Madrid Agreement	E.C. State Trade Mark Directive implemented?
AUSTRIA[5]	●	●	●	●
BELGIUM[5]	●[1]	●	●	●[6]

[8] Annex XVII.4 (b).
[9] Annex XVII.4(c).
[10] See EEA section on Enforcement of Intellectual Property, para. 7.118 *et seq.*
[11] See n. 101 (1994) pp. 131 Blanchet, et al, *The Agreement on the European Economic Area.*
[12] Y(N) represents a state which has ratified the Nice Revision but not the Stockholm Revision. All Madrid Contracting Countries have declared under Art. 3bis that protection from international registration shall not extend to them unless the proprietor of the mark so requests.

Bulgaria	●	●	●	
Czech Republic	●	●		
Denmark[5]	●		●	●[7]
Finland[5]	●		●	●
France[5]	●	●	●	●[8]
Germany	●	●	●	●[9]
Greece[5]	●		●	●[10]
Hungary	●	●	●	
Ireland[5]	●		●	
Italy[5]	●	●	●	●[13]
Luxembourg[5]	●[1]	●	●	●[6]
Monaco[5]	●	●	●	
Netherlands[5]	●[1]	●	●	●[6]
Norway	●			
Poland	●			
Portugal[5]	●	● (Nice Revision)	●	●[11]
Romania	●	●	●	
Russia	●	●	●	
Slovakia	●	●		
Spain[5]	●	●	●	
Sweden[5]	●		●	●
United Kingdom[5]	●		●[3,4]	●[12]
E.C.			●[2]	N/A

NOTES

[1] The territories of these countries are for the application of the Madrid Agreement deemed under Article 9[quarter] to be one territory.

[2] Accession under Article 14(1)(b) of the Protocol
[3] declarations under Article 5(2)(b) and (c) of Protocol permitting national offices a longer time limit for notifying refusals
[4] declaration under Article 8(7) of the Protocol allowing national offices to charge international fees equivalent to domestic fees for similar applications
[5] Member State of the European Community
[6] Benelux Trade Mark Law 2/12/1992 (not yet in force but expected soon)
[7] Danish Trade Mark Law Act 341, 6/6/1991
[8] French Trade Mark Law 92-597 of 1/7/1992 (Intellectual Property Code)
[9] German Trade Mark Law (Markengesetz) 1/1/1995●
[10] Greek Trade Mark Law Law No 2239/1994 (in force from November 1, 1994)
[11] Portuguese Trade Mark Law coming into force on June 1, 1995
[12] U.K. Trade Marks Act 1994
[13] Legislation Decree 480 4/12/1992.

TABLE B—Enactment of optional provisions of Trade Mark Directive by Member States

3.086

	3.2(a)	3.2(b)	3.2(c)	3.2(d)	3.3 (2nd sentence)	4.4(a)	4.4(b)	4.4(c)
AUSTRIA[NK]								
BELGIUM					●	●	●[11]	
DENMARK	●	●	●		●	●	●	●
FINLAND[NK]								
FRANCE	●	●	●	●	●	●	●	●
GERMANY	●			●	●[2]	●	●	●
GREECE		●	●	●		●	●	●
IRELAND[NIF]								
ITALY	NK	NK	NK	NK	●	NK	●	NK
LUXEMBOURG					●	●	●[11]	
MONACO[NK]								
NETHERLANDS					●	●	●[11]	
PORTUGAL	●	●	●	●		●	●[3]	●[4]
SPAIN[NIF]								
SWEDEN[NK]								
UNITED KINGDOM	●		●[5]	●	●	●	●	●

	4.4(d)	4.4(e)	4.4(f)	4.4(g)	4.5	5.2	9.2
AUSTRIA							
BELGIUM	●	1	●	6	●	●	
DENMARK	●	●	●		●	●	●[7]
FINLAND							
FRANCE	●	●		●	●	●	
GERMANY	●	1		●[8]		●	●
GREECE				●	●	●	
IRELAND							
ITALY	NK	NK	NK	NK	NK	●	NK
LUXEMBOURG	●	1	●	6	●	●	
MONACO							
NETHERLANDS	●	1	●	6	●	●	
PORTUGAL	●	●		●	●	●	
SPAIN							
SWEDEN							
UNITED KINGDOM	●		●[9]	●[10]	●	●	●

NOTES

NK Not Known

NIF Directive not implemented

[1] Country does not provide for certification or guarantee marks

[2] Acquired secondary meaning at date of decision upon entry is decisive

[3] Prior use of nonregistered mark confers a priority period for a maximum period of six months

[4] Firms, company names, business names, shop signs and copyright

[5] Royal arms and insignia and national flags are included.

[6] Benelux laws requires the fulfilment of certain other conditions—see 4.6.b and 14.B of draft Benelux Trade Mark Law

[7] No specific clause in Denmark but practice is clear on this point.

[8] No specific provision but general protection for bad faith applications and also protection under unfair competition laws

[9] Any trade mark that has expired within a year of the application must be taken into account unless there has been no use of the trade mark for two years prior to its expiry

[10] General protection for bad faith applications

[11] Prior users of nonregistered marks only given protection if application was made in bad faith

CHAPTER FOUR

COPYRIGHT IN EUROPE

1. INTRODUCTION

Copyright merely confers the right to prevent others copying a protected work. If one person independently writes exactly the same book as another, there is no infringement of the latter's rights. For infringement to be established, it must be shown that infringing work is derived from the copyright work. Because of this, copyright is described as a qualified monopoly as opposed to absolute monopolies such as patents, registered designs, trade marks and plant breeders' rights. In the circumstances, it might be thought that copyright was less harmful to competition, the economic development of a country and trade between countries. If a competitor wishes to produce a rival product to a copyright product, he must merely ensure that he does not copy the product but comes up with his own independent design. This should be contrasted with patents and other absolute monopolies where such a right may constitute an absolute bar to others entering a particular product market. Moreover, because copyright vests automatically, no cost is associated with copyrighting a product. In contrast, obtaining a patent can be a costly and often prohibitive venture.

The nature and extent of copyright is a complex subject. Thus, there exists copyright in literary, dramatic and artistic works, moral rights, cinematographic films, sound recording rights, musical rights, performers' rights, film producers' rights, broadcasting and cable retransmission rights. A product might be subject to many rights. Thus, a person who wishes to record a satellite broadcast of a film might require the licence of the performers in the film, the author of the novel on which the film was based, the scriptwriter, the composer of the soundtrack, the film producer and the broadcaster. If the extent and nature of all these rights differ from country to country, it can often become an impossible task to properly commercially exploit copyright work. This can result in the isolation of national markets.

4.001 Copyright protection exists in all European countries. Adherence to the Berne Convention has meant basic harmonisation. Furthermore, within the E.C., the Commission has been especially active in issuing directives which harmonise Member States' laws. In the "core" copyright area of authors' rights in literary and artistic works, total harmonisation of Member States' laws has been or will shortly be achieved. Coupled with the E.C. exhaustion of rights principle and the fact that copyright protection arises automatically out of original works and does not concern itself with "prior" rights, the internal borders of the E.C. have become transparent as to the marketing and circulation of literary and artistic works subject to copyright.

Where there is considerable divergence in Europe is in the extent and nature of neighbouring rights, *i.e.* performers' rights, sound recording rights, film producers' rights, etc. Also, the extent of protection conferred by copyright to authors to prevent unauthorised rental, home copying, cable retransmission and satellite broadcasting varies throughout Europe. However, the Commission has also been active in harmonising these rights as well. Thus, it is anticipated that by about 1997 to 1998, copyright and neighbouring rights will have been harmonised in all key respects.

This Chapter examines the protection afforded by international conventions, under the E.C. Treaty and finally under the EEA Treaty.

2. International Legislation

(a) Berne Convention

4.002 In the nineteenth century, the major industrial powers entered into a multitudinous number of bilateral agreements with each other and third countries for the protection of copyright of artistic and literary works of their nationals in each others countries. It was apparent to most countries that a far better solution was for industrialised countries to ensure protection in each other's country by way of an international convention. In 1886, several countries including the United Kingdom signed the Berne Convention for the protection of literary and artistic works. The fundamental principle of the Berne Convention was that Contracting States would not discriminate between domestic authors and authors of other Contracting States in respect of the level of protection conferred on qualifying artistic and literary works. The other principal objective of the Berne Convention was to harmonise copyright laws in Contracting States. The Berne convention has been revised several times since 1886. There has been the additional act of Paris 1896; the revised Berne Convention of Berlin 1908 and further revisions at Rome in 1928, at Brussels in 1948, at Stockholm in 1967 and at Paris in 1971.[1] Many countries did not sign the earlier versions of the Berne Convention. The Stockholm revision introduced a controversial protocol regarding developing countries which was aimed to meet the wishes of certain developing countries who considered the extent of protection provided by the Berne Conven-

[1] Minor amendments to the Administrative Sections of the Paris version were made in 1979.

tion too great in the light of the particular domestic circumstances of developing countries. These provisions were substantially altered in the Paris Act which meant that the Paris revision became acceptable to most industrial countries. Accordingly, many countries have now signed and ratified the Paris Act including all E.C. countries and the United States. A full account of the legislative history of the Berne Convention is outside the scope of this book.[2] This Chapter does not examine the provisions on developing countries as they are not relevant to Europe.

The fundamental provisions of the Berne Copyright Convention (Paris revision 1971) are set out as follows.

(i) Protection of Literary and Artistic Works

4.003 The Berne Convention provides that the rights of authors in literary and artistic works are to be protected in the countries which adhere to the convention.[3] Literary and artistic works are deemed to include every production in the literary, scientific and artistic domain. Thus the convention provides for the protection of, *inter alia*, written material, lectures, dramatic work, choreographic works, musical compositions, cinematographic works, works of drawing, painting, architecture, sculpture and photographic works.[4]

(ii) Qualifying Works

4.004 The protection of literary and artistic works under the Berne Convention is only extended to the works of those authors who are nationals of one of the countries which belong to the Berne Convention (whether those works have been published or not) or to works which were either first published in a country of the Berne Union or simultaneously published in a country outside the Union and in a country of the Union (whether or not the author is a national of one of the Contracting States).[5] Authors who are in habitual residence in a country of the Berne Union are for the purposes of the Berne Convention deemed to be nationals of that country.[6] With regard to the criteria of simultaneous publication, a work is considered to have been published simultaneously if it is published in two or more countries within 30 days of its first publication.[7]

[2] For those interested in reading about the legislative history of the Berne Convention, the following books may be of assistance—S. Ricketson, *The Berne Convention for the Protection of Literary and Artistic Works: 1886 to 1989*, (1987); Copinger and Skone James *Copyright* (1991) 13th ed. and *Stewart* International Copyright & Neighbouring Rights (2nd ed.).

[3] Arts. 1, 2(6), 3, and 5(1).

[4] Art. 2(1).

[5] Art. 3(1).

[6] Art. 3(2).

[7] Art. 3(4).

(iii) Principle of non-discriminatory protection

4.005 The Berne Convention provides that authors of works qualifying for protection under the Berne Convention have the same rights in a Contracting State as the latter's nationals.[8] Thus, the Berne Convention prevents Member States from discriminating against foreign authors of qualifying works. Furthermore, a Contracting State may not make such protection dependent on the existence of protection in the country of origin of the work.[9] Protection in the country of origin is governed by domestic law.[10] "Country of origin" is deemed to be the country where the work was first published if the country is a Contracting State or if first published outside the Union, the Contracting State where the author is a national or habitually resident.[11] The cumulative effect of the above principles being applicable in all countries of the Union is that the protection afforded to a qualifying work will depend on the domestic copyright law of the Contracting State where protection is sought and is not dependent on the national origin of the work or author.

There are four important derogations from the above principle. First, the protection of works of applied art and industrial designs can be limited to that available in the country of origin.[11a] Secondly, where a non-Contracting State fails to provide adequate protection for the works of an author of a Contracting State, the latter may restrict protection conferred under the Berne Convention to the works of authors who are nationals of that non-Contracting State. For instance, where an author of a non-Contracting State first publishes his work in a Contracting State, such a work would normally qualify for protection under the Berne Convention. However, any Contracting State may restrict protection to such work if the non-Contracting State does not confer reciprocal protection for works of that Contracting State. Furthermore, if the Contracting State where the work was first published avails itself of this right then other Contracting States can similarly restrict protection to such a work regardless as to whether or not works of their own nationals are protected adequately in the non-Contracting State.[12] Thirdly, the length of protection in a Berne Country need not exceed that available in the country of origin.[12a]

Fourthly, the inalienable right of authors (or their personal representatives if dead) to enjoy an interest in any subsequent sale of original works of art or manuscripts granted by the Berne Convention may be limited to that available in the country "to which the author belongs."[12b] Impor-

[8] Arts. 5(1) and 5(3).
[9] Art. 5(2).
[10] Art. 5(3).
[11] If neither of these conditions apply, then the work is not a work which qualifies for protection under the Berne Convention—see Qualifying Works, para. 4.004.
[11a] Art. 2(7).
[12] Art. 6.
[12a] Art. 7(8).
[12b] Art. 14ter.

tantly, many commentators doubt that such derogations are valid within the C.E.A. as such would discriminate between nationals of different member states.[12c]

(iv) Term of Protection

4.006 The Berne Convention provides that the term of copyright is the life of the author and 50 years after his death.[13] Contracting States may grant a term of protection in excess of such a period.[14] For various specific types of works, there are derogations from this general principle. For a cinematographic work, the Berne Convention permits Member States to provide that the term of protection for a cinematographic work shall expire 50 years after the work has been made available to the public with the consent of the author or if such is not made available within 50 years from the making of such a work, then the term of protection is 50 years after the making.[15] For photographic works and works of applied art, the Berne Convention allows Member States to provide for a minimum of 25 years protection but leaves it to their discretion to fix an upper limit.[16]

(v) Translations

4.007 Translations, adaptations, arrangements of music and other alterations of a literary or artistic work are under the Berne Convention protected as original works but this is without prejudice to the copyright in the original work.[17]

(vi) Collections

4.008 Collections of literary or artistic works whether encyclopaedias, anthologies or which by reason of the selection and arrangement of their contents constitute intellectual creations are protected *per se* under the Berne Convention but again without prejudice to the copyright in the works forming part of such collections.[18] The reference to literary and artistic works in this provision means that the Berne Convention only recognises copyright in a collection of works themselves capable of being protected

[12c] Case C–92/92 *Phil Collins v. Imtrat Handelsgesellschaft mbH* [1993] 3 C.M.L.R. 773, ECJ, and VerLoren van Themaat and Bettink, "Another Side of the Story" [1995] E.I.P.R. 307. Interestingly, the authors argue that Article 23a which protects and upholds rights and obligations arising from treaties entered into prior to the Treaty of Rome coming into force between one or more Member States and one or more third countries should apply, and that therefore the Berne Convention should take precedence where the relevant article predates the Member State's accession and ratification of the E.C. Treaty.

[13] Art. 7(1). In the case of joint authorship, the relevant date is the 50 years from the death of the last surviving author—Art. 7[bis].

[14] Art. 7(6). In the E.C., there is a directive which increases this to the life of the author and 70 years after his death. See para. 4.022 *et seq.*

[15] Art. 7(2).

[16] Art. 7(4).

[17] Art. 2(3).

[18] Art. 2(5).

under copyright. Thus, a railway timetable would not qualify as a collection of literary or artistic works but might qualify for copyright protection as an original literary work.

(vii) Cinematographic Works

4.009 Cinematographic works are protected under the Berne Convention as original works.[19] Such a right is without prejudice to the copyright in the original work. The issue of ownership of copyright in such a work is a matter of domestic legislation in the country where protection is claimed.[20] The Berne Convention also provides that in countries where authorship is attributed to those who have contributed to the cinematographic work, such authors may not object in the absence of any contrary or special stipulation to the exploitation of the work.[21]

(viii) Exclusive rights

4.010 The Berne Convention provides authors of qualifying works with the exclusive right to authorise the reproduction of their works in any manner and form and to authorise the translation of their works throughout the term of protection of their rights in the original works.[22]

The Berne Convention also confers secondary rights upon authors. Thus authors of qualifying works enjoy exclusive rights to authorise the cinematographic adaptation and reproduction of their works and the public performance and communication to the public by wire of such works thus adapted or produced.[23] Similarly, authors of qualifying works enjoy the exclusive right to authorise any broadcast of their protected works.[24]

Authors of literary works enjoy the exclusive right of authorising any public recitation of their works or any communication to the public of their recitation of their works.[25] Authors of dramatico-musical and musical works also enjoy the exclusive right of authorising any public performance of their works and any communication to the public of such performance of their works.[26]

The Berne Convention provides for less protection in the field of musical works. Whilst such works are protected under the Berne Convention, it permits Contracting States to allow reservations to such an exclusive right provided that such authors are not denied the right to obtain equitable remuneration for the exploitation of any sound recording incorporating a protected work.[27]

[19] Art. 14bis.
[20] Art. 14bis(2)(A).
[21] Art. 14bis(2)(b).
[22] Art. 8 and 9.
[23] Art. 14.
[24] Art. 11bis.
[25] Art. 11ter.
[26] Art. 11.
[27] Art. 13.

(ix) Moral Rights

4.011 The Berne Convention provides that the author of literary or artistic work has the right to claim authorship of the works and to object to any distortion, mutilation, modification or other derogatory action in relation to their works which will be prejudicial to the author's honour or reputation.[28] Furthermore, the Berne Convention provides that such moral rights can be enforced after the death of the author by those responsible for the enforcement of copyright protection.[29]

(x) Fair Dealing Exceptions

4.012 The Berne Convention provides certain exceptions to the exclusive right conferred on the author. Firstly it permits persons to make quotations from a work providing such is compatible with fair practice and does not exceed that justified by its purposes.[30] Furthermore, it permits countries of the Union to permit reproduction of such works in certain special cases provided such reproduction does not conflict with a normal exploitation of the work and does not unreasonably prejudice the legitimate interest of the author.[31] The Berne Convention provides for the utilisation of literary or artistic works for teaching purposes provided such utilisation is compatible with fair practice.[32] The Berne Convention permits Contracting States to allow the reproduction, the broadcasting or the communication to the public of literary and artistic works in the press or in periodicals where they relate to current economic, political or religious topics.[33] In such a case, the source of the article must always be clearly indicated.

(xi) Infringement proceedings

4.013 In order for the author of a literary or artistic work to bring infringement proceedings in a Member State, his name must appear on the work in the usual manner.[34] In relation to cinematographic works, the person or body corporate whose name appears on such a work is unless otherwise proved, presumed to be the maker of the said work.[35] The Berne Convention provides specifically that infringing copies of the work shall be liable to seizure in any country of the union.[36]

28 Art. 6bis(1).
29 Art. 6bis(2).
30 Art. 10(1).
31 Art. 9(2).
32 Art. 10(2).
33 Art. 10bis.
34 Art. 15(1).
35 Art. 15(2).
36 Art. 16.

(xii) Retroactive effect of Berne Convention

4.014 The Berne Convention applies to all works which at the moment of the Convention coming into force for a country have not fallen into the public domain in the country of origin through the expiry of the term of protection.[37]

(xiii) Miscellaneous Provisions

4.015 The Berne Convention provides for an assembly, executive committee and a financial budget. Such administrative functions are generally performed by the International Bureau of WIPO. Furthermore, there are various provisions as to ratification of the Berne Convention.[38]

(b) Universal Copyright Convention

4.016 The Universal Copyright Convention was signed at Geneva on September 6, 1952 and further revised at Paris in 1971. Its purpose was to provide a bridge between the Berne Convention countries and the Pan-American Convention countries. Its applicability in Europe is limited because it is expressed not to affect in any way the provisions of the Berne Convention.[39] In particular, it is expressed not to apply to relationships among countries of the Berne Union in so far as it relates to the protection of works having as their country of origin, within the meaning of the Berne Convention, a country of the Berne Union.[40] It is thus only relevant to works which have not been published in a Berne Union country and whose authors are not nationals or resident in a Berne Union state. Thus it is of marginal importance. Its most notable contribution was to provide that works of authors of another Contracting State were to be afforded protection without formality provided that all copies bore the symbol © accompanied by the name of the copyright proprietor and the year of first publication placed in such a manner and location so as to give reasonable notice of claim of copyright.[41]

(c) Rome and Geneva Conventions for Protection of Performers, Phonogram Producers and Broadcasting Organisations

4.017 The Convention for the Protection of Performers, Producers of Phonograms and Broadcasting Organisations was signed at Rome ("the Rome Convention") on October 26, 1961 in order to protect the rights of performers, producers of phonograms and broadcasting organisations. These rights are generally termed secondary rights in that their works will normally incorporate artistic or literary works which may be pro-

[37] Art. 18(1).
[38] Arts. 22 *et seq.*
[39] Universal Copyright Convention, Art. XVII.
[40] Appendix Declaration concerning Art. XVII.
[41] Art. III.

tected under copyright and for which the performer, producer, etc., will require permission from the author. To ensure that there is no ambiguity, the Rome Convention is expressed so as to be without prejudice to the protection of copyright in literary and artistic works.[42] The Rome Convention was unacceptable to some countries because of its provisions on performers' and broadcasting rights. Thus, a more restrictive Convention merely protecting the unauthorised duplication of phonograms was signed at Geneva on October 29, 1971. The Geneva Convention essentially makes the same provisions as to phonograms as the Rome Convention does. Both Conventions seek to prevent a state which is a signatory to one or other of the Conventions from discriminating against a national of another signatory state and also provide limited harmonising measures.

(i) Performers' rights

4.018 In relation to rights in performances, under the Rome Convention, each Contracting State must grant "national treatment" to a performance which took place in another Contracting State.[43] "National treatment" is defined as the protection that a Contracting State would give to a performance which took place in its own country and was performed by its own nationals.[44] Furthermore, the Rome Convention obliges Contracting States to grant "national treatment" to performances incorporated in a phonogram which gives rise to phonogram producers' rights under the Convention.[45] Moreover, "national treatment" must be granted to performances which are carried by a broadcast which is protected under the Convention.[46] Accordingly, "national treatment" will be granted to the performers of a performance if any of the following conditions are met;

(a) performance takes place in a Contracting State;[47]
(b) the performance is incorporated in a phonogram, where the producer of the phonogram is a national of a Contracting State or the first fixation of the phonogram was in a Contracting State or the phonogram was first published in a Contracting State;[48]
(c) the performance is broadcast, where the headquarters of the

[42] Rome Convention, Art. 1.
[43] Art. 4(a).
[44] Art. 2(1)(a). "Performers" is widely defined as including any one who performs an artistic or literary work—Art. 3(a). However, contracting states may extend performers' rights to artistes who do not perform literary or artistic works (*i.e.* impromptu performances)—Art. 9.
[45] Art. 4(b). For phonogram producers' under the Rome Convention, see para. 4.019.
[46] Art. 4(c). For broadcasts protected under the Rome Convention, see para. 4.020.
[47] Art. 4(a). Interestingly, in the U.K. performers' rights are extended to both nationals of a Contracting State and where performance takes place in a Contracting State—see Copyright Designs and Patents Act 1988, s.181. The grant of rights to nationals of another Contracting State goes beyond the obligation under the Rome Convention.
[48] Arts. 4(b) and 5—note that in certain countries, the criteria of first fixation or first publication may not apply. See para. 4.019.

broadcasting organisation are situated in a Contracting State or where it was transmitted from a transmitter situated in a Contracting State.[49]

Performers have the right to prevent the broadcast and communication to the public of their performance, the fixation of their performance and the reproduction of a fixation of their performance.[50] The term of protection lasts for 20 years from the date of the performance or if fixed in a phonogram, 20 years from the date of fixation.[51]

(ii) Rights of Producers of Phonograms

4.019 Under the Rome Convention, each Contrasting State must treat phonograms[52] which fulfil any of the following conditions, *i.e.*

(i) were produced by the national of another Contracting State;
(ii) first fixed in another Contracting State (criterion of fixation);
(iii) first published in another Contracting State (criterion of publication);

in the same manner as phonograms made by its own nationals and first fixed or published in its own territory.[53] Producers of phonograms (who are defined as the legal entity or person who first fixes the sound of a performance or other sound) have the exclusive right to authorise or prohibit the direct or indirect reproduction of their phonograms.[54] The Rome Convention makes recognition of phonogram rights only subject to the conditions that copies of the phonogram bear the symbol Ⓟ accompanied by the year of the first publication placed in such a manner as to give reasonable notice of a claim of protection and must also bear the names of the producer or owners of the phonogram rights together with the names of the principal performers or the owner of their rights.[55] The Rome Convention provides that the broadcast or other communication to the public of a phonogram shall result in a single payment of equitable remuneration to the producer of the phonogram and the performer.[56] The term of protection is 20 years from the date of fixation of the phonogram.[57] The provisions of the Geneva Convention differ in a few minor ways to that of the Rome Convention as to the protection of phonograms. Firstly, it merely requires that a Contracting State protect pro-

[49] Arts. 4(c) and 6.
[50] Art. 7.
[51] Art. 14(b).
[52] Defined as any exclusive aural fixation of sounds.
[53] Arts. 2 and 5. A phonogram is deemed first published in a Contracting State if it is published within 30 days of first publication in a non-Contracting State—Art. 5(2). Contracting States may declare that the criteria of fixation and publication do not apply—Art. 5(3).
[54] Art. 10.
[55] Art. 11.
[56] Art. 12.
[57] Art. 14(a).

ducers of phonograms who are nationals of another Contracting State.[58] Secondly, it allows the Contracting State to decide how such protection should be afforded under national law—it does not necessarily have to be under copyright.[59] Thirdly, the length of protection is a matter of domestic law but cannot be less than 20 years from the end either of the year in which the sounds embodied in the phonogram were first fixed *or* of the year in which the phonogram was first published.[60] All the countries which signed the Rome Convention have signed the Geneva Convention. Generally speaking, countries which have adhered to both have declared that the criteria of first fixation and first publication do not apply and have granted rights to producers of phonograms who are nationals or have a place of business in a Contracting State.[61]

(iii) Rights of Broadcasting Organisations

4.020 In relation to broadcasts, the Rome Convention provides that each Contracting State is to provide similar treatment under its laws to broadcasting organisations situated in another Contracting State in relation to broadcasts from a transmitter in another Contracting State as it would to domestic broadcasts by domestic organisations.[62] Contracting States can provide that such protection is only to be provided where the transmitter and broadcasting organisation are situated in the same Contracting State.[63] Broadcasting organisations have the right to authorise or prohibit the rebroadcasting, fixation or reproduction of such unauthorised fixations of their broadcast.[64] The term of protection is for a period of 20 years from the date that the broadcast took place.[65]

There are also the usual exceptions for the purposes of fair dealing and the usual administrative provisions.

3. European Community Legislation

(a) EEC Green Paper on Copyright[66]

4.021 In 1988, the European Commission produced a Green Paper on copyright and the challenge of technology. The Commission observed that the protection of artistic and literary works and other similar types of works was of growing importance to the Community. Firstly, a shift had

[58] Geneva Convention, Art. 2.
[59] Art. 3.
[60] Geneva Convention, Art. 4.
[61] See Copyright Designs and Patents Act 1988, s.185. See n. 53.
[62] Art. 2 and 6.
[63] Art. 6(2).
[64] Art. 13.
[65] Art. 14(c).
[66] COM 88 (172).

occurred in the economic activities of industrialised countries away from the production of basic goods to the production of goods to which considerable value had been added through the application of technology, skill and creativity. Secondly, it observed that the service sector of many industrialised countries had come to play a more prominent role in the recent past. It noted that such industries were particularly vulnerable to damage through unauthorised copying. In the area of technology, the Commission commented that lack of protection favours third parties who have not had to incur large research and development expenditure. Thus, the Commission said that its concerns in this field were fourfold. Firstly, the requirement of a single internal market meant that the elimination of obstacles and legal differences in copyright at a national level was necessary. Secondly, the Commission was concerned that the community should develop policies that would improve the competitiveness of its economy in relation to its trade partners. Such could be insured by a high level of protection in relation to copyright. Thirdly, the Commission observed that it was of great importance that intellectual property resulting from creative effort and substantial investment within the community should not be misappropriated by others outside the community. Fourthly, it was noted that in some areas copyright protection, for instance in the area of purely functional industrial designs and in computer programs, could have a restrictive effect on competition rather than enhance it.

For sometime, the Commission had been keeping under review the copyright field as a whole with a view to publishing a consultative document. It was becoming quite apparent to the Commission that the effective protection of authors' rights in artistic and literary works and their enforcement in the community and throughout the world were matters which had far reaching economic implications to the economic well-being of the community. Accordingly, the Commission identified certain issues which required attention at community level and which were most urgent. These issues were: piracy; home copying of sound and audio-visual material; distribution and rental rights for certain classes of work, in particular, sound and video recordings; the protection available to computer programs and databases and finally the limitations on the protection available to community right holders in non-Member States. It specifically left the problems in relation to the protection of industrial design for another green paper.[67]

The Commission pointed out that Community legislation should be restricted to that which is needed to carry out the task of the community. It observed that many issues of copyright law did not need to be the subject of action at community level. It said that since all Member States belong to the Berne Convention and also to the Universal Copyright

[67] See Chapter on Design Protection in Europe.

Convention, a certain fundamental convergence of their laws had already been achieved. Many of the differences that remained had no significant impact on the function of the internal market for the community's economic competitiveness. The Commission gave as an example the issue of author's moral rights.

The Green Paper therefore proposed the issuing of various directives on copyright law under Article 100 and 100a of the E.C. Treaty. These Articles enable the issuing of directives harmonising national law in Member States which directly affect the establishment or functioning of the Common Market.

The Green Paper has resulted in the following directives or draft directives—a directive for the legal protection of computer programs;[68] a directive on rental and lending rights and certain rights related to copyright;[69] a directive on copyright and neighbouring rights relating to satellite broadcasting and cable retransmissions;[70] a directive on the term of protection of copyright[71] and a draft directive for the legal protection of databases.[72–73]

(b) Directive harmonising the term of protection copyright and certain related rights

(i) Introduction

4.022 The Council has issued a directive harmonising the term of protection for copyright and other related rights.[74] This directive arose out of the Green Paper's statement[75] that there was a need to harmonise copyright and neighbouring rights at a high level of protection since such rights were fundamental to intellectual creation. The essence of the Directive is to extend the term of protection laid down by the Berne Convention, namely the life of the author and 50 years after his death, to the life of the author and 70 years after his death. This alteration reflected the fact that the Berne Convention originally intended to provide protection for the author and the first two generations of his descendants whereas now the average lifespan in the community has grown longer to the point where the life of the author plus 70 years would provide such protection.[76] It should be noted that there is no conflict between the Directive and the Berne Convention as the latter merely provides for a minimum period of

[68] Dir. 91/50, [1991] O.J. L122/42. Adopted January 1, 1993.
[69] Dir. 92/100, [1992] O.J. L345/61. Adopted November 19, 1992.
[70] Dir. 93/83 [1993] O.J. L248/15. Adopted September 27, 1993.
[71] Dir. 93/98, [1993] O.J. L290/9. Adopted by qualified majority October 29, 1993.
[72–73] Amended Proposal of Commission [1993] O.J. C308/1. Still under technical discussion.
[74] Dir. 93/98, [1993] O.J. L209/0.
[75] COM (90) 584, "Follow up to Green Paper—Working Program of Commission in the field of copyright and neighbouring rights".
[76] See Recital 5.

protection.[77] This directive should be read in conjunction with the directive harmonising rental, lending and allied right.[78]

(ii) Duration of copyright for literary and artistic works

4.023 The fundamental provision of the Directive is that the rights of an author of a literary or artistic work within the meaning of Article 2 of the Berne Convention now run for the life of the author and to 70 years after his death, irrespective of the date when the work was lawfully made available to the public.[79] In the case of joint authorship, the 70 year period is calculated from the death of the last surviving author.[80] In the case of anonymous or pseudonymous works, the period of protection is 70 years after the work was lawfully made available to the public.[81] This latter period of protection also applies to collective works or where a legal person is designated as the rightholder unless the author of the collective work itself is identified in the published versions.[82] This "collective" right is expressed to be without prejudice to the rights of identified authors of identifiable contributions in the collection.[83]

If a work is published in volumes, parts, instalments, issues or episodes and the term of protection runs from the time when the work was lawfully made available to the public (*i.e.* there is no identifiable author), the term of protection shall run for each item separately.[84] Finally, in the case of works for which the term of protection is not calculated from the death of the author or author(s) and which have not been lawfully made available to the public within 70 years from their creation, protection for such works ceases.[85]

(iii) Cinematographic or audiovisual works

4.024 The principal director of a cinematographic work or audiovisual work is deemed to be the author or one of its authors.[86] Member States can designate other co-authors.[87] The term of protection for such works expires 70 years after the death of the last of the following persons to survive whether or not these persons are designated as co-authors: the principal director, the author of the screen play, the author of the dialogue and the composer of music specifically created for use in the cinematographic or audiovisual works.[88]

[77] Art. 7(6).
[78] See para. 4.031.
[79] Art. 1(1).
[80] Art. 1(2).
[81] Art. 1(3).
[82] Art. 1(4).
[83] *ibid.*
[84] Art. 1(5).
[85] Art. 1(6).
[86] Art. 2(1). Member States are not required to apply this provision to works created before July 1, 1994—Art. 10 and may determine the date from which this provision applies provided that date is no later than July 1, 1997—Art. 10(5).
[87] *ibid.*
[88] Art. 2(2).

(iv) Duration of related rights

4.025 In relation to the rights of performers, the rights of performers run for 50 years from the date of the performance.[89] If a fixation of the performance is lawfully published or communicated to the public within this period, the rights expires 50 years from the date of the first such publication or communication (whichever is the earliest).[90]

The period of protection for the producer of a phonogram is 50 years from the date of fixation.[91] However, if the phonogram is lawfully published or lawfully communicated to the public during this period, the period of protection is 50 years after the date of first publication or first communication to the public (whichever is the earliest).[92] The same approach applies to the length of protection for the rights of producers of the first fixation of films.[93] Film is defined as a cinematographic or audio-visual work or moving image whether or not accompanied by sound.

The rights of broadcasting organisations expire 50 years from the first transmission of a broadcast.[94]

(v) Protection of previously unpublished works and "public domain" scientific or critical publications

4.026 If a person publishes or communicates to the public an unpublished work after the expiry of copyright protection, that person is entitled to a period of protection of 25 years from the time when the work was first published or communicated.[95] The Directive also permits Member States to protect critical and scientific publications which have come into the public domain for a period of 30 years from the time when the publication was first lawfully published.[96]

(vi) Photographs

Photographs which are original in the sense that they are the author's own intellectual creation are protected for a period equivalent to any other artistic or literary work.[97]

(vii) Protection vis-à-vis third countries

4.027 The Directive also provides that where the country of origin of a work within the meaning of the Berne Convention is a third country and the author of the work is not a Community national, the term of protection granted by Member States expires on the date of the expiry of the protec-

[89] Art. 3(1).
[90] *ibid.*
[91] *ibid.*
[92] Art. 3(2).
[93] Art. 3(3).
[94] Art. 3(4).
[95] Art. 4.
[96] Art. 5.
[97] Art. 6.

tion granted in the country of origin but can not exceed the lifetime of the author plus 70 years.[98] In the case of related rights under Article 3 where the rightholder is not a Community national,[99] the term of protection of such rights must not exceed the term of protection in the country of which the rightholder is a national without prejudice to the international obligations of Member States.[1]

(viii) Calculation of terms

4.028 The terms referred to in the Directive are calculated from the first day of January of the year following the event which gave rise to them.[2]

(ix) Transitional provisions

4.029 Where the term of protection is already running as of July 1, 1995, the Directive does not have the effect of shortening the period of protection.[3] Importantly, the term of protection provided for in the Directive applies to all works which as of July 1, 1995 were protected in at least one Member State.[4] Thus where copyright in a work has expired in one Member State, this may be revived if it is still protected in another Member State.[5] To compensate for such a provision, the directive is expressed to be without prejudice to acts of exploitation performed before July 1, 1995.[6] Member States are required to protect the acquired rights of third parties and the principle of legitimate expectation.[7] Special transitional positions apply to cinematographic works.[7a]

(x) Date for implementation of directive

4.030 Member States are required to bring into force the directive by July 1, 1995.[8]

[98] Art. 7(1). The expression "third country" in this context must mean it refers to a non-Berne Union country as opposed to a non-E.C. country otherwise such would result in discriminatory treatment contrary to Art. 5(1) of the Berne Convention. For meaning of country of origin under the Berne Convention, see above, para. 4.005.

[99] Art. 7(2). *i.e.* performer's rights, phonogram producer's rights and broadcasting organisation's rights, see para. 4.025.

[1] Art. 7(2).

[2] Art. 8.

[3] Art. 10(1).

[4] Art. 10(2).

[5] See Jorna and Martin-Prat, "New Rules in European Copyright" [1994] 4 EIPR 145, which examines the effect of this provision by giving hypothetical examples.

[6] Art. 10(3).

[7] Art. 10(3). See also Recital 27 which rehearses the principle of legitimate expectation and permits Member States to protect persons who undertook in good faith the exploitation of the works at the time when such works were in the public domain. See also, Jorna and Martin-Prat, "New Rules in European Copyright" [1994] 4 EIPR 145 at p. 153 for a detailed discussion as to the protection of acquired rights.

[7a] See para. 4.024 and n. 86.

[8] Art. 13. In the case of cinematographic and audiovisual works, there are provisions which derogate from this—see n. 86 *supra*.

(c) E.C. Rental and Neighbouring Rights

(i) Introduction

4.031 The Green Paper on Copyright examined the availability of a rental right and other allied rights for protected works throughout the Community. It noted that some Member States had or were proposing to enact a rental right whereas in others there was no right. Such divergence of national laws distorted trade between Member States as authors were better remunerated in some countries than others. The Commission commented on the fact that the rental of protected works was becoming commonplace especially for videos and, increasingly, sound recordings. This meant that the income of authors decreased as fewer sales occurred. It suggested that a certain degree of uncontentious harmonisation should be sought. In fact, the Commission's proposals in this area were considerably changed with a series of proposals and extensive discussion with parties, including a two-day hearing.[9] This has resulted in the issue of Council Directive 92/100[10] which requires Member States to enact the Directive by July 1, 1994. Because of strenuous lobbying which stressed the similarity of rental and lending rights, the Commission decided to include, contrary to the proposal of the Green Paper, a lending right in the Directive. The Directive expressly states that it in no way affects the protection of copyright.[11] The Directive also harmonises performers' rights, phonogram producers' rights, cinematographic producers' rights and broadcasting rights. In these areas, the Directive includes matter covered under the Rome and Geneva Convention. The adoption of the Directive coincided with a resolution that Member States should become, by January 1, 1995, parties to the Paris Act of the Berne Convention and the Rome Convention.[12] Member States are obliged to bring into force the necessary legislation for the implementation of the directive by July 1, 1994.[13] The following sections examine the provisions of the directive.

(ii) Rental and lending right

4.032 Article 1 of the Directive requires Member States to provide a right to authorise or prohibit the rental and lending of originals and copies of copyright works. The rental and lending right must extend to performances, phonograms and films.[14] Rental is widely defined as meaning making available for use for a limited period of time and for direct or indirect economic or commercial advantage. Lending is defined as

[9] To see how much the finally adopted directive differs from proposal, see von Lewinski "Rental Right, Lending Right and Certain Neighbouring Rights: The E.C. Commission's Proposal for a Council Directive" [1991] 4 EIPR 17. The second proposal of the Commission as set out in that Article bears little resemblance to the final directive.

[10] [1992] O.J. L346/61.

[11] Art. 14.

[12] [1992] O.J. C138/1.

[13] Art. 15.

[14] Arts. 1 and 2(1).

making available for use, for a limited period of time and not for direct or indirect economic or commercial advantage, when it is made through establishments which are accessible to the public.[15]

4.033 *Ownership of rights*—the exclusive rental and lending right is deemed to belong to the author in respect of the original and copies of his work; the performer in respect of fixations of his performance; the phonogram producer in respect of his phonograms and the producer of the first fixation of the film in respect of the original and copies of his film.[16]

4.034 *Cinematographic works*—various provisions are made as to the rental and lending of cinematographic works. Thus for the purposes of the directive, the principal director of a cinematographic work or audiovisual work is deemed to be the author but Member States can provide that others shall be considered authors.[17] As a cinematographic work often consists of several protected works, *e.g.* the book of which the film was made of or performers' rights as well as the actual cinematographic right, all of whom would have a rental right, the Directive seeks to simplify matters.Thus, a performer is to be presumed in a contract, subject to express contractual stipulations to the contrary, between him and the film producer to have transferred his rental right to the film producer.[18] Member States may also compel performers to authorise rental of a film when they conclude a contract with a film producer but must ensure that the performer is equitably remunerated.[19] In fact, the right of an author or performer to equitable remuneration is always retained and cannot be waived.[20]

4.035 *Compulsory Licence of Lending Rights*—the directive permits Member States to provide for the compulsory licensing of the lending right in respect of public lending of copyright works and their copies provided that authors are remunerated taking account of their cultural promotion objectives.[21] In respect of the public lending of phonograms, films and computer programs, Member States need only provide

[15] Art. 1(2), (3).
[16] Art. 2(1).
[17] Art. 2(2). Member States do not need to enact this provision until July 1, 1997—Art. 13(5). See equivalent provision in Dir. 93/98 which harmonises the term of copyright. Under that Dir., the term of protection is not dependent on whether or not certain persons have been designated as co-authors under a Member State's law. See above, para. 4.024.
[18] Art. 2(5). Member States may provide for a similar presumption in respect of authors—Art. 2(6).
[19] Art. 2(7).
[20] Art. 4(1), (2). Member States can delay the enactment of such an unwaivable right until July 1, 1997—Art. 13(8). Performers or authors who have concluded contracts before July 1, 1994 are only entitled to equitable remuneration for the rental or lending of such works provided that they make a request to that effect before January 1, 1997—Art. 13(9).
[21] Art. 5(1).

remuneration for authors.[22] For instance, a Member State need not remunerate a phonogram producer where his phonogram is publicly lent but must provide for remuneration of the writer of the song.

4.036 *Duration and Miscellaneous*—the Directive originally provided that the rental and lending right are to run alongside other rights provided for by the Berne Convention and to expire simultaneously as with other primary rights. This was expressed to be without prejudice to further harmonisation.[23] Directive 93/98 concerning the term of copyright and allied rights has now repealed these provisions.[24] Accordingly, the duration of the rental right must be calculated by reference to the period of protection provided by directive.[25] Transitional provisions permit Member States to deem that a rightholder has authorised the rental or lending of a work which has been made available to third parties for such purposes or has been acquired prior to July 1, 1994.[26]

(iii) Allied Rights

4.037 The Directive provides for the harmonisation of various rights allied to copyright. These can be conveniently categorised under the heading of performers' rights, phonogram producers' rights, cinematographic producers' rights and broadcasting rights. Apart from the cinematographic producers' right, the rights provided coincide with those provided under the Rome Convention.[27] Since the Directive was issued, the Directive for the co-ordination of certain rules concerning copyright and rights related to copyright applicable to satellite broadcasting and cable retransmission has been issued. This latter Directive extends the protection given to phonogram producers, performers and broadcasting organisations in this Directive to include communication to the public by satellite.[28] For ease of reference, the provisions of that Directive which apply to the above persons are discussed in the commentary on this Directive.

4.038 *Performers' rights*—the Directive compels Member States to provide that performers have the exclusive right to authorise or prohibit the fixation of their performances;[29] the right to prevent the direct or indirect reproduction of such fixations;[30] the right to a single equitable remuneration of the broadcast whether by wireless means or satellite or communication to the public of phonograms incorporating their

[22] Art. 5(2).
[23] Art. 11.
[24] Dir. 93/98, Art. 11(2).
[25] See above, para. 4.022 *et seq.*
[26] Art. 13(3). If it is a digital recording, then the rightholder must be entitled to equitable remuneration. This is essentially because such recordings do not degrade over a period of time—see Green Paper on Copyright.
[27] See above, at para. 4.017 *et seq.*
[28] See Arts. 4–7 of Dir. 93/83. For a detailed discussion on this directive, see para. 4.044 *et seq.*
[29] Art. 6(1).
[30] Art. 7(1).

performances[31] and the right to prevent the broadcasting whether by wireless means or via satellite of their performances or communication to the public of their performances unless such is already a broadcast performance or is made from a fixation.[32] Thus performers have the right to prevent live broadcasts but not broadcasts of recorded material. Also, performers have the exclusive right to distribute fixations of their performances until such is sold with the consent of the rightholder.[33] The duration of performers' rights was originally the same as that provided under the Rome Convention—that is 20 years from the date of performance or 20 years from the date of fixation if the performance is incorporated in a phonogram.[34] This has now been repealed by Directive 93/98 harmonising the term of protection for copyright and allied rights to 50 years from the date of the performance or if published or communicated to the public in this period, 50 years from the date of publication or communication to the public.[35]

4.039 *Phonogram rights*—phonogram producers are granted the exclusive right to authorise or prohibit the direct or indirect reproduction of their phonograms;[36] the right to a single equitable remuneration for the broadcast, whether by wireless means or via satellite or communication to the public, of their phonograms (such remuneration to be shared with the performers whose performance is incorporated in the phonogram)[37] and the right to distribute their phonograms until such is sold with their consent.[38] A phonogram right runs for a period of 50 years from the date of fixation or if published or communicated to the public in this period, 50 years from the date of publication or communication to the public.[39]

4.040 *Cinematographic producer's rights*—producers of the first fixation of films have the exclusive right to prevent reproduction of their film and its copies[40] and their distribution until they are sold with their consent.[41] This right should be distinguished from the director's and other

[31] Dir. 92/100, Art. 8(2) and Dir. 93/83, Art. 4(2) (in relation to broadcasting by satellite). Such remuneration is to be shared with the phonogram producer. Member States are free to provide more far-reaching protection for performers in this area—see Dir. 92/100, Recital 20 and Dir. 93/83, Art. 6(1).

[32] Dir. 93/83, Art. 8(1) and Art. 4(2) (with regard to satellite broadcasting). Member States are free to provide more protection than that provided under these Arts. See n. 31, above.

[33] Arts. 9(1) and 9(2).

[34] Dir. 93/98, Art. 12 and Rome Convention, Art. 14. See above, para. 4.018.

[35] Dir. 93/98, Art. 3(1). See para. 4.025.

[36] Art. 7(1).

[37] Dir. 93/83, Arts. 4(2) and 8(2) (with regard to satellite broadcasting). Member States are free to provide more protection for phonogram producers in this area—see Dir. 93/83, Recital 20 and Art. 6(1).

[38] Art. 9(1), (2).

[39] Dir. 93/98, Arts. 3(2), 11 repealing Dir. 92/100, Art. 12. See also Rome Convention, Art. 14 and Geneva Convention, Art. 4 which provides for a minimum protection period of 20 years from the date of fixation.

[40] Art. 7(1).

[41] Art. 9.

author's rights in a film. The period of protection is 70 years after the last death of the principal director, the author of the screenplay, the author of the dialogue and the composer of music specifically created for the film.[42]

4.041 *Broadcasting Organisations' Rights*—under the Directive, broadcasters have the exclusive right to authorise or prohibit the fixation of their broadcasts however transmitted;[43] the exclusive right to prevent reproductions and distribution of fixations of their broadcasts[44] and the exclusive right to prevent rebroadcasts by wireless means or via satellite or communication to the public of their broadcasts where such communication is made in places accessible to the public against payment of an entrance.[45] These broadcasting rights expire 50 years from the date of the first transmission.[46]

4.042 *Limitations to above rights*—the Directive permits Member States to provide for limitations to the allied rights listed above in respect of private use; use of short excerpts in connection with the reporting of current events; ephemeral fixation by a broadcasting organisation by means of its own facilities and for its own broadcasts and for use solely for the purposes of teaching or scientific research.[47] The Directive reserves the right to enact future legislation providing remuneration for reproduction for private use.[48] At present, there is a working document on home copying of sound and audiovisual recordings but no consensus has been reached and any legislation in this field is some distance away.

Member States may provide for the same kind of limitations with regard to the protection of performers, producers of phonograms, broadcasting organisations and producers of the first fixations of films as provided for with the protection of artistic or literary works. However, compulsory licences may be provided only to the extent to which they are compatible with the Rome Convention.[49]

[42] Dir. 93/98, Arts. 2(1), 11(2) which repeals Dir. 92/100, Art. 12 which provided for a term of protection of 20 years from the date of fixation.
[43] Art. 6(2). This right does not extend to cable distributors who merely retransmit the broadcasts of another—Art. 6(3).
[44] Art. 9(1).
[45] Dir. 93/83, Arts. 8(3) and 4(2) (with regard to satellite broadcasting). Member States are free to provide more far-reaching protection in this area for broadcasting organisations—see Dir. 93/83, Recital 20 and Art. 6(1). Dir. 93/98, Art. 3 makes certain provisions with regard to collective agreements between broadcasting organisations and collecting societies with regard to simulcasting via satellite and terrestrial means. See below, para. 4.045.
[46] Dir. 93/98, Art. 3(4). Art. 11(2) repealed Dir. 92/100, Art. 12 which provided for 20 years from the date of the first transmission.
[47] Dir. 92/100, Art. 10(1).
[48] Art. 10(3).
[49] Art. 10(2). The Rome Convention makes limited provision for compulsory licensing of performers' rights or broadcasting rights (see Rome Convention, Art. 12 whereby a performer or phonogram producer is entitled to a single equitable remuneration where a phonogram is broadcast which is already provided for in the directive at Art. 8(2)). Accordingly, it is submitted that member States have very little latitude to compulsorily licence such rights.

Finally, where the Directive provides for distribution rights,[50] this is exhausted once the copyright work is put on sale on the Community by the rightholder or with his consent.[51]

(iv) Transitional provisions

4.043 The Directive is to apply to all copyright works, phonograms, broadcasts and first fixations of films that on July 1, 1994 were still protected by the legislation of the Member States or which meet the criteria for protection under the Directive but without prejudice to acts of exploitation performed before that date.[52] In certain circumstances, this will mean the creation or revival of rights. In order to comply with the principle of legitimate expectation, the Directive caters for situations where exploitation has already occurred.[53] Thus, Member States can enact that rightholders who have given their consent for exploitation of their works are presumed to have "transferred their new exclusive rights".[54] Generally, contracts concluded before the date of adoption of the Directive into a Member State's laws are not to be affected by the Directive.[55]

(d) Copyright and Neighbouring Rights relating to satellite and broadcasting

(i) Introduction

4.044 In December 1990, the Commission issued a Discussion Paper, "Broadcasting and Copyright in the Internal Market", aimed at allowing a process of consultation to take place with interested parties. In this paper, the Commission suggested harmonising measures related to satellite broadcasting and simultaneous and unaltered cable retransmission. It had become apparent that communication to the public of copyright works via these media had increased immensely in the 1980s and was expected to carry on increasing. However, the transnational nature of satellite broadcasting meant that there was much legal dispute over which country's law was applicable. Was it the country where the broad-

[50] Art. 9(1).

[51] Art. 9(2). It is unclear whether the introduction of an E.C-wide exhaustion of rights principle into this Directive has meant that the general domestic principle whereby the distribution rights is exhausted in a work once it has been placed on the market *anywhere in the world* should no longer apply—see Chapter on Enforcement of Intellectual Property, para. 7.029.

[52] Art. 13(1), (2). These transitional provisions apply to satellite broadcasting rights—see Dir. 93/83, Art. 7(1).

[53] See Jorna and Martin-Prat, "New Rules in European Copyright" [1994] 4 EIPR 145 at p. 151 where the authors discuss in detail the effect of Dir. 92/100 (rental and lending rights and allied rights), Dir. 93/98 (harmonisation of term of protection of copyright and allied rights) and Dir. 93/83 (harmonisation directive of copyright applicable to satellite transmission and cable retransmission) on existing situations.

[54] Art. 13(7). This provision is rather obscure. Consent to exploitation normally means a licence to exploit and yet it would be peculiar if this was to lead to an assignment (*i.e.* transfer) of the new rights to the licensee—Jorna and Martin-Prat "New Rules in European Copyright" [1994] 4 EIPR 145 at p. 151.

[55] Art. 13(6).

caster was situated, the country where the broadcast signal was emitted or the country or countries where it was received? This issue was important because there was much disparity in European countries' laws over the protection awarded to performers, phonogram producers and film producers in relation to broadcasting whether by wireless or satellite. For example, some countries merely provided a right to equitable remuneration to performers and phonogram producers when their works were broadcast while others provided for an exclusive right. Accordingly, the issue as to which country's copyright law was applicable became an important one. Furthermore, it was clear that a minimum level of legal harmonisation should be secured to protect rightholders with regard to satellite broadcasting.

On the issue of cable retransmissions, the Commission noted that legal certainty was missing where programmes transmitted across frontiers were fed into and re-transmitted through cable networks. Cable operators were often unsure whether they had acquired all the programme rights covered by an agreement.

On July 22, 1991, the Commission submitted to the Council a Proposal for a Council Directive on the co-ordination of certain rules concerning copyright and neighbouring rights applicable to satellite broadcasting and cable retransmissions. After amendments by the European Parliament, this led to Council Directive 93/83 on the co-ordination of certain rules concerning copyright and rights related to copyright applicable to satellite broadcasting and cable retransmission.[56]

The main features of this Directive is that the relevant law is that where under the control and responsibility of the broadcasting organisation, the programme carrying signals are introduced into an uninterrupted chain of communication leading to the satellite and down towards the earth.[57] In other words, the relevant law is the *lex emissionis*. With regard to cable retransmissions rights, the Directive provides that retransmission rights in a copyright work can only be exercised through a collecting society and further provides for a mechanism to ensure that parties successfully conclude their negotiations.[58] The following sections examine the provisions of the Directive.

(ii) Satellite broadcasting

4.045 The Directive requires Member States to provide an exclusive right for the author to authorise the communication to the public by satellite of copyright works.[59] Member States are not permitted to enact a compulsory licensing scheme and must ensure that authorisation is only acquired by agreement.[60] Member States may provide that a collective agreement

[56] Council Dir. 93/83, [1993] O.J. L148/15.
[57] Art. 1(2)(b).
[58] Art. 6 *et seq.*
[59] Art. 2.
[60] Art. 3(2).

between a collecting society and a broadcasting organisation regarding a given category of works (but not cinematographic works) extends to the satellite broadcasting provided that the satellite broadcast is simultaneous with the terrestrial broadcast and the unrepresented rightholder has the possibility of excluding such an automatic extension of the agreement to include satellite broadcasting.[61]

"Satellite" is defined as meaning any satellite operating on frequency bands which under telecommunications laws are reserved for the broadcast of signals for reception by the public or which are reserved for closed point-to-point communication.[62] The act of communication to the public by satellite is deemed to occur solely in the Member State where under the control and responsibility of the broadcasting organisation, the programme carrying signals are introduced into an uninterrupted chain of communication leading to the satellite and down towards the earth.[63] It is the copyright law of this Member State (*lex emissionis*) which is relevant in considering whether the exclusive right of communication to the public by satellite has been infringed.[64] If the programme signals are introduced in a non-Member State which does not provide the same level of protection as that provided under the Directive, then where the programme carrying signals are transmitted to the satellite via an uplink station situated in a Member State, then the act of communication to the public via satellite is deemed to have occurred in the latter Member State and to have been committed by the person operating the uplink station and the relevant law will thus be the law of that Member State.[65] If both the introduction of the programme carrying signals and the uplink occurs in non-Members States, then if the broadcasting organisation which commissioned the act of communication to the public by satellite has its principal place of establishment in a Member State, then the exclusive satellite broadcasting rights may be exercised against the broadcasting organisation.[66]

Accordingly, the Directive does not provide effective and enforceable protection for rightholders where the satellite broadcast is beamed direct to a satellite from outside the Community (*i.e.* not via an uplink in the Community) and where the broadcasting organisation's principal place of establishment is outside the Community. The Commission recognised that in such circumstances, Member States would be free to treat these

[61] Art. 3(2),(3).
[62] Art. 1(1).
[63] Article 1(2)(b).
[64] The private international law of the *lex emissionis* may take into account the laws of the countries where the broadcast is received (the "footprint" countries). In both a French and Austrian case, the courts of both countries held that broadcasters must comply with the laws of the footprint countries either because they created damage or because they were intended to be received by the audience of that country—see Kern, "The E.C. Common Position on Copyright Applicable to Satellite Broadcasting and Cable Retransmission" [1993] 8 EIPR 276 at p. 280.
[65] Art. 1(2)(d)(i).
[66] Art. 1(2)(d)(ii).

broadcasts differently.[67] It has been noted that this may have the effect of encouraging satellite broadcasters to relocate outside the Community to countries where rightholder's satellite broadcasting rights are not so well protected.[68]

(iii) Harmonisation of neighbouring rights with respect to satellite broadcasting

4.046 The Commission recognised that if legal protection for rightholders differed in Member States, satellite broadcasters would be encouraged to relocate their transmitters and uplink stations so as to take advantage of such differences. Accordingly, the Directive provides a certain level of harmonisation of copyright and neighbouring rights with regard to satellite broadcasting. As mentioned in the previous paragraph, authors are granted the exclusive right to authorise the communication to the public by satellite of copyright works. This was a relatively uncontroversial proposal as most countries already protected such rights.

With regard to performers, phonogram producers and broadcasting organisations, the Directive assimilates the satellite broadcasting right of such persons to the exclusive right of communication to the public provided for in Directive 92/100 which *inter alia* harmonises the level of protection in the Community for performers, etc.[69] For ease of reference, the reader is referred to the discussion on Directive 92/100, which includes a detailed analysis of the application of this Directive to such rights.

(iv) Cable Retransmission Right

4.047 The Commission realised that legal certainty which was a prerequisite for the free movement of broadcasts was missing where programmes were transmitted via cable networks.[70] Cable operators were not sure whether they had the rights to retransmit broadcasts via cable networks. Initially, the Commission proposed a compulsory licensing scheme for cable retransmission. However, after intensive lobbying, it dropped this idea. Under the Directive, Member States must now ensure that when programmes from other Member States are retransmitted via cable in their territory, the applicable copyright and related rights are observed.[71] However, the "cable retransmission right" to grant or refuse authorisation may only be exercised through a collecting society.[72] If the rightholder has not transferred his rights to a collecting society, he is deemed

[67] See Proposal submitted on July 2, 1991 and Kern, "The E.C. Common Position on Copyright Applicable to Satellite Broadcasting and Cable Retransmission" [1993] 8 EIPR 276 at p. 277.
[68] See Kern, *ibid.*, at p. 277.
[69] Art. 4 *et seq.*
[70] See Recital 8.
[71] Art. 8.
[72] Art. 9(1). "Collecting society" is defined as meaning any organisation which manages or administers copyright or rights related to copyright as its sole purpose or as one of its main purposes—Art. 1(4).

to have transferred his rights to a collecting society which manages rights of the same category.[73] In such circumstances, he may claim any rights (*i.e.* royalties) within a period not shorter than three years from the date of the cable retransmission of his works.[74]

Two important exceptions to the compulsory "collectivisation" of the cable retransmission right applies. First, where the cable retransmission right is owned by a broadcasting organisation in respect of its own transmission, there is no obligation to transfer such rights to a collecting society.[75] Secondly, as has been pointed out, where a Member State does not provide for a right to authorise but merely a right to a single equitable remuneration, such rightholders are free to decide whether to act collectively or individually.[76]

The Directive makes important safeguards to ensure that negotiations do bear fruit. Firstly, parties are entitled to call upon the assistance of mediators whose task is to provide assistance with negotiation and submit proposals.[77] Secondly, Member States must ensure that parties enter and conduct negotiations regarding authorisation for cable retransmission in good faith and do not prevent or hinder negotiation without valid justification.[78]

(v) Abolishment of territorially limited broadcast licences?

4.048 It has long been the custom of film rightholders to license the broadcasting of films on a territorial basis In the *CODITEL* cases,[79] the ECJ upheld the principle that exclusive territorially limited broadcast licences were compatible with the Treaty of Rome.[80] With the implementation of the Directive, especially its "country of origin" principle, is there any justification to grant territorially limited licences? Clearly, with satellite broadcasting, there is a practical problem in enforcing such licences as technology does not generally permit a satellite to broadcast purely to within a country's borders. However, de-encryption devices only issued to residents of a Member State could give rise to a compartmentalisation of territories. Satellite broadcasters could refuse to give de-encryption devices to homes in Member States outside their territory. With cable retransmission, it is easy to limit such retransmission to within a country's border. Accordingly, the validity of such licences is important. Recital 13 of the Directive states that minimum rules should be laid down in order to establish and guarantee free and uninterrupted cross-border broadcasting by satellite and simultaneous cable retransmission. Article

[73] Art. 9(2).
[74] Art. 9(2).
[75] Art. 10.
[76] See Kern, "The E.C. Common Position on Copyright Applicable to Satellite Broadcasting and Cable Retransmission" [1993] 8 EIPR 276 at p. 281.
[77] Art. 11.
[78] Art. 12.
[79] CASE 62 *CODITEL I* [1986] E.C.R. 881 [1981] 2 C.M.L.R. 362; CASE 262/81 *CODITEL II* [1982] E.C.R. 3381; [1983] 1 C.M.L.R. 49.
[80] See Chapter on Licensing of Intellectual Property at para. 8.070.

7(3) of the Directive which is a transitional provision suggests that authorisation by a producer, co-producer or assignee of a copyright work who owns exploitation rights for a specific area within the Community will constitute permission for the whole Community except where the agreement was concluded prior to January 1, 1995.[81] If this is so, then it may be the decisions of *CODITEL I & II* have been implicitly repealed and licences will have to be granted on a Community-wide scale.[82] Thus agreements and licences concluded after January 1, 1995 must be on a Community scale and take into account the size of the potential audience. This may hamper the distribution of films by satellite because of the language differences in the Community which require broadcasters to dub or subtitle films for each state often require licensing to be done on a territorial basis.

(vi) Transitional Provisions

4.049 The provisions in the Directive regarding the relevant law and whom satellite broadcasting rights may be exercised against are deemed to apply to agreements in existence on January 1, 1995 as from January 1, 2000 if they expire after that date.[83]

Article 7(3) provides as follows:

> "When an international co-production agreement concluded before the date mentioned in Article 14(1) [*i.e.* July 1, 1995] between a co-producer from a Member State and one or more co-producers from other Member States or third countries expressly provides for a system of division of exploitation rights between the co-producers by geographical areas for all means of communication to the public, without distinguishing the arrangement applicable to communication to the public by satellite from the provisions applicable to the other means of communication and where communication to the public by satellite of the co-production would prejudice the exclusivity in particular the language exclusivity of one of the co-producers or his assignees in a given territory the authorisation by one of the co-producers or his assignees for a communication to the public by satellite shall require the prior consent of the holder of that exclusivity whether co-producer or assignee."

This rule has been described as an interpretation rule: "What would the contracting partners have written into their contract if they had been aware of the technological developments?".[84] Clearly, prejudice will

[81] The transitional provisions of this Article are discussed below, at para. 4.049.

[82] See Kern, "The E.C. Common Position on Copyright Applicable to Satellite Broadcasting and Cable Retransmission" [1993] 8 EIPR 276, at p. 280. See also Jorna and Martin-Prat "New Rules in European Copyright" [1994] 4 EIPR 145, at p. 151 where the authors appear to subscribe to the view that the adoption of the Dir. and country-of-origin principle would remove such "legal borders".

[83] Art. 7(2) and 14.

[84] See Jorna and Martin-Prat "New Rules in European Copyright" [1994] 4 EIPR 145 at p. 152.

occur if the satellite broadcast is in a language which can be understood by more than one country.[85] The transitional provision appears to suggest that if the agreement has specifically catered for satellite broadcasting, then the transitional provision is inapplicable. If so, the emphasis laid on the inclusion of this Article by certain parties as suggesting that it implicitly infers that agreements concluded after January 1, 1995 cannot be limited territorially within the Community may not be a valid one.[86]

Member States are permitted to retain bodies with jurisdiction over cases where the right to retransmit by cable to the public has been unreasonably refused or offered on unreasonable terms until January 1, 2003.[87]

(vii) Implementation of Directive

4.050 Member States are required to implement the Directive by January 1, 1995.[88]

(e) **Database Directive**

(i) Introduction

4.051 In its Green Paper on Copyright, the Commission considered the question of protection for databases. The 1980s had witnessed a large increase in the informational services market and in particular, in the storage of data on computer.

In 1988, the turnover in databases worldwide was $5 billion of which the United States was responsible for four-fifths and the E.C. for about $350 million. It was thus clear that databases were important both economically and for informational purposes. in order for the Community to foster growth in this area, the Commission realised that it was of paramount importance that some form of protection be conferred on the owners of databases in order to prevent unauthorised copying of data which reduces the economic incentive of creating and maintaining databases.

The Commission made several observations on the legal protection of databases. Firstly, it observed that the storage in databases of a work protected under copyright required the permission of the author of such a work. Secondly, it observed that the retrieval of such protected works were also restricted acts if it resulted in a reproduction of the work.[89] In both these cases, the laws of Member States were substantially the same.

However, the Commission observed that the greatest variety of protection afforded under Member States' laws was to the protection of the

[85] *ibid.*, where the authors give examples of where consent would be required.
[86] See section on "Abolishment of territorialy limited licences?" above at para. 4.048.
[87] Art. 12(2),(3) and 14(1).
[88] Art. 14.
[89] The Commission noted that a mere visual display of information was akin to reading and would not normally infringe copyright. Under the proposed directive, temporary reproduction of the database does infringe the copyright, if any, in the database—see Art. 5(a).

database itself as a collection of copyright works and/or non-copyright works. The vast majority of countries protected original collections and compilations of protected works as required under Article 2(5) of the Berne Convention.[90] This confers protection on:

> "Collections of literary and artistic works, such as encyclopaedias and anthologies which, by reason of the selection and arrangement of their contents, constitute intellectual creations shall be protected as such, without prejudice on the copyright in each of the works forming part of such collections."

Many countries had gone further and provided protection for collections of non-copyright works. Thus, the courts of several Member States have held that copyright exists in an original collection of non-copyright works. Where considerable variety lies is in the courts' approaches to the issue of originality. This difference of approach is most notable in considering whether collections of factual data which require considerable labour and investment but little or no creativity are protected under a country's copyright laws. Thus, in the United Kingdom, the courts define originality without reference to the level of creativity in the work but by merely saying that the work must have originated from the author and must have been the result of the author's skill and labour. Thus, trade catalogues have been found to possess copyright.[91] In other Member States, there is greater emphasis on the originality which subsists in the criteria for selecting and arranging. Thus, in Germany, copyright will only vest in a database if the selection, accumulation, arrangement and organisation has been the subject of know-how beyond that possessed by the average programmer.[92] As pointed out by one commentator, such an approach would result in the denial of copyright protection to most factual databases in Germany.[93] The laws of other Member States emphasise that some level of creativity is required in the selection or arrangement of data before copyright will vest.[94] In other countries, like Denmark, *sui generis* rights have been enacted to prevent the copying of works like catalogues, tables and similar works which did not attract genuine copyright protection because the works were not sufficiently original.[95]

In the Green Paper, the Commission proposed that protection for the compilation of copyright works in databases should be provided in the Community. It also invited comments on whether the protection should

[90] See above, at para. 4.008.

[91] See *Maple & Co. v. Junior Army and Navy Stores* [1882] 21 Ch.D. 369 and Copinger (13th Ed.) para. 3–36. See also *Victoria Park Racing and Recreation Grounds Co. Ltd v. Taylor* [1937] 58 C.L.R. 479 at 511 (decision of the Australian High Court).

[92] *Inkassaprogram*—Bundesgerichtshof, 9 May 1985.

[93] Pattison, "The European Commission's proposal on protection on Computer Databases" [1992] 4 EIPR 115.

[94] *ibid.*

[95] Art. 49 of the Danish Copyright Act which provided for an exclusive right to the creator of the work for 10 years. See s.6.4.5 of Green Paper.

be extended to databases where the material was not in itself protected by copyright and whether such protection should be copyright or a *sui generis* right. In May 1992, the Commission issued its first proposal for a Directive on the Legal Protection of Databases accompanied by an Explanatory Memorandum.[96] The Draft Directive proposed that those databases which did not qualify for copyright because they did not meet the criterion of creativity should be subject to a *sui generis* unfair extraction right to the extent that their contents were not themselves protected by copyright. The proposal was discussed by the Economic and Social Committee and by the European Parliament which voted in support of the proposals subject to a number of detailed amendments. The Commission considered the Parliament's amendments and on October 4, 1993 presented its amended proposal along with an explanatory memorandum.[97] On June 6, 1991, the E.C. Council agreed a Common Position. Accordingly, subject to further amendments from the European Parliament, it is likely to become law in the near future.

(ii) Proposed E.C. Database Directive

4.052 The proposed directive is organised into four sections—definitions, copyright, unauthorised extraction right and common provisions.

(1) Definitions

4.053 "Database" is defined as:

> "a collection of data, works or materials arranged, stored and accessed by electronic means, and the materials necessary for the operation of the database such as its thesaurus, index or system for obtaining or presenting information."[98]

The extension of the definition to include data was an amendment of the European Parliament. The definition of "database" does not apply to the computer programme used in the making of the database or operation of the database.[99] This should already be protected by domestic legislation responsible for the enactment of the Computer Harmonisation Directive.[1]

(2) Owner of Rights in a database

4.054 Under the Directive, the "owner of the rights in a database" is granted certain exclusive rights both under copyright law and under a *sui generis* right to prevent unauthorised extraction or re-utilisation of the contents of the database.[2] This phrase is defined as meaning (a) the author of a

[96] COM (92) 24.
[97] COM (93) 464 [1993] O.J. C308/1.
[98] Art. 1(1).
[99] *ibid.*
[1] See below, at para. 4.067.
[2] Arts. 6 and 10(2).

database[3] or (b) the natural or legal person to whom the author has lawfully granted the right to prevent unauthorised extraction of material from a database or (c) where the database is not eligible for protection by copyright, the maker of the database.[4]

Where the database itself is subject to copyright (see para. 4.055, below), the author of the database or (if relevant) the author's grantee of the unauthorised extraction right is the owner of rights (both copyright and unauthorised extraction right) in the database. It is questionable why the assignee of the author's copyright in the database has not been included in this definition whereas the assignee of the author's unauthorised extraction right has been included. Surely, the Directive is not intended to prevent such an assignee from exercising his copyright? Where the database itself is not subject to copyright, *i.e.* it is an electronic collection of data or it is a collection of copyright works but there is no originality in the collection and therefore the database itself does not satisfy the test of originality, the owner of the rights can be all three persons. However, in such circumstances, one is only concerned with the unauthorised extraction right. Thus, it is not appropriate to refer to the creator of the database as being an author (as such a term is only relevant in the context of copyright). Accordingly, consideration of the assignment of the author's rights are also irrelevant. Thus, one is only concerned with the maker of the database and his unauthorised extraction right.[5]

(3) Protection of database by copyright

4.055 *Article 2(5) Berne Convention*—the proposed database Directive protects databases by copyright as collections within the meaning of Article 2(5) of the Berne Convention.[6] As mentioned in the introduction, this Article does not provide for protection of a collection of non-copyright works, *i.e.* a database of data. It merely provides for protection for a collection of artistic or literary works, *i.e.* works themselves protected under copyright.

4.056 *Originality*—a database *per se* will only be protected *by copyright* under the proposed Directive:

> " . . . if it is original in the sense that it is a collection of works or materials, which by reason of their selection or their arrangement, constitutes the author's own intellectual creation. No other criteria

[3] Defined at Art. 3.
[4] Art. 1(2).
[5] In other words, the term "author" and "maker" are used as terms of art to indicate respectively the creator of the database where it possesses copyright and where it does not. See Art. 3 which is headed "Authorship: copyright", Art. 13(1) and Art. 2(5) of the original proposal of the Commission which refers to the "maker" of a database in respect of the unfair extraction right.
[6] Art. 2(1).

> shall be applied to determine the eligibility of a database for this protection."[7]

It is significant that the addition of the term "data" in the revised proposal's definition of database is not repeated in this definition. This accords with Article 2(5) of the Berne Convention. Because the protection of databases by copyright is in accordance with Article 2(5), it is submitted that "works or materials" here must be read as meaning copyrights of artistic or literary works. Accordingly, collections of data and other non-copyright works, however intellectually creative in their selection or arrangement are not protected under copyright law.[8]

The Directive underscores the above definition of originality by only granting exclusive rights to the author of the database in respect of the selection or arrangement of the contents of the database.[9] Furthermore, the Directive does not permit any other criteria to be used in determining the eligibility of a database for protection.[10] The Recitals to the Directive make it clear that no aesthetic or qualitative criteria should be applied in considering the issue of originality.[11] However, the emphasis that originality vests by reason of the selection or arrangement of the contents of the database means that if such proposals stand copyright protection will be denied to most databases. This is because most databases are useful to the public precisely because they provide *all the material* in a given subject. For example, it would be little use for a database on patent publications to have a selection of such publications. Difficulties can be envisaged here because the selection or arrangement must merely be the author's own intellectual creation but no qualitative criteria can be applied. For example, is a database which contains Court of First Instance Judgments a "selection" of European court cases? Whilst it may be a very obvious selection, it is a selection. It may be that courts will give due weight to the phrase "intellectual creation" and require more than *de minimis* intellectual effort.

Similarly, the concept of arrangement in a database has limited value. The manner in which materials are stored in the database is dependent on the computer program running the database and the operating system being used on the computer.[12]

4.057 *Interrelationship of copyright in database and copyright in contents*—any copyright in the database itself is expressed not to extend to and to be without prejudice to the protection by copyright or

[7] Art. 2(3).

[8] See Chalton, "The Amended Database Directive Proposal: A Commentary and Synopsis" [1994] 3 EIPR 94, at p. 96.

[9] Art. 6.

[10] Art. 2(3).

[11] Recital 15.

[12] See Pattison, "The European Commission's proposal on protection on Computer Databases" [1992] 4 EIPR 115.

other rights existing in the works that form part of the database.[13] The consideration of copyright to the contents of the database and to the database itself are independent.[14]

4.058 *Nonapplicability to non-electronic databases*—the Directive only applies to databases stored by electronic means and is expressed to be without prejudice to the protection of collections arranged, stored or accessed via non-electronic means which remain protected according to Article 2(5) of the Berne Convention.[15] Accordingly, a railway timetable book is not subject to the Directive or Article 2(5) (being a collection of data) and the issue as to whether it is subject to copyright is a matter of national law.

4.059 *Definition of "author"*—the author of a database for the purposes of copyright is deemed to be the natural person or group of natural persons who *created* the database or where Member State legislation permits, the legal person designated as the rightholder by that legislation.[16] Where Member State legislation deems a particular person to have created a collective work, then where such legislation deems someone to be the creator of the database, that person shall be deemed to be its author.[17] Where there are more than one creator, then the exclusive rights are owned jointly.[18] Furthermore, where the creator of the database is an employee who created the database in the execution of his duties or following the instructions given by his employer, then copyright vests in the employer unless otherwise provided.[19]

(4) Restricted Acts regarding Copyright in Database[20]

4.060 The owner of the rights in a database has, in respect of the selection or arrangement of the contents of the database and the electronic materials necessary for the operation of the database, the exclusive right to do or to authorise the temporary or permanent reproduction of the database by any means and in any form, in whole or part; the translation adaptation arrangement and any other alteration of the database; the reproduction of the results of any of the above acts; the distribution (prior to sale) or rental of the database or its copies to the public and the communication, display or performance of the database to the public.[21]

[13] Art. 2(4),15(1).
[14] See Chalton, "The Amended Database Directive Proposal: A Commentary and Synopsis" [1994] 3 EIPR 94, at p. 95.
[15] Art. 2(2).
[16] Art. 3(1). Readers should note that Art. 3 is headed "Author: copyright". Thus, author here clearly means the author for the purposes of copyright and not for the purposes of the unauthorised extraction right.
[17] Art. 3(2).
[18] Art. 3(3).
[19] Art. 3(4).
[20] Art. 6.
[21] Art. 6.

The emphasis on the exclusive rights in relation to the selection or arrangement of the contents of the database means that it may well be difficult for a court to decide whether there has been infringement. Clearly, where the database is merely "downloaded", there will be reproduction. The more difficult test is where there is "downloading" of the contents on the basis of a search by a database user. For example, where an unauthorised user selects all cases decided by a certain judge from a database of cases of the Court of First Instance, has he infringed the exclusive right in relation to the selection or arrangement of the database? Article 2(4) of the Directive makes it clear that the copyright protection of a database given by the Directive does not extend to the works or materials contained therein irrespective of whether or not they are themselves protected by copyright. This suggests that there must be more than mere extraction of material from a database which possesses copyright but some form of substantial reproduction of the selection or arrangements of the contents of the database. If so, it is rare that an extraction of material by a database user will amount to copyright infringement. In such circumstances, the rights owner must rely on his unauthorised extraction rights.

(5) Unauthorised Extraction Right

4.061 Article 10(2) states that:

> "Member States shall provide for a right for the owner of the rights in a database to prevent the unauthorised extraction or re-utilisation from that database of its contents in whole or in substantial part for commercial purposes.[22] This right to prevent unauthorised extraction shall apply irrespective of the eligibility of that database for protection under copyright. It shall not apply to the contents of a database where these are works already protected by copyright or neighbouring rights."[23]

The grant of this right is the consequence of the Commission's recognition that database makers are exposed to the risk of having the contents of their databases downloaded without their authorisation and that such would constitute misappropriation of their financial and professional investment incurred in obtaining and collecting data.[24] The Commission opted for a *sui generis* right. Importantly, the right does not apply to the contents where the *contents* are already protected by copyright. Thus, the works of living authors themselves will not be produced under the unfair extraction right.

[22] "Commercial purposes" is defined as use which is not private, personal or for non-profit making purposes—Art. 11(7).

[23] "Right to prevent unauthorised extraction" is defined as the right of the owner of the rights in a database to prevent acts of extraction and re-utilisation of part or all of the material from that database—Art. 10(1).

[24] Recital 27 and 28.

The unauthorised extraction right only extends to databases whose makers are nationals, habitually resident or in the case of businesses have their seats of business in a Member State.[25] The Directive allows for the Council to extend reciprocal protection under this right to databases produced in third countries.[26] These provisions are designed to secure reciprocal extraction rights with third countries in order to encourage wider availability of the new right.

The prohibition on re-utilisation could mean that a person who does not actually download the database can still be liable for infringement of the unauthorised extraction right if he makes uses of information downloaded without authorisation from a database by a third party. Such constitutes a form of secondary infringement and it would seem that a requirement of knowledge or "reason to believe" might be appropriate to safeguard innocent users.

The Directive provides for a system of compulsory licensing of the unauthorised extraction right where the works or materials contained in a public database cannot be independently created, collected or obtained from any other source.[27] Interestingly, the CFI has held that in circumstances where such material was unavailable from other sources, it was an abuse of a dominant position for the owners of copyright in television listings not to license others who wished to compile such listings.[28]

Such licensing would be on fair and non-discriminatory terms and must be open to arbitration. The Directive also provides for compulsory licensing of the unauthorised extraction right in relation to databases made publicly available by a public body which is either established to assemble or disclose information pursuant to legislation or is under a general duty to do so.[29] Read literally, the compulsory licence provisions do not apply to databases of data.[30]

Importantly, the compulsory licensing provisions only apply to the unfair extraction right and not to copyright in the database. Where a database enjoys both types of protection, the compulsory licensing provisions may be of little use.[31]

[25] Art. 13(1).
[26] Art. 13(3).
[27] It is not a material consideration that obtaining the information would be prohibitively expensive or time-consuming—see Recital 33.
[28] Case T-69/89 [1991] II E.C.R. 485, *Radio Telefis Eireann v. E.C. Commission* [1991] 4 C.M.L.R. 586; Case T-70/89 [1992] E.C.R. 535, *BBC v. E.C. Commission* [1991] C.M.L.R. 669; Case T-76/89 [1992] II E.C.R. 575, *Independent Television Publication Ltd. v. E.C. Commission* [1991] C.M.L.R. 745 upheld on appeal, Judgment April 6, 1995 (unreported). See Chapter on Abuse of a Dominant Position for further discussion of these cases at para. 11.053 *et seq.*
[29] Art. 11(2).
[30] See Chalton, "The Amended Database Directive Proposal: A Commentary and Synopsis" [1994] 3 EIPR 94, at p. 98.
[31] See Pattison, "The European Commission's proposal on protection on Computer Databases" [1992] 4 EIPR 115 at p. 118.

(6) Term of Protection

4.062 Copyright protection for a database is the same as that for any protected collection of literary works.[32] Normally, this will mean 70 years after the death of the author if he is identifiable. The Directive provides that a substantial change to the selection or arrangement of the contents of a database gives rise to the creation of a new database which is protected from that moment as a new copyright work.[33] "Substantial change" is defined as additions, deletions or alterations which involve substantial modifications to the selection or arrangement of the contents of a database resulting in a new edition of that database.[34] Correspondingly, insubstantial changes to the selection or arrangement of the contents of a database do not entail a fresh period of copyright protection for the database.[35]

The unauthorised extraction right runs for 15 years from 1 January following the date when the database was first made available to the public or when a substantial change was made to the database.[36] The Directive provides that any substantial change to the contents of a database will give rise to a fresh period of protection to the right to prevent unauthorised extraction.[37] "Substantial change" is defined as the successive accumulation of insubstantial additions, deletions or alterations in respect of the contents of a database resulting in substantial modifications to all or part of a database.[38] Correspondingly, insubstantial changes will not give rise to a fresh period of protection.[39] These are defined as insubstantial additions, delections or alterations which taken together do not substantially modify the contents of a database.[40] Accordingly, the term of protection for databases which are continually updated will continually start afresh.

(7) Fair Dealing Provisions

4.063 The Directive provides that the incorporation into a database of quotations, abstracts, etc., does not require the permission of the rightholder in those works.[41] Lawful users of a database may without the permission of the database maker extract and re-utilise insubstantial parts of works or materials for commercial purposes provided that acknowledgment is made of the source and for private purposes without such acknowledgment.[42] "Insubstantial parts" is defined as parts of a database made available to the public whose reproduction evaluated quantitatively and

[32] Art. 9(1).
[33] Art. 9(2)(a). Such protection does not prejudice existing rights in respect of the original database—*ibid.*
[34] Art. 9(2)(b).
[35] Art. 9(2)(c).
[36] Art. 12(1).
[37] Art. 12(2)(a).
[38] Art. 12(2)(b).
[39] Art. 12(3)(a).
[40] Art. 12(3)(b).
[41] Art. 5(2).
[42] Art. 11(5), (6).

qualitatively in relation to the database from which they are copied, can be considered not to prejudice the exclusive rights of the owner of that database to exploit the database. The lawful user must demonstrate that the extraction and re-utilisation of insubstantial parts does not prejudice such rights and is necessary to achieve the desired objective.[43] However, these provisions are not meant to weaken the rights of rightholders in the works or materials which form the contents of the database.[44] Accordingly, the lawful user of a database must ensure that his reproduction of part of the contents of a database falls within national "fair dealing" provisions in relation to the contents themselves or forms an insubstantial part of the contents.

(8) Remedies

4.064 The Directive requires that Member States provide appropriate remedies in respect of infringements of the rights provided for in the directive.[45]

(9) Transitional Provisions

4.065 In relation to transitional provisions, the Directive merely provides that it applies to databases created prior to the date of publication of the Directive but without prejudice to any contracts concluded and rights acquired before that date.[46]

(10) Copyright and Extraction Right Compared

4.066 A database may qualify both for protection by copyright by reason of its selection or arrangement of works or materials capable of protection under copyright law and for protection under the extraction right.[47] However, the extraction right does not apply to the contents of a database where these are works already protected by copyright or neighbouring rights.[48] This leads to three different scenarios:

(a) A database consisting of an original selection or arrangement of *copyrightable* works or materials in an electronic database may be protected by both copyright and unfair extraction right.
  (i) If those works or materials themselves are subject to copyright protection, then the database may be protected under copyright (if selection or arrangement is original) and the unfair extraction right but the contents will not be protected under the unfair extraction right.
  (ii) If those works or material are not subject to copyright protection, the database may possess both copyright (if selec-

[43] Art. 11(8).
[44] Art. 15.
[45] Art. 14.
[46] Art. 15(2).
[47] Art. 10(2), second sentence.
[48] Art. 10(2) third sentence.

tion or arrangement is original) and under unfair extraction right.[49]

(b) A database of data may be protected by unfair extraction right but not by copyright.

Two examples illustrate the application of the above principles.

(1) Database consists of complete compilation of novels of a living author. In this case, the contents are subject to copyright but there is no copyright in the database as there is no selection or arrangement of the works. The unfair extraction right subsists in the database but not in the contents. Thus, unlawful extraction of a novel of the author would constitute an infringement of the author's copyright but not the database owner's unfair extraction right even if the novel is clearly a substantial part of the database (*i.e.* only three novels).

(2) Database consists of collection of names and addresses of persons who have an income over £50,000. Names and addresses are not literary works. Accordingly, there is no copyright in the contents. Although the names and addresses have been selected according a particular criteria, the database is not subject to copyright because the names and addresses are not capable of being the subject of copyright. An unfair extraction right exists in relation to the database.

(f) Computer Software Protection

(i) Introduction

4.067 Prior to the enactment of specific software legislation in Europe, the laws of contract and confidentiality were primarily relied upon by licensors to control copies of their computer programs. While this was usually effective against copying by licensees, it was powerless to prevent the widespread pirating of a computer program which had been obtained illegally. In recent years, specific protection under copyright laws has been introduced in most Member States.[50] Its popularity as a means of software protection arose for the following reasons;

(i) the strong analogy between computer software and literature (although no reproduction of the work is involved before a literary work is read, reproduction is involved in the preparation of a translation) and therefore computer programs could be deemed to be literary works within the existing frame-

[49] The wording of Art. 10(2), third sentence that the unauthorised extraction right "does not apply to the contents of a database where these are works already protected by copyright or neighbouring rights" does not preclude the extraction right from applying to the database itself. Thus, if a database consists of poems of a living author, an extraction of one whole poem will only infringe the copyright in the poem but an extraction of several poems could infringe the copyright in the poems, the copyright in the database and the extraction right.

[50] All member states save for Italy and Belgium offer either statutory or common law copyright protection for computer programs as literary works.

work of copyright law avoiding the need for deriving a completely new law from scratch;

(ii) whereas any neighbouring rights or *sui generis* approach would have required the creation of a new instrument for international protection, copyright had the advantage of integrating program protection into an established system of international protection providing for national treatment and certain minimum rights such as moral rights which had been the subject of considerable international co-operation and harmonisation already, ever since the Berne Convention of 1886;

(iii) the rightholder can sue anyone under copyright whereas the privity rule in the law of contract prevents a contact being enforced against anyone other than those who are parties to it. Furthermore, copyright law has the further advantage that all rights operate automatically without the need for any formalities or incurring any cost to member states in setting up a registration system or right holders in obtaining registration;

(iv) the wide scope of protection which prohibits close copies as well as exact copies; the heavy onus which shifts on to the infringer to prove he did not copy once the copyright holder has proved his ownership, the existence of copyright and demonstrated that the infringer had an opportunity to copy;

(v) the potential for criminal sanctions which are more appropriate remedies in some circumstances, for example, where a large scale fraud has been perpetrated;

(vi) the appropriate balance between protection and encouraging development can be achieved using copyright because it protects only the expression and not the idea. Thus the protection can extend to the underlying specifications and keystroke sequences to be protected without encompassing the logic, principles, algorithms or programming languages. It also provides means for imposing precise conditions on permitted acts such as reverse engineering which are vulnerable to abuse;

(vii) several of the Member States had already embarked upon this course with varying degrees of success.

However, some commentators have queried whether copyright is an appropriate means of protection for computer software.[51] Because copyright protection did not exist in some Member States and because of the differing approaches to the protection of computer software under the various copyright laws, the E.C. Commission perceived a need to harmonise in this field. Accordingly, it has introduced the Software Protection Directive which provides for copyright protection of computer software in all Member States.

[51] Christie, "Designing Appropriate Protection for Computer Programs" [1994] EIPR 486.

(ii) History of the E.C. Software Directive

4.068 In 1985 the Commission published its white paper which was followed in June 1988 by the publication of its green paper entitled "Copyright and the Challenge of Technology".[52] The Commission's draft proposal for a Directive was presented to the Council in January 1989. It was also submitted to the European Parliament for its opinion which was delivered in July 1990.

In October 1990 the Commission published its "Amended proposal for a Council Directive on legal protection of computer programs" taking into account the European Parliament's proposals, including the addition of an Article expressly allowing reverse engineering/decompilation of programs to achieve interoperability.

Within two months the Council was able to adopt the "Common Position" which was approved without amendment by Parliament in April 1991. The Council then enacted the common position and the Directive was published in May 1991.

The deadline for its implementation was January 1, 1993.[53] It is not clear whether parties can rely directly on the provisions of the Directive in legal actions in either the national court or European Court of Justice where the Directive has not yet been implemented.[54]

(iii) Present position in member states

4.069 By February 1994 Denmark, Germany, Ireland, Italy, Greece, Spain and the United Kingdom had all implemented the Directive. Germany initially extended its copyright laws to cover computer programs as "literary works" in 1985 with additional protection being provided under trade mark and general competition law. At that stage the law was extended by merely adding programs to the list of protectable works. The Directive has now been implemented with specific computer program legislation. Spain extended copyright protection to computer programs in 1987. The legislation was modified to some extent by the implementation of the Directive. However, the earlier legislation usefully defined what constituted a computer program.[55] In the United Kingdom, the Copyright, Patents and Designs Act 1988 completely repealed the Copyright (Computer Software) Amendment Act 1985 which was the first United Kingdom Act to specifically provide for copyright protection of computer programs as literary works. The 1988 Act went much further towards protecting computer programs but further legislation was required in order to comply fully with the Directive. In December 1992

[52] COM (88) 172.

[53] Art. 10(1) of the Directive.

[54] See Introduction Chapter and in particular Guy and Barrett "The EC software directive: could it have direct effect?" [1991] *Comp. Law & Practice* 249–250.

[55] "Every sequence of instructions or indications destined to be used. Either directly or indirectly in a computer system for the purpose of carrying out a function or task or for obtaining a specific end result, whatever its method or expression or guise."

the United Kingdom government implemented the Directive in the Copyright (Computer programs) Regulations 1992 (S.I. No. 3233) which came into force on January 1, 1993. Under the Regulations the 1988 Act is amended to incorporate the provisions of the Directive not already complied with.

France has not yet implemented the Directive. However, it had already extended its copyright laws to cover computer programs in 1985. In France there is no definition of a computer program ("logiciels"). As with all copyright works, the software must be original. In a 1986 decision of the French supreme court, it held that the test of originality required "an intellectual contribution from the author". In the Netherlands, whilst there is no specific legislation relating to computer programs, caselaw has developed the principle that programs including preparatory works should be protected by copyright. The Netherlands government intends to codify the caselaw in so far as it is compatible with the Directive.

Even once the Directive has been implemented in all Member States, differences will remain. Thus, issues not dealt with by the Directive are regulated by national laws of Member States and therefore subject to variation across the European Union. These include the definition of a "computer program", the test for "originality",[56] the meaning of "adaptation"[57], the copyright in computer-generated works[58] and the authorship of commissioned software.

(iv) Terms of Directive

(1) Protection of computer programs by copyright

4.070 The Directive requires Member States to protect computer programs by copyright as literary works under the Berne Convention.[59] Preparatory design material for programs is also protected.[60] In keeping with the con-

[56] For instance, the test for originality is much stricter in Germany than it is in the United Kingdom.

[57] Under the Directive, the adaptation of a program is a restricted act. However, it is not defined. In the U.K., the making of an "adaptation" of a work is an act restricted by the copyright—Copyright Designs and Patents Act 1988, s.21. In particular, in relation to a computer program, "adaptation" means an arrangement or altered version of the programme or a translation of it. Furthermore, adaptation is deemed to include the translation of a work which in relation to a computer program is deemed to include a version of the program in which it is converted into or out of a computer language or code or into a different computer language or code—CDPA 1988, s.21 as amended by Copyright (Computer Programs) Regulation 1992 (S.I. 1992 No. 3233).

[58] Copyright in computer generated works are recognised only in U.K. The author of such a work is deemed to be the "person by whom the arrangements necessary for the creation of the work are undertaken"—CDPA 1988, s.9(3). These works are not to be confused with computer-aided works where the author is human and the computer is a mere tool. This section has not been repealed since there is nothing specific in the Directive to indicate whether or not it is allowed to remain.

[59] Art. 1(1).

[60] Art. 1(1). Recital 7 elaborates on this by stating that the term "computer program" also includes preparatory design work leading to the development of a computer program "provided that the nature of the preparatory work is such that a computer program can result from it at a later stage".

cept of copyright, the Directive specifically states that protection extends to the expression of a program "in any form".[61] Again, in keeping with the laws of copyright, the ideas and principles which underlie any element of a computer program including those which underlie its interfaces are not protected by copyright.[62]

The Directive does not include a definition of "computer program".

Only computer programs which are original in the sense that they are the author's own intellectual creation are protected.[63] The recital states that in considering the issue of originality, no tests as to the qualitative or aesthetic merits of the program should be applied.[64] Accordingly, it would appear that the test of originality is satisfied where it is shown that the program has not been copied from another source.

In keeping with the principle of protection of computer programs under national laws of copyright, the Directive specifically provides that protection shall be granted to all natural or legal persons eligible under national copyright legislation as applied to literary works.[65]

(2) Authorship

4.071 The copyright in the computer program accrues to the author. The author of the program is defined as the natural person or group of persons who created the program.[66] Importantly, the Directive permits derogation from these provisions if national legislation otherwise provides for. Thus, the author of the program may be deemed to be the owner/legal person designated as rightholder by that legislation.[67] In effect, this means that Member States have total freedom to decide who owns the copyright in a computer program. Where collective works are recognised by the legislation of a member state, the author is the person or group of persons considered by that legislation to have created the work.[68]

Where a computer program is created by an employee in the execution of his duties or following instructions given by his employer, the employer is exclusively entitled to exercise all economic rights unless otherwise provided by contract.[69] The Directive is silent on whether the employer has an exclusive licence from the employee or in fact owns the

[61] Thus, this includes programs incorporated into hardware—see Recital 7.
[62] Art. 1(2). Thus, an algorithm *per se* is not protected but the language code used to incorporate such an algorithm into a computer program is protected—see Recital 14.
[63] Art. 1(3).
[64] Recital 8.
[65] Art. 3.
[66] Art. 2(1). Where the program is created by a group of persons jointly, the exclusive rights are owned jointly—Art. 2(2).
[67] Art. 2(1).
[68] Art. 2(1). This provision is rather puzzling. A computer program is not a collection of literary works. Under Art. 2(5) of the Berne Convention, a collection of literary works which by reason of their selection or arrangement constitute the author's own creation are protected. However, it is considered that it will be rare that someone will collect and collate computer programs in the same sense as an anthology of poems.
[69] Art. 2(3).

copyright. In practice, there should be little distinction because in most member State's laws, an exclusive licensee can sue third parties for infringement of copyright.

The Directive does not specifically regulate authorship in commissioned programs. Consequently in the absence of special provision under national legislation, the position will be entirely controlled by contract.

(3) Restricted Acts

4.072 Under Article 4 of the Directive the owner is granted the exclusive right to do or authorise:

(a) the permanent or temporary reproduction of a computer program by any means an in any form in part or in whole. *Insofar as loading displaying running transmission or storage of the computer program necessitate such reproduction such acts shall be subject to authorization by the rightholder*;[70]

(b) the translation, adaptation,[71] arrangement and any other alteration of a computer program and the reproduction of the results thereof (this is without prejudice to the rights of the person who alters the program) . . .

(c) any form of distribution including rental of the program or its copies to the public . . . [72] In accordance with established E.C. jurisprudence on intellectual property and Articles 30 to 36 of the E.C. Treaty, the Directive provides that once a copy of a program has been sold in the Community by the rightholder or with his consent, his distribution rights are exhausted within the Community with the exception of the right to control its further rental.[73]

(4) Exceptions to exclusive rights

4.073 Since the restricted acts are so broadly defined in the Directive, it provides for certain exceptions. In particular, the Commission wished to preserve the following rights, namely:

(a) the right of the lawful acquirer to carry out any of the restricted acts if they are necessary for the use of the program in accordance with its intended purpose, including error correction;

[70] Art. 4(a). See also Art. 5(1) discussed below which provides a defence of "intended purpose".

[71] Art. 4(b). "Adaptation" is not defined. For U.K. definition of "adaptation" in relation to a computer program, see Copyright Designs and Patents Act 1988, s.21 as amended by Copyright (Computer Programs) Regs. (S.I. 1992 No. 3233). See n. 57 *supra*.

[72] Art. 4(c). Recital 16 specifically states that "renting" does not include public lending which remains outside the scope of the Directive. However, this right was introduced under Council Dir. 92/100 for literary works. Accordingly, as a computer program is protected as a literary work, a lending right will apply to computer programs. See para. 4.031 *et seq*.

[73] *ibid*. See Chapter on Enforcement of Intellectual Property in relation to the ECJ's jurisprudence on the interaction between Articles 30 to 36 of the EC Treaty and intellectual property.

(b) the making of back-up copies;
(c) the right to observe study and test a program to ascertain its underlying ideas and principles;
(d) the right to decompile a program to obtain interface information for the interoperability of programs;

Intended purpose

4.074 Article 5(1) provides that:

> "In the absence of specifical contractual provisions, the acts referred to in Article 4(a) and (b) shall not require authorisation by the rightholder where they are necessary for the use of the computer program by the lawful acquirer in accordance with its intended purpose including for error correction."

This Article should be read in conjunction with the proviso to Article 4(a) set out above at para. 4.072. The idea behind the "necessary for use" exception in Article 5(1) and the proviso in Article 4(a) is to make it clear that certain minimum acts involved in running a computer program and keeping it running do not require express contractual permission from an owner of the copyright to someone lawfully in possession of the software.

Can the rightholder exclude Article 5(1) by contractual provisions?

4.075 On the face of it, this seems an impertinent question because clearly Article 5(1) specifically provides that the rightholder can. However, Recitals 17 and 18 provide that:

> "Whereas the exclusive rights of the author to prevent the unauthorised reproduction of his work have to be subject to a limited exception in the case of a computer program to allow the reproduction technically necessary for the use of that program by the lawful acquirer.
>
> Whereas this means the acts of loading and running necessary for the use of a copy of a program which has been lawfully acquired, and the act of correction of its errors, may not be prohibited by contract; whereas, in the absence of specific contractual provisions, including when a copy of the program has been sold, any other act necessary for the use of the copy of a program may be performed in accordance with its intended purpose by a lawful acquirer of that copy."

On the fact of it, there is a conflict between these recitals and Article 5(1). In support of the fact that Article 5(1) prevails, Article 9(1) provides that the Directive

> "shall be without prejudice to any other legal provisions such as . . .

> the law of contract. Any contractual provisions contrary to Article 6 or to the exceptions provided for in Article 5(2) and (3) shall be void."

On the principle of *inclusio unum est exclusio alterum*, Article 9(1) specifically permits contractual derogations to Article (5)1.

Adopting the most reasonable interpretation possible of the relevant recitals and Articles, it would appear that the ban on contractual provisions in Recital 18 is intended to apply to the rather narrow case of loading and running a programme and the correction of errors *in order that the program can load and run.*[74] Thus, a lawful acquirer cannot be prevented (*i.e.* by a shrink wrap licence) from running or loading a program he has bought. However, he could be prevented by contract from doing other acts, *i.e.* reproducing, adapting, arranging, altering the program and correcting errors *in order that the program fulfil its intended purpose.* It has been suggested that the intended purpose of the program must be determined objectively, having regard to the interests of both parties.[75] With regard to a software product bought off the shelf, the intended purpose is presumably the function which the manufacturer states the program will fulfil. In relation to software specifically tailored or programmed according to a customer's specification, the intended purpose will presumably be that purpose which the customer specified he wished the program to fulfil.

In the United Kingdom, the implementing legislation does not prohibit the contracting out of Article 5(1).[76]

Back-up copies

4.076 The making of a back-up copy by a person having the right to use the computer program cannot be prevented by contract insofar as it is necessary for that use.[77] This presupposes that the making of such back-up copies would not normally constitute infringement of copyright otherwise there would be no need to prevent it by contractual means.[78]

Observation, studying and testing

4.077 Article 5(3) permits lawful user:

> "without authorisation of the rightholder, to observe study or test the functioning of the program in order to determine the ideas and principles which underlie any element of the programs if he does so

[74] Art. 4(a) suggests that loading and running a program are not restricted acts save where they necessitate reproduction (which is invariably the case as the program will be loaded into RAM memory).

[75] Smith, "EC software protection directive—an attempt to understand Art. 5(1)" [1990–91] 7 *Computer Law and Security Report* 148 at p. 150.

[76] See Copyright (Computer Programs) Regs. 1992, s.11 (S.I. 1992 No. 3233).

[77] Art. 5(2). See also Art. 9(2).

[78] See CDPA 1988, ss.50A, s.296A as inserted by Copyright (Computer Programs) Regs. ss.8, 11 for implementation of this provision in U.K.

> while performing any of the acts of loading running transmitting or storing the program which he is entitled to do."

Parties are not allowed to contract out of this provision.[79] This provision is limited in scope because the user cannot actually alter or adapt the code in order to observe, test or study the program. Indeed, there seems little reason for this provision other than for the sake of clarity because the acts of observing, studying or testing do not fall within the definition of restricted acts either in the Directive or under normal copyright laws. Indeed, such a provision would normally fall within the "fair dealing" and research provisions of national copyright laws. Thus, in the United Kingdom, no such specific defence is provided although there is a specific provision which prohibits any contractual provision which purports to ban the use of "any device or means" to observe study or test the functioning of a program in order to understand the ideas and principles which underlie any element of the program.[80]

(5) Decompilation/Reverse Engineering

4.078 Article 6 introduced a reverse engineering or decompilation defence where such is "indispensable to obtain the information necessary to achieve the interoperability of an independently created program with other programs".[81]

Computer program companies often wish to ensure that their programs are "interoperable" with third party programs. "Interoperability" is the ability to connect computer systems from different makers together, to run the same software on machines of a different design and to enable different computer programs to work together.

In order to ensure "interoperability", a company will often need to decompile a program, *i.e.* alter the machine/object code of a computer program into its source code. This can be used to derive the specifications of any interfaces where the creator has chosen not to reveal them. In order to gain knowledge about the interface one must carry out the following steps;

(a) decompile the portion of the object code which implements the interface and to collect the interface information from the source code thus obtained;
(b) write the code implementing the corresponding interface on the basis of the information thus obtained.

Initial drafts of the Directive were completely silent on the matter. As a result two powerful lobby groups developed different stances as to the effect of this omission. The first, "ECIS" (European Committee for Interoperable Systems which consists of small firms: ICL, Bull, etc.) suggested

[79] Art. 9(1).
[80] s.11 1992 Reg. amending CDPA 1988, s.296A.
[81] Art. 6(1).

that the Directive should permit reverse engineering and the other group, "SAGE" (Software Action Group for Europe made up of large firms; IBM, Microsoft, etc.) took the opposite view.

Under Article 6, a rightholder's permission is not required where reproduction of the code and translation of its form are indispensable to obtain the information necessary to achieve the interoperability of an independently created computer program with other programs provided that the following conditions are met:

(1) the acts are performed by the licensee or by another person having a right to use a copy of a program, or on their behalf by a person authorised to do so;
(2) the information necessary to achieve interoperability has not previously been readily available to the above persons;[82]
(3) these acts are confined to the parts of the original program which are necessary to achieve interoperability;[83]

In the United Kingdom, the right to reproduce and translate for the purposes of interoperability has been specifically implemented as a "decompilation" right namely a right to convert a low level language into a high level language including any incidental copying of the program done in the course of decompilation.[84]

4.079 In order to further safeguard a rightholder's rights, the Directive provides that any information obtained in such a way cannot:

(a) be used for goals other than to achieve interoperability of the independently created programs;
(b) be supplied to third parties except where that is necessary to achieve the interoperability of the independently created program;
(c) be used to develop, produce or market a program substantially similar in its expression to the decompiled program, or for any other act which infringes copyright.[85]

The above right to decompile cannot be excluded by contract.[86]

A further control on the decompilation right is Article 6(3) which states that:

> "In accordance with the Berne Convention . . . the provisions of this Article may not be interpreted in such a way as to allow its application to be used in a manner which unreasonably prejudices the rightholder's legitimate interests or conflicts with the normal exploitation of the computer program."

Whilst the application of this provision is unclear, it would seem clear

[82] *Quaere* whether a rightholder can make the information available but subject to the payment of a royalty. In such circumstances, is the information "readily" available?
[83] Art. 6(1)(a)–(c).
[84] CDPA 1988, s.50B as inserted by Copyright (Computer Program) Regulation 1992, s.8.
[85] Art. 6(2)(a)–(c).
[86] Art. 9(1).

that a rightholder cannot claim as a "legitimate interest" a general right to prevent decompilation as such would negate Article 6. Thus, it is likely that Article 6(3) is a rule of interpretation.[87]

It should be noted that the above specific provisions are exhaustive and comprehensive in nature. Accordingly, a defendant should not be able to resort to "fair use" provisions in national copyright laws to justify the carrying out of restricted acts in the course of decompilation.[88] Thus, in the United Kingdom, a defendant is not permitted to argue "fair dealing" in relation to acts of decompilation.[89]

(6) Special remedies of protection

4.080 The Directive provides that Member States must provide in accordance with their national legislation appropriate remedies against persons committing any of the following acts namely:

(a) putting into circulation a copy knowing or having reason to believe that it is an infringing copy;
(b) possessing a copy for commercial purposes knowing or having reason to believe that it is an infringing copy;
(c) putting into circulation or the possession for commercial purpose of devices designed to facilitate the unauthorised removal or circumvention of any copy protection device.[90]

Furthermore, the Directive provides that infringing copies must be liable to seizure.[91]

It should however be noted that although possession of an infringing copy for private purposes is not an infringement, such copies are subject to seizure. Moreover, on a literal interpretation of subparagraph (a) and (b), a person who puts into circulation copies he wrongly believes to be infringing is liable.

[87] In some respects similar to the Protocol on European Patent Convention, Art. 69, see Chapter on Patents in Europe.

[88] In the United States, the copying of a computer program in the context of reverse engineering is permissible under the doctrine of fair use so long as the reproduction "is strictly necessary to ascertain the balance of protected information within the work"—*Atari v. Nintendo*, Court of Appeals for the Federal Circuit, judgment dated September 10, 1992. It held that the peeling of a semiconductor chip to examine the object code and further disassembly of the object code to determine the functioning of the Nintendo locking system was "fair use" (reversing *Sega Enterprises v. Accolade*, District Court). However, copying of source code was not permitted in the context of reverse engineering because copy was obtained under false pretences and fair use required that the user have "clean hands". Note that under Recital 22, the decompilation right in the Directive is deemed to be compatible with fair practice *Quaere* whether the obtaining of source code under false pretences would prevent the application of Art. 6.

[89] CDPA 1988, s.29(4) as inserted by C(CP) Regulations 1992, s.7.

[90] Art. 7(1).

[91] Art. 7(2).

(7) Term of protection

Copyright protection in a computer programs extends for 70 years after the author's death.[92] **4.081**

(8) Miscellaneous

The Directive leaves untouched other legal provisions governing computer programs such as the laws of patents,[93] trade marks, unfair competition, trade secrets, semi-conductor product protection or the law of contract.[94] Furthermore, the use and reproduction of screen displays may be protected by artistic copyright. **4.082**

(9) Transitional Provisions

The Directive applies to programs created before January 1, 1993 without prejudice to any acts concluded and rights acquired before that date.[95] **4.083**

4. EEA LEGISLATION

The only legislation adopted in the copyright field by the cut-off date of July 31, 1991 for the purposes of the EEA Agreement is the Computer Software Directive. That Directive forms part of the *acquis communautaire* of the EEA Agreement.[96] The only material amendment to the Directive for the EEA Agreement is that the exhaustion principle set out in Article 4(c) now applies to the territories of the Contracting Parties. Accordingly, the sale of a copy of a programme in the EEA exhausts the rights of the copyright owner in that programme to prevent further movement with the EEA of that copy. However, it does not affect the right to control further rental of the program or the copy.[97] **4.084**

Since the cut-off date but prior to the entry into force of the EEA, various directives have been adopted in the field of copyright by the E.C. Council. These were the Rental and Lending Right Directive, the Directive harmonising the term of copyright and allied rights and the Satellite Broadcasting and Cable Retransmission Directive. As such, they form part of the "Additional Package" which is under discussion between E.C. and EFTA experts.

[92] Dir. 93/98, Art. 11 (the "Term" Directive) which repealed the Computer Software Dir. Art. 8. In general, see para. 4.022.
[93] For protection of computer-related inventions, see Chapter on Patents in Europe, at para. 2.050.
[94] However, see, "Can the rightholder exclude Article 5(1) by contractual provision", para. 4.075.
[95] The U.K. has legislated that the implementing legislation of the Directive applies to computer programs created before January 1, 1993 as it applied to computer programs created on or after that date but that nothing in the legislation affects any term or condition where such was entered into before January 1, 1993—Copyright (Computer Programs) Regulation 1992, s.12.
[96] Annex XVII.5, EEA agreement.
[97] Annex XVII.5.

In relation to the draft proposals of the E.C., these will be subject to the EEA legislation process before becoming part of the EEA secondary legislation.[98]

5. Table of Copyright protection in Europe

Countries	Berne Convention	Rome Convention	Geneva Convention	E.C. state
Austria	●	●	●	●
Belgium	●[1]			●
Bosnia-Hercegovina	●			
Bulgaria	●			
Croatia	●			
Czech Republic	●	●	●	
Denmark	●	●	●	●
Finland	●	●	●	●
France	●	●	●	●
Germany	●	●	●	●
Greece	●	●	●	●
Hungary	●		●	
Iceland	●	●		
Ireland	●[1]	●	●	●
Italy	●	●	●	●
Luxembourg	●	●	●	●

[98] See Introduction, para. 1.039.

Republic of Macedonia	●			
Monaco	●	●	●	●
Netherlands	●	●	●	●
Norway	●	●	●	
Poland	●			
Portugal	●			●
Romania	●			
Slovakia	●	●	●	
Slovenia	●			
Spain	●	●	●	●
Sweden	●	●	●	●
Switzerland	●	●	●	
United Kingdom	●	●	●	●
Yugoslavia	●	●		

NOTES

[1] Belgium and Ireland have not acceded to the Paris version of the Berne Convention. Both are members of the Brussels version except that they have acceded to Articles 22–28 of the Stockholm Convention.

Chapter Five

DESIGN PROTECTION IN EUROPE

1. Introduction

5.001 The extent and type of protection of designs in Europe varies more than any other form of intellectual property. In the following discussion of national laws on design and Community initiatives in the area of design law, many of the problems arise from the difficulty in defining what the word "design" means. In earlier days, designs were regarded as merely cosmetic which were applied to an article for decorative effect. A clear distinction was made between the functional article and decorative design. Nowadays, with increasing sophistication in technology, such an approach is outdated. Thus, it has been said that the design of a production can be seen as extending from colour through to the patentable basis of the article.[1] Thus, the design of the shape of a car is usually an intimate combination of function (aerodynamics) and eye-appeal. Thus the following definitions have been put forward:

> "the arrangement or layout of a product"[2];
>
> "the visual appearance of a product, whether that appearance is created by a choice of a particular shape or by surface ornamentation, or by a combination of shape and ornamentation"[3];
>
> "the design of any aspect of the shape or configuration (whether internal or external) of the whole or part of an article"[4];
>
> "the features of shape, configuration, pattern or ornament applied to an article by any industrial process, being features which in the finished article appeal to and are judged by the eye but does not include (1) a method or principle of construction or (2) features of shape or configuration of an article which (a) are dictated solely by . . . function"[5];
>
> "a product of design is what it should be at the moment when it should be and in the place where it should be. It is not fanciful nor

[1] Para 3.3, Australian Discussion Paper, August 1994, on Designs.
[2] Oxford English Dictionary.
[3] Tootal, "The Law of Industrial Designs" CCH (1990).
[4] Copyright Designs and Patents Act 1988, s.213(2), in relation to the unregistered design right created under that Act in U.K. law.
[5] Definition of "design" in Registered Designs Act 1949 (U.K.).

oriented to flatter or capture the wishes of the public. It results from logical design and engineering"[6];

"the enhanced functionality of a product by way of its design."[7]

Such definitions or explanations demonstrate that there is little consensus as to what design means. It is not surprising that protection in Europe varies so widely. The protection of designs in Europe is a rather haphazard matter with varying degrees of protection being bestowed on designs by different types of law. Thus, designs can be protected by design laws which require the registration of the design with the national industrial property office, by way of an unregistered design right, by copyright laws, utility model laws, trade mark laws and unfair competition laws.

This section compares the differences in the application of national laws of European countries to designs and then examines the proposals of the European Commission in the area of design.[8]

2. National Design Protection Laws

5.002 Neither the Paris nor the Berne Convention make any detailed provisions as to the protection of industrial designs. Article 5 quinquies of the Paris Convention requires industrial designs to be protected in all the countries of the Union. Apart from this general stipulation, the Paris Convention merely requires that the protection of industrial designs shall not be liable to be forfeited for failure to work or by reason of importation of articles imported corresponding to those which are protected or by failure to deposit the industrial design.[9] The Paris Convention applies the basic principle of non-discrimination and the priority right of six months to industrial designs.[10]

Article 2(7) of the Berne Convention leaves the extent and conditions of protection of industrial designs and works of applied art to the countries of the Union. Furthermore, it permits countries of the Union to only afford to works protected in another Berne country only "such protection as is granted in that country to designs and models; however if no such protection is granted in that country, such works shall be protected

[6] Franzosi, "The Legal Protection of Industrial Design: Unfair Competition as a Basis of Protection" [1990] 5 EIPR 155, at p. 156.

[7] Introduction to the Green Paper on the Legal Protection of Industrial Design III/F/5131/91–EN.

[8] For further reading on the protection of industrial designs in Europe, see Fellner, *The Future of Legal Protection for Industrial Design* (1985) Firth, "Aspects of Design Protection in Europe" [1993] 2 EIPR 43; Horton, "Industrial Design Law: The Future for Europe" [1992] 12 EIPR 443; Cohen, "The E.C. Green Paper on the Legal Protection of Industrial Design. Half Way down the Right track—A view from the Benelux" [1992] 3 EIPR 75: Horton, "European Design Law and the Spare Parts Dilemma: the Proposed Regulation and Directive [1994] 2 EIPR 51.

[9] Arts. 5B, 5D.

[10] Art. 2.4(c)(1)

as artistic works". In so far as designs are protected by copyright as works of applied art, Article 7(4), which Article 2(7) is expressed to be without prejudice to, provides that Berne Countries must provide a minimum term of protection of at least 25 years from the making of the work. Thus, the Berne Convention envisages the protection of industrial designs by *sui generis* laws and copyright.

Accordingly, protection of designs in Europe greatly varies. Protection is afforded by means of specific design laws, copyright, trade mark and unfair competition law.[11]

(a) Specific design laws

5.003 Eleven out of the 12 Member States of the Community have introduced specific protection for industrial designs. Greece is the only country which does not have such *sui generis* laws. Most involve a registration system whereby the design sought to be protected is applied for at the national industrial property office, published, examined as to formalities but not as to prior art and registered.[12] The design invariably must relate to the appearance of the product but such may consist of ornamental features or such combined with functional features depending on the country. Thus, the United Kingdom, Spain, Italy and Germany all require an ornamental or aesthetic contribution to the design which can be considered as a capricious addition to the function of the product. The Benelux system and France are less stringent and permit the registration of the appearance of functional products.

All countries require that the design is that of the applicant (whether in fact or by operation of law) and that the design is novel. The degree of novelty required varies from country to country. Thus, Spain and Italy require the design to be novel worldwide; Benelux and Germany require that the design is not known to trade circles in their respective countries; the United Kingdom merely requires that the design is not locally known and France only requires that the applicant does not know of other designs when he created his design.[13] Examination of applications by national industrial property offices is normally restricted to mere formal examination.

The duration of the registered design varies greatly from country to country with periods ranging from unlimited renewal of an initial five year period (Portugal) to a minimum of 15 years (Italy and Benelux) from

[11] A very useful resume of the variety of national protection afforded to industrial designs in Benelux, France, Spain, Germany, Italy and the U.K. is set out in Firth "Aspects of Design Protection in Europe" [1993] 2 EIPR 45. See also Chap. 2 and 4, Green Paper. (See n. 7).

[12] In the United Kingdom, the Registrar must examine the application to ensure that it meets all the statutory requirements including novelty. He has the power to make searches for existing prior art and to require the filing of evidence. However in practice, this rarely happens. Moreover, there is no procedure for opposition before grant and the application for registration is not even advertised.

[13] Certain developments in Spanish case law have also resulted in a similar approach being taken—see Green Paper, para. 2.3.7.

date of application. The exclusive rights afforded by a valid registration generally are to prevent any one else from using the design for commercial purposes. In all Member States but Germany and France, the monopoly afforded is absolute. In the latter two countries, the monopoly afforded is against copying, *i.e.* independent design would be a defence.

In only one country, the United Kingdom, does there also exist a specific design law which does not require the registration of the design sought to be protected. Since the enactment of the Copyright Designs and Patents Act 1988, there now exists protection for a maximum of 15 years for purely functional designs without the requirement of registration.[14]

(b) Copyright

5.004 The vast majority of European countries belong to the Berne Convention. Thus protection is afforded under copyright to design and products incorporating designs where such amount to works of applied art. Germany, Portugal, Spain and Benelux require that there is a high or marked degree of artistic merit in the work.[15] In Italy, copyright plays a small part in designs. Firstly, the application for registration of a design automatically entails the loss of copyright. Secondly, the protection under copyright of designs which have not been registered are subject to the requirement of "scindibilita", *i.e.* that the artistic work can be dissociated from the product to which it is applied.[16] In the United Kingdom, copyright vests in designs but this protection is largely negated by the fact that it is not an infringement of any copyright in a design document or model recording or embodying a design incorporating anything other than an artistic work or a typeface to make an article to the design or to copy an article made to the design.[17] Of course, copyright in the United Kingdom applies to artistic works. However, copyright in artistic works which have been applied industrially expires after 25 years from the date of first marketing.[18]

(c) Utility models

5.005 Many countries have introduced specific legal instruments to cater for functional designs which have an exclusive technical function but are not sufficiently inventive to be protected under patent law. This is available in Germany, Greece, Italy, Spain and Portugal, although the degree of inventive step differs. The usefulness of the utility patents is that examination only takes place if challenged by a potential infringer.[19]

[14] See Copyright Designs and Patents Act 1988, s.213 *et seq.*

[15] However, case law in Benelux has given a broad interpretation to this requirement, *Screenoprints Ltd v. Citroen Nederland*, Benelux Court of Justice, May 22, 1987.

[16] See Franzosi, "The Legal Protection of Industrial Design: Unfair Competition as a Basis of Protection" [1990] 5 EIPR 154 as to the weakness of this approach.

[17] CDPA 1988, s.51.

[18] CDPA 1988, s.52.

[19] See a review of utility models by Dr. Haertel, meeting on Union of European Practitioners in Industrial Property, Brussels summarised in Union Bulletin 21/3/1992.

(d) Unfair competition and trade mark laws

5.006 It is possible in most European countries (or under the law of passing-off in the United Kingdom) to invoke unfair competition laws where consumers are confused as to the trade origin of two products. Most continental countries recognise slavish imitation or exploitation of another's reputation as actionable. In France, arguments of exploitation of a design have succeeded even where confusion has been absent. The limitation of unfair competition protection for designed products is that normally they will require an element of capricious distinctiveness readily recognisable to the public. In a typical well-designed but commonplace functional object, this will often not be the case.[20]

Under most Member States' trade mark laws and in the Trade Mark Directive, shapes of objects are registrable as trade marks.[21] However, if the trade mark consists exclusively of the shape which results from the nature of the goods themselves or the shape is necessary to give a technical result, then the shape may not be registered.[22]

(e) Cumulative protection

5.007 Most European countries permit a designed product to enjoy more than one type of legal protection. There are two notable exceptions: Italy where the application for registered design deprives a product of copyright or trade mark protection and the United Kingdom where cumulative protection under copyright and the unregistered design right is prevented.[23]

3. Community Legislation

(a) Green paper on the protection of industrial design

5.008 In 1991, the Commission published a Green Paper on the Legal Protection of Industrial Design. The Commission had long recognised that national laws on design in the Member States was unsatisfactory. Firstly, they failed to provide adequate protection for designs as they only protected effectively the ornamentative features of a design rather than the salient features of a contemporary industrial design which it described as "the enhanced functionality of a product by way of its design".[24] Secondly, the Commission was concerned about the disparate protection of designs in Member States and the effect that had on the creation of an internal market.[25] Accordingly, it proposed in the Green Paper the intro-

[20] *e.g.* see *Hodgkinson & Corby Ltd v Wards* [1995] F.S.R. 189. H.C. where a passing-off action based on a slavish imitation of a functional object (an invalidity cushion) failed.
[21] Art. 2.
[22] Trade Mark Dir. Art. 3(e). See para. 3.065.
[23] See CDPA 1988, s.51, s.236.
[24] Green Paper, p. 2.
[25] See s.3.2, *et seq.*

duction of a Community Design Regulation accompanied with a limited harmonising directive of Member States' designs laws. The first proposal drew heavily on a proposal for a Community Design by the Max Planck Institute for Foreign and International Patent, Copyright and Competition Law. The proposal has been substantially altered following the European Parliament's amendments and extensive lobbying by industry and practitioners alike. The Commission has now adopted a new draft Regulation[26] and a new draft Directive.[27] It is clear that even this proposal will generate considerable discussion and argument and it will probably be some time before there is legislation in this area.[28]

(i) Proposed community design regulation

5.009 The essence of the proposal is that designs will be protected in the Community under such a regulation in two different ways:

—an Unregistered Community Design not subject to any deposit formalities with a short term of protection (three years);
—a Registered Community Design, on the basis of an application to be filed with a Community Design Office to be set up with a term of protection which could reach 25 years.

Both unregistered Community design and registered Community design would be subject to the same conditions for protection but the former would provide protection against unauthorised copying whereas the latter would provide absolute protection against any product which is of similar design. The unregistered Community Design can be compared in broad terms with the unregistered design right in the United Kingdom created by the Copyright Designs and Patents Act 1988 which vests automatically in a design and protects the owner against unauthorised copying. The Registered Community Design can be compared to the various systems of registered design protection that exist in Member States.[29]

5.010 *Definition of design*—the Commission's approach has been to perceive design as an "intimate merger of functionalism and aesthetic value".[30] It is clear that the Commission accepts that aesthetics need play no part in a design and that a good design may merely result in the enhanced functional improvement of a product. The Commission was keen to avoid giving protection to ideas rather than the shape of a product, the former being the province of patent law. It has now substan-

[26] COM DOC 93/342, [1994] O.J. C37/20.
[27] COM DOC 93/344, [1993] O.J. C345/14.
[28] Indeed, there is no real impetus to legislate in this matter because there is at present no need to secure reciprocal protection in the U.S. for E.C. nationals because the U.S. has not implemented specific design protection for essentially functional designs—see Horton "European Design Law and the Spare Parts Dilemma: the Proposed Regulation and Directive" [1994] 2 EIPR 51, at p. 57.
[29] *i.e.* see Registered Designs Act 1949, (U.K.).
[30] See Green Paper, s.5.4.1.

tially amended its definition of design from its original proposal. It now reads:

> "The appearance of the whole or part of a product resulting from the specific features of the lines, contours, shape and/or materials of the products itself and/or its ornamentation."[31]

"Product" itself is defined as "any industrial or handicraft item, including parts intended to be assembled into a complex item, sets or composition of items, packaging, get-ups, graphic symbols and typographic typefaces but excluding a computer program or a semi-conductor product."[32]

The avowed aim of the Commission is to provide a fully modern design protection system adapted to the reality of design activities and to the need of the users of the system.[33] The current definition is very different from that first proposed. The important condition is that of "appearance". The Explanatory Memorandum states that the definition of design means that any feature of appearance which can be perceived by the human senses as regards sight and tactility are features of design. It also states that weight and flexibility may be design features. However, these features do not seem to fall within the word "appearance".[34] A debatable issue is whether the regulation protects internal features. The regulation protects the appearance of parts of a product. Does this cover parts of a product which are not seen by the potential purchaser but can be seen upon disassembly? It is submitted that unless the potential purchaser can see it without disassembly, protection cannot be afforded to such a part under the Regulation. Therefore, the appearance of the engine under the bonnet of a car would be protected but not the camshaft.

5.011 *Protection in a community design*—a design (as defined above) is capable of protection as a Community Design to the extent that it is new and has an individual character.[35] A Community Design has unitary character in the Community and cannot be registered, transferred or surrendered or declared invalid save in respect of the whole Community.[36]

A Community design right cannot subsist in a design to the extent that the realisation of a technical function leaves no freedom as regards arbitrary features of appearance.[37] This provision could be dangerous. For instance, many designs are created so as to achieve maximum functional effect. Could a defendant who copies such a design claim that he is entitled to copy such a design because the design features of the original item are functional in nature and constitute the best way of achieving the

[31] Art. 3(a).
[32] Art. 3(b).
[33] Explanatory Memorandum, para. 4.5.
[34] See Horton, "European Design Law and the Spare Parts Dilemma: the Proposed Regulation and Directive" [1994] 2 EIPR 51.
[35] Art. 4(1).
[36] Art. 1(3).
[37] Art. 9(1).

desired function? The emphasis on "arbitrary" features means that a designer of a functional item will often be hard pressed to prove that certain features of his design were chosen arbitrarily rather than to assist in achieving the desired function of the product. Moreover, what is the position where two or more designs are capable of achieving the desired technical function? Is a design merely "arbitrary" because another design can achieve the same function?[38] Furthermore, design protection does not subsist in interconnections.[39]

5.012 *Novelty and originality of design*—a design is only capable of protection as a Community design if it is new and has an "individual character".[40] A design is considered new if no identical design has been made available to the public before the "date of reference" but will not be considered new if its features differ only in immaterial details to other designs.[41] "Made available to the public" is defined as a design which has been published, exhibited, used in trade or otherwise disclosed. It does not include disclosures to third parties under explicit or implicit conditions of confidentiality.[42] "Date of reference" is for an unregistered Community design, the date on which the design for which protection is claimed was first made available to the public and for a registered Community design, the date of filing the application for registration or if priority is claimed, the date or priority.[43]

A design has "individual character" if the overall impression it produces on the informed user differs significantly from the overall impression produced on such a user by any qualifying designs. A design qualifies as "prior art" for the purposes of the test of individual character if (a) it was commercialised in the market place at the date of reference whether in the Community or elsewhere or (b) published following registration as a registered Community design or as a design right of a Member State provided that protection has not expired at the date of reference.[44] The "informed user" is specifically stated in the Explanatory Memorandum not to be a designs expert.[45] In assessing individual character, the informed user should give more weight as a matter of prin-

[38] In England, see decision of *Amp Inc v Utilux Pty Ltd* [1972] RPC 103 where the House of Lords held in considering a provision in the 1949 Registered Designs Act that excluded protection for designs dictated solely by function that the fact that there were alternative but equally functional designs was irrelevant. The crucial criterion was whether a design was arrived at purely to meet functional criteria.

[39] See below, para. 5.017.

[40] Art. 4–6.

[41] Art. 5(1).

[42] Art. 5(2).

[43] Art. 7. Under the Paris Convention, any person who files an application for an industrial design in a Contracting State benefits from a six month "grace period"—Paris Convention, Art. 4(C)(1). See draft Reg. Arts. 43 *et seq.*

[44] Art. 6(2)(a), (b).

[45] See Horton, "European Design Law and the Spare Parts Dilemma: the Proposed Regulation and Directive" [1994] 2 EIPR 51, at p. 52 as to discussion on the meaning of "informed user".

ciple to common features than differences and the degree of freedom of the designer in developing the design should be taken into consideration.[46]

The regulation provides that for a 12 month "grace period" prior to the filing date (or other priority date) disclosures to the public made by the designer or his successor in title or by third parties on behalf of the designer will not be taken into account for the purposes of determining novelty or individual character.[47] This "grace period" is included to allow designers to test their products embodying the design on the marketplace before deciding whether to apply for a Community design.[48] In certain circumstances, the design may be disclosed to the public as a consequence of an abuse (*i.e.* an unauthorised disclosure). Such disclosures are also subject to a grace period of 12 months. However, if such a disclosure leads to registration of a Community design or other design right in a Member State, then the grace period does not apply and the proper course of action is to apply for a transfer of the registered right under Article 16 of the Regulation or the appropriate national provision.[49] It should be noted that the grace period is in *addition* to the priority period provided for under the Paris Convention for industrial designs of six months.[50]

5.013 *Exclusive rights*—The Commission has proposed that the protection conferred on by a Community Design shall extend to designs which in the eyes of the informed user display a significantly similar overall impression to that of the Community Design.[51] In order to assess the scope of protection, common features are as a matter of principle to be given more weight than differences and the degree of freedom of the designer in developing his design is to be taken into account.[52]

In relation to the Unregistered Community Design, a critical difference between the unregistered and registered Community design is that the former only gives protection against unauthorised reproduction of its design as opposed to an absolute monopoly which exists for a registered design.[53]

The unregistered design right merely gives the holder the right to prevent any third party from copying his design or from using a copied design.[54] The Registered design right confers on the holder the much stronger exclusive right to use the design and to prevent any third party

[46] Art. 6(3). If there is no degree of freedom in the design of a function item then no Community design right can subsist in it—Art. 9.
[47] Art. 8.
[48] Recital 19.
[49] See Horton, "European Design Law and the Spare Parts Dilemma: the Proposed Regulation and Directive" [1994] 2 EIPR 51, at p. 53.
[50] Art. 43–46.
[51] Art. 11(1).
[52] Art. 11(2). See similar approach to issue of novelty and originality above, para. 5.012.
[53] Art. 17, 18.
[54] Art. 20.

from using a design included within the scope of protection of the registered Community design.[55]

The rights do not extend to acts done privately done and for non-commercial purposes, acts done for experimental purposes, acts of reproduction for the purposes of making citations or teaching provided such does not unduly prejudice the normal exploitation of the design and that mention is made of the source.[56] In addition, the rights conferred by a Community design do not extend to the equipment on ships and aircraft registered in a third country temporarily entering the Community and spare parts for such craft.[57]

Term of Protection

5.014 **Registered community design**—it is suggested that the term of protection for the Registered Community Design be for a period of five years extendible to 25 years from the date of filing.[58]

5.015 **Unregistered community design**—The Directive provides that an unregistered design right exists for three years from the date the design was first made available to the public.[59]

5.016 *Ownership of community designs*—This belongs to the designer or his successor-in-title.[60] It is proposed that the question of a design made by an employee belongs to the employer unless otherwise provided for by contract.[61]

5.017 *Interconnections*—Article 9(b) provides that a Community design right shall not subsist in a design to the extent that it must necessarily be reproduced in its exact form and dimensions in order to permit the product in which the design is incorporated or to which it is applied to be mechanically assembled or connected with another product.[62] The purpose of such a provision has been stated by the Commission so as to enhance the interoperability of products of different makes and to prevent manufacturers of design products from creating captive markets. Thus, the Commission has stated in its Explanatory Memorandum that the dimensions of the fitting of an exhaust pipe dictated by the necessity of fitting the exhaust pipe to a specific car model cannot constitute a protectable design element since the dimensions are dictated by those of the underside of the car. To a certain extent, Article 9(a), which provides that a Community design right does not subsist in a design to the extent that

[55] Art. 21.
[56] Art. 22.
[57] Art. 22(2).
[58] Art. 13.
[59] Art. 7(a), 12.
[60] Art. 14.
[61] Art. 14(2).
[62] Art. 9(b).

the realisation of a technical function leaves no freedom as regards arbitrary features, covers this point.[63] Clearly, there is no freedom in the design of the exhaust pipe with regards to its dimensions. Moreover, in considering the scope of protection of the exhaust pipe, the degree of freedom of the designer must be taken into account.[64]

In order to allay the concerns of manufacturers of modular equipment, *e.g.* Lego, interstacking chairs, etc., Article 9(c) stated that notwithstanding Article 9(b), a Community design right shall subsist in a design serving the purposes of allowing simultaneous and infinite or multiple assembly or connection of identical or mutually interchangeable products within a modular system. Therefore, if the innovative design consists in the design of the interconnecting elements, then protection is available.[65]

5.018 *Repair*—the above exception to protection for "interconnections" does not relate specifically to spare parts. An exhaust pipe must be of a specific size and dimension in order to fit a car. In United Kingdom design law parlance, it "must fit". However, in many cases, consumers wish to purchase spare parts for repair purposes will be concerned with the overall appearance of the product and the part. For instance, a consumer purchasing a hub cap for a car will want it to match with the other hub caps. In United Kingdom design law parlance, it "must match". Whilst under English law, exceptions to protection under the unregistered design right exist for "must match" and "must fit" products, no such protection *per se* is extended to "must match" products under the proposed regulation.

However, the Commission has proposed a "right to repair" clause which in some respect equates with the "must match" provision under English law.[66] Under this clause, it is not an infringement of a Community registered design to use such a design three years after from the first putting on the market of a product incorporating the Community registered design provided that:

(a) the product incorporating the design or to which the design is applied is a part of a complex product upon whose appearance the protected design is dependent;
(b) the purpose of such a use is to permit the repair of the complex product so as to restore its original appearance; and
(c) the public is not misled as to the origin of the product used for the repair.[67]

The three year period exactly coincides with the term of protection

[63] Art. 9(a).
[64] Art. 11(2).
[65] See Horton, "European Design Law and the Spare Parts Dilemma: the Proposed Regulation and Directive" [1994] 2 EIPR 51 at p. 54.
[66] See Horton, "European Design Law and the Spare Parts Dilemma: the Proposed Regulation and Directive" [1994] 2 EIPR 51, p. 55.
[67] Art. 23.

offered under the unregistered Community design right. Accordingly, the unregistered right will have expired before use can be made of this provision by a spare part manufacturer. The Explanatory Memorandum to this Article explicitly states that because the provision makes an inroad into the rights of the right holder, it should be applicable only under strict conditions.

5.019 *Other provisions*—in respect of the prosecution of Community design applications, litigation and jurisdiction aspects, the Community Design Regulation closely mirrors the Community Trade Mark Regulation.[68] Thus, the draft Regulation sets up a Community Design Office which would be in charge of applications to register designs and issues of validity. Community Design Courts are to be established in Member States for the purposes of litigating on Community Design. National Design rights are to co-exist with Community Design rights.

(ii) Proposed harmonising directive

5.020 The Commission has also published a proposal for a Directive harmonising the design laws of Member States as a parallel measure to the proposed Community Design Regulation.[69] The proposed Directive adopts the same substantive principles as appear in the Regulation. Importantly, the draft Directive only seeks to harmonise the laws of the Member States in relation to *registered* designs. The Commission proposes that the National Design laws of Member States be approximated so that the definition of design, the criteria of novelty and distinctiveness, the grace period, the extent of protection, the exclusion of interconnections from protection, the right to repair and the term of protection coincide with the corresponding provision in the draft Regulation for a Community Design.[70]

The Directive requires that Member States must protect designs by way of a *sui generis* design protection laws and not rely exclusively upon copyright law.[71] In keeping with the concept of cumulative protection, the Directive is expressed to be without prejudice to any legal provisions of the Community or of Member States relating to unregistered design rights, trade marks or other distinctive signs, patents and utility models, typefaces, civil liability or unfair competition.[72] Moreover, Article 18 of the directive provides:

"Pending further harmonisation of the laws of copyright of the

[68] See, para. 3.031 *et seq*.
[69] COM DOC 93/344, [1993] O.J. C345/14.
[70] Art. 1, 3–7, 9–10, 12–14. The only exception is that under the definition of "design" in the Directive, semiconductor products are not excluded as they are in the Regulation. This is because the Directive on the legal protection of topographies of semiconductor products do not preclude implementation of its provisions by means of national designs legislation—see Explanatory Memorandum.
[71] Art. 3 and the Explanatory Memorandum.
[72] Art. 17.

> Member States, a design protected by a design right unregistered in or for a Member State in accordance with this directive shall also be eligible for protection under the law of copyright of that State as from the date on which the design was created or fixed in any form, irrespective of the number of products in which such design is intended to be incorporated or to which it is intended to be applied and irrespective of whether the design can be dissociated from the products in which it is intended to be applied. The extent to which, and the conditions under which, such a protection is conferred, including the level of originality required, shall be determined by each Member State.[73]

The Explanatory Memorandum explains Article 18 as making the cumulative application of copyright law and specific design protection law mandatory and that it implies that national legislation needs to be amended where it foresees that copyright protection cannot or can only under certain conditions be cumulated with protection under specific design protection law. Prima facie, this affects U.K. legislation whereby it is not an infringement of copyright in a design document or model recording or embodying a design for anything other than an artistic work or a typeface to make an article to the design or to copy an article made to the design.[74] However, the last sentence of Article 18(1) dilutes its effect although to what extent it is unclear.[75] Importantly, protection under the copyright law of a Member State may not discriminate against designs whose country of origin is another Member State even if the design does not fulfil the conditions for protection under the law of copyright of that State.[76] This rule complements the jurisprudence of the ECJ which holds that it is wrong for the intellectual property laws of one Member State to indirectly discriminate against a national of another Member State.[77] If the draft provision is enacted, it will be unlawful to discriminate both on the grounds of the nationality of the author of the design and the origin of the design.

It is intended that Member States should enact the directive by October 31, 1996.

[73] Art. 18(1). Thus, national legislation which provides that copyright protection cannot or can only under certain conditions be cumulated with protection under specific design protection must be amended—see Explanatory Memorandum.

[74] s. 51 Copyright Designs and Patents Act 1988. "Design" is designed for the purposes of s.51 as the design of any aspect of the shape or configuration (whether internal or external) of the whole or part of an article, other than surface decoration.

[75] The Explanatory Memorandum states that "the conditions of application of copyright protection and in particular, the question relating to the level of originality required for the application of copyright protection is however pending a possible future harmonisation of the originality requirement left to national law". This suggests that national laws can set the level of originality for copyright protection much higher than that for design protection but apart from that and possible formal requirements, it must confer copyright protection on designs.

[76] Art. 18(2).

[77] *e.g.* see Case C–92/92 *Phil Collins v. IMTRAT* [1993] 3 C.M.L.R. 773, ECJ.

CHAPTER SIX

PLANT VARIETY RIGHTS IN EUROPE

1. INTRODUCTION

6.001 Plant breeding in Europe is big business. The moral and financial incentives to breed agricultural crop varieties which have advantageous characteristics (*i.e.* high yield, low water requirement, winterhardiness, pest resistance, etc.) for a world with a growing population are clear. Plant breeding is also prevalent in the field of fruit, flowers and in some instances, drugs. Crops will normally be soil specific whereas flowers tend to either be more easily grown or the right soil conditions can be more easily reproduced. This means that there is greater trade in the latter than the former. Breeding new varieties is often a time-consuming and expensive business. Many attempts to come up with a new, commercially viable and advantageous variety will not succeed. Often, it can take up to 10 years before a new variety becomes commercially available. Indeed, 12 years is the average time for new cereal varieties.

Plant variety rights (or plant breeder's rights as they are often called) have a twofold purpose. First, they provide a mechanism of reward and incentive to plant breeders. Secondly, they provide a method of controlling the reproduction of varieties which breeders have created. This second aspect is peculiar to plant breeding. Commercial exploitation is not the sole rationale behind the breeding of new varieties. Many plant breeding institutions are more concerned with the improvement of existing stock through the advancement of knowledge whilst also providing necessary crops is a critical rationale behind many programmes. For these bodies, the legal ability to exclusively control the use of reproductive and propagating material of varieties that they have bred is paramount in order to maintain the variety.

Plant variety rights are confined to the protection of the *reproductive or propagating* material of a variety. No rights exist in relation to the actual produce of plant varieties provided they are not used for the purposes of reproducing the variety. Thus, a plant variety rights' owner has no control over grain produced by his variety but can prevent that grain (if capable of being propagated) from being used to reproduce more grain of the same variety.[1]

[1] However, where the holder of plant variety rights has not had reasonable opportunity to exercise his rights against the propagative or reproductive material, he may exercise his rights in relation to the harvested material—see para. 6.014.

In 1961, the International Convention for the Protection of New Varieties ("the UPOV Convention") was concluded in Paris and signed by most European countries.[2] Its objective was to provide *sui generis* protection for plant varieties for a limited period provided that certain criteria were met. It was felt to be imperative to adopt a system different to the patent system. The UPOV Convention does not provide for a single system as for example under the European Patent Convention. Rather, it simply provides the requirements which have to be adhered to by countries wishing to set up national plant variety rights. The Convention was revised at Geneva in 1972 and 1978 and has recently been revised at a Diplomatic Conference held in Geneva in March 1991. This last revision incorporated some considerable changes and was the result of extensive discussions amongst interested bodies.[3]

The 1991 Convention has been signed by most European countries but at time of writing, none have ratified it. This means that it is the 1978 version that is currently ratified in the vast majority of European countries. However, it is anticipated that the 1991 Convention will soon be ratified by several countries. Accordingly, the 1991 Convention is discussed below but reference is made to the 1978 Convention where there is a material difference.

As plant breeders' rights are of recent invention and very much *sui generis*, countries that have acceded to the UPOV Convention have not inherited any corpus of law relating to plant breeders' rights. Furthermore, under the UPOV Convention, countries that ratify the UPOV Convention are required before depositing an instrument of ratification to ask the UPOV Council to advise it in respect of the conformity of its laws with the provisions of the Convention.[4] This has resulted in a very high degree of similarity between Member States' laws.[5] Moreover, litigation is rare and thus no substantial case law has developed. The main reason for this is that the system was set up by plant breeders for plant breeders and the tribunals set up by national systems which hear disputes are made up of scientists as well as lawyers and thus problems can normally be remedied without recourse to full trial. Thus, there is little to be gained from carrying out a comparison of the law of plant breeders' rights in European countries. Of course, application and interpretation of the UPOV Convention as enacted nationally by national tribunals and states has and shall vary.[6]

[2] Belgium, France, Federal Republic of Germany, Italy and Holland adopted it in 1961; the United Kingdom and Sweden in 1962 and Ireland, Hungary, Spain and Switzerland in 1969.

[3] See Greengrass, "The 1991 Act of the UPOV Convention" [1991] 12 EIPR 466.

[4] *e.g.* see 1991 Convention, Art. 34(3).

[5] For U.K., see the Plant Varieties and Seeds Act 1964 (as amended by the Plant Varieties Act 1983).

[6] There will often be considerable variation is the extent of *ex officio* testing of varieties by national offices prior to the grant of rights. Thus, in *Daehnfeldt v. Controller of Plant Varieties* [1976] FSR 94, an appeal from a decision of the Controller to the Plant Variety Rights Tribunal, the issue was whether the Italian ryegrass variety named PREGO was

Recently, plant variety rights have become more important in the light of the failure of the Community directive on the legal protection of biotechnology and the requirement under Article 27(3) of the GATT/TRIPS agreement that all countries should provide either patent or plant variety rights protection for new plant varieties.

At a Community level, the Commission has been active in seeking to harmonise plant variety protection within the European Union. On July 27, 1994, the European Council adopted the Regulation on Community plant variety rights and it is due to come into force on April 27, 1995.[7] This will affect the whole structure of plant variety rights within the EU. The object of the Regulation is to create a Community regime which although coexisting with national regimes, allows for the grant of a Community Plant Variety Right valid throughout the Community.

The effect of the EC Regulation and the 1991 UPOV Convention is that the authorities of most European countries will shortly be amending their existing PVR legislation to comply with their international obligations.

2. 1991 UPOV Convention

(a) Introduction

6.002 The 1991 UPOV Convention is the most recent revision of the original 1961 UPOV Convention. The previous revision was the 1978 revision and most European countries have enacted that into domestic legislation.[8] The 1991 Convention has been signed by 16 countries of which 11 are European. No European country has so far ratified it.[9] The 1991 Convention will come into force one month after five states have deposited instruments of ratification provided that at least three of such instruments are deposited by existing member states of UPOV.[10] Once it comes into force, the 1978 Act will be closed to further accessions.

The 1991 Convention will become of greater international importance than the 1978 Convention because of the GATT/TRIPS Agreement which requires countries to provide patent or plant variety rights protection for plant varieties. Prior to the agreement, the UPOV Convention

sufficiently distinct from TIARA and VEJRUP. The British examiners had been unable to distinguish clearly between these varieties and had refused registration. In contrast, plant breeders' rights had been granted in Germany and Denmark because in the former, the German authority had not compared PREGO against VEJRUP and the tests in Denmark had been very bare and uninformative. The appeal was unsuccessful and it is believed that the German authorities then revoked the rights—an example of cooperation between the national authorities. See Byrne, "The Agritechnical Criteria in Plant Breeders' Rights Law" [1983] Industrial Property 293 at p. 299.

[7] E.C. Council Regulation 2100/94 [1994] L227/1.

[8] There is a table at the end of this chapter which sets out those countries which have signed and/or ratified the various revisions of the UPOV Convention. See para. 6.046, below.

[9] Australia is the first country to ratify it and has only just done so.

[10] Art. 37.

was seen as essentially European in content and context. With non-European countries looking to comply with their obligation under the GATT/TRIPS agreement, the 1991 UPOV Convention will provide a tried and tested route.

(b) Fundamental principles of 1991 UPOV Convention

6.003 The 1991 Convention does not alter the fundamental principles of the previous conventions, namely that contracting parties are to grant and to protect breeders' rights in the reproductive and propagating material of plant varieties.[11] Under the system of the Convention, breeders who have produced a new variety that is distinct, uniform and stable may apply for registration of its variety at a national level. If registration is obtained, the proprietor has the exclusive right to commercially exploit the reproductive or propagative material of variety. The UPOV Convention lays down that such protection shall last for a minimum of 20 years and shall not be shorter than 25 years for trees and vines. In some cases, like potatoes, the rights can last up to 30 years. It is important to emphasise that all the UPOV Conventions only protect the reproductive material of a variety and not the variety itself. This is often why many refer to the system as plant *breeders'* rights rather than variety rights.

(c) Conditions for protection for plant varieties

6.004 Protection is only granted to plant "varieties". Varieties should be distinguished from genera and species which are higher orders.[12] Such varieties must be new, distinct, uniform and stable.[13] Apart from this requirement, the grant of a breeder's right can only be subject to the requirement that it is designated by a denomination and that the application complies with the formalities provided for by the law of the state where the application has been filed.[14] The aim of the 1991 Convention is that protection is granted to plant varieties of all genera and species. However, the 1991 Convention provides for a transitional period up to 10 years whereby Contracting States need not provide protection for all genera.[15]

[11] Art. 2.

[12] By way of example, "cats" are genera, "domestic cats" constitute a species of cats and "tabby cats" constitute a variety of domestic cats. Because the definition of "variety" in the 1991 UPOV Convention is that of a plant grouping within a single botanical taxon of the "lowest known rank", then, using the example above, if there were clearly recognisable subvarieties of tabby cats, *i.e.* long-haired and short-haired tabby cats, the grouping "tabby cat" would not constitute a "variety" for the purposes of an animal equivalent to the 1991 UPOV Convention as it would not be a grouping at the lowest known rank.

[13] Art. 5.

[14] Art. 5(2).

[15] Art. 3. Thus, states already members of UPOV must provide protection for all plant species and genera after the end of five years from the date of ratification and new UPOV states must do so within 10 years from the date of ratification.

(i) Variety

6.005 "Variety" is defined under the 1991 UPOV Convention as

> "A plant grouping within a single botanical taxon of the lowest known rank, which grouping irrespective of whether the conditions for the grant of a breeder's rights are fully met, can be:
> — defined by the expression of the characteristics resulting from a given genotype or combination of genotypes;
> — distinguished from any other plant grouping by the expression of at least one of the said characteristics and;
> — considered as a unit with regard to its suitability for being propagated unchanged."[16]

In the 1978 Convention, there is no definition of "variety". The 1961 Convention defined "variety" as "any cultivar, clone, line, stock or hybrid which is capable of cultivation" and which is homogeneous and stable.[17] Whether a definition of variety was required or even desirable caused considerable discussion. This was because under Article 53(b) of the European Patent Convention, patents cannot be granted for "plant or animal *varieties* or essentially biological processes for the production of plants or animals".[18] Thus, any definition of "variety" by UPOV was likely to affect the patentability of a plant invention. Indeed, in *Ciba-Geigy*,[19] the Technical Board of Appeal of the European Patent Office interpreted the meaning of "plant variety" by reference to the 1961 UPOV Convention.[20] It was thus a concern that the definition of "variety" did not adversely affect the patentability of plant innovations.[21] Recently, the EPO has said that the concept of plant varieties under A. 53(b) EPC refers to any plant grouping within a single botanical taxon of the lowest known rank which irrespective of whether it would be eligible for protection under the UPOV Convention is characterised by at least one single transmissible characteristic distinguishing it from other plant groupings and which is sufficiently homogeneous and stable in its relevant characteristics (referring to the above definition of variety).[22]

The definition of "variety" means that it merely defines variety at a scientific level and is irrespective as to whether or not the conditions for the grant of a breeder's rights are fully met. This differs from previous UPOV conventions where the definition of variety was almost equivalent to a variety capable of being protected under the Convention. In framing

[16] Art. 1(vi).
[17] "Homogeneous" tends to be interchanged with "uniform". For the purposes of plant variety rights, the two mean the same.
[18] See Chap. Two at para. 2.051 *et seq.*
[19] [1979–1985] EPOR, Vol. C 758.
[20] The TBA's approach was confirmed in *Lubrizol I* [1990] EPOR 177.
[21] Thus, patent circles were concerned that the definition of "variety" in the 1991 UPOV Convention might embrace a plant cell line—see Greengrass, "The 1991 Act of the UPOV Convention" [1991] 12 EIPR 466, at p. 467.
[22] T356/93 Plant Genetic System and Biogen EPOR [1995] 357 at para. 23. See also para. 2.053.

a definition for the 1991 Convention, it was considered that the definition of variety should be less stringent than the requirements for a variety to be protected.[23] Thus, the three indents in the definition correspond respectively to the requirements of uniformity, distinctness and stability but are considered to set these requirements at a lower level than that necessary for protection.[24] The effect of this is that when considering whether a plant variety satisfies the requirements under the UPOV Convention, due regard can be taken of varieties which themselves do not qualify for protection. For example, a variety will only qualify for protection under the Convention if it is clearly distinguishable from any other variety whose existence is a matter of common knowledge at the time of filing of the application. If the variety in issue is not distinguishable from another variety then it does not qualify for protection even if the latter variety does not itself qualify for protection. In relation to agricultural and some vegetable varieties, in the United Kingdom, this distinction may not count for much as these must be entered on a national list before they can be commercially used. The requirements for registration on the national list (which normally takes place at the same time as assessment for the purposes of plant variety rights) are similar to that for plant variety rights. Thus, these varieties will not be commercially exploitable *i.e.* become commonly known unless they qualify for PVR. However, in relation to other types of plants (*i.e.* horticultural varieties), there is no requirement of national registration.

(ii) National treatment

6.006 The 1991 UPOV Convention, as with the previous conventions, provides that Contracting States must not discriminate in the grant of breeders' rights between their own nationals and nationals of another Contracting State.[25]

(iii) Cumulative Protection

6.007 The 1991 UPOV Convention abolishes the ban on double protection under both patent and plant variety law in the 1978 Convention.[26] Applicants now will be able to obtain both patent protection and plant variety rights for a plant variety. The effectiveness of the abolishment of such a requirement will be rather one-sided because of the ban under the EPC of the patenting of "plant varieties". Such double protection in

[23] See Greengrass, "The 1991 Act of the UPOV Convention" [1991] 12 EIPR 466, at p. 467.

[24] *ibid.*

[25] Art. 4. Where the state is an intergovernmental organisation, "nationals" means nationals of the states belonging to that organisation—Art. 4(2).

[26] See 1978 UPOV Convention, Art. 2(1). Greengrass, "The 1991 Act of the UPOV Convention" [1991] 12 EIPR 466 at p. 467, states that Member States are free to enact legislation that an applicant must decide between patent or plant breeders' rights. This seems to conflict with Art. 2 which baldly states that Contracting States *shall* grant breeders rights to those varieties protectable under the Convention.

countries which adhere to the EPC and the 1991 UPOV Convention will only be possible where the EPO or a national patent office takes the view that a plant innovation is not a "plant variety" but the corresponding national plant varieties office holds that such is a "plant variety". This is unlikely.[27]

(iv) Protection of plant genera and species

6.008 Under the 1978 Convention, no requirement was placed on Contracting States to protect varieties in all plant genera and species. It merely required that acceding states protect five genera or species on accession and that they should protect a minimum of 24 genera or species within eight years.[28] The 1991 Convention distinguishes between States which have already ratified the UPOV Convention and new members of UPOV. In the former case, such states must extend protection to all genera and species by the end of five years from the date that the state is bound by the 1991 Convention. In the latter case, new members must initially protect a minimum of 15 plant genera and species and within 10 years from being bound by the Convention, all plant genera and species.[29] This will mean that a Contracting State will have eventually to confer protection even on species that cannot be grown in that country.

(v) Conditions of protection

6.009 As mentioned earlier, breeders' rights can be granted where the variety is new, distinct, uniform and stable and has been designated by a denomination which is called its generic designation.[30] Each variety must be examined prior to the grant of plant variety rights in order to demonstrate that it fulfils the above requirements. In comparing varieties for the purposes of whether such criteria are met, UPOV at Geneva provides guidelines which are intended to provide Contracting States with a common basis for testing varieties and establishing varietal descriptions in a standardised form. These guidelines are prepared for each plant species and regularly updated to take account of technical progress and new insights on species. Furthermore, they provide information on the relevant characteristics for each species which should be taken into account in deciding whether plant breeders' rights should be granted. For instance, relevant characteristics for a flower could include plant height, colour of stem, leaf width, thickness and type of flower head. Clearly, relevant characteristics for flowers will be different to those for crop varieties.

[27] This is even more so because the EPC have referred to the UPOV Convention in order to determine the meaning of "variety"—see T49/83, *CIBA-GEIGY* [1984] OJEPO 112, [1979–1985] EPOR Vol. C 758.

[28] 1978 Convention, Art. 4. There is a provision in Art. 4 that Contracting States should progressively expand protection to as many genera and species as possible although it is not a binding provision.

[29] 1991 Convention, Art. 3.

[30] Art. 5, 20.

(1) Novelty

6.010 The 1991 UPOV Convention states:

> "The variety shall be deemed to be new if, at the date of filing of the application for a breeder's right, propagating or harvested material of the variety has not been sold or otherwise disposed of to others, by or with the consent of the breeder, for the purposes of exploitation of the variety:
> (i) in the territory of the Contracting Party in which the application has been filed earlier than one year before that date and
> (ii) in a territory other than that of the Contracting Party in which the application has been filed earlier than four years or, in the case of trees or of vines, earlier than six years before the said date."[31]

The novelty test for plant variety rights is a very different concept from that of novelty in patent law. The only concern is whether the plant variety *in issue* has been marketed before by or with the consent of the breeder. In patent law, the invention in issue must have novel features when compared to the prior art which is a much broader concept and incorporates all knowledge about the relevant invention at the date of filing. However, under plant variety rights law, the applicant must also show that the variety right is distinguishable from other varieties.[32] The novelty test for patents is broadly analogous to the combination of the novelty and distinctness test under the 1991 Convention. The 1991 Convention also includes the requirement of "*for the purposes of exploitation of the variety*" when considering novelty which is absent in the 1978 Convention. This additional requirement relaxes the test of novelty. If the applicant can show that propagating material of the variety applied for has been previously only used for the purposes of creating another variety, then the variety applied for is not invalid for want of novelty. For instance, an inbred line "variety" which has only been used for the purposes of producing an F1 hybrid has not *itself* been commercially exploited. Thus, where the applicant wishes now to commercially exploit the inbred line variety itself, he can still apply for plant variety rights according to the 1991 Convention even if he has for many years been using the variety to produce the F1 hybrid.[33]

In contrast, the addition of "propagating or harvested material of the variety" in the 1991 Convention in contrast to just "variety" in the 1978

[31] Art. 6(2).
[32] See 6.011.
[33] An F1 hybrid is the immediate progeny of two different parent varieties often inbred lines so that the characteristics of the hybrid are predictable—see Byrne, "The Agritechnical Criteria in Plant Breeders' Rights Laws", *Industrial Property*, October 1983, 293 at p. 296. Often the F1 hybrid is sterile and cannot reproduce itself. Accordingly, breeders must always use the parent varieties to produce it. Hybrids are often commercially popular because they produce strong plants. For instance, many wheat varieties are sterile hybrids.

Convention tightens the test of novelty. For instance, if a breeder has marketed parent inbred lines for the purposes of production and subsequent exploitation of an F1 variety, then the breeder has provided propagating material for an F1 variety and he will not be able to obtain breeders' rights for the F1 variety under the 1991 Convention. Under the 1978 Convention, the breeder could have obtained breeders' rights provided the F1 variety itself had not been commercially exploited. However, if the breeder had marketed the parent inbred lines for use by third parties, then an application for plant variety rights for the F1 hybrid will not fail unless it can be shown that the parent inbred lines were marketed in order to commercially exploit the F1 hybrid.

It should be noted that the test of novelty only concerns acts done by or with the consent of the breeder and not varieties put on the market by third parties. However, the variety must, to qualify for protection, be distinctive from varieties placed on the market by third parties also.[34] The application will not fail for want of novelty if the variety was marketed later than one year before the date of application in the applicant's territory or a maximum of six years in other territories. This "grace period" should be distinguished from that in patents where the applicant has a one year period of protection from possible disclosures of the invention from the date of first filing. This permits the breeder to place the variety on the market in order to ascertain its commercial worth before applying for plant breeders' rights.

Where a Contracting Party applies the 1991 Convention to a plant genus or species to which it had not previously applied it to, it may extend the grace periods referred to above for the purposes of novelty.[35]

(2) Distinctness

6.011 Under the 1991 UPOV Convention, a variety is distinct if it is clearly distinguishable from any other variety whose existence is a matter of common knowledge at the time of filing of the application.[36] The 1991 Convention differs from the 1978 version in that the requirement that the variety be distinguishable by one or more *important characteristic* from any other variety has been abandoned since it was thought to be needlessly ambiguous. The word "important" had frequently suggested to persons reading the 1978 Act that a variety must, to be protectable, be distinct from existing varieties by some feature related to merit.[37] The notion of common knowledge is not refined further in the 1991 Convention but it deems that the filing of an application for the grant of breeders' rights or the entering of a variety in an official register shall make such a variety a matter of common knowledge from the date of

[34] See below, para. 6.011.
[35] Art. 6(2).
[36] Art. 7.
[37] See Greengrass, "The 1991 Act of the UPOV Convention" [1991] 12 EIPR 466, at p. 468.

application or filing provided such leads to the grant of breeders' rights.[38] In considering the issue of distinctness, the national office will examine the claimed characteristics of the variety as against other "commonly known" varieties. National plant variety offices will not seek to examine the actual internal genetic structure of the variety in order to determine whether it differs from other varieties but merely whether the variety expresses differing characteristics from other varieties. This historical approach to distinctness now closely accords with the definition of variety in the 1991 Convention.

(3) Uniformity

6.012 The variety must be uniform for protection to be granted. The 1991 Convention deems this to be so if "subject to the variation that may be expected from the particular features of its propagation, it is sufficiently uniform in its relevant characteristics."[39] The wording is somewhat different from the 1978 version but it is not intended that there should be any change in substance.[40] The above wording emphasises that absolute uniformity is not required. Clearly, the criteria of uniformity is linked with that of distinctness and stability. Without a sufficiently homogeneous variety, it may be difficult to satisfy the distinctness criteria between similar varieties of plants.

Furthermore, a uniform first-generation cross-pollinating variety may produce a heterogeneous second-generation variety. Similarly, an F1 hybrid which consists of a dominant and recessive gene may be homogeneous because of the dominant gene but when it self-pollinates, the second generation will produce 25 per cent twin-recessive gene plants which will exhibit the recessive gene characteristics as opposed to the 75 per cent which will exhibit the dominant characteristics. In such cases, an apparently uniform variety is not truly so because it is unstable.[41]

(4) Stability

6.013 The 1991 Convention deems a variety to be stable if its relevant characteristics remain unchanged after repeated propagation or in the case of a particular cycle of propagation, at the end of each such cycle.[42] Again, there is a change of wording from the 1978 Act but no substantive change was intended.[43] The UPOV Guidelines suggest that where a sample of the variety proves homogeneous, the variety can be considered stable.[44] However, as seen above, this may not be the case and thus

[38] Art. 7, second sentence.
[39] Art. 8.
[40] See Greengrass, "The 1991 Act of the UPOV Convention" [1991] 12 EIPR 466, at p. 469.
[41] In *Zephyr* [1967] FSR 576, the Controller of the Plant Variety Tribunal emphasised that in such matters, the real criteria to consider is that of stability as essentially it is a condition precedent to the issue of uniformity.
[42] Art. 9.
[43] Greengrass, "The 1991 Act of the UPOV Convention" [1991] 12 EIPR 466, at p. 469.
[44] UPOV TG/1/2, General Introduction to Guidelines.

where there is reason to doubt it, stability must be tested by growing a further generation or new seed stock to verify that it exhibits the same characteristics as those shown by the previous sample of the variety.[45]

(vi) Scope of breeders' rights

6.014 The owner of plant variety rights under the 1991 Convention has the exclusive right in relation to the *reproductive or propagating* material of the protected variety, to produce or reproduce; condition for the purposes of propagation; offer for sale, market, export, import or stock for any of these purposes.[46] This differs from the 1978 Convention which included the condition "for the purposes of commercial marketing".[47] This had the effect of implicitly creating "farmers' rights" to replant on their farms propagating material from the previous year's harvest. The 1991 Convention deals with the issue of such farmer's privileges in a different way. It makes no mandatory provisions but permits Contracting Parties "within reasonable limits and subject to the safeguarding of the legitimate interests of the breeder" to restrict the breeder's rights so as to protect the "farmer's privilege".[48] The Diplomatic Conference formally recommended that such a provision "should not be read so as to be intended to open the possibility of extending the practice commonly called "farmer's privilege" to sectors of agricultural or horticultural production in which such a privilege is not a common place."[49] The 1991 Convention makes it clear that the breeder's right does not extend to acts done privately and for non-commercial purposes, acts done for experimental purpose and importantly, it retains the right of plant breeders to use a protected variety to produce other varieties without infringing a plant breeder's rights.[50] As will be seen, this exemption does not apply to the creation of varieties which are "essentially derived" from the protected variety.[51]

The 1991 Convention makes provision for the protection of harvested material ("second generation material") including entire plants and parts of plants derived from the protected variety and also for products made directly from the harvested material ("third generation material"). Such protection was seen as necessary because often the plant breeder would not have had an opportunity to exercise his rights in relation to the initial

[45] ibid.
[46] Art. 14(1). Contracting Parties may extend this list of rights to cover other acts—Art. 14(4).
[47] 1978 UPOV Convention, Art. 5.
[48] Art. 15(2).
[49] See Greengrass, "The 1991 Act of the UPOV Convention" [1991] 12 EIPR 466, at p. 469. This provision can be implemented in many ways. In the Community Plant Variety Rights Regulation, detailed provisions have been enacted in relation to the exact nature and scope of the farmers' exemption. In the United Kingdom, proposed changes to the Plant Varieties and Seeds Act 1964 in order to comply with the 1991 Convention states that the farmers' exemption be enacted upon lines similar to that adopted in the Community Plant Variety Rights Regulation.
[50] Art. 15(1)(i)–(ii).
[51] Art. 15(1)(ii) and see below, para. 6.015.

propagating material.[52] In both cases, the extension of breeders' rights is dependent on the breeder not having had "reasonable opportunity to exercise his right" in relation to material of an earlier generation.[53] Thus the 1991 Convention provides for a "cascade" of rights in relation to a variety, namely propagating material, harvested material of propagating material, and products directly derived from such harvested material whereby the exercise of rights against one type is dependent on the rights owner not being able to exercise his rights against the breeder or user of an earlier generation. Clearly, the rights owner must have had an opportunity to exercise his rights against the propagating material actually used for making the harvested material *in casu* rather than any propagating material and a similar argument applies to products directly derived from harvested material.

The 1991 UPOV Convention also extends a plant breeder's exclusive rights to varieties which are not clearly distinguishable from the protected variety and "varieties whose production requires the repeated use of the protected variety".[54] Thus, in the latter case, where the production of a sterile F1 hybrid requires the repeated use of the protected variety, the plant breeder can prevent the commercial exploitation of the F1 hybrid.

Protection starts from the date of grant of plant breeders' rights although Contracting Parties must enact that the holder of such rights is entitled to at least equitable remuneration for acts which would otherwise infringe the owner's rights but carried out between the date of applicant and that of grant.[55]

(vii) Essentially Derived Varieties

6.015 A breeder cannot prevent another breeder from using the former's protected variety to breed another variety. This exception applies in both the 1978 and 1991 Conventions.[56] It was felt that as the level of distinctness was so low, a breeder need only introduce a minor variant into the protected variety in order to breed another variety in order to avail himself of this provision which unfairly prejudiced plant breeders. The 1991 Act thus introduces an extension of breeders' rights to cover varieties which are "essentially derived" from the protected variety where the protected variety is not itself an essentially derived variety.[57] The Convention defines an "essentially derived" variety as meaning:

> "(i) it is predominantly derived from the initial variety, or from a variety that is itself predominantly derived from the initial

[52] *i.e.* where harvested material of a protected variety is imported from a country where there is no plant variety protection or where the owner of the rights was unaware of the existence of the propagating material used to make the harvested product.

[53] Art. 14(2), (3).

[54] Art. 14(5)(a)(ii), (iii).

[55] Art. 13.

[56] 1978 Convention, Art. 5(3); 1991 Convention, Art. 15(1)(iii).

[57] Art. 14(5)(a)(i).

variety, while retaining the expression of the essential characteristics that result from the genotype or combination of genotypes of the initial variety

(ii) it is clearly distinguishable from the initial variety and

(iii) except for the differences which result from the act of derivation, it conforms to the initial variety in the expression of the essential characteristics that result from the genotype or combination of genotypes of the initial variety."[58]

Article 14(5) provides that essentially derived varieties may be obtained, for example, by the selection of a natural or induced mutant, or of a somaclonal variant, the selection of a variant individual from plants of the initial variety, backcrossing or transformation by genetic engineering. There is a resolution on Article 14(5) which calls for the immediate establishment of draft standard guidelines for adoption by the Council of UPOV on essentially derived varieties. It will be observed that the second requirement set out above states that a variety is only deemed an essentially derived variety if it is clearly distinguishable from the initial variety. Thus, if the derived variety is not clearly distinguishable, then it is not an essentially derived variety but still infringes the exclusive rights of the initial variety.[59] The above means that an essentially derived variety is capable of being subject to plant breeders' rights because it satisfies the distinctness test. However, the owner of such a right will require the permission of the initial variety rights' owner in order to exploit it.[60] Thus, the situation is analogous to that of the proprietor of an improvement patent under patent law. Article 14(5) makes it clear that protection does not exist against essentially derived varieties of essentially derived varieties. Such a provision prevents a proliferation of plaintiffs suing for instance a breeder of an F3 variety essentially derived via several generations from an initial variety.[61] Essentially derived clearly means that it must have been *causally* derived from the protected variety. This means that a variety which has been arrived at independently of the protected variety will not fall within Article 14(5) even if it shares a majority of essential characteristics of the initial variety. Thus, such a right is similar to copyright where there is the dual requirement of copying and a substantial similarity for an infringement action to be successful.[62] The specific mention of "genotype" means that the mere coincidence of observable features is not sufficient even where there has been a causal

[58] Art. 14(5)(b).

[59] Art. 14(5)(a)(ii)—see first paragraph of 6.014.

[60] During discussions of the 1991 Convention, it was suggested that the breeder of an essentially derived variety should be able to force the breeder of the initial variety to grant a licence. However, no such provision appears in the 1991 Convention. In the Community Plant Variety Regulation, there is more detailed provision for a compulsory exploitation licence for the breeder of an essentially derived variety—see 6.030.

[61] F3 means a third-generation variety.

[62] Arts. 14(5)(b)(i) and (iii) are similar to the requirements of copying and substantial similarity in copyright.

derivation—the features must be derived from the particular genotype.[63] For instance, if a breeder inserts genetic material into an initial variety which results in similar characteristics, he could show that the similarities are because of the inserted new genetic material and not the genotype of the initial variety. Accordingly, the variety would not retain the essential characteristics that result from the genotype and thus it would not fall under the definition of an "essentially derived" variety.

(viii) Exhaustion of the breeder's rights

6.016 The 1991 UPOV Convention deems the plant breeder's rights to have been exhausted in relation to any material of the protected variety or any material derived from such material or an essentially derived variety once it has been sold or otherwise marketed by the breeder or with his consent in the territory of the Contracting Party concerned.[64] This provision mirrors the jurisprudence of the ECJ in relation to the free movement of goods and intellectual property rights.[65] The ECJ has held that competition law must be applied to the marketing of the seeds of protected varieties.[66] Interestingly, the ECJ's jurisprudence deems a rights owner to have exhausted his rights even if he has marketed it in a Member State where the owner has no protection.[67] The 1991 Convention merely deems a plant breeders' rights owner to have exhausted his rights if he has marketed it in the country where he has rights.

The 1991 Convention provides that no exhaustion of rights shall be deemed to have taken place in relation to acts which involve further propagation of the variety in question or involve an export of material of the variety, which enables the propagation of the variety, into a country which does not protect varieties of the plant genus or species to which the variety belongs except where the exported material is for final consumption purposes.[68] This protects third parties from corrupting a variety by further breeding and emphasises the importance of the fact that a plant breeder has control over a variety so that it does not degenerate.[69] In relation to export of a variety, the measure is aimed at preventing propa-

[63] Genotype means a particular version (allele) of a gene. A *genotype* will often produce observable characteristics (*a phenotype*) which result from the interaction between the genotype and its environment.

[64] Art. 16.

[65] See Chap. Seven.

[66] See Case 258/78, *L. C. Nungesser KG & Eisele v. E.C. Commission* [1982] E.C.R. 2015; [1983] 1 C.M.L.R. 278, at para. [41] *et seq.* The ECJ takes a more lenient view as to the application of competition law to the distribution of basic seeds merely used to produce first and second generation seeds—Case 27/87, *Louis Erauw-Jacquery v. La Hesbignonne*, [1988] E.C.R. 1919; [1988] 4 C.M.L.R. 576. See Chap. Eight and paras. 8.095 to 8.097.

[67] See Case 187/80, *Merck v. Stephar*, [1981] E.C.R. 2063, [1981] 3 C.M.L.R. 463 and see Chap. Seven at para. 7.014 *et seq.* In relation to Exhaustion of rights under the CPVR regime, see para. 6.031.

[68] Art. 16(2).

[69] See Case 27/87, *Louis Erauw-Jacquery v. La Hesbignonne* [1988] E.C.R. 1919; [1988] 4 C.M.L.R. 576 at para. [10] where the ECJ emphasises that a breeder must have the right to prevent improper handling of a variety.

gation of a variety in a country where the breeder is not able to own rights. Those varieties such as hybrids which rely upon a continuous supply of a basic line in order to be reproduced would clearly not come within this exemption.

(ix) Procedure

6.017 The 1991 Convention provides for a procedure whereby a qualifying person under the Convention applies to the appropriate office of a Contracting Party.[70] The Convention provides for a 12 month priority period whereby an applicant can claim a priority date which equates to the date of filing of the first application.[71] The relevant authority must examine the application for compliance with the requirements of the UPOV Convention and must grow the variety or carry out other necessary tests or take into account results of trials in order to ascertain whether such requirements have been met.[72] Rights may be revoked if the requirements of novelty, distinctness, uniformity or stability have been proved not to have been satisfied.[73]

(x) Miscellaneous

6.018 The 1991 Convention contains the usual administrative provisions.[74] It does not permit Contracting States to make any reservations except that where states provide for protection for varieties that reproduce asexually via rights other than the plant breeders' right, they may continue to do so and need not apply the 1991 Convention.[75–77]

3. Community Regulation on Plant Variety Rights[78]

6.019 As with other forms of intellectual property, the EC Commission has been active in seeking to create a Community regime for the grant of plant variety rights throughout the Community. In 1990, it proposed a regulation which would set up a Community Plant Variety Right ("CPVR") which would be independent of but coexist with national plant variety rights. After a four year period of consultation between the Commission and the European Parliament, on July 27, 1994, the EC Council adopted a Regulation on Community Plant Variety Rights. A CPVR is valid throughout the Community. The Regulation establishes a

[70] Art. 10.
[71] Art. 11.
[72] Art. 12.
[73] Arts. 21, 22.
[74] Arts. 21 *et seq.*
[75–77] This provision was specifically designed for the U.S. which provides a type of plant patent protection for such varieties—see Greengrass, "The 1991 Act of the UPOV Convention" [1991] 12 EIPR 466. It is not thought to affect European countries.
[78] Regulation 2100/94 [1994] O.J. L227/1.

CPV Office ("CPVO") with a legal personality which is responsible for the administration of the granting of CPVRs. The substantive law of the Regulation closely mirrors the 1991 UPOV Convention which it expressly takes into account and it will be re-examined if there are future developments in the 1991 Convention.[79] The CPVO is intended to be fully functioning by April 27, 1995. At present, no decision has been made on the actual location of the CPVO. In the meanwhile, the CPVO will be temporarily located in Brussels.

(a) Fundamental provisions

6.020 The CPVR Regulation establishes a plant variety right which is effective throughout the Community.[80] As with the Community Trade Mark and the proposed Community Patent and Registered Design, the CPVR can only be granted, transferred or terminated in respect of the whole Community.[81] The Regulation establishes a Community Plant Variety Office ("CPVO") for the purpose of administration and implementation of the regulation.[82]

(b) Definition of "variety"

6.021 The definition of "variety" is exactly the same as that under the 1991 UPOV Convention.[83] As with the 1991 UPOV Convention, the definition of "variety" is irrespective of whether the conditions for the grant of a PVR can be fully met. However, the regulation provides two important additions to the UPOV definition. First, the expression "plant grouping" applies to either entire plants or parts of plants "as far as such parts are capable of producing entire plants".[84] The Regulation refers to both as "variety constituents". Secondly, the Regulation states that the requirement that the plant grouping be defined by "the expression of the characteristics that results from a given genotype or combination of genotypes" (echoed in the first indent of the definition of "variety" in the 1991 Convention) is satisfied regardless as to whether the characteristics are invariable or variable provided that the level of variation results from the genotype or combination of genotypes.[85] Therefore, provided the variety is distinguishable *as a whole* from other plant groupings,[86] then the fact that it has variable characteristics does not prevent it from being defined a variety for the purposes of the CPVR Regulation.

[79] See Recitals.
[80] Art. 1, 2.
[81] Art. 2.
[82] Art. 4.
[83] Art. 5(2). See 6.005.
[84] Art. 5(3).
[85] Art. 5(4).
[86] This is the requirement set out at the second indent of the definition of "variety" in both the 1991 Convention and the Regulation.

(c) Protectable varieties

6.022 Varieties of all botanical genera and species including hybrids between genera and species may form the object of CPVRs.[87] The substantive requirements for a plant variety to qualify for registration are similar to that under the 1991 Convention. Thus, the variety must be new, distinct, stable and uniform and must be designated by a denomination.[88]

6.023 *Distinctness*—This test is the same as under the 1991 Convention except that, unsurprisingly, "common knowledge" is deemed to include varieties which, at the date of application, are the subject of a CPVR or an application for a CPVR which has in the meantime led to the granting of a CPVR.[89] The Regulation permits the implementation of rules which would specify further cases as examples which would be deemed to be a matter of common knowledge.

6.024 *Novelty*—The Regulation provides for the same test of novelty as under the 1991 Convention including the same "grace periods" whereby the applicant may test the commercial value of the variety prior to the date of application. Thus, under Article 10(1), a variety is deemed to be new if, at the date of application,[90] variety constituents or harvested material of the variety have not been sold or otherwise disposed of to others, by or with the consent of the breeder, for purposes of exploitation of the variety:

> "(a) earlier than one year before the date of application within the Community
> (b) earlier than four years, or in the case of trees or of vines, earlier than six years before the date of application outside the territory of the Community."[91]

These "grace periods" are extended under the transitional provisions of the Regulation. Thus, where an application for a CPVR is made within one year of the entry into force of the Regulation (by September 1, 1995),[92] then the "grace periods" are four years prior to the entry into force of the Regulation or in the case of trees or vines, six years.[93] Furthermore, in order to encourage owners of national PVRs to apply for a CPVR, these transitional "grace periods" also apply where national

[87] Art. 5(1).
[88] Art. 6. Art. 17 compels persons offering or disposing variety constituents of a protected variety to use the variety denomination even after termination of the CPVR.
[89] Art. 7.
[90] For the determination of "date of application", see Art. 51 and 6.033.
[91] Art. 10.
[92] Art. 18 of the Regulation deems that the Regulation entered into force on the day of its publication in the Official Journal of the European Communities which was September 1, 1994.
[93] Art. 116(1).

PVRs have been granted in one or more Member States before the entry into force of the Regulation.[94]

As with the 1991 UPOV Convention, in considering novelty, the emphasis is on whether or not there has been commercial exploitation by the applicant or with his consent. Unlike patent law, novelty is not destroyed by the fact that third parties are fully aware of the variety, its pedigree or its characteristics before the date of application. Because the drafters of the Regulation anticipated problems with whether a variety has been "disposed of to others", Article 10 of Regulation clarifies the position in relation to certain cases where the 1991 Convention is silent. The exemptions listed below in relation to whether or not a disposal is deemed to be a novelty-destroying disposal reflect the broad emphasis that a disposal is only relevant if it is a disposal for commercial gain.

First, where the breeder gives variety constituents to a statutory body or other bodies solely for production, reproduction, multiplication, conditioning or storage, this is not deemed to be a disposal provided that the breeder preserves the exclusive right of disposal of these and other variety constituents and no further disposal is made.[95] Accordingly, where a breeder subcontracts the growing and testing of the variety to a third party, this will not constitute a disposal. However, the breeder must maintain legal control over the variety and the subcontractor or other third party must not be able to sell or dispose the variety (whether variety constituents or harvested material) to third parties. In this regard, the Regulation makes it clear that if the third party repeatedly uses the variety constituents of a parent variety to make a hybrid variety and then sells or disposes the variety constituents or the harvested material of the hybrid variety, that will destroy novelty in the parent variety.

Secondly, a disposal of variety constituents by one company or firm to another company or firm which belongs to the same economic unit is not deemed a disposal.[96]

Thirdly, where variety constituents or harvested material are produced from plants grown for experimental purposes or for the purposes of breeding or discovering other varieties, then their disposal will not be deemed to be for the purposes of exploitation of the variety provided that they are not used for further reproduction or multiplication.[97] For instance, where grain is produced by a new cereal plant pursuant to experimental research, the disposal of that grain to a farmer for use as animal feed would not constitute a novelty-destroying disposal. However, if the farmer used that grain to produce further grain, it would be a novelty-destroying disposal as the grain is then used for further reproduction or multiplication. The exception to the general rule is that if refer-

[94] Art. 116(2). This provision is somewhat obscure because the grant of a national PVR has no effect on the issue of novelty for the purposes of the CPVR Regulation.
[95] Art. 10(2).
[96] Art. 10(2).
[97] Art. 10(3).

ence is made to the variety for the purposes of disposal, that will constitute a novelty-destroying disclosure.

The three exceptions operate by deeming the disposals referred to not to be a disposal for the purposes of Article 10(1). Where the disposals are by way of sale, do the three exceptions apply? The reference in Article 10(1) to " . . . sold or *otherwise* disposed of to others" suggests that a sale does constitute a disposal. Therefore, it is submitted that the three above exceptions apply where the disposal is by way of sale.

6.025 *Uniformity*—The definition of uniformity in the Regulation is very similar to that in the 1991 UPOV Convention. Under both, the applicant must show that the plant's characteristics are "sufficiently uniform" subject to the variation that may be expected from the particular features of its propagation.[98] The difference is that the Convention merely requires the "relevant characteristics" to be sufficiently uniform whereas the Regulation requires "the expression of those characteristics which are included in the examination for distinctness, as well as any others used for the variety description" to be sufficiently uniform. In essence, the Regulation spells out what characteristics are relevant. In case there was any doubt, the Regulation makes it clear by the reference to "expression of those characteristics" that the CPVO is interested in tangible, observable features in considering the issue of uniformity and not uniformity in relation to the underlying genetic structure.

6.026 *Stability*—The definition of stability in the Regulation is also very similar to that in the 1991 Convention. The applicant must show that the expression of the characteristics which are included in the examination for distinctness as well as any others used for the variety description remains unchanged after repeated propagation, or in the case of a particular cycle of propagation, at the end of each such cycle.[99] Again, as with the Regulation's definition of uniformity, it spells out that the "relevant characteristics" referred to in Article 9 of the Convention are those included in the examination for distinctness and those in the variety description.

(d) Entitlement to CPVR

6.027 The person who bred or discovered and developed the variety is entitled to the CPVR for that variety.[1] As with other rights, if the above activities were carried out by more than one person, they are jointly entitled to the CPVR. If one person discovered the variety and the other developed it, the CPVR vests jointly in the discoverer and developer.[2] The Regulation permits persons declared in writing to be entitled to a CPVR to apply for

[98] Art. 8, CPVR Reg.; Art. 8, 1991 UPOV Convention.
[99] Art. 9.
[1] Art. 11.
[2] Art. 11(2).

a CPVR. If the breeder is an employee, the entitlement to the CPVR is determined in accordance with the national law applicable to the employment relationship in the context of which the variety was bred or discovered and developed. A court seised of an employer-employee dispute will have to resort to its private international laws in order to determine the relevant domestic law.[3]

Only persons or legal persons who are nationals of a Community state or nationals of a UPOV Convention country or who are domiciled or have their seat or establishment within such a country can apply for a CPVR.[4] In addition, the Commission may extend the right to apply for a CPVR to nationals of states where reciprocal protection is provided.[5]

(e) Scope and effect of CPVR

6.028 A CPVR holder has the right to prevent the production or reproduction (multiplication), conditioning for the purpose of propagation, offering for sale, selling or other marketing, exporting from the Community, importing to the Community or stocking for any of the above purposes of the variety constituents or the harvested material of the variety.[6] This is identical to the 1991 UPOV Convention.

The Regulation only permits the exercise of the above rights in relation to the harvested material if the holder has not had reasonable opportunity to exercise his rights in relation to the unauthorised use of the parent variety constituents.[7] In this respect, the Regulation is identical to the Convention. In relation to products obtained directly from "material of the protected variety", the Regulation permits the implementation of rules that, in specific cases, the CPVR holder may enforce his rights in respect of such products.[8] The wording differs slightly from the equivalent measure in the 1991 Convention which refers to "products made directly from harvested material of the protected variety".[9] The Regulation deems products obtained directly from the variety to be "material".[9a] In other words, the CPVR holder could enforce his rights once the necessary rules had been implemented against products directly obtained from products directly obtained from the protected variety. As with the Convention, the rules can only confer such rights on the CPVR holder if he has not had a reasonable opportunity to exercise his rights against the parent material. Thus, as with the Convention, the Regulation provides for a "cascade" of rights.[10]

The CPVR holder's rights extend to "essentially derived" varieties,

[3] *cf.* the approach under the European Patent Convention to choice of law issues regarding entitlement to a European patent. See 13.058 *et seq.*
[4] Art. 12.
[5] Art. 12(1)(b).
[6] Art. 13.
[7] Art. 13(3).
[8] Art. 13(4).
[9] See 6.014.
[9a] Art. 13(4), last sentence.
[10] See 6.014.

varieties which are not distinct from the protected variety and varieties whose production requires the repeated use of the protected variety.[11] These provisions are virtually identical to those in the Convention.[12] Where a CPVR is granted pursuant to the transitional provisions of the Regulation,[13] the CPVR does not extend to cover essentially derived varieties whose existence was a matter of common knowledge in the Community before the date of entry into force of the Regulation.[14]

The CPVR does not extend to acts done privately and for non-commercial purposes; acts done for experimental purposes or acts done for the purpose of breeding or discovering and developing other varieties.[15]

The Regulation also prohibits the exercise of rights which would violate any provisions adopted on the grounds of public morality, public policy or public security, the protection of health and life of humans, animals or plants, the protection of the environment, the protection of industrial or commercial property or the safeguarding of competition, of trade or of agricultural production.[16] This provision which has no counterpart in the 1991 UPOV Convention is broad in scope. It should be contrasted with the European Patent Convention which prevents the grant of a European patent which is contrary to "*ordre public*" or morality.[17] The Regulation only prohibits the *exercise* of a CPVR in such circumstances. This shifts the emphasis from whether the right in itself is contrary to public policy to whether in certain circumstances, its exercise is contrary to provisions adopted on the grounds of public policy. For example, where a breeder obtains a CPVR for a variety whose harvested material has life-saving properties, then, if national legislation exists whereby the variety is subject to a compulsory licence, the CPVR holder cannot exercise his rights against a harvester of unauthorised variety constituents but is merely entitled to a royalty. It should be noted that for this derogation to apply, the exercise of the CPVR must contravene a provision. It is not a defence merely to allege that the exercise of the CPVR is contrary to public policy *per se*.

(f) Farmers' privilege

6.029 The Regulation provides a "farmers' privilege" which permits farmers to use the product of the harvest of a protected variety for replanting. The exact nature and extent of the farmer's privilege is set out in detail and discussed below. The provisions relating to farmers' privilege should be

[11] Art. 13(5), (6).
[12] See 6.015.
[13] As to CPVRs granted under the transitional provisions, see 6.045.
[14] Art. 116(4). The Reg. entered into force on September 1, 1994 (Art. 118).
[15] Art. 15.
[16] Art. 13(8).
[17] See 2.049.

contrasted with the corresponding and far less detailed and optional provision in the 1991 UPOV Convention.[18]

Article 14(1) authorises farmers to use for propagating purposes in the field, on their own holding the product of the harvest which they have obtained by planting on their own holding, propagating material of a variety other than a hybrid or synthetic variety which is covered by a CPVR. However, this privilege only applies to certain agricultural plant species specified in Article 14(2).[19] The Regulation distinguishes between small and large farmholdings. Farmers who grow plants on an area less than the area required to produce 92 tonnes of cereals are not required to pay any remuneration to the CPVR holder.[20] Other farmers are required to pay an equitable remuneration to the CPVR holder which shall be "sensibly lower than the amount charged for the licensed production of propagating material of the same variety in the same area".[21] However, in the case of a CPVR granted under Article 116,[22] if farmers have used and continue to use a variety protected under such a CPVR as part of their farmers' privilege before September 1, 1994 without payment, they may continue to do so without payment until June 30, 2001.[23] The Regulation provides for the introduction of rules for the purposes of defining the exact nature and scope of the farmers' privilege based on the above criteria.[24]

(g) Compulsory exploitation right

6.030 The CPVR Regulation permits persons to apply to the CPVO for compulsory licences to exploit a protected variety on the grounds of public interest.[25] Member States may not grant compulsorily licences in respect of a CPVR.[26] This provision mirrors Article 17 of 1991 UPOV Convention which permits Contracting Parties to compulsorily license PVRs on the basis of public interest. The Recitals state that public interest may include the need to supply the market with material offering specified features or to maintain the incentive for continued breeding of improved varieties. The former reason is analogous to a compulsory licence granted under patent law where the patentee fails to adequately work the invention. Clearly, if the CPVR holder grows sufficient quantities (whether himself or through licensees) to satisfy market demand, this could not

[18] See 6.014.

[19] These are fodder plants (chickpea milkvetch, yellow lupin, lucerne, field pea, Berseem/Egyptian clover, Persian clover, field bean, common vetch and Italian ryegrass); cereals (oats, barley, rice, canary grass, rye, triticale, wheat, durum wheat and spelt wheat); oil and fibre plants (swede rape, turnip rape and linseed (but not flax)) and potatoes.

[20] Art. 14(3). The calculation of the area is based upon Art. 8(2), Reg. 1765/92 [1992] O.J. L181/12 as last amended by Reg. 1552/93 [1993] O.J. L154/19. Comparable criteria will apply to farmers who grow other plant species.

[21] Art. 14(3).

[22] See 6.045.

[23] Art. 116(4) second indent, Art. 14(3) fourth indent, Art. 118.

[24] Art. 14(3).

[25] Art. 29.

[26] Art. 29(7).

constitute a ground. However, the CPVO will probably consider other factors such as whether the plant variety is supplied at a reasonable price, whether there are proper distribution channels and whether the produced variety is of a proper quality.[27]

The latter reason would appear to relate to the situation where a breeder wishes to improve a protected variety for the purposes of commercial exploitation. If the improved variety is an "essentially derived" variety of a protected variety, then the breeder would need a licence to commercially exploit his variety from the holder of the CPVR in the initial variety.[28] He will be entitled to one if he can show that there is a public interest.[29]

If the CPVO grants a compulsory licence, it must stipulate the type of acts covered and reasonable conditions. Normally, this will provide for the payment of an appropriate royalty. If the compulsory licence is applied for in relation to an "essentially derived" variety, the licence must provide for payment of a reasonable royalty.[30]

The Regulation permits the implementation of rules setting out specific examples of public interest.[31]

(h) Exhaustion of CPVR

6.031 Once material of the protected variety has been disposed of in the Community, Article 16 provides that the CPVR holder is deemed to have exhausted his rights in such material.[32] Moreover, his rights are exhausted as against "material derived from the said material". Thus, the CPVR holder has no rights against harvested products or products derived from harvested products of varieties placed on the market in the Community by him or with his consent. However, the marketing of the protected variety does not exhaust the CPVR holder's rights in relation to varieties "essentially derived" from a protected variety, varieties which are not distinct from the protected variety or varieties whose production requires the repeated use of the protected variety.[33] The same principles would apply to the marketing of varieties in the grace periods prior to the date of application for a CPVR.

In the case of CPVRs granted pursuant to transitional provisions, the

[27] *cf.* Plants Varieties and Seeds Act 1964, s.7(3) (as amended by Plant Varieties Act 1983, s.3) which states that the Controller in considering whether or not to grant a compulsory licence should have regard to the desirability of securing that the plant variety is available to the public at reasonable prices, is widely distributed and is maintained in quality.

[28] See 6.028.

[29] Art. 29(5).

[30] Art. 29(3), (5).

[31] Art. 29(6).

[32] Art. 16.

[33] The wording of Art. 16 suggests that whereas the CPVR holder's rights are exhausted as against "material derived" from a variety marketed by him, this does not extend to varieties derived from the marketed variety.

Regulation retrospectively enacts the exhaustion of rights principle to acts concerning the disposal of any material of the variety prior to the date of entry into force of the Regulation.[34] Whilst normally EC legislation does not enact retrospectively because of the EC principle of "legitimate expectation", for many years there has existed the exhaustion of rights principle as developed by the ECJ in relation to national intellectual property rights.

A buyer of a protected variety does not have the right to further propagate the variety except "where such propagation was intended when the material was disposed of".[35] This permits CPVR holders to contractually prevent propagation once the protected variety has been sold and merely sell the variety for the purpose of producing harvested material. Where the protected variety constituents, having been marketed in the Community, are destined for export to a third country which does not protect varieties of the plant genus or species to which the variety belongs, the CPVR holder may exercise his rights to prevent such export unless the "exported materials" is for final consumption purposes.[36]

(i) Duration and termination of CPVR

6.032 A CPVR lasts for 25 years or in the case of varieties of vine and tree species, for 30 years.[37] The EC Council may extend these terms up to a period of five years for specific genera or species. The CPVO can cancel CPVRs if, after grant, it is established that the variety has ceased to remain uniform or stable.[38] Where a CPVR is granted under Article 116,[39] the duration of the CPVR is reduced by the longest period during which variety constituents or harvested material thereof has been sold or otherwise disposed of to others by or with the consent of the breeder within the territory of the Community for the purposes of exploitation of the variety or for the period in which national PVRs have been effective but for not more than five years.[40]

[34] Art. 116(4) third indent. For CPVRs applied for under transitional provisions, see 6.045.

[35] Art. 16(a). In relation to CPVRs granted under Art. 116 (see 6.045), where material was disposed prior to September 1, 1994 by the breeder or with his consent to third parties for the purposes of propagation, the breeder is not deemed to have exhausted his rights in perpetuity in relation to further propagation of that variety. Instead, the breeder's authorisation is required for any further propagation after September 1, 1996 or in the case of tree or vine varieties, after September 1, 1998—Art. 116(4) third indent, second para.

[36] Art. 16(b). It is unclear whether the expression "for final consumption purposes" permits the growing of the exported variety constituents to produce food (as opposed to further propagation of the variety) or merely means that the exported materials themselves must be consumed. For holders of CPVRs who wish to prevent any form of propagation or reproduction of the protected variety in such countries, practical problems may arise as clearly, variety constituents can be subsequently used for propagation purposes.

[37] Art. 19.

[38] Art. 21.

[39] See 6.045.

[40] Art. 116(4) fourth indent.

(j) Application for CPVR: practice and procedure

6.033 Applications for a CPVR can be filed directly with the CPVO or a designated national office.[41] The application must contain a request for the grant of a CPVR, identification of the botanical taxon, information identifying the applicant(s), the name of the breeder and an assurance regarding entitlement to the CPVR, provisional designation of the variety, technical description of the variety, geographic origin of the variety, the credentials of the procedural representative, details of any previous commercialisation of the variety and of any other application made in respect of the variety.[42] The date of application is deemed to be the date which a valid application was received by the CPVO subject to payment of the relevant fees.[43]

An application which is filed within 12 months of the filing of an earlier application for the same variety in a Community state or UPOV state will enjoy a right of priority based on the date of the earlier application. The claim for priority is dependent on the applicant filing within three months of the date of application copies of the earlier application certified by the authority responsible for such an application.[44] The application then undergoes a three part examination test. The first examination is purely formal. In the second part called the "substantive examination", the CPVO examines for novelty, whether the variety applied for is a "variety" for the purposes of the CPV Regulation; for entitlement and whether the denomination is suitable.[45] The final examination is the technical examination to see if the variety meets the DUS requirements (distinctness, uniformity and stability).[46] This examination is carried out by national offices designated by the CPVO called "Examination Offices". These offices must grow the variety or carry out any other investigations that are required. However, where there are available findings resulting from proceedings for the grant of national PVRs, the technical examination may be carried out by the CPVO on the basis of such findings with the agreement of the relevant authority.[47]

Third parties may file written objections but only on the grounds that either novelty or the DUS criteria are not satisfied or that there is an impediment under Article 63(3) or (4) to the proposed variety denomination.[48] It should be noted that a third party cannot object on the basis of entitlement.[49]

[41] Art. 49.
[42] Art. 50.
[43] Art. 51.
[44] Art. 52(4).
[45] Art. 54. As to whether the denomination is suitable, see Art. 63.
[46] Art. 55, 56.
[47] Art. 116(3).
[48] Art. 63(3) and (4) are discussed below.
[49] See para. 6.041.

6.034 *Variety denomination*—The chosen denomination must be suitable. It is not suitable if a third party has a prior right over the name; if it may commonly cause its users difficulties as regards recognition or reproduction; if it is identical or may be confused with a variety denomination under which another variety of the same or of a closely related species is entered in an official register of plant varieties or under material of another variety has been marketed in a Member State or in a Member of the International Unit for the Protection of New Varieties of Plants unless the other variety no longer remains in existence and its denomination has acquired no special significance; if it is identical or may be confused with other designations which are commonly used for the marketing of goods or which have to be kept free under other legislation or if it is liable to give offence in one of the Member States or is contrary to public policy.[50] Furthermore, if the proposed variety denomination has already been entered on a national plant variety register under a different name, then it is deemed not to be suitable.[51]

6.035 *Fees*—Applicants for CPVRs are required to pay fees for the various stages in the application. Also, CPVR holders must pay annual renewal fees.[52]

6.036 *Appeal*—In relation to most decisions of the CPVO, an appeal lies to the Board of Appeal. Such an appeal has a suspensory effect on proceedings. A further appeal to the ECJ lies from the decisions of the Boards of Appeal on grounds of lack of competence, infringement of an essential procedural requirement, infringement of the Treaty, of the Regulation or of any rule of law relating to their application or misuse of power.[53] The latter grounds are the same as under Article 173 of the EC Treaty.[54] A direct appeal lies to the ECJ from a decision of the CPVO in relation to applications for compulsory licences.[55]

6.037 *Conditions governing proceedings*—The Regulation makes the usual provisions regarding the need for reasoned decisions, oral proceedings, taking of evidence and the award of costs.[56] These provisions are virtually identical to that for the Community Trade Mark and the proposed Community Registered Design.[57]

[50] Art. 63.
[51] Art. 63(4).
[52] Art. 83. Regs. specifying the level of fees are to be issued under Art. 113.
[53] Arts. 67 to 75.
[54] See 1.028.
[55] Art. 74.
[56] Arts. 75 to 86.
[57] See 3.052 vis à vis C.T.M.

(k) Prohibition on cumulative protection

6.038 Whilst the CPVR is designed to coexist with national plant variety rights,[58] the holder of a CPVR is not permitted to enforce national plant variety rights or patent rights for the same variety.[59] Once a CPVR has been granted, such national rights become ineffective. Accordingly, an applicant must choose whether he requires national protection or CPVR protection. There is nothing to stop the applicant from initially pursuing both routes. It is only upon grant of the CPVR that the national PVR becomes ineffective.

(l) Infringement and remedies

6.039 The owner of a CPVR may sue for an injunction and/or reasonable compensation where his exclusive rights have been infringed in relation to the protected variety. Moreover, he may seek similar relief in respect of incorrect usage of the variety denomination or use by a third party of an identical or confusingly similar denomination on another variety of the same botanical species or a species regarded as related pursuant to a CPVO publication.[60] The CPVR owner may also claim as against a person who acts intentionally or negligently for any further damage resulting from the act in question. The Regulation states that in cases of "slight negligence", such claims may be reduced according to the degree of such negligence but not however to the extent that they are less than the advantage derived therefrom by the person who committed the infringement.[61] The distinction between an entitlement to reasonable compensation *per se* and an entitlement to further damages on proof of intention or negligence means that an action for infringement of a CPVR may have different monetary consequences than that of a corresponding national PVR. For instance, in the United Kingdom, entitlement to damages for infringement of a UK PVR is not conditional on the proof of negligence or intention but is absolute.[62] Moreover, the concept of "slight negligence" is not known in the United Kingdom. For instance, if a PVR holder wishes to sue a person for having exported protected seedstock to a third country where no protection is available and which has had disastrous financial consequences to the PVR holder, he may wish to use national PVRs where in the absence of consent, the exporter will be liable for all foreseeable consequent damage flowing from the infringement rather than under the CPVR regime, where he will be entitled to reasonable compensation but will have to show negligence to claim in damages and may have his damages reduced according to the degree of "slightness". As the grant of a CPVR renders corresponding national PVRs ineffective, this constitutes a deterrent to seeking protection via the CPVR

[58] See Recitals.
[59] Art. 92.
[60] Art. 94.
[61] Art. 94(2).
[62] See Plant Varieties and Seeds Act 1964, s.4.

route. However, the Regulation permits national courts to apply national laws regarding restitution where the infringing party has made any gain out of his infringement.[63]

For infringing acts between the publication date of the application for the CPVR and the grant, the holder is entitled to reasonable compensation.[64]

6.040 *Limitation periods*—The holder of a CPVR must sue for infringement within three years of the following three events (whichever occurs latest):

(a) grant of the CPVR
(b) knowledge of the infringing acts
(c) knowledge of the party liable for the acts.[65]

In any event, there is an absolute bar on proceedings brought after 30 years from the termination of the offending acts.

(m) Disputes on entitlement to CPVR

6.041 Where a person considers that he is entitled to be the holder (whether jointly or not) or be named as an applicant for the grant of a CPVR, he must make a claim in the court of the appropriate Member State.[66] Such a claim must be made within five years from the publication of the grant of the CPVR unless the holder knew that he was not entitled to the CPVR whether solely or at all.[67] If the appropriate court adjudicates that there should be a complete change in the ownership of the CPVR, any exploitation or other rights which arose from the previous holder lapse upon entry of the person on the CPVR Register.[68] However, persons owning such rights (including the previous holder) can apply for a non-exclusive exploitation rights from the new holder or, in the absence of agreement, from the CPVO where they have effected any prohibited acts or made "effective and genuine arrangements" to do so prior to the commencement of the entitlement proceedings unless the previous or other persons enjoying exploitation rights acted in bad faith.[69]

[63] Art. 97.
[64] Art. 95.
[65] Art. 96.
[66] Art. 98. As for the appropriate state, see 6.042.
[67] Art. 98(3).
[68] Art. 100(1).
[69] Art. 100(2). The Regulation is unclear as to whether "the proceedings" referred to are the proceedings relating to entitlement or proceedings following a change in ownership for infringement. It is submitted that it is the former as clearly everyone is on notice once proceedings for entitlement are brought that there is a genuine dispute over ownership and also the use of the definite article in "the proceedings" suggests an implicit reference to the proceedings concerning entitlement rather than possible future proceedings for infringement.

(n) Jurisdiction in infringement or entitlement disputes

6.042 The Regulation sets out jurisdictional rules as to where actions for infringement of CPVRs or disputes as to the entitlement to a CPVR are to be brought. The general rule is that the Lugano Convention applies.[70] However, the Regulation also sets out complementary jurisdictional provisions which apply as well.[71] Thus, the Regulation provides that proceedings must be brought:

(a) in the court of the Member State or other Contracting Party of the Lugano Convention in which the defendant is domiciled or has his seat[72] or in the absence of such, has an establishment

failing which

(b) in the court of the Member State where the plaintiff is domiciled or has his seat or in the absence of such, has an establishment

failing which

(c) in the court of the Member State where the CPVO is located.

Unlike the Community Trade Mark Regulation, the CPVR Regulation does not designate specific courts but merely refers to the "competent courts". It is assumed that these will be the same courts as would deal with the infringement of national PVRs. A competent court which is seised of an infringement action under the above rules has jurisdiction in respect of infringements committed in all Member States.[73]

A CPVR holder can also bring an action for infringement in the Member State where the harmful event occurred. However, the competent court in that state will only have jurisdiction in respect of acts of infringement committed in that state.[74]

The above jurisdictional rules can be waived if the parties have agreed in writing to try the dispute in a particular jurisdiction or the defendant submits to the jurisdiction of a court in a particular state.[75]

National courts seised of disputes relating to CPVRs must apply the same rules of procedure as applicable to corresponding national property

[70] Art. 101. For commentary on the Lugano Convention, see 13.052 *et seq*.
[71] The wording of Art. 101 suggests that unless expressly excluded, both the Lugano Convention and the Regulation's jurisdictional provisions apply.
[72] For definition of domicile or seat, Art. 102 states that the definition in Arts. 52 and 53 of the Lugano Convention shall apply. See 13.012 and 13.003.
[73] Art. 101(2).
[74] Art. 101(3). This ground is similar to Art. 5(3) of the Brussels and Lugano Convention. *Quaere* whether Art. 5(3) of the Lugano Convention also applies to acts of infringements of CPVR. This may be important because there is no express limitation in the Lugano Convention that the court shall have jurisdiction only in respect of infringement alleged to have been committed in the jurisdiction. As to whether courts seised under Art. 5(3) in relation to an infringement action would have extra-territorial jurisdiction, see 13.052 and 13.010 to 13.011. The supplementary jurisdictional rules under Art. 5(3) and 5(4) of the Lugano Convention do not apply to disputes over entitlement to a CPVR (Art. 102(1)).
[75] Art. 102(2).

rights.[76] In the case of employer-employee disputes, the relevant national law is that applicable to the relationship in the context of which the variety was bred, or discovered and developed.[77]

(o) Entitlement to sue

6.043 Actions for infringement may be brought by the holder of the CPVR. Under Article 104, persons enjoying exploitation rights may also bring such actions "unless that has been expressly excluded by agreement with the holder in the case of an exclusive exploitation right or by the Office pursuant to Articles 29 or 100(2)".[78] This provision differs markedly from other forms of intellectual property that only the holder of the right or an exclusive licensee can sue for infringement. It means that anyone who has any authorisation (whether via permission of the holder or via a compulsory exploitation right) to exploit the variety may sue for infringement. This could lead to a multiplicity of plaintiffs. Even where the holder has initiated an action for infringement, any person enjoying exploitation rights is entitled to intervene in such an action for the purpose of obtaining compensation for damage suffered by him.[79] The wording of Article 104 suggests that this right to sue can be excluded by agreement with the holder or by the CPVO in the case of a compulsory exploitation right.

(p) Validity of CPVR in national proceedings and stays

6.044 In actions for infringement of a CPVR, national courts are obliged to treat the CPVR as valid.[80] If the CPVR is in the process of being challenged for validity in the CPVO, the national court may stay the proceedings if it is dependent on the validity of the CPVR.[81] If there is a dispute over the entitlement to be named as an applicant for an application for a CPVR, then the national court must stay proceedings until the CPVO has decided on the merits of the application.[82]

(q) Transitional provisions

6.045 Where variety constituents or harvested material have been sold or otherwise disposed of to others, by or with the consent of the breeder, within the territory of the Community for purposes of exploitation of the variety no earlier than four years or in the case of trees or vines, no earlier than six years prior to September 1, 1994, this will not destroy novelty in an

[76] Art. 103.
[77] Art. 11(4).
[78] Art. 104. Art. 29 concerns the grant of compulsory exploitation rights by the CPVO—see 6.030—and Art. 100(2) concerns the grant of a non-exclusive exploitation right to the former holder of a CPVR where it has been transferred to the new holder following judgment in a dispute over entitlement to a CPVR.
[79] Art. 104(2).
[80] Art. 105.
[81] Art. 106(2).
[82] Art. 106(1).

application for a CPVR for that variety if applied for by September 1, 1995.[83] In case there was any doubt, this provision applies even if there exists national plant variety rights which were granted prior to September 1, 1994.[84] This transitional provision is much more generous than the normal rule of novelty and is clearly designed to encourage early use of the CPVR route for plant variety protection.

Where a CPVR is granted pursuant to this route, there are a number of other provisions designed to safeguard the acquired rights of third party. These concern exclusive rights over essentially derived varieties, farmer's privileges, exhaustion of rights and the duration of the right. In relation to each of these, the exact effect of the transitional provisions are dealt with in the appropriate section.[85]

4. Table of European Countries who are Members of UPOV

6.046

Contracting State	1978 Convention[1]	1991 Convention[2]
Belgium[1]	●	●
Czech Republic	●	
Denmark	●	●
France	●	●
Germany	●	●
Hungary	●	
Ireland	●	●
Italy	●	●
Netherlands	●	●
Poland	●	
Slovak Republic	●	

[83] Art. 116(1).
[84] Art. 116(2).
[85] For transitional provisions regarding "essentially derived varieties", see 6.028; regarding farmers' privileges, see 6.029; regarding exhaustion of rights, see 6.031 and regarding duration of right, see 6.032.

SPAIN[1]	●	●
SWEDEN	●	●
SWITZERLAND	●	●
UNITED KINGDOM	●	●

NOTES

[1] All the above countries except Belgium and Spain that are signatories of the 1978 Convention have ratified it. Belgium and Spain have only ratified the 1961 Convention and the Additional Act of 1972.

[2] The 1991 Convention has yet to come into force.

CHAPTER SEVEN

ENFORCEMENT OF INTELLECTUAL PROPERTY

1. INTRODUCTION

7.001 It is often said that there is an inherent conflict between the enforcement of intellectual property rights and the free movement of goods across national boundaries. By Article 3(a) of the Treaty of Rome, one of the activities of the Community is the "elimination as between Member States, of customs duties and of quantitative restrictions on the import and export of goods, and of all other measures having equivalent effect". It is thus not surprising that the European Court of Justice and Commission have developed a body of case law in an attempt to reconcile this conflict. In doing so, they have sought to prevent intellectual property rights from being improperly used to artificially divide up the Common Market.

Articles 30 and 34 ban quantitative restrictions on imports and exports and all measures having equivalent effect in the Member States. However, Article 36 derogates from the above principle in that the free movement of goods provisions do not apply where, *inter alia*, such behaviour is justified on the grounds of the protection of industrial and commercial property. This derogation has a proviso that it does not apply where "such prohibitions or restrictions constitute a means of arbitrary discrimination or a disguised restriction on trade between Member States".[1] The main provision, its derogation and the latter's proviso reflect the Member States' attempt to reconcile this inherent conflict.

In seeking to resolve the inherent conflict, the Commission and European Court of Justice have sought to look behind the mere territorial monopolistic nature of intellectual property and have examined the reason that patents, copyright, trade marks, etc., exist so as to be sure that the owner of a monopoly granted under a country's laws exercises his rights in a proper and fair manner. Patents, trade marks, copyright, plant breeders' rights, design rights, semiconductor topographical rights, and other forms of intellectual property all possess common characteristics. These are that they are creatures of law which confer on the owner the exclusive right to commercially exploit goods, processes or services protected by the intellectual property within a defined territory. The

[1] Art. 36, 2nd sentence.

grant of such a monopoly permits the owner to reap a greater financial reward from such exploitation than if he had to compete in the open market. There are essentially two reasons for the creation of intellectual property rights. Firstly, there is the doctrine of *private justification*. This rationalises the existence of intellectual property as being a reward for the creative endeavours of the inventor (in the case of patents), the author or artist (in the case of copyright), the designer (in the case of industrial design), the plant breeder (in the case of plant breeder's rights), the owner of branded goods with a high reputation (in the case of trade marks). Secondly, there is the doctrine of *public justification*. This justifies the existence of intellectual property as necessary to encourage technical and artistic progress in society. Thus, the lure of a 20 year patent monopoly will encourage companies to invest in research and development which may lead to an invention. Similarly, plant breeders need a considerable time for propagating before seeds can be brought to the market. Without a monopoly, there would be little incentive to develop new strains. Trade marks can also be publicly justified as being necessary to prevent confusion in the marketplace and encourage competition between rival concerns. In most examples of intellectual property, both doctrines are capable of applying, though on particular facts, only one may apply. For instance, the person who invented the wheel probably did not do a large amount of research into circular dynamics but had a brainwave. In such circumstances, there is no public justification for granting a 20 year patent, merely the private justification. In relation to registered trade marks, the use of a similar mark on similar goods which confuses will be injurious to the public as they will be confused, whereas the use of a similar mark on dissimilar goods may merely cause the public to associate (but not confuse) the two marks. This would not be against the public interest but merely be against the private interest of the trade mark owner and it would dilute the goodwill of the mark.[2]

In considering the relationship between intellectual property and competition law, there has been much emphasis on the public justification theory. Thus, intellectual property monopolies are often defended in a competition context as encouraging technological and artistic progress and increasing consumer choice.[3] In contrast, in relation to Articles 30 to 36 and the use of intellectual property rights, the Commission and the ECJ have adopted the private justification theory. In other words, the aim of intellectual property is to *reward* the inventor or creator and if exercise of the intellectual property rights is for an ulterior purpose, this is not *justified* under Article 36. The theory has been refined so that the rights owner is only permitted to be rewarded once and cannot subsequently be rewarded again as protected goods cross national boundaries. The case law has sought to reconcile the need for the free movement of goods (whether protected by rights or not) and the right of an inventor or

[2] See para. 3.073 *et seq.*
[3] See para. 8.011 *et seq.*

author to be rewarded for his creation. Accordingly, the ECJ has ruled that once a good has been placed on the market by the owner of the rights or with his consent, he can not prevent further movement of those goods within the Community.[4] The public justification theory is more applicable to the field of competition law and has played little part in the jurisprudence of Articles 30 to 36 in relation to intellectual property.

7.002 *Plan of chapter*—this chapter is concerned with whether or not the exercise of intellectual property rights may be contrary to the free movement of goods provisions and Article 85 of the Treaty of Rome. The chapter examines the application of Articles 30 to 36 to intellectual property and unfair competition law. At the end, it examines the effect of Article 85 on the *exercise* of intellectual property rights. The reader should be aware that the exercise of intellectual property rights may also amount to an abuse of a dominant position. This is discussed in Chapter Eleven.[5]

2. Free Movement of Goods between Member States—E.C. Treaty Provisions

7.003 The general provision for the free movement of goods is Article 3(a). This provides that:

> "For the purposes set out in Article 2, the activities of the Community shall include, as provided in this Treaty and in accordance with the timetable set out therein:
> (a) the elimination as between Member States of custom duties and of quantitative restrictions on the import and export of goods, and of all other measures having equivalent effect . . . "

The Articles that implement Article 3(a) in relation to quantitative restrictions are Articles 30 to 37 of the Treaty of Rome. Articles 31, 32, 33, 35 and 37 are transitional provisions which do not concern the reader.[6]

Article 30 states that:

> "Quantitative restrictions on imports and all measures having equivalent effect shall, without prejudice to the following provisions, be prohibited between Member States."

Article 34(1)[7] states very much the same with regard to exports:

> "Quantitative restrictions on exports, and all measures having equivalent effect, shall be prohibited between Member States."

[4] Note that under Arts. 30 to 36, the ECJ has not concerned itself with the level of reward which is a competition concern.

[5] See para. 11.042 *et seq.*

[6] These provisions provide for the phasing out of restrictions, quotas and state monopolies which discriminate between nationals and undertakings of Member States.

[7] Art. 34(2) is a transitional provision.

One should note that Article 34 unlike Article 30 does not state that such restrictions and measures are without prejudice to the following provisions (*i.e.* the free movement provisions).

Article 36 provides that:

> "The provisions of Articles 30 to 34 shall not preclude[8] prohibitions or restrictions on imports, exports or goods in transit justified on grounds of public morality, public policy or public security; the protection of health and life of humans, animals or plants; the protection of national treasures possessing artistic, historic or archaeological value; or the protection of industrial and commercial property. Such prohibitions shall not however constitute a means of arbitrary discrimination or a disguised restriction on trade between Member States."[9]

Unlike Articles 85 and 86, there is no "appreciable effect" rule for Article 30.[10]

Also of importance for the purposes of discussion below is Article 222 which provides that:

> "The Treaty shall in no way prejudice the rules in Member States governing the system of property ownership."

If the prohibition or restriction is *justified* on the grounds of the protection of industrial or commercial property then it is not a prohibition or restriction contrary to the Treaty of Rome's free movement of goods provisions.

The phrase "*justified*" in Article 36(1) would appear to mean that the mere exercise of intellectual property rights so as to prevent imports or exports is not sufficient to bring such a prohibition within Article 36(1). It must be justified on grounds of the protection of industrial and commercial property. Secondly, the phrase "*such prohibitions*" in Article 36(2) refers to the prohibitions in the first sentence. Thus, on a strict literal analysis of Article 36, *even* if the prohibitions or restrictions *are justified* for the protection of industrial and commercial property, they must not constitute a means of arbitrary discrimination or a disguised restriction on trade between Member States.[11] Thus, on the literal word-

[8] Thus this phrase renders inconsequential the fact that Art. 34 fails to mention "without prejudice to the following provisions".

[9] For convenience's sake, the two sentences will hereafter be referred to as Art. 36(1) and Art. 36(2).

[10] See *Van der Haar* [1984] E.C.R. 1797; Oliver, *Free Movement of Goods*, p. 81; Reindl, "The Magic of Magill: TV Program Guides as a Limit of Copyright Law?" IIC 1993 1 60 at p. 70; Case 16/83 *Criminal Proceedings against Karl Prantl*: [1984] E.C.R. 1299, [1985] 2 C.M.L.R. 238 at Point 20.

[11] See Case 119/75, *Terrapin v. Terranova*: [1976] E.C.R. 1039, [1976] 2 C.M.L.R. 482, Point 4 of the ECJ's judgment where it was stressed that the national court should concern itself as to whether the rights in question are exercised with the same strictness against all whatever the national origin of any possible infringer. See also para. 7.033 on Art. 36(2).

ing of Article 36, the owner of intellectual property rights has a limited scope to exercise his rights.

The European Court of Justice has on several occasions repeated that Article 36, as it constitutes a derogation from the basic rule that all obstacles to the free movement of goods between Member States shall be eliminated, must be interpreted strictly.[12] However, in contrast, the European Court has interpreted the expression "industrial and commercial" policy widely. The expression is one more familiar to continental lawyers and has been held to apply to patents, trade marks, industrial designs, copyright and plant variety rights. However, it does not apply to unfair competition and fair trading laws which are to be considered under Article 30.[13] Service marks probably fall within the expression "industrial property" but are not used in relation to goods and are thus not affected by Articles 30 to 36.[14]

The European Court has issued numerous judgments on the meaning of Articles 30, 34 and 36 in relation to the use of intellectual property rights to prevent inter-State trade. Certain doctrines have developed from such case law and these are discussed below. To facilitate such a discussion, two landmark cases which firmly established three of the most important doctrines in this field are set out below, at para. 7.005 to 7.009.

3. Articles 30 to 36: Intellectual Property Doctrines

7.004 Early cases on the application of Articles 30 to 36 on the import and export of goods which were alleged to infringe intellectual property rights under national law were few and alluded to the free movement provisions rather than directly applied them.[15] This is despite the fact that nowadays the facts of the cases would be recognised as falling within Article 36. It seems that the parties involved in these early disputes were slow to realise that their facts came within the free movement provisions. Most defendants tried to argue that the exercise of property rights were prohibited by virtue of Articles 85 and 86.[16] When these cases were referred under Article 177 to the European Court, the latter only con-

[12] Case 46/76, *Bauhuis v. Netherlands*: [1977] E.C.R. 5; Case 95/81, *E.C. Commission v. Italy*: [1980] E.C.R. 2187 and Case 103/84, *E.C. Commission v. Italy*: [1986] E.C.R. 1759.

[13] See Case 120/78, *Rewe-Zentral AG v. Bundesmonopolverwetungfur Branntwein*: [1979] E.C.R. 649, [1979] 3 C.M.L.R. 494 (commonly known as the *Cassis de Dijon* case). See also Beier, "Industrial Property and Internal Market" IIC 1990 2 131 at p. 145 for criticism of the exclusion of such laws from Art. 36.

[14] See Beier, "Industrial Property and Internal Market" IIC 1990 2 131 at p. 145, n. 33.

[15] Case 56/64, *Etablissements Consten SA and Grundig-Verkaufs-GmbH v. EC Commission*: [1966] E.C.R. 299, [1966] C.M.L.R. 418, 476; Case 24/67, *Parke-Davis v. Probel*: [1968] E.C.R. 55, [1968] C.M.L.R. 47, 59; Case 40/70, *Sirena SRL v. Eda SRL*: [1971] E.C.R. 64, [1971] C.M.L.R. 260, 273.

[16] For the success of such arguments, see para. 8.052.

cerned itself with resolving the specific questions that had been referred. The European Court often strained the meaning of Articles 85 and 86 so as to find the practice contrary to the Articles.

In the early 1970s, the European Court of Justice gave a series of landmark judgments on Article 30 to 36 in relation to intellectual property. These judgments established certain doctrines and laid the foundations for the reconciliation of intellectual property with the free movement of goods. To facilitate the discussion of such doctrines, two landmark cases are set out in detail below. These two cases established three important doctrines.

(a) Deutsche Grammophon

7.005 The first landmark judgment of the European Court which directly ruled on the application of Article 36 was the *Deutsche Grammophon*[17] case. In this case, the reference was from the Hanseatische Oberlandesgericht.

Facts—Deutsche Grammophon is a German company which produces gramophone records. In Germany, it supplied records under the "Polydor" mark directly to retailers. The retail prices of the records were controlled. Retailers contracted, *inter alia*, that they could only import Deutsche Grammophon records from abroad with the authorisation of Deutsche. This was given if the retailer undertook to observe the resale price maintenance scheme with respect to these imported goods as well.

Deutsche Grammophon in Germany exported records to its Paris subsidiary in France. These were then re-exported back to Germany where Metro, a German wholesaler and not part of the Deutsche Grammophon network, purchased them. These records were then sold by Metro to retail customers at a price below that fixed by Deutsche in Germany.

Deutsche Grammophon obtained an injunction in Germany for infringement of its exclusive right under German law, as manufacturer of sound recording to reproduce and to distribute the recording in Germany. The matter went on appeal to the Hanseatische Oberlandesgericht who referred the matter under Article 177 to the European Court on questions concerning the interpretation of Articles 85 and 86.

7.006 *Judgment*—the European Court although it had not been asked as to the compatibility of Articles 30 to 36 with the legality of the German action held that the enforcement of such a right was incompatible with the provision regarding the free movement of goods.

The European Court said that:

> " . . . although the Treaty does not affect the *existence* of industrial property rights conferred by the national legislation of a Member-State, the *exercise* of these rights may come within the prohibitions

[17] Case 78/70, *Deutsche Grammophon GmbH v. Metro-SB-Grossmarkte GmbH & Co., KG*: [1971] E.C.R. 487, [1971] 1 C.M.L.R. 631.

of the Treaty. Although Article 36 permits prohibitions or restrictions on the free movement of goods that are justified for the protection of industrial and commercial property, it only allows such restriction on the freedom of trade to the extent that they are *justified* for the protection of the rights that form the *specific object* of this property.

If a protection right analogous to copyright is used in order to prohibit in one Member State, the marketing of goods that have been brought onto the market by the holder of the right or with his consent in the territory of another Member-State solely because this marketing has not occurred in the domestic market, such a prohibition maintaining the isolation of the national markets conflicts with the essential aim of the Treaty, the integration of the national markets into one uniform market. This aim could not be achieved if by virtue of the various legal systems of the Member States private persons were able to divide the market and cause *arbitrary discriminations or disguised restrictions in trade between the Member-States.*

Accordingly, it would conflict with the provisions regarding the free movement of goods in the Common Market if a manufacturer of recordings exercised the exclusive right granted to him by the legislation of a Member-State to market the protected articles in order to prohibit the marketing in that Member-State of *products that had been sold by himself or with his consent in another Member-State* solely because this marketing had not occurred in the territory of the first Member-State"[emphasis added].[18]

(b) Centrafarm v. Sterling & Winthrop

7.007 The next landmark decision in this area was the decision in the joined cases of *Centrafarm BV v. Sterling Drug Inc.* and *Centrafarm BV v. Winthrop BV.*[19]

7.008 *Facts*—Sterling Drug Inc. held parallel national patents for a drug for urinary tract infections in, *inter alia*, Holland and Great Britain. Furthermore, Sterling-Winthrop Group Ltd held the trade mark "Negram" for the drug in the United Kingdom and its wholly-owned subsidiary Winthrop BV held it in Holland.

Centrafarm imported into Holland without the consent of Sterling Drug Inc. the drug from the United Kingdom where it had been properly put on the market by subsidiaries of Sterling Drug Inc. (whom were licensed by Sterling Drug Inc.), thus benefitting from a considerable price difference for the drug in the two countries. Some of the drug packaging bore the mark "Negram".

[18] Point 13.
[19] Cases 15/74, [1974] E.C.R. 1147, [1974] 2 C.M.L.R. 480.

Sterling Drug Inc. and Winthrop BV brought patent and trade mark infringement proceedings in Holland against Centrafarm. Proceedings eventually went to the Hoge Raad (the Dutch Supreme Court) who referred to the European Court (*inter alia*) the question of whether the use of the trade mark and patent rights was contrary to Articles 30 to 36.

7.009 JUDGMENT: The European Court stated that such an exercise of rights was incompatible with Articles 30 to 36. It said that:

> "In so far as it makes an exception to one of the fundamental principles of the Common Market, Article 36 allows derogations to the free movement of goods only to the extent that such derogations are *justified for the protection of the rights which constitute the specific object of such property.*

As regards patents, the *specific object* of the industrial property is *inter alia* to ensure to the holder, so as to recompense the creative effort of the inventor, the exclusive right to utilise an invention with a view to the manufacture and first putting into circulation of industrial products, either directly or by the grant of licences to third parties, as well as the right to oppose any infringement."[20]

In relation to the trade mark action, the Court came to the same conclusion and said:

> "As regards trade marks, the specific object of commercial property is *inter alia* to ensure to the holder the exclusive right to utilise the mark for the first putting into circulation of a product, and to protect him thus against competitors who would take advantage of the position and reputation of the mark by selling goods improperly bearing the mark."[21]

The court said that:

> "The existence in national laws on industrial and commercial property of provisions that the right of a patentee is not exhausted by the marketing in another Member State of the patented product, so that the patentee may oppose the import into his own State of the product marketed in another State, may continue an obstacle to the free movement of goods.
>
> While such an obstacle to free movement may be justifiable for reasons of protection of industrial property when the protection is invoked against a product coming from a Member-State in which it is not patentable and has been manufactured by third parties without the consent of the patentee or where the original parties are legal and economically independent of each other, the *derogation to the*

[20] Para. 829, p. 503 (*Sterling* case) (*Winterby* case).
[21] p. 509.

> *principle of free movement of goods is not justified when the product has been lawfully put by the patentee himself or with his consent on the market of the Member-State* from which it is being imported *e.g.* in the case of a holder of parallel patents."[22]

The court also said that it was immaterial whether the patentee and licensee belonged to same group or not. The essential factor was whether the product had been marketed by the patentee himself or with his consent.[23] Furthermore, the Court said that this was regardless as to whether there were price differences between the countries resulting from measures taken by the public authorities in the exporting country (United Kingdom) to control prices.

The above cases introduced or clarified three doctrines in regard to intellectual property and Article 3 which for convenience's sake are described as the "existence v. exercise" doctrine; the "specific object" doctrine and the "consent" doctrine.

(c) Existence v. Exercise

7.010 The "*existence v. exercise*" doctrine mentioned in *Deutsche Grammophon* had been mentioned previously by the Court in relation to Article 85.[24] It was however the first time that it had been applied by the Court in relation to an Article 36 ruling. This doctrine distinguishes between two aspects, the existence and the exercise, of an intellectual property right. The former is unaffected by the Treaty of Rome whereas the latter *may* come within the prohibitions of the Treaty.

Such a distinction has been forcefully criticised by several authors.[25] The origin of the "existence v. exercise" doctrine derives from the ECJ's judgment in *Consten & Grundig v. E.C. Commission*[26] in response to Consten's argument that applying Article 85 to a particular use of a trade mark would violate Article 222 of the Treaty of Rome. The ECJ responded by saying that the challenged decision of the Commission did not affect the grant of the right but only limited their exercise to the extent necessary to give effect to the prohibition under Article 85. However, legal commentators have noted that Article 222 was derived from Article 83 of the ECSC Treaty which was intended only to ensure that Member States would be free to determine whether enterprises subject to the

[22] Paras. 10–11, p. 503.

[23] Paras. 18–21.

[24] Case 56/64, *Etablissements Consten & Grundig v. E.C. Commission*: [1966] E.C.R. 299, [1966] C.M.L.R. 418; Case 24/67, *Parke Davis v. Probel*: [1968] E.C.R. 55, [1968] C.M.L.R. 47; Case 40/70, *Sirena Srl v. Eda Srl*: [1971] E.C.R. 69, [1975] C.M.L.R. 1.

[25] Beier, "Industrial Property and Internal Market" IIC 1990 2 131; Reindl, "The Magic of Magill: TV Program Guides as a Limit of Copyright Law?" IIC 1993 1 60; Korah, *EEC Competition Law*, (4th Ed. 1991).

[26] Case 56/64, [1966] E.C.R. 299, [1966] C.M.L.R. 418.

ECSC Treaty are publicly or privately owned.[27] Thus, critics argue that Article 222 provides no basis for the existence v. exercise doctrine.[28]

If the existence v. exercise doctrine owes its origin to Article 222, then "system of property ownership" in that Article would have to be construed narrowly as not including that part of the legislation which confers private rights on individuals. Such analysis is unhelpful and contributes little to resolving the conflict between the principle of the free movement of goods and the protection of industrial property.[29] The conferring of private rights on individuals by intellectual property statutes is the essential part of intellectual property law. A prohibition on the *exercise* of such rights means that the essential part of the relevant law is unenforceable and as such, the prohibition constitutes an attack on the very *existence* of such laws. Articles 30 to 36 are concerned with state measures. If a state measure constitutes a quantitative restriction and is not justifiable under Article 36, it is void. Thus, Articles 30 to 36 are only concerned with the validity (*i.e.* the existence) of national laws.[30] If a law is found to be prohibited under Articles 30 to 36, it no longer has any valid existence at a Community level. Accordingly, to introduce a distinction between the existence and exercise of rights for the purposes of Articles 30 to 36 is illogical and wrong. On a more pragmatic basis, the existence of intellectual property rights are valueless unless the owner is prepared to exercise them. At best, the "existence" of rights may have a deterrent value on potential infringers. However, the moment they are used to found a cause of action against another (or even where the other party is threatened with court action), they are being exercised. Accordingly, from a private party's viewpoint (and hence his legal advisers), the distinction serves no purpose.

Accordingly, it is submitted that the application of the existence v. exercise doctrine is of little value.[31] Recently, the doctrine has been far less invoked in the analysis of intellectual property cases under Article 36. Indeed, in a recent seminal case, it was not mentioned at all.[32] In a recent important case on the application of Article 86 to a refusal to

[27] See Vinje, "Magill: Its Impact on the Information Technology Industry" [1992] 11 EIPR 397 at p. 398. See also Marenco and Banks, "Intellectual Property and the Community Rules on Free Movement: Discrimination Unearthed" [1990] 15 ELR, n. 8 at pp. 224 and 226; Myrick, "Will IP on Technology Still be Viable in a Unitary Market?" [1992] 9 EIPR 298 at p. 299.

[28] *e.g.* see Vinje, *ibid.* at p. 398.

[29] Beier, "Industrial Property and Internal Market" IIC 1990 2 131 at p. 147.

[30] See René Joliet "Trade Mark Law and the Free Movement of Goods: the overruling of HAG I" 311C/1992 at p. 313 ". . . it is not the exercise of the right, *i.e.* the national legislation that constitutes the obstacle to free movement; it is the national legislation making it possible to exercise the right in such circumstances by instituting infringement proceedings."

[31] See Reindl, "The Magic of Magill: TV Program Guides as a Limit of Copyright Law?" IIC 1993 1 60 at p. 68, n. 30.

[32] *SA CNL-Sucal NV v. Hag GF AG ("Hag 2")* [1990] 3 C.M.L.R. 571.

licence, the CFI stated that the *exercise* of an exclusive right in principle corresponds to the *substance* of the relevant intellectual property.[33] Such suggests that it is implicitly recognised that it serves little purpose to talk of the existence of rights as opposed to their exercise.

What is clearly true is that the ECJ has stated several times in relation to Articles 30 to 36 and intellectual property that, in the absence of Community standardisation or harmonisation of laws, the determination of the conditions and procedure under which protection is granted is a matter for national rules.[34] In such a sense, it could be said that the existence of intellectual property rights is inviolate from attack under the Treaty of Rome. However, such a principle does not support the *existence v. exercise* doctrine because the exercise of intellectual property rights cannot be prohibited under Articles 30 to 36 purely on the ground that there *exists* disparity in the respective laws of Member States which would favour one undertaking over another.[35] A rights owner is not prohibited from exercising his rights against an imported product merely because a parallel right in another Member State has expired.[36]

(d) Specific object

7.011 In *Deutsche Grammophon v. Metro-Grossmarkte*,[37] the ECJ stated that Article 36 permits prohibitions or restrictions of industrial and commercial property to the extent that they are justified for the protection of the rights that form the *specific object* of the property.[38] Such a formulation immediately begged the question as to what the specific object of a particular intellectual property was. The answer for patents and trade marks was provided in the joined cases of *Centrafarm BV v. Sterling Drug Inc.* and *Centrafarm v. Winthrop*.[39] The ECJ said that the specific object of a patent is *inter alia* to ensure to the holder so as to recompense the creative effort of the inventor, the exclusive right to utilise an invention with a

[33] Case T-69/89, *Radio Telefis Eireann v. E.C. Commission*: [1991] II E.C.R. 485, [1991] 4 C.M.L.R. 586; Case T-70/89, *BBC v. E.C. Commission*: [1992] II E.C.R. 535, [1991] C.M.L.R. 669; Case T-76/89, *Independent Television Publication Ltd v. E.C. Commission*: [1992] II E.C.R. 575, [1991] C.M.L.R. 745; at para. 72 in RTE.

[34] *e.g.* see Case 35/87, *Thetford Corporation v. Fiamma SpA*: [1988] E.C.R. 3585, [1988] 3 C.M.L.R. 549; Case 341/87, *EMI Electrola GmbH v. Patricia Im und Export*: [1989] 2 C.M.L.R. 413; Case 144/81, *Keurkoop v. Nancy Kean Gifts*: [1982] E.C.R. 2853, [1983] 2 C.M.L.R. 47; Case C-235/89, *Compulsory Patent Licences: E.C. Commission v. United Kingdom & Italy*: [1992] I E.C.R. 777, [1992] 2 C.M.L.R. 709; *Deutsche Renault v. Audi*: [1993] I–E.C.R. 6227. See below, para. 7.031.

[35] *e.g.* see Case 341/87, *EMI Electrola GmbH v. Patricia Im und Export*: [1989] E.C.R. 79, [1989] 2 C.M.L.R. 413.

[36] *ibid.*

[37] Case 78/70, *Deutsche Grammophon v. Metro-Grossmarkt*: [1971] E.C.R. 487, [1971] C.M.L.R. 631.

[38] Para. 11.

[39] Joined Cases 15–16/74, *Centrafarm BV v. Sterling Drug Inc & Centrafram v. Winthrop*: [1974] E.C.R. 1147, [1974] 2 C.M.L.R. 480.

view to the manufacture and first putting into circulation of industrial products either directly or through licensees.[40] Similarly, for trade marks, the specific object was the exclusive right to utilise the mark for the first putting into circulation of a product and to protect the trade mark owner against competitors who would take advantage of the position and reputation of the mark by selling goods improperly bearing the mark.

It has been said that the "specific object" test is conceptually more consistent with the effects of a court judgment than the existence/exercise doctrine, *i.e.* the unenforceability or non-existence of a national intellectual property law.[41] However, the ECJ has never attempted to develop the theory of the "specific object" of a right in the abstract without reference to the right itself. Indeed, there would appear to be no underlying implicit theoretical basis to be derived from the ECJ's decisions in relation to the meaning of specific object. Certainly, neither the Treaty of Rome nor its secondary legislation provide a sufficient legal basis for such a definition.[42] Instead, the ECJ has several times "magically" invoked the phrase "justified under the specific object" in order to rationalise a particular finding.[43] This failure to develop a proper theory of the specific object of a right has meant that as a legal analytical tool, it must be used with caution. This is perhaps best illustrated by the ECJ's failure to properly analyse the application of the doctrine of specific object to the assignment of intellectual property rights in the E.C.[44]

It has been suggested that the specific object is essentially the right to be rewarded. For instance, the words:

> " . . . the specific object of the industrial property is *inter alia* to ensure to the holder, so as to recompense the creative effort of the inventor, the exclusive right to . . . first putting into circulation of industrial products . . . "

in *Centrafarm v. Sterling* suggest such an interpretation. However, whilst a right to reward may be included in the specific object, such an analysis

[40] For reiteration of this principle, see *Compulsory Patent Licences: EC Commission v. United Kingdom & Italy*: [1992] I E.C.R. 777, [1992] 2 C.M.L.R. 709; Case 434/85, *Allen & Hanbury's Ltd v. Generics (UK) Ltd*: [1988] E.C.R. 1245, [1988] 1 C.M.L.R. 701.

[41] Reindl, "The Magic of Magill: TV Program Guides as a Limit of Copyright Law?" IIC 1993 1 60 at p. 66.

[42] See Beier, "Industrial Property and Internal Market" IIC 1990 2 131 at p. 148.

[43] For an interesting example of this, the reader is referred to Case 193/83, *Windsurfing International v. E.C. Commission*: [1986] E.C.R. 611, [1986] 3 C.M.L.R. 489, a case concerning the validity under Art. 85 of clauses of a patent licence. Here, the ECJ held that certain clauses were unenforceable or not by reference to whether such clauses fell within the "specific subject matter" of a patent without any attempt to define what was meant by such a phrase. See para. 8.060 *et seq.*

[44] See C–9/93 [1994] 3 C.M.L.R. 857 *Ideal Standard*, Judgment of ECJ, June 24, 1994, [1995] FSR 1–72; Tritton, "Articles 30 to 36 and Intellectual Property: Is the jurisprudence of the ECJ now of an Ideal Standard" [1994] EIPR 423.

is oversimplistic when one reviews the case law of the ECJ. In *Windsurfing*,[45] quality control relating to products covered by the patent were held to fall within the specific subject matter of a patent.[46] Similarly, a contractual clause stipulating that a notice stating that licensed products had been licensed by Windsurfing International was held to fall within the specific subject matter of a patent.[47] The ECJ held in a case concerning a compulsory licence that the specific object had been altered to ensure a fair return to the patentee, *i.e.* normally the specific object of a patent is more than mere reward to the patentee.[48]

Others have suggested that the doctrine of specific object is in effect the same as the doctrine of exhaustion.[49] Once the rights owner or someone with his consent has "first put" the protected project on the market, he has "consented" to its marketing throughout the E.C. However, as seen later, where the two doctrines are compared, the two doctrines are not identical.[50]

Accordingly, the doctrine of "specific object" must be considered a fluid concept which is defined and refined on a case by case basis. As has been commented, the main advantage of this formula is that it allows subtle distinctions to be made depending on the type of intellectual property in issue.[51] The disadvantage of this flexibility is that its application to a set of facts different to that of a decided case may be uncertain.

The specific object of each type of intellectual property is examined in detail later on in this Chapter.

(e) Consent/exhaustion

7.012 Both *Deutsche Grammophon* and *Centrafarm v. Sterling & Winthrop* emphasise that where a protected product has been placed on the market by the rights owner or with his consent in a Member State, then Article 36 cannot be invoked and thus the owner cannot use his rights to prevent further trading in the product. This is known as the *doctrine of consent.* The doctrine of consent is sometimes referred to as the *doctrine of exhaustion* in that the owner of the right has "exhausted" his rights in the intellectual property once the protected product had been placed on

[45] Case 193/83, *Windsurfing International v. E.C. Commission*: [1986] E.C.R. 611, [1986] 3 C.M.L.R. 489. This case concerned the application of Art. 85 to a patent licence and is discussed in detail at para. 8.060 *et seq.*
[46] Para. 45.
[47] Para. 72.
[48] See Case 19/84, *Pharmon v. Hoechst*: [1985] E.C.R. 2281, [1985] 3 C.M.L.R. 775 and Case 434/85, *Allen & Hanburys Ltd v. Generics (UK) Limited*: [1988] E.C.R. 1245, [1988] 1 C.M.L.R. 701.
[49] See below, para. 7.012.
[50] See below, para, 7.027.
[51] Advocate-General Jacobs in *SA CNL-Sucal NV v. Hag GF AG ("Hag 2")*: [1990] 3 C.M.L.R. 571 at p. 580.

the market by himself or with his consent.[52] The doctrine of consent has been applied numerous times by the European Court and now must be considered a cast-iron rule of law.[53] It prevents the owner of the right in effect being remunerated more than once for the marketing of a protected good. It also prevents the owner from hindering the free movement of goods and partitioning the common market.[54]

It is tempting as with the doctrine of specific object to view the doctrine of consent as one recognising the right of the proprietor to be rewarded. However, such is not the case.[55] In *Centrafarm v. Sterling*, the doctrine merely defines the limit that intellectual property rights can be used to derogate from the free movement of goods. Thus, where a patent was subject to compulsory licensing subject to a reasonable royalty and patented products had been placed on the market pursuant to such provisions, the patentee was deemed not to have consented to its marketing although he had been financially remunerated.[56] Conversely, where patent protection was denied to pharmaceuticals in Italy but patent protection existed in Germany, the ECJ held that the patentee in Germany was not entitled to prevent the importation of a pharmaceutical from Italy to Germany as the product had been put on the market in Italy by the patentee or with his consent. In such case, it is arguable that the patentee had not obtained the substance of the exclusive rights that flow from the patent.[57] Certainly, the patentee was not in a position to recoup his research and development costs as effectively as if there had been no competition. Furthermore, in *Ideal Standard*,[58] the rights owner sought to exercise his trade mark rights in Germany against a parallel importer of goods bearing an identical French mark which had previously been assigned by the rights owner to a French company. The ECJ in ruling in favour of the rights owner ignored the fact that the rights owner had been in effect rewarded for goods bearing the French trade mark being placed

[52] That the two concepts are essentially the same has been recognised by the Court, *e.g.* see Case 19/84, *Pharmon BV v. Hoechst AG*: [1985] E.C.R. 2281, [1985] 3 C.M.L.R. 775 at Point 20. The principle of exhaustion is recognised in the national laws of several Member States—see Beier, "Industrial Property and Internal Market" IIC 1990 2 131, at pp. 151–152.

[53] The doctrine was recently re-emphasised in *SA CNL-Sucal NV v. Hag GF AG ("Hag 2")*: [1990] 3 C.M.L.R. 571, para. 15. See also Case 19/84, *Pharmon v. Hoechst*: [1985] E.C.R. 2281, [1985] 3 C.M.L.R. 775 and Case 187/80, *Merck v. Stephar*: [1981] E.C.R. 2063, [1981] 3 C.M.L.R. 463.

[54] Of course, in any event, the artificial partitioning of the market is prohibited under Art. 36(2).

[55] See Roudard, "Direct Exports in Community Law" *Patent World*, May 1989, p. 34 where she discusses the ECJ's progress from emphasis on the reward criterion to emphasis on the consent criterion.

[56] Case 19/84, *Pharmon v. Hoechst*: [1985] E.C.R. 2281, [1985] 3 C.M.L.R. 775.

[57] Demaret, "Compulsory Licence and the Free Movement of Goods under Community Law" 18 IIC 161, 176; Case 187/80, *Merck v. Stephar*: [1981] E.C.R. 2063, [1981] 3 C.M.L.R. 463.

[58] *Ideal Standard*, Judgment of ECJ, June 24, 1994. See n. 44 above.

on the market. The connection between the right to reward and the doctrine of consent/exhaustion is that the former is an argument for justifying the principle of exhaustion but does not determine the latter's scope.[59]

It is clear that a rights owner cannot limit his consent to the marketing of a protected product in a Member State. Thus, even if the rights owner contractually bans a party from marketing a product other than in a Member State, the ECJ will not permit him to exercise his rights against a parallel importer importing products so marketed into another Member State.[60] Once the product has been lawfully marketed, he can no longer exercise his rights and prevent the subsequent movement within the Common Market of such goods.

The doctrine of consent has been consistently applied and refined by the European Court of Justice since *Deutsche Grammophon* and the *Sterling* cases.[61] The application of the doctrine of consent and the doctrine of specific object is now discussed in relation to particular factual circumstances.

(f) Parties economically or legally linked

7.013 If a protected product is placed on the market by a party who is economically or legally linked to the owner of the right then the owner's rights are exhausted.[62] Legal links suggest licensing arrangements whereby the licensor exercises control over the licensed products and the placing of them on the market. Economic links will generally be links that exist as a result of belonging to the same group of companies. In such circumstances, there will be no need to investigate whether one party actually consented to the marketing of the product by the other party. Parties will be deemed to have consented to the marketing and thus their rights are exhausted. Nowadays, with multi-national conglomerates, the actual links between subsidiaries may be tenuous and remote.[63]

[59] See Beier, "Industrial Property and Internal Market" IIC 1990 2 131, at p. 156 where he puts this view forward in criticism of early German writers' views of the predominance of the reward theory.

[60] Case 58/80, *Dansk Supermarked v. Imerco*: [1981] E.C.R. 181, [1981] 3 C.M.L.R. 590.

[61] See Case 119/75, *Terrapin v. Terranova*: [1976] E.C.R. 1039, [1976] 2 C.M.L.R. 482; Cases 55/80 & 57/80, *MEMBRAN & K-TEL v. GEMA*: [1981] E.C.R. 147, [1981] 2 C.M.L.R. 44; Case 187/80, *Merck v. Stephar*: [1981] E.C.R. 2063, [1981] 3 C.M.L.R. 463; Case 58/80, *Dansk Supermarked A/S v. Imerco A/S*: [1981] E.C.R. 181, [1981] 3 C.M.L.R. 590; Case 144/81, *Keurkoop v. Nancy Kean Gifts*: [1982] E.C.R. 2853, [1983] 2 C.M.L.R. 47; Case 19/84, *Pharmon v. Hoechst*: [1985] E.C.R. 2281, [1985] 3 C.M.L.R. 775; *SA CNL-Sucal NV v. Hag GF AG ("Hag 2")*: [1990] 3 C.M.L.R. 571; *Ideal Standard*, Judgment of ECJ, June 24, 1994, [1994] 3 C.M.L.R. 857.

[62] See Point 11 in Joined Cases 15–16/74, *Centrafarm BV v. Sterling Inc.*: [1974] E.C.R. 1147, [1974] 2 C.M.L.R. 480 and *Ideal Standard* at paras. [34] to [36].

[63] In the English case concerning parallel import *Revlon v. Cripps* [1980] FSR 85, C.A., it was held that each member of a multinational group must be deemed to have consented to the marketing of products by other members pp. 105–106.

(g) Differing protection in Member States

7.014 It is for the intellectual property owner to decide, in the light of all the circumstances, under what conditions he will market his product, including the possibility of marketing it in a Member State where the law does not provide protection or the same rate of remuneration for the product. As said in *Merck v. Stephar*,[64] the Court said that:

> "It is for the proprietor of the patent to decide, in the light of all the circumstances, under what conditions he will market his product, including the possibility of marketing it in a Member State where the law does not provide patent protection for the product in question. If he decides to do so he must then accept the consequences of his choice as regards the free movement of the product within the Common Market, which is a fundamental principle forming part of the legal and economic circumstances which must be taken into account by the proprietor of the patent in determining the manner in which his exclusive right will be exercised."[65]

Thus, he cannot exercise his rights to prevent the import into Member State A of a protected product first put on the market by himself or with his consent in Member State B merely because the commercial return for the protected products in B is less than in A. In *Musik vertrieb*,[66] a case concerning the licensing of sound recordings, sound recordings were manufactured in England and a parallel importer imported them into Germany. A royalty had been negotiated on the basis of 6.25 per cent of the retail price as, under English legislation a party could obtain a statutory licence to manufacture sound recordings on payment of 6.25 per cent. Accordingly, 6.25 per cent represented a ceiling on negotiated royalty rates. Sound recordings produced in Germany were subject to a higher royalty which was collected by GEMA, the German collecting society. GEMA sought to exercise sound recording rights in Germany on behalf of the author. Even though it was submitted that such constituted a type of compulsory licence, the ECJ paid scant regard to such submissions and held that the fact that GEMA could not exercise its rights because the rights owner had consented to the marketing of the recordings in England. The fact that the rights owner could have obtained a higher rate under German laws was irrelevant. It was for the owner to decide under what circumstances he would market the goods.

Where the differing level of remuneration is because a product has been compulsorily licensed in a Member State, such considerations do not apply because the proprietor has not consented to the marketing of the product.[67] This leads to commercial absurdities. For instance, in

[64] Case 187/80, [1981] E.C.R. 2063, [1981] 3 C.M.L.R. 463.
[65] Para. 11.
[66] Case 55/80, *Musik Vertrieb Membran GmbH v. GEMA*: [1981] E.C.R. 147, [1981] 2 C.M.L.R. 44.
[67] See Case 19/84, *Pharmon v. Hoechst*: [1985] E.C.R. 2281, [1985] 3 C.M.L.R. 775.

Musik Vertrieb, if the rights owner had refused to license the other party, then the latter would have obtained a statutory licence paying the same royalty rate of 6.25 per cent. However, in such a case, the licensee would not have been able to export the sound recordings to Germany without the consent of the German rights owner.

In contrast, a parallel importer cannot argue that where a product has come on the market in one Member State because its laws do not provide for protection of such a product or because certain conditions have not been fulfilled, that it is entitled to import such a product into a Member State where protection does exist for such a product if the owner of such protection has not consented to the marketing of the product in the first Member State.[68]

(h) "Placed on the market"

7.015 Under the doctrine of consent, a rights owner has exhausted his rights in a protected product once he has placed the product on the market. Similarly, under the doctrine of specific object, a rights owner is not justified in exercising his rights in a product once he has put it into circulation within the Community. There is little authority on what is meant by placing on the market or putting into circulation and each case will depend on its facts. However, the Bundesgerichtshof, applying the European Court's judgment in *MEMBRAN & K-TEL v. GEMA*[69] held that where a German importer imported records from its English sister company which had acquired a licence from the Mechanical Copyright Protection Society to distribute the records in Great Britain, there was no question of the applicability of Articles 30 to 36 in the case of mere movements within a group of enterprises and where the goods have not yet left the group's internal field of operation.[70]

It should be noted that the distinction between a parallel import and a direct import into a Member State is often not made. Thus, in *Ideal Standard*,[71] the ECJ treated a case concerning direct exports to Germany by a French company as a case of parallel imports.[72] In fact, the goods were never placed in circulation in France.[73] Strictly speaking, a parallel importer buys goods in one country and exports to another whereas with a direct export, there is no purchase in the country of export.

[68] See para. 7.031 on Determination of Conditions for Protection a matter of National Law.

[69] Cases 55/80 & 57/80, [1981] E.C.R. 147, [1981] 2 C.M.L.R. 74 (ECJ); [1982] 1 C.M.L.R. 630 at p. 687 (Bundeisgerichtschof).

[70] The Court said that this accorded with the ECJ's judgment in Case 15/74, *Centrafarm BV v. Sterling Drug Inc.*: [1974] E.C.R. 1147, [1974] 2 C.M.L.R. 480.

[71] *Ideal Standard*, Judgment of ECJ, June 24, 1994, [1994] 3 C.M.L.R. 857.

[72] A parallel imported good is a good which has placed on the market (*i.e.* sold) in one State and subsequently exported to another State.

[73] Tritton, "Articles 30 to 36 and Intellectual Property: Is the jurisprudence of the ECJ now of an Ideal Standard" [1994] EIPR 423.

(i) Constructive consent

7.016 Whilst the issue of whether a product has been placed on the market or not is a relatively simple factual issue, the issue as to whether a person has *consented* to a product being placed on the market is more complicated. As discussed above, the rights owner cannot limit his consent to the marketing of a protected good in a particular state but must accept the subsequent free movement of that good within the Community.[74] To what extent is a person deemed to have consented to the marketing of a product? For instance, is the owner of a national right in marketing a product taken to have accepted the national legislation as a whole including all its consequences, adverse or otherwise? Does the failure to enforce rights against a third party mean that a rights owner has consented to the marketing of such products? Where a licensee places a product on the market in another licensee's territory in breach of his licence, is such a product placed on the market with the licensor's consent even though the licensee will be in breach of contract? Where a person assigns a trademark to a third party for a particular territory, has he consented to the marketing of goods bearing the trade mark by the assignee in his own territories? In these situations, it is normally clear that the rights owner has not consented to the *actual* marketing of the product. The issue is whether the owner of the right is *deemed* by the operation of Community law to have consented to the marketing of the product.

In general, the ECJ has rejected the concept of constructive consent. For instance, when a patent is subject to compulsory licensing provisions of a Member State and a product is placed on the market by virtue of such legislation, it is arguable that the patentee by obtaining a patent in that Member State, accepts all possible legislative consequences including the possibility of compulsory licensing. However, in *Pharmon v. Hoechst*,[75] the Court held that the party is not deemed to have consented to the lawful marketing of a product in a Member State by another person where the latter has marketed the product pursuant to a compulsory licence.[76]

7.017 In relation to trade marks, the ECJ has said that the decisive factor in considering the issue of consent is the possibility of control over the quality of the goods bearing the trade marks and not the actual exercise of that control.[77] The ECJ specifically rejected a submission by the Commission that by assigning a trade mark to a third party, the assignor has implicitly consented to the marketing of goods bearing the trade mark by the assignee, reiterating that in such circumstances where the assignee is

[74] See Case 58/80, *Dansk Supermarked v. Imerco*: [1981] E.C.R. 181, [1981] 3 C.M.L.R. 590.

[75] Case 19/84, *Pharmon v. Hoechst*: [1985] E.C.R. 2281, [1985] 3 C.M.L.R. 775.

[76] In *Pharmon v. Hoechst*, *ibid.*, the product was compulsorily licensed as a result of U.K. legislation which extended the length of protection of patents granted before the 1977 Patents Act came into force from 16 to 20 years but which permitted third parties to obtain licenses of right for the last four years of the patent term.

[77] *Ideal Standard*, Judgment of ECJ, June 24, 1994, [1994] 3 C.M.L.R. 857.

not economically or legally linked to the assignor, the assignor cannot exercise control over the assignee's goods.[78]

Also, Member States may provide for differing types of protection and differing periods. In such circumstances, the European Court has rejected the concept of constructive consent. For instance, where copyright in sound recordings expired in Denmark prior to its expiry in Germany, the Court held in *EMI Electrola v. Patricia*[79] that the German owner of the rights was not prohibited from exercising its rights against importers of the protected products from Denmark.[80] Similarly, where one Member State (U.K.) did not provide for a video rental right but another (Denmark) did, the Court held in *Warner Bros v. Christiansen* that the marketing of videos in the United Kingdom marketed by the copyright owner did not exhaust the rental right in Denmark.[81] In such cases, the absence of actual consent has been critical.

In certain circumstances, there may be a fine distinction between whether a patentee has consented to the marketing of patented products or not. For instance, where a product has been compulsorily licensed as a result of the failure of the patentee to work the patent, he is in effect responsible for any such products coming on the market. In such situation, it might be open for a parallel importer of such products to argue that the patentee has consented to such products being put on the market because of his own failure to work the patent. In these "grey" scenarios, a court's decision could turn on subtle findings of fact. For instance, if the patentee, in response to a letter from a person who has written to him claiming that he has not worked the patent and that therefore he will apply for a compulsory licence if he is not permitted to exploit the patent, informs the writer that he is content to take a royalty of five per cent on the turnover of the patented product manufactured and sold by the former, does this constitute consent?[82]

(j) Licensees and imports

7.018 The Court in *Centrafarm v. Sterling* emphasised that once a sales licence has been granted in a Member State by the patentee, the latter can no longer oppose the marketing of any protected product sold under the sales licence throughout the Common Market.[83] The patentee is deemed

[78] Paras. 42–43. See Tritton, "Articles 30 to 36 and Intellectual Property: Is the jurisprudence of the ECJ now of an Ideal Standard" [1994] EIPR 423 and para. 7.057 *et seq.*

[79] Case 341/87, *EMI Electrola GmbH v. Patricia Im und Export*: [1989] E.C.R. 79, [1989] 2 C.M.L.R. 413.

[80] Case 341/87, *EMI Electrola GmbH v. Patricia Im und Export*: [1989] E.C.R. 79, [1989] 2 C.M.L.R. 413.

[81] Case 156/86, *Warner Bros v. Christiansen*: [1988] E.C.R. 2605, [1990] 3 C.M.L.R. 684.

[82] *e.g.* see Case 55/80 & 57/80, *MEMBRAN & K-TEL v. GEMA*: [1981] E.C.R. 147, [1981] 2 C.M.L.R. 44 discussed above, at para. 7.014, where a licence was entered into against the implicit threat of the licensee obtaining a compulsory licence.

[83] Point 20.

to have consented to its marketing throughout the E.C. It was irrelevant as to whether the patentee and the licensees belonged to the same group or not for the purposes of Articles 30 to 36.[84] However, the situation becomes less clear when it is not the owner of the right but the licensee seeking to enforce the right. Can Licensee A prevent the importation by parallel importers into his licensed territory of protected products lawfully marketed in another Member State by O, the owner of the right or another licensee B?[85] The European Court has not yet ruled on such a point.[86]

Upon a literal interpretation of the ECJ's judgment in *Centrafarm v. Sterling & Winthrop*, because such products have been placed on the market by the patentee or in the case of Licensee B, with the consent of the patentee, their subsequent circulation within the Community cannot be impeded by exercise of any rights. Thus licensee A would not be permitted to exercise his rights against such imported goods.

It could be said that in relation to goods marketed by B, that A has not "consented" to the marketing of such goods by B as B has no privity of contract with A. It is submitted that such is an invalid argument because it is not B's consent which is important but the patentee's. A must be deemed to accept all the consequences of the patentee licensing B to market the protected product within the terms of B's licence provided that the grant of B's licence does not constitute a breach of the patentee's licence with A.[87] Alternatively, this situation can be analysed in terms of the specific object. The right to first place the protected product on the market has been exhausted by O or B.

A patentee may decide to license his patent and impose particular conditions on the licence which prevent the licensee from marketing its goods outside an assigned territory. For instance, the licence may ban the marketing of the invention outside a particular territory. It may be that the ban is contrary to Article 85 and not exempted by the patent block exemption. In this case, it would be void and unenforceable.[88] If it is void and unenforceable, can the patentee exercise his rights against a licensee who places the protected goods in another territory where the patentee owns a parallel patent? Technically, Articles 30 to 36 and 85 are independent of each other—the former falling with the free movement of goods provisions and the latter within the competition provisions of the EC Treaty. As has been commented on, the validity of a contractual

[84] This is a material consideration in Art. 85 proceedings.

[85] "Lawfully" here means placed on the market in accordance without breaching any conditions in a licence.

[86] For the present purposes, it is assumed that Licensee A is able to exercise the right in his licensed territory.

[87] *i.e.* where the patentee grants A an exclusive licence for the whole Community and then subsequently grants B a licence.

[88] See Chapter Eight. For instance, an export ban unlimited in time is contrary to Art. 85 and not exempted under the Patent Block Exemption.

clause under Article 85 is a different matter to the validity of the exercise of rights.[89] Thus, the patentee might submit that although the export ban is void under Article 85, he has not *actually* consented to the marketing of the protected product in another territory. No doubt the ECJ would find the submission unattractive. It is possible that the ECJ will deem the patentee to have consented to the marketing of any protected products if his lack of consent is based upon an unenforceable condition. Put another way, the ECJ could argue that the licence must be treated as authorising exports of the protected product to other Member States.[90]

If the export ban does not infringe Article 85(1) or is exempted under Article 85(3) (whether individually or via a block exemption), what is the position? For instance, an exclusive licensee, A, chooses to disregard such a clause and markets the invention outside his allotted territory into territory C. The invention is then imported into the territory of another exclusive licensee, B. Can the patentee bring infringement proceedings against the importer? Can the importer argue that although the product was marketed in breach of A's licence, the patentee has exhausted his rights in the patent? Although the point has not been decided, it is submitted that such a conclusion would distort the concept of consent. Clearly, the patentee has indicated to licensee A that he only consents to the marketing of the invention upon strict adherence to the terms of the licence. If the licensee does not adhere to such terms, it cannot be said that the licensee has marketed the invention with the consent of the patentee.[91] Any suggestion that the grant of *any* licence constitutes a general licence to sell throughout the Common Market as it has been suggested is the Commission's view[92] is simplistic.

(k) Consent and direct exports

7.019 In the preceding section the situation was considered where a protected product is lawfully placed on the market and then exported to another Member State. However, what is the position where a protected product is directly exported by a rights owner or his licensee into the territory of another licensee or territory reserved to the rights owner? For instance, what is the position, say, where E is an exclusive licensee of O in Member State A and Member State B is a reserved territory of O? Can O exercise

[89] See *Roudard* "Direct Reports in Community Law" Patents World May 1989, p. 34, at p. 37. See also *Reindl* at pp. 69 to 71 where he considers the impact of Art. 36 on competition law and concludes that concepts developed under Art. 36 provide little guidance to examine a private party's behaviour in a competition law case.

[90] An interesting scenario occurs if it is held that the export ban is not severable from the licence *in toto* and therefore the licence is void—see para. 12.080. If this is the case, the patentee could submit that as the licence is void *ab initio*, he had not consented to the licensee marketing any protected products let alone in another territory.

[91] See Roudard at p. 38.

[92] See Roudard at p. 35.

his rights against E where E directly exports to O? The European Court of Justice has not ruled on this point.[93]

The concept of exhaustion of rights is not applicable to direct exports because the goods have not been previously marketed in a Member State. The more relevant approach is whether the owner of the rights has consented to the marketing of the licensed products by E. For the present purposes, one must distinguish between two situations. Firstly, where E has been contractually banned from direct exporting into Member State B. Secondly, where there is no contractual ban on direct exports.

7.020 *Ban on direct export into B*—where there is a ban on direct exports in Member State B, it is perverse to say that O has consented to their marketing in B. He clearly has only consented to the marketing of goods in A. For the purposes of Articles 30 to 36, the specific object of the right namely the right to put on the market has been reserved for O in State B. In such circumstances, a finding that O cannot exercise his rights against E would seem to undermine the specific object of the right.[94–96] Thus, it is submitted that, contrary to the Commission's view that the grant of a licence to sell in a Member State is a general licence to sell throughout the Common Market, a rights owner is entitled to limit his consent to the marketing of products through a ban on direct exports.[97]

It may be that such a ban is contrary to Article 85 or falls outside the Patent or Know-How Block Exemption or proposed Technology Transfer Block Exemption.[98] Under Article 85, the European Court of Justice and Commission has considered the validity of contractual prohibitions on direct sales by licensor/licensees into each other's territories. For instance, in the Patent Block Exemption, a ban on passive sales by one licensee into another's territory is only permissible for a period not exceeding 5 years from the date when the product was first marketed within the common market.[99] Thus, the direct export ban may be void under Article 85. If it is void, it is unlikely that O could exercise his rights against E in Member State B.[1]

[93] In *Pharmon v. Hoechst*, the case concerned the direct export of compulsory licensed goods from England to Holland. The Commission took the view that direct exports were subject to the application of Art. 30 but the Court did not comment on this aspect as it held that the owner of the patent had not consented to the marketing of the goods at all, regardless of whether they were direct exports or parallel imports.

[94–96] See para. 7–021, n. 79, of Bellamy and Child, *Common Market Law Competition*, (3rd ed.). Sweet & Maxwell.

[97] See Roudard at pp. 35 and 38.

[98] See Chapter on Licensing of Intellectual Property.

[99] See Art. 1(1)(6) and Art. 3(11) Reg. 2349/84. See also Know-How Block Exemption, where there is a similar provision (Art. 1(1)(6) and Art. 3(11)). For Patent and Know-How Block Exemption, see Chapter Eight. Both Block Exemptions are shortly to be replaced by the Technology Transfer Block Exemption.

[1] See preceding section.

7.021 *No ban on direct exports into B*—where there is no export ban, is the exclusive licensee E entitled to directly sell the licensed products into O's territory? The issue again is whether or not O has consented to the marketing of the protected products in his territory. Often, a ban on direct exports clause can be implied into a licence which merely grants the licensee the right to manufacture and sell in a particular territory. *A fortiori*, such a licence prohibits the licensee from selling in other Member States where there is a parallel protection. Such an approach emphasises the territorial nature of intellectual property. It may be argued that such an approach is contrary to the free movement of goods provisions. However, such an argument ignores the fact that O decided to exercise his rights to stop the goods being placed on the market *in the first place* and *not to* affect the free movement of goods *already in circulation* in the Community. To find in favour of such an argument means that the grant of a simple licence to manufacture and sell a patented product in one state is a licence to sell in all states in the Community. Thus the absence of a direct export ban is not determinative of the issue. It is submitted that a national court should determine by reference to its domestic laws of contract, intellectual property and canons of construction whether O has consented to the exporter, E, directly exporting his goods in O's territory.

In England, the High Court has intimated that there will be no exhaustion of rights where direct exports are involved. In *Lowenbrau Munchen v. Grunhalle Lager International Ltd.*[3] in an English passing-off action, the Plaintiff manufactured Lowenbrau lager in Germany and sold it directly in England. The Plaintiff could not restrain the use of the word "Lowenbrau" in Germany but had reputation and goodwill in England in the word. The High Court stated that there was no exhaustion of rights and therefore the Plaintiff could sue for passing-off against the defendant for marketing in the United Kingdom beer called "Grunhalle Lowenbrau". Mr Justice Graham said that this was not a case where the Plaintiff had put parcels of their lager on the market of Germany and then sued when they were imported into England.

(l) Assignment and consent

7.022 Often, concerns will divest or acquire rights through commercial transactions. Thus, a company may sell its patent rights in the various Member States in order to finance other commercial deals. This raises the issue of whether the assignor has "consented" to the placing on the market and subsequent export of protected goods by the assignee. What is the situation where O, the owner of the parallel rights in Member States A and B assigns the rights in B to X, the assignee and then seeks to prevent the import by a parallel importer into O's territories of the protected goods marketed by X in B?

[3] [1974] F.S.R. 1; [1974] 1 C.M.L.R. 1.

The only case on this point concerns the assignment of trade marks in the Community. The case is discussed in detail later on in this Chapter.[4] Briefly, the owner of a parallel German and French registered trade mark, "Ideal Standard", assigned the latter mark to a third party with whom it had no legal or economic connection. Subsequently, goods bearing the French mark were imported into Germany whereby the owner of the German mark sought to exercise his trade mark rights against the importer. The ECJ, ruling in favour of the German trade mark owner, rejected a submission by the Commission that by assigning in France the trade mark to a third company, the plaintiff gave implied consent to that third company to put goods bearing the mark into circulation in France and therefore could not prevent the marketing in Germany of goods bearing the assigned mark. The ECJ said that:

> "the consent implicit in any assignment is not the consent required for application of the doctrine of exhaustion of rights. For that the owner of the right in the importing State must, directly or indirectly, be able to determine the products to which the trade mark may be affixed in the exporting State and to control their quality. That power is lost if, by assignment, control over the trade mark is surrendered to a third party having no economic link with the assignor."[5]

It is not clear where in making the above statement, the ECJ intended that the principle should apply to other forms of intellectual property. The reference to the need to control the quality of the goods was derived from previous discussion by the ECJ about the need to maintain the essential function of a trade mark by ensuring that a trade mark indicates a single "point of control of manufacture".[6] Such considerations do not apply to other types of intellectual property. Thus, it remains to be seen whether the ECJ will apply such reasoning to assignments of other forms of intellectual property.[7]

7.023 If the ECJ's ruling is to be applied to other rights, its application may well be overly generous to the assignor and overly restrictive of the free movement of goods. Considering patents, the ECJ in *Centrafarm v. Sterling*[8] specifically referred to the specific object of a patent being to recompense the creative effort of the inventor. The assignment for value of a parallel patent in one Member State to a third party would mean that the patentee had been compensated for his creative efforts in relation to patented products placed into circulation in that Member State. Consequently, any exercise of his patent rights against such products would not have been justified under Article 36 as they would not have related to the

[4] See para. 7.057 on Trademarks and Assignment.

[5] Para. 43, *Ideal Standard*, Judgment of ECJ, June 24, 1994, [1994] 3 C.M.L.R. 857.

[6] See paras. 37–39, *Ideal Standard*, Judgment of ECJ, June 24, 1994, *ibid.*

[7] See Tritton, "Articles 30 to 36 and Intellectual Property: Is the jurisprudence of the ECJ now of an Ideal Standard" [1994] EIPR 423.

[8] Case 15/74, *Centrafarm BV v. Sterling Drug Inc.*: [1974] E.C.R. 1147, [1974] 2 C.M.L.R. 480.

specific object of the patent. Considerations of control over the manufacture of products and their quality are irrelevant because there is no likelihood of the public being deceived as to the origin of the assignor's and assignee's products. It is difficult to say that in such circumstances, the patentee has not "consented" to the marketing of patented products in France. Clearly, the patentee would have exhausted his rights in relation to products marketed under a patent licence. In such circumstances, to make a distinction between a licence (that is a controlling enduring consent) to an assignment (a once-and-for-all consent) appears artificial.[9]

It has been pointed out that the principle should not apply in reverse where the assignor exports to the assignee's territories. Certainly, whilst the specific object of the patent for the marketing of future goods has been satisfied *qua assignor*, it has not been satisfied *qua assignee*. In layman's terms, the assignee has not been compensated for the marketing of the patented goods by the assignor. Such is clearly the case where the assignor seeks to *directly* export to the assignees territory as the assignor has specifically assigned the right to first market in the assignee's territories.[10] Furthermore, it is submitted that the assignee should be able to prevent patented products which are parallel imports from the assignor's territories because the assignee has not consented to their marketing in his territory nor has he received any form of reward for their marketing in the assignor's territory.

7.024 The above considerations become even more complicated when both assignor and assignee have subsequently assigned their rights to others. For instance, can a third generation assignor and a third generation assignee prevent the importation of each other goods into their territories? For instance, where the owner X of parallel patents in Member States A and B assigns the latter patent to Y who subsequently assigns it to Z, can X exercise his patent rights against a parallel importer into Member State A of products marketed in Member State B by Z? In the *Ideal Standard*[11] case, the trade marked products *in casu* had been placed on the market in France by a subsequent purchaser of the assigned French mark.[12] However, as mentioned above, it is not clear that the

[9] See Tritton, "Articles 30 to 36 and Intellectual Property: Is the jurisprudence of the ECJ now of an Ideal Standard" [1994] EIPR 423. Kunze, "Waiting for Sirena II—Trademark Assignment in the Case Law of the European Court of Justice" (1991) 3 IIC 319 at p. 328 states that once assignment has taken place, there is no further need for consent and that the assignment cannot be construed as implying such consent for the future. Accordingly, he concludes that in the case of trademarks, it cannot be said that the assignor or assignee have consented to the marketing of each others' goods after assignment has taken place. Strictly speaking this is correct but there is no doubt that the assignor has "permitted" the marketing of protected goods by another when before such was not permitted. In the author's opinion, the nature of assignment is a one-and-for-all act and as such is a single event that gives consent to the assignee for all future products to be marketed by the assignee in his territories.

[10] See Joliet, "Trade Mark Law and the Free Movement of Goods: The overruling of HAG I" 3 IIC/(1992) at 317 at p. 319.

[11] *Ideal Standard*, Judgment of ECJ, June 24, 1994, [1994] 3 C.M.L.R. 857.

[12] For the facts of the case, see para. 7.017 on Assignment and Trade Marks.

ECJ's reasoning in that case applies to other forms of intellectual property. It is submitted that courts should apply the doctrines of consent and specific object in attempting to determine the answer to such second and subsequent generation assignments. Thus, in the example given, it is submitted that the reasoning given in the previous paragraphs applies equally to purchasers of an assigned patent as it does to the original assignee. In other cases, the application of the doctrines may be more difficult.

7.025 *Example A*—Owner X of parallel patents A and B in Member States A and B assigns the latter patent to Y who subsequently assigns it to Z. Owner X then assigns patent A to XA. Can XA exercise his patent rights against a parallel importer into Member State A of patented products marketed in Member State B by Z? In this case, X has surrendered the right to first put products on the market in Member State B (and thus their subsequent movement within the Community) and hence "consented" to the marketing of such products in B and therefore it is submitted that XA should be in no better position than X.

7.026 *Example B*—The converse of the above example where a parallel importer imports patented products of XA in Member State A to Member State B. Can Z enforce his rights against the parallel importer? Firstly, Z's rights have never extended to Member State A and so he has not been rewarded by the placing on the market of the patented products in Member State A. Secondly, Z has not "consented" to the marketing of XA's products in A. Accordingly, he should be allowed to exercise his rights against the parallel importer.

If the owner of the rights has assigned the rights in order to partition the Common Market, such will amount to artificial partition or a disguised restriction on trade between Member States and any exercise of rights will be prohibited under Article 36(2). Finally, the assignment may be contrary to Article 85. The reader is referred to the section on Article 85, Parallel Imports and Intellectual Property Rights.[13]

(m) Doctrines of specific object and consent compared

7.027 The doctrine of specific object and the doctrine of consent are closely related. The latter is defined *inter alia* as the right to first put a patented or trade marked product on the market. In such circumstances, the *specific object* of a patent or trade mark is exhausted once the owner of the right has *consented* to its marketing. Historically, the ECJ has chosen consent as being the decisive factor. In doing so, the development of the doctrine of specific object became somewhat arrested. For instance, in *Ideal Standard*,[14] the Court rehearsed the doctrine of the specific object

[13] See para. 7.113 *et seq.*
[14] *Ideal Standard*, Judgment of ECJ, June 24, 1994, *supra.*

of a trade mark and then proceeded to ignore its application and merely analysed the facts of the case by reference to the doctrine of exhaustion of rights.

If the doctrine of specific object of a patent, trade mark or other right is in essence the right to first put a protected product on the market, then it is the doctrine of consent by another name. Indeed, the ECJ has recently said that "the right of the proprietor of a protected design to prevent third parties from manufacturing and selling or importing, *without its consent*, products incorporating the designs *constitutes the very subject-matter of his exclusive rights*".[15] However, the case law of the ECJ suggests that although this is the most important aspect of the specific object of an intellectual property right, it is not the only aspect. For instance, the ECJ's judgment in *Centrafarm v. Sterling*[16] clearly envisaged that a patentee's creative effort could be protected in other ways than merely having the right to first put patented products on the market. In *Windsurfing*,[17] a quality control clause relating to products covered by the patent was held to fall within the specific object of a patent.[18] Similarly, a contractual clause stipulating that a notice stating that licensed products had been licensed by Windsurfing International should be displayed was held to fall within the specific object of a patent.[19] In *Centrafarm v. Winthrop*, the specific object of trade mark also includes the trade mark owner's right to be protected against competitors who would take advantage of the position and reputation of the mark by selling goods improperly bearing the mark.

7.028 That the two doctrines are different is graphically expressed where the application of the two doctrines to a case will lead to opposing results. Where a patented product was compulsorily licensed in the United Kingdom so that third parties could manufacture and market it on the payment of a reasonable royalty to the patentee, the ECJ held that the patentee could exercise his rights against the importation of such licensed products into Holland where a parallel patent existed.[20] In these circumstances, the specific subject matter had altered so as to provide a fair return to the patentee.[21] Accordingly, the specific object of the patent had been discharged but the patentee was not prevented from exercising his rights because he had not consented to the products being placed on the market. Similarly, where patent protection for pharmaceuticals existed in

[15] Case 238/87, *Volvo AB v. Erik Veng (UK) Ltd*: [1988] E.C.R. 6211, [1989] 4 C.M.L.R. 122, para. [8].
[16] Case 15/74, *Centrafarm BV v. Sterling Drug Inc.*: [1974] E.C.R. 1147, [1974] 2 C.M.L.R. 480.
[17] Case 193/83, *Windsurfing International v. E.C. Commission*: [1986] E.C.R. 611, [1986] 3 C.M.L.R. 489.
[18] Para. [45].
[19] Para. [72].
[20] Case 19/84, *Pharmon v. Hoechst*: [1985] E.C.R. 2281, [1985] 3 C.M.L.R. 775.
[21] Case 434/85, *Allen & Hanburys Ltd v. Generics (UK) Limited*: [1988] E.C.R. 1245, [1988] 4 C.M.L.R. 701.

Germany but not in Italy, the ECJ held that the patentee in Germany was not entitled to exercise his patent rights against a pharmaceutical imported from Italy to Germany as the product has been put on the market in Italy with his consent. In such case, it is arguable that the patentee had not obtained the substance of the exclusive rights, *i.e.* the specific object that flows from the patent.[22] Certainly, the lack of a patent monopoly in Italy would have affected the price of the pharmaceutical. Therefore, where there is a conflict, the ECJ has always favoured the doctrine of consent over the doctrine of specific object.[23]

(n) International or E.C.-wide exhaustion of rights principle?

7.029 The ECJ case law has meant that the courts of Member States must recognise the principle that once a protected product has been placed on the market in a Member State by the rights owner or with his consent, the rights owner has exhausted his rights. As regards patents, this has generally meant an "upgrading" of the exhaustion of rights principle from a national level to an E.C. level. As regards copyright and trade mark rights, invariably the principle of international exhaustion applies such that once a protected product is marketed anywhere in the world, the owner has exhausted his rights.

Where the E.C. has harmonised intellectual property laws, it has included provisions on the exhaustion of rights. Thus, in the Trade Mark Directive, the trade mark proprietor is not entitled to exercise his rights once he has placed a product under the mark on the market in the Community or with his consent.[24] Similarly, the Community Trade Mark regulation makes similar provisions.[25] In the field of copyright, the Directive on Rental and Lending Rights and Neighbouring Rights provides that the distribution right shall not be exhausted "within the Community . . . except where the first sale in the Community of that object is made by the rightholder or with his consent".[26] In the field of software, there is a similar provision in relation to copies of programmes.[27]

7.030 Concern has been raised, primarily in the context of the EEA Agreement, as to whether codification of an EEA-wide exhaustion principle obliges Member States to "downgrade" their national international exhaustion of rights principles for trade marks and copyright.[28] The

[22] Demaret, "Compulsory Licence and the Free Movement of Goods under Community Law" 18 IIC 161, 176.

[23] See Tritton, "Articles 30 to 36 and Intellectual Property: Is the jurisprudence of the ECJ now of an Ideal Standard" [1994] EIPR 423 at p. 425.

[24] Dir. 89/104, Art. 7(1).

[25] CTM Regulation, Art. 13 [1984] O.J. L 11.

[26] Dir. 92/100, Art. 9(2) [1992] O.J. L 346/61.

[27] Dir. 91/250, Art. 4(c) on the legal protection of computer programs [1991] O.J. L 122.

[28] See Blanchet et al, *The Agreement in the European Economic Area* (1994), at p. 124. According to this book, all EEA States have an international doctrine of exhaustion for trademarks and copyright. The same considerations apply to the E.C. Treaty.

chance of a conflict between this doctrine and the EEA-exhaustion doctrine will only apply where the product comes from outside the EEA into its own state.[29] In such circumstances, there is no effect on trade between Member States and Article 30 to 36 or their parallel provisions in the EEA Agreement are inapplicable.[30] However, can a rights owner argue in civil proceedings that a Member State's international exhaustion of rights principle is in breach of Community or EEA legislation where a directive or regulation has provided exhaustive legislation which only permits an E.C. or EEA-wide exhaustion principle?

Whilst many readers may consider that this is a preposterous suggestion and that a domestic principle of international exhaustion which is more liberal than an E.C.-wide exhaustion principle cannot be capable of infringing a Treaty designed to ensure free movement of goods, it should be remembered that in many respects, the E.C. adopts a "Fortress Europe" approach. Upon a strict analysis of the E.C. Directive on Harmonisation of Trade Marks, Member States are not free to legislate in areas where the Directive specifically provides for. Moreover, in the Community Trade Mark Regulation, the Commission sought, but failed, to introduce an international exhaustion principle.[31] Indeed, it appears that in both the Directive and the CTM Regulations, a deliberate decision was taken to exclude an international exhaustion of rights principle.[31a] The Commission has stated that the restriction to Community—wide exhaustion does not prevent the national courts from extending this principle in cases of a special nature, in particular where, even in the absence of a formal agreement reciprocity is guaranteed.[31b] Thus, the adoption of an international exhaustion of rights principle may now be in breach of Community law in relation to trade marks. However, it is unlikely, as one commentator put it, that a national rule which for 20 years was never expressly considered as contrary to E.C. jurisprudence should all of a sudden become an infringement of Community law merely because the said E.C. jurisprudence had become incorporated into a directive.[32]

(o) Scope and nature of protection is a matter of national law

7.031 The ECJ has stated quite clearly that in the absence of Community standardisation or harmonisation of laws that the determination of the con-

[29] If it comes from an EEA state, then there will be exhaustion of rights both under the EEA Agreement and domestic law.
[30] Case 51/75, *EMI Records Ltd v. C.B.S.*: [1976] E.C.R. 811, [1976] 2 C.M.L.R. 235.
[31] See draft Council Regulation on the CTM, Working Document, July 11, 1978, III/S/753/78.
[31a] See Rasmussen, "Exhaustion of Trade Mark Rights pursuant to Directive 89/109" [1995] EIPR 174. See also para. 3.075. See also Shea, "Does the First Trade Marks Directive know International Exhaustion of Rights?" [1995] 10 EIPR 763.
[31b] Explanatory Memorandum to CTM proposal at VT Com (89) 470. See also Rasmussen, *ibid.*
[32] See Blanchet at p. 124.

ditions and procedure under which protection is granted is matter for national rules.[33] Such an approach implicitly recognised the importance of Article 222 which prevents the Treaty from prejudicing the rules in Member States governing the system of property ownership.

However, such national laws must not discriminate directly or indirectly between Member States or their nationals. In some cases, the discrimination will be directly based on the nationality of the author. In this case, the relevant law or its application by a national court is contrary to Article 7 of the Treaty of Rome.[34] In other cases, the discrimination is less obvious. This has most recently been seen in a series of cases concerning United Kingdom and Italian patent legislation. Thus, a provision that where a patentee did not manufacture the patented invention in the United Kingdom, it was liable to be subject to be compulsorily licensed was held contrary to Articles 30 to 36, as it encouraged the patentee to manufacture within the United Kingdom rather than manufacture the patented invention in another Member State and import the patented product from the territory of another Member State.[35] The ECJ chose to consider such provisions as not falling within Article 36 at all as the object of compulsory licensing rules were not to ensure the protection of industrial and commercial property but on the contrary to limit the rights conferred by such property.[36] It held that such provisions constituted measures having an effect equivalent to quantitative restrictions on imports within the meaning of Article 30.[37]

[33] Case 35/87, *Thetford v. Fiamma*: [1988] E.C.R. 3585, [1988] 3 C.M.L.R. 549 discussed in detail at para. 7.073. See also in relation to copyright, Case 341/87 *EMI Electrola GmbH v. Patricia Im und Export*: [1989] E.C.R. 79, [1989] 2 C.M.L.R. 413 discussed later at para. 7.094. Also see Case 144/81, *Keurkoop BV v. Nancy Kean Gifts BV*: [1982] E.C.R. 2853, [1983] 2 C.M.L.R. 47, para. [18] in relation to industrial designs. This doctrine has recently been affirmed in Cases C-30/90–C235/89, *Compulsory Patent Licences: E.C. Commission v. United Kingdom & Italy*: [1992] E.C.R. I 829, [1992] 2 C.M.L.R. 709, para. 17. In relation to trade marks, see the recent decision of *Deutsche Renault v. Audi*: [1993] I E.C.R. 6277.

[34] *e.g.* see Case C.92/92, *Phill Collins v. IMTRAT Handels-GmbH*: [1993] 3 C.M.L.R. 773, ECJ. However, see van Themaat and Beltink "Another side of the story: why the Phil Collins judgment does not necessarily mean the end of the reciprocity principle" [1995] EIPR 307. See also para. 4.005 for further discussion".

[35] Cases 30/90 and 235/89, *Compulsory Patent Licences: E.C. Commission v. United Kingdom & Italy*: [1992] I E.C.R. 829, [1992] 2 C.M.L.R. 709. In relation to compulsory licences, see also *Generics (U.K.) Limited v. Smith Kline and French Laboratories*: [1993] 1 C.M.L.R. 89 and Case 434/85, *Allen & Hanbury v. Generics*: [1988] E.C.R. 1275, [1988] 1 C.M.L.R. 701.

[36] See Cases 30/90 and 235/89, *Compulsory Patent Licences: E.C. Commission v. United Kingdom & Italy*: [1992] I E.C.R. 829, [1992] 2 C.M.L.R. 709, para. 14. See also application of the principles developed in this case in Case 191/90, *Generics v. Smith Kline & French Laboratories Limited*: [1992] I E.C.R. 5335, [1993] 1 C.M.L.R. 89, ECJ.

[37] Para. 27. Compulsory Patent Licences, *ibid.*

4. Ancillary Doctrines Developed in Relation to Article 36

(a) Community secondary legislation and Articles 30 to 36

7.032 If Community secondary legislation provides complete and exhaustive measures designed to guarantee protection of a particular interest set out in Article 36, then recourse to Article 36 is not permitted.[38] Furthermore, where there exists such a comprehensive and exhaustive regime, Member States are not free to adopt any measures which might undermine or create exceptions to that legislation.[39] Such doctrines will be mainly applicable in the field of unfair competition and passing-off. A good example of the application of the above principle is in the *Prantl* case.[40] This case, which is discussed later in this Chapter at para. 7.099, concerned, *inter alia*, the issue of whether a provision of German law which reserved the use of a particular shape of bottle (called the Bocksbeutel) as an indication that the wine came from Franconia and Baden in Germany was valid or not. Mr Prantl imported wine from Italy bottled in the same shape. The Commission argued that the German provision of the law was invalid as there was existing Community legislation on the marketing of wines and such was exhaustive and complete. The European Court held that the legislation was exhaustive with regard to prices, regulation of production and of technical methods, naming and labelling but could not be regarded as exhaustive in relation to the shape of bottle as such was ancillary to the main objects of a common organisation. Therefore, member States were free to legislate in this area unless such legislation contravened Articles 30 to 36.[41] However, if the Commission had exhaustively legislated for the shape of bottles for wines, then the relevant provision of German law would have been void. Furthermore, any person with private intellectual property rights who sought to exercise them against the importation of wine, packaged inside a Bocksbeutel on

[38] See Case 35/76, *Simmenthal v. Ministero delle Finanze*: [1976] E.C.R. 1871, [1977] 2 C.M.L.R. 1, Case 5/77, *Tedeschi*: [1977] E.C.R. 1555, [1978] 1 C.M.L.R. 1; Case 72/83, *Campus Oil Limited and others v. Minister for Industry and Engergy and others*: [1984] E.C.R. 2727, [1984] 3 C.M.L.R. 544. For a recent confirmation of this doctrine, see Case C-347/89, *Bavaria v. Eurim-Pharm GmbH*: [1991] E.C.R. 1747, [1993] 1 C.M.L.R. 616, para. 26.

[39] See Case 40/69, *Bollman*: [1970] E.C.R. 69, [1970] C.M.L.R. 141; Case 34/70, *Syndicat National Céréales*: [1970] E.C.R. 1233; Case 31/74, *Galli*:]1975] 1 C.M.L.R. 211, [1975] E.C.R. 47; Case 83/78, *Redmond*: [1979] 1 C.M.L.R. 177, [1978] E.C.R. 2347; Case 20/79, *Danis*: [1979] E.C.R. 3327, [1980] III C.M.L.R. 492.

[40] Case 16/83, *Criminal Proceedings against Karl Prantl*: [1984] E.C.R. 1299, [1985] 2 C.M.L.R. 238.

[41] The finding that there was not exhaustive legislation was despite the fact that Reg. 997/81, Art. 18 protected the use of the traditional *Flute d'Alsace* but no other shape of bottle. For a case comment, see Turner, "The Prosecution of Karl Prantl Bottles on the Incoming Tide" [1985] 4 EIPR 113.

the basis that the shape was an infringement of his rights would have been prohibited from doing so.[42]

Thus, an action for trade mark infringement or passing-off in relation to the import of a good which has a confusing name or get-up will be prohibited by Article 30 and not permissible under Article 36 if the Community has implemented comprehensive legislation in this area. Importantly, a series of E.C. Regulations on the protection of geographical indications and designations of origin for agricultural products and foodstuffs have been issued which in this area provide for comprehensive and exhaustive legislation.[43]

b. Article 36(2)

7.033 Even if the exercise of rights are justified under Article 36(1), they may be prevented under Article 36(2).

The Court has said in relation to Article 36 that:

> "Article 36 is thus intended to emphasise that the reconciliation between the requirements of the free movement of goods and the respect to which industrial and commercial property rights are entitled must be achieved in such a way that protection is ensured for the legitimate exercise, in the form or prohibitions on imports which are 'justified' within the meaning of that Article, of the rights conferred by national legislation, but is refused, on the other hand, in respect of any improper exercise of the same rights which is of such a nature as to maintain or establish artificial partitions within the Common Market. The exercise of industrial and commercial partitions within the Common Market. The exercise of industrial and commercial property rights conferred by national legislation must consequently be restricted as far as is necessary for that reconciliation."

Thus, the first and second sentence of Article 36(2) represents the demarcation between legitimate and improper use.[44] However, as has been pointed out, the ECJ has not provided any objective criterion for determining what is legitimate or abusive and that classification of some use of

[42] For instance, the First Trade Mark Harmonisation Directive provides that shapes are capable of registration as trade marks. Thus, if there had been exhaustive legislation, then the owner of a registered trade mark for the Bocksbeutel would not have been able to bring infringement proceedings.

[43] Council Reg. 2081/92. This reg. must be read in conjunction with Council Reg. 2082/92 on certificates of specific character for agricultural products and foodstuffs (and its implementing Reg. 1848/93 which lays down detailed rules for the application of Reg. 2082/92 on certificates of special character for agricultural products and foodstuffs. See also Commission Decision 93/53 setting up a scientific committee for designation of origins, geographical indications and certificates of special character, and Commission Reg. 2037/93 which lays down detailed rules of application of Council Reg. 2081/92. See para. 3–080 *et seq*.

[44] See Beier, "Industrial Property and Internal Market" IIC 2/1990 131 at pp. 149–150.

an intellectual property rights as abusive or legitimate may be "the result of an analysis but it cannot be the instrument of the analysis".[45] Thus, one is forced to resort back to the wording of Article 36(2).

7.034 The ECJ has not given much illumination as to what will amount to an "arbitrary discrimination" or "disguised restriction" on trade between Member States. Where rights are exercised so as maintain or effect artificial partitions within the Common Market, then such will amount to improper exercise of rights and will not be permissible under the free movement of goods provisions.[46]

The exercise of rights must be in such a manner as not to discriminate against importer or imports of another Member State. The Court in *Terrapin v. Terranova*[47] (in which none of the above doctrines were held to prevent the exercise of the right) stated that it was for the national court with regard of Article 36(2) to consider whether the rights in question are in fact exercised by the proprietor with the same strictness whatever the national origin of any possible infringer. In this respect, as the Court is concerned with the free movement of goods, it is submitted that this principle applies in relation to the national origin of the infringing product as well as the infringer.[48]

The Court has primarily dealt with the relationship of Article 36(2) with intellectual property in two contexts: national patent legislation and repackages of pharmaceutical goods. With regard to the latter, the ECJ is somewhat ambiguous on the effect of Article 36(2) and the reader is referred to the relevant section.[49]

With regard to the former, in *Thetford Corporation v. Fiamma*,[50] the ECJ ruled that a national patent measure will not amount to an "arbitrary discrimination" if the measure applies to both domestic and imported products.

7.035 Furthermore, it said in the context of the validity of a provision of United Kingdom patent legislation that it will not be a "disguised restriction" if there is a legitimate reason for it.[51] A more difficult scenario is where differences in national legislation result in unequal protection throughout the Community. In such cases, the general rule is that in the absence of Community harmonisation, this is merely a matter of national law (see para. 7.031). However, it may be that the effect of such

[45] Joliet, "Trade Mark Law and the Free Movement of Goods: The Overruling of the Judgment in HAG I" IIC 2/1991 at p. 315.

[46] Case 119/75, *Terrapin v. Terranova*: [1976] E.C.R. 1039, [1976] 2 C.M.L.R. 482, para. 7. Whether such behaviour could not be said to be justified under Art. 36(1) or falls within Art. 36(2) is academic.

[47] Point 4. *ibid.*

[48] Art. 7 prohibits discrimination on the grounds of nationality.

[49] See para. 7–062 *et seq.*

[50] Case 35/87, [1988] E.C.R. 3585, [1988] 3 C.M.L.R. 549.

[51] Case 35/87, *Thetford v. Fiamma*: [1988] E.C.R. 3585, [1988] 3 C.M.L.R. 549, ECJ. See also Case 156/86, *Warner Bros v. Christiansen*: [1988] E.C.R. 2605, [1990] 3 C.M.L.R. 684, para 12 in relation to rental rights.

inequality of protection is to favour nationals of one Member State over another. If so, do such national provisions fall within Article 36(2)? Is such inequality an "arbitrary discrimination"? Generally, it is submitted that this does not fall within Article 36(2). Provided that the measure does not discriminate between products or nationals from differing Member States, it does not fall within Article 36(2). However if the national legislative measures, by their nature, prefer the nationals of one Member State over another, this may constitute covert discrimination and fall within Article 36(2).[51a]

An important question in this regard is whether an objective or subjective test applies to Article 36(2) in relation to intellectual property. Is it necessary that there is intended to be an arbitrary discrimination or disguised restriction or is it merely sufficient that such occurs? The Court has never made a definitive ruling on this point. The wording of Article 36(2) implies that even if quantitative restrictions on free trade are *justified* for the protection of industrial and commercial property, Article 36(2) may be applicable. The word "justified" connotes that something is permissible by reference to an external reasonable tribunal and not by reference to a person's subjective morality. As Article 36(2) is a derogation to Article 36(1), it would seem that the wording of Article 36 favours an objective interpretation.[52]

(c) Trade with non-E.C. countries

7.036 The free movement of goods provisions under the Treaty of Rome are only concerned with quantitative restrictions which affect trade between Member States. This was highlighted in the case of *EMI Records v. CBS*.[53]

In this case, the mark "Columbia" was held by EMI Records Ltd in various Member States whilst CBS held the rights to the mark in the United States and other non Member States. The mark had once been in common ownership a long time before the Common Market was estab-

[51a] See *Berkeley Administration v. McClelland* [1990] 2 Q.B. 407 and *Biotrading v. Biohit* Judgment, July 31, 1995, H.C. unreported. In the latter case, the judge gave the example of procedural obstacles in the way of non-residents who are predominantly non-nationals which could, if not objectively justifiable, constitute covert discrimination. See also *Hagen v. Fratelli* [1980] 3 C.M.L.R., where the Court of Appeal held that a rule of English patent law that prior was in England invalidates a patent but not prior use in other Member States was arguably contrary to Arts. 30–36. In that case, the provision does not overly discriminate between foreign and domestic products and indeed probably prefers foreign products.

[52] See the opinion of Advocate-General Caportorti in *Pfizer Inc v. Eurim-Pharm GmbH*: [1981] E.C.R. 2913, [1982] 1 C.M.L.R. 406 where he stated that it was not necessary to ascertain whether there is a subjective intention to act unlawfully, it being sufficient to establish that as a result of the exercise of that right, an artificial partitioning of the markets within the Community takes place.

[53] Case 51/75, *EMI Records Ltd v. CBS United Kingdom Ltd and others*: [1976] E.C.R. 811, [1976] 2 C.M.L.R. 235. The doctrine was repeated in Case C-191/90, *Generics v. Smith Kline & French Laboratories Limited*: [1992] I E.C.R. 5335, [1993] 1 C.M.L.R. 89, ECJ.

lished. CBS sought to import goods bearing the Columbia mark into the E.C. Furthermore, they sought to manufacture goods and subsequently affix the mark on them in the E.C. EMI sued for infringement of trade mark in various Member States.

Upon reference under Article 177 from various Member States' courts, the ECJ held that the exercise of a trade mark right in order to prevent the import of goods from a non-Member State bearing an identical mark could not come within the free movement of goods provisions as such exercise of rights did not apply "between Member States" as required under Article 30 and 36(2).[54] Furthermore, it held that Articles 9 and 10 of the Treaty were inapplicable.[55] As Articles 30 to 36 were inapplicable, the doctrine of common origin was not relevant.

The situation is unaffected even if the rights owner seeks to exercise his rights against imports from another Member State if such imports originally came from outside the E.C. and were marketed by the patentee or with his consent. Thus, where a patentee had put protected products onto the market in a country outside the E.C. and these were then exported to Holland and then further exported to Germany, a German court has interpreted this as meaning that the patentee has not exhausted its rights and can sue for infringement.[56] Furthermore, on a variation of the above situation, a German court has held that the patentee has not exhausted its rights where the patentee does not possess a parallel patent in the intermediate Member State.[57]

7.037 However, trade between Member States can be affected even though the ostensible nature of legislation is aimed against non-Member States. Thus, in a case concerning the settlement of conditions for compulsory licences by the United Kingdom authorities, it was the practice of the Patent Office in a compulsory licence to permit the importation of the patented product from non-Member States where the proprietor of the patent did not manufacture the product within the United Kingdom but imported from other Member States. The ECJ held that such a practice encouraged proprietors of patents to manufacture patented products within the United Kingdom rather than to import them from other Member States so as to avoid competition from imports from non-Member States and thus affected trade between Member States.[58] Accordingly, it was prohibited by Articles 30 to 36.

[54] Paras. 9 and 10.

[55] Art. 9 governed the effect of compliance with custom formalities on products which had come from third countries but which were already in circulation in the Common Market. Art. 10(1) states that products shall be considered to be in free circulation in a Member State if the import formalities have been complied with and custom duties or charges had already been levied in the importing Member State.

[56] See *Re Tylosin*: [1977] 1 C.M.L.R. 460 (Bundesgerichtshof).

[57] See *Re Patented Bandages Material*: [1988] 2 C.M.L.R. 359; [1988] F.S.R. 505 (Hanseatisches Oberlandesgericht Hamburg). See also *Re Tylosin*, *ibid* where the Bundesgerichtshof held that unsanctioned imports from Italy (where patents for veterinary medicines were not permissible) infringed German patent rights in the veterinary medicine.

[58] Case C-191/90, *Generics v. Smith Kline & French Laboratories Limited*: [1992] I E.C.R. 5335, [1993] 1 C.M.L.R. 89, ECJ, [1993] F.S.R. 592 at 612.

(d) EFTA Countries

7.038 The above reasoning is no different where the third country has a Free Trade Agreement with the E.C. In the case of *Polydor Limited v. Harlequin Records*,[59] gramophone records had been lawfully made in Portugal by licensees of the copyright owner. These records were exported to the United Kingdom where the British licensee sought to prevent such imports as being unlawful under British copyright law. At that time, Portugal was not a member of the E.C. but had a Free Trade Agreement with it. Articles 14(2) and 23 of that agreement were virtually identical to Articles 30 and 36. However, the Court held that the case law on Articles 30 to 36 was peculiar to the E.C. and did not apply to third countries who were the subject of a FTA agreement with the E.C. Similarly, courts in FTA countries have held that the doctrine of consent is not applicable to Free Trade Agreements.[60]

Where the country concerned is a member of EFTA and has ratified the EEA Agreement, the EEA now provides for an EEA-wide exhaustion of rights principle.[61] However, in relation to countries such as Switzerland and central and eastern European countries, who are not members of the EEA but who have entered into FTAs with the Community, the principle will still apply.

Recently, in *Eurim-Pharm Bundesgesundheisamt*,[62] the ECJ considered the application of the free movement of goods provisions of a FTA between the E.C. and Austria to parallel imports. At that time, Austria was not a member of the E.C. In this case, a German law prevented the importation into Germany of medical products unless authorised by the relevant German authorities. To obtain authority, it was necessary to lodge certain information concerning the product which in practice would only be readily available from the manufacturer. Bayer AG manufactured a medical product in France and was authorised to import it into Germany. It also exported the product to Austria. Eurim-Pharm, a parallel importer, purchased the product in Austria and sought to import it into Germany. The German authorities refused to allow the importation because Eurim-Pharm could not deposit the relevant papers eventhough they already had the information because of Bayer's application. Under E.C. case law, such a law constituted a clear infringement of Article 30.[63] On reference to the ECJ, the German court asked whether such principles applied to the E.C.-Austria agreement. The ECJ simply concluded that the German law was contrary to the E.C.-Austria agree-

[59] Case 270/80, *Polydor Limited and RSO Records Inc. v. Harlequin Records Shops Limited and Simons Records Limited*: [1982] E.C.R. 329, [1982] 1 C.M.L.R. 677.
[60] See *Bosshard Partners Intertrading AG v. Sunlight AG*: [1980] 3 C.M.L.R. 664 (Switzerland) and *Austro Mechana v. Gramola Winter & Co.*: [1984] 2 C.M.L.R. 626 (Austria)
[61] See below, para. 7.118 *et seq*.
[62] Case 207/91, [1993] E.C.R. 3723.
[63] *e.g.* Case 104/75, *Officier van Justitie v. De Peijper*: [1976] E.C.R. 613, [1976] 2 C.M.L.R. 271.

ment. The Advocate-General however considered the *Polydor* case. He stated that the principle in that case could not be *per se* transposed to a corresponding provision in a FTA. This reflected a general principle of judicial interpretation contained in the Vienna Convention on the Law of Treaties according to which a rule must be interpreted in its general context. The aims of the E.C.-Austria FTA were much more limited than that of the E.C. Treaty. However, whilst accepting this principle, he said that there would need to be a reason to depart from established jurisprudence where substantially the same facts were involved. He concluded that the restriction on parallel imports was purely formal without any underlying rationale. Whilst such an approach appears to undermine *Polydor*, a commentator has pointed out that nothing in the judgment or opinion was said which suggested that the *Polydor* judgment was flawed and indeed the facts were materially different.[64]

(e) Transitional provisions for acceding states

7.039 In many cases, there will be transitional provision for countries that accede to the European Community. These provisions will seek to provide a gradual transition so that Community law is not instantaneously applicable in relation to the acceding State. In such cases, it may be that the application of the provisions of Articles 30 to 36 and its case law are delayed. In one case, the United Kingdom Court of Appeal referred to the ECJ as to whether a ban in a compulsory licence against pharmaceutical imports from Spain and Portugal was contrary to Articles 30 to 36 because although both were Member States, Articles 47 and 209 of the Acts of Accession of Spain and Portugal expressly permitted the holders of pharmaceutical patents in the Community to exercise their rights against products from Spain and Portugal even if the products had been placed on the market by the patentee or with his consent provided such rights were exercised prior to the expiry of the third year after Spain or Portugal had made pharmaceutical products patentable. The ECJ held that the terms of the licence may on the basis of those provisions prohibit the licensee from importing from Spain and Portugal a patented pharmaceutical product if national law conferred upon the patent owner the right to prevent imports and if the proprietor demonstrated an intention to exercise the right conferred upon him by Articles 47 and 209.[65]

[64] See Worth, "Free Trade Agreements and the Exhaustion of Rights Principle: Eurim Pharm v. Bundesgesundheitsamt" [1994] 1 EIPR 40 at p. 41.

[65] See *Generics v. Smith Kline & French Laboratories Limited*: [1993] 1 C.M.L.R. 89, ECJ, [1993] F.S.R. 592 at p. 615. See also *The Wellcome Foundation Ltd v. Discpharm and Others* (a U.K. decision on similar facts) and its Case Comment by Jones, "Exhaustion of Rights: Pharmaceutical Marketed in Spain—a Wellcome Exception" [1993] March EIPR 107.

5. Individual Types of Intellectual Property

7.040 In the previous sections, the doctrines developed by the ECJ, the Commission and national courts in relation to Articles 30 to 36 were examined. However, each form of intellectual property differs slightly from each other. In this section, the application of the above doctrines to specific forms of intellectual property is examined.

(a) Trade marks

(i) Role of trademarks

7.041 Trademarks play an essential role in a market economy. By conferring exclusive rights on a registered trade mark owner, the latter is given an incentive to promote the reputation of the mark and goods or services sold under the mark in the knowledge that others will not be able to exploit the mark's reputation.[66]

Trade marks also permit the public to distinguish between goods of varying sources at the point of sale. This is valuable both from the consumer viewpoint and the seller viewpoint. The former can distinguish between goods on the market and by being able to do so gives the supplier of goods under the mark an incentive to produce high quality goods sold under a mark. Of course, the public is primarily interested in the *quality* of goods rather than the *trade source* of goods. Normally, a uniform quality will only be guaranteed if the goods are produced under the control of a single undertaking to which responsibility for their quality can be attributed.[67] However, sometimes, a manufacturer will permit goods of widely differing quality to be sold under one trade mark. It is unlikely that a manufacturer will permit this to occur in one territory. In such circumstances, the value of that trade mark to the public becomes worthless. However, a manufacturer may use the same trade mark in differing territories to goods of differing quality. This does not compromise the essence of a trade mark as the trade mark would indicate to consumers in each territory goods of a particular quality.

From the above, it is clear that a trade mark has two functions, which complement each other. Firstly, a trade mark enables a consumer to distinguish between goods from differing sources. Normally, a guarantee of trade origin is sufficient for consumer purposes although sometimes, this may not be sufficient where trade marked products coming from a single origin are of widely varying quality. Secondly, it is essential that the owner of the trade mark has the exclusive right to market specified goods or services under the mark in order to safeguard this guarantee of origin.

[66] Para. 19, Advocate-General Jacobs' Opinion in *Hag No. 2*, 1990 3 C.M.L.R. 571, [1990] I E.C.R. 371.

[67] See Joliet, "Trade Mark law and the Free Movement of Goods: The Overruling of the Judgment in HAG I" IIC 2/1991 at p. 311.

The ECJ has recognised that trade marks have these two functions. The first is called the "essential function" of the trademark and the second is the "specific object" of the trade mark.

(ii) Specific object

7.042 The specific object of a trade mark has been defined as follows:

> "The specific object of a trade mark right consists particularly in granting the owner the exclusive right to use the trade mark when *first* [emphasis added] putting a product into circulation, and in thereby protecting him against competitors seeking to abuse the position and reputation of the trade mark by selling products which have been unlawfully furnished with the trade mark."[68]

Such a right provides protection against competitors wishing to take advantage of the status and reputation of the mark by selling products illegally bearing the trade mark.[69] As mentioned before, the specific object of the trade mark means that once the goods have been lawfully placed on the market, the owner of the right has exhausted its rights in the trade marked product. The concept of specific object and its relevance to Articles 30 to 36 has been discussed earlier in this Chapter.[70]

(iii) Essential function

7.043 The second function of a trade mark as mentioned briefly above is to guarantee the identity of the origin of the trade marked product to the consumer or ultimate user. This enables the consumer to distinguish a particular trade marked product from another of a differing provenance.[71] This is known as the "essential function" of the trade mark. The ECJ said in *HAG No. 2* that:

[68] Joined Case 15–16/74, *Centrafarm BV v. Sterling Drug Inc. and Winthrop*: [1974] E.C.R. 1147, [1974] 2 C.M.L.R. 480. See also Case 102/77, *Hoffmann-La Roche v. Centrafarm*: [1978] E.C.R. 1139, [1978] 3 C.M.L.R. 217; Case 1/81, *Pfizer Inc. v. Eurim-Pharm GmbH*: [1981] E.C.R. 2913, [1982] 1 C.M.L.R. 406; Case 119/75, *Terrapin v. Terranova*: [1976] E.C.R. 1039, [1976] 2 C.M.L.R. 482; Case 3/78, *American Home Products Corporation v. Centrafarm*: [1978] E.C.R. 1823, [1979] 1 C.M.L.R. 326; Case 58/80, *Dansk Supermarked A/S v. Imerco A/S*: [1981] E.C.R. 181, [1981] 3 C.M.L.R. 590; *SA CNL-Sucal NV v. Hag GF AG ("Hag 2")*: [1990] 1 E.C.R. 3711, [1990] 3 C.M.L.R. 571; *Ideal Standard*, Judgment of ECJ, June 24, 1994, [1994] 3 C.M.L.R. 857.

[69] See Case 3/78, *American Home Products Corporation v. Centrafarm*: [1978] E.C.R. 1823, [1979] 1 C.M.L.R. 326, paras. 11 to 14.

[70] See para. 7.011.

[71] Case 102/77, *Hoffmann-La Roche v. Centrafarm*: [1978] E.C.R. 1139, [1978] 3 C.M.L.R. 217, para. 7; Case 3/78 *American Home Products Corporation v. Centrafarm*: [1978] E.C.R. 1823, [1979] 1 C.M.L.R. 3326, paras. 11–12; *SA CNL-Sucal NV v. Hag GF AG ("Hag 2")*: [1990] 1 E.C.R. 371, [1990] 3 C.M.L.R. 571, para. 14.

> " . . . the essential function of the mark would be compromised if the owner of the right could not exercise his option under national law to prevent the importation of the similar product under a name likely to be confused with his own mark because, in this situation, consumers would no longer be able to identify with certainty the origin of the marked product and the bad quality of a product for which he is in no way responsible could be attributed to the owner of the right."[72]

The ECJ's statement which was based upon a fully argued and lucid Opinion of the Advocate-General clearly proves the link between the essential function and the specific object of a trade mark. Where trademarked goods have been placed on the market by the owner of the trademark, he will not be able to rely on the essential function of the trademark to prevent further trade of these particular goods.

In *Ideal Standard*,[73] the ECJ refined the concept of "essential function". In the course of its judgment,[74] the Court emphasised that the function of a trade mark is not called into question where a product is marketed by a subsidiary, licensee or exclusive distributor as "for the trade mark to be able to fulfil its role, it must offer a guarantee that all goods bearing it have been produced under the control of a single undertaking which is accountable for their quality".[75] The Court said that the "decisive factor is the possibility of control over the quality of goods and not the actual exercise of that control".[76]

7.044 Accordingly, the essential function of a trade mark is a guarantee of unitary control and not merely of actual origin. By defining the essential function in such a way, the ECJ recognised that in certain circumstances, products of differing quality may be marketed under a single point of control. Such an approach would permit consumer confusion. Thus, the ECJ in *Ideal Standard* said that where subsidiaries in each of the Member States manufactured products whose quality was geared to the particularities of each national market, then each subsidiary cannot exercise its rights against the importation of products from another Member State on grounds that quality differences exist. Articles 30 to 36 required the group to bear the consequences of its choice.[77] It is questionable whether consumer confusion as to quality is less important than consumer confusion as to trade origin.[78] The issue of consumer confusion as to quality is discussed below.[79]

[72] Para. 16. This case is discussed in detail below, at para. 7.053 *et seq*.
[73] *Ideal Standard*, Judgment of ECJ, June 24, 1994, [1994] 3 C.M.L.R. 857.
[74] The case concerns the assignment of trade marks and is considered in detail below, at para. 7.057.
[75] Para. 37.
[76] Para. 38. This concept appears to be derived from Benelux Law (see statement of grounds for the Benelux Convention and the Uniform Law, *Bulletin Benelux* 1962–2, p. 36).
[77] Para. 38.
[78] See Tritton, "Articles 30 to 36 and Intellectual Property: Is the jurisprudence of the ECJ now of an Ideal Standard" [1994] EIPR 423.
[79] See para. 7.047.

(iv) Confusion and Article 36

7.045 In *HAG No. 2*, Advocate-General Jacobs noted that the number of confusingly similar marks could be in the region of several hundred thousand. Thus, if a trade marks owner could prevent the import of goods bearing confusingly similar trade marks, then it was obvious that trade mark conflicts could constitute a considerable hindrance to intra-Community trade.[80] This was especially so because the concept of confusion varied from one Member State to another and such could lead to distortions of trade. Thus he mentioned the fact that in the *Terrapin v. Terranova*[81] case, it was questionable whether an English court would have held that there was a danger of confusion and thus the German manufacturer could export to Britain but not vice versa.

Advocate-General Mayras said in *Terrapin v. Terranova* that it was a matter for the national authorities to decide whether a similar mark constituted infringement or not, *i.e.* this was a matter of national law and not Community law.[82] The Court had not been asked to rule on this point but stressed that the question of confusion and similarity may involve Community law and in particular consideration of the second sentence of Article 36.[83]

In a recent case, *Deutsche Renault v. Audi*,[84] the ECJ said that:

> "the determination of the criteria allowing the conclusion to be drawn that there is a risk of confusion is part of the detailed rules for protection of trade marks, which . . . are a matter for national law . . .
>
> Community law does not lay down any criterion requiring a strict interpretation of the risk of confusion."[85]

As pointed out in *Ideal Standard*, the relevant period in *Renault v. Audi* was the period before the entry into force of the First Council Directive approximating Trade Mark Laws.[86]

[80] See p. 591.
[81] Case 119/75, [1976] E.C.R. 1039, [1976] 2 C.M.L.R. 482.
[82] This argument was based by analogy to the decision of the ECJ in Case 41/74, *Van Duyn v. Home Office*: [1974] E.C.R. 1337, [1975] 1 C.M.L.R. 1 wherein the Court referred to the concept of public policy in the context of Art. 36 and said that it is necessary to allow the competent national authorities an area of discretion within the limits imposed by the Treaty.
[83] Para. 4. The Commission had submitted that the concepts of the danger of confusion and of similarity of goods must, in the interests of free movement of goods, be reduced to a minimum necessary to guarantee national trade mark protection. However, the ECJ did not associate itself with the Commission's viewpoint. Thus the Bundesgerichtshof when applying the ECJ's judgment did not consider that Arts. 30–36 required it to take a more restricted view of the concepts of similarity and confusion than national law dictated—[1978] 3 C.M.L.R. 102. See also Advocate-General Jacobs' Opinion in *SA CNL-Sucal NV v. Hag GF AG ("Hag 2")*: [1990] 1 E.C.R. 371, [1990] 3 C.M.L.R. 571 at p. 596.
[84] Case C-317/91, *Deutsche Renault v. Audi*: [1993] I-E.C.R. 6277.
[85] Paras. 31, 32.
[86] See para. 18 of *Ideal Standard*, Judgment of ECJ, June 24, 1994, [1994] 3 C.M.L.R. 857.

7.046 Now that the Trade Mark Directive has entered into force, national courts will be required to interpret domestic legislation which enacts the directive so as to give effect to the objectives of the directive.[87] In the Recitals of the Directive, the Directive makes specific reference to factors which should be taken into account in considering the likelihood of confusion, namely the recognition of the trade mark on the market, the association which can be made with the registered sign and the degree of similarity between the marks and the goods as constituting the specific condition of such protection. The Recital continues that the ways in which likelihood of confusion is established and in particular the onus of proof are matters for national *procedural* rules. This suggests strongly that the way a court applies the *substantive* test of confusion is intended to be a matter of Community law and if necessary, the court should make a reference under Article 177 to the ECJ for clarification of the application of the test of confusion.[88] However, it is more likely that national courts will consider the wording plain in the national implementing legislation but apply differing standards based upon previous national practice and case law. Such has certainly been the practice of national patent courts in construing the width of patent claims although the European Patent Convention was intended to harmonise the law in this area.[89]

The ECJ emphasised in *Deutsche Renault v. AUDI* and *Ideal Standard* that application of national law continued to be subject to the limits set out in the second sentence of Article 36 of the Treaty of Rome. Thus, there must be no arbitrary discrimination or disguised restriction on trade between Member States in applying the test of confusion. In *Ideal Standard*, the ECJ said that such would be the case if a national court conducted an arbitrary assessment of the similarity of products.[90]

(v) Guarantee of quality?

7.047 Trade marks do not provide a *legal* guarantee of quality.[91] The trade mark owner is free to provide trade marked goods of widely varying quality if he wishes. However, if he does so, he will undermine the very essence of a trade mark—namely as a *de facto* guarantee of quality. A consumer will usually buy trade marked goods because he knows that such goods will be of a consistent quality. The fact that they come from

[87] *e.g.* see Case 14/83, *Von Colson v. Land Nordrhein-Westfalen*: [1984] E.C.R. 1891, ECJ. See Introduction Chapter, at para. 1.021.

[88] See Tritton, "Articles 30 to 36 and Intellectual Property: Is the jurisprudence of the ECJ now of an Ideal Standard" [1994] EIPR 423.

[89] See Chap. 2, para. 2.025.

[90] Under German law, infringement was established if the defendant had applied the plaintiff's mark to goods of a similar nature to those falling in the specification of goods.

[91] See Advocate-General Jacobs' Opinion in *SA CNL-Sucal NV v. Hag GF AG ("Hag 2")*: [1990] 1 E.C.R. 371, [1990] 3 C.M.L.R. 571. See also Advocate-General Mayras' Opinion in Case 119/75, *Terrapin v. Terranova*: [1976] E.C.R. 1039, [1976] 2 C.M.L.R. 482 at p. 358.

one source will normally ensure this. Rarely will a trade mark owner apply the same trade mark in a particular territory to goods of differing quality. However, a trade mark owner may apply the same trade mark in differing countries to goods of differing quality. In such circumstances, it can be said that the trade mark's essential function is no longer that of origin but of quality.[92]

Consider the following scenario: P owns the trade mark "X" in Member States "A" and "B" for toothpaste. In A, its subsidiary sells the toothpaste without fluoride under the mark whereas in B, another subsidiary sells toothpaste with fluoride under the same mark. A parallel importer seeks to take advantage of potential confusion and imports the non-fluoride toothpaste from State A to B. P and its subsidiary in B brings trade mark infringement proceedings against the importer in State B.[93]

In this case, the marks in their respective States indicate a product from the same source and of the same quality but once exported to the other State will indicate a product to consumers in that state of the same origin but of differing quality. The consumers in State A and B will have very differing expectations from the trade mark X. If imports are allowed, there is a danger of confusion for the consumer.

7.048 The ECJ said in *Ideal Standard*[94] that the decisive factor in considering the function of a trade mark is the possibility of control over the quality of goods and not the actual exercise of that control. Therefore, a national law which enabled one subsidiary of the group to oppose the marketing in the territory of that state of products manufactured by an affiliated company on grounds of quality differences would not be permissible under Articles 30 to 36.[95] This ruling would permit consumer confusion as to quality but not as to trade origin. It is questionable whether the former is less important than the latter.[96] In this respect, the ECJ's decision in *Ideal Standard* has been criticised as inconsistent and illogical.[97] It appears to ignore the territorial nature of trade marks. Indeed the ECJ said in *Ideal Standard* that "since trade marks are territorial, the function of a trade mark is to be assessed by reference to a particular territory".[98] However, it is consistent with the decision in *Dansk Supermarked v. Imerco*.[99]

[92] See Case 434/85, *Allen & Hanburys*: [1988] E.C.R. 1275, [1988] 1 C.M.L.R. 701 where the ECJ stated that in that case (concerning a compulsory licence), the substance of the patent had changed. Thus the ECJ is not adverse to recognising that the function of a particular type of intellectual property can change.

[93] The facts of this example are derived from a U.K. case, *Colgate Palmolive v. Markwell Finance* [1989] RPC 497, C.A. which concerned importation from a non-Member State.

[94] *Ideal Standard*, Judgment of ECJ, June 24, 1994, [1994] 3 C.M.L.R. 857.

[95] *ibid*, para. 38.

[96] See Tritton, "Articles 30 to 36 and Intellectual Property: Is the jurisprudence of the ECJ now of an Ideal Standard" [1994] EIPR 423.

[97] *ibid.*

[98] Para. 48.

[99] Case C–10/89. *SA CNL-Sucal NV v. HAG GF AG ("Hag 2")*: [1990] 3 C.M.L.R. 571; Case 58/80, *Dansk Supermarked A/S v. Imerco A/S*: [1981] E.C.R. 181, [1981] 3 C.M.L.R. 590. See Tritton *ibid.*

The ECJ's approach in this field should be compared with the courts' approaches in the United Kingdom and Germany. In Germany, a similar approach has been adopted. Thus, if a group pursues a policy of making products of different quality for different national markets, it must suffer the consequences of its policy and accept the free movement of goods although the importer may be required to conspicuously indicate that the product differs from the other same branded product.[1] In England, the courts have adopted a different approach in a case where Community law was not applicable.[2] In *Colgate Palmolive v. Markwell Finance*,[3] a United States company owned trade marks in the United Kingdom and Brazil. These marks were licensed to Colgate-U.K. and Colgate-Brazil, subsidiaries of the United States company. The products in each country looked the same but there were marked differences in quality between the products from the two countries. The Brazilian product was markedly inferior in composition and therapeutic benefit, principally because it contained no fluoride. Markwell, a parallel importer, imported Brazilian Colgate toothpaste into the U.K. Colgate-U.S. sued for trade mark infringement. The Court of Appeal held that the trade marks applied on the Brazilian imports were different trade marks indicative of differing goods although they were of the same name. The Brazilian trade mark "Colgate" was different to the U.K. trade mark "Colgate" as each was a creature of national laws. Accordingly, the Court held that there was no implied or express consent to their marketing in the U.K. It was clear that the difference in quality of the goods and the possibility of consumer confusion of a therapeutic substance was of paramount importance in the Court's mind.

(vi) Are trade marks less worthy of protection than other forms of intellectual property?

7.049 In *Sirena Srl v. Eda Srl*,[4] the European Court of Justice held that:

> "The exercise of trade mark rights is particularly liable to contribute to the division of markets and therefore to prejudice the free movement of goods between States which is essential for the Common

[1] *Francesco Cinzano GmbH v. Java Kaffeegeschafte GmbH*: [1974] 2 C.M.L.R. 20, Bundesgerichtshof (importer of alcoholic drink of differing quality in differing Member States permitted to import trade marked drink from French and Spanish subsidiary of Cinzano into Germany provided conspicuous indication that product differed from product of plaintiff (the German subsidiary of Cinzano).)

[2] In *Champagne Heidsieck et Cie Monopole Sa v. Buxton* (1930) 1 Ch. 330; [1929] RPC 28, an English decision, a plaintiff who sold champagne which tasted differently and was marketed under slightly different labels in both France and England, sued a parallel importer in passing off and trade mark infringement. It was held that the plaintiff had exhausted his rights and that the consideration of free trade outweighed the protection of the public from confusion.

[3] [1989] RPC 497, C.A.

[4] Case 40/70, [1971] E.C.R. 69, [1975] C.M.L.R. 1.

Market. Trade mark rights are distinguished from other industrial and commercial property rights in so far as the object of the latter is often more important and worthy of greater protection than the object of the former.[5]

A similar lacklustre approach to trademarks was taken in *HAG No. 1*[6] where the ECJ held that trade marks were merely useful for indicating the trade origin of a product but stated that other means should be used so as not to affect the free movement of goods.[7] Such derisory treatment of trade marks was eventually rectified in *Hag No. 2* where Advocate-General Jacobs said:

> "The truth is that at least in economic terms, and perhaps also 'from the human point of view', trade marks are no less important, and no less deserving of protection, than any other form of intellectual property. They are in the words of one author, 'nothing more nor less than the fundament of most market-place competition'."[8]

The ECJ supported this view and said that:

> "With regard to trade mark rights, it should be observed that such rights constitute an essential element of the system of undistorted competition which the Treaty aims to establish and maintain. In such a system enterprises must be able to gain customers by the quality of their products or services, which can be done only by virtue of the existence of distinctive signs permitting identification of those products and services. For a trade mark to be able to play this part, it must constitute a guarantee that all the products bearing it have been manufactured under the supervision of a single enterprise to which responsibility for their quality may be attributed."[9]

Thus, it would seem that trade marks are not to be treated as lesser forms of intellectual property.[10]

(vii) Common origin and trade marks

7.050 In the 1970s, the ECJ considered the exercise of trade mark rights against imports where the mark on imports and that used by the trade mark owner has once been in common ownership but in which ownership of the marks had been divided as a result of wartime legislation.

[5] Para. 7. The ECJ followed Advocate-General Dutheille de Lamothe who observed that the debt owed to the inventor of the name "Prep Good Morning" is certainly not of the same nature as that which humanity owes to the discoverer of penicillin.

[6] [1974] E.C.R. 731, [1974] 2 C.M.L.R. 127.

[7] Case 192/73, *Van Zuylen v. HAG*: [1974] E.C.R. 731, paras. 13, 14.

[8] p. 583.

[9] Para. 13.

[10] The rehabilitation of trade marks by the ECJ in *HAG No. 2* [1990] 3 C.M.L.R. 171 as being essential in a market economy is discussed in Joliet, "Trade Mark Law and the Free Movement of Goods: The Overruling of the Judgment in HAG I" IIC 2/1991 at p. 311.

HAG NO. 1[11]

7.051 *FACTS*—HAG AG invented decaffeinated coffee. It marketed the coffee under the trade mark HAG which it had registered in various countries including Luxembourg and Belgium. These latter countries' marks were owned by Cafe HAG SA, a subsidiary of HAG AG. In 1935, the international registration of HAG was struck out in relation to Belgium and Luxembourg and new registrations of HAG in those states were effected in the name of Cafe HAG SA. From then on until 1944, Cafe HAG SA produced decaffeinated coffee for the Belgo-Luxembourg market under the "HAG" trade mark. In 1944, all the shares in Cafe HAG SA were sequestrated as enemy property and sold to the Van Oevelen family. In 1971, the HAG marks were assigned to the firm Van Zuylen Freres. HAG AG subsequently acquired registrations in Belgium and Luxembourg in the Cafe HAG marks of its own accord. In 1972, HAG AG decided to export decaffeinated coffee under the mark HAG to Luxembourg. Van Zuylen Freres brought trade mark infringement proceedings and a parallel action to cancel HAG AG's registrations in Belgium and Luxembourg.

The matter was referred to the European Court on the question as to whether Article 85 and 30 to 36 prohibited Van Zuylen Freres from bringing an infringement action given the fact that though the parties in the action had no legal, economic, financial or technological ties between each other, the trade marks had a common origin.

7.052 The Court of Justice held in a short judgment:

> "It could not therefore be accepted that the exclusiveness of the trade mark right, which can be the consequence of the territorial limits of the national laws, should be relied on by the holder of a mark with a view to prohibiting trading, in one Member State, in goods lawfully produced in another Member State under an identical mark which has the same origin. In fact such a prohibition, establishing the isolation of the national markets would come into conflict with one of the fundamental aims of the Treaty, the fusion of the national markets into one single market. While in such a market, the indication of the origin of a trade-marked product is useful, informing consumers thereon can be done by means other than those which would affect the free circulation of goods.
>
> Therefore to prohibit trading in one Member State in a product which lawfully bears a trade mark in another member-state, for the sole reason that an identical mark, sharing the same origin, exists in the first State is incompatible with the provisions laying down the free circulation of goods within the Common Market."[12]

[11] Case 192/73, [1974] E.C.R. 731, [1974] 2 C.M.L.R. 127.
[12] Point 15 in the Judgment.

The Court thus held in the formal part of the judgment that:

> "To prohibit trading in one Member State, in a product which lawfully bears a trade mark in another Member State, for the sole reason that an identical mark, *sharing the same origin*, exists in the first State, is incompatible with the provisions laying down the free circulation of goods within the Common Market."

7.053 The decision in *HAG No. 1* which gave rise to the doctrine of "common origin" was severely criticised.[13] The judgment is short and unhelpful. Clearly, it took no notice of the essential function of a trade mark. In relation to this, the Court merely said that "while the indication of the origin of a trade marked product is useful, informing consumers thereon can be done by means other than those which would affect the free circulation of goods."[14]

It took 16 years for the European Court to recognise the suspect reasoning in *Van Zuylen Freres v. HAG AG*. This was done ironically in a case[15] concerning the successor-in-title to Van Zuylen Freres (SUCAL) who started to export decaffeinated coffee under its mark HAG to Germany. This was opposed by HAG AG who brought trade mark infringement proceedings against SUCAL. Thus the boot was on the other foot. The European Court stated that the decision in *Van Zuylen* (now known as *HAG No. 1*) had to be reconsidered in the light of the subsequent case law.

Advocate-General Jacobs delivered a lengthy Opinion for the case. He initially reviewed the relevant Treaty provisions, the principles established by the Court in relation to intellectual property and the nature and function of trade marks. He then went on to consider the *HAG No. 1* case and confessed that he did not find the reasoning at all convincing. In particular, he criticised the judgment in that the Court did not explain anywhere why the fact that the trade marks were of common origin was relevant in the absence of any market-sharing arrangement.

He concluded that the doctrine of common origin was not a legitimate creature of Community law. He noted that the doctrine had been developed when the Court's case law on intellectual property had been in its infancy and before the Court had established the doctrine of the specific subject matter and essential function of a trade mark. Furthermore, he

[13] For criticism of the logic of *HAG No. 1*, see Morcom Q.C., "Trademarks in the European Community after Café HAG II" *Trademark Reporter*, Vol. 81, No. 5 *Trade Mark World*. Also see discussion of *HAG No. 1* in Advocate-General Jacobs' Opinion in *HAG No. 2* discussed below. See also Joliet, "Trade Mark Law and the Free Movement of Goods: The Overruling of the Judgment in HAG I" IIC 2/1991 and the list of reviewers at n. 2 and Kunze, "Waiting for Sirena II—Trademark Assignment in the Case Law of the European Court of Justice" 1991 IIC 319.

[14] Para. 14.

[15] Case C-10/89, [1990] 3 C.M.L.R. 571; *HAG GF AG v. SA CNL-SUCAL NV*.

found that the case of *Pharmon v. Hoechst*, a case analogous but pertaining to patent was irreconcilable with *HAG No. 1.*[16]

7.054 Having dismissed the proposal that confusingly similar trade marked goods should be distinguished by the addition of additional matter as not feasible,[17] he concluded that the owner of a trade mark must be allowed to exclude from his territory goods on which an identical trade mark had been placed by another, unrelated person who is the owner of the mark in another Member State and that such a view was both justified by the specific subject-matter of the right and the essential function of the mark. Finally, he recognised that there were differences between *HAG Nos. 1 & 2* and that the injustice in *HAG No. 2* was more obvious but considered it healthier to recognise that *HAG No. 1* was wrongly decided rather than make spurious distinction between the two cases.

7.055 The Court in effect followed the Advocate-General's Opinion. The Court said that it was necessary "to reconsider" the interpretation given in *HAG No. 1* in the light of the subsequent developments in the case law in the field of industrial and commercial property in relation to the free movement of goods provisions. The Court emphasised the doctrine of consent, the specific subject matter of the trade mark and the essential function of a trade mark as a guarantee to the consumer of the identity of origin of the product. The Court then went on:

> "[15] In assessing in the light of the foregoing considerations a situation such as that described by the national court, the decisive fact is the absence of any element of consent, on the part of the owner of the trade mark right protected by national legislation, to the marketing in another Member State, under a mark which is identical or may cause confusion, of a similar product manufactured and marketed by an enterprise which has no tie of legal or economic independence with that owner.
>
> [16] Under these circumstances the essential function of the mark would be compromised if the owner of the right could not exercise his option under national law to prevent the importation of the similar product under a name likely to be confused with his own mark because, in this situation, consumers would no longer be able to identify with certainty the origin of the marked product and the bad quality of a product for which he is in a way responsible could be attributed to the owner of the right.
>
> [17] This conclusion cannot be altered by the fact that the mark protected by national legislation and the similar mark borne by the

[16] Case 19/84, *Pharmon v. Hoechst*: [1985] E.C.R. 2281, [1985] 3 C.M.L.R. 775, concerned patented goods that had been compulsorily licensed in the U.K. and directly exported to Holland without the consent of the owner of the Holland and U.K. patents. Thus, a common origin existed. This case is discussed elsewhere, see para. 7.077.

[17] See para. 7.060.

> imported product pursuant to the legislation of the Member State of provenance originally belonged to the same owner, which was dispossessed in one of the marks as a result of expropriation by one of the two States in question before the Community was established.
>
> [18] In fact since the date of expropriation and in spite of their common origin, each of the marks has independently fulfilled within its own territorial limits, its function of guaranteeing that the marked products come from a single source."[18]

The Court thus concluded that:

> "Articles 30 and 36 of the EEC Treaty do not preclude national legislation from allowing an undertaking which is the holder of a trademark in a Member State from opposing the importation from another Member State of similar products lawfully bearing an identical trade mark in the latter State or liable to confusion with the protected mark even though the mark under which the contested products are imported originally belonged to a subsidiary of the undertaking which opposes the importation and was acquired by a third undertaking as a result of the expropriation of that subsidiary."

7.056 Thus, the doctrine of common origin was annulled in respect of expropriated marks. It was finally laid to rest in *Ideal Standard*,[19] where the Court held in concluding that the free movement of the goods *in casu* would undermine the essential function of the trade mark, that its reasoning equally applied to the splitting of the market whether through the act of a public authority or as a result of a contractual assignment. Thus, it can now be said that the fact that a trade mark has a common origin is now irrelevant in considering the application of Articles 30 to 36 to the exercise of trade mark rights.

(viii) Assignments of trademark

7.057 In *Terrapin v. Terranova*,[20] the Court stated that a trade mark owner cannot exercise his rights against imports from another state when the right relied on was a result of the subdivision whether by voluntary act or as a result of public restraint of a trade mark right which originally belonged to one and the same proprietor.[21] It said that in such cases, the basic function of the trade mark, *i.e.* that of a guarantee of origin had been undermined. The reasoning suggested that once a mark had been assigned, a trade mark owner could not exercise his rights against imports bearing the assigned mark from another Member State.

[18] Paras. [15] to [18].
[19] *Ideal Standard*, Judgment of ECJ, June 24, 1994, [1994] 3 C.M.L.R. 857.
[20] Case 119/75, *Terrapin v. Terranova*: [1976] E.C.R. 1039, [1976] 2 C.M.L.R. 482.
[21] See para. 6.

Recently, in *Ideal Standard*,[22] the ECJ considered the issue of the assignment of trade marks in the context of Articles 30–36. The facts of this case were that until 1984, the American Standard group held through its French and German subsidiaries—Ideal-Standard GmbH ("IS Germany") and Ideal-Standard SA ("IS France")—the trade mark "Ideal Standard" in Germany and France for sanitary fittings and heating equipment. In July 1984, IS France which had been in financial difficulties sold the "Ideal Standard" French trade mark for heating equipment (retaining it for sanitary fittings) to Societe Generale de Fonderie ("SGF") who later assigned the mark to Compagnie Internationale de Chauffage ("CICh"). CICh had no legal or economic links with American Standard. CICh continued to manufacture heating equipment and marketed it under the Ideal Standard trade mark.

7.058 IHT, a German company, began marketing heating equipment made by CICh in France, its parent company, and bearing the "Ideal Standard" mark in Germany. IS Germany brought proceedings for trade mark infringement against IHT although the former had stopped manufacturing and marketing heating equipment in 1976. The Landgericht Dusseldorf found in IS Germany's favour. It held that there was a risk of confusion between the use of the mark on sanitary fittings and heating equipment. IHT appealed to the Oberlandesgericht which referred under Article 177 to the ECJ the following question:

> "Does it constitute an unlawful restriction of intra-Community trade, within the meaning of Articles 30–36 of the EEC Treaty, for an undertaking carrying on business in Member State A which is a subsidiary of a manufacturer of heating systems based in Member State B to be prohibited from using as a trade mark the name "Ideal Standard" on the grounds of risk of confusion with a mark having the same origin, where the name "Ideal Standard" is lawfully used by the manufacturer in its home country by virtue of a trade mark registered there which it has acquired by means of a legal transaction and which was originally the property of a company affiliated to the undertaking which is opposing, in Member State A, the importation of goods marked Ideal Standard?"

7.059 The ECJ held that in such circumstances, Articles 30 to 36 did not prevent the exercise of trade mark rights. The decisive factor was whether the trade mark owner had the possibility of control over the quality of the goods.[23] It held that in the case of an assignment, the owner did not have such control if the mark was surrendered to a third party having no

[22] *Ideal Standard*, Judgment of ECJ, June 24, 1994, [1994] 3 C.M.L.R. 857.

[23] In making this statement, the Court was following a proposal put forward in Joliet, "Trade Mark Law and the Free Movement of Goods: The overruling of HAG I" IIC 3/2992 at p. 317. Coincidentally, the Rapporteur in the case was a Professor Rene Joliet—a case of a self-fulfilling prophecy! See Tritton, "Articles 30 to 36 and Intellectual Property: Is the jurisprudence of the ECJ now of an Ideal Standard" [1994] EIPR 423 for discussion on the *Ideal Standard* case.

economic link with the assignor. Furthermore, it rejected the Commission's viewpoint that the consent implicit in any assignment is the consent required for application of the doctrine of exhaustion of rights. It also rejected the Commission's argument that the owner of a trade mark who assigns the trade mark in one Member State while retaining it in others must accept the consequences of the weakening of the identifying function of the trade mark following from that assignment. It said that the argument failed to take account of the fact that since trade mark rights are territorial, the function of the trade mark is to be assessed by reference to a particular territory.[24] A detailed analysis of the ECJ's finding in this regard and its application to assignment of other types of intellectual property is discussed elsewhere in this Chapter, at para. 7.022.[25]

It should be noted that if the assignment is done for the purposes of market-sharing, then such will be prohibited under Article 85.[26]

(ix) Addition of additional distinguishing matter

7.060 In *HAG No. 1*, the Court had said that consumers could be informed as to the origin of a trade marked product by means other than those which would affect the free circulation of goods.[27] The ECJ did not discuss this in *HAG No. 2*[28] but emphasised that the essential function of the mark was to enable one product to be distinguished from another product of a different origin. Could it be argued that if an importer adds additional distinguishing matter to an imported trade marked product that clearly indicates that the product is not of the same origin as products bearing an otherwise confusingly similar trade mark in the Member State to which it is being imported, then the trade mark owner is prohibited from exercising its rights due to the free movement of goods provision.[29]

7.061 Whilst this was not discussed by the ECJ in *HAG No. 2*, such an approach was canvassed by the Advocate-General in his Opinion.[30] He noted that certain doctrines like the "honest concurrent user" doctrine in English law allowed confusingly similar trade marks to co-exist. Simi-

[24] Para. 47, 48. In doing so, the ECJ implicitly overruled the Court's ruling in Case 119/75, *Terrapin v. Terranova*: [1976] E.C.R. 1039, [1976] 2 C.M.L.R. 482 referred to at the beginning of this section, para. 7.057.

[25] See para. 7.022 on Consent and Assignment.

[26] See Case 56/64, *Etablissements Consten & Grundig v. E.C. Commission*: [1966] E.C.R. 299, [1966] C.M.L.R. 418; Case 40/70, *Sirena Srl v. Eda Srl*: [1971] E.C.R. 69, [1975] C.M.L.R. 1; Case 51/75, *EMI Records Ltd v. CBS*: [1976] E.C.R. 811, [1976] 2 C.M.L.R. 235; Case 28/77, *Tepea v. E.C. Commission*: [1978] E.C.R. 1391, [1978] 3 C.M.L.R. 392.

[27] Para. 14.

[28] *SA CNL-Sucal NV v. Hag GF AG ("Hag 2")*: [1990] 1 E.C.R. 371, [1990] 3 C.M.L.R. 571.

[29] It should be noted that where Art. 36 does not apply, the ECJ has ruled many times under Art. 30 that national unfair competition laws concerning the get-up and packaging of food and drink cannot be enforced where there are alternative less restrictive means of ensuring that consumer confusion does not occur, *i.e.* labelling. See para. 7.106.

[30] pp. 592–595.

larly, the German Act on the Integration of the Saarland provided for the peaceful co-existence of confusingly similar trade marks in Germany and the Saarland by the addition of distinguishing matter. The Advocate-General distinguished between identical marks and confusingly similar marks. With the former, he doubted whether additional distinguishing matter would ever dispel consumer confusion giving the example of blue and green packets of Persil on a supermarket shelf. With regard to confusingly similar marks, he accepted that in certain circumstances, the addition of distinguishing matter could overcome confusion but thought that such was the exception rather than the rule.

It is submitted that the trade mark owner should not be prohibited from exercising its rights. To do so would undermine the *specific object* of the trade mark (if not its *essential function*), namely to first market a product bearing the trade mark within the territory covered by the trade mark. Whilst a consumer may not be confused as to trade origin, it is likely that the reputation of one mark will affect the other. For instance, even if a product bearing the mark "Persil" and manufactured by A was imported into a Member State where the mark was owned by B and the imported product said that it was not manufactured by B and/or there was additional distinguishing matter, it is likely that consumers would import some of B's reputation to A's product. In such circumstances, A is unfairly appropriating the reputation of B's product to its own.

(x) How much can you interfere with a trade mark if you are a parallel importer?

7.062 Parallel importers who wish to import trade marked products from one Member State into another may often be interested in the product rather than the brand. Whilst a parallel importer may remove the trade mark and merely import the underlying goods, it may be that it merely wishes to repackage the goods and then re-affix the mark in order to comply with national legislation.

The ECJ has ruled on this question with regard to parallel importers repackaging pharmaceuticals when importing a product but leaving the original trade mark on.

(1) ***Hoffmann-La Roche & Co. v. Centrafarm***[31]

7.063 *FACTS*—Hoffmann, who owned the trade mark "Valium", licensed a British company and a German company to market Valium tablets in their respective countries. The price of Valium in the United Kingdom was considerably less than in Germany. Centrafarm imported the British Valium tablets into Holland, re-packaged the tablets, re-affixed the mark "Valium" and exported them to Germany. A notice was inserted that the drug had been "marketed by Centrafarm GmbH".

[31] Case 102/77, [1978] E.C.R. 1139, [1978] 3 C.M.L.R. 217.

Hoffmann-La Roche and its German company brought infringement proceedings against Centrafarm in Germany. The matter was referred to the ECJ under Article 177 as to whether the exercise of their trade mark rights was, *inter alia*, contrary to Articles 30–36.

JUDGMENT—The ECJ was clearly in some difficulties on this case. **7.064** Reasoning that a trade mark was primarily a guarantee of origin, the consumer was entitled to know that the product that he bought, which bore a trade mark, had not been interfered with such as to affect the original condition of the product. Thus, the ECJ held that the owner was justified under Article 36(1) in preventing the importer of a trade marked product from affixing the trade mark after re-packaging without authorisation of the trade mark owner.

However, the ECJ felt it was necessary to consider the second sentence of Article 36. Did the exercise of the trade mark owner's rights amount to a "disguised restriction on trade between Member States". They decided that it did if the following conditions had been fulfilled, namely:

(a) That it is established that the use of the trade mark right by the proprietor, having regard to the marketing system which he has adopted, will amount to an artificial partition of the markets between the member States.
(b) The re-packaging cannot adversely interfere with the original condition of the product.
(c) The proprietor of the mark receives prior notice of the re-packaging.
(d) It is stated on the new packaging that the product has been re-packaged.

It may be difficult to prove that condition (a) is fulfilled, *i.e.* that the marketing system of the owner of the right causes an artificial partitioning of the market between Member States.[32]

(2) *Centrafarm BV v. American Home Products Corporation*[33]

FACTS—AHP sold a tranquilliser under the "Seresta" mark in **7.065** Holland, France and Belgium and under "Serenid D" in the United Kingdom. The only difference between the Seresta and Serenid D drug was one of taste. The therapeutic effect was the same. Centrafarm imported Serenid D into Holland and re-packaged it so that it bore the mark "Seresta" and "marketed by Centrafarm BV".

[32] See *e.g. Hoechst AG v. Centrafarm BV*: [1980] 1 C.M.L.R. 650; *The Boots Co. Ltd v. Centrafarm*: [1979] 2 C.M.L.R. 495; (both cases were in the District Court Rotterdam) and the application of the ECJ's ruling in *Hoffmann-La Roche v. Centrafarm* by the German Federal Supreme Court to the case—[1984] 2 C.M.L.R. 561. See below, para. 7.068.

[33] Case 3/78, [1978] E.C.R. 1823, [1979] 1 C.M.L.R. 326.

7.066 *JUDGMENT*—The ECJ held that this was going too far. However, rather than over-refine its previous decision with Centrafarm, it returned to first principles and said that a trade mark owner must have the right to prevent:

> " . . . an unauthorised third party from usurping the right to affix one or other marks to any part whatsoever of the production or to change the marks affixed by the proprietor to different parts of the production."

Thus, it held that the proprietor of a trade mark which is protected in one Member State is accordingly justified by Article 36(1) in exercising its rights to prevent the import of a product bearing the mark even if the product had been lawfully marketed in another Member State under another mark in the latter State by the same proprietor.[34]

However, it said that such a practice may fall within Article 36(2) and that it was for the national court to settle in each particular case whether the proprietor had followed the practice of using different marks for the same product for the purpose of partitioning the markets.[35]

(3) *Pfizer Inc. v. Eurim-Pharm GmbH*[36]

7.067 *FACTS*—A parallel importer had merely replaced the outer covering of trade marked pharmaceuticals with its own smaller pack without touching the inner packing and, by using a transparent window on the outer packing, permitted the trade mark affixed by the manufacturer to be visible. Thus the only material difference in fact to the *Hoffman-La Roche* case was that in the latter the parallel importer had actually re-affixed the mark "Valium" on the packaging.

JUDGMENT—The Court held that where repacking does not affect the condition of the product and does not misrepresent the origin of the product, then Article 36 cannot be invoked by the trade mark owner.

7.068 *COMMENT*—The three cases give rise to the following doctrines:

(a) If the mark if *first* affixed by a repackager, then the owner is justified under Article 36(1) in preventing its importation. However, Article 36(2) may apply. *Centrafarm v. American Home Products*[37] modifying *Centrafarm v. Hoffmann-La Roche*.[38]
(b) If the trade mark is re-affixed to a product during repackaging then the owner is justified under Article 36(1) in preventing its

[34] *ibid*, para. 18.
[35] *ibid*, para. 23.
[36] Case 1/81, [1981] E.C.R. 2913, [1982] 1 C.M.L.R. 406.
[37] [1984] 2 C.M.L.R. 561.
[38] Case 3/78, [1978] E.C.R. 1823, [1979] 1 C.M.L.R. 326.

importation. However, Article 36(2) may apply *Hoffmann La Roche v. Centrafarm.*[39]

(c) However, where the product is merely repackaged but the trade mark is not re-affixed then Article 36 does not apply and the owner of the mark cannot prevent importation of the repackaged trade marked goods—*Pfizer v. Eurim-Pharm.*[40]

The importance of the above distinctions is that in case (c) Article 36 does not apply at all. In cases (a) and (b), Article 36(2) is applicable and the effect of such considerations can be seen in the application of the preliminary ruling of *Hoffmann-La Roche v. Centrafarm*[41] in the German courts. On appeal, the Bundesgerichtshof (the German Federal Supreme Court), ruled that as Hoffmann-La Roche had not deliberately introduced different packaging sizes and different prices for different Member States (these were the result of external market and legislative factors) then the enforcement of La Roche's trade mark rights did not contribute to the artificial partitioning of the market. Thus the enforcement of the trade mark rights did not fall within Article 36(2). It seems that the Bundesgerichtshof followed the statement in *Centrafarm v. American Home Products*[42] that use of a trade mark right constituted a disguised restriction only if it had the *purpose* [emphasis added]—together with its marketing system—of artificially partitioning the markets.

This should be contrasted to Advocate-General Capotorti's opinion in *Pfizer Inc. v. Eurim-Pharm GmbH,*[43] where he stated that in order to show whether the exercise of a trade mark right is contrary to Article 36(2), it is not necessary to show whether there is a subjective intention to act unlawfully, it being sufficient to establish that as a result of the exercise of that right, an artificial partitioning of the market had taken place. He stated that the precedent set by *Centrafarm v. American Home Products* should be confined to its specific facts it being an unusual situation.[44]

(xi) Nature and scope of trade mark law is a matter for Member State

7.069 The ECJ has recently confirmed that it is a matter of national law to determine what the requirements for registration of a mark are.[45] Thus, where a German company brought an action for infringement of its trade mark "QUATTRO" against a German subsidiary of a French company for importing cars with the mark "QUADRA", the defendant claimed

[39] Case 102/77 [1978] E.C.R. 1139, [1978] 3 C.M.L.R. 217.
[40] Case 102/77 [1978] E.C.R. 1139, [1978] 3 C.M.L.R. 217.
[41] Case 1/81, [1981] E.C.R. 2913, [1982] 1 C.M.L.R. 406.
[42] The European Court in *Pfizer v. Eurim-Pharm* declined to answer the question of whether Art. 36(2) was subjective or objective in nature, as they had already decided that *Pfizer Inc.* could not avail itself of Art. 36.
[43] Case 1/81 [1981] E.C.R. 2913, [1982] 1 C.M.L.R. 906.
[44] Case 3/78, [1978] E.C.R. 1823, [1979] 1 C.M.L.R. 326.
[45] *Deutsche Renault v. Audi* [1993] I–E.C.R. 6277.

that it was contrary to Articles 30–36 to permit the registration of a representation of a number (*i.e.* the number four) which has a significant meaning in the automobile trade (*i.e.* four cylinder engine). The ECJ held following its line of reasoning adopted in previous decisions for other types of intellectual property that Member States are not prevented from relying on their own trade mark registration criteria provided that the measures adopted do not lead to arbitrary discrimination or a disguised restriction on trade between Member States.[46]

(xii) "Fair and traditional practice"

7.070 The Court in *Prantl*[47] stated in the context of the bringing of criminal proceedings in Germany against an importer marketing an Italian drink in a bottle protected under German laws for a particular beverage from a particular part of Germany, that Article 36 could never be used to prevent imports of wines bottled according to a fair and traditional practice. This would seem to imply that a trade mark owner cannot bring infringement proceedings against imports where the mark or other identifying symbol was applied according to a fair and traditional practice. However, this judgment must be considered suspect.[48]

(b) Patents

(i) Role of patents

7.071 Unlike trade marks, patents do not have an essential function. Patents only exist to reward the inventor for his creative efforts and to encourage innovation in technology. Thus patents merely have a specific object.

(ii) Specific object and consent

7.072 As discussed earlier, the ECJ has said that the specific object of a patent is:

> "*inter alia* to ensure to the holder, so as to recompense the creative effort of the inventor, the exclusive right to utilise an invention with a view to the manufacture and first putting into circulation of industrial products, either directly or by the grant of licences to third parties, as well as the right to oppose any infringement."[49–50]

[46] See para. 7.031 on Scope and Nature of Protection is a Matter of National Law.

[47] Case 16/83, *Criminal Proceedings against Karl Prantl*: [1984] E.C.R. 1299, [1985] 2 C.M.L.R. 238.

[48] See para. 7.111 *et seq.* on Unfair Competition law and criticism of such a finding in Turner, "The Prosecution of Karl Prantl on the Incoming Tide" [1985] 4 EIPR 113 at p. 116. It would appear that the recent emphasis of the essential function of trade mark (see *SA CNL-Sucal NV v. Hag GF AG ("Hag 2")*: [1990] 1 E.C.R. 371, [1990] 3 C.M.L.R. 571) as a guarantee of origin would further weaken the effect of this *obiter dicta* remark.

[49–50] Case 15/74, *Centrafarm v. Sterling Drug Inc.*: [1974] E.C.R. 1147, [1974] 2 C.M.L.R. 480, para. 9.

Thus, the specific object of a patent is similar to that of a trade mark. Once goods bearing the mark have been marketed by the trade mark owner or with his consent, the owner has exhausted his rights in such products. Thus, the doctrine of consent applies to patents.[51]

In the case of compulsory licences, the ECJ has held in *Allen & Hanburys v. Generics*[52] that the specific object of a patent alters to the entitlement to a fair reward. However, if a patented product is marketed pursuant to a compulsory licence, a patentee of a parallel patent in another Member State is entitled to enforce his patent right to prevent the importation of such products.[53] The decisive criterion is that of actual consent to the marketing of a protected product even if the patentee has received a royalty for its marketing.[54]

(iii) Differences in Member States' patent laws

7.073 Often, differences in national patent laws of the Member States will affect trade in patented products in the Community. As discussed before, the scope and nature of protection of intellectual property rights is a matter of national law and is not affected by Articles 30–36.[55] Thus, an infringer cannot submit in a patent litigation action in a Member State that the patentee is not entitled to rely on a provision in national patent law which does not exist in other Members States' laws as such would constitute an attack on national patent rights. The ECJ has said that:

> "as the existence of patent rights is at present a matter solely of national law, a Member State's patent legislation . . . is covered in principle by the derogations from Article 30 which are provided for in Article 36."[56]

Thus, in *Thetford v. Fiamma*,[57] a provision in English patent law stated that an invention is not anticipated by publication of a specification of a patent more than 50 years before the filing date of the patent for the invention.[58] This meant that a patent existed in the United Kingdom for a

[51] See Case 15/74, *Centrafarm BV v. Sterling Drug Inc.*: [1974] E.C.R. 1147, [1974] 2 C.M.L.R. 480; Case 187/80, Merck v. Stephar: [1981] E.C.R. 2063, [1981] 3 C.M.L.R. 463 and Case 19/84, *Pharman v. Hoechst*: [1985] E.C.R. 2281, [1985] 3 C.M.L.R. 775.

[52] Case 434/85, *Allen & Hanbury v. Generics Ltd*: [1988] E.C.R. 1275, [1988] 1 C.M.L.R. 701.

[53] See Case 19/84, *Pharmon v. Hoechst*: [1985] E.C.R. 2281, [1985] 3 C.M.L.R. 775. See also Case C-191/90, *Generics (U.K.) Ltd v. Smith Kline & French Laboratories Ltd*: [1992] I E.C.R. 5335, [1988] 1 C.M.L.R. 701, paras. 35 to 37 where the ECJ rejected the submission that a compulsory licenced patent is a "weak" patent which did not fall within the context of Arts. 47 and 209 of the Act of Succession of Spain and Portugal which permitted a derogation from the general principle of the doctrine of consent for a limited period—for the details of this case, see Acceding Countries, para. 7.039.

[54] See para. 7.076.

[55] See para. 7.031.

[56] per the ECJ at para. 15 in Case 35/87, *Thetford Corporation v. Fiamma SpA*: [1988] E.C.R. 3585 [1988] 3 C.M.L.R. 549.

[57] [1988] 3 C.M.L.R. 549.

[58] Patent Act 1949, s. 50(1).

portable toilet but not in other countries. An importer sought to import portable toilets from Italy. A reference to the ECJ was sought on the question of whether the free movement of goods provisions prevented the owner of the patent from exercising his rights.

7.074 The Court held that the "50 year" provision was part of United Kingdom patent law and thus covered by Article 36. It then considered the application of Article 36(2). The Court held that it must be shown that the legislative measure does not discriminate between national and imported products and that there is a bona fide reason for the measure for Article 36(2) to be inapplicable. It held that there was no arbitrary discrimination on the grounds that the application of the legislation applied to nationals of all Member States. Furthermore, it held that there was a legitimate reason for the 50 year rule and thus it was not a disguised restriction on trade between Member States.

The importance of a national rule of patent law not directly or indirectly discriminating against products from another Member State has been emphasised in a series of cases on compulsory licences which are discussed below. Whether a national provision does discriminate can often be open to doubt. In *Hagen v. Fratelli*,[59–60] the Court of Appeal held that it was arguable that a rule of English patent law that prior use in England invalidates a patent but not prior use in other Member States was contrary to Articles 30 to 36.[61]

(iv) Marketing of products by patentee in country where no patent exists exhausts patentee's rights

7.075 It has been stated earlier in the context of the doctrine of consent/exhaustion that it is for the intellectual property owner to decide in the light of all the circumstances under what conditions he will market his product including the possibility of marketing it in a Member State where the law does not provide protection or the same rate of remuneration for the product.[62]

Thus, in *Merck v. Stephar*,[63] a patent case, a drug was not patentable in Italy but was in other Member States. The holder of the patents had marketed the drug in Italy knowing that it was not patentable. A parallel importer sought to import the drug into Holland. On reference to the ECJ on the question as to whether Articles 30–36 prevented the exercise of the patent in Holland to prevent importation, it was held that a patentee cannot exercise his rights to prevent importation of a product from a Member State where it has been marketed by himself or with his consent.

[59–60] [1980] 3 C.M.L.R. 253 (English Court of Appeal).

[61] [1980] 3 C.M.L.R. 253; [1980] F.S.R. 517. The decision was prior to *Thetford v. Fiamma*: [1988] 3 C.M.L.R. 549.

[62] See above, para. 7.014.

[63] Case 187/80, [1981] E.C.R. 2063, [1981] 3 C.M.L.R. 463.

It is arguable that in that case, the application of the doctrine of consent undermined the patentee's right to reward by first placing the product on a market where there is a patent, *i.e.* the patentee had not obtained the exclusive rights that flowed from the patent.[64] But the ECJ said that such a reward is not always guaranteed in all circumstances.[65] It is likely that the patentee will receive a fair profit for the marketing of the goods even where the invention is unpatentable.[66]

(v) Compulsory patent licences

7.076 The patent laws of Member States provide for compulsory licences in a variety of situations. Thus, their patent laws have permitted such licences where the patentee has failed to work the invention. Furthermore, under United Kingdom patent legislation, once 16 years of an "old" (*i.e.* pre-1977) patent's term had expired, a compulsory licence (providing for a reasonable royalty) could be obtained by any person. The ECJ rejected a submission that such patents were "weak" patents which should not be subject to the same rules as normal patents.[67] Two main issues arise out of compulsory licences and their interaction with Articles 30–36. The first is whether products marketed pursuant to a compulsory licence are free to circulate in the Community. The second issue is whether provisions in Member State's patent laws dealing with compulsory licences can distinguish between the domestic manufacture of the patent invention as opposed to its manufacture in another Member State.

(1) Compulsory licences and free movement of goods

7.077 The ECJ in *Pharmon v. Hoechst*[68] rejected the principle that a patentee with parallel patents must be deemed to have consented to the free movement of products throughout the Community which were marketed in a Member State pursuant to a compulsory licence.[69] In *Pharmon v. Hoechst,*[70] a German company, Hoechst AG, owned parallel patents in England and Holland. Pharmon, a Dutch company, obtained a compulsory licence in England which stipulated that any goods manufactured under the licence were not to be exported from the United Kingdom. However Pharmon BV disregarded the rule and directly exported goods

[64] Demaret, "Compulsory Licence and the Free Movement of Goods under Community Law" 18 IIC 161, 176.

[65] Case 187/80, *Merck v. Stephar*: [1981] E.C.R. 2063, [1981] 3 C.M.L.R. 463, para. 10.

[66] Competitive manufacturers may experience a substantial delay as they work out the associated knowhow to produce effectively the invention. Furthermore, their goods will not be exportable to States where the patent exists and so will not have the economics of scale that the patentee will have.

[67] Case C-191/90, *Generics (U.K.) Ltd v. Smith Kline & French Laboratories*: [1992] I E.C.R. 5335, [1993] 1 C.M.L.R. 89, paras. 35 to 37.

[68] Case 19/84, *Pharmon v. Hoechst*: [1985] E.C.R. 2281, [1985] 3 C.M.L.R. 775.

[69] The reader is referred to the section on Constructive Consent earlier in this Chapter for a discussion on the ECJ's approach generally to this area, see para. 7.016.

[70] Case 19/84, [1985] E.C.R. 2281, [1985] 3 C.M.L.R. 775.

into Holland. Hoechst sued for patent infringement. The European Court in a preliminary ruling said that Hoechst cannot be deemed to have consented to the marketing of the goods manufactured under the compulsory licence. Further, it said that the substance of a patent rights lies essentially in according the inventor an exclusive right of first placing the product on the market so as to allow him to obtain the reward for his creative effort. Thus Articles 30–36 did not prevent Hoechst from enforcing its rights against Pharmon even though it had received a royalty for the marketing of the patented products in issue. In a later case, in *Allen & Hanburys Ltd v. Generics*,[71] the ECJ said that in the circumstances of a compulsory licence, the substance of the exclusive right has been altered so as to ensure a fair return for the patentee as opposed to the right to first market the invention. Accordingly, the decisive issue is whether the patentee has consented to the marketing of the goods *in casu*. Whether or not the patentee has already been remunerated for the marketing of these goods is irrelevant. Furthermore, in accordance with the decision of the ECJ for other types of intellectual property, the issue is one of *actual* consent and not *deemed* consent that is of paramount importance.[72]

(2) Compulsory licences laws: discrimination between manufacture of invention in domestic state as against other Member States

7.078 The ECJ has recently adjudicated on several cases concerning the compatibility of Member State's laws on compulsory licensing with Articles 30 to 36. In doing so, the ECJ has said that compulsory licensing laws cannot be justified by the derogating provisions of Article 36 because the object of the rules is not to ensure the protection of industrial and commercial property but on the contrary to limit the rights conferred by such property.[73] Thus, provisions in United Kingdom and Italian law that granted compulsory licences where the patentee failed to work the patent in the United Kingdom and Italy fell to be considered under Article 30. The ECJ held that such laws were contrary to Article 30 as they encouraged the patentee to manufacture in the United Kingdom and Italy rather than in other Member States. Consequently, they discriminated against foreign manufacturers.[74]

[71] [1988] E.C.R. 1275, [1988] 1 C.M.L.R. 701.

[72] See para. 7.016 on Constructive Consent. See also para. 7.014 on "Differing Protection in Member States" where the distinction between actual and deemed consent can be a fine one as in the case of *Musik Vertrieb*. See also Demaret, "Compulsory Licence and the Free Movement of Goods under Community Law" 18 IIC 161, at p. 173, where he discusses the *Pharmon* judgment and its consistency with previous case law of the ECJ and points out that a blind application of the consent test without regard to the issue of remuneration of the rights owner for the marketing of the invention can produce bizarre results.

[73] *Compulsory Patent Licences*: Case C-30/90, *E.C. Commission v. United Kingdom & Italy*: [1992] I E.C.R. 777, [1992] 2 C.M.L.R. 709 at para. 14.

[74] See Demaret, "Compulsory Licence and the Free Movement of Goods under Community Law" 18 IIC 161 where he analyses the compatibility of a domestic manufacturing requirement with Art. 30–36 and predicted accurately that such a requirement was prohibited by the same.

7.079 Other provisions in the compulsory licensing laws of Member States which have the effect of indirectly discriminating between manufacturers of different Member States also fall foul of Articles 30–36. In *Allen & Hanburys Ltd v. Generics (U.K.) Ltd*,[75] a person was entitled to a licence of right for "old" patents (pre-1977) after 16 years of the patent had expired. The law further provided that an injunction would not be granted for infringement of the patent if the defendant undertook to enter into a licence by right. However, under United Kingdom law, an injunction could be granted against an importer of an infringing article and the licence of right could be endorsed with a ban on importation of the patented product. On reference to the ECJ, it was held that such provisions discriminated against manufacturers in other Member States and was contrary to Articles 30–36. In a more recent case, *Generics (U.K.) Ltd v. Smith Kline and French Laboratories Ltd*,[76] what was at issue was whether it was compatible with Articles 30–36 to refuse an English licensee of right authorisation to import products covered by the patent from non-Member States where the patentee worked and manufactured in the United Kingdom but to grant such authorisation where the patentee worked the patent by importing from another Member State. The ECJ held that in such circumstances, the proprietor of the patent may be exposed to competition from imports from non-Member States to which he is not exposed when he works the patent by manufacturing the product within the national territory. Thus, such a practice was discriminatory because it encouraged proprietors of patents to manufacture patented products within the United Kingdom rather than to import them from other Member States. The ECJ importantly said in that case that the adverse effects for the economy and for consumers arising out of the disparity in the legislation of the Member States and from the absence of common rules applicable to patents could not in any event justify discriminatory national practices contrary to Articles 30–36. These cases must be seen as an application of the general principle in the Treaty of Rome that national laws must not discriminate against nationals or goods of other Member States.[77]

Where transitional provisions for acceding States derogate from the Treaty's provisions on free movement of goods, such discriminatory legislation is permissible in relation to imports from the acceding States.[78]

[75] *ibid.*

[76] [1993] 1 C.M.L.R. 89.

[77] Case C-92/92, *Phil Collins v. IMTRAT Handels-GmbH*: [1993] 3 C.M.L.R. 773, ECJ. Article 7 E.C. Treaty.

[78] See *Generics (UK) Ltd v. Smith Kline & French* [1992] I E.C.R. 5335; [1993] 1 C.M.L.R. 89 and also a decision of the English Patents County Court in *The Wellcome Foundation Ltd v. Discpharm Ltd and others* [1993] F.S.R. 433, Pat. County Ct. and an article on that decision by Jones, "Exhaustion of Rights: Pharmaceuticals Marketed in Spain—A Wellcome Exception" [1993] 3 EIPR 107.

(c) Copyright and industrial design

(i) Introduction

7.080 Copyright and industrial design are the least harmonised sectors of intellectual property law in the Community. Certainly, in the field of industrial design, the protection conferred on industrial products varies greatly in the E.C. The nature and extent of copyright and neighbouring rights varies considerably between Member States. Furthermore, many rights may exist in one work. For instance, in a sound recording, there will normally exist performers' rights, composer's rights and phonogram producers' rights. These rights will extend from reproduction of the sound recording to supplying, selling, broadcasting and cable retransmissions rights. In the face of such complexity and variety of law, it was inevitable that cases were referred to the ECJ on the issue of the enforcement of copyright or related rights against the importation of goods into a Member State or the performance of works in a Member State.

For the purposes of the Treaty of Rome, a distinction is drawn between the exclusive rights of reproduction and the exclusive rights of performance. For instance, the right of reproduction applies to books, sculptures, paintings, sound recordings, video cassettes, etc. Such goods are protected by copyright in that it confers the right of reproduction, distribution and sale to the owner of the copyright. Secondly, there is the right of performance. This consists of the communication of the work to the public whether by performers at the theatre, by film at a cinema or by land and satellite broadcasts. These rights of performance differ materially from the rights embodied in goods because they are not concerned with goods but more specifically, services. As such, they do not fall within Articles 30–36 but Articles 59–60 which concern services.[79] The ECJ has confirmed that the same principles that apply to Articles 30–36 and intellectual property rights apply to Articles 59–60.[80]

7.081 Theoretically, there can be any number of performances of a work. Thus, a discothèque can play a tape recording work as many times as it wishes. With goods subject to copyright, the reward in relation to the reproduction right is based on the number of goods sold. In relation to the performance rights, the reward for the author is based on the number of performances and the size of the audience. Thus, the reproduction right is materially different from the performance right. This section examines copyright firstly in terms of copyright materialised in goods and secondly for performance rights.

[79] See Case 62/78, *CODITEL I*: [1980] E.C.R. 881, [1981] 2 C.M.L.R. 362 and Case 262/81, *CODITEL II*: [1982] E.C.R. 3381, [1983] 1 C.M.L.R. 49.

[80] See Case 62/79, *CODITEL I*: [1980] E.C.R. 881 at 903, [1981] 2 C.M.L.R. 362 and Defalque, "Copyright-Free Movement of Goods and Territoriality: Recent Developments" [1989] 12 EIPR 435 at p. 435.

(ii) Copyright materialised in goods

7.082 The phrase "for the protection of industrial and commercial property" in Article 36 applies to goods subject to artistic and literary copyright.[81] Thus sound recordings,[82] industrial designs[83] and video cassettes[84] have all been held to be goods subject to Articles 30–36. Indeed, the ECJ has said in so far as the commercial exploitation of a copyrighted work is concerned, there is no reason to make any distinction between copyright work and other forms of industrial and commercial property.[85]

(1) Doctrine of specific object and consent

7.083 The Court has confirmed that the doctrine of consent in this area and has held that neither a copyright owner, nor a copyright management society acting in the owner's or licensee's name, may rely on the exclusive exploitation right conferred by copyright to prevent or restrict the importation of sound recordings which have been lawfully marketed in another Member State by the owner himself or with his consent.[86] Thus, once the owner has placed his work on the market, he cannot prevent the importation distribution or sale of that good in another Member State. It should be noted that the ECJ will not permit a party to consent to the placing of a product on a market only for a particular Member State. Thus, a contractual stipulation that a party may only place a copyright product on the market in a particular Member State does not entitle the copyright owner to bring copyright infringement proceedings against the importation of such products into another Member State.[87]

Furthermore, such a rule applies even if different Member States provide for differing rates of remuneration. In *Musik Vertrieb*,[88] English copyright law provided that anyone may reproduce sound recordings on payment of a 6.25 per cent royalty to the rights owner. Such a law provided a "ceiling" to the level of negotiated royalties between parties. An

[81] Case 55/80, *Musik-Vertrieb Membran GmbH v. GEMA*: [1981] E.C.R. 147, [1981] 2 C.M.L.R. 44, per ECJ at 64 and Case 262/81, CODITEL II: [1982] E.C.R. 3381, [1983] 1 C.M.L.R. 49.

[82] Case 78/70, *Deutsche Grammophon v. Metro-Grossmarkte*: [1971] E.C.R. 487, [1971] C.M.L.R. 631; *Musik Vertrieb membran v. GEMA, ibid.*; Case 270/80, *Polydor v. Harlequin Record Shops*: [1982] E.C.R. 329, [1982] 1 C.M.L.R. 677; Case 34/87, *EMI Electrola GmbH v. Patricia Im und Export*: [1989] E.C.R. 79, [1989] 2 C.M.L.R. 413.

[83] Case 144/81, *Keurkoop BV v. Nancy Kean Gifts BV*: [1982] E.C.R. 2853, [1983] 2 C.M.L.R. 47.

[84] Case 156/86, *Warner Bros v. Christiansen*: [1988] E.C.R. 2605, [1990] 3 C.M.L.R. 684.

[85] See Case 58/80, *Dansk Supermarked v. Imerco*: [1981] E.C.R. 181, [1981] 3 C.M.L.R. 590; Case 55/80, *Musik-Vertrieb Membran v. GEMA*: [1981] 2 C.M.L.R. 44 at para. 11–12.

[86] Case 78/70, *Deutsche Grammophon v. Metro-Grossmarkte*: [1971] E.C.R. 487, [1971] C.M.L.R. 631; *Musik Vertrieb, ibid.*, per ECJ at para. 15. See also Case 58/80, *Dansk Supermarked v. Imerco*: [1981] E.C.R. 181, [1981] 3 C.M.L.R. 590.

[87] Case 58/80, *Dansk Supermarked A/S v. Imerco A/S*: [1981] E.C.R. 181, [1981] 3 C.M.L.R. 590.

[88] Case 55/80, *Musik-Vertrieb Membran v. GEMA*: [1981] E.C.R. 147, [1981] 2 C.M.L.R. 44.

importer imported into Germany sound recordings that had been put on the market in England with the consent of the copyright owner. The German copyright collecting society sued the importer for copyright infringement, seeking payment of the higher royalties that were charged in Germany. It argued that the aforesaid provision of United Kingdom law amounted to a statutory licence and that the free movement of goods provisions could not apply to sound recordings emanating from the United Kingdom.

7.084 The ECJ disagreed and held that an author is free to choose the place in which to put his copyright product on the market in the Community and that the fact that one Member State's laws in effect provided for a lower level of remuneration did not affect the fact that the copyright owner had exhausted his rights in the product once placed on the market.

Thus where sound recordings, having been distributed on the national market[89] in one Member State by the owner of the copyright or with his consent and then imported into another Member State, a copyright management society of the latter State cannot claim the difference between the royalties paid on the Member State less the lower royalties paid in the state of manufacture.[90]

This judgment emphasises the importance of the consent of the rights owner to the placing of the product on the market. Thus, where the sound recording has been placed on the market as a result of a compulsory licence, the owner is not deemed to have consented to the marketing of the product and can bring an action for copyright infringement.[91]

7.085 As stated earlier, a product may have several rights attached to it. For instance, a right of reproduction and performance will arise in an original audiovisual work. The ECJ has ruled that the exhaustion of one right does not lead to the exhaustion of allied rights. Thus, the consent of the rights owner to the placing of a protected product on a market does not constitute consent to the renting of that work if such a right is protected by a Member State's law.[92] The relevant distinction is between rights embodied in a good and rights which can be properly characterised as performance-type rights.

It would appear by analogy with the rulings on patents given by the

[89] The Bundesgerichtshof (the German Federal Supreme Court) applying the ruling in *Musik Vertrieb*, *ibid.* See *Musik Vertrieb MEMBRAN v. GEMA*: [1982] 1 C.M.L.R. 630 interpreted the phrase "having been put on the national market" as meaning that if the sound recordings had been manufactured but had only been internally distributed before export to Germany, then GEMA (the copyright management society) were not prohibited from enforcing the copyright. This is despite the fact that the importer had paid a licence fee in the United Kingdom to distribute the records in Great Britain. See "Placed on the market" at para. 7.015.

[90] *ibid*, at Point 27.

[91] See *Pharmon v. Hoechst* (patent case) and see 7.016, [1985] E.C.R. 2281; [1985] 3 C.M.L.R. 571.

[92] *Warner Bros v. Christiansen*: [1990] 3 C.M.L.R. 684 discussed later in more detail, at para. 7.090.

ECJ that the specific subject-matter of the author is the right to first market the protected goods.[93]

(iii) Copyright in performances

7.086 It was mentioned in the introduction to this section that Member States' laws will often confer copyright protection for the performance of works and their onward transmission whether by terrestrial broadcast, satellite broadcast or cable retransmission. Thus, the playing of a sound recording in a discothèque is a performance of a sound recording and will normally be a restricted act subject to copyright. In Member States' countries, the broadcast of a film will only be permissible with the consent of the owners of copyright and neighbouring rights in the film. In such cases, one is not concerned with protected goods but the provision of services. In such cases, Articles 59–60 rather than Articles 30–36 are applicable.

Article 59 provides that:

> " . . . Restrictions on freedom to provide services within the Community shall be progressively abolished during the transitional period in respect of nationals of Member States who are established in a State of the Community other than that for whom the services are intended."[94]

Article 60 states that:

> "services shall be "services" within the meaning of the Treaty where they are normally provided for remuneration, in so far as they are not governed by the provisions relating to freedom of movement for goods, capital and persons."
>
> In particular, they are stated as including, activities of a commercial, industrial nature and those of craftsmen and professionals. Thus anything which is provided for money but cannot be categorised as goods, capital or persons will be governed by Articles 59 to 66.

(1) Application of articles 59–66 to services

7.087 The first case that the ECJ had to consider the question of copyright in public performances in relation to Articles 59–66 was in *Coditel v. S.A. Ciné Vog Films* (CODITEL I").[95]

[93] See Advocate-General Darmon's Opinion in case 34/87 *EMI Electrola GmbH v. Patricia Im und Export*: [1989] 2 C.M.L.R. 413 at p. 418. See also, in England, Mr Justice Foster's judgment in *British Leyland Motors v. Armstrong Patents* [1982] 3 C.M.L.R. 603 at para. 4 where he states that the specific object of copyright was in the case of industrial design drawings to ensure that the skill and effort of the draughtsmen are rewarded by the grant of an exclusive right to copy and make for sale three dimensional reproductions by the grant of licences and to prevent others from infringing that right.

[94] The Article actually states that restrictions on freedom to provide services within the Community shall be progressively abolished during the transitional period. This transitional period has ended. Thus the restrictions on freedom to provide services are now contrary to Community law.

[95] Case 62/79, [1980] E.C.R. 881, [1981] 2 C.M.L.R. 362.

In this case, Ciné Vog had the exclusive distribution rights in Belgium to the film *Le Boucher* which it obtained from a French company called Les Fils la Boetie. Coditel was a Belgium cable television distribution service. Its central aerial in Belgium picked up a transmission of the film *Le Boucher* being broadcast in Germany by German television. This broadcast was with the consent of the original owner of the copyright in the film but confined under contract to Germany. Coditel then transmitted the film on its cable network in Belgium. At the time of transmission, Ciné Vog was showing the film in cinemas. It was stipulated in its contract with les Fils la Boetie that the right to transmit the film by television could not be exercised until 40 months after the first showing of the film in Belgium. Only seven months of this period had expired before the events in question.

Ciné Vog sued Coditel for infringement of copyright. The Cour d'Appel then referred to the European Court the question as to whether in the light of such facts Ciné Vog was prohibited from exercising its rights against Coditel by virtue of Article 59

7.088 The European Court stated that:

> "a cinematographic film belongs to the category of literary and artistic works made available to the public by performances which may be infinitely repeated. In this respect the problems involved in the observance of copyright in relation to the requirements of the treaty are not the same as those which arise in connection with literary and artistic works the placing of which at the disposal of the public is inseparable from the circulation of the material form of the works, as in the case of books or records.
>
> In these circumstances the owner of the copyright in a film and his assigns have a *legitimate interest in calculating the fees due in respect of the authorisation to exhibit the film on the basis of the actual or probable number of performances* and in authorising a television broadcast of the film only after it has been exhibited in cinemas for a certain period of time."[96]

The ECJ said that the essential function of copyright in performances was to require fees for any showing of a film. Imputing the wording of Article 36 to Article 59.[97] It then continued:

> "Whilst Article 59 of the Treaty prohibits restrictions upon freedom to provide services, it does not thereby mean restrictions upon the exercise of certain economic activities which have their origin in the application of national legislation for the protection of intellectual property, save where such application constitutes a means of arbitrary discrimination or a disguised restriction on trade between

[96] *ibid.* at paras. 12 and 13.

[97] See also Cases 395/87 & 110 & 241–242/88, *Ministere Public v. Tournier* and *Lucazeau v. SACEM*: [1991] 4 C.M.L.R. 248, at para. 10 to 15.

> Member States. Such would be the case if that application enabled parties to make an assignment of copyright to create artificial barriers to trade between Member States.[98]

Thus they held that Ciné Vog was entitled to exercise its exclusive distribution right against Coditel as the fact that the broadcast was limited to Germany was not incompatible with the Treaty of Rome as it was often impracticable to impose any other limitation. In CODITEL II,[99] the ECJ confirmed that Articles 59–60 and not Articles 30–36 were applicable and that the distinction underlying Article 36 between the existence and exercise of a right applied equally where the right is exercised in the framework of the provision of services.[1]

7.089 The recognition that the rights owner can place geographical limits to a broadcast of his works should be contrasted with the inability under Community law of a rights owner to limit the marketing of goods to a particular territory within the Community by contract.[2] The ECJ in *CODITEL I* stated that Article 59 does not prohibit the imposition of a geographical limit on any licence to broadcast. The ECJ stated that the fact that such geographical limits coincided with national boundaries did not lead to a different conclusion. Thus the ECJ would seem to be recognising the fact that the amount of reward for a performance is dependent on the size of the audience. This must be so. The reward of an author for his creative endeavour in a performance of his work is based upon the number of showings and the size of the audience. Thus the specific object of the copyright in performance can be said that he should receive reward concomitant with such a formula. In CODITEL I, if Coditel had been allowed to transmit the film in Belgium without recompense to Ciné Vog, then the latter as licensee of the copyright owner in Belgium, would not have received a fair or proportionate reward for his rights. Another way of looking at it is that if the copyright owner or his licensee in Germany had realised that Belgium would retransmit the German broadcast such that it would reach a much larger audience than was anticipated, then no doubt the fee to the copyright owner would have been substantially larger. Thus, he cannot be said to have *consented* to the showing of the film in Belgium and it was only due to lack of technological sophistication that it was able to be shown in Belgium.

Finally, it should be noted that the recently passed Council Directive on the coordination of certain rules concerning copyright and neighbouring rights applicable to satellite broadcasting and cable retransmissions may have implicitly banned Member States from permitting parties to include in broadcasting licences contractual provisions placing geogra-

[98] *ibid*, Para. 15.
[99] Case 262/81, [1982] E.C.R. 3361, [1983] 1 C.M.L.R. 49.
[1] Para. 13.
[2] Case 58/80, *Dansk Supermarked A/S v. Imerco A/S*: [1981] E.C.R. 181, [1981] 3 C.M.L.R. 590.

phical limits on licences concerning satellite broadcasting for licences concluded after January 1, 1995.[3]

(2) Exhaustion of reproduction right does not exhaust performance right

7.090 The European Court in the application of the doctrine of exhaustion, distinguishes between differing rights in the protected good. The marketing of a copyright product by the owner of the right or with his consent in one Member State does not exhaust the owner of a performance or quasi-performance right in another Member State from enforcing such a right. This is even if the law of first Member State does not provide for the performance right in question. This can be seen in the context of the ECJ's decisions on performance rights and rental rights.

Performance rights

7.091 In *Basset v. Sacem*,[4] the ECJ was concerned with the collection of a supplementary mechanical right royalty from a French discothèque owner when he played sound recordings in his nightclub. Under French law, a copyright owner or his assigns can authorise reproduction to a specific end. Thus, reproduction can be authorised for private purposes only. Thus, if the work is publicly performed then the permission of the owner is required and a further royalty can be recovered. It is this which is called the supplementary mechanical right royalty. This should be distinguished from the performance right royalty which also exists under French law. Thus the author or his assigns, in this case, it was the French copyright company, SACEM, can receive two types of royalty when a sound recording subject to copyright is publicly performed. The owner of the discothèque refused to pay the supplementary right royalty on the grounds, *inter alia*, that the supplementary mechanical right royalty did not exist in other countries, notably the United Kingdom, where many of the records were reproduced. On reference to the ECJ, the Court ruled that the supplementary right royalty, could be described as forming part of the royalty payment for public performance of a recorded musical work.[5] Thus even if the records which the discothèque played had been manufactured in a Member State where no such right existed, the right which applied to both domestic and national products was not exhausted as it was a performance-type right and not embodied in a product.[6]

Basset v. SACEM[7] was recently followed in *Ministere Public v.*

[3] See Chap. Four, para. 4.078.
[4] Case 402/85, [1987] 3 C.M.L.R. 173.
[5] The royalty was calculated on the basis of the discotheque's turnover and not on the number of discs purchased.
[6] It seemed that if the supplementary right royalty had been declared exhausted, SACEM would have increased the performance royalty to compensate for the shortfall. Thus the effect would have been negligible.
[7] Case 402/85, [1987] 3 C.M.L.R. 173.

Tournier and *Lucazeau v. SACEM.*[8] In the joined cases, Mr Tournier and Mr Lucazeau, the complainants, felt that it was a real injustice that they were paying considerably higher royalties for the playing of a largely Anglo-American repertoire than they would have done in the United Kingdom. The complainants relied upon the ECJ's judgment in *Musik Vertrieb v. GEMA*[9] that a copyright management society cannot seek to prevent the marketing of a recording which had been lawfully placed on the market in another Member State even if its practice was to levy a higher royalty rate than effectively done in the Member State where it was placed on the market. The ECJ held that a distinction between the marketing and performance rights must be maintained and held that the rate of royalty charged by copyright management society was not a matter for Articles 36 or 59 but must be appraised in relation to the competition rules contained in Articles 85 and 86.[10]

Rental rights

7.092 In *Warner Bros v. Christiansen,*[11] video cassettes of a film were imported by a Danish trader from England where they had been marketed by the copyright owner. Danish copyright law, unlike United Kingdom law at that time,[12] conferred on the author the exclusive right to rent as well as to place the video on the market. The Danish trade offered the videos for hire and the owner of the exclusive rights to hire in Denmark sued for infringement. The case was referred to the ECJ on the issue of whether in such a situation Articles 30–36 prohibited the owner of the rental right in Denmark from exercising his rights against the renter of the video cassette.

Advocate-General Mancini in *Warner Bros v. Christiansen*[13] had proposed that the ECJ find that Articles 30–36 did prevent the holder of the Danish exclusive rental right from suing for infringement. He held that rental rights cannot be assimilated to performance type rights. He put much emphasis on the fact that in the United Kingdom there was no rental right and relied upon the *Musik Vertrieb v. GEMA*[14] case in that the owner of a right who has put his work into circulation may not take advantage of the "disparities which continue to exist in the absence of any harmonisation of national rules on the commercial exploitation of copyrights so as to impede the free movement of goods in the Common Market".[15]

[8] Cases 395/87 & 110 & 241–242/88, *Ministere Public v. Tournier* and *Lucazeau v. SACEM*: [1991] 4 C.M.L.R. 248.
[9] Case 55/80, [1981] E.C.R. 147, [1981] 2 C.M.L.R. 44.
[10] See Chap. Eight at para. 8.146 *et seq.* and Chap. Eleven at para. 11.074.
[11] Case 156/86, [1988] E.C.R. 2605, [1990] 3 C.M.L.R. 684.
[12] The situation had now changed in the U.K., see Copyright Designs and Patent Act 1988 s. 18(2). See also Dir. on Rental Rights, Lending Rights and Allied Rights which provides for a rental right for Member States—see para. 4.031.
[13] Case 156/86, [1988] E.C.R. 2605, [1990] 3 C.M.L.R. 684.
[14] Case 55/80, [1981] E.C.R. 147, [1981] 2 C.M.L.R. 44.
[15] Case 55 & 57/80, *MEMBRAN and K-TEL v. GEMA:* [1981] E.C.R. 147, [1981] 2 C.M.L.R. 44, para. 26.

7.093 The ECJ did not follow the Advocate-General. The ECJ stated that the two essential rights of the author, namely the exclusive right of performance and the exclusive right of reproduction are not called into question by the rules of the Treaty.[16] The Court noted that there was a specific market for the hiring-out of records. Furthermore, the collection of royalties on sales could not provide a remuneration to the author which reflected the number of occasions on which a video cassette had been hired out. The ECJ rejected the contention by the importer that a maker of a video cassette who has offered it for sale in a Member State where there is no exclusive right of hire must accept the consequences of his choices and the exhaustion of his right to restrain hiring-out in any other Member State. The ECJ said that such a submission would render worthless the right to hire out. Thus, the marketing of a video cassette in a Member State which did not protect the right to rental, did not exhaust the right of the author granted to him by the laws of another Member State to oppose the rental in the latter State.

It is submitted that the Court was right and the Advocate-General was wrong. The rental of a video can take place repeatedly. Therefore, the exclusive right to rent will be infringed *every time* a video is rented and not merely the *first* time. Thus, even if in England there had been a rental right at the time and the video had been rented out, this would not have exhausted the owner of the Danish exclusive rental right. To rule otherwise would have meant that the rental right only pertains to the first rental and that subsequently the right must be deemed to have been exhausted. Thus, a rental right is similar to a performance right and is not capable of exhaustion. It should be noted that the importer was not sued for importing the video cassettes, merely for offering them for hire. In essence, the case did not concern the difference in national laws but the nature of a rental right being a very different animal to that of a marketing right.

(iv) Scope and nature of protection is a matter of national law

7.094 As with other forms of intellectual property, the ECJ has held that in the present state of Community law and in the absence of Community standardisation or of a harmonisation of laws, the determination of the conditions and procedures under which protection of copyright and designs is granted is a matter for national rules.[17] As mentioned in the previous section, it is for the copyright owner to decide in the light of all the circumstances, under what market conditions he will place his product on the market. In certain circumstances, a copyright product may come on the market as a result of differences in national copyright laws.

[16] *ibid.*, para. 12.

[17] *Keurkoop BV v. Nancy Kean Gifts BV*: [1983] 2 C.M.L.R. 47: *EMI Electrola GmbH v. Patricia Im- & Export Verwaltungs-GmbH*: [1989] 2 C.M.L.R. 413. See para. 7.031.

In *EMI Electrola GmbH v. Patricia Im und Export*,[18] the ECJ confirmed that if a copyrighted product comes on the market as a result of a difference in national laws and not with the consent of the copyright owner, then the latter could enforce his rights in another Member State against such a product. In that case, differing periods of copyright protection existed in Denmark and Germany such that the copyright protection existed in sound recordings expired earlier in Denmark than in Germany. Patricia imported sound recordings into Germany. EMI Electrola as owner of the exclusive rights of distribution for the sound recordings sought an injunction for copyright infringement. On reference to the ECJ on the question as to whether this was contrary to Articles 30–36, the ECJ said that as the sound recordings had been marketed lawfully in Denmark due to the expiry of the period of copyright and not due to an act of consent by the copyright owner or his licensee, then the owner of the distribution right was not precluded from exercising his rights by virtue of Articles 30–36.

In this regard, the ECJ's approach to copyright is consistent with that to patents.[19] Furthermore, it adopts the reasoning in *Pharmon v. Hoechst*[20] in relation to patents by rejecting the concept of constructive consent.[20a]

(d) Passing-off and unfair competition

(i) Introduction

7.095 Generally speaking, unfair competition law has two objectives. Firstly, it is to prevent the consumer against confusion in the market place; secondly, it is to protect the trader against other traders' business practices that are intended or have the effect of damaging the trader's business other than those founded on free market economics.

Article of the Paris Convention for the Protection of Industrial Property 1883[21] defines unfair competition as any act of competition contrary to honest industrial or commercial practice. In particular, Article 10 *bis* states that [as part of the general obligation of the countries of the Union to assure effective protection against unfair competition] that the following are prohibited:

(i) All acts of such a nature as to create confusion by any means whatever with the establishment, the goods, or the industrial or commercial activities, of a competitor.

[18] *EMI Electrola GmbH v. Patricia Im und Export*: [1989] 2 C.M.L.R. 413.
[19] See Case 35/87, *Thetford Corporation v. Fiamma SpA*: [1988] 3 C.M.L.R. 549.
[20] Case 19/84, [1985] E.C.R. 2281, [1985] 3 C.M.L.R. 775.
[20a] *i.e.* that anyone who decides to take out protection in a State is thereby accepting the consequences of that State's legislation as a whole and is thus deemed to have consented to any marketing of a product brought about by such measures. It is unclear whether EMI had previously marketed records in Denmark when the copyright was in force. See para. 7.016 on Constructive Consent.
[21] As revised in Stockholm on July 14, 1967.

(ii) False assertions, in the conduct of business, which might discredit the establishment, the products, or the industrial or commercial activity of a competitor.

(iii) Indications or allegations the use of which in the course of trade is liable to mislead the public as to the nature, the manufacturing process, the characteristics, the suitability for the purpose, or the quantity, of the goods.

7.096 E.C. countries all have laws, whether by statute or case law, that implement such obligations. In the United Kingdom which, unlike other Member States, has no comprehensive law of unfair competition, there are piecemeal provisions of which the most important is the case law doctrine of passing-off,[22] trade libel, malicious falsehood and Trade Descriptions Act 1968. These areas are now sufficiently developed so as to encompass most acts which constitute unfair competition in civil law countries.

From the intellectual property practitioner's viewpoint, the law of unfair competition is important. Often a distinctive[23] attribute of a good or service is not adequately protected by copyright, patent, trade mark or industrial design laws. This is especially so in the get-up, design and shape of products. The enforcement of unfair competition laws can often result in an enterprise owning a monopoly in a particular name, get-up or design. The European Court has dealt with the problems of unfair competition and the free movement of goods provision mainly in relation to well-known national brand names and shapes of food and wine products.

The main difference between this area and patents, trade marks and copyright is that unfair competition law does not necessarily fall within Article 36. Whether a particular aspect does fall within the meaning of "industrial or commercial property" will depend on the facts. The Court has developed the following principles in relation to Article 30 in the realm of unfair competition law.

(ii) The "Dassonville" principle

7.097 In the case of *Procureur du Roi v. Dassonville*,[24] the ECJ was concerned with criminal proceedings instituted in Belgium against traders who duly acquired a consignment of Scotch whisky in free circulation in France and imported it into Belgium without being in possession of a certificate

[22] Five characteristics must be present in order to create a valid cause of action for passing-off—"(1) a misrepresentation (2) made by a trader in the course of trade (3) to prospective customers of his or ultimate consumers of goods or services supplied by him (4) which is calculated to injure the business or goodwill of another trader (in the sense that it is a reasonably foreseeable consequence) and (5) which causes actual damage to the business to goodwill of the trader by whom the action is brought or (in a *quia timet* action) will probably do so . . . ", per Lord Diplock in *Warninck v. Townend ("Advocaat")* [1980] R.P.C. 31 at 93.

[23] Distinctive is used in the sense of indicative of trade origin or of a particular product.

[24] Case 8/74, [1974] E.C.R. 837, [1974] 2 C.M.L.R. 436.

of origin from the British customs authorities, thereby infringing Belgium rules. It transpired that a trader wishing to import whisky from a country other than the producer country could only obtain such a certificate with great difficulty. The ECJ ruled that such a provision was contrary to Articles 30–36. It went on to say that:

> "All trading rules enacted by Member States which are capable of hindering, directly or indirectly, actually or potentially, intra-Community trade are to be considered as measures having an effect equivalent to quantitative restrictions."[25]

This is called the "Dassonville" principle.

Recently, the ECJ has said that:

> "It is established by the case law beginning with *Cassis de Dijon* that in the absence of harmonisation of legislation, obstacles to free movement of goods which are the consequences of applying to goods coming from other Member States where they are lawfully manufactured and marketed, rules that lay down requirements to be met by such goods (such as those relating to designation, form, size, weight, composition, presentation, labelling, packaging) constitute measures of equivalent effect prohibited under Article 30. This is even if those rules apply without distinction to all products unless their application can be justified by a public-interest objective taking precedence over the free movement of goods.[25a]

(iii) Application of the "Dassonville" principle

7.098 If a national measure intentionally discriminates between imported products and domestic products, it is contrary to Article 30.[26] If the national measure discriminates against nationals then it is contrary to Article 7. Furthermore, if the procedural requirements of a national measure are such as to cause discrimination then this too will be contrary to Article 30.[27]

However, in many cases, it is not so obvious that a national law or legal provision has the effect of hindering trade between Member States. This is especially the case where the relevant provision applies equally to both domestic and imported products. Thus, a national law that states that all eggs must be sold in six-egg boxes does not appear to be a law capable of hindering trade between Member States. However, whilst in England, the sale of eggs in such containers is commonplace, it may not be so in other Member States. Thus, producers of eggs in those countries

[25] *ibid.*, point 5.

[25a] C267 268/91 Keck & Mithouard [1995] C.M.L.R. 101 at para. 15.

[26] See Case 434/85, *Allen & Hanburys Ltd v. Generics (U.K.) Limited*: [1986] 1 C.M.L.R. 101; see also Case 788/79, *Gilli and Andries*: [1980] E.C.R. 2071 and *Re Irish Souvenirs: E.C. Commission v. Ireland*: [1982] E.C.R. 4005.

[27] See Case 8/74, *Procureur du Roi v. Dassonville*: [1974] E.C.R. 837, [1974] 2 C.M.L.R. 436.

would have to bear additional costs in packaging eggs for the United Kingdom market so as to comply with United Kingdom law. He would thus be competing unfavourably with domestic United Kingdom egg producers who would not have to pack in two different ways. Similarly, United Kingdom egg producers would be at a disadvantage with French producers if there was a French law which provided that eggs must be sold in circular containers. In these cases, the importer or the foreign producer is often disadvantaged as compared to the domestic producer.

In applying the Dassonville principle, the ECJ has widely applied Article 30 to national laws which disadvantage suppliers of products from other Member States. However, until recently, the ECJ gave the impression of taking the view that *any* idiosyncratic national provision which was not duplicated in other States and which was capable of affecting trade between Member States was prohibited under Articles 30–36 unless there was a good reason for it. This led traders to invoke Article 30 in relation to national provisions which had no ostensible effect on trade between Member States. However, in the recent case of *Keck v. Mithouard*,[28] the ECJ has retreated from this extreme stance. The ECJ's application of the *Dassonville* rule is now considered in three cases.

(1) Criminal proceedings against Karl Prantl[29]

7.099 Section 17 of the Wein-Verordnung 1971 stated that only wine produced in Franconia could be marketed in a traditional bottle known as the Bocksbeutel (a bulbous shaped bottle). This legislative measure was actually enacted as the Bundesgerichtshof had found that the Bocksbeutel was an indirect indication of geographical origin and thus its use might mislead consumers if used for wine not produced in Franconia. Furthermore, anyone who marketed Bocksbeutel not containing such wine was guilty of a criminal offence. Mr Prantl imported Italian red wine into Germany which was traditionally bottled in a bottle virtually identical to the Bocksbeutel. The matter was referred to the ECJ as to whether such a provision was contrary to Articles 30–36. The Court held that:

> "A provision such as section 17 of the Wein-Verordnung, allowing a specific shape of bottle to be used only by certain producers of domestic wine, *has protective effects* inasmuch as it favours those producers compared to producers in other Member States who traditionally bottle their wine in bottles of identical or very similar shape."[30]

Thus the Court said that although the legislation applied to national and imported products alike, *in practice* it had protective effects. Therefore, it came within the scope of the prohibition of Article 30.

[28] C267–268/91 [1995] C.M.L.R. 101.
[29] Case 16/83, *Criminal Proceedings against Karl Prantl*: [1985] 2 C.M.L.R. 238.
[30] *ibid.*, point 22.

(2) *Theodar Kohl KG v. Ringelhan & Rennett SA*[31]

7.100 Ringelhan and Rennet were an old German company who used the logo "r + r". They had a French subsidiary, Ringelhan and Rennett SA. However, in 1982, the German company was wound up and the French subsidiary was sold to a third party. The French company carried on using the logo for their pharmaceutical equipment in Europe. Theodore Kohl, another pharmaceutical equipment manufacturer, brought an action against R. & R. SA under a provision in German unfair competition law which prohibited misleading statements. It alleged that the use of the mark without a clarifying statement misled customers into believing that R. & R. SA were connected with the defunct German company (who had an excellent reputation). On reference to the ECJ, it was held that although the German provision applied to both German and imported products, it had been interpreted and applied by the German Courts in such a way as to discriminate against imported products.

Thus the ECJ extended the concept of discrimination even further than in *Prantl* because it ruled that even if a law does not have a protective effect, it can be contrary to Article 30 if it is applied so as to give a *de facto* protective effect.[32]

(3) *Keck v. Mithouard*[33]

7.101 Recently, the ECJ has attempted to narrow the application of the *Dassonville* principle. This followed an increasing tendency of traders to invoke Article 30 as a means of challenging any rule whose effect was to limit their commercial freedom even where such rules were not aimed at products from other Member States. This tendency had been encouraged in the light of decisions by the ECJ which tended to find that apparently innocuous measures infringed Article 30 merely because they directly or indirectly made free trade more difficult.[34] In *Keck v.*

[31] Case 177/83, [1985] 3 C.M.L.R. 340.

[32] As the headnote says, this ruling should be analysed with care. In appearance it is extremely wide. It appears from both the Advocate-General and the Court that the section had never been applied in a purely domestic context. Thus it is the practical application of the German law and not the actual legislation which appeared to have determined the issue.

[33] Joined Cases 267, 268/91, *Keck v. Mithouard*: [1994] O.J. C1/9, T.L.R., November 25, 1993, [1995] C.M.L.R. 101.

[34] In particular, the Court's severe application of the *Dassonville* principle can be seen in its case law condemning national legislation which regulates prices where such legislation clearly did not have the intention of preventing imports—*e.g.* see *Cullet v. Sodinord & Sodirev*: [1985] 2 C.M.L.R. 524, ECJ (fixed minimum price of petrol in France prevented importers of petrol of lower cost price from passing on the competitive advantage to consumers and thus contravened Art. 30) Case 65/75, *Tasca*: [1976] E.C.R. 291 (fixed maximum prices forced importers of more highly priced goods to cut their profit margins or be forced to sell at a loss); *Procureur General v. Buys*: [1979] E.C.R. 3203 (national price freeze rules induced dealers of products to prefer domestic products to imported products because of the higher prices generally of imported products).

Mithouard,[35] the applicants were prosecuted for reselling products in an unaltered state at prices lower than their actual purchase price contrary to French law. The Court of Justice said in a short judgment that it was not the purpose of such legislation to regulate trade in goods between Member States. It continued that such legislation may admittedly restrict the volume of sales and hence the volume of sales of products from other Member States. However, it said that the question was whether such a possibility is "sufficient to characterise the legislation in question as a measure having equivalent effect to a quantitative restriction on imports".[35a] The Court said that in view of the tendency described above, it was necessary to re-examine and clarify its case law on this matter.

7.102 It then recited the *Cassis de Dijon* principle. It then went on to say:

> "However, contrary to what has previously been decided, the application to products from other Member States of national provisions restricting or prohibiting certain selling arrangements is not such as to hinder directly or indirectly actually or potentially trade between Member States within the meaning of the Dassonville judgment . . . provided that those provisions apply to all affected traders operating within the national territory and provided that they affect in the same manner, in law and in fact, the marketing of domestic products and of those from other Member States.
>
> Where those conditions are fulfilled, the application of such rules to the sale of products from another Member State meeting the requirements laid down by that State is not by nature such as to prevent their access to the market or to impede access any more than it impedes the access of domestic products. Such rules therefore fall outside the scope of the Article 30 of the Treaty."[36]

In this judgment, the ECJ places considerable doubt on much of its earlier case law in this area where patently the above proviso was fulfilled. In particular, the continuing principles discussed below are now subject to considerable doubt. The decision undoubtedly represents a retreat from the previously held case law where almost any law which was capable of affecting imports or exports fell within Article 30 unless it was capable of satisfying the *Cassis de Dijon* exceptions discussed below, at para. 7.103. It would appear from the judgment that it is not enough for the measure to have the *possibility* of affecting trade between Member States. Instead, the measure in issue must have some defining purposive characteristic that affects imports and exports. It is not clear whether the ECJ in *Keck*[37]

[35] Joined Cases 267, 268/91, *Keck v. Mithouard*, [1994] O.J. C1/9, T.L.R., November 25, 1993, [1995] C.M.L.R. 101.
[35a] para. 13.
[36] *ibid.*, paras. 16, 17.
[37] *ibid.*

intended to make a statement of general principle or purely to confine it to selling arrangements.

(iv) The "Cassis de Dijon" principle

7.103 In the "Cassis de Dijon"[38] case, German law provided that fruit liqueurs could only be sold in Germany if they contained a minimum of 32 per cent wine-spirit content. To this general rule, certain beverages were exempted. A trader attempted to import "Cassis de Dijon" liqueur, a well known French liqueur but whose alcoholic strength was below 32 per cent from France. Thus the German provision prevented the sale of Cassis de Dijon in Germany. The trader sought a ruling from the ECJ that the measure was contrary to Article 30 in that it prevented the import of drinks traditionally and lawfully produced in another Member State. The ECJ stated that:

> "In the absence of common rules[39] relating to the production and marketing of alcohol . . . it is for the Member State to regulate all matters relating to the production and marketing of alcohol and alcoholic beverages on their own territory. *Obstacles of movement within the Community resulting from disparities between the national laws relating to the marketing of the products in question must be accepted in so far as those provisions may be recognised as being necessary in order to satisfy mandatory requirements relating in particular to the effectiveness of fiscal supervision, the protection of public health, the fairness of commercial transaction and the defence of the consumer.*"[40]

The underlined phrase is traditionally called the "Cassis de Dijon" principle. The German Government argued that it was in the interests of the consumer for the latter to know that fruit liqueurs were of a certain alcoholic content and to prevent unfair trade practices developing.[41] However, the ECJ said that the labelling of products stating their alcoholic

[38] Case 120/78, *Rewe-Zentral AG v. Bundesmonopolverwaltung fur Branntwein*: [1979] E.C.R. 649, [1979] 3 C.M.L.R. 495.

[39] This is interpreted as meaning "in the absence of comprehensive (or exhaustive) legislation"—see Case 16/83, *Criminal Proceedings against Karl Prantl*: [1985] 2 C.M.L.R. 238.

[40] This principle has been applied often by the ECJ, *e.g.* see Case 6/81, *Industrie Diensten Group v. Beale*: [1982] E.C.R. 1625, [1982] 1 C.M.L.R. 102; Case 220/81, *Robertson*: [1982] E.C.R. 2349, [1983] 1 C.M.L.R. 556; Case 286/81, *Oosthoek*: [1982] E.C.R. 4575, [1983] 3 C.M.L.R. 428. One must now include "protection of the environment" in the Cassis de Dijon list—see Case 302/86, *Re Disposable Cans: E.C. Commission v. Denmark*: [1989] 1 C.M.L.R. 619.

[41] This latter argument was based on the fact that the lowering of the alcohol content secures a competitive advantage in relation to beverages of a higher alcoholic content because alcohol, being taxed heavily, is by far the most expensive constituent of such beverages.

content would suffice to ensure that consumers were not prejudiced. Thus, the German law was not necessary. It therefore concluded that the German measures did not serve the general interest and did not take precedence over the requirements of the free movement of goods. Thus where alcoholic beverages had been lawfully produced in one Member State, they could not be prevented from being exported to other Member States. Such an argument applied even though the German law applied to both domestic and imported products.[42]

7.104 The "Cassis de Dijon" principle prohibits any national measure which has the effect of preventing the sale of a product lawfully marketed in another Member State, even if the national measure applies indiscriminately to both domestic and imported products, unless the measure falls within the exceptions described above. After the judgment, the Commission sent a letter to the Member States containing some policy conclusions.[43] In that communication, the Commission said that where products are manufactured according to a customarily and traditionally accepted way, then exceptions to the principle of free movement of such products would only be admissible under strict conditions. These were that the rules were necessary, appropriate and not excessive in order to satisfy mandatory requirements; they served a purpose in the general interest which was compelling enough to justify an exception to the principle of free movement of goods and the rules were essential for such a purpose, *i.e.* were the means most appropriate and at the same time least hindered trade.

This approach can be seen in *Prantl*[44] discussed above. Having set out the law in that case, the Court then considered whether the "Cassis de Dijon" exceptions applied. The German government argued that the legislative measure was necessary to prevent consumer confusion. However, the Court said that regard must be had to the fair and traditional practices observed in the Member States. It held that an exclusive right to use a certain type of bottle could not be used to prevent imports or wines originating in another Member State in accordance with a *fair and traditional practice* [emphasis added]. It held that the Community provisions on labelling were sufficient to prevent confusion. It further held that Article 36 could not be invoked as well.

7.105 The "Cassis de Dijon" principle must be reconsidered in the light of

[42] However, national case law will be presumed to apply without distinction to domestic and imported products unless the contrary is show. See Case 6/81, *Industrie Diensten Groep v. Beele Handelmaatschappij*: [1982] E.C.R. 707, [1982] 3 C.M.L.R. 102.

[43] Communication from the Commission concerning the consequences of the judgment given by the Court of Justice on February 20, 1979 in *Cassis de Dijon* [1979] O.J. C 256/2.

[44] Case 16/83, *Criminal Proceedings against Karl Prantl*: [1985] 2 C.M.L.R. 238. See para. 7.099 for the facts of this case.

Keck v. Mithouard.[45] In *Cassis de Dijon*, obstacles to the free movement of the goods which result from disparities between national laws are prima facie prohibited. In *Keck*, the judgment suggests that if national laws merely affect in the same manner, in fact and in law, both domestic and foreign products, then they are compatible with Articles 30 to 36. Thus, under *Keck*, even if there are disparities between national laws which do hinder trade between Member States, it is sufficient merely that there is no legal or actual discrimination between domestic and foreign products. It is submitted that the judgment in *Keck* is aimed at those laws which have no defining characteristic which could be said to affect trade between Member States as opposed to those laws which have a more obvious and direct effect on trade between Member States. Thus, laws like in *Prantl*[46] which clearly had a *protective effect* and which do discriminate in practice between Italian and German wine will still be governed by the "Cassis de Dijon" principle.

(v) The "reasonableness" rule

7.106 In *Dassonville*, the Court emphasised that a Member State may take measures to prevent unfair practices provided that such measures are reasonable.[46a] By virtue of *Cassis de Dijon*, the measure must be "justified as necessary in order to satisfy mandatory requirements".[47]

The European Court has applied the reasonableness rule in a severe way. In fact, the rule whilst it has been known as the reasonableness rule, can be described as embodying two principles. Firstly, there is the principle of proportionality. This means that where the restrictive effect on the free movement of goods is out of proportion to its purpose, then the measure is not permissible.[48] Secondly, there is the principle of alternative means. This means that where the same objective can be attained by other means which are less of a hindrance to trade, then the measure is not permissible.[49] These principles have been especially applied in the field of food and alcoholic drinks where the Court has constantly held that if labelling can prevent confusion of the consumer, then a national measure prohibiting imports of certain types of food or drinks on

[45] [1994] O.J. C1/9. See para. 101.
[46] Case 16/83, *Criminal Proceedings against Karl Prantl*: [1985] 2 C.M.L.R. 238.
[46a] *Dassonville*, para. 6.
[47] See also Case 788/79, *Gilli and Andres*: [1980] E.C.R. 2071, [1981] 1 C.M.L.R. 146.
[48] *e.g.* Case 302/86, *Re Disposable Beer Cans: E.C. Commission v. Denmark*: [1989] 1 C.M.L.R. 619.
[49] See Advocate-General Van Themaat in Case 6/81, *Industrie Diensten Groep v. Beele*: [1982] E.C.R. 707, [1982] 3 C.M.L.R. 102. Advocate-General Slynn again emphasised the principle of alternative means in Case 341/82 and 189/83, *Re the Packaging of Margarine: E.C. Commission v. Belgium*: (this case was settled after he delivered his opinion).

account of their packaging or bottling on the grounds of danger of public confusion is contrary to Article 30.[49a]

7.107 However, where a marked or packaged good is imported which is misleading to consumers, then an action for a misleading statement will not be contrary to Articles 30 to 36 if the importer has failed to counteract the confusion.[50] The Court has upheld the principle of reasonableness in several cases concerning Article 30 that a generic name for a product cannot be reserved by means of national laws for a national variety to the detriment of other varieties lawfully produced in other Member States.[51] A Dutch rule prohibiting slavish imitation of someone else's product if there is no compelling practical reason for such imitation and the imitation causes confusion was held to fall within the scope of the "Cassis de Dijon" mandatory requirements of protection of consumer and fairness of commercial transactions and to be reasonable.[52] A rule of the United Kingdom Pharmaceutical Society requiring dispensing chemists to dispense medicines only as named by the doctor and not to substitute therapeutically identical brands was held to fall within Article 30 but covered

[49a] *e.g. Prantl* supra; *Cassis de Dijon* supra; Case 182/82, *Miro BV*: [1985] E.C.R. 3731, [1986] 3 C.M.L.R. 545 (sale of low alcohol *Genever* lawfully and traditionally marketed in Belgium could not be prohibited in Netherlands as confusion could be prevented by labelling); Case 261/81, *Walter Rau Lebensmittelwerke v. De Smedt*: [1983] 2 C.M.L.R. 946 (Belgium rules which required all margarine to be sold in cuboid shapes so as to distinguish it from butter were contrary to Art. 30 as other means such as labelling were less harmful to inter-state trade.); Case 179/85, *Re the Use of Champagne Bottles: E.C. Commission v. Germany*: [1986] E.C.R. 3879, [1988] 1 C.M.L.R. 135 (German legislation allowing the use of champagne bottles and stoppers only for sparkling wines could not be invoked to prevent the import of *petillant de raisin* which was not a sparkling wine but had been traditionally marketed in champagne style bottles as labelling would prevent confusion); Case 128/84, *Re German Purity Requirements for Beer: E.C. Commission v. Germany*: [1988] 1 C.M.L.R. 780 (German legislation restricting the use of the word "Bier" for beer produced according to strict rules which was only met by German manufacturers was contrary to Art. 30 as labelling could protect German public expectations); Case 286/86, *Ministere Public v. Deserbais*: [1989] 1 C.M.L.R. 516 (French provision which prevented EDAM cheese being marketed with a fat content of less than 40 per cent could not be invoked against German EDAM cheese as consumer confusion could be prevented by labelling nb EDAM admitted not to be an indication of origin) Case 274/87 *Re German Sausages: E.C. Commission v. Germany*: [1989] 2 C.M.L.R. 733 (ban on import of low fat sausages contrary to Art. 30 as confusion could be prevented by labelling); Case 196/89, Case 210/89. *Re Low Fat Cheese: E.C. Commission v. Italy*: [1992] 2 C.M.L.R. 1 (Italian provision that dairy products whose fat content was lower than 45 per cent could not be called cheese (*formaggio*) was contrary to Art. 30 as consumer confusion could be cured by labelling).

[50] See the decision of the Oberlandesgericht Koln in *Re labelling of Dutch poultry* [1990] 2 C.M.L.R. 104 (Dutch poultry sold in Germany bore labels specially translated into German that give consumer the impression that produce was local and not foreign, there being no other indication on get-up to counteract such an impression constituted a misleading statement and was not covered by Art. 30).

[51] *e.g.* see Case 12/74, *"Sekt" und "Weinbrand" case, E.C. Commission v. Germany*: [1975] E.C.R. 181, [1975] 1 C.M.L.R. 340; Case 193/80, *E.C. Commission v. Italy (the vinegar case)*: [1981] E.C.R. 3019; *Ministere Public v. Deserbais, ibid.*

[52] Case 6/81, *Industrie Diensten Groep v. Beele Handelmaatschappij*: [1982] E.C.R. 707, [1982] 3 C.M.L.R. 102.

Article 30 but covered by the public health grounds in Article 36.[53] A provision in German unfair competition laws which prohibited the circulation of goods with the ® symbol where the mark was not protected was held to be contrary to Article 30 and not justifiable under the principles established in *Cassis de Dijon*.[54]

(vi) Ancillary principles

7.108

(1) The above four principles are all subject to the general rule (as intimated in *Cassis de Dijon*) that Member States cannot take or enact any measures which are contrary to or frustrate legislation implemented by the Community pursuant to the Treaty of Rome's objectives. Thus if the Community has introduced a comprehensive and exhaustive regime of legislation in a particular sphere, then Member States have no powers to enact or maintain legislation in that sphere.[55]

(2) The law of unfair competition usually exists to prevent consumer confusion. As such, it need only be applicable when goods are offered for sale. Thus importation *per se* of goods lawfully marketed in another Member State would not be classified as an unfair practice. The ECJ has recognised this and has held that an unfair competition law provision which is used to prevent imports (rather than their offering for sale) lawfully marketed in another Member State is contrary to Article 30.[56]

(3) Measures which prima facie impede imports will not fall within the "Dassonville" principle regardless as to whether they fall within Article 36 if they constitute a means of arbitrary discrimination or a disguised restriction on trade between Member States.[57]

(vii) Consent and Article 30

7.109 An important residual question is whether the doctrine of consent applies to Article 30. It should be remembered that the doctrine of consent arose out of the interrelationship between intellectual property and Article 36. Thus, if a party wishes to invoke an unfair competition law provision which falls outside Article 36 against a seller, does it matter if he originally placed the complained of goods on the market?

[53] *R. v. Pharmaceutical Society of GB ex parte Association of Pharmaceutical Impoters*: [1989] 2 C.M.L.R. 751. In this case, the ECJ did not consider whether the provision fell within the Cassis de Dijon exception of public health but there seems little reason why such would not have applied.

[54] Case C-238/89, *Pall v. Dahlhausen*: [1990] E.C.R. 4827.

[55] *e.g.* see Case 83/78, *Pigs Marketing Board*: [1978] E.C.R. 2347, [1979] 1 C.M.L.R. 177; *Prantl, ibid. Re Low Fat Cheese: E.C. Commission v. Italy*: [1992] 2 C.M.L.R. 1. See also para. 7.032 on Community secondary legislation.

[56] This principle was established in Case 22/71, *Begeulin*: [1971] E.C.R. 181, [1972] C.M.L.R. 81 and applied in *Dansk Supermarked v. Imerco* [1981] E.C.R. 181, [1981] 3 C.M.L.R. 590 at Point 2.

[57] *Dassonville* [1974] E.C.R. 837; [1974] 2 C.M.L.R. 436, C58/80, para 7.

In *Industrie Diensten v. Beele*,[58] a case concerning Dutch laws on slavish imitation and their validity under Article 30, Industrie Diensten was seeking to import cable ducts from Germany which were a slavish imitation of a Swedish product whose patent had just expired. The ECJ commented that there was no indication of an agreement or of dependence between Beele and Diensten, the plaintiff and defendant.[59] This observation implies that where legal and/or economic ties do exist between the parties then Beele would not have been able to prevent the imports and that if Beele had placed the imitation product on the German market, it would have been deemed to have consented to its marketing in Belgium.

7.110 However, unfair competition laws exist essentially to protect the consumer. In such circumstances, the consumer is little interested in whether a party has marketed the goods in another Member State. Often, the importer will not be sued by a private party but by a state organ responsible for trading standards.[60] In those cases, the laws are not enforced by persons who can be said to "consent" to the placing of the product on the market. In such cases, the issue of consent becomes less important. Thus, it cannot be a case of a rights owner seeking to partition the common market. Accordingly, in cases involving prosecution under unfair competition laws by the state, it is highly arguable that the issue of consent is irrelevant. However, where a private individual is seeking to bring proceedings for unfair competition against an importer, it is submitted that as with Article 36 and its case law, the importer should be allowed to import goods which have been placed on the market with the plaintiff's consent. Moreover, the ECJ has demonstrated that the issue of consent takes priority over possible consumer confusion.[60a]

(viii) Article 36, unfair competition and indications of origin

7.111 If the "unfair competitive" feature relates to, *inter alia*, the protection of industrial or commercial property then Article 36 is applicable. This affords more protection for the rights owner than the *Cassis de Dijon* exceptions under Article 30 because there is no reasonableness criteria.[61]

[58] Case 6/81, *Industrie Diensten Groep v. Beele Handelmaatschappij*: [1982] E.C.R. 707, [1982] 3 C.M.L.R. 102.
[59] *ibid.*, Point 12.
[60] *e.g.* see C16/83 *Prantl* [1985] 2 C.M.L.R. 238.
[60a] See para. 7.047.
[61] A rule of proportionality has been held to exist before a State can avail itself of the protection of the "human health" exemption in Art. 36—see Case 174/82, *Criminal Proceedings against Sandoz BV*: [1983] E.C.R. 2445, [1984] 3 C.M.L.R. 43. However, this should be seen as a condition precedent before Art. 36 is applicable. It thus would not appear to pertain to rights based on the specific objects of intellectual property rights.

In *Theodor Kohl KG v. Ringelhan und Rennett*,[62] the Court held that the protection of the consumer does not fall within Article 36.[63] Thus it will be rare that unfair competition laws fall within Article 36. Importantly for the intellectual property practitioner, is whether features indicative of origin but which are not registered trade marks come within Article 36. Such could be an unregistered trade mark, get-up or design.

This point has never been conclusively determined. In the *Sekt und Weinbrand* case,[64] the ECJ implied that true indications of origin could be protected under Article 36.[65] English and German courts have assumed that distinctive names (not amounting to a trade mark) and get-ups of products come within Article 36.[66] In *Sekt und Weinbrand*, the ECJ analysed the effect of Directive 70/50 and stated that designation of origin and indications of origin as used in that Directive always indicate a product coming from a given geographical area. It continued to say that in so far as such are protected, they fulfil their specific function only if the product which they designate in fact possesses qualities and characteristics due to the geographic locality of its origin. The court concluded that the term "Sekt" and "Weinbrand" were not indications of origin and therefore were not protected by Article 36. However, in *Exportur*[66a] the ECJ rejected such a narrow interpretation. It said that such a concept would mean depriving of all protection those geographical names used for products in respect of which it could not be proved that they owed their particular flavour to the soil. Such names could nevertheless enjoy great renown with customers and represent for the producers established in the places they designated, an essential means of obtaining customers and should be protected. Accordingly, provided the designation or indication of origin had not become generic, they were protected under Article 36.

[62] Case 177/83, *Theodor Kohl KG v. Ringelhan und Rennett*: [1984] E.C.R. 3651, [1985] 3 C.M.L.R. 339.

[63] *ibid.*, paras. 18 and 19.

[64] Case 12/74, at para. 19. *Re German Sparkling Wine: EC Commission v. Germany* [1975] E.C.R. 181, [1975] 1 C.M.L.R. 339.

[65] The Court said that: "The fact that the terms "Sekt" und "Weinbrand" do not constitute "indications of origin" prevents the measures in issue—the wine laws—being able to rely on Art. 36 of the treaty for the protection of industrial and commercial property" (at point 15). This implies that where terms do indicate origin, then Art. 36 is applicable.

[66] *e.g.* in England, *Maxims Limited v. Dye* [1977] FSR 364, [1977] 1 W.L.R. 1155, [1978] 2 All E.R. 55, [1977] 2 C.M.L.R. 410, the Court held that the rule in the English law of passing-off that the proprietor of a business locally situated in England can bring a claim for passing-off against someone not in that locality (provided his reputation is nationwide) but that this would not be true if the proprietor's business was situated in another Member State was contrary to Art. 36(2). In Germany, the Hanseatische Oberlandesgericht held in *Re Cointreau Bottles:* [1976] 1 C.M.L.R. 268 that Art. 36 meant that the owners of a distinctive bottle get-up (the distinctive Cointreau bottle) could obtain an injunction against the importation of a triple sec liqueur called "Breton". It is apparent from the report that the liqueur had been on the market since at least 1922.

[66a] C–3/91, *Exportur SA v. Lor SA and Confiserie du Tech*, Judgment November 10, 1992.

7.112 In *Prantl*, the Court declined to determine whether the Bocksbeutel was "industrial or commercial property" within Article 36. However, in an alarming paragraph of its judgment, it ruled in effect that Article 36 will not assist industrial or commercial property rights owners to prevent imports of wines originating in another Member State bottled according to a fair and traditional practice. As has been pointed out,[67] this would seem to conflict with the Court's judgment in *Terrapin v. Terranova*,[68] where the Court held that an industrial or commercial property right legally acquired in one Member State could legally be used against products from another under a name giving rise to confusion if those rights had been independently acquired. As has been commented on,[69] there is no obvious reason for restricting the ruling in *Terrapin v. Terranova* to word marks or non-traditional trade mark use. Article 36, unlike Article 30 (of which the case was primarily concerned with) explicitly states what are to be considered the exceptions for Article 36. Importantly, the *HAG No. 2*[70] case upholds the *Terrapin* ruling and holds that the essential function of a trade mark is to distinguish goods from one trade origin and another so that the consumer is not confused. Whether a wine has been bottled according to a fair and traditional practice is not relevant concern for consumers. Accordingly, it is submitted that if the right being enforced constitutes commercial or industrial property, then Article 36 is applicable regardless of whether a product has been made according to a fair and traditional practice in another Member State.

6. Article 85, Parallel Imports and Intellectual Property Rights

(a) Introduction

7.113 Article 85(1) prohibits all agreements between undertakings, decisions by associations of undertakings and concerted practices which may affect trade between Member States and which have as their object or effect the prevention, restriction or distortion of competition within the common market.[71] Prima facie, it is not apparent how the exercise of an intellectual property right falls within Article 85. Indeed, the Court of Justice has held that a patent taken by itself does not constitute an agreement or con-

[67] See Turner, "The Prosecution of Karl Prantl Bottles on the Incoming Tide" [1985] EIPR 113.
[68] Case 119/75, *Terrapin v. Terranova*: [1976] E.C.R. 1039, [1976] 2 C.M.L.R. 482.
[69] Turner, "The prosecution of Karl Prantl Bottles on the Incoming Tide" [1985] 4 EIPR 113.
[70] *SA CNL-Sucal NV v. Hag GF AG ("Hag 2")*: [1990] 3 C.M.L.R. 571.
[71] The relationship of Art. 85 and intellectual property to licensing agreements is discussed in depth Chapter Eight.

certed practice but results from a grant by a state.[72] Similarly, the Court has ruled the same in relation to trade marks[73] and in relation to industrial design rights.[74]

In spite of the above, the European Court has consistently ruled that the *exercise* of a right may fall within Article 85(1) if it is the object, the means or the result of an agreement, decision or concerted practice whose object or effect is to distort competition within the Common Market.[75] This is discussed elsewhere in this book.[76] This aspect of Article 85 is not contentious. Clearly, the effect of Article 85 would be undermined if the exercise of intellectual property rights could defeat a finding that there was an anti-competitive practice.[77]

However, in a case in the 1970s, the ECJ in *Sirena v. Eda*[78] sought to prevent the exercise of trade mark rights by recourse to Article 85 which had a common origin and which had the effect of establishing rigid frontiers between Member States. The *Sirena* case and its consequences for parallel imports are discussed below, and in particular, whether the "common origin" doctrine has survived under Article 85.

(b) Sirena v. Eda[79]

7.114 Rights to a trademark in Italy had been assigned by the original American proprietor in 1937 to Sirena. Subsequently, a German company had been permitted to use the mark in Germany by the American proprietor. A parallel importer imported goods from Germany bearing the trade mark into Italy. Sirena sought to exercise its trade mark rights against the parallel importer but the national court referred to the ECJ the question of whether the exercise of the rights was contrary to Articles 85 and 86.

The ECJ held that the simultaneous assignment to several concessionaires of national trade mark rights for the same product if it has the effect of re-establishing rigid frontiers between Member States may prejudice trade between Member States and distort competition. It held that:

[72] Case 24/67, *Parke Davis v. Probel*: [1968] C.M.L.R. 70.
[73] Case 40/70, *Sirena Srl v. Eda Srl*: [1971] C.M.L.R. 260 [1971] E.C.R. 69. Also *EMI records Ltd v. CBS (UK) Ltd*: [1976] C.M.L.R. 235, point 26.
[74] *Keurkoop BV v. Nancy Kean Gifts BV*: [1983] 2 C.M.L.R. 47 at point 27.
[75] *Sirena v. Eda, supra* at point 9. This has been re-iterated in several judgments of the ECJ, *e.g. Deutsche Grammophon v. Metro*: [1971] 1 C.M.L.R. 631, point 6; *Centrafarm v. Sterling*: [1974] 2 C.M.L.R. 238, points 38–41; *EMI Records v. CBS (U.K.) Ltd*: [1976] 2 C.M.L.R. 235, point 27; *Keurkoop BV v. Nancy Kean Gifts BV*: [1983] 2 C.M.L.R. 47, point 278.
[76] See Chap. Eight, para. 8.052.
[77] As recognised by the ECJ in *Etablissements Consten & Grundig v. E.C. Commission*: [1966] E.C.R. 299, [1966] C.M.L.R. 418.
[78] Case 40/70 *Sirena Srl v. Eda Srl*: [1971] E.C.R. 69, [1971] C.M.L.R. 260.
[79] Case 40/70 *Sirena Srl v. Eda Srl*: [1971] E.C.R. 69; [1971] C.M.L.R. 260.

> "Article 85 therefore applies[80] where by virtue of trade mark rights, imports of products originating in other Member States, bearing the same trade mark because their owners have acquired the trade mark itself or the right to use it through agreements with one another or with third parties, are prevented . . . If the agreements have been concluded before the entry into force of the Treaty it is necessary and sufficient that their effects continue after this date."[81]

The decision fits uneasily into the framework of Article 85. It appears to prohibit any exercise of trade mark rights which have a common origin against products bearing the same trade mark and origin. As has been commented on, neither the Advocate General nor the Court ever really examined the true nature of an outright trademark assignment in the context of the provisions of Article 85.[82] This may be of importance because there may be legitimate reasons for the division of trade mark rights.[83]

7.115 The ECJ's decision in *Sirena* has been criticised and distinguished by subsequent courts and Advocate-Generals. The difficulties which the *Sirena* case give rise to can be illustrated as follows. Suppose Sirena had sued a genuine pirate as well as the parallel importer who affixed illegally the "Prep" mark to shaving foam products. As Article 85 was applicable against the parallel importer, then Article 85(2) meant that the assignment was void, being the only voidable agreement in issue. Thus, the pirate could argue that as the assignment was void, the Italian undertaking did not have title to the Italian trade mark rights. In reality, there was no underlying anti-competitive agreement which the Court could point to as being anti-competitive.

In *HAG No. 1*,[84] Advocate-General Mayras said in relation to *Sirena* that:

> " . . . in the case of assignment pure and simple of the trademark right, it is more difficult to discern, in the absence of special circumstances, an agreement which has the object or effect of restricting competition. It is in fact of the very nature of such an assignment to constitute a total transfer of the right and to confer on the transferee the very prerogatives held by the transferor."

[80] It has been suggested that the word "applies" here should be read in the context of paras. 9 to 12 of the case to mean that such an assignment is capable of being prohibited under Art. 85 but is not necessarily so prohibited—see Kunze, "Waiting for *Sirena II*—Trade Mark Assignment in the Case Law of the European Court of Justice" IIC 1991 319 at p. 331.

[81] Paras. 11 and 12.

[82] See Morcom, "Trade Marks in the European Community After Café HAG II" *Trade Mark Reporter*, Vol. 81, No. 5 (USTA) at p. 549. See also Kunze, "Waiting for *Sirena II*—Trade Mark Assignment in the Case Law of the European Court of Justice" IIC 1991 319.

[83] *e.g.* liquidation of subsidiary companies of trade mark owner.

[84] *Van Zuylen Frères v. HAG AG ("HAG 1")*: [1974] E.C.R. 731, [1974] 2 C.M.L.R. 127.

He thus considered that the Court in *Sirena* had gone too far and concluded that it seemed that there were certain factual elements in the court file which revealed the presence of concerted practices condemned by Article 85. However, the Advocate-General rejected an argument that an assignment contract fully executed, having exhausted all its efforts in the past could not fall under the prohibition of Article 85 as the mere fact that a party was seeking to exercise its rights which it owned by virtue of the assignment established it was capable of producing legal consequences.

7.116 In *EMI v. CBS*,[85] the Court again considered whether Article 85 could prevent the exercise of rights by one party against another where both derived their rights from a common origin. The assignments which had brought about a division of rights had occurred a long time before the Treaty of Rome came into force. Advocate-General Warner said that he found the decision of *Sirena* difficult to understand and that, at the date of giving his opinion, it would have been decided under Articles 30–36. He held that the prohibition in Article 85 could not extend to an agreement made and terminated before the entry into force of the Treaty because the Treaty did not have retroactive effect nor could it extend to the mere consequences of such an agreement such as the exercise of trade mark rights. The Court agreed with the Advocate-General and held that:

> "For Article 85 to apply to a case, such as the present one, to agreements which are no longer in force, it is sufficient that such agreements continue to produce their effects after they have formally ceased to be in force.
>
> An agreement is only regarded as continuing to produce its effects if from the behaviour of the persons concerned there may be inferred the existence of elements of concerted practice and of co-ordination peculiar to the agreement and producing the same result as that envisaged by the agreement.
>
> This is not the case when the said effects do not exceed those flowing from the mere exercise of the national trade mark rights."[86]

7.117 Thus *Sirena* was tacitly overruled[87] in relation to assignments which occurred before the Treaty of Rome entered into force. Recently, in *Ideal Standard*,[88] the ECJ stated that:

[85] *EMI Records Ltd v. CBS*: [1976] E.C.R. 811, [1976] 2 C.M.L.R. 235.

[86] p. 267.

[87] See also Advocate-General Jacobs in *SA CNL-Sucal NV v. Hag GF AG ("Hag 2")*: [1990] 3 C.M.L.R. 571 where he said that the rule in *Sirena* had been importantly modified by the ECJ's decision in *EMI v. CBS*. See also Morcom, "Trade Marks in the European Community After Cafe HAG II", *Trade Mark Reporter*, Vol. 81, No. 5 (USTA) and Kunze, "Waiting for *Sirena II*—Trade Mark Assignment in the Case Law of the European Court of Justice" IIC 1991 319.

[88] *Ideal Standard*, Judgment of ECJ, June 24, 1994, [1994] 3 C.M.L.R. 857.

> "where undertakings independent of each other make trade mark assignments following a market sharing agreement, the prohibition of anti-competitive agreements under Article 85 applies and assignments which give effect to that agreement are consequently void. However, before a trade mark assignment could be treated as giving effect to an agreement prohibited under Article 85, it was necessary to analyse the context, the commitments underlying the assignment and the intention of the parties and the consideration for the assignment.[89]

Although *obiter dicta*, such a ruling means that an assignment *per se* can never be allowed to result in an adverse finding under Article 85 where one party seeks to exercise its trade mark rights against the import of products bearing the same mark from another Member State. As such, the decision would appear to tacitly overrule *Sirena* in its entirety.[90]

7. EEA and Free Movement of Goods

(a) Adoption of the ECJ's approach in relation to Articles 30–36?

7.118 Articles 11 and 12 of the EEA Agreement are identical in substance to Articles 30 and 34. Article 13 is identical in substance to Article 36. Under Article 6 of the EEA Agreement, the EEA Articles must be interpreted in conformity with rulings given by the ECJ prior to May 2, 1992 in relation to Articles 30–36. In relation to judgments given by the ECJ after that date, the EFTA Court must pay "due account" of them.[91] Prima facie, this would appear to mean that the fundamental principles developed by the ECJ in relation to Articles 30–36 and intellectual property apply as much to the EEA Treaty as to the E.C. Treaty. However, such may be a dangerous assumption.

Firstly, as mentioned in the Opinion of the ECJ,[92] the objectives of the EEA and E.C. treaties are different. In the landmark case of *Deutsche Grammophon*, much reliance was placed by the ECJ on the effect that the exercise of rights would have in maintaining the isolation of national markets thus conflicting with the essential aim of the Treaty, the integration of national markets into one uniform Treaty.[93]

[89] Para. 59.

[90] See Tritton, "Articles 30 to 36 and Intellectual Property: Is the jurisprudence of the ECJ now of an Ideal Standard" [1994] E.I.P.R. 423.

[91] ESA/Court Agreement, Art. 3(2). See Chap. One, para. 1.044.

[92] Opinion 1/91, December 14, 1991, [1991] I E.C.R. 6079.

[93] *e.g.* see Case 78/70, *Deutsche Grammophon v. Metro-Grossmarkte*: [1971] E.C.R. 487, [1971] C.M.L.R. 631.

7.119 Indeed, in *Polydor v. Harlequin Record Shops*,[94] a case in the early 1980s, gramophone records had been lawfully made in Portugal by licensees of the copyright owner. These records were exported to the United Kingdom where the British licensee sought to prevent such imports as being unlawful under British copyright law. At that time, Portugal was not a member of the E.C. but had a Free Trade Agreement with it. Articles 14(2) and 23 of that agreement were virtually identical to Articles 30 and 36. The Court in holding that the exhaustion of rights principle did *not* apply, said:

> "However, such similarity of terms is not a sufficient reason for transposing to the provisions of the Agreement the above-mentioned case law, which determines in the context of the Community the relationship between the protection of industrial and commercial property rights and the rules on the free movement of goods.
>
> The scope of that case law must indeed be determined in the light of the Community's objectives and activities as defined in Articles 2 and 3 of the EEC Treaty. As the court has had occasion to emphasise in various contexts, the Treaty, by establishing a common market and progressively approximating the economic policies of the Member States seeks to unite national markets into a single market having the characteristics of a domestic market.
>
> Having regard to those objectives, the Court, *inter alia* in its judgment of June 22, 1976 in *Terrapin v. Terranova*,[95] interpreted Articles 30 and 36 of the Treaty as meaning that the territorial protection afforded by national laws to industrial and commercial property may not have the effect of legitimising the insulation of national markets and of leading to an artificial partitioning of the markets and that consequently the proprietor of an industrial or commercial property right protected by the law of a Member State cannot rely on that law to prevent the importation of a product which has lawfully been marketed in another Member State by the proprietor himself or with his consent.
>
> The considerations which led to that interpretation of Articles 30 and 36 of the Treaty do not apply in the context of the relations between the Community and Portugal. It is apparent from an examination of the Agreement that although it makes provision for the unconditional abolition of certain restrictions on trade between the Community and Portugal, such as quantitative restrictions and measures having equivalent effect, they do not have the same purpose as the EEC Treaty, inasmuch as the latter, as has been stated

[94] Case 270/80, [1982] E.C.R. 329, [1982] 1 C.M.L.R. 677.
[95] Case 119/75, *Terrapin v. Terranova*: [1976] E.C.R. 1039, [1976] 2 C.M.L.R. 482.

above, seeks to create a single market reproducing as closely as possible the conditions of a domestic market."

7.120 Such a ruling emphasises that the ECJ's principles in relation to Articles 30 to 36 are derived in large part from the objectives of the E.C. As the *Polydor* case forms part of the ECJ jurisprudence incorporated into the EEA under Article 6, it is submitted that there is considerable doubt on whether the ECJ's principles apply to the EEA. In terms of integration, the objectives of the EEA Agreement must be considered to fall between the limited aims of the Portugal-E.C. Free Trade Agreement (the consolidation and extension of economic relations existing between the Community and Portugal and harmonious development of commerce between the two parties) and the fully integrative objectives of the E.C. Treaty. In a recent decision, the ECJ has veered towards adopting a similar approach to free movement of goods provisions in FTAs as that adopted under the E.C. Treaty.[96]

In relation to the exhaustion of rights principle, the EEA Agreement specifically imposes an obligation on Contracting Parties to enact an EEA-wide exhaustion of rights principle.[97] Accordingly, it is irrelevant whether Articles 11 to 13 of the EEA Treaty should be interpreted as giving rise to an exhaustion of rights doctrine.

(b) EEA and national legislation on exhaustion of rights

7.121 Article 2 of Protocol 28 to the EEA provides that:

> "To the extent that exhaustion is dealt with in Community measures or jurisprudence, the Contracting Parties shall provide for such exhaustion of intellectual property rights as laid down in Community law. Without prejudice to the future developments of case law, these provisions shall be interpreted in accordance with the meaning established in the relevant rulings of the Court of Justice of the European Communities given prior to the signature of the Agreement.
>
> As regards patent rights, its provision shall take effect at the latest one year after the entry into force of the Agreement."

The reference to Community measures in addition to Community jurisprudence refers to E.C. secondary intellectual property legislation which expressly enact the exhaustion of rights principle. The above article suggests that the doctrine of exhaustion of rights as developed by the ECJ must become part of the Contracting States' domestic law (whether expressly enacted or implicitly enacted). The wording of the article suggests that for the purposes of the EEA, an EEA-wide exhaustion principle must apply and that accordingly, the ECJ's decision in *Polydor v. Harlequin*[98] is inapplicable.

[96] See *Eurim Pharm v. Bundesgesundheitsamt* [1993] E.C.R. 3723. See para. 7.038.
[97] See below, para. 7.121.
[98] Case 270/80 [1982] E.C.R. 329, [1982] 1 C.M.L.R. 677.

This approach is confirmed in the amendments to the *acquis communautaire* relating to E.C. secondary legislation concerning intellectual property. Thus, under the semiconductor directive, the trade mark directive and the software directive, Annex VII of the EEA Agreement amends their exhaustion provisions so as to provide for an EEA-wide exhaustion of rights principle.

Chapter Eight

LICENSING OF INTELLECTUAL PROPERTY

1. Introduction

8.001 Few intellectual property owners have the resources to manufacture, distribute and sell their works themselves in many countries. The vast majority of intellectual property owners license their rights to other parties in order to maximise their financial potential. This involves the negotiating of and entering into agreements which reflect the licensor and licensees' commercial concerns.

This Chapter examines the competitive effect of the licensing of intellectual property rights. For the sake of completeness, this necessitates a two stage analysis. The first stage is to establish the effect that intellectual property monopolies have on competition. Analysis at this stage establishes how intellectual property affects competition in the marketplace and whether such an effect is positive or negative. Thus, intellectual property often promotes innovation and enhances consumer welfare but sometimes, the exercise of intellectual property rights can be generally detrimental to competition (*i.e.* where rights are merely used to partition markets). The second stage is to examine the effect that licensing of intellectual property has on competition in market economies where intellectual property rights exist. Economic analysis at the second stage concerns itself with how the licensing of intellectual property rights affects competition in the marketplace. Generally licensing is procompetitive because it encourages the exploitation of protected technology or works and ensures that there is more than one potential supplier of the protected technology. However, licensing can also be anti-competitive. For instance, cross-licensing arrangements between competitors in the state of the art technology will often reduce competitiveness between such parties as there is less incentive to gain a technological lead. Analysis at this stage examines the economic situation with and without licensing. Any competitive analysis of the competitive effect of licences must start on the premise that intellectual property itself is inviolate. To do otherwise is to mount an attack on intellectual property rights themselves. When considering the competitive effect of licences, one accepts the validity of intellectual property rights and a market where such rights exist. Therefore, whilst the first stage analysis may be interesting, it is not relevant in considering the competitive effect of licences.

8.002 Under Community law, Article 85 prohibits agreements and concerted practices between undertakings which may affect trade between Member States that prevent, restrict or distort competition within the Common Market. The Commission and European Court of Justice have applied Article 85 to intellectual property licences in many cases. In considering the competitive effect of licences, both institutions have often failed to distinguish between the two stage analysis described above. In combining the two stages, Community law has implicitly considered the competitive effect of intellectual property laws themselves as well as their licensing. In doing so, they have historically tended to take a restrictive view as to the procompetitive effects of licensing by questioning the validity of intellectual property rights themselves with regard to competition. Recently, the Court and Commission's approach has been more similar to the United States on licensing, where a "rule of reason" approach is taken in which the economic analysis of competitive effect of licenses in the relevant market is of much greater importance than the development and application of competition law jurisprudence relating to the validity of licenses and their clauses.

This chapter examines the effect of Article 85 on the validity of intellectual property licences in the European Community. As such it is restricted to those licences which affect trade between Member States. It does not concern itself with the effect of national competition laws on Member States. It first examines the principles underlying competition theory, intellectual property and its application to licences. This section is not strictly relevant to the competition law practitioner although it is recommended that he read it. Secondly, it looks at the European Court of Justice and the Commission's approach to Article 85. Thirdly, it examines the ECJ and Commission's approach to individual clauses in licences. Finally, it examines the block exemptions that the Commission has introduced or is proposing to introduce in the field of intellectual property.

2. Competition Law and Intellectual Property: Principles

(a) Introduction

8.003 Intellectual property grants a monopoly to a particular person for a defined period which reserves the right to exploit a protected work. Broadly speaking, the principle of a competitive market is that there must be no artificial restraints on trading between persons such as to inhibit trading or distort the marketplace. It is not surprising therefore that the relationship between intellectual property monopolies and a competitive market has often been described as one of inherent conflict. In order to probe this relationship, one must first examine what is meant by competition. Secondly, one must examine the economic and social reasons for the existence of intellectual property monopolies. It will be seen that in many cases, the two do not conflict with each other and that intellectual property monopolies are capable of enhancing competition. In other cases, there may be conflict and competition laws must be established to prevent an overall detrimental effect on an economy.

The principle of unfettered competition between businesses is one of the sacred cows of today's democratic economies. The theory is that a market economy based on genuine competition benefits the consumer (and thus the voter!) by preventing artificially high prices and encouraging the development and availability of high quality goods and services. Comparisons with the highly centralised non-competitive economies of the Soviet Union and Eastern Bloc countries, where there exists stagnant growth and a poor supply of essential goods which are invariably of inferior quality, reinforces this theory.[1]

(b) Meaning of competition

8.004 What is meant by a truly competitive economy is far from clear.[2] Competition suggests a struggle for superiority. The belief is that man's desire to better himself will characterise itself in the marketplace by seeking to make a profit. To do so, he will need to obtain the custom and business of people in the marketplace. The economic theory is that consumer welfare is maximised in conditions of perfect competition.[3] Perfect competition exists where on a particular market, there are a large number of buyers and sellers all producing identical products; consumers have perfect information about market conditions; resources can freely flow from one area of economic activity to another: there are no "barriers to entry" which might prevent the emergence of new competition and there are no "barriers to exit" which might hinder firms wishing to leave the market.[4] Generally, perfect competition never exists on the marketplace. There will be often be only a few buyers and sellers; products will invariably be different to each other and capital investment costs may mean that there are high "barriers to entry".

The aim of competition law is often complex. Its purposes are often several: to maximise consumer welfare by the most efficient allocation of resources and the reduction of costs; to protect traders against the collective power of other traders; the protection of the small firm against the big firm and to promote technological and artistic progress. The simplistic view of competition law is that it should prohibit artificial restraints on a person's freedom to trade in the marketplace. This means the freedom of, having the right to buy goods from any source and sell them to

[1] Even recently, with legislation allowing for the formation of market economies in the new republics, one can see how difficult it is to achieve the benefits of a truly competitive economy.

[2] A detailed analysis of the theory of competition and the role of competition law is given in Whish, *Competition Law* (3rd Ed.).

[3] For the meaning of perfect competition, see *ibid*, at p. 2.

[4] *ibid*.

any source. In this sense, it could be said that a contract for sale of goods or supply of services is anti-competitive. If A contracts to pay £1,000 to B for X widgets, then B is restricted from selling those widgets to another for a greater price and A is restricted from buying the same number of widgets from another cheaper supplier. However, legally binding agreements encourage business relations and provide for certainty in business, ultimately facilitating the supply of widgets to the consumer. The consumer is interested in buying widgets and not competition theories. Thus the current tendency in considering what is meant by competition is to look at it from the consumer's viewpoint. This analysis assumes that an increase in consumer satisfaction is an increase in competition. A consumer (whether trade purchaser or end-user) is usually interested in being able to find on the market the highest quality widgets on the market place at the lowest price possible. The above connotes that three factors are relevant. These are:

(i) availability of supply;
(ii) price;
(iii) quality.

8.005 In an ideal world, the consumer would be able to obtain a limitless supply of very cheap high quality widgets. However, manufacturers will only make widgets if they are commercially viable. The consumer interest combined with the manufacturer's commercial interest controls the above three factors. For instance, the two factors of availability of supply and price are interrelated. Obviously, the price per widget must be sufficiently high enough so as make it financially worthwhile for manufacturers to make them and thus satisfy demand. Similarly, a high quality good may cost more to make than a low quality good and thus its price will be greater. Thus, a truly competitive market in widgets is that which:

(a) can provide widgets in sufficient quantity and of varying quality so as to meet all consumer demand; and
(b) for a widget of a given quality, sell it at the "optimum" price.

The "optimum" price is the lowest price that can be endured by a manufacturer so as to ensure that he will deem it commercially worthwhile producing such widgets to meet the foreseeable demand in the future. If the cost of manufacture is so high that no consumer will buy it, then the product is commercially unviable no matter how good its quality.[5] Other matters are often of importance to a consumer, *e.g.* after-sale maintenance, guarantees, ease of access to goods (*i.e.* location of shop), etc. These all emphasise that in our consumerist society, it is unrealistic to examine the meaning of competition without considering the demands of the consumer.

Generally speaking, the more businesses that are making and selling

[5] *e.g.* a nuclear fission kettle which boils cold water in 2 seconds costing £100,000 (although NASA might!).

widgets, the easier the above two conditions are achieved. Similarly, the absence of artificial restraints will usually enable the market to optimise at a level most beneficial to the consumer. It is in that sense that the achievement of a competitive market is helped by the presence of a number of businesses in a particular field and the lack of artificial restraints. Thus by reason of the above, restrictive practices which limit either the number of businesses or their freedom to respond to consumer demand may thus be defined as anti-competitive as they make it more difficult for the above two conditions to be achieved. However, the means and the end should not be confused. It is the above two conditions which are the goal and not necessarily a large number of businesses or a complete laisser-faire policy. This is emphasised here because it is sometimes forgotten in the fog of discussion on competition law and its application to a particular set of facts. For example, joint ventures between manufacturers to develop or manufacture a new product in a particular market are often entered into because the manufacturers do not have the resources to develop the product on their own. Such ventures often impose legal obligations on each party, *i.e.* an obligation not to compete against each other. These agreements have the effect of reducing the number of undertakings in a particular field, contractually restrict the parties' freedom to compete but will provide the consumer with more choice in that market. Accordingly, on our above analysis, they are increasing consumer choice by providing a greater range of widgets than existed before.

Before proceeding further in our discussion, it is important to introduce the reader to several concepts in competition theory.

(c) Levels of competition

8.006 Competition can exist at various levels. Firstly, there can be competition between businesses which deal with the same product. Thus, retailers can compete with each other to sell Widget X. This type of competition is called intra-brand competition. Competition can also exist between different products, *i.e.* Widget X and Widget Y. This is called inter-brand competition. Inter-brand competition is normally between different economic concerns. However, the emphasis is on competition between goods not undertakings. Thus, it is a well-known fact that some washing powder manufacturers create their own inter-brand competition by selling differently branded washing powders manufactured by themselves.

(d) Kinds of competition

8.007 At a pure intra-brand level, the goods are all the same and therefore quality is an irrelevant factor. Thus the price per product and its availability become important when considering the level of effective competition. However, at an inter-brand level, consumers are interested in the quality of goods as well. Some consumers may place more emphasis on price, others on quality. Thus, a competitive market should provide a range of high quality, high priced products as against low quality, low priced products to maximise consumer choice. Also, consumers are often interested in other factors like after-sales service, customer relations, geographical location, etc. As these are important to a consumer, then they constitute areas in which competition can exist. Thus, competition can exist in many fields in relation to a good.

(e) Types of competitors: horizontal and vertical relationships

8.008 Generally speaking, competition is between parties at one level of trading. Thus, manufacturers may complete with each other; distributors may compete with each other and retailers may complete with each other. This is called horizontal competition. Agreements which restrict competition between horizontal competitors are considered the more blatant forms of anti-competitive practices. Agreements between a manufacturer and distributor, distributor and retailer and importantly, licensor and licensee are termed vertical agreements as the persons trade at different levels in the marketplace. The capacity for competition between these parties is usually limited. However, restrictive agreements between vertical parties can affect free market forces operating on a product.

(f) "Ancillary restraints"

8.009 In several situations, it is necessary to impose conditions that restrict the competitive freedom of parties to an agreement in order to ensure that the transaction is commercially viable. An example of this are distribution networks. These ensure a reliable supply of goods to the consumer and are thus generally pro-competitive. However, many distributors will not enter into agreement unless the agreement is an exclusive distributorship agreement, *i.e* the manufacturer agrees not to enter into any other distributorship agreements for a designated territory. Such a restriction is often necessary as otherwise the potential distributor will not be inclined to make the appropriate investment into setting up the distribution network. Clearly, in such circumstances, the exclusivity provision is a necessary "ancillary restraint" in order to bring about a net gain in competition. The lesser evil (the exclusivity) is outweighed by the greater good (the greater availability of the goods).

(g) Rule of reason approach

8.010 In investigating the competitive effect of an agreement, the most logical approach is to consider the economic situation on the relevant market with and without the agreement or behaviour. If a detailed economic analysis shows that the agreement or behaviour increases competition, then it should not be prohibited under antitrust laws. This approach is termed the "rule of reason" approach. It emphasises an economic analytical approach to facts and not a legal approach.

The "rule of reason" approach is often applied to determine whether a restraint is ancillary in an agreement. If the agreement is *in toto* pro-competitive, then if the restraints are necessary to make the agreement economically viable, then the restraints are ancillary and should be permitted.

(h) Incentive to progress: justification for intellectual property

8.011 In many situations, the marketplace alone is unable to confer the benefits of technology and progress on society. A peasant economy based on bartering can be truly competitive yet still backwards. Technological and artistic progress is deemed important by most societies. One way that this can be achieved is by the grant of commercial monopolies to investors and authors. The monopolies provided by patents, copyright, design rights, plant breeder rights, etc., are nowadays generally justified as being essential to encourage progress in the fields of science and foster talent in the arts. Without such protection, companies would not invest time and money into research as, if the invented widget is reproduced by others who have not spent such time and money, the company which invented the widget will be financially worse off than the imitators. This is often termed the "public justification" for intellectual property. Similarly, artists or authors will not be able to pursue careers in their chosen artistic field if plagiarisers prevent them from receiving sufficient remuneration for their endeavours. However, the monopoly is granted for a fixed term. The theory behind granting a monopoly for a fixed term rather than in perpetuity is that the carrot (the fixed term) need only be long enough so as not to impair technological and artistic progress. Thus, the lure of a 20 year manufacturing monopoly in an invented product is usually enough for a business to deem it worthwhile committing funds for research and development with the hope of inventing a commercially lucrative invention.[6] Once the fixed term monopoly has expired, the widget can be exposed to market forces.

The "public justification" theory is rather Anglo-Saxon and utilitarian in concept. Another justification for intellectual property rights is as a "reward" for the inventor's rights owner creativity and endeavours. This is called the "reward" theory or "private justification" theory. Thus, the award of a patent to an inventor is a measure of society's gratitude for his inventiveness. Similarly, copyright can be justified in such a way as well. In continental Europe, much more emphasis is given to the "reward"

[6] However, in very large-scale, long term projects, clearly such a period will not be long enough and state-assisted collaborative ventures are neeeded, *e.g.* the development of artificial intelligence. Also, pharmaceutical firms often have to delay placing a drug on the market because of the extensive need to test the drug. Thus, the E.C. has introduced a regulation to permit the extension of the period of protection for patents where there has been a substantial delay in placing a product on the market because of the need for governmental approval. See Chap. 2 at para. 2.115.

theory. For instance, in England, the first statute for copyright was the 1709 Copyright Act which was introduced to protect the commercial concerns of stationers who printed books. In France, copyright is known as "author's right" and is based on the concept of reward.[7] Thus, many continental laws conferred moral rights on an author's works.[8]

8.012 Trade marks differ from other types of intellectual property. They are concerned with product-differentiation rather than product-innovation. Trade mark law, by making it illegal for imitators to put the trade mark on products reassures the public that a good with the trade mark affixed comes from the same trade source. Furthermore, a trade mark monopoly not only rewards a trader who has developed a reputation in a particular mark (usually through promotion of the mark and the quality of the trade marked product) but also serves as a valuable indicator of trade origin (and thus quality) for the consumer. Trade marks assist competition because they permit consumers to differentiate between products in the marketplace thus encouraging suppliers to improve and promote their own products. From an economic viewpoint, trade marks are different from other forms of intellectual property because trade mark rights do not give their owner a monopoly in a product. Accordingly, they cannot be used to provide market power in a particular product market. Thus, cases on the exercise of trade mark rights constituting an abuse of a dominant position are rare.

However, trade mark rights can often be used to partition markets. Thus, it is not surprising that the interface of trade marks and competition law often differs to that of other intellectual property rights. Any competition theory must safeguard the right of the trade mark owner to be rewarded for the promotion of his mark and products bearing the mark and also safeguard the right of the public to be protected against confusion in the marketplace.

(i) Money or monopoly: which is important?

8.013 Leaving aside trade marks, intellectual property monopolies are ultimately there to provide financial remuneration to their owners. Thus, if a rights owner could be provided with the same amount of money as he would have earned if he exploited the right for its duration whether by himself or by licensing then there would still be the same incentive to create, invent and innovate. Innovative products would reach the market and the rights owner would be rewarded. Thus, many have questioned the need for a monopoly right rather than the right to remuneration.

[7] e.g. *droit d'auteur*.

[8] These included the right to be named as author; the right to object to revisions affecting honour and reputation. Moral rights have been introduced into English Law by the Copyright, Designs and Patent Act 1988.

Alternatively, others have said that intellectual property is fundamentally concerned with the right of reward. These people argue that competition would be improved by rewarding the inventor or author rather than granting him exclusive rights to control a particular product or service market.

The difficulty with such an approach is threefold. Firstly, it ignores the fact that almost all countries through international agreement have chosen to confer exclusive rights rather than the right to remuneration. It is far simpler and more manageable for an inventor or author to control and exploit the market in his product than for countries to provide for a complex, enforceable, unwieldly compulsory licensing system. Secondly, it is very difficult to ascertain the correct level of remuneration. Should the level be based on notions of reasonableness? Many tribunals have great difficulties in applying the concept of a "reasonable" royalty in compulsory licensing cases. For instance, technological firms often only make a profit out of a small fraction of their patented inventions. Is it permissible to take into account the cost of past failures in calculating a reasonable royalty for a successful intention? A refusal to do so could jeopardise future innovation as firms would be less willing to innovate, preferring to wait for competitions to innovate. If the remuneration is based on the full "unreasonable" value of the invention to the rights owner on the basis that he had exclusive rights in it, it will be very difficult to assess the level of remuneration. For instance, it may be important commercially for a patentee to deprive a fellow competitor from exploiting the invention. In that case, a reasonable rate to the licensor would be a rate so punitively high that the potential licensee could not profitably work the invention. Similarly, it is difficult to hypothesise what royalty rate willing licensees would have paid over a 20 year period. Thirdly, a monopoly allows an owner to maintain tight quality control on the manufacture of protected works and preserve their reputation.

8.014 It can be concluded from the above that competition is usually best served by an exclusive right system and not a compulsory licensing system. In effect, the above reasoning is predicated on the fact that an inventor or author knows far better how to exploit his invention or works than cumbersome legislative machinery. Of course, the system sometimes breaks down. For instance, most countries' patent legislation provides for a system of compulsory licences if a patent is not worked. Clearly, in such circumstances, the justification for a patent, namely to encourage the bringing of inventions onto the marketplace, has failed. However, generally if the exploitation of an invention is commercially feasible, it will be exploited.

The above argument is important because some might argue that the inherent conflict between intellectual property and competition law could be resolved by compulsory licensing. Such notions to some extent appear to have been entertained by the European Court of Justice in relation to Article 86.

(j) Intellectual property and competition: inherent conflict?

8.015 It has often been said that there is an inherent conflict between intellectual property and competition law. However, does this adage survive under close examination? Must any legal or economic system balance the conflicting aims of a truly competitive economy with the exclusive rights of intellectual property?

Once one accepts as argued above that the only meaningful interpretation of competition is by looking at the market place from the consumer's viewpoint, then intellectual property is generally procompetitive. Whilst it restricts the freedom of competitors to imitate the protected product or in the case of trade marks, to appropriate the goodwill of the trade mark, it usually provides for greater inter-brand competition by enabling the introduction of innovative products on the market or, in the case of trade marks, permitting greater choice for the discerning consumer. Therefore, consumer choice increases and a greater number of goods in a particular product market will facilitate the optimisation of market prices.[9] In effect, the monopoly right is a state-granted ancillary restraint necessary to improve competition.

8.016 In some situations, there will be an apparent inherent conflict. This will be the case when a protected product requires little or no initial research, development or investment such that it would still have arrived on the market even if no monopoly existed. Thus, the invention and marketing of a patented revolutionary paperclip may be the result of a five minute flash of inspiration but involve no perspiration. In such circumstances, it would be difficult to say that if no patent existed, the owners of the right would not have invented or marketed the product. Clearly, in these circumstances, the practical effect of the patent monopoly is to ensure that only one person can exploit the invention and not several. This means that it is likely that there will be a detrimental effect on the economy. In such circumstances, the patent merely "rewards" the inventor for his creative endeavours rather than acts as an incentive to progress. One may argue: why permit patents of the latter type if they are detrimental to the economy? Firstly, it would be almost impossible to determine whether a patent should be granted on the basis of economic criteria, *i.e.* would the product have come to the marketplace if no patent protection existed. Secondly, it would make the grant of a patent a more costly and lengthy matter than it is now. Thirdly, patents are there to reward inventors as much as to improve the economy. Fourthly, the certainty that a patent will be granted for a new and inventive product capable of industrial application constitutes a spur to invention and innovation which would not exist if each inventor knew that he had to economically justify the award of a patent. Accordingly, whilst some people might suggest a "rule of reason" approach in considering whether a

[9] See above, para. 8.004 *et seq*.

patent should be awarded, it is submitted that such an approach would be clearly wrong.

(k) Intellectual property rights and competition laws: both creatures of law

8.017 Intellectual property rights derive from the laws of sovereign states. In enacting such laws, it is clearly the legislature's intention that they are exercised. A prohibition on the exercise of rights would constitute an attack on the very existence of such laws.[10] Thus, a prohibition *per se* by national competition laws on the exercise of rights by their owner constitutes a direct attack on the validity of legislation. In such a case, to rule that national competition laws can invalidate the exercise of intellectual property rights is to confer a "superior" status on competition laws as against intellectual property laws.

Antitrust laws normally sidestep this constitutional problem by attempting to define some form of anti-competitive behaviour which is extraneous to the exercise of rights but which the latter is used to implement. A classic example is a prohibition on the exercise of intellectual property rights in order to partition markets.[11] The Department of Justice of the United States' view is that:

> "... The same general antitrust principles to conduct involving intellectual property that they apply to conduct involving any other form of tangible property. That is not to say that intellectual property in all respects the same as any other form of property. Intellectual property has important characteristics such as ease of misappropriation, that distinguish it from other forms of property. These characteristics can be taken into account by standard antitrust analysis, however and do not require the application of fundamentally different principles."[12]

In the E.C., the problem is less because Community competition law takes precedence over national intellectual property laws, *i.e.* they are superior.

3. Intellectual Property Licences and Competition

(a) Introduction

8.018 In the previous section, the relationship between competition and intellectual property was discussed. In this section, the relationship between intellectual property licences and competition is examined. Intellectual

[10] See Beier, "Industrial Property and Internal Market" IIC 1990 2 131 at p. 147; Tritton, "Articles 30 to 36 and Intellectual Property: Is the jurisprudence of the ECJ now of an Ideal Standard" [1994] EIPR 423.

[11] See *Tepea v. Commission*: [1978] 3 C.M.L.R. 392 for a Community case on this fact.

[12] Para 2.1 of the *U.S. Antitrust Guidelines for Intellectual Property*, issued by the Department of Justice. These are set out in July 1995 EIPR Supplement.

property rights *per se* are assumed to be incapable of attack from competition laws. Thus, analysis is restricted to comparing the competitive situation with and without the licence.

Generally, licensing must be considered pro-competitive. Firstly, if the licensor is a manufacturer of the protected product, it will bring extra competitors to bear on the licensed technology's market at an intra-brand level. Whilst such competitors will usually be at a competitive disadvantage to the licensor because of the obligation to financially remunerate the latter, at the least, there will be an increased availability of supply from differing sources. More often, the licensor will not be able to provide manufacturing and distribution facilities, workforces and interlocking intellectual property. In these circumstances, the licensing of intellectual property to companies or persons who are able to provide complementary resources and skills in order to efficiently exploit the intellectual property plays a crucial role in bringing innovative products to the marketplace. Sometimes, the exploitation of intellectual property requires access to another intellectual property. An example of this is an improvement patent. In these circumstances, licensing promotes the coordinated development of technologies.

The following sections discuss in detail principles applied in considering the competitive effect of licences. Much of the analysis is based on the development of antitrust law in the United States in relation to intellectual property. The United States has immense wealth of experience in considering the competitive effect of licences. The Department of Justice recently has issued Antitrust Guidelines for Intellectual Property which provides invaluable assistance in considering the competitive effect of licences. These Guidelines replace the 1988 Antitrust Guidelines.

(b) "Pure" and "hybrid" licences

8.019 It is rare that a licence will merely provide for exploitation of intellectual property on the payment of a royalty (a "pure" licence"). Such a licence is pure in the sense that it is purely permissive and does not place any restraints on the licensor or licensee. It is very rare that a pure licence will cause any antitrust concerns. The exception is where the licensor and licensee(s) are competitors. In these circumstances, licensing is capable of reducing competition between the two concerns especially at an *inter-brand* level. The more common licence is the "hybrid" licence which places restrictions on either or both the licensor and licensee. Normal "rule of reason" economic analysis should be applied to such restrictive clauses in order to determine how the licence will affect competition.

Furthermore, in considering provisions in licences, one should distinguish between permissive clauses and restrictive clauses. Clauses which partially lift the prohibitive effects of a monopoly are permissive clauses. Thus, clauses which limit a licensee to exploiting a patent in a particular way (*i.e.* manufacture, sale, distribution); limit the quantity of patented products to be exploited; limit the period of exploitation and limit the patented area where exploitation is permissible are all permissive clauses. Whilst certain clauses such as a limit on the quantity of products a licensee can manufacture, appear ostensibly as a restriction on the licensee, they are properly characterised as permissive clauses. Once it is accepted that the existence of the intellectual property monopoly is immune to the rules of competition law, permissive clauses will rarely be anti-competitive. This principle is known as the "*limited licence*" principle. This principle is based on the concept that a rights owner is not obliged to create competition within his protected technology. A licensor could quite clearly refuse to license the protected product and limit himself accordingly. By granting a person the right to partially exploit an invention which otherwise he as prohibited from doing so, one is introducing one more competitor at an intra-brand level in the market for the patented product. Thus such clauses in licences will generally increase competition. The exception to this rule is if the licensing of the protected technology itself has anti-competitive effects.

8.020 Licences will usually contain other clauses that restrict licensor and/or licensee. For instance, examples of restrictions that bind the licensee are no-challenge clauses (which prevent the licensee from challenging the validity of the licensed right), tying-in clauses (*e.g.* the licensee must buy unprotected parts from the licensor), minimum royalty clauses, export bans, grant-backs of improvement patents clauses, obligations to keep know-how secret, obligations not to assign or grant sub-licences, etc. Clauses that bind the licensor can be obligations not to license other undertakings or for himself to exploit the licensed invention in the licensee's territory (an exclusive licence), export bans into licensee's territory, obligations to grant licenses for improvement patents to licensees, obligation to grant a licensee the most favourable terms that the licensor has granted to other licensees, obligations to enforce rights against parallel, importers, etc. A restrictive clause will generally reduce the independence of the licensor and/or the licensee to determine its method of exploitation of the technology and bind each or both party to a particular course of action. To determine whether such a restraint is anti-competitive, it is necessary to conduct a rule of reason approach to the restraint.[13]

(c) Appropriation of full inherent value of intellectual property

8.021 In the *1988 International Antitrust Guidelines*, the Department stated that:

> "because they hold a significant procompetitive potential, unless the underlying transfer to technology is a sham, the Department analyses restrictions in intellectual property licensing arrangement under a rule of reason. That analysis is conducted with two fundamental principles in mind. First, the Department will not challenge

[13] See para. 8.024.

licensing arrangements the represent simply an effort by the creator of intellectual property *to appropriate the full inherent value of that property* [emphasis added]. The potential for appropriating that value provides the economic incentive to engage in risky and costly research and development in the first place. Second, the Department will not require the owner of technology to *create competition in its own technology* [emphasis added]."

The first italicised remark in the above quotation means, for instance, that a rights owner is entitled to demand as high a royalty as the market will bear. The second italicised remark means that there is no obligation on a rights owner to licence. The new 1995 Guidelines do not repeat this passage *verbatim*. Instead it states:

> "If a patent other form of intellectual property does confer market power, that market power does not by itself offend the antitrust laws. As with any other tangible or intangible asset that enables its owner to obtain significant supracompetitive profits, market power (or even a monopoly) that is solely "a consequence of a superior product, business acumen or historic accident" does not violate the antitrust laws. Nor does such market power impose on the intellectual property owner an obligation to licence the use of that property to others. As in other antitrust contexts, however, market power could be illegally acquired or maintained or, even, if lawfully acquired or maintained, would be relevant to the ability of an intellectual property owner to harm competition through unreasonable conduct in connection with such property."[13a]

Both passages are clearly derived from the exclusive rights inherent in intellectual property.

(d) Relevant market

8.022 In considering the competitive effect of a licence, the evaluation of the relevant product and geographical market or markets that the licence will affect is necessary.[14] Restraints in licences may affect the "downstream" market for final or intermediate goods made using the intellectual property or may have effects upstream, in markets for goods that are used for the production of raw materials to be used in the manufacture of the licensed goods. In considering the relevant market, account must also be taken of whether the protected products are interchangeable with other products on the marketplace. If the licence is licensed royalty free in exchange for the right to use other technology, the relevant market will include the product market in which that technology competes.

[13a] *Antitrust Guidelines for the Licensing of Intellectual Property* [1995] EIPR Supplement, para. 2.2.

[14] For a full discussion of the relevant market, see Chap. 11 at para. 11.006, where the concept of relevant market is axiomatic in determining whether an undertaking has a dominant position.

The Department of Justice and American antitrust law has developed the concept of an "innovation market". Where the capacity for research and development activity that is likely to produce innovation in technology is scarce and can be associated with identifiable specialised assets or characteristics of specific firms, it may be appropriate to consider separately the impact of the conduct in question on competition in research and development among those firms. The firms identified as possessing these specialised assets or characteristics can be thought of as competing in a separate innovation market. Once an innovation market has been defined, the competitive significance of licensing can be determined. For instance, if two rival competitors cross-license existing and future patents in a state-of-the-art technology, it could be appropriate to define the innovation market in that technology. This would involve considering the ability of other firms to innovate in this area or which in future gain the required capability. If the innovative market is small, the cross-licensing arrangement will diminish rivalry between the firms and reduce the incentives of its members to compete in their research and development efforts. Unless there are offsetting efficiency gains, such arrangements may restrict competition in the innovative market.[14a]

(e) Horizontal and vertical relationships

8.023 Licences may have horizontal or vertical components.[15] Generally, licences will be vertical in nature. Thus, a licence granted by a research company to a manufacturer is a vertical licence. Such licences are common because they permit the integration of intellectual property with manufacturing and other disciplines in order to bring the product to a market. Accordingly, they are generally procompetitive.

A horizontal licence will exist where the licensor or licensees would be actual or potential competitors in the relevant market absent the licence. Generally, licensors and licensees fall into this category. Whilst obviously licensees would not be able to exploit the protected technology absent the licence, generally only companies who are active in similar or neighbouring technologies to the licensor are able to effectively exploit the licensed technology.[16] In such circumstances, competition may be reduced by a licence. For instance, if the licensee was the manufacturer of a substitutable technology to the licensed product which it abandoned once it became a licensee, *inter-brand* competition is reduced. Where the licensor and licensees are in a horizontal relationship, the potential for competitive harm is generally proportionate to the proportion of the licensor's and licensees' market share in the relevant market the difficulty of entry

[14a] *ibid*, para. 32.3.
[15] See para. 8.008 for an explanation as to horizontal or vertical arrangements.
[16] Hence the fact that non-competition clauses in both the Patent and Know-How Block Exemption are banned.

into the market and is also exacerbated where there is substantial inelasticity of supply and demand in markets.[17]

(f) Ancillary restraints in licences

8.024 Many licences may contain prima facie anti-competitive restraints. However, such restraints may be ancillary in nature.[18] Restraints in licences often play an important role in making licences commercially attractive to licensor and licensee and ensuring the protected technology is exploited as efficiently and quickly as possible. In order to ascertain whether a restraint is ancillary, the restraint must produce offsetting procompetitive effects, such as facilitating the efficient development and exploitation of intellectual property. The restraint must be causative of the offsetting procompetitive effects and be proportionate in nature.

For example: a licence may contain a "tie-in" clause which binds the licensee to purchase certain unprotected goods from the licensor. The licence does not charge royalties as the licensor makes his profits from the purchase of the unprotected goods. Such a clause prima facie appears restrictive of competition because it prevents other rival firms which supply the unprotected product from supplying the licensee and thus reduces competition in the unprotected goods. However, such an obligation may have procompetitive effects because a normal licence including the payment of royalties could reduce the licensee's profit margin to such an extent that the licence becomes commercially unattractive to the licensee.[19] Economic analysis shows that the licensee is one of many users of the unprotected goods and thus the "tie-in" clause does not foreclose sales outlets for rival firms. The tribunal concludes that the benefit of having licensees in the protected technology outweighs the foreclosure effect of the "tie-in" clauses on rival suppliers. There is no obvious simple alternative way of making the licence attractive to licensees and accordingly, the clause is deemed an ancillary restraint.

(g) "Rule of reason" approach adopted by United States

8.025 Many of the principles discussed in this section are used in the Department of Justice's approach to considering whether intellectual property licensing is restrictive of competition which has issued the following statement in its old 1988 International Antitrust Guidelines:

> "The Department's rule of reason analysis of intellectual property licensing arrangement involves four steps. Step 1 is designed to determine whether the licence restrains competition between the licensor and licensee (or licensees) in a relevant market for techno-

[17] Para. 4.1.1., *US Antitrust Guidelines for Intellectual Property*, issued by the Department of Justice, April 6, 1995 [1995] EIPR 7 Supplement.

[18] See para. 8.009 on discussion of ancillary restraints.

[19] *i.e.* if the licensee had to buy the unprotected product and pay royalties rather than merely pay for the unprotected product.

logy and, if it does, whether it would likely create enhance, or facilitate the exercise of market power.[20] Step 2 is designed to determine whether the license expressly or implicitly restrains competition in any other market in which the licensor and licensee (or licensees) do or would compete in the absence of the license. Step 2 covers both express restrictions in a license relating to competition in some product market that incorporates the licensed technology as well as implicit "spill-over" effects. Step 3 is a vertical analysis to determine (i) whether a license (or licenses) would result in anti-competitive exclusion (beyond that exclusion provided by the intellectual property rights themselves); or (ii) whether, even if the licence does not restrain competition between the licensor and licensee (or licensees), it would likely serve to facilitate collusion in a technology market or some other market. In Step 4, the Department determines whether any risk of anti competitive effects revealed under the first three steps is outweighed by the procompetitive efficiencies generated by the license restrictions."

These guidelines have been replaced but they represent a sophisticated analysis of the relationship between intellectual property and competition law.[21] In its 1995 Guidelines, the U.S. Department of Justice sets out its current approach to intellectual property licensing and competition concern. It recognises that the owner of intellectual property is not required to create competition in its own technology. However it recognises that antitrust concern may arise when a licence harms competition among entities that would have been actual or likely potential competitors in a relevant market in the absence of the licence.

If it appears that such competition may be adversely affected it will adopt a rule of reason analysis. It will examine what is the relevant goods market, the relevant technology market and (if applicable) the relevant innovation market.

It will look at restraints in intellectual property licences according to the rule of reason. Firstly, the Department of Justice considers whether the restraint has an anticompetitive effect. Secondly, it considers whether the restraint is reasonably necessary to achieve pro-competitive benefits that outweigh the anticompetitive effects.

This requires an analysis as to whether the restraint can be expected to contribute to an efficiency—enhancing integration of economic activity.

A horizontal licence may increase the risk of co-ordinated pricing, con-

[20] This step is expanded upon. The guidelines state that Step 1 applies if licensor and its licensees own or control access to competing technologies and the licence either implicitly or explicitly restricts their independent decisions with respect to the price or output of these technologies. This might be the case in a joint venture co-operation agreement involving cross-licensing or patent pools. However it will not apply to the usual licence agreement where the licensee would not have had access to the licensed technology but for the licence.

[21] See *US Antitrust Guidelines for Intellectual Property*, issued by the Department of Justice April 6, 1995 [1995] July EIPR Supplement.

tent restriction or the acquisition of market power. Harm may also occur if the arrangement poses a significant risk of restricting the development of new or improved goods or processes.[21a] A vertical licence may harm competition amongst entities in a horizontal relationship at either the level of the licensor or the licensee. Thus, harm to competition from a restraint may occur if it anticompetitively forecloses access to the market in which the licensor and licensee operate.

The Department of Justice generally will not challenge licences if there are no anticompetitive restraints and the licensor and its licensees' accounts for no more than 20 per cent of each relevant product market significantly affected by the restraint. Similarly in analysing the effect of the constraint on the relevant technology or innovation market the Department will not challenge such constraints if they are not obviously anticompetitive and there are four or more independently controlled technologies or parties who possess the required specialised assets and incentive to engage in research and development.

The Department of Justice considers the effect of specific constraints but these are dealt with later in the chapter when considering particular constraints.

(h) European approach

8.026 In Europe, there exists both national and Community competition laws. The principles regarding the interrelationship of competition law to intellectual property licences in Europe have been derived from both the Commission and the European Court of Justice. The situation differs from the U.S.A. in three material ways. Firstly, there is no equivalent to Article 85(3) which exempts agreements found to be anti-competitive under Article 85(1) where such agreements contribute to the improvement of the production or supply of goods and promote technical or economic progress. Hence, European regulatory authorities have to concern themselves with an artificial dichotomy whereby such considerations as the improvement of the production or supply of goods are impliedly not relevant to considerations of competition. Secondly, the Community unlike the United States is not a single market and thus there is a need to prohibit agreements which artificially partition the Common Market. Hence, the Commission has emphasised that one of the main aims of competition laws is to integrate national markets into one common market.[22] Thirdly, the conflict is between Community competition law and national intellectual property law. In the United States, the conflict is invariably between laws of an equal status, namely federal laws.

The Court and the Commission's approach to the issue of licences is discussed below. For the present purposes, it suffices to say that the Court and Commission have not exhibited the sophisticated economic "rule of reason" analysis that exists in the United States. This is mainly

[21a] See also para. 8.023.
[22] *SNPE v. LEL* [1978] 2 CMLR 758 at para. 13.

due to the fact that antitrust laws have existed for a much longer period in the United States. Analysis by the Court and Commission has too often been conducted without the benefit of an established and sophisticated jurisprudence. The European Court of Justice has not been involved to any great extent with intellectual property licences. In two cases concerning the question of Article 85 and exclusive licences, it has favoured a liberal approach which has acknowledged the "pro-competitive" effects of exclusive licences.[23] However, the sparse case law has meant that the European Court of Justice has not been able to develop a sophisticated jurisprudence in the application of competition laws to licences. Accordingly, the burden has fallen on the Commission and to a lesser extent, the national courts.

8.027 More troubling, the European Commission has not favoured the United States' tolerant approach to licences. The Commission which is the executive body responsible for enforcement of the competitive provisions of the Treaty of Rome has applied a very restrictive interpretation of the meaning of anti-competitive provisions as meaning those which restrict the contractual freedom of the licensor/licensee. Where licences have tended to be "procompetitive", they have been exempted under Article 85(3) as promoting technical or economic progress or for improving the production and distribution of goods.

4. Community Law and Intellectual Property Licences

(a) Article 85

8.028 The competition provisions of the Treaty of Rome are contained in Articles 85 to 94. Article 85 is concerned with anticompetitive agreements. It states that:

> "The following shall be prohibited as incompatible with the common market:
>
> 1. all agreements between undertakings, decisions by associations of undertakings and concerted practices which may affect trade between Member States and which have as their object or effect the prevention, restriction or distortion of competition within the common market, and in particular those which:
>   (a) directly or indirectly fix purchase or selling prices or any other trading conditions;
>   (b) limit or control production, markets, technical development or investment;
>   (c) share markets or sources of supply;
>   (d) apply dissimilar conditions to equivalent transactions with

[23] Case 258/78, *L.C. Nungesser KG & Eisele v. E.C. Commission*: [1983] 1 C.M.L.R. 278; CODITEL II (*Coditel v Cine Vog Films (No. 2)*): [1982] E.C.R. 3381, [1983] 1 C.M.L.R. 49.

other trading parties, thereby placing them at a competitive disadvantage;

(e) make the conclusion of contracts subject to acceptance by the other parties of supplementary obligations which, by their nature or according to commercial usage, have no connection with the subject of such contracts.

2. Any agreements or decisions prohibited pursuant to this Article shall be automatically void.

3. The provisions of paragraph 1 may, however, be declared inapplicable in the case of:

— any agreement or category of agreements between undertakings;

— any decision or category of decisions by associations of undertakings;

— any concerted practice or category of concerted practices;

which contributes to improving the production or distribution of goods or to promoting technical or economic progress, while allowing consumers a fair share of the resulting benefit, and which does not:

(a) impose on the undertakings concerned restrictions which are not indispensable to the attainment of these objectives;

(b) afford such undertakings the possibility of eliminating competition in respect of a substantial part of the products in question."

8.029 The four essential elements of Article 85(1) are:

(1) An agreement, concerted practice or decision;
(2) Between undertakings;
(3) Which affects trade between Member States and;
(4) Has as its object or effect the prevention restriction or distortion of competition within the common market

These elements are discussed in detail below.[24]

(b) Court and Commission's approach to Article 85(1)

(i) Agreement, decisions and concerted practices

8.030 The expression "agreements between undertakings, decisions by associations of undertakings and concerted practice" covers practically any form of co-operative behaviour between undertakings. Agreements need not be legally binding. It is merely sufficient if the undertakings in question have expressed their joint intention to conduct themselves on the

[24] For further reading on the law relating to Art. 85, see Bellamy and Child *Common Market Law of Competition* 4th Ed.; *Butterworth's Competition Law*; Whish *Competition Law* (3rd Ed.); Goyder *E.C. Competition Law* (2nd Ed.); Korah *EEC Competition Law and Practice* (3rd Ed.).

market in a specific way.[25] Whilst unilateral action taken by an undertaking without reference to another does not infringe Article 85(1), the Commission and ECJ will infer readily that apparently unilateral action is pursuant to some "understanding" between undertakings.[26]

Where an agreement is no longer in force, Article 85(1) will apply if it continues to product effects.[27] With regard to assignments of intellectual property where there is no evidence on continuing co-operation, the ECJ said that an agreement is only regarded as continuing to produce its effects if, from the behaviour of the persons concerned, there may be inferred the existence of elements of concerted practice and of co-ordination peculiar to the agreement and producing the same result as that envisaged by the agreement but that such was not the case when the assignee merely exercised his trade mark rights.[28] Certainly, an assignment *per se* does not bind the assignor after the event and in itself cannot be evidence of co-operative behaviour.[29]

The concept of a "decision" and "association" in the phrase "a decision between an association of undertakings" is widely applied by the Commission and Court.[30]

8.031 The meaning of "concerted practices" was explained in the *Dyestuffs* case as

> "a form of co-ordination between undertaking which without having reached the stage where an agreement properly so called has been concluded, knowingly substitutes practical co-operation between them for the risks of competition."[31]

In most cases concerned the meaning of "concerted practices", undertakings have argued that the allegedly anti-competitive behaviour was unilateral, parallel behaviour and not the result of co-operation.[32] However,

[25] Case T-7/89, *Hercules v. Commission*: [1992] 4 C.M.L.R. 84.

[26] *e.g. AEG Telefunken v. E.C. Commission*: [1983] E.C.R. 3151, [1984] 3 C.M.L.R. 325; *Metro-SB-Grossmarkte v. E.C. Commission*: (1977) E.C.R. 1875, (1978) 2 C.M.L.R. 1. See also *Franco-Japanese Ballbearings*: [1975] C.M.L.R. D8 at para. 25 where the Commission held that where an undertaking "voluntarily undertakes to limit its freedom of action with regard to the other", such constitutes an agreement. However, in that case, it was clear that the apparently unilateral action resulted from a series of correspondence and meeting between the parties. Accordingly, the Commission concluded that there was in principle an agreement.

[27] *Binon*: [1985] 3 C.M.L.R. 800; *EMI Records Ltd. CBS*: [1976] E.C.R. 811, [1976] 2 C.M.L.R. 235.

[28] *EMI Records Ltd v. CBS*: [1976] E.C.R. 811, [1976] 2 C.M.L.R. 235. See Art. 85, Parallel Imports and Intellectual Property in Chap. 7, para. 7.113.

[29] See *Ideal Standard*, Judgment of ECJ, June 24, 1994 [1994] 3 C.M.L.R. 857.

[30] *e.g.* see *IAZ v. Commission*: [1984] 3 C.M.L.R. 276.

[31] *ICI v. E.C. Commission "Dyestuffs"*: [1972] C.M.L.R. 557, para. 64.

[32] The leading cases on "concerted practice" are *ICI v. E.C. Commission "Dyestuffs"*: [1972] C.M.L.R. 557; Case 4/73, *Suiker Unie v. E.C. Commission* [1975] E.C.R. 1663, [1976] 1 C.M.L.R. 295; Case 100/80, *Musique Diffusion Francaise v. E.C. Commission,* [1983] E.C.R. 1825, [1983] 3 C.M.L.R. 221 and the *Polyproplene* cases, *e.g. Hercules v. Commission*: [1992] 4 C.M.L.R. 84.

the Court has been quick to find that whilst parallel behaviour did not, by itself, constitute a concerted practice, it might however amount to strong evidence to such a practice if it led to conditions of competition which did not correspond to the normal conditions of the market.[33] Thus where rival undertakings make direct or indirect contact between themselves if the object or effect is to influence each other's market behaviour, then a concerted practice will readily be inferred.[34] Where mere disclosure to a rival of market information, *e.g.* prices leads the rival to maintain or alter its conduct as a result of such information, this will constitute a concerted practice.[35]

In practice, a concerted practice will be readily inferred if parallel behaviour in the market is established and contact between the parties is proved. In such cases, parties must put forward evidence to explain why such parallel behaviour was not the result of a concerted practice.[36] Expert economic analysis in this regard will often be invaluable.[37]

(ii) Undertakings

8.032 The word "undertaking" which is not defined in the Treaty of Rome has been given a broad meaning by the Commission and the Court. It includes any type of person, natural or legal, whose activities are of an economic or commercial nature. This does not necessarily mean that the activity must be profit-orientated.[38] Member States themselves are not as a rule considered undertakings for the purposes of Article 85.[39] However, this is construed narrowly and reflects the fact that many activities of Member States are concerned with the performance of administrative

[33] *ICI v. Commission*: [1972] C.M.L.R. 557, para. 65–68.

[34] *e.g.* see Case 4/73, *Suiker Unie v. E.C. Commission*: [1975] E.C.R. 1663, [1976] 1 C.M.L.R. 295.

[35] *e.g.* see *Hercules v. E.C. Commission* [1992] 4 C.M.L.R. 84, paras. 259–261.

[36] *e.g.* see Case T-2/89, *Petrofina v. E.C. Commission*: [1991] II E.C.R. 1087, para. 128 (one of the *Polypropylene* cases).

[37] *e.g.* see *Woodpulp*: [1993] 4 C.M.L.R. 407, para. 73 to 127 where the Court overturned a Commission's finding as to a concerted practice between parties as a result of expert evidence.

[38] See Cases 209–215/78 & 218/78, *Heintz van Landewyck Sarl v. E.C. Commission*: [1980] E.C.R. 3125, [1981] 3 C.M.L.R. 134, ECJ; *Re Cast Iron and Steel Rolls*: [1984] 1 C.M.L.R. 694, E.C. Commission; *Interpar and others v. Gesellschaft zur Berwetung von Leistungsschutzrechten mbH* [1982] 1 C.M.L.R. 221. Also see recent decision of *Film Purchasers by German TV stations* [1989] O.J. L284/36 at 41. A "one-off" inventor who forms a company to exploit his invention commercially and to which he gives a licence to work his patent is himself an "undertaking" for the purposes of Art. 85 in addition to his company—Case 79/86, *H. Vaessen BV v. Alex Moris and other*: [1979] 1 C.M.L.R. 511. See also *Case 76/743 Gottfried Reuter v. BASF* (E.C. Commission) [1976] 2 C.M.L.R. D44, [1976] O.J. L254/40.

[39] Art. 90 of the Treaty of Rome governs the competitive behaviour of Member States. See *AROW/BNIC*: O.J. 1982 L379/1, [1983] 2 C.M.L.R. 240 (a decision by a government commission laying down minimum prices for sale of cognac was not a decision given by an undertaking).

and non-commercial duties. Thus where a public body or even a government department is involved in a commercial or economic enterprise, it may be deemed to be an undertaking.[40] Conversely, where a public body is merely carrying out its public duties and awarding public service contracts to private concessionaires, then the public body is not an undertaking for the purposes of Article 85.[41] However, public contracts for a concession which contains terms requiring or encouraging concession holders to act in a manner contrary to Article 85 may fall within the scope of Article 90.[42]

8.033 For the purposes of Article 85 and 86, "undertaking" designates an economic unit rather than a legal person.[43] Thus agreements between legal bodies which form a single economic unit will not fall within Article 85. In the 1960s and 1970s the Commission emphasised that the criteria for determining whether they do form an economic unit is whether competition is possible between the parties.[44] The ECJ refined this by saying that:

> "With regard to the applicability of Article 85 to relations between holders of concessions belonging to the same group of undertakings it must be borne in mind that, as the Court has held (Case 15/74, *Centrafarm v. Sterling Drug*),[45] that provision is not concerned with agreements or concerted practices between undertakings belonging to the same concern and having the status of parent company and subsidiary, if the undertakings form an economic unit within which the subsidiary has no real freedom to determine its course of action on the market, and if the agreements of practice are concerned merely with the internal allocation of tasks as between the undertakings."[46]

[40] *e.g.* see *9th Annual Report on Competition Policy*, points 114–115 (*French State/Suralmo*) where a patent licence agreement between a French government department and Suralmo was deemed to fall withihn Art. 85. See also Case 123/83, *BNIC v. Clair*: [1985] E.C.R. 391 [1985] 2 C.M.L.R. 430, at point 16–19 where the European Court stated that the classification given to an agreement by a Member State's law was irrelevant in relation to the applicability of Art. 85 (agreement between two associations of undertakings done under the aegis of an institution of public law did not take the agreement outside Art. 85).

[41] Case 30/87, *Bodson v. PFRL* [1988] E.C.R. 2479, [1989] 4 C.M.L.R. 984.

[42] See Opinion of Advocate-General da Cruz Vilaça in *Bodson v. PFRL*: [1989] 4 C.M.L.R. 987 at p. 1005–1006. Art. 90(1) requires Member States neither to enact nor maintain in force any measure in favour of public undertakings to which they grant special or exclusive rights which run counter to the rules of the Treaty.

[43] See Case 170/83, *Hydrotherm Geratebau GmbH v. Compact de Dott Ing. Mario Andreoli & C.S.A.S.* [1984] E.C.R. 2999, [1985] 2 C.M.L.R. 244. Also see decision of Commission in *Re: Racal Group Service*: [1990] 4 C.M.L.R. 627.

[44] See *Christiani and Nielsen*: [1969] C.M.L.R. D36 (E.C. Commission) and *KODAK*: [1970] C.M.L.R. D19.

[45] Case 15/74, [1974] E.C.R. 1147, [1974] 2 C.M.L.R. 480. See also *VIHO v. Commission* T/120–/92 (unreported, 1995).

[46] Case 30/87 *Bodson v. PFRL*: [1984] E.C.R. 2999, [1989] 4 C.M.L.R. 984.

Thus, an agreement between a parent company and a wholly owned subsidiary will normally fall outside Article 85(1).

The phrase "association of undertakings" applies to regulatory bodies, *e.g.* trade associations, which can affect the trading behaviour of their members.

An undertaking need not be resident in the E.C. for Article 85 to be applicable. It is sufficient that such an undertaking is responsible for anti-competitive behaviour within the E.C.[47]

(iii) Effect on trade between Member States

8.034 This aspect of Article 85 is often considered a jurisdictional one. The Court of Justice in *Commercial Solvents v. E.C. Commission*[48] said the expression is intended to define the sphere of application of Community rules in relation to national laws. Thus if an agreement[49] only affects trade in one Member State, then it is a matter for the relevant national competition authorities and Article 85 law is inapplicable.

However, it is clear that the Commission and the Court interpret the phrase in a very broad manner. In *Consten & Grudig v. E.C. Commission*,[50] the Court stated in respect of this condition that:

> "it is necessary to know whether the agreement is capable of endangering, either directly or indirectly, in fact or potentially, freedom of trade between Member States in a direction which could harm the attainment of the objects of a single market between States."

This formula which was originally stated in *Technique Minière v. Maschinenbau Ulm*[51] has been re-iterated many times by both the Court and the Commission. The Court and Commission has demonstrated in its decisions that it will readily conclude that the above criteria have been fulfilled especially where it is clear that the object of the agreement was to restrict competition.[52]

[47] See para. 8.039 below. The E.C.J. has ruled that according to Community law, jurisdiction is established against undertakings responsible for anti-competitive behaviour in the E.C. regardless of whether or not they are established inside the Community.

[48] Cases 6 & 7/73, [1974] E.C.R. 223, [1974] 1 C.M.L.R. 309, ECJ, at 342. This was a decision on Art. 86 but both Arts. contain the same condition.

[49] Hereinafter the phrase "agreement" is used to refer to agreements, concerted practices and decisions.

[50] Cases 56 & 58/64, [1966] E.C.R. 299, [1966] C.M.L.R. 19.

[51] Case 56/65, [1966] E.C.R. 235, [1966] C.M.L.R. 357.

[52] *e.g.* in Case 123/83, *BNIC v. Clair*: [1985] E.C.R. 391 [1985] 2 C.M.L.R. 430 at 425, the Court stated that any agreement whose object or effect is to restrict competition by fixing minimum prices for an intermediate product is capable of affecting intra-Community trade, even if there is no trade in that intermediate product between the Member States, where that product constitutes the raw material for another product marketed elsewhere in the Community.

8.035 An alternative formula was stated in *Commercial Solvents*.[53] The Court stated that the prohibitions of Article 85 and 85 must be in fact interpreted and applied in the light of Article 3(f).[54] It went on to say:

> "The Community authorities must therefore consider all the consequences of the conduct complained of for the competitive structure in the Common Market without distinguishing between production intended for sale within the market and that intended for export. When an undertaking in a dominant position within the Common Market abusively exploits its position in such a way that a competitor in the Common Market is likely to be eliminated, it does not matter whether the conduct relates to the latter's exports or its trade within the Common Market, once it has been established that this elimination will have repercussions on the competitive structure within the Common Market (emphasis added)."[55]

Trade between Member States is capable of being affected even where some or all of the undertakings who are party to the agreement or concerted practice are not resident in the Community. The test is still the same regardless of the locations of the economic seats of the undertakings concerned.[56] This test is often called the "effects" doctrine. It applies even if the economic seat of an undertaking is in a country which has entered into a free trade agreement with the E.C.[57] The converse to this is that if the clause's effects are only operative outside the E.C., this will usually cause the clause to fall outside Article 85 even if the undertakings to the agreement are based in the Community.[58]

[53] Case 6 & 7/73, *Istituto Chemioterapico Italiano spa and Commercial Solvents Corp. v. E.C. Commission*: [1974] E.C.R. 223, [1974] 1 C.M.L.R. 309. See also Case 22/79, *Greenwich Film Production v. SACEM* [1979] E.C.R. 3275, [1980] 1 C.M.L.R. 629 (E.C. Commission) which applied this doctrine to a performing rights' society's behaviour under Art. 86.

[54] This provides that the activities of the Community shall include the institution of a system ensuring that competition in the Common market is not distorted.

[55] Case 6 & 7/73, *Istituto Chemioterapico Italiana spa and Commercial Solvents Corp. v. E.C. Commission*: [1974] E.C.R. 223, [1974] 1 C.M.L.R. 309.

[56] See Case 80/95 etc., *Re Woodpulp Cartel*: [1988] E.C.R. 5193, [1988] 4 C.M.L.R. 901; Case 51/75, *EMI Records Ltd v. CBS (UK) Ltd* [1976] E.C.R. 811, [1976] 2 C.M.L.R. 235, ECJ (a restrictive agreement between traders within the E.C. and competitors in non-member countries that would bring about an isolation of the Common Market as a whole thus reducing the supply of products originating outside the E.C. could be of such a nature as to affect adversely the conditions of competition within the Common Market—at point 28); see also Case 22/71, *Beguelin Import v. GL Import Export*: [1971] E.C.R. 949, [1972] C.M.L.R. 81, ("the fact that one of the undertakings which are parties to the agreement is situated in a third country does not prevent the agreement of Art. 85 since the agreement is operative on the territory of the Common Market").

[57] See *RE the LdPE Cartel*: [1990] 4 C.M.L.R. 382.

[58] Thus an agreement between two undertakings situated in the E.C. prohibiting the export of patented products to Spain and Portugal (then not part of the E.C.) fell outside Art. 85, since it was unlikely, given the facts that the products would be re-exported back to the E.C.—*Re the Agreement between Kabel and Luchaire SA*: [1975] 2 C.M.L.R. D40 (E.C. Commission).

Appreciable effect[59]

8.036 Even if the above criteria are fulfilled, the agreement or concerted practice will not fall within Article 85 if it has no appreciable effect on trade in the Community.[60] This requirement must be assessed by the effect of the agreement or clause on the competitive structure of the Community in the relevant product and geographic market. In determining whether there is an appreciable effect on trade between Member States, it is the market shares of the undertakings in the relevant market that are of importance rather than the actual level of imports or exports in the relevant goods between Member States that is capable of being restricted by the agreement.[61] Thus if at least one of the undertakings has a large market share in the Member State in a product, an agreement with an undertaking in another Member State prohibiting imports into the former's country will have an appreciable effect on trade between Member States even if the latter's imports were negligible prior to the agreement.[62] However, the Commission and ECJ will sometimes consider the level of trade between Member States rather than the market share of the undertakings in question. Thus, it held that a contract which affected 10 per cent of French exports in a particular good to Germany had an appreciable effect on trade between Member States.[63] When considering whether or not there is an appreciable effect on trade between Member States, the Commission has tended to construe the relevant product or service market restrictively.[64]

As a first approximation figure, the Commission has said, in its Notice

[59] For a recent detailed examination of this doctrine, see "The De Minimis Doctrine in EEC Competition Law: Agreements of Minor Importance" [1993] 3 ELR 97.

[60] See *e.g.* Case 56/65, *Technique Minière v. Maschinenbau Ulm GmbH*: [1966] E.C.R. 235, [1966] C.M.L.R. 357, ECJ; Case 5/69, *Volk v. Vervaecke* [1969] E.C.R. 295, [1969] C.M.L.R. 273, ECJ; Case 22/71, *Beguelin Import v. Gl Import Export SA*: [1971] E.C.R. 949, [1972] C.M.L.R. 81, ECJ.

[61] *e.g.* see Case 19/77, *Miller v. E.C. Commission*: [1977] E.C.R. 131, [1978] 2 C.M.L.R. 334 which involved an agreement between a German record manufacturer (Miller) and its French distributor in Alsace-Lorraine that prohibited the latter from exporting to other countries. There was no discussion of the potential export market share from Alsace-Lorraine but only Miller's market share in records in Germany. See also Case 30/78, *Distillers v. E.C. Commission* [1980] E.C.R. 229, [1980] 3 C.M.L.R. 121 which concerned an agreement which related to a particular alcoholic drink which had minimal sales outside the U.K. The Court stated at point 28 that "although an agreement may escape the prohibition in Art. 85(1) when it affects the market only to an insignificant extent, having regard to the weak position which those concerned have in the market in the products in question, the same considerations do not apply in the case of a product of a large undertaking responsible for the entire production. In those circumstances there is no reason to distinguish between Pimm's and the other drinks produced by the applicant."

[62] See *Compagnie Royale Asturienne des Mines SA v. E.C. Commission*: [1985] 1 C.M.L.R. 688, points 28–30, ECJ. See also Notice on Agreements of Minor Importance, para. 8.038, below. As for the determination of market share and the concepts of relevant product and geographic market, see Chap. 11 at para. 11.006.

[63] Case 319/82, *Ciments et Betons* [1985] E.C.R. 4173.

[64] See *Fisher Price/Quaker Oats—Toyco*: [1988] O.J. L44/4; *Jourdan*: [1989] O.J. L35/31.

on Agreements of Minor Importance,[65] that goods or services which are the subject of agreement must not represent more than five per cent of the total market for such goods or services in the Common Market affected by the agreement. Where an undertaking had a market share of five per cent in the relevant market in a Member State, then an agreement with an undertaking in another Member State which included an export ban to the former Member State fell within Article 85.[66] The Commission's approach to agreements where the relevant market share is below five per cent is less consistent. Thus, an agreement between two undertakings whose market share in hi-fi equipment was below five per cent in the Community but had a greater share of a fragmented market than most other competitors was held to be capable of having an effect on trade between Member States.[67] At the other end, if a manufacturer holds less than one per cent of the market share in a product in a Member State then an exclusive concession agreement between manufacturer and distributor will invariably fall outside Article 85(1).[68] However, this is not a hardfast rule.

8.037 The doctrine of appreciable effect must be viewed in the context of the *Consten & Grundig* doctrine whereby agreements having a potential effect on competition fall within Article 85.[69] Thus, where a British manufacturer granted a Dutch dealer the exclusive right to use its trade mark in Holland and impose an export ban on its British dealers, the Commission held that the agreement could fall within Article 85 and have an appreciable effect on trade between Member States even though the known quantities of parallel imports were small because the restriction on potential competition was considerable.[70] Conversely, where there is no normal pattern of trade between Member States that can be disrupted and there is no likelihood of trade between Member States in the absence of the competitive agreement, then there is no appreciable effect on trade between Member States. Thus, where a Swedish supplier refused to supply spare parts to a London service/repairer, there was no effect on trade between Member States because the latter would not find it in his interests to buy spare parts from other Member States.[71]

The Commission will be more likely to conclude that an agreement is capable of having an appreciable effect upon trade between Member

[65] See below, at para. 8.038.

[66] Case 19/17, *Miller International v. E.C. Commission*: [1977] E.C.R. 131, [1978] 2 C.M.L.R. 334, ECJ. In this case, Miller's percentage of the German market in records (the relevant market) was actually 3.75 per cent *in value* whereas it was about 5 per cent *in quantity*.

[67] Case 100–103/80, *Musique Diffusion Française SA and Pioneer v. E.C. Commission* [1993] E.C.R. 1825, [1983] 3 C.M.L.R. 221.

[68] Case 5/69, *Volcke v. Ets Vervaecke* [1969] E.C.R. 295, [1969] C.M.L.R. 273, ECJ. Volcke had 0.2 per cent and 0.05 per cent of the market in washing machines in Germany in 1963 and 1966 respectively.

[69] See para. 8.039, above.

[70] Case 28/77, *Tepea v. E.C. Commission*: [1978] E.C.R 1391, [1978] 3 C.M.L.R. 392.

[71] Case 22/78, *Hugin Kassaregister v. E.C. Commission* [1979] E.C.R. 1869, [1979] 3 C.M.L.R. 345.

States when the agreement or concerted practice has as its object (*i.e* price fixing or export bans) the restriction of trade.[72]

An agreement or concerted practice is not viewed in isolation. Thus if there are a series of agreements whose cumulative effect is to cause an appreciable effect on trade between Member States, then the agreement will fall within Article 85.[73] Thus, the Notice on Agreements of Minor Importance does not apply where competition is restricted by the cumulative effect of parallel networks of similar agreements established by several manufacturers or dealers.[74] Conversely, one need not show that each individual clause in an agreement is capable of affecting intra-Community trade. Rather, only if the agreement as a whole is capable of affecting trade is it necessary to examine which are the clauses of the agreement which have as their object or effect a restriction or distortion of competition.[75]

Notice on agreements of minor importance

8.038 The Commission has issued a Statement on its stance with regard to agreements of minor importance.[76] In order to facilitate co-operation between small and medium sized undertakings and prevent them having to notify every agreement entered into to the Commission, it has given quantitative criteria that it applies to determine if an agreement is capable of having an appreciable effect on trade between Member States. Those agreements which fall below the threshold do not have to be notified to the Commission for negative clearance or exemption.[77] Where cases are covered by the Notice, the Commission, as a general rule, will not open proceedings under Regulation 17 either upon application or of its own initiative. It is important to understand that the Notice has no legally binding effect on the Commission, European Court or national courts. The Commission will in exceptional circumstances start proceedings against undertakings even if the agreement falls within the Notice.

[72] *e.g.* see Case 19/17, *Miller v. E.C. Commission GmbH* [1978] E.C.R. 131, [1978] 2 C.M.L.R. 334, points 11–12; Case 77/129, *Wilkes v. Theal NV and Watts Ltd*: [1977] 1 C.M.L.R. D44.

[73] See Case 56/65, *Technique Minière v. Maschinenbau Ulm*: [1966] E.C.R. 235, [1966] C.M.L.R. 357, ECJ; see also *Distillers v. E.C. Commission*: [1980] E.C.R. 2229, [1980] 3 C.M.L.R. 121. See also *Re the "Toltecs" and "Dorcet" Trade Mark*: [1983] 1 C.M.L.R. 412 at points 51–53 (E.C. Commission). In this case, BAT had entered into similar trade mark settlement agreements with numerous other firms besides the complainant. The Commission held that it was entitled to consider the cumulative effect of these arrangements on competition. See also Case C-234/89 *Delimitis v. Henninger Brau*: [1991] I E.C.R. 935, [1992] 5 C.M.L.R. 210 ECJ.

[74] para. 16.

[75] *Windsurfing International v. Commission* [1986] 3 C.M.L.R. 489 at para. 96.

[76] [1986] O.J. C 312/2, dated September 3, 1986. This Notice replaced the previous Commission Notices of 19/12/77 ([1977] O.J., C 313/3) with itself revoked the Commission Notice of 1970 ([1970] O.J. C64/1).

[77] See Chap. 12.

However, the Notice states that in such circumstances, it will not impose fines.[78] The criteria for an agreement to fall within the Notice are:

(i) The goods or services which are the subject of the agreement together with the participating undertakings[79] other goods or services which are considered by users to be equivalent in view of their characteristics, price and intended use, do not represent more than five per cent of the total market for such goods or services in the area of the common market affected by the agreement; and

(ii) the Aggregate annual turnover of the participating undertakings does not exceed 300 million ECU.[80]

The total market is a combination of the relevant product and geographical market.[81]

Jurisdictional aspects of Article 85

8.039 It has already been stated that an agreement can affect trade between Member States irrespective of whether the undertakings to the agreement are situated inside or outside the Community or whether the effects of an agreement are intended to take place outside the Community.[82] This has raised certain questions as regards the Commission's jurisdiction with regard to undertakings situated outside the Community. The jurisdictional aspect should be distinguished from the "effects" doctrine.[83] The

[78] Thus although the Notice is not legally binding, arguably the Commission would be acting contrary to the principle of legitimate expectation if they sought to impose a fine on an agreement (even a seriously anticompetitive one) which falls within the criteria if the undertakings can prove that they would have notified the agreement in the absence of the Notice.

[79] Defined in the Notice as (a) undertakings party to an agreement or (b) undertakings in which a party to the agreement, directly or indirectly:

— owns more than half the capital or business assets or

— has the power to exercise more than half the voting rights or

— has the power to appoint more than half the members of the supervisory board, board of management or bodies legally representing the undertakings or

— has the right to manage the affair;

(c) undertakings which directly or indirectly have in or over a party to the agreement the rights or powers listed in (b); (d) undertakings in or over which an undertaking referred to in (c) directly or indirectly has the rights or powers listed in (b).

[80] The agreement will also fall within the Notice if the five per cent market shares stated are exceeded by not more than one tenth during two successive financial years. If the undertakings have wrongly calculated that their market share and turnover is such that the agreement is covered by the Notice, the Commission will not impose fines provided the mistake was not due to negligence. The recent Commission Notice on Minor Agreement [at 1994 C368/20] increased the limit from 200 to 300 million ECU.

[81] The Notice expands on the meaning of these two requirements. The concept of relevant product and geographical market is considered in Chap. 11 at para. 11.006 *et seq.*

[82] See para. 8.035.

[83] *ibid.*

latter is concerned with whether certain behaviour is capable of satisfying the conditions under Article 85. The former is concerned with the jurisdictional competence of the Commission or national courts to make findings under Article 85 against undertakings resident outside the E.C. In reality, the difference is a practical one. If the Commission or Court holds that an agreement falls within Article 85(1) by reason of the "effects" doctrine, the important question becomes whether it is capable of enforcement both from a legal and practical viewpoint.

In order to deal with this point and the sensitive question of enforcement, the Court has decided that the behaviour of a subsidiary can be imputed to a parent company.[84] Thus where a non-member undertaking has a subsidiary within the E.C., the establishment of jurisdiction against the non-member undertaking is not based solely on the effects of actions committed outside the E.C. but also on activities attributable to the undertaking by virtue of its subsidiary being situated within the E.C.[85]

8.040 Recently, the Court of Justice sought to expand the jurisdictional power of the Community in ruling that where producers of a particular product are established outside the Community and sell directly to purchasers within the Community, then where those producers act in concert in fixing prices, such behaviour falls within Article 85(1) and the competence of Community institutions.[86]

It said

> "It should be observed that an infringement of Article 85, such as the conclusion of an agreement which has had the effect of restricting competition within the Common Market, consists of conduct made up of two elements, the formation of the agreement, decision or concerted practice and the implementation thereof. If the applicability of prohibitions laid down under competition law were made to depend on the place where the agreement, decision or concerted practice was formed, the result would obviously be to give undertakings an easy means of evading those prohibitions. The decisive factor is therefore the place where it is implemented.
>
> The producers in the case implemented their pricing agreement within the Common Market. It is immaterial in that respect whether or not they have recourse to subsidiaries, agents, sub-agents or branches within the Community in order to make their contacts with purchasers within the Community.

[84] See Cases 48/69, *ICI v. E.C. Commission*: [1972] E.C.R. 619, [1972] C.M.L.R. 557, 629; Case 6/72, *Continental Can v. E.C. Commission*: [1973] E.C.R. 215, [1973] C.M.L.R. 199.

[85] See Case 52/69, *Geigy AG & Sandoz AG v. E.C. Commission*: [1972] C.M.L.R. 640, point 51 (a case related to the ICI case in n. 81, above).

[86] *Re the Woodpulp Cartel*: [1988] 4 C.M.L.R. 901. For a commentary on the effect of this, see "EC Jurisdiction in Antitrust Matters: The Wood Pulp Judgment" [1989] Fordham Corp. Law Institute.

> Accordingly, the Community's jurisdiction to apply its competition rules to such conduct is covered by the terrotoriality principle as universally recognised in public international law."[87]

The effect of this judgment is to give jurisdiction to Community institutions whenever an agreement has anticompetitive effects in the Community. Thus, if the "*effects*" doctrine applies to an agreement, then Community institutions have *jurisdiction* over the undertakings concerned regardless of their location.

Inevitably, such a finding gives rise to enforcement problems. Will non-Member States courts recognise any decisions of the Commission in such cases? This will be a matter for the relevant national court. However, from the point of Community law, the European Court has held that the Commission cannot be denied the right on the basis on public international law to safeguard its measures against conduct distorting competition in the Common Market even where those responsible for the said conduct are resident outside the Common Market. Thus where the Commission served complaint proceedings against a Swiss undertaking at its Swiss address, this was held to be valid service in accordance with Community law even if it was not according to Swiss law.[88] Recently, the Commission has fined several undertakings situated outside the Community for anti-competitive behaviour.[89]

The Court has held that the existence of Articles prohibiting restrictive practices in the Free Trade Agreements between the EEC and a non-Member State did not oust the Community's jurisdiction under Article 85 and 86.[90]

(iv) "*Object or effect the prevention, restriction or distortion of competition within the common market*"

8.041 The problems posed by the licensing of intellectual property has played a key role in the evolution of the European Court and Commission's case law on Article 85. Many of the doctrines developed by the Court and Commission have resulted from cases concerning the assignment and licensing of patents, trade marks, copyright, plant breeder's rights and Article 85. This requirement of Article 85 is its essence. The reader is advised to read the section on Competition Law and Intellectual Property for a study of the conceptual problems that this topic brings.[91]

No attempt by the Court of Justice or the Commission has been made to refine or elaborate what is meant by the term "competition". It is not defined in the Treaty. Article 85 gives examples of what is to be considered anti-competitive practices which are deemed not exhaustive. The

[87] See *Woodpulp*, *ibid*, paras. 16–18.
[88] See Case 52–53/69 *Geigy Ag and Sandoz AG v. Commission* [1972] CMLR 637.
[89] *Re: the LdPe Cartel* [1990] 4 CMLR 382 (Commission).
[90] *Woodpulp* at pts. 30–31. See also *Re the LdPe Cartel ibid.*
[91] See para. 8.003 *et seq.*

Court of Justice and Commission have approached this subject rather differently.

Commission

8.042 From the outset, the Commission has appeared to subscribe to a simplistic view of anti-competitive agreements, namely anything which restricts the contractual freedom or conduct of the parties in the marketplace. An example of this can be seen in relation to patent and know-how licensing decisions of the Comission in the early 1970s and which is discussed below.[92] Where there were beneficial effects for the consumer, then the Commission exempted the agreement under Article 85(3). This however is an unsatisfactory approach from the viewpoint of national litigants as only the Commission has the right to exempt agreements.[93] Thus, if a court finds that an agreement falls within Article 85(1), it is void unless the Commission has exempted it.[94] An analysis of the Commission's decisions to evaluate how it interprets the phrase "competition" is beyond the scope of this book. Suffice to say that the Commission's approach has historically gone from a restrictive analysis to a more "rule of reason" approach. It has not attempted to evaluate the meaning of competition in the abstract but by application to particular set of facts. The Commission's approach to licences and clauses in licences is discussed later.[95]

European Court of Justice

8.043 The Court of Justice has been less dogmatic and has appeared to adopt a "rule of reason" approach. It will look at any possible anti-competitive effects of an agreement in its economic rather than legal context.[96] It has thus realised that certain contractual restrictions are necessary so as to increase competition or facilitate its growth in the future and make transactions commercially viable.[97] The Court will look at the competitive position before the undertakings have signed the agreement and determine whether an undertaking is deterred from entering the market place without the agreement.

For example, the Court has ruled that certain clauses restrictive of competition in a distribution franchise agreement were essential to the

[92] See para. 8.051 *et seq.*

[93] See Reg. 17, Art. 9.

[94] Which can involve lengthy delays.

[95] See para. 8.054 *et seq.*

[96] Case 56 & 58/64, *Etablissements Consten & Grundig v. E.C. Commission*: [1966] E.C.R. 299, [1966] C.M.L.R. 418.

[97] *e.g.* see Case 56/65 *Technique Minière v. Maschinenbau Ulm*: [1966] E.C.R. 235, [1966] C.M.L.R. 357; Case 258/78, *L.C. Nugesser KG & Eisele v. E.C. Commission*: [1982] E.C.R. 2015, [1983] 1 C.M.L.R. 278; Case 262/81, *Coditel v. Cine Vog Films (No. 2)* (CODITEL II): [1982] E.C.R. 3381, [1983] 1 C.M.L.R. 49; Case 42/84, *Remia v. E.C. Commission*: [1985] E.C.R. 2547, [1987] 1 C.M.L.R. 1; Case 161/84, *Pronuptia v. Schillgalis*: [1986] E.C.R. 353, [1986] 1 C.M.L.R. 414.

working of the franchise. As a franchise was a system which allowed the opening up of markets (*i.e.* procompetitive), these clauses fell outside Article 85(1).[98] These clauses included prohibitions on franchisees opening shops with an identical or similar purpose to the franchise where he would be in competition with other franchisees; bans against sale of shops; bans on sale of merchandise in shops other than that covered in agreement; obligations that the decoration of premises be according to the franchise agreement and bans against assignment of the franchise. However, clauses which have as their object the partitioning of the market will fall within Article 85(1) even if they may be essential to a procompetitive agreement.[99]

Horizontal and vertical agreements

8.044 Both vertical and horizontal agreements can fall within Article 85.[1] This is important as usually a vertical agreement will involve undertakings who do not compete against each other whereas a horizontal agreement will invariably be between competing undertakings. Thus, it is not surprising that horizontal agreements are far more likely to fall within Article 85(1) and not be exempted under Article 85(3) than vertical agreements. However, where vertical agreements restrict competition between the undertakings and third parties, then such agreements will fall within Article 85(1).[2]

Inter-brand and intra-brand competition

8.045 For the purposes of Article 85, both inter-brand and intra-brand competition must be considered.[3] Furthermore, a vertical agreement which restricts intra-brand competition does not necessarily fall outside Article 85(1) even if it might increase inter-brand competition.[4]

[98] See Case 161/84 *Pronuptia v. Schillgalis*: [1986] E.C.R. 353, [1986] 1 C.M.L.R. 414, 474 (distribution franchise selling wedding apparel). Franchise agreements are dealt with in detail—see para. 8.075 and Chap. 10.

[99] *ibid* at point 24—the Court held that these could be exempted under Art. 85(3); see also Case 56 & 58/64 *Etablissements Consten & Grundig v. E.C. Commission*: [1966] E.C.R. 299, [1966] C.M.L.R. 418.

[1] See Case 58 & 58/64 *Etablissements Consten & Grundig v. E.C. Commission*: [1966] E.C.R. 299, [1966] C.M.L.R. 418. For the meaning of horizontal and vertical agreements, see para. 8.008.

[2] Case 58 & 58/64 *Etablissements Consten & Grundig v. Commission*: [1966] E.C.R. 299 C.M.L.R. 234, 286.

[3] *Etablissements Consten & Grundig v. E.C. Commission*: [1966] E.C.R. 299, [1966] C.M.L.R. 418. For the meaning of inter-brand and intra-brand competition, see para. 8.006 *et seq*.

[4] *ibid*, at 473. However, this must now be seen in the light of the decision of the Court of Justice in Case 258/78, *L.C. Nungesser KG & Eisele v. E.C. Commission*: [1983] 1 C.M.L.R. 278. See para. 8.066 *et seq*.

Division of markets

8.046 Any agreement which reinforces the compartmentalisation of the markets of the Member States thus preventing the economic interpenetration of national markets falls within Article 85(1).[5] Such agreements clearly conflict with the fundamental aim of the Treaty of Rome to establish a Common Market.

Competitive effect of agreements considered in toto

8.047 Agreements are not viewed in isolation. Thus if an agreement is one of a series of agreements, whose cumulative effect is such as to restrict competition, then the agreement will fall within Article 85(1).[6] This principle is applied widely so that where an agreement is similar to many other agreements concluded between different undertakings, *i.e.* reflects a trade practice, then the competitive effect of the agreements *in toto* will be considered when appraising the competitive effect of the agreement *in casu*.

Types of competition

8.048 The Court of Justice has accepted that competition can occur in several ways.[7] The obvious one is price competition can occur in other areas as well, *e.g.* with regards to the quality of service to customers. Thus, where a manufacturer operates a selective distribution system such that resellers are only eligible if they have suitable technical qualifications and premises so as to be able to provide a high quality after-sales service to the consumer, then such an agreement will fall outside Article 85(1) as the quantitive restriction on competitors is outweighed by the qualitative increase in competition in terms of high quality service.[8] Thus, a restriction in potential competitors may be compatible with Article 85 if there is a corresponding increase in quality.

"Object or effect"

8.049 In a series of landmark cases, the European Court has examined what is meant by the phrase "whose object or effect is to prevent, restrict or distort competition". The Court has distinguished between the phrase "object or effect".

[5] See *Etablissements Consten & Grundig v. E.C. Commission*: [1966] E.C.R. 299, [1966] C.M.L.R. 418; Case 8/72, *Vereeniging van Cementhandelaren v. E.C. Commission*: [1972] E.C.R. 977, [1973] C.M.L.R. 7.

[6] See *Technique Minière v. Maschinenbau Ulm GmbH*: [1966] C.M.L.R. 357. It does not matter if different undertakings are involved in each agreement—see *Brasserie de Haecht v. Wilkin et al*: [1967] E.C.R. 407 (concerning the widespread practice in the brewery industry to provide financial support to a trader in return for imposing an obligation on the trader to buy its beverages from the brewery). See also *Distillers v. E.C. Commission*: [1980] E.C.R. 2229, [1980] 3 C.M.L.R. 121 and recently *De Limitis v. Henninger Brau*: [1992] 5 C.M.L.R. 216.

[7] See para. 8.007 as to a discussion as to the theory of competition and the kinds of competition.

[8] See *Metro v. E.C. Commission*: [1977] E.C.R. 1875, [1978] 2 C.M.L.R. 1 (cash-and-carry wholesaler excluded from selective distribution because unable to meet require-

(i) Where the object of the agreement is to restrict competition, then one does not need to look at the effects of the agreement in order to establish that it falls within Article 85.[9] Thus the Court of Justice said:

> "Finally, to be hit by the prohibition of Article 85(1), the agreement in the proceedings should be designed to prevent, restrict or distort competition within the Common Market or have that effect. The fact that these are not cumulative but alternative conditions, indicated by the conjunction [or], suggests first the need to consider the very object of the agreement, in the light of the economic context in which it is to be applied. The alterations in the play of competition envisaged by Article 85(1) should result from all or part of the clauses of the agreement itself. Where, however, an analysis of the said clauses does not reveal a sufficient degree of harmfulness with regard to competition, examination should then be made of the effects of the agreement and if it is to be subjected to the prohibition, the presence of those elements which establish that competition has in fact been prevented, restricted or distorted to a noticeable extent should be required."[10]

Thus whether an agreement has as it "object" the restriction of competition does not mean that one looks at the subjective intentions of the parties to the agreement. It is sufficient if the arrangement by its nature prevents, restricts or distorts competition.[11] Whether an agreement by its nature restricts or distorts competition seems rather circular in argument—how does one know whether a clause by it nature restricts or distorts competition unless one looks at its effect? The Court has taken the view that certain clauses can have no other effect than to restrict competition and thus by their nature fall within Article 85(1). Thus, price fixing, clauses granting absolute territorial protection from internal and external competition[12] and export bans,[13] have been found to fall within Article 85(1). In contrast, exclusive licences which do not contain prohi-

ment); see also *AEG-Telefunken Ag v. E.C. Commission*: [1984] 3 C.M.L.R. 325. The Court stated that the entry requirements of a selective distribution system must be based on objective criteria. See also Case 161/84, *Pronuptia v. Schillgalis*: [1985] C.M.L.R. 446 which concerned a franchise agreement.

[9] *Etablissements Consten & Grundig v. E.C. Commission*: [1966] E.C.R. 299, [1966] C.M.L.R. 418, ECJ.

[10] *Technique Minière v. Maschinenbau Ulm*: [1966] E.C.R. 235, [1966] C.M.L.R. 357, at 375.

[11] See Case 56/65, *Technique Minière v. Maschinebau Ulm*: [1966] E.C.R. 235, [1966] C.M.L.R. 357; Case 19/77, *Miller v. Commission*: [1977] E.C.R. 131 [1978] 2 C.M.L.R. 334. *Co-operative Stremsek- en Kleurselfabriek v. E.C. Commission*: [1981] E.C.R. 851, points 12, 13; Case 123/83 *BNIC v. Clair*: [1985] E.C.R. 391, [1985] 2 C.M.L.R. 430 at 399, per A-G Slynn.

[12] *i.e.* where an exclusive licence for a particular territory is granted to an undertaking which prohibits parallel imports. This is usually effected by the licensor prohibiting other licensees in other territories from exporting or by the assignment of an intellectual property right to an exclusive licensee in a Member State. See Case 28/77, *Tepea v. E.C. Commission*: [1978] E.C.R. 1391, [1978] 3 C.M.L.R. 392, ECJ.

[13] Case 28/77, *Tepea v. Commission*: [1978] E.C.R. 1391, [1978] 3 C.M.L.R. 392.

bitions against parallel imports[14] and agreements tying a retailer to buy beverages from a particular brewer in return for a loan[15] have been found not to be of their nature restrictive of competition. It would seem that the examples given in Article 85 have as their object the restriction of competition.

8.050 (ii) If a clause by its nature does not have the object of restricting or distorting competition, then one must look at the effects of the clause on the competitive structure of the Community. In order to determine whether the effect of an agreement is to restrict competition, one must look at the competitive position in the absence of the agreement.[16] If the agreement has the effect of increasing competition in the relevant market (*i.e.* by being necessary for the penetration of an undertaking into an area in which it was not operating), then it will fall outside Article 85(1). This exercise must be done with regard to the actual circumstances in which the agreement was made. Thus where a contract contained an exclusive distributorship clause, the Court stated that it is necessary to take into account:

> "The competition in question should be understood within the actual context in which it would occur in the absence of the agreement in question. In particular, the alteration of the conditions of competition may be thrown in doubt if the said agreement appears precisely necessary for the penetration of an undertaking into an area in which it was not operating. Therefore to judge whether a contract containing a clause 'granting an exclusive right of sale' should be regarded as prohibited by reason of its object or its effect, it is necessary to take into account, in particular, the nature and the quantity, whether limited or not, of the products which are the object of the agreement, the position and size of the grantor and concessionaire on the market for the products concerned, the isolated nature of the agreement in question or, on the contrary, its position in a series of agreements, the severity of the clauses aiming at protecting the exclusive right or on the contrary, the possibilities left for other commercial currents upon the same products by means of re-exports and parallel imports."[17]

Where a sauce-making business was assigned, the Court held that a clause preventing the assignor from trading in sauces for 10 years did not have as its object or effect the restriction of competition. Without such a clause, it was held that the assignment would be devoid of any value as

[14] Case 258/78, *L.C. Nungesser KG & Eisele v. E.C. Commission*: [1982] E.C.R. 2015, [1983] 1 C.M.L.R. 278.

[15] Case 23/67, *Brasserie de Haecht SA v. Wilkin*: [1967] E.C.R. 407, [1968] C.M.L.R. 26, ECJ.

[16] Case 56/65, *Technique Minière v. Maschinenbau Ulm*: [1966] E.C.R. 235, [1966] C.M.L.R. 357; Case 42/84, *Remia v. E.C. Commission*: [1985] E.C.R. 2547; [1987] 1 C.M.L.R. 1.

[17] *Technique Minière*, *ibid* at p. 375.

the assignor could effectively prevent the assignee from building up a client base. However, 10 years was held to be long.[18] In such circumstances, it was clear that the restraint of trade clauses was an ancillary restraint necessary for the working of the agreement.

The dichotomy between "object" and "effect" is mirrored in the United States where a tribunal is entitled to rule a restraint so plainly anticompetitive that it can be treated as unlawful *per se* without an elaborate inquiry into the restraint's purpose and effect on the market.[19]

(c) Intellectual property and Article 85(1)

8.051 This section is concerned with the Court of Justice and Commission's application of Article 85 to the validity of clauses in intellectual property licences. It is assumed that the reader has read the above parts of this chapter and is thus familiar with the general principles applied by the Court to Article 85.

The licensing of intellectual property often forms part of a greater agreement. Thus an agreement between two competitors to undertake a joint research and development program will often include a cross-licensing clause allowing each undertaking to disclose and work the other's know-how and patents in the field of research. Similarly, a franchise agreement will often include the licensing of trade mark rights to franchisees. Thus, the analysis of the competitive aspects of licences will often be part of an overall study of the competitive effect of business arrangements between undertakings. However, the Court and Commission have established several principles relating to licences and individual clauses which can be applied to more complex licensing arrangements.

The Commission has played the major role in determining the validity of licensing clauses under Article 85. Whilst the Commission is only an executive body of the E.C., whose decisions on the interpretation of the Treaty of Rome are not binding on any national court of law, its decisions are important. Firstly, its decisions are binding on parties until overruled by the European Court. Secondly, they provide a valuable indicator as to how it will decide in future cases. Thirdly, its decisions will have a strong persuasive effect in the absence of a European Court judg-

[18] Case 42/84, *Remia v. E.C. Commission*: [1985] E.C.R. 2547, [1987] 1 C.M.L.R. 1.

[19] *e.g. National Society of Professional Engineers v. United States* 435 U.S. 679, 692 (1978). In relation to whether an intellectual property licence is *per se* anticompetitive or not, see para. 3.4 of the *US Antitrust Guidelines for Intellectual Property*, Issued by the Department of Justice, April 6, 1995 [1995] 7 EIPR Supplement. The examples given of restraints that are *per se* unlawful are market price-fixing, unlawful restraints and market division among horizontal competition as well as certain group boycotts and resale price maintenance. In the other copy the Department of Justice will deem restraints in licences to be *per se* unlawful if they cannot be expected to contribute to an efficiency exchange activity.

ment on national court.[20] Fourthly, the Court can only review the legality of the acts of the Commission's decision on the grounds of lack of competence, infringement of an essential procedural requirement, infringement of the Treaty of Rome or of any rule of law relating to its application or misuse of powers.[21] Fifthly and most importantly, it is the Commission that is responsible for the enforcement of Article 85 and 86. Firms seeking negative clearance or exemption of any agreement must apply to the Commission.[22]

(i) Exercise of intellectual property rights falling with Article 85(1)

8.052 At the outset, the reader should clearly distinguish between, on the one hand, the validity of intellectual property licences (or specific clauses in it) under Article 85 and on the other hand, the validity of the exercise of intellectual property rights under Article 85. The mere exercise of rights does not infringe Article 85(1).[23] However, if there is an agreement or restrictive practice between undertakings which infringes Article 85(1) and is thus void, then the use of intellectual property rights in furtherance of such an illegal restrictive practice is prohibited.

In *Consten & Grundig v. Commission*,[24] the Court of Justice held that an exclusive distributorship coupled with export bans so as to provide absolute territorial protection fell within Article 85(1) and that consequently the exercise of trade mark rights to enforce such absolute protection was invalid. Similarly, in *Tepea BV v. E.C. Commission*,[25] a British manufacturer had an exclusive distributorship agreement with a Dutch dealer. The agreement included the grant of an exclusive licence to the Dutch dealer to use the former's trade marks in Holland and was supported by export prohibitions on the British manufacturer's dealers in the United Kingdom. All orders received by the manufacturer for Holland were to be passed onto the Dutch dealer. It was apparent from the evidence that the object was to create absolute territorial protection for the Dutch dealer from internal or external competitors and that the Dutch dealer was to exercise trade mark rights in order to achieve such an aim. The ECJ held that such absolute territorial protection has as its object or effect the prevention of competition within Holland and thus fell within Article 85(1). Trade mark rights could not be exercised so as to achieve absolute territorial protection.

[20] In fact, in the U.K., it is arguable that it is binding on national court—see European Community Act 1972, s.2. See also *British Leyland v. Wyatt Interpart Co. Ltd* [1979] 3 C.M.L.R. 79 where it was held that a Commission's decision which was not appealed ought to be considered as having the same effect as a Court of Justice's decision.

[21] Treaty of Rome, Art. 173.

[22] As to the meaning of negative clearance, exemption and the procedure for notifying the Commission, see Chap. 12, on Enforcement of EEA Competition Law.

[23] See *Parke Davis v. Probel*: [1968] E.C.R. 55, [1968] C.M.L.R. 47; *EMI v. CBS (UK) Ltd*: [1976] E.C.R. 811, [1976] 2 C.M.L.R. 235.

[24] [1966] C.M.L.R. 19.

[25] [1978] E.C.R. 1391, [1978] 3 C.M.L.R. 392.

In both the above cases, it was intended that intellectual property rights be exercised to maintain absolute territorial protection. Clearly, the courts were concerned that if the mere exercise of rights could not infringe Article 85(1), then a finding that the exclusive distributorship agreement was void would be ineffectual if the dealer could exercise his rights so as to achieve the same effect, Thus, whilst the mere exercise of intellectual property rights does not fall within Article 85(1), the exercise of intellectual property rights pursuant to an agreement or concerted practice is contrary to Article 85(1). In such circumstances, the exercise of such rights are merely the instrument of enforcing such an illegal agreement and as such can be injuncted.

8.053 In an early case, the ECJ stated that the exercise of trade mark rights can be prohibited under Article 85 to prevent parallel imports of products lawfully bearing the same trade mark.[26] This decision must now be considered of dubious authority. It is discussed in the Chapter on Enforcement of Intellectual Property Rights, at para. 7.113 *et seq*.

In *Hydrotherm v. Geratebau*,[27] the ECJ held (in the context of Article 3 of Regulation 67/67 [the former exclusive distributorship block exemption] which prevented the application of the Regulation where contracting parties use intellectual property rights to prevent parallel imports) that the fact that an agreement between licensor and licensee permitted the latter to register the former's trade mark in the latter's country and thus allowing the latter the mere possibility of abuse did not bring the agreement within Article 3. Thus, the complainant must bring proper evidence to bear of the misuse of intellectual property rights by a party. Before a trade mark assignment can be treated as giving effect to an agreement prohibited under Article 85, it is necessary to analyse the context, the commitments underlying the assignment, the intention of the parties and the consideration for the assignment.[28]

(ii) Article 85(1) and licences

8.054 The principles affecting the interrelationship of competition and intellectual property licences have already been discussed and the reader is advised to read the relevant section.[29] The Commission has adopted a favourable approach to simple "pure" licences whereby a licensee is granted the right to exploit the licensor's intellectual property in return for payment of royalty. Such an agreement is clearly pro-competitive as at the very least, it increases intra-brand competition.[30] What has concerned the Court and Commission is the existence of contractual restraints in a licence on either licensee or licensor. The approach by the

[26] Case 40/70, *Sirena Srl v. Eda Srl*: [1971] E.C.R. 69, [1975] C.M.L.R. 1.
[27] Case 170/83, *Hydrotherm v. Compact* [1984] E.C.R. 2999, [1985] 3 C.M.L.R. 276.
[28] C9/93 *Ideal Standard*, Judgment of ECJ, June 24, 1994 [1994] 3 C.M.L.R. 857.
[29] See para. 8.018.
[30] *e.g.* see *Re the Agreements between Schlegell CPIO Agreements*: [1984] 2 C.M.L.R. 179 (Commission) (a seven year non-exclusive know-how licence granted to licensee in return for royalty payments fell outside Art. 85(1)).

Commission has been to find that generally such restrictions prima facie restrict competition and thus fall within Article 85(1) and to only use market analysis in order to determine whether such licences should be exempted under Article 85(3). The Court has favoured a more "rule of reason" approach to determine whether restrictive clauses infringe Article 85(1).

Historically, the Commission and the Court has approached the relationship of intellectual property and Article 85(1) from four different angles—the "limited licence", the "specific subject matter", the "rule of reason" and the "unified market" approach.

The "limited licence" approach

8.055 Clauses which partially lift the prohibitive effects of an intellectual property monopoly ("permissive clauses") should never be deemed to be anti-competitive. This principle is known as the "*limited licence*" principle and is based on the concept that a rights owner is not obliged to create competition within his protected technology.[31] The Commission and Court's approach to the compatibility of permissive clauses with Article 85(1) has varied over time.

Initially, the Commission adopted the "limited licence" approach to intellectual property licensing. In 1962, it issued a Notice on Patent Licensing Agreements.[32] This Notice permitted restrictions (*inter alia*) as to the form of exploitation of the patent (*i.e.* manufacture or sale), the duration of the licence, geographical restrictions and restrictions against assignment and sub-licensing.[33] It pronounced that such clauses in patent licences did not, in the Commission's view, fall within Article 85(1).

[31] See para. 8.018 *et seq*.

[32] O.J. No. 139, December 24, 1962, p. 2922. This has been called the "Christmas" Message.

[33] The important aspects of the Notice are set out below (NB it has now been revoked).

"1. On the basis of the facts known at present, the Commission considers that the following clauses in patent licensing agreements are not caught by the prohibition laid down in Article 85(1) if the Treaty:

A. Obligations imposed on the licensee which have as their object:

1. Limitation of the exploitation of the invention to certain of the forms which are provided for by patent law (manufacture, use, sale).
2. Limitation:
   (a) of the manufacture of the patented product,
   (b) of the use of the patented process, to certain technical application.
3. Limitation of the quantity of products to be manufactured or of the number of acts constituting exploitation.
4. Limitation of exploitation: (a) in time (a licence of shorter duration than the patent); (b) in space (a regional licence for part of the territory for which the patent is granted, or a licence limited to one place of exploitation or to a specific factory); (c) with regard to the person (limitation of the licensee's power of disposal, *e.g.* prohibiting him from assigning the licence or from granting sub-licenses).

Other permitted clauses in the Notice related to obligation to mark the product with an indication of the patent, quality standards, disclosure of know-how learnt whilst exploiting the patent (provided it was non-exclusive) and undertakings by the licensor not to authorise anyone else to exploit the invention or to exploit the invention himself.

The Notice was not applicable to agreements relating to the joint ownership of patents, reciprocal licensing and multiple parallel licensing.

8.056 Of interest was that the Commission expressly explained the Notice by application of the "limited licence" doctrine to the relationship of patents and Article 85(1). It stated that such limitations fell within the patent monopoly as:

> "they entail only the partial maintenance of the right of prohibition contained in the patentee's exclusive right in relation to the licensee, who in other respects is authorised to exploit the invention."

It became clear from the earliest decisions and pronouncements on patent licences in the 1970s that the Commission virtually ignored or forgot its initial "limited licence" approach.[34] Subsequently, it has virtually played no part in the Commission or Court's reasoning. In the 1980s the approach of both the Commission and the Court has undermined any possible application of the doctrine. Thus territorial restrictions[35] and quantitative restrictions[36] are considered to fall within Article 85(1) whereas field-of-use restrictions and temporal restrictions on licences are not.[37] Other examples of its irrelevance to licences can be given. The Commission in its Patent Block Exemption has prohibited any clause in patent licences which attempts to restrict the quantity of licensed products produced.[38] In *Boussois v. Interpane*,[39] the Commission held that a clause in a patent/know-how licence which only allowed a licensee to manufacture in one Member State fell within Article 85(1) as it prevented the licensee from manufacturing elsewhere in the Common Market. This was despite the fact that parallel patents existed in most of the other Member States and thus the manufacturer would have been prohibited from manufacturing in those countries by the patents.

The Court of Justice has never referred to the limited licence doctrine in its judgments preferring to emphasise the "specific subject matter' and the "ancillary restraints" doctrine. Indeed in the *Windsurfing* case,[40] some of its findings arguably conflict with the "limited licence" approach.[41]

The decline in the application of the limited doctrine eventually resulted in the 1962 Notice being revoked.[42] It is thus only of historical interest. Recently, the Commission has appeared to relax its whole approach to licensing. Thus, in know-how licences, it has recognised that bans on the use of know-how after the expiry of the licence do not gener-

[34] See *4th Report on Competition Policy*, (1974), points 22 *et seq*; *5th Report on Competition Policy*, (1975), point 11.
[35] See *Windsurfing International v. E.C. Commission*: [1986] 3 C.M.L.R. 489.
[36] See Quantitative Restrictions, para. 8.130.
[37] See para. 8.129. Field-of-Use and para. 8.125 for temporal restrictions.
[38] Regulation 2349/84, Art. 3(5). See also Art. 3(1) of draft Technology Transfer Block Exemption.
[39] [1987] O.J. L50/30, [1988] 4 C.M.L.R. 124.
[40] *Windsurfing International v. E.C. Commission*: [1986] 3 C.M.L.R. 489.
[41] See *ibid*, below. See also submissions of United Kingdom in *Windsurfing* where arguments based on the doctrine of limited licence were put forward.
[42] It was revoked just before the Patent Block Exemption came into force.

ally fall within Article 85(1).[43] However, whilst such would appear implicit recognition of the limited licence doctrine as such a restriction is a temporal restriction, the Commission has justified such an approach as being necessary to encourage know-how owners to licence their technology.[44] Thus, the "limited licence" approach must be considered redundant in analysing whether a licence falls within Article 85(1).

The failure to apply the limited licence doctrine constitutes a direct attack on the existence of intellectual property. It gives rise to the contradiction that a rights owner cannot be forced to license others but if he chooses to do so, he cannot choose the extent to which he wishes to create more competition in his technology. Such an approach may have an adverse effect and prevent the owner from licensing at all. In this respect, the United States' approach that it will not force an owner to technology to create competition in its own technology seems preferable.[45]

8.057 It should be added that even if the "limited licence" doctrine becomes more acceptable again in Community law as it may do, care must be taken to apply it properly. This is illustrated by the Commission's decision in *IMA AG v. Windsurfing International*,[46] where patent licensees were restricted to manufacturing in one place in Germany. Patents did not exist in the United Kingdom or other countries. The Commission took the view that this made it impossible for German licensees to engage in royalty-free manufacture in areas not covered by the patent and thus "indirectly" sought to secure for the patentee a regard for his invention in areas not covered by the patent. It thus considered that clause 4(b) in the 1962 Patent Notice (then in force) by which the prohibition in Article 85(1) did not apply to a territorial restriction of the licensees which limited the licence to a specific factory was not applicable.[47] The effect of the clause was to *inter alia* restrain the licensees from manufacturing in countries where there were no patents. Therefore, such a clause did not fall purely within the "limited licence" doctrine.

"Specific subject matter" doctrine

8.058 In the early 1970s the European Court tackled the question as to when a rights owner could exercise its rights against parallel importers of goods subject to such rights. It developed the "existence v. exercise" doctrine in relation to Article 30–36. This doctrine stated that whilst the existence of intellectual property rights were not affected by the Treaty of Rome provisions, the exercise of such rights were. As few owners of intellectual property are interested in anything other than the right to exercise such

[43] See Know-How Block Exemption at para. 8.234. See also similar position in draft Technology Transfer Block Exemption, Art. 2(1)(3).
[44] See Reg. 556/89, Recital 14 (Know-How Block Exemption).
[45] See para. 8.021.
[46] [1984] 1 C.M.L.R. 1, points 100–101. Upheld on appeal, *Windsurfing International v. E.C. Commission*: [1986] 3 C.M.L.R. 489.
[47] A Notice issued by the Commission is not binding.

rights, this doctrine was further elaborated by the ECJ so as to determine whether an intellectual property right was exercised in relation to the specific subject matter of the right or not. Where a right was exercised in relation to the specific subject matter of industrial or commercial property, then (but not otherwise) the exercise of such a right was not contrary to the free movement of goods provisions of the Treaty of Rome. For instance, the specific subject matter of a patent has been held to be "*inter alia*" to ensure to the holder, so as to recompense the creative effort of the inventor, the exclusive right to utilise an invention with a view to the manufacture and first putting into circulation of industrial products".[48] Thus, once a patentee has been financially rewarded by the first placing of his patented product in the Common Market, he has exhausted his rights in that product and is forbidden by Articles 30 to 36 from exercising his right to prevent subsequent inter-State trade in the product.[49]

8.059 The Commission sought to adopt such concepts into Article 85. Thus in its 4th Report on Competition Policy, the Commission stated:

> "On a legal plane, the Commission faces the problems of definition exposed by the Court of Justice in its distinction between the existence of nationally protected industrial property rights, which is not to be affected by Community law, and the exercise of these rights, which can be subject to the Treaty rules. Accordingly, any appraisal of particular patent licensing provisions requires prior differentiation between terms which are germane to the existence, and those which relate to the exercise, of patent rights, in order to establish upon which provisions the Commission may properly rule. While the differentiation remains to be more fully worked out by future decisions of the Court, it is clear that patent licensing agreements are not automatically within Article 85(1) if the agreements simply confer rights to exploit patented inventions against payment of royalties, but that questions of applicability of Article 85(1) arise if a grant is accompanied by terms which go beyond the need to ensure the existence of an industrial property right, or where the exercise of such right is found to be object, means or consequence of a restrictive agreement."[50]

Whilst such a remark was helpful, it was clear that the Commission was not prepared to provide any theoretical basis as to whether patent licences provisions were "germane to the existence" of the patent. In all cases, the Commission asserted but never explained the meaning of such a phrase. For instance, soon after this statement, the Commission held that an exclusive licence "did not relate to the existence of the patent, for

[48] See *Centrafarm BV v. Sterling Drug Inc.*: [1974] 2 C.M.L.R. 1.
[49] The doctrine of "specific subject matter" and "existence and exercise" in relation to Arts. 30–36 is discussed in Chap. 7 at para. 7.010 and 7.011.
[50] At point 20.

a contractual obligation which restricts the holder of a right in his exercise thereof cannot call into question the very existence of that right".[51] However, it is arguable that an exclusive licence is virtually identical to a patent and falls within the specific subject matter of a patent. Each national patent gives the owner an exclusive right to exploit the patent. Granting an exclusive licence of a national patent is virtually equivalent to assigning the patent.[52] Indeed, one Advocate-General has said that the specific subject matter of the copyright in a film covers exploitation by a single person whether the owner or an exclusive licensee.[53] It puts the licensee into the exact position an assignee would have been in. Such an assignment of the patent to the licensee would have been unimpeachable under Article 85(1) unless it was intended to artificially partition the market. Similarly, in the context of a patent licence which restricted the licensee's capacity, the Commission said that it was "not of the essence of his rights as patent-holder . . . there might be justification for differences in royalties but there is none for a restriction of capacity".[54] In another licence with export bans, no-challenge and non-competition clauses imposed on a licence, this fell within Article 85(1) as "the existence of the patent-right [was] not in issue."[55]

In the 1980s, the Court of Justice distilled the doctrine of existence v. exercise into the specific subject matter or specific object doctrine in relation to the compatibility of the exercise of intellectual property rights and the free movement of goods provisions of the Treaty of Rome.[56] In *Windsurfing International*, the Commission and Court applied for the first time the more sophisticated concept of the specific object to the compatibility of a patent licence with Article 85.

Windsurfing International

8.060 An American company had invented a rig for a sailboard. Patents were applied for in several countries. In Germany, a patent was applied for and granted which was deemed to be for a rig for a sailboard. Licences were entered into by the patentee with two German undertakings for the exploitation of the German patent. These non-exclusive licences had several clauses which restricted the freedom of licensees. The Commission brought proceedings under Regulation 17 against the patentee.

At the heart of the dispute was that many restrictions imposed on the licensees by the patentee concerned the sailboard rather than the rig. The Commission took the viewpoint that the evidence strongly suggested that

[51] See *AOIP v. Beyrard*: [1976] 1 C.M.L.R. D14, at para. 20. See also *Re Kabelmetal's Agreement*: [1975] 2 C.M.L.R. D40.

[52] Thus in England, exclusive licensee as well as patentees can sue for patent infringement (Patents Act 1977, ss. 66–67).

[53] See Advocate-General Reischl in *Coditel v. Cine Vog Films (No. 2)* CODITEL II: [1982] E.C.R. 3381, [1983] 1 C.M.L.R. 49 at 62.

[54] See *Zuid-Nederlandsche Bronbemaling en Grondboringen BV v. Heidemaatschappij Beheer NV*: [1975] 2 C.M.L.R. D67 at para. 18.

[55] *AOIP v. Beyrard*: [1976] 1 C.M.L.R. D14 at paras. 22–25, 30.

[56] See Chap. 7, para. 7.011.

the patent only related to the rig and not the sailboard (although this was disputed by the patentee).

The Commission found that certain clauses, *inter alia*, fell within Article 85(1).[57]

(a) The obligation on the licensees to exploit the invention only for the purposes of mounting the patented rig on certain types of board specified in the licence and the accompanying obligation to submit for the licensor's approval, prior to their being placed on the market, any new board types on which the licensees intended to use the rigs.

Windsurfing International (WSI) submitted that such was an assertion of the right to exercise quality control over board and rig combinations. The Commission held that such a right could only be recognised as forming part of the specific subject matter of the patent right if it was confined to the protected rig.

(b) The obligation on the licensees to only sell the rig in conjunction with the board, *i.e.* as a complete sailboard.

The Commission held that such restricted the right of licensees to act as distributors of rigs to third parties and did not fall within the specific subject matter of the patent.

(c) The obligation to affix to the sailboards manufactured a notice stating "licensed by Windsurfing International (the patentee)".

The Commission held that this gave rise to the erroneous impression that the boards were covered by industrial property rights.

(d) An obligation on the licensees to restrict production of the licensed product to a specific manufacturing plant in Germany coupled with the right of the patentee to terminate the license if the licensee changed its production site.

The Commission held that this prevented licensees from manufacturing in countries where there was no patent protection. It said that it was not part of the specific subject matter of the patent if conditions were so formulated as to secure for the patentee a reward for invention even in places where he does not enjoy any patent protection at all.

(e) An obligation on the licensee not to challenge the validity of the licensed patents or the trade marks.

The Commission held as it had done several times before that such clauses were not in public interest and therefore restricted competition.

(f) An obligation to pay royalties calculated on the net selling price of the complete sailboard. This obligation applied even if the licensees chose to sell the rig and sailboard separately such that it was punitive to attempt to sell rigs or sailboards separately as

[57] *IMA AG v. Windsurfing International*: [1984] 1 C.M.L.R. 1.

> the royalty charged was still based on the sale of a complete sailboard.
>
> The Commission held that such an arrangement meant that producers of boards were prevented from selling their boards as complete boards with rigs and licensees were forced to sell boards and rigs as combination only even though there was a demand for the two parts separately.

Thus, the Commission was concerned that the above provisions were an attempt to extend the scope of the patent monopoly and thus did not fall within the specific subject matter of the patent. Whilst it did not in its decision expand on what is meant by the specific subject matter, it would appear that it saw it as only meaning the right of a patentee to remuneration for the exploitation of the protected product (*i.e.* the rig) and also the right to exercise quality control over production of the protected product.

8.061 On appeal under Article 173, the Court agreed with the Commission's view that the patent only covered the rig and not the sailboard. It went on to state that:

> "The clauses contained in the licensing agreements, in so far as they relate to parts of the sailboard not covered by the German patent or include the complete sailboard within their terms of reference, can therefore find no justification on grounds of the protection of an industrial property right."[58]

The Court on all but a few points upheld the Commission's decision.

With regard to Clause (a), the Court stated that such controls (which were said by the patentee to be quality controls) did not fall within the subject matter of the patent unless they related to a product covered by the patent since their sole justification is that they ensure that the technical instructions as described in the patent and used by the licensee may be carried into effect. Furthermore, such controls had to be effected according to quality and safety criteria agreed upon in advance and on the basis of objectively verifiable criteria.[59]

With regard to Clause (b), the Court said that such an obligation was not indispensable to the exploitation of the patent. Accordingly, Windsurfing's argument that such a restriction was covered by the specific subject matter of the patent failed.

8.062 With regard to Clause (c), the Court said such a clause is covered by the specific subject matter of the patent provided that the notice is placed on the components covered by the patent.

With regard to Clause (d), it was noted that the principle reason behind this clause was to prevent licensees from manufacturing in coun-

[58] At point 36.

[59] This test of objectively verifiable criteria for quality controls has been applied in relation to selective distribution networks—see *Metro-SB-Grossmarkte v. Commission*: (1977) E.C.R. 1875, (1978) 2 C.M.L.R. 1.

tries where no patent existed. The Court held that the patentee cannot rely on the specific subject matter of the patent in order to gain the protection afforded by the patent in a country where there is no patent protection.

With regard to Clause (e), it stated that such a clause clearly does not fall within the specific subject matter of the patent in view of the fact that it is in the public interest to eliminate any obstacle to economic activity which may arise where a patent was granted in error.

With regard to Clause (f), the Court held that such restricted competition with regard to the separate sale of boards but not rigs as it was accepted that it was equitable for the patentee to charge a higher royalty rate in its new agreements based on the selling price of rigs alone as opposed to the complete sailboards.

8.063 In relation to Clause (c), the ECJ said:

> "It should then be noted that such a clause may be covered by the specific subject matter of the patent provided that the notice is placed only in components covered by the patent. Should this not be the case, the question arises whether the clause has as its object or effect the prevention, restriction or distortion of competition."[60]

Clearly, it is implicit that if a clause falls within the subject matter of the right then even if it does restrict or distort competition, it falls outside Article 85(1). Thus, it is a *condition precedent* to the application of Article 85(1) and not a factor to be taken into account in weighing up the pro and anticompetitive effects of the agreement. The "specific subject matter" doctrine concerns itself more with the *purpose and reason* for patent and allied rights legislation and the reader should refer to the case law developed in relation to it with the free movement of goods provisions[61] whereas the "limited licence" concept concerns itself more with the *nature and extent* of the patent monopoly.

What is precisely meant by the specific subject matter of an intellectual property right in relation to licenses and Article 85 has never been clarified. The doctrine was borrowed from the ECJ's jurisprudence under Articles 30–36 in the context of parallel imports of protected products. Its suitability to the competitive effect of individual clauses in licences is questionable. The Court gives the impression in *Windsurfing* of applying the "specific subject matter" doctrine only to clauses that relate either to remuneration for the exploitation of the patented product alone or which are necessary for the proper exploitation and manufacture of the patented product. It is submitted that the doctrine of specific object cannot replace a proper "rule of reason" approach to licences and clauses in licences. If it has any value at all, it is that certain clauses which are germane to a licence like the payment of royalties and quality control restric-

[60] At point 72.
[61] See Chap. 7, on Enforcement of Intellectual Property.

tions may be considered *per se* to fall outside Article 85 without the need for market analysis.

Rule of reason

8.064 In order to determine whether an agreement restricts or distorts competition, the Court has stated that one must examine the competitive situation in the absence of the agreement.[62] The Court has shown that it will thus accept ancillary restraints on the conduct of parties to an agreement where such is necessary for the commercial viability of the agreement.[63] In particular, the Court has accepted that exclusive licenses, *i.e.* a restriction on the licensor not to licence others in a designated territory are necessary to the dissemination of technology.[64]

Conversely, the Commission generally has merely examined whether the contractual freedom of the parties to trade has been restricted. If so, the agreement usually is held to infringe Article 85(1). Only where the Commission has been constrained by a specific decision of the Court has it adopted an ancillary restraints approach. Where there are clear benefits to the consumers, it has preferred to exempt under Article 85(3) rather than clear the licences under Article 85(1).

The Commission has sought to emphasise that it does not seek to undermine the existence of intellectual property rights. Thus it said in its 5th Report on Competition Policy:

> "One comment has been that the Commission regards some clauses in patent licences as *per se* infringements of Article 85(1). This is not so. The facts of each case have to be examined before it can be decided whether Article 85(1) has been infringed. The terms of the Article must be satisfied in each case. These in turn require the consideration of such features as the economic power of the parties, the nature of the market or business in which they are engaged, their share of the market, the number of competitors and the significance of the licensed invention or know-how.
>
> The recent decisions do not mark a new departure in the Commission's policy, which continues to stem from the Treaty of Rome. The Treaty does not oppose the existence of intellectual property rights, but if used in a manner which infringes Article 85(1), the Commission will take appropriate action. The use of industrial property rights for the purposes of restrictive business practices does not alter the character of the infringement and cannot render such practices any less liable to attack from the Commission."[65]

[62] See *Technique Minière v. Maschinenbau Ulm*: [1966] E.C.R. 235, [1966] C.M.L.R. 357 and para. 8.050, above.
[63] See para. 8.024, as to the meaning of ancillary restraints.
[64] See Case 258/78, *L.C. Nungesser KG & Eisele v. E.C. Commission*: [1983] 1 C.M.L.R. 278 and *Coditel v. Cine Vog Films (No. 2)*: [1982] E.C.R. 3381, [1983] 1 C.M.L.R. 49; *Pronuptia v. Schillgalis*: [1986] E.C.R. 353, [1986] 1 C.M.L.R. 414.
[65] Points 10–11.

This comment is perhaps more notable by what it did not say rather than what it does. The criteria which the Commission state must be met before a licence is capable of falling within Article 85(1) relate to the issue of appreciable effect. Such an analysis is borne out in practice where the only market analysis done in relation to Article 85(1) has been to determine whether an agreement has an appreciable effect on trade. Badly put, the Commission acknowledged that such rights exist but that is all. Article 85 applies to licensing agreements as to any other agreement.

8.065 The above excerpt does not mention anything of the "procompetitive" effect of some agreements. The need for certain clauses, *i.e.* exclusivity in order to encourage undertakings to become licensees, *e.g.* because of the need to invest, is only undertaken as to the question of exemption under Article 85(3). This was unsatisfactory because it meant that an undertaking had to either bring his agreement within a relevant block exemption or had to notify the Commission for individual exemption.[66] By taking such an approach, it meant that the Commission was able to control which agreements it authorised.

Accordingly, the Commission in the 1980s did not show itself willing to examine in detail the effect of an agreement on competition in a particular market for the purposes of Article 85(1). Recently, the Commission has shown that it will apply a "rule of reason" approach. For instance, it accepts in relation to joint venture and research and development agreement that certain clauses are necessary ancillary restraints.[67] However, in other respects, it has only applied the "rule of reason" approach as taken by the Court of Justice where constrained by authority. This can be particularly seen in its approach to exclusive licensing.

In the early 1980s, the European Court of Justice was given the chance to review the Commission's approach to Article 85(1) and intellectual property licences in two landmark cases. In *Nungesser v. E.C. Commission (the "Maize Seed" case)*,[68] a decision was given by a full Chamber of the European Court to rule on the application of Article 85(1) to exclusive licences.

(1) Nungesser v. Commission

8.066 A French botanical institution, INRA, had developed varieties of maize seed capable of being cultivated under temperate climactic conditions. Mr Eisele was a supplier of seeds in Germany. In 1961, INRA assigned the breeder's rights in Germany for four varieties of maize seed to Mr Eisele. Mr Eisele successfully achieved registration of these varieties with the Bundessortenamt (the Plant Varieties Register in Germany). In 1965, INRA and Eisele entered into a new agreement relating to six varieties of maize seed. INRA granted a Mr Eisele an exclusive licence to produce

[66] Only the Commission can grant exemption—Reg. 17, Art. 9. See generally Chapter 12.

[67] *e.g.* see *Elopak v. Tetra Pak*: [1988] O.J. L272/27; [1990] 4 C.M.L.R. 47; *Notice regarding restrictions ancillary to concentrations* [1990] O.J. 203.

[68] Case 258/78, [1982] E.C.R. 2015, [1983] 1 C.M.L.R. 278.

and market a hybrid maize seed in Germany. This agreement conferred on Mr Eisele the exclusive right to produce and distribute INRA varieties in Germany. Furthermore, INRA undertook to do everything in its power to ensure that INRA maize varieties were not exported to Germany other than through Mr Eisele. These rights were then assigned to Nungesser KG but the registrations remained in Eisele's name.

Eisele sought to prevent parallel importers of INRA seeds into Germany by threatening action for infringement of breeder's rights. Eventually, a parallel importer lodged a complaint under Regulation 17, Article 3 to the Commission.

8.067 *Commission's decision*—The Commission held that the exclusive nature of the licence granted by INRA to Eisele infringed Article 85(1) as it deprived the licensor of the right to issue licences to other undertakings in the same territory. Similarly, it held that the obligation on INRA to prevent parallel importers was contrary to Article 85(1). It refused to grant an exemption under Article 85(3).

8.068 *Court's decision*—On appeal under Article 173, the Court overruled the judgment in part. The Court of Justice distinguished between an "open" and a "closed" exclusive licence. The first allows parallel imports of the protected product into the designated territory whereas the second provides for absolute territorial protection.

The Court of Justice upheld the well-established principle that the exercise of an industrial or commercial property right cannot be used to prevent genuine parallel imports and thus ensure absolute territorial protection.[69] This principle, it should be remembered, arose from the decision in *Counsten & Grundig* where it was held that trade mark rights could not be exercised to render ineffective a finding that an exclusive distributorship agreement was void under Article 85. Thus it held that a "closed" exclusive licence fell within Article 85(1). The Court then went on to consider whether the grant of an "open" exclusive licence fell within Article 85(1). It stated that:

> "In fact, in the case of a licence of breeder's rights over hybrid maize seeds newly developed in one Member State, an undertaking established in another Member State which was not certain that it would not encounter competition from other licensees for the territory granted to it, or from the owner of the right himself, might be deterred from accepting the risk of cultivating and marketing that product; such a result would be damaging to the dissemination of a new technology and would prejudice competition in the Community between the new product and similar existing products."[70]

[69] See *Etablissements Consten & Grundig v. E.C. Commission*: [1966] E.C.R. 299, [1966] C.M.L.R. 418; *EMI Records Ltd v. CBS*: [1976] E.C.R. 811, [1976] 2 C.M.L.R. 235; *Tepea v. E.C. Commission*: [1978] E.C.R. 1391, [1978] 3 C.M.L.R. 392.

[70] *Nungesser*, point 57.

Such an approach adopts the "rule of reason" approach. The Court of Justice acknowledged that an "open" exclusive licence was a necessary ancillary restraint which increased competition at the inter-brand level where it concerned the introduction of new technology in the Community.

Why did the Court make the distinction between "open" and "closed" licence when it came to considering the question of whether an exclusive licence had a procompetitive effect? In certain situations, licensees might be deterred from taking a licence unless they can be assured of absolute territorial protection. This would especially be the case where transport costs would be negligible (as would be the case for seeds) and which would thus undermine the effect of an "open" exclusive licence.

8.069 Some commentators have stated that where there is a new technology, it is desirable to have some intra-brand competition (*i.e.* via parallel imports) as it is unlikely that there will be effective inter-brand competition (because it is a new technology).[71] Thus an "open" exclusive licence achieves a compromise. However, if a potential licensee is deterred from taking a licence, then both inter and intra brand competition will be adversely affected.

It is clear that this was too large a step for the Court to take. The Court said that Articles 30–36 did not allow a licensor to prevent parallel imports from licensees' territory. Secondly, the Court said that it was well-established since *Consten & Grundig v. E.C. Commission* that absolute territorial protection amounts to artificial maintenance of separate national markets and distorts competition.[72] It is unfortunate that it sought not to distinguish *Consten* and others as being trade mark cases which did not concern new technologies and significant investment.[73] It would have thus been inconsistent with its previous rulings if it had ruled that a "closed" exclusive licence fell outside Article 85(1) if the right bestowed by the licence could be used to provide absolute territorial protection to the licensee.

Thus the Court declined to analyse the effect on competition in *Nungesser* by the grant of a closed exclusive licence. The judgment may be seen as one of policy. It balances its ancillary restraints approach with a

[71] See Hoffmann and O'Farrell, "The 'Open' Exclusive Licence—Scope and Consequence" [1984] 4 EIPR 107.

[72] However the Court in special circumstances have ruled that absolute territorial protection is not contrary to Art. 85(1), see CODITEL II: *Coditel v. Cine Vog Films (No. 2)* [1982] E.C.R. 3381, [1983] 1 C.M.L.R. 49; *Louis Erauw-Jacquery v. La Hesbignonne*: [1988] 4 C.M.L.R. 576.

[73] The cases which established the principle that industrial and commercial property rights could not be used to provide absolute territorial protection were usually cases which concerned trade marks (see *Etablissements Consten & Grundig v. E.C. Commission*: [1966] E.C.R. 299; *Tepea v. E.C. Commission*: [1978] 3 C.M.L.R. 392). It is much more difficult to argue that the grant of an exclusive "closed" trade mark licence is procompetitive than that of a similar patent or plant breeder's right where often considerable investment and money must be made by the licensee before he can expect to reap any financial rewards.

desire to avoid partitioning of the common market. The compromise is the "open" exclusive licence.

The Court adopted a similar approach in a case concerning film rights.

(2) Cine Vog v. CODITEL (No. 2) ("CODITEL II")[74]

8.070 A French film producer granted to a Belgian film distributor (Cine Vog) the exclusive right to exhibit a film in Belgium for seven years. Various Belgian cable television companies picked up transmission of the film in Germany (where it was lawfully transmitted by the German licensee) and distributed it by cable in Belgium. Cine Vog sued CODITEL, a cable company, for copyright infringement in Belgium. The matter was referred to the European Court under Article 177 as to whether an exclusive right granted to Cine Vog was compatible with Article 85(1).[75]

8.071 *Advocate-General Reischl's Opinion*—The Advocate-General noted that if there were several distributors in one territory, each would undercut the other in endeavouring to find buyers and would be unable to pay the original owner of the rights earnings equal to those he could have obtained by exploiting the film himself. He thus said that seen in such a way he said it was possible to say that the:

> "specific subject matter of the copyright in a film covers not only the exclusion of unauthorised outsiders from exploiting it, but also where necessary, exploitation by a single person, whether the owner of the right himself or an exclusive licensee, to whom the right is assigned against payment."[76]

He also pointed out that often distributors advanced sums of money so that the film could be made in return for being granted an exclusive licence. Secondly, films often involved considerable expenditure on publicity and dubbing before being brought to the market. Thus, if the practice was to cease, he noted that film production would largely cease as distributors would not be prepared to take anything other than an exclusive licence. Thus, he drew a parallel with *Nungesser* and held that Article 85 did not apply to the assignment of exclusive performance right for a new film.

8.072 *Judgment*—The Court broadly followed the Advocate-General's Opinion. It held that such a right did not infringe Article 85(1). It said that:

> "[15] The mere fact that the proprietor of a film copyright has

[74] [1982] E.C.R. 3381, [1983] 1 C.M.L.R. 49.

[75] This matter also went to the European Court on the question of whether Cine Vog was prevented from enforcing its copyright against CODITEL by virtue of Articles 30–36. See Case 62/79, *Cine Vog v. CODITEL (No. 1)*: [1980] E.C.R. 881, [1981] 2 C.M.L.R. 362 and Chap. 7. *Enforcement of Intellectual Property*, para. 7.087.

[76] [1983] 1 C.M.L.R. 49, 62.

granted to a single licensee the exclusive right to exhibit the film in the territory of a Member State, and therefore to prohibit its diffusion by others, for a specified period, is not sufficient however for a finding that such a contract must be considered as the object, means or consequences of an agreement, decision or concerted practice prohibited by the Treaty.

[16] Indeed the characteristic features of the cinematograph industry and markets in the Community, particularly those relating to dubbing or subtitling for audiences belonging to different languages, to the possibilities of television broadcasting, and to the system for financing film production in Europe, show that a licence for exclusive exhibition is not in itself likely to prevent, restrict or distort competition

Although, therefore, the copyright in a film and the right, arising from the copyright, to exhibit a film do not by their nature fall within the prohibitions of Article 85, the exercise of such rights may nevertheless, under economic or legal circumstances which have the effect of substantially restricting the distribution of films or distorting competition in the film market having regard to its special characteristics, fall within those prohibitions."[77]

Thus the Court analysed the competitive effect of the agreement by referring to the facts and the effect the agreement had on the relevant market. Such an approach so quickly after *Nungesser* suggested that the Court had adopted a "rule of reason" approach to Article 85(1) in the context of licensing and disapproved of the strict approach favoured by the Commission. Furthermore, this decision was taken by the Court despite the fact that the *de facto* position would be that Cine Vog had a "closed" territorial licence (as the exhibition right granted was not one which could be embodied in goods capable of being imported by third parties).[78] The Court has maintained its "rule of reason" approach when examining whether contractual restrictions in licences are necessary in order to give commercial efficacy to an agreement and whether such restrictions are a necessary ancillary restraint which fall outside Article 85(1).[79]

8.073 After *Nungesser* and *CODITEL II*, it was hoped that the Commission would adopt a more "rule of reason" approach to intellectual property licences. However, this proved not to be the case with the Commission interpreting the cases restrictively.[80] Recently, the Commission appears to have moderated its view and appears to be prepared to examine the

[77] Paras. 15–17.

[78] See also Case 27/87, *Louis Erauw Jacquery v. La Hesbignonne* [1988] E.C.R. 1919, [1988] 4 C.M.L.R. 576 where an absolute exclusive manufacturing licence was held to fall outside Art. 85(1) on very special facts.

[79] Case 27/87, *Louis Erauw-Jacquery v. La Hesbignonne* [1988] E.C.R. 1919, [1988] 4 C.M.L.R. 576; Case 65/86, *Bayer v. Sullhöfer*: [1988] E.C.R. 5249, [1990] 4 C.M.L.R. 182; *Ottung v. Klee*: [1990] 4 C.M.L.R. 915.

[80] See para. 8.099 *et seq* and in particular, para. 8.103.

economic impact of restrictions.[81] For instance, the Commission will consider whether the grant of licences are ancillary restrictions necessary to make workable an agreement which gives rise to a concentration of undertakings.[82]

Unlike the specific subject matter approach, the rule of reason approach is not restricted to intellectual property licences but can be applied to any agreement. It is clear that particular clauses may be permissible under the rule of reason approach but not under the specific subject matter. Thus, the grant of an exclusive patent licence will often be a necessary ancillary restraint but will not fall within the specific subject matter of a patent. However, this does not give rise to a conflict between the two doctrines. As seen in the *Windsurfing* case, the correct approach is to consider whether the clause falls within the specific subject matter of a patent. It if does, then one does not need to consider the competitive effect of the clause. If it does not, then one must go on to ask whether the clause has as its object or effect the prevention restriction or distortion of competition.[83]

"Unified market" approach

8.074 The development of an internal market in Europe free from internal barriers has always been an overriding concern of the Treaty of Rome and its institutions.[84] It is clear that in the early 1970s, the Commission in adopting a tougher approach to licensing agreement sought to prohibit any licence that artificially partitioned the Common Market. This change in stance can be seen from the Commission's 4th Report on Competition Policy:

> "The assessment of patent licensing agreements under the Treaty rules calls upon a consideration of interests and issues which go beyond the field of competition policy. Patents conferred by national laws as incentives and rewards to inventors have traditionally created monopoly rights which restrict competition. Against this, the evolution of rules based on policies which underlie the establishment of the Community is designed to stimulate competition so as to achieve an integrated common market. It is the Commission's continuing concern to set standards for permitted licensing provision which can reconcile a legitimate exercise of the monopoly rights conferred by patent grants with the requirements of a unified market."[85]

This difference in approach emphasises the need not to artificially parti-

[81] *e.g.* see *Elopak v. Tetra Pak*: [1988] O.J. L272/27, [1990] 4 C.M.L.R. 4.
[82] See *E.C. Commission Notice* regarding restrictions ancillary to concentrations, para. IIIB. O.J. [1990] C203/5.
[83] See *Windsurfing International v. E.C. Commission* [1986] 3 C.M.L.R. 489 at point 72 and para. 8.063.
[84] Art. 5 of the Treaty.
[85] Para. 19.

tion the common market ("the unified market") and de-emphasises the inherent monopoly effect of intellectual property.

The Commission's approach followed a series of decisions by the Court which prohibited the use of intellectual property rights to prevent parallel imports as being contrary to the attainment of a common market.[86] Later on, the Court in *Nungesser* appeared to counterbalance the "rule of reason" approach with the need for a unified market in permitting an "open" exclusive licence but not a "closed" licence.[87]

8.075 In *Pronuptia v. Schillgalis*,[88] the Court again emphasised this balancing act. The case concerned a franchise agreement and is discussed in detail elsewhere. Of interest was the grant of an exclusive licence for use of the business name to franchisee in the given territory. The Court said that:

> "It must be emphasised that . . . certain provisions restrict competition between the members of the network. That is true of provisions which share markets between the francisor and franchisees or between franchisees or prevent franchisees from engaging in price competition with each other.
>
> In that regard, the attention of the national court should be drawn to the provision which obliges the franchisee to sell goods covered by the contract only in the premises specified therein. That provision prohibits the franchisee from opening a second shop. Its real effect becomes clear if it is examined in conjunction with the franchisor's undertaking to ensure that the franchisee has the exclusive use of his business name or symbol in a given territory. In order to comply with that undertaking the franchisor must not only refrain from establishing himself within that territory but also require other franchisees to give an undertaking not to open a second shop outside their own territory. A combination of provisions of that kind results in a sharing of markets between the franchisor and the franchisees and thus restricts competition within the network. As is clear from the judgment of 13 July 1966,[89] a restriction of that kind constitutes a limitation of competition for the purposes of Article 85(1) if it concerns a business name or symbol which is already well-known. It is of course possible that a prospective franchisee would not take the risk of becoming part of the chain, investing his own money, paying a relatively high entry fee and undertaking to pay a substantial annual royalty, unless he could hope, thanks to a degree of protec-

[86] See *Etablissements Consten & Grundig v. E.C. Commission*: [1966] E.C.R. 299, [1966] C.M.L.R. 418; *Sirena Srl v. Eda Srl*: [1971] E.C.R. 69, [1975] C.M.L.R. 1; also see in relation to Art. 30–36, *Deutsche Grammophon v. Metro-Grossmarkte*: [1971] E.C.R. 487, [1971] 1 C.M.L.R. 631; *Centrafarm v. Sterling Drug*; *Centrafarm v. Winthrop*: [1974] E.C.R. 1183, [1974] 2 C.M.L.R. 480.

[87] See para. 8.066.

[88] Case 161/84, [1986] E.C.R. 353, [1986] 1 C.M.L.R. 414.

[89] Cases 56 & 58/64, *Consten and Grundig v. E.C. Commission* [1966] E.C.R. 299.

tion against the competition on the part of the franchisor and other franchisees, that his business would be profitable. That consideration, however, is relevant only to an examination of the agreement in the light of the conditions of Article 85(3)."[90]

Thus, where there appear to be provisions in an agreement which might hinder the achievement of a common market and result in the division of markets, then the rule of reason doctrine is relegated to Article 85(3).

(d) Article 85(2)—effect of finding that agreement falls within Article 85(1)

8.076 If an agreement or decision falls within Article 85(1), it is automatically void. It is a matter of national law what the effect of a finding that a clause is invalid has on the validity of the whole agreement. Generally, only those elements of an agreement which are prohibited by Article 85(1) are annulled unless they are inseparable from the agreement as a whole.[91] The effect of Article 85(2) on an agreement is examined in more detail elsewhere.[92]

(e) Article 85(3) and exemption

8.077 Article 85(1) may be declared inapplicable by virtue of Article 85(3). Exemption for a restrictive practice which infringes Article 85(1) can either be obtained by the licence falling within a block exemption or the Commission granting exemption upon notification of a particular agreement.

(i) Individual exemption

Introduction

8.078 Only the Commission can, subject to the review of the Court of Justice, grant exemption under Article 85(3).[93] In order for a restrictive practice which does not fall within a block exemption to be exempted, it must be notified to the Commission unless it falls within certain categories.[94] This section concerns itself with the substantive requirements of Article 85(3). The procedural requirements of obtaining exemption and its effect are discussed elsewhere.[95]

There are four limbs to Article 85(3) which must be satisfied. These are that the agreement, decision or concerted practice:

[90] Paras. 23–24.

[91] *Technique Minière v. Maschinenbau Ulm*: [1966] E.C.R. 235, [1966] C.M.L.R. 357; Case 319/82, *Societé de Vente de Ciments et Bentons de l'Est v. Kerpen and Kerpen* [1983] E.C.R. 4173, [1985] 1 C.M.L.R. 511 and in English law, *Chemidus Wavin Ltd v. TERI*: [1976] 2 C.M.L.R. 387, H.C., [1978] 3 C.M.L.R. 514, C.A.

[92] See Chap. 12 on Enforcement of EEA Competition Law, para. 12.080.

[93] Reg. 17/62, Art. 9(1).

[94] Reg. 17/62, Art. 4. These categories are discussed in the Chap. 12 on Enforcement of EEA Competition Law, para. 12.013.

[95] See Chap. 12.

"(i) contributes to improving the production or distribution of goods or to promoting technical or economic progress;
(ii) while allowing consumers a fair share of the resulting benefit; and
(iii) does not impose on the undertakings concerned restrictions which are not indispensable to the attainment of these objectives;
(iv) nor afford such undertakings the possibility of eliminating competition in respect of a substantial part of the products in question."

These conditions are cumulative and must all be satisfied. As mentioned already, in applying the above criteria, the Commission has tended to exempt agreements which are "procompetitive" under Article 85(3) rather than clearing them under Article 85(1). Thus, it will often conduct extensive market analysis of the relevant market which the agreement affects in order to determine whether there is a general increase in competition. In fact, the Commission has justified the exemption of a franchise agreement on the express ground (*inter alia*) that it increases inter-brand competition.[96]

The burden of proof lies on the party seeking exemption.[97] As the Commission has stated in the context of economic progress:

> "The fundamental principle in this respect, established at the time the Common Market was formed, lays down that fair and undistorted competition is the best guarantee of regular supply on the best terms. Thus the question or a contribution to economic progress within the meaning of Article 85(3) can only arise in those exceptional cases where the free play of competition is unable to produce the best result economically speaking."[98]

Similarly, the Court has said in the context of whether an exclusive distribution agreement contributed to an improvement in the distribution of goods that "the improvement should in particular present noticeable objective advantages to compensate for the inconveniences resulting therefrom on the level of competition".[99]

Thus, a party seeking exemption whose licence does not fall within a block exemption must prepare a full and extensive analysis so as to justify exemption.

8.079 Generally, the issue of exemption will be resolved in the light of the economic circumstances of the agreement in question. Clauses in the licence which are essential to ensure that licensees obtain a sufficient

[96] See *Re the Franchise Agreements of Yves Rocher*: [1988] 4 C.M.L.R. 592.
[97] See *Etablissements Consten & Grundig v. E.C. Commission*: [1966] E.C.R. 299, [1966] C.M.L.R. 418; *Remia v. E.C. Commission*: [1985] E.C.R. 2547, [1987] 1 C.M.L.R. 1.
[98] *Re Bayer & Gist-Brocades*: [1976] 1 C.M.L.R. D98 at para. 57.
[99] *Etablissements Consten & Grundig v. E.C. Commission*: [1966] C.M.L.R. 19 at p. 294.

return on their investments so as to make the licence worthwhile will usually be exempted if it is clear that the licensor does not have the economic power to exploit his rights himself. The Commission views the agreement as a whole in deciding whether to exempt it. Thus, particular obligations may be exempted in one agreement and not in another. However, the Commission has developed in relation to specific clauses in licences a consistent policy of non-exemption.[1] Also, the Commission will only exempt an agreement *in toto*. Thus if certain clauses which fall within Article 85(1) are capable of exemption but others are not, then the Commission will refuse to exempt the agreement.[2]

Improving the production or distribution of goods

8.080 This is generally self-explanatory. Thus, the Commission, in the case of a franchise licence which fell within Article 85(1), granted exemption as the franchise agreements contributed to improving the distribution of goods, since they helped the producer to penetrate new markets by enabling him to expand his network without having to undertake any investment in the fitting out of new shops.[3] A producer who seeks to expand his production and rationalise his distributive network by means of granting production and sales licences will be favourably treated by the Commission. Thus, if such licences have clauses which infringe Article 85(1), then if the clauses are necessary so as to provide a sufficient return for a licensee and thus make the licence worthwhile, then the Commission will grant exemption.[4]

Technical or economic progress

8.081 These two criteria overlap. In the context of exclusive patent/know-how licences between an American licensor and European licensees, the Commission in granting exemption held that such licences contribute to promoting economic progress by permitting the exploitation of a manufacturing process previously unworked in the Community.[5] The Commission held that a licence which fostered the cross-flow of technical knowledge and encouraged joint improvements of licensed techniques

[1] See Specific Clauses, para. 8.087 *et seq.*

[2] *e.g.* see *AOIP v. Beyrard*: [1976] 1 C.M.L.R. D14. The Court has impliedly upheld this approach—see *L.C. Nungesser KG & Eisele v. E.C. Commission*: [1983] 1 C.M.L.R. 278 at para 78. However, the Commission will usually give the concerned undertaking the opportunity to remove those clauses incapable of exemption before its final decision—*e.g.* see *Re the Agreements of Davide Campari-Milano SpA*: [1978] 2 C.M.L.R. 397.

[3] *Re the Franchise Agreements of Yves Rocher*: [1988] 4 C.M.L.R. 592 at para. 58.

[4] *Re the Agreements of Davide Campari-Milano SpA*: [1978] 2 C.M.L.R. 397 (trade mark licence).

[5] *Re the Agreements of Davidson Rubber Company*: [1972] C.M.L.R. D52.

contributed to promoting technical progress.[6] Thus, any licence which permits the exploitation of a technical process in new territories will tend to be exempted even if such a process is not new and is worked in other countries.[7]

Consumers have a fair share of the resulting benefit

8.082 If the above categories are satisfied, it seems that the Commission will be ready to infer that this requirement is fulfilled. In a licensing context, consumers mean anyone (not just end-users) who might use products manufactured under the licence. Thus, in the case of a licence for the matching of parts made by the cold-extrusion process, electrical-equipment and motor-vehicle manufacturers were held to be consumers.[8]

This provision means that parties to a licence cannot argue that it provides advantages to both licensor and licensee but must justify the licence on objective grounds.[9] In the case of new technologies, the Commission will deem that the consumer has benefitted by having access to such technology.[10] The Commission has indicated in the context of patent licences that consumers will generally experience a fair share of the benefit by an improvement in the supply of goods.[11]

Indispensable restrictions

8.083 For an agreement to fall within Article 85(3), only restrictions which are necessary to ensure that the parties enter into the agreement will be allowed. Thus, an "open" exclusive licence has been exempted where it acts as an incentive for would-be licensees.[12] This requirement is important when the Commission decides the period of exemption.[13] Generally, the greater the investment or the longer the delay in returns, the longer the period of exemption will be. A licensor will find it difficult to justify a

[6] *Re Kabelmetal's Agreement*: [1975] O.J. L222/34, [1975] 2 C.M.L.R. D40.

[7] *e.g.* see *Re the Agreements between Jus-Rol Ltd. and Rich Products Corp.* [1988] O.J. L69/21, [1988] 4 C.M.L.R. 527; *Re the Agreement between Boussois SA and Interpane mbH*: [1987] O.J. L50/30, [1988] 4 C.M.L.R. 124.

[8] *Re Kabelmetal's Agreement*: [1975] O.J. L222/34, [1975] 2 C.M.L.R. D40. See also *Re The Agreements of Davidson Rubber Company*: [1972] O.J. L143/31, [1972] C.M.L.R. D52; *GEC/Weir*: [1977] O.J. L327/26, [1978] 1 C.M.L.R. D42; *Rockwell/Iveco*: [1983] O.J. L224/19, [1983] 3 C.M.L.R. 709.

[9] See *Etablissements Consten & Grundig v. E.C. Commission*: [1966] C.M.L.R. 19.

[10] *Re The Agreements of Davidson Rubber Company*: [1972] O.J. L143/31, [1972] C.M.L.R. D52; *Re Kabelmetal's Agreement*: [1975] O.J. L222/34, [1975] 2 C.M.L.R. D40.

[11] See Patent Block Exemption (Reg. 2349/84).

[12] *e.g.* see *Re The Agreements of Davidson Rubber Company*: [1972] O.J. L143/31, [1972] C.M.L.R. D52; *Re Kabelmetal's Agreement*: [1975] O.J. L222/34, [1975] 2 C.M.L.R. D40; *Re The Agreements of Davide Campari-Milano SpA* [1978] 2 C.M.L.R. 397; *Re the Agreement between DDD Ltd and Delta Chemie*: [1988] O.J. L309/34, [1989] 4 C.M.L.R. 535.

[13] See Reg. 17, Art. 8.

particular restriction as indispensable if he has concluded other licences with other licensees which do not contain such a restriction.[14]

Elimination of competition in substantial part of goods in question

8.084 Despite its wording, it is clear that the Court and the Commission interpret competition here to mean both intra-brand and inter-brand competition.[15] This requirement will often be important in the area of new technology where inter-brand competition is minimal. However, the Commission has readily inferred that inter-brand competition exists even with regard to new technologies. Furthermore, the Commission has been prepared to exempt an agreement if it does eliminate competition in a substantial part of the goods provided that the participating undertakings will become competitors at the end of the agreement.[16]

This section sometimes involves analysis of the relevant product and geographical market.[17] Where it is difficult to isolate the Community market from the world market for a particular product, the Commission will take the relevant geographical market as being the world.[18]

(ii) Block exemptions

8.085 In the 1960s, after the enactment of Regulation 17, the Commission received a flood of notifications of agreements. Many of these agreements related to intellectual property, especially patents and contained similar clauses. It became apparent to the Commission that it was desirable to declare by way of regulation that certain categories of these agreements were exempted without the need for individual notification. To this end, the Council has passed two empowering regulations that allow the Commission to issue "block exemptions" to certain categories of agreements. Regulation 19/65[19] empowers the Commission to issue block exemptions in relation to exclusive dealing agreements and to restrictions imposed in industrial property licences. Regulations 2821/71[20] similarly empowers the Commission to issue block exemptions in relation to whole categories of agreements relating to the research and development of products and exploitation of the results thereof and specialisation. Such block exemptions must state what types of restrictive clauses are unexemptable ("black-listed") and those which are exemptible ("white-listed") and must be for a finite period.

The Commission has since issued block exemptions for exclusive dis-

[14] *Re Agreements on Video Cassette Recorders*: [1978] 2 C.M.L.R. 160.
[15] *e.g.* see *Re Kabelmetal's Agreement* [1975] O.J. L222/34, [1975] 2 C.M.L.R. D40; *Re the Agreement beween Boussois SA and Interpane mbH* [1987] O.J. L50/30, [1988] 4 C.M.L.R. 124.
[16] See *Re United Reprocessors GmbH*: [1976] O.J. L51/7, [1976] 2 C.M.L.R. D1.
[17] This is discussed in detail in relation to Art. 86—see para. 11.006 *et seq.*
[18] *e.g. Re Bayer & Gist-Brocades*: [1976] 1 C.M.L.R. D98.
[19] O.J. [1965–66] p. 35.
[20] O.J. L285/46 as modified by Reg. 2743/72, O.J. L291/144.

tribution,[21] exclusive purchasing,[22] patent licences,[23] motor vehicle distribution and servicing,[24] specialisation,[25] research and development agreements,[26] franchise licences,[27] know-how licences[28] and mergers.[29] These block exemptions have played an invaluable role for businesses who have neither the time nor resources to individually notify agreements yet need to know that their agreements are valid. Furthermore, the Commission, which is usually over-worked, no longer has to devote its time and resources to dealing with a large number of agreements with similar clauses. The dramatic effect of such block exemptions were demonstrated in relation to patent licences. In 1979, 63 per cent of agreements notified were patent licences.[30] After the introduction of the patent licence block exemption in 1984, this dropped to a dozen.[31]

8.086 Generally, in order for a licence to come within a block exemption, it must come within the subject matter of the block exemption and contain only "white-listed" clauses. A mixture of black-listed and white-listed clauses will prevent the agreement *in toto* from being exempted. If an agreement contains clauses not specifically white or black-listed, many of the block exemptions provide that the agreement will be covered by the block exemption provided that the agreement is notified to the Commission and it does not oppose exemption within a period of six months.

This book examines in detail the patent licence, know-how, franchise and research and development block exemptions. All these are relevant to the intellectual property practitioner.

(f) Specific types of intellectual property licence

8.087 Intellectual property licences will often have similar clauses, *i.e.* exclusivity, export bans, no-challenge, quality control, etc., that are common to all. In considering specific clauses in the next section, these are considered generally unless a distinction needs to be or has been made by the Court or Commission in relation to differing types of intellectual property. In this section, the Court and Commission's approach to licences of differing intellectual property is discussed.

[21] Reg. 1983/83, [1983] O.J. L173/1. Expires on December 31, 1997.
[22] Reg. 1984/83, [1983] O.J. L173/5. Expires on December 31, 1997.
[23] Reg. 2349/84, July 24, 1984. Expires on December 31, 1994. This has recently been extended firstly to June 30, 1995 and secondly to December 31, 1995 because of the delay in implementing the Technology Transfer Block Exemption.
[24] Reg. 123/85, [1985] O.J. L15/16. Expires on June 30, 1995.
[25] Reg. 417/85, [1985] O.J. L53/1. Expires on December 31, 1997.
[26] Reg. 418/85, December 19, 1984 O.J. Expires on December 31, 1997.
[27] Reg. 4087/88, November 30, 1988. Expires on December 31, 1999.
[28] Reg. 556/89, November 30, 1988. Expires on December 31, 1999. It is intended that the draft Technology Transfer Block Exemption will replace this regulation.
[29] Reg. 4064/89, [1989] O.J. L395/1.
[30] 9th Report on Competition Policy, paras. 20 to 27.
[31] See Introduction to 15th Report on Competition Policy.

(i) Patents

8.088 A patent licence is a technological licence. Usually, a patent licence ensures that the invention is commercially exploited. Once the patent has expired, the licensor and licensees usually will have a lead-time over third parties who have yet to begin manufacturing and learn the necessary know-how for an efficient and economic operation. Patent licences will often involve ancillary know-how for better production in the licensed technology. Furthermore, as patents are granted for inventions, the technology will often be state-of-the-art and advanced in its field of application. This maybe important in the question as to whether an exclusive licence falls within Article 85(1).

The Commission and the Court have principally been concerned with patent licences. However, in their judgments, they have not sought to differentiate patent licences from other intellectual property licences but have restricted their analysis to particular clauses in patent licences. The Commission and Court have used the concept of the specific subject matter of a patent in the context of patent licences.[32] In 1984, the Commission issued a block exemption for Patent Licences. This is discussed below.[33]

(ii) Know-how

8.089 Know-how licences, like patent licences, are often technological licences. However, know-how licences can exist in other areas like business, financial and marketing. They differ from other intellectual property licences in one key aspect. This is that the monopoly that a know-how owner has is a *de facto* monopoly and not one granted by the law. Thus, licensing know-how is a potentially hazardous venture as it may result in the know-how entering the public domain. Parties to know-how licences will only have contractual remedies against each other rather than the ability to enforce a statutory right. Thus, a licensor may be able to sue a licensee who releases the information into the public domain for damages for disclosure, but cannot bring a cause of action against third parties unless such are under a duty of confidence to the licensor.[34] The Commission and the Court have treated know-how licences as fundamentally similar to patent licences. In 1989, the Commission issued a Know-How Block Exemption. This is discussed below.[35]

[32] See above, para. 8.060.

[33] See para. 8.170. This is shortly to be replaced by the draft Technology Transfer Block Exemption.

[34] Under English law, a plaintiff may sue third parties who receive confidential information knowing that it is confidential—see *Carl Zeiss Stiftung v. Herbert Smith*: [1969] 2 All E.R. 367.

[35] See para. 8.209. This is shortly to be replaced by the draft Technology Transfer Block Exemption.

(iii) Trade mark

8.090 Trade marks differ in certain key respects from patent and know-how licences. Firstly, the latter licences are usually technological in nature. A trade mark licence merely permits a licensee to use the mark in the course of trade. Thus, it does not relate to manufacture (although there will often be ancillary trade mark licences in patent and know-how licences). Secondly a trade mark serves two purposes. Firstly, it grants the exclusive right to its owner to first market the trade marked goods. This is similar to patent and know-how licences. However, it is also an indication of origin so as to prevent confusion in the public. This role is not mirrored in other intellectual property licences.

Historically, the ECJ has considered trade mark rights as being less "worthy" than other forms of intellectual property.[36] This view has changed and the ECJ now appears to recognise the worth of trade marks and their importance from a competition viewpoint.[37] A pure trade mark licence whereby a licensee is permitted to use the trade mark of the licensor is rare. In brief, there are three types of trade mark licences—manufacturing licences whereby the licensee is permitted to apply the licensor's mark; distribution and sales licences whereby the licensee is permitted to sell goods under a mark and franchise licences whereby the licensee is permitted to trade under a trade mark.

8.091 *Manufacturing trade mark licences*—Often, a know-how or patent licence or mixed patent/know-how licence will have ancillary provisions relating to trade marks. These ancillary licences will fall within the Patent and Know-How Block Exemption and are discussed below.[38] However, where a trade mark was of crucial importance to the parties, the Commission held that a mixed know-how/trade mark licence fell outside the Know-How Block Exemption.[39]

8.092 *Distribution/sales trade mark licences*—Trade mark licences will often be merely distribution/sales licences. In such circumstances, they may fall within Regulation 1983/83—the block exemption on exclusive distribution agreements.[40] This exempts exclusive distributorship agreements even though there is an obligation to sell the contract goods under trade marks.[41] However, the benefit of the exclusive distribution block

[36] See Chap. 7, on Enforcement of Intellectual Property, para. 7.049.
[37] *e.g.* see *SA CNL-Sucal NV v. Hag GF AG ("Hag 2")*: [1990] 3 C.M.L.R. 571 at 583 where Advocate-General Jacobs said that trade marks are "nothing more nor less than the fundament of competition".
[38] See para. 8.170 and 8.209.
[39] *Moosehead/Whitbread*: [1990] O.J. L100/32, [1991] 4 C.M.L.R. 391.
[40] Reg. 1983/83: [1983] O.J. L173/1 and [1983] O.J. L281/24–25.
[41] Art. 2(3)(b).

exemption is removed if it contains any restrictions on competition other than the following:

(a) An obligation not to manufacture or distribute goods which compete with the contract goods;
(b) An obligation not to obtain the contract goods for resale only from the other party;
(c) An obligation to refrain, outside the contract territory and in relation to the contract goods, from seeking customers, from establishing any branch and from maintaining any distribution depot.[42]

Thus, most trade mark licences will not fall within Regulation 1983/83 and must be notified individually for exemption if there are obligations that fall within Article 85(1).

8.093 *Franchise licences*—Franchise agreements generally involve the transfer of know-how and the licensing of a business name. The latter will involve a registered or non-registered trade mark licence. This particular type of trade mark licence is discussed in Chapter Ten on Franchises.[43]

(iv) Copyright and industrial design

8.094 Copyright and industrial design right are similar to patents in that both give the owner the exclusive right to exploit the right. There have been few cases on copyright and design licences but the principles developed by the Court and Commission for patent licences will be generally relevant to copyright licences.

Copyright differs in one aspect to other types of intellectual property in that it can exist as a performance copyright as well as a reproductive right. This difference is discussed in full in relation to Articles 30–36.[44] Performance copyright relates to the exclusive right of an author to prevent broadcasts, performances, exhibition and other communications to the public of his work. It differs from the reproduction right because the performance right is capable of separation from goods embodying the work and its marketing is a matter of the provision of services rather than the supply of goods. With regard to performance copyright licences, *i.e.* a broadcasting licence for a film, the right of a film copyright owner to require fees for any showing of the film is part of the essential function of copyright.[45]

[42] Reg. 83/83, Art. 2.
[43] See Chap. 10.
[44] See Chap. 7, para. 7.086.
[45] *Coditel v. Cine Vog Films (No. 2)*: [1982] E.C.R. 3381, [1983] 1 C.M.L.R. 49 at 65.

(v) Plant breeder's rights

8.095 Plant varieties are protected in most industrialised countries by appropriate *sui generis* legislation.[46] The general requirement is that the plant variety must be new, distinct, uniform and stable.[47] The holder of a plant breeder's right has the exclusive right to sell or offer or expose for sale the "reproductive material" for his plant variety and to produce such reproductive material for the purpose of selling it.[48]

A distinction must be made between basic seeds and seeds intended to be sold for the use in production of plants (usually cereals). Basic seed must be propagated for about eight years under very stringent conditions before it finds its definitive form and thus becomes certified seed which can be marketed. It is produced under the responsibility of the breeder according to accepted practices for the maintenance of a variety and is intended for the production of certified seeds (*i.e.* for direct or indirect sale to farmers for sowing.[49] Certified seed is of direct descent from basic seed and is generally intended for purposes other than the production of seeds. Certified seeds must exhibit characteristics of uniformity, distinctness and stability in order to be entitled to protection under plant breeders' rights.

8.096 *Certified seeds*—The European Court of Justice and Commission have dealt with the problem of plant breeder's rights licences in several cases. In *Nungesser v. E.C. Commission*,[50] a landmark case on the compatibility of exclusive licences with Article 85, the Court of Justice was concerned with a licence granting exclusive propagating and selling rights over certain varieties of protected hybrid maize seeds. These were certified seeds and not basic seeds. However, being hybrid seeds, their stability could only be guaranteed if the seeds were cultivated every time from basic lines.

The Court held that whereas the development of basic seeds may involve considerable financial sacrifice, that risk is encountered at the time of the production of the basic seeds but not when the newly-developed variety has found its definitive form, in the sense that it may be used for the production of seeds capable of being certified and marketed. In the latter case, competition law must in principle be applied to their marketing.[51] It therefore concluded that whilst certified seeds are subject to quality controls relating to maintenance of the stability of the variety, such meant that "the legal position of a breeder of seeds is not different from that of the owner of patent or trade mark rights over a product sub-

[46] See Chap. 6 on Plant Variety Rights in Europe.
[47] See para. 6.004.
[48] *e.g.* in U.K., see Plant Varieties and Seeds Act 1964, s. 4(1).
[49] See *Re Comasso*: [1990] 4 C.M.L.R. 259, [1990] O.J. C6/3 at paras. 12 and 13 where the Commission sets out its definition of basic and certified seed.
[50] Case 258/78, [1982] E.C.R. 2015, [1983] 1 C.M.L.R. 278.
[51] *ibid*, para. 33.

ject to strict control by the public authorities, as is the case with pharmaceutical products".[52]

Thus, it concluded that breeders' rights are not so special as to require a differing treatment in relation to competition rules as other rights.[53]

8.097 *Basic seeds*—Whilst *Nungesser*[54] was concerned with certified seeds, *Louis Erauw-Jacquery v. La Hesbignonne*[55] was a licence concerned with the propagation of basic seeds. Under the licence, the propagator was prohibited from selling E2 basic seeds to anyone other than the farmer propagating them.

Advocate-General Mischo held that "basic seeds" are comparable to a manufacturing process protected by a patent as it is merely the vehicle for producing what are called first and second generation seeds which are intended to be marketed.[56] He went on to say that:

> "The situation of the breeder or his agent therefore in some respect resembles that of a franchisor, of whom the Court has said that 'he must be able to communicate his know-how to the franchisees and provide them with the necessary assistance in putting his methods into effect, without running the risk that this know-how and assistance will aid his competitors, even directly. It thus follows that those clauses which are essential to prevent this risk do not constitute restrictions of competition in the sense of Article 85(1) (Pronuptia)'."

The Court placed a different emphasis and said:

> "On this point it should be emphasised that, as the Court found in Case 258/78, *Nungesser*, the development of basic lines may involve considerable financial sacrifices. Consequently, it should be accepted that anyone who makes considerable investments in developing basic seed varieties, which may be the subject of plant breeder's rights must be able to obtain protection against improper handling of those seed varieties. For this purpose the breeder must have the right to reserve propagation for the propagating establishments chosen by him as licensees. To that extent, the clause prohibiting the licensee from selling the exporting basic seeds does not come within the prohibition laid down by Article 85(1) of the Treaty."[57]

[52] *ibid*, para. 41.
[53] *ibid*, para. 43.
[54] *ibid*.
[55] Case 27/87, [1988] 4 C.M.L.R. 576.
[56] See Opinion of Mischo A.G. in Case 27/87. *Louis Erauw-Jacquery v. La Hesbignonne* [1988] 4 C.M.L.R. 576.
[57] Case 27/87, *Louis Erauw-Jacquery v. La Hesbignonne*: [1988] 4 C.M.L.R. 576, para. 10.

(g) Specific clauses in intellectual property licences

8.098 The Commission and Court's approach to specific clauses in intellectual property licences is now discussed. Many clauses are common to all type of intellectual property licences and are governed by the same principles. Other obligations (*e.g.* an obligation in a know-how licence not to disclose the know-how) are peculiar to certain categories and are discussed separately.

(i) Exclusivity

8.099 A pure exclusive licence merely imposes an obligation on the licensor not to exploit the right himself in a designated territory and not to license others in that territory. In certain circumstances, an exclusive licence without more may be practically indistinguishable from an assignment of the right. Thus, where the term of the licence is the same as that of the right, no practical distinction can be made.[58] Certainly, the grant of an exclusive licence will often not be anti-competitive as a rights owner is not obliged to license his rights and accordingly, should not be obliged to license more than one person. To deem such an exclusive licence as anti-competitive is to attack the nature of intellectual property rights themselves. In the United States, the grant of exclusivity will generally only raise concerns if the licensees themselves, or the licensor and its licensees are actual or potential competitors in a relevant technology market or goods market in the absence of the licensing arrangement.[59] Often exclusivity is a prerequisite from the potential licensee's viewpoint because it provides protection from other licensees and thus encourages a licensee to penetrate and consolidate a market in a particular territory.

A simple exclusive licence is called an "open" exclusive licence. Often, an exclusive licence will seek to provide more territorial protection from other licensees and parallel imports. These exclusive licences may contain export bans, direct sales bans and protection against parallel imports. Such licences are described as "closed" exclusive licences[60] because they seek to prevent trade between territories of licensees and licensor. Some exclusive licences will be more "closed" than others.

From a Community viewpoint, where the patentee has many parallel patents in different countries, exclusive licences in each country may contribute to greater market partitioning then if the patentee merely exploited the patent himself. This is particularly the case where the exclu-

[58] See Advocate-General's Opinion in *Coditel v. Cine Vog Films (No. 2)* ("CODITEL II"): [1982] E.C.R. 3381, [1983] 1 C.M.L.R. 49 where he rejected a submission from the U.K. government that no distinction can be drawn between an assignment and an exclusive licence and that such a distinction depended on whether the licence was shorter than the right and who bore the risk of exploitation.

[59] Para 4.1.2, *US Antitrust Guidelines for Intellectual Property*, issued by the Department of Justice, April 6, 1995.

[60] These terms were first used in Case 258/78, *L.C. Nungesser KG & Eisele v. E.C. Commission*: [1983] 1 C.M.L.R. 278.

sive licence is "closed". In this section, exclusive licences are generally discussed and then exclusive licences containing export bans, direct sales bans and protection against parallel imports are considered.

European Court

8.100 In *Nungesser v. E.C. Commission*,[61] *Ciné Vog v. CODITEL (No. 2)*[62] and *Pronuptia*,[63] the Court examined the effect of "open" and "closed" exclusive licences on competition. The facts of these cases have already been discussed.[64] These decisions followed a series of decisions by the Commission on exclusive licences that such fell within Article 85(1).

A "closed" exclusive licence will rarely be permitted under Article 85(1) or be exemptible under Article 85(3). Since *Consten & Grundig v. E.C. Commission*,[65] the Court has ruled that "closed" exclusive licences which give absolute territorial protection are contrary to the Treaty.[66] However, the circumstances of the case may mean that absolute territorial protection arises merely by the grant of an exclusive licence. Such was the case in *Ciné Vog (No. 2)*[67] where the grant of an exclusive broadcasting right amounted to de facto absolute territorial protection. Recently, in *Louis Erauw-Jacquery v. La Hesbignonne*,[68] the Court was concerned with a licence for the propagation and sale of certain varieties of cereal seeds protected by plant breeder's rights in Belgium. The licence contained a clause prohibiting the sale or transfer of the basic seeds to anyone other than the farmer propagating them and a ban on exporting them to any country. There were many such agreements. The Court considered the special characteristics of basic seed varieties and held that the breeder must have the right to reserve propagation for the propagating establishments chosen by him as licensees. Such was necessary to prevent improper handling of seed varieties which were the result of considerable investment.[69]

8.101 In *Nungesser*, the Court, reversing the Commission's decision in part, held that in the context of plant breeder's rights and a new product, an "open" exclusive licence might be necessary so as not to deter an undertaking from accepting the risk of cultivating and marketing the product

[61] Case 258/78, *L.C. Nungesser KG & Eisele v. E.C. Commission*: [1983] 1 C.M.L.R. 278.
[62] [1982] E.C.R. 3381; [1983] 1 C.M.L.R. 49.
[63] Case 161/84 *Pronuptia v. Schillgalis* [1986] E.C.R. 353, [1986] 1 C.M.L.R. 414.
[64] See above, paras. 8.066 to 8.075.
[65] [1966] E.C.R. 299, [1966] C.M.L.R. 418.
[66] *e.g.* see *Tepea v. Commission*: [1978] E.C.R. 1391, [1978] 3 C.M.L.R. 392 and Case 258/78, *L.C. Nungesser KG & Eisele v. E.C. Commission*: [1983] 1 C.M.L.R. 278.
[67] [1982] E.C.R. 3381, [1983] 1 C.M.L.R. 49.
[68] Case 27/87, [1988] 4 C.M.L.R. 576.
[69] Advocate-General Mischo also considered a clause preventing indirect exports of seeds of any variety which Erauw-Jacquery was the agent or breeder as prohibited under Art. 85(1) as helping to maintain absolute territorial protection. The Court did not consider this clause as the national court had not asked under Art. 177 for a ruling on its validity.

and would thus fall outside Article 85(1).[70] In *Ciné Vog Films (No. 2)*, a case which concerned the grant of an exclusive exhibition right, the Court adopted a "rule of reason" approach to such exclusive licences. It held that such a licence is not in itself likely to infringe Article 85(1). The Court stated that it had to consider whether exercise of the exclusive right would lead to artificial and unjustified barriers with regards to the requirements of the film industry, the possibility of excessive royalties and whether the geographical scope and duration of the exclusive right was excessive and thus likely to prevent, restrict or distort competition.[71] It is clear that the Court had in mind the fact that distributors were required to make considerable advance investment in financing films, dubbing them and marketing them.[72] In the later case of *Pronuptia*, a case concerned with retail franchises providing a combination of wedding goods and services, the Court appeared to resile from an entirely "rule of reason" approach and held that the combination of the grant of an "open" exclusive licence and the obligation on a franchisee only to trade from the premises stipulated in the contract would result in artificial partitioning of the Common Market and could thus only be exempted under Article 85(3) even if such protection was required to entice undertakings to enter into the franchise.[73]

Thus the European Court will apply a "rule of reason" approach in considering the competitive effect of an "open" exclusive licence but will balance such an approach against a need to ensure that the markets of the Community are not artificially partitioned. In relation to "closed" exclusive licences, the artificial partitioning effect on the Community means that such licences are incompatible with Article 85(1).

Commission

8.102 Historically, the Commission has taken an illiberal view of the compatibility of exclusive licences with Article 85(1). In the 1962 Notice on Patent Licensing Agreement (now annulled), the Commission stated that the undertaking by a licensor not a license other applicants for the same territory was outside Article 85(1) as "leaving out of account the controversial question whether such exclusive undertakings have the object or effect of restricting competition, they are not likely to affect trade between Member States as things stand in the Community at present [*i.e.* 1962]". This tolerant approach soon disappeared. In the 1970s, the Commission consistently ruled that exclusive licences of any type fell within Article 85(1) as they restricted the licensor's freedom to compete

[70] Case 258/78, [1982] E.C.R. 2015, [1983] 1 C.M.L.R. 278, paras. 57–58. The Court held that plant breeder's rights were not conceptually different to other rights.
[71] Case 262/81, [1982] E.C.R. 3361, [1983] 1 C.M.L.R. 49, paras. 18–19.
[72] See Advocate-General Reischl's remarks at p. 62.
[73] See above for detailed discussion of this case, para. 8.074 and Chap. 10 at para. 10.007.

and to grant licences to other competitors in the relevant territory.[74] Similarly, clauses which have the effect of granting an exclusive licence were held to infringe Article 85(1). Thus an obligation on a patentee/licensor not to exploit its rights in a Member State where the licensee was active constituted an infringement of Article 85(1).[75]

After the decisions of the Court in *Nungesser*[76] and *CODITEL II*[77] in the early 1980s, it might have been hoped that the Commission would have followed the Court's "rule of reason" approach. At that time, the Commission had been preparing a block exemption for patent licences.[78] It delayed issuing the block exemption in order to await the outcome of the Court's decision in *Nungesser*. When it was finally issued, it stated that:

> "Exclusive licensing agreement, *i.e.* agreements in which the licensor undertakes not to exploit the 'licensed' invention, *i.e.* the licensed patented invention and any know-how communicated to the licensee, in the licensed territory himself or to grant further licences there, are not in themselves incompatible with Article 85(1) where they are concerned with the introduction and protection of a new technology in the licensed territory, by reason of the scale of research which has been undertaken and of the risk that is involved in manufacturing and marketing a product which is unfamiliar to users in the licensed territory at the time the agreement is made. This may be the case where the agreements are concerned with the introduction and protection of a new process for manufacturing a product which is already known."[79]

It is noticeable that the Commission instead of adopting the general "rule of reason" approach intimated at by the Court to exclusive patent licences, strictly construed the Court's particular justification for an "open" exclusive licence as applying only to new technology similar to the facts in *Nungesser*.[80] Similarly, in relation to non-technological licences, the Commission has not adopted a general "rule of reason" approach but instead adopted a strict approach unless restrained by authority.

[74] Patent/Know-How: *Re The Agreements of Burroughs AG & Delplanque*: [1972] C.M.L.R.; *Re The Agreement of Burroughs and Geha-Werke GmbH*: [1972] C.M.L.R. D73; *Re the Agreement of the Davidson Rubber Company*: [1972] C.M.L.R.; *Re the Agreement of A. Raymond & Company*: [1973] C.M.L.R.; *Bronbemaling v. Heidemaatschappij*: [1975] C.M.L.R. D67; *Re Kabel's Agreement*: [1975] C.M.L.R. D40; *AOIP v. Beyrard*: [1976] C.M.L.R. D141; *Re the Peugeot-Zimmern Agreement*: [1977] C.M.L.R. D22; Trade marks: *Re the Agreement of Davide Campari-Milano Spa*: [1978] 2 C.M.L.R. 397.

[75] *Re the Complaint by Yoshida Kogyo KK*: Commission Press Release, June 9, 1978; [1978] 3 C.M.L.R. 44.

[76] Case 258/78 [1982] E.C.R. 2105, [1883] 1 C.M.L.R. 278.

[77] Case 262/81 [1982] E.C.R. 3361, [1983] 1 C.M.L.R. 49.

[78] Reg. 2349/84 of July 23, 1984. See para. 8.170.

[79] Patent Block Exemption, Recital 11.

[80] Case 258/78 [1982] E.C.R. 2015, [1983] 1 C.M.L.R. 278.

8.103 Early proof that the Commission was to take a restrictive interpretation of *Nungesser*[81] and *Coditel (No. 2)*[82] came with its decision in *Velcro/Aplix*.[83] Velcro was a Swiss company that had been founded by a Mr Mestral who had invented the "Velcro" fastener. Velcro granted Aplix an exclusive manufacturing and exploitation rights in the patents in France. In 1977, the basic patents expired although the certain improvement patents were still in force. Under the licence, *inter alia*, Aplix was obliged to sell all products derived from the patent under the mark "Velcro". The Commission held that the exclusive licence was contrary to Article 85(1) in as far it related to the period after the expiry of the basic patents. It held that the exclusive licences could only fall outside Article 85(1) if it concerned the introduction and protection of new technology following *Nungesser*.

More recently, the Commission has continued to resist the application of a general "rule of reason" approach to Article 85(1). It continues to favour the interpretation of Article 85(1) in terms of whether the trading freedom of parties is restricted or not.[84] However, the Commission has sporadically shown that it will conduct a detailed analysis of the effect of the agreement on market conditions.[85] Where the Commission has cleared an exclusive licence, it is because it has applied either the ruling in *Nungesser*[86] that an exclusive licence is often required to encourage the establishment of new technologies in territories or the ruling of the Court in *Ciné Vog (No. 2)*,[87] where the Court sanctioned an approach that took into account the fact that an exclusive licence was often granted to the licensee where the latter needed to make a significant investment before the product could be marketed. The application of these two criteria are examined below.

[81] *ibid.*
[82] Case 262/81 [1982] E.C.R. 3361, [1983] 1 C.M.L.R. 49.
[83] [1985] O.J. L233/22; [1989] 4 C.M.L.R. 157.
[84] For recent Commission decisions where exclusive licences were found to infringe Art. 85(1), see Knoll/Hille *13th Annual Report on Competition Policy*, p. 91, (exclusive manufacturing and distribution rights for various furniture designs); *Re the Agreement between Boussois SA v. Interpane*: [1985] 4 C.M.L.R. 124 (patent/know-how exclusive licence); *Re the Agreement between JusRol and Rich Products Corporation*: [1988] 4 C.M.L.R. 527 (exclusive know-how licence); *Re The Agreement between DDD Limited and Delta Chemie* [1989] 4 C.M.L.R. 535 (exclusive know-how licence); *Re the Agreements between BBC Brown Boveri and NGK Insulators Limited*: [1989] 4 C.M.L.R. 610 (exclusive joint research and development know-how licence); *Re German TV Films*: [1989] O.J. L284/36; [1990] 4 C.M.L.R. 841 [exclusive television rights in Germany]; *Moosehead/Whitbread*: [1990] O.J. L100/32; [1994] 4 C.M.L.R. 391 (exclusive trade mark/know-how brewing licence). In contrast, the grant of exclusive licences were cleared in Spitzer/Van Hool *12th Report on Competition Policy*, para. 86; RAI/Unitel *12th Report on Competition Policy*, (exclusive performance contracts for opera singers) where Commission took a favourable view of an exclusive licence once Unitel agreed to waive its exclusive rights for important cultural events.
[85] *e.g.* see *Re German TV Films*: [1989] O.J. 1284/36; [1990] 4 C.M.L.R. 841, discussed below, para. 8.109.
[86] Case 258/78, [1982] E.C.R. 2015, [1983] 1 C.M.L.R. 278.
[87] Case 262/81, [1982] E.C.R. 3361, [1983] 1 C.M.L.R. 49.

8.104 *"New technology"*—The Commission has taken a restrictive view of the Court's ruling in *Nungesser* that exclusive technological licences only fall outside Article 85(1) if they concern "new technology". However, in this context, what is meant by "new"? Firstly, it could mean that the technology is new because it breaks new ground. The second interpretation is that "new" refers to the novelty of the patent, plant breeder's right, know-how, etc., that gives it its validity. The second view would seem to be the correct one.[88] However, the Commission appears to favour the first view. This can be seen by the following decisions:

8.105 *Re the agreement between Jus-Rol and Rich Products Corp.*[89]—Rich Products granted Jus-Rol an exclusive know-how licence for the manufacture of frozen yeast dough products. The Commission held that as other processes existed which provided the means for freezing the yeast, the licence was not concerned with the introduction of new technology necessitating territorial protection. Thus the licence fell within Article 85(1).

8.106 *Re the agreement between Boussois and Interpane*[90]—Interpane granted an exclusive know-how/patent licence to Boussois in connection with the sale of a production plant for application of a "special and novel coating" process to glass. The Commission held that such an agreement fell within Article 85(1), baldly re-iterating that the exclusive licence restricted competition because it prevented the licensor or other potential licensees from competing with the exclusive licensee in the designated territory.

8.107 *Re the agreement between DDD Limited and Delta Chemie*[91]—Delta Chemie granted DDD an exclusive know-how licence to manufacture and sell stain-removing products in the United Kingdom. The agreement allowed DDD to import the products until, depending on the commercial success of the patent, DDD decided to manufacture the products in the UK. In fact, the licensee imported the product for a considerable period before it took the risk of manufacturing the product. The licensee only started to manufacture when sales had reached a substantial volume. The Commission held that the agreement fell within Article 85(1) as it did not concern the introduction of a new technology within the meaning of *Nungesser*.

[88] In point 57 of Case 258/78, *Nungesser*, [1983] 1 C.M.L.R. 278, the Court refers to competition "between the new product and similar existing products". Thus, it would appear that the Court is not referring to technology which is breaking new ground. Secondly, in *Nungesser*, maize seed was already well-known in Europe but the strain was new. Thus, the Court implies that it was the novelty of the maize seed *in casu* and not the newness of maize seed in Europe. See Hoffmann and O'Farrell, " '*Open Exclusive' Licence*" [1984] 7 EIPR 206, and a letter in reply to that article from Professor Korah.

[89] [1988] 4 C.M.L.R. 527.

[90] [1988] 4 C.M.L.R. 124.

[91] [1989] 4 C.M.L.R. 535.

8.108 *Re the agreement between BBC Brown Boveri and NGK Insulators Ltd*[92]—A German company and a Japanese company agreed to set up a joint venture to develop sodium-sulphur high performance batteries. The agreement provided that an exclusive licence to use technical knowledge which arose out of the joint venture would be granted to the Japanese company in Japan and far eastern countries and to the German company in respect of the E.C., USA and other countries. The Commission held that the partners had thereby reserved exploitation of their combined technical knowledge for themselves and prevented other firms having access to that knowledge. Thus the licence fell within Article 85(1). The Commission did not refer to *Nungesser*.[93]

8.109 *Significant investment*—The Commission has been reluctant to follow the Court's lead in *CODITEL II*[94] and consider whether exclusive licences that involve significant initial investment by licensees fall outside Article 85(1) as such exclusivity is required to lure potential licensees. In two cases, it has taken the issue of significant investment into consideration.[95]

In applying the criteria of "significant investment", the Commission will also consider whether the length of the exclusive licence is justified under Article 85(1). In *Re German TV Films*,[96] the Commission considered the application of *CODITEL II* an agreement whereby one of the world's leading film producers granted a group of German broadcasting organisations exclusive television rights within Germany and surrounding German-speaking areas to a selection of films from its library and all new ones produced for 15 years. The Commission held that the number of films involved in the agreement were too many and that the duration of the exclusive licence was too long. Such was disproportionate and would result in an artificial barrier to other.[97]

Medium and small sized licensors

8.110 The Commission will be more disposed to grant negative clearance for an exclusive licence if the licensor is a medium or small sized undertaking.[98] Such an approach underlies the Commission's commitment to fostering

[92] [1989] 4 C.M.L.R. 610.
[93] Case 258/78, [1983] 1 C.M.L.R. 278.
[94] Case C262/81, [1982] E.C.R. 3381, [1983] 1 C.M.L.R. 49.
[95] See Knolle/Hille, Form *13th Report on Competition Policy*, paras. 90 *et seq*., and Spitzer/Van Hool, *12th Report on Competition Policy*, para. 72.
[96] *Re German TV Films*: [1989] O.J. 1284/36; [1990] 4 C.M.L.R. 841.
[97] Para. 44. See also Knolle/Hille, *13th Report on Competition Policy*, p. 91, where the Commission had serious doubts as to whether an exclusive licence which related to furniture "programmes" covered by a mixture of patents, registered designs, trade mark and copyright was valid since neither the "newness" of the product nor the amount of investment seemed to indicate the exclusivity granted was indispensable to the launching of the product in the relevant market, at any rate not for the length of time originally envisaged (eight years).
[98] See Spitzer/Van Hool, *12th Report Competition Policy*, para. 86.

small and medium sized undertakings so as to maintain competition with large undertakings.

Assignment and exclusive licences

8.111 An assignment and exclusive licence have similar effects. Where the holder of parallel patents assigns a patent to an undertaking, this has very similar effects to granting an exclusive licence to the undertaking. Indeed such is recognised by many countries in that an exclusive licensee as well as the owner is given the right to sue infringers.[99] Can an owner avoid the effects of Article 85 by assigning rather than granting an exclusive licence?

Generally speaking, where rights are assigned as opposed to exclusively licensed, it is doubtful whether such an assignment *per se* is capable of falling within Article 85(1).[1] An assignment of intellectual property amounts to a mere substitution of owner of the right. It cannot be said to bind the assignor's hand. In *Coditel II*,[2] Advocate-General Reischl said it was certainly possible to justify the view that the specific subject matter of copyright in a film covered not only the exclusion of unauthorised outsiders from exploiting it but also, if necessary, exploitation by a *single person*, whether the owner of the right himself or an exclusive licensee.[3] However, where the rights owner has parallel rights in several states, substitution of different exclusive licensees for his own rights in differing states in effect would mean exploitation by several persons rather than one person. In such circumstances, concerns about artificial partitioning of the Community may arise. Certainly, where the assignment forms part of an agreement whose object or effect is to restrict competition, it will fall within Article 85(1). Such will be the case if it can be inferred that the object of the assignment was to partition markets.[4]

The European Court will look at the assignment in the context of the economic and legal relationship between assignor and assignee. If it amounts to in economic terms an exclusive licence then it will be construed as such. Thus in *Nungesser*,[5] INRA authorised Mr Eisele to register himself as owner of the relevant breeder's rights of INRA in Germany.

[99] *e.g.* in the U.K., see Patents Act 1977, s.67; also see Copyright Designs and Patent Act 1988 where s.101 states that "an exclusive licensee has, except against the copyright owner, the same rights and remedies in respect of matters occurring after the grant of the licence as if the licence had been an assignment".

[1] See para. 7.113, Chap. 7.

[2] C262/81 [1982] E.C.R. 338, [1983] 1 C.M.L.R. 99.

[3] At p. 62.

[4] See *Etablissements Consten & Grundig v. E.C. Commission*: [1966] E.C.R. 299, [1966] C.M.L.R. 418; *Sirena Srl v. Eda Srl*: [1971] E.C.R. 69, [1975] C.M.L.R. 1; *Tepea v. E.C. Commission*: [1978] E.C.R. 1391, [1978] 3 C.M.L.R. 392; *EMI Records Ltd. v. CBS*: [1976] E.C.R. 811; [1976] 2 C.M.L.R. 235. See also *Advocaat Zwarte kip*; [1974] 2 C.M.L.R. D79 (E.C. Commission).

[5] Case 258/78, *L.C. Nungesser KG & Eisele v. E.C. Commission*: [1983] 1 C.M.L.R. 278.

There were three contracts. Firstly, there was the contract of 1960 which initiated co-operation between INRA and Eisele; secondly, there was the 1961 contract which assigned the plant breeder's rights and thirdly the contract of 1965 which concerned the distribution of INRA seeds in Germany. The Court said that the agreement formed an indivisible whole and that in economic terms, Mr Eisele was an exclusive licensee.[6]

Where an assignment of intellectual property continues to produce effects, such an assignment may be more in the nature of an exclusive licence. This will rarely be the case unless there is evidence of continuing co-operation between the assignor and assignee.[7] For instance, where the assignee is contractually bound in any way whatsoever post-assignment, such an assignment continues to produce effects and is thus capable of falling within Article 85(1). Thus, where there is a ban against further assignment, it is submitted that the true situation is more analogous to an exclusive licence.

Exclusive manufacturing licences

8.112 It is rare that an exclusive licence will be granted which only permits the licensee to manufacture the protected product and not to onwardly sell it. If such is the case, the licence will normally be a sub-contracting licence. The Commission has indicated in its Notice on Subcontracting Agreements that such licences fall outside Article 85(1).[8] Thus where a party is licensed to use industrial property rights for the purposes of manufacturing licensed goods and these goods are to be supplied back to the licensor, the Commission considers that such a license falls outside Article 85(1).[9]

Exclusive sales licence

8.113 Most intellectual property rights give the owner the right to prohibit distribution or the offering for sale of the protected product. However, Community law and most domestic laws provide that once a protected product has been put on the market by the owner or with his consent, the rights owner cannot interfere with further dealings in the product. Thus, when one refers to an exclusive sales licence which is not coupled with the production of the protected product or the first affixing of a trade

[6] See also *Moosehead/Whitbread*: [1990] O.J. L100/32, [1991] 4 C.M.L.R. 391 where an assignment by a Canadian brewing firm of the trade mark to Whitbread and Moosehead jointly was treated by the Commission as being in fact an exclusive licence.

[7] See *EMI Records Ltd v. CBS*: [1976] E.C.R. 811, [1976] 2 C.M.L.R. 235. In general, as to whether a rights owner can enforce his rights in the context of assignments, see para. 7.022 *et seq* and 7.113 *et seq*.

[8] [1979] O.J. C1/2. See para. 8.168.

[9] *ibid*.

mark, it is in essence an exclusive distributorship agreement for which the distributor does not require a licence. Exclusive distributorship agreements are exempted by the Block Exemption on Exclusive Distribution Agreements which exempts agreement whereby one party agrees with the other to supply certain goods for resale within the whole or a defined area of the common market only to that other.[10]

"Closed" exclusive licences

8.114 An exclusive licence does not itself restrict trade between the territories of licensees or the territory of the licensor and that of a licensee. Thus, a licensor will often seek to provide further territorial protection for licensees and himself as against each other. There are many good reasons for doing so. For instance, the grant of an exclusive licence for Germany may not be sufficient incentive to a potential licensee seeking to establish a market for the licensed product in Germany if there is already a well-established licensee in France who is keen to trade in Germany and who can undercut the German licensee because of the latter's initial start-up costs. This section looks at compatibility of measures designed to ensure further territorial protection with Article 85(1).

How can further protection be provided? The first way is to contractually ban "direct sales" by one licensee into another licensee's or the licensor's territory. Direct sales may be "passive sales" into other licensees' territories, *i.e.* sales which have not been solicited or "active sales" that is sales which have resulted from active promotion by a licensee and might include stockpiling of goods in another licensees' territory.

Secondly, the licence may seek to prevent parallel imports between licensees and licensor's territories. Clearly, this is more difficult to achieve contractually. The exercise of rights to prevent parallel imports is contrary to Articles 30–36.[11] However, provisions such as a ban on any licensee selling goods to someone whom he knows intends to onward sell them in another territory can help to achieve such protection. On a semantic note, the term "export ban" is often used without clarifying whether it is merely a "direct sale" ban or a ban intended to cover parallel imports as well. In the following discussion, the term "export ban" is used where absolute protection against exports to other territories is intended.

[10] Reg. 1983/83, Art. 1. A detailed discussion of this reg. is outside the scope of this book and the reader is referred to *Butterworth's Competition Law* and Bellamy and Child *Common Market Law of Competition* (4th Ed., Sweet & Maxwell). See also *Re the Agreement between DDD Ltd and Delta Chemie*: [1988] O.J. L309/34, [1989] 4 C.M.L.R. 535 where there existed a distributorship agreement which gave the importer an option to start its own manufacturing. Such an agreement was given individual exemption.

[11] See Chap. 7 on Enforcement of Intellectual Property.

8.115 *Exclusive licences and export bans*—The Court and Commission has consistently held that export bans infringe Article 85(1).[12] There is no doubt that any agreement or practice which seeks to impose absolute territorial protection by preventing any imports infringes Article 85(1).[13] However, when the Court or Commission condemns "export bans" as falling within Article 85(1), it is often not clear in each case whether the Court or the Commission was concerned with or had in mind a "direct sales" ban or an attempt to provide absolute territorial protection.

8.116 *Exclusive licences and direct sales bans*—The European Court has not directly considered the compatibility of Article 85(1) for an exclusive licence coupled with a direct sales ban. As discussed before, the Court in *Nungesser* held that an "open" but not a "closed" exclusive licence may fall outside Article 85(1). The latter is not permitted as it seeks to affect trade between licensees and third parties. However, when considering exclusive licenses containing direct sales bans, it is less clear as to what is the distinction between the two as the grant of an exclusive licence means that only the exclusive licensee is permitted to sell in the designated territory. Strictly speaking, any other person seeking to sell the protected product in the territory would be infringing the exclusive licensee's rights.[14] Thus, one must study the decision in *Nungesser* in order to establish what precisely is meant by an "open" and "closed" licence. The reader is referred above for the facts of the case.[15]

The Commission in its decision declared that:

> "(a) An obligation upon INRA or those deriving rights through INRA to refrain from having the relevant seeds produced or sold by other licensees in Germany, and;
>
> (b) An obligation upon INRA or those deriving rights through INRA to refrain from producing or selling the relevant seeds in Germany themselves;"

infringed Article 85(1). Furthermore it held that:

> "(c) An obligation upon INRA or those deriving rights through INRA to prevent third parties from exporting the relevant seeds

[12] The Court has constantly stated that clauses that attempt to give absolute territorial protection fall within Art. 85(1). *E.g.* see *Nungesser v. E.C. Commission* and *Tepea v. Commission*: [1978] E.C.R. 1391, [1978] 3 C.M.L.R. 392 where the Court held that an export ban imposed by a manufacturer on its wholesalers fell within Art. 85(1). Similarly, the Commission has ruled that export bans fall within Art. 85(1)—*e.g.* see *Re the Application of Bayerische Motoren Werke AG*: [1975] 1 C.M.L.R. D44; *AOIP v. Beyrard*: [1976] 1 C.M.L.R. D14; *Peugeot v. Zimmern*: [1977] 1 C.M.L.R. D22; *Re the Plant Royalty Bureau Limited*: *8th Annual Report on Competition Policy*, point 120; *Velcro/Aplix Agreement*: [1985] O.J. L233/22.

[13] *Etablissements Consten & Grundig v. E.C. Commission*: [1966] C.M.L.R. 19; Case 258/78 and *Tepea v. Commission*: [1978] E.C.R. 1391, [1978] 3 C.M.L.R. 392.

[14] Indeed, many Member States' laws permit exclusive licensees to sue for infringement.

[15] See para. 8.066 above.

to Germany without the licensee's authorisation for use or sale there, and;

(d) Mr Eisele's concurrent use of his exclusive contractual rights and his own breeder's rights to prevent all imports into Germany or exports to other Member States of the relevant seeds;"

infringed Article 85(1). On appeal, the Court of Justice distinguished the two situations stating that obligations (a) and (b) gave rise to an "open" exclusive licence and declaring that such obligations fell outside Article 85(1). It upheld the Commission's findings on obligations (c) and (d). On a literal reading of obligations (a) and (b), such meant that INRA was permitted to contractually ban licensees from directly selling in each other's territories. However, contradicting the declaratory part of the judgment is a passage in the Court's judgment that:

> "the grant of an open exclusive licence, that is to say a licence which does not affect the position of third parties such as parallel importers and licensees for other territories, is not in itself incompatible with Article 85(1) of the Treaty."[16]

Such a statement suggests that a licence which does affect the ability of licensees to sell in each other's territory is incompatible with Article 85(1). This appears to contradict the Court's annulment of the Commission's findings at (a) and (b). However, it could be said that if a licensee has not been licensed to sell into the territories of other licensees, then a "direct sales" ban does not "affect" his position.

8.117 It is submitted that "direct sales" bans are permissible and to permit exclusive licensees to directly sell in each other's territories undermines the very nature of an exclusive sales licence. If one exclusive licensee cannot be permitted to manufacture in another's territory, why should he be permitted to sell in another's territory. In reality, an exclusive licensee which is investing considerable sums of money requires protection on the marketplace in his territory from licensees inside and outside his territory. It is submitted that it is the declaratory part of the judgment that should prevail over the text and "direct sales" ban in the context of exclusive sales bans should be permitted.

It may be that the European Court will permit "active sales" bans but not "passive sales" bans in the context of intellectual property licences. A "passive sales" ban can often be similar to an export ban which has been disapproved of by the Court and Commission.[17] However, an "active sales" campaign could include stockpiling goods in another licensee's territory for distribution and as such would not seem to be an export ban. In

[16] Para. 58.

[17] For instance, a passive sales ban is a ban which prevents a licensee from fulfilling unsolicited orders from outside his territory.

practice, much will depend on the facts of a case and the Court should balance the procompetitive effects of a direct sales ban for a potential exclusive licensee against the requirement for a unified market which does not recognise internal barriers. In this respect, the Court may compromise and rule that an active sales ban in an exclusive licence does not infringe Article 85(1) but that a passive sales ban does so.

The Commission considers that a ban on a licensor or licensees from engaging in active or passive sales ban in other licensees' territories falls within Article 85(1).[18] It appears that the Commission regards direct sales as one form of export and thus are a type of export ban.[19]

Exclusive licence for the entire Community

8.118 Whilst there is no clear authority on this point,[20] the general principles are the same. Thus, if an exclusive licence for the whole Community is capable of affecting trade between Member States, then if it does not concern the introduction of new technology or involve significant investment, it will probably be held to fall within Article 85(1).

Exclusive licences—exemption

8.119 The Commission has generally exempted "open" exclusive licences which infringe Article 85(1) where such licences are required as an incentive for licensees to penetrate new markets and need to make significant investments.[21] The Commission takes a more lenient view of exclusive

[18] *Re the Agreements of Davide Campari-Milano*: [1978] 2 C.M.L.R. 397; *Re the Agreement between Boussois Sa and Interpane*: [1988] 4 C.M.L.R. 124. *Moosehead/Whitbread*: [1990] O.J. L100/32, [1991] 4 C.M.L.R. 391 (active sales ban outside territory of licensee was an appreciable restriction of competition as licensee had production capacity to supply other markets within the Common Market). See also Patent Block Exemption and Know-How Block Exemption which do not include active and passive sales ban in the category of obligations generally not restrictive of competition. See also Art. 1 of draft Technology Transfer Block Exemption.

[19] See *AOIP v. Beyrard*: [1976] 1 C.M.L.R. D14 where the Commission stated (in the context of exemption) that exemption can be granted in an appropriate case "on bans on exports applicable to the first sale only . . . ". (at para. 39). Such would appear to mean direct sales bans.

[20] Though see *Re "Tyler" Trade Mark* [1982] 3 C.M.L.R. 613, (E.C. Commission) where a 10 year exclusive licence for the whole of Europe in relation to the transfer of business was held to infringe Art. 85(1).

[21] *Re the Agreements of Davidson Rubber Company*: [1972] O.J. L143/31, [1972] C.M.L.R. D52 (exclusive patent licence); *Re Kabelmetal's Agreement*: [1975] O.J L222/34, [1975] 2 C.M.L.R. D40 (exclusive patent licence); *Re the Agreements of Davide Campari-Milano SpA* [1978] 2 C.M.L.R. 397 (exclusive trademark/know-how); *Re the Agreement between Boussois SA and Interpane mbh*: [1987] O.J. L50/30, [1988] 4 C.M.L.R. 124 (patent/know-how licence); *Re the Agreements between Jus-Rol Ltd and Rich Products Corp.*: [1988] O.J. L69/21, [1988] 4 C.M.L.R. 527 (know-how licence); *Re the Agreement between DDD Ltd and Delta Chemie*: [1988] O.J. L309/34, [1989] 4 C.M.L.R. 535 (know-how licence); *Moosehead/Whitbread*: [1990] O.J. L100/32; [1991] 4 C.M.L.R. 391 (trademark/know-how licence).

manufacturing licences than exclusive sales licences. Thus the Commission in 1978 has said that exclusive manufacturing licences may be given exemption

> "Where it is found that the licensed territory is not too extensive, that there are similar products which compete in that territory and that parallel imports are still possible.
>
> But exclusive sales licences and export bans constitute direct barriers to the free movement of goods in the Common Market and the Commission will consider giving exemption only in special circumstances, as where new products are to be manufactured and sold or a new market is to be penetrated, entailing heavy investment and hence considerable risks."[22]

This approach is reflected in the Patent and Know-How Block Exemptions. Thus undertakings by licensors not to grant further licences or to exploit the protected work in a designated territory (*i.e.* "open" exclusive licences) are "white-listed" in the patent, know-how and franchise block exemptions. Similarly, obligations on the licensee not to manufacture or use the licensed products or process within other territories are "white-listed".

Closed exclusive licences which seek to provide absolute territorial protection are invariably unexemptible. The Commission takes the view that such protection prevents the consumer from deriving advantages from effective intra-brand competition which might arise from increased outlets.[23] The Court has endorsed such a viewpoint by baldly stating that absolute territorial protection has no connection with the improvements in distribution.[24] Any requirement that a patent or know-how licensee refuse or make it difficult to supply a user or reseller in their territory is black-listed under the Patent and Know-How Block Exemption.[25]

"Direct sales" bans (which are often called "export bans") in exclusive licences are usually unexemptible[26] but may be justified when

> "the exclusivity is needed to protect small or medium-sized undertakings in their attempts to penetrate a new market or promote a

[22] *7th Report on Competition Policy*, point 133.

[23] *Wilkes v. Theal NV*: [1977] 1 C.M.L.R. D44, at para. 56. Upheld on appeal—*Tepea v. E.C. Commission*: [1978] E.C.R. 1391, [1978] 3 C.M.L.R. 392. See also *Re the Eisele-INRA Agreement*: [1978] O.J. L286/23, [1978] 3 C.M.L.R. 434 (plant-breeder's licence) upheld on appeal, Case 258/78, *L.C. Nungesser KG & Eisele v. E.C. Commission*: [1983] 1 C.M.L.R. 278.

[24] *Etablissements Consten & Grundig v. E.C. Commission*: [1966] C.M.L.R. 418, at 296.

[25] See Reg. 2349/84, Art. 3(11) and Reg. 556/89, Art. 3(12).

[26] *Etablissements Consten & Grundig v. E.C. Commission*: [1966] C.M.L.R. 19, ECJ; Case 258/78, *L.C. Nungesser KG & Eisele v. E.C. Commission*: [1983] 1 C.M.L.R. 278, ECJ; *Re Sirdar's Agreement*: [1975] 1 C.M.L.R. D93, (E.C. Commission) (trade mark litigation settlement that prohibited exports by each party to the other's territory).

new product, provided that parallel imports are not restricted at the same time."[27]

The Commission will grant exemption to 'passive sales' bans where an active sales ban would not adequately protect a licensee during the initial launch of a licensed product.[28] The Patent Block Exemption grants exemption to clauses in patent licensing agreements which prevent a licensee from making active sales for the duration of the patent and in respect of passive sales for a period of five years from the product first being placed on the market.[29] Similarly, the Know-How Block Exemption exempts bans on active and passive sales of licensed know-how products in know-how licences for the duration of 10 years and five years respectively from signing of the licence agreement or until the know-how enters the public domain.[30]

The draft Technology Transfer Block Exemption provides for similar exemption for active and passive sales bans.

Export bans, direct sales bans and articles 30–36

8.120 Regardless of the validity of contractual bans under Article 85(1) or 85(3), the enforcement of intellectual property rights against direct sales by a licensee into another licensee's or the licensor's territory may be contrary to Articles 30–36. According to the case law of the ECJ on the relationship between the free movement of goods provisions and the exercise of intellectual property rights, the exercise of a rights by their owner against the marketing of protected goods where such goods have been marketed by the rights owner or with its consent is contrary to Article 30–36.[31] It is not clear whether this principle prevents the exercise of rights where a licensed product is directly exported to the licensor or another licensee's territory.[32] However, if a licensee is contractually banned from directly selling to another's territory, he is unlikely to risk

[27] *Re the Eisele-INRA Agreement*: [1978] 3 C.M.L.R. 434, para. 54. This finding was upheld by the Court of Justice in *L.C. Nungesser KG & Eisele v. E.C. Commission*: [1983] 1 C.M.L.R. 278. See also *AOIP v. Beyrard*: [1976] 1 C.M.L.R. D14 (exemption for a prohibition on exports applicable to the first sale only and of limited duration may be granted where the object is the mutual protection of the parties or of other licensees); *Velcro S.A. v. Aplix S.A.*: [1985] O.J. L233/22, [1989] 4 C.M.L.R. 157, para. 69 (export bans may be exemptible during the life of a patent on account of the novelty of the technology and the investment required); *Re the Agreement between DDD Ltd and Delta Chemie*: [1988] O.J. L309/34, [1989] 4 C.M.L.R. 535 (exclusive manufacturing and distribution licence of "Stain Devils" product exempted); *Re the Agreements between BBC Brown Boveri and NGK Insulators Limited*: [1989] 4 C.M.L.R. 610 (export ban exempted as licensee ran unusually high risk of failure at the marketing stage). See also 7th Report on Competition Policy, *point 133*.

[28] See *Re the Agreement between Boussios SA and Interpane mbH*: [1987] O.J. L50/30, [1988] 4 C.M.L.R. 124, para. 20 (products sold to well-informed trade buyers).

[29] See Reg. 2349/84, Art. 1(1)(6).

[30] Reg. 556/89, Art. 1(4) & (5).

[31] See Chap. 7 on Enforcement of Intellectual Property.

[32] See Chap. 7 on Enforcement of Intellectual Property, para. 7.019.

termination of his licence even if Community law prevents the licensee to whom he is exporting from exercising his rights. In such circumstances, does Article 30–36 place any limits on the validity of a direct sales ban? It is submitted that Articles 30–36 which are concerned with the free movement of goods cannot affect the validity of "direct sales" bans under Article 85 especially where such bans are clearly valid in certain circumstances.[33]

(ii) Geographical restrictions

8.121 Licensors will often seek to restrict licensees from manufacturing goods or supplying services outside their territories. These clauses (which should be distinguished from export bans) can be divided into two categories—those where the licensor possesses parallel rights in territories outside the designated territory and those where no such parallel rights exist. In the latter case, the Court of Justice has held in *Windsurfing*[34] that such restrictions are not of the essence of the patent and fall within Article 85(1).[35]

In the former case, such restrictions would appear to fall within the "limited licence" doctrine as they constitute a partial lifting of the prohibitive territorial effect of the right. However, as has been seen, the Commission and the Court have paid little attention to this doctrine.[36] In general, it is the essence of the grant of a licence for a territory that the licensee is not permitted to exploit the protected work outside the territory. Accordingly, implicit geographical restrictions are the natural corollary of a licence for a particular territory where parallel rights exist in other territories. As such, express geographical restrictions in such a licence merely underscore the nature of such a licence.

The European Court and Commission are not tolerant of geographical restrictions which could result in market partitioning. The European Court in *Pronuptia*[37] held that a restriction on a licensee only to trade

[33] For a useful résumé of this issue, see Roudard, "*Exports in Community Law: The compatibility of the block exemption of patent licences with the exhaustion of rights principle*," *Patent World*, May 1989, p 34. In Roudard's article at p. 36, the authoress infers from the case law of the ECJ that it is tempting to conclude that Arts. 30–36 permit a licensor to impose geographical limits on the placing of licensed goods on the market through contractual obligation in a licence.

[34] [1986] 3 C.M.L.R. 48.

[35] For discussion on *Windsurfing v. E.C. Commission*, see para. 8.060, above. See also the Commission's decision in *Velcro S.A. v. Aplix S.A.*: [1985] O.J. L233/22, [1989] 4 C.M.L.R. 157 where it held that a restriction in a patent licence which was a mixture of basic and improvement patents (the former having expired) that prevented a licensee from manufacturing products for which the patents had expired outside its designated territory fell within Art. 85(1) as it prevented the licensee from making the expired patent product in the Member State where it could manufacture most advantageously.

[36] See para. 8.055.

[37] Case 161/84, *Pronuptia v. Schillgalis*, [1986] E.C.R. 353, [1986] 1 C.M.L.R. 414.

from the outlet permitted in the franchise when coupled with clauses preventing other franchisees from opening a second shop outside the designed territory resulted in an artificial partitioning of the Common Market and was not permissible.[38]

Recently, the Commission in *Boussois/Interpane*[39] has demonstrated that it will consider geographical restrictions in manufacturing and selling licences as falling within Article 85(1) even where parallel patents exist. In this case, Interpane, a German undertaking granted to Boussois a French firm an exclusive mixed know-how and patent manufacturing licence in France for the first five years and thereafter on a non-exclusive basis for an indefinite period. Interpane possessed parallel patents in various other European countries but not all. Furthermore, Interpane gave Boussois an exclusive sales licence in France for five years and thereafter on a non-exclusive basis. Outside France, Boussois had a non-exclusive sales licence for an indefinite period but this was without prejudice to the right of Interpane (who at that time had not licensed anyone else besides Boussois) to grant exclusive sales licences to other undertakings in other territories in the future.

The Commission held that the prohibition on Boussois manufacturing outside France restricted potential sales in other Community countries because the cost of transportation increased the sales price of the protected product and thus fell within Article 85(1). Also, the prohibition on sales outside France where and when Interpane appointed an exclusive licensee fell within Article 85(1) as it prevented Boussois from supplying such territories.[40]

8.122 *Exemption*—Where it is clear that geographical restrictions are necessary so as to encourage would-be licensees to take licences then such geographical restrictions will be exempted.[41] Obligations that licensees do not exploit the licensed invention in territories reserved to the licensor or other patentees in patent licences are exempted under the Patent Block Exemption.[42] A similar provision is exempted in the Know-How Block Exemption.[43] An obligation that a franchisee only exploit the franchise from the contract premises is exempted under the Franchise Block Exemption.[44] These "white-listing" of such clauses are repeated in the draft Technology Transfer Block Exemption.

[38] *ibid*, at para. 24.
[39] [1987] O.J. L50/30, [1988] 4 C.M.L.R. 124.
[40] See also *Re the Agreements between Jus-Rol Ltd and Rich Products Corp.*: [1988] O.J. L69/21, [1988] 4 C.M.L.R. 527, where a similar clause fell within Art. 85(1).
[41] See *Agreement between Boussios and Interpane mbH*: [1987] O.J. L50/30, [1988] 4 C.M.L.R. 124 and *Re the Agreements between Jus-Rol Ltd and Rich Products Corp.*: [1988] O.J. L69/21, [1988] 4 C.M.L.R. 527.
[42] Reg. 2349/84, Art. 1(3).
[43] Reg. 556/89, Art. 1(3) and 1(4).
[44] Reg. 4087/88, Art. 2(c).

(iii) *Export and direct sales bans*

8.123 Export bans and direct sales bans have already been discussed when associated with exclusive licences. This section is only concerned with clauses in the context of non-exclusive licences.

Both the Court and the Commission have held that export bans are contrary to Article 85(1).[45] Such an approach extends to licences which expressly or impliedly have the effect of restricting exports. Thus, recently, the Commission held that a ban on sale of branded dental products to third parties except in unopened form and a provision that the products were intended for distribution solely in Germany fell within Article 85(1) as such constituted an export ban.[46] The Commission has held that export bans do not form part of the essential function of a patent rights[47] nor of trade marks.[48] In the context of plant breeders' rights, the Commission will view favourably export bans on basic seeds and first generation seeds but not second generation certified seeds.[49]

Export bans or direct sales bans are rarely included in non-exclusive licences. In non-exclusive licences, it will be very difficult to justify an export ban or direct sales ban by reference to the need for protection for the licensee if a licensee is not protected from domestic competition by way of an exclusive licence. Such would lead to an artificial partitioning of the market and distortion of competition.

A ban on exports to countries outside the Common Market (including EFTA countries) will not fall within Article 85(1) where re-importation into the E.C. is unlikely.[50]

8.124 *Exemption*—Export bans or direct sales bans in non-exclusive licences would discriminate against foreign licensees and will rarely be justifiable as indispensable to improving technological progress or improving the

[45] The Court has constantly stated that clauses that attempt to give absolute territorial protection fall within Art. 85(1). *E.g.* see *Nungesser v. E.C. Commission* and *Tepea v. Commission* where the Court held that an export ban imposed by a manufacturer on its wholesalers fell within Art. 85(1). Similarly, the Commission has ruled that export bans fall within Art. 85(1)—*e.g.* see *Re the Application of Bayerische Motoren Werke AG*: [1975] 1 C.M.L.R. D44; *AOIP v. Beyrard*: [1976] 1 C.M.L.R. D14; *Peugeot v. Zimmern*: [1977] 1 C.M.L.R. D22; *Velcro S.A. v. Aplix S.A.*: [1985] O.J. L233/22, [1989] 4 C.M.L.R. 157. See also in relation to copyright *Re BBC*: [1976] 1 C.M.L.R. D89; *Dutch Publishers Association*: [1976] 1 C.M.L.R. D2; *6th Report on Competition Policy*, point 152; Ernest Benn Ltd: *9th Report on Competition Policy*, point 118–119; *Re STEMRA*: *11th Report on Competition Policy*, point 98; in relation to plant breeder's rights, see *Re Plant Royalty Bureau*: *8th Report on Competition Policy*, point 120.

[46] *The Community v. Bayer AG*: [1990] O.J. L351/46, [1992] 4 C.M.L.R. 61 (E.C. Commission). See also *Re "The Old Man and the Sea"*: [1977] 1 C.M.L.R. D121 where an implied export ban was held to fall within Art. 85(1) in relation to a copyright licence.

[47] See *Velcro S.A. v. Aplix S.A.* [1985] O.J. L233/22, [1989] 4 C.M.L.R. 157.

[48] *Wilkes v. Theal & Watts*: [1977] 1 C.M.L.R. D44 upheld on appeal *Tepea v. Commission*: [1978] E.C.R. 1391, [1978] 3 C.M.L.R. 392.

[49] *Re Comasso*: [1990] 4 C.M.L.R 259, [1990] O.J. C6/3. In this agreement, there were complex provisions in relation to export bans of basic, first and second generation seeds in order to ensure that control over breeding lines was not lost.

[50] *Re the Agreement of Davide Campari-Milano SpA*: [1978] 2 C.M.L.R. 397 (E.C. Commission).

distribution of goods. The position on the exemption of export and direct sales bans in exclusive licences is discussed elsewhere.[51]

(iv) *Temporal restrictions*

8.125 Generally, licensors seek to impose a specific period for the duration of the licence. This could be shorter than the period of protection. Such would appear to fall within the "limited licence" doctrine as constituting a partial lifting of the prohibitive effect of patents and copyright.[52] The European Court and Commission view favourably temporal restrictions which are shorter than the period of protection. Thus the Commission considers that an obligation on a licensee not to exploit a patent after termination of the agreement whilst the patent remains in force falls outside Article 85(1).[53]

In know-how licences, it is important that a licensor be able to limit the period as he has no rights at law other than in contract to sue the licensee if he carried on using the know-how after expiry or termination of the agreement. The Commission recently seems to have relaxed its stance on clauses banning post-term use of know-how in a know-how licence where the know how remains secret. Thus, it has recently recognised that a ban on the use of know-how after the expiry of a know-how licence generally falls outside Article 85(1) as it is "a normal feature of the licensing of know-how as otherwise the licensor would be forced to transfer his know-how in perpetuity and this could inhibit the transfer of technology".[54] Similarly, an obligation to pay royalties for the use of secret know-how after the termination of a licence also falls outside Article 85(1).[55]

Greater difficulties occur where a licensee is obliged to pay royalties after the expiry of the intellectual property or the entering of the licensed know how into the public domain. Licensors may often seek to lock-in a licensee into a licence agreement even after expiry of the relevant intellectual property. Normally, this will mean that the licensee will have to continue paying royalties. Historically, the Commission had viewed these

[51] See para. 8.119.

[52] See para. 8.055.

[53] Reg. 2349/84, Art. 2(1)(4) and Art. 2(1)(3) draft Technology Transfer Block Exemption.

[54] Reg. 556/89, Recital 14 and Art. 2(1)(3) ("the Know-How Block Exeption") where such a clause is "super-white-listed" and "Notice on Post Term Use Bans in Know-How Licensing Agreements" Commission Press Release, October 12, 1988 [1989] 4 C.M.L.R. 851. See also Art. 2(1)(3) draft Technology Transfer Block Exemption. See also decisions on know-how licences made prior to the commencement of the Know-How Block Exemption—*Re the Agreement between DDD Ltd, and Delta Chemie*: [1989] 4 C.M.L.R. 535. A 10 year post-term ban on use of know-how unless terminated through the fault of the licensee was held to fall outside Art. 85(1)—*Re the Agreement between Jus-Rol and Rich Products Corporation*: [1988] 4 C.M.L.R. 527. *Cf.* earlier and stricter approach prohibiting total post-term use of know-how bans—*Constructions Normalisées A. Cartoux S.A. v. Terrapin (Overseas) Limited*: [1981] 1 C.M.L.R. 182.

[55] *Re Kabelmetal's Agreement*: [1975] O.J. L222/34, [1975] 2 C.M.L.R. D40; *Constructions Cartoux v. Terrapin Overseas Limited*: [1981] 1 C.M.L.R. 182.

obligations as falling within Article 85(1).[56] However, where the licensee is able to freely terminate the licence, then an obligation to pay a royalty throughout the validity of the agreement will not fall within Article 85(1).[57]

8.126 Recently, the Commission has taken a more favourable stance on schemes whereby the licensee is obliged to pay royalties after the expiry of the intellectual property in order to facilitate payment. Thus, in a know-how licence where the know-how enters into the public domain through no fault of the licensor prior to the end of the agreement, the Commission now has relaxed its attitude to such an obligation and views such an obligation as an appropriate way of financially structuring the licence.[58] However, an indefinite period will rarely be permitted as it is difficult to say that an obligation to pay an indefinite sum of money *in toto* constitutes a method of financial structuring. Thus, if the period for which the licensee is obliged to continue paying royalties after the know-how has become publicly known by the action of third parties and substantially exceeds the lead time acquired because of the headstart in production and marketing, then the Commission may consider such an obligation as restrictive of competition and unexemptible.[59] Similarly, in patent licences, the Commission will allow the payment of royalties over a period extending beyond the life of the licensed patents in order to facilitate payment by the licensee.[60] By analogy, it is submitted that a similar approach should be taken in trade mark and copyright licences.

8.127 The European Court has also adopted a tolerant approach to an obligation to pay royalties after the expiry of the licensed intellectual property. In *Ottung v. Klee*,[61] the European Court considered such an obligation. Under a patent licence entered into before the patent was granted, the licensee was obliged to pay a royalty on the sale of each patented product even after expiry of the patent. Furthermore, the licensee was obliged under the agreement to pay royalties on a complementary non-patented product. The licensee could terminate the agreement but if he did so was contractually prohibited from manufacturing or marketing the patented products. The Court held that:

> "the reason for the inclusion in a licensing agreement of a clause imposing an obligation to pay royalty may be unconnected with a patent. Such a clause may instead reflect a commercial assessment of the value to be attributed to the possibilities of exploitation granted by the licensing agreement. That is even more true where, as in the main proceedings, the obligation to pay royalty in respect of two devices, one being patented after the agreement was entered into and

[56] See *UARCO 14th Report on Competition Policy*, point 93. See Reg. 2349/84, Art. 3(4).
[57] *Ottung v. Klee*: [1990] 4 C.M.L.R. 915, para. 13.
[58] See also Art. 2(1)(7) of draft Technology Transfer Block Exemption and Recital 16.
[59] Reg. 556/89, Art. 7(7).
[60] See proviso to Patent Block Exemption, Art. 3(4).
[61] [1990] 4 C.M.L.R. 915.

the other being complementary to the first, was embodied in a licensing agreement entered into before the patent was granted."[62]

The Court continued and said that an obligation to pay a royalty for an indeterminate period does not in itself constitute a restriction of competition within the meaning of Article 85(1) where the agreement was entered into after the application was submitted and immediately before the grant of the patent. The Court's judgment is short and not particularly illuminating. For instance, they do not explain the significance of entering into the licence before the patent was granted. Once granted, a patent is effective as of the date of application. Accordingly, it would be foolhardy of a party not to enter into a licence prior to a patent being granted for the period from the date of application unless there were good grounds for believing that the application will never become a patent. Moreover, a party will not voluntarily pay a royalty unless he needs a licence (whether patent or mixed patent/know-how) to exploit protected technology. Accordingly, it should be very rare that an obligation to pay a royalty is not connected with some form of protected technology. The Advocate-General's Opinion goes into the issue in more detail. He remarks that payment of royalties after expiry of the patent may represent part of the remuneration granted to the inventor for the exploitation of the patent during its validity.[63] He stated that it was for the national court to determine whether the payment of the royalty after the expiry of the patent constituted a special arrangement for discharging the obligation to pay the reward due to the inventor or a supplementary payment to which the inventor is not entitled after the entry of the patent into the public domain.[64] It is submitted that such is a better approach. Thus, an obligation to pay royalties indefinitely is unlikely to represent a special arrangement to facilitate payment.[65]

In *Ottung v. Klee*, the Court held that where the licence was terminated, a ban on manufacturing or marketing the licensed product once the patent had expired weakened the licensee's competitive position since it placed him at a disadvantage in relation to its competitors.[66] Accordingly, if such a clause appreciably affected trade between Member States, it was likely to fall within Article 85(1). Such a finding rather weakens and contradicts the Court's earlier reasoning in this case. If an obligation to pay royalties is enforceable once expiry of the patents has occurred, then the licensee is at a disadvantage compared to his competitors from then on. Thus, on the basis of this reasoning, one would have expected the Court to conclude that an obligation to pay royalties after the expiry of patents was anticompetitive as others would not have to pay them. Clearly, if the licensee can freely prematurely terminate the licence, a ban

[62] *ibid*, para. 11.
[63] At p. 920.
[64] At p. 920.
[65] See Advocate-General's remarks on Patent Block Exemption, Art. 3(4) at p. 920.
[66] [1990] 4 C.M.L.R. 915, para. 18.

on manufacturing the licensed product until the end of the licence period is essential where there was originally an obligation to pay royalties until the end of the licence period.

A licensor may seek to prolong a licence by stipulating that it will terminate upon the expiry of the last patent or additional know-how. An obligation that a licence remains in force until expiry of the most recent improvement patent will fall within Article 85(1) unless the licensee has a right to terminate.[67] Thus, in *Velcro S.A. v. Aplix S.A.*,[68] the Commission said where there was, at the time of consideration, a licence which concerned a mixture of expired patents and patents in force, the Commission saw no justification for restrictions on marketing or importation of products manufactured using processes that were no longer protected.[69]

8.128 *Exemption*—An obligation to pay royalties in a patent licence beyond the expiry of the patent after the expiry of intellectual property is black-listed under the Patent Block Exemption unless it constitutes an arrangement to facilitate payment by the licensee.[70] However, the Commission's view in the later Know-How Block Exemption is that such arrangements are not anti-competitive.[71] Accordingly, it is submitted that if such an obligation is not to facilitate payment and does not genuinely relate to the exploitation of the licensed technology, this would render the agreement ineligible for exemption. The Commission has "black-listed" clauses which seek to prolong the licence by inclusion of improvement patents in patent licences and further know-how in know-how licences unless they provide each party with an annual (or triennial in the case of know-how) right to terminate the licence.[72]

(v) Field-of-use

8.129 Generally, field of use restrictions do not fall within Article 85(1) unless it is shown that they are the result or means of implementing an agreement to eliminate competition between licensees.[73] An obligation in a patent or know-how licence which restricts the exploitation to one or more technical fields of application will generally fall outside Article 85(1).[74]

The Commission considers that an obligation in a know-how licence that a licensee use the licensed product only in the manufacture of its own

[67] *AOIP v. Beyrard* [1976] 1 C.M.L.R. D14; *Re the Agreement between Peugeot and Zimmern*: [1977] 1 C.M.L.R. D22; *Velcro/ Aplix*: [1989] 4 C.M.L.R. 157.

[68] [1985] O.J. L233/22, [1989] 4 C.M.L.R. 157.

[69] Para. 63–64.

[70] Patent Block Exemption, Art. 3(4).

[71] Know-How Block Exemption, Art. 3(5).

[72] With regard to the obligation to pay royalties on know-how in know and mixed patent/ know-how licences, see Patent Block Exemption, Art. 3(2) and Know-How Block Exemption, Art. 3(10).

[73] See *4th Report on Competition Policy*, s.28.

[74] Reg. 2349/84, Art. 2(1)(3); Reg. 556/89, Art. 2(1)(8).

products falls outside Article 85(1)[75] as such gives the licensor an incentive to disseminate the technology in various applications. Similarly, a requirement that the licensee should only use the licensed know-how solely for the purposes of manufacturing the licensed product falls outside Article 85(1).[76]

(vi) Quantitative restrictions

8.130 A licence often includes restrictions on the quantity of products that can be produced by the licensee.These can either be restrictions on the minimum or maximum number of products which a licensee can manufacture or sell.

In relation to patents, copyright and trade marks, ceiling restrictions on the manufacture of products fall within the "limited licence" doctrine as constituting a partial lifting of the prohibitive effect of intellectual property. However, such an approach has not been taken by the Court or Commission. Thus, although, quantitative restrictions were included in the 1962 Notice on Patent Licensing Agreements as falling outside Article 85(1), the Commission has indicated that such clauses fall within Article 85(1).[77] Furthermore, such restrictions in patent and know-how licences are non-exemptible.[78]

"Minimum" quantity clauses in patent and know-how licences are considered by the Commission to generally fall outside Article 85(1) as they encourage the exploitation of technology.[79] Such clauses can be by way of minimum royalty payments.[80] In non-exclusive licences, justification for minimum royalty clauses is more difficult because if there is inadequate exploitation of the technology, the licensor can license another. If the minimum royalty clause is too high, it may be anti-competitive as it could deter small or possibly medium-sized firms from entering into licences. Such reasoning is not valid under a "rule of reason" approach because a licensor is not obliged to create competition in his own technology.[81]

(vii) Tie-in and quality control clauses

8.131 Many manufacturing licences oblige licensees to exclusively buy unprotected products or material necessary for the exploitation of the licensed technology from the licensor or his appointed supplier. These obligations

[75] See the Know-How Block Exemption, Recital 7 and Art. 1(8) and Art. 2(1)(8) of draft Technology Transfer Block Exemption.
[76] See *Re the Agreements between Jus-Rol Ltd and Rich Products Corp.*: [1988] O.J. L69/21, [1988] 4 C.M.L.R. 527, para. 35.
[77] See *4th Report on Competition Policy*, para. 31.
[78] Reg. 2349/84, Art. 3(5); Reg. 556/89, Art. 3(7). See also Art. 3(9) of draft Technology Transfer Block Exemption.
[79] See Patents and Know-How Block Exemption, Reg. 23489/84, Art. 21(1); Reg. 556/89, Art. 2(1)(9). See also Art. 2(1)(10) of draft Technology Transfer Block Exemption.
[80] A minimum royalty generally encourages a licensee to exploit the licensed technology.
[81] See para. 8.021.

are called "tie in" clauses. Such clauses can be procompetitive to licensees if they are a substitute for the payment of royalties because exploitation of the licence will generally be cheaper provided that the cost of the products or the material are similar or cheaper to those of other rival suppliers. However, such a restraint can have the effect of foreclosing rival suppliers of sufficient outlets for exploiting their technologies and thus be anticompetitive.[82] A licence may give rise to an implicit "tie in" effect if it is structured to make it costly for licensees to use competing technology.[83]

The Court of Justice has not had to deal with the competitive effects of tie-in clauses in the context of licences. The Commission considered the question of tie-in clauses in a patent licence in *Vaessen BV v. Moris*.[84] This concerned a patent relating to a process and device for manufacturing meat sausages. The patent existed only in Belgium, was owned by Mr Moris and licences to ALMO, a company of which Mr Moris was principal shareholder. ALMO manufactured and sold synthetic casings for all types of sausages but these casings were not protected by patents. ALMO sublicensed others to work the patent. The right to use the process was royalty-free provided that the sublicensees undertook to obtain all their supplies of casing from ALMO. Vaessen, a rival manufacturer of synthetic sausage casings similar to those sold by ALMO in Belgium complained to the Commission that its attempt to penetrate the Belgian market had been impeded by the exclusive purchasing commitment in ALMO's sublicenses. The Commission held that such a clause had the object and effect of restricting competition since it deprived the sublicensee of its business freedom to obtain supplies from other undertakings perhaps on more favourable terms.

Importantly, the Commission said that it was not a "requirement imposed by the industrial property right" since its deletion did not jeopardise the patent holder's exclusive right to work his invention himself or through others as the products supplied by ALMO were not covered by the patent. Thus, the Commission held that the clause constituted "an unlawful extension by contractual means of the monopoly".[85] The Commission has also held that an obligation on a patent licensee to obtain manufacturing equipment for making the patented product from a

[82] See the U.S. approach in para. 5.4, *US Antitrust Guidelines for Intellectual Property*, issued by the Department of Justice, April 6, 1995.

[83] *e.g.* see para. 4.3.2 in *US Antitrust Guidelines for Intellectual Property*, issued by the Department of Justice, April 6, 1995 where the guidelines comment on the Complaint in *United States v. Microsoft Inc* Civ No. 94–1564 (D.D.C. filed July 15, 1994); Competitive Impact Statement, *id* (filed July 27, 1994) where it says that a royalty arrangement based on total sales of a licensee's product regardless of whether it was made using the licensed technology may increase the cost to a licensee of substituting alternative technologies.

[84] [1979] O.J. L19/32; [1979] 1 C.M.L.R. 511.

[85] *ibid*, para. 15.

named third party falls within Article 85(1).[86] In this case, whilst such did not recompense the patent owner, the patentee had given the third party the responsibility for developing the equipment for manufacturing the patented product on the implicit promise that it would include an exclusive purchasing clause in its licences.

8.132 *Quality control and "tie-in" clauses*—Where quality control clauses are closely associated with the nature of the intellectual property, then they fall outside Article 85(1). Thus, in the case of patent licences, clauses requiring mandatory quality control specifications, checks and inspections to be carried out by the licensor are indispensable to the proper exploitation of the licensed process and fall outside Article 85(1).[87] With regard to know-how licences, the Commission has indicated that such clauses are not generally restrictive of competition.[88] In trade mark licences, it is important to ensure that the reputation of the mark is not damaged by the sale of trade marked products of poor quality or the supply of services of a poor standard.

Often, the owner of a right will seek to maintain quality control by imposing obligations on the licensee to purchase certain stock or raw material from the licensor or an approved outlet. Where such a clause is intrinsic to the nature of the intellectual property, it will fall outside Article 85(1). Thus, in patent licences, the Commission takes the view that obligation on licensees to purchase goods or services from the licensor fall outside Article 85(1) where they are necessary for a technically satisfactory exploitation of the licensed invention.[89] That tie-in clauses will only be permissible in licences where they are germane to the intellectual property itself is demonstrated by the Commission's approach to such clauses in the Franchise Block Exemption. This removes exemption for any tie-in clause if the franchisor refused to designate third parties as suppliers of goods for reasons other than protecting the franchisor's industrial or intellectual property rights or to maintain the common identity and reputation of the franchised network.[90]

In *Campari*,[91] the Commission showed that in the context of a trade mark/know-how licence it will take a tolerant view of tie-in obligations if such is necessary to maintain the reputation and goodwill of the trade mark. The facts were that manufacturing licensees of the well-known drink "Campari" were obliged to restrict the manufacture of the drink to plants which were capable of guaranteeing the quality of the product.

[86] See *Velcro/Aplix SA*: [1989] 4 C.M.L.R. 157.
[87] See *Re the Agreement of Raymond & Company*: [1972] C.M.L.R. D45. See also Reg. 2349/84, Art. 2(1)(9) in relation to patent licences.
[88] Reg. 556/89, Art. 21(5) and 3(3) (Know-How Block Exemption).
[89] Reg. 2349/84, Art. 21(1) (Patent Block Exemption).
[90] Reg. 4087/88, Art. 5(c).
[91] *Re the Agreements of Davide Campari-Milano SpA*: [1978] 2 C.M.L.R. 397.

The Commission cleared such a condition as "maintenance of the quality is referable to the existence of the trade mark right".[92] Similarly, obligations to purchase albumin and bitter orange essence from manufacurers who were capable of providing such products of a sufficiently high standard and to purchase colouring matter and herbal mixtures from the licensor fell outside Article 85(1). The Commission said that it was a legitimate concern of the licensor to ensure that the product manufactured under licence had the same quality. The composition of the two products determined the characteristic of Bitter Campari and being a trade secret, the licensor could not be required to reveal it to its licensees.[93]

In *Moosehead/Whitbread*,[94] which concerned a trade-mark/know-how licence concerning the brewing of "Moosehead" beer between a Canadian brewery (Moosehead) and an English brewery, the Commission held that an obligation to purchase yeast from Moosehead or a third party designated by it fell outside Article 85(1) as it was necessary to ensure a "technically satisfactory exploitation of the licensed technology and a similar identity between the lager produced originally by Moosehead and the same lager produced by Whitbread".[95]

8.133 *Exemption*—If a tie-in clause is found to infringe Article 85(1), it will generally not be exemptible.[96] Once it is accepted that such clauses are anti-competitive, it is difficult to say that it fulfils the criteria under Article 85(3). In the context of patent and know-how manufacturing licences, obligations to use goods or services which the licensee does not want unless such are necessary for a technically satisfactory exploitation of the patent or know-how are black-listed.[97] The arguments generally put forward in relation to exclusive purchasing agreements that they improve distribution of the purchased goods are not applicable to tie-in clauses in manufacturing licences as the exclusive supplies are not sold on but incorporated into manufactured goods.[98]

Where the licence is not a manufacturing licence, tie-in clauses are not strictly relevant. Instead, clauses which oblige parties to buy exclusively from a party or his appointed suppliers' are in effect exclusive purchasing clauses. An exclusive purchasing agreement between two parties which obliges the purchaser to sell contract goods under trademarks, or packed

[92] *ibid.* para. 61.
[93] *ibid*, para. 62.
[94] [1990] O.J. L100/32; [1991] 4 C.M.L.R. 391.
[95] *ibid*, p. 398.
[96] *H Vaessen BV v. Moris*: [1979] O.J. L19/32; [1979] 1 C.M.L.R. 511, para. 23.
[97] See Patent Block Exemption, Art. 3(9); Know-How Block Exemption, Art. 2(5), 3(3). These provisions do not appear in the draft Technology Block Exemption.
[98] Thus the Exclusive Purchasing Block Exemption (1984/83) only applies whereby one party undertakes to exclusively purchase from another *for resale only* (Art. 1).

and presented as specified by the supplier will fall within the Exclusive Purchasing Block Exemption.[99]

(viii) Resale price maintenance and other "downstream" restrictions

8.134 The expression "downstream restrictions" is used to refer to contractual constraints on a licensee relating to the onward sale of protected products. A typical downstream restriction is resale price maintenance.

Both the Court and Commission view "downstream restrictions" as infringements of Article 85(1). The Court of Justice in *Windsurfing*[1] upheld the Commission's argument that a licensor is not entitled to control the market in the products under licence. Thus, an obligation that licensees only sell patented products, namely rigs for sailboards, in conjunction with boards as approved by the licensor fell within Article 85(1). The Commission has held that provisions in licensing agreements which restrict the licensee's right to fix sales prices fall within Article 85(1).[2]

In certain situations, downstream restrictions may be necessary so as to maintain the commercial strength of the intellectual property. The Court in *Pronuptia*[3] held that an obligation on franchisees only to sell merchandise covered by the franchise agreement fell outside Article 85(1) and to decorate their shops according to the franchisor's specifications had as their purpose to guarantee a uniform image. Similarly, the Commission held that an obligation on dealers to use a licensor's trade mark without additions or alternations and only in such a manner as justified by the method and scope of business falls outside Article 85(1) as such an obligation is an incident of the protection under the law of trade marks.[4] The Commission has held that an obligation on a franchisee that it exploit the franchisor's industrial property rights and know-how in a manner in keeping with their subject matter are inherent in the very existence of the rights and fall outside Article 85(1).[5]

Resale price maintenance clauses are "black-listed" under the Patent, Know-How and Franchise Block Exemptions[6] and must be considered unexemptible in other licences. However, recommendations as to resale prices are permissible.[7] With respect to other "downstream" restrictions, such generally constitute interference in market forces and will rarely be

[99] Reg. 1984/83, Art. 2(3)(c).
[1] See *Windsurfing International v. E.C. Commission* [1986] 3 C.M.L.R. 489. This is discussed in detail at para. 8.060.
[2] *Re the Complaint by Yoshida Kogyo KK*: Commission Press Release, June 9, 1978; [1978] 3 C.M.L.R. 44.
[3] Case 161/84, *Pronuptia v. Schillgalis* [1986] E.C.R. 353, [1986] 1 C.M.L.R. 414.
[4] *Re the Application of Bayerische Motoren Werke AG*: [1975] 1 C.M.L.R. D44. See also *Re the Agreement between DDD Ltd and Delta Chemie*: [1989] 4 C.M.L.R. 742.
[5] See *Re the Franchise Agreements of Yves Rocher*: [1988] 4 C.M.L.R. 592.
[6] Reg. 2349/84, Art. 3(6); Reg. 556/89, Art. 3(8); Reg. 4087/88, Art. 5(e). See Art. 3(1) of draft Technology Transfer Block Exemption.
[7] *e.g.* see Reg. 4087/88, Art. 5(e).

exemptible unless they relate to the maintenance of quality control or reputation of products.

(ix) Grantback clauses

8.135 A grantback is an arrangement under which a licensee agrees to extend to the licensor the right to use to the licensee's improvements to the licensed technology and vice versa. The United States considers that grantbacks can have procompetitive effects, such as providing a means for the licensee and the licensor to share risks and reward the licensor for making possible further innovation based on or informed by the licensed technology. Such arrangements can both promote innovation in the first place and promote the subsequent licensing of the results of the innovation. Grantbacks may adversely affect competition, if they substantially reduce the licensee's incentive to engage in research and development and limit rivalry in innovation markets.[8] This may often be the case where the grantback of improvements is to the exclusion of the licensee. The United States' Department of Justice will consider the extent as to which, compared with no licence at all, the licence with the grantback provision may diminish total research and development investment or lessen competition in innovation or technology markets.[9]

In Europe, the Commission has held that an obligation on a licensee to assign or grant-back an exclusive licence in improvement patents or know-how developed during the licence to the licensor will fall within Article 85(1).[10] However, an obligation on a licensee to grant a non-exclusive licence to the licensor and other licensees will generally fall outside Article 85(1).[11]

However, the Commission takes the view that an obligation to grant-back non-exclusive licences may restrict competition in a oligopolistic market as such would prevent one party ever gaining a competitive advantage over another which might result from such improvements and thus discourage any efforts which the company might normally make to obtain such an advantage.[12] Thus the Commission has held that provisions in a patent/know-how licence granting the two chief producers of zips in the Common Market the use in a substantial part of the common market of all future patents and know-how developed by the licensor who was a major competitor infringed Article 85(1) as it helped the two

[8] For the meaning of "innovation markets", see para. 8.022.

[9] Para. 5.6, *US Antitrust Guidelines for Intellectual Property*, issued by the Department of Justice, April 6, 1995 [1995] 7 EIPR Supplement.

[10] See *Re the Agreement of Raymond & Company*: [1972] C.M.L.R. D45.

[11] See *The Agreements of Davidson Rubber Company*: [1972] O.J. L143/31, [1972] C.M.L.R. D52; *Re Kabelmetal's Agreement*: [1975] O.J. L222/34, [1975] 2 C.M.L.R. D40; *Re the Agreement between Jus-Rol and Rich Products*: [1988] 4 C.M.L.R. 527 (know-how); *Re the Agreement between Boussois SA and Interpane*: [1988] 4 C.M.L.R. 124 (know-how). See also Reg. 2349/84, Art. 2(1)(11), and Art. 3(2) in the context of patent and know-how licences. See also Art. 2(1)(4) of draft Technology Transfer Block Exemption.

[12] See *Re Kabelmetal's Agreement*: [1975] O.J. L222/34, [1975] 2 C.M.L.R. D40, para. 33.

manufacturers to secure a broader control in the field of zip technology.[13] In the context of joint ventures, the Commission, in a patent cross-licensing co-operation agreement between two large undertakings with big market shares, found that an obligation on each to licence each other for new, independently developed processes infringes Article 85(1) as neither of the two firms would be able to obtain a competitive advantage over the other in research nor can either gain individually by keeping research results to itself.[14] It is submitted that in an oligopolistic market, analysis of the competitive effects of non-exclusive grantback clauses should examine whether the procompetitive effects of increasing *intra-brand* competition and increasing technology between licensor and licensee in the improvement technology is balanced against possible anti-competitive effects in the innovation market.[15]

8.136 *Exemption*—An obligation to assign or grant an exclusive licence in rights in technology developed by the licensee is "black-listed" in both patent and know-how licences.[16] Where improvement know-how is not severable from the licensor's know-how, the Know How Block Exemption has complicated provisions.[17]

(x) Non-competition clauses

8.137 Licensors may seek to prevent competition between licensees and licensor. Where this is achieved by way of exclusive licences and export bans, this has already been discussed.[18] However, often a licensor will seek to merely impose blanket non-competition clauses. Not surprisingly, such blanket clauses prohibiting one party from competing with another will fall within Article 85(1).[19] However, in the case of an exclusive performance contract involving opera singers, the Commission took a favourable position on a non-competition clause as its duration was not intended to be long.[20] The perceived need for non-competition clauses in licences reflects the fact that licensors and licensees are generally actual or potential competitors.[21]

Licensors also seek to prevent competition between the licensed tech-

[13] *Re the Complaint by Yoshida Kogyo KK*, Press Release of the Commission, June 9, 1978; [1978] 3 C.M.L.R. 44.

[14] *Re the Agreement between Bayer AG and Gist-Brocades NV*: [1976] 1 C.M.L.R. D94.

[15] See para. 8.022 for meaning of innovation market.

[16] Reg. 2349/84, Art. 3(8); Reg. 556/89, Art. 3(2). See also Art. 3(6) of draft Technology Transfer Block Exemption.

[17] See para. 8.239 *et seq.*

[18] See para. 8.099 *et seq.*

[19] See *4th Report on Competition Policy*, para. 30; *AOIP v. Beyrard*: [1976] 1 C.M.L.R. D14; *Neilson-Hordell/Richmark*: *12th Report on Competition Policy*, point 89.

[20] *RAI/Unitel*: *12th Report on Competition Policy*, point 90 (Unitel undertook to ensure that the making of a film was not delayed unnecessarily so that the non-competition clause was not overly extended).

[21] *cf* exemption of non-competition clauses in the Exclusive Dealing Block Exemption (1983/83) which reflects the fact that manufacturer and distributor are rarely competitors.

nology and rival technology. Thus, a licensor will often ban a licensee from dealing or selling competing goods.[22] This is often an exclusive dealing clause. In the U.S.A., the Department of Justice considers that exclusive dealing may be achieved expressly or by other provision such as compensation terms or other economic incentives. In considering the competitive effect of such clauses, the Department will take into account the extent to which the arrangement (1) promotes the exploitation and development of the licensor's technology and (2) anticompetitively forecloses the exploitation and development of or otherwise restrains competition among competing technologies.[22a] Such exclusive dealing obligations have been held to infringe Article 85(1) in know-how/trade mark licences.[23] Similarly, clauses in a patent licence which have the effect of restricting a licensee to only manufacturing the licensor's patented product infringe Article 85(1).[24] Such clauses will invariably be non-exemptible.[25] However, non-competition clauses are exemptible in the context of specialisation agreements.[26] In the context of franchise agreements, non-competition obligations are considered necessary by the Commission in so far as they protect the franchisor's industrial and intellectual property rights or to maintain the common identity and reputation of the franchised network.[27]

Transfer of business

8.138 When a rights owner wishes to sell a business which contains intellectual property rights, the buyer often demands that the assignor be prevented from competing with him. Clauses prohibiting the seller of a business competing with the purchaser after sales will normally fall within Article 85(1) unless they are necessary to preserve the worth of the transferred

[22] This should be distinguished from a tie-in clause which obliges the licensee to purchase non-licensed products only from the licensor—see para. 8.131.

[22a] U.S. Antitrust Guidelines for the Licensing of Intellectual Property, para. 5.4.

[23] *Re the Agreements of Davide Campari-Milano SpA*: [1978] 2 C.M.L.R. 397 (E.C. Commission); *Moosehead/Whitbread*: [1990] O.J. L100/32; [1991] 4 C.M.L.R. 391.

[24] See *Re the Agreements on Video Cassette Recorders*: [1978] 2 C.M.L.R. 160. A patent licence obliged licensees to observe particular technical standards for the manufacture and distribution of video cassette recorders and video cassettes which meant that licensees could only manufacture VCR equipment which constituted the licensed technology.

[25] See *AOIP v. Beyrard*: [1976] 1 C.M.L.R. D14; reg. 2349/84, Art. 3(3); Reg. 556/89, Art. 3(9). In the latter there is a right for the licensor to terminate licence if licensee deals in competing goods. See Art. 3(2) draft Technology Transfer Block Exemption.

[26] Para. 30, *4th Report on Competition Policy*. There is a Specialist Block Exemption (Reg. 417/85) which exempts agreements whereby undertakings accept reciprocal obligations not to manufacture certain products for the purposes of specialisation provided that the participating undertakings do not possess more than 20 per cent of the market in the specialised products or goods equivalent to them in the Community or a substantial part of it—Art. 1 and 3. Such agreements may contain intellectual property provisions to facilitate such specialisation but contain little of interest to the intellectual property practitioner and are not dealt with in this book. For further discussion, see Bellamy and Child 4th Ed. Common Market Law of Competition, Butterworth's *Competition Law* and Harding *Notices and Group Exemptions in EEC Competition Law*.

[27] Reg. 4087/88, Art. 3, Franchise Block Exemption. See Chap. 10 on Franchises in Europe.

business and to protect the purchaser.[28] Thus a non-competition clause in an agreement to sell a business which involved the transfer of know-how and goodwill did not fall within Article 85(1).[29] However, a personal non-competition clause was held to be more restrictive than was justified when it covered non-commercialised research in the field concerning the transferred technological rights as it was not necessary to safeguard the worth of the transferred business.[30]

The period of non-competition must not exceed what is necessary for the preservation of the transferred business. Factors to be taken into account for determining the duration of the non-competition clause on the transfer of know-how are the nature of the transferred know-how, the opportunities for its use and the knowledge possessed by the purchaser. Such a clause must not extend beyond the relevant geographical market in which the seller was active before the transfer.[31] However, if a ban on competition would have the effect of closing down the seller's business, he may be allowed the manufacture within the area in which he was previously active provided the goods are intended for direct export only outside the area.[32] Such covenants are often necessary to ensure that the agreement is commercially viable.[33]

Where an exclusive licence of a trade mark is given to the purchaser of a business regarding a trade marked product such that it has the effect of the seller entering into a non-competition agreement, then the Commission will treat it accordingly. Thus, in such a case, it held that a 10 year exclusive licence of a trade mark in relation to the transfer of a business for the whole of Europe constituted protection against competition for an unreasonable length of time.[34]

Research and development

8.139 In the context of research and development joint ventures, the Commission held that a clause prohibiting the parents of a joint venture from competing with the joint subsidiary in the field covered by their co-operation fell within Article 85(1).[35] Similarly, restrictions on the right to exploit know-how belonging to a joint venture subsidiary after withdrawal from the joint venture fell within Article 85(1).[36]

[28] See Case 42/87, *Remia v. E.C. Commission*: [1985] E.C.R. 2547, [1987] 1 C.M.L.R. 1.
[29] *Reuter v. BASF AG*: [1976] 2 C.M.L.R. D45.
[30] *ibid* at para. 49.
[31] *ibid* at para. 47.
[32] *Sedamel/Precilec*, point 95, *11th Report on Competition Policy*.
[33] See Case 42/84, *Remia v. E.C. Commission*: [1985] E.C.R. 2547, [1987] 1 C.M.L.R. 1.
[34] *Re the "Tyler" Trade Mark*: [1982] 3 C.M.L.R. 613.
[35] *Re Carbon Gas Technologie GmbH*: [1984] 2 C.M.L.R. 275. See Chap. 9 on Intellectual Property and Joint Ventures.
[36] *ibid*, para. 9. For exemption of such clauses, see Research and Development Block Exemption and Chap. 9.

(xi) Legal action clauses

8.140 The Commission considers licences that obligations to inform a licensor of infringements, take legal action against infringers and assist the licensor in any infringement action fall outside Article 85(1).[37]

(xii) Assignment and sub-licences

8.141 An obligation on a licensee not to assign or to sub-licence is not restrictive of competition within Article 85(1). Such an obligation safeguards the right of the licensor to select its licensees.[38] In know-how licences, a ban on assignment and sublicensing is important in order to control the dissemination of the know-how.[39]

(xiii) Most-favoured licensee

8.142 A clause stipulating that the licensor will not grant other licences on terms more favourable than that applying to the licensee will fall outside Article 85(1).[40] However, where such terms are so onerous that the licensor might find it difficult to find other licensees, such a term may constitute a restriction of competition within Article 85(1).[41]

A commercially more flexible clause is an obligation on the licensor to grant a licensee any more favourable terms subsequently granted to other licensees. The Commission has indicated that such a clause generally does not infringe Article 85(1) in the context of patent and know-how clauses.[42]

(xiv) No-challenge clauses

8.143 A no-challenge clause is an obligation on the licensee not to contest the validity of the intellectual property of the licence. It used to be the case that under English and United States' law a licensee was estopped from challenging the validity of the right. This rule has now been abolished in

[37] Reg. 2349/84, Art. 21(8). Reg. 556/89, Art. 2(1)(6); Reg. 418/85, Art. 5(1)(e). See Art. 2(1)(6) of draft Technology Transfer Block Exemption.

[38] *Re the Contract of Burroughs AG and Geha-Werke*: [1972] O.J. L13/53, [1972] C.M.L.R. D72; *Re the Contract of Burroughs AG and Delplanque*: [1972] O.J. L13/50, [1972] C.M.L.R. D67; *Re The Agreements of Davidson Rubber Company*: [1972] O.J. L143/31, [1972] C.M.L.R. D52; *Re the Agreements of Davide Campari-Milano SpA*: [1978] 2 C.M.L.R. 397. See also Reg. 2349/84, Art. 21(5) (Patent Block Exemption); Reg. 556/89, Art. 2(1)(2) (Know-How Block Exemption). See however *French State/Suralmo*, point 114, *9th Report on Competition Policy* where an obligation that a patent licensee obtain the licensor's consent for sub-licensing for military purposes existed, no such consent being required for civil use, fell within Art. 85(1) as it was discriminatory and Art. 223 was not relevant as the patent was intended primarily for non-military use.

[39] *e.g.* see *Re the Agreements of Davidson Rubber Company*: [1972] O.J. L143/31, [1972] C.M.L.R. D52.

[40] *Re Kabelmetal's Agreement*: [1975] O.J. L222/34, [1975] 2 C.M.L.R. D40.

[41] *ibid.*

[42] See Patent Block Exemption, Art. 2(11); Know-How Block Exemption, Art. 2(1)(10). See also Art. 2(1)(11) draft Technology Transfer Block Exemption.

the United States on the grounds that it is not in the national interest to prohibit challenge of a possibly invalid patent and that licensees are often the only individuals with enough economic incentive to challenge the patentability of an inventor's discovery.[43] The rule in England is also subject to doubt.[44]

The Commission has since the 1970s ruled that no-challenge clauses in patent and know-how licences,[45] trade mark licences,[46] copyright[47] and plant breeder's rights[48] infringe Article 85(1). Such rulings were based on the grounds that public policy required that everyone including the licensee ought to be able to bring proceedings for the revocation of patents which had been wrongly granted.[49] Alternatively, it was said that the clause was a restriction on the licensee's freedom of action which did not come within the monopoly granted by the patent right.[50]

This view was endorsed by the Court of Justice in *Windsurfing*[51] where it said:

> "It must be stated that such a clause clearly does not fall within the specific subject matter of the patent, which cannot be interpreted as also affording protection against actions brought in order to challenge the patent's validity, in view of the fact that it is in the public interest to eliminate any obstacle to economic activity which may arise where a patent was granted in error."[52]

Similarly, the Court held that a clause which required licensees to acknowledge the validity of *Windsurfing's* trade marks infringed Article 85(1).[53] Thus, the Court and the Commission have treated the matter as one of "public policy" and have not historically examined the competitive justifications for no-challenge clauses. Until recently, the Court and

[43] See *Lear v. Adkins* 23 L, Ed. 2d. 610, para. 12 (U.S. Supreme Court).
[44] See Singleton, "Intellectual Property Disputes: Settlement Agreements and Ancillary Licences under E.C. and U.K. Competition Law" [1993] 2 EIPR 48.
[45] See *Re the Agreements of the Davidson Rubber Company*: [1972] C.M.L.R. D52; *Re the Agreement of Raymond & Company*: [1973] C.M.L.R. D45; *Re the Agreement between Kabel AG and Luchaire*: [1975] 2 C.M.L.R. D40; *Re Bayer Ag and Gist-Brocades*: [1976] 1 C.M.L.R. D94 (joint venture specialisation agreement; *AOIP v. Beyrard*: [1976] 1 C.M.L.R. D14; *Vaessen v. Moris*: [1979] 1 C.M.L.R. 511; *Ateliers de Construction de Compiègne v. Fabry*: [1979] 3 C.M.L.R. 77.
[46] See *Re the "Toltecs" and "Dorcet" Trade Marks*: [1982] O.J. L379/19 [1983] 1 C.M.L.R. 412 upheld on appeal by the ECJ—see Case 35/83, *BAT Cigaretten Fabriken v. E.C. Commission (ECJ)* [1985] E.C.R. 363, [1985] 2 C.M.L.R. 470; *Goodyear Italiano*: [1975] 1 C.M.L.R. D31 (Commission).
[47] See *Neilson-Hordell/Richmark*, point 89, *12th Report on Competition Policy.*
[48] See *Royon v. Meilland*: [1985] O.J. L369/9, [1988] 4 C.M.L.R. 193.
[49] See *AOIP v. Beyrand*: [1976] 1 C.M.L.R. D14 at para. 24.
[50] See *Re the Agreement of Raymond and Company* [1972] O.J. L143/49, [1973] C.M.L.R. D45.
[51] Case 193/83, *Windsurfing International v. E.C. Commission* [1986] E.C.R. 611, [1986] 3 C.M.L.R. 489.
[52] Para. 92.
[53] See para. 81.

Commission had not permitted except in one instance "no-challenge" clauses in litigation settlement disputes.[54]

Recently, in *Bayer AG v. Sullhöfer*,[55] the Court of Justice reconsidered the question of no-challenge clauses in a litigation settlement. In 1967, Sullhöfer had applied and obtained a utility model and applied for a patent for the manufacture of polyurethane foam-based panels. In 1967, Sullhöfer issued warnings to Hennecke, a wholly-owned subsidiary of Bayer that it was infringing its utility model. Hennecke sought a declaration that the utility model was invalid and issued opposition proceedings against the patent. In 1968, both parties reached a settlement whereby Sullhöfer granted Hennecke a non-exclusive free licence to use the patent and utility model and the right to sub-licence. He also granted a licence subject to payment of royalties to use the corresponding industrial property rights in other Member States. Bayer granted Sullhöfer a non-exclusive and non-transferable licence subject to payment of royalties for the manufacture of foam panels under a German patent it held. Further, it undertook not to challenge the validity of Sullhöfer's patents and to withdraw its legal proceedings. Later on, further disputes arise and Sullhöfer sought to terminate the agreement for fraudulent misrepresentation. The matter eventually went to the ECJ as to whether a no-challenge clause was incompatible with Article 85(1).

8.144 The Commission suggested that such a clause should not be incompatible with Article 85(1) if the following conditions were fulfilled:

(1) The clause was included in a settlement putting an end to litigation pending before a national court;
(2) There were no other clauses restricting competition;
(3) The clause related solely to the right in issue;
(4) That right was manifestly unlikely to be revoked.

The Court rejected the Commission's argument. It stated that Article 85(1) made no distinction between settlement agreements and other types of agreements. It went on to say that a no-challenge clauses may fall within Article 85(1) depending on the legal and economic context. However, it would not restrict competition when the licensee paid no royalties or when the licence was granted subject to payment of royalties but related to a technically outdated process which the undertaking accepting the no-challenge clause did not use.

[54] See Case 35/83, *BAT Cigaretten-Fabriken GmbH v. E.C. Commission*: [1985] E.C.R. 363, [1985] 2 C.M.L.R. 470 (ECJ) upholding *Re the "Toltecs" and "Dorcet" Trade Marks*: O.J. L379/19; [1983] 1 C.M.L.R. 412; see *Vaessen BV v. Moris*: [1979] 1 C.M.L.R. 511 (Commission); *Zoller & Frohlich/Telemecanique*, point 109, *8th Report on Competition Policy*. The exception was in *Re Penney's Trade Mark*: [1978] 2 C.M.L.R. 100 where the Commission held in a trade mark settlement dispute that a no-challenge clause limited in duration for five years constituting a period which in most countries was reasonable for establishing use under the Paris Convention and that the likelihood of the trade marks being liable to be struck off was remote and therefore such a restriction did not have an appreciable effect on competition.

[55] Case 65/86, [1988] E.C.R. 5249, [1990] 4 C.M.L.R. 182.

Thus the virtually irrefutable presumption that no-challenge clauses fall within Article 85(1) and are unexemptable has now gone. The Court in *Bayer v. Sullhöfer* made no mention of the public interest aspect as it had in *Windsurfing* and this remains a valid consideration. Clearly, the grant of a royalty-free licence does not remove the public interest in ensuring that wrongly granted patents are revoked especially as the licensee is often best-placed to evaluate whether the patent is invalid. Thus the legal validity of a licence with a no-challenge clause is unclear and each case must be reviewed on its facts.[56]

Also, recently, in *Moosehead/Whitbread*,[57] the Commission considered the question of a trade mark no-challenge clause in a trade mark/know-how licensing agreement for the brewing of "Moosehead" beer by Whitbread, the English brewers, in England. The agreement stipulated that Whitbread would not challenge the validity or ownership of the registered trade mark "Moosehead". The Commission distinguished between ownership and validity. In the case of ownership, it stated that a no-challenge clause does not fall within Article 85(1) as "whether or not the licensor or licensee has the ownership of the trade mark, the use of it by any other party is prevented in any event, and competition would thus not be affected".[58]

The Commission said in relation to an attack on the validity of a trade mark that a successful challenge would result in the trade mark falling into the public domain. In such case, a no challenge clause could restrict competition "because it may contribute to the maintenance of a trade mark that would be an unjustified barrier to entry into a given market". However, the Commission went on to say that:

> "The ownership of a trade mark only gives the holder the exclusive right to sell products under that name. Other parties are free to sell the product in question under a different trade mark or trade name. Only where the use of a well-known trade mark would be an important advantage to any company entering or competing in any given market and the absence of which therefore constitutes a significant barrier to entry, would this clause which impedes the licensee to challenge the validity of the trade mark, constitute an appreciable restriction of competition within the meaning of Article 85(1)."[59]

[56] See Ferry "*Patent Agreements: No-Challenge Clauses*" [1989] 4 EIPR 139. Also see Singleton "*Intellectual Property Disputes: Settlement Agreements and Ancillary Licences under E.C. and U.K. Competition Law*" [1993] 2 EIPR 48 which considers the context of no-challenge clauses in litigation settlement agreements under E.C. and U.K. competition law.

[57] [1990] O.J. L100/32; [1991] 4 C.M.L.R. 391.

[58] *ibid* p. 398. It does not mention the position if the licensee challenges ownership on the basis that a third party is the owner. In such circumstances, the result may be that the trade mark is struck off the register and not the third party declared as the owner. In this case, under trade mark law (as opposed to passing-off), no party can be prevented from using the mark. In such circumstances, it is difficult to say that there has not been a challenge to the validity of the mark.

[59] *ibid* pp. 398–399.

Thus, the Commission held that as the trade mark "Moosehead" was comparatively new to the lager market in the United Kingdom, the no-challenge clause could not have an appreciable effect on competition. Whilst this decision appears to merely apply the requisite criterion that Article 85(1) only applies to appreciable restrictions on trade between Member State, the Commission's statement suggests that only no-challenge clauses in licences for well-known marks are susceptible of attack under Article 85.

Exemption

8.145 If a no-challenge clause is held to infringe Article 85(1), the Commission will rarely exempt it.[60] "No-challenge" clauses are "black-listed" in the Patent and Know-How Block Exemptions.[61] Thus, where licences include any restrictions in Article 1 of each Block Exemption, a no-challenge clause (even one which would fall outside Article 85(1) by virtue of the Court's judgement in *Bayer/Sullhöfer*) will cause such exemption to be removed. Parties must therefore apply for individual exemption. The uncertainty of such a ruling may mean that most advisors will continue to treat agreements with "no-challenge" clauses as falling within Article 85(1) unless they fall specifically within the Court's two examples in *Bayer* and no other restrictive clauses exist.

(xv) Royalty clauses

8.146 Remuneration in licences by way of royalty payments represents the traditional method of payment and as such does not fall within Article 85(1).[62] An obligation on a licensee to pay a minimum royalty will usually not infringe Article 85(1).[63] Obligations to pay royalties after the expiry of patents or copyright or the entry into the public domain of know-how are considered as relating to the permitted duration of a licence and are discussed elsewhere.[64]

Royalties on products not covered by intellectual property

8.147 Generally, an obligation to pay royalties on products not protected by intellectual property in the general context of a licence falls within Article 85(1). Thus in *Windsurfing*,[65] the licensor required that the licensee pay royalties for the sale of sailboards as well as the patented rigs on the basis of the fictitious net selling price of the complete sailboard. The Court

[60] *AOIP v. Beyrard*: [1976] 1 C.M.L.R. D14; *Royon v. Meilland*: [1985] O.J. L369/9, [1988] 4 C.M.L.R. 193.
[61] See Reg. 2349/84, Art. 3(1) and Reg. 556/889, Art. 3(4).
[62] See *4th Report on Competition Policy, para 21 and AOIP v. Beyrard*: [1976] 1 C.M.L.R. D14.
[63] See section on Quantitative Restrictions, para. 8.130.
[64] See para. 8.125 *et seq.*
[65] Case 193/83, *Windsurfing International v. E.C. Commission*: [1986] E.C.R. 611, [1986] 3 C.M.L.R. 489.

upheld the Commission's finding that such a clause distorted competition as it forced the licensees to sell boards and rigs as a combination only and prevented supply of rigs to board manufacturers who wished to sell the completed sailboard.[66] Such an approach emphasises that the charging of royalties on unpatented products often has anti-competitive spill-over effects into ancillary markets.

The European Court is more tolerant of royalties based on unprotected products where such merely represents a *method* of calculating remuneration for exploitation of the protected product. Thus, in *Windsurfing*, the Court held that the calculation of royalties for the sale of patented rigs based upon the net selling price of the complete sailboards (*i.e.* rig and unpatented board combined) was in effect merely a method of calculation for royalties based on the sale of rigs and thus fell outside Article 85(1).[67] This was even though the parts were easily separated. The Court acknowledged that the licensees accepted that it was equitable for the licensor to charge a higher percentage if the royalty was based on the sale price of the rig as opposed to the complete and more expensive sailboard. More recently, the Advocate-General in *Ottung v. Klee*,[68] in considering whether an obligation to pay royalties on an unpatented product, stated that such fell within Article 85(1) unless the payment was merely a factor in the calculation of the amount already decided upon for the patent product.[69] He emphasised the difference between the quantum of total payment being based upon a percentage of an unpatented product as opposed to the method of payment. In the former case, it was difficult to deny the existence of a tie-in.[70–71]

8.148 The Court's approach appears to be in conflict with the Commission's approach to such clauses. The Commission has indicated that a clause in a copyright licence that charges royalties for the sale of non-copyright items infringed Article 85(1) and is unexemptible.[72] Clauses which seek to charge royalties on products not entirely or partially protected by patents or know-how are "black-listed" in the case of patents and know-how licences.[73] In future, it may be that the Commission will take a similar view on the obligation to pay royalties on non-patented products as it did for an obligation to pay royalties after the expiry of a patent.[74]

[66] *IMA AG v. Windsurfing International* [1983] O.J. L229/1, [1984] 1 C.M.L.R. 1 at para. 97 (E.C. Commission). On appeal to the ECJ, Case 193/83, *Windsurfing International v. E.C. Commission*: [1986] E.C.R. 611, [1986] 3 C.M.L.R. 489 at para. 67.

[67] Case 193/83, *Windsurfing International v. E.C. Commission*: [1986] E.C.R. 611, [1986] 3 C.M.L.R. 489, at para. 69. This implicitly overturned the Commission's finding that the royalty rate cannot be linked to the sale price of products not covered by the patent unless the value of the component patented product is difficult to establish. See Stone "Some Thoughts on the Windsurfing Judgment" [1986] 8 EIPR 242.

[68] Case 320/87, [1989] E.C.R. 1177, [1990] 4 C.M.L.R. 915.

[69] *ibid*, at p. 923 where the Advocate-General analysed the effect of *Windsurfing*. The Court did not rule on this point having decided the case on other points.

[70–71] *ibid.*

[72] *Neilson-Hordell/Richmark*, point 89, *12th Report on Competition Policy*.

[73] Reg. 2349/84, Art. 31 (4); Reg. 556/89, Art. 3(4).

[74] See section on Temporal Restrictions, para. 8.125 *et seq*.

Namely, that such an obligation is permissible if it merely goes to the method of payment rather than the quantum of payment.

Considerable difficulties may arise for a national court in considering whether such a clause goes to quantum or mere calculation or royalty.[75] In many respects, it is submitted that such a distinction is a legal refinement which bears little relationship to commercial reality. It is arguable that every licensee who enters into an agreement with such clauses is aware of the amount and duration for which it will be paying royalties. Accordingly, it is arguable that the *quantum* of payment is always agreed from the start and that such clauses merely relate to the method of payment. If the licensee knows what royalties he will be paying and still decides it is profitable to enter into a licensing arrangement, the competition in the market place has most likely been improved. In fact, it is the market in the unpatented product where examination of the competitive effects of such a clause should be concluded. For instance, a royalty based on total sales of a licensee's products regardless as to whether or not they include unlicensed parts will normally increase the cost to licensees of using rival firms' technology in relation to the unlicensed parts.[76]

Discriminatory/arbitrary royalties

8.149 The Commission has shown it will interfere if the charging of royalties discriminates against imports as opposed to domestically produced goods. Thus where all manufacturing companies in Germany of television sets had pooled their patents on a royalty-free basis so that the practical effect was that only imports were subject to royalties, such a practice fell within Article 85(1).[77] Similarly, the Commission intervened to prevent national performing right societies from charging manufacturers of records from paying royalties based upon the average retail price of records rather than the manufacturer's published selling price.[78] The Commission said that such meant that manufacturers had to pay widely differing royalties depending on the country of sale. Such a practice also prevented the cost or price advantages that arose in the country of manufacture from being passed on to consumers in the country of sale. The Commission thus said that such a system did not have an objective

[75] In *British Leyland Motor Corporation v. T.I. Silencers* [1981] 2 C.M.L.R. 75, C.A., an English case pre-dating *Windsurfing*, the High Court held that where the owner of industrial design right offers prospective manufacturing licensees a royalty clause which covered either items subject to copyright at a higher rate or all items, whether covered by the copyright or not, at a lower rate, such did not infringe Article 85 as the reason for the alternative was that it might be very difficult to be absolutely certain whether a particular item was or was not the subject of copyright. Such an approach appears to fall properly into the *method* of calculation category and thus fall outside Article 85(1).

[76] See U.S. case of *United States v. Microsoft* at note 83 at p. 464.

[77] See *IGR/Stereo TV*, para. 62, *11th Report on Competition Policy* and para. 75, *14th Report on Competition Policy* (royalty rate was subsequently dropped so that effect on competition was no longer appreciable).

[78] *Re Performing Right Societies*: [1984] 1 C.M.L.R. 308; Press Release IP(84)7 (January 9, 1984).

basis of assessment. An arbitrary assessment of royalties may have anti-competitive effects on adjacent markets.

(xvi) Secrecy and post-term use ban clauses in know-how licences

8.150 Know-how presents its own problems in the case of licensing. The licensing of know-how is only of value to the licensee provided the know-how has not entered the public domain. Thus, it is of paramount concern to a licensor that it ensures that know-how does not enter the public domain even after the expiry of the licence.

The Commission considers that clause in know-how licences which require the licensee to maintain the secrecy of technical know-how during or after the termination of the licence do not fall within Article 85(1) if the know-how has not failed into the public domain.[79] Bans on exploitation of know-how after termination of the licence are now considered by the Commission to fall outside Article 85(1) provided the know-how is still secret.[80] Where the know-how has entered the public domain, the Know-How Block Exemption black-lists a ban on use of the licensed know how after termination of the agreement where the know how has become publicly known other than by action of the licensee.[81]

(h) Special categories of agreements

(i) Patent and know-how pools

8.151 Sometimes, several businesses "pool" together their patents and know-how. For instance, they may agree to grant all the others in the pool a royalty-free, non-exclusive licence to work the patents. Such arrangements should be distinguished from joint venture arrangements whereby parties seek by way of a commercial vehicle (usually a jointly-owned subsidiary) to research and develop technology more economically and efficiently than if pursued separately.[82] Cross-licensing and pooling arrangements can be procompetitive by integrating complementary technologies, reducing transaction costs, clearing blocking positions and in the case of settlement agreement, preventing costly litigation. The United States' Department of Justice consider that such arrangements can be

[79] *Re the Agreement of Burroughs Ag and Deplanque et Fils; Re the Agreement between Jus-Rol Limited and Rich Products*: [1988] 4 C.M.L.R. 527; *Re the Agreement between Boussois and Interpane*: [1988] 4 C.M.L.R. 124; *Re the Agreement between DDD Ltd and Delta Chemie*: [1988] 4 C.M.L.R. 535. In the context of mixed patent/know-how agreement see Reg. 2349/84, Art. 2(1)(7). In the context of pure know-how agreements, see Art. 2(1)(1).

[80] See para. 8.125 *et seq.*

[81] Reg. 556/89, Art. 3(1). See also Case 320/87, *Ottung v. Klee* [1989] E.C.R. 1177, [1990] 4 C.M.L.R. 915 where the ECJ held that a post-termination ban on manufacture in relation to an expired patent fell within Art. 85 but that an obligation to pay royalties after the expiry of the patents in a licence did not fall within Art. 85(1)—see Temporal Restrictions, para. 8.125 *et seq.*

[82] See Chap. 9 on Joint Ventures in Europe.

anti-competitive in certain circumstances.[83] Firstly, where such arrangements are a mechanism to price fixing or customer allocation. Secondly, where the parties have large market shares in the relevant technological market, cross-licensing may harm competition by putting competitors at a significant disadvantage. Thirdly, pooling arrangements may deter or discourage participants from engaging in research and development, thus retarding innovation. Thus, cross-licensing for minimal costs between the majority of participants in a particular area of research and development would reduce the incentive of each member to conduct their own research and development.

In Europe, the Commission has had little experience of patent pools and know-how pools. Until recently, such arrangements were excluded from the Patent and Know-How Block Exemption.[84] However, it has issued several decisions on the question of cross-licensing and pooling arrangements.

8.152 *Brombemaling/Heidemaatschappij*[85]—A Dutch patent holder granted licences to four Dutch undertakings in consideration of them withdrawing their opposition to the grant of the patent. Included in the agreement was an obligation that the patent holder could not grant licences to other firms in Holland without the consent of a majority of the licensees. The Commission in a preliminary decision under Article 15(6) of Regulation 17[86] held that such an obligation infringed Article 85(1) and was unexemptible as "there might be a justification for differences in royalty but there is none for a restriction of capacity".[87]

8.153 *Concast/Mannesmann*[88]—Where two market leaders whom between them held 60 per cent of the market share in continuous casting technology, the Commission held that a know-how pooling arrangement eliminated competition between them and in effect forced purchasers to purchase from the two concerns because of the substantial amount of know-how that the two owned.

8.154 *IGR/Stereo TV*[89]—Where two German research institutes who together owned the patents for stereo television assigned their patents to a pool of firms who were all German TV manufacturing firms such that

[83] Para 5.5, draft *US Antitrust Guidelines for Intellectual Property*, issued by the Department of Justice, April 6, 1995.

[84] See Reg. 2349/84, Recital 8 and Reg. 556/89, Recital 5.

[85] *Zuid-Nederlandsche Brombemaling en Grondboringen BV v. Heidemaatschappij Beheer NV*: [1975] O.J. L249/27, [1975] 2 C.M.L.R. D67.

[86] Which removes immunity from fines being imposed upon undertakings after notification.

[87] However, the patent holder could have achieved such by merely unilaterally refusing to licence others. Thus, one could argue that it is of the essence of a patent that one can restrict capacity. However, the Court and Commission have not followed such a path—see para. 8.055.

[88] Point 92, *11th Report on Competition Policy*.

[89] Point 92, *11th Report on Competition Policy* and point 76, *14th Report on Competition Policy*.

foreign firms were excluded from importing TV sets with stereo into Germany, such a practice constituted an infringement of Article 85(1).[90]

8.155 *Re Video Cassette Recorders*[91]—Phillips, a larger Dutch electronics undertaking, marketed video cassette recorders using the VCR system that it had developed. Other manufacturers of video cassette recorders were interested in marketing the equipment and had decided to use Phillips' VCR system. The parties agreed to grant each other royalty-free, non-exclusive and non-transferable licences under their patents and patent applications where such was required to ensure compatibility between the parties' goods. Other manufacturers of VCR machines were free to become parties to the agreement. In the event of termination by a party, that party forfeited any licence for the patents of the other parties granted under the agreement but the remaining partners retained their licences granted by the terminating partner.

The Commission held that the termination arrangements fell within Article 85(1). It stated that if a party was contemplating manufacturing another system after withdrawing from the agreement, its decision was rendered more difficult by the knowledge that it would no longer be able to use investments it had already made for the manufacture of the VCR system and that its patents which might be of use in manufacturing another system would be exploited free of royalties by its former partners.[92] In view of the pre-eminent position of Phillips on the market, the restrictions were particularly marked and would effectively dissuade the parties from any attempt to adopt another system. The Commission also refused to exempt the agreement as it felt that it led to the exclusion of other, perhaps, better systems.[93]

Comment:

8.156 *Brombemaling* was an early decision of the Commission and was prior to the Court ruling that exclusive licences may fall outside Article 85. Clearly, as the same objection can be levelled at exclusive licences, this decision will have to be reconsidered. Certainly, the fact that it was an attempt to settle litigation and may well have fostered competition by permitting undertakings to exploit patented technology when they might not otherwise have been able to do so does not seem to have been considered.[94]

The decision of *Concast/Mannesmann* demonstrates that in an oligo-

[90] The Commission withdrew its opposition when a licence was granted to the complainant (A Finnish firm). However, the matter later came to the Commission's attention when there were further complaints that royalties being raised by the poll system on foreign manufacturers constituted a type of import tax. The royalties were then drastically reduced such that the Commission held that there were no appreciable effect on competition.

[91] [1978] O.J. L47/42, [1978] 2 C.M.L.R. 160.

[92] *ibid* para. 24.

[93] *ibid* para. 29.

[94] See Patent Litigation Settlements, para. 8.163.

polistic market, the Commission is concerned that there is effective competition between undertakings and that incentives to gain a technological advantage on a competitor are not removed.[95] Similarly, the decision in *Video Cassette Recorders*[96] shows the concern the Commission has in state-of-the-art technology to ensure that technological progress and effective *inter-brand* competition is not stultified. Different considerations should apply to pooling arrangements between undertakings in a non-oligopolistic market. Thus, it is arguable that patent/know-how pool schemes between undertakings with small shares in a market fall outside Article 85(1) as they enable such parties to effectively compete with undertakings who possess large shares of the market and its patent/know-how.

8.157 *Exemption*—As mentioned before, reciprocal licensing of patents and know-how were until recently excluded from the Patent and Know-How Block Exemption. Recently, the Commission had adopted the view that the pooling of resources is commercially beneficial for small undertakings who have not got the resources to undertake new ventures individually and that such should be encouraged in order to make the Community more competitive. In furtherance of this, the Commission has amended the Patent and Know-How Block Exemption so that certain types of reciprocal licensing arrangements are exempted. This is discussed in detail later.[97]

(ii) Litigation settlement agreements

Trade mark settlements

8.158 Litigation disputes are more often than not settled rather than pursued to trial. In many cases, where it is clear that the defendant has infringed, the latter submits to the relief that the plaintiff is seeking and undertakes not to infringe the plaintiff's mark. These settlements play a vital part in a country's economy by relieving pressure on courts and clarifying at an early stage each party's rights. However, often the extent of the plaintiff's rights are in dispute. Thus, in a trade mark dispute, an undertaking not to infringe the plaintiff's trade marks often does not define the forbidden activities sufficiently clearly. Thus, plaintiffs will seek an undertaking prohibiting particular activities rather than mere undertakings not to infringe. In these circumstances, the plaintiff may seek an undertaking from the defendant which goes beyond his trade mark rights.[98]

[95] For Commission's approach to obligations in oligopolistic situation, see also *Re Kabelmetal's Agreement*: [1975] O.J. L222/34, [1975] 2 C.M.L.R. D40; *Re Bayer & Gist-Brocades*: [1976] 1 C.M.L.R. D98; *Re the Complaint by Yoshida Kogyo KK*, Press Release of the E.C. Commission, June 9, 1978; [1978] 3 C.M.L.R. 44.

[96] [1978] O.J. L47/42, [1978] 2 C.M.L.R. 160.

[97] See para. 8.171 for patents and 8.215 for know how licences. See similar provisions in draft Technology Transfer Block Exemption (Art. 5(2)).

[98] See Singleton, "Intellectual Property Disputes: Settlement Agreement and Ancillary Licences" [1993] 2 EIPR 48.

In other cases, there are genuine conflicting rights. For instance, two independent businesses own trade marks for different territories which are identical or confusingly similar. Rather than endless litigation, the two firms often prefer to negotiate an agreement that preserves each undertaking's right to trade under their mark. Alternatively, an opposition to registration of a trade mark may be abandoned on the basis of a grant of a licence.

From a competition viewpoint, most trade mark settlement agreements will contain clauses apparently restrictive of trade, *e.g.* each party is confined to using its trade mark within defined territories or to certain types of goods. Moreover, such agreements often contain reciprocal no-challenge clauses. Whether such agreements are truly anti-competitive depends on what the outcome of the litigation would have been if no settlement had taken place. It may be that the contractual obligations imposed on the parties by the settlement agreement coincide with the legal obligations on the parties which would have resulted from the litigation. For instance, if A owns a trade mark X in Territory A which is identical to B's trade mark X in Territory B, then under Community and national law, neither will be able to export to each other's territory if there are no economic or financial links between A and B.[99] In such a case, a settlement agreement which restricts each party from using the trade mark Z in the other's territory merely reflects the legal position and is procompetitive because it prevents expensive litigation and clarifies the parties' positions from an early stage thus often ending a "deadlock" situation.

The difficulties arise where (as is normally the case) the legal outcome of litigation is uncertain. Thus, in the above example, it may be unclear as to who has the right to use the mark X in countries besides A and B. In this case, analysis based upon "but for the settlement what would the position have been" becomes speculative and difficult. In such cases, the Court and Commission's viewpoint has veered between two doctrines. The first doctrine is that the parties must reach an agreement which least restricts competition and the use of the marks regardless of the possible outcome of the litigation. The second doctrine is that it is appropriate to consider the likely outcome of the litigation in examining whether the settlement agreement restricts competition.

8.159 *European Court of Justice*—The ECJ has said that for the purposes of Article 85(1), no distinction should be drawn between agreement whose purposes is to put an end to litigation and those concluded with other aims in mind.[1] Thus, if a patent licence is granted pursuant to a settlement, it will be subject to the patent block exemption. Similarly,

[99] Case 119/75, *Terrapin v. Terranova* [1976] E.C.R. 1039, [1976] 2 C.M.L.R. 482.
[1] Case 65/86, *Bayer v. Sullhöfer* [1988] E.C.R. 5249 [1990] 4 C.M.L.R. 182, para. 15. See also Case 258/78, *L.C. Nungesser KG & Eisele v. E.C. Commission* [1982] E.C.R. 2015, [1983] 1 C.M.L.R. 278.

blatant protective measures will infringe Article 85(1) even in the context of a settlement. The issue is always whether competition has been restricted.[2] In *BAT v. E.C. Commission*,[3] the Court of Justice considered the question of delimitation agreements.

BAT, the second-largest tobacco firm in Germany was the registered owner of the trade mark "Dorcet" for raw tobacco, tobacco products and cigarette paper in Germany. This trade mark had not been used for more than five years and was thus liable to be struck off the register. Segers, a small Dutch firm, owned the trade mark "Toltecs Special" and had it registered internationally including Germany for raw tobacco and tobacco products. Segers sought to take advantage of the growing market in Germany for fine cut tobacco (used for rolling one's own cigarettes). BAT challenged the registration of "Toltecs Special" in Germany as being confusingly similar under German law to "Dorcet". The two parties entered into an agreement which provided that (a) Segers would not use or promote its "Toltecs Special" mark as being suitable for rolling cigarettes, (b) Segers would not challenge the validity of BAT's "Dorcet" mark and (c) BAT would withdraw its opposition to the grant of protection to the Segers' "Toltecs Special" mark.

8.160 The Commission held that such an agreement fell within Article 85(1) and was not exemptible under Article 85(3). The Commission acknowledged that delimitation agreements can promote competition but held in the instant case, this was not so especially as it included a no-challenge clause. It stated:

> "In the present state of Community law, in cases where the products are similar, there is a serious likelihood of confusion and the owner of the prior mark is therefore more likely to be a position to prevent registration and use of the later mark, restrictions on the use of a later mark do not restrict competition within the meaning of Article 85(1), for in accordance with the case law of the Court of Justice the right to prevent marketing relates to the existence of the prior mark.
>
> However, the greater the difference in the product or the less likely the risk of confusion, the more the agreement must take account of the overriding goal of the Common Market unity. Of all the possible solutions to the conflict, the parties therefore have to adopt that which least restricts the use of both marks throughout the whole of the Common Market. This includes agreements to reproduce the disputed mark only in a certain way (colour, form of lettering, inclusion of trade name, etc.) or possibly to use it for certain products only."[4]

On appeal, the Court of Justice, upholding the Commission, held that:

[2] Case 56/65 *Technique Minière v. Maschinenbau Ulm* [1966] E.C.R. 235, [1966] C.M.L.R. 357.
[3] Case 35/83, [1985] E.C.R. 363; [1985] 2 C.M.L.R. 470.
[4] *ibid*, para. 40–41.

> "it recognises the legality and usefulness of so-called "delimitation agreements" under which in the reciprocal interests of the parties the respective spheres of application of their marks are defined in order to avoid confusion or conflicts. But that view does not mean that the application of *Article 85* of the EEC Treaty to such agreements is excluded if they are also for the purpose of market-sharing or other restrictions of competition. As the Court has already stated in *Consten*, it is incompatible with the Community competition system to allow the improper use of rights under any national trade mark law in order to frustrate the Community's law on cartels."[5]

The Court upheld the Commission's decision principally on the grounds that the agreement was not a genuine delimitation agreement and in effect served no other purpose than to enable BAT to control and prevent distribution of tobacco produced by Segers in Germany.

The Court and Commission both considered that the unequal bargaining strengths of the parties had meant that an agreement had been foisted on Segers and did not reflect a genuine attempt to resolve differences and consequently increase competition. If the object of the agreement is to restrict competition, then the Community provisions of free movement of goods and competition may take priority over national trade mark law. Thus Advocate-General Slynn said that the Commission:

> "is entitled, in my view, to scrutinise critically a delimitation agreement to see whether it is regulating a real dispute in a reasonable way or whether in essence it is restricting competition. If the agreement is essentially to prevent the entry of a competitor on to the market, that is to be considered in the light of the rules on Community competition law, *whatever the position may be in terms of national trade mark law*. [emphasis added]."

Such an opinion would appear to mean that even if a party can legally exclude by use of trade mark law the entry of a competitor onto a national market, a delimitation agreement which has the same effect may still fall within Article 85(1).

8.161 *Commission*—The Commission's approach to settlement agreements has been one of gradual acceptance of the importance that such agreements have in the commercial world and that such agreements will often open up trade and prevent the waste of time and resources in fruitless litigation.

In the 1970s and early 1980s, the Commission took a strict view of settlement agreements. Agreements which restricted circulation of goods or partitioned markets infringed Article 85(1). The Commission paid scant regard to the actual effects of litigations and the possible outcome.

[5] *ibid*, at point 33.

For example, the Commission held that an agreement between an English and French firm who possessed the trade marks "SIRDAR" and "PHILDAR" which prevented each from selling its goods under its trade mark in the other's territory fell within Article 85(1). The Commission said in that case that even if the trade marks were similar and likely to be confused, such did not justify market sharing.[6] Parties were under a duty at Community law to settle any dispute in a way which was least restrictive of competition and the free movement of goods.[7] When looking at the competitive effects of a delimitation agreement, the Commission was more likely to conclude that an agreement was anticompetitive when it was clear that the strong party had forced the agreement on the weaker as was the case in *BAT v. Commission*.[8] However, the converse did not necessarily apply so that it was not a relevant consideration in considering whether a delimitation agreement fell within Article 85(1) that there was a common intention to enter into the agreement.[9]

Conversely, the Commission has ruled that agreements which generally foster competition by allowing each party to freely circulate their trade marked goods and thus avoid market partitioning will fall outside Article 85(1) even if there are ancillary restraint clauses. Thus where two competing enterprises held identical trade marks but in different countries such that neither was capable of marketing goods under the trade mark in the other's countries, a clause in a settlement of a litigation agreement which was generally pro-competitive but prohibited one undertaking from challenging for five years the other's registration fell outside Article 85(1).[10] Similarly, an agreement between two owners of a trade mark with a common origin which permitted the circulation of each's trade marked products in the other's territories subject to distinctive colouring being used fell outside Article 85(1).[11] Where a German firm obtained an injunction against a Japanese firm for the latter's use of a trade mark confusingly similar to the former's trade mark according to German law, an agreement that the Japanese company could use its mark

[6] *Re the Agreement of Sirdar Limited*: [1975] 1 C.M.L.R. D93 at para. 21. The Commission held that the agreement was not capable of exemption under Art. 85(3). See *Sirdar Limited v. Les Fils de Louis Mulliez et al* [1975] 1 C.M.L.R. 378, H.C. where the High Court refused to grant an interlocutory injunction brought by Sirdar for trade mark infringement and breach of contract based on the agreement as the agreement as the Commission had found it was void under Art. 85(2). See also *Re the Persil Trade Mark*: [1978] 1 C.M.L.R. 395 (Commission held that concerted practice between two undertakings owning a trade mark "Persil" in different territories [the two trade marks being of common origin] to prevent exports of their trade marked goods to each other's territories fell within Art. 85(1)).

[7] *e.g.* see *Bramley/Gilbert* point 128, *10th Report on Competition Policy*; *Zoller & Frohlich/Telemecanique*, point 109, *8th Report on Competition Policy*.

[8] Case 35/83, [1985] E.C.R. 363, [1985] 2 C.M.L.R. 470.

[9] Cases 29–30/83, *Cie Royale Asturienne Des Mines & Rheinzink v. E.C. Commission* [1984] E.C.R. 1679, [1985] 1 C.M.L.R. 688, para. 26.

[10] See 78/193/EEC, *Re Penney's Trade Mark*: [1978] 2 C.M.L.R. 100 (E.C. Commission).

[11] *ibid.*

unchanged for three years and then only in conjunction with its own name was held not to infringe Article 85(1).[12] In *Hershey/Schiffers*,[13] a more recent case, an American company, Hershey Foods Corporation, which owned the mark "Hershey" for chocolate products worldwide and a Dutch company, Schiffers, which owned the mark "Herschi" for drinks settled prolonged litigation whereby Schiffers sold their mark to Hershey and in return, received a renewable exclusive licence for five years for a defined group of products. Furthermore, Schiffers undertook not to introduce new products with the trade mark and not to use Herschi as a corporate name for a certain number of years. The Commission held that the agreement fell outside Article 85(1) as it was designed to avoid confusion and did not artificially partition the Common Market.

8.162 The Commission's most recent decision is *Syntex/Synthelabo*.[14] Synthelabo and Syntex came to an agreement to prevent confusion whereby the marks "Synthelabo" or "Synthelab" would not be used in the U.K. and certain non-Member States. The Commission held that the risk of confusion between Synthelabo's trade marks and Syntex's trade marks (the former owning Synthelabo and the latter owning Syntex, Syntrex, Syndrex, Synodex and Synlexan) was not such as to justify the partitioning of the market and because of the size of the companies, the agreement fell within Article 85(1).

However, it did say that:

> "In principle national jurisdictions usually have the right to decide on issues where there is risk of confusion between differing trade marks. However, Article 85(1) is applicable to trade mark delimitation agreement in case where *it is not evident that the holder of the earlier trade mark could have recourse to national law to prevent the holder of a later mark from using it in one or more member-States* [emphasis added]."[15]

The above excerpt suggests that the Commission will now consider the likely outcome of legal proceedings in considering whether the settlement is restrictive of competition. This represents a change from its earlier view that parties must settle a dispute in the least restrictive way regardless of the likely outcome of the litigation. In one case, the Commission initially intended to grant negative clearance of a trade mark delimitation agreement whereby each party restricted itself to use of their identical marks to their own respective spheres of operation. Later on, it became clear that one party's mark had become vulnerable to cancellation

[12] *Tanabe Seiyaku Company v. Bayer AG 8th Report on Competition Policy*, point 125 (E.C. Commission).

[13] Press Release IP (90)87.

[14] Commission Press Release, February 23, 1989, *The Community v. Synthex and Synthelabo* [1990] 4 C.M.L.R. 343, point 59, *19th Report on Competition Policy*.

[15] *ibid*, para. 5.

because of non-use. Upon notification of this fact, the Commission changed its mind and issued a statement of objections.[16]

The present situation as regards trade mark delimitation agreements may be tentatively summarised as follows

(a) Where it is likely (or evident) that one party may succeed in preventing another importing trade marked goods into a Member State, then a *bona fide* delimitation agreement will fall outside Article 85(1) even if such has the effect of restricting imports.

(b) The less evident that one party may exercise its trade mark right successfully against another, then the greater the need to ensure that the agreement encourages the flow of trade marked goods between countries if necessary by adopting distinguishing features.

Patent and other IP litigation settlements

8.163 Whilst the above agreements relate to trade mark settlement disputes, the Commission has shown that it will interfere in patent litigation settlements although in one case, the Commission appears to have ignored the fact that certain restrictive clauses resulted from a patent litigation settlement.[17] The same principles as for trade mark delimitation agreements would seem to apply. Thus the Commission has interfered in a settlement dispute relating to joint ownership of a patent as the interests of the party could have been protected in ways less restrictive of competition.[18] The Commission considered that a patent compromise settlement in which a French concern gave a German concern a licence to manufacture under the patent in exchange for the latter withdrawing its revocation action could not be interpreted as preventing the German company exporting its licensed products to France.[19]

It would seem reasonable to expect the above principles to apply to settlement agreements in the fields of copyright and industrial design.[20]

[16] *Apple Corps Ltd v. Apple Computer Inc* [1991] 3 C.M.L.R. 49, C.A. In this case, the Court of Appeal held in relation to a claim that a trade mark delimitation agreement was in breach of Art. 85 because of the weakness of one's party registrations through non-use and that European law and English law are not concerned with the validity of registrations except to a very slight extent but rather the actual facts. However, the Court of Appeal appeared to be of the opinion that the parties' litigation strengths *vis-à-vis* each other were not enhanced by the fact of registration, *i.e.* the extent of use of each mark was the important criteria. Whilst this is true in many respects in first-to-use countries, it is not true in first-to-file countries where the party to register first a trade mark often gains superior rights over the party to use the mark first. In such cases, registration of a mark will make a considerable difference to the party's relative strengths.

[17] *H. Vaessen BV v. Moris* [1979] 1 C.M.L.R. 511.

[18] *Bramley/Gilbert*, point 128, *10th Report on Competition Policy*.

[19] *Zoller & Frohlich/Telemecanique*, point 109, *8th Report on Competition Policy*, Under Arts. 30–36, the French concern would not have been able to prevent imports of goods from the German licensee into France.

[20] In relation to copyright, see *Neilson-Hordell/Richmark*, point 89, *12th Report on Competition Policy*.

No-challenge clauses in settlement agreements

8.164 Often in intellectual property litigation, an action for infringement involves a counterclaim for revocation of the right as being invalid. Thus, settlement agreements may include no-challenge clauses often coupled with the other party granting a licence (often royalty-free). Such clauses are intrinsic parts of settlement clauses. The effect of such clauses must be judged in the context of the competitive effect of the whole agreement. Thus, whilst normally a no-challenge clause will infringe Article 85, it may fall outside Article 85(1) in a settlement dispute.[21]

(iii) National collecting societies and agreements

8.165 Most countries have national copyright collecting societies which are responsible for levying royalties on the performance of copyright works for their members. The latter will usually have assigned to the copyright collecting society the exclusive world-wide rights of public performance. Such arrangements facilitate the collection of royalties as individual members will rarely have the resources to demand royalties for all performances of their works.

The Court and Commission have several times had to consider agreements and practices of these soceties. Whilst the essence of these societies is to grant performance licences, in effect they are essentially royalty collection agencies. As such, the case law on the compatibility of the societies' practices must be considered *sui generis*. Generally, the Commission and Court will seek to ensure a balance between the requirements of maximum freedom for authors, composers and publishers to dispose of their works and that of the effective management of their rights by an undertaking which in practice they cannot avoid joining.[21a] Thus, contracts between copyright management society and users, whereby the former refuses to grant authorisation for partial use of the repertoire such that the user has to pay high royalties corresponding to the use of the whole repertoire when they only play part of it, does not infringe Article 85(1) unless access to a part of the protected repertoire could entirely safeguard the interests of authors, composers and publishers of music without increasing the costs of managing contracts and mailing the use of protected musical works.[21b]

8.166 *Custom pressing: Re GEMA (Commission)*[22]—Where a royalty-paying licence has been granted by a national performing right society of one Member State to a sound recording supplier, such will be

[21] See No-Challenge Clauses, para. 8.143.
[21a] *BRT v. SABAM* [1974] 2 C.M.L.R. 238 at para. 8.
[21b] *Ministere Public v. Tournier*, at p. 33. In this case, a French discotheque sought access only to Anglo-American music. See n. 24, below.
[22] *Re GEMA*, Notice of the Commission, (February 6, 1985); [1985] 2 C.M.L.R. 1.

valid throughout the Community. Therefore another national performing right society is not entitled to charge supplementary royalties if the supplier seeks to have the records manufactured by an independent pressing firm ("custom pressed") in the latter's country. This is so even if the royalties differ between Member States.[23] The copyright society can carry out checks to ensure that the custom presser has a licence granted by a Member State.

8.167 *Refusal by copyright-management society to grant access to its repertoire to user established in another Member State: Ministere Public v. Tournier and Lucazeau v. SACEM: ECJ*[24]—These combined cases concerned complaints by French discothèque owners about the royalties charged by SACEM, the French national copyright collecting society. Various complaints under Articles 30–36, 59–60 and 85 and 86 were made. For present purposes, we are concerned with the Article 85 case. Such concerned the practice of national copyright-management societies to give each other the right to grant for their respective territories the appropriate licence for any public performance of copyright works. Such reciprocal agreement also stipulated that each society was to collect royalties for the appropriate society as agent but that they were to charge the royalty rate that they would for their own repertoire. Combined with these agreements was a collective practice amongst national copyright management societies that they would refuse to grant licences to their respective territories to users established in other Member States. Such meant that discotheque owners were required to pay SACEM's royalty rates (which were high) for music which they played that was predominantly Anglo-American rather than pay American or British national copyright management societies direct. The Commission held that any concerted practice between national copyright management societies which has as its object of effect the refusal by each society to grant direct access to its repertoire for users established in another Member State was contrary to Article 85.[25]

(iv) Sub-contracting agreements

8.168 Often, undertakings, especially small and medium-sized ones, will for financial reasons prefer to sub-contract out the manufacture of goods or the supply of services rather than manufacture themselves. If intellectual property is involved, this will usually involve licensing the sub-contractor to manufacture the goods.

[23] See Case 55 & 57/80, *MEMBRAN and K-TEL v. GEMA*, [1981] E.C.R. 147; [1981] 2 C.M.L.R. 44.
[24] Cases 395/87 and 110 & 241–242/88, [1989] E.C.R. 2251 [1991] 4 C.M.L.R. 248.
[25] *ibid*, para. 26.

The Commission has issued a Notice on the Application of Article 85(1) to certain Sub-Contracting Agreements[26] in which it states that:

> "The Commission considers that agreements under which one firm, called the 'contractor', whether or not in consequence of a prior order from a third party, entrusts to another called 'the subcontractor', the manufacture of goods, the supply or services or the performance of work under the contractor's instructions, to be provided to the contractor or performed on his behalf, are not of themselves caught by the prohibition in Article 85(1)."

Thus, in the Commission's view, Article 85(1) does not apply to clauses which:

(a) restrict the use of technology or equipment provided by the contractor except for the purposes of the subcontracting agreement; or
(b) prohibit the making available of technology or equipment provided by the contractor to third parties; or
(c) "tie-in" the sub-contractor to supplying the goods or services resulting from the use of such technology or equipment to the contractor

if and only if such technology or equipment is necessary to enable the subcontractor under reasonable conditions to manufacture the goods or supply the services.[27]

The Notice provides that such restrictions are not justifiable where the sub-contractor could under reasonable conditions obtain access to the technology or equipment needed to produce the goods or provide the services. Generally, this will be the case where the contractor provides no more than information which merely describes the work to be done as in such circumstances, the restrictions could deprive the subcontractor of the possibility of developing his own business in the fields covered by the agreement.

The following obligations are also considered to fall outside Article 85(1): An obligation on the sub-contractor not to disclose confidential information or know-how; a ban on use of know-how after the expiry of the agreement and an obligation to licence back on a non-exclusive basis any improvement know-how or patents.[28] A contractor may forbid a subcontractor to apply the former's trade mark or get-up on goods or services which are not to be supplied to the contractor.[29]

[26] O.J. [1979] 1/2.
[27] Notice on Sub Contracting Agreements, para. 2.
[28] *ibid*, para 3. The undertaking may be exclusive in so far as improvements and inventions made by the subcontractor during the currency of the agreement are incapable of being used independently of the contractor's secret know-how. However, any ban on the right to dispose of results of his own research and development where such results are capable of being used independently may restrain competition.
[29] *ibid*, para. 4.

(v) Mergers and acquisitions

8.169 In certain circumstances, an agreement to merge two undertakings can restrict competition.[30] The implementation of such an agreement will often involve the transfer to the acquirer with a view to the full exploitation of the assets transferred, of rights to industrial or commercial property or know-how. However, the vendor may remain the owner of the rights in order to exploit them for activities other than those transferred. In these cases, the usual means for ensuring that the acquirer will have the full use of the assets transferred is to conclude licensing agreements in his favour. In such circumstances, the grant of simple or exclusive licences of patents, similar rights or existing know-how will often be acceptable as ancillary restrictions necessary for the completion of the transaction, and likewise agreements to grant such licences. Thus, the determination of whether the ancillary restriction is anticompetitive or not will depend on whether the merger or acquisition itself is anticompetitive. They may be limited to certain fields of use, to the extent that they correspond to the activities of the undertaking transferred. Normally, it will not be necessary for such licences to include territorial limitations on manufacture which reflect the territory of the activity transferred. Licences may be granted for the whole duration of the patent or similar rights or the duration of the normal economic life of the know-how. As such licences are economically equivalent to a partial transfer of rights, they need not be limited in time.[31] Similarly, where patent undertakings set up a concentrative joint venture, similar provisions aimed at implementing the concentration will be considered necessary and ancillary to such an aim.[32] Such clauses clearly assist the transfer of business and must be considered in the same light as non-competition obligations on the vendor of a business.[33]

(i) Patent Block Exemption[34]

(i) Introduction

8.170 It become apparent in the 1960s and 1970s to an overworked Commission that there was an urgent need for a Patent Block Exemption. Regulation 19/65[35] empowered the Commission to issue block exemp-

[30] *See* Case 6/72, *Europemballage Corp. & Continental Can v. E.C. Commission* [1973] E.C.R. 215, [1973] C.M.L.R. 199. This case is discussed in more detail in the Chapter on Abuse of a Dominant Position—see para. 11.034. Generally, see *Butterworth's Competition Law*; *Bellamy and Child on Common Market Law of Competition* (4th Ed., Sweet and Maxwell). The acquisition of intellectual property via a merger may constitute an abuse of a dominant position, see para. 11.076.

[31] Commission Notice regarding restrictions ancillary to concentrations [1990] O.J. C203/5, para. IIIB.

[32] *ibid* para. VB. See also Chap. 9 on Intellectual Property and Joint Ventures.

[33] *e.g.* see *ibid* para. IIIA and Non-competition obligations, para. 8.138.

[34] This Block Exemption is extensively reviewed by P.A. Stone in his two-part Article "*The EEC Block Exemption—Part I and II*" [1985] 6 EIPR 173 and [1985] 7 EIPR 199. See also Korah "Monograph on Patent Block Exemption".

[35] [1965] O.J. 36, 6.3, p. 533/65.

tions in relation to licences of industrial property rights and know-how.[36] However, such a block exemption was not to be issued until sufficient experience had been gained in the light of individual decisions such that it became possible to define categories of agreements which fell within Article 85(3).[37] A series of decisions by the Commission on patent licences and a considerable amount of consultation in the 1970s between various bodies and the Commission's own Advisory Committee on Restrictive Practices on Dominant Positions led to a draft Patent Block Exemption being published in 1979.[38] By 1979, 63 per cent of all agreements notified to the Commission had been patent licences and thus the need for such an exemption was paramount.[39] The high number of notifications reflected precisely the uncertainty of the application of Article 85 to such agreements.

The Commission decided to wait for the Court's decision in *Nungesser v. E.C. Commission*[40] before officially issuing the Patent Block Exemption which entered into force on January 1, 1985 for a period of 10 years. The effect was dramatic and the number of notifications reduced dramatically.[41]

The Patent Block Exemption was due to expire on December 31, 1994. The Commission has published a preliminary draft Technology Transfer Block Exemption. This is intended to replace both the Patent and the Know How Block Exemption by providing a single combined regulation covering pure patent licensing, pure know how licensing and mixed agreements. The transitional provisions of the draft regulation at present permit patent licences to benefit from the Patent Block Exemption from January 1 to June 30, 1995 provided the agreement was in force on January 1, 1995.[42] Because of a delay in implementing this block exemption, the Patent Block Exemption has again been extended to December 31, 1995.

(ii) Scope of Patent Block Exemption

8.171 The Block Exemption only applies to agreements between two parties whereby one undertaking (the licensor) permits another (the licensee) to exploit the patented invention.[43] It applies to licenses for patents which have been applied for but not granted, utility models and their appli-

[36] *ibid*, Art. 1(b).
[37] *ibid*, Recital 4.
[38] See [1979] O.J. No C 58, 3.3, p. 12.
[39] *9th Report on Competition Policy*, points 20–27.
[40] Case 258/78, [1982] E.C.R. 2015, [1983] 1 C.M.L.R. 278.
[41] See Introduction to *15th Report on Competition Policy*.
[42] Art. 9, draft Technology Transfer Block Exemption—a copy of this draft appears in the August version of 1994 EIPR.
[43] The Regulation specifically includes licensing agreements where the licensor is not the patentee; assignments of a patent where payment is based on turnover by the assignee in respect of the patented products and where the rights and obligations of the licensor or licensee are assumed by undertakings connected with them—Art. 11. "Connected undertakings" are defined at Art. 12.

cations.[44] In case there was any doubt, licences of plant breeder's rights are specifically excluded.[45]

Until recently, patent pools, licensing agreement entered into in relation to joint ventures and reciprocal licensing/distribution agreements[46] were not covered by the Block Exemption.[47] The Commission has recently issued an amending regulation which allows for exemption of joint venture and reciprocal licensing agreements subject to certain criteria.[48] Where a patent undertaking grants the joint venture a patent licence, the block exemption applies provided that the contract products and the other products of the participating undertakings, which are considered by users to be equivalent in view of their characteristics, price and intended use, represent in the case of a licence limited to production not more than 20 per cent and in the case of a licence covering production and distribution note more than 10 per cent of the market for all such products in the Common Market or a substantial part thereof. Furthermore, the Patent Block Exemption applies to patent reciprocal licences provided that the parties are not subject to any territorial restriction within the Common Market with regard to the manufacture, use or putting on the market of the contract products or on the use of the licensed processes.[49]

Patent licensing agreements often contain ancillary know-how provisions as such mixed agreements are commonly concluded to allow the transfer of a complex technology. Such agreements will only fall within the Patent Block Exemption:

> "where the communicated technical knowledge is secret and permits a better exploitation of the licensed patents . . . [and] only in so far as the licensed patents are necessary for achieving the objects of the licensed technology and as long as at least one of the licensed patents remain in force."[50]

Accordingly, mixed licensing agreements will often fall outside the Patent Block Exemption.[51] Ancillary provisions relating to trade marks come within the scope of the Regulation provided that the trade mark licence is

[44] Art. 10(1). In fact, the Block Exemption applies to licences entered into for the exploitation of an invention prior to an application for a patent provided such an application is made within a year of the date when the agreement was entered into—Art. 10(2).

[45] Recital 8, Art. 5(1)(4).

[46] Unless both parties are not subject to any territorial restrictions in the Common Market—original Regulation Art. 5(2).

[47] Recital 2, 8, Art. 5.

[48] Group Exemptions (Amendment) Regulation 1992 [1993] O.J. L21/8, [1993] 4 C.M.L.R. 151.

[49] Art. 5(2) as amended.

[50] Recital 9.

[51] See *Re the Agreement between Boussois and Interpane mbh*: [1987] O.J. L50/30, [1988] 4 C.M.L.R. 124 where the Commission held that a mixed licence was not covered by the Patent Block Exemption because the know how formed the dominant element and there were no patents in some areas of the licensed technology.

not used to extend the effects of the patent licence beyond the life of the patents.[52]

(iii) Scheme of Block Exemption

8.172 The Regulation lists three types of clauses. The first category of clauses (Article 1) are those to which Article 85(3) is deemed to apply. The clauses are thus said to be "white-listed". The second category (Article 2) are those clauses ("super-white-listed") which are not considered by the Commission to generally fall within Article 85(1) but which, if included in a licence will not cause it to fall outside the Block Exemption. This category is deemed not be exhaustive. The third category (Article 3) are those clauses which if included in a licence will cause it to fall outside the Block Exemption. They are said to be "black-listed". Thus any licence which *only* contains clauses in the first two categories will be covered by the Block Exemption. Any licence which contains even one clause from the third category falls outside the Block Exemption and must be notified for individual exemption. Where a licence contains clauses *restrictive of competition* but not mentioned in Articles 1, 2, or 3, then the opposition procedure must be used if the licence is to benefit from the Block Exemption.[53] Furthermore, the Commission may withdraw the benefit of the Block Exemption where a licence which is covered by it has certain effects incompatible with Article 85(3).[54]

(iv) Justification for Block Exemption

8.173 The Commission in its 14th Report on Competition Policy said in relation to the block exemption:

> "The obligations listed in Article 1 generally contribute to improving the production of goods and to promoting technical progress; they make patentees more willing to grant licences and licensees more inclined to undertake the investment required to manufacture, use and put on the market a new product or to use a new process, so that undertakings other than the patentee acquire the possibility of manufacturing their products with the aid of the latest techniques and of developing those techniques further. The result is that the number of production facilities and the quantity and quality of goods produced in the common market are increased."[55]

(v) Duration of Patent Block Exemption

8.174 The Patent Block Exemption entered into force on January 1, 1985 and was due to expire on December 31, 1994. Very recently, the Commission has twice extended the regulation to give it time to rework the technology

[52] Recital 10.
[53] See Opposition Procedure, para. 8.207. Whether such a clause infringes Art. 85(1) will depend on the case law.
[54] See para. 8.208 below.
[55] Recital 12.

transfer draft block exemption.[55a] Accordingly, at present, it is due to expire as of December 31, 1995.

(vi) Transitional provisions

8.175 If a licence was entered into after January 1, 1985 and is covered by the Block Exemption, then Article 85(1) is deemed inapplicable to the licence. The Regulation also applies with retroactive effect to "old" patent licences in existence on January 1, 1985 if the licence fulfilled the conditions of the Block Exemption though it is not entirely clear whether or not retroactive exemption applies to non-notified "old" exclusive licences.[56] The recent amendments to the Patent Block Exemption on its applicability to certain types of joint venture licensing arrangement and reciprocal licensing arrangements are retrospective and thus apply to agreements entered into before 1st April 1993.[57] At present, according to the draft Technology Transfer Block Exemption which is intended to replace the Patent Block Exemption, the latter will continue to apply to patent licences until June 30, 1995 which were in force on January 1, 1995.[58]

(viii) Check-list

White-listed clauses

8.176
—Exclusive licence
—Exploitation ban in licensor's territory
—Manufacuring ban in other licensees' territory
—Active competition ban in other licensees' territory
—Passive sales ban in other licensees' territory for five year period
—Obligation to use only licensor's trade mark or get-up on licensed product

Super-white-listed clauses

8.177
—Exclusive Purchasing Restrictions necessary for technically satisfactory exploitation of licensed invention
—Minimum royalty/working obligations
—Field-of-use restrictions
—Post-term exploitation bans

[55a] O.J. [1994] C313/6; O.J. [1995] C141/6.

[56] Arts. 6–8 and Recital 26. There appears to be a lacuna. The Arts (the binding part of the Regulation—*cf.* Recital 26) do not cover "old licences" in existence on January 1, 1985 which were not notified to the Commission unless they fall within Reg. 17 Art. 4(2)(2)(b), which does not apply where restrictions ar placed in the licensor *i.e.* exclusive licences. Thus there may be some scope for argument that an "old" non-notified exclusive licence is not covered by the Block Exemption and hence void for the period preceding January 1, 1985.

[57] See Group Exemptions (Amendment) Regulation 1992, Art. 5 [1993] O.J. L21/8, [1993] 4 C.M.L.R. 151.

[58] Art. 9, draft Technology Transfer Block Exemption—a copy of this draft appears in the August version of 1994 EIPR.

—Assignment/sub-licence bans
—Marking obligations
—Maintenance of secrecy of know-how obligations
—Obligation to legally assist licensor
—Quality control specifications
—Non-exclusive licensing to licensor of improvement patents and know-how
—"Most favourable term" provisions

Black-listed clauses

8.178

—No-challenge clauses
—Artificial prolongation of licence
—Non-competition bans
—Royalties on unprotected goods or services
—Quantitative restrictions
—Resale Price Restrictions
—Customer restrictions
—Compulsory assignment of improvement patents to licensor
—"Tie-in" packages not referable to technical exploitation of invention
—Bans on sales into other licensee's territory where not white-listed
—Parallel import restrictions

(viii) Effect of Patent Block Exemption on individual clauses

(a) Territorial obligations of licensor and licensees

Relevant provisions

White-listed clauses

8.179

1(1)(1) An obligation on the licensor not to license other undertakings to exploit the licensed invention in the licensed territory, covering all or part of the common market, in so far as and as long as one of the licensed patents remains in force.

1(1)(2) An obligation on the licensor not to exploit the licensed invention himself in the licensed territory in so far and as long as one of the licensed patents remains in force.

1(1)(3) An obligation on the licensee not to exploit the licensed invention in territories within the common market which are reserved for the licensor, in so far and as long as the patented product is protected in those territories by parallel patents.

1(1)(4) An obligation on the licensee not to manufacture or use the licensed products, or use the patented process or the communicated know-how, in territories within the common market which are licensed to other licensees, in so far and as long as the licensed product is protected in those territories by parallel patents.

1(1)(5) An obligation on the licensee not to pursue an active policy of putting the licensed product on the market in the territories within the common market which are licensed to other licensees, and in particular not to engage in advertising specifically aimed at those territories or to establish any branch or maintain any distribution depot there, in so far as and as long as the licensed product is protected in those territories by parallel patents.

1(1)(6) An obligation on the licensee not to put the licensed product on the market in the territories licensed to other licensees within the common market for a period not exceeding five years from the date when the product is first put on the market within the common market by the licensor or one of his licensees, in so far as and for as long as the product is protected in these territories by parallel patents.

1(2) The exemption for restrictions on putting the licensed product on the market resulting from obligations referred to in paragraph 1(2)(3)(5) and (6) shall apply only if the licensee manufactures the licensed product himself or has it manufactured by a connected undertaking or by a subcontractor.

Black-listed clauses

8.180 3(10) Without prejudice to Article 1(1)(5), the licensee is required to for a period exceeding that permitted under Article 1(1)(6), not to put the licensed product on the market in territories licensed to other licensees within the common market or does not do so as a result of a concerted practice between the parties.

3(11) One or both of the parties are required (a) to refuse without any objectively justified reason to meet demand from users or resellers in their respective territories who would market products in other territories within the common market; (b) to make it difficult for users or resellers to obtain the products from other resellers within the common market and in particular to exercise industrial or commercial property rights or take measures so as to prevent users or resellers from obtaining outside, or from putting on the market in, the licensed territory products which have been lawfully put on the market within the common market by the patentee or with his consent—or do so as a result of concerted practice between them.

The above clauses essentially deal with three types of clauses: those that confer exclusivity on the licensee, those that seek to prevent sales between licensees and licensor and thirdly, parallel imports of patented products.

8.181 *Exclusive licences*—At Recital 11, the Commission said that:

> "Exclusive licensing agreements, *i.e.* agreements in which the licensor undertakes not to exploit the 'licensed invention', *i.e.* the licensed patented invention and any know-how communicated to the licensees in the licensed territory himself or to grant further licences there, are not in themselves incompatible with Article 85(1) where they are concerned with the introduction and protection of a new technology in the licensed territory, by reason of the sale of the research which has been undertaken and of the risk that is involved, in manufacturing and marketing a product which is unfamiliar to users in the licensed territory at the time the agreement is made. This may also be the case where the agreements are concerned with the introduction and protection of a new process for manufacturing a product which is already known."[59]

Thus, exclusive licences will often fall outside Article 85(1). Where such is not the case, an exclusive licence is now exempted. The effect of Articles 1(1) to 1(4) is to permit a licensor to grant exclusive licences for designated territories and to prevent the manufacture of patented products by licensees or licensor in each other's territories.

The licensor is advised to include a clause which gives it the right to terminate the exclusivity granted to the licensee if the licensee fails to exploit the patent adequately or at all as the Commission can withdraw the effect of the Block Exemption if such a clause is omitted.[60]

8.182 *Direct sales—licensee/licensee*—It is notable that the above clauses do not allow absolute territorial protection for licensees or licensor. Article 1(1)(5) exempts bans against a licensee conducting an "active sales" policy in other licensees' territory for the duration of the patent. Article 1(1)(6) exempts "passive sales" bans in other licensees' territory (*i.e.* where "the licensee of a territory simply responds to requests which he has not solicited from users or resellers established in the territories of other licensees"[61]) for a period of five years from the "date when the product is first put on the market within the common market by the licensor or one of his licensees". It should be noted that this period refers to the product first being marketed in the Community not the start of the licence. Thus, once five years has expired from the date of first marketing, established licensees may make passive sales into a new licensee's territory even if the latter has just entered into a licence. This seems a rather anomalous effect as often the later licensees need more protection from aggressive established licensees than the original licensees ever did. Any bans of longer duration are specifically black-listed by Article 3(10).

[59] Recital 11.
[60] Art. 9(3). See para. 8.208, below.
[61] Recital 12. Recital 13 seems to contradict the limited "passive sales" exemption by stating that Art. 1 does not apply where the licensee is obliged to refuse to meet unsolicited demand from the territory of other licensees.

8.183 *Direct sales—licensee/licensor*—It should be noted that the active and passive sales bans only apply to licensees selling into other licensees' territories. With regard to licensees selling into territories reserved to the licensor,[62] Article 1(1)(3) exempts obligations on the licensee not to "exploit" the licensed invention in territories reserved to the licensor. This provision would appear to include bans on exports into the licensor's territory.[63] Accordingly, a licensor is better protected from his licensees than the latter are from each other. Furthermore, Article 1(1)(2) exempts reciprocal obligations on the licensor but in this case, it is less clear whether or not this includes export bans into licensees' territory.[64]

8.184 *Parallel imports*—Article 3(11)(a) black-lists any requirement that one or both parties without objectively justified reason refuse to meet demand for licensed products from users or resellers (*i.e.* parallel importers) *in their respective territories* who would market products in other territories by contractual means.[65] For this condition to be applicable, it would appear that the user or reseller must be established in the party's territory.[66]

Article 3(11)(b) also "black-lists" any requirement that a party hinders the obtaining of products from other resellers within the common market and in particular to exercise intellectual or industrial property rights so as to prevent users or resellers from obtaining outside or from putting on the market in, the licensed territory products which have been lawfully put on the market within the common market by the patentee or with his consent whether by the use. This provision does not cover "direct sales" by licensees but products which have already been sold and is designed to prevent licensor and licensees from preventing the free circulation of "franked" goods. It is designed to mirror the doctrine of exhaustion that the Court of Justice has established in relation to Articles 30–36 (the free movement of goods provisions) whereby one party is not allowed to exercise its rights against another in relation to the import of protected goods where they have been placed on the market with the former's consent.[67]

8.185 *Exclusive sales licence*—The effect of Article 1(2) is that an exclusive sales licence (*i.e.* a distribution agreement) is not covered by the Block Exemption unless coupled with an exclusive manufacturing licence.[68]

[62] *i.e.* territories for which licence have not been granted—Recital 12.
[63] Recital 12.
[64] Recital 12 is silent on the issue of exports into licensees' territory from the licensor.
[65] Art. 3(11) and Recital 13.
[66] See Recital 12 which refers in respect of the "passive sales" exemption (Art. 1(1)(6)) that it applies to "users or resellers *established* in the territories of other licensees"; See also Art. 3(11) of the French text of the Patent Block Exemption refers to users and resellers *established* in the licensor or licensee's territory.
[67] See Chap. 7 on *Enforcement of Intellectual Property*.
[68] Article 1(2). For meaning of "connected undertaking", see Art. 12.

(b) Marking clauses

Relevant provision

White-listed

1(1)(7) An obligation on the licensee to use only the licensor's trade mark or the get-up determined by the licensor to distinguish the licensed product, provided that the licensee is not prevented from identifying himself as the manufacturer of the licensed product. **8.186**

Super-white-listed

2(1)(6) An obligation on the licensee to mark the licensed product with an indication of the patentee's name, the licensed patent or the patent licensing agreement. **8.187**

(c) Tie-in clauses

Relevant provisions

Super-white-listed

2(1)(1) An obligation on the licensee to procure goods or services from the licensor or from an undertaking designated by the licensee to procure goods or services from the licensor or from an undertaking designated by the licensor, in so far as such products or services are necessary for a technically satisfactory exploitation of the licensed invention. **8.188**

Black-listed

3(9) The licensee is induced at the time the agreement is entered into to accept further licences which he does not want or to agree to use patents, goods or services which he does not want, unless such patents, products or services are necessary for a technically satisfactory exploitation of the licensed invention. **8.189**

(d) Royalty clauses

Relevant provisions

Super-white-listed

2(1)(2) An obligation on the licensee to pay a minimum royalty or to produce a minimum quantity of the licensed product or to carry out a minimum number of operations exploiting the licensed invention. **8.190**

Black-listed

8.191 3(4) The licensee is charged royalties on products which are not entirely or partially patented or manufactured or manufactured by means of a patented process, or for the use of know-how which has entered into the public domain otherwise than by the fault of the licensee or an undertaking connected with him, without prejudice to arrangements whereby, in order to facilitate payment by the licensee, the royalty payments for the use of a licensed invention are spread over a period extending beyond the life of the licensed patents or the entry of the know-how into the public domain.

The minimum royalty provision is self-explanatory. However, it should be noted that the Commission has the right to withdraw the benefit of the Block Exemption if the patent is not adequately exploited after five years.[69] Thus, it may be advisable to include a minimum working provision as well.[70] With regard to a requirement to pay royalties on products where all licensed patents have expired, it is likely that such an obligation will be construed as constituting an arrangement to facilitate payments.[71]

(e) Field-of-use provisions

Relevant provisions

Super-white-listed

8.192 2(1)(3) An obligation on the licensee to restrict his exploitation of the licensed invention to one or more technical fields of application covered by the licensed patent.

(f) Temporal provisions

Relevant provisions

Super-white-listed

8.193 2(1)(4) An obligation on the licensee not to exploit the patent after termination of the agreement in so far as the patent is still in force.

Black-listed

8.194 3(2) The duration of the licensing agreement is automatically prolonged beyond the expiry of the licensed patents existing at the time the agreement was entered into by the inclusion

[69] Art. 9(3).
[70] See para. 8.181, above.
[71] See section on Temporal Restrictions, para. 8.125.

in it of any new patent obtained by the licensor, unless the agreement provides each party with the right to terminate the agreement at least annually after the expiry of the licensed patents existing at the time the agreement was entered into, without prejudice to the right of the licensor to charge royalties for the full period during which the licensee continues to use know-how communicated by the licensor which has not entered into the public domain, even if that period exceeds the life of the patents.

The ban on post-term exploitation of intellectual property is now standard Commission policy. Article 3(2) is aimed at preventing licensees from being "locked in" once the patents have expired. Such a clause may be ineffective though to prevent a licensee from paying royalties for products whose patents have expired if such an arrangement is merely to facilitate payment by the licensee in relation to royalty payments for the prior exploitation of the expired patents.[72]

(g) Assignment/sub-licensing provisions

Relevant provisions

Super-white-listed

8.195 2(1)(5) An obligation on the licensee not to grant sub-licenses or to assign the licence.

(h) Know-how secrecy provisions

Relevant provisions

Super-white-listed

8.196 2(1)(7) An obligation on the licensee not to divulge know-how communicated by the licensor; the licensee may be held to this obligation after the agreement has expired.

(i) Legal assistance provisions

Relevant provisions

Super-white-listed

8.197 2(1)(8) Obligations (a) to inform the licensor or infringements of the patent (b) to take legal action against an infringer (c) to assist the licensor in any legal action against an infringer—provided that these obligations are without prejudice to the licensee's right to challenge the validity of the licensed patent.

[72] See Art. 3(4) and Temporal Restrictions, para. 8.125.

(j) Quality control clauses

Relevant provisions

Super-white-listed

8.198 2(1)(9) An obligation on the licensee to observe specifications concerning the minimum quality of the licensed product, provided that such specifications are necessary for a technically satisfactory exploitation of the licensed invention, and to allow the licensor to carry out related checks.

(k) Grant-back provisions

Relevant provisions

Super-white-listed

8.199 2(1)(10) An obligation on the parties to communicate to one another any experience gained in exploiting the licensed invention and to grant one another a licence in respect of inventions relating to improvements and new applications, provided that such communications or licence is non-exclusive.

Black-listed

8.200 3(8) The licensee is obliged to assign wholly or in part to the licensor rights in or to patents for improvements or for new applications of the licensed patents.

(l) Most-favourable term clauses

Relevant provisions

Super-white-listed

8.201 2(1)(11) An obligation on the licensor to grant the licensee any more favourable terms that the licensor may grant to another undertaking after the agreement is entered into.

(m) No-challenge clauses

Relevant provisions

Black-listed

8.202 3(1) The licensee is prohibited from challenging the validity of licensed patents or other industrial or commercial property rights within the common market belonging to the licensor or undertakings connected with him, without prejudice to the right of the licensor to terminate the licensing agreement in the event of such a challenge.

The fact that the block exemption permits a licensor to terminate the licence in the event of a challenge renders the "black-listing" of no-challenge clauses largely ineffective. Few licensees will be prepared to risk the loss of a licence to embark upon a challenge to the validity of the patent unless they are absolutely sure of its invalidity. Conversely, licensors would usually be content merely to terminate a licence if the licensee challenges the validity of the rights. Few would seek damages for breach of the no-challenge clause as such would be difficult to quantify. It may well be that the "no-challenge" clauses falls outside Article 85(1) if the licence is part of a settlement agreement.[73] In such circumstances, the licence would have to be individually notified.[74]

(n) Non-competition clauses

Relevant provisions

Black-listed

3(3) One party is restricted from competing with the other party, with undertakings connected with the other party or with other undertaking within the common market in respect of research and development, manufacture, use or sales, save as provided in Article 1 and without prejudice to an obligation on the licensee to use his best endeavours to exploit the licensed invention. **8.203**

This bans blanket competition bans which seek to restrict competition more than permitted in Article 1. Article 3(10) also black-lists obligations on parties not to put the licensed product on the market in territories licensed to other licensees without prejudice to Article 1(1)(5) and Article 1(1)(6). Thus, Article 3(3) black-lists those competitions bans which are not of a territorial nature. The proviso permitting a "best endeavours" clause is of interest. If a licensee was exploiting another product, a licensor may seek to invoke the best endeavours clause and allege that the licensee is not concentrating all his efforts on marketing the licensed product. Thus, a best endeavours clause can play the part of a non-competition clause.

(o) Quantitative restrictions

Relevant provisions

Black-listed

3(5) The quantity of licensed products may manufacture or sell or the number of operations exploiting the licensed invention he may carry out are subject to limitations. **8.204**

This clearly only applies to restrictions which place a ceiling on the number of goods to be manufactured. Article 2(2) "super-white-lists" minimum quantitative restrictions.

[73] See No-Challenge Clauses, para. 8.143 and Case 65/86, *Bayer AG v. Sullhöfer* [1988] E.C.R. 5249, [1990] 4 C.M.L.R. 182.
[74] The opposition procedure would not work as that only pertains to licences that do not contain "black-listed" clauses. See Art. 4.

(p) Resale price restrictions

Relevant provisions

Black-listed

8.205 3(6) One party is restricted in the determination of prices, components or prices or discounts for the licensed products.

(q) Customer restrictions

Relevant provisions

Black-listed

8.206 3(7) One party is restricted as to the customers he may serve, in particular by being prohibited from supplying certain clauses of user, employing certain forms of distribution or, with the aim of sharing customers certain types of packaging for the products, save as provided in Article 1(1)(7) and Article 2(1)(3).

Article 1(1)(7) merely exempts an obligation on the licensee to use only the licensor's trade mark or get-up as prescribed by the licensor. Article 2(1)(3) permits field-of-use restrictions. Clearly, the latter restriction *de facto* restricts the customers that will be interested in the licensee's products.

(ix) "Opposition" procedure

8.207 The Patent Block Exemption provides for a procedure for exemption of licences that contain obligations restrictive of competition not listed in Article 1, 2 or 3.[75] Such licences must be notified to the Commission as if the party were seeking individual exemption.[76] If the Commission does not oppose exemption within six months of receiving the notification, then the licence is deemed to be exempted. Express references must be made to the fact that exemption is being sought under the Patent Block Exemption and that complete information on the licence and its economic context is provided. The Commission has a discretion to oppose exemption but must do so if requested to do so by a Member State. In the latter case, the Commission may only withdraw its opposition after consultation with the Advisory Committee on Restrictive Practices and Dominant Positions.

If the Commission does not oppose exemption, then the licence is covered by the Patent Block Exemption and thus is deemed to have been exempt for the life of the licence. If the Commission opposes and then withdraws its opposition, exemption applies from the date of notification.[77] If amendments are made so as to satisfy the Commission that

[75] Art. 4.
[76] See Chap. 12 on Enforcement of EEA Competition Law.
[77] Art. 4(7).

the agreement falls within Article 85(3), then exemption applies as from the date of the amendments.[78] If the opposition is not withdrawn, then the effects of the notification is covered by Regulation 17.[79]

The effects of notification via the opposition procedure are discussed in more detail later on.[80]

(x) Right of commission to withdraw benefit of Patent Block Exemption

8.208 The Commission may withdraw the benefit of the Block Exemption where an agreement has certain effects incompatible with Article 85(3). These are where such effects arise from an arbitration award; the licensed products are not exposed to effective *inter-brand* competition in a licensee's territory;[81] there is no clause allowing the licensee to rescind the exclusivity of a licence if the patent has not been worked adequately or at all; the licensee refuses to meet unsolicited demand from users or resellers in other licensee's territories after the five year "passive sales" ban period has expired or the licensee/licensor refuse to meet demand from users or parallel importers in their respective territory or make it difficult for them to market licensed products already on the market.[82]

(j) Know-How Block Exemption[83]

(i) Introduction

8.209 It became apparent early on in the life of the Patent Block Exemption that many technological licensing agreements were not covered by it. In *Boussois v. Interpane*,[84] the Commission took a restrictive view of the application of the Patent Block Exemption to mixed know-how/patent licences. It held that a mixed patent/know-how licence did not fall within the Patent Block Exemption because the know-how formed the "dominant element" of the licensing package and there were no patents in certain areas of the technology licensed. Furthermore, the Commission stated that a prohibition on the licensee manufacturing in Member States outside France where there were no parallel patents did not fall within the Patent Block Exemption because it only covered territorial restrictions on the exploitation of technology in territories where there were parallel patents and there were no patents in five Member States.

[78] Art. 4(8).
[79] Art. 4(9). See Chap. 12 on Enforcement of EEA Competition Law.
[80] See Chap. 12.
[81] This provision can cause problems if the technology is very new and inventive and there is no effective competition. Note however that the Commission considers that "new technology" agreements fall outside Art. 85(1) if they involve manufacturing and marketing a product which is unfamiliar to users in the licensed territory at the time the agreement was made—see Recital 11 and also Case 258/78, *L.C. Nungesser KG & Eisele v. E.C. Commission* [1982] E.C.R. 2015, [1983] 1 C.M.L.R. 278.
[82] Art. 9.
[83] Reg. 556/89.
[84] *Re the Agreement between Boussois and Interpane mbh*: [1987] O.J. L50/30, [1988] 4 C.M.L.R. 124.

Most technological licences invariably include know-how. Furthermore, most businesses do not take out patents in all Member States because of the cost. Know-how licences provides a cheaper although more risky way of exploiting technology. Thus there arose a great need for a know-how block exemption. As the Commission said:

> "The increasing economic importance of non-patented technical information (*e.g.* descriptions of manufacturing processes, recipes, formulae, designs or drawings) commonly termed "know-how", the large number of agreements currently being concluded by undertakings including public research facilities solely for the exploitation of such information (so-called "pure" know-how licensing agreements) and the fact that the transfer of know-how is in practice frequently irreversible make it necessary to provide greater legal certainty with regard to the status of such agreements under the competitions rules, thus encouraging the dissemination of technical knowledge in the Community."[85]

The Commission first considered the possibility of a know-how block exemption in 1984. In August 1987, a draft regulation was published.[86] A considerable amount of consultation with Member States, industry and the Advisory Committee on Restrictive Practices and Monopolies was undertaken. Furthermore, the Commission had taken several decisions in the field of know-how licences since the entry into force of the Patent Block Exemption.[87] Such licences were treated favourably for exemption purposes although the Commission still applied Article 85(1) restrictively to such licences.

Such experience empowered the Commission under Regulation 19/65 to issue a block exemption regulation in relation to "rights arising out of contracts for assignment of, or the right to use, a method of manufacture or knowledge relating to the use or to the application of industrial processes".[88]

The Commission has recently issued a draft Technology Transfer Block Exemption which is intended to replace the Know-How and Patent Block Exemption for new agreements. However, the Know-How Block Exemption is intended to continue to apply until December 31, 1999 to agreements which were in force on January 1, 1995.[89]

[85] Recital 1, para. 2.

[86] [1987] O.J. C214/2.

[87] *Re the Agreements between Jus-Rol Ltd and Rich Products Corp.*: [1988] O.J. L69/21, [1988] 4 C.M.L.R. 527; *Agreement between Boussois and Interpane mbh*: [1987] O.J. L50/30, [1988] 4 C.M.L.R. 124; *Re the Agreement between DDD Ltd and Delta Chemie*: [1988] O.J. L309/34, [1989] 4 C.M.L.R. 535.

[88] Reg. 19/65, Art. 1(b). Recital 4 stipulates that the Commission may issue a block exemption after sufficient experience has been gained in the light of individual decisions.

[89] Art. 9, draft Technology Transfer Block Exemption—a copy of this draft appears in the August version of 1994 EIPR.

(ii) Relaxation in commission's stance on intellectual property licences

8.210 The passing of the Know-How Block Exemption reveals a clear moderation of the Commission's views since the Patent Block Exemption was passed as to clauses that fall within Article 85(1) and what can be exempted under Article 85(3). Three examples demonstrate this.

Firstly, the Commission appears to be relaxing its attitude to the question of remuneration of the licensor. As has been argued already, as licences are essentially "pro-competitive", allowing for the dissemination of technology and increasing the number of competitors in a field, it would seem correct to allow both licensor and licensee to negotiate freely the terms in a licence relating to remuneration. The Commission in the Patent Block Exemption "black-lists" an obligation to pay royalty payments after the patent has expired or the know-how has entered the public domain.[90] In the Know-How Block Exemption, the Commission "super-white-lists" an obligation to pay royalties after the know-how has entered the public domain until the end of the licence. In its explanation of this, it implies that such an obligation reflects one method of payment and is thus generally unrestrictive of competition.[91]

Secondly, it "white-lists" an obligation on the licensee to limit production of the licensed product to the quantities required only in the manufacture of his own products and to sell the licensed product only as an integral part or replacement part for his own products.[92] Such is "white-listed" because "it gives the licensor an incentive to disseminate the technology in various application while reserving the separate sale of the licensed product to himself or other licensees."[93] This must be contrasted with the Commission's previous opposite stance. Such a quantitative restriction is "black-listed" in the Patent Block Exemption.

Thirdly, an obligation on the licensee only to exploit the know-how for a particular product market is "super-white-listed" and thus considered by the Commission to be generally unrestrictive of competition. In the Patent Block Exemption, restrictions as to technical fields of application are "super-white-listed" but no mention is made of product markets. It is likely that under the Patent Block Exemption such a restriction amounts to a customer restriction and is thus "black-listed".[94] The Com-

[90] Art. 4(4). This ban on such clauses was expressed to be without prejudice to arrangements whereby in order to facilitate payment by the licensee by the spreading of royalty payments.

[91] Recital 15. However if this obligation to pay royalties for know-how that has entered the public domain is excessive in relation to the lead-time gained by the licensee over other non-licensed manufacturers then the Commission may withdraw exemption if such is detrimental to competition—Art. 7(7).

[92] Art. 1(1)(8).

[93] Recital 7.

[94] See Reg. 2349/84, Arts. 2(3) and 3(7). The equivalent provision re: customer restriction in the Know-How Block Exemption specifically restricts itself to "black-listing" customer restrictions within a particular product market—see Art. 3(6).

mission justifies such clearance because the licensor can be regarded as having the right to transfer the know-how only for a limited purpose.[95]

The new approach in the Know-How Block Exemption recognises that a licensor is under no obligation to create competition in his own technology and that the competitive effect of a clause must be examined by comparing the economic situation with and without a licence.

(iii) Duration of Know-How Block Exemption

8.211 The Know-How Block Exemption came into force on April 1, 1989 and remains in force until December 31, 1999.[96] The draft Technology Transfer Block Exemption intends to replace the Know-How Block Exemption for agreements which came into force after January 1, 1995. Where agreements were in force on that date, the Know-How Block Exemption will continue to apply until December 31, 1999.[97]

(iv) Scope of Know-How Block Exemption

8.212 Know-how licences must fulfil the following conditions in order to fall within the Know-How Block Exemption.

(a) Secret, substantial and identified

8.213 The Block Exemption only covers know-how licences where the know-how is secret, substantial and identified in any appropriate form.[98] These four conditions are defined as follows:[99]

> *know-how*—means a body of technical information that is secret, substantial and identified in any appropriate form.
>
> *secret*—means that know-how package as a body or in the precise configuration and assembly of its components is not generally known or easily accessible, so that part of its value consists in the lead-time the licensee gains when it is communicated to him; it is not limited to the narrow sense that each individual component of the know-how should be totally unknown or unobtainable outside the licensor's business.
>
> *substantial*—means that the know-how includes information which is of importance for the whole or a significant part of (i) a manufacturing process or (ii) a product or service or (iii) for the development thereof and excludes information which is trivial. Such know-how must thus be useful, *i.e.* can reasonably be expected at the date of conclusion of the agreement to be capable of improving the competi-

[95] Recital 16.
[96] Art. 12.
[97] See Art. 9, draft Technology Transfer Block Exemption—a copy of this draft appears in the August version of EIPR 1994.
[98] Recital 1, Art. 1(3).
[99] Art. 1(7) (1)–(4).

tive position of the licensee, for example by helping him to enter a new market or giving him an advantage in competition with other manufacturers or providers of services who do not have access to the licensed secret know-how or other comparable secret know-how.

identified—means that the know-how is described or recorded in such a manner as to make it possible that it fulfils the criteria of secrecy and substantially and to ensure that the licensee is not unduly restricted in his exploitation of his own technology. To be identified the know-how can either be set out in the licence agreement or in a separate document or recorded in any other appropriate form at the latest when the know-how is transferred or shortly thereafter, provided that the separate document or other record can be made available if the need arises.

Subsequent improvements to know-how must be identified and communicated to the other party as well.[1]

(b) Pure know-how and mixed patent/know-how licences

8.214 The Block Exemption encompasses pure know-how licences and *only* those mixed patent/know-how licences not covered by the Patent Block Exemption.[2] Thus all mixed know-how licences where the know-how is secret, substantial and identified will be covered by either the Patent or Know-How Block Exemption. In case of doubt, Recital 2 of the Block Exemption says that in the case of mixed agreements, it covers:

> "—mixed agreements in which the licensed patents are not necessary for the achievement of the objects of the licensed technology containing both patented and non-patented elements; this may be the case where such patents do not afford effective protection against the exploitation of the technology by third parties;
>
> —mixed agreements which regardless of whether or not the licensed patents are necessary for the achievement of the objects of the licensed technology, contain obligations which restrict the exploitation of the relevant technology by the licensor or the licensee in Member States without patent protection, in so far and as long as such obligations are based in whole or in part on the exploitation of the licensed know-how and fulfil the other conditions set out in this Regulation."

Thus Recital 2 re-iterates the Commission's ruling in *Boussois/Interpane*.[3] The relative benefits and drawbacks of the Patent and Know-How Block Exemptions are discussed below.[4]

[1] Art. 1(3).
[2] Art. 1(1), Recital 2, 3.
[3] See para. 8.209.
[4] See para. 8.253.

(c) Excluded know-how licences

8.215 The Block Exemption does not cover exclusive know-how licenses unless the licensee manufactures or proposes to manufacture the licensed product himself or has it manufactured by a connected undertaking or by a subcontractor. Thus, exclusive know-how sales licence are not covered by the Block Exemption.[5] Licences relating to marketing know-how in the context of franchise agreements are not covered by the Block Exemption.[6]

Agreements between members of a patent or know-how pool which relate to the pooled technologies are not covered by the Block Exemption.[7] The Commission has recently issued an amending regulation which allows for exemption of joint venture and reciprocal licensing agreements subject to certain criteria.[8] Where a parent undertaking grants the joint venture a know-how licence, the block exemption now applies provided that the contract products and the other products of the participating undertakings which are considered by users to be equivalent in view of their characteristics, price and intended use represent in case of a licence limited to production not more than 20 per cent and in the case of a licence covering production and distribution not more than 10 per cent of the market for all such products in the Common Market or a substantial part thereof. Furthermore, the Know-How Block Exemption applies to reciprocal licences provided that the parties are not subject to any territorial restriction within the Common Market with regard to the manufacture, use or putting on the market of the contract products or on the use of the licensed processes.[9]

(d) Ancillary licence (other than patents)

8.216 Licences of trademarks, copyright, design rights, software or other intellectual property rights are not covered by the Block Exemption unless they are of assistance in achieving the object of the licensed technology and contain no obligations restrictive of competition other than those also attached to the license know-how and which are block-exempted.[10]

[5] Art. 1(5). *Quaere* whether the Know-How Block Exemption covers licences where the licensee only intends to manufacture if and only if there is sufficient demand for the licensed products. In *Re the Agreement between DDD Ltd and Delta Chemie*: [1988] O.J. L309/34, [1989] 4 C.M.L.R. 535, the licensee entered into an exclusive sales licence in order to *determine* whether there was sufficient demand to justify setting up a manufacturing base in the licensed territory. The Commission exempted such an agreement. It should be noted that the exclusive distributorship block exemption (Reg. 83/83) does not apply to such an agreement which must be classified as a know-how licence—see *DDD/Delta Chemie*, para. 40. "Connected undertaking" is defined at Art. 1(7)(13). For meaning of sub-contractor, see Notice on Sub-Contracting, para. 8.168.

[6] Recital 4.

[7] Art. 5(1)(1).

[8] Group Exemptions (Amendment) Regulation 1992: [1993] O.J. L21/8, [1993] 4 C.M.L.R. 151.

[9] Art. 5(2) as amended.

[10] Art. 5(4).

In *Moosehead/Whitbread*,[11] the Commission held, in the context of a trade mark/know-how licence relating to the production and selling of Canadian lager in England under the trade mark "Moosehead", that as the parties viewed the Canadian origin of the mark as crucial to the success of the marketing campaign which promoted the product as Canadian beer, the trade mark aspect of the agreement was not ancillary to the know-how and thus fell outside Regulation 556/89.

(e) Non-Member State provisions

8.217 The application of the Block Exemption is not affected where there are obligations relating to territories outside the Common Market or if the know-how licences are for non-Member States but which have effects within the Common Market.[12]

(v) Scheme of Block Exemption

8.218 The structure of the Know-How Block Exemption is similar to the Patent Block Exemption and reflect the dictates of Regulation 19/65. Thus Article 1 "white-lists" certain obligations mainly territorial and exclusivity restrictions) in know-how licences. Article 2 "super-white-lists" obligations which generally fall outside Article 85(1) for the sake of certainty. Article 3 "black-lists" certain obligations. Article 4 provides for an opposition procedure where a know-how licence contains clauses restrictive of competition not in Article 1 to 3.

(vi) Transitional provisions

8.219 The transitional provisional of the Know-How Block Exemption[13] are similar to the Patent Block Exemption. Thus, Recital 21 states that the Regulation applies with retroactive effect to know-how licences in existence when the Regulation came into force (April 1, 1989). Existing "old" licences can be divided into three categories—those which fall within Article 4(2)(2)(b) of Regulation 17; those not falling within Article 4(2)(2)(b) which either (i) existed on March 13, 1962 ("ancient" licences) or (ii) which came into being after that date ("old" licences).

Article 4(2)(2)(b) licences—Where know-how licences fall within Article 4(2)(b) of Regulation 17, then the Block Exemption applies retroactively to such licences to the date when the conditions for the Regulation were fulfilled.[14]

"Ancient" licences—If the licence does not fall within Article 4(2)(2)(b) of Regulation 17,[15] existed on March 13, 1962 *and* was noti-

[11] [1991] O.J. L100/32, [1991] 4 C.M.L.R. 391.
[12] Recital 4.
[13] Arts. 8 to 10.
[14] Art. 8. Article 4(2) Regulation 17/62 is discussed in the Chapter on Enforcement of EEA Competition Law at para. 12.013.
[15] See note *supra*.

fied before February 1, 1963[16] then the licence is retroactively exempted from the date as and when it fulfilled the conditions of the Block Exemption.

"Old" licences—If the licence does not fall within Article 4(2)(2)(b) *and* is not an "ancient licence" *and* has been notified, then the Block Exemption applies retroactively to the date when the conditions for the Regulation were fulfilled or the date of notification, whichever is the later.[17]

Article 9 stipulates transitional provisions where the above agreements are amended prior to July 1, 1989 to bring them within the Block Exemption. This leaves a residue of "old" and "ancient" licences which are not notified and do not fall within Article 4(2)(2)(b). Whilst Recital 21 appears to retroactively exempt such licences, the Articles of the Block Exemption do not include them. In any event, such licences will be exempt as of April 1, 1989 provided the conditions of the Block Exemption are fulfilled.

The draft Technology Transfer Block Exemption is intended to replace the Know-How Block Exemption. However, the latter will still apply to know how licences entered into on or before January 1, 1995.[18]

(vii) Check-list

8.220 The following provides a rough guide to specific obligations in know-how licences. The reader is advised to read the appropriate section for full information on the effect of the Block Exemption on the obligation.

White-listed clauses

8.221

—Exclusive Licence
—Exploitation ban in Licensor's territory
—"10 year" manufacturing ban in other licensees' territory[19]
—"10 year" active competition ban in other licensees' territory[20]
—"5 year" passive sales ban in other licensees' territory[21]
—Obligation to use only licensor's trade mark or get-up on licensed product

[16] If the know-how licence falls under Art. 85(1) as a result of an act of accession, then these dates are modified to the date of accession of the relevant Member State—see Art. 10.

[17] Art. 8(2).

[18] Art. 9, draft Technology Transfer Block Exemption—a copy of this draft appears in the August version of 1994 EIPR.

[19] 10 years from the date of signature of the first licence agreement entered into by the licensor within the E.C. in respect of the same technology.

[20] The 10 year period is calculated as in previous footnote.

[21] The five year period starts from the date of the signature of the licence agreement entered into by a licensor within the E.C. in respect of the same technology.

Super-white-listed clauses

8.222

—Secrecy obligations
—Assignment/sub-licence bans
—Post-term exploitation bans
—Non-exclusive licensing to licensor of improvement know-how
—Quality control specifications
—Exclusive Purchasing Restrictions necessary for technically satisfactory exploitation of licensed technology
—Obligation to legally assist licensor
—Obligations to pay royalties until end of agreement even if know-how becomes publicly known
—Field-of-use restrictions
—Minimum royalty/working obligation
—"Most favourable term" provisions
—Marking obligations
—Obligation not to use licensed know-how to construct facilities for third parties

Black-listed clauses

8.223

—Ban on use of licensed know-how once it has become publicly known
—Compulsory assignment of improvement patents to licensor
—"Tie-in" packages not referable to technical exploitation of invention
—No-challenge clauses
—Royalties on unprotected goods or services
—Customer restrictions within same technological field of use/product market
—Quantitative restrictions
—Resale Price Restrictions
—Non-competition bans
—Artificial prolongation of licence
—Bans on sales into other licensee's territory where not white-listed
—Parallel importer restrictions

(viii) Effect of Block Exemption on individual clauses

(a) Territorial restrictions

Relevant provisions

White-listed Clauses

Article 1(1)(1) to Article 1(1)(6), Article 1(2), Article 1(4). **8.224**

Black-listed Clauses

Article 3(11), Article 3(12). **8.225**

8.226 *Exclusive licence*—As in the Patent Block Exemption, the Commission includes exclusive licences in the Know-How Block Exemption. It re-iterates the Court's judgment in *Nungesser*[22] that exclusive licences may not fall within Article 85(1) where they are concerned with:

> "the introduction and protection of new technology by reason of the scale of the research which has been undertaken and of the increase in competition, in particular inter-brand competition, and in the competitiveness of the undertakings concerned resulting from the dissemination of innovation within the Community."[23]

In order to grant an exclusive licence to a licensee, it is necessary to impose obligations on both licensor and other licensees.

(1) **Licensor/licensee restrictions**—Vertical obligations between the licensor and the licensee whereby (i) the licensor is obliged not to grant other know-how licences in the licensed territory and/or (ii) to exploit[24] the licensed technology himself in the licensed territory and/or (iii) the licensee is obliged not to exploit the technology in territories reserved to the licensor are exempted.[25] Such obligations must not extend for a period greater than 10 years from the date of signature of the first licence entered into by the licensor for that territory and the same technology.[26] This limited protection clause which has no analogy in the Patent Block Exemption is justified by the Commission because of the difficulty of determining the point at which the know-how is no longer secret and the frequent licensing of a continuous stream of know-how especially where the technology is rapidly evolving.[27]

(2) **Licensee/licensee restrictions**—An obligation on the licensee not to manufacture or use the licensed product or use the licensed process in territories licensed to other licensees is exempted. Furthermore, a ban on a licensee conducting an "active sales" campaign in a territory licensed to another licensee is exempted.[28] However, such bans are only exempted for a period of 10 years from the date of signature of the first licence agreement entered into by the licensor *within the E.C.* in respect of the

[22] Case 258/78 [1982] E.C.R. 2015 [1983] 1 C.M.L.R. 278.

[23] Recital 6.

[24] This is defined as "any use of the licensed technology in particular in the production, active or passive sales in a territory even if not coupled with manufacture in that territory, or leasing of the licensed products"—Art. 1(7)(10).

[25] Art. 1(1)(1)–(3). "Territories reserved to the licensor" means territories in which the licensor has not granted any licences and which he has expressly reserved for himself—Art. 1(7)(12).

[26] Art. 1(2). "Same technology" is defined at Art. 1(7)(8) as "the technology as licensed to the first licensee and enhanced by any improvements made thereto subsequently, irrespective of whether and to what extent such improvements are exploited by the parties or the other licensees and irrespective of whether the technology is protected by necessary patents in any Member States."

[27] Recital 7.

[28] Art. 1(1)(4)–(5).

same technology.[29] A "passive sales" ban is exempted for a period of five years from the date of signature of the first licence agreement entered into by the licensor *within the* E.C. in respect of the same technology.[30]

(3) **Parallel imports**—Article 3(12) "black-lists" obligations which tend to restrict or prevent parallel imports.

Article 3(12)(a) "black-lists" any obligation whereby one or both parties are required without objectively justified reason to refuse to meet demand from "users or resellers in their respective territories who would market products in other territories within the common market". The wording is exactly the same as the corresponding provision in the Patent Block Exemption and it is submitted as before that at the very least, the user or parallel importer must be *established* in the licensee's territory.'[31]

Article 3(12)(b) prohibits any agreement or concerted practice whereby the parties seek to prevent trade in licensed products which have already been placed on the market.[32] It is exactly the same provision as Article 3(11)(b) of the Patent Block Exemption.[33] If there are no obligations or concerted practices to restrict parallel imports but the licensor or licensee attempts unilaterally to prevent or restrict imports, then the Commission may withdraw the benefit of the Block Exemption.[34]

As mentioned earlier, the Know-How Block Exemption does not apply to exclusive sales licences.[35]

(b) Marking/packaging obligations

Relevant provisions

White-listed

1(1)(7) An obligation on the licensee to use only the licensor's trade mark or the get-up determined by the licensor to distinguish the licensed product during the term of the agreement, provided that the licensee is not prevented from identifying himself as the manufacturer of the licensed products. **8.227**

[29] As opposed to date of signature for first licence *within the territory* for licensor/licensee restrictions (Art. 1(1)(1) to (3)). For definition of "same technology", see note 26 above.
[30] Art. 1(1)(6), 1(2).
[31] See para. 8.184. It is interesting to note that as in the Patent Block Exemption, the French text of the Know-How Block Exemption contains the word "established" after "resellers" in Art. 3(12)(a). As the Commission had attempted to remove this from the French version of the Patent Block Exemption, its inclusion demonstrates the French fears over possible problems with Art. 3(12).
[32] See discussion of this section in relation to the Patent Block Exemption, para. 8.184, above.
[33] See para. 8.184.
[34] Art. 7(5).
[35] See para. 8.215.

Super-white-listed

8.228 2(11) An obligation on the licensee to mark the licensed product with the licensor's name.

An obligation to use certain types of packaging for the aim of sharing customers is "black-listed" under Article 3(6).[36] However, such is expressed to be without prejudice to Article 1(1)(7). The Commission has indicated that it will clear packaging obligations that are necessary to ensure the strict *conformity* of products manufactured by the licensor and licensees. Thus packaging restrictions relating to usability by purchasers of the product have been cleared.[37] However, the licensor is recommended to use the opposition procedure unless such packaging can be described as get-up within the meaning of Article 1(1)(7).

(c) Assignment/sub-licence bans

Relevant provisions

Super-white-listed

8.229 2(2) An obligation on the licensee not to grant sub-licences or assign the licence.

The situation is not clear as to bans on the licensee licensing its own improvement know-how to third parties. Where such know-how is non-severable, licensing to third parties would disclose the know-how and thus a ban on sub-licensing would be "super-white-listed" under Article 2(1)(1).[38] Where the know-how is severable, Article 3(2)(b) "black-lists" the grant of an exclusive licence of severable know-how to the licensor where (*inter alia*) such would prevent the licensee licensing its severable know-how to third parties.[39] Such suggests that a licensee must be able to license its own severable improvement know-how and that a ban on such sub-licensing will remove the protection of the Block Exemption. However, a ban on the licensee from licensing severable improvement know-how to third parties is not mentioned in Articles 1, 2 and 3. Thus any licence with such a clause would have to be notified under the opposition procedure.[40–41]

[36] See Downstream Restrictions, para. 8.245.
[37] See *Re the Agreement between DDD Ltd and Delta Chemie*: [1988] O.J. L309/34, [1989] 4 C.M.L.R. 535.
[38] See para. 8.243.
[39] See para. 8.240.
[40–41] See also Grant-Back Clauses, para. 8.239.

(d) Quantitative restrictions

Relevant provisions

White-listed

1(1)(8) An obligation on the licensee to limit his production of the licensed product to the quantities he requires in manufacturing his own products and to sell the licensed product only as an integral part of or a replacement part for his own products or otherwise in connection with the sale of his own products, provided that such quantities are freely determined by the licensee. **8.230**

Black-listed

3(7) The quantity of the licensed products one party may manufacture or sell or the number of operations exploiting the licensed technology he may carry out are subject to limitations, save as provided in Article 1(1)(8) and Article 4(2). **8.231**

Article 9(2) states that where an obligation on a licensee to supply only a limited quantity of the licensed product to a particular customer exists where the licence is required by the customer in order to provide him with a second source of supply within a licensed territory, then the opposition procedure must be used. The Block Exemption permits clauses which stipulate that a minimum quantity of the licensed product must be produced. This is discussed in the next section, para. 8.237.

(e) Royalty provisions

Relevant provisions

Super-white-listed

2(9) An obligation on the licensee to pay a minimum royalty or to produce a minimum quantity of the licensed product or to carry out a minimum number of operations exploiting the licensed technology; **8.232**

2(7) An obligation on the licensee, in the event of the know-how becoming publicly known other than by action of the licensor, to continue paying until the end of the agreement the royalties in the amounts, for the periods and according to the methods freely determined by the parties, without prejudice to the payment of any additional damages in the event of the know-how becoming publicly known by the action of the licensee in breach of the agreement.

Black-listed

3(5) The licensee is charged royalties on goods or services which are not entirely or partially produced by means of the **8.233** licensed technology or for the use of know-how which has become publicly known by the action of the licensor or an undertaking connected with him.

As in the Patent Block Exemption, the Commission has the right to withdraw the effect of the Block Exemption if the licensor does not have the right to terminate the exclusivity granted to the licensee at the latest five years from the date of the agreement and annually thereafter if the licensee fails, without legitimate reason to adequately exploit the licensed technology.[42] Furthermore, the Commission may withdraw exemption if the parties were competitors before the grant of the licence and such an obligation has the effect of preventing the licensee from using competing technologies.[43] Thus, the usual "minimum royalty" clause that a licensee pay a certain percentage of items sold/made or a flat fee whichever is the greatest may not be sufficient if there is no right to terminate for insufficient exploitation.

With regard to payment of royalties until the end of the licence even if the know-how has entered the public domain, the Commission has said:

> "As a rule, parties do not need to be protected against the foreseeable financial consequences of an agreement freely entered into and should therefore not be restricted in their choice of the appropriate means of financing the technology transfer. This applies especially where know-how is concerned since here there can be no question of an abuse of a legal monopoly and, under the legal systems of the Member States, the licensee may have a remedy in an action under the applicable national law. Furthermore, provisions for the payment of royalties in return for the grant of a whole package of technology throughout an agreed reasonable period independently of whether or not the know how has entered into the public domain are generally in the interest of the licensee in that they prevent the licensor demanding a high initial payment up front with a view to diminishing the financial exposure in the event of premature disclosure. Parties should be free in order to facilitate payment by the licensee to spread the royalty payments or the use of the licensed technology over a period extending beyond the entry of the know-how into the public domain. Moreover, continuous payments should be allowed throughout the term of the agreement in cases where both parties are fully aware that the first sale of the product will necessarily disclose the know-how. Nevertheless, the Commission may where it was clear from the circumstances that the licensee would have been able and willing to develop the know-how himself in a short period of time in comparison with which the period of continuing payments is excessively long, withdraw the benefit of the exemption under Article 7 of this Regulation."[44–45]

The last sentence is particularly important for advisors.

[42] Art. 7(3).
[43] Art. 7(8).
[44–45] Recital 15.

(f) Temporal provisions

Relevant provisions

Super-white-listed

2(3) An obligation on the licensee not to exploit the licensed know-how after termination of the agreement in so far as the know-how is still secret. **8.234**

Black-listed

3(1) The licensee is prevented from continuing to use the licensed know-how after the termination of the agreement where the know-how meanwhile become publicly known, other than by the action of the licensee in breach of the agreement. **8.235**

3(10) The initial duration of the licensing agreement is automatically prolonged by the inclusion in it of any new improvements communicated by the licensor, unless the licensee has the right to refuse such improvements or each party has the right to terminate the agreement at the expiry of the initial term of the agreement and at least every three years thereafter.

Article 3(1) should be considered alongside Article 2(7) which permits the payment of royalties until the expiry of the agreement even after the know-how has entered the public domain.[46] Similar to Article 3(2) of the Patent Block Exemption, Article 3(10) is designed to prevent the *indefinite* payment of royalties and/or other restrictions continuing after the end of the initial term where the know-how has entered the public domain.[47]

(g) Field-of-use restrictions

Relevant provisions

White-listed

1(1)(8) An obligation on the licensee to limit his production of the licensed product to the quantities he requires in manufacturing his own products and to sell the licensed product only as an integral part of or a replacement part for his own products or otherwise in connection with the sale of his own products provided that such quantities are freely determined by the licensee. **8.236**

[46] See para. 8.232.
[47] See *Velcro S.A. v. Aplix S.A.* [1985] O.J. L233/22, [1989] 4 C.M.L.R. 157 where such behaviour was individually condemned by the Commission.

Super-white-listed

8.237 2(1)(8) An obligation on the licensee to restrict his exploitation of the licensed technology to one or more technical fields of application covered by the licensed technology or to one or more product markets.

2(1)(12) An obligation on the licensee not to use the licensor's know-how to construct facilities for third parties; this is without prejudice to the right of the licensee to increase the capacity of its facilities or to set up additional facilities for its own use on normal commercial terms, including the payment of additional royalties.

Article 1(1)(8) and 2(1)(8) combined will permit very stringent restrictions on use of the licensed technology. The Commission justifies the former obligations as it "gives the licensor an incentive to disseminate the technology in various applications while reserving the separate sale of the licensed product to himself or other licensees".[48]

(h) No-challenge clauses

Relevant provisions

Black-listed

8.238 3(4) The license is prohibited from contesting the secrecy of the licensed know-how or from challenging the validity of licensed patents within the common market belonging to the licensor or undertakings connected with him, without prejudice to the right of the licensor to terminate the licensing agreement in the event of such a challenge.

This is similar to the equivalent black-listed "no-challenge" obligation in the Patent Block Exemption and the reader is referred to the commentary on it.[49]

(i) Grant-back provisions

Relevant provisions

Super-white-listed

8.239 2(1)(4) An obligation on the licensee to communicate to the licensor any experience gained in exploiting the licensed technology gained in exploiting the licensed technology and to grant him a non-exclusive licence in respect of improvements to or new applications of that technology, provided that:

(a) the licensee is not prevented during or after the term of the agreement from freely using his own improvements, in

[48] Recital 7.
[49] See paras. 8.202 and generally, 8.143.

so far as these are severable from the licensor's know-how, or licensing them to third parties where licensing to third parties does not disclose the know-how communicated by the licensor that is still secret; this is without prejudice to an obligation on the licensee to seek the licensor's prior approval to such licensing provided that approval may not be withheld unless there are objectively justifiable reasons to believe that licensing improvements to third parties will disclose the licensor's know-how, and

(b) the licensor has accepted an obligation, whether exclusive or not, to communicate his own improvements to the licensee and his right to use the licensee's improvements which are not severable from the licensed know-how does not extend beyond the date on which the licensee's right to exploit the licensor's know-how comes to an end, except for termination of the agreement for breach by the licensee; this is without prejudice to an obligation on the licensee to give the licensor the option to continue to use the improvements after that date, if at the same time he relinquishes the post-term use ban or agrees, after having had an opportunity to examine the licensee's improvements to pay appropriate royalties for their use.

Black-listed

8.240 3(2) The licensee is obliged either:

(a) to assign in whole or in part to the licensor rights to improvements to or new applications of the licensed technology;

(b) to grant the licensor an exclusive licence for improvements to or new applications of the licensed technology which would prevent the licensee during the currency of the agreement and/or thereafter from using his own improvements in so far as these are severable from the licensor's know-how, of[50] from licensing them to third parties, where such licensing would not disclose the licensor's know-how or

(c) in the case of an agreement which also includes a post-term use ban to grant back to the licensor, even on a non-exclusive and reciprocal basis, licences for improvements which are not severable from the licensor's know-how, if the licensor's right to use the licensor's know-how, except for termination of the agreement for breach by the licensee.

The provisions in Article 2 and 3 relating to improvement know-how are

[50] This appears to be a typographical error and should be "or".

complicated and require analysis. Article 2(1)(4) and Article 3(2) must be read together. A distinction is made in both Articles between severable and non-severable improvement know-how. This distinction is not defined in the Block Exemption. Recital 14 suggests that non-severable improvement know-how is know-how that cannot be exploited without using the original licensed know-how. In certain instances, it may be difficult to classify which category improvement know-how goes into.

The Commission takes the view that the sharing of improvement know-how is beneficial and unrestrictive of competition. However, where a post-term use ban is coupled with an obligation on the licensee to license his non-severable improvement know-how to the licensor, a restrictive effect on competition arises because the licensee has no possibility of inducing the licensor to authorise him to continue exploiting the originally licensed know-how and hence the licensee's own improvements as well, after the expiry of the agreement.[51]

The following sets out in relation to severable and non-severable know-how the effect of the above articles.

(a) Severable improvement know-how

8.241

a. Obligations to assign/grant exclusive licences of a licensee's severable improvement know-how to the licensor are "black-listed"
b. Obligations on licensee to communicate or grant a non-exclusive licence of severable improvement know-how to the licensor are "super-white-listed" *provided* that
   (i) There is no ban on licensee using his severable improvement know-how before or after the termination of the agreement, and
   (ii) There is a reciprocal obligation on the licensor to communicate his improvements to the licensee, and
   (iii) The licensee can license his severable improvement know-how to third parties if such licensing does not disclose the licensor's know-how (such licensing can be subject to an obligation to seek prior approval which must be given unless there are objectively justifiable reasons for believing that such licensing will disclose the licensor's know-how).

(b) Non-severable improvement know-How

8.242

a. An obligation to assign to the licensor rights to non-severable improvements to or new applications of the licensed technology is "black-listed".
b. An obligation to grant the licensor an exclusive licence for non-severable improvements would seem not to be covered by

[51] Recital 14.

Article 3(2). Nor does Article 2(1)(4)(a) apply. Thus such an obligation is not covered by Article 1, 2 and 3 and must be notified under the opposition procedure. It is highly unlikely such a clause would ever be permitted by the Commission. Such an exclusive licence is "black-listed" by Article 3(2)(b) if it lasts longer than the licensee's right to use the licensor's know-how.

c. An obligation to grant a non-exclusive licence to the licensor of non-severable improvement know-how is "super-white-listed" provided that
   (i) There is a reciprocal obligation on the licensor to communicate his improvements to the licensee, and
   (ii) Where there is a post-term use ban on the licensee, the licensor is banned from exploiting the non-severable improvement know-how of the licensee for the duration of the post-term use ban[52] (this is without prejudice to a clause in the licence permitting the licensor to use the improvements after expiry of the licence by waiving the post-term use ban *or* paying appropriate royalties for their use[53]).

If the above conditions are not fulfilled, Article 3(2) "black-lists" the obligation.

(j) Secrecy obligations

Relevant provisions

Super-white-listed

2(1) An obligation on the licensee not to divulge the know-how communicated by the licensor; the licensee may be held to this obligation after the agreement has expired. **8.243**

(k) Most-favourable clauses

Relevant provisions

Super-white-listed

2(10) An obligation on the licensor to grant the licensee any more favourable terms that the licensor may grant to another undertaking after the agreement is entered into. **8.244**

[52] Such an obligation is permitted if the licence is brought to a premature end because of disclosure by the licensee of the know-how.

[53] Art. 2(1)(4)(b) and Art. 3(2)(c) are somewhat confusing. The latter suggests that an obligation on the licensee to accept royalties for its non-severable inprovement know-how in a period after the expiry of the licence when it is itself banned from using the licensor's know-how is black-listed whilst such is clearly "super-white-listed" in the former Article.

(l) "Downstream" restrictions[54]

Relevant provisions

Black-listed

8.245 3(6) One party is restricted within the same technological field of use or within the same product market as to the customers he may serve, in particular by being, prohibited from supplying certain classes of user, employing certain forms of distribution or, with the aim of sharing customers, using certain types of packaging for the products, save as provided in Article 1(1)(7) and Article 4(2);

3(8) One party is restricted in the determination of prices, components of prices or discounts for the licensed products.

Customer restrictions that arise indirectly because of field-of-use restrictions or product market restrictions imposed on the licensee are white-listed or super-white-listed.[55] Article 1(1)(7) permits marking and packaging for the purposes of distinguishing customers. Article 4(2) requires an obligation on the licensee to supply only a limited quantity of the licensed product to a particular customer, where the know-how licence is granted at the request of such a customer in order to provide him with a second source of supply within a licensed territory to be notified under the opposition procedure.[56] Thus, where the customer restriction falls within Article 4(2), it is not automatically black-listed but may be permitted by the Commission. Other express customer restrictions are black-listed.

(m) Competition bans

Relevant provisions

Black-listed

8.246 3(9) One party is restricted from competing with the other party, with undertaking connected with the party or with other undertakings within the common market in respect of research and development, production or use of competing products and their distribution, without prejudice to an obligation on the licensee to use his best endeavours to exploit the licensed technology and without prejudice to the right of the licensor to terminate the exclusivity granted to the licensee and cease communicating improvements in the event of the licensee's engaging in any such competing activities and to require the licensee to prove that the licensed know-how is not used for the production of goods and services other than those licensed.

[54] *i.e.* resale price maintenance, customer restrictions, etc.

[55] Art. 1(1)(8) and Art. 2(1)(8). See Field-of-Use Restrictions, para. 8.236.

[56] See Recital 18.

Article 3(9) covers bans in respect of manufacturing or dealings in products that compete with the licensed products. Bans in relation to *intra-brand* competition between licensees and licensor in relation to the licensed products are dealt with in Article 1(1)(1) to (6) and 3(11) and 3(12).[57] The double proviso to Article 3(9) is so powerful as to have a *de facto* effect of preventing a licensee deal in competing products.

(n) Quality control/exclusive dealing clauses

Relevant provisions

Super-white-listed

2(1)(5) An obligation on the licensee to observe minimum quality specifications for the licensed product or to procure goods or services from the licensor or from an undertaking designated by the licensor, in so far as such quality specifications, products or services are necessary for: **8.247**

(a) a technically satisfactory exploitation of the licensed technology, or

(b) for ensuring that the production of the licensee conforms to the quality standards that are respected by the licensor and other licensees,

and to allow the licensor to carry out related checks.

Black-listed

3(3) The licensee is obliged at the time the agreement is entered into to accept quality specifications or further licences or to procure goods or services which he does not want, unless such licences, quality specifications, goods or services are necessary for a technically satisfactory exploitation of the licensed technology or for ensuring that the production of the licensee conforms to the quality standards that are respected by the licensor and other licensees. **8.248**

Articles 2(1)(5) and Articles 3(3) must be read together. Obligations to observe minimum quality specifications or to procure goods or services from the licensor are only permissible so as to allow a technically satisfactory exploitation of the licensed technology or for ensuring that the production of the licensee conforms to the quality standards that are respected by the licensor and the other licensees. Anything which exceeds such conditions are "black-listed".

One difficulty that may arise in this field is whether a licensee can be obliged to buy goods from the licensor necessary for a technically satisfactory exploitation of the licensed technology if such goods could be included in the transferred know-how and the licensee thus permitted to

[57] See para. 8.226 *et seq.*

manufacture the secret product. Are such goods "necessary" for a technically satisfactory exploitation of the know-how when they can be included in the transferred know-how? The Commission's decisions in this area prior to the Know-How Block Exemption coming into force suggest that the Commission will not object to such an obligation.[58]

(o) Legal assistance provisions

Relevant provisions

Super-white-listed

8.249 2(6) Obligations:

(a) to inform the licensor of misappropriation of the know-how or of infringements of the licensed patents, or

(b) to take or to assist the licensor in taking legal action against such misappropriation or infringement

provide that these obligations are without prejudice to the licensee's rights to challenge the validity of the licensed patents or to contest the secrecy of the licensed know-how except where he himself has in some way contributed to its disclosure.

(ix) Contractual restrictions after entry of know-how into public domain

8.250 Certain contractual restrictions on the licensee for the period of the licence (*e.g.* obligation to restrict his exploitation to certain fields of application, to use know-how only for licensee's products, to pay royalties, to produce a minimum quantity, mark the licensor's name, bans against using the licensor's know-how to construct facilities for third parties) are "white-listed" or "super-white-listed" by the Know-How Block Exemption. The Block Exemption is silent on the permissibility of such clauses even after the know how has entered the public domain except in respect of the question of an obligation to pay royalties.[59] Prima facie, the Block Exemption would permit the continuation of such restrictions beyond entry of the know-how into the public domain.

Thus, most know-how licensees should insist on the right to terminate the licence once the know-how has entered to public domain if such restrictions could become oppressive. If the licensor is reluctant to concede such an obligation, then the licensee must have due regard to the

[58] *Re the Agreements of Davide Campari-Milano* SpA [1978] O.J. L157/39, [1978] 2 C.M.L.R. 397 (obligation to buy secret herbs from Campari exemptible because of the need to ensure uniform flavour and quality of the product); *Re the Agreements between Jus-Rol Ltd and Rich Products Corp.*: [1988] O.J. L69/21, [1988] 4 C.M.L.R. 527 (obligations to buy secret pre-mix from know-how licensor did not infringe Art. 85(1)).

[59] See para. 8.232.

likelihood of the know-how entering the public domain in negotiating the term of the licence.[60]

(x) "Opposition" procedure

8.251 The Know-How Block Exemption provides a similar procedure as that in the Patent Block Exemption for the exemption of licences that contain obligations restrictive of competition not listed in Article 1, 2 or 3.[61] Such licences must be notified to the Commission as if the party were seeking individual exemption.[62] If the Commission does not oppose exemption within six months of receiving the notification, then the licence is deemed to be exempted. Express reference must be made to the fact that exemption is being sought under the Patent Block Exemption and that complete information on the licence and its economic context is provided. The Commission has a discretion to oppose exemption but must do so if requested to do so by a Member State. In the latter case, the Commission may only withdraw its opposition after consultation with the Advisory Committee on Restrictive Practices and Dominant Positions.

If the Commission does not oppose exemption, then the licence is covered by the Know-How Block Exemption and thus is deemed to have been exempt for its life. If the Commission oppose and then withdraw its opposition, exemption applies from date of notification.[63] If amendments are made so as to satisfy the Commission that the agreement falls within Article 85(3) then exemption applies as from the date of the amendments.[64] If the opposition is not withdrawn, then the effects of the notification is covered by Regulation 17.[65]

(xi) Right of Commission to withdraw benefit of Know-How Block Exemption

8.252 As in the Patent Block Exemption, the Commission may withdraw the benefit of the Know-How Block Exemption from an agreement otherwise covered by it where it has certain effects incompatible with Article 85(3). These are where such effects arise from an arbitration award; the licensed products are not exposed to effective *inter-brand* competition in a licensee's territory;[66] there is no clause allowing the licensee to rescind the exclusivity of a licence if the patent has not been worked adequately or at all; the licensee refuses to meet unsolicited demand from users or resellers

[60] It may be of course that a licensee will seek to terminate the agreement unilaterally. Whilst the consequence of this is that they cannot be prevented from using the know-how, they may be liable for substantial damages under the licence.
[61] Art. 4.
[62] See Chap. 12 on Enforcement of EEA Competition Law.
[63] Art. 4(7).
[64] Art. 4(8).
[65] Art. 4(9). See Chap. 12 on Enforcement of EEA Competition Law.
[66] This provision can cause problems and has been discussed already in relation to the Patent Block Exemption—see para. 8.208, above.

in other licensee's territories after the five year "passive sales" ban period has expired or the licensee/licensor refuse to meet demand from users or parallel importers in their respective territory or makes it difficult for them to market licensed products already on the market; the operation of a post-term use ban on secret know-how prevents the licensee from working an expired patent which can be worked by all other manufacturers; the period for which the licensee is obliged to continue paying royalties is excessively long in comparison to the period of the licence or where the parties were competitors before the grant of the licence and obligations on the licensee to produce a minimum quantity or use his best endeavours to exploit the licensed technology have the effect of preventing the licensee from using competing technologies.[67]

(k) Comparison of Patent and Know-How Block Exemptions

8.253 As discussed already, whether a mixed patent/know-how licence falls within the Patent or Know-How Block Exemption will depend essentially as to whether the licensed patents are necessary for the achievement of the licensed technology or not and whether there are obligations restricting the exploitation of technology in Member States where no patents exist.[68] In practice, this will mean that the majority of technological licences will fall within the Know-How Block Exemption as there will usually be some technology in a licence which can be exploited without infringing a patent. In this respect, it is useful to compare the two block exemptions as it may be desirable to split a technology licence which would fall into the Know-How Block Exemption into two—one where the patents are necessary for the exploitation of the technology and thus falling under the Patent Block Exemption and the other where the residual know-how and patents falling under the Know-How Block Exemption.

In this section, the two block exemptions are compared in relation to contractual obligations where they produce a different effect.[69]

(i) Territorial restrictions

8.254 Exclusive licences and bans on licensees manufacturing in other licensees' territories under the Patent Block Exemption until the expiry of the patents are white-listed. Under the Know-How Block Exemption, exclusive licences and manufacturing bans are only exempted for 10 years

[67] Art. 7.

[68] See Recital 2 and Art. 1 of the Know-How Block Exemption and Recital 9 of the Patent Block Exemption.

[69] A very helpful side-by-side comparison of the two block exemptions is provided by Whaite "Licensing in Europe" [1990] EIPR 88.

from the date of signature of the first licence agreement entered into by the licensor for that territory (or within the E.C., in the case of licensee/licensee bans) in respect of the same technology.

Active sales bans in the Patent Block Exemption are exempted for the life of the patents but in the Know-How Block Exemption the ban must not be greater than 10 years from the date of signature of the first licence agreement entered into by the licensor within the EEC in respect of the same technology.

Passive sales bans in the Patent Block Exemption are exempted for five years from the date the licensed product was first put on the market by the licensor or licensees but in the Know-How Block Exemption for five years from the date of signature of the first licence agreement entered into by the licensor within the E.C.

It should be noted that the "white-listing" in the Patent Block Exemption of the above territorial restrictions only applies if the product is protected in the relevant territories. In the Know-How Block Exemption, no such restriction exists. Thus where patents are near to expiring, it is better to bring an agreement within the Know-How Block Exemption. However, as the lifetime of a patent is 20 years, where licences are entered early on in the life of the patent, it is better to bring the agreement within the Patent Block Exemption as it means that the duration of permitted territorial restrictions can be longer than under the Know-How Block Exemption.

(ii) Tying-in clauses

8.255 The Know-How Block Exemption super-white-lists obligations on the licensee to buy goods and use services of the licensor where such is necessary for a technically satisfactory exploitation of the licensed technology *and* for ensuring that product of the licensee conforms to quality standards that are respected by the licensor and other licensees. The Patent Block Exemption does not specifically "super-white-list" for the latter condition (although it is unlikely that such a clause falls within Article 85(1)).

(iii) Royalties

8.256 An obligation to continue paying royalties even where the know-how has entered the public domain (unless fault of licensor) until the end of the license is "super-white-listed" in the Know-How Block Exemption. In the Patent Block Exemption, an obligation to pay royalties where the know-how has entered the public domain is "black-listed" unless it is in order to facilitate payment by the licensee. Recital 22 of the Patent Block Exemption refers to this as meaning "arrangements for spreading payments in respect of previous use of the licensed invention". Whilst this will be the case for instalment payments, it is unclear whether this will be satisfactory for the normal form of payment, namely royalties based on a percentage of turnover. Thus, the practicality is that invariably the licence will have to be notified under the opposition procedure of the Patent Block Exemption for the Commission to determine whether such a clause falls within the proviso or not.

(iv) Field-of-use and quantitative restrictions

8.257 The Know-How Block Exemption "white-lists" an obligation on the licensee to limit his production to the quantities he requires in manufacturing his own products and to sell the licensed product only as an integral part of or a replacement part for his own products or otherwise in connection with the sale of his own products. The Patent Block Exemption has no such provision which is probably black-listed under Article 3(5) as constituting a quantitive restriction.

(v) Third party facilities

8.258 The Know-How Block Exemption "super-white-lists" an obligation on the licensee not to use the licensor's know-how to construct facilities for third parties. No mention of such an obligation is made in the Patent Block Exemption which would have to be notified under the Opposition Procedure.

(vi) Non-competition ban

8.259 Both Regulations black-list non-competition obligations. However, the Know-How Block Exemption provides three important qualifications to the black-listing in the event of the licensee engaging in competing activities. Firstly, the licensor may terminate the licensee's exclusivity. Secondly, he may cease communicating improvements to the licensee. Thirdly, he may require the licensee to prove that the licensed know-how is not used for the production of goods and services other than those licensed. The powerful effect of such conditions mean that it will be rare for a licensee of a licence covered by the Know-How Block Exemption to engage in competing activities.

(vii) Automatic prolongation of licence

8.260 Where a licence's term is automatically prolonged by the inclusion of improvement patents and know-how, the Patent Block Exemption black-lists such an effect unless the licensee has the right to terminate the agreement at the expiry of the initial licensed patents and *annually* thereafter. In the Know-How Block Exemption, there is similar provision but there must be the right to terminate the agreement at the expiry of the initial term of the agreement and at least every *three* years thereafter.

(viii) Grant-back clauses

8.261 The Patent Block Exemption "super-white-lists" reciprocal non-exclusive licences for improvement know-how between parties. The Know-How Block Exemption provides more stringent conditions for non-exclusive licensing of know-how.[70]

(l) Technology Transfer Block Exemption

(i) Overview

The Commission intends to consolidate the Patent and Know-How Block Exemption to be called the Technology Block Exemption. The Commission considers that the two block exemptions ought to be combined into a single Regulation covering technology transfer agreements and the rules governing patent licensing agreements and agreements for the communication of know how to be harmonised and simplified as far as possible in order to encourage the dissemination of technical knowledge in the Community and to promote the manufacture of technically more sophisticated goods. Accordingly, the Block Exemption would cover "pure" patent licences, "pure" know how licences and "mixed" patent/know how licences.

The Technology Transfer Block Exemption broadly adopts the same approach as the Patent and Know-How Block Exemptions. Territorial restraints of limited duration on licensor and licensees are white-listed. Most clauses which were "super-white-listed" in the former block exemptions are "super-white-listed". Blatant anticompetitive clauses which were black-listed in the Patent and Know-How Block Exemptions are black-listed in the Technology Transfer Block Exemption.

The main difference is that the draft Technology Transfer Block Exemption does not apply where the product manufactured by the licensee in the same field as products to be manufactured under the licence constitute more than 40 per cent of the relevant product market and in an oligopolistic market, account for more than 10 per cent of the relevant product market. Also, territorial restrictions were not covered by the Technology Transfer Block Exemption where the licensee to be protected had a market share exceeding 20 per cent. Since publication of the draft block exemption,[71] it has been the subject of intensive lobbying and study by industry, Member States and the Economic and Social Committee.[72] This has resulted in certain changes to the market share provisions and the reinstatement of the opposition procedure.

At present (September 1995), discussions on the Technology Transfer Block Exemption still continue. The Patent Block Exemption which initially expired on December 31, 1994 has been extended until

[70] See Grant-Back Clauses, para. 8.239.
[71] [1994] O.J. C178/3 as corrected [1994] O.J. C187/16.
[72] ESC Opinion, [1995] O.J. C102/1.

December 31, 1995. The Technology Transfer Block Exemption is intended to replace the Know-How Block Exemption which does not expire until December 31, 1999. It remains to be seen what transitional provisions the regulation will contain.

(ii) Substantive Provisions of draft Technology Transfer Block Exemption

A brief description of the substantive parts of the draft Block Exemption is now carried out.

White-listed clauses

(1) Exclusive and sole licences within a particular territory—Permitted duration of exclusivity
- "pure" patent licences for duration of parallel patents
- "pure" know how licences for 10 years from the date when the licensed product is first put on the market in the Community by the licensor or one of its licensees
- "mixed" licences for duration of "necessary" patents.

(2) Protection between licensees regarding manufacturing and actively selling in each other's territories
- "pure" patent licences for duration of parallel patents
- "pure" know how licences for 10 years from the date when the licensed product is first put on the market in the Community by the licensor or one of its licensees
- "mixed" licences for duration of "necessary" patents.

(3) Protection between licensees from passively selling in each other's territories
- "pure" patent licences for five years from the date when the product is first put on the market within the common market by the licensor or one of his licensees (provided patents still in force)
- "pure" know how licences for five years from the date when the product is first put on the market within the common market by the licensor or one of his licensees
- "mixed" licences for five years from the date when the product is first put on the market within the common market by the licensor or one of his licensees provided the necessary patents are in force.

(4) Obligation on licensee to use the licensor's trade mark or get up.

(5) Obligation on licensee to limit his product of the licensed product to the quantities he requires in manufacturing his own products and to sell the product only as an integral part or replacement part in relation to his products provided that licensee is free to determine the quantities.

Condition for "white-listed" clauses to qualify under block exemption

(1) Where the parties are competing manufacturers, the block exemption will not apply if a sole licence is granted to an undertaking who has more than 40 per cent market share in the product market in which the licensed product falls.
(2) Other territorial restrictions such as exclusivity, bans on passive or active sales will not fall within the block exemption if the market share of the person to be protected is greater than 40 per cent and the licensor and licensees are competitors.

Super-white-listed clauses

Confidentiality
Ban on sub-licences
Post-term use ban
Non-exclusive grant back clauses *re*: improvement technology
Minimum quality
Legal assistance
Obligation to pay royalties until expiry of agreement or the regular expiry of the patents
Field of use restrictions
Mutual cross-licensing of improvement technology after expiry of agreement
Minimum royalty
Most favoured licensee clause
Obligation to mark product with licensor's name
Obligation on licensee not to construct facilities for third parties
Obligation on licensee to only supply a limited quantity of licensed products to a particular customer

Black-listed clauses

Price restrictions
Competition bans
Parallel imports restraints
Customer restrictions
Quantity limits
Obligation on licensee to assign to licensor improvements in technology

Exclusion of Technology Transfer Block Exemption

The Regulation does not cover patent or know how pools; joint ventures between competitors; reciprocal licensing between competitors or the licensing of trademarks, copyright and design rights or licensing of software except where these rights or the software are of assistance in achieving the object of the licensed technology.

The Technology Transfer Block Exemption will apply to licences to Joint Ventures companies provided that the licensed products and the other products of the participating undertakings do not exceed 20 per cent (for production licences) and 10 per cent (for productions and distribution licences). Also the Technology Transfer Block Exemption will apply to patent or know how pools or reciprocal licences where there are territorial restrictions within the common market.

Withdrawal of block exemption

The block exemption may be withdrawn where the Commission finds that the effect of the agreement is to prevent the licensed products from being exposed to effective competition in the licensed territories; where the licensee refuses without valid reason to meet unsolicited demand from users or resellers in the territory of other licensees (without prejudice to a valid passive sale ban[73]); where the parties seek to prevent or restrict parallel trade in the licensed products or where there is an agreement between competitors, minimum quality or best endeavours clauses have the effect of preventing the licensee from using competing technologies.

Opposition procedure

It is intended that there be an opposition procedure in the Technology Transfer Block Exemption as with the Patent and Know-How Block Exemption but with a more limited period of four months for the Commission to raise objections. The opposition procedure expressly applies to "tie-in" clauses imposed on the licensee; quality specifications and no-challenge clauses.

5. EEA Agreement and Competition Rules

8.262 The competition provisions in the EEA Agreement broadly mirror those in the E.C. Treaty. The objectives of the EEA Agreement and E.C. Treaty in the competition field are the same namely that a system ensuring that competition is not distorted should be set up and that effective competition should be maintained with the EC and EEA. Article 53 EEA reflects almost exactly Article 85. The only differences are that "incompatible with the common market" has been replaced by "incompatible with the functioning of this [EEA] Agreement"; "trade between Member States" has become "trade between the Contracting Parties" and "within the common market" has become "within the territory covered by this Agreement". Thus, it is likely that Article 53 will be interpreted in exactly the same way as Article 85.[74]

[73] See "White-Listed Clauses".

[74] Indeed, all decisions that the ECJ has given in relation to Art. 85 prior to May 2, 1992 are deemed to apply to Art. 53 EEA Agreement—Art. 6 EEA Agreement. The EFTA Court must pay due account of decisions given after that date—Art. 3(2) ESA/Court Agreement. These provisions are discussed in the Introduction Chapter, para. 1.044.

Article 55 places an obligation on the E.C. Commission and the EFTA Surveillance Authority (ESA) to ensure the application of the EEA competition provisions. The enforcement of the EEA competition provisions by the E.C. Commission and ESA is dealt with in another Chapter.[75]

The EEA incorporates via the *acquis communautarie* method certain E.C. regulations adopted prior to the cut off date of July 31, 1991 into the EEA Agreement. Of relevance to this Chapter are the Patent Block Exemption, the Specialisation and Research and Development Block Exemptions, the Franchise Block Exemption and the Know-How Block Exemption.[76] Each regulation has been amended so that it fits into an EEA context. Three amendments are of note. The first amendment concerns the splitting of the regulations between substantive rules which remain and procedural rules which are transferred to another part of the EEA Agreement. This reflects the two pillar system and the rules of Protocol 21 EEA which specially empower the surveillance authorities to enforce the EEA competition rules. The second amendment is that the transitional provisions concerning existing or already notified agreements are declared not applicable in the EEA context.[77] The third amendment is that the block exemptions do not refer to the so-called "enabling" regulations whereby the E.C. Council enables the Commission to adopt group exemptions. This is due to the fact that these regulations have been considered by the negotiators as belonging to internal Community decision-making procedure and being therefore irrelevant for the EEA.

Importantly, Regulation 151/93 (the Block Exemption which amends the Patent, Know-How, Specialisation and Research and Development Block Exemption to cover certain types of joint ventures) has been put in the "Additional Package" to be adopted by the EEA Joint Committee after the EEA comes into effect.

[75] See Chap. 12.

[76] Annex XIV, EEA.

[77] Mainly because these instances are taken care of by the transitional rules of Protocol 21 EEA, notably Art. 7, 11, 12.

CHAPTER NINE

INTELLECTUAL PROPERTY AND JOINT VENTURES

1. INTRODUCTION

9.001 With the ever increasing complexity of technology, many concerns no longer have the ability to innovate and develop state-of-the-art technology themselves. Increasingly, companies are looking to co-operate with each other in joint ventures (JVs). A considerable amount of technological innovation is now generated by joint ventures between companies. Often this will result in new patents and associated know-how. Thus, most research and development joint ventures are intended to generate innovative technology and permit its commercial exploitation via intellectual property licences. However, there are other forms of co-operation which may be of importance to the intellectual property advisor from a licensing angle. For instance, specialisation agreements whereby two undertakings seek to rationalise their manufacturing concerns in a particular field will often involve the cross-licensing of rights. Other joint ventures may be concerned with the acquisition and granting of licences for the use of intellectual property rights.

Joint ventures may be considered either co-operative or concentrative in nature. The latter occur when two or more undertakings merge their business interests into a discrete business. Thus, a joint venture is co-operative and not concentrative in nature where the activities of the JV are not to be performed on a lasting basis, especially those limited in advance by the parents to a short time period and, where JVs do not perform all the functions of an autonomous economic entity, especially those charged by their parents simply with the operation of the particular functions of an undertaking and also where JVs perform all the functions of any autonomous economic entity where they give rise to co-ordination of competitive behaviour by the parents in relation to each other or to the JV.[1] This Chapter is concerned with co-operative joint ventures. The appraisal of the competitiveness of concentrative joint ventures is concerned with the need to maintain effective competition within the com-

[1] See Reg. 4064/89 (Merger Regulation), Art. 3(2) [1989] O.J. L 395/1 and para. 10 of Commission Notice on the Assessment of Co-operative Joint Ventures, [1993] O.J. C43/2. For more detailed examination of these three conditions, see Commission Notice on Concentrative and Co-operative Co-operations [1990[O.J. C203/10. See also *Butterworth's Competition Law*; Bellamy and Child *Common Market Law of Competion*; Whish, *Competition law*, (3rd ed.).

mon market. In this regard, intellectual property only plays a subordinate role.[2]

There exist many varieties of co-operative JVs. Thus, co-operation might be limited to the mere exchange of technological information. More extensive co-operation might involve the setting up of an autonomous joint venture company (JVC) which is aimed at entering new markets in which the parent undertakings do not operate. The assessment of the competitive effect of a co-operative JV does not depend on the legal form which the parents choose.[3] Furthermore, it is difficult, in view of the variety of JVs, to make any general pronouncement on the compliance of JVs with competition law.[4]

In many joint ventures, intellectual property concerns will be subsidiary to general competition concerns. For the purposes of this book, a study of every case which includes licensing provisions would be unproductive—the competitive analysis of such agreements does not consider such provisions in isolation but in the context of the competitive effect of the joint venture *in toto* on the market. This Chapter discusses the Commission's approach to joint ventures in general but concentrates on Research and Development agreements because of their importance to the intellectual property practitioner.

2. Joint Ventures and Competition

9.002 The Commission generally takes a favourable view of JVs. They enable undertakings to adapt to the new conditions of the single market. Moreover, they help contribute to a number of the Community's general economic objectives—the integration of the internal market; the facilitation of risky investments; the promotion of innovation and transfer of technology; development of new markets; improvement in the competitiveness of Community industry; the strengthening of the competitive position of small and medium sized firms and the elimination of structural overcapacity.[5] Recently, the Commission has recognised the need for certainty as to whether or not a co-operative JV infringes Article 85 and to this end, has issued the Notice on Co-operative Joint Ventures.[6] This notice along with the amendment of the patent, know-how licence, specialisation and Research and Development block exemption[7] to include

[2] In general, for the compatibility of concentrative joint ventures with Art. 85 and 86, see *Butterworth's Competition Law*; Bellamy and Child *Common Market Law of Competition* (3rd ed.). For the application of Art. 85 to licences which are ancillary to merger agreements, see para. 8.169. For the application of Art. 86 where a dominant undertaking strengthens its position by acquiring intellectual property, see para. 11.076.

[3] Notice on the Assessment of Co-operative Joint Ventures [1993] O.J. C 43/2, para. 3.

[4] *ibid*, para. 5.

[5] Draft Joint Venture Guidelines issued by Commission's DG IV in 1985.

[6] Notice on the Assessment of Co-operative Joint Ventures [1993] O.J. C 43/2.

[7] See Commission Reg. 151/93. The amending provisions of this reg. exempt, via the relevant block exemption, the licensing of JVs where the market share of the JVs products and the parents' competing products do not exceed a specified market share. For patent licences, see para. 8.171. For know-how licences, see para. 8.215.

certain JVs represents a concerted effort on the behalf of the Commission to foster co-operation between undertakings in the Community.

The Commission's main concerns are whether the creation of the JV is likely to restrict, prevent or distort competition between the parent undertakings and secondly, affect appreciably the competitive position of third parties.[8]

Competition between parent companies—Competition between parent companies will normally only be affected by a JV if they are actual or potential competitors. In this regard, the Commission has said that: 9.003

> "the assumption of potential competitive circumstances presupposes that each parent alone is in a position to fulfil the tasks assigned to the JV and that it does not forfeit its capabilities to do so by the creation of the JV. An economically realistic approach is necessary in the assessment of any particular case."[9]

In considering whether the parents have the ability to perform the tasks of the JV individually, the Commission will look at the financial and managerial resources of the parents; whether the parents know the production technique of the JV; whether the parents make the upstream or downstream products themselves and have access to the necessary production facilities; whether actual or potential demand is such as to enable each parent company to manufacture the product on its own; whether the parent companies have access to the distribution channels needed to sell the product manufactured by the JV; whether each parent company can on its own bear the technical and financial risks associated with the production operations of the JV and whether each parent company is capable of entering the JV's market on its own and can overcome existing barriers within a reasonable time and without undue effort and cost.[10] In considering the competitive position between the parent companies and the JV, the Commission may intervene if the JV is a joint venture vehicle which is in competition with or is a supplier or customer of the parent undertakings.[11]

Moreover, the Commission will look at the level of co-operation. Generally, co-operation at a Research and Development stage is less likely to be anticompetitive than at a production and distribution stage.[12]

Competitive effect of a JV on third parties—Whether the JV has a competitive effect on the activities of third parties will generally depend on the combined market power of the parent undertakings. Thus, where parent companies leave it to the JV to handle their purchases or sales, the choice available to suppliers or customers may be appreciably restricted. 9.004

[8] Notice on the Assessment of Co-operative Joint Ventures [1993] O.J. C 43/2, para. 17.
[9] *ibid*, para. 18.
[10] See *ibid*, para. 19 and *13th Annual Report on Competition Policy*, point 55.
[11] *ibid*, para. 21.
[12] *ibid*, para. 20.

Similarly, this applies where the parents arrange for the JV to manufacture primary or intermediate products or to process products which they themselves have produced. The creation of a JV may even exclude from the market the parents' traditional suppliers and customers especially in an oligopolistic market.[13]

9.005 *Competitive effect of JV between non-competitors*—Even though a JV may be between non-competitors, it may still affect competition in the market place. Generally, this will not be the case. However, market access by third parties may be significantly affected by the JV. Moreover, in a JV between parents of large market shares, the JV may not leave sufficient numbers of independent operators in the area of economic activity of the JV.[14]

9.006 *Competitive effect of JV between competitors*—Generally, where a JV restricts competition between parents who are competitors (and the possible ensuing secondary effects on third parties), such JVs will fall within Article 85.[15] Where the parents concentrate their manufacturing activities in the JV, this will often lead to a standardisation of manufacturing costs and the quality of the products and thus a weakening of competition.[16] However, economic analysis must be carried out to see whether in fact there is a restriction or distortion of competition. Thus, where co-operation in the form of JV can objectively be seen as the only possibility to enter a new market or to remain in their existing market, then provided that its presence will strengthen competition or prevent it from being weakened, the JV will not fall within Article 85.[17]

9.007 *Competition and Joint Venture Companies*—Often the parent undertakings set up a fully functioning joint venture company (JVC) which is independent of the parents. Normally, where the JVC operates on the same market as its parents, competition between all participating undertakings will be restricted.[18] Where the JVC operates on a market upstream or downstream of that of the parents with which it has supply or delivery links, then restrictions of competition can occur to third parties who are suppliers or distributors of the parents especially where the JVC acts as a vertical multilevel integration instrument.[19] Where the JVC operates on a market adjacent to that of its parents, competition can only be restricted when there is a high degree of interdependence between the two markets. This is especially the case where the JVC manufactures products which are complementary to those of its parents.[20]

[13] Notice on the Assessment of Co-operative Joint Ventures [1993] O.J. C43/2, para. 24.
[14] *ibid*, para. 33–35.
[15] *ibid*, para. 37. As to whether competition is restricted between parents, see para. 9.003.
[16] Notice on the Assessment of Co-operative Joint Ventures [1993] O.J. C43/2, para. 40.
[17] *ibid*, para. 42.
[18] *ibid*, para. 41.
[19] *ibid*, paras. 35 and 41.
[20] *ibid*, para. 41.

Exemption of joint ventures—JVs which infringe Article 85(1) may be exemptable either under a block exemption or through individual exemption. In the former case, the JV may fall in the specialisation regulation;[21] the research and development regulation[22] or the patent and know-how regulations.[23] In the case of individual exemption, the applicant must satisfy the Commission of the conditions in Article 85(3). Any JV which opens up a market, develops new technologies, leads to a sales expansion of the parent undertaking in new territories or the enlargement of its supply range by new products will normally be assessed favourably.[24] However, each case will turn on specific consideration of whether the four factors in Article 85(3) are fulfilled.[25] **9.008**

Ancillary restrictions—The Commission makes a distinction between restrictions of competition which arise from the creation and operation of the JV and additional agreements which would, on their own, also constitute restrictions of competition by limiting the freedom of action in the market of the participating undertakings. Additional agreements which are directly related to the JV and necessary for its existence must be assessed together with the JV. They are treated under the rules of competition as ancillary restrictions if they remain subordinate in importance to the main object of the JV. In considering the necessity of the restriction, it is proper not only to take account of its nature but equally to ensure that its duration, subject matter and geographical field of application do not exceed what the creation and operation of the JV normally requires.[26] Ancillary restrictions will not cause a co-operative agreement to fall within Article 85 if the JV does not fall within the scope of Article 85. **9.009**

The Commission considers that obligations imposed on JVCs not to manufacture or market products competing with the licensed products are normally ancillary vehicles.[27] Restrictions as to the field of activity of the JV are also normally ancillary. Obligations in a production JV on the JVC to purchase from or supply its parents may also be regarded as ancillary at least during the JV's start up period.[28]

Restrictions on parent companies from competing with the JV or from actively competing with it in its area of activity may be regarded as ancillary at least during the JVs start up period.[29] Where non competition is

[21] Reg. 417/85. Discussed at para. 9.066.
[22] Reg. 418/85—discussed at para. 9.032 below.
[23] Reg. 2349/84; Reg. 556/89. For further discussion on whether either regulation is applicable, see paras. 8.171 (patent block exemption) and 8.215 (Know-How Block Exemption).
[24] Notice on the Assessment of Co-operative Joint Ventures [1993] O.J. C43/2, para. 55.
[25] See *ibid*, paras. 52 *et seq*.
[26] Notice on the Assessment of Co-operative Joint Ventures [1993] O.J. C 43/2, paras. 65, 66.
[27] See *ibid*, para. 72, *Mitchell Cotts/Sofiltra* [1987] O.J. L 41/31, [1988] 4 C.M.L.R. 111.
[28] Notice on the Assessment of Co-operative Joint Ventures [1993] O.J. C 43/2, para. 74.
[29] *ibid*, para. 75.

achieved by the grant of exclusive licences to the JV in the field of activity in which the JV is intended to operate, such exclusive licences will normally be considered as ancillary restrictions.[30]

3. Research and Development Joint Ventures

9.010 Research and development is presently important because of the increasing cost of invention and innovation. The accelerating pace of technological change means that companies must invest large portions of their profits into research and development. In the Common Market, the danger of businesses duplicating each other's research and development efforts is greater than any other large trading bloc because of national rivalry, language barriers and the existence of many centres of excellence. The fragmentation of national markets in the Community often mean that the small size of a potential market for a research and development product discourages many firms from investing in research and development.

It is not surprising therefore that from early on the Commission has taken a keen interest in encouraging research and development collaboration between enterprises. Thus, in 1968, it took the view, issuing a Notice to that effect, that certain research and development agreements did not infringe Article 85(1).[31] Fifteen years later, it stated that:

> "Competition has never been a matter of only quantities and prices for existing goods and services. Today, it relies increasingly on innovation, that is: the creation of new or improved products and services. The introduction of new processes and products on the market stimulates competition within the common market, and helps to strengthen the ability of European industry to compete internationally. In both contexts, research and development (R & D) plays an essential role. In fact, R & D promotes and maintains dynamic competition, characterised by initiation and imitation and in doing so assures economic growth.
>
> Although innovative efforts should be regarded as a normal part of the entrepreneurial spirit of individual undertakings, it can not be denied that in many cases the synergy arising out of co-operation is necessary because it enables the partners to share the financial risks involved and in particular to bring together a wider range of intellectual and mental resources and experience, thus promoting the transfer of technology. In the absence of such cooperation, the innovation may not take place at all, or otherwise not as successfully or

[30] Notice on the Assessment of Co-operative Joint Ventures [1993] O.J. C 43/2, para. 76. See also, *Mitchell Cotts/Sofiltra* [1987] O.J. L 41/31, [1988] 4 C.M.L.R. 111 and *ODIN* [1990] O.J. L209/15, [1991] 4 C.M.L.R. 832.

[31] Commission's Notice of July 29, 1968 on Co-operation Agreement [1968] O.J. C75/3. See also *Eurogypsum* [1968] O.J. L57/9, [1968] C.M.L.R. D1.

efficiently. Also, the present situation in the Community demands a more rapid and effective transformation of new ideas into marketable products and processes, which may be facilitated by joint efforts by several undertakings.

The Commission has always shown a favourable attitude towards R & D cooperation, provided that competition is maintained by the *existence of different independent poles of research*."[32]

Such an approach is consistent with the Commission's policy of supporting small and medium-sized firms to compete with large undertakings in the Common Market.[33] In support of this approach, the Commission has issued a Block Exemption for research and development agreements which automatically exempt many such agreements between firms with combined market shares of the relevant product market less than 20 per cent.[34]

9.011 Recently, the importance of research and development initiatives in the EC has been recognised in the Treaty on European Union. This has modified Article 130(f) of the Treaty of Rome which now reads:

"The Community shall have the objective of strengthening the scientific and technological bases of Community industry and encouraging it to become more competitive at international level, while promoting all the research activities deemed necessary by virtue of other Chapters of this Treaty.

For this purpose the Community, shall throughout the Community, encourage undertakings, including small and medium-sized undertakings, research centres and universities in their research and technological development activities of high quality; it shall support their efforts to co-operate with one another aiming, notably, at enabling undertakings to exploit the internal market potential to the full, in particular through the opening of national public contracts, the definition of common standards and the removal of legal and fiscal obstacles to that cooperation."[35]

This Article is substantially similar to the old Article 130(f) and emphasises the Community's positive approach to research and development. In this context, the Council of Ministers has allocated 5.6 billion ECU to E.C. research programmes for 1990 to 1994.[36] Furthermore, the Commission has assisted in Community-wide research and development programmes via funding and the approval of state aids.

It is the aim of any commercial research and development programme to produce a product or process that will be technologically innovative

[32] *14th Annual Report on Competition Policy*, para. 28.
[33] For recent emphasis by Commission on the need to support small and medium sized firms, see *16th* through to *20th Annual Reports on Competition Policy*.
[34] Reg. 418/85.
[35] Treaty on European Union, Art. G(38).
[36] Council Decision April 4, 1990, [1990] O.J. L 117/28.

compared to existing products or processes. It is thus vitally important that the results of such programmes are properly protected by patents, industrial designs and confidential know-how. Furthermore, the intellectual property practitioner will often be involved in the negotiation and formulation of JV agreements. It is crucial that he knows with certainty the effect of Article 85 on provisions relating to the exploitation of intellectual property generated by the JV.

Research and development ventures can either be "pure" with no element of joint exploitation or "applied" where the parties agree to jointly exploit the results of such co-operative ventures, whether by manufacturing or marketing.

This Chapter is not concerned with the parents or JVC's licensing of their results with third parties *per se* which is covered elsewhere save as where this is affected by obligations between the parties to the research and development agreement. The reader is referred to the Chapter on Licensing of Intellectual Property for an examination of the effect of Article 85 on such licences.

4. Commission's Approach and Case Law: Article 85(1)

9.012 The ECJ and CFI have not considered the competitive effect of research and development agreements. This is because the Commission has invariably granted negative clearance or exempted research and development agreements.[37] The Commission has generally favoured research and development agreements. In 1985, the Commission completed a study into the competitive effect of research and development agreements. It stated that research and development collaboration had recently proliferated and noted that there were two types of agreement: those providing for short-term co-operation on specific projects, and joint ventures (which may or may not be legally independent entities) doing research and development work on a longer-term basis. It summarised its findings as follows:

9.013 "*Legal and economic aspects of R & D collaboration*

> [282] R & D collaboration agreements are difficult to negotiate and to keep working smoothly, for the following main reasons:
> (i) it may be difficult to work out arrangements for sharing costs and exploitation of results, which are not always foreseeable;
> (ii) collaboration between firms in different Community countries may be hampered by differences of national objectives, strategies and methods.
>
> R & D collaboration has various economic advantages:

[37] Indeed, it has only once refused exemption and that was in an early case, *Research and Development* [1971] C.M.L.R. D31. However, the Commission has often insisted on amendments to agreements before it grants exemptions.

(i) investment in R & D can be kept to a minimum. Economies of scale can be achieved;
(ii) research budgets can be made to go further and risks spread by sharing the costs and benefits of a project between several firms or spreading a given sum over a series of relatively independent projects;
(iii) cross-frontier R & D collaboration within the Community can help to open up national markets. The Community's poor performance in high technology is mainly due not to too low a level of expenditure on R & D, but to the low productivity of such expenditure because of the fragmentation of markets and supply. Governments' nationalistic support of national champions in their procurement policies checks or prevents the growth of new enterprises and limits the potential supply of high technology products. International R & D collaboration can enlarge markets and supply the products (high technology or otherwise) incorporating the results of joint research to a Community or even world scale.

But the economic benefits of R & D are not always beneficial:
(i) Powerful firms may enter into R & D agreements with potentially very innovative rivals in order to be able to control technological progress. In other cases, R & D collaboration may raise entry barriers to non-participating competitors.
(ii) R & D collaboration can also facilitate coordination of pricing and production and enable abnormal profits to be made from innovations. Such dangers are greatest where, as is frequently the case in the Community, there are non-tariff barriers between national markets. In such cases, cross-frontier collaboration at the R & D stage may give way to geographical division of the market on national lines for the product resulting from the R & D.

Implications for competition policy

[284] Research and development collaboration can have several important pro-competitive effects, notably that of stimulating research and development by making it more profitable and of creating units capable of overcoming national barriers.

However, there is also an inherent danger of research and development arrangements being used for anti-competitive purposes. This danger is a real one in that a large proportion of such links are horizontal, *i.e.* between firms at a similar level of production in the same industry, involve firms with large turnovers, and concern development of a finished product. These facts highlight the importance of the Commission's policy towards research and development co-operation agreements embodied in block exemption Regulation No

418/85. This seeks to maintain workable competition and to ensure that the technical progress resulting from the research does not merely serve to produce monopoly profits."[38]

The above statement was made in 1985 when the Block Exemption for research and development agreements was introduced. In its decisions on research and development agreements and from the block exemption, it is clear that the Commission's approach to such agreements depends broadly on two factors.

9.014 Firstly and historically, it has emphasised that research and development agreement often fall within Article 85(1) because they prevent the maintenance of independent research and development centres. In this context, it has distinguished between research and development ventures between undertakings who compete with each other in relevant product market to those undertakings which do not compete.[39] It is more suspicious of the former research and development agreements because of the elimination of competion between undertakings.[40] However, even with a JV between non competitors, the Commission will examine whether there remains room for a sufficient number of research and development centres.[41]

Secondly, the Commission distinguishes between parties to a research and development agreement who possess small or medium sized shares in the relevant product market and of limited resources as opposed to parties with large shares and large resources. The Commission is more favourable to the former entering into research and development agreements because often such parties would often be unable to develop a product on their own and also because such agreements help the parties to compete with undertakings with large market shares in the relevant product market. In an oligopolistic market, the Commission has historically emphasised the need for independent research and development centres. However, recently it has adopted a more "rule of reason" approach which examines the *actual* effects of the agreement on the marketplace rather than whether the parties' freedom to maintain independent research and development centres has been restricted.[42]

9.015 The Commission also considers the extent of the co-operation between the parties. It distinguishes between agreements which relate purely to research and development ("pure research and development") as opposed to those which extend to joint production and marketing ("applied research and development"). Generally, it views the latter as

[38] *15th Annual Report on Competition Policy*, para. 282 *et seq*.
[39] See Notice on Co-operative Ventures discussed at para. 9.002 *et seq*.
[40] *e.g.* see Notice on the Assessment of Co-operative Joint Ventures [1933] O.J. C 43/2, para. 37.
[41] *ibid*, para. 33.
[42] *e.g.* see *ODIN* [1990] O.J. L209/15, [1991] 4 C.M.L.R. 832 discussed at para. 9.020, below.

more anti-competitive than the former because collusion between the parties is greater and carries on into the marketplace.[43]

The following sections set out in detail the Commission's approach to research and development agreements.

(a) Competition best served by independent research and development centres

(i) Parties are competitors

9.016 The Commission in several decisions on research and development agreements have emphasised that such agreements infringe Article 85(1) because they prevent either party obtaining a competitive advantage over the other via the maintenance of independent research and development centres and thus potentially restrict consumer choice of competing products.[44] Various examples of the Commission's decisions where the undertakings competed are given below:

> *Beecham/Parke-Davis*[45]—Two large pharmaceutical firms entered into a collaborative venture for the development of a product to control the impairment of blood circulation. The Commission held that the collaboration between the parties at every stage of the research and development meant that neither party could obtain a competitive advantage over the other at any point in the innovative cycle.
>
> *Bayer/Gist-Brocades*[46]—Two large companies involved in penicillin manufacture notified a hybrid r & d/specialisation agreement to the Commission. The latter held that an obligation on both parties to the agreement to licence each other for new, independently developed processes (as opposed to pursuant to the agreement) restricted competition because it prevented either of the two firms from obtaining a competitive advantage over the other in research.[47]

[43] *e.g.* see Notice on the Assessment of Co-operative Joint Ventures [1993] O.J. C 43/2 para. 20.

[44] See *Henkel/Colgate* [1972] O.J. L14/14, *8th Annual Report on Competition Policy*, paras. 89–91; *Re Bayer & Gist-Brocades* [1976] 1 C.M.L.R. D98; *Vacuum Interrupters (No. 1) [1977]* O.J. L48/32, [1977] 1 C.M.L.R. D67; *GEC/Weir* [1978] 1 C.M.L.R. D42; *SOPELEM/Vickers (No. 1)* [1978] O.J. L70/47, [1978] 2 C.M.L.R. 146; *Beecham/Parke Davis* [1979] O.J. L70/11, [1979] 2 C.M.L.R. 157; *Carbon Gas Technologie* [1983] O.J. L376/17, [1984] 2 C.M.L.R. 275; *Continental Gummi-Werke and Michelin* [1988] O.J. L305/33, [1989] 4 C.M.L.R. 920; *Alcatel Espace/ANT* [1990] O.J. L32/19; [1991] 4 C.M.L.R. 208. See also Recital 8 of the Research and Development Block Exemption where the Commission express their concern that several independent poles of research are maintained in any given economic sector.

[45] [1979] 2 C.M.L.R. 157.

[46] [1976] 1 C.M.L.R. D98.

[47] The *practical consequence* of cross-licensing provisions in an agreement is that it will discourage parties from conducting its own research and development program. It will thus infringe Art. 85(1)—see *Henkel/Colgate* [1972] O.J. L14/14, *8th Report on Competition Policy,* Paras. 89–91, (an obligation on a party to communicate the results of its own research to the other party in an agreement between parties who were amongst the largest washing powder/detergent manufacturers prevented one party from obtaining a competitive advantage over the other).

ICI/Enichem[48]—An Italian and British company concluded an agreement establishing a joint venture company for research, development, production and distribution of PVC. The main reason for the agreement was that it allowed the activities of the parent companies to be rationalised in the PVC sector. The joint venture company set up (EVC) was barely independent of the parent companies. There was no transfer of assets to EVC and each parent company retained full ownership of production facilities, patents, know-how and research centres. Thus the effective co-operation of the joint venture company was highly dependent upon the close co-operation of the parent companies. This restricted the parent companies's ability to maintain effective independent research efforts and thus fell within Article 85(1).

Alcatel Espace/ANT[49]—Alcatel and ANT were rival manufacturers of satellite communications equipment. They entered into a co-operation agreement providing for joint research and development, production and marketing in this field. Essentially, the agreement was to ensure that the parties did not duplicate their research and development efforts and combined their resources for the exploitation of the results through rationalisation of manufacturing servicing and testing of such systems as well as co-operation in bidding and negotiations for contracts in the field. Both parties agreed to license all necessary patents and know-how to each other on a royalty free and non-exclusive basis. Exploitation of the results was to be on a co-operative basis including one party sub-contracting to the other party as much as possible. The parties's combined market share was less than 20 per cent of the Community product market. The Commission held that the effect of the agreement was to "alter the previously autonomous position of the parties relating to planning, financing, research and development, production and marketing of the equipment covered by the agreement, the parties no longer being able to act independently".

Thus, where the parties to a research and development agreement are competitors, the Commission will readily assume that Article 85(1) is infringed and the parties must look for exemption for the agreement. The Commission's concern to maintain independent poles of research in an oligopolistic market has meant that the Research and Development Block Exemption does not apply to competing undertakings with a combined market share of 20 per cent or more of the relevant market.[50] However, even where undertakings are not competitors, the Commission will often deem Article 85 to be applicable because of the need for independent

[48] [1988] O.J. L50/18.
[49] *Alcatel Espace/ANT* [1990] O.J. L32/19; [1991] 4 C.M.L.R. 208.
[50] Research and Development Block Exemption, Recital 8, Art. 3.

research and development efforts.[51] Thus, the Commission had held that Article 85(1) applies to research and development agreements even where the parties at the time of entering into the agreement were not involved in research or development in the field of the agreement if they were potentially capable of developing the product.[52]

(ii) Parents are not competitors

9.017 Where the parties are neither competitors or potential competitors in the field of research and development, the Commission's approach has been somewhat inconsistent in deciding whether such agreements fall within Article 85. In *BP/Kellogg*,[53] BP had developed a catalyst for use in the production of ammonia. It entered into a joint development agreement with Kellogg, an important process plant designer and constructor to jointly develop a process plant for the production of ammonia utilising its catalyst. The parties were not actual or potential competitors of each other. The Commission in a short decision stated that various restrictions imposed on the parties in a co-operation agreement fell within Article 85(1) as they restricted the parties' "freedom of action".[54]

In *SOPELEM/Vickers*,[55] both parties notified an agreement establishing a joint venture company for the research, development and production of *elementary to sophisticated microscopes*. The parties' combined market share of microscopes in the Common Market was about 3.5 per cent. Furthermore, competition in the field of microscopy was strong with three manufacturers holding a combined market share of 50 per cent in the Common Market. SOPELEM would have abandoned the production of microscopes if the agreement with Vickers had not been entered into. Nevertheless, the Commission held that the technical cooperation and exchange of expertise in research and development would eliminate *inter-brand* competition between the parties in research and development, preferring to exempt the agreement.[56]

(iii) Restrictions on parent companies's independent research and development efforts

9.018 In a research and development joint venture, restrictions on parties' independent research efforts or a requirement that expertise independently

[51] Notice on the Assessment of Co-operative Ventures [1993] O.J. C43/2 para. 33.

[52] See *Vacuum Interrupters Ltd* [1977] 1 C.M.L.R. D67 (neither party to the research and development agreement to manufacture vacuum interrupters were involved in the production of such before entering into the agreement). The Commission has set out a step by step process for examining whether parent companies are actually or potential competitors in the field of the JV—see paras. 19 *et seq* of Notice on the Assessment of Co-operative Joint Ventures [1993] O.J. C43/2 discussed at para. 9.003 above.

[53] *BP/Kellogg* [1985] O.J. L369/6; [1986] 2 C.M.L.R. 619.

[54] *ibid*, para. 15. However, the agreement was exempted.

[55] [1978] O.J. L70/47, [1978] 2 C.M.L.R. 146.

[56] See also Notice on the Assessment of Co-operative Joint Ventures [1993] O.J. C43/2, para. 33 which emphasises even where the parents are non-competitors, the need for a sufficient number of research and development centres.

developed be communicated to other participating parties will often be a necessary ancillary restraint in that it gives each party the confidence that the other will be fully committed to the joint venture. The Commission considers that such restrictions fall within Article 85(1) preferring to exempt them, again demonstrating its concern that independent research centres be maintained in the Community.[57] However, such restrictions are not exemptable where they seek to restrict research and development in unconnected fields to the research and development venture.[58] Even where there are no express contractual restrictions, the very fact of co-operation will often mean that it is unlikely that the parties will in fact engage in any independent research and development efforts in that field and accordingly such an agreement will normally be restrictive of competition in an oligopolistic market.[59]

It is possible that the Commission may now consider bans on parents' research and development efforts as ancillary restrictions which are directly related to the JV and necessary for its existence.[60]

(iv) Undertakings with small market shares

9.019 The Commission's desire that there exist several independent poles of research in the Community has meant that it has often been wary of research and development agreements between undertakings with large market shares in oligopolistic markets. Not surprisingly, the Commission's attitude to research and development agreements between undertakings with small or medium sized shares has been more welcoming as often such undertakings are not able to maintain their own independent research and development efforts.[61] Thus, the Research and Development Block Exemption only applies to competing undertakings with a combined market share which does not exceed 20 per cent of the relevant market because of the necessity to maintain independent research and development poles of research.[62] Similarly, patent and know-how licences granted to joint venture vehicles by parent companies will be covered by the Patent and Know-How Block Exemption provided the contract products and competing products of the parents do not exceed at the very most, 20 per cent of the market share.[63]

Historically, the Commission's approach to research and development

[57] See Research and Development Block Exemption and Notice on Co-operation Agreements [1968] O.J. C75/3, Art. 4(1)(a).

[58] This is blacklisted under Research and Development Block Exemption, Art. 6(a)

[59] See *1st Annual Report on Competition Policy*, para. 32 and *GEC/Weir* [1978] 1 C.M.L.R. D42 at para. 21; *Carbon Gas Technologie* [1983] O.J. L376/17, [1984] 2 C.M.L.R. 275 at para. 8.

[60] See Notice on the Assessment of Co-operative Joint Ventures [1993] O.J. C43/2, para. 66. Ancillary restrictions are discussed above at para. 9.009.

[61] See *1st Annual Report on Competition Policy*, para. 31. See also the new Art. 130(f) of Treaty of Rome with its emphasis on the need to encourage undertakings, including small and medium sized undertakings in their research and development efforts.

[62] Recital 8 and Art. 3 of Research and Development Block Exemption.

[63] See para. 8.171 for Patent Block Exemption and para. 8.215 for Know-How Block Exemption.

agreements between undertakings with small or medium sized market shares was to find rather formalistically that they fell within Article 85(1) but to exempt them.[64] However, the more "rule of reason" approach shown in *ODIN*[65] suggests that if it is highly unlikely that the undertakings would have developed the products of the intended research and development agreements by themselves, then such agreements would fall outside Article 85(1).[66] Moreover, research and development agreements between small or medium sized undertakings will normally not involve any risk of foreclosure of the relevant technology to third parties as the latter will be more likely to be able to develop the technology themselves.[67]

(v) Licensing in JV's—ODIN

9.020 As discussed above, the Commission has recently become more positive towards joint ventures including research and development agreements.[68] Thus, where the parties to joint research and development agreements which extend to joint production are not competitors, actual or potential and the development of the product by either party on its own is highly unlikely, the Commission will generally view the formation of a joint venture research and development vehicle as falling outside Article 85(1) as clearly such an arrangement increases *inter-brand* competition.[69] This can be seen in its decision in *ODIN*.[70] Elopak and Metal Box were manufacturers of food packaging containers. Elopak primarily supplied cartons for use in the dairy and food industries and integrated systems equipment for filling, packaging and handling these cartons. Metal Box was active in the canning business. The two parties entered into an agreement establishing a joint venture company, ODIN, to carry out research and development of a container with a carton base and separate closure which could be filled by an aseptic process with UHT processed foods. ODIN was also to undertake production and distribution of the new containers and their filling machines. Both parent companies granted licences to ODIN to exploit all their intellectual property rights relevant to the agreement and ODIN was granted an exclusive licence for those rights relating to ODIN's project. The parents were entitled to obtain from ODIN non-exclusive licences but could not use such licences

[64] *SOPELEM/Vickers (No. 1)* [1978] O.J. L70/47, [1978] 2 C.M.L.R. 146—see para. 9.017, above.

[65] *ODIN* [1990] O.J. L209/15; [1991] 4 C.M.L.R. 832 discussed at para. 9.020, below.

[66] See also *Carbon Gas Technologie* [1983] O.J. L376/17, [1984] 2 C.M.L.R. 275 at paras. 7 to 10 where the Commission considered it relevant in concluding that an agreement setting up a joint subsidiary for the purposes of research and development infringed Art. 85(1) was that the participating parties were able to achieve independently the object of the co-operation.

[67] See *ODIN* [1990] O.J. L209/15, [1991] 4 C.M.L.R. 832.

[68] See para. 9.014.

[69] *ODIN* [1990] O.J. L209/15; [1991] 4 C.M.L.R. 832; *Konsortium ECR 900* [1990] O.J. L228/31. See also Notice on the Assessment of Co-operative Joint Ventures [1993] O.J. C43/2, para. 33.

[70] *ODIN* [1990] O.J. L209/15, [1991] 4 C.M.L.R. 832.

in the field where ODIN was active. The market for the proposed new package was oligopolistic in structure with several undertakings with large market shares and resources.

The Commission held that Elopak and Metal Box were not competitors in activities outside the joint venture and were highly unlikely to develop the proposed product on their own. Furthermore, the Commission held that the existence of other substantial undertakings in the product market meant that there was little risk of foreclosure to third parties. The Commission considered the compatibility of certain clauses in the agreement in order to determine whether such clauses were necessary ancillary restraints designed to ensure the starting up and proper functioning of the joint venture. In relation to the licensing clauses, the Commission held that the licensing provisions included the grant of exclusivity to ODIN by the parent companies was necessary and did not go beyond what was required as there were no restrictions on the joint venture in respect of pricing, volume, customers and territory and because the exclusivity was limited to the narrowly defined field relevant to the manufacture of the new product.[71] In particular, it distinguished the grant of exclusivity in the joint venture from that of the grant of an exclusive licence in a licensor/licensee situation or where the licensor was a partner in a joint production venture which competed directly.[72]

(b) "Pure" research and development agreements

9.021 In 1968, the Commission issued a Notice on Co-operation Agreements.[73] The Notice was issued primarily to encourage co-operation between small and medium sized enterprises where such co-operation enabled them to work more rationally and increase their productivity and competitiveness in a larger market.[74] The Notice said that agreements on the joint execution of research work or the joint development of the results of research up to the stage of industrial application did not affect the competitive position of the parties.[75] This view was reiterated recently in the Notice on Co-operative Joint Ventures which states that in the Commission's view, agreements which have as their sole object co-operation in fields removed from the market do not fall within Article 85(1).[76]

[71] *ibid*, paras. 30–31

[72] *i.e.* see *Re the Agreement between Boussois and Interpane mbh* [1987] O.J. L50/30, [1988] 4 C.M.L.R. 124 (know-how licence discussed in Chap. 8 on Licensing of Intellectual Property); *Mitchell Cotts/Sofiltra* [1987] O.J. L41/31, [1988] 4 C.M.L.R. 111 (production joint venture discussed in section of joint ventures para. 9.068).

[73] Notice of July 29, 1968 on Co-operation Agreements [1968] O.J. C75/3.

[74] The effect of the Notice was reaffirmed in the *1st Annual Report on Competition Policy*, para. 31.

[75] Notice of July 29, 1968 on Co-operation Agreements [1968] O.J. C75/3, para. 3.

[76] Notice on the Assessment of Co-operative Joint Ventures [1993] O.J. C43/2, para. 15. The Commission considers that the 1968 Notice complements the Research and Development Block Exemption in relation to pure Research and Development agreements. For Commission decisions on pure Research and Development agreements, *Eurogypsum* [1968] O.J. L57/9, [1968] C.M.L.R. D1; *Beecham/Parke Davis* [1979] O.J. L70/11, [1979] 2 C.M.L.R. 157.

However, pure research and development agreements will not always fall outside Article 85(1). Article 2 of the Research and Development Block Exemption states:

> "As stated in the Commission's 1968 Notice concerning agreements decisions and concerted practices in the field of co-operation between enterprises, agreements on the joint execution of research work or the joint development of the results of the research, up to date but not including the stage of industrial application, generally do not fall within the scope of Article 85(1) of the Treaty. In certain circumstances, however, such as where the parties agree not to carry out other research and development in the same field thereby forgoing the opportunity of gaining competitive advantages over the other parties, such agreements may fall within Article 85(1) and should therefore not be excluded from this Regulation."[77]

Accordingly, in an oligopolistic market where few undertakings have the resources to conduct research and development, collaborative JVs may restrict competition as the parents will not be supporting independent research and development efforts. Even if there is no contractual restriction on the carrying out of independent research and development by the parties, the practical effect of the joint venture will be to discourage parties to carry out their own research and development. If this is so, the agreement will infringe Article 85(1).[78] "Pure" research and development agreements between undertakings with small market shares in the relevant product market will normally be exemptable under the Research and Development Block Exemption provided that all participating parties have access to the results.[79] However, where the parties have a substantial share of the relevant product market, the Commission's concern to maintain independent poles of research is more acute and the Research and Development Block Exemption does not apply.[80] Despite this, the Commission has recently said that even where a pure research and development JV does not fulfil the conditions for group exemption under the block exemption, such arrangement can normally be viewed positively especially where the parents entrust the JV with the further task of granting licences to third parties.[81]

(c) "Applied" research and development ventures

9.022 Generally, pure Research and Development agreements are rare and most are "applied" *i.e.* provide for joint exploitation of the results. Indeed the Commission has said that such is the natural consequence of

[77] Research and Development Block Exemption, Recital 2.
[78] See *Beecham/Parke Davis* [1979] O.J. L70/11, [1979] 2 C.M.L.R. 157 at para. 33.
[79] See Reg. 418/85, Art. 2(c).
[80] See Recital 8 of the Research and Development Block Exemption and Art. 3. See also *16th Annual Report on Competition Policy*, para. 9.
[81] Notice on the Assessment of Co-operative Joint Ventures [1993] O.J. C43/2, para. 59.

joint research and development.[82] Exploitation can either be through co-operation in the manufacture and marketing of products which are the results of the research and development or through the joint licensing of third parties. This section deals with the competitive effect of any contractual provisions in relation to the exploitation of results of research and development.

Historically, the Commission has been much more circumspect about agreements which include provisions relating to joint exploitation of the results of research and development ventures. Such agreements fall outside the Notice on Co-Operation Agreement. In *Beecham/Parke Davis*, the Commission said:

> "that joint research co-operation can only be admitted if the results of such joint research can be used by both parties freely and without any territorial or other restrictions or other restrictions on production or marketing within the Common Market."[83]

Recently, the Commission has expressed the view that the economic pressure towards co-operation at the research and development stage does not normally eliminate the possibility of competition between the participating undertakings at the production and distribution stages. Even where the pooling of the production capacity of several undertakings, is economically unavoidable and thus unobjectionable as regards competition law, this does not necessarily imply that these undertakings should also co-operate in the distribution of the products concerned.[84] In general, any research and development agreement which provides for joint exploitation of the results will fall within Article 85(1) because the parties collude as to the manufacture and licensing of results rather than compete against each other in the marketplace and thus the parties must seek exemption.[85] Below, various licensing arrangements are considered.

(i) Licensing relationship between joint venture vehicle and parent companies

9.023 Where the parties to a research and development agreement set up a joint venture company ("JVC"), the agreement will often contain licensing provisions between the parents and the JVC. In practice, parent companies will often have to licence a joint venture vehicle set up for the purposes of research and development and exploitation. Such in itself will not constitute a restriction of competition. Often, the parent firms will

[82] Research and Development Block Exemption, Recital 7.

[83] *Beecham/Parke-Davis* at para. 47. See also *Henkel/Colgate* [1972] O.J. L14/4, *8th Report on Competition Policy,* paras. 89 to 91. The Research and Development Block Exemption has moderated the above view and exempts certain territorial restrictions.

[84] Notice on the assessment of Co-operative Joint Ventures [1993] O.J. C43/2, para. 20.

[85] See Research and Development Block Exemption, Recital 3. Where the parents are not actual or potential competitors, the Commission will be more tolerant of such arrangement, see Notice on the Assessment of Co-operative Joint Ventures [1993] O.J. C43/2, para. 33.

seek to grant exclusivity in the relevant field on the joint venture company so as to make it commercially viable and prevent the parent companies from competing with it. The Commission has said that the grant to a joint venture company formed to manufacture a new product of the exclusive right to exploit the know-how of both parent companies is not caught by Article 85(1), even though that protection extends beyond any initial starting up period for new technology and may apply for the life of the joint venture where:

(a) the existing know-how of both parents plus further research and development are necessary to develop, manufacture and market the new product as well as the machinery and technology linked to it;
(b) there are no explicit restrictions on the joint venture's activities with respect to pricing, volume, customers and territory even though the new product may compete to some extent with the output of one of the parents;
(c) the exclusivity is limited to the narrowly defined field relevant to the manufacture of the new product and the parents are free to develop closely related and possibly competing products.[86]

Recently, the Commission has amended its Patent and Know-How Block Exemption so that where in a joint venture arrangement where the parents are competitors, the Block Exemptions will be applicable to the grant of a patent or know-how licence by the parent to the joint venture provided that the combined market share of the participating undertakings is not more than 20 per cent in the case of joint production or not more than 10 per cent in the case of joint production and distribution.[87] Accordingly, in these circumstances, the grant of an exclusive licence to a joint venture company will be exempted under these Block Exemptions. The Commission has said that restrictions on parent companies competing with the area of activity of a JV may be regarded as ancillary at least during the JV's start up period.[88]

9.024 Restrictions on the back licensing by the JVC of results generated by the research and development project to the parent companies are often permissible to ensure the proper working of the joint venture. Thus, restrictions on a JVC from licensing its parents where such use was likely to conflict with the purposes of the joint venture vehicle was not anti-competitive.[89] In another case, the Commission exempted an arrangement whereby the joint venture vehicle granted the parent companies

[86] *ODIN* [1990] O.J. L209/15, [1991] 4 C.M.L.R. 832, at para. 30–31. The judgment is somewhat confusing (see para. 32) as to whether the parent companies granted exclusive or non-exclusive licences to the joint venture company. In fact, within the field of the agreement, the parents granted exclusive rights to the joint venture company—see p. 837. See also the incorporation of this decision into the Notice of the Assessment of Co-operative Joint Ventures [1993] O.J. C43/2 at para. 76.
[87] Reg. 2349/84 (as amended), Art. 5(2); Reg. 556/89 (as amended), Art. 5(2).
[88] Notice on the Assessment of Co-operative Joint Ventures [1993] O.J. C43/2, para. 75.
[89] *ODIN* [1990] O.J. L209/15, [1991] 4 C.M.L.R. 832 at para. 30.

exclusive licences of the results of the research and development venture such that the European partner was given an exclusive licence for the Community and America.[90]

Often, a JV agreement will cater for the use of the results of a research and development agreement when the agreement terminates. The Commission is keen to ensure that the parents are not denied use of know-how that they previously had access to. Thus a ban on parties who withdrew from a joint venture from exploiting for five years know-how belonging to the joint research and development venture including know-how that the retiring party had transferred to the joint venture company was held to restrict competition because it made it more difficult for the party to compete in the field of co-operation once it had left the joint venture.[91] Conversely, a more limited restriction on parent companies that upon the breakup of the joint venture vehicle company, they would only be able to use the other party's know-how in the field of the research and development agreement was held to be a necessary consequence of such an agreement and thus fell outside Article 85(1).[92] It is submitted that a prohibition on a parent who withdraws from a research and development JV from using the technology generated by the JV will normally constitute an ancillary restriction necessary for the existence of the JV and thus not per se objectionable under Article 85.

(ii) Payment of royalties between participating undertakings

9.025 JV agreements will sometimes provide for the cross payment of royalties between undertakings for exploitation of the research and development technology. In effect, this amounts to co-operation at the market stage and the Commission's stance is that provisions relating to profit sharing from sales of the licensed products infringe Article 85(1) and are not exemptable although remuneration for expenditure and risks taken in the research and development agreement are permissible. In *Beecham/Parke-Davis*[93] the Commission took the view that equal contributions to joint research expenditure did not necessarily justify sharing the profit from mutual marketing exploitation and insisted on the removal of a clause which provided for fixed royalties to be paid by one party to the other for sales of the licensed product. The Commission said that it might be fair for one party to pay royalties to the other where one party is unable, particularly for technical reasons, to exploit the results. The Commission held that as both parties manufactured and sold world-wide, there was no reason why results should not be exploited by both parties and thus

[90] *Re the Agreements between BBC Brown and Boveri and NGK Insulators Limited* [1988] O.J. L301/68, [1989] 4 C.M.L.R. 610 (see para. 9.031, below).

[91] *Carbon Gas Technologie* [1983] O.J. L376/67, [1984] 2 C.M.L.R. 275. However, the provision was exempted as it afforded a limited degree of protection against competition from former shareholder or from outside companies without which the object of the co-operation could not have been attained—para. 15.

[92] *ODIN* [1990] O.J. L209/15, [1991] 4 C.M.L.R. 832 at para. 33.

[93] *Beecham/Parke Davis* [1979] O.J. L70/11, [1979] 2 C.M.L.R. 157.

such cross-royalty payments were unnecessary. If the cross-royalty payments are so structured as to be likely to result in the partitioning of markets, then such a provision will fall within Article 85(1) and be unexemptable.[94]

The Commission's stance above appears partly contradicted by the fact that under Research and Development Block Exemption, an obligation to share royalties received from third parties is considered generally unrestrictive of competition.[95] Such an obligation appears to moderate the effect of the Commission's decision in *Beecham/Parke-Davis* which views unfavourably such a provision in relation to the sales of the research and development products by the parties themselves. Obligations to share royalties received from third parties provisions could be seen to be anti-competitive where the parties individually license out the results of the research and development as such an obligation acts as a disincentive to competitive licensing between the participating parties and punishes the party best able and/or who makes the greatest effort to exploit the licensed technology via licensing.

Furthermore, Regulation 418/85 considers that an obligation to pay royalties to the other party where there is "unequal exploitation" of the results of the research and development agreement generally falls outside Article 85(1).[96] Such a provision obscures the issue and its finding in *Beecham/Parke-Davis* and it remains to be seen what the Commission means by "unequal exploitation."

(iii) Restrictions on licensing of third parties

9.026 The Commission generally disapproves of restrictions on the parties licensing third parties. A general limitation on a party's freedom to grant licences to third parties for patents developed through the joint development infringes Article 85(1).[97] This will be invariably the case where one party requires the consent of the other in order to license third parties. The anti-competitive effect of such restrictions will be enhanced in an oligopolistic market where there are few manufacturers in the relevant product market. However, each case will depend on its facts. Thus in *EMI/Jungheinrich*,[98] EMI, a manufacturer of electronic control systems and Jungheinrich, a manufacturer of bulk handling systems entered into a joint research and development agreement for the development of electronic control devices for use by Jungheinrich in the field of driverless tractor and forklift systems. Under the agreement, Jungheinrich was to

[94] *Research and Development* [1971] C.M.L.R. D31 (parties obliged to pay royalties to each other if they marketed research and development products in territories reserved to the other).

[95] Reg. 418/85, Art. 5(1)(g).

[96] Reg. 418/85, Art. 5(1)(f). Discussed at para. 9.059.

[97] See *Henkel & Colgate, 8th Report on Competition Policy*, paras. 89–90. For original decision granting exemption, see *Henkel & Colgate* [1972] O.J. L14/14; *Beecham/Parke Davis* [1979] O.J. L70/11, [1979] 2 C.M.L.R. 157; *Continental Gummi-Werke and Michelin* [1988] O.J. L305/33, [1989] 4 C.M.L.R. 920.

[98] *EMI/Jungheinrich* [1978] 1 C.M.L.R. 395, Press Release, December 2, 1977.

make financial contributions to research undertaken by EMI. The Commission approved a provision that EMI would not be able to grant licenses to third parties without Jungheinrich's approval in relation to patents which would be obtained from the joint development for use in relation to driverless tractor and forklift systems but disapproved of such consent being required for use outside such a field. In *Continental Gummi-Werke and Michelin*,[99] the Commission held that where a joint venture company in a research and development agreement was required to consult with both parent companies before it granted licences to third parties, such had the practical effect of ensuring that the consent of both parties was required before a third party was licensed and thus fell within Article 85(1) although it was exempted under Article 85(3) as it meant a simplification of administrative procedure.[1]

(iv) Joint marketing

9.027 A research and development agreement may seek to make arrangements in relation to the marketing of any products that are manufactured under the joint venture scheme. For instance, a joint venture company may be charged with the distribution and sale of the research and development products. Alternatively, the parties to research and development agreement may agree to jointly tender for contracts. Until recently, the Commission had been wary of such agreements. Thus, such agreements used to fall outside the Research and Development Block Exemption because the degree of co-operation at such a stage involved implicit restrictions on each party's freedom to determine prices and the customers that they serve.[2] The Commission may exempt such arrangements in special circumstances. For instance, the Commission exempted a joint marketing arrangement where close co-operation was required between the parties and the subject of the research and development agreement was highly technical, such that individual marketing was not possible.[3] The Commission will only permit under Article 85(3) that period of co-operation during the marketing phase which is necessary to ensure that the research

[99] [1988] O.J. L305/33, [1989] 4 C.M.L.R. 920.

[1] It would appear that any third party interested in obtaining a licence for the RHT (flat tyre) which was the subject of the joint venture would have had to obtain licences from the parent companies as well and thus in any event, the consent of the parents was necessary. See also *Re the Agreements between BBC Brown and Boveri and NGK Insulators Limited* [1988] O.J. L301/68, [1989] 4 C.M.L.R. 610 where a provision requiring the consent of the parties before sub-licences were granted was exempted—discussed at para. 9.031, below.

[2] See Art. 6(d) and (e) of the Block Exemption. See also *Alcatel Espace/ANT* [1990] O.J. L32/19, [1991] 4 C.M.L.R. 208 where the Commission held that the requirement that the parties jointly tender meant that they were restricted as to the determination of prices and accordingly, the agreement fell outside the Research and Development Block Exemption.

[3] *Alcatel Espace/ANT* [1990] O.J. L32/19, [1991] 4 C.M.L.R. 208 at para. 20. See also *Vacuum Interrupters (No. 1)* [1977] O.J. L48/32, [1977] 1 C.M.L.R. D67; *GEC/Weir* [1978] 1 C.M.L.R. D42.

and development agreement is workable.[4] Recently, the Commission has granted negative clearance to an agreement where the joint venture company was to market any results of the research and development although the decision was firmly based on the facts of the cases.[5]

Very recently, the Commission appears to have become more tolerant of joint distribution arrangements within the context of research and development ventures. It has issued the Group Exemptions (Amendment) Regulation 1992[6] which extends the Research and Development Block Exemption to agreements between undertakings with a combined market share of 10 per cent or less which contain arrangements as to joint distribution.

5. Commission's Approach: Article 85(3)

9.028 The vast majority of decisions by the Commission on research and development have resulted in exemptions, sometimes after the removal of clauses considered unexemptable. Such an approach reflects the Commission's sympathetic treatment to research and development ventures. In 1984, the Commission issued a Research and Development Block Exemption.[7] This along with the Notice on Co-operative Joint Ventures now provides the principal guide to the Commission's policy.[8] The Commission will base individual exemptions upon the guidelines set out in the Research and Development Block Exemption.[9] Thus, the Commission will not only take account of the criteria specified in Article 85(3) but also world competition and the particular circumstances prevailing in the manufacture of high-technology products.[10] However, the Block Exemption is not as well-drafted as later Block Exemptions and there are many ambiguities in it. Thus, agreements will often have to be notified either using the opposition procedure in the Block Exemption or in the normal way under Regulation 17.

The Commission's application of Article 85(3) is based on the economic facts surrounding the notified agreement. Often the exemption is accompanied by detailed market analysis of the competitive effect of the agreements. As the Commission's approach to Article 85(3) is highly dependent on the facts of the case, it is not helpful to try and deduce various principles that the Commission applies. The reader is referred to the

[4] See *Continental Gummi-Werke and Michelin* [1988] O.J. L305/33, [1989] 4 C.M.L.R. 920. See para. 9.029 below.

[5] *ODIN* [1990] O.J. L209/15, [1991] 4 C.M.L.R. 832. See also *Konsortium ECR 900* [1990] O.J. L228/31.

[6] [1993] O.J. L21/8, [1993] 4 C.M.L.R. 151.

[7] Reg. 418/85 of December 19, 1984 considered at para. 9.032, below.

[8] Notice on the Assessment of Co-operative Joint Ventures [1993] O.J. C43/2 which applies generally to joint ventures, see para. 9.001 to 9.009.

[9] See *Continental Gummi-Werke and Michelin* [1988] O.J. L305/33, [1989] 4 C.M.L.R. 920 at para. 32.

[10] See Reg. 418/85, 10th Recital and *Continental Gummi-Werke and Micheli* [1988] O.J. L305/33, [1989] 4 C.M.L.R. 920.

Notice on Co-operative Joint Ventures which helpfully sets out the Commission's approach to exempting joint venture arrangements.[11] Below, various decisions of the Commission in relation to the exemption of research and development agreements are set out below to give the reader a flavour of the Commission's approach.

(a) Research and development agreement between companies with large market shares

9.029 *Continental/Michelin*[12]—Michelin and Continental entered into a co-operation agreement to develop the new run-flat tyre system—the RHT (Reverse Hook Tyre). The agreement was limited in scope merely providing for exchange of information and division of research and development efforts. Each party was to remain owner of its own work products. However, the agreement did envisage the setting up of a common entity whose sole function was to exploit the patents and know-how that resulted from the research and development. Each party was to have a worldwide non-exclusive licence covering all such patents and know-how. Third parties would be granted a licence upon request by one of the parties and after consultation. The parties submitted that the purchasing power of the motor vehicle industry was so great and the latter's insistence upon having several independent sources meant that in practice licences would be granted upon reasonable terms. The parties' combined share of the market was over 20 per cent and thus it was not covered by the Research and Development Block Exemption.

The Commission held that the agreement fell within Article 85(1) because without the agreement, both parties might have proceeded to develop competing run-flat systems themselves and because of the intended co-ordination on the marketing of the product and the grant of licences to third parties.

The parties managed to convince the Commission that joint research was necessary and that Continental alone would not have been able to solve the numerous technical problems. Also, the Commission accepted the fact that the motor vehicle industry would not tolerate a single supplier so as to avoid supply bottlenecks, so that even if Continental had produced the RHT themselves, they would have had to grant a licence to Michelin. The Commission did not consider that there would have been any difference if Continental had developed the RHT alone and licensed Michelin. Either way, the consumer benefitted from the introduction of a run-flat tyre.

The agreement provided for two different periods of co-operation. The Commission exempted in relation to the research and development agreement a provision that extended the agreement for five years after the

[11] Notice on the Assessment of Co-operative Joint Ventures [1993] O.J. C43/2, paras. 43 *et seq.*

[12] *Continental Gummi-Werke and Michelin* [1988] O.J. L305/33, [1989] 4 C.M.L.R. 920.

first marketing of the RHT, with automatic annual renewal unless terminated. In relation to the exploitation of the RHT, the Commission considered that two years after first marketing was the longest period necessary for attainment of the objectives of the agreement as the two parties were competitors with strong market positions and co-operation must be restricted particularly strictly to the period essential for the implementation of the programme.

There was no risk of the elimination of competition in respect of a substantial part of the products in question as the RHT tyre would compete with other conventional tyres produced by other manufacturers and it was not certain that RHT tyres would replace conventional tyres. Furthermore, the demands of the motor vehicle industry meant that the parties would offer licences to all interested competitors on reasonable terms.

(b) Research and development agreement between companies with small market shares

9.030 *SOPELEM/Vickers*[13]—This agreement has already been discussed.[14] Both parties manufactured a wide range of microscopes, of which some were competing with each other but most were complementary. There was only overlapping of the parties' instruments at an elementary level. However, the Commission held that both parties were capable of extending their range of activities and becoming competitors. The parties set up a joint venture agreement which aimed at setting up technical co-operation as well as establishing a future common means of distribution. Furthermore, the parties agreed to standardise their microscopes so that their parts were interchangeable. Each party continued carrying out concurrently its own research and development activities.

The Commission exempted the agreement holding that such an agreement would enable SOPELEM and Vickers to secure the development and maintenance of a more comprehensive and advanced range of microscopes. Furthermore, the agreement prevented the parties duplicating each other's results. The distribution system helped rationalise the parties' own distribution costs which were disproportionately high because of the parties' small market shares. Such would lead to a reduction in costs of the microscopes and this would benefit the consumer. The Commission noted that both parents were free to exploit the results of the research and development without restriction after the termination of the agreement. Due to the presence of other manufacturers, the agreement did not eliminate competition in a substantial part of the relevant products.

[13] *SOPELEM/Vickers (No. 1)* [1978] O.J. L70/47, [1978] 2 C.M.L.R. 146.
[14] See para. 9.017 above.

(c) High risk research and development agreement

9.031 *BBC/Brown Boveri*[15]—This was an agreement between a German company (BBC) and a Japanese company (NGK) setting up a Joint Venture (NEWCO) to develop sodium-sulphur high performance batteries. These batteries were to be used for powering cars and for providing off-peak power in power stations. BBC was the main party having brought the sodium-sulphur battery to an advanced stage. Such batteries included ceramic parts which BBC was unable to manufacture satisfactorily. Thus, it sought to co-operate with NGK, which was experienced in ceramics. Each parent company granted NEWCO an exclusive licence for existing patents and know-how in the research and development field. NEWCO then granted NGK an exclusive sub-licence for patents and know-how for Japan and the Far East and a similar exclusive sub-licence for BBC in the Community, America and some other countries, both for 15 years. These included active sales bans in each other's territory for 10 years. The granting of sub-licences in each party's territory was subject to the prior consent of the other party which could not be refused without reasonable grounds. NGK and NEWCO were prohibited from carrying out research and development with third parties without BBC's consent.

The Commission exempted the agreement. The co-operation was aimed at developing a fundamental technological innovation which could be done more quickly and cheaply on a collaborative basis. The consumer's quality of life would be enhanced as electrically-driven cars were beneficial to the environment and the battery would play an important role in power stations. The ban on third party research and development was exempted as being necessary to secure the benefits from the joint research and development. The exclusive sub-licence to BBC was deemed indispensable because of the high-risk in marketing the batteries successfully. Competition was not substantially eliminated as electrically driven cars competed with conventional cars.

6. The Research and Development Block Exemption: Regulation 418/85

(a) Introduction

9.032 The Commission's sympathetic approach to research and development agreements led invariably to such agreements being exempted. The Notice on Co-operation Agreements had become unreliable as a guide especially where the agreement provided for commercial exploitation of the results. It thus became clear that a Research and Development Block Exemption would be useful. The Commission was empowered to issue a Block Exemption for the research, development and subsequent exploitation of the results including provisions regarding industrial property

[15] *Re the Agreements between BBC Brown and Boveri and NGK Insulators Limited* [1988] O.J. L301/68, [1989] 4 C.M.L.R. 610.

and confidential technical knowledge under Article 1(1)(b) of Regulation 2821/71. Thus in the early 1980s the Commission began its consultation procedure[16] with a view to issuing such a Block Exemption.

The Commission's concern that competition be maintained by the existence of different poles of research meant that the Commission found it very difficult to draw the line between obligations which reinforced the competitiveness of European industry and those which had the effect of stultifying economic and technological progress.[17] Thus, the Commission in drafting the Research and Development Block Exemption regulation distinguished between agreements between competitors with small market shares and those with large market shares in the relevant product market. The Research and Development Block Exemption does not automatically exempt the latter.[18]

(b) Justification for block exemption

9.033 The Commission supported the issue of a Research and Development Block Exemption as follows:

> "Co-operation in research and development and in the exploitation of the results generally promotes technical and economic progress by increasing the dissemination of technical knowledge between the parties and avoiding duplication of research and development work, by stimulating new advances through the exchange of complementary technical knowledge, and by rationalising the manufacture of the products or application of the processes arising out of the research and development. These aims can be achieved only where the research and development programme and its objectives are clearly defined and each of the parties is given the opportunity of exploiting any of the results of the programme that interest it."[19]

(c) Agreements covered by block exemption

(i) Types of R & D agreement

9.034 The Block Exemption applies to: (a) agreements for joint research and development of products or processes excluding joint exploitation of the results,[20] (b) agreements for the joint research and development of pro-

[16] As provided for in Reg. 2871/71.

[17] See *13th Annual Report on Competition Policy*, para. 42.

[18] Interestingly, in the draft block exemption, it was provided that the latter type of agreements could be exempted via the opposition procedure which exempts the agreement unless the Commission objects within six months of notification. The actual Research and Development Block Exemption does not allow such an accelerated exemption process for such agreements which must be individually notified.

[19] Reg. 418/85, Recital 4.

[20] "Research and development of product or processes" is defined as "the acquisition of technical knowledge and the carrying out of theoretical analysis, systematic study or experimentation, including experimental product, technical testing of products or processes, the establishment of the necessary facilities and the obtaining of intellectual property rights for the results;" —see Art. 2(a). "Technical knowledge" is further defined at Art. 1(2)(e).

ducts or processes and joint exploitation of the results and; (c) agreements for the joint exploitation of the results of research and development jointly carried out pursuant to a prior agreement between the same undertakings.[21] Thus, it does not cover joint exploitation of parties' individual research and development efforts. "Exploitation" is widely defined as including manufacturing products arising out of the research and development or the application; the application of processes arising out of the research and development; the assignment or licensing of intellectual property rights or the communication of know-how required for such manufacture or application.

Until recently, the Research and Development Block Exemption did not cover arrangements for the joint distribution and sale of contract products.[22] In 1992, the Commission issued a Group Exemptions (Amendment) Regulation which extended the application of the block exemption to joint distribution and sale of the contract products. The Commission explained the amendment as intended to facilitate co-operation between firms and to bring the treatment of co-operative joint ventures assessed under Article 85 in line with that of concentrative joint ventures.[23] Now, where one of the parties, a joint undertaking, a third undertaking or more than one joint undertaking or third undertaking are entrusted with the distribution of the products, the Research and Development Block Exemption will apply provided that the market share of the parties in the relevant product market is small.[24]

The Block Exemption covers a variety of different vehicles for setting up research and development agreements from those establishing an independent Joint Venture company for the purposes of research and development and exploitation to those which merely allocate the research and development efforts between the parties.[25]

(ii) Agreements with a research and development element

9.035 Agreements between commercial concerns may comprise many areas of interest including specialisation of manufacture, distribution and licensing of results. The Research and Development Block Exemption realises this and states that research and development agreements may be covered by other Block Exemptions as well.[26] Thus, a Joint Venture Company set up to carry out research and development may wish to exploit the results by licensing to third parties. Whilst the Research and Development Block

[21] Art. 1(1)(a) to (c). The last type of agreement gives the parties the option to decide whether to exploit the results of a research and development agreement.

[22] See Research and Development Block Exemption, Art. 1(2)(d); *14th Report on Competition Policy*, para. 30; *ODIN* [1990] O.J. L209/15; [1991] 4 C.M.L.R. 832 at para. 21; *Alcatel Espace/ANT* [1990] O.J. L32/19; *Konsortium ECR 900* [1990] O.J. L228/31; [1991] 4 C.M.L.R. 208; *KSB/Gould/Lowara/ITT* [1991] O.J. L19/25 and 20th Report on Competition Policy, para. 44.

[23] *22nd Annual Report on Competition Policy*, para. 265.

[24] This requirement is discussed in more detail below, para. 9.039.

[25] Art. 1(3).

[26] Recital 14.

Exemption would cover the agreement setting up the Joint Venture company, it would not cover patent or know-how licences entered into by third parties and the Joint Venture company (which will be covered by the Patent and Know-How Block Exemption). Similarly, a research and development may contain provisions relating to the allocation of manufacturing of any of the Research and Development products. Such provisions will be covered by the Specialisation Block Exemption.[27] In certain circumstances, there will be grey areas, *e.g.* where the Joint Venture agreement attempts to restrain the JVs power to negotiate licences with third parties (*i.e.* where consent of both parents is needed for a licence) or where there are provisions for the redistribution of royalties between the parties to a co-operation agreement from third parties. In these cases, if the Research and Development Block Exemption contains specific rules on the clause in question, then the other Block Exemptions are inapplicable.[28]

Recently, the Commission has amended its Patent and Know-How Block Exemption so that in a joint venture arrangement where the parents are competitors, the Block Exemptions will be applicable to the grant of a patent or know how licence by the parent to the joint venture provided that the combined market share of the participating undertakings is not more than 20 per cent in the case of joint production or not more than 10 per cent in the case of joint production and distribution.[29] Accordingly, the grant of an exclusive licence to a joint venture company will be exempted under these Block Exemptions as the Research and Development Block Exemption does not contain a specific rule on this point.

(iii) "Article 2" Conditions

9.036 Furthermore, a research and development agreement must also fulfil various other conditions before it is deemed to fall within the Block Exemption.

(a) The research and development work must be carried out within the framework of a programme defining the objectives of the work and the field in which it is to be carried out.[30] The objectives may be widely drawn but must be specific.[31]
(b) All parties must have access to the results of the work.[32]
(c) Where the agreement provides only for joint research and development, each party is free to exploit the results of the joint research and development and any pre-existing technical

[27] Reg. 417/85.
[28] Recital 14.
[29] Reg. 2349/84 (as amended), Art. 5(2); Reg. 556/89 (as amended), Art. 5(2).
[30] Art. 2(a).
[31] See *KSB/Gould/Lowara/ITT* [1991] O.J. L19/25; *GEC-ANT-Telettra/ITT* [1988] O.J. C180/13 for application of this condition.
[32] Art. 2(b).

knowledge necessary therefor independently.[33] This clause means that any attempt to restrict the individual use or exploitation of results emanating from such an agreement will cause the agreement to fall outside the Block Exemption. However, where such restrictions are exempted under Article 4 or 5 of the Block Exemption, the parties are advised to characterise the agreement as one of joint exploitation to avoid the effects of this clause. It may be agreed that universities and research institutes may use the results solely for the purpose of further research.[34]

(d) Joint exploitation must relate only to results which "are protected by intellectual property rights or constitute know-how which substantially contributes to technical or economic progress and that the results are *decisive* for the manufacture of the contract products or the application of the contract processes".[35] Such a formulation will include the joint exploitation of technical information that existed before the co-operation began if it has become a component part of the joint development to such an extent that it is necessary for the manufacture, use and sale of the contract goods as such technical knowledge is deemed to be part of the "contract processes" and "contract products".[36]

(e) This provision provided that any joint undertaking or third party charged with manufacture of the contract processes is required to supply them only to the parties.[37] Its application was rather obscure and has now been repealed.[38]

(f) Undertakings charged with manufacture by way of specialisation in production are required to fulfil orders for supplies from all the parties.[39]

(d) Duration of exemption for particular agreements

9.037 The Research and Development Block Exemption distinguishes between agreements between competing manufacturers, non-competing manufacturers and agreements concerning joint distribution.

[33] Art. 2(c).
[34] Recital 4.
[35] Art. 2(d) (For the definition of contract products or contract processes, see Art. 1(2)). See *KSB/Gould/Lowara/ITT* [1991] O.J. L19/25 for application of this requirement.
[36] *Continental Gummi-Werke and Michelin* [1988] O.J. L305/33, [1989] 4 C.M.L.R. 920 at para. 32.
[37] Art. 2(e).
[38] Reg. 151/93.
[39] Art. 2(f). Such a clause envisages the application of the Specialisation Block Exemption (Reg. 417/85) which permits reciprocal undertakings by parties as the allocation of manufacturing tasks in a certain field or production.

Non-competing parties—If the parties are not competing manufacturers of products capable of being improved or replaced by the research and development programme, then Article 3(1) provides that the exemption under Article 1 will apply for the duration of the Research and Development programme and, if jointly exploited, for five years from the time the contract products[40] were first put on the market within the Common Market. **9.038**

Competing parties—Where the parties are competing manufacturers of products capable of being improved or replaced by the research and development programme, then the period of exemption provided for by Article 3(1) applies if and only if at the time the agreement is entered into, the parties' combined production of the products capable of being improved does not exceed 20 per cent of the market for such products in the common market or a substantial part thereof.[41] **9.039**

In many research and development programmes, the agreement may anticipate a "rolling program" of continuous research and development alongside the exploitation of results already provided by the programme. After five years of joint exploitation of results, does the exemption provided for by Article 3(1) cease in relation to the continuous research and development programme? The Research and Development Block Exemption is unclear on this point. As "pure" research and development agreements fall outside Article 85(1) prior to the industrial application of results, it is likely that once the contract products have been on the market for five years then Article 3(3) will govern the subsequent situation.[42]

Expiry of initial period—Once the above period in Article 3(1) has expired, then Article 3(3) provides that exemption under the Research and Development Block Exemption only lasts as long as the parties' combined production of the research and development products and other products considered by users to be equivalent in view of their characteristics, price and intended use does not exceed 20 per cent of the total market for such products in the common market or a substantial part thereof.[43] *This is regardless of whether the parties are or are not competitors.* Such exemption continues to apply where the parties's combined market share during any period of two consecutive years increases to 22 per cent.[44] Otherwise, where the parties' combined market share exceeds such amounts, the Research and Development Block Exemption will only continue exemption for a period of six months following the end of the **9.040**

[40] Defined at Art. 1(2).
[41] Thus, one must examine the relevant product market for the pre-existing goods. See para. 11.006 *et seq* on Relevant Product Market in Chap. 11 on Abuse of a Dominant Position.
[42] See next section, para. 9.040.
[43] Art. 3(3). The Commission thus will look to the relevant product market. See para. 11.606 *et seq* below and for the meaning of "substantial" see para. 11.083.
[44] Art. 3(4).

financial year during which it was exceeded.[45] Where there is doubt as to whether the parties' market share exceeds 20 per cent, the Commission will treat the agreement on an individual basis applying the principles of the Research and Development Block Exemption.[46]

9.041 *Research and development agreements with provisions as to distribution*—In 1992, the Research and Development Block Exemption was amended so that certain provisions as to distribution were capable of exemption.[47] Until then, the Commission had taken the view that research and development agreements which involved joint distribution fell within Article 85 and outside the Block Exemption.[48] Now, agreements containing certain provisions as to joint distribution[49] fall within the Block Exemption for five years from the time the contract products are first put on the market within the Common Market provided that the parties' combined production of the product capable of being improved or replaced by the contract products does not exceed 10 per cent of the market for all such products in the Common market or a substantial part thereof.[50] Exemption continues after this initial period provided that market shares in the contract products together with the parties combined production of other products which are considered by users to be equivalent in view of their characteristics, price and intended use does not exceed 11 per cent in any two consecutive financial years.[51] If it does, exemption shall cease after six months following the end of the financial year when such shares were exceeded.[52]

(e) Transitional provisions — article 11

9.042 The transitional provisions for the Research and Development Block Exemption are somewhat complicated and now mainly of historical interest. The Block Exemption came into force on March 1, 1985 and stays in force until December 31, 1997. Article 11 makes provisions for agreements notified prior to March 1, 1985 which will be only of historical interest. Articles 11(3) to (6) cover agreements which Article 85 applies as a result of the accession of a Member State. The transitional provisions also cater for the rare occasions where agreements were notified prior to the accession of a country to the Community. The more common situation is where agreements in existence prior to the accession of the relevant country have not been notified. In these circumstances, Recital 16 states that the Regulation should apply with retroactive effect

[45] Art. 3(5).
[46] *KSB/Gould/Lowara/ITT* [1991] O.J. L19/25.
[47] Group Exemptions (Amendment) Regulation 1992 [1993] O.J. L21/8, [1993] 4 C.M.L.R. 151.
[48] See para. 9.034.
[49] These provisions are discussed in para. 9.060 below.
[50] Art. 3(3a).
[51] Art. 3(4).
[52] Art. 3(5).

to agreements in existence when the Regulation comes into force where such agreements already fulfil its conditions or are modified to do so.

(f) Scheme of block exemption

9.043 If an agreement meets all the above criteria, then such an agreement is *capable* of being automatically exempted.[53] In order for it to be so exempted, it must only contain clauses which are "white-listed" (clauses restrictive of competition but exempted) under Article 4 or those "super-white-listed" (clauses generally not restrictive of competition but exempted anyway) under Article 5. Exemption will not be granted if the agreement contains any clauses "black-listed" under Article 6. If the agreement contains obligations restrictive of competition which are not "white-listed" or "super-white-listed" and do not contain any "black-listed" clauses, it may be exempted by notification under Article 7 (the opposition procedure).

(g) Opposition procedure

9.044 Where a qualifying agreement contains obligations restrictive of competition that are neither white-listed, super-white-listed (if applicable) or black-listed, the agreement will be exempted if it is notified to the Commission and the Commission does not oppose exemption within six months. The procedural requirements are the same as the Know-How and Patent Block Exemption and the reader is referred to the relevant sections.[54] Notifiers should make sure that they provide fully detailed applications otherwise the notified agreement will not benefit from the opposition procedure.[55]

(h) Withdrawal of exemption

9.045 Article 10 empowers the Commission to withdraw the benefit of the Block Exemption where it finds in a particular case that the agreement has certain effects incompatible with the conditions laid down in Article 85(3) of the Treaty and in particular where:

(a) the existence of the agreement substantially restricts the scope for third parties to carry out research and development in the relevant field because of the limited research capacity available elsewhere;
(b) because of the particular structure of supply, the existence of the agreement substantially restricts the access of third parties to the market for the contract products;
(c) without any objectively valid reason, the parties do not exploit the results of the joint research and development;

[53] Art. 1.
[54] See para. 8.207 for opposition procedure under Patent Block Exemption.
[55] See *20th Annual Report on Competition Policy*, Art. 7(3) and para. 47.

(d) the contract products are not subject in the whole or a substantial part of the common market to effective competition from identical products or products considered by users as equivalent in view of their characteristics, price and intended use.[56]

(i) Duration of block exemption

9.046 The Block Exemption came into force on March 1, 1985 and expires on December 31, 1997.

(j) Block exemption and individual clauses

Check-list

Article 4—white listed clauses

9.047

—Ban on independent research and development in connected fields during programme
—Ban on research and development ventures with third parties in connected fields during programme
—Obligation to procure contract products from a party
—Ban on manufacture of contract products or use of contract processes in reserved territories
—"Field of use" restrictions except where parties are competitors
—"Active sales" in reserved territories from five years from first marketing
—Certain joint distribution clauses
—Obligation to communicate the results to each other and grant non-exclusive licences

Article 5—super-white-listed clauses

9.048

—Obligation to communicate technical knowledge
—Ban on use of other party's know-how except for purposes of research and development programme
—Obligation to obtain and maintain intellectual property rights
—Obligation to preserve confidentiality of know-how
—Legal assistance obligations
—Obligation to pay royalties to other parties as compensation for unequal contributions or unequal exploitation of its results
—Obligation to share royalties received from third parties
—Obligation to supply minimum quantities of contract products to other parties
—Obligation to observe minimum standards of quality

[56] Arts. 10(a) to (d).

Article 6—black listed clauses

9.049

—Ban on independent research and development in unconnected fields to research and development programme
—No-challenge clauses
—Quantitative restrictions
—Price restrictions
—Customer restrictions
—Active sales bans after five year period from initial marketing
—Bans on manufacture by third parties
—Restrictions on sales of contract products to intermediate parties/ resellers

(a) Research and development restrictions

Relevant provisions

"White-Listed" Clauses

9.050

4(1)(a) An obligation [on the parties] not to carry out independently research and development in the field to which the programme relates or in a closely connected field during the execution of the programme;

4(1)(b) An obligation [on the parties] not to enter into agreements with third parties on research and development in the field to which the programme relates or in a closely connected field during the execution of the programme;

"Black-Listed" Clauses

6(a) Obligation [on the parties] restricting the freedom to carry out research and development independently or in co-operation with third parties in a field unconnected with that to which the programme relates or, after its completion, in the field to which the programme relates or in a connected field;

The above three provisions are self-explanatory and clear. Article 6(a) tightly circumscribes Articles 4(1)(a) and (b). Thus, there will rarely be need to use the Opposition Procedure for such clauses. Difficulties may arise out of the meaning of "closely connected". It is unclear whether the reference to the completion of the "programme" in Article 6(a) refers to the end of the period of the joint research and development period or the end of the period for the joint exploitation of the agreement which may include the exploitation of results. It seems that the former will probably be the case as there seems no justification for preventing parties from doing their own research once they are no longer committed to joint research.

(b) Communication provisions

Relevant provisions

"White-Listed" Clauses

9.051 4(1)(g) An obligation on the parties to communicate to each other any experience they may gain in exploiting the results and to grant each other non-exclusive licences for inventions relating to improvements or new applications.

"Super-White-Listed" Clauses

9.052 5(1)(a) An obligation [on the parties] to communicate patented or non-patented technical knowledge necessary for the carrying out of the research and development programme for the exploitation of its results; (Article 5(1)(a)).

It is interesting to note that the provision in Article 4(1)(g) is treated as falling within Article 85(1). In the later Patent and Know-How Block Exemptions, such a provision is treated as generally not restrictive of competition (*i.e.* "super-white-listed"). Such may reflect the concern that often the parties in research and development agreements are actual or potential competitors and the sharing of improvements would discourage each party from obtaining a competitive edge on each other. In normal licensing situations, this will rarely be the case and thus there is no need for concern.

(c) Know-how provisions

Relevant provisions

"Super-White-Listed" Clauses

9.053 5(1)(b) An obligation not to use any know-how received from another party for purposes other than carrying out the research and development programme and the exploitation of its results.

5(1)(c) An obligation to preserve the confidentiality of any know-how received or jointly developed under the research and development programme; this obligation may be imposed even after the expiry of the agreement.

The above terms are self-explanatory. A general restriction on the use of the parties' know-how to that of the field of research and development will not be permitted by the Commission.[57] Parties will often wish to have the right to license third parties in relation to jointly developed know-how. A legitimate concern of the parties may be that the jointly developed know-how is only communicated to responsible third parties,

[57] *20th Report on Competition Policy*, para. 44.

who can be trusted not to disclose the know-how, as obligations on the third parties not to disclose the know-how may be ineffectual and if breached, very damaging. To combat such problems, parties to an agreement may insist on a clause that know-how only be communicated to a third party with the consent of the others. In an early case, the Commission has considered that such a term is restrictive of competition and unexemptable.[58] However, recently the Commission has held in a decision granting individual exemption that a procedure for licensing third parties whereby the joint vehicle could grant licences after consultation with the parents that such was exemptable because it constituted a simplification of administrative procedures for licensees and was the economic correlative to the joint research and development.[59] Parties are advised to notify such clauses under the opposition procedure.

(d) Manufacturing restrictions

Relevant provisions

"White-Listed" Clauses

9.054

4(1)(c) An obligation [on the parties] to procure the contract products exclusively from parties, joint organisations or undertakings or third parties, jointly charged with their manufacture;

4(1)(d) An obligation [on the parties] not to manufacture the contract products or apply the contract processes in territories reserved for other parties;

4(1)(e) An obligation [on the parties] to restrict the manufacture of the contract products or application of the contract processes to one or more technical fields of application, except where two or more of the parties are competitors within the meaning of Article 3 at the time the agreement is entered into;

"Black-Listed" Clauses

9.055

6(c) Parties are restricted as to the quantity of the contract products they may manufacture or sell or as to the number of operations employing the contract they may carry out.

6(g) Parties are prohibited from allowing third parties to manufacture the contract products or apply the contract processes in the absence of joint manufacture;[60]

Where the parties decide to jointly manufacture, Article 4(1)(c) permits the parties to decide how this should be achieved. Thus, a provision

[58] *Beecham/Parke Davis* [1979] O.J. L70/11, [1979] 2 C.M.L.R. 157 at para. 42.
[59] *Continental Gummi-Werke and Michelin* [1988] O.J. L305/33, [1989] 4 C.M.L.R. 920 at para. 35.
[60] See Art. 1(3) for definition of "jointly".

whereby one party manufactures all the contract products for the other parties falls within the Block Exemption.[61] Similarly, the parties can subcontract the manufacture of the contract products to a third party. Article 6(g) ostensibly appears to prohibit a ban on a party who does not wish to manufacture the contract products or process itself but intends to licęnse the manufacturing to a third party. However, Article 6(g) should be read in conjunction with Article 2(c) which provides that the block exemption only applies if the agreement provides only for joint research and development, each party is free to exploit the results independently. Accordingly, Article 6(g) is somewhat otiose.

Article 4(1)(e) permits non-competing parties to restrict manufacture to different technical fields of application.[62] If such a restriction is accompanied by an obligation on each party not to grant licences in the other party's field of use, then such is considered by the Commission as an ancillary restriction to the field of use restriction and will be permitted if notified under the Opposition procedure.[63]

Article 4(1)(d) permits territorial restrictions on manufacturing by the parties. This combined with the white-listing of a limited active sales ban in each parties' territories affords a degree of territorial protection to each party.[64] An interesting situation arises where parties to the research and development venture have reserved territories and wish to licence third parties to manufacture and onwardly sell the contract products. Such licences will not be governed by the Research and Development Block Exemption but by the Patent and Know-How Block Exemptions which allow considerably greater territorial protection between licensees and licensee/licensor.[65] Thus, one may have the paradoxical situation that the licensees of the parties will be better protected *vis-à-vis* each other than the original parties.[66]

(e) Sales restrictions

Relevant provisions

"White-Listed" Clauses

9.056 4(1)(f) An obligation not to pursue, for a period of five years from the time the contract products are first put on the market within the common market, an active policy of putting the products on the market in territories reserved for other par-

[61] See Art. 1(3) and *KSB/Gould/Lowara/ITT* [1991] O.J. L19/25.

[62] *17th Annual Report on Competition Policy*, para. 31.

[63] *ibid.*

[64] See Sales Restrictions, para. 9.056.

[65] See sections on Know-How and Patent Block Exemption, paras. 8.182 *et seq* and 8.224 *et seq*

[66] The astute advisor may suggest that parties set up small companies which then licence their rights to so as to obtain the greater territorial protection provided by the Patent and Know-How Block Exemption. However, the Commission may hold that such arrangements fall foul of Art. 5(1)(2) of the Block Exemptions.

ties and in particular not to engage in advertising specifically aimed at such territories or to establish any branch or maintain any distribution depot there for the distribution of the products, provided that users and intermediaries can obtain the contract products from other suppliers and the parties do not render it difficult for intermediaries and users to thus obtain the products;

"Black-Listed" Clauses

9.057 6(f) The Parties are prohibited from putting the contract products on the market or pursuing an active sales policy for them in territories within the common market that are reserved for other parties after the end of the period referred to in Article 4(1)(f);

Thus, the Block Exemption covers bans on active selling in reserved territories for a limited period. Where a variety of differing products are produced over several years in a research and development venture, it is not clear whether the period referred to in Article 4(1)(f) starts afresh for each new product. Where it is anticipated that the active sales ban will be longer than five years in total because of a rolling programme, the agreement should be notified under the opposition procedure.[67] If the agreement confers "marketing exclusivity", such will not be permitted as it envisages protection against both active and passive marketing.[68]

(f) "Downstream restrictions"

Relevant provisions

Black-Listed Clauses

9.058 6(d) Parties are restricted in their determination of process, components of prices or discounts when selling the contract products to third parties;

6(e) Parties are restricted as to the customers they may serve, without prejudice to Article 4(1)(e);

The exception in Article 6(e) means that *implicit* customer restrictions are permissible if a party has been restricted to manufacturing in a particular technical field of the field of research and development.

[67] The Commission has granted individual exemption where there was an active sales ban for the duration of the agreement—see *Re the Agreements between BBC Brown and Boveri and NGK Insulators Limited* [1988] O.J. L301/68, [1989] 4 C.M.L.R. 610.

[68] *17th Report on Competition Policy*, para. 31.

(g) Royalty provisions

Relevant provisions

"Super-White-Listed" Clauses

9.059 5(1)(f) An obligation to pay royalties or render services to other parties to compensate for unequal contributions to the joint research and development or unequal exploitation of its results;

5(1)(g) An obligation to share royalties received from third parties with other parties.

In *Beecham/Parke-Davis*,[69] the Commission insisted on the removal of a royalty-sharing clause for sales of products where there had been equal contributions to the joint research and development. The Commission took the view that equal contribution did not necessarily justify sharing the profit from mutual marketing exploitation.[70] It stated that such a provision might be acceptable where for technical reasons, the results could only be exploited by one party.[71] The Commission stated that such a provision was:

> "likely to create a considerable disincentive for the parties to compete with one another, particularly where marketing raises difficulties, since substantial returns through royalties would have been obtained without production of marketing expenditure."[72]

Such a provision clearly would favour one party if there had been more sales by one party than the other, *i.e.* unequal exploitation. By the introduction of Article 5(1)(f), the Commission has relaxed its stance such that unequal exploitation *for whatever reason* is super-white-listed. Clearly, the easiest way to compensate for unequal exploitation is by way of payment of a royalty per article sold by each party to the other,[73] it would appear that the Commission would allow such a clause although it is recommended that such a clause be notified under the opposition procedure because of the Commission's decision in *Beecham/Parke-Davis*. Parties should be aware of not making payment of royalties dependent on sales of contract products in a particular territory as the Commission

[69] *Beecham/Parke Davis* [1979] O.J. L70/11, [1979] 2 C.M.L.R. 157.

[70] *ibid*, para. 43(c).

[71] *ibid*. Such was not the case as the parties were world-wide manufacturers and sellers of pharmaceutical products.

[72] *ibid*. In *Re Research and Development* [1971] C.M.L.R. D31, the Commission refused to exempt an obligation that parties to a research and development venture pay royalties for exploitation of patents in other parties' territories but not in their own, saying that "there is no obvious compelling reason why the contracting partners should have a further artifical advantage in order to attain the objectives of the joint research besides the natural advantage which they possess in the primary marketing areas through their important position on the market, the particular structure of the market and the previous absence of the other partner from these markets."

[73] Clearly if both parties sell the same number of contract products, there will be no net payment of royalties.

considers such to be unexemptable as it contributes to partitioning of the market.[74]

Article 5(1)(g) permits the sharing of royalties received from third parties who have been licensed to manufacture or sell the contract products or apply the contract processes. It is perhaps surprising that such a universal approval of such a provision has been permitted by the Commission. Such a provision could deter active competition as both parties are equally rewarded for the efforts of one party. Where the research and development mechanism is a joint venture company, obviously there will have to be a royalty-sharing provision between the parents of the joint venture for royalties received by the joint venture company from third parties and the Commission may have had that in mind in drafting this clause.

(h) Joint distribution provisions

Relevant provisions

White-Listed Clauses

9.060

4(fa) An obligation to grant one of the parties the exclusive rights to distribute the contract products, provided that the party does not distribute products manufactured by a third producer which compete with the contract products;

4(fb) An obligation to grant the exclusive right to distribute the contract products to a joint undertaking or a third undertaking, provided that the joint undertaking or third undertaking does not manufacture or distribute products which compete with the contract products;

4(fc) An obligation to grant the exclusive right to distribute the contract products in the whole or a defined area of the Common Market to joint undertakings or third undertakings which do not manufacture or distribute products which compete with the contract products, provided that users and intermediaries are also able to obtain the contract products from other suppliers and neither the parties nor the joint undertaking or third undertakings entrusted with the exclusive distribution of the contract products render it difficult for users and intermediaries to thus obtain the contract products.

These provisions "white-list" certain contractual provisions as to joint distribution. However, they are only permissible provided that the combined market share of the parties in the relevant product market is small.[75] Until recently, provisions as to joint distribution caused the agreement to fall outside the block exemption. Now, Article 4(fa) and

[74] *Research and Development* [1971] C.M.L.R. D31.
[75] See para. 9.041 above.

4(fb) provides that the grant of the exclusive right to distribute the contract products to a party, joint undertaking or third undertaking are "white-listed" provided that the concern exclusively charged with distribution does not distribute products manufactured by a third party and in the case of joint undertaking or third party, it does not manufacture or distribute competing products.

Article 4(fc) permits the grant of the exclusive distribution rights for particular territories within the Common Market on parties who do not manufacture or distribute competing products. This permits the appointment of several exclusive distributors for certain territories. To offset the effect of such exemption, Article 4(fc) stipulates that users and intermediaries must be able to obtain the contract products from other suppliers and are not interfered with in doing so by anyone. There is no limitation on the duration of the exclusive distribution agreement. Accordingly, this route affords more protection between exclusive distributors who qualify under Article 4(fc) than exists between the parties themselves where they have reserved territories.[76]

(i) Parallel import restrictions

Relevant provisions

"Black-Listed" Clauses

9.061 6(h) Parties are required:

- to refuse without any objectively justified reason to meet demand from users or dealers established in their respective territories who would market the contract product in other territories within the common market, or
- to make it difficult for users or dealers to obtain the contract products from other dealers within the common market, and in particular to exercise intellectual property rights or take measures so as to prevent users or dealers from obtaining, or from putting on the market within the common market, products which have been lawfully put on the market within the common market by another party or with its consent.

This provision confirms the Commission's concern that parallel imports are not impeded. In the first indentation of Article 6(h), it provides that the users or dealers be "established" in the parties territories. Thus, a party would be entitled to refuse to meet demand from a parallel importer established in another party's territory (even if he was intending to sell in a third party's territory). This differs from the Patent and Know-How Block Exemption where the requirement of establishment is omit-

[76] Because of the limited period that an active selling ban is exempted under the Block Exemption—see para. 9.056 above.

ted.[77] Thus, the Research and Development Block Exemption is less favourable to parallel importers wishing to take advantage of price differences between parties than the Patent and Know-How Block exemption.

A similar obligation to Article 6(h) appears in the proviso to Article 4(1)(f) which white-lists a limited period active sales bans.[78]

(j) No-challenge clause

Relevant provisions

Black-Listed Clauses

6(b) Parties are prohibited from completion of the research and development programme from challenging the validity of intellectual property rights which the parties hold in the common market and which are relevant to the programme or, after the expiry of the agreement, from challenging the validity of intellectual property rights which the parties hold in the common market and which protect the results of the research and development; **9.062**

Following the decision of the European Court in *Bayer v. Sullhofer*,[79] it may be that a no-challenge clause does not infringe Article 85(1).

(k) Maintenance of intellectual property and legal assistance provisions

Relevant provisions

"Super-White-Listed" Clauses

5(1)(c) Obligation to obtain and maintain in force intellectual property rights for the contract products or processes; **9.063**

5(1)(e) An obligation (i) to inform other parties of infringements of their intellectual property rights (ii) to take legal action against infringers, and (iii) to assist in any such legal action or share with the other parties in the cost thereof:

These are self-explanatory.

(l) Minimum quantities and quality control

"Black-listed" Clauses

5(1)(h) An obligation to supply other parties with minimum quantities of contract products and to observe minimum standards of quality. **9.064**

This is self-explanatory.

[77] Except for in the French text.
[78] See para. 9.056 above.
[79] Case 65/86, *Bayer v. Sullhofer* [1988] E.C.R. 5249, [1990] 4 C.M.L.R. 182. See para. 8.143.

7. Licensing in non Research and Development Joint Ventures

9.065 Many undertakings enter into joint ventures where there is no element of research and development. Such ventures may involve joint manufacture and/or joint distribution of products using existing technology. Such agreements may include intellectual property licences but these will normally be ancillary to the main aim of the agreement. The approach of the Commission in general to joint ventures has already been discussed.[80] Below, the Commission's approach to specialisation agreements and licensing in a non research and development context are discussed.

(a) Specialisation joint ventures

9.066 Parties may often wish to co-operate on the manufacturing and distribution of products by way of specialisation. Thus, competing parties may agree that only one party should manufacture a particular product in return for supplying the product to the other. Alternatively, a party could agree the exclusive supply of a product to one party in return for the other exclusively purchasing from the former party. Such agreements will often involve technical co-operation and technology licensing. Invariably, the parties will be actual or potential competitors. Accordingly, such agreements restrict competition at a horizontal level and will normally fall within Article 85(1). Agreements may be covered by the Specialisation Block Exemption[81] provided there are reciprocal manufacturing specialisation obligations, the turnover threshold of the parties does not exceed 500 million ECU or the market share of the parties in the relevant product market is no more than 20 per cent.[82] If the Block Exemption is applicable, then certain restrictions as to the grant of exclusive distribution rights will be exempted under the regulation.[83]

(b) Two case studies

9.067 Two examples are given here of non research and development joint ventures where a substantial degree of licensing existed.

9.068 *Mitchell Cotts/Sofiltra*[84]—This was a joint venture between Mitchell Cotts, a United Kingdom company and Sofiltra, a French company for the establishment of a joint venture in the United Kingdom for the manufacture of high efficiency air filters. The parties competed on a distribution level but not on a manufacturing level because Mitchell Cotts did not have the technological know-how and capability to manufacture such air filters. The joint venture was granted an exclusive manufacturing

[80] See para. 8.001 *et seq.*
[81] Reg. 417/85, [1985] O.J. L53/1.
[82] Reg. 417/85, Arts. 1, 3(1)(a) and 3(1)(b).
[83] See Art. 2(a) to (f).
[84] [1987] O.J. L41/31, [1988] 4 C.M.L.R. 111.

licence in the United Kingdom and exclusive sales licence in the United Kingdom, Ireland and seven non-E.C. countries. The combined market share of the parties was 17 per cent. The Commission held that the exclusive manufacturing licence infringed Article 85(1) but granted exemption for a ten year period (the duration of the joint venture) as the exclusivity was required to enable the joint venture to establish itself without experiencing competition from its parent companies or other licensees.

9.069 *Optical fibres*[85]—Corning Technology was the owner of optical fibre know-how. It entered into three joint ventures, one in each of France, Germany and the United Kingdom to manufacture fibres using its technology. Each of the partners were already experienced specialist cable manufacturers which had already been working with Corning. Between the three parties, they owned 48 per cent of the total E.C. production capacity. Territorial protection was granted to each joint venture by the grant of exclusive sales licence. The Commission considered that such an agreement fell within Article 85(1) but granted exemption on the condition that: (a) the exclusive sales licences were diluted to non-exclusive licences so that Corning itself could sell or manufacture within the E.C.; (b) that each joint venture was given the right to make active sales in the territories of other joint ventures and that; (c) each joint venture was obliged to sell their products to all users without discrimination. The Commission considered the agreement made available high technology to E.C. undertakings, and that sufficient competition between the parties was possible once the amendments to the agreement were implemented.

[85] [1986] O.J. L236/30 (Commission).

Chapter Ten

FRANCHISING

1. Introduction

10.001 In the last ten years, the franchising concept has become very popular in Europe. It was introduced into Europe in the early 1970s, having been developed in America. The sharp rise in franchises within the E.C. was noted by Advocate-General VerLoren van Themaat in his opinion in the *Pronuptia*[1] case where he noted that in Germany alone, by 1982, there were 200 franchises with 120,000 franchisees and a total turnover of 100 thousand million deutschmarks. It is thus not surprising that recently, the competitive aspects of this marketing style has attracted much comment.

The expression is used to cover a multitude of different type of vertical agreements. This chapter is only interested in those agreements where the franchisor licenses the franchisee to use the franchisor's trade name, trade mark and know-how for the sale of goods or provision of services and where the franchisor exercises continuing control over the franchisee's business. These are called "business format" franchises. Other agreements which are sometimes called franchise agreements are "pure" distributorship agreements (*i.e.* no element of licensing or control)[2] and manufacturing licences which include an ancillary licence for the manufacturer to affix the licensor's trade mark.[3] Where the expression "franchise" is used in this chapter, it refers to a business format franchise.

From a commercial viewpoint, a franchise is a very efficient way of exploiting a marketing concept or scheme developed by the franchisor. From a legal viewpoint, a franchise agreement has in essence four features:[4]

(1) The independence of the franchisor and franchisee;
(2) The existence of a contractual licence for the use of the franchisor's trade name, trade mark, emblems, symbols, etc.;
(3) The provision of continuing assistance to the franchisee by the franchisor;

[1] Case 161/84 *Pronuptia v. Schillgalis* [1986] E.C.R. 353, [1986] 1 C.M.L.R. 414.

[2] These fall outside the scope of this book. See *Butterworth's Competition Law* and Bellamy and Child, *Common Market Law of Competition* (4th Ed.).

[3] See *Re the Agreements of Davide Campari-Milano SpA* [1978] O.J. L70/69, [1978] 2 C.M.L.R. 397.

[4] See for instance, Advocate VerLoren van Themaat A.-G.'s Opinion in case 161/84, *Pronuptia v. Schillgalis* [1986] E.C.R. 353, [1986] 1 C.M.L.R. 414. Also, see Adams and Prichard Jones, *Franchising: Practice and Precedents in Business Format Franchising* (3rd Ed., 1990), p. 18.

(4) Contractual control by the franchisor over the way in which the franchisee conducts the business (usually so that there is uniform presentation by all franchisees).

"Business format" franchise agreements can be for goods or services. Where they concern goods, they will tend to be retail distribution franchises whereby trade-marked goods of the franchisor are sold through special outlets. The franchise agreement will usually ensure that these franchise outlets provide a uniform method of selling the goods and ensure that ancillary services are provided to their customers. The advantage of such systems of selling is that the customer can go to any franchised outlet and know that the standard of goods and ancillary services will be the same. Service franchises concern the provision of services under a trade name. Invariably, it will include the communication of technical know-how to the franchisee. Thus, fast food chains, estate agencies, holiday agencies, maintenance and service of domestic appliances and picture-framing franchises are all examples of service franchises. Remuneration of the franchisor in both types of franchises is usually by an initial joining fee and then by way of royalty payments or management fees or service fees.

2. Franchise: Type of Trade Mark Licence

10.002 From an intellectual property practitioner's viewpoint, a business format franchise is a trade mark or name and know-how licence between two independent undertakings with supplementary contractual controls. In fact, it could be said that a franchise licence represents the ideal registered trade mark licence because it ensures by means of quality control provisions that the trade mark does not lose its distinctiveness.[5] With a bare trademark or service mark licence, differing standards of service and manufacturing may be applied by licensees and thus the essential function of a trade mark as an indicator of quality will be compromised.

With regard to the licensing of unregistered trade mark, trade names, etc., it is the control exercised by the licensor which ensures that the goodwill and reputation of the trade mark or name accrues to the licensor. Only a licence which allows considerable and identical control over licensees will ensure that the licensor does not lose the goodwill of the trade mark or name.

3. Competitive Aspects of Franchising Agreements

10.003 From a competition viewpoint, it is clear that the principle of franchising can foster competition. The European Court of Justice in *Pronuptia*,[6] a case concerning a distribution franchise (but was in many respects a business format franchise), said:

[5] As suggested *ibid*, Adams at p. 25.
[6] Case 161/84, [1986] E.C.R. 353, [1986] 1 C.M.L.R. 414.

> "In a distribution franchise system such as this, an enterprise which has established itself as a distributor in a market and which has thus been able to perfect a range of commercial methods gives independent business men the chance, at a price, of establishing themselves in other markets by using its mark and the commercial methods that created the franchisor's success. More than just a method of distribution, this is a manner of exploiting financially a body of knowledge, without investing the franchisor's capital. At the same time, this system gives business men who lack the necessary experience access to methods which they could otherwise only acquire after prolonged effort and research and also to profit from the reputation of the mark. . . . Such a system which permits the franchisor to take advantage of his success, is not itself restrictive of competition."

Contractual controls which ensure the quality and uniformity of the network and thus maintain the reputation and goodwill of the franchise's trading names are necessary ancillary restraints because it is precisely the attraction of setting up business under a name which possesses a substantial reputation that encourages persons to take out franchises.[7] If such controls were held to be anti-competitive and hence illegal then the franchise's reputation would fragment because of the inability of the franchisors to impose effective quality control measures and other control measures to maintain the identity and reputation of the franchise network. Such would discourage potential franchisees and franchisor from franchising. There may be restrictions on the franchisee which are not necessary to the maintenance of the reputation of the network. One particular area of concern has been "tie-in" clauses in franchise which oblige franchisees to buy products from the franchisor.[8]

(a) Franchises and other distributor agreements

10.004 In assessing the competitive effects of franchise, it is appropriate to compare franchise networks with other distribution arrangements, in particular exclusive distributorship and selective distributorship agreements. The ECJ has said that retail franchises can be distinguished from other distribution agreements because the former uses a single mark, the application of uniform commercial methods and payment of royalties in consideration of the advantages such a system confers.[9] Franchise agreements are predominantly characterised by the effort, by means of licences for trade names, marks and know-how, to assimilate the commercial practices of the franchisee as closely as possible to those of the franchisor or its subsidiaries whilst maintaining the economic independence of the parties. Exclusive supply and purchase obligations play a subordinate role and from the point of view of competition policy, can

[7] For the meaning of the expression "ancillary restraints" in the context of competition law, see Chap. 8 on Licensing of Intellectual Property at para. 8.009.
[8] This is discussed later at para. 10.035 *et seq*.
[9] Case 161/84 *Pronuptia v. Schillgalis* [1986] E.C.R. 353, [1986] 1 C.M.L.R. 414.

only be assessed in the context of the objective pursued, namely the thorough integration of franchisees in the franchisor's network. In contrast, licensing arrangements in exclusive distributorship agreements are subordinate to the grant of exclusivity.[10] In particular, exclusive distributorships are rarely concerned with the transfer of know-how to the franchisee.

Franchises also have similarities with selective distributorship agreements. Both seek to distribute products or provide services through selected outlets in order that stringent quality control can be maintained in the area of ancillary services related to the sale of goods or supply of services. Thus, a company might wish only to supply its goods to outlets which can provide an adequate level of after sales repair and maintenance of its goods. The ECJ and Commission look favourably at selective distributorship agreements if it is established that the properties of the products in question necessitate the establishment of such a system in order to maintain the quality of the products and ensure their proper use provided that distributors are chosen on the basis of objective criteria of a qualitative nature relating to the technical qualifications of the distributor and his staff and suitability of his trading premises and that such conditions are laid down uniformly for all potential distributors and are not applied in a discriminatory fashion.[11] Also, both types of arrangements will often involve the licensing of a trade mark.

10.005 The main difference is that a franchise is a far more highly developed and sophisticated arrangement than a selective distributorship. For instance, in selective distributorship agreements, obligations that exclude firms from a network that are able to meet the objective uniform qualitative selection criteria are held as restrictive of competition.[12] On the other hand, the more highly controlled nature of franchise means that Community law recognises the right of a franchisor to select its franchisees as it sees fit.[13] Accordingly, the Commission will accept restrictions in franchises more readily than selective distributorship. For instance, it has recognised that obligations to pay a minimum royalty, order in

[10] See A.-G. VerLoren van Themaat in Case 161/84 *Pronuptia v. Schillgalis* [1986] E.C.R. 353, [1986] 1 C.M.L.R. 414 at 437.

[11] *Metro v. E.C. Commission* [1977] E.C.R. 1875, [1978] 2 C.M.L.R. 1; *L'Oreal v. De Nieuwe* [1980] E.C.R. 3775, [1981] 2 C.M.L.R. 235; Case 99/79 *Lancome v. Etos*, [1980] E.C.R. 2511, [1981] 2 C.M.L.R. 164 and *Hasselblad v. E.C. Commission* [1984] E.C.R. 883, [1984] 1 C.M.L.R. 559. See A.-G.'s Opinion in Case 161/84, *Pronuptia v. Schillgalis* [1986] E.C.R. 353, [1986] 1 C.M.L.R. 414 at p. 430–431. For a typical Commission decision exempting a selective distributorship, see *Yves Saint Laurent* [1993] 4 C.M.L.R. 120 (selective distribution network for cosmetic goods).

[12] See *Metro v. E.C. Commission* [1977] E.C.R. 1875, [1978] 2 C.M.L.R. 1; *L'Oreal v. De Nieuwe* [1980] E.C.R. 3775, [1981] 2 C.M.L.R. 235; *AEG Telefunken v. E.C. Commission* [1983] E.C.R. 3151, [1984] 3 C.M.L.R. 325; *Re the Agreements of Villeroy and Boch* [1985] O.J. L376/15, [1988] 4 C.M.L.R. 461. The selection criteria must be made known to the public. See *Butterworth's Competition Law* and Bellamy and Child on *Common Market Law of Competition* (4th Ed.).

[13] In *Yves Rocher* [1987] O.J. L8/49, [1988] 4 C.M.L.R. 592, the Commission held that Yves Rocher were entitled to choose its franchisees freely and turn down applicants who did not, in its view, have the personal qualities and business qualifications (at para. 41).

advance 50 per cent of last year's sales and to hold stocks might restrict competition in a selective distribution system in that they could exclude from the network firms that were unwilling to accept such further obligations and their effect would be to force distributors to push certain products to the detriment of other items. However, in distribution franchises, the exclusion of others from the territory allotted to the franchise and the obligation to promote the franchised products is inherent in the very system of franchising and as such does not restrict competition.[14]

(b) Franchise agreements and trade mark licences

10.006 Franchises are often exclusive trade mark licences plus a high degree of contractual control. However, from a competitive viewpoint, trade mark licences and franchises differ markedly because of the pro-competitive aspects of franchising. In exclusive trademark licences, the Commission has held that the grant of an exclusive licence infringes Article 85(1) because it prevents the licensor licensing others in the same territory.[15] In contrast, the commercial attractiveness of franchises to a potential franchisor and franchisee mean that the ECJ and Commission consider franchises as a versatile mechanism for setting up efficient distribution networks for the medium and small business and accordingly help foster competition. Only where a franchise contributes to market sharing will Article 85(1) be applicable.[16]

4. Community Law and Franchise

(a) Pronuptia[17]

10.007 The European Court of Justice in *Pronuptia de Paris v. Schillgalis*,[18] had the opportunity to rule on the compatibility of Article 85 and franchising agreements. It observed that the compatibility of distribution franchise agreements with Article 85(1) could not be assessed in the abstract but depended on the clauses contained in such contracts. The case was a reference under Article 177 from the Bundesgerichtshof in a German action. Thus, the Commission had not examined the agreement.

10.008 *Facts*—The franchise agreement in question was a business format agreement (although the franchise was called a distribution franchise by ECJ) for the distribution of wedding dresses and other clothes under the

[14] *Re the Agreements of Pronuptia de Paris SA* [1987] O.J. L13/39; [1989] 4 C.M.L.R. 355 (Commission).

[15] *Re the Agreements of Davide Campari-Milano SpA* [1978] O.J. L70/69 [1978] 2 C.M.L.R. 397 (exemption renewed—see *Campari* [1989] IV 139). It is usually arguable that an exclusive licence is not anticompetitive when compared to no party being licensed but the Court and Commission have not adopted such an analysis.

[16] Para. 24 of Case 161/84 *Pronuptia v. Schillgalis* [1986] E.C.R. 353, [1986] 1 C.M.L.R. 414.

[17] Case 161/84 *Pronuptia v. Schillgalis* [1986] E.C.R. 353, [1986] 1 C.M.L.R. 414.

[18] *ibid.*

"Pronuptia" name. Litigation had occurred regarding non-payment of fees based on sales figures. The Bundesgerichtshof referred two main questions to the ECJ. The first question was whether or not Article 85(1) applied to franchise agreements. The second question was whether such agreements if they did fall within Article 85(1), were covered by Regulation 67/67 (the Block Exemption for exclusive dealing agreements).

The actual franchise agreement gave Mrs Schillgalis the exclusive right to use the mark "Pronuptia" in the areas of Hamburg, Oldenburg and Hanover. The franchisor agreed to provide training and assistance to the franchisee. The franchisee agreed to only trade under the name Pronuptia in the shop specified in the agreement; to purchase 80 per cent of its wedding dresses and accessories from the franchisor; to pay an initial fee and a 10 per cent royalty on all sales and to refrain from any act of competition including opening any business with an identical or similar purpose and a ban against assignment of the franchise.

10.009 *Court's judgment*—The Court held that distribution franchise agreements similar to Pronuptia were not per se restrictive of competition.[19] It stated that:

> "In a distribution franchise system such as this, an enterprise which has established itself as a distributor in a market and which has thus been able to perfect a range of commercial methods gives independent businessmen the chance, at a price, of establishing themselves in other markets by using its mark and the commercial methods that created the franchisor's success. More than just a method of distribution, this is a manner of exploiting financially a body of knowledge without investing the franchisor's own capital. At the same time this system gives businessmen who lack the necessary experience access to methods which they could otherwise only acquire after prolonged effort and research and allows them also to profit from the reputation of the mark. Distribution franchise agreements are thus different from either dealership agreements or those binding approved resellers appointed under a system of selective distribution which involve neither use of a single mark nor application of uniform commercial methods nor payments of royalties in consideration of the advantages thus conferred. Such a system, which permits the franchisor to take advantage of his success, is not by itself restrictive of competition. For it to function two conditions must be satisfied.

It stated that in order for the franchise to operate effectively the franchisor must be able:

(1) to communicate its know-how to the franchisees and provide them with the necessary assistance in putting its method into

[19] *ibid*, para. 15.

effect without running the risk that the know-how and assistance would aid its competitors;

(2) to take appropriate measures to preserve the identity and reputation of the network which is symbolised by the mark.[20]

It then set out the restrictions which were necessary to be included in a franchise agreement so as to enable the franchisor to fulfil these requirements. It concluded that all restrictions bar the requirement that the franchisee only trade under the franchise name at the location specified in the agreement were necessary ancillary restrictions designed to ensure that the franchise system was successful. Thus, such clauses fell outside Article 85(1). However, it held that the ban on the franchisee opening other shops in conjunction with the exclusivity clause resulted in a kind of market partitioning between the franchisor and a franchisee and between franchisees themselves. Thus such an obligation fell within Article 85(1).[21] The Court stated that a prospective franchisee might not want to take the risk of taking a franchise if his business was not afforded a certain amount of protection from other franchisees and/or the franchisor but that was a matter for exemption under Article 85(3).

The Court further stated that franchise agreements concluded between enterprises in the same Member State may affect trade between Member States if they prevent franchisees from setting themselves up in another Member State.

It ruled that franchise agreements did not fall within the exclusive distribution block exemption (Regulation 67/67).[22]

(b) Exemption: commission's decisions post-Pronuptia

10.010 In *Pronuptia*, the Court was not able to examine whether Article 85(3) was applicable to the agreements as the agreements had not been notified to the Commission. Soon afterwards, the Commission issued several exemptions in relation to notified franchise agreements.[23] All these

[20] *ibid*, para. 16.

[21] The Court followed its decision in *Etablissements Consten & Grundig v. EC Commission* [1966] E.C.R. 299; [1966] 19 C.M.L.R. Note that the Court followed that decision because the "Pronuptia" Cases 56/64 and 58/64 mark was well-known ("répandu") as in *Grundig*. Where the mark is not well-known, it would seem that an exclusive trade mark licence may not have an appreciable effect on competition—see *Moosehead/Whitbread* [1990] O.J. L100/32, [1991] 4 C.M.L.R. 391 (Commission—mixed trademark/know-how manufacturing licence). For discussion of this case or an example of the "unified market" approach by ECJ and Commission—see para. 8.074.

[22] This Reg. has now been replaced by Regs. 1983/83 (block exemption for exclusive distribution agreements) and 1984/83 (block exemption for exclusive purchasing agreements). See *Re the Franchise Agreements of Charles Jourdan* [1989] O.J. L35/31, [1989] 4 C.M.L.R. 591 where the Commission held that Reg. 1983/83 is inapplicable to franchise agreements.

[23] *Re the Franchise Agreements of Yves Rocher* [1987] O.J. L8/49, [1988] 4 C.M.L.R. 592; *Re the Franchise Agreements of Computerland Europe* [1987] O.J. L222/12, [1989] 4 C.M.L.R. 259; *Re the Agreements of Pronuptia de Paris* [1987] O.J. L13/39, [1989] 4 C.M.L.R. 355 (exemption granted to Pronuptia franchise); *Re the Franchise Agreements of Service Master* [1988] O.J. L332/38, [1989] 4 C.M.L.R. 581; *Re the Franchise Agreements of Charles Jourdan* [1989] O.J. L35/31, [1989] 4 C.M.L.R. 591;

decisions must now be seen in the light of the Franchise Block Exemption.[24]

The Commission's decision after *Pronuptia* followed the guidelines set out in that case as to whether a franchising clause was necessary for "an effective transfer of the business formula".[25] All the franchises notified were found to fall within Article 85(1) mainly because the franchise agreements imposed a protected zone for each franchisee which led to artificial partitioning of the market. The following two cases are given by way of example of the Commission's approach to franchise agreement after *Pronuptia* but before the introduction of the Franchise Block Exemption.

(i) Yves Rocher: distribution of goods franchise[26]

10.011 This was the first "business format" franchise to be exempted by the Commission. Yves Rocher was a well-known cosmetic manufacturer. It held a 7.5 per cent market share in France, six per cent in Belgium and elsewhere in the Community, its share was less than five per cent. However, there were many competitors and the largest firm held 15 per cent of the European market. It sold by mail order and through franchised retailers. It selected its franchisees in the light of their personality, aptitude and their performance in a training programme. Furthermore, it chose the exact location of the franchisee's shop after careful study. Each franchisee was granted an exclusive right in a defined marketing area to exploit the Yves Rocher's trade marks. Considerable know-how and assistance, both commercial and technical was provided by Rocher to its franchisees. It recommended resale prices to its franchisees but these were not binding. Sale to resellers was not permitted but was (after amendment) permitted between franchisees. Franchisees were not permitted to carry on a competing business for the duration of the franchise or for a year after termination of the contract. Payment was by way of an initial joining fee and royalties on sales.

The Commission held that only the agreements' effects of restricting one franchisee per given territory fell within Article 85(1). In particular, it held that the ban on sale to resellers did not fall within Article 85(1) as it would completely devalue the reputation and originality of the Rocher franchise network if resellers could sell goods bearing the franchisor's marks without constraint.[27] Interestingly, it considered the horizontal anti-competitive effects of the Yves Rocher network to see whether it was

[24] Reg. 4087/88—see para. 10.014 below.

[25] See *Re the Franchise Agreements of Computerland Europe* [1987] O.J. L222/12, [1989] 4 C.M.L.R. 259 at p. 269.

[26] *Re the Franchise Agreements of Yves Rocher* [1987] O.J. L8/49, [1988] 4 C.M.L.R. 592.

[27] Note that in *Re the Franchise Agreements of Computerland Europe* [1987] O.J. L222/12, [1989] 4 C.M.L.R. 259, the ban on sale to resellers was held to fall within Article 85(1) because in that case, the franchisor did not manufacture the franchise goods and the franchise was effectively a service franchise which provided to the customer computer products of many different manufacturers.

capable of freezing the structures of distribution and thus rendering access to the market appreciably more difficult to competing producers but concluded that there was no appreciable effect.

The Commission exempted the agreements. It held that the franchise contracts contributed to improving distribution of the goods since they helped the producer to penetrate new markets without having to undertake any investment. Furthermore, it held that development of a chain of identical retail outlets strengthened competition *vis-à-vis* large retail organisations with a branch network. Consumers benefitted from the know-how passed on by the franchisor. The contractual obligations, especially those of exclusivity, were indispensable as franchisees would be unlikely to have taken up their franchises without a certain amount of protection from other franchisees or the franchisor itself. Competition in the field of cosmetics was not substantially eliminated either at an *intra-brand level* because the areas allotted were sufficiently small and there was a mail order service and the fact that franchisees could sell to any customer or at an *inter-brand level* because of the smallness of Yves Rocher's market share.

(ii) ServiceMaster: service franchise

10.012 This franchise concerned the supply of housekeeping, cleaning and maintenance services to commercial and domestic customers and the supply of ancillary goods related to those services. The Commission stated that service franchises showed strong similarities to distribution franchises. However, it considered that the know-how element of services franchises was often more important than in distribution franchises. There were many provisions similar to those in *Yves Rocher* which fell outside Article 85(1) as they related to the protection of know-how and the safeguarding of the common identity and reputation of the network. Particular provisions included the obligation to buy products from ServiceMaster or approved third party suppliers and the franchisee's obligation to resell homecare products only with the consent of ServiceMaster and only to customers serviced by the franchisee. Both were held to fall outside Article 85(1).[28]

The Commission held that the ban on the franchisee setting up outlets and conducting an active sales policy (but not passive) outside the franchisee's territory fell within Article 85(1) as such amounted to market partitioning. The Commission held that whilst ServiceMaster at the time of the decision only had a substantial market (six per cent) in the United Kingdom, it was envisaged that its E.C. share would exceed five per cent in the future. Thus the Commission held that there was a *sufficient prob-*

[28] The second provision acts as a ban against sales to resellers. Whereas in *Computerland*, another service franchise, such a provision was held to fall within Article 85(1), the Commission stated in *ServiceMaster* that such a restriction was based on the legitimate concern that the franchisee concentrated on the primary business which was the provision of services [1989] 4 C.M.L.R. 581 at p. 588.

ability that the restrictions in the agreements would affect trade between Member States. It exempted the agreement for 10 years upon similar grounds as given in *Yves Rocher*.[29]

(iii) "Appreciable effect": trade between Member States

10.013 It will be difficult to show that a franchise does not have an appreciable effect on competition. In *Charles Jourdan*,[30] the Commission held that whilst Charles Jourdan's share of the show market in the E.C. was negligible and only one per cent in France, its share of the medium and top quality shoe market was two per cent in the E.C. and 10 per cent in France. Such would appear to fall within the Notice on Agreements of Minor Importance and fall outside Article 85(1).[31] However, the Commission, as in *ServiceMaster* and *Computerland*, held that the franchise network was likely to spread and thus would be likely to appreciably affect trade between Member States. Furthermore, any argument that the franchise is purely local and thus unlikely to affect trade between Member States will not succeed as both the European Court and the Commission have held that agreements which prevent franchisees setting up in other territories are *per se* capable of affecting trade between Member States.[32] It is important to remember that the competitive effect of a franchise agreement will be considered in the light of the whole franchise network.[33]

(c) Franchise Block Exemption: Regulation 4087/88

(i) Introduction

10.014 The rapid growth in franchises in the 1980s and the finding in *Pronuptia* that exclusive franchise agreements infringed Article 85(1) led to pressure on the Commission to prepare a draft Franchise Block Exemption under the empowering Regulation 19/65. A draft regulation was issued in 1987 after the Court's judgment in *Pronuptia* and the Commission's decision in *Yves Rocher* and *Pronuptia*. The Regulation came into force on February 1, 1989 and remains in force until December 31, 1999. It only covers retail distribution and service franchises. However, the definition of such is to include most business format franchises.

In the Regulation, the Commission takes the view that franchise agreements are essentially licences of industrial or intellectual property rights

[29] See above, para. 10.011.

[30] *Re the Franchise Agreements of Charles Jourdan* [1989] O.J. L35/31, [1989] 4 C.M.L.R. 591.

[31] See para. 8.038 on Notice on Agreements of Minor Importance in Chap. 8 on Licensing of Intellectual Property.

[32] *e.g.* see Case 161/84 *Pronuptia* [1986] E.C.R. 353, [1986] 1 C.M.L.R. 414. (ECJ) at para. 26 and Recital 6 of Reg. 4087/88 (Franchise Block Exemption).

[33] See Case 56/65, *Technique Miniere v. Maschinenbau Ulm* [1966] E.C.R. 235, [1966] C.M.L.R. 357.

of trade marks, signs and know-how combined with restrictions to supply or purchase of goods.[34]

(ii) *Justification*

10.015 The Commission states in the Recitals that franchise agreements normally improve the distribution of goods and/or the provision of services:

> "as they give franchisors the possibility of establishing a uniform network with limited investments, which may assist the entry of new competitors on the market, particularly in the case of small and medium sized competitors on the market, particularly in the case of small and medium sized undertakings, thus increasing inter-brand competition. They also allow independent traders to set up outlets more rapidly and with higher chance of success than if they had to do so without the franchisor's experience and assistance. They have therefore the possibility of competing more efficiently with large distribution undertakings."[35]

It further stated that the consumer received a fair share of the benefit:

> "as they combined the advantage of a uniform network with the existence of traders personally interested in the efficient operation of their business. The homogeneity of the network and the constant co-operation between the franchisor and the franchisees ensures a constant quality of the products and services."[36] However, as in other Block Exemptions, the Commission stressed the importance of horizontal cross supply.

(iii) *Qualifying agreements*

10.016 Only franchise agreements which concern the provision of goods or services to end users are covered by the Regulation.[37] Industrial franchises are specifically excluded[38] as are wholesale franchises.[39] The Regulation only covers bipartite agreements and thus does not include multi-partite agreements. In particular, franchise agreements entered into between competing undertakings are specifically excluded from the Block Exemption.[40] On the other hand, the Regulation cover both master franchise agreements and agreements between a master franchisee and its sub-franchisees.[41]

The Regulation defines a franchise as:

[34] Recital 2, Art. 1(3)(a).
[35] Recital 7.
[36] Recital 8.
[37] Recital 4.
[38] Industrial franchises are those which consist of manufacturing licences based on patent and/or know-how combined with trade mark licences—Recital 4 (e.g. see *Re the Agreements of Davide Campari-Milano SpA* [1978] O.J. L70/69, [1978] 2 C.M.L.R. 397).
[39] Recital 5.
[40] Art. 5(1).
[41] Recital 5, Art. 1(2).

> "a package of industrial or intellectual property rights relating to trade marks, trade names, shop signs, utility models, designs, copyrights, know-how or patents, to be exploited for the resale of goods or the provision of services to end users."[42]

A franchise agreement is defined as:

> "an agreement whereby one undertaking, the franchisor, grants the other, the franchisee, in exchange for direct or indirect financial consideration, the right to exploit a franchise for the purposes of marketing specified types of goods and/or services; it includes at least obligations relating to:
> — the use of a common name or shop sign and a uniform presentation of contract premises and/or means of transport;
> — the communication by the franchisor to the franchisee of know-how;
> — the continuing provision by the franchisor to the franchisee of commercial or technical assistance during the life of the agreement.[43]

It would appear that the above conditions are cumulative.[44] Of the above provisions, the know-how one may cause problems. Know-how is defined as a package of non-patented practical information resulting from experience and testing by the franchisor which is secret, substantial and identified.[45] However, these last three terms are widely defined.[46] For instance, the definition of substantial includes, *inter alia*, know-how which is of importance concerning the sale of goods or provision of services to end-users dealing with presentation of goods for sale, methods of dealings with customer and administration and financial management. Thus, it is likely that most business format franchises will possess enough know-how to fall within the scheme.

(iv) Scheme of regulation

10.017 Prima facie, Article 1 exempts qualifying franchise agreements if such agreements meet the conditions of Article 4.[47] Article 2 "white-lists" obligations which are expressly stated to be restrictive of competition. Article 3(1) conditionally "white-lists" certain obligations "in so far as they are necessary to protect the franchisor's industrial or intellectual property rights or to maintain the common identity and reputation of the franchised network". Article 3(2) "super-white-lists" obligations that generally fall outside Article 85(1). Article 5 "black-lists" certain obligations. Article 6 and 7 provides for an opposition procedure for those

[42] Art. 1(3)(a).
[43] Art. 1(3)(b).
[44] See Korah *Monograph on Franchising and hte EEC Competition Regulation* (1989).
[45] Art. 1(3)(f).
[46] Art. 1(3)(g) to (i).
[47] See next section, para. 10.018.

agreements with obligations not covered by Articles 2, 3 and 5. Article 8 empowers the Commission to withdraw the benefit of the Block Exemption if certain conditions are fulfilled.

(v) Requirements for qualifying agreements to be exemptible

10.018 A qualifying agreement will only be capable of exemption if it fulfils three conditions as set out in Article 4. Firstly, the franchisee must be free to obtain the franchise goods from other franchisees or other authorised distributors of the franchisor.[48] Secondly, if the franchisor obliges the franchisee to honour guarantees for the franchisor's goods, this must be applied to all such goods whether marketed by other franchisees or other authorised distributors.[49] Thirdly, it must be stipulated in a franchise agreement that the franchisee indicate its status as an independent undertaking.[50] The Commission considers that these conditions are essential so as to ensure that competition is not eliminated for a substantial part of the goods and that consumers receive a fair share of the resulting benefit.[51]

(vi) Opposition procedure

10.019 Like others, the Franchise Block Exemption provides a procedure whereby a qualifying agreement which meets the conditions of Article 4 but contains obligations restrictive of competition not listed in Articles 2, 3 or 5 can be notified to the Commission for exemption.[52] The agreement will be exempted by default if the Commission does not oppose exemption within six months of receipt of notification.[53] If the Commission opposes exemption[54] then the effects of the notification are governed by the provisions of Regulation 17.[55] If is important that express reference be made to Article 6 and that the information supplied is complete and in accordance with the facts.[56] Information supplied via Article 6 is confidential.[57]

[48] Art. 4(1).
[49] Art. 4(b).
[50] Art. 4(3).
[51] Recital 12.
[52] The agreements must be notified in accordance with Reg. No 27. See Chap. 12 on Enforcement of EEA Competition Law.
[53] If notification is sent by registered post, the date or receipt is the postmark date—Art. 6(2).
[54] It must oppose exemption if a Member State requests it to but can withdraw after consultation with the Advisory Committee on Restrictive Practices and Dominant Positions—Art. 6(5) and (6).
[55] See Chap. 12 on Enforcement of EEA Competition Law.
[56] Art. 6(3).
[57] Art. 7.

(vii) Withdrawal of Benefit of Block Exemption

10.020 Article 8 empowers the Commission to withdraw the benefit of the Block Exemption where an agreement has certain effects incompatible with Article 85(3). Article 8 states that it may be withdrawn in particular where territorial protection is awarded to the franchisee. Certain of these situations are dealt with below.[58] Other situations include where access to the relevant market or competition therein is significantly restricted by the cumulative effect of parallel networks of similar agreement established by competing manufacturer or distributors.[59] Also, if there is no effective competition in a substantial part of the Common Market then the Commission may withdraw the effect of the Block Exemption.[60]

(viii) Transitional provision

10.021 The Block Exemption makes no transitional provision other than that those agreements notified prior to February 1, 1989 (the commencement of the Franchise Block Exemption) may take advantage of the opposition procedure if so entitled by communicating to the Commission referring expressly to Article 6.[61] This raises doubts as to the validity of existing agreements which fall within the Block Exemption prior to its commencement.

(ix) Duration of Regulation 4087/88

10.022 The Franchise Block Exemption came into force on February 1, 1989 and remains in force until December 31, 1999. Decisions about its renewal and possible extension are now underway.

(x) Individual clauses

(1) Check list

10.023 Is it a franchise within terms of Regulation 4087/88?

Article 2—"white-listed" clauses

10.024
- —Exclusive franchise
- —Exclusive master franchise
- —Exploitation of franchise restricted to contract premises
- —Active selling ban
- —Ban on sale of competing goods (unless spare parts or accessories)

[58] See Territorial Restrictions, para. 10.028, for Art. 8(c), Resale Price Maintenance, para. 10.046, for Art. 8(d) and Location Restrictions, para. 10.039, for part of Art. 8(e).

[59] Art. 8(a). In *Re the Franchise Agreements of Yves Rocher* [1987] O.J. L8/49, [1988] 4 C.M.L.R. 592, the Commission considered this point but held that as the Yves Rocher network was small there was no danger of freezing the structures of distribution and rendering access to the market appreciably more difficult for competing producers.

[60] Art. 8(b).

[61] Art. 6(4).

Article 3(1)—conditionally white-listed

—Exclusive selling of franchised goods based on objective quality criteria **10.025**
—Exclusive purchasing clauses where impracticable to apply objective quality criteria
—"Similar business" ban for duration of franchise and for one year afterwards in franchised territory
—Competing financial interest bans
—Restrictions to sell goods only to end-users, other franchisees or resellers of franchisor in other distribution channels
—Best endeavours clauses
—Obligation to contribute to advertising fund of franchisor

Article 3(2)—super-white-listed

—Ban on disclosure of know-how **10.026**
—Communication of experience to franchisor and non-exclusive licence of improvement know-how
—Legal assistance obligations
—Restriction of use of know-how to franchise
—Training obligations
—Obligations to apply commercial method of franchisor
—Equipment/presentation/transport obligations
—"Checking" rights of franchisor
—Ban on change of franchised premises
—Assignment ban

Article 5—"black-listed" obligations

—Agreements between competing undertakings **10.027**
—Clauses preventing franchisee from obtaining supplies of goods of equivalent quality to those offered by franchisor
—Franchisee restrictions on obtaining goods where not relevant to protection of its intellectual property or for maintenance of identity and reputation of the franchised network
—Post-term use of know-how where know-how has become known or easily accessible
—Resale price maintenance
—No-challenge clauses
—Discrimination based on residence of end-user

(a) Territorial Protection

Relevant provisions

White-Listed Clauses

2(*a*) *Exclusive franchise* An obligation on the franchisor in a defined area of the common market, the contract territory, not to: **10.028**

— grant the right to exploit all or part of the franchise to third parties
— itself exploit the franchise, or itself market the goods or services which are the subject-matter of the franchise under a similar formula.
— itself supply the franchisor's goods to third parties;

2(b) *Exclusive master franchise* An obligation on the master franchisee not to exploit franchise agreement with third parties outside its contract territory;

2(d) *Active selling ban* An obligation on the franchisee to refrain, outside the contract territory from seeking customers for the goods or the services which are the subject matter of the franchise.

Conditionally White-Listed Clauses

10.029 *3(1)(e)* *Sales Restrictions* An obligation to sell only the goods which are the subject-matter of the franchise only to end-users, to other franchisees and to resellers within other channels of distribution supplied by the manufacturer of these goods or with its consent.

Black-Listed Clauses

10.030 *5(g)* *Customer Discrimination* An obligation on franchisees not to supply within the common market the goods or services which are the subject-matter of the franchise to end users because of their place of residence.

Possible withdrawal of Block Exemption

10.031 *8(c)* The parties or one of them prevent end users because of their place or residence from obtaining directly or through intermediaries, the goods or services which are the subject-matter of the franchise within the common market, or use differences in specifications concerning those goods or services in different Member States, to isolate markets.

10.032 *Franchisor/franchisee protection*—Article 2(a) white-lists the grant by a franchisor of an exclusive licence to a franchisee. The grant of an exclusive licence is one of the more common reasons (tying clauses are the other common reason) why a franchise falls within Article 85(1) and thus Article of the Block Exemption must be considered the keystone of the regulation. Importantly, it permits a clause preventing the franchisor from supply third parties outside the franchise network within the franchisee's territory. It is difficult to reconcile this provision with Article 8(c). A refusal by a franchisor to meet a demand from an end-user established in a franchisee's territory asking the franchisor to supply his goods would fall within the ambit of Article 2(a) but might cause exemption to be withdrawn.

10.033 *Active and passive sales*—Article 2(d) white-lists franchisees from actively selling outside their territories. However, Article 5(g) "black-lists" any attempt to contractually ban a franchisee from providing goods or supplying services to an end-user outside the franchisee's territory. Thus, a ban on passive sales (*i.e.* an unsolicited order) to end-users in other territories is not permitted.

10.034 *Parallel Imports*—Article 5(g) only black-lists an obligation not to supply goods to end-users situated outside the franchisee's territory. The position with resellers, *i.e.* parallel importers is different. Article 3(1)(e) "conditionally white-lists" a restriction that franchisees only sell to end-users, resellers within other channels of distribution supplied by the manufacturers of the franchised goods or with its consent. In *Yves Rocher*,[62] the Commission held that such a prohibition is necessary and fell outside Article 85(1) as otherwise:

> "Yves Rocher franchisees could freely pass over the goods covered by the contract to resellers who by definition have no access to the Yves Rocher know-how and are not bound by the same obligations, which are necessary in order to establish and maintain the originality and reputation of the network and its identifying marks."[63]

In the case of *Computerland Europe*,[64] an obligation to sell products only to end-users or to other Computerland franchisees fell within Article 85(1) as the franchise only covered the business format as such and not the microcomputer goods being sold which bore various manufacturers' trade marks. Such a clause was however exempted as it was necessary to ensure that franchisees put all their efforts into the franchise and did not expend their efforts on activities other than retail sales and servicing. Under the Block Exemption, it is arguable that such a justification does not come within protection of the franchisor's industrial or intellectual property rights or maintenance of the common identity and reputation of the franchised network and is thus not "white-listed".[65] Thus, it is advised that in service franchises, such an obligation be notified under the opposition procedure for individual exemption.

Exemption can be rescinded under Article 8(c) where one party unilaterally seeks to discriminate against end-users or intermediaries (*i.e.* resellers) because of their place or residence within the common market. As Article 3(1)(e) conditionally white-lists an obligation only to sell the contract goods to resellers within other channels of distribution supplied by the manufacturer of franchised goods or with its consent, it would

[62] [1987] O.J. L8/49, [1988] 4 C.M.L.R. 592.
[63] *ibid*, para. 46.
[64] [1987] O.J. L222/12, [1989] 4 C.M.L.R. 259.
[65] See Art. 3(1).

appear that Article 8(c) is only intended to cover a refusal to supply such resellers rather than independent parallel importers.

(b) Exclusive dealing provisions

Relevant provisions

Conditionally White-Listed Clauses

10.035 *3(1)(b)* *Sale of franchisor's goods only* An obligation to sell, or use in the course of the provision of services, goods which are manufactured only by the franchisor or by third parties designated by it, where it is impracticable, owing to the nature of the goods which are the subject-matter of the franchise, to apply objective quality specifications.

White-Listed Clauses

10.036 *2(e)* *Competition ban* An obligation on the franchisee not to manufacture, sell or use in the course of the provision of services, goods competing with the franchisor's goods which are the subject matter of the franchise; where the subject-matter of the franchise is the sale or use in the course of the provision of services both certain types of goods and spare parts or accessories therefor, that obligation may not be imposed in respect of these spare parts or accessories.[66]

Black-Listed Clauses

10.037 *5(b)* *Purchase of Goods Restrictions* without prejudice to Article 2(e) and Article 3(1)(b), the franchisee is prevented from obtaining supplies of goods of a quality equivalent to those offered by the franchisor;

5(c) *Sales of Goods Restrictions* without prejudice to Article 2(e), the franchisee is obliged to sell—or use in the process of providing services, goods manufactured by the franchisor or third parties designated by the franchisor and the franchisor refuses, for reasons other than protecting the franchisor's industrial or intellectual property rights, or maintaining the common identity and reputation of the franchised network, to designated as authorised manufacturers third parties proposed by the franchisee.

The above provisions deal with the validity of contractual obligations whereby the franchisor "ties-in" the franchisee to only using or selling goods that it provides whether via itself or an approved manufacturer.

Where it is impracticable to specify objective quality specifications,

[66] It appears there should be a comma after "sell" and "of" before "certain types of goods" for this Art. to make sense.

then Article 3(1)(b) conditionally white-lists such a clause. As the provision of goods of a uniform nature and quality must be necessary to maintain the common identity and reputation of the franchised network, it is unlikely that Article 3(1)(b) will ever be inapplicable. Where it is practicable, the effect of Article 5(b) and 5(c) is that the franchisor must allow and approve manufacturers and suppliers of goods which are of an equivalent quality to those offered by the franchisor where such is practicable.

10.038 Article 2(e) white-lists a ban on the manufacture, sale or use in the provision of services of competing goods. This Article sits uneasily with Articles 5(b) and 5(c) which are expressed to be without prejudice to Article 2(e). If "competing goods" means goods as supplied by or manufactured under a licence from a competing firm, then on a literal analysis, a franchisor could refuse to designate any independent supplier or manufacturer to provide a franchisee with goods of a quality equivalent in quality to those offered by the franchisor as such would mean the franchisee handling competing goods which is white-listed by Article 2(e). This would render ineffectual Articles 5(b) and 5(c). If "competing goods" in Article 2(e) means qualitatively differing goods and not the franchise goods as supplied by a nominated third party who is possibly a competitor, such would prevent any conflict.[67]

The proviso to Article 2(e) prevents the white-listing of bans on manufacturing, using or selling competing accessories or spare parts. As such are deemed to be restrictive of competition, such bans must be individually notified under the opposition procedure. There is the issue of whether a product is an essential product of the franchise or an accessory or spare part. It is submitted that where a good provides the franchise with an element of distinctiveness, a ban on the provision of competing goods is permissible as such does not constitute a spare part of accessory. Thus tangy sauces used in fast food franchises would not be a spare part or accessory but needles and threads used in a clothing franchise would be. Accordingly, in this example, the clothing franchisor must allow the franchisee to sell needles from any source.

(c) Location restrictions

Relevant provisions

White-Listed Clauses

10.039 *2(c) Confinement to contract premises* An obligation on the franchisee to exploit the franchise only from the contract premises.

[67] Recital 9 favours such an explanation as it explains the basis for Art. 2(e) that it makes it possible to establish a coherent network which is identified with the franchised goods. Such would be possible with goods of an equivalent quality which are provided by competitors.

Possible withdrawal

10.040 *8(e)* The franchisor uses its right to check the contract premises and means of transport or refuses its agreement to requests by the franchisee to move the contract premises for reasons other than protecting the franchisor's industrial or intellectual property rights, maintaining the common identity and reputation of the franchised network or verifying that the franchisee abides by its obligations under the agreement.

(d) Similar business ban

Relevant provisions

Conditionally White-Listed Clauses

10.041 *3(1)(c)* *Business Competition Ban* An obligation not to engage, directly to indirectly, in any similar business in a territory where it would compete with a member of the franchised network, including the franchisor; the franchisee may be held to this obligation after termination of the agreement, for a reasonable period which may not exceed one year, in the territory where it has exploited the franchise;

3(1)(d) *Ban on financial interests in competing business* An obligation not to acquire financial interests in the capital of a competing undertaking, which would give the franchisee the power to influence the economic conduct of such undertaking.

This provision concerns bans on franchisees providing competing business services. To the extent that Article 3(1)(c) covers the sale of competing goods, this is already white-listed under Article 2(e).[68] It should be noted that Article 3(1)(c) is conditionally white-listed. The Court in *Pronuptia* justified such a "similar business" ban because the franchisor must be able to communicate his know-how to franchisees without running the risk that this know-how will aid his competitors.[69] Thus, it will be rare that such a provision does not fall within the Article 3(1) condition.

With regard to post-termination bans, the period must be reasonable but at the most a year. Thus, it is important to establish what a reasonable period is. In considering the question, it is helpful to look at the Commission's decisions. The Commission will consider the time for the franchisor to establish a new franchised outlet.[70] Thus, the Commission

[68] See Exclusive Dealing, para. 10.035, above.

[69] Case 161/84, [1986] E.C.R. 353, [1986] 1 C.M.L.R. 414, para. 16. See also *Re the Franchise Agreements of Computerland Europe* [1987] O.J. L222/12, [1989] 4 C.M.L.R. 259 at para. 22; *Re the Agreements of Pronuptia de Paris SA* [1987] O.J. L13/39, [1989] 4 C.M.L.R. 355 (Commission) at para. 25; *Re the Franchise Agreements of Charles Jourdan* [1989] O.J. L35/31, [1989] 4 C.M.L.R. 591 at para. 27.

[70] *Re the Agreements of Pronuptia de Paris SA* [1987] O.J. L13/39, [1989] 4 C.M.L.R. 355 (Commission) at para. 25.

in *Computerland* considered that a franchisee's obligation not to engage in competing activities for one year after termination of the agreement within a radius of 10 kilometres of his previous outlet fell outside Article 85(1) as such constituted a

> "reasonable compromise between the franchisor's concern to protect the confidentiality of his business formula and to open a new outlet in the ex-franchisee's former exclusive territory on the one hand, and the ex-franchisee's legitimate interest in continuing to operate in the same field on the other hand."[71]

However, where the know-how includes a large element of general commercial techniques or the franchisee is already experienced in the field of the franchise, a post-term non-competition ban may not be justifiable.[72]

(e) Quality control

Relevant provisions

Conditionally White-Listed Clauses

3(1)(a) *Minimum Objective Quality Provision* An obligation to sell, or use in the course of provision of services, exclusively goods matching objective quality specifications laid down by the franchisor. **10.042**

(f) Best endeavours/minimum royalty/customer and warranty services

Relevant provisions

Conditonally White-Listed Clauses

3(1)(f) *Best endeavours, etc.,* An obligation to use best endeavours to sell the goods or provide the services that are the subject-matter of the franchise; to offer for sale a minimum range of goods, achieve a minimum turnover, plan its orders in advance, achieve a minimum turnover, plan its orders in advance, keep minimum stocks and provide customer and warranty services. **10.043**

[71] *Re the Franchise Agreements of Computerland Europe* [1987] O.J. L222/12, [1989] 4 C.M.L.R. 259 at para. 22(ii). The Commission specifically said in this case that such a finding is without prejudice to any provision of national law which may bestow rights on franchisees after termination. Thus mere clearance of an agreement under Community law does not prevent a finding of invalidity under national law.

[72] See *Re the Franchise Agreements of Charles Jourdan* [1989] O.J. L35/31, [1989] 4 C.M.L.R. 591 at para. 27.

(g) Advertising payments

Relevant provisions

Conditionally White-Listed Clauses

10.044 *3(1)(g) Advertising Payments* An obligation to pay to the franchisor a specified proportion of its revenue for advertising and itself carry out advertising for the nature of which it shall obtain the franchisor's approval.

(h) Know-how provisions

Relevant provisons

Black-Listed Clauses

10.045 *5(d) Use of Public Know-How* An obligation preventing the franchisee from continuing to use the licensed know-how after termination of the agreement where the know-how has become generally known or easily accessible other than by breach of obligation by the franchisee.

(i) Resale price maintenance

Relevant provisions

Black-Listed Clauses

10.046 *5(e) Resale Price Restrictions* the franchisee is restricted by the franchisor, directly or indirectly, in the determination of sale prices for the goods or services which are the subject-matter of the franchise, without prejudice to the possibility for the franchisor of recommending sale prices.

Possible withdrawal

10.047 *8(d) Resale Price Concerted Practices* Franchisees engage in concerted practices relating to the sale prices of the goods or services which are the subject matter of the franchise.

The ease by which the Commission has found there to be a concerted practice where there is parallel behaviour may cause concern to advisors[73] but it would have to be shown that there was actual or tacit *horizontal* collusion between franchisees rather than just the fact that many franchisees sold at the price recommended by the franchisor.[74]

[73] See para. 8.031 on Agreements, Decisions and Concerted Practices in Chap. Eight on Licensing of Intellectual Property.

[74] This seems clear from Art. 8(d) where it states "franchisees engaged in concerted practices" rather than "franchisor and franchisees engage in concerted practices".

(j) No-challenge clauses

Relevant provisions

Black-Listed Clauses

> *5(f) No-challenge Clauses* the franchisor prohibits the franchisee from challenging the validity of the industrial or intellectual property rights which form part of the franchise without prejudice to the possibility for the franchisor of terminating the agreement in such a case. **10.048**

This provision is similar to that in the Patent block Exemption and the reader is referred to the discussion there.[75]

(k) Super-white-listed clauses

10.049 The obligations in Article 3(2) are considered by the Commission to generally not affect competition.[76] They include restrictions on the disclosure and use of know-how; communication of improvements; obligations to inform the franchisor of infringements; the training of franchisees; compliance with the franchisor's standards; application of the franchisor's commercial methods; allowance of the franchisor to carry out checks of premises,[77] stocks, accounts and inventory and bans on the franchisee changing premises and against assignment of the contract without the consent of the franchisor.[78] Where such obligations do fall within Article 85(1), they are exempted.[79]

[75] Para. 8.202.
[76] For a full list of the obligations listed in Art. 3(2), see the Block Exemption.
[77] Although see Art. 8(e) where such a right is used arbitrarily.
[78] Consent must only be withheld for reasons relating to the protection of the franchisor's industrial or intellectual property rights, maintaining the common identity and reputation of the franchised network or verifying that the franchisee abides by its obligations under the agreement—Art. 8(e) *supra*.
[79] Art. 3(3).

Chapter Eleven

ABUSE OF A DOMINANT POSITION

1. Introduction

11.001 According to general economic theory, the behaviour of a monopolist must be scrutinised. This is because a monopolist is able to maximise his profit on the product he sells. Thus the price of his product will usually be higher than the marginal cost price (*i.e.* the cost of the product plus a sufficient profit margin to encourage the investor but no more than absolutely necessary) which could exist in a perfectly competitive market. A dominant undertaking can be inefficient and still be able to make a profit. The theory is that such inefficiency benefits only the monopolist and not the consumer, his welfare or the economy in general.[1] The theory is that a monopoly is an unnatural economical condition brought about by factors other than market forces and is generally detrimental to an economy. However, in reality, a monopoly may be a natural market condition. For instance, in a particular market, it may be that a minimum efficient scale of operation is achieved only by a firm with a market share of more than 50 per cent because of the need to recoup high capital investment and because of economies of scale. In these circumstances, a suspicion of firms with large market shares is unjustified.

Article 86 of the E.C. Treaty prohibits the abuse of a dominant position by one or more undertakings within a substantial part of the Common Market in so far as it affects trade between Member States. Both Article 85 and 86 thus complement each other in order to ensure that competition in the Common Market is not distorted as required by Article 3(f) of the Treaty.

The main difference between the analysis and application of Article 86 and 85 is that the former requires and has involved a much greater understanding and application of economic theory. For instance, in order to establish whether an undertaking has a dominant position, the Commission and the European Court has drawn extensively on economic concepts such as relevant product and geographic market, elasticity of supply and demand, barriers to entry and other economic analytical tools. For the lawyer, this will mean that in many cases, the outcome of a case will not be as predictable as in Article 85 proceedings and will often mean having to employ an economic expert.

Once it is established that the undertaking has a dominant position,

[1] See Whish *Competition Law* (3rd ed.) at p. 3, 4.

the question of what amounts to an abuse is often difficult to ascertain. Certain schools of thought emphasise concepts of efficiency and the right of a dominant undertaking to reap the rewards of gaining dominance in a market. They argue that a firm that has acquired dominance may have done so because of its superior economic financial and marketing strategy and possibly by sacrifice. Thus, it would be wrong to penalise such a firm for being supracompetitive. On the other hand, it is generally recognised that abusive monopolistic behaviour is detrimental to a market economy regardless of the historical reasons for the monopoly. Community law applies what is termed the jurist approach which emphasises the interests of the consumer, small and medium-sized undertakings and fairness in commercial dealings. The difficulty about such an approach is that it often undermines certainty in the application of the law. This has recently been highlighted in a number of cases concerning the application of Community law to intellectual property.

2. Intellectual Property and Abuse of a Dominant Position

11.002 The approach by the European Court of Justice, the Court of First Instance and the Commission in relation to the relationship between intellectual property and Article 86 must be divided into two parts. Firstly, the existence of a legal monopoly conferred on a person by intellectual property laws for a particular good, process or service may be relevant to the issue as to whether an undertaking has a dominant position in the relevant product and geographic market but will not necessarily be decisive. Usually, there will be other goods, processes or services that will be interchangeable with the protected property. Thus, the relevant product market will be often larger than the market in the protected good or service. Only in the case of a highly innovative patented product which is not interchangeable with other products will the relevant product market be the same as the market in the patented product.

Much greater difficulty arises when considering whether the exercise of intellectual property rights constitutes an abuse of a dominant position. *Inherent* in the nature of intellectual property is a legal monopoly which gives the owner the right to exclude others from doing a variety of acts in relation to the protected goods. For instance, a patentee may refuse to licence others or only on certain onerous conditions. That such intrinsic rights are likely to lead to difficulties with Article 86 can be seen by the fact that Article 86(b) specifically mentions that an abuse may consist of the limitation of production, markets or technical developments.

In order to resolve conflicts such as these, it is perhaps not surprising that Community law has drawn legal inspiration from the dichotomy of Article 36 and its decisions under Articles 30 to 36. Thus, the European Court has distinguished between on one hand, the exercise of rights for legitimate reasons associated with the specific subject matter of the intellectual property itself and on the other hand, as an instrument for committing acts of abuse of a dominant position extrinsic to its specific subject matter. It is this area which has recently caused considerable case law. In this area as others, certainty of the law has now been replaced by notions of fairness. The European Court and the CFI will have regard to the economic justification and the undertaking's reasons for the enforcement and exploitation of intellectual property rights. If an undertaking seeks to charge high prices or royalties for its protected goods, this may constitute an abuse if it is merely to maximise profits rather than so as to reimburse research, development and investment costs. Such an approach strikes at the heart of the rationale for intellectual property that the rights owner is permitted to maximise his profits arising out of his legal monopoly in a good or service as he chooses. The intrinsic conflict between the exercise of intellectual property rights and the abuse of a dominant position is considered later in this Chapter.[2]

3. Plan of Chapter

11.003 One cannot understand the application of Article 86 to intellectual property without first studying its general principles as developed by the Court and Commission. Thus, each aspect of Article 86 is examined firstly, on a general level and secondly with regard to intellectual property.

4. Article 86

11.004 Article 86 states that:

> "Any abuse by one or more undertakings of a dominant position within the common market or in a substantial part of it shall be prohibited as incompatible with the common market in so far as it may affect trade between Member States. Such abuse may, in particular, consist in:
> (a) directly or indirectly imposing unfair purchase or selling prices or other unfair trading conditions;
> (b) limiting production, markets or technical development to the prejudice of consumers;
> (c) applying dissimilar conditions to equivalent transactions with other trading parties, thereby placing them at a competitive disadvantage;
> (d) making the conclusion of contracts subject to acceptance by the other parties of supplementary obligations which, by their nature or according to commercial usage, have no connection with the subject of such contracts.

[2] See para. 11.042 *et seq.*

The above list as suggested by the wording is not exhaustive of what may constitute an abuse.[3]

The requirements of Article 86 can be categorised as so:

(a) Dominant position,
(b) Abuse of,
(c) In a substantial part of the Common Market,
(d) Which affects trade between Member States,
(e) By one or more undertakings.

Unlike Article 85, Article 86 has no equivalent of Article 85(3) and thus an abuse of a dominant position cannot be exempted.

5. Dominant Position

11.005 In order to determine whether an undertaking has a dominant position, it is necessary to define the relevant market which it is alleged to be dominant in. Thus, one must define the product market and also the geographic market.[4] As the ECJ said in *United Brands v. E.C. Commission.*[5]

> "The opportunities for competition under Article 86 of the Treaty must be considered having regard to the particular features of the product in question and with reference to a clearly defined geographic area in which it is marketed and where the conditions of competition are sufficiently homogeneous for the effect of the economic power of the undertaking concerned to be able to be evaluated."[6]

The issue of what is the relevant market is of crucial importance in Article 86 proceedings. The larger the relevant market, the easier it is to prove that one does not have a dominant position.

(a) Relevant product or service market

11.006 In order to determine what is the relevant product or service market, one must consider the nature of the product or service which is in issue. It is of crucial importance for courts and tribunals to properly analyse and define the relevant product market. Thus, the European Court annulled a decision of the Commission where it failed to state in detail the peculiarities which distinguished three markets from each other, that of the market for light containers for preserved meat; the market for light

[3] Case 6/72, *Europemballage and Continental Can v. E.C. Commission* [1973] E.C.R. 215; [1973] C.M.L.R. 199.

[4] Case 27/76, *United Brands v. Commission* [1978] E.C.R. 287; [1978] 1 C.M.L.R. 429; Case 88/76, *Hoffmann La Roche v. E.C. Commission* [1979] E.C.R. 461; [1979] 3 C.M.L.R. 211.

[5] *ibid.*

[6] [1978] 1 C.M.L.R. 429 at para. 11.

containers for preserved fish and the market for metal closures for the canning industry.[7]

What are the important criteria in determining the relevant market? The crucial criterion is whether other products are capable of competing with the product in question. If this is so, then the relevant market must include the markets which these competing products fall within. In order to determine whether a product is capable of competing with the relevant product, prime regard must be had as to whether a consumer would consider the products to be interchangeable.

(i) Interchangeability

11.007 In *Hoffmann La Roche v. E.C. Commission*,[8] the Court said that:

> "The concept of the relevant product market in fact implies that there can be effective competition between the products which form part of it and this presupposes that there is a sufficient degree of interchangeability between all the products forming part of the same market . . ."[9]

This concept of interchangeability has other economic labels, namely cross-elasticity of demand and demand substitutability. All three terms have been used by the Court and Commission and essentially mean the same.[10]

Interchangeability depends principally upon three factors: the intrinsic nature of the product, the nature of the goods as perceived by consumers and the price of the products. A good illustration of the factors which will be taken into account in considering the interchangeability of a product is in *United Brands*.[11] The issue was whether other fruit products competed with bananas. The Commission maintained that there was a demand for bananas which was distinct from the demand for other fresh fruit produce. Features of the banana were that

(a) It was an all-year fruit as it could be ripened at any time. Thus there was no unavoidable seasonal substitution with other fruits.
(b) It had certain characteristics, *e.g.* appearance, taste, softness, seedlessness, easy handling and a constant level of production which enables it to satisfy the very young, the old and the sick.

These characteristics distinguished the banana from other fruits and was

[7] Case 6/72, *Europemballage Corp. & Continental Can v. E.C. Commission* [1973] E.C.R. 215; [1973] C.M.L.R. 199, at para. 33.
[8] Case 88/76 [1979] E.C.R. 461; [1979] 3 C.M.L.R. 211.
[9] See para. 28.
[10] See Case 27/76, *United Brands v. E.C. Commission* [1978] E.C.R. 287; [1978] 1 C.M.L.R. 429 at paras. 22–28 where all three terms are used. If there is a difference, it is that interchangeability is used more often in relation to the characteristics of products and cross-elasticity of demand is used in relation to the effect that price variations have on sales of similar competing products.
[11] Case 27/76, [1978] E.C.R. 287; [1978] 1 C.M.L.R. 429.

borne out in surveys which showed that the seasonal arrival of other fruits did not appreciably effect demand for bananas. Further, it was found that because of the flexible way in which imports were controlled and their marketing was adjusted, the price of bananas was also not seasonally affected. Thus, the Court held that fresh fruit was only to a very limited extent substitutable for bananas and that the banana market constituted a market sufficiently distinct from other fresh fruit markets.

(ii) Application of doctrine of interchangeability

11.008 *Spare Parts*—The concept of interchangeability can sometimes cause the relevant product market to be defined in very narrow terms. In *Hugin Kassaregister v. E.C. Commission*,[12] a London firm, Liptons, which repaired cash registers, complained to the Commission that Hugin, a manufacturer of cash registers had refused to supply them with spare parts for its machines as they were not part of Hugin's dealer network. The Court, upholding the Commission,[13] said that the relevant product market was that of Hugin spare parts as such were not interchangeable with spare parts of cash registers of other makes.[14] Hugin had argued that the supply of spare parts could not be considered a separate market but rather an essential parameter of competition in the market for cash registers as a whole. The Court also distinguished between the market for the provision of *services* relating to maintenance and repair work and that of the *product* market for spare parts.[15]

In *British Leyland v. Armstrong*,[16] an English case, Foster J. held in an action by British Leyland against a spare parts manufacturer for infringement of its industrial design rights in its exhaust for its cars, that the relevant market was that of exhausts for all makes of car.[17]

11.009 *Prices*—Where there is a considerable divergence between the price of comparable products, this may reflect the fact that one product is a luxury or high quality good and the other is a budget good. In such circumstances, the question of interchangeability relates more to the intrinsic or perceived quality of the good than the price which merely reflects such characteristics. In other situations where the difference in the characteristics of the goods are less obvious, a significant price difference may be evidence of the fact that there is little cross-elasticity of demand between the two products and thus they belong to separate markets. Where similar products have similar prices, the interchangeability of the two can be

[12] Case 22/78, [1979] E.C.R. 1869; [1979] 3 C.M.L.R. 345.

[13] Although it reversed the Commission's decision on other grounds.

[14] [1978] 3 C.M.L.R. 345 at para. 7. See also *Hilti AG v. E.C. Commission* [1992] 4 C.M.L.R. 16 where the Court held that the Commission's finding that a relevant product market was nails produced for a specific nail gun manufactured by Hilti was correct.

[15] See also Advocate-General Mischo's Opinion in Case 238/87, *Volvo AB v. Erik Veng (UK) Ltd* [1988] E.C.R. 6211; [1989] 4 C.M.L.R. 122 and Case 53/87, *CICRA v. Regie Nationale des Usines Renault* [1990] 4 C.M.L.R. 265.

[16] [1982] 3 C.M.L.R. 603, H.C.—on appeal [1984] 3 C.M.L.R. 102, C.A.

[17] The Court appeared not to be referred to *Hugin Kassaregister v. E.C. Commission*.

measured by raising the price of one product and seeing the effect on the sales of the other. A large increase in sales of the other means that there is a high degree of cross-elasticity and thus they can be considered interchangeable to a large degree. A small increase will suggest that other factors besides obvious characteristics are relevant in determining the relevant product market. However, rarely are undertakings prepared to tinker with the market merely for the purposes of legal proceedings! Thus, survey evidence or other evidence to determine consumer reaction to a change in prices may be useful.[18] Generally, where similar products have similar prices, this will be evidence that the relevant product market encompasses both products.

11.010 *Legal Monopolies*—Where an undertaking has a legal monopoly for the manufacture of certain goods or for the supply of certain services, there has been a tendency for the Commission and the Court to define the relevant market restrictively.

An illustration of this can be seen in *British Leyland plc v. E.C. Commission.*[19] In this case, a person in the United Kingdom seeking to import a British Leyland car had to obtain a certificate of conformity from B.L. certifying that the vehicle conformed to a previously approved type vehicle. A trade had developed in the re-importation of Metro cars from Belgium due to the price difference between the two countries. The Commission claimed that BL was operating its monopoly in an abusive manner.

The European Court held that the relevant market was that of services which are indispensable to dealers who wish to sell the vehicles manufactured by B.L. in a specific geographical area. In such circumstances, there is clearly no interchangeability between certificates for B.L. cars and other makes of cars. Similarly, other manufacturers could not provide certificates for B.L. cars. Thus they could not enter into the market. This analysis favoured the conclusion of a restrictive relevant market.[20]

11.011 *Market Hierarchies*—The relevant product market does not have to be a market for a finished product. Competition and thus product markets are capable of existing at all levels of a manufacturing process. In *Commercial Solvents v. E.C. Commission,*[21] the applicants manufactured nitropropane and aminobutanol which were intermediary products for the manufacture of ethambutanol. The latter was used as an anti-

[18] However, the ECJ has said in *Hilti AG v. Commission* [1992] 4 C.M.L.R. 16 that the mere fact that consumers refer to price as a decisive factor without elaborating on the impact which a change in price would have on the choice of products cannot prove that there is a high degree of cross price elasticity particularly where the choice of the consumer depends to a large extent on unquantifiable circumstances (at para. 75–76).

[19] Case 226/84, [1987] 1 C.M.L.R. 185.

[20] See also Case 26/75, *General Motors Continental NV v. E.C. Commission* [1975] E.C.R. 1367; [1976] 1 C.M.L.R. 95 where the Court had previously upheld a finding of a similar relevant product market on similar facts.

[21] Cases 6–7/72, [1974] E.C.R. 224; [1974] 1 C.M.L.R. 309.

tuberculosis drug and was in competition with other drugs. The matter came to the Commission's attention because the applicants had refused to sell aminobutanol to a competitor because the applicants themselves wished to enter the marked for the derivative product, ethambutanol.

The Court, upholding the Commission, held that for the purposes of defining the relevant product market, it was in fact possible to distinguish the market in the raw materials, nitropropane and aminobutanol from the market on which the product is sold, *i.e.* anti-tuberculosis drugs of which ethambutanol was but one of several. Clearly, if there were raw products which went to make up nitropropane and aminobutanol, then the relevant product market would be the raw products if the issue of supply of those raw products was at issue. Thus, there may exist many levels of product markets in a manufacturing chain.

(iii) Supply-side substitutability

11.012 In considering the relevant product market, it may be that one product which is interchangeable with others is preferred by consumers to other products. In a truly competitive world, one would expect manufacturers to start producing the preferred product in order to increase their sales. However, it may be that there are considerable obstacles in the way of doing so, *e.g.* the purchase of costly plant machinery, the establishment of distribution channels and legal monopoly rights. In other words, there may be certain factors which prevent manufacturers or suppliers from producing the relevant good. These are often called "barriers to entry [of the product market]"—an expression which is more commonly used in order to determine the market power of an undertaking. However, it has become common practice to use such criteria in determining what the relevant product market is. Can other suppliers enter a particular market for goods or services or are they prevented by these barriers to entry? In terms of the relevant product market, this concern is called rather cumbersomely "supply-side substitutability". Where there is little supply-side substitutability, there are high barriers to entry and it will be uneconomic or unfeasible for manufacturers to start supplying products the same or similar to the relevant product. Where there is high supply-side substitutability, it will cost little for competing manufacturers to produce identical or competing goods.

In *Michelin v. E.C. Commission*,[22] the European Court of Justice said:

> " . . . for the purposes of investigation the possibly dominant position of an undertaking on a given market, the possibilities of competition must be judged in the context of the market comprising the totality of the products which, with respect to their characteristics, are particularly suitable for satisfying constant needs and are only to a limited extent interchangeable with other products. However, it must be noted that the determination of the relevant market is useful

[22] Case 322/81, [1983] E.C.R. 3461; [1985] 1 C.M.L.R. 282.

in assessing whether the undertaking concerned is in a position to prevent effective competition from being maintained and behave to an appreciable extent independently of its competitors and customers and consumers. For these purposes, therefore, an examination limited to the objective characteristics only of the relevant products cannot be sufficient: the competitive conditions and the *structure of supply and demand* on the market must also be taken into consideration."[23]

As can be seen from this passage, the issue of supply-side substitutability can be considered an indicator of market power in a relevant product market rather than being concerned with the latter's definition. The distinction is a fine one.

Thus, in *Continental Can v. E.C. Commission*,[24] the European Court stated that:

> "a dominant position in the market for light metal containers for canned meat and fish cannot be decisive in so far as it is not proved that competitors in other fields in the market for light metal containers cannot, by a mere adaptation, enter this market with sufficient strength to form a serious counterweight."[25]

Again, the Court's analysis relates more to market power than the relevant product market. However, later on in its decision, it pointed out that there was contradictory evidence in the Commission's file as to whether competition by other undertakings in producing metal containers had been ruled out because of the size of the investment necessary for integrated production facilities and the technological lead of Continental Can in this area. It said that such confusion was further evidence as to the Commission's uncertainty regarding the delineation of the markets concerned.[26]

11.013 The level of supply-side substitutability will often correspond to the level of demand substitutability (*i.e.* interchangeability) of a product. If the relevant product is A, the existence of several competing products mean that there is high interchangeability. Furthermore, such will normally demonstrate that there is high supply-side substitutability as other manufacturers have found it economical to enter the market and produce competing products. Furthermore, if all the competing products are broadly similar in price and other characteristics, there will be little desire for manufacturers to start manufacturing their competitors' product. Thus, the issue of supply-side substitutability to the definition of the relevant product market is irrelevant. Conversely, if one product is vastly preferred to other products, then normally this suggests that there are barriers to manufacturers producing the clearly favoured product or

[23] [1985] 1 C.M.L.R. 282, at para. 37.
[24] Case 6/72, [1973] E.C.R. 215; [1973] C.M.L.R. 199.
[25] [1973] C.M.L.R. 199 at para. 33.
[26] *ibid*, para. 36.

comparables to it (otherwise they would have done so). In other words, there is low supply-side substitutability. In such a case, clear consumer preference for one produce would suggest that the other products are not particularly interchangeable with the preferred product. In such a case, there would be little interchangeability and supply-side substitutability.

However, in some cases, the two concepts of demand-side (*i.e.* interchangeability) and supply-side substitutability can serve as important complementary analytical tools. This is illustrated in *Michelin v. E.C. Commission.*[27] The Dutch subsidiary of Michelin brought an appeal against a Commission's finding that it had abused its dominant position in the market for replacement tyres for lorries, buses and other heavy vehicles. It argued that the Commission had defined the relevant market:

(a) Too widely in that it failed to distinguish between the market for differing types and sizes of tyre which were not interchangeable in the eyes of the consumer;
(b) Too narrowly in that it had excluded car and van tyres although they occupied similar positions on the market.

The Commission defended its position in respect of the above arguments by saying that:

(a) It was not possible to distinguish between the differing types and dimensions because the elasticity of *supply* between differing types and dimensions must be taken into account;
(b) The criteria of interchangeability and elasticity of *demand* allowed a distinction to be drawn between the market in heavy vehicles and the market in car tyres owing to the structure of demand and the presence of experienced trade buyers in the case of tyres for heavy vehicles.[28]

11.014 The Court, whilst generally upholding the Commission found also that there was no elasticity of supply between tyres for heavy vehicle and car tyres owing to significant production techniques and plant and tools needed for their manufacture. Interestingly, overruling the Commission, the Court also held that there was also no elasticity of supply between different types and dimensions of tyres for heavy vehicles due to differences in the conditions of productions. However, it said that neither that nor the absence of interchangeability meant that the relevant product market should be construed more narrowly. Instead it said, harking back to the definition in *United Brands*,[29] that in view of the fact that no undertaking specialised in manufacturing a particular type or dimension, such differences were not crucial in assessing the market position of the undertaking because in view of their similarity and the manner in which

[27] Case 322/81, [1983] E.C.R. 3461; [1985] 1 C.M.L.R. 287.
[28] [1985] 1 C.M.L.R. 287 at para. 36.
[29] Case 27/76, [1978] E.C.R. 287; [1978] 1 C.M.L.R. 429. See para. 11.005 above.

they complemented one another, the conditions of competition on the market were the same for all types and dimensions.

The Commission increasingly has demonstrated a willingness to fully utilise the concept of supply substitutability together with demand substitutability.[30]

(b) Relevant geographic market

11.015 For Article 86 to apply, it must be shown that an undertaking is dominant in a substantial part of the Common Market. This condition clearly envisages that an undertaking's power may not only be restricted to a relevant product or service market but also may be restricted territorially. In *United Brands*,[31] the Court said that:

> "The conditions for the application of Article 86 to an undertaking in a dominant position presuppose the clear delimitation of the substantial part of the Common Market in which it may be able to engage in abuses which hinder effective competition and this is an area where the objective conditions of competition applying to the product in question must be the same for all traders."[32]

Thus in *United Brands*, the Court upheld the Commission's decision that the relevant geographic market was Germany, Denmark, Ireland, the Netherlands, Belgium and Luxembourg as the banana markets in these countries were completely free, although the applicable tariff provisions and transport costs were of necessity different but not discriminatory and thus the conditions of competition were the same for all. On the other hand, France, Italy and the United Kingdom were excluded because of special circumstances relating to import arrangements and trading conditions and the fact that bananas of various types and origin were sold there.

Often the relevant geographic market will be the region over which the alleged abuse is capable of affecting. Where an alleged dominant undertaking has a statutory monopoly which it is accused of abusing, then clearly the relevant geographic market can be no wider than its territorial extent.[33] In *TV Listings*,[34] RTE, the Irish State Television was accused of abusive behaviour by bringing actions for infringement of copyright against independent publishers of weekly TV listings. The relevant geo-

[30] See *Elopak v. Tetra Pak* [1988] O.J. L272/27; [1990] 4 C.M.L.R. 47 for an analysis of the relevant product market where a high degree of sophisticated analysis using both concepts is applied by the Commission.

[31] Case 27/76, [1978] E.C.R. 287; [1978] 1 C.M.L.R. 429.

[32] *ibid*, para. 44.

[33] See Case 26/75, *General Motors Continental NV v. E.C. Commission* [1975] E.C.R. 1367; [1976] 1 C.M.L.R. 95.

[34] Case T–69/89, *Radio Telefis Eireann v. E.C. Commission* [1991] 4 C.M.L.R. 586; Case T–70/89, *BBC v. E.C. Commission* [1991] C.M.L.R. 669; Case T–76/89, *Independent Television Publication Ltd v. E.C. Commission* [1991] C.M.L.R. 745. Upheld on appeal to ECJ, Judgment April 6, 1995; Case C241–242/91P, *TV Listings* [1995] 6 C.M.L.R. 718.

graphic market was held to be the area in which the programmes could be broadcast to. Furthermore, the area in which the abuse itself occurs rather than where it is capable of operating may determine the relevant geographic market.[35] Another factor which will affect the determination of the relevant geographic market are the costs of transport of the relevant product.[36]

A party accused of a dominant position will often be caught between trying to define the relevant geographical market as small as possible to show that it does not constitute a substantial part of the Common Market and widely as possibly to show that it does not have a dominant position in such an area.

(c) Intellectual property and relevant market

11.016 Intellectual property laws grant a legal monopoly to a person to exclusively exploit a product or service. Where a person manufactures a product under a patent, the existence of the patent *per se* is irrelevant in determining the relevant product market. Often a rights owner will license several parties to manufacture a protected product. Often, this product will be very innovative and there will not be much interchangeability with other products. Again, in these circumstances, in examining the relevant product market, economic analysis will concentrate on the product and not the existence of the patent. This approach is adopted by the Department of Justice in their 1995 Antitrust Guidelines for the Licensing of Intellectual Property where it states that there will often be sufficient actual or potential close substitutes for such products or processes as work to prevent the exercise of market power.

It has been urged, essentially in cases involving a refusal to licence, that the relevant product market is in licences granted by the rights owner. Clearly, any such finding would make it difficult for the intellectual property owner not to have a dominant position. Recently, in the United Kingdom, there have been several cases where one party has submitted that the relevant market is that of granting licences under a patent. This submission is normally coupled with an argument that the plaintiff's refusal to licence is an abuse of a dominant position. For such an argu-

[35] See Case 4/73, *Suiker Unie v. E.C. Commission* [1975] E.C.R. 1663; [1976] 1 C.M.L.R. 295.

[36] *Eurofix-Bauco v. Hilti AG* [1988] O.J. L65/19, [1989] 4 C.M.L.R. 677 (E.C. Commission)—high value of product and low transport costs—relevant geographic market held to be the E.C. (upheld on appeal in *Hilti AG v. E.C. Commission* [1992] 4 C.M.L.R. 16); *Napier Brown-British Sugar* [1988] O.J. L284/41 (E.C. Commission)—high transport costs of sugar and other factors led Commission to hold that relevant geographic market was Great Britain. In *Re Italian Flat Glass* [1990] 4 C.M.L.R. 535, the Commission held that where the cost of transport is an important factor and sources of supply in a Member State are controlled by local group, then the relevant geographical market is the territory of a Member State (at para. 77).

ment to succeed, the defendant must often show that the relevant service market is purely that of licences granted under the patent.

The English courts have been reluctant to conclude that the relevant product market is that of licences granted by the patentee.[37] Thus, the English Court of Appeal rejected a submission that the relevant market was licences to make car exhausts as opposed to exhausts.[38] Defendants have argued that the granting of licences under a patent is analogous to the granting of certificates pursuant to a statutory monopoly.[39] In doing so, the defendants were seeking to draw an analogy with *General Motors Continental NV v. E.C. Commission*.[40] In that case, the ECJ held that General Motors had a dominant position in the grant of certificates of approval for its cars as Belgium law required that certificates were required to be provided by each manufacturer in respect of their vehicles.[41] The Patents Court rejected a submission that *General Motors* was similar to a patentee granting licences as a patentee was not required to grant licences.[42] However, one judge has said that it is arguable that the relevant product market could be the grant or transfer of patent licences.[43] Also, the English Court of Appeal has said that there are no doubt cases *e.g.* the granting of licences for musical works where the licensor can be said to be engaged in the provision of a service.[44]

11.017 It is submitted that it is wholly artificial to determine a market as that for licences granted by a licensor of rights. Licences are not sold, marketed, traded in or subject to the marketplace. In short, they are purely legal in nature. For instance, to rule that the relevant market is that of licences granted by the patentee is *ipso facto* to rule that a patentee always has a dominant position by the very nature of owning the patent and thus the market in licences. This is contrary to the ECJ's clear approach that intellectual property rights *per se* are not conclusive of a dominant position.[45] In cases concerning a refusal to licence, it is submitted that the proper course if for the court to ascertain the relevant product or service market which the rights owner operates in. A refusal to licence merely goes to the issue of abuse and not the determination of the relevant market.

[37] *e.g.* see *British Leyland Motor Corp. Ltd v. Armstrong Patents Company Ltd et al* [1984] 3 C.M.L.R. 102 (C.A.); *Chiron Corp. v. Organon Teknika Ltd* [1993] F.S.R. 324; *Intergraph Corp. v. Solid Systems CAD* Judgment of Mr Justice Ferris, December 7, 1993, unreported.

[38] *British Leyland v. Armstrong* [1984] 3 C.M.L.R. 102, C.A.

[39] *Intergraph Corp. v. Solid Systems CAD* Judgment of Mr Justice Ferris, December 7, 1993, unreported.

[40] Case 26/75, [1975] E.C.R. 1367; [1976] 1 C.M.L.R. 95.

[41] See Legal Monopolies, para. 11.010, above.

[42] *Chiron Corp. v. Organon Teknika Ltd* [1993] F.S.R. 324.

[43] *Intergraph Corp v. Solid Systems CAD* Judgment of Mr Justice Ferris, December 7, 1993, unreported (the allegation was that Intergraph was using its copyright in its computer programs to stifle competition in ancillary markets, namely the sale of second-hand Intergraph equipment and hardware maintenance).

[44] *British Leyland v. Armstrong Patents* [1984] 3 C.M.L.R. 102 at para. 100.

[45] See para. 11.027.

(d) Dominant position

11.018 Once the relevant product and geographic market has been established, one must ascertain whether the relevant undertaking has a dominant position. The European Court of Justice said in *United Brands*:[46]

> "The dominant position referred to in this Article relates to a position of economic strength enjoyed by an undertaking which enables it to prevent effective competition being maintained on the relevant market by giving it the power to behave to an appreciable extent independently of its competitors, customers and ultimately of its consumers."[47]

The definition of a dominant position has been reiterated in several important subsequent cases on Article 86.[48]

It is not necessary that there is a complete absence of competition in order for an undertaking to have a dominant position. As said in *Michelin*,

> " . . . it is not a precondition for a finding that a dominant position exists in the case of a given product that there should be a complete absence of competition from other partially interchangeable products as long as such competition does not affect the undertaking's ability to influence appreciably the conditions in which that competition may be exerted or at any rate to conduct itself to a large extent without having to take account of that competition and without having to take account of that competition and without suffering any adverse effects as a result of its attitude."[49]

To prove that an undertaking is in a dominant position, many factors must be taken into account. Principally, one must examine the undertaking's market share of the relevant market. An undertaking with a small market share will never be able to dictate market conditions. Where an undertaking has a substantial market share, it may be in a position to dictate market conditions. Whether this is so will depend on how difficult it is for other undertakings to enter the relevant market. There may be many obstacles like the initial cost of plant and machinery; intellectual property rights and the need to set up distribution networks. These are called "barriers to entry". If these barriers are high, then an undertaking with a substantial market is likely to be able to behave independently of others and thus be in a dominant position.

[46] Case 27/76, [1978] E.C.R. 287; [1978] 1 C.M.L.R. 429.
[47] [1978] 1 C.M.L.R. 429 at para. 65–66.
[48] Case 88/76, *Hoffmann La Roche v. E.C. Commission* [1979] E.C.R. 461; [1979] 3 C.M.L.R. 211; Case 322/81, *Nederlandsche Banden-Industrie Michelin N.V. v. E.C. Commission* [1983] E.C.R. 3461; [1985] 1 C.M.L.R. 287.
[49] [1985] 1 C.M.L.R. 282 at para. 48. See also Case 88/76, *Hoffmann La Roche v. E.C. Commission* [1979] E.C.R. 461; [1979] 3 C.M.L.R. 211 at para. 39.

(i) Market shares

11.019 The existence of a dominant position may be inferred from several factors which taken separately are not necessarily determinative. Among these factors a highly important one is the existence of very large market shares. As said in *Hoffmann La Roche v. E.C. Commission*,

> "Furthermore although the importance of the market shares may vary from one market to another the view may legitimately be taken that very large shares in themselves, and save in exceptional circumstances, are evidence of the existence of a dominant position. An undertaking which has a very large market share and holds it for some time, by means of the volume of production and the scale of the supply which it stands for—without those having much smaller market shares being able to meet rapidly the demand from those who would like to break away from the undertaking which has the largest market share—is by virtue of that share in a position of strength which makes it an unavoidable trading partner and which already because of this secures for it, at the very least during relatively long periods, that freedom of action which is the special feature of a dominant position."[50]

11.020 What precise percentage amounts to a "very large market share" is unclear. In *Hoffmann La Roche*, the Court and Commission considered the markets for different groups of vitamins.

(a) The Court held that Roche's market share in vitamin B2, which was 86 per cent, was so large as to be in itself evidence of a dominant position.

(b) In the vitamin B6 and H category, the Court said that even on Roche's figures of 65 per cent to 70 per cent market share, this would nevertheless be so large as to "prove the existence of a dominant position".

(c) In the vitamin C market, a 65 per cent market share was "evidence" of the existence of a dominant position which was "confirmed" by the gap between Roche's shares and those of its next largest competitors (14.8 per cent and 6.3 per cent).

(d) In the vitamin E group, Roche held an agreed market share of 54 per cent to 64 per cent over three years. Roche's competitors' market shares were estimated at 16 per cent, 6 per cent and 1 per cent and 19 per cent for importers. The Court held that:

> "Such a position as that which has been established conforms even more typically than that established in the case of Vitamin A to the pattern of a narrow oligopolistic market in which Roche's share is much larger than the com-

[50] Case 88/76, [1979] E.C.R. 461; [1979] 3 C.M.L.R. 211 at para. 41.

bined shares of the two largest competitors. Therefore, the Commission was right to find that there was a dominant position on this market."[51]

11.021 Thus the relative market strength of an undertaking compared to other undertakings is an important indicator of market strength. In *Michelin*,[52] the Court held that a market share of 57 to 65 per cent when compared with its main competitors' market shares of 4 to 8 per cent constituted a "valid indication of Michelin NV's preponderant strength in relation to its competitors".[53] The Court found that Michelin did have a dominant position although the existence of several barriers to entry was important to its finding.

In *United Brands*,[54] the Court held that a market share of 40 per cent did not permit the conclusion that an undertaking had control of the market but that one must have regard to the strength and number of competitors.[55] In this case, the Court said that as United Brands' share was several times greater than that of its nearest competitor, that along with other factors afforded evidence of its preponderant strength.

It would seem that where a market share is below 60 per cent, other factors must exist before there will be a valid finding of dominance. In the vitamin B market, Roche held market shares of 28.9 per cent, 34.9 per cent and 51 per cent in the period from 1972 to 1974. Such figures were held not to be a "factor sufficient" to establish the existence of a dominant position. The Court said that as the Commission had not indicated what other additional factors might establish a dominant position, its finding that a dominant position existed was unsustainable.

(ii) Barriers to entry

11.022 Once it is established that an undertaking has a substantial market share, one must establish whether there are any barriers to entry. As has been seen, where an undertaking has a very large market share, that will be evidence of a dominant position without more. On the other hand, where an undertaking does not have a substantial market share, it is very unlikely that he will be in a dominant position even if there are high barriers to entry preventing further competitors into the relevant market. Thus the consideration of the issue of barriers to entry must be subsidiary to the issue of market shares. However, the Court and Commission frequently refer to the existence of barriers to entry and they must be considered as important evidence in establishing whether an undertaking has a dominant position when his market shares can neither be said to be

[51] [1979] 3 C.M.L.R. 211 at para. 66.
[52] Case 322/81, *Nederlandsche Banden-Industrie Michelin N.V. v. E.C. Commission* [1983] E.C.R. 3461; [1985] 1 C.M.L.R. 287.
[53] *ibid*, para. 52.
[54] Case 27/76, *United Brands v. E.C. Commission* [1978] E.C.R. 287; [1978] 1 C.M.L.R. 429.
[55] [1978] 1 C.M.L.R. 429 at para. 109.

very large nor insubstantial. The following are examples of barriers to entry.

Capital investment—Where a potential competitor has to invest large capital sums before it is able to manufacture the relevant product, this is a barrier to entry.[56] **11.023**

Economies of scale—Certain products may have to be manufactured and distributed on a large scale before they become profitable commodities. Thus, potential competitors would have to undergo a period of unprofitability if they wished to enter the relevant market until their manufacture of the product is sufficiently considerable to make a profit. This is a barrier to entry. It is somewhat controversial because the alleged dominant undertaking may often undergo the same period of unprofitability as well. However, clearly if the economy of scale barrier to entry is allied with an undertaking having a substantial market share then it may be that there is only room for one profitable undertaking in the relevant market and that will enhance the market power of the incumbent undertaking.

Technological lead—If an undertaking has a substantial technological lead in the products in question which is a result of investment and research, then this will constitute a barrier to entry. Clearly, if a competitor has to commit itself to a substantial and lengthy investment and research program, this will mean that there will be a lag time before it can start to manufacture the product in issue.[57]

Distribution networks—The existence of an existing distribution network with commercial contacts which gives the undertaking concerned direct access to end-users facilitates the sale of goods. If a competing undertaking does not have access to such a network, he may have to invest considerable sums of money setting up such a network. Furthermore, this may be difficult if the alleged undertaking has exclusive contracts with existing dealers. Distribution and dealer networks are very important for a product which requires after-sales support and maintenance.[58]

Marketing barriers to entry—Some markets require much more advertising and promotion than others. Thus, the beer, clothing and cigarette market is very dependent on the promotion of image. Also in some markets, the existence of brand name products is much more important than in other markets. In these markets, a potential competitor **11.024**

[56] Case 27/76, *United Brands v. E.C. Commission* [1978] E.C.R. 287; [1978] 1 C.M.L.R. 429 at para. 122.

[57] Case 322/81, *Nederlandsche Banden-Industrie Michelin N.V. v. E.C. Commission* [1983] E.C.R. 3461; [1985] 1 C.M.L.R. 287, at para. 55.

[58] *ibid*, paras. 58–59.

will have to spend substantial sums of money promoting its product in order to gain market share. This is another barrier to entry.[59]

Market saturation—Where the relevant market concerns the sale of capital items as opposed to perishables, then if a market has become saturated (*i.e.* all or nearly all consumers have already purchased the capital item) then it will be more difficult for a newcomer to enter the market. Thus in relation to a case concerning the supply of milk packaging machinery, the Commission held that as most dairies were already equipped with packaging machinery which had an average life span in excess of 10 years, it made it difficult for newcomers to enter the market since in order to sell their products, they had either to compete in the limited market for renewing old equipment or persuade dairies to replace existing equipment.[60]

11.025 *Legal monopolies*—The existence of a legal monopoly for the manufacture and sale of a product or supply of a service in a relevant market will obviously be an insuperable barrier to entry for the period of its duration. This area is clearly of importance to the intellectual property practitioner.[61] If the legal monopoly is co-terminous with the relevant product or service market, then the undertaking who owns the legal monopoly has a dominant position. If the legal monopoly is not co-terminous and only covers one particular product or service in the relevant market, it will not be particularly relevant to any finding of any dominance as competing suppliers can supply interchangeable products which are not covered by the legal monopoly. Where there is limited interchangeability between goods in a product market, then a legal monopoly in a preferred good may be relevant as a barrier to entry.

(iii) Behaviour suggesting dominance

11.026 Certain behaviour by an undertaking may be evidence of a dominant position. Thus, if it makes excessive profits on the sale of products, then this may be evidence that it is in a dominant position. Whilst this might be suggested that the above argument is logically backwards, it is true that certain behaviour can only happen if the undertaking is in a dominant position.

The converse does not apply. Thus, even if an undertaking is operating at a loss in the relevant market, this does not bar a finding of dominance. Thus, in *United Brands*, the Court held that a finding that despite the fact that United Brands made losses on its banana sales, the fact that the customers continued to buy more goods from it and that it was the dearest

[59] *e.g.* see Case 27/76, *United Brands v. E.C. Commission* [1978] E.C.R. 287; [1978] 1 C.M.L.R. 429, at para. 122.

[60] *Elopak v. Tetra Pak* [1988] O.J. L272/27; [1990] 4 C.M.L.R. 47 at para. 44. On appeal to the ECJ, see Case T–51/89, *Tetra Pak Rausing SA v. E.C. Commission* [1991] 4 C.M.L.R. 334.

[61] See Intellectual Property and Dominant Position, para. 11.027.

seller was more significant and in fact was a particular feature of a dominant position.[62]

(e) Intellectual property and dominant position

11.027 *Intellectual Property Rights not conclusive per se of dominant position*—The existence of intellectual property rights does not necessarily mean that the owner has a dominant position. Whilst such rights give their owner absolute power in the protected product or service, rarely will that product or service be the only product or service in the relevant product or service market. As the Court of Justice said in *Deutsche Grammophon v. Metro*:[63]

> "A manufacturer of recordings who has a protection right analogous to copyright does not however have a dominant position within the meaning of Article 86 of the Treaty merely because he exercises his exclusive right to market the protected articles."[64]

In *Sirena Srl v. Eda Srl*,[65] the Court said, in the context of trade marks, that for a dominant position to be proved, it is necessary to show that:

> "the trade mark owner should have the power to prevent the maintenance of effective competition in a considerable part of the market in question, taking into account, in particular, the possible existence and the position of producers or distributors who market similar or substitute products."[66]

This doctrine has been re-iterated several times. Thus, in *EMI Records Ltd v. CBS (UK) Ltd*,[67] the Court emphasised that in the context of trade marks, where there are several competing undertakings whose economic strength is comparable to that of the owner of the mark and who operate in the market for the products in question, then the existence of trade mark rights for a particular product does not imply the existence of a dominant position.[68] Similarly, the English Court of Appeal in *British Leyland v. Armstrong*,[69] held that the mere refusal to grant licences for exhausts cannot by itself prove that the owner of the right had a dominant position.[70]

11.028 Recently, the ECJ in *TV Listings*[71] has re-emphasised that so far as dominant position is concerned, mere ownership of an intellectual property rights cannot confer such a position.[72] In that case which concerned

[62] Case 27/76, [1978] E.C.R. 287; [1978] 1 C.M.L.R. 429 at para. 128.
[63] Case 78/70 [1971] E.C.R. 487; [1971] C.M.L.R. 631.
[64] *ibid*, para. 15.
[65] [1971] E.C.R. 69; [1975] C.M.L.R. 1.
[66] *ibid*, para. 16.
[67] [1976] E.C.R. 811; [1976] 2 C.M.L.R. 235.
[68] *ibid*, para. 36.
[69] [1984] 3 C.M.L.R. 102 at para. 99 (*per* Oliver L.J.)
[70] *ibid*, para. 99.
[71] C241–242/91P [1995] C.M.L.R. 718.
[72] *ibid*, para. 46.

the publication of weekly television guides covering all channels, the television companies used their copyright to prevent such guides being published.[73] The owner of the weekly television guides complained to the Commission who upheld his complaint under Article 86. On appeal to the CFI, the CFI held that the television companies enjoyed a dominant position in the relevant market (weekly guides) as a consequence of their copyright in the programme listings. On appeal of this decision to the ECJ, the ECJ upheld the CFI but on a slightly different ground. The ECJ said that the television companies enjoyed a *de facto* monopoly over the information used to compile listings for the television programmes. In other words, the ECJ de-emphasised the fact that copyright gave the companies a dominant position and emphasised that they had a monopoly over the raw material used to compile the listings. This was a necessary gloss because copyright is a qualified monopoly and not an absolute monopoly. It only prevents third parties from *copying* the copyright material. It does not prevent third parties from compiling exactly the same material from a common source. Accordingly, copyright alone will rarely give a party a dominant position unless others are precluded from accessing the raw material. If this is the case, then the dominant position is derived from the *de facto*, monopoly and not the *de jure* monopoly.

The above approach is mirrored in the United States where the Department of Justice will not presume that patent, copyright or trade secret necessarily confers market power upon its owner because there will often be sufficient actual or potential close substitutes for such product, process or work to prevent the exercise of market power.[74]

11.029 *Intellectual property and market share*—Intellectual property rights are not relevant in considering the market share of an undertaking in a relevant market. One possible area of difficulty is whether the market share of licensees should be taken into account in calculating the market share of an alleged dominant undertaking. Prima facie, provided licensees are independent undertakings and not economically or financially connected with the party being investigated, their market share should not be taken into account. In *British Leyland v. Armstrong*,[75] Foster J. held, in an English case concerning British Leyland bringing proceedings for copyright infringement against manufacturers of spare parts for its exhausts, that if the relevant market was restricted to the after-sales market for B.L. exhausts then there was no dominant position where B.L. had a 24 per cent market share while its four licensees had a total of 36 per cent and the market was highly competitive and on several occasions the manufacturer had to reduce the price of its exhausts in order to remain competitive.[76]

[73] For a detailed account of the facts in this case, see para. 11.053 *et seq*.
[74] See para. 2.2 of *US Antitrust Guidelines for Intellectual Property*, issued by the Department of Justice, April 6, 1995 [1995] 7 EIPR Supplement.
[75] [1982] 3 C.M.L.R. 603.
[76] *ibid*, para. 15.

11.030 *Intellectual Property as Barriers to Entry*—In considering market power, intellectual property rights are relevant as they can constitute a barrier to entry. Intellectual property as with any legal monopoly may constitute a barrier to entry in a particular market.

In the field of spare parts, the relevant market will usually be construed narrowly as spare parts for a particular machine.[77] Sometimes, the design of the spare parts will be protected by design rights. In such circumstances, the rights owner will have a dominant position as such rights constitute an insuperable barrier to entry in the relevant market.[78]

The existence of a registered trade mark with a high quality reputation will often be treated as a barrier to entry. In *United Brands*,[79] the existence of the "Chiquita" trade mark was seen by consumers as a guarantee of high quality bananas. Thus consumers were prepared to spend between 30 to 40 per cent more for "Chiquita" bananas than unlabelled and 7 to 10 per cent more than for other brand names.[80]

As mentioned earlier, a technological lead can constitute a barrier to entry.[81] Such a lead will invariably comprise know-how which other competitors will not be privy to. The existence of a body of know-how will thus constitute a barrier to entry.[82] Furthermore, such a lead could be protected by the existence of patents or could be the result of expired patents.[83] If an undertaking does not have a technological lead, the existence of know-how and patents becomes less important because of the interchangeability of other products in the relevant product market.

6. Abuse

(a) Concept of abusive behaviour

11.031 Many legal practitioners would say that it is much easier to recognise an abuse than to define what is an abuse of a dominant position. Such a statement indicates that there is a lack of fundamental theory underpinning the concept of abuse in Article 86. This Article gives four non-exhaustive examples of what constitutes abuse. The prohibited acts in

[77] See Spare Parts, para. 11.008, above.

[78] See Advocate-General's Opinion in Case 238/87, *Volvo AB v. Erik Veng (UK) Ltd* [1988] E.C.R. 6211; [1989] 4 C.M.L.R. 122 and Case 53/87, *CICRA v. Regie Nationale des Usines Renault* [1990] 4 C.M.L.R. 265. In neither case did the Court have to decide the question as to whether a rights owner had a dominant position in its spare parts market.

[79] Case 27/76, *United Brands v. E.C. Commission* [1978] E.C.R. 287; [1978] 1 C.M.L.R. 429.

[80] *ibid*, para. 88.

[81] See para. 11.023, above.

[82] See *Re United Brands* [1976] 1 C.M.L.R. D28 (E.C. Commission) at para. 85. This decision was appealed in Case 27/76 *United Brands v. E.C. Commission* [1978] E.C.R. 287; [1978] 1 C.M.L.R. 429 but no mention was made by the Court of the know-how.

[83] As was the case in Case 88/76, *Hoffmann La Roche v. E.C. Commission* [1979] E.C.R. 461; [1979] 3 C.M.L.R. 211 at 278. See also *Elopak v. Tetra Pak* [1988] O.J. L272/27; [1990] 4 C.M.L.R. 47 at 70 (E.C. Commission) upheld in Case T–51/89, *Tetra Pak Rausing SA v. E.C. Commission* [1991] 4 C.M.L.R. 334.

these examples are only *economically possible* where the relevant undertaking has a dominant position in a particular market. For instance, a dominant undertaking can charge very high prices or limit production to the prejudice of consumers in an effort to increase profits but the result of a non-dominant undertaking, doing the same thing in a competitive environment would merely be economic suicide. Is the carrying out of economic acts which are only possible if one is dominant an abuse of a dominant position? An economist might answer that an abuse of a dominant position requires three elements. Firstly, the allegedly abusive act must economically prejudice other consumers or competing traders (potential or actual). Secondly, it must be committed by the dominant undertaking. Thirdly, the act is only possible (*i.e.* economically feasible as opposed to theoretically possible) because of the dominance of the undertaking. Such would permit a dominant undertaking to behave as any other competitive trader would have done in a normal competitive market but not otherwise if such results in economic harm to traders or consumers.

11.032 A more radical school of thought starts on the assumption that the ideal economy is a competitive economy where no one has a dominant position. In other words, the mere existence of a dominant undertaking is inherently anti-competitive. According to such a school, if a dominant position is a bar to a competitive market but is not *per se* illegal, then dominant undertakings must not commit any acts which further reduce the competitiveness of the market. Thus acts which if committed by a non-dominant undertaking would be unobjectionable will be illegal if committed by a dominant undertaking if such is to weaken the competitiveness of the market. A classic example of abuse according to this definition would be the acquisition of a company producing competitive goods by a dominant undertaking. Clearly, this would weaken competition whether committed by a dominant or non-dominant undertaking. This approach differs from the previous one in that the abusive behaviour is not made possible by the dominance of the undertaking—it is merely classified abusive because the undertaking is in a dominant position.

11.033 This radical approach is controversial. The acquisition of a rival company by a dominant company would merely mean that a dominant undertaking becomes even more dominant. Such an act in itself would not harm a rival company or consumer. In fact, it could benefit the general public. For instance, a dominant undertaking in a particular market will often be able to produce and market a widget cheaper than a small competitor because of economies of scale and established distribution channels. It may have acquired dominance by an aggressive low pricing campaign over its competitors. The purchase of another company may help to improve its manufacturing or distribution business thus ensuring that the consumer can buy its widgets cheaper as well as ensuring greater profit to the dominant undertaking. Such an act would clearly damage existing competitors because their product prices will be less attractive than they were before the acquisition but will benefit consumers. However, competition is not an aim in itself but so as to ensure that the purchaser of the product benefits by low prices and high quality. Many economic analysts would consider that it is difficult to say that the acquisition of the company in this example is an abuse in itself even if it reduces "competition" in a product market.[84]

Often the reason behind the establishment of the monopoly will be that the undertaking's goods or services are superior in quality, cheaper or more readily available than other competitors (or a combination of the three). In other words, at the time, its goods and services were *more competitive* than others in a competitive market. This resulted in it becoming dominant in a particular market. Thus, some schools of thought would argue that the inherent suspicion of dominant positions is unjustified and is such as to penalise super-competitive efficient firms. In other circumstances, the undertaking may have a dominant position merely because it was the first on the market; it has a legal monopoly or a *de facto* monopoly[85] or for other reasons not related to the prior super-competitiveness of the undertaking concerned. Many would argue that a court or tribunal should be quicker to make a finding of abusive behaviour in the latter cases than otherwise.

In the author's opinion, it is wrong to confuse the concept of abuse with the reduction of competitiveness in the marketplace. Firstly, such a definition does not take into account the consumer's viewpoint. As argued elsewhere in this book, the consumer is not interested *in the abstract* that there exist several equally competing undertakings in the marketplace but that he can find on the market the highest quality widgets at the lowest price possible.[86] Secondly, if it is intended that an abuse by a dominant undertaking is equivalent to a reduction in competition, then it presupposes that being a dominant undertaking is in itself an abuse. For instance, why should the acquisition of a company with a 5 per cent shareholding in the market by an undertaking with a 70 per cent shareholding in the market be illegal but not the mere existence of an undertaking with a 75 per cent shareholding? There may well be good reasons for not allowing dominant undertakings on the market. The result is often an unattractive homogeneity of products in a product market. However, if the *mere existence* of a dominant position is an abuse, then the relevant legislative body should have the courage to state clearly that dominant undertakings are prohibited.

[84] At this point, the reader is referred to the section called Competition Law and its Principles, para. 8.003 *et seq* in Chap. 8 on Licensing of Intellectual Property. In the section, the author argues that competition has little meaning as a workable economic tool if it merely means the presence of competing rivals but is much more relevant if it is viewed by reference to the consumer.

[85] *e.g.* ownership of the only quarry in the world that produces a particular mineral.

[86] See section on Meaning of Competition, para. 8.003 in Chap. 8 on Licensing of Intellectual Property.

(b) Abuse in Community Law

11.034 The European Court of Justice sought to define what an abuse of a dominant position was in *Europemballage Corp. & Continental Can v. E.C. Commission*,.[87] The facts were that Continental Can Co. Inc. of New York, via a holding company, Europemballage Corporation, acquired 91.07 per cent of the shares in a Dutch company, Thommassen. The Commission held that Continental Can had a dominant position in the market in light containers for preserved meat and other products and also, in the market for metal closures for glass containers through its previous acquisition of an 85.8 per cent holding in a German company. It alleged that the acquisition of the shares in the Dutch company was an abuse of a dominant position in that such an acquisition eliminated competition in a substantial part of the Common Market. The Court interpreted Article 86 in the light of Article 3(f) of the Treaty which provides for the establishment of a system which will protect competition from the Common Market from distortion and thus held that there may be abusive behaviour if an undertaking in a dominant position strengthens that dominant position so that the degree of control achieved substantially obstructs competition.[88]

The Court in *Hoffmann La Roche* refined the above concept. It said that:

> "The concept of abuse is an objective concept relating to the behaviour of an undertaking in a dominant position which is such as to influence the structure of a market, where as a result of the very presence of the undertaking in question, the degree of competition is weakened and which, through recourse to methods different from those which condition normal competition in products or services on the basis of the transactions of commercial operators, has the effect of hindering the maintenance of the degree of competition still existing in the market or the growth of that competition."[89]

11.035 The Court appears to emphasise the fact that the *mechanism* of the abuse must be through methods which could not be used in a normal competitive market. However, this emphasis should be seen in the light of the actual abuse in *Hoffmann La Roche* which was that it was forcing its vitamin buyers to exclusively purchase from it by means of giving customers a "fidelity rebate" or by express contractual provision. In *Continental Can*,[90] the abuse, namely the acquisition of shares was an act that any undertaking could effectively accomplish in a normal competitive market and whose achievement did not depend on the fact that the undertaking was in a dominant position.

[87] Case 6/72, [1973] E.C.R. 215; [1973] C.M.L.R. 199.
[88] *ibid*, para. 26.
[89] Case 88/76, [1979] E.C.R. 461; [1979] 3 C.M.L.R. 211 at para. 91.
[90] Case 6/72, [1973] E.C.R. 215; [1973] C.M.L.R. 199.

Indeed, the ECJ's approach is to impose a higher duty upon dominant undertakings. Thus, in *Michelin*, the ECJ said:

> "the finding that an undertaking has a dominant position is not in itself a recrimination but simply means that irrespective of the reasons for which it has such a dominant position, the undertaking concerned has a special responsibility not to allow its conduct to impair genuine undistorted competition on the market."[91]

Deciding whether an abuse has had the effect of weakening competition is difficult. The examples given in Article 86 provide a starting point and most cases of abuse will come within one of the four categories. Each case will turn on its facts.[92]

For the purposes of this book, it is not intended to examine in detail abuses which do not relate to intellectual property. The following acts have been found to be abuses of a dominant position.

(i) Merger/Acquisition

11.036 The merger/acquisition of another undertaking by or with a dominant undertaking.[93]

(ii) Unfair prices

11.037

(a) Charging prices excessive in relation to the economic cost or value of the product or service provided.[94]
(b) The imposition of differing prices in different Member States by a seller when selling its products to an intermediate based on the market conditions that apply to the market that governs the sale of those goods to the consumer.[95]
(c) Where a dominant undertaking lowers its prices for a period so as to force another undertaking out of business (known as "predatory pricing"), this constitutes an abuse.[96]

[91] Case 322/81, *Nederlandsche Banden-Industrie Michelin N.V. v. E.C. Commission* [1983] E.C.R. 3461; [1985] 1 C.M.L.R. 287, at para. 57.

[92] Bellamy and Child *Common Market Law of Competition*, (4th Ed.) at para. 8–037 provides a useful checklist of considerations in considering whether behaviour constitutes abuse.

[93] Case 6/72, *Europemballage Corp. & Continental Can v. E.C. Commission* [1973] E.C.R. 215; [1973] C.M.L.R. 199.

[94] Case 27/76, *United Brands v. E.C. Commission* [1978] E.C.R. 287; [1978] 1 C.M.L.R. 429; Case 26/75, *General Motors Continental NV v. E.C. Commission* [1975] E.C.R. 1367; [1976] 1 C.M.L.R. 95. In relation to unfair prices in the context of intellectual property, see para. 11.070.

[95] Case 27/76, *United Brands v. E.C. Commission* [1978] E.C.R. 287; [1978] 1 C.M.L.R. 429 at paras. 227–230. In this case, United Brands on the basis of information fed to it by local representatives of market conditions in a country would fix the sale price of bananas by them to the intermediate ripener/distributor.

[96] *ECS/AKZO* [1985] O.J. L374/1; [1986] 3 C.M.L.R. 271 (E.C. Commission).

(iii) Refusal to supply

11.038 (a) Refusal to sell essential raw material to competitor.[97] Similarly, in the context of services, a dominant undertaking who refuses for no good reason to supply a service to another undertaking and reserves the service for itself constitutes an abuse of a dominant position.[98]

(b) An undertaking may not stop supplying a long-standing customer even if the latter has engaged in conduct which is against the interest of the dominant undertaking as sanctions must be proportionate to the circumstances and will normally fall short of a cessation of supplies.[99]

(iv) Resale restrictions

11.039 A blanket prohibition on distributors of a dominant undertaking reselling goods to anyone other than retailers.[1]

(v) Tying-in arrangements

11.040 A clause stipulating that a purchaser exclusively buy from a dominant undertaking.[2]

(vi) Loyalty rebates

11.041 The application of a fidelity rebate whereby loyal customers who purchased all or most of their goods from the dominant undertaking receive financial advantages constitutes an abuse of a dominant position because it in effect ties-in the purchaser.[3] This should be contrasted with a quantity discount which is linked solely to the volume of purchases from the manufacturer concerned which is not an abuse.[4] In deciding whether the

[97] Cases 6–7/72, *Commercial Solvents v. E.C. Commission* [1974] E.C.R. 224; [1974] 1 C.M.L.R. 309.

[98] Case 311/84, *Centre Belge D'Etudes de Marche-Telemarketing SA v. Compagnie Luxembourgeoise De Telediffusion and Information Publicite Benelux SA* [1986] 2 C.M.L.R. 558. This case concerned the refusal by IPB, the advertising arm of CLT, which ran a television station in Belgium to allow CBEMT to conduct telemarketing sales on its channel.

[99] Case 27/76, *United Brands v. E.C. Commission* [1978] E.C.R. 287; [1978] 1 C.M.L.R. 429 at paras. 182–194. The offending distributor/ripener was an exclusive distributor for another banana supplier and had advertised for a rival competitor of United Brands.

[1] Case 27/76, *United Brands v. E.C. Commission* [1978] E.C.R. 287; [1978] 1 C.M.L.R. 429 at paras. 152–162.

[2] Case 88/76, *Hoffmann La Roche v. E.C. Commission* [1979] E.C.R. 461; [1979] 3 C.M.L.R. 211 at paras. 89–120.

[3] Case 4/73, *Suiker Unie v. E.C. Commission* [1975] E.C.R. 1663; [1976] 1 C.M.L.R. 295; *Hoffmann La Roche v. E.C. Commission*; *ibid*, Case 322/81, *Nederlandsche Banden-Industrie Michelin NV v. E.C. Commission* [1983] E.C.R. 3461; [1985] 1 C.M.L.R. 287 at paras. 62 to 86.

[4] Case 322/81, *Nederlandsche Banden-Industrie Michelin N.V. v. E.C. Commission* [1983] E.C.R. 3461; [1985] 1 C.M.L.R. 287 at para. 71.

discount system operated is an abuse, the Court will have regard as to whether:

> "in providing an advantage not based on any economic service justifying it, the discount tends to remove or restrict the buyer's freedom to choose his sources of supply, to bar competitors from access to the market, to apply dissimilar conditions to equivalent transactions with other trading partners or to strengthen the dominant position by distorting competition.[5]

7. Intellectual Property and Abuse

(a) Introduction

11.042 In the cases of *General Motors Continental NV v. E.C. Commission*[6] and *British Leyland v. E.C. Commission*,[7] both General Motors and British Leyland were exclusively responsible by operation of law for the issue of certificates that entitled cars respectively made by them to be driven on, respectively, Belgium and United Kingdom roads. In both cases, it was held that they had a dominant position in the relevant market, namely the issue of those certificates. Also, in both cases, it was held that they had abused their dominant position by not charging prices which related to the economic value of the service provided. In neither case did the Court of Justice consider the alleged abuse in the light of the nature of the legal monopoly. The issue of abuse was treated independently from the fact that a national law had *purposively* given an undertaking a monopoly which resulted in a dominant position in the relevant market.

As intellectual property is merely one example of monopolies that are derived from law rather than fact should the question of abuse be treated any differently from any other abuse? Various reasons can be proposed why in fact it should be:

(i) Intellectual property monopolies are often justified in that they are there to reward the author. Other legal monopolies exist usually in order that some duty can be carried out efficiently.
(ii) The owner of an intellectual property is not statutorily bound to commercially exploit it for the benefit of others. Other legal monopolies usually impose (impliedly or expressly) a duty to operate the monopoly.
(iii) Intellectual property monopolies exists to encourage further creative work in artistic field and investment in research and development in industry.

[5] Case 322/81, *Nederlandsche Banden-Industrie Michelin N.V. v. E.C. Commission* [1983] E.C.R. 3461; [1985] 1 C.M.L.R. 287 at para. 73.
[6] Case 26/75, [1975] E.C.R. 1367; [1976] 1 C.M.L.R. 95.
[7] Case 226/84, [1987] 1 C.M.L.R. 185.

(iv) National laws have specifically granted exclusive rights and not merely rights to reasonable remuneration. This implies that the owner is entitled to exploit the market to maximise his profit.

The European Court has implicitly recognised this and has sought to make a distinction between the mere exercise of intellectual property rights and the exercise of rights as an instrument of abuse of a dominant position.

11.043 The distinction between the mere exercise of rights as against the exercise of rights as an instrument of abuse is a difficult one. No undertaking merely exercises its rights for the fun of it. They are exercised for a reason. The underlying motive for exercising one's rights is that it make commercial sense to enforce a monopoly in a protected name, product, process or service. For instance, the enforcement of intellectual property rights to stop imports of pirate copies; to maintain the reputation of a trade mark by preventing its dilution and, ultimately, to refuse to grant a licence for the protected product/process/service to potential competitors is made with the intention of reserving the right of exploitation in the protected products to oneself. Such a reservation will permit the owner of a monopoly to maintain high prices for a protected product (if there is a demand for it) and, if necessary, to impose commercially lucrative and if necessary, onerous conditions on potential licensees.

In this respect, there appears to be three schools of thought as to what should amount to an abuse. The first school is that the exercise of intellectual property rights can never amount to an abuse. This is because intellectual property rights are not a manifestation of a superiority derived from dominance in the marketplace but derived from national laws. As intellectual property rights may prevent restrict or distort competition without using market power, then even if an undertaking is dominant, there can be no abuse because there is no use of market power.[8] This approach is radical but ignores the fact that the exercise of rights may result in serious distortions of the marketplace when they are exercised by a dominant undertaking but would not so adversely affect the marketplace if exercised by an undertaking with relatively little market share. This goes back to the general principle that *ordinary* behaviour when carried out by a dominant undertaking may be damaging to the marketplace. Thus, U.S. competition laws recognise that as in other antitrust contexts, market power could be illegally acquired or maintained, or, even if lawfully acquired and maintained, would be relevant to the ability of an intellectual property owner to harm competition through unreasonable conduct in connection with such property.[9] For instance, in

[8] Miller "Magill: Time to Abandon the Specific Subject Matter Concept" [1994] EIPR 415, 416.

[9] See *US Antitrust Guidelines for Intellectual Property*, issued by the Department of Justice, April 6, 1995.

the E.C., the acquisition of market share may be an abuse if committed by a dominant undertaking but not if done by a non-dominant undertaking.[10]

11.044 The second more moderate school says that the grant of a monopoly to an intellectual property rights owner is in effect a state-granted sanction to the owner to exploit the market in the protected product to the full extent that the market place can bear. Such would allow high prices[11] and a refusal to licence unless the party enters into a licence which involves paying large royalties or submits to other onerous clauses.[12] In effect, this school argues that the exercise of intellectual property rights designed to extract the maximum commercial benefit from the protected goods can never amount to an abuse. Thus, the new Antitrust Guidelines state that the owner of intellectual property is not required to create competition in its own technology.[12a] Thus, improper exploitation of an intellectual property rights would only exist in those cases where this was not true, *i.e.* discriminatory licensing designed to eliminate a competitor or use of intellectual property rights to influence an adjacent or ancillary market where the rights owner has no protection. In these circumstances, the rights are being used for an ulterior purpose than merely the extraction of commercial benefit from the sale of the protected goods.

The third school of thought is that the exercise of intellectual property rights by a dominant undertaking must be subject to the same controls as the exercise of any other type of economic power by a dominant undertaking. Dominance however obtained, enables the imposition of unfair prices, the ability to limit production in a product market to the prejudice of the consumer, etc. and must thus be controlled. This approach means that owners of intellectual property rights are not necessarily allowed to appropriate the full inherent value of that property but must economically *justify* any exercise of their rights and show that such does not adversely affect the consumer or residual competition. In particular, they must make sure that they do not infringe Article 86 by charging unfair purchase or selling prices or by limiting production, markets or technical development to the prejudice of consumers. This approach permits a patentee to control and regulate the production, price, distribution, etc., of his *patented product* but not the *product market* in which the invention finds itself in. It is this school of thought that appears to have been adopted by the European Court of Justice and the Court of First Instance and which is discussed below.

[10] Case 6/72, *Europemballage Corpn & Continental Can v. E.C. Commission* [1973] E.C.R. 215; [1973] C.M.L.R. 199.
[11] See V. Korah "No Duty to License Independent Repairers to Make Spare Parts: The Renault, Volvo and Bayer & Hennecke Cases" [1988] EIPR 381.
[12] The imposition of onerous clauses may infringe Art. 85. However, if an undertaking considers that the prohibition of onerous clauses under Art. 85 means that his own exploitation would be more profitable, then he may refuse to licence others.
[12a] Para. 3.1.

(b) Intellectual property, article 86 and community law

(i) Exercise of rights per se not abuse

11.045 In *Parke Davis v. Probel*,[13] the European Court of Justice had to consider for the first time whether the exercise of patent rights could be an abuse of a dominant position. It said that:

> "Although a patent confers on its holder a special protection within the framework of a State, it does not follow that the exercise of the rights so conferred implies the existence of the three elements mentioned. It could only do so if the utilisation of the patent could degenerate into an improper exploitation of the protection."[14]

The principle that the mere exercise of intellectual property rights cannot constitute an abuse has been re-iterated by the Court of Justice.[15]

(ii) Exercise of rights as an instrument of abuse may be prohibited

11.046 In the passage quoted above, the Court warned that exercise of patents rights could constitute an abuse of a dominant position. This was reiterated in *Hoffmann La Roche v. E.C. Commission* where the Court said that the exercise of intellectual property rights could constitute an abuse where such was used as an "instrument of abuse".[16] Whilst such a doctrine is easy to state, its particular application to a set of facts is difficult to predict.[17]

The Court of Justice in a series of recent cases has sought to elaborate on the difference between the exercise of rights *per se* and as in instrument of abuse. Three important landmark cases are set out below.

Volvo AB v. Erik Veng (U.K.) Ltd[18]

11.047 *Facts*—Erik Veng was a United Kingdom company which imported automobile body panels for sale to the automobile repair market in the United Kingdom. In particular, it imported front wing body panels for the Volvo 200 series from Italy and Denmark, which had been manufactured without Volvo's authority. Volvo commenced proceedings against Veng alleging infringement of its U.K. registered design in the front wing body panel. Veng's defence alleged that Volvo's refusal to grant a licence to the defendant or others constituted an abuse of a dominant position when Veng and others were willing to pay a reasonable royalty. Further-

[13] [1968] C.M.L.R. 47.
[14] *ibid*, para. 4.
[15] *e.g. EMI Records Ltd v. CBS* [1976] E.C.R. 811; [1976] 2 C.M.L.R. 235, at para. 37; Case 238/87, *Volvo AB v Erik Veng (U.K.) Ltd* [1988] E.C.R. 6211; [1989] 4 C.M.L.R. 122, at paras. 7, 8; C241–242/91P, *TV Listings*, ECJ, Judgment April 6, 1995 [1995] 6 C.M.L.R. 718 at para. 49.
[16] Case 88/76, [1979] E.C.R. 461; [1979] 3 C.M.L.R. 211, at para. 16.
[17] See para. 11.042 *et seq*.
[18] Case 238/87, [1988] E.C.R. 6211; [1989] 4 C.M.L.R. 122.

more, it contended that the front wings were sold by Volvo at exaggeratedly high prices although this point was not at issue before the ECJ.

The High Court referred three questions to the European Court of Justice. The first concerned whether Volvo could be said to be in a dominant position. The second question was whether it was prima facie an abuse of a dominant position to refuse to licence others. The third question concerned whether such refusal was capable of affecting trade between Member States. The Advocate-General's Opinion and the Court's judgment to the second question are considered below.

Advocate-General Mischo's Opinion

11.048 The Advocate-General in considering the second question drew inspiration from the case law developed under Article 36[19] that the substance of a patent right lay essentially in according the inventor an exclusive right of first placing the product on the market so as to allow him to obtain the reward for his creative effort.[20] He noted that compulsory licences are only granted in exceptional circumstances. Thus, he inferred from such considerations that:

> "the proprietor of a registered design would also be deprived of the substance of his right if he were obliged to grant a licence to every person who requested one and offered to pay a reasonable royalty."[21]

Thus, he said that the refusal to grant a licence cannot amount to an abuse of a dominant position. He further considered the question of unfair pricing by Volvo although the European Court had not been asked to rule on this point by the national court. This is discussed below.[22]

Court's judgment

11.049 The Court first emphasised that in the absence of harmonisation and standardisation of laws, the determination of the conditions and procedures under which protection of designs and models is granted was a matter for national rules.[23]

The Court adopted the Advocate-General's opinion and emphasised that an obligation to grant to third parties a licence for the supply of products incorporating the design would lead to the proprietor being deprived of the substance of the exclusive right and that a refusal to grant such a licence cannot in itself constitute an abuse of a dominant position.[24]

[19] In particular, Case 19/84, *Pharmon v. Hoechst* [1985] E.C.R. 2281; [1985] 3 C.M.L.R. 775.
[20] As stated in *Pharmon v. Hoechst, ibid.*
[21] Case 238/87, *Volvo AB v. Erik Veng (U.K.) Ltd* [1988] E.C.R. 6211; [1989] 4 C.M.L.R. 122 at 131.
[22] See, para. 11.070, below.
[23] See *Keurkoop v. Nancy Kean Gifts* [1982] E.C.R. 2853; [1983] 2 C.M.L.R. 47.
[24] Case 238/87, *Volvo AB v. Erik Veng (U.K.) Ltd* [1988] E.C.R. 6211; [1989] 4 C.M.L.R. 122, para. 8.

It however said that:

> "the exercise by the proprietor of an exclusive right in a registered design in respect of car body panels may be prohibited by Article 86 if it involves, on the part of an undertaking holding a dominant position, certain abusive conduct such as the arbitrary refusal to supply spare parts to independent repairers, the fixing of prices for spare parts at an unfair level or a decision no longer to produce spare parts for a particular model even though many cars of that model are still in circulation, provided that such conduct is liable to affect trade between Member States."[25]

As there was no instance of any such conduct in the facts as referred from the national court, the Court did not consider the matter any further.

CICRA v. Renault[26]

11.050 *Facts*—Various independent Italian manufacturers of spare parts for bodywork of cars sought a declaration that the manufacture of spare parts for Renault cars did not infringe Renault's design rights. The Italian Court referred to the European Court of Justice, inter alia, the question as to whether the *registration* of such protective rights in respect of ornamental models for car bodywork components constituted an abuse of a dominant position.

Advocate-General Mischo's Opinion

11.051 The Advocate-General mainly considered whether the assertion of designs rights was contrary to Articles 30–36. He specifically referred to his opinion in *Volvo v. Veng*. In relation to the above question he again emphasised that:

> "the mere acquisition of an industrial or commercial property right (and the exercise of the corresponding rights without which proprietorship of the ornamental design would be deprived of any practical utility) does not therefore constitute abuse of a dominant position. A further element is required."

Court's Judgment

11.052 The Court first emphasised that it is a matter for national legislation whether a design is to be afforded protection.[27]

The Court emphasised that the mere fact of registration could not be regarded as an abuse. It then said that the exercise of the right could amount to an abuse and gave examples of where this might be the case by

[25] *ibid*, para. 10.

[26] Case 53/87, [1990] 4 C.M.L.R. 265. This case was heard together with *Volvo v. Veng*, *ibid*.

[27] *ibid*, para. 10 thus following *Keurkoop v. Nancy Kean Gifts* [1982] E.C.R. 2853; [1983] 2 C.M.L.R. 47.

re-iterating those given in *Volvo v. Veng* as set out in the extracted passage above.

"TV Listing" cases[28]

Facts—Various broadcasting companies issued weekly programme listings magazines for their channels in Ireland and Northern Ireland. Copyright vested in such listings because under Irish law, copyright vests in compilations. These companies refused to license others to reproduce these weekly listings and adopted a vigorous policy of suing anyone who did for infringement of copyright. One undertaking who sought to produce a comprehensive weekly list incorporating all the channels' programmes complained to the Commission that such amounted to an abuse of a dominant position. The Commission held that it was an abuse of a dominant position and ordered the lists to be made available to third parties on request under terms approved by the Commission. The broadcasting companies appealed to the Court of First Instance. **11.053**

The CFI dismissed the appeals whereupon the appellants brought the case before the ECJ.

On the question of abuse, the applicants argued that the refusal to licence and the bringing of infringement proceedings could not amount to an abuse, relying on the Court's judgment in *Volvo AB v. Erik Veng (UK) Ltd.*[29] and saying that the case was virtually indistinguishable from it. The Commission argued that the conduct complained of was equivalent in effect, to an arbitrary refusal to supply spare parts to independent repairers who depended on such supply for their business. Such conduct was prohibited in *Volvo v. Veng*. Furthermore, it said that the fact that the applicants published their own weekly listings and allowed daily listings to be published by third parties meant that their refusal was arbitrary and discriminatory. Furthermore, it said that the applicants were exploiting a dominant position in one market (the market in information in its programmes) in order to obtain advantages in the publishing market, a separate economic activity and an ancillary market.

CFI's Judgment

The Court of First Instance considered the question of whether the refusal to licence could constitute an abuse. It reviewed the relationship of intellectual property law and Community law by examining the case law under Article 36. It concluded that it was common ground that in principle the protection of the "specific subject-matter" of copyright entitles **11.054**

[28] Case T–69/89, *Radio Telefis Eireann v. E.C. Commission* [1991] 4 C.M.L.R. 586, CFI; Case T–70/89, *BBC v. E.C. Commission* [1991] C.M.L.R. 669, CFI; Case T–76/89 *Independent Television Publication Ltd v. E.C. Commission* [1991] C.M.L.R. 745, CFI. The three cases were decided by the same Chamber and rely on almost identical analysis. The cases are thus not discussed separately. Citations always refer to the first case, *RTE v. E.C. Commission*. The decisions of the CFI were appealed to the ECJ-Judgment, April 6, 1995, C241–242/91P [1995] 6 C.M.L.R. 718. The ECJ dismissed the appeal.

[29] Case 238/87, [1988] E.C.R. 6211; [1989] 4 C.M.L.R. 122.

the copyright-holder to reserve the exclusive right to reproduce the protected work. It cited *Warner Bros v. Christiansen*[30] that the exclusive right of performance and the exclusive right of reproduction was not called into question by the rules of the Treaty.[31]

It then said:

> "However, while it is plain that the exercise of the exclusive right to reproduce a protected work is not in itself an abuse, that does not apply when, in the light of the details of each individual case, it is apparent that right is exercised in such ways and circumstances as in fact to pursue an aim manifestly contrary to the objectives of Article 86. In that event, the copyright is no longer exercised in a manner which corresponds to its essential function, within the meaning of Article 36 of the Treaty, which is to protect the moral rights in the work and to ensure a reward for the creative effort, while respecting the aims of, in particular, Article 86. In that case, the primacy of Community law, particularly as regards principles as fundamental as those of the free movement of goods and freedom of competition, prevails over any use of a rule of national intellectual property law in a manner contrary to those principles.
>
> That analysis is borne out by the case of the Court of Justice which in its above-mentioned judgments—*Volvo v. Veng*, on which the Commission relies, and *CICRA v. Renault*—held that the exercise of an exclusive right which, in principle, corresponds to the substance of the relevant intellectual property right may nevertheless be prohibited by Article 86 if it involves, on the part of the undertaking holding a dominant position, certain abusive conduct."[32]

11.055 The Court endorsed the Commission's arguments. The Court stated that the broadcasting companies were using their copyright in the programme listings to secure a monopoly in the derivative market of weekly television guides. It also noted that they authorised free of charge daily listings to be published in the press. Furthermore, it noted that they authorised the weekly listings in other member-states without charging royalties.

It thus ruled that:

> "Conduct of that type—characterised by preventing the production and marketing of a new product for which there is potential consumer demand, on the ancillary market of television magazines and thereby excluding all competition from that market solely in order to secure the applicant's monopoly—clearly goes beyond what is necessary to fulfil the essential function of the copyright as permitted in Community law. The applicant's refusal to authorise third parties

[30] Case 156/86, [1988] E.C.R. 2605; [1990] 3 C.M.L.R. 684.

[31] Case T–69/89, *Radio Telefis Eireann v. E.C. Commission* [1991] 4 C.M.L.R. 586, CFI, para. 70.

[32] *ibid*, para. 71–72.

> to publish its weekly listings was, in this case, arbitrary in so far as it was not justified either by the specific needs of the broadcasting section, with which the present case is not concerned, or by those peculiar to the activity of publishing television magazines. It was thus possible for the applicant to adapt to the conditions of a television magazine market which was open to competition in order to ensure the commercial viability of its weekly publication. The applicants conduct cannot therefore be covered in Community law by the protection conferred by its copyright in the programme listings."[33]

It distinguished the case from the ECJ's decisions in *Volvo v. Veng* and *CICRA v. Renault* as the applicants' refusal to authorise any third party to publish its programme listings was comparable to an arbitrary refusal by a car manufacturer to supply spare parts to an independent repairer carrying on his business in the derivative market of automobile maintenance and repair. Furthermore, the TV magazines concerned not the TV stations' main business (broadcasting activities) but only a downstream market. It thus held that the applicant's conduct was not related to the actual substance of its copyright.

ECJ's Judgment[34]

11.056 The ECJ confirmed the CFI's decision. It said that in the absence of Community standardisation or harmonisation of law, determination of the conditions and procedures for granting protection of an intellectual property right is a matter for national rules. It further stated that the exclusive right of reproduction formed part of the author's rights so that a refusal to grant a licence even if it is the act of an undertaking holding a dominant position cannot *in itself* constitute abuse of a dominant position.[35]

It then stated that the exercise of an exclusive right by the proprietor may, in exceptional circumstances, involve abusive conduct.[36] It then went on to consider the facts. Having rehearsed the reasoning of the CFI, the ECJ emphasised that the television companies were the only sources of the basic information on programme scheduling which is the indispensable raw material for compiling a weekly television guide. This meant that viewers who wished to obtain information on the choice of programmes for the week ahead had no choice but to buy the weekly guides from each television company. The companies' refusal to provide basic information by relying on national copyright provisions thus prevented the appearance of a new product, a comprehensive weekly guide to TV programmes, which the companies did not offer and for which there was consumer demand. The ECJ said that such refusal constituted an abuse under heading (b) of second paragraph of Article 86 (limiting

[33] See, *e.g. ibid*, para. 73.
[34] Judgment, April 6, 1995, C241–242/91P [1995] 6 C.M.L.R. 718.
[35] *ibid*, paras. 49, 50.
[36] *ibid*, para. 50.

production, markets or technical development to the prejudice of consumers). The ECJ further held that there was no justification for such a refusal. Thirdly, the ECJ confirmed the CFI's analysis that the companies had reserved to themselves the secondary market of weekly television guides by excluding all competition on that market since they denied access to the basic information which was the raw material indispensable for the compilation of such a guide.[37]

Thus, the ECJ confirmed the CFI's decision that the television companies had abused their dominant position by their conduct. The ECJ also confirmed that the Commission was entitled in order to ensure that its decision was effective to require the television companies to provide the information if necessary on payment of royalties.[38]

(iii) Present state of community law: Abuse and the exercise of intellectual property rights

11.057 The cases of *Volvo v. Veng*, *CICRA v. Renault* and *TV Listings* emphasise that the mere exercise of rights cannot amount to an abuse but that in exceptional circumstances, they could constitute abusive conduct. What are these "exceptional circumstances"? In *Hoffman La Roche v. E.C. Commission*,[39] the Court had said that the exercise of intellectual property rights could constitute an abuse where such was used as an "instrument of abuse". This choice of phrase suggests that there must be some conduct (actual or intended) which is *extraneous* to the use of the intellectual property rights which constitutes an abuse. This approach suggests that the relevant tribunal or court should identify the abusive conduct *without reference to the use of intellectual property rights* and if such is prohibited under Article 86 then any exercise of intellectual property rights to further such an abuse is also prohibited. This approach accords with the ECJ's approach under Article 85 whereby the exercise of rights is prohibited if such is used to implement an agreement or concerted practice that is contrary to Article 85.[40] In other words, under Article 85, the ECJ first identifies the anti-competitive agreement and then rules that the use of intellectual property rights to implement such an agreement is also prohibited under Article 85.

11.058 CFI's approach in *TV Listings* did not fully distinguish between the exercise of the rights as an exercise of the rights as an instrument of abuse as opposed to being an abuse in itself. In *TV Listings*, the CFI had to distinguish *Volvo* and *Renault* and show that the broadcasting companies were doing more than merely refusing to licence magazine companies.

[37] *ibid*, paras. 54–56. The third reason was based on the decision of the ECJ in Cases 6–7/72, *Commercial Solvents v. E.C. Commission* [1974] E.C.R. 223; [1974] 1 C.M.L.R. 309. See para. 11.038.
[38] *ibid*, paras. 88–94.
[39] See para. 11.046.
[40] See Chap. 8 on Licensing of Intellectual Property and para. 8.052.

However, it is questionable whether any of the factors that the CFI cited do in fact distinguish *TV Listings* from *Volvo* or *Renault*. For instance, one legal writer points out that the CFI's statement that the TV stations' refusal to license was similar to a refusal to supply spare part to independent repairers and thus prohibited according to *Volvo* is not a proper analogy. In *Volvo*, the car companies sought to extend their design right to the derivative market of automobile maintenance where Volvo or Renault had *not* been granted exclusive rights. However, in *TV Listings*, the television companies sought to extend their copyright to the derivative market *i.e.* TV journals, which *was protected by copyright*. Thus there was no extension of market power to an adjacent market in which the broadcasting companies did not enjoy the protection of an exclusive intellectual property right.[41] The refusal to authorise the reproduction of works protected by copyright did not go beyond that of merely securing the exclusive reproduction right. If the abuse is to be extraneous to the mere exercise of rights, it must be shown that the extraneous abusive conduct affects a product or service market *larger* than that covered by the intellectual property monopoly because such a market is reserved to the rights owner in any event. The CFI failed to identify the additional abusive element in the TV stations' conduct that went beyond the mere enforcement of an exclusive right.[42]

11.059 In *TV Listings*, the CFI examined the justification for the broadcasting companies in not giving the necessary information to the magazine companies and held that where there was consumer demand in an ancillary market of television magazines, this went beyond "the essential function" of copyright. It said that the applicant's refusal to authorise third parties to publish its weekly listings was not "justified" by the "specific needs" of the broadcasting section or by those peculiar to the activity of publishing television magazines. The CFI appears to be saying that it will examine all the circumstances involving a refusal to licence others even where there is no extraneous abusive conduct other than the refusal to licence. It was the aspect which troubled commentators and caused many to consider that the CFI had attacked the power of a rights owner to exercise his rights so as to appropriate the full commercial value of his rights and without due regard to the economic effect such exercise has on third parties. Many regard this to be the economic corollary of reserving exclusive rights of reproduction to the rights owner. However, the ECJ had already partly undermined this principle in *Volvo* by stating that unfair prices could constitute an abuse. Clearly, if the rights owner has a monopoly, charging high prices for products covered by the monopoly is merely extracting the full commercial value of a state-granted monopoly.

[41] See Reindl "The Magic Of Magill: TV Program Guides as a Limit of Copyright Law?" IIC 1993. 1, p. 60 at p. 76.
[42] *ibid*, at p. 76.

11.060 The decision of the CFI in the *TV Listings* case was heavily criticised.[43] The Advocate-General recommended that the decisions be overturned. Although the ECJ did not overturn it, the ECJ's emphasis in its judgment is interesting. It de-emphasises the copyright aspect and instead emphasises the fact that the television companies had a *de facto* monopoly over the raw material and had abused this monopoly. Copyright is not an absolute monopoly but allows every designer of identical or similar works the right to exploit those works provided no designer copied the work from another. In *TV Listings*, copyright existed in the weekly programme schedules because Irish law deemed that the skill and labour expended in compiling the listings from the raw material was sufficient to make the listings original works. This gave the companies a *legal monopoly* preventing others from copying their listings as opposed to listings compiled by others. However, the television companies also had a *de facto* monopoly in the raw material and the actual selection procedure which led to the listings. Thus, third parties like Magill who were clearly prepared to spend considerable sums of money were never able to independently compile the listings themselves. Thus, in reality, it was the *de facto* monopoly that prevented Magill and others from publishing the listings.[44] In effect, the exercise of copyright by the TV companies transformed the qualified monopoly of copyright into an absolute monopoly. The ECJ ignored all the arguments about when a refusal to licence can amount to an abuse. Instead, in effect, the ECJ identified an abuse *extraneous* to the exercise of copyright and then held that any exercise of intellectual property rights to reinforce this abuse was illegal. In the author's submission, this approach is exactly right. In *TV Listings*, the exercise of copyright was being used as an instrument of abuse. It is a pity that the ECJ never expressly said.

11.061 It is also unfortunate that the ECJ did not see fit to discuss the CFI's judgment more fully. In particular, the ECJ considered it unnecessary to examine the reasoning of the CFI's decision in so far as it was based on Article 36.[45] In this regard, it will be remembered that the CFI held that a dominant undertaking may only exercise its copyright in a manner corresponding to the essential function within the meaning of Article 36 which is to protect the moral rights in the work and to ensure a reward for the author's creative effort.[46] By failing to examine this aspect of the CFI's decision, the latter's reasoning is unimpeached. In *TV Listings*, the CFI considered that the creative effort of compiling the listings was negligible. Will the validity under Article 86 of the exercise of rights depend on the

[43] See Reindl "The Magic Of Magill: TV Program Guides as a Limit of Copyright Law?" IIC 1993 1, p. 60; Ronald Myrick "Will Intellectual Property on Technology still be viable in a Unitary Market" [1992] EIPR 298; Thomas C. Vinje "Magill: Its Impact on the Information Technology Industry" [1992] EIPR 397.

[44] It must be remembered that Magill and others were prepared to pay royalties for the use of listings.

[45] See para. 11.054.

[46] *ibid.*

amount of creativity that an author is entitled to? In the second extract above in *TV Listings*, the CFI stated that the refusal to licence was arbitrary in that it was not justified by the specific needs of the broadcasting section or by those peculiar to the activity of publishing television magazines. As has been said, the value and enforceability of a right cannot depend on the appreciation of the market which is affected by the exclusive right.[47] Such an approach would override national laws which specifically do not make the exercise of the exclusive reproduction right conditional on economic circumstances.[48]

11.062 It is unlikely that *TV Listings* will dramatically reform the application of Article 86 to straightforward intellectual property licensing or its refusal. The facts were unusual and only the United Kingdom and Ireland protected such factual information. It sets out markers as to when a refusal to licence may constitute an abuse. These are:

(a) no actual or potential substitute for the product for which licence is sought,
(b) demand for a product not provided by rights owner,
(c) no justification for refusal to licence,
(d) interference in an adjacent/secondary market.

However, it is not difficult to envisage other facts where the Commission or courts would be tempted to apply Article 86 if the rights owner refused to licence. Thus, there is much concern in the information technology market that the decision in *TV Listings* will be used to force dominant vendors to licence "interfaces" to third parties so that they can enter adjacent or downstream markets where reproduction of the interface is technologically necessary so that the third parties' product can interact with the dominant firm's product. For instance, in the computer market, manufacturers of peripheral products such as disk drivers must standardise their product to mainframe computer systems so that they are operable.[49]

(iv) Specific abuses and intellectual property

11.063 The above section considers the impact of the judgments of the ECJ and CFI on the issue as to whether the exercise (or threatened exercise) of rights can amount to an abuse of a dominant position. In this section, specific abuses relating to intellectual property are considered. In many cases, for instance a refusal to licence, the charging of excessive royalties

[47] See Reindl "The Magic Of Magill: TV Program Guides as a Limit of Copyright Law?" IIC 1993. 1, p. 60 at p. 76.

[48] Ronald Myrick "Will Intellectual Property on Technology still be viable in a Unitary Market" [1992] EIPR 298 at p. 302 states that such would allow Art. 86 to override Art. 222.

[49] See Thomas C. Vinje "Magill: Its Impact on the Information Technology Industry" [1992] EIPR 397 at p. 401. The Computer Software Directive already provides for a decompilation rights in relation to interfaces—see para. 4.078. See also *IBM* [1984] 3 C.M.L.R. 147 discussed at para. 11.068.

or the imposition of onerous clauses in a licence, there is an underlying threat that the rights owner will bring infringement proceedings. If such in itself is an abuse, then clearly the refusal to licence, etc., is irrelevant. Thus, the reader is recommended to read the above sections on the exercise of rights before considering the specific allegations of abuse involving abuse of intellectual property rights.

(1) Refusal to licence

11.064 The cases of *Volvo AB v. Erik Veng (UK) Ltd* and *CICRA v. Regie Nationale des Usines Renault* established the principle that mere refusal to licence a third party is not an abuse of a dominant position.[50] However, the absolute nature of this doctrine has been undermined by the CFI and ECJ's decision in *TV Listings*.[51] In that case, the CFI said that:

> "In confirmation of that finding, it must also be stressed that, contrary to its assertions, the applicant's refusal to authorise third parties to publish its weekly programme listings may be distinguished from the refusal of Volvo and Renault . . . to grant third parties licence to manufacture and market spare parts. In the present case, the aim and effect of the applicant's exclusive reproduction of its programme listings was to exclude any potential competition from the derivative market represented by information on the weekly programmes broadcast on BBC channels, in order to maintain the monopoly enjoyed, through the publication of the *Radio Times*, by the applicant on that market. From the point of view of outside undertakings interested in publishing a television magazines, the applicant's refusal to authorise, on request and on a non-discriminatory basis, any third party to publish its programme listings is therefore comparable as the Commission rightly stresses to an arbitrary refusal by a car manufacturer to supply spare parts—produced in the course of his main activity of car making—to an independent repairer carrying in his business on the derivative market of automobile maintenance and repair."[52]

The Court's ruling was necessary as the applicants invoked the doctrine in *Volvo* and *Renault* which stated that the refusal to licence third parties to manufacture and market automobile spare parts was not an abuse but which also stressed that an arbitrary refusal to supply spare parts to automobile repairers would be an abuse of a dominant position. On appeal, the ECJ sidestepped this point. It held that the refusal to supply basic

[50] Case 238/87, [1988] E.C.R. 6211; [1989] 4 C.M.L.R. 122; Case 53/87, [1990] 4 C.M.L.R. 265.

[51] Case T–69/89, *Radio Telefis Eireann v. E.C. Commission* [1991] 4 C.M.L.R. 586; Case T–70/89, *BBC v. E.C. Commission* [1991] C.M.L.R. 669; Case T–76/89, *Independent Television Publication Ltd v. E.C. Commission* [1991] C.M.L.R. 745. On appeal to the ECJ, Judgment dated April 6, 1995, C241–242/91P [1995] 6 C.M.L.R. 718.

[52] See Case T–70/81, *BBC v. E.C. Commission*, [1991] C.M.L.R. 669, para. 61.

information by relying upon national copyright laws which the TV companies did not provide and for which there was a demand constituted an abuse under paragraph (b) of Article 86 (limitation of markets to the prejudice of consumers).

11.065 Can the decision in *Volvo* and *Renault* be reconciled with the *TV Listings* decision, the latter suggesting that compulsory licensing may in certain circumstances be justified?[53] It has already been commented that the comparison that the refusal to licence in *TV Listings* to a refusal to supply spare parts is not an appropriate analogy.[54] Clearly, in the former two cases, an obligation to supply spare parts did not result in the grant of a licence to manufacture and reproduce. In *TV Listings*, it clearly did.[55] The CFI's and ECJ's judgment in *TV Listings* stresses the fact that the TV companies' use of its rights had prevented competition in a derivative market and thus was an abuse. Thus, it may be that where a refusal to licence an undertaking in an ancillary market would have the *practical* effect of eliminating competition in an ancillary market, then that is an abuse of a dominant position.[56] However, care must be taken in defining an ancillary market. If the market clearly falls within the monopoly of the intellectual property rights, then legally it is reserved to the rights owner in any event. Thus, if the "ancillary markets" doctrine is to be applied properly, then the ancillary market must fall outside the intellectual property monopoly. In *Volvo* and *Renault*, the refusal to licence was not fatal because they could buy spare parts from the car companies and remain in business. In *TV Listings*, this was not an option available to the complainants. In the information technology market, a refusal to licence an "interface" of one product could have a damaging effect on the emergence of other products in ancillary markets which are designed to link in with that product. Thus, a refusal to licence the copyright in that part of a computer program which controls the linkage of a computer to peripheral products would prevent such products from being manufactured by parties other than the copyright owner. It is submitted that in such cases, the refusal to licence (and thus the threat to bring proceedings for infringement of copyright) is truly being used as an

[53] The ECJ never ordered the television companies to licence their copyright. Instead, it merely ordered the companies to provide the basic information as that was the only way to curtail the abuse. When a finding of infringement of E.C. law has been made, E.C. regulatory and judicial bodies must ensure that any order is appropriate and necessary to attain the objective sought—*e.g.*, CFI decision in *TV Listings* (ITP) at para. 80.

[54] See para. 11.058. See Advocate-General's Opinion in the appeal discussed in Haines "Copyright Takes the Dominant Position" [1994] EIPR 401.

[55] If the television magazine market were to physically "supply" a list of weekly programmes for every copy of TV magazines, such would have constituted a direct factual analogy to the supply of spare parts. However, such does not make commercial sense and it clearly is sensible to licence interested parties.

[56] See discussion above at para. 11.060 as to the *de facto* monopoly that the television companies had with regard to the source of the television listings material.

instrument of abuse so that the copyright owner can dominate the adjacent peripheral market where he has no legal monopoly.[57]

11.066 What is the situation under Article 86 if the rights owner refuses to licence a party unless the latter enters into a licence upon unreasonable terms? Alternatively, is it an abuse to bring infringement proceedings for the purpose of forcing a party to enter into an unreasonable licence? If a refusal to grant a licence is not an abuse of a dominant position then *a fortiori* it should follow that a refusal to grant except on unreasonable terms is not an abuse. Clearly, any licence is better than no licence. At present, there is no decision of the ECJ or CFI on this point. In the United Kingdom, the courts in following *Volvo* have said that if a refusal to grant a licence *per se* cannot amount to an abuse then such a refusal except on terms involving excessive and unfair prices cannot be an abuse.[58] However, the Patents Court has held that in the absence of a decision from the ECJ, it may be an abuse of a dominant position not to licence a patent for a process which is life-saving.[59] Working from the other direction, the ECJ has suggested that the charging of excessive royalties and unfair prices for protected products may be an abuse of a dominant position.[60] Extrapolating this approach, it is logical to conclude that a refusal to licence except on excessive royalty terms or unfair price term would be an abuse. Certainly, the Commission has suggested that where the bringing of infringement proceedings against a competitor was suspended on condition that the latter entered into an agreement which was void under Article 85, then such was an abuse of a dominant position under Article 86.[61] However, the CFI has stated that Articles 85 and 86 constitute two independent legal instruments addressing different situations and the issue of the validity of a licence under Article 85 should not affect the consideration of the matter under Article 86.[62]

11.067 *Compulsory licences under national intellectual property laws*—Most national intellectual property laws provide for compulsory licensing in certain circumstances. In the United Kingdom, the Patents Act 1977 provides for licences of right where the patent is not worked in

[57] See para. 11.058, above. In the U.K. see *Intergraph Corp. v. Solid Systems CAD*, Judgment of Mr Justice Ferris December 7, 1993 (unreported) where the judge held that it was arguable that the refusal of the owner of copyright in computer programs to licence third parties in the adjacent maintenance market and secondhand markets was by analogy to the *TV Listings* case an abuse of a dominant position. See also *Postal Franking Machines*, Cmnd. 9747 (1986) paras. 9.69, 9.71 where the MMC held that in such circumstances, the refusal to licence is a matter of concern to the MMC. See also *IBM* [1984] 3 C.M.L.R. 147 (refusal of IBM to supply technical information on their interfaces objected to by the Commission and dealt with by way of undertakings).

[58] See *Chiron Corp. v. Organon Teknika Ltd* [1993] F.S.R. 324 at 335 (Patents Court). See also *Pitney Bowes Inc v. Francotyp Postalia* [1990] 3 C.M.L.R. 466, at para. 20 (H.C.).

[59] *Chiron Corp v. Organon Teknika Ltd* [1993] FSR 324, (Patents Court).

[60] See sections on Excessive Royalties and Unfair Prices, paras. 11.070 and 11.074.

[61] *Re the Complaint by Yoshida Kogyo KK* [1978] 3 C.M.L.R. 44, Press Release of the Commission IP(78) 111, June 9, 1978.

[62] See Case T–51/89, *Tetra Pak Rausing SA v. E.C. Commission* [1991] 4 C.M.L.R. 334 at para. 22.

the United Kingdom, where demand for the patented product is not being met; where a market for the export of the product made in the United Kingdom is not being supplied; where the working or efficient working of another patented product which makes a substantial contribution to the art is prevented or hindered; where the establishment or development of commercial or industrial commercial activities is unfairly prejudiced or where by reason of conditions imposed by the proprietor of the patent on the grant of licence under the patent or on the use or disposal of the product, the manufacture, use or disposal or materials not protected by the patent or the establishment or development of commercial or industrial activities in the United Kingdom is unfairly prejudiced.[63] Moreover, where the MMC concludes that a monopoly situation exists in relation to a patented product and that its operation is contrary to the public interest, the Minister to whom the report is made may apply to the Comptroller for an order that the patent be endorsed "licence of right".[64]

In these circumstances, national law has circumscribed and curtailed the exclusive right of the patentee. In these circumstances, a complainant may apply for a compulsory licence rather than argue that under Community law, he is entitled to a compulsory licence. It is submitted that where clearly national laws (many based upon international conventions) have clearly defined when compulsory licences may be obtained, the corollary of this is to emphasise that national intellectual property legislation intended that the essence of intellectual property is the grant of an exclusive right and not merely the right to reward. Therefore, it is submitted that Community law should be wary of concluding that the "core rights" of intellectual property is anything other than an exclusive right. Accordingly, if a complainant argues that he is prepared to pay even an unreasonable royalty to a dominant undertaking and this would generously reward the rights owner, courts should be wary of concluding that an abuse has occurred under Article 86 precisely because it was clearly the intention of national laws not to merely confer a right to reward on intellectual property owners except in exceptional circumstances.

(2) Refusal to supply

11.068 In normal circumstances, a refusal to supply goods or services by a dominant undertaking is an abuse.[65] This is regardless as to whether or not the goods or services are protected by intellectual property rights. Therefore, a refusal by a dominant undertaking to supply spare parts for cash registers to an existing customer because he had an independent business in the repair and servicing of the undertaking's product was held to be abus-

[63] Patents Act 1977, s.50.
[64] Patent Act 1977, s.51.
[65] See para. 11.038.

ive even though the spare parts were themselves the subject of United Kingdom design rights.[66] A refusal to supply information can amount to an abuse to a dominant position. Thus, in *TV Listings*,[67] the ECJ held that it was an abuse for television companies to refuse to supply by relying upon national copyright laws basic information relating to programme scheduling to third parties who wished to prepare weekly listings covering all channels which the companies did not offer and for which there was a clear demand.[68] Similarly, in *IBM*,[69] the Commission objected to IBM's refusal to supply technical information to other manufacturers which was needed to make their systems interface with IBM's technology.[70]

The ECJ has said that where a dominant undertaking "arbitrarily" refuses to supply spare parts to independent car repairers, the exercise of registered designs rights may be prohibited by Article 86.[71] The question therefore is what amounts to an "arbitrary" refusal. This should be distinguished from merely supplying spare parts to independent repairers at high prices which is dealt with elsewhere.[72] It is submitted that whether a refusal to supply is an abuse should be considered without regard to the existence of intellectual property rights. If it is an abuse, then it is submitted that it is an arbitrary abuse within the meaning of *Volvo*. However, where a dominant undertaking has arbitrarily refused to supply protected spare parts, this will not necessarily result in a court granting a compulsory licence. Generally, the principle of proportionality means that the burdens imposed on undertakings in order to bring an infringement of competition law to an end must not exceed what is appropriate and necessary to attain the objective sought namely re-establishment of compliance with the rules infringed.[73] Therefore, it is submitted that where such an abuse has been found by a court, then the dominant undertaking should be merely ordered to cease and desist its abusive behaviour. This permits the dominant undertaking to determine whether he will supply spare parts or licence the repairer.

[66] Case 22/78, *Hugin Kassaregister v. E.C. Commission* [1979] E.C.R. 1869; [1979] 3 C.M.L.R. 345. The ECJ appeared to accept the Commission's submission that Hugin could use the U.K. Design Copyright Act 1968 to prevent independent manufacturers from making the required spare parts.

[67] *TV Listings*, C241–242/91P [1995] 8 C.M.L.R. 718.

[68] *ibid*, para. 54.

[69] [1984] 3 C.M.L.R. 147.

[70] IBM subsequently gave undertakings to meet the Commission's objections.

[71] Case 238/87, *Volvo AB v. Erik Veng (U.K.) Ltd* [1988] E.C.R. 6211; [1989] 4 C.M.L.R. 122; Case 53/87, *CICRA v. Regie Nationale des Usines Renault* [1990] 4 C.M.L.R. 265 and repeated in Case T–69/89, *Radio Telefis Eireann v. E.C. Commission* [1991] 4 C.M.L.R. 586; Case T–70/89, *BBC v. E.C. Commission* [1991] C.M.L.R. 669; Case T–76/89, *Independent Television Publication Ltd v. E.C. Commission* [1991] C.M.L.R. 745.

[72] See para. 11.070.

[73] *TV Listings*, ECJ at para. 93. See also *AKZO v. E.C. Commission* [1991] I E.C.R. 3359; [1993] 5 C.M.L.R. 215, ECJ.

11.069 A supplier may be able to justify a refusal where he is concerned about maintaining reputation in the protected goods/services. Under Article 85, the Commission has sanctioned distribution franchisers being permitted to choose its retail franchisees as the former are entitled to turn down applicants who do not have the personal qualities and business qualifications they deem important and thus to decide to whom it supplies its trade-marked goods.[74] Such sanction clearly envisages that a refusal to supply those who do not meet such criteria would be permissible. Whilst Articles 85 and 86 although complementary are independent of each other,[75] it would be strange if a dominant undertaking was not permitted to refuse to supply to parties who did not meet its requirements (applied in a non-discriminatory fashion) on the basis that such constituted an abuse of a dominant position.[76] Similarly, in the field of spare parts, the above reasoning would entitle a dominant undertaking to refuse to supply a repairer where the latter was not capable of providing the necessary standard of repair service.

(3) Unfair prices

11.070 The European Court of Justice and the Commission has not resiled from applying the prohibition of unfair prices under Article 86 to goods or services protected by intellectual property rights. In *Renault*, it stated that:

> "With reference more particularly to the difference in prices between components sold by the manufacturer and those sold by the independent producers, it should be noted that the Court has held (Case 24/67, PARKE DAVIS) that a higher price for the former than for the latter does not necessarily constitute an abuse since the proprietor of protective rights in respect of an ornamental design may lawfully call for a return on the amounts which he has invested in order to perfect the protected design."[77]

In both *Volvo v. Veng* and *Renault*, Advocate-General Mischo concluded from *Parke Davis v. Probel*[78] that an inventor was entitled to recover not only his production costs in the strict sense and a reasonable profit margin but also his research and development expenditure.[79]

In relation to trade marked products, research and development

[74] *Re the Franchise Agreements of Yves Rocher* [1987] O.J. L8/49, [1988] 4 C.M.L.R. 592.
[75] See Case T–51/89, *Tetra Pak Rausing SA v. E.C. Commission* [1991] 4 C.M.L.R. 334.
[76] Selective distributorship agreement which exclude distributors who are unable to fulfil certain objective qualitative criteria are considered generally not to infringe Art. 85—see *Metro-SB-Grossmarkte v. E.C. Commission* (1977) E.C.R. 1875, (1978) 2 C.M.L.R. 1; *L'Oreal v. De Nieuwe* [1980] E.C.R. 3775, [1981] 2 C.M.L.R. 235; Case 99/79, *Lancome v. Etos* E.C.R. 2511, [1981] 2 C.M.L.R. 164; *Hasselbald v. E.C. Commission* [1984] E.C.R. 883, [1984] 1 C.M.L.R. 559.
[77] Case 53/87, *CICRA v. Regie Nationale des Usines Renault* [1990] 4 C.M.L.R. 265, para. 17.
[78] [1968] E.C.R. 55, [1968] C.M.L.R. 47.
[79] p. 132 (CMLR). See also ECJ in Case 78/70, *Deutsche Grammophon v. Metro-Grossmarkte* [1971] E.C.R. 487; [1971] C.M.L.R. 631, at para. 19.

expenditure is not relevant. However, the owner of a trade mark may have incurred considerable expense in promoting and advertising it and in ensuring that the trademarked product is of a high quality. In *Sirena*,[80] the Court held that the higher price of a trade-marked product "although it does not *per se* constitute sufficient proof, may nevertheless become so, in view of its size, if it does not seem objectively justified."[81]

11.071 In considering the issue of unfair prices for goods protected by an intellectual property right, one should distinguish between the situation where a dominant undertaking is able to charge unfair prices because of its intellectual property rights and where he is able to do so because of his market power. For instance, if a dominant undertaking sells a new and revolutionary patented diamond cutter which uses Element X, he may be able to charge very high prices *inter alia* because he owns the only quarry in the world which produces Element X. In these circumstances, the existence of the patent is irrelevant because even if the dominant undertaking did not enforce his patent rights, other undertakings would have to buy the diamond cutter from the dominant undertaking. If, however, other undertakings can economically and profitably make the diamond cutter *but for* the dominant undertaking's patent, then the high prices are consequent upon the threat of the dominant undertaking enforcing his patent rights. In the following analysis, it is assumed that one is referring to the latter situation.

In fact, a patentee can only charge high prices because of his market power and not because of his patent. If his patented product is not dominant in a product market but readily interchangeable with other products, then the patentee will not be able to charge high prices because purchasers will buy interchangeable products. Accordingly, the ability to charge high prices is because of the patentee's market power. However, often the market power is derived from the patent itself especially where it is a technologically innovative product and hence not readily interchangeable with others. In this sense, the patented product provides market power, the patent causes an insuperable barrier to entry and thus permit the patentee to charge high prices. In this sense, the patent permits the charging of high, possibly unfair, prices.

11.072 It is perhaps unfortunate that unfair prices for protected goods or services can constitute an abuse as such often represents an attempt to appropriate the full value of the right.[82] It has been pointed out that the factors in *Volvo* and *Renault* do not take into account the need to encourage innovation.[83] Clearly, some innovations, designs and inventions fail and if one is forced to justify prices by the above formulae without taking into account the ability to accommodate past and future

[80] [1971] E.C.R. 69; [1975] C.M.L.R. 1.
[81] *ibid*, para. 17.
[82] See para. 11.044.
[83] See Professor Korah "Case Comment" [1988] 12 EIPR 381.

commercial failures, such will have a deleterious effect on the development of technology, design and artistic and literary works.[84]

English courts have accepted that unfair prices for protected products can amount to an abuse of a dominant position.[85] An English court has held that a net profit of 15.7 per cent cannot be in any way regarded as unreasonable in the context of whether the price of a product was unfair within the meaning of Article 86.[86]

It is more clear that an abuse has occurred where a rights owner conducts discriminatory pricing. In an action for infringement of a dominant undertaking's copyright in spare parts relating to the fork lift industry, the English Court of Appeal held that where an instruction had been given to the dominant undertaking's agents to charge full retail price to traders selling spare parts for the dominant undertaking's fork lift trucks so that the traders would be unable to make an ordinary commercial profit, that such did disclose a defence under Community Law.[87] In a patent infringement action, the English High Court permitted the defendant leave to amend its defence to plead that the patentee was infringing Article 86 by exporting protected products at a lower price than it sold the products in its home market.[88]

11.073 It is submitted that it is correct to find that there has been unfair pricing where there is evidence that a firm's pricing practice is an instrument of abuse, *i.e.* intended to discriminate against some traders or to partition markets in the Community or to adversely affect firms in an adjacent market (*i.e.* the charging of independent repairers by a car manufacturer of excessive prices for spare parts in the derivative market of car maintenance so as to prevent unfranchised repairers carrying out repairs to a car manufacturer's cars). However, where the rights owner is merely seeking to appropriate the full value of its intellectual property, *i.e.* by charging prices as high as the market can afford, such is the economic corollary of the grant under national laws of the exclusive rights of exploitation to a qualifying person and should not *per se* amount to an abuse of a dominant position. It is hoped that the ECJ will clarify between the illegality of charging unfair prices as an instrument of abuse as opposed to analyzing whether prices are *per se* unfair by reference to the costs of research and development and allied costs.

[84] Described by Professor Korah, *ibid*, as "Heads I only make a profit and tails, I lose my investment."

[85] See, *e.g. Pitney Bowes Inc. v. Francotyp-Postalia GmbH* [1990] 3 C.M.L.R. 466, (H.C.). See also *Chiron Corp. v. Organon Teknika Ltd* [1993] FSR 324, (Patents Court) where the Court rejected an argument that as it was not an abuse to exploit a patent, it was not an abuse to charge a particular price for a patented article, citing *Volvo* as authority for the proposition that charging excessive prices could amount to an abuse of a dominant position.

[86] *Hoover plc v. George Hulme (STO) Ltd* [1982] 3 C.M.L.R. 186 (H.C.).

[87] *Lansing Bagnall Ltd v. Buccaneer Lift Parts Ltd* [1984] 1 C.M.L.R. 224. See also *Pitney Bowes v. Francotyp-Postalia GmbH* [1990] 3 C.M.L.R. 466 (discrimination against smaller customers by unjustifiably charging high prices can amount to an abuse).

[88] See *Pitney Bowes v. Francotyp-Postalia GmbH* [1990] 3 C.M.L.R. 466, paras. 5 and 13.

(4) Excessive royalties

11.074 In *Basset v. SACEM*,[89] the ECJ said that "it was possible that the level of the royalty fixed by a copyright society is such that Article 86 may be applied".[90] This was said in a case where the applicant was arguing that a "supplementary mechanical reproduction royalty" should not be charged in France for the performance of United Kingdom records as no such right existed in the United Kingdom. The Court held that the mere existence of such a fact did not mean that Article 86 applied and the royalty complained of was akin to a performance royalty. Thus, the complainant was in reality complaining about the level of royalty.

In *Ministere Public v. Tournier* and *Lucazeau v. SACEM*,[91] the Court of Justice ruled that a national copyright-management society which has a dominant position in a substantial part of the Common Market and imposes trading conditions was guilty of abuse of a dominant position where the royalties which it charges to discotheques were appreciably higher than those charged in other Member States. However, it stated that such would not be the case if the copyright-management society was able to justify differences by reference to objective and relevant dissimilarities between copyright-management in the differing Member States.[92] The Court's decision was concerned with differing royalty rates in Member States. As copyright management societies manage the collection of royalties on behalf of the copyright owner, it is arguable that the copyright owner is through the society charging differing royalty rates depending on the Member States. Such behaviour would fall within Article 7 of the Treaty of Rome which prohibits discrimination and the distortion of competition that results within the Common Market if discrimination occurs. However, the ECJ has not dealt with the question of whether the charging of excessive royalties *per se* can be unfair.

11.075 One school of thought is that if the refusal to licence is not *per se* an abuse of a dominant position, then the refusal to licence except on payment of excessive royalties cannot be an abuse of a dominant position.[93] If there is even one licensee, the effect is to create more competition than otherwise might have been the case and thus such cannot constitute an abuse.

However, the ECJ has held that in certain circumstances, the charging of unfair prices for protected goods could constitute an abuse of a dominant position.[94] Such a finding suggests that the ECJ could find that the non-discriminate charging of excessive royalties *per se* could also be an abuse of a dominant position. At present, one awaits a decision to clarify the relationship between Article 86 and a refusal to licence except on

[89] [1987] 3 C.M.L.R. 173.
[90] *ibid*, at para. 19.
[91] Cases 395/87 and 110/88 & 241–242/88, [1991] 4 C.M.L.R. 248.
[92] *ibid*, para. 46.
[93] See para. 11.064 on Refusal to Licence.
[94] See para. 11.070 on Unfair Prices.

unreasonable terms. The ECJ might rule that whilst the mere reservation to oneself of the exploitation of a protected product by refusing to licence cannot amount to an abuse, any actual exploitation whether by licence or manufacture and sale by the owner is capable of falling within Article 86. Such a finding would be unsatisfactory because it would persuade patentees and other rights owner to exploit their rights themselves rather than enter into licensed subject to a reasonableness criteria. It may often be the case that both patentee and licensee would prefer to enter into licences containing excessive royalty terms rather than no licence at all. In such cases, the ECJ's finding would be damaging to the spread of technology via licensing.

It is hoped that the ECJ will recognise that there is an inherent conflict in the two principles that a mere refusal to licence is not an abuse but that the charging of excessive royalties or unfair prices is such an abuse. Again, it is submitted that the ECJ having recognised that the exclusive right to exploit falls within the specific subject matter of copyright and other rights, it should accept that a rights owner is entitled to any royalty rate that the market will bear save to the important exception that he cannot charge excessive royalties where such is an instrument intended to achieve some *extraneous abuse*, *i.e.* an attempt to partition markets in the Community by charging certain undertakings with excessive royalties such that licensing is unprofitable.[95]

In one case, the English Court of Appeal appeared to accept that unreasonable royalties can amount to an abuse of a dominant position but held that no case had been made out.[96] However, subsequently, English courts have said that a mere refusal to licence except on unreasonable terms cannot constitute an abuse.[97]

(5) Acquisition of intellectual property rights and licences ancillary to mergers

11.076 In *Elopak v. Tetra Pak*,[98] the Commission held that an undertaking had abused its dominant position when it purchased via the acquisition of a group an exclusive licence which strengthened its position in the relevant

[95] In *Pitney Bowes v. Francotyp-Postalia GmbH* [1990] 3 C.M.L.R. 466 (H.C.), at para. 22, a judge of the High Court held that he was not prepared to hold that discrimination between licensees without objective justification was an abuse of a dominant position. However, it would seem that the judge's remarks were directed to a bare allegation in a proposed amendment to the pleadings that it was an abuse of a dominant position not to offer to a party the same terms as another licensee.

[96] *British Leyland v. Armstrong* [1984] 3 C.M.L.R. 102 at paras. 101–105. The Court of Appeal held that a "blanket" royalty rate whereby a royalty was charged on British Leyland's exhausts regardless as whether they were protected by copyright or not was not an abuse because it constituted a convenient way of calculating a royalty of 7 per cent on infringing items—para. 105. However, a blanket royalty rate can distort competition and be prohibited under Article 85—see para. 8.147 *et seq*.

[97] See para. 11.064 on Refusal to Licence.

[98] [1988] O.J. L272/27; [1990] 4 C.M.L.R. 47 (E.C. Commission). On appeal Case T–51/89, *Tetra Pak Rausing SA v. E.C. Commission* [1991] 4 C.M.L.R. 334.

market. Such a finding must be seen as an application of the general rule established in *Continental Can*[99] that an abuse under Article 86 is that which strengthens the dominant undertaking and substantially weakens the residual competition.[1]

In the context of the mergers of undertakings, concentrations are often achieved by the transfer of an undertaking to the acquirer. In these circumstances, the vendor may often remain the owner of the rights in order to exploit them for activities other than those transferred. In these cases, the usual means for ensuring that the acquirer will have the full use of the assets transferred is to conclude licensing arrangements between vendor and purchaser. In such circumstances, the grant of exclusive licences, similar right or existing know how can be accepted as necessary for the completion of the transaction and thus not anticompetitive. Limitations as to certain fields of use, to the extent that they correspond to the activities of the undertaking transferred similarly and temporal restrictions are acceptable as they are economically equivalent to a partial transfer of rights.[2]

It is important that in infringement proceedings that a defendant show that there is a credible nexus between the prohibited strengthening of the plaintiff's position and the bringing of infringement proceedings. Thus, in *Pitney Bowes*,[3] a postal franking manufacturer brought patent infringement proceedings against a rival German manufacturer. The defendant pleaded a defence under Community law which included the fact that the plaintiff had entered into a cross-licensing agreement with another company whereby it acquired a "pick" option allowing it to use the other's technology and thus strengthen its dominant position. Mr Justice Hoffmann held that the mere strengthening of a dominant position does not necessarily amount to an abuse unless procured by an abuse of a dominant position and therefore held that there had been no infringement of Article 86.[4] However, it would have been more true to have held that there was no nexus between the alleged abusive behaviour and the infringement proceedings as it was not suggested that Pitney Bowes was suing the German manufacturer on the basis of patents acquired from the other company.[5]

[99] Case 6/72, *Europemballage Corp. v. Continental Can v. E.C. Commission* [1973] E.C.R. 215; [1973] C.M.L.R. 199.

[1] See also para. 11.034.

[2] See Commission Notice August 14, 1990, regarding restrictions ancillary to concentrations, [1990] O.J. C 203/5, para. IIIB.

[3] [1990] 3 C.M.L.R. 466, H.C.

[4] The judge's remark that strengthening a dominant position cannot constitute an abuse in itself is *per incuriam* in the light of the *Continental Can* decision.

[5] Counsel for the plaintiff had argued that there was no causal link between the grant of the relief which the plaintiff sought and the alleged abuses. The judge appears not to have dealt with this submission merely saying that the strengthening of a dominant position could not amount to an abuse in itself. For further discussion on the need for nexus in Euro-defences, see para. 12.083.

(6) Defensive registration of trademark

11.077 In *Renault*,[6] the ECJ said that the mere fact of registration of a design could not constitute an abuse. However, the Commission has held that where a firm in a dominant position registers a trademark which it knew or ought to have known that the mark was already being used by a competitor in another Member State, this may constitute an abuse of a dominant position.[7]

(7) Imposition of unduly onerous clauses in licences

11.078 Where an undertaking is in a dominant position, it will usually be in a position to dictate terms to parties who wish to do business with it. This is true in the area of intellectual property as in any other. Often these clauses will be prohibited under Article 85 and thus the application of Article 86 will be irrelevant. However, in other circumstances, the imposition of clauses by a dominant undertaking which are permissible under Article 85(1) or Article 85(3) may constitute an abuse of a dominant position. In such cases, the permissibility of such clauses under Article 85 is irrelevant to its consideration under Article 86.[8]

In many respects, the compatibility of unduly onerous clauses in licences is similar to the issue of excessive royalties and the reader is referred to that section.[9] An example of an unduly onerous clause can be seen in the Commission's decision in *Eurofima*[10] to withdraw proceedings under Article 86 against an organisation which had a dominant position as a buyer of railway rolling stock. The undertaking had a requirement that as a condition of a contract for the development of a new type of rolling stock with its contractors, it was to have unlimited right of use of the resultant patent rights without payment of additional compensation to the contractors. Upon the Commission bringing proceedings under Article 86, it withdrew the requirement. The Commission held that it was "materially improper" that the dominant undertaking was free to give licences for future patent rights to third parties without consulting or giving additional compensation to the contractor.

(8) Threats and conduct of infringement proceedings

11.079 It will be rare that the mere initiation of infringement proceedings will amount to an abuse of a dominant position as such amounts to a mere exercise of intellectual property rights. As rights are exercised by the bringing of infringement proceedings, in general, the issue will be the

[6] Case 53/87, [1990] 4 C.M.L.R. 265.
[7] *OY Airam AB v. Osram GmbH* [1982] 3 C.M.L.R. 614, *11th Report on Competition Policy*, para. 66 (E.C. Commission).
[8] *Elopak v. Tetra Pak* [1988] O.J. L272/27; [1990] 4 C.M.L.R. 47 upheld an appeal *Tetra-pak v. E.C. Commission* [1991] 4 C.M.L.R. 334 (ECJ).
[9] See para. 11.074.
[10] *Re Eurofima Press Release* IP (73) 67 of April 16, 1973, [1973] C.M.L.R. D217 (E.C. Commission).

same. Thus, if the exercise of rights is permissible under Article 86 then the *means* of exercising those rights should be permissible. This principle should apply whatever the intention of the rights owner in bringing infringement proceedings is.[11]

However, will the making of threats amount to an abuse of a dominant position? An English court has said that the making of threats will rarely amount to an abuse even if such were made in bad faith.[12] It is submitted that whilst it is tempting to conclude that it is an abuse of a dominant position to threaten infringement proceedings where it is clear that on the merits it has no case, such should be dealt with under national laws relating to the bringing of frivolous or vexatious cases.[13] Similarly, such an approach should relate to the conduct of proceedings for infringement of rights. In *Hoover plc v. George Hulme*,[14] Mr Justice Whitford said that:

> "If the conduct of the plaintiffs in connection with this or any other litigation were such as to amount to an abuse it could be and would be dealt with as an abuse of the process of the court. The consideration of litigation against persons infringing statutory rights and the institution and conduct of such litigation cannot, however, be an abuse within Article 86."[15]

In an early case, the Commission held that where the commencement of actions for patent infringement against a competitor by a dominant undertaking was suspended on condition that it entered into a restrictive agreement contrary to Article 85 with the dominant undertaking, such constituted an abuse of a dominant position.[16] However, the Commission did not say what the situation would have been if the dominant undertaking had merely continued its patent infringement actions. This decision preceded the CFI's decision in *Tetra Pak Rausing SA v. E.C. Commission*[17] which held that Articles 85 and 86 are independent of each other. It is submitted that such behaviour is permissible under Article 85, unless there were any extraordinary factors.

[11] *e.g.* see *Ransburg-Gema Electrostatic Plant Systems Ltd* [1989] 2 C.M.L.R. 712 (English H.C.) at para. 15 and 28.

[12] *Pitney Bowes v. Francotyp-Postalia GmbH* [1990] 3 C.M.L.R. 466, H.C., at para. 16. Mr Justice Hoffmann said that if such threats were made in bad faith, it would merely have amounted to a threat to commit an independent tort (malicious prosecution) unrelated to a dominant position. In the United States, an infringement action brought by a plaintiff where he knows that the rights are invalid may violate U.S. antitrust laws—see para. 6 *US Antitrust Guidelines for Intellectual Property*, issued by the Department of Justice, April 6, 1995 [1995] EIPR 7 Supplement.

[13] Under many national intellectual property laws, making groundless threats to bring proceedings is actionable as a statutory tort.

[14] [1982] 3 C.M.L.R. 186.

[15] *ibid*, para. 86.

[16] *Re the Complaint by Yoshida Kogyo KK* [1978] 3 C.M.L.R. 44, Press Release of the Commission, IP (78) 111, June 9, 1978.

[17] Case T–51/89, *Tetra Pak Rausing SA v. E.C. Commission*, [1991] 4 C.M.L.R. 334 (CFI).

8. Which affects trade between Member States

11.080 This condition of Article 86 is shared with Article 85 and has been discussed in the Chapter on Licensing. The classic statement on what abuse may be considered to affect trade between Member States was given in *Commercial Solvents.*[18] The Court held that this condition was to be interpreted and applied in the light of Article 3(f) which provides that competition in the Common Market is not to be distorted. Thus one had to consider abuse which might indirectly prejudice consumers by impairing the effective competitive structure as envisaged by Article 3(f).

The Court said that:

> "When an undertaking in a dominant position within the Common Market exploits its position in such a way that a competitor in the Common Market is likely to be eliminated, it does not matter whether the conduct relates to the latter's exports or its trade within the Commons Market, once it has been established that this elimination will have repercussions on the competitive structure within the Common Market."[19]

With such a definition, it is rare that the Commission will find that an abuse by an undertaking in a dominant position in a substantial part of the Common Market has not affected trade between Member States. It is not necessary to show that the conduct in question has affected trade between Member States. It is sufficient to establish that the conduct is capable of having such an effect.[20] More recently, the ECJ has said that in order to determine whether trade between Member States is capable of being affected by an abuse of a dominant position, within the meaning of Article 86, account must be taken of the consequences for the effective competitive structure in the Common Market.[21]

11.081 The notable exception to this broad interpretation is *Hugin Kassaregister v. E.C. Commission.*[22] The facts of this case have been reported above.[23] The Court, emphasising that the condition defined the boundary between the application of Community law and national law whilst essentially reiterating the above definition, stated that conduct the effects of which are confined to the territory of a single Member State is governed by the national legal order.

In that case, the applicant, Liptons was a London-based firm and it appeared from the file that there were large numbers of small, local

[18] Cases 6–7/72, [1974] E.C.R. 224; [1974] 1 C.M.L.R. 309.

[19] [1974] 1 C.M.L.R. 309 at para. 33.

[20] Case 322/81, *Nederlandsche Banden-Industrie Michelin NV v. E.C. Commission* [1983] E.C.R. 3461; [1985] 1 C.M.L.R. 287; Case C–41/90, *Hofner and Elser v. Macrotron* [1991] I E.C.R. 1979; *TV Listings*, Judgment, April 6, 1995, ECJ, C241–242/91P [1995] 6 C.M.L.R. 718.

[21] *Bodson v. PFRL* [1989] 4 C.M.L.R. 984 at para. 24, applying *GVL v. E.C. Commission* [1983] 3 C.M.L.R. 645.

[22] Case 22/78, [1979] E.C.R. 1869; [1979] 3 C.M.L.R. 345.

[23] See para. 11.008.

undertakings which specialised in the provision of cash register repair services. Such was also the case in other Member States.

11.082 The Court held that the commercial value of spare parts were in themselves insignificant and thus there was no trade between Member States. The Court asked what would be the case if the alleged abuse, namely refusal to supply outside its dealer network, did not exist. It said that in such circumstances, each independent dealer would obtain its spare parts from its own country and thus there would still be no significant trade between Member States. Furthermore, they would look to Hugin itself (which was a Swedish company which was not then part of the European Community) rather than an undertaking in the Common Market for its parts. Thus the Court said that:

> "In those circumstances, Hugin's conduct cannot be regarded as having the effect of diverting the movement of goods from its normal channels, taking account of the economic and technical factors peculiar to the sector in question. It must therefore be concluded that Hugin's conduct is not capable of affecting trade between Member States."[24]

Thus, the Court demonstrated that it will sometimes look at the effect on actual trade between Member States and consider the question of channels of trade with emphasis on imports and exports rather than apply the more abstract concept of whether there have been repercussions on the competitive structure within the Common Market.

It should be remembered that the complainant must show that the *conduct* affects trade between Member States.[25] Accordingly, in an infringement action, it is not sufficient to show that the relief sought affects trade between Member States. The complainant must show that the abuse itself affects trade between Member States. Accordingly, in a patent infringement action where the defendant alleged that the charging of high prices amounted to an abuse of a dominant position, it was not sufficient to show that the relief sought (*i.e.* an injunction) would affect trade between Member States.[26]

9. Substantial Part of the Common Market

11.083 The question as to what amounts to a substantial part of the Common Market is ultimately a question of fact. The two factors that are important are the land area where the abuse is operative and the density of the population in that area. Furthermore, the Court will have regard to the patterns and volume of production and consumption of the said product as well as the habits and economic opportunities of vendors and pur-

[24] Case 22/78, [1979] E.C.R. 1869; [1979] 3 C.M.L.R. 345, para. 25.

[25] *e.g.*, see Case 238/87, *Volvo AB v. Erik Veng (UK) Ltd* [1988] E.C.R. 6211; [1989] 4 C.M.L.R. 122.

[26] *Chiron v. Murex* [1994] F.S.R. 187 at p. 198, *per* Staughton L.J. (C. of A.).

chasers.[27] The Court has held the following to be a substantial part of the Common Market:

(i) Eire and a small part of Northern Ireland;[28]
(ii) Belgium and Luxembourg;[29]
(iii) Southern Germany;[30]
(iv) Netherlands.[31]

In *Suiker Unie v. E.C. Commission*, the Court, having stated that Belgian consumption of sugar was 350,000 tonnes against Community consumption of 6,500,000, said that such market shares were sufficiently large for the alleged abuses of Suiker Unie to be said to be operating on a substantial part of the Common Market.[32] Thus, in considering whether the abuse occurs in a substantial part of the Common Market, the Commission and courts will consider many economic matters other than the actual territory in which the abuse operates.

10. One or More Undertakings

11.084 This requirement of Article 86 suggests that two or more undertakings can abuse a dominant position. In this respect, one must distinguish between undertakings which are economically and financially linked, which are for the purposes of Community Law treated as a single economic unit and undertakings which are independent of each other.

(a) Economically linked undertakings

11.085 Undertakings are economically linked usually in the form of a parent-subsidiary relationship. In such situation, it is clear that if the parent company can exercise effective control over the activities of its subsidiary, then the parent and subsidiary will be treated as one economic unit for the purposes of Article 86.[33] Separate undertakings might be treated for a particular purpose as a single economic unit. This could be in the case of joint ventures where actual control vests in the parents.

[27] Case 4/73, *Suiker Unie v. E.C. Commission* [1975] E.C.R. 1663; [1976] 1 C.M.L.R. 295, at para. 371.
[28] Case T–69/89, *Radio Telefis Eireann v. E.C. Commission* [1991] 4 C.M.L.R. 586.
[29] Case 4/73, *Suiker Unie v. E.C. Commission* [1975] E.C.R. 1663; [1976] 1 C.M.L.R. 295.
[30] Case 4/73, *Suiker Unie v. E.C. Commission* [1975] E.C.R. 1663; [1976] 1 C.M.L.R. 295. This finding was made when there were only the original six members in the Common Market.
[31] Case 322/81, *Nederlandsche Banden-Industrie Michelin NV v. E.C. Commission* [1983] E.C.R. 3461; [1985] 1 C.M.L.R. 287.
[32] Case 4/73, *Suiker Unie v. E.C. Commission* [1975] E.C.R. 1663, [1976] 1 C.M.L.R. 295, at para. 371.
[33] Cases 6–7/72, *Commercial Solvents v. E.C. Commission* [1994] E.C.R. 224; [1974] 1 C.M.L.R. 309. See also *Beguelin* [1971] E.C.R. 949 and *Centrafarm* [1974] E.C.R. 1147.

(b) Economically and financially independent undertakings

11.086 The CFI Court in *Italian Flat Glass*[34] said:

> "That there is nothing, in principle, to prevent two or more independent economic entities from being, on a specific market, united by such economic links that, by virtue of that fact together they hold a dominant position *vis-à-vis* the other operators on the same market. This could be the case for example where two or more independent undertakings jointly have through agreement or licences, a technological lead affording them the power to behave to an appreciable extent independently of their competitors, their customers and ultimately of their consumers."[35]

It stated that such followed from the phrase "one or more undertakings" in Article 86. In this case, proceedings had been brought by the Commission against three Italian producers of automotive and non-automotive glass for operating a cartel in contravention of Article 85 and for abusing their collective dominant position in breach of Article 86. The Commission (and the CFI on appeal) found that there was sufficient proof that two of the producers had engaged in concerted practices as regards prices, discounts and customer classification. The CFI annulled the Commission's decision under Article 86 because the latter had failed to properly analyse and define the relevant product and geographic market.

It is clear from *Flat Glass* that undertakings can collectively dominate a market. The CFI emphasised that collective dominance was possible between economically independent undertakings where economic links existed. However, where there is clear evidence of anti-competitive collusion between undertakings, Article 85 rather than 86 is the appropriate article even if the undertakings collectively dominate the relevant market. The Court has said that Article 86 is not concerned with collusive parallel conduct.[36]

11.087 What is less clear is whether two or more independent undertakings with no links at all can collectively dominate a market. Some economists argue that the frequent absence of competition in oligopolistic markets is not necessarily due to collusive behaviour but rather the nature of oligopolistic markets. In such circumstances, Article 85 would be inapplicable. The question as to whether non-collusive oligopolistic behaviour can fall within Article 86 has yet to be decided by the European Court of Justice. The Court of Justice in *Hoffmann La Roche*[37] stated that:

> "a dominant position must also be distinguished from parallel courses of conduct which are peculiar to oligopolies in that in an oligopoly the courses of conduct interact, while in the case of an under-

[34] [1992] 5 C.M.L.R. 302 (CFI).
[35] *ibid*, para. 358.
[36] Case 172/80, *Zuchner v. Bayerische Vereinsbank* [1981] E.C.R. 2021.
[37] Case 88/76, [1979] E.C.R. 461; [1979] 3 C.M.L.R. 211, para. 39.

> taking occupying a dominant position the conduct of the undertaking which derives profits from that position is to a great extent determined unilaterally."

This suggests that where a few undertakings with no links with each other collectively own a very substantial share of an oligopolistic market, this does not mean that they collectively are in a dominant position for the purposes of Article 86.

The Commission has asked the Court to consider whether parallel behaviour on the part of several independent undertakings, in particular with regard to prices and trading conditions, which does not leave their customers any possibility of negotiating the terms of the contracts to be concluded may place those undertakings collectively in a dominant position coming within the scope of Article 86.[38]

[38] See Case 247/86, *Alsatel v. Novasam* [1990] C.M.L.R. 434 at p. 447. The Court declined to consider the possibility because it was unconnected with the facts for the reference under Art. 177 from the national court.

Chapter Twelve

ENFORCEMENT OF E.C. AND EEA COMPETITION LAW

1. Introduction

12.001 This Chapter is primarily concerned with the enforcement of Community law both by the European Commission and by the national courts. In this regard, the role of these two bodies differ. The Commission acts as an investigative authority with powers to gather evidence, mediate and make decisions on the compatibility of undertakings' activities within the Community with the competition Articles 85 and 86 of the Treaty of Rome. It derives its authority to enforce Community law from the Treaty of Rome and secondary legislation. If the undertakings' activities are found to be anti-competitive, the Commission has the power to order the parties to cease and desist and to fine the undertakings concerned. In the case of the enforcement of Community law by the national courts, they are only concerned with Community law where it is raised in the course of proceedings by a party. The court itself is merely concerned with determining whether a party has successfully proved an infringement of the Treaty of Rome.

This Chapter is only concerned with the provisions of the Treaty of Rome which relate to free movement of goods and services and to competition articles. The Commission's powers to enforce Articles 85 and 86 are derived from Regulation 17. There is no such corresponding regulation in relation to Articles 30–36, the provisions on the free movement of goods within the Community. Accordingly, there is no legislation empowering the Commission to investigate infringements of Articles 30–36. Parties must seek redress for such infringements through the national courts.[1] This Chapter is also concerned with the enforcement of EEA competition law by the EFTA Surveillance Authority.

2. Plan of this chapter

12.002 This chapter first compares the merits and disadvantages of the enforcement of Community law in the national courts and through the Commission. It then examines the law, practice and procedure arising out of notification of an agreement to the Commission for negative clearance

[1] Articles 30–36 have direct effect.

and/or exemption and the consequences of the Commission's investigation and findings. It also examines the law, practice and procedure relating to complaints made to the Commission about anti-competitive practices.

In the second section, it considers the law, practice and procedure where an issue of Community law is raised in a national court and the consequences of a party successfully proving an infringement of Community law. In particular, it looks at the situation where there are concurrent proceedings before a national court and with the Commission. In the final section it considers the enforcement of ESA Competition law.

3. Comparison of enforcement of Community law by Commission and national courts

12.003 The enforcement of Community law by the national courts and by the Commission differs in many respects. The fundamental difference has been described as being that:

> "the Commission is the administrative authority responsible for the implementation and for the thrust of competition policy in the Community and for this purpose has to act in the public interest. National courts, on the other hand, have the task of safeguarding the subjective rights of private individuals in their relations with one another."[2]

The Commission has recently issued a Notice on Co-operation Between National Courts and the Commission in Applying Articles 85 and 86 of the EEC Treaty[3] which examines the enforcement of Articles 85 and 86 by the two bodies and sets out many of the salient features that distinguish enforcement by the Commission and national courts. Such a notice is not binding and is merely issued for guidance.[4] However, it provides a useful analysis of the relationship between the Commission and the national courts in the field of enforcement of Article 85 and 86. As noted in the Introduction, the Commission has no investigative or decision-making powers in relation to infringements of Article 30–36. Accordingly, the enforcement of such articles lies solely with the national courts.

The Commission derives its powers to enforce Articles 85 and 86 from provisions adopted pursuant to Articles 87 and 89. National courts derive their power to enforce these Articles from the direct effect of such

[2] See Notice on Co-operation Between National Courts and the Commission in Applying Article 85 and 86 of the EEC Treaty, para. 4 [1993] O.J. C 39/05, which was derived from the CFI's judgment in Cases 24 & 28/90, *Automec Srl v. E.C. Commission (No. 2)* [1992] II E.C.R. 367, [1992] 5 C.M.L.R. 431.

[3] [1993] O.J. C 39/05.

[4] *ibid*, Para. 45. However, it is based to a large part on case law which is obviously binding.

provisions.[5] Although in certain continental jurisdictions, national courts will have the power to investigate through its own initiative whether or not there has been a breach of the competition rules, generally parties in an action must raise a "Euro" point before the court will consider it. In contrast, the Commission is continually supervising and monitoring the observance of competition policy within the Community. Investigations are carried out either at the request of parties or on its own initiative. Because the Commission's resources are limited, the Commission is not required to investigate every complaint but is entitled to concentrate its limited resources on notifications and complaints having particular economic or legal significance to the Community.[6] Indeed, the Commission has stated that it considers that there is not normally a sufficient Community interest in examining a case when the plaintiff is able to secure adequate protection of his rights before the national courts.[7] Accordingly, where a party wishes to raise a point of Community law in relation to acts which have little effect within the Community, his only effective redress may be through the national courts.[8]

12.004 The main difference between the Commission and national courts is that the Commission alone has the right to exempt an agreement under Article 85(3).[9] If an agreement or concerted practice infringes Article 85(1), it is void under Article 85(2). However, if a party has notified the agreement to the Commission, the latter may grant exemption to it under Article 85(3). However, if it is proved in a court that an agreement infringes Article 85(1), it is prima facie void under Article 85(2) and a court cannot exempt it.

If there are concurrent proceedings in the national courts and with the Commission, the Notice on Co-operation envisages the national court assessing the likelihood of negative clearance and/or exemption being granted in the light of the relevant criteria as developed by case law and legislation.[10] Recently, the ECJ has ruled that a national court only has jurisdiction to rule on the lawfulness of an agreement notified to the Commission where the court considers that the conditions for application of Article 85(1) are *clearly* not satisfied.[11] If it concludes that

[5] Case 127/73, *BRT v. SABAM* [1974] E.C.R. 51, [1974] 2 C.M.L.R. 238. For the meaning of "direct effect", see Introduction Chapter at para. 1.012.

[6] Cases 24 & 28/90, *Automec Srl v. E.C. Commission (No. 2)* [1992] II E.C.R. 367, [1992] 5 C.M.L.R. 431, (CFI).

[7] Notice on Cooperation between national courts and the Commission in applying Article 85 and 86 of the EEC Treaty, para. 14 [1993] O.J. C 39/05.

[8] Although it may be difficult for the Commission to show that he can obtain adequate protection of his rights before a national court. See "More Radicalism, Please: The Notice on Co-operation between National Courts and the Commission in applying Articles 85 and 86 of the EEC Treaty" [1993] ECLR 91.

[9] Reg. 17, Art. 9(1).

[10] Notice on Cooperation, para. 29. The position where there are concurrent proceedings before national courts and the Commission is discussed in more detail—see para. 12.097 *et seq.*

[11] *Gottrup-Klim v. Dansk Landbrugs Judgment* (unreported, 1994) ECJ at para. 60.

exemption is not possible, it must apply Article 85(1) and 85(2).[12] If it concludes that exemption is possible, it should stay the proceedings until determination by the Commission of whether the agreement is capable of exemption.[13]

Where the alleged competitive practice is capable of being exempted, the alleged infringer will invariably notify the agreement to the Commission in case the court finds that Article 85(1) is infringed. In such cases, the Commission will in practice take over the investigation of the alleged anti-competitive practice. Furthermore, the effect of the Commission granting exemption to an agreement where a court has decided that there was no possibility of exemption is to retroactively reverse a national court's decision. In such cases, many parties will prefer to only use the Commission route. Even the Commission has accepted that the above procedure where there are concurrent proceedings is complex and sometimes insufficient to enable the courts to perform their judicial function properly.[14]

12.005 The Notice lists the advantages that the application of Community competition law by the national courts has. Firstly, the Commission cannot award compensation for loss suffered as a result of an infringement of Article 85 of 86. Secondly, national courts can usually adopt interim measures and order the ending of infringements more quickly than the Commission is able to do. Thirdly, it is possible to combine a claim under Community law with a claim under national law in a national court. Fourthly, in some Member States, the courts have the power to award legal costs to the successful applicant. This is never possible in the administrative procedure before the Commission.[15]

However, there are many advantages to using the Commission route. Firstly, a complaint to the Commission is cheap and anonymous. It is cheap because the Commission will often take over the investigation once the complainant has proved that there is a prima facie case against an undertaking. It is anonymous thus safeguarding the complainant who is threatened by the practices of a much larger competitor. The Commission's evidential gathering powers are normally much greater than those of an individual. The Commission has considerable fact-finding powers including the power to carry out "dawn raids". The legal and financial power of the Commission often has the effect of causing a party to terminate the alleged anti-competitive practices. Furthermore, the privilege against self-incrimination and the right to legal privilege is more restricted in Commission proceedings as opposed to civil proceedings. The Commission has the power to fine undertakings and such fines will often be very substantial.[16] The threat of large fines will usually be far

[12] *ibid*, para. 30.
[13] *ibid*.
[14] *ibid*, para. 32.
[15] *ibid*, para. 16.
[16] *e.g.* British Steel was fined c.£25 million in a recent investigation into anti-competitive practices by the Commission.

more effective to deter a potential infringer than the threat of a potential claim in damages which the complainant will have to prove arises out of breach of the particular provision of the Community law.

Furthermore, the Commission has much greater experience and capability than national courts in determining whether certain activities are anti-competitive. This normally means that the Commission is more ready to find that conduct is anti-competitive than a national court which is often unfamiliar with competition law concepts. Consequently, a national court will pay more regard to the results of a Commission investigation or decision than to the complainant's own evidence or submissions. Thus, a party raising an issue of Community law is often best advised to notify the Commission in order to buttress its case with observations of the Commission and evidence gathered by the Commission. The Commission has sought to reduce the discrepancy between the Commission's powers on one hand and the courts and private individual's powers on the other hand by permitting national courts to consult the Commission on points of procedure, practice and law.[17] More importantly, the court can ask for information from the Commission regarding factual data *e.g.* statistics, market studies and economic analyses.[18] However, the Commission's powers to convey such information will often be hampered by information which is of a confidential nature and its obligation to be neutral so that only requests from the court rather than individuals will be dealt with.[19]

12.006 In contrast, in civil proceedings, a party who relies upon European law (who will normally be a small or medium-sized undertaking) will often be against a large undertaking who will have the financial resources to prosecute or defend a lengthy action. The complainant will be responsible for proving at its own expense that the large undertaking is guilty of anti-competitive practices. Gathering evidence will be difficult as the complainant does not have the legal and financial resources of the Commission. In such circumstances, the fact that it may be able to recover its costs if successful is often of academic interest because it will not have the financial resources to be able to prosecute the action to trial or alternatively, be able to prove the infringement.

12.007 In the circumstances, a complainant will often be best advised to notify the Commission of alleged anti-competitive practices rather than bring an action in the national courts for breach of Community law and it is unlikely that the Notice on Co-operation between the Commission and National Courts will alter this.[20] It remains to be seen to what extent the Commission will refuse to initiate an investigation into anti-competitive

[17] Notice on Co-operation between national courts and the Commission in applying Article 85 and 86 of the EEC Treaty, paras. 36–39, [1993] O.J. C 39/05.

[18] *ibid*, para. 40.

[19] *ibid*, para. 41–42.

[20] See "More Radicalism, Please: The Notice on Co-operation between National Courts and the Commission in applying Articles 85 and 86 of the EEC Treaty" [1993] ECLR 91 at p. 94.

practices following a complaint. The complainant will often be advised to notify as early as possible if he suspects that he is soon to be the victim of anti-competitive practices. This is because the Commission may be more reluctant to pursue a complaint if proceedings have already been brought in a national court and the latter has already obtained considerable information as to the alleged anti-competitive practice.[21]

4. Notification of agreements to Commission

(a) Introduction

12.008 If an agreement infringes Article 85(1), then it is null and void unless it is exempted under Article 85(3). In order to ensure that Articles 85 and 86 are enforced uniformly and effectively throughout the Common Market, Article 87 allows the Commission to implement legislation to meet such requirements. Pursuant to this, the Commission has issued Regulation 17/62[22] which governs the enforcement of the Articles by the Commission. The Regulation does not suspend the effect of Article 85(1) and 86, specifically stating that such agreements, decisions and concerted practices which fall within Article 85(1) and the abuse of a dominant position within the meaning of Article 86 are prohibited without the need for a prior decision.[23] However, Regulation 17/62 removed the jurisdiction of national courts to exempt an agreement and reserved it exclusively to the Commission.[24] Accordingly, where there are doubts about the compatibility of an agreement with Article 85, it is often necessary to notify the agreement to the Commission for exemption.

(b) Notification, negative clearance and exemption

(i) Introduction

12.009 A party may seek to notify an agreement or practice to the Commission for two reasons. Firstly, it may wish to obtain the view of the Commission as to whether it infringes Article 85(1) or Article 86. The Commission may decide that the agreement is compatible with Article 85(1) or 86 and requires no action on its part. Such an opinion is useful in proceedings in national courts because of the weight that a court will normally give to the Commission's view.[25] Secondly, it may wish to obtain

[21] See para. 64 in Cases 24 & 28/90, *Automec Srl v. E.C. Commission* (No. 2) [1992] II E.C.R. 367, [1992] 5 C.M.L.R. 431, (CFI).

[22] [1962] O.J. 13/204, [1959–62], O.J. 87.

[23] Reg. 17, See Art. 1.

[24] Reg. 17, Art. 9.

[25] *e.g.* in England, see *British Leyland v. Wyatt Interpart Co Ltd* [1979] 3 C.M.L.R. 79 and Notice on Cooperation between national courts and the Commission in applying Article 85 and 86 of the EEC Treaty [1993] O.J. C 39/05 at para. 18 where it is stated that the court must take account of the Commission's powers in order to avoid conflicting decisions.

exemption for an agreement if it appears clear that it does infringe Article 85(1). A decision by the Commission to grant exemption has effect *erga omnes* and thus no party can submit that the agreement is invalid under Article 85(2).

To this purpose, Regulation 17/62 provides the regulatory framework for notifying agreements to the Commission. An agreement may be notified to the Commission by the undertakings concerned for a certificate that the Commission, on the basis of the facts in its possession, has no grounds under Article 85(1) or Article 86 for action on its part.[26] This is termed "negative clearance". It should be noted that the effect of such a certificate is limited. It is binding on no-one except the Commission itself. It does not prevent the Commission taking further action if it comes across further information which suggests that the agreement does infringe Article 85(1). Unlike notification for exemption, it does not provide any interim protection from fines.[27] Thus, it is common and sensible practice to notify for both negative clearance and exemption.

Only the Commission has the power to exempt an agreement under Article 85(3).[28] The general rule is that agreements must be notified in order for the Commission to grant exemption.[29] There are certain agreements whereby the requirement for notification has been dispensed with. These are called "Article 4(2)" agreements. The exact legal effect and requirements of notification depends on what category or categories an agreement falls into. There are five types of agreement for the purposes of notification—"new" agreements, "old" agreements, "accession" agreements, "Article 4(2)" agreements and "opposition procedure" agreements. These are discussed below.

(ii) Notification of "new" agreements

12.010 Agreements, decisions and concerted practices which came into existence after the entry into force of Regulation 17, namely February 6, 1962, (known as "new" agreements) must be notified to the Commission if the party seeks exemption under Article 85(3) for the agreement.[30] The Commission cannot exempt such agreements until they have been notified. The only exception to this rule is that the requirement of notification is dispensed with for those "new" agreements which fall within Article 4(2) (and are thus called "Article 4(2)" agreements).[31]

[26] Reg. 17, Art. 2.

[27] See Reg. 17, Art. 15(5), Section IV of Complementary Note to Form A/B and *John Deere* [1985] O.J. L35/58, [1985] 2 C.M.L.R. 554.

[28] Reg. 17, Art. 9(1).

[29] Reg. 17, Art. 4(1).

[30] Art. 4(1). For purposes of brevity, the rest of this chapter will just refer to agreements although the same considerations apply to concerted practices and decisions.

[31] Art. 4(2). This category which is important to intellectual property practitioners is discussed more fully below, para. 12.013.

(iii) Notification of "old" agreements

12.011 Those agreements which existed at the date of entry into force of Regulation 17, namely February 6, 1962, are called "old" agreements and are now of marginal interest to the reader. The importance of classifying an agreement as "old" rather than "new" is that a national court in civil proceedings may have to treat the former agreements, if notified, as provisionally valid until the Commission has taken a decision.[32]

Importantly, where a standard form agreement has been used for a long period of time and the first standard form agreement concluded was an "old" agreement, then other agreements which have been concluded on the same standard form may be treated as "old" agreements even though they have been concluded after the entry into force of Regulation 17.[33]

(iv) Notification of "accession" agreements

12.012 An agreement to which Article 85 applies by virtue of the accession to the Community by a state and which existed at the date of accession is known as an "accession" agreement. Since several Member States have joined the Community in the last 10 years, these agreements are important. For the United Kingdom, Denmark and Ireland, the accession date was January 1, 1973; for Greece, the accession date was January 1, 1981; for Spain and Portugal, the accession date was January 1, 1986. Furthermore, Austria, Finland and Sweden acceded to the Community as of January 1, 1995. It is likely that the Community will be expanded in the near future. In many respects, they are treated by Regulation 17 as being equivalent to "old" agreements.[34]

"Accession" agreements which were notified to the Commission for exemption within six months of the date of the accession will be entitled to exemption ab initio rather than from the date of notification.[35] Furthermore, if the agreement has been notified within such a time limit and is found to be unexemptable, the Commission shall determine the period of prohibition of the agreement provided that the undertakings concerned have ceased to give effect to the anti-competitive provisions of agreement or modified it so that it becomes exemptible.[36] The Commission cannot impose fines on acts performed prior to the date of notification and done pursuant to "accession" agreements where the

[32] Case 48/72, *Brasserie de.Haecht v. Wilkin (No. 2)* [1973] E.C.R. 77, [1973] E.C.R. 287. The meaning of provisional validity and the effect that notification has on the validity of agreements under Article 85 in civil proceedings is discussed below. See para. 12.072 *et seq.*

[33] See Case 1/70, *Parfum Marcel Rochas v. Bitsch* [1970] E.C.R. 515, [1971] C.M.L.R. 104, ECJ. However Case 48/72, *Brasserie de Haecht v. Wilkin (No. 2)* [1973] E.C.R.77, [1973] C.M.L.R. 287 appears to tacitly overrule *Parcel Rochas* by stating that notification of standard form agreements outside the time limits for notification of "old" agreements does not confer upon such contracts the character of "old" agreements.

[34] See Reg. 17, Art. 25, (as amended by the various accession agreements).

[35] Reg. 17, Arts. 5, 6 and 24.

[36] Arts. 7, 24.

agreements have been notified within six months of the date of accession.[37] As with "old" agreements, it would appear that "accession" agreements are provisionally valid in civil proceedings in national courts until a decision has been taken by the Commission regarding exemption.[38]

Advisors should be aware that the definition of an "accession" agreement for the above purposes is that Article 85 *applies by virtue of accession.* Article 85 applies to agreements entered into between undertakings from non-Member States provided that the effects of such agreements are capable of affecting trade between Member States.[39] Accordingly, Article 85 may have already been applicable to agreements between undertakings from accession countries entered into prior to accession if they had an effect on trade between existing Member States. It would appear that standard form agreements concluded after the date of accession may like "old" standard form agreements be treated as "accession" agreements if the standard form was first used before accession.[40]

(v) Article 4(2) agreements—exemption from notification

12.013 The general rule that agreements must be notified for exemption is waived in relation to certain types of agreements which are considered by the Commission to be less prejudicial to the development of the common market.[41] These are set out in Article 4(2) of Regulation 17 and are agreements, decisions or concerted practices where:

(i) the only parties thereto are undertakings from one Member State and the agreements, decision or practices do not relate either to imports or to exports between Member States;

(ii) not more than two undertakings are party thereto, and the agreements only

   (a) restrict the freedom of one party to the contract in determining the prices or conditions of business upon which the goods which he has obtained from the other party to the contract may be resold; or

   (b) impose restrictions on the exercise of the rights of the assignee or user of intellectual property rights—in particular patents, utility models, designs or trade marks—or of the person entitled under a contract to the assignment, or grant, of the right to use a method of manufacture or knowledge relating to the use and to the application of industrial processes;

(iii) they have as their sole object;

[37] Art. 24.
[38] See para. 12.072 *et seq.*
[39] See Chap. 8 on Licensing of Intellectual Property.
[40] See para. 12.011.
[41] Recitals to Reg. 17.

(a) the development or uniform application of standards or types; or
(b) joint research and development; or
(c) specialisation in the manufacture of products, including agreements necessary for achieving this:
   — where the products which are the subject of specialisation do not in a substantial part of the common market, represent more than 15 per cent of the volume of business done in identical products or those considered by consumers to be similar by reason of their characteristics, price and use, and
   — where the total annual turnover of the participating undertakings does not exceed 200 million units of account.

As with other agreements, only the Commission can grant exemption to "Article 4(2)" agreements. However, the Commission may grant exemption to such agreements even though they have not been notified. For the interests of certainty, such agreements may be notified in the ordinary way.[42] The greatest benefit of bringing an agreement within Article 4(2) is that the Commission may retroactively exempt the agreement *ab initio*, as opposed to from the date of notification.[43] However, it is difficult to prove that an agreement falls within Article 4(2). Where such an agreement has not been notified, there is no protection from fines being imposed if the agreement is found to fall within Article 85(1) and is unexemptible.[44] However, it is unlikely that parties will be fined because such agreements are not considered to be particularly damaging to the Community.

If an Article 4(2) agreement is found not to be exemptible, it would appear that the agreement is void *ab initio*.[45] Where an unexempted Article 4(2) agreement is also an "accession" agreement, is notified to the Commission within six months of the date of accession and the parties have desisted from giving effect to the anti-competitive provisions of the agreement or modified it so that it is exemptible, the Commission shall state the period that the prohibition under Article 85(1) shall apply for if the agreement is not exempted.[46]

The provisions of Article 4(2) are now considered in detail.

[42] Reg. 17, Art. 4(2).
[43] Art. 6(2).
[44] Case 240/82, *SSI v. E.C. Commission* [1985] E.C.R. 3831, [1987] 3 C.M.L.R. 661, ECJ.
[45] See Case 48/72, *Brasserie de.Haecht v. Wilkin (No. 2)* [1973] E.C.R. 77 [1973] C.M.L.R. 287 (decision dated February 6, 1973) at paras. 24–27 overturning tacitly Case 43/69, *Brauerei A. Bilger v. Jehle* [1970] E.C.R. 127 [1974] 1 C.M.L.R. 382 (decision dated March 18, 1970) at para. 10–11 in so far as it relates to "new" Art. 4(2) agreements.
[46] Reg. 17, Arts. 7, 25. The wording of Art. 7(1) suggests that the Commission's decision under this Article is binding *erga omnes* and thus can be relied upon in civil proceedings.

12.014 *Article 4(2)(i)*—It will usually be obvious that the parties are from one Member State. The more difficult question is whether an agreement "relates to either imports or exports". The Court has held that whilst, in the context of an exclusive purchasing brewery contract, an agreement may affect trade between Member States (if taken together with a number of similar contracts), it is nonetheless exempted from notification where the agreement does not concern either imports or exports.[47] Thus the agreement itself must be concerned with the importation and export of goods and not merely have an effect on trade between Member States. This is regardless of whether the goods in question have at a former stage been imported from another Member State.[48]

The Commission has in the context of a patent licence with an exclusive purchasing clause and no-challenge clause concluded between two nationals from the same Member State, ruled that such an agreement falls within Article 4(2)(i).[49] If it appears that the agreement is intended to protect a national market from imports, then it will be unlikely that parties will be able to rely upon Article 4(2)(i).[50]

12.015 *Article 4(2)(ii)(a)*—This is of little interest to the intellectual property practitioner.

12.016 *Article 4(2)(ii)(b)*—This exception is of the greatest interest to intellectual property practitioners. However, it will be difficult to bring an agreement within this category. If an agreement contains restrictions which go beyond the scope of the rights conferred by a patent, then the agreement will not fall within Article 4(2).[51] Thus, where a patent licence agreement contained a no-challenge clause and tie-in clauses relating to objects not covered by the patent, the agreement did not "only impose restrictions on the exercise of the rights of the assignee or user".[52] An exclusive licence would fall outside Article 4(2)(ii)(b) as such constitutes a restriction on the licensor rather than the licensee.

In the Notice on Patent Licensing Agreements,[53] the Commission listed various restrictions which it considered did not fall under the prohibition of Article 85(1) because they were covered by the patent. It said that such restrictions "entail only the partial maintenance of the right of

[47] *43/69, Brauerei A. Bilger v. Jehle* [1970] E.C.R. 127, [1974] 1 C.M.L.R. 382, (ECJ). In England, see *Esso Petroleum v. Kingswood Motors* [1974] 1 Q.B. 142, H.C.

[48] Case 63/75, *Fonderies Roubaix v. Fonderies Roux* [1976] E.C.R. 111, [1976] 1 C.M.L.R. 538 at para. 8.

[49] *Vaessen BV v. Moris* [1979] O.J. L19/32, [1979] C.M.L.R. 511.

[50] See also Case 96/82 *IAZ v. E.C. Commission* [1983] E.C.R. 3369 [1984] 3 C.M.L.R. 27; Case 240/82, *SSI v. E.C. Commission* [1985] E.C.R. 3831 [1987] 3 C.M.L.R. 661 and Commission decisions of *The Community v. Melkunie* [1986] O.J. L348/50, [1989] 4 C.M.L.R. 853 at para. 74 and *Roofing Felt* [1991] 4 C.M.L.R. 130.

[51] Case 193/89, *Windsurfing International v. E.C. Commission:* [1986] E.C.R. 611, [1986] 3 C.M.L.R. 489.

[52] *ibid.* See also *Vaessen BV v. Moris* [1979] O.J. L19/323, [1979] 1 C.M.L.R. 511 (Commission).

[53] [1962] O.J. 139, 2922 (now revoked).

prohibition contained in the patentee's exclusive right in relation to the licensee, which in other respects is authorised to exploit the invention."[54] Whilst this Notice has been revoked in relation to what infringes Article 85(1), it can be considered helpful in deciding whether an agreement merely restricts the exercise of rights of an assignee or user. Thus quantitative, field-of-use (*i.e.* manufacture, use or sale), geographical restrictions, duration of licence restrictions and bans on assignments would fall within Article 4(2)(ii)(b). However, the addition of other restrictions may cause the agreement to fall outside Article 4(2)(ii)(b). As such simple agreements are not usually considered to infringe Article 85(1),[55] the exemption from notification becomes otiose.

It is more likely that an intellectual property licence will fall within Article 4(2)(i) than Article 4(2)(ii)(b).[56]

12.017 *Article 4(2)(iii)*—The exemption for research and development and specialisation has become rather redundant because in both areas, the Commission has passed block exemptions and thus the usefulness of this provision is limited.[57]

(vi) "Opposition procedure" agreements and notification

12.018 Certain block exemptions provide for a procedure whereby agreements whose subject matter in principle falls within a block exemption but contain obligations restrictive of competition not specifically mentioned in the block exemption may be notified to the Commission for exemption.[58] The reader must refer to the relevant block exemption in order to establish whether this is the case. The legal effects of notification of an agreement via the "opposition procedure" of a block exemption are common to all block exemptions and are dealt with here. The effect of notification upon the validity of an agreement in civil proceedings is dealt with later in this Chapter.[59]

An agreement which is notified to the Commission via the opposition procedure of a block exemption will automatically become exempt if the Commission does not oppose such exemption within a period of six months upon receipt of the notification of the agreement.[60] Where a

[54] *ibid*, para. IV.

[55] *e.g.*for patent licences, see Reg. 2349/84 (Patent Block Exemption), Art. 2.

[56] *e.g.* see *Vaessen BV v. Moris* [1979] 1 C.M.L.R. 511 where an exclusive patent licence fell outside Art. 4(2)(ii)(b) but fell within Art. 4(2)(i).

[57] See Chap. Nine on Joint Venture and Intellectual Property.

[58] *e.g.* Reg. 417/85 (Research and Development Block Exemption), Art. 7; Reg. 2349/84 (Patent Licensing Block Exemption), Art. 4; Reg. 4087/88 (Franchise Block Exemption), Art. 6; Reg. 556/89 (Know-How Block Exemption) Art. 4.

[59] See para. 12.074 for effect of notification upon the validity of an agreement in civil proceedings.

[60] See sub-paras. (1) of the Articles mentioned in n. 57.

qualifying agreement has already been notified before the block exemption came into effect, a communication to the Commission referring to the appropriate article of the block exemption will suffice to treat the agreement as having been notified under the opposition procedure.[61]

If the Commission does oppose exemption but then withdraws its opposition, then exemption will apply only from the date of notification.[62] If the opposition is withdrawn because the undertakings concerned have amended the agreement, the exemption shall apply from the date on which the amendments take effect.[63] There appears some doubt as to whether an agreement notified to the Commission but unopposed within six months is exempted *ab initio* or from the date of notification. On the one hand, there seems no reason to distinguish between an agreement unopposed and that of an agreement where the Commission initially opposes but then withdraws its opposition. Such analysis would favour exemption of the notified agreement as of the date of notification. On the other hand, the wording of the Block Exemptions suggests that an unopposed notified "opposition" agreement is to be treated as falling within the block exemption and would thus be exempt *ab initio*.[64]

12.019 If the opposition is not withdrawn, then the effects of the notification will be governed by Regulation 17.[65] Thus, the notification under the opposition procedure will be treated as an individual notification for exemption. It is not clear at what stage in the process, an "opposition" notification turns into an individual notification under Regulation 17. This may be important as the "opposition" procedure unlike Regulation 17 does not provide for immunity from fines after the date of notification and has different provisions (*e.g.* confidentiality). However, in practice, parties will notify using Form A/B for both individual exemption under Regulation 17 and via the opposition procedure and thus such matters become academic. As the requirements for the information to be furnished under the opposition procedure are more burdensome than under Regulation 17, there is very little argument for not doing so.

[61] *e.g.* see Patent Block Exemption, Art. 4(4).

[62] *e.g.* see Patent Block Exemption, Art. 4(3), Know-How Block Exemption, Art. 4(8).

[63] It would appear from the provisions in the "opposition procedure" Articles of the block exemptions that where the opposition is withdrawn after amendments have been made, the "opposition procedure" has not turned into a notification under Regulation 17. Thus there would appear to be no power for the Commission to fine the undertakings as their power to fine is derived from Regulation 17.

[64] *e.g.* see the Patent Block Exemption, Art. 4(1) which provides that "the exemption provided for in Articles 1 and 2 shall also apply to agreements containing obligations restrictive of competition . . . on condition that the agreement in question are notified to the Commission in accordance with the provision of Regulation 27 and that the Commission does not oppose such exemption within a period of six months". Reg. 27 is merely procedural and it appears clear that Reg. 17 (which provides that exemption for "new" agreement cannot be backdated earlier than the date of notification—Art. 6) does not apply to unopposed agreements notified under the opposition procedure (*e.g.* see Art. 4(9) of Reg. 2349/84).

[65] *e.g.* Patent Block Exemption, Art. 4(9).

12.020 *Vires*—There has been some discussion as to whether the opposition procedure is *ultra vires.*[66] The Commission derives its power to enact block exemptions from Regulation 19/65 and 2821/71. Neither makes express provision for opposition procedures. The opposition procedure does not initially allow complainants to register their interests or be heard. Whilst complainants cannot complain about agreements which fall within a block exemption, Regulation 19/65 and Regulation 2821/71 obliges the Commission to initiate an extensive consultative process with trade, industry and the Advisory Committee on Restrictive Practices and Monopolies before issuing by block exemption.[67] Thus, it would be difficult to say that natural justice has been denied. In relation to individual exemptions, the Commission cannot take a decision granting exemption without publishing a summary of the relevant application and inviting all interested parties to submit their observations.[68] However, with regard to the opposition procedure, which should only be used where there are obligations restrictive of competition (*i.e.* which infringe Article 85(1)) but are not mentioned in the Block Exemption, there is no requirement that the Commission initiates a consultative procedure or allows complainants to protect their interest. Such would appear to be contrary to the principle of natural justice.[69] Furthermore, Regulation 2821/71 and 19/65 do not specifically empower the Commission to enact an opposition procedure.[70]

[66] See Professor Korah in *Monograph on Know-How Licensing*; Kerse *AntiTrust Procedure* (2nd Ed. 1988); Venit "The Commission's opposition procedure—between the Scylla of *ultra vires* and the Charybdis of Perfume: legal consequences and tactical considerations" [1985] CMLRev 167.

[67] Art. 5, 6 of both Regulations.

[68] Reg. 17, Art. 19(3).

[69] The principles of the European Convention for the Protection of Human Rights and Fundamental Freedoms are part of Community law. See the Joint Declaration on Fundamental Rights signed on April 5 by the Presidents of the European parliament, the Commission and the Council, [1977] O.J. C103. Art. 6 requires that civil rights and obligations be determined by a "fair and public hearing by an independent and impartial tribunal".

[70] See Reg. 2821/71, Art. 1(2) which states that "The Regulation shall define the categories of agreements to which it applies and shall specify in particular: (a) the restrictions or clauses which *may* or *may not* be contained in the agreements, decisions and concerted practices: (b) the clauses which *must* be contained in the agreements, or the other conditions which must be satisfied." [emphasis added]. Such a requirement is exhaustive and thus does not appear to allow block exemptions enacted under this Reg. to benefit agreements which contain clauses not specified in the Block Exemption. This is precisely what the opposition procedure seeks to do. However, it may be that it comes within "other conditions to be satisfied" of Art. 1(2)(b) (although this would seem to be referring to substantive conditions rather than procedural). With regard to Reg. 19/65, Art. 1(2) is somewhat different as it only requires that the block exemption specifies the clauses which *must* or *must not* be contained in the agreements or the other conditions which *must* be satisfied. Art. 1(2) of Reg. 19/65 is clearly not exhaustive of the clauses which may appear in a block exemption. Thus, the Franchise Block Exemption lists obligations restrictive of competition in Art. 2 which may appear in an agreement without removing the exemption provided for under Art. 1. As the opposition procedure is concerned with whether clauses restrictive of competition may appear in agreements, it clearly does not contravene Art. 1(2) of Reg. 19/65. However, as with Reg. 2821/71, there is no specific provision in Reg. 19/65 empowering the Commission to enact an opposition procedure.

(c) Termination of notification proceedings

12.021 Notification proceedings may be terminated in the following ways:

1. A formal decision granting negative clearance.
2. A formal decision granting exemption.
3. A comfort letter is issued to the parties stating that the Commission intends to take no further action.
4. An agreement which has been notified is granted exemption under the opposition procedure by the failure of the Commission to oppose the agreement or by the withdrawal of its opposition.
5. The Commission refuses to grant negative clearance or exemption and issues a "cease and desist" order and financial penalties.

(i) Negative clearance

12.022 The Commission may certify that, on the basis of the facts in possession, there are no grounds under Article 85(1) or Article 86 for action on its part in respect of an agreement, decision or concerted practice. However, as has been discussed, this certificate is of limited value and not binding on national courts.[71] Paradoxically, this would put the notifier in a worse position than if the agreement had been exempted as a decision granting exemption is effective *erga omnes*. In such a case, it could not be argued in civil proceedings that the agreement is void under the Article 85(2). However, it is unlikely that a national court would come to a different conclusion on the same facts to a fully investigated and reasoned decision by the Commission. If it is clear that the agreement clearly does not fall within the scope of the prohibition of Article 85(1), the Commission will not normally issue a formal negative clearance decision.[72]

(ii) Exemption

12.023 The Commission has the power to retrospectively exempt agreements falling within Article 85(1). If the agreement is a "new" one, exemption cannot be declared earlier than the date of notification.[73] If the agreements are not "new" agreements but "old", "accession" or "4(2)" agreements, the Commission has the power to grant exemption prior to the date of notification.[74]

The exemption of an agreement must be specified for a fixed period and conditions and obligations may be attached thereto.[75] If a party commits a breach of these conditions, the Commission may fine the undertakings concerned up to 1,000,000 units of account or a maximum of 10 per cent of its previous year's turnover.[76] Parties may apply for the

[71] See para. 12.009.
[72] See Part II to Complementary Note to Form A/B Reg. 27/62 (as amended).
[73] Reg. 17, Art. 6(1).
[74] See the relevant sections on "old", "accession" and "4(2)" agreements at para. 12.011 *et seq*.
[75] Reg. 17, Art. 8(1).
[76] Art. 15(2)(b).

exemption to be continued.[77] The Commission may revoke or amend its decision granting exemption including revoking its decision with retroactive effect where there has been a basic change in any of the facts basic to the making of the decision; where the parties commit a breach of any obligation attached to the decision; where the decision is based on incorrect information or was induced by deceit or where the parties abuse the exemption from the provision of Article 85(1).[78]

(iii) Comfort letters

12.024 After notification of the agreement, the Commission may decide not to issue a formal decision granting exemption or negative clearance but send a letter to the undertakings concerned that the Commission does not intend to take further action in relation to the notified agreement. This procedure is adopted in the majority of cases as the Commission does not have the resources to grant many individual expemptions.[79]

A comfort letter does not amount to a decision granting negative clearance under Article 2 or exemption under Article 6 of Regulation 17.[80] In civil proceedings, a national court should give regard to but is not bound by a comfort letter.[81] Difficulties may arise in this regard to a comfort letter which declares that the agreement appears to qualify for exemption. It would appear that in such circumstances, the national court should stay proceedings and inform the Commission that the issue of exemption is axiomatic to an action.[82] The Commission will give priority to cases which are the subject of national proceedings suspended in this way, particularly if the outcome of the action depends on it.[83] The effect of comfort letters on civil proceedings is discussed in more detail later in this Chapter.[84]

Where a party is seeking negative clearance or exemption of an agreement, the Commission will sometimes issue a "formal" comfort letter by publishing the essential contents pursuant to Article 19(3) of Regulation 17 so as to give interested third parties an opportunity to make known

[77] Art. 8(2).
[78] Art. 8(3).
[79] The Commission sets out the number of individual exemption decisions and "comfort letters" given each year in its Annual Reports on Competition Policy. In 1992, 17 decisions of individual exemption were given and 553 cases were settled without formal decision because such agreements had been altered to conform with the competition rules, were terminated or had expired and a further 176 cases were dealt with by way of administrative letter—see *22nd Annual Report on Competition Policy* at paras. 80 and 126.
[80] See Case 253/78, *Procureur de la Republique v. Giry et Guerlain* [1980] E.C.R. 2327, [1981] 2 C.M.L.R. 99; Case 37/79, *Marty v. Launder* [1980] E.C.R. 2481, [1981] 2 C.M.L.R. 143.
[81] *Procureur de la Republique v. Giry et Guerlain, ibid.*
[82] See Notice on Cooperation between national courts and the Commission in applying Article 85 and 86 of the EEC Treaty [1993] O.J. C 39/05 at paras. 30, 37.
[83] *ibid*, para. 37.
[84] See para. 12.071.

their views.[85] Such letters will not have the status of a decision and thus will not be capable of appeal to the ECJ. They will state that the Directorate-General for Competition does not consider it necessary to pursue the formal procedure through to the adoption of a decision granting negative clearance and/or exemption. The Commission has taken this step in order to enhance the declaratory value of a comfort letter. Whether the legal effects of a formal comfort letter are any greater than an informal comfort letter is uncertain although a national court will probably pay more regard to a formal comfort letter rather than an informal one.

12.025 The effect of a comfort letter is that the agreement remains notified. It has been held that the Community institutions are bound by the doctrine of legitimate expectation.[86] Thus it is submitted that the Commission cannot renege on its stance set out in a comfort letter unless there has been a material change in circumstances.[87] However, in many cases, the Commission will issue a comfort letter on the basis of the information supplied to it. In such circumstances, can the Commission revoke its comfort letter if it subsequently obtains information about the agreement and the undertakings which causes it to change its mind? Article 8(3) of Regulation 17 lists conditions which if applicable permit the Commission to revoke a formal decision of exemption under Article 6. It is likely that any of these conditions would amount to "a material change in circumstances" permitting the Commission to revoke its comfort letter. However, these conditions do not include the provision of insufficient information (as opposed to incorrect or misleading information). Furthermore, the Commission is entitled under Article 11 to obtain further information on an undertaking. Thus if it instead chooses to issue a comfort letter rather than to carry out an investigation, it is submitted it is bound by that decision and cannot alter its mind if it learns of further information. In effect, the Commission is estopped by its *conduct*. However, if the party fails to provide all relevant information in its possession, such might be termed misleading or deceitful and the Commission would be entitled to revoke its previously favourable stance.[88] The Commission has stated that if, after the grant of exemption, additional or different information comes to light that *could and should* have been in the notification, then the benefit of the exemption will be lost.[89] This suggests that the Commission considers that there is a duty on the notifier to gather all relevant information and communicate it to the Commission.

Importantly, the signatory of the comfort letter may not be authorised

[85] See Notice on procedures concerning applications for negative clearance pursuant to Art. 2 of Reg. 17, [1982] O.J. C343/4 and Notice on Procedures concerning notifications pursuant to Art. 4 of Reg. 17 [1983] O.J., C295/6. For an example, see *Campari* [1989] 4 C.M.L.R. 139 (application to renew exemption).

[86] Case 81/72, *E.C. Commission v. E.C. Council* [1973] E.C.R. 575, [1973] C.M.L.R. 639.

[87] See in Case 31/80 *L'Oreal v. De Nieuwe:* [1980] E.C.R. 3775, [1981] 2 C.M.L.R. 235.

[88] See Case 28/77, *Tepea v. E.C. Commission:* [1978] E.C.R. 1391, [1978] 3 C.M.L.R. 392.

[89] Part IV, Complementary Note, Form A/B, Reg. 27/62.

to issue a comfort letter and legal advisors are advised to check whether the signatory has apparent authority.[90] Furthermore, a letter from the Commission may not be sufficiently precise so as to bind the Commission.[91]

(iv) Discomfort letter

12.026 The Commission may issue a preliminary letter which states that after preliminary examination it is of the opinion that Article 85(1) applies and that the agreement is not exemptible. This has the effect of removing the protection that an undertaking has from being fined after notification. In such circumstances, the undertakings continue with the agreement at risk of the Commission imposing fines or the agreement being found invalid in civil proceedings. If the undertakings concerned are not content with such a letter, they may wish the Commission to investigate further or appeal the letter.[92]

(vi) Exemption via the opposition procedure

12.027 This has already been discussed above and the reader is referred to the appropriate section.[93]

(vi) Agreement found to be prohibited under Article 85(1) and incapable of exemption

12.028 If the Commission finds that an agreement infringes Article 85(1) and does not fulfil the criteria for exemption, it may impose fines and require the undertakings concerned to bring such infringement to an end (known as a "cease and desist" order).[94] During the proceedings, it may suggest amendments to the agreement to the undertakings concerned so as to enable it to issue a decision of exemption, negative clearance or so as to prevent the necessity for a formal "cease and desist" order.[95] However, the Commission's powers to order affirmative action is limited. Thus, the Commission does not possess the power to order a party to enter into a contractual relationship where there exist several means for the parties to end an infringement.[96]

(a) Fines

12.029 The Commission may impose by decision on undertakings or association of undertakings fines from 1,000 to 1,000,000 units of account or if greater a fine up to 10 per cent of the turnover in the preceding business

[90] See Case 71/74, *Frubo v. Commission*, [1975] E.C.R. 563, [1975] 2 C.M.L.R. 123, (ECJ).
[91] *ibid.*
[92] See Art. 15(6). Such a step would have to be reasoned and is appealable—see Case 8–11/66, *Re Noordwijks Cement Accoord* [1967] E.C.R. 75, [1967] C.M.L.R. 77, ECJ.
[93] See Opposition Procedure and Notification, para. 12.018 *et seq*.
[94] Art. 3(1).
[95] Reg. 17, Art. 3(2).
[96] Cases T24 & 28/90 *Automec Srl v. E.C. Commission (No. 2)* [1992] II E.C.R. 367, [1992] 5 C.M.L.R. 431, (CFI).

year of each of the undertakings participating where they intentionally or negligently infringe Article 85(1) or Article 86.[97] Such fines can not be imposed for infringing acts occurring after the notification of a "new" agreement if the acts fall within the limits of the activity described in the notification.[98] If the agreements are "old" or "accession" agreements and were duly notified within the time limits, the Commission additionally cannot impose fines before notification.[99] If the Commission has issued a "discomfort letter" under Article 15(6), then the interim protection is removed.[1] The Commission cannot impose fines for anti-competitive behaviour where it failed to notify its objections to such behaviour to the undertakings concerned.[2] Any such fines are stated not to be of a criminal nature.[3]

In fixing the amount of fine the Commission will have regard to the gravity and duration of the infringement and the general principles of proportionality and equity.[4] In practice, the amount the Commission fines has varied considerably.[5] The Commission may impose fines on a punitive basis (provided it does not exceed the legal limit) so as to deter others from breaking the rules on competition in the Treaty of Rome.[6] Ignorance of Article 85 or 86 is no excuse where it is clear that the behaviour complained of has had as its object the restriction of competition.[7] Ultimately, the question of fines is very much in the discretion of the Commission.

Limitation periods—The imposition of fines is subject to limitations periods.[8] The Commission may not impose fines for substantive infringements after five years.[9] Time begins to run on the day on which the infringement is committed. However, where the infringement is repeated **12.030**

[97] Reg. 17, Art. 15(2).
[98] Art. 15(5)(a).
[99] Art. 15(5)(b). The time limits are February 1, 1963 for "old" agreements; January 1, 1967 for "old" Article 4(2) agreement; six months from the date of accession for "accession" agreements. See Reg. 17, Arts. 5(1), 7(2), 15(5) and 25(3).
[1] Art. 15(6).
[2] Reg. 99/63, Art. 2(3).
[3] Art. 15(4). However, in England, the House of Lords has held that a person can claim the privilege of self-incrimination where he may be exposed to fines under Article 85 or 86—see *Westinghouse Uranium* [1978] A.C. 547, H.L. In relation to intellectual property claims, see Supreme Court Act 1981, s. 72(2) which removes the privilege of self-incrimination in relation to a related offence for proceedings for infringement of rights pertaining to any intellectual property or for passing off. See also para. 12.077.
[4] Reg. 17, Art. 15(2).
[5] See Bellamy and Child, 4th Edition, for a useful schedule of fines awarded. See also *Butterworth's Competition Law.*
[6] See Case 100/80, *Musique Diffusion Francaise v. E.C. Commission* [1983] E.C.R. 1825, [1983] 3 C.M.L.R. 221.
[7] Case 19/77, *Miller v. E.C. Commission* [1978] E.C.R. 131, [1978] 2 C.M.L.R. 334.
[8] Reg. 2988/74, [1974] O.J. L319/1.
[9] Reg. 2988/74, Art. 1(b). For procedural infringements, it is three years—Art. 1(a).

or continuing, time runs on the day on which the infringement ceases.[10] Thus, in the case of an anti-competitive agreement, the relevant date will be the date when the undertakings concerned ceased to implement the agreement.[11] Where any action is taken by the Commission for the purpose of the preliminary investigation or proceedings in respect of an infringement, this will start time running afresh.[12] However, even allowing for interruptions, the Commission cannot impose fines for substantive infringements which occurred greater than 10 years earlier.[13] Time is suspended (as opposed to interrupted) where the Commission's decision is subject to appeal to the Court of Justice.[14]

12.031 *Payment and Enforcement of Fines*—Payment of the fine is usually stipulated to be within three months and the offender is invariably given the option of paying in its national currency as well as in ECU. Commission fines are enforceable by virtue of Article 192 of the Treaty. A decision of the Commission may be registered with the High Court in England (or the Court of Session in Scotland) whereupon it will have the same legal effect as a judgment or order made or given by that Court on the date of registration.[15] Enforcement proceedings cannot be commenced after five years from the date that the decision was made final.[16] The limitation period is suspended if time to pay is allowed or enforcement of payment is suspended pursuant to a decision of the ECJ.[17] However, any action taken by the Commission or Member State for the purpose of enforcing the fine starts time afresh.[18]

(b) "Cease and desist" orders and affirmative relief

12.032 The Commission may, upon application[19] or on its own initiative, order the concerned undertakings to terminate the infringements.[20] This is known as a "cease and desist" order.

The Commission also has the right to order positive action by under-

[10] Art. 1(2).
[11] See *Re the "Toltecs" and "Dorcet" Trade Marks* [1983] O.J. L379/19, [1983] 1 C.M.L.R. 412.
[12] Art. 2 which gives specific examples of what will cause an interruption of the running of the period.
[13] Art. 3(3). It appears that where the infringement is continuing, the Commission may impose fines for behaviour more than ten years earlier as Art. 1(2) deems time to run only from the day on which the infringement ceases.
[14] Art. 3.
[15] The European Communities (Enforcement of Community Judgments) Order 1972 (S.I. 1590).
[16] Reg. 2988/74, Art. 4.
[17] Reg. 2988/74, Art. 4–6.
[18] Art. 5.
[19] Only Member States or natural or legal persons who claim a legitimate interest may apply. See Complaints at para. 12.055 *et seq.*
[20] Reg. 17, Art. 3(1).

takings who have been found to infringe Article 85 or 86.[21] Such orders would appear limited to having the effect of placing the parties in the position as if the infringement has never occurred.[22] For instance, the Commission has ordered that specific provisions be included in a copyright collective association's contracts with copyright owners.[23] Recently, the CFI has ruled on the Commission's powers to put an end to infringements of Article 85 in the context of a party seeking an order from the Commission compelling a car manufacturer to resume supplies to it. It stated that the Commission cannot in principle be acknowledged to possess in the framework of its powers to put an end to infringements of Article 85, a power to order a party to enter into a contractual relationship where as a general rule the Commission has suitable means at its disposal for compelling an enterprise to end an infringement. In particular, the CFI stated that it is not for the Commission to impose upon the parties its own choice among the different potential courses of action which all conform with the Treaty of Rome.[24] However, the principle of proportionality means that the burdens imposed in undertakings in order to bring an infringement of competition law to an end must not exceed what is appropriate and necessary to attain the objective sought namely re-establishment of compliance with the rules infringed.[25]

(c) Periodic penalty payments

12.033 Where undertakings fail to give effect to a "cease and desist" order, the Commission may by decision impose on undertakings or association of undertakings periodic penalty payments of 50 to 1,000 units of account per day.[26] These may also be imposed for failure to abide by conditions imposed upon exemption.[27] The Commission has the right to fix the total amount of the payment to be made at a lower figure than that arrived at under the original order where the undertakings have satisfied the obligation which it was the purpose of the penalty payments to enforce.[28] Periodic penalty payments may be imposed for procedural violations as well.[29]

[21] Case 6/73, *Commercial Solvents v. Commission* [1974] E.C.R. 223, [1974] 1 C.M.L.R. 309.

[22] Case 228, etc., *Ford v. E.C. Commission (No. 1)* [1984] E.C.R. 1129, [1984] 1 C.M.L.R. 649; Cases 6–7/72 *Commercial Solvents v. E.C. Commission* [1974] E.C.R. 224, [1974] 1 C.M.L.R. 309; Case 210/81, *Demo-Studio Schmidt v. E.C. Commission* [1983] E.C.R. 65, [1984] 1 C.M.L.R. 63.

[23] Case 125/78, *GEMA v. E.C. Commission* [1971] E.C.R. 79, [1980] 2 C.M.L.R. 177.

[24] Cases 24 & 28/90, *Automec Srl v. E.C. Commission (No. 2)* [1992] II E.C.R. 2223 [1992] 5 C.M.L.R. 431, (CFI) at paras. 51–52.

[25] *TV Listings*, C241–242/91P [1995] 6 C.M.L.R. 718.

[26] Reg. 17, Art. 16.

[27] Art. 16.

[28] Art. 16(2). The Commission must be consulted before taking any decision to impose penalty payments—Art. 16(3).

[29] *e.g.* failing to submit to an investigation under Art. 14 of Reg. 17.

5. Notification for exemption or negative clearance: procedure and practice

12.034 This section deals with the mechanics of notification for negative clearance and exemption. A fully detailed discussion of this is outside the scope of this work.[30] Regulation 3385/94 governs the procedure for notification.[31]

(a) Who may notify?

12.035 An application for negative clearance or exemption may be made by any undertaking which is party to the agreement, decision or concerted practice in question.[32] Where the application is not made by all, the other parties must be given notice of the application.[33] Where there is a representative of an undertaking (as will always be the case for companies, firms and other nonhuman legal entities), the representative must provide written proof that they are authorised to act.[34] An application may be made to seek negative clearance under Article 86 of potential abusive behaviour under Article 86.[34a]

(b) Compulsory form for notification

12.036 Applications for negative clearance, individual exemption or exemption via the opposition procedure of a block exemption (but not complaints) must be submitted on the Form A/B which is appended to the Regulation 3385/94.[35] This form can be obtained from the Commission's United Kingdom office at 8 Storey's Gate, London SW1 (tel: 0171–222–8122) or from DG IV, Rue de la Loi, 200, B–1049, Belgium. Seventeen copies of each application and three copies of the Annexes must be provided in one of the official languages of the Community.[36] Documents must be submitted in their original language accompanied by translations in one of the official languages.[37] The date of submission of an application is deemed to be the date on which it was received by the Commission or the date shown on the postmark if posted.[38] However, where the Commission finds that the information provided is incomplete in a material respect, it will inform the applicant and ask for complete information to

[30] See Kerse *AntiTrust Procedure* (2nd Ed. 1988); Bellamy and Child *Common Market Law of Competition* (4th Ed. 1987) and *Butterworth's Competition Law*.

[31] Commission Regulation 3385/94 [1994] O.J. L377/28. This replaces the old Regulation 17/62.

[32] Reg. 3385/94, Art. 1.

[33] *ibid.*

[34] Art. 11.

[34a] Art. 1(2).

[35] Reg. 3385/94, Art. 2(1). This form must be used for any type of notification involving negative clearance or exemption. See Case 30/78, *Distillers v. E.C. Commission* [1980] E.C.R. 229, [1980] 3 C.M.L.R. 121, ECJ.

[36] Reg. 3385/94, Art. 2(2).

[37] Reg. 3385/94, Art. 2(1).

[38] Reg. 3385/94, Art. 4(1).

be provided. In such cases, the effective date is the date on which the complete information is received by the Commission.[38a]

(c) Information required under form A/B

12.037 Applications and notifications must contain all information asked for under Form A/B.[39] The applicant is recommended to read both and ensure that the information supplied is complete and correct. Failure to do so may cause the applicant to incur fines for the supply of incorrect or misleading information.[40] The Commission has the power where incorrect information has been supplied to invalidate a decision of exemption.[41]

Any negative clearance may be of little effect if based upon incomplete information.[42] Regulation 17/62 permits the Commission to revoke or amend any decision based on incorrect information or induced by deceit.[43] Furthermore, the Commission has stated that it will usually base its decision on the information provided by the applicant and has stated that any decision taken on the basis of incomplete information could be without effect in the case of a negative clearance or voidable in the case of an exemption.[44] Any material changes to a notifier's arrangements after notification should be communicated to the Commission. The Commission will accept estimates where accurate information is not readily available.[45]

If it is established that the party has provided full and frank disclosure but subsequently after the grant of exemption, the Commission comes across information not available to the notifier which the Commission could have discovered through investigation during prosecution of the application, such does not necessarily invalidate a decision granting exemption. In Form A/B Regulation 3385/94, a valid application is one which is not incomplete. This is subject to two qualifications—firstly, if the information required by Regulation 3385/94 is not readily available, secondly, where the Commission dispenses with the obligation to provide certain information.[46]

In the case of a notification under the opposition procedure of a block exemption, the failure to provide information that is complete and in

[38a] Art. 4(2), Reg. 3385/94.
[39] Art. 3 and para. 13 of Form A/B.
[40] Reg. 17, Art. 15(1). See Case 28/77, *Tepea v. E.C. Commission* [1978] E.C.R. 1391, [1978] 3 C.M.L.R. 392 where the Court of Justice upheld a decision by the Commission fining parties to an oral exclusive distributorship agreement for failure to notify an ancillary concerted practice effecting an exclusive trade mark licence in a Member State.
[41] Reg. 17, Art. 8(3).
[42] See Reg. 17, Art. 2 and Part VI of the Complementary Note to Form A/B. Article 3(1) Reg. 3385/94—Section E, Form A/B.
[43] Art. 8(3)(c).
[44] Section E, Form A/B.
[45] *ibid.*
[46] S.6, Form A/B, Regulation 3385/94.

accordance with the facts will invalidate exemption achieved by non-opposition by the Commission.[47]

The Commission has the power to fine from 100 to 5,000 units of accounts undertakings which intentionally or negligently supply incorrect or misleading information pursuant to a notification.[48]

12.038 The information required is listed below:

1. *Identity of the parties*—The applicant must identify himself and any other parties to the agreement. However, this is not required in respect of parties who have signed standard form contracts.
2. *Purposes of the application*—The applicant must specify whether negative clearance and/or exemption is being sought. Furthermore, he must state whether he is claiming exemption via the opposition procedure of a block exemption.[49] The applicant is asked whether he would be satisfied with a comfort letter. This will be inappropriate if the validity of the agreement under Article 85 is in issue in a national court.
3. *Agreements*—Where agreements are notified, the applicant must attach copies of the agreements to the Form A/B and include translations into one of the official languages.[50] A brief description of the agreements including 3 copies of the text and details of provisions in the agreement which may restrict competition must be included.[51] Where a standard form contract is used, the applicant need only attach the text of the standard form and not every agreement concluded between the parties.[52] If a standard agreement is notified, parties should ensure that the form identifies the agreement as a standard form.[53]
3. *Economic information*—Form A/B lists the economic information required. It permits estimates where exact information is not readily available. This includes a brief description of the agreements; the market of the goods or services affected by the agreements; details of the parties including their financial and economic relationships, both their total turnover and in the market affected by the arrangement; the parties' market shares of the

[47] *e.g.* see Art. 4(4) of Know-How Block Exemption (Reg. 556/89). See also Section E of Form A/B.

[48] Reg. 17/62, Art. 15(1)(a).

[49] The applicant cannot avail himself of the opposition procedure unless he makes "express reference" to the Article and the Block Exemption he is claiming exemption under.

[50] See para. 12.036.

[51] In Case 106/79, *VBBB v. Eldi Records BV* [1980] E.C.R. 1137, [1980] 3 C.M.L.R. 719, (ECJ), the Court of Justice held that where the applicant failed to draw attention to provisions which were restrictive of competition but the full text of the agreement was annexed to Form A/B, the agreement will be deemed properly notified provided there was no evident intention to mislead.

[52] See Case 1/70, *Parfum Marcel Rochas v. Bitsch*: [1970] E.C.R. 515, [1971] C.M.L.R. 104, ECJ; Case 48/72, *Brasserie de Haecht v. Wilkin (No. 2)* [1973] E.C.R. 77, [1973] E.C.R. 287.

[53] *Burns Tractors v. Sperry New Holland*: [1985] O.J. L 276/21, [1988] 4 C.M.L.R. 306.

relevant market and which Member States' trade may be affected by the arrangements.

4. *Reason for negative clearance*—The applicant should outline the areas where he considers there may be incompatibility of the agreement with Article 85 or 86 and why he considers that the Articles are inapplicable.
5. *Reason for exemption*—The applicant must explain how the arrangements satisfy the conditions under Article 85(3) if exemption is sought.

(d) Secrecy obligations

12.039 The notification procedure provides for strict respect of the secrets of undertakings. The Commission is obliged not to disclose information obtained via the notification procedure without prejudice to their obligation to publish.[54] Where the Commission is obliged to publish its intention to make a decision granting negative clearance and its actual decision to do so, the publication must have regard to the legitimate interests of undertakings in the protection of their business secrets.[55]

Form A/B advises notifiers to annex all information claimed to be confidential and mark it as "Business Secrets". Claims as to confidentiality are important because under the Notice on Co-operation between national courts and the Commission in applying Article 85 and 86 of the EEC Treaty, it is envisaged that national courts may apply to the Commission for factual information relevant to a civil dispute.[56] In such circumstances, the Commission will not disclose confidential information.

6. Commission's investigative powers

12.040 Under Article 11–14 of Regulation 17, the Commission has certain investigative powers. These may be used in proceedings relating to notifications for exemption, negative clearance or when the Commission is conducting its own investigations into anti-competitive practices.

(a) Requests for information: Article 11

12.041 The Commission is empowered under Article 11 of Regulation 17 to obtain all necessary information from governments, competent authorities and undertakings in order to carry out its investigations.[57] The

[54] Reg. 17, Art. 20(2). See also Art. 214 of the Treaty of Rome.
[55] Arts. 19, 20 and 21 of Reg. 17. The Commission may be liable under Art. 215 of the Treaty of Rome for inadvertent disclosure of secrets which damage the interests of undertakings—see *Adams v. E.C. Commission* [1986] 1 C.M.L.R. 506.
[56] See Notice of Cooperation between national courts and the Commission in applying Article 85 and 86 of the EEC Treaty, 1993 O.J. C 39/05, paras. 40–42.
[57] Reg. 17, Art. 11.

Commission must state the legal basis for the request and the penalties for the supply of incorrect information. However, the Commission has the right to decide what information is necessary to prove infringement of Article 85 or 86 and thus parties will rarely be able to refuse a request on the basis that the Commission is not entitled to such information.[58] The Commission will stipulate a time period for the supply of the information.

If the undertaking refuses to comply with the request, the Commission may take a decision requiring the information to be supplied. This decision must specify the information required, fix a time limit, indicate the penalties provided for under Article 15 (fines) and Article 16 (periodic penalty payments) and the right to have the decision reviewed by the Court of Justice.[59] The Commission must forward any copies of requests or orders for information to the competent authority where the undertaking is situated.[60] If the parties then fail to comply with the decision or supply incorrect information either intentionally or negligently, the Commission may fine the parties concerned up to 1,000 units of account and impose, if necessary, periodic penalty payments on the offending parties.[61]

The Commission will often follow up an investigation under Article 14 with requests for information under Article 11. The ECJ has confirmed that the Commission has the right to do and rejected a submission that its power under Article 11 must be exercised prior to Article 14.[62]

(b) Inquiries into sectors of the economy: Article 12

12.042 The Commission may conduct a general inquiry into an economic sector and may request undertakings (not necessarily parties to the notified agreements) to supply economic and other information necessary for deciding whether such behaviour is anti-competitive. In particular, it may request all undertakings in an economic sector to communicate to it all agreements, decisions and concerted practices which are exempt from notification (*i.e.* Article 4(2) agreements). The Commission may require information to be supplied in relation to the structure and behaviour of undertakings potentially occupying a dominant position within the Com-

[58] Joined Cases 274/87 & 27/88, *Orkem SA v. E.C. Commission; Solvay & CIE v. E.C. Commission* [1989] E.C.R. 3283 [1991] 4 C.M.L.R. 502 following Case 155/79, *AM & S v. E.C. Commission* [1982] E.C.R. 1575, [1982] 2 C.M.L.R. 264.

[59] Art. 11(5). A decision under Art. 11(5) is properly served if it reaches the addressee and he is in a position to take cognizance of it—see Joined Cases 274/87 & 27/88, *Orkem SA v. E.C. Commission; Solvay & CIE v. E.C. Commission* [1989] E.C.R. 3282, [1991] 4 C.M.L.R. 502.

[60] Art. 11(2) and (6).

[61] Arts. 15(1)(b), 16.

[62] Joined Cases 274/87 and 27/88, *Orkem SA v. E.C. Commission; Solvay & CIE v. E.C. Commission* [1989] E.C.R. 3283, [1991] 4 C.M.L.R. 502.

mon Market.[63] The Advisory Committee on Restrictive Practices and Monopolies must be consulted according to Article 10 of Regulation 17 before such an inquiry is initiated.[64]

(c) Investigative powers of the Commission: Article 14

12.043 The Commission is empowered under Article 14 to conduct all necessary investigations into potentially anti-competitive behaviour of undertakings. The Commission has the right to examine books and other business records; take copies of or extracts from such books and records; ask for oral explanations on the spot and enter any premises, land and means of transport of undertakings.[65] It is for the Commission to decide for the purposes of an investigation under Article 14 whether particular information is necessary to enable it to bring to light an infringement of the competition rules.[66]

Article 14 provides two procedures for carrying out investigations. Article 14(2) enables authorised officials of the Commission to exercise their powers upon production of an authorisation in writing specifying the subject matter and purpose of the investigation and the penalties under Article 15(1)(c) for the production of books or records which are incomplete. The undertaking is not obliged to submit to an Article 14(2) investigation and may refuse it.[67] Officials of the competent authority of the Member State where the investigation is to be carried out must be informed in good time before the investigation. Such officials may be present at the investigations and usually will be.[68]

Article 14(3) provides that undertakings must submit to an investigation if ordered by a decision of the Commission. The decision must stipulate the subject matter and purpose of the investigation; the appointed day for the investigation; the penalties provided in Article 15 for non-compliance or the supply of incomplete records and the right to have the decision reviewed by the European Court of Justice.[69] Where questions are asked, a company cannot remain silent unless such would

[63] Art. 12.
[64] Art. 12(4).
[65] Reg. 17/62, Art. 14(1).
[66] Case 155/79, *AM & S v. E.C. Commission* [1982] E.C.R. 1575, [1982] 2 C.M.L.R. 264; Joined Cases 274/87 & 27/88, *Orkem SA v. E.C. Commission; Solvay & CIE v. E.C. Commission* [1989] E.C.R. 3283, [1991] 4 C.M.L.R. 502 at 553.
[67] See para. 3 of Explanatory Note to authorization to investigate under Art. 14(2) of Reg. 17/62 reported at *13th Annual Report on Competition Policy*, pp. 270–272.
[68] *ibid.* In England, the competent authority is the Office of Fair Trading.
[69] The information must clearly indicate the presumed facts on which it intends to investigate—see Case 46/87R, *Hoechst v. E.C. Commission* [1987] E.C.R. 1549, [1991] 4 C.M.L.R. 410; Case 85/87, *Dow Benelux NV v. E.C. Commission* [1989] E.C.R. 3283, [1991] 4 C.M.L.R. 502; Case 97/87, *Dow Chemical Iberia Sa v. E.C. Commission* [1989] E.C.R. 2859, [1991] 4 CMLR 410 at 470 although it does not need to set out a precise legal analysis of the alleged infringements, see p. 483.

amount to an admission at law of infringing behaviour under Article 85 or 86.[70] Similar provisions apply in relation to the assistance of the competent national authority as in Article 14(2). The authorities of the Member State must assist the officials of the Commission to enable them to make their investigations.[71]

The Article 14(2) and Article 14(3) procedures are independent of each other. Thus the Court of Justice has confirmed that a decision under Article 14(3) can be taken without having earlier authorised officials to make an investigation under Article 14(2).[72] The Commission has provided 2 explanatory notes to Article 14(2) and Article 14(3) procedures.[73]

12.044 For sometime now, the Commission has ordered on-the-spot investigations without giving prior notice to the undertakings concerned (known as "dawn raids"). This practice has been validated by the Court of Justice as necessary to the practical application of the Community's competition laws.[74] Furthermore, the Court has stated that the Commission has a right to carry out "dawn raids" when "there is need for an appropriate inquiry having regard to special features of the case".[75] Thus the Commission has a wide discretion in deciding whether to make a dawn raid. Furthermore, the Commission need not give the reasons for carrying out the investigation.[76] It need only comply with the conditions in Article 14(2) and 14(3). Thus, one is not entitled to ask the Commission what their reasons for carrying out the investigation are.[77] The right to privacy and family life as provided by Article 8(1) of the European Convention on Human Rights cannot prevent a Commission from

[70] See Case 46/87R, *Hoechst v. E.C. Commission* [1987] E.C.R. 1549, [1991] 4 C.M.L.R. 410; Case 85/87, *Dow Benelux NV v. E.C. Commission* [1989] E.C.R. 3283, [1991] 4 C.M.L.R. 502; Case 97/87, *Dow Chemical Iberia Sa v. E.C. Commission* [1989] E.C.R. 2859, [1991] 4 C.M.L.R. 410; Case 374/87, *Orkem SA v. EC Commission* [1989] E.C.R. 3283, [1991] 4 C.M.L.R. 502; Joined Cases 274/87 & 27/88, *Solvay & CIE v. E.C. Commission* [1991] 4 C.M.L.R. 502 at paras. 18 to 35. The question of whether a party can remain silent in Article 14 investigations is discussed in more detail at para. 12.047.

[71] Art. 14(6). In England, the Treasury Solicitor may by an *ex parte* application to the High Court ask for an order that the undertaking be forced to submit to the investigation. A breach of such an order would amount to a contempt of court carrying with it possible imprisonment.

[72] Case 136/79, *National Panasonic v. E.C. Commission* [1980] E.C.R. 2033, [1980] 3 C.M.L.R. 169, paras. 8–16.

[73] See *13th Annual Report on Competition Policy*, pp. 270–272.

[74] Case 136/79, *National Panasonic v. E.C. Commission* [1980] E.C.R. 2033, [1980] 3 C.M.L.R. 169, paras. 8–16.

[75] *ibid.*

[76] Although it must specify the subject-matter and purpose of the investigation—see Case 46/87R, *Hoechst v. E.C. Commission* [1989] E.C.R. 1549, [1991] 4 C.M.L.R. 410; Case 85/87, *Dow Benelux NV v. E.C. Commission* [1989] E.C.R. 3137, [1991] 4 C.M.L.R. 410; Case 97/87, *Dow Chemical Iberia Sa v. E.C. Commission* [1989] E.C.R. 2859, [1991] 4 C.M.L.R. 410, at p. 467.

[77] See Case 136/79, *National Panasonic v. E.C. Commission* [1980] E.C.R. 2033, [1980] 3 C.M.L.R. 169.

carrying out an investigative raid at business premises even if that happens to be someone's home.[78]

During an investigation under Article 14(3), the Commission has the power to have shown to them the documents they request, to enter such premises as they choose and to have shown to them the contents of any piece of furniture which they indicate. If the undertaking concerned opposes the Commission's investigation, the Commission may search for any information necessary for the investigation with the assistance of the national authorities.[79] The Commission must follow and respect a Member State's law laid down for such investigations.[80] The competent body cannot substitute its own assessment of the need for investigations for that of the Commission but can consider whether the measures sought are arbitrary or excessive having regard to the subject-matter of the investigation.[81] Similarly, a decision taken under Article 14(3) is not rendered invalid because it conflicts with a Member State's law as such cannot affect the validity of Community measures.[82]

12.045 It will be difficult to ascertain until later whether the Commission is "fishing" or not. However, the Court of Justice has indicated that the Commission will not be entitled to use papers or documents received by way of investigation pursuant to a decision by the Commission which is subsequently annulled by the Court of Justice under Article 173 for the purposes of establishing an infringement of Article 85 or 86.[83] An appeal to the Court of Justice for an interim order temporarily suspending the decision of the Commission is unlikely to succeed.[84]

During an investigation, the Commission considers that there is a positive duty on the undertakings to assist the Commission officials in the carrying out of the investigation including the identification of relevant documents.[85] Undertakings do not have the right to have a lawyer present during the investigation. However the Commission will allow the

[78] *Case 46/87, Hoechst v. E.C. Commission* [1989] E.C.R. 1549, [1991] 4 C.M.L.R. 410; Case 85/87, *Dow Benelux NV v. E.C. Commission* [1989] E.C.R. 3137, [1991] 4 C.M.L.R. 410; *Dow Chemical Iberia Sa v. E.C. Commission* [1989] E.C.R. 2859, [1991] 4 C.M.L.R. 410 at p. 465.

[79] See Article 14(6) and Case 46/87R, *Hoechst v. E.C. Commission* [1989] E.C.R. 1549, [1991] 4 C.M.L.R. 410; Case 85/87, *Dow Benelux NV v. Commission* [1989] E.C.R. 3137, [1991] 4 C.M.L.R. 410; Case 97/87, *Dow Chemical Iberia Sa v. E.C. Commission* [1989] E.C.R. 2859, [1991] 4 C.M.L.R. 410 at p. 468.

[80] Case 46/87R, *Hoechst v. E.C. Commission*, [1989] E.C.R. 1549, [1991] 4 C.M.L.R. 410, at para. 34.

[81] *ibid*, para. 35.

[82] Case 97/87, *Dow Chemical Iberica v. E.C. Commission* [1989] E.C.R. 2859, [1991] 4 C.M.L.R. 410, at p. 481 applying Case 11/70, *Internationale Handelsgesellschaft v. Einfuhr- und Vorratsstelle fur Getriede und Futtermittel* [1970] E.C.R. 1125, [1972] C.M.L.R. 250.

[83] Case 87/87R, *Dow Chemical v. Commission* [1988] 4 C.M.L.R. 439.

[84] Case 46/87R, *Hoechst v. E.C. Commission* [1989] E.C.R. 1549, [1988] 4 C.M.L.R. 410; Case 87/87R, *Dow Chemical v. E.C. Commission* [1988] 4 C.M.L.R. 439. The Court said that it would be difficult to say that irreparable harm would be caused by such a decision (a condition for the award of interim relief) and would amount to prejudging a decision on the main issue of the case.

[85] *Fabricca Pisana et al* [1980] O.J. L 75/30, [1980] 2 C.M.L.R. 354.

undertakings time to summon their lawyers unless there are in-house lawyers present upon appropriate undertakings as to non-interference with business records.[86]

If a party does not comply with a decision under Article 14(3), he may be fined up to 5000 units of account and subject to periodic penalty payments of 1000 units of account per day.[87]

(d) Legal privilege

12.046 The application of Article 11 to 14 by the Commission must have regard to the rights of the defence.[88] Thus the Court of Justice has held that a form of legal privilege applies to communications between a lawyer and his client in relation to possible or actual proceedings against the latter under Regulation 17.[89] Such communications must be made for the purposes of the client's defence and emanate from an independent lawyer.[90] Thus privilege will apply to all communications entered into between an independent lawyer and the client after the initiation of an administrative procedure which may lead to a decision on the applicability of Article 85 and 86 and earlier written communications which have a relationship to the subject matter of that protection.[91] Communications between an "in-house" lawyer and the client will not attract privilege from the Commission's investigation.[92] However, internal documents confined to reporting the text or the content of external independent legal advice are subject to privilege.[93]

[86] Case 136/79, *National Panasonic v. E.C. Commission* [1980] E.C.R. 2033, [1980] 3 C.M.L.R. 169. See Explanatory Note to Art. 14(2) and 14(3) proceedings, *supra.* Also see Case 46/87R, *Hoechst v. E.C. Commission* [1989] E.C.R. 1549, [1989] 4 C.M.L.R. 410; Case 85/87, *Dow Benelux NV v. E.C. Commission* [1989] E.C.R. 3137, [1991] 4 C.M.L.R. 410; *Dow Chemical Iberia Sa v. E.C. Commission* [1989] E.C.R. 2859, [1991] 4 C.M.L.R. 410 at para. 16 where the ECJ held that the Commission must respect the right to legal representation as from the preliminary-inquiry stage.

[87] As was done in Case 46/87R, *Hoechst v. E.C. Commission* [1989] E.C.R. 1549, [1988] 4 C.M.L.R. 430 (maximum periodic penalty payment order made).

[88] See Case 322/81, *Nederlandsche Banden-Industrie Michelin NV v. E.C. Commission* [1983] E.C.R. 3461, [1985] 1 C.M.L.R. 282, at para. 7; Case 46/87R, *Hoechst v. E.C. Commission* [1987] E.C.R. 1549, [1989] 4 C.M.L.R. 430; Case 85/87, *Dow Benelux NV v. Commission* [1989] E.C.R. 3137, [1991] 4 C.M.L.R. 410; Case 97/87; *Dow Chemical Iberia Sa v. E.C. Commission* [1989] E.C.R. [1991] 4 C.M.L.R. 410 at para. 14 (p. 465).

[89] Case 155/79, *AM & S v. E.C. Commission* [1982] E.C.R. 15756, [1982] 2 C.M.L.R. 264; Case 46/87, *Hoechst v. E.C. Commission* [1987] E.C.R. 1549, [1989] 4 C.M.L.R. 430; Case 85/87, *Dow Benelux NV v. E.C. Commission* [1989] E.C.R. 3137, [1991] 4 C.M.L.R. 410; Case 97/87, *Dow Chemical Iberia Sa v. E.C. Commission* [1989] E.C.R. 2859, [1991] 4 C.M.L.R. 410 at para. 16.

[90] Case T–30/89, *Hilti AV v. E.C. Commission* [1990] 4 C.M.L.R. 602, CFI applying Case 155/79, *AM & S v. E.C. Commission* [1982] E.C.R. 1575, [1982] 2 C.M.L.R. 264. This rule differs from the English rule where communications between solicitor and client are privileged regardless of the purpose of the communication.

[91] Case T–30/89, *Hilti AV v. E.C. Commission* [1990] II E.C.R. 163, [1990] 4 C.M.L.R. 602, CFI at paras. 13 and 14.

[92] Case 155/79, *AM & S v. E.C. Commission* [1982] E.C.R. 1576, [1982] 2 C.M.L.R. 264.

[93] Case T–30/89, *Hilti AV v. E.C. Commission* [1990] II E.C.R. 163, [1990] 4 C.M.L.R. 602, CFI, at para. 18.

The independent lawyer must be qualified under a Member State's laws.[94] Whilst the communications must be in relation to the initiation of proceedings by the Commission under Regulation 17, this will be interpreted widely.[95] The undertaking may be required to show documentation to the Commission which confirms that it is privileged.[96]

(e) Self-incrimination

12.047 The Commission does not recognise the right to self-incrimination which is an Anglo-Saxon legal concept.[97] However, recently the Court of Justice has in *Orkem SA v. E.C. Commission*[98] considered whether an undertaking has the right to remain silent in the face of a request for information under Article 11(5). It held that:

> "Accordingly, whilst the Commission is entitled, in order to preserve the useful effect of Article 11(2) and (5) of Regulation 17, to compel an undertaking to provide all necessary information concerning such facts as may be known to it and to disclose to it, if necessary, such documents relating thereto as are in its possession, even if the latter may be used to establish, against it or another undertaking, the existence of anti-competitive conduct, it may not, by means of a decision calling for information, undermine the rights of defence of the undertaking concerned.
>
> Thus, the Commission may not compel an undertaking to provide it with answers which might involve an admission on its part of the existence of an infringement which it is incumbent upon the Commision to prove."[99]

The above right is more narrow than the English rights against self-incrimination. The latter provides a right to remain silent if the answer would be likely to expose a person to criminal proceedings whilst the former only provides a right to remain silent if the answer would involve an admission. Thus, in *Orkem & Solvay*, a case which concerned suspected cartels in the PVC trade, the ECJ held that questions which related to meetings of the producers, which were intended only to discover the circumstances in which the meetings were held, the capacity in which the participants attended them and as to what price level measures were

[94] Case 155/79, *AM & S v. E.C. Commission* [1982] E.C.R. 1575, [1982] 2 C.M.L.R. 264. Thus, communications with a lawyer qualified in *e.g.* the United States will not qualify for legal privilege.

[95] In *AM & S* the Court held that legal privilege attached to communications in 1972 prior to the U.K.'s accession in relation to proceedings started by the Commission in 1979.

[96] Case 155/79, *AM & S v. Commission* [1982] E.C.R. 1575, [1982] 2 C.M.L.R. 264.

[97] See *17th Annual Report on Competition Policy*, p.55.

[98] Joined Cases 274/87 & 27/88, *Orkem SA v. E.C. Commission; Solvay & CIE v. E.C. Commission* [1991] 4 C.M.L.R. 502.

[99] *ibid*, para. 34–35. See also Case 46/87R, *Hoechst v. E.C. Commission* [1987] E.C.R. 1549, [1989] 4 C.M.L.R. 439; Case 85/87, *Dow Benelux NV v. Commission* [1989] E.C.R. 3137, [1991] 4 C.M.L.R. 410; Case 97/87, *Dow Chemical Iberia Sa v. E.C. Commission* [1989] E.C.R. 2859, [1991] 4 C.M.L.R. 410.

taken and how they were to be implemented were permissible, but that questions which sought an acknowledgment of the undertakings' involvement in price-fixing and production-control agreements were not permissible.[1] The difference between questions relating to facts which may expose an undertaking to fines under Article 15 and those requiring actual admission of anti-competitive behaviour will often be a fine one.

7. Termination of Notification: Practice and Procedure

12.048 As already discussed, there are four ways which a notification can come to an end. The practice and procedure of those four ways are discussed here.

(a) Formal decision granting exemption or negative clearance

12.049 Prior to the Commission taking a favourable decision, it must transmit copies of the application and notification to the competent authorities of the Member States.[2] The Commission must maintain close and constant liaison with the competent authorities of the Member States.[3]

The Commission must publish a summary of the relevant application or notification and invite all interested third parties to submit their observation within a fixed time limit (not less than a month) before taking a formal decision.[4] Furthermore, the Commission must allow those parties with "sufficient interest"[5] the opportunity of making known their views in writing within a fixed time limit.[6] If a party with sufficient interest wishes to put forward its arguments orally, it has the right to do so.[7]

Furthermore, the Advisory Committee on Restrictive Practices and Monopolies must be consulted prior to the taking of any formal decision.[8]

Finally, any formal decision of negative clearance or exemption must be published giving the names and the main content of the decision having regard to the legitimate interest of undertakings in the protection of their business interests.[9]

Generally speaking, where a favourable decision is to be made, the applicant does not have the right to be heard as the Commission has not taken objection.[10]

[1] See para. 38–41.
[2] Reg. 17, Art. 10.
[3] Art. 10(2).
[4] Art. 19(3).
[5] This concept is discussed in relation to complaints. See para. 12.055 *et seq.*
[6] Reg. 17, Art. 19(2); Reg. 99/62, Art. 5.
[7] Reg. 99/63, Art. 7.
[8] Reg. 17/62, Art. 10(3).
[9] Reg. 17/62, Art. 21.
[10] See Art. 19(1) and Reg. 99/63 which hangs upon Art. 19(1).

(b) Comfort letter

12.050 There is no fixed procedure for issuing a comfort letter. The Commission has standard letters which are issued. However, the letter must be authorised and approved by Members of the Commission if it is to be capable of estopping the Commission from subsequently asserting to the contrary.[11] Sometimes, the Commission will issue a "formal" comfort letter and publish the essential content of the agreement so as to give interested parties an opportunity to make known their views.[12]

(c) Exemption via "opposition" procedure

12.051 Where an agreement has been notified via the opposition procedure of a block exemption, all block exemptions state that it becomes automatically exempt after six months if the Commission does not oppose such an exemption. Time runs from the date on which the notification was received or if registered post, the date on the postmark.[13] However, such automatic exemption will be invalid if the applicant has failed to provide information which is complete and in accordance with the facts.[14] The Commission may oppose the exemption but must oppose if it receives a justified request to do so from a Member State within three months of the transmission of the notification.[15] It may withdraw its opposition to the exemption at any time but must consult the Advisory Committee on Restrictive Practices and Dominant Positions if it was requested to oppose exemption by a Member State.[16] Where opposition is raised, the undertakings will be given the opportunity to show why the conditions of Article 85(3) are fulfilled or to amend the agreement so that they are fulfilled.[17] If the opposition is maintained then the effects of the notification become governed by the provisions of Regulation 17.[18]

(d) Adverse decision

12.052 Where the Commission does not intend to grant exemption or negative clearance but intends to issue a cease and desist order, impose fines or periodic penalty payments or revoke or amend a prior decision granting exemption or even impose onerous conditions on the grant of exemp-

[11] Case 71/74, *Frubo v. E.C. Commission* [1975] E.C.R. 563, [1975] 2 C.M.L.R. 123.
[12] See Notice on Procedures concerning applications for negative clearance pursuant to Article 2 of Regulation 17, [1982] O.J. C 343/4; Notice on Procedures concerning notifications pursuant to Article 4 of Regulation 17, [1983] O.J. C295/6. See para. 12.071 for more detailed discussion on the legal effect of comfort letters in national proceedings.
[13] *e.g.* Reg. 2349/84, Art. 4(2).
[14] *e.g.* see Reg. 2349/84, Art. 4(3).
[15] *e.g.* see Reg. 2349/84, Art. 4(5).
[16] *e.g.* see Art. 4(6).
[17] *e.g.* Reg. 2349/84, Art. 4(7) and (8).
[18] See Procedure for taking an adverse decision, para. 12.082.

tion,[19] the procedure as set out in Regulation 99/63 is put into motion. Regulation 99/63 effectively gives the undertakings concerned the right to be heard and the Commission should use it whenever it intends to take a decision which is potentially adverse to an undertaking.[20] Once the Commission has initiated the procedure for taking an adverse decision, the authorities of the Member States are not competent to apply Article 85(1) and Article 86.[21] However, "authorities" has been held not to include ordinary national courts.[22]

Firstly, the Commission must inform the undertakings of the objections raised against them. This is known as the Statement of Objections.[23] This must set out the essential facts and the objections and the parties must be provided with "the details necessary to the defence".[24] The Commission cannot deal in its decision with objections that it has not afforded undertakings the opportunity of making known their views.[25] Documents that the Commission relies upon as evidence of infringement must be sent to the undertakings concerned.[26] If it fails to do so and the document contains information it has taken into account coming to its decision, then it is precluded from relying upon that document in proceedings brought before the CFI or ECJ in an action for annulment of the decision.[27] Thus, if a Commission cannot disclose a document it relies upon because of its confidential nature, it will be prevented from relying on it to support its case.[28]

Undertakings then must within the time limit fixed by the Commission make known in writing its views concerning the objections raised against them.[29] Such views may contain comments, documentation and may propose that the Commission hear persons who may corroborate the facts.[30] Where other persons showing a sufficient interest apply to be heard, the Commission must allow them to make known their views in writing.[31]

[19] See Case 17/74, *Transocean Marine Paint v. E.C. Commission* [1974] E.C.R. 1063, [1974] 2 C.M.L.R. 459, (ECJ).
[20] See Reg. 17, Art. 19(1), Recitals to Regulation 99/63.
[21] Reg. 17/62, Art. 9(3).
[22] Case 127/73, *BRT v. SABAM* [1974] E.C.R. 51, [1974] 2 C.M.L.R. 238. Confirmed in Case 209/84 etc. *Ministere Public v. Asjes* [1986] E.C.R. 1425, [1986] 3 C.M.L.R. 173.
[23] Reg. 99, Art. 2.
[24] See Case 45/69, *Boehringer Mannheim v. E.C. Commission* [1970] E.C.R. 767 at 795.
[25] Reg. 99/63, Art. 4.
[26] See Case 88/76, *Hoffmann La Roche v. Commission* [1979] E.C.R. 461; [1979] 3 C.M.L.R. 211; Case 107/82, *AEG Telefunken v. E.C. Commission* [1983] E.C.R. 3151, [1984] 3 C.M.L.R. 325; Case 100/80, *Musique Diffusion Francaise v. Commission* [1983] E.C.R. 1825, [1983] 3 C.M.L.R. 221; Case 106/79, *VBBB v. Eldi Records BV* [1980] E.C.R. 1137, [1980] 3 C.M.L.R. 719, (ECJ).
[27] Case C–62/86, *AKZO Chemie v. E.C. Commission* [1991] I E.C.R. 3359, [1993] 5 C.M.L.R. 215 at para. 21, (ECJ).
[28] e.g. see Case C–62/86, *AKZO v. E.C. Commission* [1993] 5 C.M.L.R. 215, (ECJ);Case 106/79, *VBBB v. Eldi Records BV* [1980] E.C.R. 1137, [1980] 3 C.M.L.R. 719, (ECJ).
[29] Reg. 99, Art. 3(1).
[30] Reg. 99/63, Art. 3(2), 3(3).
[31] Reg. 19, Art. 19(2), Reg. 99, Art. 5.

12.053 Undertakings concerned have a limited right of access to the Commission's file. As a general principle, the Commission is not required to divulge the contents of its files to the parties concerned.[32] In 1982, the Commission announced that undertakings involved in Article 85 proceedings have the right to inspect all documents, whether in their favour or not, which the Commission has obtained during the course of an investigation except where these relate to business secrets of third parties, the internal documents of the Commission or other confidential information.[33] The CFI has recently held that the Commission is now bound by this policy and must adhere to it.[34]

Generally, the Commission's procedure is written. However, if requested, the matter may go to an oral hearing if the party requesting shows a sufficient interest or if the Commission proposes to impose on them a fine or periodic penalty payments.[35] Member States may appoint an official to attend the hearing as well.[36] Each oral hearing will be organised and regulated by a specially appointed Hearing Officer.[37]

Prior to any decision being taken by the Commission, it must consult the Advisory Committee on Restrictive Practices and Monopolies who will deliver an opinion on the proceedings.[38]

Where a complaint from a third party has caused the Commission to initiate an investigation under Regulation 17, the complainant may apply to be heard under Article 19(2), Regulation 17 and, if he does not, cannot complain that he was not afforded the opportunity to make oral representations at a hearing.[39]

Parties who consider that the Commission has infringed its rights of defence can only bring an action for annulment of an adverse decision after the final decision has been taken.[40]

8. To notify or not to notify?

12.054 Notification of an agreement has many advantages. Firstly, it is the only method of obtaining exemption of an agreement. Notification provides for immunity from fines for acts after the date of notification. If a civil

[32] Case C–62/86, *AKZO v. E.C. Commission* [1991] I E.C.R. 3359, [1993] 5 CMLR 215; Case 106/79, *VBBB v. Eldi Records BV* [1980] E.C.R. 1137, [1980] 3 C.M.L.R. 719 (ECJ).

[33] See *12th Annual Report on Competition Policy*, paras. 34–35.

[34] Case T–71/89, *Hercules Chemicals NV v. E.C. Commission* [1991] II E.C.R. 1711, [1992] 4 C.M.L.R. 84, (CFI).

[35] Reg. 99, Art. 7.

[36] Reg. 99, Art. 8(2).

[37] For the principal duties of the Hearing Officer, see *12th Annual Report on Competition Policy* at para. 36, *13th Annual Report on Competition Policy* at p. 273.

[38] Reg. 17, Art. 10.

[39] Case 43/85, *ANCIDES v. E.C. Commission* [1987] E.C.R. 3131, [1988] 4 C.M.L.R. 821.

[40] Case T–10/92, *Cimenteries CBR v. E.C. Commission* [1992] E.C.R. II 2667, [1993] 3 C.M.L.R. 243, (CFI). See also Case 608/81, *IBM v. E.C. Commission* [1981] E.C.R. 2639, [1981] 3 C.M.L.R. 635 (Issue of Statement of Objections not a decision capable of challenge before the ECJ under Article 173).

action is started which claims that an agreement or practice infringes Article 85, a failure to notify an agreement for exemption prior to the issue of writ will jeopardise a party's chances of success as the Commission only has the power for most agreements to exempt the agreement from the date of notification. Furthermore, a court will generally be more reluctant to stay proceedings if the undertaking concerned has not at the date of the hearing notified the agreement in issue.

The main disadvantages of notification is that it brings the agreement and surrounding circumstances to the Commission's attention although because of its limited resources, the Commission may often choose to ignore an infringement of Article 85 which has a limited effect on trade between Member States. Secondly, the costs of preparing and prosecuting a notification to a final decision is high.

9. Complaints

12.055 A person or Member State may apply to the Commission complaining about an infringement of Article 85 or 86 by a third party asking them to issue a "cease and desist" order.[41] A person(natural or legal) may only apply if he has a "legitimate interest".[42] However as the Commission may, on its own initiative, take proceedings following a complaint, it may be sufficient just to alert the Commission, in which case the requirement of legitimate interest becomes academic.[43]

Unlike notification of an agreement for negative clearance or exemption, there is no prescribed form. However, the Commission has issued a Form C which can be used as an official complaints form.[44] Such an application must contain full information on the alleged infringements.

A complainant does not have the right to demand that the Commission give a decision on the existence or otherwise of the alleged infringement.[45] Upon receipt of the complaint, the Commission has a duty to examine the facts put forward by the complainant in order to decide whether they indicate behaviour likely to distort competition in the Common Market.[46] However, the Commission is not under a duty to investigate the complaint even if there appears to be grounds to believe that an infringement has occurred.[47] In considering whether to initiate an investigation, the Commission is entitled to accord different degrees of

[41] Reg. 17, Art. 3(1).
[42] Reg. 17, Art. 3(2).
[43] *ibid.*
[44] [1989] O.J. C 26/6; [1989] 1 C.M.L.R. 617.
[45] Case 125/78, *GEMA v. E.C. Commission* [1979] E.C.R. 3173, [1980] 2 C.M.L.R. 175.
[46] See Case 210/81, *Demo-Studio Schmidt v. E.C. Commission* [1983] E.C.R. 65, [1984] 1 C.M.L.R. 63; Case 298/83, *CICCE v. E.C. Commission* [1985] E.C.R. 1105, [1986] 1 C.M.L.R. 486; Cases 24 & 28/90, *Automec Srl v. E.C. Commission (No. 2)* [1992] II E.C.R. 2223, [1992] 5 C.M.L.R. 431, (CFI) at para. 78, 79.
[47] Cases 24 & 28/90, *Automec Srl v. E.C. Commission (No. 2)* [1992] II E.C.R. 2223, [1992] 5 C.M.L.R. 431, (CFI) at para. 76.

priority to examining the complaints it receives according to the Community interest.[48] It must take account of the circumstances of the particular case, the importance of the alleged infringement for the functioning of the Common Market, the probability of being able to establish the existence of the infringement and the extent of the investigation measure necessary in order to fulfil successfully its task of securing compliance with Article 85 and 86.[49] Furthermore, it is entitled to consider whether the complainant has begun proceedings in a national court and whether such protection as he seeks can be awarded by such a court.[50]

12.056 If the Commission considers that on the basis of the information in its possession there are insufficient grounds for granting the application, either because the information contained in the complaint does not disclose an infringement or because the Commission decides that there is not sufficient Community interest, it must inform the applicants of its reason and fix a time limit for them to submit any further comments in writing.[51] This step may be taken after the Commission's preliminary investigation or even after the Commission has initiated its adverse decision procedure. It does not have to issue a Statement of Objections or initiate a formal procedure pursuant to taking an adverse decision against the complainant.[52] Moreover, such a step is not appealable because it does not constitute a "decision" under Article 173. However, a letter confirming the Commission's stance after receipt of further comments from the complainant does constitute a decision which is appealable.[53] Conversely, such a letter will constitute a definition of position within the meaning of Article 175 and thus the Commission cannot be reviewed before the Court of Justice for its failure to act.[54]

If the Commission decides to pursue the complaint, the Commission will then inform the undertakings concerned of the objections raised against them. This procedure then becomes that for taking an adverse decision.[55] If the complainant has "sufficient interest", the complainant may then expand upon its application and, has the right to apply to put

[48] Cases 24 & 28/90, *Automec Srl v. E.C. Commission (No. 2)* [1992] 5 C.M.L.R. 431, (CFI). See also Commission's position as stated in *Notice on Cooperation between national courts and the Commission in applying Article 85 and 86 of the EEC Treaty* [1993] O.J. C 39/05 at paras. 13–16.

[49] Case 24 & 28/90, *Automec Srl v. E.C. Commission (No. 2)*: [1992] II E.C.R. 2223, [1992] S.C.M.L.R. 431, at para. 86.

[50] *ibid*, paras. 87–98.

[51] Reg. 99/62, Art. 6.

[52] Case 43/85, *ANCIDES v. Commission* [1987] E.C.R. 3131, [1988] 4 C.M.L.R. 821.

[53] See Cases 142 & 156/84, *BAT & Reynolds v. E.C. Commission* [1987] E.C.R. 4487, [1988] 4 C.M.L.R. 24, ECJ; Case 210/81, *Demo-Studio Schmidt v. E.C. Commission* [1983] E.C.R. 65, [1984] 1 C.M.L.R. 63.

[54] Case 125/78, *GEMA v. E.C. Commission* [1979] E.C.R. 3173 [1980] 2 C.M.L.R. 177, (ECJ).

[55] See para. 12.052.

its arguments.[56] In practice, the complainant is provided with the substance of the replies and observations regarding the complaint.[57]

10. Interim relief

12.057 Whilst Regulation 17 does not specifically empower the Commission to make interim orders against parties who are subject to Regulation 17 proceedings, the Court of Justice has held that under Article 3 of Regulation 17, the Commission has the power to order such relief.[58] A decision granting interim relief can only be made when it is shown that: (i) the need for such an order is urgent; (ii) the acts complained of are likely to cause serious and irreparable damage; or (iii) the behaviour complained of is intolerable to the public.[59] Damage which is purely financial is not serious and irreparable for the purposes of interim measures unless in the event of success in the main action, it cannot be recouped.[60]

The relief ordered must be temporary and conservatory and restricted to what is required.[61] The Commission has said that such an order must not exceed the framework of the Commission's powers to make such an order in a final decision.[62] The party requesting interim measures may be required to give a cross-undertaking as to damages to the party against which interim measures are sought if at a later stage that the latter party was found not to infringe Article 85 or 86.

As an order granting interim relief is an order under Article 3, Regulation 17, the Commission must give those undertakings affected by the decision the opportunity of being heard.[63] In practice, a shortened form of the Regulation 99/63 procedure for taking an adverse decision is followed. The Commission has considerable discretion as to whether or not to grant interim relief and the CFI will be reluctant to interfere in the exercise of that discretion.[64]

[56] Reg. 99, Arts. 5, 7. It is unlikely that a party which has a legitimate interest within the meaning of Reg. 17, Art. 3(1) does not have sufficient interest. On the other hand, the Commission may have acted upon its own initiative after receiving the complaint in which case the question as to whether the complainant has a legitimate interest becomes academic. In such case, the question as to what amounts to "sufficient interest" becomes pertinent.

[57] *13th Annual Report on Competition Policy,* para. 74. Difficulties may arise on the disclosure of business secrets and commercially sensitive information, see Case 53/85, *AKZO v. E.C. Commission* [1986] E.C.R. 1965, [1987] 1 C.M.L.R. 231.

[58] Case 792/79R, *Camera Care v. E.C. Commission* [1980] E.C.R. 119, 131, [1980] 1 C.M.L.R. 334.

[59] *ibid.*

[60] Case 229/88R, *Cargill v. E.C. Commission* [1989] 1 C.M.L.R. 304, (ECJ).

[61] *ibid.*

[62] *Brass Band Instruments v. Boosey & Hawkes plc* [1987] O.J. L286/36, [1986] 4 C.M.L.R. 67.

[63] Reg. 17, Art. 19(1); Case 792/79R, *Camera Care v. E.C. Commission* [1980] E.C.R. 119, 131, [1980] 1 C.M.L.R. 334.

[64] Case T–131/89R, *Cosimex v. E.C. Commission* [1990] II E.C.R. 1, [1992] 4 C.M.L.R. 395.

11. Judicial review of commission

(a) Introduction

12.058 Acts of the Commission may be subject to judicial challenge by the Court of Justice and the Court of First Instance. A decision of the Commission may be challenged by way of judicial review under Article 173. Furthermore, the Court under Article 172 has unlimited jurisdiction with regard to penalties imposed by the Commission. Article 175 makes the Commission liable to judicial review where it fails to act in infringement of the Treaty of Rome.[65]

Any review of the Commission's decision will usually lie to the Court of First Instance. It has jurisdiction in the following circumstances:

(i) to annul decisions of the Commission imposing fines and cease and desist orders;
(ii) Application by parties to annul conditions imposed in decisions otherwise favourable to them;
(iii) Application by parties to annul decision favourable to third parties;
(iv) The rejection of complaints by the Commission;
(v) The Commission's failure to act under Article 175.

(b) Article 173

12.059 Under Article 173 of the Treaty of Rome, the Court can review the legality of acts of the Council and the Commission other than recommendations or opinions. Any natural or legal person may review the decision of the Commission which is addressed to him or is of direct and individual concern to it.

The Court may review a decision on the grounds of lack of competence, infringement of an essential procedural requirement, infringement of the Treaty of Rome or of any rule relating to its application or misuse of powers.[66] Thus, the appeal is by way of judicial review and not a rehearing.

(i) Direct and individual concern

12.060 Where a decision of the Commission is addressed to the applicant for judicial review, he has the right of appeal. If it is not addressed to the appellant, he must demonstrate that it is of "direct and individual concern" to him. The Court of Justice has held that a complainant with a legitimate interest under Article 3 of Regulation 17 may appeal to the European Court. The ECJ has said that:

> "The Court has consistently held that persons other than those to whom a decision is addressed may claim to be concerned within the

[65] For a general discussion as to Art. 173 & Art. 175, see para. 1.028 to 1.031.
[66] Treaty of Rome, Art. 173(1).

> meaning of Article 173(2) only if that decision affects them by reason of certain attributes which are peculiar to them, or by reason of circumstances in which they are differentiated from all other person, and by virtue of these factors distinguishes them individually just as in the case of the person addressed."[67]

(ii) Decision?

12.061 Where it is expressly provided for by Community legislation that a particular act must be made by a decision of the Community, then such will be capable of appeal. Thus, in Regulation 17, the following are expressly stated to be decisions: "cease and desist" orders, grants of exemption, fixings of a period of prohibition for "old" and "accession" agreements under Article 7, orders that information be supplied under Article 11(5), orders that undertakings shall submit to an investigation under Article 14(3) and orders imposing a fine or periodic penalty payments on an undertaking. Furthermore, orders under Article 15(6) removing an undertakings's interim protection from fines for a notified agreement constitutes a "decision";[68] decisions refusing to grant an interim order;[69] decisions granting an interim order[70] and a letter formally rejecting a complaint after the complainant has made further submissions pursuant to Article 6, Regulation 99,[71] have been held by the Court of Justice to constitute a decision within the meaning of Article 173.

The ECJ has said that where "a measure has affected the interests of the undertakings by bringing a distinct alteration to their legal position", such is to be deemed a decision.[72] The ECJ refined this doctrine in *IBM v. E.C. Commission*.[73] In relation to whether the initiation of a procedure by the Commission under Regulation 17 and the issue of a Statement of Objections constituted a "decision" under Article 173, the ECJ said after confirming the general rule outlined above:

> "In the case of acts or decision adopted by a procedure involving several stages, in particular where they are the culmination of an internal procedure, it is clear from the case law that in principle an act is open to review only if it is a measure definitively laying down

[67] Case 75/84, *Metro-SB-Grossmarkte v. E.C. Commission* [1986] E.C.R. 3021, [1987] 1 C.M.L.R. 118, at para. 20.

[68] Case 47/76, *De Norre v. Brouwerij Concord* [1977] E.C.R. 65, [1977] 1 C.M.L.R. 378.

[69] Case 792/79R, *Camera Care v. E.C. Commission* [1980] E.C.R. 119, 131, [1980] 1 C.M.L.R. 334. However, see Case T–131/89R, *Cosimex v. E.C. Commission* [1990] II E.C.R. 1 [1992] 4 C.M.L.R. 395.

[70] Case 2228, etc., *Ford v. E.C. Commission (No. 1)* [1984] E.C.R. 1129, [1984] 1 C.M.L.R. 649.

[71] Case 298/83, *CICCE v. E.C. Commission* [1985] E.C.R. 1105, [1986] 1 C.M.L.R. 486. However the original letter sent under Art. 6 is not a decision as it does not definitively lay down the position of the Commission—see A.-G. in *CICCE* and see also Case T–64/89, *Automec Srl v. E.C. Commission* [1991] 4 C.M.L.R. 177, (CFI).

[72] Case 8–11/66, *Re Noordwijks Cement Accoord* [1967] E.C.R. 75, [1967] C.M.L.R. 77, (ECJ).

[73] Case 60/81, *IBM v. E.C. Commission* [1981] E.C.R. 2639, [1981] 3 C.M.L.R. 635.

the position of the Commission or the Council on the conclusion of that procedure, and not a provisional measure intended to pave the way for the final decision."[74]

The final decision must be capable of altering the provisional step. Thus the Court in *IBM v. E.C. Commission* held that where a decision was taken in the course of proceedings, it would amount to a decision if it was the "culmination of a special procedure distinct from that intended to permit the Commission or the Council to take a decision on the substance of the case".[75]

12.062 *Comfort Letters*—The question as to whether a comfort letter constitutes a decision capable of judicial review is not clear. Firstly, such a letter does not amount to a decision under Article 2 or 6 of Regulation 17 whereby negative clearance or exemption is granted.[76] Recently, the CFI has ruled that a letter from the Commission stating that it does not consider that an agreement falls within Article 85(1) and was unexemptible was not a decision as the facts and circumstances implied that the Commission was still examining the file.[77] Where the letter informs the parties that the Commission is not intending to take action, a third party may wish to appeal the comfort letter. In such circumstances, does the letter "definitively lay down the position of the Commission"? As such letters usually say that the Commission intends to take no further action, such may be the position. Generally speaking, the third party should complain under Article 3 and, if his complaint is rejected under Article 6 of Regulation 99, he may appeal to the CFI or ECJ.[78]

(iii) Grounds for review

12.063 The four categories in Article 173 which allows the CFI or ECJ to review a decision of the Commission have been set out above. A full review of these grounds are outside the scope of this book.

The four grounds for review in Article 173 overlap considerably and provide a broad basis on which to review a decision of the Commission. As Article 173 merely empowers the ECJ to judicially review the Commission's decision, the Court will not approach the matter as a rehearing. However, the CFI has shown that it is prepared to examine in detail evidence used by the Commission in reaching its decision and will check

[74] *ibid.* para. 10.

[75] *ibid*, para. 11. This thus confirms the validity of the decision in Case 8–11/66, *Re Noordwijks Cement Accoord* [1967] E.C.R. 75, [1967] C.M.L.R.77, (ECJ) that a decision under Art. 15(6) of Reg. 17/62 ("discomfort" letter) is a decision reviewable under Art. 173, as such is a special procedure designed to be final.

[76] See Case 253/78, *Procureur de la Republique v. Giry et Guerlain* [1980] E.C.R. 2327, [1981] 2 C.M.L.R. 99 and para. 12.024.

[77] *Nefarma v. E.C. Commission,* December 13, 1990 as yet unreported, CFI.

[78] Case 298/83, *CICCE v. E.C. Commission* [1985] E.C.R. 1105, [1986] 1 C.M.L.R. 486. See para. 12.056.

meticulously the nature and import of such evidence that is taken into consideration by the Commission.[79]

The ECJ have found there to be good grounds for review where the Commission has afforded the concerned undertakings a right to be heard;[80] failed to give adequate reasoning;[81] made an error of law[82] or where the facts as established are not capable of supporting the Commission's decision.[83] It would seem that failure by the Commission to observe any of the procedural requirements in Regulation 17 or 99 would amount to an infringement of an essential procedural requirement.[84]

(c) Article 175

12.064 Where the Commission has failed to address an act to a natural or legal person and such constitutes an infringement of the Treaty, he may bring an action before the Court to have it so established under Article 175.[85] However, he must first call upon the Commission to act. If the Commission fails to define its position within two months of being so called upon, the person may bring its action within a further period of two months. In *GEMA v. E.C. Commission*,[86] the Court held that a letter under Article 6 of Regulation 99 which informed a complainant that there were insufficient grounds for granting its application and giving it a time limit to submit further observations, constituted a definition of position within Article 175 and thus was there were no grounds to review the Commission's failure to act.[87]

There is little case law on the effect of Article 175. Is it appropriate to use Article 175 where the Commission is guilty of inordinate delay in issuing a decision under Regulation 17 granting exemption or negative clearance? Can a concerned undertaking use the procedure under Article 175 to force the Commission to act?

Firstly, Article 175 merely refers to infringement of the Treaty and not its secondary legislation. It is unclear as to whether this refers to infringements of basic rights under the Treaty like the right to a decision within a

[79] Case 89/93, *Re Italian Flat Glass v. E.C. Commission* [1990] 4 C.M.L.R. 535, at para. 95.

[80] Case 100/80, *Musique Diffusion Francaise v. E.C. Commission* [1983] E.C.R. 1825, [1983] 3 C.M.L.R. 221.

[81] Case 8–11/66, *Re Noordwijks Cement Accoord* [1967] E.C.R. 75, [1967] C.M.L.R. 77, (ECJ); *Remia v. E.C. Commission* [1985] E.C.R. 2547; [1987] 1 C.M.L.R. 1. Art. 190 of the Treaty of Rome stipulates that decisions must be reasoned.

[82] Case 4/73, *Suiker Unie v. E.C. Commission* [1975] E.C.R. 1663, [1976] 1 C.M.L.R. 295.

[83] *SABAM* [1977] E.C.R. 1875.

[84] A. G. Gand in Case 41/69, *ACF Chemiefarma v. E.C. Commission* [1970] E.C.R. 661, considered that a failure by the Commission to consult the Advisory Committee on Restrictive Practices and Monopolies pursuant to Art. 10 of Reg. 17 would justify annulment of its decision.

[85] For general discussion as to Art. 175, see para. 1.030.

[86] Case 125/78, *GEMA v. E.C. Commission* [1979] E.C.R. 3173 [1980] 2 C.M.L.R. 177.

[87] If after further submissions, the Commission maintains its position, this is a decision capable of review under Art. 173—*CICCE v. E.C. Commission* [1985] E.C.R. 1105, [1986] 1 C.M.L.R. 486.

reasonable period of time.[88] Secondly, the Commission merely has to define its position. In such circumstances, it may issue a comfort letter saying it does not intend to take any action under Articles 85 or 86. Such would probably constitute a definition of position within Article 175 but might be appealable as a decision under Article 173.[89] Furthermore, would a communication to the effect that it is investigating the matter constitute a definition of position within Article 175? This has yet to be resolved by the European Court.

The problem is compounded by the fact that a decision of negative clearance under Article 2, Regulation 17 and the grant of exemption under Article 85(3) are discretionary and not compulsory. Thus, the Commission is not required under the Treaty or any secondary legislation to make such decision and thus could be said not to have infringed the Treaty.[90]

(d) Article 175 and 173

12.065 Ideally, Articles 173 and 175 should complement each other. The ECJ's definition of what amounts to a decision within Article 173 being "an act which definitively lays down the position of the Commission" closely mirrors the "definition of position" provision in Article 175.[91] Thus, one may be advised to apply under both Article 173 and 175 if there is doubt as to whether or not an act of the Commission amounts to a definition of position. However, the requirements for Article 173 and 175 differ (principally in that the failure to act under Article 175 must be an infringement of the Treaty) and it has been held that a definition of position under Article 175 is not necessarily reviewable under Article 173.[92]

(e) Article 172

Under Article 172, the Court can review de novo matters of fact and law in relation to the imposition of fines or periodic penalty payments.[93]

12. National Courts and Article 85 and 86

(a) Civil proceedings in national court without concurrent proceedings before the Commission

12.066 Private individuals can rely upon Article 85 and 86 in proceedings in national courts in Member State. The Court of Justice has repeatedly held that both Article 85(1) and 86 have direct effect and thus can be

[88] This would be especially so where an application for exemption has been made as only the Commission may grant exemption.

[89] See Comfort letters and Article 173, para. 12.062.

[90] See also Case 125/78, *GEMA v. E.C. Commission* [1979] E.C.R. 3173, [1980] 2 C.M.L.R. 177.

[91] See Case 608/81, *IBM v. E.C. Commission* [1981] E.C.R. 2639, [1981] 3 C.M.L.R. 635.

[92] See Case 48/65, *Lutticke v. E.C. Commission* [1966] E.C.R. 19, [1966] C.M.L.R. 378.

[93] Art. 172 of the Treaty of Rome; Reg. 17, Art. 17.

relied upon in civil proceedings.[94] Thus any legal person may rely upon them in any action in a national court. A national court has the jurisdiction to find that the agreement is void under Article 85(2) or that anti-competitive behaviour is prohibited under Article 86.

Where an agreement has not been notified to the Commission, a court need not concern itself whether the agreement is capable of being individually exempted.[95] A court itself is not competent to exempt an agreement.[96] However, a national court is competent to rule on the question as to whether or not an agreement which falls within Article 85(1) is covered by a block exemption.[97] Agreement which fall within the scope of a block exemption are automatically exempted without the need for a Commission decision or comfort letter.[98]

(b) Concurrent proceedings in national court and before the Commission

12.067 In many cases, there will be concurrent proceedings in the national courts and before the Commission. There are several reasons for this. Firstly, if the validity of an agreement is disputed under Article 85(1), a party to the proceedings may have notified the agreement to the Commission for negative clearance or exemption. As only the Commission can grant exemption, it will often be imperative that the party relying on the validity of the agreement has notified it. Secondly, a party which is the victim of anti-competitive practices may have already complained to the Commission. The merits of bringing an action in a national court and/or before the Commission and the relationship between the enforcement of Article 85 and 85 by the Commission and national courts has already been discussed.[99]

[94] Case 127/73, *BRT v. SABAM* [1974] E.C.R. 51, [1974] 2 C.M.L.R. 238. Case T–51/89*Tetra Pak Rausing SA v. E.C. Commission* [1991] 4 C.M.L.R. 334; *Delimitis v. Henninger Brau* [1991] 4 C.M.L.R. 329, (ECJ). In England, see *Garden Cottage Foods v. Milk Marketing Board* [1984] A.C. 130; [1983] 3 C.M.L.R. 43, [1984] F.S.R. 23, H.L.

[95] Reg. 17, Art. 9; *Notice on Co-operation between national courts and the Commission in applying Article 85 and 86 of the EEC Treaty* [1993] O.J. C 39/05, at para. 28.

[96] Reg. 17, Art. 9(1). Ironically, the Commission favours giving national courts the jurisdiction to determine whether an agreement falls within Art. 85(3) when Community law and practice is absolutely clear on the point. See Commission's submissions in Case 47/76, *De Norre v. Brouwerij Concordia* [1977] E.C.R. 65, [1977] 1 C.M.L.R. 378 and *Procureur de la Republique v. Giry et Guerlain* [1980] E.C.R. 2327, [1981] 2 C.M.L.R. 99. As there is a discretion in Art. 85(3)as whether to grant exemption even if the conditions in Art. 85(3) are fulfilled, it does not seem arguable that Art. 85(3) has direct effect and thus cannot be relied upon in a national court by an individual.

[97] Case C–234/89, *Delimitis v. Henninger Brau* [1991] 1 E.C.R. 935 [1991] 4 CMLR 329, (ECJ); Case 63/75, *Roubaix v. Fonderies Roux* [1976] E.C.R. 111 [1976] C.M.L.R. 531, Case 59/77, *De Norre v. Brouwerij Concordia* [1977] E.C.R. 65, [1977] 1 C.M.L.R. 378; *de Bloos v. Bouyer* [1978] E.C.R. 2359, [1978] 1 C.M.L.R. D52; Case 170/83, *Hydrotherm v. Compact.*[1984] E.C.R. 2999, [1985] 3 C.M.L.R. 276; in England, see *Cutsforth v. Mansfield Inns* [1986] 1 W.L.R. 558, 1 All E.R. 577.

[98] *Notice on Co-operation between national courts and the Commission in applying Article 85 and 86 of the EEC Treaty* [1993] O.J. C 39/05 at para. 26.

[99] See para. 12.003 *et seq.*

(i) Proceedings in national court and before the Commission: agreement not notified

12.068 Where it is alleged that an agreement or behaviour of a party is anti-competitive in civil proceedings, it is often the case that proceedings before the Commission have also been initiated whether by way of formal complaint or the Commission on its own initiative launching an investigation. If the agreement had not been notified for exemption at the relevant date for the purpose of the civil proceedings, then the issue of exemption is irrelevant.

In such circumstances, if invited to do so by a party to the proceedings, the national courts should consider the application of Article 85(1) and 86 but must, when exercising its powers, take account of the Commission's powers and try and avoid a decision which could conflict with that taken by the Commission.[1] In order to comply with this requirement, the national court should ascertain whether the agreement has already been the subject of a decision, opinion or other official statement issued by an administrative authority and in particular by the Commission.[2] If the Commission has not ruled on the agreement, the national court should be guided by the case law of the ECJ, CFI and the Commission. If it forms the opinion that the agreement clearly falls within Article 85(1), it should take the appropriate measures including those relating to the consequences that attach to infringement of a statutory prohibition under the relevant civil law.[3] If the Commission has initiated a procedure in a case relating to the same conduct, they may seek to stay the proceedings until the outcome of the Commission' action.[4] If the national court wishes to consult the Commission on questions of procedure, law or wishes to make a request for legal and factual information, it may do so and stay proceedings.[5]

Finally, it should be noted that once the Commission has initiated a procedure into alleged anti-competitive behaviour of an undertaking, specialist competition law tribunals no longer remain competent to apply Article 85(1) and 86 in relation to such behaviour.[6]

[1] *Notice on Co-operation between national courts and the Commission in applying Article 85 and 86 of the EEC Treaty* [1993] O.J. C 39/05 at para. 17; Case C–234/89, *Delimitis v. Henninger Brau* [1991] I E.C.R. 935, [1992] 5 C.M.L.R. 210 at para. 47. A decision of a national court does not overrule a decision of the Commission and vice versa—they are independent jurisdictions. However, it is clearly undesirable to have conflicting judgments.

[2] *Notice on Co-operation between national courts and the Commission in applying Article 85 and 86 of the EEC Treaty* [1993] O.J. C 39/05 at para. 20. This includes "comfort letters"—see Case 99/79, *Lancome v. Etos* [1980] E.C.R. 2511, [1981] 2 C.M.L.R. 164.

[3] *Notice on Co-operation between national courts and the Commission in applying Articles 85 and 86 of the EEC Treaty* [1993] O.J. C 39/05, at para. 23.

[4] *ibid*, para. 22.

[5] *ibid*, para. 22 and 33 *et seq*.

[6] Reg. 17/62, Art. 9(3), Case 127/73, *BRT v. SABAM* [1974] E.C.R. 51, [1974] 2 C.M.L.R. 238 (which held that "authorities" in this Article did not include ordinary national courts).

(ii) Proceedings in national court and before Commission: agreement notified to Commission

12.069 Where there are concurrent proceedings before a national court and the Commission, the legal situation becomes more complex if the agreement has been notified to the Commission pursuant to Regulation 17 for negative clearance and/or exemption. The validity of an agreement under Community law depends on whether the agreement is a "new", "old", "accession", "Article 4(2)" or an agreement notified under the opposition procedure of a block exemption. In the latter four cases, the national court may be required to regard the agreement as valid if the Commission has not reached a decision.

(a) "New" agreements

As discussed earlier, a new agreement is an agreement which is defined as having come into existence after the entry of Regulation 17/62 or, if the agreement becomes subject to Article 85 or 86 due to the accession of a Member State, after the date of accession to the EEC by the relevant Member States. It does not include agreements falling within Article 4(2) of Regulation 17 which are exempted from notification.

Where a "new" agreement has been notified for negative clearance or exemption to the Commission but no decision has been made with regard to exemption,[7] a national court is still under a duty to determine whether the agreement is void under Article 85(2).[8] If a "new" agreement has merely been notified for negative clearance, then the court's position is the same as where the agreement has not been notified. Thus, a court's decision is not affected by the Commission's finding because a "negative clearance" decision by the Commission that an agreement does not infringe Article 85(1) is not binding on a national court.[9] However, it should endeavour to avoid reaching a contrary finding to that of the Commission and may seek to stay proceedings until the Commission has reached its decision.

Where the agreement has been notified for negative clearance and exemption (which will invariably be the case), greater difficulties arise because of the sole power of the Commission to retroactively exempt a "new" agreement from the date of notification.[10] In such circumstances, there is an overlap of jurisdiction between the national court and the Commission because a court's finding that the agreement is void under Article 85(2) will be rendered null and void by a grant of exemption by a Commission where the relevant date of exemption predates the relevant

[7] A "comfort letter" stating that the Commission does not intend to take any further action as it considers that the agreement merits exemption is not a "decision in application of Art. 85(3)" as set out in Reg. 17, Art. 8. See para. 12.024.

[8] Case 127/73. *BRT v. SABAM* [1974] E.C.R. 51, [1974] 2 C.M.L.R. 238; Case 48/72, *Brasserie de Haecht v. Wilkin (No. 2)* [1973] E.C.R. 77, [1973] E.C.R. 287; Case 37/79, *Marty v. Lauder* [1980] E.C.R. 2481, [1981] 2 C.M.L.R. 143.

[9] *John Deere* [1985] O.J. L35/58, [1985] 2 C.M.L.R. 554.

[10] Reg. 17/62, Art. 9(1) [1995] 2 C.M.L.R. 437.

date for the purposes of the civil proceedings. Where the date of notification postdates the relevant date for the purposes of the civil proceedings, the national court is entitled to consider separately the matter before and after the date of notification.[11]

12.070 In such circumstances, the court has the power to stay proceedings until resolution of the question of exemption by the Commission where it considers it "necessary for reasons of legal certainty".[12] The Commission has recently issued guidelines as to what a national court should do. Firstly, it must examine whether the procedural conditions necessary for securing exemption are fulfilled. Then, it must consider the likelihood of exemption being granted. If it concludes that it is not possible that the Commission will grant exemption or that the agreement clearly falls outside Article 85(1), it must apply Article 85(1) and 85(2). If it concludes that there is a possibility of exemption, it should stay proceedings pending the Commission's decision on exemption.[13] The national court may ask the Commission for an interim opinion. If the Commission states that it is unlikely to grant exemption, national courts may waive a stay of proceedings and rule on the validity of the agreement.[14] If it needs any assistance from the Commission on legal, procedural or factual matters, it may request such help from the Commission.[15]

Where a "new" agreement is notified after the relevant date for the purposes of civil proceedings (*i.e.* the date of issue of writ) and it is clear that the agreement infringes Article 85(1), then it is submitted that a court should rarely stay proceedings as the Commission has only the power to exempt the agreement from the date of notification.

12.071 *Comfort letters and "new" agreements*—A "comfort letter" is not binding on a national court but a Court may take it into account in determining whether an agreement falls within Article 85(1) or outside Article 85(3).[16] A comfort letter does not constitute a decision granting negative clearance or exemption under Articles 2 and 6 of Regulation 17.[17] Comfort letters can indicate that the Commission considers that (i)

[11] As was done in *MTV Europe v. BMG and others* [1995] 1 C.M.L.R. 437 English High Court where Plaintiff sought summary judgment for damages for breach of Art. 85 against the Defendant up to the date of notification by the Defendant of their arrangements.

[12] Case 127/73, *BRT v. SABAM* [1974] E.C.R. 51, [1974] 2 C.M.L.R. 238 at para. 20.

[13] *Notice on Co-operation between national courts and the Commission in applying Article 85 and 86 of the EEC Treaty* [1993] O.J. C 39/05 at paras. 28–30. See also, *Delimitis v. Henninger Brau AG* [1991] ECR I–935, para. 50 and Case C–250/92 *Gottrup-Klin and ors v. Dansk Landbrugs* (unreported, 1994) at para. 58. In the latter case, the ECJ appear to treat the issue as one of jurisdiction. Thus, the national court only has jurisdiction to rule on the lawfulness of an agreement notified to the Commission where the conditions for application of Art. 85(1) are clearly not satisfied.

[14] *Notice on Co-operation between national courts and the Commission in applying Article 85 and 86 of the EEC Treaty* [1993] O.J. C 39/05, para. 38.

[15] *ibid*, paras. 37 *et seq.*

[16] Case 253/78, *Procureur de la Republique v. Giry et Guerlain* [1980] E.C.R. 2327 [1981] 2 C.M.L.R. 99; Case 37/79, *Marty v. Lauder* [1980] E.C.R. 2481, [1981] 2 C.M.L.R. 143; Case 31/80, *L'Oreal v. De Nieuwe* [1980] E.C.R. 3775, [1981] 2 C.M.L.R. 235.

[17] Case 31/80, *L'Oreal v. De Nieuwe* [1980] E.C.R. 3775, [1981] 2 C.M.L.R. 235.

the agreement falls outside Article 85(1)(ii) falls within Article 85(1) and (ii) is unexemptable or falls within Article 85(1) but merits exemption. In the first two cases, a court will be unlikely to stay proceedings. However, the third case may cause difficulties because, as stated, a comfort letter does not grant exemption for an agreement. This can cause problems for a national court because the Commission often terminates proceedings with a comfort letter. If such a letter indicates that the agreement falls within Article 85(1) but merits exemption under Article 85(3), then one must obtain a formal decision from the Commission pursuant to Article 8 of Regulation 17 in order for the agreement to be exempted. In such circumstances, the Commission has indicated that it will take an appropriate decision quickly.[18] It has been suggested that in such circumstances a national court may uphold the validity of an agreement on the basis that the agreement does not infringe Article 85 as a whole and that such a finding does not amount to granting an exemption.[19]

(b) "Old" and "accession" agreements: doctrine of provisional validity

12.072 "Old" agreements are those which existed at the time of entry of Regulation 17/62. "Accession" agreements are those agreements to which Article 85 applies by virtue of accession and existed at the time of accession.[20] Where "old" agreements were notified by at the latest February 1, 1963, the ECJ has held that such agreements must be treated as valid by national courts until a decision has been taken by the Commission.[21] This is called the doctrine of "provisional validity". Such agreements are provisionally valid until the Commission has made a decision pursuant to Regulation 17.[22]

"Accession" agreements would appear to be provisionally valid if they were notified within six months from the date of accession.[23] Thus, a national court is barred from finding that an "old" or "accession" agreement that has been properly notified pursuant to Regulation 17 is void

[18] See *Notice on Co-operation between national courts and the Commission in applying Article 85 and 86 of the EEC Treaty* [1993] O.J. C 39/05 at para. 37.

[19] See Stephen Kon 1982 Common Market Law Review p. 141 and Valentine Korah *Know-how Licensing Agreements and the EEC Competition Rules Regulation 556/89* at 1.1.1. (1989).

[20] See para 12.009 *et seq* above as to discussion as to the definitions of "old" and "accession" agreements.

[21] Case 10/69, *Portelange* [1969] E.C.R. 309 [1974] 1 C.M.L.R. 397, 418; Case 48/72, *Brasserie de Haecht v. Wilkin (No. 2)* [1973] E.C.R. 77, [1973] C.M.L.R. 287; Case 59/77, *de Bloos v. Bouyer* [1978] E.C.R. 2359, [1978] 1 C.M.L.R. 511. See also Notice on Co-operation between national courts and the Commission in applying Article 85 and 86 of the EEC Treaty [1993] C 39/05 at para. 31.

[22] See Art. 5 and 7 of Reg. 17 and the ECJ's judgment on the effect of such Articles in civil proceedings in Case 48/72, *Brasserie de Haecht v. Wilkin (No. 2)* [1973] E.C.R. 77, [1973] C.M.L.R. 287.

[23] See Reg. 17, Art. 25; Commission's statement in the *3rd Annual Report on Competition Policy* at para. 5 and Notice on Co-operation between national courts and the Commission in applying Article 85 and 86 of the EEC Treaty [1993] O.J. C 39/05 at para. 31. In England, see *Esso Petroleum v. Kingswood Motors* [1974] 1 Q.B. 142, H.C.

under Article 85(2) until the Commission has made a decision under Regulation 17.

A comfort letter which states that the Commission does not consider that the notified agreement comes within the prohibition of Article 85(1) will terminate the provisional validity accorded to "old" agreements (and presumably "accession" agreements).[24] Thus a court is competent to rule on the application of Article 85(1) once this has occurred. Difficulties may arise where the Commission's comfort letter states in closing its file, that in its opinion, the agreement falls within Article 85(3) but that there is no need for a formal decision. In such circumstances, the agreement is no longer provisionally valid but the Commission's opinion suggests that it might be void unless exempted. In such a case, it is suggested that the court stay the proceedings and ask the Commission for a speedy decision.[25]

It may be arguable that the doctrine of provisional validity applies even to "old" and "accession" agreements even if the agreements have not been notified according to Article 5 or Article 24 of Regulation 17.[26]

(c) Article 4(2) agreements

12.073 Agreements which fall within Article 4(2) of Regulation 17 are exempt from notification as they are generally considered not to be anti-competitive. However, only the Commission may grant exemption to such agreements. It would appear although it is not entirely clear that Article 4(2) agreements must be treated as provisionally valid until the Commission has made a decision on the agreement.[27] This is regardless of whether the agreement has actually been notified or not.[28] In English

[24] See Case 99/79, *Lancome v. Etos* [1981] E.C.R. 2511, [1981] 2 C.M.L.R. 164. See *Notice on Co-operation between national courts and the Commission in applying Article 85 and 86 of the EEC Treaty* [1993] O.J. C 39/05 at para. 31.

[25] See para. 37, *Notice on Co-operation between national courts and the Commission in applying Article 85 and 86 of the EEC Treaty* [1993] C 39/05.

[26] Para. 8 of the Court's decision in Case 48/72, *Brasserie de Haecht v. Wilkin (No. 2)* [1973] E.C.R. 77, [1973] C.M.L.R. 287 states that "As far as old agreements are concerned, certainty of law as regards contracts requires that a court cannot, *particularly when an agreement has been notified in accordance with Regulation 17*, establish nullity until after the Commission has made a decision under the regulation [emphasis added]." Such a statement implies that a national court should treat an unnotified agreement as valid until a contrary determination by the Commission. Such an interpretation is reinforced by the fact that the primary concern to the Court was the principle of certainty of law which applies regardless as to whether the "old" or "accession" agreements were notified or not. However, the ECJ in Case 59/77, *de Bloos v. Bouyer* [1978] E.C.R. 2359, [1978] 1 C.M.L.R. 511 suggests that the doctrine of provisional validity is derived from Arts. 5, 6 and 7 of Reg. 17/62 which require notification within certain time limits.

[27] Case 43/69, *Brauerei A. Bilger v. Jehle* [1970] E.C.R. 127, [1974] 1 C.M.L.R. 382 confirmed in Case 59/77, *de Bloos v. Bouyer* [1978] E.C.R. 2359, [1978] 1 C.M.L.R. 511. However, see para. 13 of Case 48/72, *Brasserie de Haecht v. Wilkin (No. 2)* [1973] E.C.R. 77, [1973] C.M.L.R. 287 where the ECJ states that a national court is under a duty to decide whether the agreement falls within Art. 85.

[28] See Case 43/69, *Brauerei A. Bilger v. Jehle* [1970] E.C.R. 127, [1974] 1 C.M.L.R. 382 at para. 12 and in the declaratory part of the judgment.

proceedings, it will be difficult to assert that a "new" Article 4(2) agreement is not provisionally valid.[29]

(d) Agreement notified under the opposition procedure

12.074 A national court is competent to decide whether an agreement falls within a block exemption.[30] It may apply the block exemption if it is clear that the agreement in every respect falls within the block exemption.[31]

Often, the agreement will prima facie fall within the block exemption but contain clauses restrictive of competition not listed in block exemption. In such circumstances, a party may seek to notify the agreement to the Commission under the opposition procedure contained in the relevant block exemption. This procedure provides that where an agreement has been notified under the opposition procedure, then provided the Commission does not object within six months from the date of notification, the agreement is to be treated as covered by the Block Exemption. Where an agreement has been notified under the opposition procedure of a block exemption but the six month period has not expired,[32] is the agreement provisionally valid in civil proceedings in a national court? The agreement can be described as subject to a condition subsequent. In English law, such agreements are considered valid until the condition subsequent is fulfilled.[33]

Such an agreement may be subject to the Community law principle of provisional validity? The reason for conferring provisional validity on "old" or "accession" agreements was that the principle of legal certainty required such agreements to be considered valid because when the undertakings concerned entered into the agreements Articles 85 and 86 were inapplicable. Such considerations do not apply to agreements notified under the opposition procedure. In these circumstances, it is submitted that a court should stay the proceedings until the expiry of the six month period for the purposes of legal certainty.[34] If the Commission does raise an objection, then the national court should apply the same principles as

[29] In *Esso Petroleum v. Kingswood Motors* [1974] 1 Q.B. 142, a decision by Bridge J. considered both *Bilger Jehle* and *Brasserie de Haecht v. Wilkin (No. 2)* in relation to an "accession" Art. 4(2) agreement. He followed *Bilger Jehle* and found that a 4(2) agreement was provisionally valid. He also held that as the agreement was an "accession" agreement, it was provisionally valid by virtue of the rule in *Brasserie (No. 2)*. His following of the rule in *Bilger/Jehle* was not dependent upon the fact that the agreement in casu was an "accession" agreement. Thus, it may be difficult to argue in an English court that a 4(2) agreement is not provisionally valid.

[30] *Notice on Co-operation between national courts and the Commission in applying Article 85 and 86 of the EEC Treaty* [1993] O.J. C 39/05, para. 26.

[31] Case C–234/89, *Delimitis v. Henninger Brau* [1991] I E.C.R. 935 [1991] 4 C.M.L.R. 329, E.C.J. at para. 55.

[32] See para. 12.018 above, for an explanation of opposition procedure and the relevant Block Exemptions.

[33] See para. 798 *Chitty on Contracts*, (26th ed.) para. 798. See *Head v. Tattersall* (1871) L.R. 7 Ex. 7. It appears that this is true in continental systems as it is derived from Roman law.

[34] On staying proceedings generally, see para. 12.090.

for agreements notified under regulation 17 for individual exemption as to whether or not to stay proceedings until a final decision by the Commission.[35]

(c) Consequences of finding of infringement of Article 85 or 86

12.075 This section considers the legal effect where a party successfully proves in civil proceedings that Article 85 or 86 has been infringed by another party. In some cases, the party may bring an action based upon an infringement of Article 85 or 86. In other cases, a defendant may seek to rely upon Article 85 or 86 as a defence to an action by another party.

(i) Article 85 and 86 as a Cause of Action

12.076 Whilst Article 85 and 86 prohibit certain forms of anti-competitive behaviour, it was less clear whether such behaviour could give rise to a cause of action against an offending party.[36] The ECJ had said that Article 85 and 86 creates direct rights in respect of individuals which the national courts must safeguard.[37] However, it said that national courts must be free to decide how those rights should be enforced. To this general principle, the ECJ has added two important qualifications to this rule. Firstly, the rights available for the enforcement of Article 85 and 86 must be as extensive as for similar rights existing at national law.[38] Secondly, the conditions for their application must not be less favourable then for similar claims under the national law.[39]

In *Garden Cottage Foods v. Milk Marketing Board*,[40] the House of Lords considered the question as how to categorise Article 85 and 86 for the purposes of civil proceedings in England. Lord Diplock said:

> "A breach of the duty imposed by Article 86 not to abuse a dominant position in the common market or in a substantial part of it, can thus be categorised in English law as a breach of statutory duty that is imposed not only for the purpose of promoting the general economic prosperity of the common market but also for the benefit of private individuals to whom loss or damage is caused by a breach of duty.

[35] Note that all opposition procedures provide that if the Commission maintains its opposition to an agreement notified under the opposition procedure of a block exemption, the notification is to be treated as having been converted into one made under Reg. 17.

[36] This question is often referred to whether Art. 85 and Art. 86 can be used as a "sword" as opposed to merely defensive, as a "shield".

[37] Case 127/73, *BRT v. SABAM* [1974] E.C.R. 51, [1974] 2 C.M.L.R. 238.

[38] Case 158/80, *Rewe v. Hauptsollamt Kiel* [1981] E.C.R. 1805; [1982] 1 C.M.L.R. 449.

[39] Case 199/82, *Amminnistrazione della Finance dello Stato v. San Giorgio* [1983] E.C.R. 3595; see also Case 33/76, *REWE v. Landwirtschaftkammer fur der Saarland* [1976] E.C.R. 1989 [1977] 1 C.M.L.R. 533; Case 45/76, *Comet v. Produktschap voor Siergewaassen* [1976] E.C.R. 2043; [1477] 1 C.M.L.R.; Case 68/74 *Just v. Ministry for Fiscal Affairs* [1980] E.C.R. 501 [1981] 2 C.M.L.R. 714; [1977] 1 C.M.L.R. 533 *Amminnistrazione della Finance dello Stato v. MIRECO* [1980] E.C.R. 2559.

[40] [1984] A.C. 130; [1983] 3 C.M.L.R. 43; [1984] F.S.R. 23.

> If this categorisation be correct, and I can see none other that would be capable of giving rise to a civil cause of action in English private law on the part of a private individual who sustained loss or damage by reason of a breach of a directly applicable provision of the Treaty of Rome, the nature of the cause of action cannot, in my view, be affected by the fact that the legislative provision by which the duty is imposed takes the negative form of a prohibition of particular kinds of conduct rather than the positive form of an obligation to do particular acts."[41]

Thus the House of Lords held that damages were available as a remedy for a breach of Article 86.[42]

The House of Lords did not consider in *Garden Cottage* whether Article 85 as opposed to Article 86 gave rise to a statutory duty. There seems no particular reason to distinguish between the two. Both Article 85(1) and 86 prohibit certain anti-competitive behaviour. However, the matter is complicated by the fact that agreements under Article 85 are void and probably illegal under English law. A party cannot bring an action under English law based on an illegal agreement and is deprived of any contractual remedy it might have due to the doctrine of *ex turpi causa non oritur actio*.[43] This problem is discussed below in relation to an action for an action for damages.

Injunctions

12.077 It is well settled law that injunctive relief can be obtained for breaches of Article 85 and 86.[44] The cases which establish this have concerned the granting of interlocutory relief although there is no reason to doubt that the courts would treat the grant of a permanent injunction any differently. An injunction will have to be precise as to what behaviour is prohibited and this may cause problems for the court.[45]

Damages

12.078 The House of Lords in *Garden Cottage* ruled that damages were recoverable in an action for breach of Article 86.[46] Prima facie, there appears no reason why a plaintiff should not be able to recover damages for breach of Article 85. However, a difficulty may arise in this situation.

[41] [1984] A.C. 130, 141.

[42] The appeal concerned the grant of an interlocutory injunction rather than the final trial. Lord Diplock casts doubt on the doctrine that Art. 85 and 86 gave rise to new torts as stated by Lord Denning in *Application des Gaz SA v. Falks Veritas Ltd* [1974] Ch. 381 C.A. and Lord Roskill's *obiter dicta* in *Valor International Ltd v. Application des Gaz Sa* [1978] 3 C.M.L.R. 87 C.A.

[43] See *Chitty on Contracts*, (26th ed.) Chap. 6.

[44] See *Garden Cottage Foods v. Milk Marketing Board* [1984] A.C. 130; [1983] 3 C.M.L.R. 43; [1984] F.S.R. 27; *Cutsforth v. Mansfield Inns* [1986] 1 W.L.R. 558, 1 All E.R. 577; *Holleran v. Thwaites* [1989] 2 C.M.L.R. 917, (CLD.).

[45] See *Gordon Cottage Foods v. Milk Marketing Board* [1984] A.C. 130.

[46] However, the case was an appeal from an interlocutory decision and accordingly, full argument on this issue was not given.

Article 85(2) deems agreements prohibited under Article 85(1) as void. In England, it has been held that the privilege of self-incrimination applies to actions under Article 85 and 86 as the party concerned may be exposed to penalties under Regulation 17.[47] In such circumstances, the principle of *ex turpi causa non oritur actio* would apply and prevent the plaintiff from being able to directly enforce an illegal contract.[48] However, the English courts have mitigated the severity of this doctrine by not prohibiting causes of action which are collateral to the contract.[49] It is submitted that where a plaintiff is alleging an infringement of Article 85 in relation to a contract to which he is a party to, he is not seeking to enforce the contract but suing for breach of a statutory duty imposed by Article 85(1) in relation to the contract. Such is a collateral action on the contract and would thus be permissible.

Recovery of monies

12.079 A party to a contract found to be void under Article 85(2) may wish to recover monies paid pursuant to the void contract. Under English law, recovery of monies paid under an illegal contract are irrecoverable.[50] However, this rule may be found not to apply to agreements found void under Article 85(2). Firstly, a claim for recovery of monies may be "disguised" as a claim for damages for breach of a statutory duty.[51] Secondly, the ECJ has said, in the context of health inspection charges levied contrary to Community law, that any requirement of proof which has the effect of making it virtually impossible or excessively difficult to secure repayment of charges levied contrary to Community law would be incompatible with Community law.[52] By analogy, it is submitted that any requirement of substantive national law which prevents the repayment of monies under a contract void pursuant to Article 85(2) is incompatible with Community law.

Furthermore, it may be that the parties are not *in pari delicto* (*i.e.* whereby each party is as guilty as the other). In such circumstances, the weak party may recover monies paid under an illegal contract.[53] Thus, the imposition of an anti-competitive standard term contract on a weak economic undertaking may mean that the latter may recover monies paid under the contract.

[47] See *Rio Tinto Zinc Corporation v. Westinghouse Electric Corporation* [1978] 1 All E.R. 434, H.L. [1977] 3 All E.R. 703. The recent decision of the ECJ in *Otto BV v. Postbank NV* (unreported judgment) casts doubt on whether a party can claim the priviledge of self-incrimination in national proceedings in relation to the production of documents which might expose it to fines under Arts. 85 or 86. See section on Discovery and Self-incrimination para. 12.089, below.

[48] See s. 1257 of *Chitty on Contracts* (26th ed.).

[49] See *ibid*, s. 1267.

[50] See Goff and Jones, *Law of Restitution* (1986, 3rd Ed.).

[51] See para. 12.108.

[52] Case 199/82, *Amminnistrazione dell Finance dello Stato v. San Giorgio* [1983] E.C.R. 3595, 3613.

[53] See *Browning v. Morris* (1778) 2 Cowp. 790 and Chap. 16, N. 26, p. 1272, in *Chitty on Contracts* (26th ed.).

(ii) Article 85 as a defence

12.080 Where a plaintiff brings an action based upon an agreement which a court finds infringes Article 85, then the agreement is void under Article 85(2). However, what is the position in English law with regard to the validity of the whole contract?

Article 85(2) provides that "any agreements or decisions prohibited pursuant to this Article shall automatically be null and void". A finding of nullity is retrospective and thus any agreement is unenforceable. However, in *Technique Miniere v. Maschinenbau Ulm*,[54] the ECJ held that a finding of nullity only applies to "those elements of the agreement which are subject to the prohibition, or to the agreement as a whole if those elements do not appear severable from the agreement itself".[55] In the operative part of the decision, it said that the consequences of nullity on those contractual provisions which are not incompatible with Article 85(1) are not the concern of Community law.

The effect of Article 85(2) on agreements governed by English law has been discussed in *Chemidus Wavin Ltd v. TERI*.[56] In an important judgment, Buckley L.J. in the Court of Appeal said:

> "So the position appears clearly to be this, that where in a contract there are certain clauses which are annulled by reason of their being in contravention of Article 85, paragraph (1), of the Treaty, one must look at the contract with those clauses struck out and see what the effect of that is in the light of the domestic law which governs the particular contract. In the present case, we have to consider what effect the invalidity, if any, of the clauses in the licences agreement by reason of Article 85 would have upon that contract as a whole. Whether it is right to regard the matter as one of severance of the contract or not, I do not think it is necessary for us to consider now. I doubt whether it is really a question of severance in the sense in which we in these courts are accustomed to use that term on considering whether covenants contained in contracts of employment and so forth are void as being in restraint of trade, and if they are to any extent void, whether those covenants can be severed so as to save part of the covenant, although another part may be bad. It seems to me that in applying Article 85 to an English contract, one may well have to consider whether, after the excisions required by the Article of the Treaty have been made from the contract, the contract could be said to fail for lack of consideration or on any other ground, or whether the contract would be so changed in its charac-

[54] Case [1966] E.C.R. 235, [1966] C.M.L.R. 357. See also Case 319/82, *Societe de Vente de Ciments et Betons de l'Est v. Kerpen and Kerpen* [1983] E.C.R. 4173, [1985] 1 C.M.L.R. 511.

[55] Case 56/65, *Technique Miniere v. Maschinenbau Ulm* [1966] E.C.R. 235, [1966] C.M.L.R. 357.

[56] [1976] 2 C.M.L.R. 387, H.C., [1978] 3 C.M.L.R. 514, C.A.

ter as not to be the sort if contract that the parties intended to enter into at all."[57]

Goff L.J. gave a concurring judgment. He endorsed Salter J.'s judgment in *Putsnam v. Taylor*[58] that:

> "If a promisee claims the enforcement of a promise, and the promise is a valid promise and supported by consideration, the court will enforce the promise, notwithstanding the fact that the promisor has made other promises, supported by the same consideration, which are void, and has included the valid and invalid promises in one document."

Both judgments suggest that one should "blue pencil" (*i.e.* excise) the offending provisions. However, only Buckley L.J.'s judgment goes on to consider whether the agreement as a whole is valid or not. This approach accords with the ECJ's decision in Technique Miniere which requires the court to consider whether the "blue pencilled" clauses are severable. Clearly, if they are not, it is submitted that the whole agreement is void. Accordingly, it would appear that Buckley L.J.'s judgment provides a more complete guide as to the validity of an agreement as a whole.

12.081 The effect of Article 85(2) is to render an agreement void *erga omnes* and not just *inter partes*. Thus, a defendant in civil proceedings may plead that the plaintiff is not entitled to the relief being sought as the relief sought is contrary to Article 85 even though the defendant is not party to an agreement with the plaintiff. However, the defendant must show that there is a nexus between the relief sought by the plaintiff and the alleged infringement of Article 85.[59]

(iii) Article 86 as a Defence

12.082 A party may plead in its defence that the relief that the plaintiff is seeking is an abuse of a dominant position and thus contrary to Article 86. If this is proved, then the relief sought is prohibited. However, it must still be shown that there is a nexus between the relief sought and the alleged abuse of a dominant position.[60]

(iv) Nexus between alleged infringement and relief sought

12.083 In cases where it has been alleged that a party's behaviour or the relief that it is seeking is an infringement of Article 85 or 86, the English courts have been concerned with the issue as to whether or not there is a nexus between such behaviour or relief sought and the alleged infringement. This has normally risen in cases where the plaintiff is seeking to enforce intellectual property rights and the defendant avers that the plaintiff is not entitled to such relief because it infringes Article 85 or 86.

[57] *ibid*, at para. 18.
[58] [1927] 1 K.B. 639.
[59] See para. 12.083, below.
[60] See para. 12.083, below.

In *ICI v. Berk Pharmaceuticals*,[61] Megarry V.-C. said:

> "Article 86 prohibits any abuse which falls within the ambit of the Article. Many other acts by the plaintiffs are also prohibited, whether by statute, common law or equity, or under the Treaty. I do not think that it could be said that a person in breach of some statutory or other prohibition thereupon becomes an outlaw, unable to enforce any of his rights against anyone. If the plaintiffs are imposing unfair selling prices in that they charge too much for their product, I cannot see why this breach of the prohibition of Article 86 means that the Defendants are thereby set free from any liability to the plaintiffs, if they, the defendants, commit the tort of passing off (or indeed, any other tort) against them."

In *British Leyland v. Armstrong*,[62] British Leyland, the British motor manufacturer sued the defendant who manufactured motor car exhausts for infringement of the former's design copyright. The defendant pleaded *inter alia* that British Leyland was debarred from exercising its design copyright against it because it had entered into licences with third parties which were void under Article 85(2). The Court of Appeal rejected this defence stating that the judgment of Megarry V.-C. in *ICI v. Berk Pharmaceuticals*[63] in relation to Article 86 (which they interpreted as meaning that there was a lack of nexus between the abuse pleaded and the right claimed by the defendants) applied also to Article 85.[64] The confirmation that there must be a nexus between the relief sought and the Euro-defence reinforces the concept of such defences being treated as breaches of statutory duties.[65]

12.084 It may be the case that the plaintiff is only entitled to partial relief where Article 85 or 86 is alleged by way of defence. In *Langsing Bagnall Ltd v. Buccaneer Lift Parts Ltd*,[66] an action for breach of copyright in spare parts was brought against the defendant who claimed that the plaintiff was abusing a dominant position under Article 86. It was alleged that the plaintiffs had abused their dominant position by restricting the number of agents who could sell spare parts, charging excessive prices for the spare parts and instructing their agents to charge retail prices to other traders in spare parts not authorised by the plaintiffs.

Templeman L.J. considered this matter and said:

> "If the enforcement by the plaintiffs of their copyright monopoly, including enforcement by means of the present litigation against the defendants, amounts to an infringement of the Treaty of Rome, the English court will be faced with the dilemma of preventing that

[61] [1981] F.S.R. 1, [1981] 2 C.M.L.R. 75.
[62] [1984] 3 C.M.L.R. 102 C.A.
[63] [1981] F.S.R. 1, [1981] 2 C.M.L.R. 75.
[64] *ibid*, at para. 93.
[65] See *Garden Cottage Foods v. Milk Marketing Board* [1984] A.C. 130; [1983] 3 C.M.L.R. 43; [1984] F.S.R. 23.
[66] [1984] 1 C.M.L.R. 224 C.A.

> infringement or upholding the copyright monopoly granted to the plaintiffs by the national law. In the present case, if that dilemma ever presents itself as a result of the evidence and findings of the judge at the trial, it is possible that the English court may be able to resolve the dilemma by declining to grant an injunction to enforce the copyright monopoly, awarding damages in lieu of an injunction so as to give effect to the law and damages to a reasonable royalty on the infringing articles so as to prevent the plaintiffs abusing their copyright protection in such a way as to infringe the Treaty of Rome."[67]

It is submitted that the above reasoning is somewhat flawed because it appears to deny that Community law on competition takes precedence over national law of copyright. However, if it is only claimed that part of the relief itself sought is an infringement of Article 85 or 86, this should not affect the remainder of the relief sought. Thus, where a defendant claimed that a claim in an infringement of copyright action for conversion damages would constitute an abuse of a dominant position, this did not affect the plaintiff's claim for relief by way of an injunction or damages for infringement of copyright as there was no nexus between the abuse and the relief sought.[68] If the plaintiff is seeking injunctive relief and an enquiry into damages for infringement of an intellectual property right, it may be that the grant of injunctive relief but not damages based on a reasonable royalty would amount to an abuse of a dominant position. This will often be the case as an order that the defendant pay a reasonable royalty rate is less restrictive of competition than the grant of an injunction.[69]

12.085 The requirement of nexus should be distinguished from the principle as enunciated by Aldous J in *Ransburg-Gema*[70] that for Article 86 to provide a defence, it must be shown that the plaintiff is in a dominant position and that the relief claimed would be an abuse of that dominant position. In considering the issue of nexus, it is presupposed that an abuse of a dominant position has already been established. The relevant issue is whether such an abuse prevents the plaintiff from obtaining the relief it seeks. The same approach applies in considering the issue of nexus under Article 85. It is presupposed that the agreements in issue infringe Article 85. In *Ransburg*, Aldous J. was concerned with the issue as to whether or not the relief sought *itself* constituted an abuse of a dominant position. This is a matter of substantive law and the reader is referred to the relevant chapter.[71]

[67] *ibid*, para. 14. Reiterated in *Ransburg-Gema AG v. Electrostatic Plant Systems Ltd* [1989] 2 C.M.L.R. 712 (Patents Court), para. 21.
[68] *Ransburg-Gema AG v. Electrostatic Plant Systems Ltd* [1989] 2 C.M.L.R. 712 (Patents Court) at para. 23.
[69] See Chap. 11 on Abuse of a Dominant Position.
[70] *Ransburg-Gema AG v. Electrostatic Plant Systems Ltd* [1989] 2 C.M.L.R. 712 (Patents Court).
[71] See Chap. 11 on Abuse of a Dominant Position.

More recently, in *Chiron v. Murex*,[72] which concerned a biotechnological patent where the plaintiff claimed infringement and the defendant alleged that the plaintiff was abusing its dominant position by refusing to licence, charging unfair prices, etc., the Court of Appeal suggested that where a defendant can seek damages for a breach of Article 86 or complain to the E.C. Commission, then it may be disproportionate to deny relief to patentees where there is an Article 86 defence.[73] Thus, the court said that only in extraordinary circumstances where clearly the grant of relief would infringe Article 86 should the patentee be denied the relief he is seeking. It is submitted that this approach is plainly wrong and contrary to Community law. The existence of other remedies should not mean that a Euro-defence should fail where clearly it has been made out and there is a clear nexus. Thus, the fact that the plaintiff can go to the Commission is irrelevant.[74]

It is submitted that as always, a defendant must show nexus. Thus, where a defendant is pleading refusal to licence is an abuse of a dominant position (as he was in *Chiron*), then clearly if such an abuse is made out, the grant of an injunction would be wrong. If the defendant is entitled to a licence, he should not be injuncted. In such a case, a nexus is made out between the abuse and the relief sought. The difficulty is that Euro-defences raised in intellectual property actions are often general and desperate in nature and not linked to the relief sought by the plaintiff. However, that does not discharge the duty on a court to consider a Euro-defence in its entirety especially as to whether it is made out or not.

(d) Practice and procedure in English courts where Article 85 or 86 is in issue

12.086 In general, there should be little difference between the procedure for an action for statutory duty and one for breach of Article 85 or 86. Particular points are noted below. Thus a party alleging such a breach must particularise the breaches, show causation and if used as a cause of action show that the damage is reasonably foreseeable. Similarly, the raising of Article 85 or 86 as a defence in an action does not materially affect the practice and procedure of such an action.

(i) Jurisdiction

12.087 The party issuing proceeding under Article 85 or 86 must consider whether he is entitled to bring an action in the English courts. It is likely that the Brussels Convention on Civil Jurisdiction applies. This is dealt with in the Chapter on Jurisdiction.[75]

[72] [1994] F.S.R. 187. C.A.

[73] See *ibid*, p. 200 *per* Staughton I.J. and Balcombe L.J.

[74] Indeed, in Notice on Co-operation between national courts and the Commission in applying Article 85 and 86 of the EEC Treaty [1993] O.J. C 39/05, national courts have a duty to apply Articles 85 and 86. See para. 12.003 *et seq*.

[75] See Chap. 13 on Intellectual Property and Jurisdiction.

(ii) Pleadings

12.088 In English proceedings, a party must include full particulars of any breach of Article 85(1) or 86.[76] Where parties anticipate a reference to the ECJ under Article 177, the Court has indicated that pleadings should from the outset be in a form which will enable the defendants to lay the factual ground for the arguments which they would want to present to the ECJ.[77] The court may order that such particulars be given after mutual discovery because of the difficulty of a party in knowing what particular breaches of Article 85 and 86 have been committed.[78]

In general, parties are advised to give full particulars of any pleadings alleging breaches of Article 85 or Article 86. English courts have been quick to strike out Euro-defences which are not adequately particularised.[79] The nexus between Article 85 and 86 and the relief sought must be properly pleaded.[80]

(iii) Discovery and self-incrimination

12.089 In civil proceedings in England, it has been held that the privilege of self-incrimination applies to Article 85 and 86 civil proceedings.[81] The Court of Appeal in *Rio Tinto Zinc Corporation v. Westinghouse Electric Corporation* held that RTZ (Court of Appeal) companies might be entitled to claim the privilege from production under section 14 of the Civil Evidence Act 1968 if such exposed the companies to the danger of being fined by the Commission. This point was conceded by Westinghouse on appeal. However, it may be that this does not apply to proceedings for infringement of intellectual property.[82]

Recently, in *Otto BV v. Postbank NV*,[83] the defendant in Dutch proceedings sought to claim that it was not obliged to give evidence on the basis that such evidence might well be brought to the attention of the Commission and thus incriminate it. The ECJ held that whilst such evidence might be brought to the attention of the Commission, the latter

[76] *Aero Zipp Fasteners Ltd v. Y.K.K. Fasteners (U.K.) Ltd* [1973] F.S.R. 580, H.C.

[77] *Hagen v. Fratelli & Moretti* [1980] 3 C.M.L.R. 253, C.A.

[78] *ibid.*

[79] For intellectual property cases where the court has struck out Euro-defences, see *ICI v. Berk Pharmaceuticals* [1981] F.S.R. 1, [1981] 2 C.M.L.R. 75; *Ransburg-Gema AG v. Electrostatic Plant Systems Ltd* [1989] 2 C.M.L.R. 712 (Patents Court); *Pitney Bowes v. Francotyp-Postalia GmbH* [1990] 3 C.M.L.R. 466, H.C.; for cases where a party failed to strike out pleadings see *Lansing Bagnall Ltd v. Buccaneer Lift Parts Ltd* [1984] 1 C.M.L.R. 224; *British Leyland v. T.I. Silencers Ltd* [1981] 2 C.M.L.R. 75 C.A. and *Chiron v. Murex* [1994] F.S.R. 187, C.A.

[80] *Ransburg-Gema AG v. Electrostatic Plant Systems Ltd* [1989] 2 C.M.L.R. 712 (Patents Court), para. 31.

[81] *Rio Tinto Zinc Corporation v. Westinghouse Electric Corporation* [1978] 1 All E.R. 434, H.L., [1977] 3 All E.R. 703, C.A.

[82] In proceedings in the High Court, s. 172 of the Supreme Court Act 1981 prevents any person from raising the privilege of self-incrimination in "proceedings for infringements relating to intellectual property". *Quaere* if a defendant asserts that the plaintiff is exercising his rights in contravention of Art. 85 or 86 as to whether the privilege of self-incrimination pertains to the plaintiff.

[83] Unreported judgment of November 10, 1993.

could not use such information as a means of evidence of an infringement of Article 85 or 86 or as a means of evidence for justifying the initiation of an inquiry. Accordingly, the reasoning in *Rio Tinto Zinc* would no longer apply and it is submitted is overruled by the ECJ's judgment in *Otto v. Postbank*. Furthermore, the privilege against self-incrimination in English law may be invalid on the basis that such a rule or its extensiveness is incompatible with Community law as it makes it very difficult for a party to establish that a party is in breach of Articles 85 or 86 and makes the enforcement of Article 85 and 86 more difficult than domestic breaches of statutory duty.[84]

The Court will not order discovery in Article 85 or 86 proceedings which amounts to a fishing expedition.[85]

(iv) Stay of proceedings

12.090 The Court may order a stay pending a decision by the Commission relating to a notified agreement where a Euro-defence is raised and there is a danger of a conflicting decision by the Commission.[86] Furthermore, the national court may seek to stay the proceedings pending a request for assistance from the Commission.[87] In certain circumstances, a stay may be ordered because the Commission's ability to investigate any alleged infringement may be much greater than a national court.[88] In *British Leyland v. Wyatt*, the High Court recognised the fact that a combination of a possible claim to privilege for self-incrimination and the Commission's wide powers of investigation meant that justice might only be done by ordering a stay. The Court said that:

> "I think also, although it is not expressly stated in the [1972 European Community] Act, that in the circumstances envisaged, a decision of the Commission which is not appealed ought to be treated by the courts here as having the same effect as one of the Court of Justice itself."[89]

The Commission is often much better placed than a national court to

[84] See Case 199/82,*Amminnistrazione dell Finance dello Stato v. San Giorgio* [1983] E.C.R. 3595, 3613 where it was held that national evidential rules must not render the application of Community law impossible or highly impracticable.

[85] *British Leyland v. Wyatt Interpart Co Ltd (No. 1)* [1979] 1 C.M.L.R. 395, H.C.

[86] *British Leyland v. Wyatt Interpart Co Ltd (No. 2)* [1979] 3 C.M.L.R. 79, H.C. See also Notice on Co-operation Between national courts and the Commission in applying Article 85 and 86 of the EEC Treaty [1993] O.J. C 39/05 and Case C–234/89, *Delimitis v. Henninger Brau* [1991] E.C.R. 935, [1991] 4 CMLR 329, ECJ. As for when the national court should grant a stay when there are concurrent proceedings before the Commission and court, see para. 12.067 *et seq.*

[87] See Notice on Co-operation between national courts and the Commission in applying Article 85 and 86 of the EEC Treaty [1993] O.J. C 39/05 at paras. 33 *et seq.*

[88] See Comparison of Enforcement of Community Law by National Court and Commission at para. 12.003 *et seq.*

[89] *British Leyland v. Wyatt (No. 2)* [1979] 3 C.M.L.R. 79, H.C., para. 14.

conduct a Community-wide investigation into anti-competitive practices.[90] Moreover, as mentioned earlier, recent caselaw from the ECJ suggests that where there are parallel proceedings before the Commission, a national court only has *jurisdiction* to determine potential abuses under Article 85 and 86 where the issue is *clear* either way.[91] Thus, even where the national court is concerned with matters occurring prior to the date of notification by a defendant of possible anti-competitive arrangements, so that there is no danger of *legally* conflicting decisions, a national court will be reluctant to form a view on whether an agreement clearly falls within or without Article 85(1) where there are parallel proceedings before the Commission.[92] Thus, in practice, it will be rare for a national court not to order a stay where there are parallel proceedings before the Commission. However, in one case, where the Plaintiff sought summary judgment and the Defendant asked for a stay of the proceedings pending the Commission's decision, the English High Court ordered that proceedings should continue until the setting down of the case for trial whereupon they should be stayed pending the Commission's decision.[93]

If proceedings have not been initiated, such a stay may be on terms including a provision compelling a party raising the Euro-defence to institute the appropriate proceedings before the Commission.[94] Other reasons for asking for a stay is that the Commission may be able to look at documents which would be covered by legal privilege in national proceedings.[95] If the Commission has not initiated an investigation and the parties are able to secure adequate protection in the national court or there is not sufficient Community interest, then the Commission may refuse to investigate the matter itself.[96] It is submitted that the national

[90] *e.g.* see *MTV Europe v. BMG and others* [1995] 1 C.M.L.R. 437 (High Court of England) where Mr. Justice Evans-Lombe held that he was in no position to form a concluded view that there was scarcely any risk that the Commission and the appellate courts from it would decide the Plaintiff's complaint of anti-competitive abuses in its favour finding support for his view from Advocate-General Jacobs' Opinion at para. 35 in *Ministere Public v. Tournier* [1989] ECR 2521, ECJ (both cases concerned alleged anti-competitive behaviour by copyright collecting societies).

[91] See para. 12.069 *et seq.*

[92] See *MTV Europe ibid.* where the court rejected a submission of the Plaintiff that there was no danger of conflict between a decision of the Commission granting negative clearance and a national court's decision. Strictly speaking, the submission was correct—there is no formal, legal barrier to a national court finding that an agreement infringes Article 85 and the Commission granting negative clearance to the same agreement. However, it is clear from the decision of Mr Justice Evans Lombe that in practice, such a conflict was highly undesirable because the Commission was in much better position than a national court to determine the issue.

[93] *MTV Europe ibid.*

[94] *ibid*, para. 20.

[95] See section on Legal Privilege in relation to proceedings brought by the Commission, para. 12.046.

[96] See *Notice on Co-operation between national courts and the Commission in applying Article 85 and 86 of the EEC Treaty* [1993] O.J. C 39/05 at paras. 13–16 and Case T–64/89 *Automec Srl v. EC Commission (No. 2)* [1990] E.C.R. 367, [1992] 5 C.M.L.R. 431, CFI.

court should consider such matters when deciding whether to stay proceedings.

(v) Burden and standard of proof

12.091 The burden of proof will lay upon the party alleging the breach.[97] The standard of proof in a civil case is on the balance of probabilities. However, the High Court has said that the standard of proof in Article 85 proceedings would be that of a "high degree of probability"[98] as such a finding carried with it a liability to fines. Such a view appears somewhat erroneous as a finding by a national court does not bind the Commission who is the only body that can impose fines and because it makes the enforcement of Article 85 and 86 more difficult than that of a domestic breach of statutory duty which would be contrary to Community law.[99]

(vi) Participation of the Commission

12.092 The Court of Appeal has the power to direct that a notice of appeal be served upon the Commission even if it is not party to the proceedings.[1] Such a direction will only be made where there are very good reasons for doing so. To the writer's knowledge, only one such order has been made where service of a notice of appeal on the Commission was ordered in a case of alleged libel contained in a letter of complaint to the Commission.[2]

(vii) Article 177 reference

12.093 Where the Court considers that it is necessary to enable it to give judgment, it may refer a question of interpretation of the Treaty, Community secondary legislation or its validity to the European Court of Justice under Article 177 if the issue has been raised in proceedings. If there is no judicial remedy under national law from the court's decision, that court must refer the matter to the Court of Justice.[3]

The procedure for this is governed by R.S.C. Ord. 114. The court may order a reference of its own motion or on application by a party before or at the trial or hearing. If a party wants to make an application before the trial date, the application must be made by motion. An order for reference can only be made by a judge in person.[4] A schedule should be drawn

[97] See *Potato Marketing Board v. Robertsons* [1983] 1 C.M.L.R. 93.
[98] *Shearson Lehman Hutton Inc v. MacLaine Watson & Co Ltd.* [1989] 3 C.M.L.R. 429, Webster J.
[99] See Art. 85 and 86 as a statutory duty, para. 12.076.
[1] R.S.C. Ord. 59, r.8.
[2] *Hasselblad v. Orbinson* [1985] Q.B. 475; [1985] 1 All E.R. 173; [1985] 3 C.M.L.R. 679, C.A.
[3] Art. 177(3).
[4] R.S.C., Ord. 14, r. 2.

up by the parties setting out the request for the preliminary ruling.[5] Proceedings will usually be stayed pending the ruling from the ECJ.[6]

Appeal from a High Court order making a reference under Article 177 lies to the Court of Appeal. Leave is not required.[7] Notice of appeal must be served within 14 days of making the order.

13. Enforcement of Competition Law under EEA Agreement

(a) Introduction

12.094 Under the EEA Agreement, a system must be set up which ensures that its competition rules are equally respected.[8] During the negotiations of the EEA Agreement, one central issue was who would enforce the EEA competition laws and how to divide the competencies. The negotiators finally opted for a two pillar system allocating the enforcement of the EEA competition laws between the E.C. Commission and EFTA Surveillance Authority (ESA). The actual allocation of responsibilities as set out in the EEA is quite complicated.

In summary, they are as follows:

(a) In relation to cases falling under Article 53 EEA (the Article 85 equivalent)

(i) *Pure cases*—"EFTA" pure cases where only trade between EFTA States is affected is dealt with by the ESA;[9] "E.C. pure" cases where only trade between E.C. Member States is affected do not fall under the EEA Agreement and will be dealt with by the E.C. Commission solely on the basis of Articles 85 and 85 of the E.C. Treaty.[10]

(ii) *Mixed cases*—"Mixed cases" where both trade between E.C. Member States and trade between E.C. and one or more EFTA states is affected are to be dealt with by the Commission;[11] "De minimis" cases where the effect on trade and competition within the Community are not appreciable are dealt with by the ESA.[12]

[5] As to the content and form of such a schedule, see the prescribed form, App. A No. 109, para. 110, Vol. 2 of the White Book (Rules of the Supreme Court). For examples, see *ex p. The Association of Pharmaceutical Importers* [1987] C.M.L.R. 951; *Factortame* [1989] 2 C.M.L.R. 353. The ECJ has given guidance as to the content of such references—see *Union Laitiere Normande* [1979] E.C.R. 2663; Case 244/80, *Foglia v. Novello* [1981] E.C.R. 3045. [1982] 1 C.M.L.R. 506, see also Note 114/1–6/18 R.S.C., Ord. 114.

[6] R.S.C. Ord. 114, r. 4.

[7] R.S.C. Ord. 114, r. 6. Leave to appeal is probably required if the Court refuses to make an order of reference as such a refusal is interlocutory in character—see 114/1–6/1 note to Ord. 114.

[8] Article 1(2)(e) EEA Agreement.

[9] Art. 56(1)(a) EEA Agreement.

[10] *ibid.*

[11] Art. 56(1)(c)

[12] Art. 56(3).

For cases, where *trade* between E.C. Member States is not affected but potentially there may be an effect on *competition* within the E.C.

(i) If at least 33 per cent of the turnover of the undertakings concerned comes from EFTA states, then the ESA has jurisdiction regardless of whether the effects on competition within the E.C. are or are not appreciable;[13]

(ii) If the above turnover is less than 33 per cent, then the ESA only has jurisdiction if the effects on competition within the EC are not appreciable.[14]

(b) In relation to cases falling under Article 54 EEA (the Article 86 equivalent)

(i) Cases where the dominance only exists within the EFTA territory will be dealt with by the ESA;[15]

(ii) Cases where the dominance exists only in the Community will be dealt with by the E.C. Commission;[16]

(iii) Cases where the dominance exists within both E.C. and EFTA territories, the rules concerning mixed cases set out above in relation to Article 53 apply.[17]

(b) Procedural rules of ESA

12.095 Under Protocol 21 of the EEA Agreement, the ESA in effect is entrusted with equivalent powers and similar functions to those of the E.C. Commission. Under Article 3 of Protocol 21 to the EEA Agreement and Protocol 4 to the ESA/Court Agreement, the procedural E.C. regulations relating to the enforcement of Articles 85 and 86 are incorporated into the EEA Agreement. In particular, Regulation 17/62 on the general procedural rules implementing Articles 85 and 86; Regulation 27/62 on the form, content and other details concerning applications and notification; Regulation 99/63 on hearings provided for in Article 19 of Regulation 17/62; and Regulation 2988/74 on limitation periods apply. Accordingly, the enforcement of EEA competition laws by the ESA will be very similar to that of the E.C. Commission which has been described in this Chapter.

(c) Co-operation between the E.C. Commission and ESA

12.096 The EEA Agreement provides for close co-operation between the ESA and E.C. Commission.[18] This co-operation extends to both handling of individual cases and to general policy issues. Under Protocol 23 of the

[13] Art. 56(1)(b).
[14] Arts. 56(1)(b), 56(3).
[15] Art. 56(2).
[16] Art. 56(2).
[17] Art. 56(2), final sentence.
[18] Art. 58.

EEA Agreement, co-operation in individual cases will extend to the forwarding of notifications and complaints, comfort letters, consultation of each other prior to decisions being made, transmission of cases and mutual assistance in fact-finding.

CHAPTER THIRTEEN

JURISDICTION AND INTELLECTUAL PROPERTY

1. INTRODUCTION

13.001 In the Community and to a lesser extent, in Europe, substantive intellectual property laws have been to a large extent harmonised. However, the enforcement of such laws varies greatly between different countries. Firstly, the interpretation and application of such harmonised laws differs greatly. Thus, the construction of a patent claim in one country will often depend on national cultural and jurisprudential factors which differ considerably between countries. Secondly, there may be procedural differences. Some jurisdictions permit extensive examination of a case including discovery, interrogatories, experiments, oral cross-examination of witnesses whilst others are much more restricted. Similarly, certain jurisdictions offer more far reaching interim measures than others. The above considerations will often mean that certain jurisdictions are more attractive than others for litigating intellectual property disputes. Also, there will be commercial considerations which will affect the choice of forum, *e.g.* the language of the proceedings, the costs of litigation, the speed of litigation and the basis of assessment of damages.

The Community institutions realised a long time ago that it was important that there should be a single uniform system of jurisdiction in the Community. In 1968, the Brussels Convention for Civil Jurisdiction and the Enforcement of Judgments was signed by the original members of the Community. New members joining the European Union since then have acceded to the Convention or are in the process of doing so. Since then, the Lugano Convention on Jurisdiction and Enforcement of Judgments which closely parallels the Brussels Convention in relation to EFTA countries has come into force. This chapter looks at jurisdictional issues in litigating in Europe, in particular concentrating on these conventions.

From the outset, it is important to distinguish between jurisdictional considerations as opposed to "choice of law" considerations. Both will be relevant to the litigator and forum shopper. A Member State may have *jurisdiction* to hear in action but it may be that under that Member State's private international law the applicable substantive law should be that of another Member State. This chapter does not deal with such choice of law issues which will be a matter of private international law of the Contracting State whose court has jurisdiction and is seised of an action. In intellectual property disputes, this will be invariably the domestic law of the state from which the right is derived. But, in considering the meaning of a concept in an issue of jurisdiction, a court may often have to decide which law it uses in order to determine the meaning of such a concept. For example, under the Brussels Convention, the courts of the Contracting State where the defendant is domiciled has primary jurisdiction. In order to determine the issue of domicile, the seised court must apply the putative *lex domicilis*. In England, the situation is further complicated by the double actionability rule which although deemed to be a rule as to choice of law, possesses jurisdictional characteristics.[1]

2. Brussels Convention

(a) Background

13.002 Article 220 of the E.C. Treaty requires Member States to enter into negotiations with each other with a view to securing for the benefit of their nationals, *inter alia*, the simplification of formalities governing the reciprocal recognition and enforcement of judgments of courts, tribunals and arbitration awards. It became quickly apparent that a treaty which sought to regulate and harmonise the recognition and enforcement of judgments in the Community would be incomplete if differing jurisdictional rules applied in the Community. For instance, it was important to ensure that conflicting judgments could not be obtained in differing Member States. Furthermore, it was realised that Member States' rules on jurisdiction often discriminated on the basis of nationality.[2] Accordingly, a working party was set up by the Member States to draft a treaty that standardised jurisdiction and the recognition and enforcement of judgments in the six original Member States. In furtherance of this, the Convention on Jurisdiction and the Enforcement of Judgments in Civil and Commercial Matters was signed by them at Brussels in 1968. The treaty was not a Community legislative measure but a multilateral treaty. Accordingly, a protocol providing for the interpretation of the Convention by the European Court of Justice was signed at Luxembourg by the Six Member States' representatives. Since then, the United Kingdom, Ireland and Denmark acceded to the Brussels Convention in 1978 and the Convention came into force into those countries on January 1, 1987. In the United Kingdom, the convention was brought into force by the Civil Jurisdiction and Judgments Act 1982 [CJJA] which provides that the Brussels Convention is to have the force of law in the United Kingdom.[3] Greece, Spain and Portugal have also acceded to the 1968 Conven-

[1] This is discussed below at para. 13.047. Note that it is proposed that this rule be abolished under the Private International Law (Miscellaneous Provisions) Bill.

[2] Thus, Art. 14 of the French Civil code permitted plaintiff French Nationals to sue foreigners in the French courts regardless of the absence of any connection between the dispute and France.

[3] Civil Jurisdiction and Judgments Act 1982, [CJJA 1982], s.2.

tion. New Members, Austria, Sweden and Finland are in the process of ratifying the Brussels Convention. The Accession Conventions have all modified the 1968 Convention. In particular, the Accession of Spain and Portugal to the 1968 Convention and to the 1971 Protocol in 1989 ("the San Sebastian Convention") modified the 1968 Convention to bring it into line with the recently agreed Lugano Convention on jurisdiction and the enforcement and recognition of judgments in civil matters for E.C. States and EFTA States.[4] The 1968 Convention, the 1971 Protocol and the subsequent amendments to them by the Accession Conventions are hereafter collectively referred to as the Brussels Convention.

The Brussels Convention splits into two parts. On the one hand, it is concerned with jurisdiction and on the other hand with the recognition and enforcement of judgments. This chapter is primarily concerned with jurisdictional aspects of the Brussels Convention as it applies to intellectual property. However, the enforcement of judgments is examined in outline.[5]

(b) Fundamental rule: defendant's domicile

13.003 The Brussels Convention harmonises jurisdictional rules in Contracting States. It applies only to civil and commercial matters but specifically not to revenue, customs, administrative matters, certain types of matrimonial proceedings, bankruptcy and insolvency, social security or arbitration.[6] Such areas are known as excluded grounds. Under the Brussels Convention, the basic rule of the Convention is that actions must be brought in the Contracting State where the proposed defendant is domiciled.[7] A party's domicile is determined according to the law of the relevant state. Thus, in the United Kingdom, "domicile" for an individual for the purposes of the Brussels Convention means that he must be resident in the United Kingdom and have a "substantial connection" with the United Kingdom.[8] If according to the court which is seised of the matter, it concludes that the party is not domiciled in that court's State, in order to determine whether the party is domiciled in another Member State, the court must apply the law of the state of putative domicile (*lex domicilis*).[9]

[4] See below, para. 13.052.

[5] For detailed analysis of the system of recognition and enforcement of judgments, see Kaye *Civil Jurisdiction and Enforcement of Foreign Judgments*, (1987); O'Malley & Layton *European Civil Practice* (1989), p. 702; Hartley *Civil Jurisdiction and Judgments* (1984). For ease of reference, the Brussels Convention is appended to the Civil Jurisdiction and Judgments Act 1982.

[6] Art. 1.

[7] Art. 2. Generally for a detailed analysis of this primary rule, see Kaye *Civil Jurisdiction and Enforcement of Foreign Judgments*, p. 278 (1987) 798; O'Malley & Layton *European Civil Practice* (1989), p. 702.

[8] CJJA 1982, s.41–46.

[9] Art. 52, 2nd sentence.

If the defendant is found not to be domiciled in any Contracting State, then the court of the seised Contracting State will determine whether it has jurisdiction by reference to its own national law.[10]

Domicile for entities other than natural persons is treated differently under the Brussels Convention. This deems that the Contracting State where the "seat" of a company or other legal person or association of legal persons is situated is to be treated as its domicile.[11] In contrast to the approach taken for individuals the court seised of the matter applies its own rules of private international law in order to determine where that seat lies.[12] Thus, if the seised court determines that the seat of a company is not in that court's State, then it must consider whether the seat falls within any other Contracting State. In doing so, it must apply its own private international laws. This is different from the situation when the court considers the question of domicile in another Contracting State for a natural person where the seised court must apply the law of the putative Contracting State in determining domicile. In the United Kingdom, a corporation or association has its seat in the United Kingdom if it was incorporated or formed under the law of a part of the United Kingdom and has its registered office or some other official address in the United Kingdom *or* its central management and control is exercised in the United Kingdom.[13] Under English private international law, a company only has its seat in another Contracting State if the law of that Contracting State would so regard it as having its seat there *and* either (i) it was incorporated or formed under the law of that state and has its registered office or some other official address there or (ii) its central management and control is exercised in that state.[14] If the seised court determines that the seat of the defendant company does not fall within any Contracting State, then it falls back on its own national jurisdictional rules.[15]

(c) Derogations from the defendant's "domicile" rule

13.004 In certain circumstances, the Brussels Convention provides for supplementary grounds of jurisdiction where the putative defendant is domiciled in a Contracting State. Moreover, in certain circumstances, the Brussels Convention confers exclusive jurisdiction on a state regardless of the defendant's domicile.[16]

[10] Art. 4.
[11] Art. 53.
[12] Art. 53, 2nd sentence.
[13] CJJA 1982, s.42(3).
[14] CJJA 1982, s.42(6), (7).
[15] Art. 4.
[16] The exclusive jurisdictional rules of the Brussels Convention apply even where the defendant is domiciled in a non-Contracting State—see Art. 4(1).

(i) Supplementary grounds of jurisdiction

13.005 Besides the primary rule in the Brussels Convention that an action is to be brought in the state where the defendant is domiciled, the Convention provides for supplementary grounds of jurisdiction where the defendant is domiciled in a Contracting State.[17] Thus the plaintiff will often have the option of suing in more than one jurisdiction. The principal of these are as follows:

(1) Article 5 affords supplementary grounds of jurisdiction for disputes relating *inter alia* to contract, tort, maintenance obligations, trusts, salvage of cargo and freight. Of particular importance in the intellectual property context is Article 5(3) which confers jurisdiction on the court of the Contracting State "in matters relating to tort, delict and quasi-delict in the Contracting State where the harmful event occurred".[18]
(2) In insurance and consumer contracts, the policy-holder is entitled to sue in the courts of the state where he is domiciled.[19]
(3) Where there are a number of defendants, a defendant may be sued in the courts where any one of them is domiciled.[20]
(4) A third party in a guarantee or warranty action may be sued in the court seised of the original proceedings.[21]
(5) In the case of a counterclaim, a person may be sued in the same state as where the original claim is pending.[22]
(6) Where a defendant submits to the jurisdiction of a court.[23] Where a defendant enters an appearance at a court other than to solely contest jurisdiction, then that court has jurisdiction. This rule does not apply where another court has exclusive jurisdiction other than pursuant to an agreement.[24]
(7) Where an interlocutory order is being applied for, the courts of any Contracting State have jurisdiction, even if under the Convention, the courts of some other state have jurisdiction as to the substantive matter.[25]

In all the above instances, the jurisdictional rules are additional to the primary rule based on domicile.

[17] Thus, these supplementary rules do not apply if the defendant is not domiciled in a Contracting State.
[18] See para. 13.010.
[19] Art. 7–16.
[20] Art. 6(1). See below, para. 13.013.
[21] Art. 6(2).
[22] Art. 6(3). Where there is a counterclaim for revocation of a registered right in an infringement action, see para. 13.031.
[23] Art. 18.
[24] Art. 18, 2nd sentence.
[25] Art. 24.

(ii) Exclusive jurisdiction

13.006 In certain cases, exclusive jurisdiction will be conferred on the courts of a particular Contracting State regardless of the defendant's domicile. The Brussels Convention rules on exclusive jurisdiction apply even where the defendant is domiciled in a non-Contracting State.[26] In such circumstances, jurisdiction based on the defendant's domicile is excluded. These are as follows.[27]

Article 16

13.007

(1) In proceedings concerned with immovable property, the court of the Contracting State in which the property is situated.
(2) In proceedings which concern the validity, nullity of dissolution of a company, the court of the Contracting State in which the company has its seat.
(3) In proceedings which concern the validity of public entries, the court of the Contracting State in which the register is kept.
(4) In proceedings which concern the registration or validity of registered intellectual property rights, the court of the Contracting State where deposit or registration has taken place or is deemed to have taken place under the terms of an international convention.[28]
(5) In proceedings concerned with the enforcement of judgments, the court of the Contracting State in which the judgment has been or is to be enforced.[29]

Article 17

13.008

Where parties, one or more of whom are domiciled in a Contracting State, have agreed that a court of a Contracting State should have jurisdiction subject to the requirements that such an agreement conferring jurisdiction is either in writing or evidenced in writing or, in international trade or commerce, in a form which accords with practices in that trade or commerce of which the parties are or ought to have been aware and which in such trade or commerce is widely known to, and regularly observed by, parties to contracts of the type involved in the particular trade or commerce concerned.[30]

[26] Art. 4(1).
[27] Art. 16(1)–(5).
[28] See para. 13.026.
[29] A post-judgment Mareva order given by an English court purporting to cover assets in an E.C. state falls within Art. 24 and does not fall within Art. 16(5) as such an order is not concerned specifically with enforcement—see *Babanaft International Co SA v. Bassatne and another* [1989] 2 W.L.R. 232, C.A., *per* Kerr L.J. at p. 249. See para. 13.039.
[30] Art. 17(1)(a)–(c) as amended by Art. 7 of the San Sebastian Convention. Where none of the parties are domiciled in a Contracting State, then the wording of Art. 17 implies that the court whose jurisdiction is founded on the parties' agreement may decline jurisdiction—see Kaye *Civil Jurisdiction and Enforcement of Foreign Judgments* (1987) p. 1099 *et seq*.

The primary difference between Article 16 and 17 is that the court of Contracting State other than that agreed to in accordance with Article 17 can obtain jurisdiction by the submission of the defendant to its jurisdiction; by contrast, submission to a court's jurisdiction is ineffective to overcome another Contracting State's exclusive jurisdiction under Article 16.[31]

(d) Intellectual property and Brussels Convention

13.009 For the purposes of intellectual property litigation, there are several important provisions other than the primary rule based on the domicile of the defendant.

(i) Infringement actions—Article 5(3)

13.010 Article 5(3) allows a defendant who is domiciled in a Contracting State to be sued instead at the plaintiff's option "in matters relating to tort, delict or quasi-delict, in the courts of the place where the harmful event occurred". This rule is in addition to the primary rule of jurisdiction based on domicile of the defendant. However, it is important not to overlook the fact that Article 5(3) only applies if the defendant is domiciled in a Contracting State. Accordingly, Article 5(3) does not confer jurisdiction on an English court to try the infringement of an English patent by a person domiciled in America.[32] The term "matters relating to tort, delict or quasi-delict" is to be regarded as an autonomous concept which is to be interpreted by reference to the scheme and objectives of the Convention in order to ensure that the latter is given full effect. Accordingly, it covers all actions which seek to establish the liability of a defendant and which is not related to a "contract" within the meaning of Article 5(1).[33] Generally intellectual property actions are brought in the state where the infringement took place and not in the state of the defendant's domicile because the substantive law governing the infringement will be the former's state and not the latter's.

The infringement of intellectual property rights is either a statutory tort or a common law tort. Thus, in a patent infringement action, the action may be brought in the state where the infringement took place.[34] The European Court of Justice in *Bier BV v. Mines de Potasse d'Alsace SA*[35] held that the expression "place where the harmful event occurred" must be understood as being intended to cover both the place where the

[31] Art. 18.

[32] In practice, this makes little difference because all national jurisdictional rules will permit a person domiciled out of the jurisdiction to be sued for infringement occurring within the jurisdiction, *e.g.* see Rules of the Supreme Court Order 11, r. 1(1)(f).

[33] *Kalfelis* [1988] E.C.R. 5565, ECJ.

[34] See *Jenard* "Report on the Convention of September 1968 on Jurisdiction and the Enforcement of Judgments in Civil and Commercial Matters" [1979] O.J. C 59/1. This is persuasive in interpreting the Convention under English law—see CJJA 1982, s.3. See also *Napp Lab v. Pfizer Inc* [1993] F.S.R. 151.

[35] Case 21/76, [1976] E.C.R. 1735.

damage occurred *and* (if different) the place of the event giving rise to it. Thus, the defendant may be sued under Article 5(3) at the option of the plaintiff, either in the courts of the state where the damage occurred or in the courts of the Contracting State where the origin of the damage is situated. Pure economic loss is not recognised as an appropriate damage for the purposes of Article 5(3) as such would be tantamount to saying that the plaintiff may sue in the state of his domicile.[36] However, where the essence of the tortious wrongdoing is in fact financial and economic loss and the latter is not merely a consequence of physical damage, then the damage must be taken to have occurred wherever financial or, as the case may be, economic loss has actually been suffered.[37] As the infringement of an intellectual property right is an economic tort, it is arguable that this would mean the place where the financial centre of the business which owns the intellectual property rights in question is situated. This would in effect provide a supplementary ground of jurisdiction of the plaintiff's domicile in any infringement action. It is submitted that in the case of infringement of a purely territorial right, a proper and common sense interpretation of the expression "where the harmful event occurred" refers to the territory where the actual act that gave rise to the infringement occurred.[38]

It should be noted that the effect of *Bier BV v. Mines de Potasses* is that where infringing goods are circulating in several Contracting States, the plaintiff will additionally be able to choose the courts of these States as places where damage has occurred. However, where jurisdiction is based merely on the fact that the goods are circulating in the jurisdiction, a court can rule only on the harm *i.e.* the damage that occurs within its jurisdiction.[39] Where a court has jurisdiction because it is situated in the State where the event giving rise to the harm occurred, it would seem that the court can award damages for *all* the harm caused by the infringement, if the factory in question is the sole relevant source of infringing goods.[40]

Where jurisdiction is disputed on the basis that the conditions in Article 5(3) are not satisfied, at a preliminary stage, the plaintiff must

[36] See Advocate-General Warner's Opinion in Case 814/79, *Netherlands v. Ruffer* [1980] E.C.R. 3807; [1981] 3 C.M.L.R. 293.

[37] See Kaye *Civil Jurisdiction and Enforcement of Foreign Judgments* (1987), p. 584 and *Jouets Eisenmann v. Geobra Brandstatter GmbH* [1985] E.C.C. 246; [1984] 12 E.L.D. 129 (Belgium) which concerned the plaintiff's inability to resell goods bought from the German defendant because they infringed a registered industrial design in Belgium.

[38] In *Shevill and ors v. Presse Alliance* Case C–68/93 [1995] All E.R. (EC) 289, the ECJ ruled that in the case of a libel the place of the event giving rise to the damage could only be the place where the publisher of the newspaper in question was established since that was the place where the harmful event originated. By analogy, in a patent infringement action, this would mean the place where the factory making the infringing goods were made if situated in a Contracting State.

[39] *Shevill and ors v. Presse Alliance* Case C–68/93 [1995] All E.R. (EC) 289.

[40] *Shevill and ors v. Presse Alliance* Case C–68/93 [1995] All E.R. (EC) 289.

show that there is a good arguable case that such conditions are satisfied.[41]

(1) Extraterritorial pan-European injunctions

13.011 Intellectual property rights are territorial in nature. Accordingly, a defendant is only capable of infringing a patent of Contracting State A by acts done in that state. Thus, an injunction to prevent the defendant from infringing a patent in State B would be nonsensical because the patent does not exist in other states and the defendant is free to do as he pleases there. But, considering the case of patents, a patentee will often have parallel patents in many states. Moreover, often these patents will result from the grant of a European patent. In such circumstances, the patents will be identical in phrasing bar translational differences and technically, are subject to a common test of interpretation.[42] If a defendant infringes parallel European patents in several countries, can the court of one Contracting State make a pan-European injunction against infringement in other states on the basis that the rights are in effect harmonised and identical in nature? Certainly, courts in some Contracting States have already done so.[43] In particular, since a landmark decision by the Dutch Supreme Court in the *Interlas* case,[44] the courts of the Netherlands in both patent and trade mark infringement cases have regularly granted extraterritorial injunctions. The Dutch Supreme Court emphasised in *Interlas* that where a defendant is obliged by virtue of a legal obligation to a plaintiff not to do certain acts, there is "no reason to assume that such an order cannot be given when the case is about an obligation under the law of a foreign country—which has to be fulfilled outside the Netherlands".[45] The Court continued that a more restricted vision found no support in law and would at a time of increasing international contact, lead to the undesirable result that in the case of torts with an international character such as intellectual property infringement, the injured party would be compelled to go to court in every country concerned.[46] Thus, in a European patent case, a Dutch court has enjoined the defendant from infringing the plaintiff's European patent in 10 jurisdictions representing the countries designated in the European patent.[47] In a European patent, the patent laws of the designated countries are derived from the European

[41] See para. 13.041.

[42] Art. 59, European Patent Convention. See Chapter 2 on European Patents, para. 2.025.

[43] *e.g.* in England, see *AMP Incorporated v. Lan Technology Ltd* unreported September 28, 1991; in Holland, see *Verdo v. Samson* unreported January 6, 1992.

[44] Hoge Raad, November 24, 1989, Nederlandse Jurisprudentie 1992, 404 (Lincoln).

[45] *Interlas*, Hoge Raad, November 24, 1989, BIE 1991 at 86 *et seq.*

[46] For commentary on the Dutch practice of issuing extra-territorial injunctions, see Brinkhof "Could the President of the District Court of the Hague Take Measures concerning the Infringement of Foreign Patents?" [1994] EIPR 361 and Gielen & Ebbink "First Europe-wide Biotech Patent Injunction" [1994] EIPR 243.

[47] *Applied Research Systems v. Organon International BV* Court of Appeals, the Hague. February 3, 1994, not yet reported; *Kirin-Amgen v. Boehringer Mannheim GmbH* not yet reported. These cases are discussed in Gielen & Ebbink, *supra.*

Patent Convention. Thus, theoretically, the test of infringement should be the same.[48]

It is submitted that the mere fact that there is harmonisation of the substantive patent or other intellectual property law is irrelevant and that recourse must be made to the normal jurisdictional rules of the Convention. For instance, if a defendant who is responsible for acts of infringement in several Contracting States of parallel patents is domiciled in Contracting State A, then the court of State A has jurisdiction to hear infringement actions in relation to all the parallel patents provided the issue of validity or registration of the patent is not principally in dispute.[49] If infringement is found to have occurred, then the Court may order the defendant to cease infringement of the parallel patents in all the Contracting States. If jurisdiction is purely founded on Article 5(3), then it is submitted that the seised court has no jurisdiction to try the infringement action of a foreign patent.[50]

13.012 Where the court has jurisdiction to concern itself with acts of infringement in other states, *i.e.* where jurisdiction is based on the defendant's domicile, then, when considering the substantive issue of infringement, the court must apply the relevant substantive law. Thus, where an English court is seised of jurisdiction in a patent infringement action, *inter alia*, because the defendant is domiciled, in England, it has jurisdiction to try matters relating to acts in Germany which infringe a parallel German patent.[51] However, it must apply German case law as the substantive law and not English case law even though the rights are harmonised. This is because the German patent derives its existence from German law and no other law. Moreover, acts committed in Germany can never infringe an English patent and vice versa. Unlike many other torts, the location of an act of infringement of an intellectual property rights is crucially important. Even in a European patent case where there is a temptation for a court to consider that the jurisprudence of a German court as to infringement of a German European patent is the same as that of a Dutch or English court is to infringement of a Dutch or English European patent, in fact the approach may differ considerably as to the scope and extent of the claims of a patent.[52]

Whilst it might be thought that the above approach would be expensive, in fact under English law of evidence, a foreign law is presumed to be the same as English law unless evidence to the countrary is provided. Accordingly, in England, it could be very convenient to try all matters

[48] See the Protocol to Art. 169, EPC which provides a harmonised approach to the issue of infringement.

[49] See para. 13.026 and in England, CJJA 1982, s.30.

[50] See *Plastus Kreativ AB v. Minnesota Mining* (1994) H.C.; (unreported).

[51] See CJJA 1982, s.30 applying Article 5(3) in relation to immovable property.

[52] See Chap. 2 on Patents in Europe where the approach of states party to the European Patent Convention to the construction of European patent claims is discussed.

together.[53] Once all matters are tried, a court may issue an injunction relating to acts done in those states where it has determined that infringement has occurred. The injunction would be enforceable against the defendant *in personam* and in relation to actual infringing products, *in rem* in all other Contracting States.

In England, even though a court has jurisdiction to try actions for infringements of foreign patents, such actions may not be "actionable" under the "double actionability" rule.[54]

(ii) Co-defendants

13.013 Under Article 6(1),

> "A person domiciled in a Contracting State may also be sued . . . where he is one of a number of defendants, in the courts for the place where any one of them is domiciled."

The application of this rule is limited. For instance, Article 6(1) confers jurisdiction on a French court in relation to an English co-defendant where the other co-defendant is French. However, Article 6(1) will not apply to give jurisdiction over a co-defendant who is American or any other person not domiciled in a Contracting State. Article 6(1) must be construed restrictively. Accordingly, there must exist such a link between the various actions brought by the same plaintiff against different defendants such that it is expedient to determine those actions together in order to avoid the risk of irreconcilable judgments resulting from separate proceedings.[55] Moreover, the nature of the link must be determined independently and is a Community concept.[56]

In England, under Order 15, defendants may be properly joined without leave of the Court where there is some common question of law or fact which would arise in all the action and all rights to relief claimed in the actions (whether they are joint, several or alternative) are in respect of or arise out of the same transaction or series of transactions.[57] The Court of Appeal has said that where Article 6(1) is concerned, the test for joinder is that which would have applied under Order 11 where a plaintiff seeks leave to serve out of the jurisdiction.[58] Accordingly, a plaintiff would have to show that there was a good arguable case that there exists

[53] In *Alfred Dunhill v. Sunoptic* [1979] F.S.R. 337, C.A., at p. 369, *per* Roskill L.J., (a passing off case), the Court of Appeal said without the benefit of full argument that it would be wrong to grant an injunction worldwide on the basis that foreign law must be presumed to be the same as English law. However, there was no evidence of passing off other than in England and Switzerland which weighed on the court's mind see p. 369 lines 6 to 7. Interestingly, upon motion for judgment given in default, the Court permitted a worldwide passing off injunction (see p. 379).

[54] See para. 13.047.

[55] *Kalfelis* [1988] E.C.R. 5565, ECJ.

[56] *ibid.*

[57] R.S.C., Ord. 15, r. 4. See footnotes to Ord. 15, rr. 4 and 5 for considerations as to how this rule is applied.

[58] *Molnlycke v. Procter & Gamble* [1992] R.P.C. 21, C.A., *per* Dillon L.J. at p. 27 applying the test in *Kalfelis* [1988] E.C.R. 5565, ECJ.

such a link between the various actions brought by the same plaintiff that it is expedient to determine those actions together in order to avoid the risk of irreconcilable judgments resulting from separate proceedings.[59] Moreover, as in Order 11, the plaintiff must satisfy the court that it is proper for it to exercise its discretion in favour of permitting joinder of the defendant.[60] In intellectual property litigation, it is rare that jurisdiction is only founded on the basis of Article 6(1) because actions are normally brought under Article 5(3) in the state where the harmful event occurred because of the territorial rights of intellectual property. However, it can occur. For instance, if a plaintiff sues in England for infringement of copyright in relation to acts done in France by a French and English person on the basis of the domicile of the latter, then the English court plainly has jurisdiction over the English domiciled defendant but neither Article 2 or 5(3) enables the English court to have jurisdiction over the French defendant. Accordingly, under Article 6(1), the plaintiff would have to convince the English court that there was a good arguable case and that it was proper to join the French defendant.

13.014 In *Molnlycke v. Procter & Gamble*,[61] a patent infringement action, the plaintiff brought an action in England against an English and American defendant for acts done in England which it alleged infringed its UK patents. It then realised that a German sister company of the defendants had important documentation relating to the action and sought to join that company as a further co-defendant to the action merely for the purposes of obtaining discovery against it. The plaintiff based its claim under the Convention under Article 5(3) and Article 6(1) on the basis that the German defendant and English defendant had a common intention to infringe in England. This case is discussed in detail later as to the evidential burden that a plaintiff has to discharge to show that jurisdiction is well founded.[62] The Court permitted joinder on the basis that there was a good arguable case that the German company was a joint tortfeasor. However, the Court said that if jurisdiction had been purely on the basis of Article 6(1), it would have been improper in the circumstances to join the German company as such discovery could have been obtained under the 1970 Hague Convention by an application in Germany.[63]

[59] Applying the test in *Kalfelis* above.

[60] See *Molnlycke* [1992] R.P.C. 21, C.A., at p. 27, lines 38–43. *Quaere* whether the Brussels Convention and Art. 7 of the EC Treaty permits a court of a Contracting State to apply a more stringent national rule as to joinder of defendant where the Brussel Convention does apply as opposed to when it does not. Under Ord. 15, r. 4, if the conditions are complied with, the Court has no discretion not to permit joinder (save in the limited circumstances under Ord. 15, r. 5) where under Ord. 11 there is a discretion. Moreover, the standard of proof under Ord. 11 is higher than under Ord. 15.

[61] [1992] R.P.C. 21, C.A.

[62] See para. 13.041.

[63] *Molnlycke v. Procter & Gamble* [1992] R.P.C. 21, C.A., per Dillon L.J. at p. 27. This remark is *obiter dicta* and was made without submissions from counsel for the plaintiffs. As to 1970 Hague Convention on taking of evidence abroad in civil and commercial matters, see McLean *International judicial assistance* (1992) at p. 852.

(iii) Provisional measures—Article 24

13.015 Interlocutory orders feature highly in intellectual property disputes. In the field of piracy, *ex parte* injunctions and preservation of property orders are common. Often disputes will in practice be finally determined by whether or not an interlocutory injunction restraining infringement is obtained. In such cases, it is vital to know about the jurisdictional grounds that the Brussels Convention provides in relation to interim relief.

Article 24 of the Brussels Convention provides that:

> "Application may be made to the courts of a Contracting State for such provisional, including protective measures as may be available under the law of that State, even if, under the Convention, the courts of another Contracting State have jurisdiction as to the substance of the matter."

In order for a court of a Contracting State to have jurisdiction under Article 24, the interim measure must be ancillary to the main proceedings on the substantive issue, must afford the plaintiff provisional (including protective) relief and must depend for their continuance upon the outcome of the proceedings on the main issue.[64] Article 24 also applies to *ex parte* proceedings.[65]

The use of the phrase "even if" in Article 24 means that *at the very least*, the fact that the courts of one Contracting State have jurisdiction under the Convention in the substantive matter is no bar to a court of another Contracting State assuming jurisdiction for the purposes of awarding provisional measures. However, what is not clear is the application of Article 24 when a Contracting State does not have jurisdiction as to the substantive matter *under the Brussels Convention.*

(1) Subject matter of the substantive action excluded from Brussels Convention

13.016 The fact that the substantive matter is excluded from the Convention under Article 1 does not *per se* prevent a party seeking ancillary protective relief in a Contracting State under Article 24 of the Convention in a Contracting State. The ECJ has held that the general scheme of the Con-

[64] Kaye *Civil Jurisdiction and Enforcement of Foreign Judgments* (1987), p. 1140 modifying a proposal put forward by a German commentator on the Convention. See also Case 120/79, *de Cavel v. de Cavel (No. 2)* [1980] E.C.R. 1553 at 1572—"provisional, including protective measures are by definition, ancillary measures." However, the English Court of Appeal has said that a post-judgment *Mareva* provisional order pending final enforcement of a judgment falls within Art. 24, see *Babanaft International Co. SA v. Bassatne and another* [1989] 2 W.L.R. 232, C.A., *per* Kerr L.J. at 249 which would appear to conflict with the requirement that the order depends on the outcome of the final proceedings.

[65] Case 125/79, *Denilauler v. Couchet Freres* [1980] E.C.R. 1553; [1981] 1 C.M.L.R. 62. See also CJJA 1982, s.25 (which seeks to enact Art. 24) which specifically confers jurisdiction on the High Court of England and Wales or Northern Ireland where proceedings have been or are to be commenced in a Contracting State other than the U.K.

vention does not necessarily link the treatment of an ancillary claim to that of a principal claim.[66] Thus, ancillary matters come within the scope of the Convention according to the subject matter with which they themselves are concerned with and not according to the subject matter involved in the principal claim.[67] Thus, it has been said that the provisional proceedings are only excluded from the Convention's scope where they themselves concern or are closely connected with subject matter excluded under the Convention.[68] Whilst the intellectual property practitioner will rarely be concerned with substantive matters excluded from the Convention,[69] it demonstrates the width and usefulness of Article 24.

(2) Substantive action in or to be brought in another Contracting State

13.017 Article 24 specifically allows a party to pursue interim measures in Contracting States other than where the substantive action is taking place. Thus, a party which conducts an infringement action in Contracting State B can obtain a discovery order in State A provided that such an order is available under the law of the latter State. It is submitted that as a matter of common sense, "such measures as may be available under the law of that State" in Article 24 means that in deciding what interim relief is available under the national law of the court seised of the application for interim relief, one must disregard any rules of national law which say that relief or certain types of relief are not available in cases where the courts of a foreign country have jurisdiction as to the substance of the dispute.[70] Thus, Article 24 would take priority over inconsistent national laws.[71] However, there is considerable support for the opposite view, namely, that national laws are to govern both the power of a court of a Contracting State to grant provisional relief in respect of foreign substantive proceedings and also its jurisdictional rules for granting such relief.[72]

The United Kingdom has specifically enacted that the High Court in England and Wales or Northern Ireland has power to grant interim relief where proceedings have been or are to be commenced in a Contracting State other than the United Kingdom or in a part of the United Kingdom other than in which the High Court in question exercises jurisdiction.[73]

[66] See Case 120/79, *de Cavel (No. 2)* [1980] E.C.R. 731 (at 740–741), [1980] 3 C.M.L.R. 1.

[67] *ibid*, at p. 741.

[68] Kaye *Civil Jurisdiction and Enforcement of Foreign Judgments* (1987) at p. 1174. However, note somewhat contradictory remarks by Kaye at p. 1144 where he states that Art. 24 only applies "to confer jurisdiction in respect of provisional including protective relief measures when under the Convention courts of a Contracting State are entitled to exercise jurisdiction over the substance of the dispute".

[69] One example would be a fight over intellectual property rights in a matrimonial dispute.

[70] See Kaye *Civil Jurisdiction and Enforcement of Foreign Judgments* (1987), p. 1148.

[71] See *ibid*, n. 53, p. 1148, where it notates decisions of the Belgian, German and Luxembourg courts which ruled as such.

[72] *ibid*, p. 1148 and n. 54.

[73] CJJA 1982, s.25(1)(a).

This is subject to the rule that the proceedings must relate to subject matter which falls within the Brussels Convention.[74] In *ex parte* proceedings, it may mean that apart from another Contracting State, the proposed plaintiff has a non-Contracting State where he is entitled to bring the substantive action. If he brought the substantive action in a non-Contracting State it is considered that Article 24 is inapplicable.[75] Thus, if Article 24 is to be relied upon, the Court should insist on an undertaking that the substantive action be brought in a Contracting State.

13.018 It may be that the defendant or putative defendant is not domiciled in a Contracting State. Under the Brussels Convention, the jurisdiction of a court is then determined according to national laws.[76] If a Contracting State holds that it is entitled to exercise jurisdiction under its national rules, then by virtue of Article 4 that state has determined that it has jurisdiction *under the Convention* but by reference to its national laws. Thus, as has been pointed out, such would mean that the proviso in Article 24 would apply and that therefore Article 24 would be applicable regardless of the domicile of the defendant.[77] Thus, one could invoke Article 24. For example if, in England, in a licensing dispute where the proposed defendant is American, jurisdiction is conferred via Order 11, r. 1(1)(d)(iii) of the Rules of the Supreme Court, which gives a plaintiff leave to serve outside the jurisdiction where the contract's proper law is English, then Article 24 would allow a party to seek interim relief in another Contracting State.

The English court has a discretion to refuse interim relief where its only basis of jurisdiction other than under section 25 is it makes it inexpedient for court to grant it.[78]

(3) Substantive action not being brought in a Contracting State

13.019 Does Article 24 entitle a plaintiff to seek interim relief where the substantive action is not brought in another Contracting State?

The ECJ has said that Article 24 expressly envisages the case of provisional measures in a Contracting State where under this Convention the courts of another Contracting State have jurisdiction as to the substance of the matter.[79] It may be considered that it was not the intention of the

[74] CJJA 1982, s.25(1)(b). Thus, this overturns the rule in *The Siskina* [1979] A.C. 210, H.L. where the Brussels Convention is applicable. See *Babanaft International Co. SA v. Bassatne and another* [1989] 2 W.L.R. 232, C.A. The rule that the main proceedings must concern proceedings whose subject matter falls within the Convention would appear to be contrary to the ECJ's rulings on Art. 24—see Substantive matter excluded from Convention, para. 13.016.

[75] See para. 13.019 below.

[76] Art. 4.

[77] Kaye *Civil Jurisdiction and Enforcement of Foreign Judgments* (1987), p. 1144.

[78] CJJA 1982, s.25(2) *Quaere* whether determination of expediency can include the fact that applicant could have brought proceedings in another Contracting State as this would appear to undermine Art. 24.

[79] See Case 143/78 *de Cavel (No. 1)* [1979] E.C.R. 1055, (at 1066) [1979] 2 C.M.C.R. 547.

legislators to confer jurisdiction for interim measures on the courts of the Contracting State where the plaintiff has not brought and never sought to bring an action in a Contracting State. Such would be more the concern of bilateral treaties between countries where the substantive action is situate and the country where the interim relief is sought. However, the ECJ has said that the provisions of the Convention do not necessarily link the treatment of an ancillary claim of that of a principal claim.[80] As seen above, the mere fact that the principal claim concerns subject matter excluded under the Brussels Convention does not prevent Article 24 from applying.[81] Accordingly, by way of analogy, it could be argued that the mere fact that the principal claim is not subject to the jurisdiction of the court of a Contracting State does not prevent Article 24 from being applicable provided the interim relief itself falls within the Brussels Convention.

The position is unclear. It would certainly seem strange that an order made by a Contracting State under Article 24 would be enforceable in all Convention countries but that the final judgment made in a non-Contracting State would not be enforceable under the Convention. However, exactly the same complaint could be made about interim orders made under Article 24 where the substantive action concerns matter excluded from the Convention. In such circumstances, an interim preservative order would have to be recognised by Convention countries but judgment in the substantive matter would not have to be so recognised.

(4) Extra-territorial interim orders

13.020 The main effect of Article 24 is to permit a plaintiff whose substantive action is brought or to be brought in Contracting State A to seek interim relief in the courts of Contracting State B. The classic example is where the defendant has assets in State B which the plaintiff desires to preserve pending determination of the action in State A. However, a plaintiff will often seek an interim order in one State which is intended to have effect in anther State. For instance, a plaintiff obtains an interim injunction in State A which is directed at activities of the defendant or proposed defendant in State B. Alternatively, a plaintiff obtains an asset freezing order in State A which is intended to have effect in all Contracting States.

13.021 From a jurisdictional viewpoint, there are two issues. Firstly, does the court in State A have the power to make such an extraterritorial order? Secondly, is a court in the State where the order is intended to have effect obliged to recognise such a judgment? In general, the Convention makes no distinction between orders which only purport to affect activities or property in the Contracting State where the order was made and those purporting to have extra-territorial effect.[82] Indeed, the Convention was clearly aimed at *inter alia* ensuring the easy enforcement of judgments in

[80] See Case 120/79 *de Cavel (No. 2)* [1980] E.C.R. 731.
[81] See above para. 13.016.
[82] Arts. 25, 26.

one Contracting State which were given in another Contracting State. Thus, the Convention envisages that judgments would have extra-territorial effect. For instance, a money judgment made in State A can be easily enforced against assets of the defendant in State B. Accordingly, in several ECJ cases concerning pre-judgment orders made by the courts of one state preserving assets of the Defendant pending judgment in another state, there was no suggestion that there was any basis for criticising the orders of the French court on the grounds that they purported to operate extraterritorially.[83] Indeed, the English Court of Appeal in commenting on these cases said that such is not surprising as the object of the Convention was to create something analogous to a single law district for the whole of the E.C.[84]

13.022 However, any order which purports to have effect extraterritorially, should not purport to operate directly upon assets, etc. Instead, the effectiveness of the order derives from its recognition and enforcement by the local courts and such should be made clear in the terms of the orders to avoid any misunderstanding suggesting an unwarranted assumption of extraterritorial jurisdiction.[85]

In considering the power of a court to make an extra-territorial order, the legal advisor should be careful to distinguish between whether a court can make the order and whether the order should be made. This can be illustrated by way of example. O is the owner of a patent in State A. X manufactures infringing products in State A. Y manufactures identical products in State B where there is no patent. Some of X's products are exported to State B. Under Article 24, O can seek to obtain an interim injunction affecting X's products in both State A and B. However, O is not entitled to an interim injunction in relation to Y's products because they have not infringed any right of O.

What is the position where the plaintiff seeks interim injunctive relief in relation to acts of infringement in several Contracting States where he owns parallel patents? The ability of a court to grant *final* relief has already been discussed.[86] Does Article 24 permit a court to grant interim extra-territorial relief where it could not grant corresponding relief at the final disposal of the action? For instance, O, the owner of a patent in State A, sues in State A a defendant domiciled in State B for acts of infringement carried out in State A under Article 5(3) of the Convention. It has already been submitted that the court seised under that rule has no

[83] See *de Cavel (No. 1)* [1979] E.C.R. 1055, *Denilauler v. Couchet Freres* [1980] E.C.R. 1553 (both cases concerned the issue of pre-judgment *saisie conservatoire* by the French court).

[84] *Babanaft International Co. SA v. Bassatne and another* [1989] 2 W.L.R. 232, C.A., *per* Kerr L.J. at p. 246.

[85] See Kerr L.J.'s remarks in *Babanaft International Co. SA v. Bassatne and another* [1989] 2 W.L.R. 232, C.A. at 246. However, nothing prevents, under English law regardless of the Convention, a court making an order *in personam* against a defendant which imposes a personal obligation on him not to move or deal in assets abroad—*per* Kerr L.J. at p. 247.

[86] See para. 13.011.

jurisdiction at the final determination of the matter to grant final injunctions in relation to acts of infringement occurring in other Contracting States where O has parallel patents. However, under Article 24, does it have jurisdiction to grant interim injunctions in relation to acts of infringement occurring in other Contracting States where O has parallel patents? It would seem strange if Article 24 confers wider powers on a seised court than it would have at final determination of the matter. However, Article 24 was clearly intended to facilitate the obtaining of provisional and protective orders. In the above example, the court might be inclined to grant such extra-territorial preservative relief upon an undertaking by the plaintiff to issue proceedings in the courts of the state of the defendant's domicile (that latter court would then have jurisdiction in relation to all acts of infringement carried out in Contracting States).[87] It should be noted that courts in the Netherlands have used Article 24 to grant extraterritorial injunctions where parallel rights exist.[88]

The second issue as to whether a court in which the extraterritorial order is sought to be enforced is discussed below in relation to recognition and enforcement of judgments. In particular, where an order is given without the other party being summoned to appear, the court of another Contracting State is not obliged under the Convention to recognise the judgment.[89]

(iv) Lis alibi pendens—conflicts of forum

13.023 Two Articles of the Brussels Convention deal with the issue where there is a possibility of two identical or similar actions running in parallel in differing Contracting States.

Article 21 states that:

> "Where proceedings involving the same cause of action and between the same parties are brought in the courts of different Contracting States, any court other than the court first seised shall of its own motion stay proceedings until such time as the jurisdiction of the court first seised is established.
>
> Where the jurisdiction of the court first seised is established, any court other than the court first seised shall decline jurisdiction in favour of that court."[90]

Article 22 states that:

> "Where related actions are brought in the courts of different Con-

[87] See para. 13.011.

[88] This is done under the "kort geding" (summary procedure) law, see *Brinkhof* [1993] 26 IIC No 6761 and *Brinkhof* "Could the President of the District Court of the Hague Take Measures concerning the Infringement of Foreign Patents" [1994] EIPR 360.

[89] See para. 13.037 *et seq*.

[90] This is the new version of Art. 21 as amended by Art. 8 of the Accession of Spain and Portugal to the Brussels Convention ("the San Sebastian Convention"). This rule applies regardless of the domicile of the parties—see Case C–351/89, *Overseas Union Insurance Ltd v. New Hampshire Insurance* [1992] 2 W.L.R. 586, ECJ.

tracting States, any court other than the court first seised may, while the actions are pending at first instance, stay its proceedings.

A court other than the court first seised may also, on the application of one of the parties, decline jurisdiction if the law of that court permits the consolidation of related actions and the court first seised has jurisdiction over both actions.

For the purposes of this Article, actions are deemed to be related where they are so closely connected that it is expedient to hear and determine them together to avoid the risk of irreconcilable judgments resulting from separate proceedings."

There are two principal differences between the two articles. First, Article 21 requires the court seised second to decline jurisdiction altogether if the first court is seised and its jurisdiction established whilst Article 22 only empowers (*i.e.* does not require) the court later seised to stay its proceedings.[91] Secondly, a court must act of its own motion in Article 21 whereas this does not apply in Article 22.[92] A court is deemed seised of a matter once proceedings have definitely been issued or if earlier, when an *ex parte* order is made prior to service.[93]

(1) Related Actions—Claims for infringement and revocation

13.024 An important issue to intellectual property practitioners is whether an action for infringement of an intellectual property right and a counterclaim for revocation of the same right fall within Article 21 or 22? The ECJ in *Gubisch v. Palumbo*[94] gave this Article a broad interpretation, rejecting the need for a formal identity between the two sets of proceedings and saying that the Article should be given an autonomous European meaning. Thus, proceedings to enforce a contract and one to annul were held to fall within Article 21. Such proceedings are analogous to a patent infringement action and an action to revoke the patent. However, in *Gubisch*, no question of exclusive jurisdiction arose. It has been said that the underlying rationale of Article 21 is to avoid incompatible judgments in different States.[95] Irreconcilable judgments could arise if the court trying the infringement action found that infringement had occurred but the other court found that the patent was valid. The difficulty is that a defendant can only bring an action for revocation in the state of registration of the right.[96] Thus, where for example a plaintiff issues proceedings in State A (being the domicile of the defendant) for

[91] In Case C–351/89, *Overseas Union Insurance Ltd v. New Hampshire Insurance Co.* [1992] 2 W.L.R. 586, the ECJ held that the second seised court could not examine the jurisdiction of the first court seised.

[92] *e.g.* see *LA Gear v. Gerald Whelan & Sons* [1991] FSR 670, H.C.

[93] See *Zegler v. Salinitri* [1984] E.C.R. ; *Dresser v. Falcongate* [1992] 1 Q.B. 502 C.A.

[94] [1987] E.C.R. 4861, ECJ.

[95] Burnside and Burnside, "Patents Litigation under the Judgment Convention" *Patent World*, March 1988, p. 18 at p. 23.

[96] Art. 16(4).

infringement of a patent registered in State B, then if the court of the state of registration, State B, declined jurisdiction in relation to a subsequent action to revoke the right, then the defendant would not be able to seek revocation of the right.

It is thought that the better view is that in that situation, the actions are related under Article 22 and that the court trying the infringement action should stay the action pending determination of the revocation action. However, where the court seised of the infringement action is the first seised court (which will often be the case), Article 22 suggests that the first seised court cannot grant a stay. However, in most jurisdictions, courts have an inherent right to stay proceedings.[97] Whether such inherent jurisdictional rules are still valid in the context of the Brussels Convention is unclear. Certainly, Articles 21 and 22 do not seem to have been drafted with Article 16 in mind. It is hoped that the ECJ will hold that the inherent jurisdictional rules enabling a stay in many Contracting States have not been overruled by Articles 21 and 22.[98] As has been suggested, a stay should not always be granted as such a policy would give the defendants too great a scope for delaying tactics.[99] Thus such factors as the likelihood of the patent being found invalid, the likely delay, the cost of the proceedings and the financial resources of the parties would be taken into account.

Indeed, a preferable route would be for the court trying the infringement action to decline jurisdiction and for both actions to be consolidated in the court of the state of registration (where jurisdiction for the infringement action will be provided under Article 5(3)). However, as discussed before, if the court trying the infringement action is the first seised, Article 22 does not provide a basis for that court to decline jurisdiction.

(2) Are parallel actions related actions under Article 22?

13.025 Where there are parallel claims in several jurisdictions relating to infringement of parallel intellectual property rights, should a court other than the first seised stay its proceedings or alternatively, decline jurisdiction on the application of a party on the basis that the court first seised has jurisdiction over the actions and its law permits consolidation of related actions. Because of the territorial nature of patents, a judgment

[97] *e.g.*, in England, see *Amersham International plc v. Corning Limited et al* [1987] R.P.C. 53—stay of European patent infringement action refused pending outcome of opposition proceedings before European Patent Office.

[98] The difficulty with this approach is that the Brussels Convention only envisages courts of a Contracting State resorting to national jurisdictional rules if the defendant is not domiciled in a Contracting State—see Art. 4. *Quaere* whether a stay is a national *jurisdictional* rule or merely a *procedural* rule.

[99] See Burnside & Burnside "Patents Litigation under the Judgment Convention", *Patent World*, March 1988, p. 18, at p. 23.

on an English patent is never irreconcilable with a judgment on a French patent on the same facts because each judgment only relates to acts done within a national border. Thus, under Article 22, it could never be said that such parallel actions do not fall within the definition of "related actions" as there is no "danger of irreconcilable judgments". Accordingly, it could be submitted that Article 22 is inapplicable. However, it may be that a more liberal interpretation of "irreconcilable judgments" is taken. Thus, in parallel actions on a European patent, it is highly undesirable that differing judgments should be given.

If such parallel actions are "related" for the purposes of Article 22, it is clearly highly desirable that a court other than the first seised should stay its proceedings pending determination of the issue of infringement by the court first seised if there is clearly a common issue. For instance, where parallel European patents are sued upon, it would be desirable for the court first seised to determine all factual issues and then permit the courts of other states to rely upon these findings of fact in determining the legal issues.

Where a defendant in a court other than the first seised applies to the court that all parallel actions be *consolidated* under second paragraph of Article 22 to the court first seised, the first seised court will only have jurisdiction over parallel infringement actions where the defendant is domiciled in the state of the first seised court.[1] Thus an application to consolidate parallel proceedings in differing jurisdictions was rejected in England because an English court did not have jurisdiction to hear claims for infringement of foreign rights in foreign territories where the defendant was not domiciled in England.[2] However, where a defendant is domiciled in a Contracting State and a plaintiff sues the defendant in that state for acts committed in several Contracting States which infringe parallel rights, the court of that Contracting State will have jurisdiction for all such parallel infringing acts.[3] In such circumstances, should a court not first seised favour consolidation of all the parallel actions in one State? Certainly, it would be expedient to do so. As discussed above, there is no objection to a court trying parallel actions for infringement in several states provided one court has jurisdiction for all matters.[4] Of course, the substantive law of each country would have to be applied in relation to the infringement of the relevant national right. However, in England, there is a presumption that a foreign law is the same as an English law unless proven otherwise.[5] Accordingly, where there is a high degree of harmonisation, *i.e.* all the parallel patents are derived from a European patent, then there is much to commend consolidation.

[1] See para. 13.010 *et seq* on Art. 5(3).
[2] See *LA Gear v. Gerald Whelan & Sons* [1991] FSR 670 at 676, H.C.
[3] *e.g.* in England, see CJJA 1982, s.30.
[4] See Extraterritorial pan. European injunctions in Intellectual Property, para. 13.011.
[5] See para. 13.012.

(v) Proceedings concerned with registration or validity of intellectual property rights

13.026 Under Article 16, exclusive jurisdiction, regardless of the domicile of the parties,[6] is conferred on the courts of a particular Contracting State. The effect of Article 16 cannot be ousted by a jurisdiction agreement or submission to another jurisdiction by the entry of appearance.[7] If a court accepts jurisdiction in breach of Article 16, its judgment will not be recognised or enforced in another Contracting State.[8] Where a court of a Contracting State is seised of a claim which is principally concerned with a matter over which the courts of another Contracting State have exclusive jurisdiction by virtue of Article 16, the court must declare of its own motion that it has no jurisdiction.[9] In the rare instances that actions come within the exclusive jurisdiction of several courts, then any court other than the court first seised must decline jurisdiction in favour of that court.[10]

(1) Registered rights

13.027 Article 16(4) confers exclusive jurisdiction regardless of domicile:

> "in proceedings concerned with the registration of validity of patents, trade marks, designs, or other similar rights required to be deposited or registered, the courts of the Contracting State in which the deposit or registration has been applied for, has taken place or is under the term of an international convention deemed to have taken place."

The Jenard Report gives fruit and vegetable variety rights as an example of "similar rights".[11]

The ECJ has construed the extent of Article 16 very restrictively. Thus, in the case of *Sanders v. Van der Putte*[12] which was concerned with whether a dispute over a lease of a florist's business was within Article 16(1) (which confers exclusive jurisdiction in proceedings which have as their object right *in rem* in immoveable property to the courts of the Contracting State in which the property is situated), the ECJ held:

> " . . . the assignment, in the interests of the proper administration of justice, of exclusive jurisdiction to the courts of one Contracting State in accordance with Article 16 of the Convention results in depriving the parties of the choice which would otherwise be theirs and, in certain cases, results in their being brought before a court

[6] Even where the defendant is domiciled in a non-Contracting State, see Art. 4(1).
[7] Arts. 17(3) and 18.
[8] Arts. 28 and 34.
[9] Art. 19.
[10] Art. 23.
[11] The Jenard Report on the 1968 Convention and the 1971 Protocol [1979] O.J. C59/1 and 66.
[12] Case 73/77, [1977] E.C.R. 2383, [1979] 1 C.M.L.R. 331.

> which is not that of the domicile of any of them. Having regard to that consideration the provisions of Article 16 must not be given a wider interpretation than is required by their objective.[13]"

Professor Jenard in his report states that the reason for Article 16(4) is that the grant of a registered intellectual property right is an exercise of national sovereignty.

The ECJ's restrictive analysis of Article 16 was applied to Article 16(4) in the case of *Duijnstee v. Goderbauer*.[14] In this case, the dispute arose as to whether either Goderbauer, the inventor of a mounting for a rail, or the liquidator of his employer company, was entitled to the patents that he had applied for the invention. The dispute as to ownership thus arose on the legal relationship between Goderbauer and the insolvent company.[15] The Hoge Raad considered of its own motion whether it had jurisdiction to hear the action because of Article 16(4) and made a reference to the ECJ.

13.028 The ECJ held that the term "proceedings concerned with the registration or validity of patents" in Article 16(4) must be regarded as an independent concept intended to have uniform application in all the Contracting States.[16] It then went on to define what this meant. It first stated that the reason for Article 16(4) was that the courts of a Contracting State are best placed to adjudicate upon cases in which the dispute itself concerns the validity of the patent or the existence of the deposit or registration. It then said that Article 16(4) must be construed restrictively and that:

> "proceedings concerned with the registration or validity of patents must be regarded as proceedings in which the conferring of exclusive jurisdiction on the courts of the place in which the patent was granted *is justified* in the light of the factors mentioned above, such as proceedings relating to the validity, existence or lapse of a patent or an alleged right of priority by reason of an earlier deposit."[17]

The above passage does not clarify the application of Article 16(4) but instead confuses. It suggests that a court seised of a jurisdictional issue under Article 16(4) should examine whether it is justified that a court of another Contracting State should have exclusive jurisdiction. The justification that the ECJ gives, namely that courts of a Contracting State are best placed to adjudicate upon cases where registration or validity of its

[13] However, in Case 241/83, *Rösler v. Rotwinkel* [1985] E.C.R. 99, [1985] 1 CMLR 806, the ECJ gave a contrasting wide interpretation of Art. 16(1) on the facts but without making any general statement.

[14] Case 288/82, [1983] E.C.R. 3663, [1985] 1 C.M.L.R. 220.

[15] The patent applications were not derived from a European patent application. If they had been, different jurisdictional rules would have applied—see para. 13.058.

[16] Thus the suggestion by Schlosser (para. 168) that the various concepts should be decided by reference to the *lex situs* would not seem applicable. See Schlosser "Report on the Convention of October 9, 1978 on the Accession of the Kingdom of United Kingdom, Ireland and Denmark to the Brussels Convention" [1979] O.J. C 59/71.

[17] Para. 24.

patents are in issue seems a poor one. As has been pointed out, it substantially amounts to saying that justice would be best served if national law as to validity was applied by the courts of that nation.[18] Such is a truism and would apply as much to infringement actions as to questions of validity. Yet, infringement actions are subject to the primary rule of the defendant's domicile and clearly do not fall within Article 16(4).[19] Thus, the matter is no clearer.

In *Duijnstee v. Goderbauer*, the court held that Article 16(4) did not include the instant dispute, noting the fact that a clear distinction between jurisdiction in disputes concerning the right to a patent and that of registration or validity of a patent was drawn in the European Patent Convention and the draft Community Patent Convention.[20]

(2) Unregistered rights

13.029 Article 16(4) does not cover unregistrable rights like copyright, unregistered design rights or common law rights. Article 16(1) provides that "in proceedings which have as their object rights *in rem* in, or tenancies of, immovable property, the courts of the Contracting State in which the property is situated" have exclusive jurisdiction. As seen, Article 16(1) is construed restrictively. It was not sufficient merely that a right *in rem* in immovable property was involved in an action or that the action had a link with immovable property but that the action had to be based on a right *in rem* and not on a right *in personam*.[21] Under English law, proceedings for trespass or any other tort relating to immovable property situated abroad is justiciable in England provided the proceedings are not principally concerned the question of title or right to possession of the property.[22]

Is unregistered intellectual property "immovable property" within the meaning of Article 16(1)? Neither the Jenard nor the Schlosser report mention anything about the relationship between Article 16(1) and intellectual property rights. Nor is there any definition of "immovable property" in the Convention. Under English law, intellectual property rights are generally analogous to immovables.[23] Firstly, the monopoly has no effect beyond the territory of the State under whose laws it is granted. Secondly, the title to intellectual property rights devolves according to

[18] Wadlow, ELR, October 1985, p. 305 at 310.
[19] See para. 23 of *Duijnstee* referring to Jenard Report.
[20] The patents in issue were not European patents. Disputes as to ownership of European patents are subject to special jurisdictional rules, see para. 13.058.
[21] *Webb v. Webb* [1994] 3 W.L.R. 801, ECJ.
[22] CJJA 1982, s.30.
[23] See *Tyburn Productions Ltd v. Conan Doyle* [1990] 1 All E.R. 909 (Ch.D.) applying *Potter v. Broken Hill Pty Co. Ltd [1906]* 3 C.L.R. 479, (High Court of Australia). See Richard Arnold "Can One Sue in England for Infringement of Foreign Intellectual Property Rights" [1990] 7 EIPR 255.

the laws imposed by the state where it was created.[24–25] Even a vital ingredient in the tort of passing-off, namely goodwill, is territorial. Thus there are good arguments for holding that unregistered intellectual property rights are equivalent to immoveables and fall, for the purposes of jurisdictional law, within Article 16(1). If this is so, argument as to the applicability of Article 16(4) will apply equally to unregistered intellectual property under Article 16(1).

(3) Infringement actions where validity in issue

13.030 In many intellectual property actions, the validity of the right is put in issue by the defendant. Thus, in a patent infringement action, the defendant will often counterclaim for revocation of the patent. In such a case, the plaintiff will usually have two jurisdictional options—one based on the domicile of the defendant and one based on where the infringement occurred. The latter will always be in the same Contracting State as where the right is situated but the former may often be in a different Contracting State. Thus where an infringement action is brought in a state other than where one or more of the patents sued upon are registered (*i.e.* that of the defendant's domicile), is the court of that state prevented by Article 16(4) from deciding upon any issues as to validity?

As discussed earlier, the ECJ has said that Article 16(4) must be interpreted restrictively.[26] Furthermore, Article 19 states that a court of a contracting State should declare of its own motion that it has no jurisdiction to hear a claim which is "principally" concerned with a matter over which the courts of another Contracting State have exclusive jurisdiction by virtue of Article 16. Thus, in deciding whether another court has exclusive jurisdiction under Article 16(4), the seised court must determine whether the claim is principally concerned with proceedings relating to the registration or validity of intellectual property.[27]

The Jenard Report states that the court is not obliged to declare of its own motion that it has no jurisdiction if the matter within the jurisdiction of the other court is raised as a preliminary or incidental matter.[28] However, the question of validity in an infringement action is neither the principal one (it acts as a defence but does not constitute an action in itself) nor could it be realistically called preliminary or incidental.[29] How

[24–25] See observations by Griffith C.J. in *Potter v. Broken Hill Pty Co. Ltd* [1906] 3 C.L.R. 479, (High Court of Australia), at 494. For more detailed discussion of the immovable v. moveable distinction and its applicability to intellectual property, see para. 13.044 below.

[26] See para. 13.027, above.

[27] *e.g.* see *Jenard*, A1.153; Kaye *Civil Jurisdiction and Enforcement of Foreign Judgments* (1987), p. 874 and reference to opinions of commentators, n. 20; O'Malley & Layton *European Civil Practice* (1989), p. 702, para. 20.04 at p. 520.

[28] The Jenard Report on the 1968 Convention and the 1971 protocol [1979] O.J. C 59/1 and 66. The Jenard Report must be taken into account in ascertaining the meaning or effect of any provision of the Convention and given due weight in the United Kingdom—CJJA 1982, s.3.

[29] See Wadlow, p. 314.

then does Article 16 and 19 affect a defence of invalidity in an infringement action?

In such circumstances, a court has potentially three options:

(1) to decline jurisdiction to try the issue of validity and thus assume that the patent is valid;
(2) to stay infringement proceedings until validity has been determined in the state of registration;
(3) to assume jurisdiction and try the issue of validity *inter partes* as well as infringement.

13.031 *Counterclaim for revocation*—Before answering such a question, it should be noted that there is no basis under the Convention for a court other than that of the state of registration for ordering revocation of a patent. Where a defendant counterclaims for revocation, Article 6(3) extends the jurisdiction of the court of the claim to that of the counterclaim. Prima facie, Article 6(3) would appear to give the right to the court trying the infringement proceedings to assume jurisdiction over the counter-claim of invalidity. However, in *Salotti v. RUWA*[30] and *Galeries Segoura v. Rahim Bonakdarian*,[31] the ECJ held that Article 17 (which gives exclusive jurisdiction to the courts of a Contracting State in cases where the parties had elected a choice of jurisdiction clause), should take precedence over Article 6(3). By analogy, it is submitted that Article 6(3) should not be allowed to derogate from Article 16.[32] This would prevent any difficulties on irreconcilable judgments and prevent one state ordering revocation of a patent in another state. Accordingly, a defendant is limited to contend the validity of the patent and cannot outside the state of registration, counterclaim for revocation.

13.032 (1) **Decline jurisdiction**—A court could hold that it has no power to rule on validity. Thus, if a patent has been granted, it would have to presume that it was valid. Such would require a defendant who disputed validity to either concede it or bring a separate revocation action in another state. This would put the defendant to considerable expense and inconvenience, as pointed out, thus going against the golden rule of the Convention, namely that the defendant comes first.[33] The danger of this approach is that the presumption that the patent is valid may be wholly wrong. If a subsequent revocation action brought in the state of registration proves successful, then there are two conflicting judgments. Commentators have pointed out the dangers that such pose.[34]

[30] Case 24/76, [1976] E.C.R. 1831; [1977] 1 C.M.L.R. 345.
[31] Case 25/76, [1976] E.C.R. 1851; [1971] 1 C.M.L.R. 361.
[32] See also Kaye *Civil Jurisdiction and Enforcement of Foreign Judgments* (1987), p. 1022, n. 331.
[33] Wadlow, p. 312.
[34] See Tritton/Tritton "The Brussels Convention and Intellectual Property" [1987] 12 EIPR 349; Wadlow *op. cit.*

(2) **Stay proceedings**—Normally, an infringement action will be brought and the defendant will then be obliged to seek to revoke the patent. Where the defendant has brought or intends to bring an action for revocation, the court could decide to stay the infringement action pending resolution of the validity of the patent in the state of registration. The issue as to whether a court would or could order a stay or consolidate proceedings to the state of registration in such a case is discussed elsewhere.[35] **13.033**

(3) **Court tries issue of validity**—A court decide to try the issue of invalidity. As mentioned above, this will be an available option if it holds that the proceedings are not principally concerned with validity. However, if the proceedings are principally concerned with validity, Article 16(4) would oust the jurisdiction of the court in favour of the courts of the state of registration. Furthermore, there is the danger of irreconcilable judgments if the patent is revoked in the state of registration after a finding that the patent is valid and has been infringed.[36] Because of this risk of irreconcilable judgments, commentators have suggested that wherever any ruling on validity in an infringement action is made in a Contracting State where the right is not registered, it should be restricted to an *inter partes* ruling and would not be intended to have any legal effect outside the ambit of the action.[37] Thus, a patent which was revoked would be recognised throughout all Contracting States but, for the purposes of the infringement action, the revocation of the patent would be deemed to have no effect.[38] **13.034**

(vi) Effect of Brussels Convention when intellectual property is registered in a non-Contracting State

What is the situation when the proceedings concern an intellectual property registered in a non-Contracting State? In such circumstances, do the general rules of the Convention apply? For instance, does an English court have jurisdiction under the Brussels Convention where a plaintiff sues a person domiciled in England for the infringement of an American patent? If the matter is purely one of infringement, then it would appear **13.035**

[35] See para. 13.024.

[36] The Brussels Convention permits courts to refuse to recognise judgments "if it is irreconcilable with a judgment given in a dispute between the same parties in the State in which recognition is sought."—Art. 27(3). Commentators have pointed out that Art. 27(3) only covers a specific situation. It does not assist in which judgment takes priority in other States. Also, it means that the revocation judgment will not be recognised in the state where the infringement proceedings occurred and vice versa the infringement judgment will not be recognised in the state of registration where the revocation action took place—see Tritton/Tritton "The Brussels Convention and Intellectual Property" [1987] 12 EIPR 349, p. 352.

[37] See Wadlow *op. cit* and Tritton/Tritton, *op. cit.*

[38] Indeed, there is precedent for this in England—see *Poulton v. Adjustable Corp. and Boiler Block* [1908] RPC at 529.

that an English court has jurisdiction under the primary rule of domicile although American law would apply to the proceedings.[39]

If the matter purely or principally concerns the validity of the registered right, the matter is less clear. Most jurisdictions will be very reluctant to determine the validity of a right which has been granted pursuant to legislation in another country.[40] However, there is no express provision in the Brussels Convention requiring courts to decline jurisdiction in such circumstances. Article 16(4) only applies where the right is registered in a Contracting State.[41] As Article 16 is interpreted restrictively, it would appear that there is no derogation from the primary rule of domicile. However, as has been pointed out, this would be contrary to the basic principle of exclusive jurisdiction, namely that the courts of states concerned with actions dealt with under Article 16 should have exclusive jurisdiction in such proceedings.[42] Thus, the policy ground for conferring exclusive jurisdiction under Article 16(4) on the court where the intellectual property is registered is that those courts are best placed to adjudicate[43] and that reason applies equally to non-Contracting States.

13.036 Commentators tend to the view that the seised court should resort to its national jurisdictional rules.[44] The arguments in favour of a court applying national jurisdictional grounds are that national jurisdictional rules akin to Article 16 which provide that the court is not the appropriate place for determination of the issue could be exercised.[45] A difficulty with this approach is that Article 4, which permits the courts to apply their national jurisdictional rules, only applies where the defendant is not domiciled in a Contracting State.

As the purpose of Article 16 is to ensure that courts which have the closest and most real connection with a dispute are alone competent to decide it, such a principle ought equally to apply to disputes where the connecting factor is outside all the Contracting States. Thus, it is sug-

[39] See Brussels Convention, Art. 24 and CJJA 1982, s.30.

[40] English law prevents courts from exercising jurisdiction in such cases—in *Tyburn Productions Ltd v. Conan Doyle* [1990] 1 All E.R. 909 (Ch. D.) which purely concerned a question of title to United States copyright, the defendant (Lady Bromet) resided in England and thus her domicile was in England. Whilst the court held that it did not have jurisdiction to hear the claim (see below) on national jurisdictional grounds, it does not seem to have been argued that the Brussels Convention applied on the basis of her domicile in a Contracting State. As the matter concerned a question of title, it would appear that Art. 16(4) was inapplicable and the normal Convention rules applied—see Case 288/82, *Duijnstee v. Goderbauer* [1983] E.C.R. 3663, [1985] 1 C.M.L.R. 220.

[41] Art. 16 applies regardless of domicile of the defendant. Thus, Art. 16 applies where the right is registered in a Contracting State even if the defendant is domiciled in a non-Contracting State—see Art. 4(1).

[42] See Kaye *Civil Jurisdiction and Enforcement of Foreign Judgments* (1987), p. 881.

[43] See Case 288/82, *Duijnstee v. Goderbauer* [1983] E.C.R. 3663, [1985] 1 CMLR 220.

[44] See Kaye *Civil Jurisdiction and Enforcement of Foreign Judgments* (1987), p. 880. O'Malley & Layton *European Civil Practice* (1989), p. 702, para. 20.06 and p. 521; Droz paras. 165–169.

[45] See Kaye *Civil Jurisdiction and Enforcement of Foreign Judgments* (1987), p. 882. Thus in the United Kingdom, the jurisdictional rule of *forum non conveniens* is similar to the policy underlying Art. 16—namely that there is another court better placed to adjudicate on the matter—see para. 13.046.

gested that the courts of Contracting States should decline to accept jurisdiction where the following conditions are fulfilled:

(1) the subject-matter of the case is the same as subject-matter which is governed by Article 16;
(2) the connection envisaged by Article 16 exists only with a non-Contracting State;
(3) the national jurisdictional law of the seised court permits it to decline jurisdiction.[46]

(e) Recognition and enforcement of judgments under Brussels Convention

13.037 The basic rule under the Brussels Convention is that a judgment given in a non-Contracting State must be recognised in another Contracting State without any special procedure being required. A judgment shall not be recognised if it is contrary to public policy in the State in which recognition is sought[47]; where the judgment was given in default of appearance and the defendant was not duly served with the document which instituted the proceedings or with an equivalent document in sufficient time to enable him to arrange for his defence[48]; if the judgment is irreconcilable with a judgment given in a dispute between the same parties in the state in which recognition is sought[49]; if the judgment is based on a preliminary question regarding the status or legal capacity of natural persons, rights in property arising out of a matrimonial relationship, wills or succession in a way that conflicts with a rule of the private international law of the State in which recognition is sought[50] or where the judgment is irreconcilable with an earlier judgment given in a non-Contracting State involving the same cause of action and between the same parties provided that this latter judgment fulfils the conditions necessary for its recognition in the state addressed.[51] A foreign judgment cannot be reviewed by the courts of another Contracting State as to substance.[52] If the judgment is being appealed, the court of the Contracting State in which recognition is sought may stay proceedings.[53]

A judgment given in another Contracting State and enforceable in that state can be enforced in any other Contracting State once an order for its enforcement has been given in the latter state.[54] In England, a judgment becomes enforceable upon registration of that judgment. The documents

[46] O'Malley & Layton European Civil Practice (1989), p. 702, Para. 20.08.
[47] *e.g.* Art. 27(1), see *Interdesco SA v. Nullfire Ltd* [1992] 1 Lloyds Rep. 180.
[48] Art. 27(2).
[49] Art. 27(3)(4).
[50] Art. 27(4).
[51] Art. 27(5).
[52] Art. 29.
[53] Art. 30.
[54] Art. 31.

required for registration include an authentic copy of the judgment and proper proof of service if the judgment was given in default.[55–56]

(i) "Extraterritorial" Interim orders

13.038 In principle, interim judgments which seek to affect property or activities in another Contracting State are enforceable. The Convention makes no distinction for the purposes of enforceability between interim and final judgments. However, under Article 27(2), a judgment shall not be recognised:

> "where it was given in default of appearance, if the defendant was not duly served with the document which instituted the proceedings or with an equivalent document in sufficient time to enable him to arrange for this defence."

Such a provision is important to intellectual property practitioners who often obtain *ex parte* orders against persons who have not been present when the order was made and had not been properly served with notice of the proceedings. In *Denilauler v. Couchet Freres*,[57] the ECJ said that the provisions of Article 27(2) and Article 46[58] clearly prevented *ex parte* judgments, where the defendant had not been duly summoned, from being enforceable in another Contracting State.[59] Thus, where a party seeks *ex parte* relief in a Contracting State which is not seised of the substantive matter, he should seek protective relief in that state directly under Article 24.[60]

(ii) "Extraterritorial" Post-judgment provisional preservative orders

13.039 It has been held in England that where judgment is given and a party seeks an order, *e.g.* a MAREVA injunction, seeking to preserve assets in all Convention states pending enforcement of the judgment, such an order falls within Article 24 and does not fall within the exclusive jurisdictional provision of Article 16(5) which confers exclusive jurisdiction in relation to proceedings concerned with the enforcement of judgments on the courts of the Contracting State in which the judgment has been or is to be enforced.[61]

[55–56] Art. 46 and R.S.C., Ord. 71.

[57] Case 125/79, [1980] E.C.R. 1553, [1981] C.M.L.R. 62, ECJ.

[58] Which requires a party seeking recognition or enforcement of a judgment given in default to produce a copy of the document which establishes that the party in default was served with the document instituting the proceedings or with an equivalent document.

[59] See also *EMI Records Ltd v. Modern Music Karl-Ulrich* [1991] 3 W.L.R. 663 where Hobhouse J. rejected an argument in O'Malley & Layton that where a defendant had an opportunity to subsequently discharge an *ex parte* order then Art. 27(2) and Art. 46 did not prevent such an order from being recognised in another Contracting State.

[60] See above and Case 125/79, *Denilauler v. Couchet Freres*, [1980] E.C.R. 1553; [1981] C.M.L.R. 62.

[61] *Babanaft International Co. SA v. Bassatne and another* [1989] 2 W.L.R. 232, C.A., at p. 249. *Quaere* whether with regard to whether such an order falls within Art. 24, this is consistent with the ECJ's rulings on Art. 24—see Art. 24 above.

(iii) Pan-European injunction orders

13.040 It has already been seen that in principle there is nothing under the Convention to prevent the court of a Contracting State making a pan-European injunction intended to prevent infringement in several states where there are parallel rights.[62] Under the Brussels Convention, such an order should be recognised in the courts of other states and cannot be reviewed as to its substance.[63] It might be argued that the recognition of such a judgment is contrary to public policy as it purports to apply the sovereign law of a foreign country. However, it is submitted that as in other areas, there is no reason why one court cannot decide whether infringement of a patent or other right has occurred in a Contracting State other than its own *provided* that under the Convention the court had jurisdiction as to the dispute.

Indeed, where a Dutch court had temporarily injuncted a party from infringing a European patent with effect for all relevant countries, a French court held that the fact that French law did not provide for a similar form of interlocutory relief was irrelevant. The court said that it is not incumbent on the court of the state where execution is sought to examine whether the foreign court's decision itself is conformable to public policy of the country where execution is sought, but only whether recognition of the foreign decision would conflict with public policy in the country of execution. This test does not leave room for examination whether the foreign rules of procedure correspond to public policy in the country where execution is requested.[63a]

(f) Determination of jurisdictional issues under Brussels Convention

13.041 Where a party disputes the jurisdiction of a court of Contracting State under the Brussels Convention, the ECJ has said that that court is entitled to look at evidence behind the pleadings in order to determine whether the conditions on which jurisdiction is based have been established. In *Effer v. Kantner*,[64] the Court said that in relation to Article 5(1) (which gives jurisdiction in "matters relating to a contract, in the courts for the place of performance of the obligation in question") a court called upon to decide a dispute arising out of a contract may examine of its own motion the essential preconditions for its jurisdiction having regard to "conclusive and relevant evidence adduced by the party concerned" establishing the existence or the inexistence of the contract.[65] However, in the same case, the ECJ also said that the plaintiff may invoke the juris-

[62] See para. 13.011.
[63] Art. 29.
[63a] BIE 1994, no. 11, Recognition [1995] 3 E.I.P.R. D–73.
[64] [1982] E.C.R. 825.
[65] *ibid*, pp. 834–835.

diction of the Court under Article 5(1) even where the existence of the contract on which the claim is based is in dispute between the parties.[66]

In England, this judgment has been interpreted as meaning that a plaintiff must show that there is serious issue to be tried that a contract exists in order for jurisdiction to be founded under Article 5(1).[67] This approach to jurisdictional issues in England has been extended to intellectual property litigation. In *Molnlycke v. Procter & Gamble*,[68] the plaintiff sued an English and American defendant for patent infringement. In the course of proceedings, it was realised that a German sister company of the defendants had important documentation in its hand relating to the action. The plaintiff sought to establish jurisdiction in England against the additional German defendant on the basis that it was a joint tortfeasor of the infringements committed in England although it was accepted that the only reason was to obtain discovery. The plaintiff based its application to join the German company on Article 6(1) and Article 5(3) of the Brussels Convention. The Court of Appeal held that as a good arguable case had been established against the German defendant as joint tortfeasor in relation to infringements committed in England, then there was no abuse in joining the German defendant to the action.[69]

13.042 If the preliminary jurisdictional issue is not one which is likely to be tried at the trial of the action, then the plaintiff may have to prove the conditions relied upon for establishing jurisdiction, so that the court is provisionally satisfied that the "plaintiff is probably right".[70] For instance, in an infringement action, where jurisdiction is founded on the domicile of the defendant, the plaintiff would have to show that "it was probably right" on the evidence that the defendant was domiciled in the state of the seised court as the issue of domicile would not be an issue at trial. However, in an infringement action, where jurisdiction is only based on Article 5(3), then because infringement is likely to be an issue at trial, the plaintiff need only show a good arguable case.

Where jurisdiction against a co-defendant is purely based only on Article 6(1), the plaintiff must show that there is a good arguable case

[66] *ibid*, pp. 835–846.

[67] See *Tesam Distribution Ltd v. Schuh Mode Team GmbH* [1989] L.S.Gaz, Times Law Reports, October 24, 1989, C.A., *per* Nicholls L.J.

[68] [1992] RPC 21, C.A.

[69] *ibid*, *per* Dillon L.J. at p. 35. Woolf L.J. appeared to endorse the slightly more stringent test of Staughton L.J. in *Attcock Cement v. Romanian Bank* [1989] 1 All E.R. 1189 (the plaintiff must be "probably right"); Leggatt L.J. reserved his position on the issue of the standard of proof. It would appear that in *Molnlycke v. Procter & Gamble* [1992] RPC 21, C.A., the Court of Appeal merely determined the issue on the basis of pleadings and not evidence—see submissions of appellant's counsel at p. 24. For the standards of proof where jurisdiction is based purely on Art. 6(1) see para. 13.013.

[70] See Staughton L.J. in *Attcock Cement v. Romanian Bank* [1989] 1 All E.R. 1189. C.A. and explained in *Molnlycke v. Procter & Gamble* [1992] RPC 21, C.A. *per* Dillon L.J. at p. 33. Note that this was the standard of proof which Woolf L.J. felt was correct in *Molnlycke*.

and it must persuade the Court that it is proper that joinder should occur.[71]

(g) Intellectual property, English law and Brussels Convention

13.043 The Brussels Convention has been enacted into English law by the Civil Jurisdiction and Judgments Act 1982. Similarly, the English rules of Supreme Court have been amended to give effect to the Convention. For instance, leave is not required to serve out of the jurisdiction if the claim is by virtue of the Civil Jurisdiction and Judgments Act 1982 one which the Court has power to hear and determine.[72] Similarly, judgments of other Convention countries are recognised in England following compliance with a simple procedure.[73]

Where the defendant is not domiciled in a Contracting State, *under the Brussels Convention*, a court must resort to its national rules on jurisdiction unless the proceedings principally concern the validity or registration of an intellectual property right in a Contracting State.[74] This section looks at national jurisdictional rules in England in relation to intellectual property. Also, it examines the effect of the "double actionability" rule whereby even if the proceedings are *justiciable* in England, the infringement proceedings may well not be *actionable* in England.[75]

(i) Immoveable v. moveable distinction

13.044 Several times, the English courts have been asked to decide whether they have jurisdiction to try an action based on a dispute relating to foreign land. In *British South Africa Co. v. Companhia de Mocambique*,[76] the House of Lords distinguished between actions arising out of a transaction abroad which were on one hand, in essence, transitory and on the other hand, local. Thus, the House of Lords held that it had no jurisdiction to entertain actions relating to foreign land. This led to the rule as expressed in Rule 77 of the 10th edition of Dicey & Morris on the *Conflict of Laws*.[77]

> "Subject to the exceptions hereinafter mentioned, English courts have no jurisdiction to entertain an action for:
> (1) the determination of the title to, or the right to the possession of, any immoveable situate out of England (foreign land); or
> (2) the recovery of damages for trespass to such immoveable."

This rule was expressly approved in *Hesperides Hotels Ltd v. Mufti-*

[71] See para. 13.013.
[72] Ord. 6, r. 7 and Ord. 11, r. 1(2)(a).
[73] Ord. 71.
[74] Art. 4 and Art. 16. See para. 13.026, above.
[75] See para. 13.047.
[76] [1893] A.C. 602.
[77] Dicey & Morris on the *Conflicts of Laws* (12th ed, 1993).

zade.[78] It was not certain until recently whether Rule 77 applied to intellectual property. The matter recently came to court in *Tyburn Productions Ltd v. Conan Doyle.*[79] Tyburn, an English film and television production company, brought an action in England seeking a declaration that Lady Bromet, the daughter of Sir Arthur Conan Doyle, the creator of the Sherlock Holmes and Dr Watson characters, was not entitled to any rights in those characters under the copyright, unfair competition or trade mark laws of the USA which would entitle her to prevent distribution in the USA of any film or television programme produced by Tyburn from an original story and an injunction preventing her from asserting that she was entitled to prevent the distribution of such films or programmes in the USA.[80] Lady Bromet applied to strike out the statement of claim. Vinelott J. held that the English courts had no jurisdiction. In doing so, he followed a decision of the High Court of Australia in *Potter v. The Broken Hill Pty Co. Ltd*[81] that the rule in the *Mocambique* case applied to patent infringement proceedings. In that case, the High Court of Australia held that the courts of the state of Victoria had no jurisdiction to hear proceedings brought against a defendant for infringement of a New South Wales patent. The High Court of Australia held that the action was not justiciable in Victoria as a patent was to be considered as analogous to an immoveable because it was a result of an act of State and because the patent monopoly had no effective operation outside the territory of the state where it was granted.[82] The judge in *Tyburn* followed this decision without expressly holding that patent was an immoveable.

(ii) Civil Jurisdiction and Judgments Act 1982, section 30

13.045 The then Rule 77(2) of Dicey and Morris was largely repealed by virtue of section 30 of the Civil Jurisdiction and Judgments Act 1982. This provides that:

> "The jurisdiction of any court in England and Wales or Northern Ireland to entertain proceedings for trespass to or any other tort affecting immovable property shall extend to cases in which the property in question is situated outside that part of the United Kingdom unless the proceedings are principally concerned with a question of the title to, or the right to possession of, that property."

The section is expressed to be subject to the Brussels Convention.[83]

[78] [1979] A.C. 508, H.L.
[79] [1990] 1 All E.R. 909 (Ch.D.).
[80] Under USA law, she was unable to obtain such declaratory relief.
[81] [1906] C.L.R. 479 on appeal from the Supreme Court of Victoria; [1905] V.L.R. 612.
[82] See *ibid*, in particular, the judgment of Griffith C.J. at p. 494. For a suggested approach as to how a court should approch whether an intellectual property right is an immoveable, see Richard Arnold, "Can One Sue in England for Infringement of Intellectual Property Rights?" [1990] 7 EIPR 254.
[83] CJJA 1982, s.30(2).

Accordingly, jurisdiction must still be established under the Brussels Convention even where the property is situated in another Contracting State.

Several points can be made about section 30 in relation to intellectual property. Firstly, it is likely to be held to be applicable to intellectual property.[84] Accordingly, it would appear to give jurisdiction to an English court to hear infringement proceedings based on a French American patent provided there were no issues as to validity.[85] The proviso in the rule relating to proceedings principally concerned with a question of title to the property means that the same jurisdictional difficulties arise under English law as under the Brussels Convention where in infringement proceedings, there is a defence or counterclaim that the right is invalid.[86] As has been commented on, it will often be very expensive and time-consuming in many cases for a court to decide whether a case is "principally" concerned with validity or infringement.[87]

(iii) Forum non conveniens

13.046 Under English common law, where a party can show that there is prima facie another forum which is clearly or distinctly more appropriate than the English forum for the trial, then the English court will normally grant a stay or decline jurisdiction unless there are special circumstances by reason of which justice requires that the trial should nevertheless take place in England.[88] In actions concerning foreign intellectual property rights, it will usually be the case that there is a more appropriate forum. Firstly, the law applicable will be a foreign law. Secondly, the acts occurred in the same foreign country. Thus, normally an English court should grant a stay. However, English courts cannot stay, strike out or dismiss proceedings before it on the ground of *forum non conveniens* where to do so is inconsistent with the Brussels Convention.[89] Thus, where the Brussels Convention applies and has the effect of conferring jurisdiction on the English court, the English court is generally bound to accept that jurisdiction and has no discretion to decline it, except as permitted by the Court itself (Articles 21 to 23). Accordingly, if a plaintiff brings an action in England for the infringement of intellectual property rights situate in another Contracting State, the doctrine of *forum non*

[84] This follows from *Tyburn Productions Ltd v. Conan Doyle* [1990] 1 All E.R. 909 (Ch.D.).

[85] Thus, implicitly overruling the Australian judgment in *Potter v. The Broken Hill Pty Co. Ltd* [1906] C.L.R. 479 as it related to infringements of foreign patents. *Quaere* whether it gives an English court the right to hear infringement proceedings relating to a patent situated in another Contracting State, *i.e.* America. As the rule is subject to the Brussels Convention, it is submitted that the plaintiff must still establish a ground of jurisdiction under the Brussels Convention, *i.e.* domicile of defendant in Contracting State.

[86] See para. 13.030 *et seq.*

[87] See Arnold, "Can One Sue in England for Infringement of Intellectual Property Rights" [1990] 7 EIPR 254, at p. 259.

[88] The doctrine of *forum non conveniens* was reviewed and restated in *Spiliada Maritime Corp. v. Consulex Ltd* [1987] A.C. 460, H.L.

[89] CJJA 1982, s.49.

conveniens is inapplicable. However, as will be seen, under English law, it is arguable that such proceedings are not actionable under the double actionability rule.

(iv) Double actionability rule

13.047 Rule 203 of Dicey and Morris,[90] derived from the judgment of Willes J. in *Phillips v. Eyre*[91] provides that:

(1) As a general rule, an act done in a foreign country is a tort and actionable as such in England, only if it is both
  (a) actionable as a tort according to English law, or in other words is an act which, if done in England, would be a tort: and
  (b) actionable according to the law of the foreign country where it was done
(2) But a particular issue between the parties may be governed by the law for the country which, with respect to that issue, has the most significant relationship with the occurrence and the parties.

This rule is known as the "double actionability" rule. In effect, it means that the *lex fori* plays the dominant role and the *lex loci delicti* plays a subordinate role. In relation to intellectual property torts and unlike other torts, the alternative wordings "actionable as a tort according to English law" and "an act which, if done in England, would be a tort" in paragraph 203(1)(a) may produce different answers. For instance, where a patentee claims that acts done in France constitute an infringement of a French patent, then under Rule 203(1)(a), such an act is not actionable as a tort under English law (French patent law does not form part of English patent law) because the right is derived from a foreign law. However, if the act had been done in England, it might have constituted infringement of a parallel United Kingdom patent. Accordingly, the alternative phrasing of Rule 203(1)(a) would produce a differing result. If the latter prevailed, clearly the act is actionable according to the law of the foreign country under Rule 203(1)(b) and as such would be actionable in England.

13.048 In *Boys v. Chaplin*, Lord Wilberforce stated that:

> "I would therefore restate the basic rule of English law with regard to foreign torts as requiring actionability as a tort according to English law, subject to the condition that civil liability in respect of the relevant claim exists as between the actual parties under the law of the foreign country where the act was done."[92]

[90] See Dicey & Morris *The Conflict of Laws*, (12th ed, 1993) p. 1487 *et seq*.

[91] [1870] L.R. 6 Q.B. 1. This rule has been considered in great detail in *Boys v. Chaplin* [1971] 1 A.C. 356 H.L.; see also *Coupland v. Arabian Gulf Oil Co.* [1983] 1 W.L.R. 1151, C.A.; *Armagas Ltd. v. Mundogas SA* [1986] A.C. 717.

[92] [1971] 1 A.C. 356, H.L.; at 389F. It would seem that therefore ultimately the applicable law is the *lex fori, i.e.* English law—see Dicey & Morris *op. cit.* at p. 1373.

Whether he knew it or not, this restatement of Rule 203 subtly altered the application of the rule to intellectual property torts by not referring to the alternative phrasing of paragraph Rule 203(1)(a) in the second half. In *Deff Lepp v. Stuart-Brown*,[93] the plaintiff brought proceedings for the infringement of U.K. copyright against, *inter alia*, two defendants for acts done by them in Luxembourg and Holland. The plaintiffs pleaded that these acts would have constituted an infringement of copyright if they had been done in England and were "not justifiable" in Luxembourg and Holland.[94] The Vice-Chancellor said that it was clear that the 1956 Copyright Act did not have any application outside the U.K. and that copyright under the act was strictly defined in terms of territory. He held, in effect, that the second limb of Rule 203(1)(a) could not extend to making acts unlawful that were otherwise lawful in England. He held, following *Boys v. Chaplin* that Rule 203 was a rule for regulating the choice of law to be applied. Thus, Rule 203 stipulated that effect should be given to the substantive law of England (*lex fori*) rather than the law of the place where the act was committed (*lex loci delicti*). He then held that once having established that English law is applicable, one must then consider whether under English law, those acts constituted an actionable wrong.[95] He held that they clearly did not as the acts occurred outside England and thus English law was not applicable. The judge was fortified by his conclusion from the decisions in Australia.[96]

This decision was followed in *Tyburn Productions Ltd v. Conan Doyle*.[97] Vinelott J. held that what is now Rule 203 of Dicey and Morris was authority for the proposition that a claim that acts done outside the United Kingdom which were an infringement of the copyright law of a foreign country were not justiciable in the English courts. He thus said that the first limb of the rule could not be satisfied because an infringement of a foreign copyright could not constitute a tort under English law and the fact that the act complained of, if done in England, would have constituted a breach of English copyright law was irrelevant.[98] Similarly, in *James Burroughs Distillers plc v. Speymalt Whisky Distributors Ltd*, a Scottish court in an action for infringement of an Italian trade mark by acts done in Italy, held that the Scottish equivalent of the double action-

[93] [1986] RPC 273 (Ch.D.).

[94] The phrase "not justifiable" is an older version of para. (b) of Rule 203(1) as stated above. The phrase "not justifiable" which was derived from *Phillips v. Eyre*, *Machado v. Fontes* [1897] 2 Q.B. 231, C.A.; *Carr v. Fracis Times & Co.* [1902] A.C. 176 was rejected by the majority of House of Lords in *Boys v. Chaplin* [1971] 1 A.C. 356, H.L. who stated that it was necessary that the defendant's act be civilly actionable by the *lex loci delicti* and not merely unjustifiable. Thus, the decision in *Machado* that it was sufficient that the defendant's act was a criminal act meant that it was unjustified although no civil liability attached to it was overruled.

[95] [1886] RPC 273 (Ch.D.), at p. 276.

[96] *Potter v. Broken Hill Pty Co. Ltd* [1906] 3 C.L.R. 479; *Norbert Steinhardt & Son Ltd v. Meth* [1960] 105 C.L.R. 440.

[97] [1990] 1 All E.R. 909 (Ch.D.).

[98] [1990] 1 All E.R. 909 (Ch.D.), at p. 917.

ability rule applied so that the matter was not justiciable in Scotland.[99] Thus, in relation to intellectual property, Rule 203(1)(a) must now be considered modified so that the words "or in other words is an act which if done in England, would be a tort" is removed.[1] Accordingly, under the double actionability rule, an action for infringement of foreign intellectual property rights is not actionable in England.[2]

(v) Double actionability rule and passing-off

13.049 In *Tyburn*, Vinelott J. said,[3] as *obiter dicta*, that although goodwill is local, an action for passing-off is an application of the tort of misrepresentation and the court could grant an injunction to restrain passing-off in a foreign jurisdiction if the threatened conduct of the plaintiff is unlawful in that jurisdiction.[4] In *James Burroughs Distillers plc v. Speymalt*, discussed above, at paragraph 13.048, the Scottish court having held that the trade mark action failed, held that the double actionability rule applied was satisfied in relation to a parallel passing-off claim.

On the one hand, it has been argued that no distinction should be drawn between passing-off cases and trade mark cases based on foreign acts.[5] The *jus actionis* for passing off in Italy involves a misrepresentation which damages goodwill in Italy, whereas the *jus actionis* for passing off in England involves a misrepresentation which damages goodwill in England. Thus the two are quite distinct. Thus, it is submitted that the true distinction should be made between actions which depend on their locality like passing-off and other intellectual property infringements (*i.e.* torts to immoveable property) and actions which do not rely upon the

[99] See [1989] S.L.T. 561.

[1] See also Dicey & Morris *op. cit.*, p. 1516 where the editors accept that Rule 203(1)(a) requires explanation in relation to patents, trade marks and copyright. See also Floyd/Purvis "Can an English Court restrain infringement of a foreign patent" [1995] E.I.P.R. 110 where they review the cases of *Deff Lepp Music v. Stuart Brown* and *Tyburn Productions v. Doyle*.

[2] See also *LA Gear v. Gerald Whelan & Sons* [1991] FSR 670 where the High Court followed *Tyburn* and said that it was difficult to see how any claim in Ireland could be made in relation to the infringement of an English registered trade mark.

[3] At p. 917G.

[4] The case of *Alfred Dunhill Ltd v. Sunoptic* [1979] FSR 337 was quoted. In the cases of *Dunhill* and *John Walker & Sons Ltd v. Henry Ost & Co. Ltd* [1970] RPC 489, which both concerned actions for passing-off in a foreign country, the applicability of Rule 205(1)(a) was never fully adjudicated on (see Tritton/Tritton "Brussels Convention and Intellectual Property" [1987] EIPR 349 at 349). See also *Intercontex v. Schmidt* [1988] FSR 575 (Ch.D) where Gibson J. stated that the double actionability rule applied in relation to passing off outside the jurisdiction but held that the motion for interlocutory relief failed because no evidence had been provided that it was a tort under the *lex loci delicti*. See also *An Bord Trachtala v. Waterford Foods plc* [1994] FSR 316, Irish High Court where proceedings in Ireland were brought in relation to passing off in England. The judge held that the double actionability rule applied but that there was no evidence that the activities complained of amounted to passing off in England.

[5] See Arnold, "Can One Sue in England for Infringement of Intellectual Property Rights?" [1990] 7 EIPR 254, at p. 262.

territory where they happen like the duty to drive carefully as in *Boys v. Chaplin.*[6]

On the other hand, it is arguable that the sole question under Rule 203 is whether an act of passing-off in another country is actionable under English law (provided that such is actionable in the other country). Here a distinction can be drawn between common law rights and statutory rights. In *Potter v. Broken Hill Pty Co. Ltd,*[7] Griffith C.J. supported his ruling that a patent was analogous to immoveable property by referring to the fact that the title, as in land, devolved according to the laws imposed by the state. He rejected an argument that the grant of a patent right was not an act of government. In contrast, goodwill is not based on an act of government and the argument for treating it as an immoveable weakens. Similarly, in *Deff Lepp*, the Vice Chancellor drew a distinction between rights conferred by statute and common law.[8] In these cases, and *Tyburn,*[9] it is submitted that the courts were giving effect to the fundamental principle that foreign law forms no part of English law. Where an action based on a foreign intellectual property statute is brought in England, then for it to be actionable according to English law under the first limb of Rule 203(1)(a) would require English law to recognise a foreign law as part of its law. As it does not do this, then Rule 203 is not satisfied. However, for an act of foreign passing-off to be recognised in England would merely mean that under English law, the three requirements of reputation, deception and damage be proved.[10] No recognition of foreign law is required. The fact that the goodwill is situated abroad rather than in England should not matter in the same way that the fact that the accident in *Boys v. Chaplin* occurred in Malta was not relevant. The important matter is whether English law would entertain a claim for passing-off *on the facts but without regard to foreign law*. On this analysis, a claim for passing-off in a foreign state would satisfy the double actionability rule.

(vi) Brussels Convention, effect of double actionability rule and Rule 203(2)

13.050 What is the interaction of the double actionability rule with the Brussels Convention? In this regard, it is important to consider whether the rule is a jurisdictional rule or a choice of law rule. If the rule is a jurisdictional rule, it is subject to the Brussels Convention.[11] Thus, as the Brussels Convention clearly envisages that infringement of an intellectual property

[6] Support for this proposition comes from Vinelott J. in *Tyburn Productions v. Conan Doyle* [1980] 1 All E.R. 909, (Ch.D.), at p. 917 where he states, in ruling on the first limb of Rule 172 (the old rule 203) that the "locality of the act is inseparable from the wrong."

[7] [1906] 3 C.L.R. 479. See para. 13.044.

[8] [1986] RPC 273 (Ch.D.), p. 276.

[9] [1990] 1 All E.R. 900, (Ch.D.).

[10] See *Reckitt & Colman v. Borden* [1987] F.S.R. 228, C.A.

[11] See also CJJA 1982, s. 49.

rights can be sued in a Contracting State other than where it is registered, it would overrule any common law jurisdictional rule to the contrary. If it is a choice of law rule, then it supplements the Brussels Convention. In *Boys v. Chaplin*,[12] Lord Wilberforce stated, giving full reasons, that he adhered to the orthodox judicial view that paragraph (a) of Rule 203(1) was a choice of law rule and not a jurisdictional rule.[13]

If the rule is a choice of law rule, then even if an English court has *jurisdiction* to here a claim, then the plaintiff must still satisfy the double actionability rule in order to have a cause of action. Conversely, if he fails to satisfy it, he does not have a cause of action. Accordingly, if a plaintiff seeks to sue a person domiciled in England for infringement of a right registered in another Contracting State, he is able to do so under the Brussels Convention but will have no cause of action because of the double actionability rule. In such a context, the rule appears as a jurisdictional bar although expressed as a choice of law clause. It remains to be seen whether the ECJ will decide that such a rule has jurisdictional aspects such that it is overruled by the Brussels Convention.[14]

A way around this may be to say that only the *lex loci delicti* should apply to intellectual property rights pursuant to Rule 203(2). In *Boys v. Chaplin*,[15] whence Rule 203(2) was derived, both Lord Hodson and Lord Wilberforce held that whilst the basic law should be the *lex fori*, justice may well be served by solely applying the law which because of its relationship of contact with the occurrence or the parties, had the greatest concern with the specific issue raised in the litigation.[16] Lord Wilberforce referred to the fact that there remains great virtue in a general well-understood rule (*i.e. lex fori*) which was flexible enough to take account of the varying interests and considerations of policy which may arise when one or more foreign elements are present.[17] Thus, Lord Hodson held that the law of England should be applicable because whilst the accident took place in Malta, it occurred between two British subjects temporarily visiting Malta. Recently, the Privy Council has confirmed the applicability of Rule 203(2) where a dispute has hardly any connection with the state of the *lex fori*.[18] Conversely, it is difficult to think of an action which is more linked to a particular state and its laws than intellectual property disputes. The approach that the applicable law is that which the facts have the most significant relationship (known in England

[12] [1971] A.C. 260.

[13] [1971] A.C. 356, 385–287; see also Dicey & Morris (12th Ed., 1993) and *Deff Lepp v. Stuart Brown* [1986] RPC 273 where the Vice Chancellor restated that Rule 203 was a choice of law rule.

[14] The importance that English law gives to the *lex fori* would appear not to be mirrored in other European countries—see Dicey & Morris pp. 1358–1359.

[15] [1971] 1 A.C. 356, H.L.

[16] *ibid*, *per* Lord Hodson at p. 380B–E, Lord Wilberforce 390H–391H.

[17] *ibid*, p. 391D.

[18] *Red Sea Insurance v. Bouygues SA* [1994] 3 All E.R. 749 on appeal from the Court of Appeal of Hong Kong. Discussed in Floyd/Purvis "Can an English Court restrain infringement of a foreign patent" [1995] 3 E.I.P.R. 110.

as the "proper law") has been adopted in many American cases and has been favoured in a Working Paper produced by the Law Commission in 1984.[19] Thus, it is submitted, that in intellectual property disputes, only the *lex loci delicti* would apply. If this is the case, then Rule 203 will never conflict with the Brussels Convention.

(vii) The Private International Law (Miscellaneous Provisions) Bill

13.051 In this Bill, it is proposed to abolish the double actionability rule in relation to any claim in tort or delict. It is intended to replace this rule with the general rule that the applicable law is the law of the country in which the events constituting the tort or delict occur. Thus, in intellectual property disputes, this would invariably be the *lex loci delicti*.

3. Lugano Convention

13.052 With the success of the Brussels Convention in providing a uniform set of jurisdictional rules throughout the E.C., E.C. States sought to secure a similar convention with EFTA States which reflected the principles of the Brussels Convention. The intention was that an EFTA multi-partite convention on jurisdiction and the recognition and enforcement of judgments would extend the beneficial effects of the Brussels Convention to EFTA states. Furthermore, such a convention would replace a mass of existing bilateral agreements between E.C. states and EFTA states which were often outdated or patchy in their coverage. The simple solution would have been to have secured the accession of EFTA states to the Brussels Convention and the 1971 Protocol whereby the ECJ was vested with the jurisdiction to give interpretative rulings on the Convention. The acceptance of the compulsory jurisdiction of the ECJ and of the binding effect of its interpretative judgments was unpalatable to most EFTA states as such would have caused constitutional difficulties. Correspondingly, E.C. states were reluctant to change the Brussels Convention to accommodate such concerns. Accordingly, it was decided that both E.C. and EFTA states should enter into a new convention which supplemented the Brussels Convention.

On September 16, 1988 at Lugano, the E.C. and EFTA states entered into a Convention on jurisdiction in civil matters and the recognition and enforcement of judgments ("the Lugano Convention").[20] The Lugano Convention almost exactly replicates the Brussels Convention. The num-

[19] See Dicey & Morris (11th Ed.), p. 1378, 1417. See also Floyd/Purvis above where the authors submit that there are very strong arguments for applying only the *lex loci delicti* to infringements of foreign patents (at p. 114).

[20] *i.e.* Belgium, Denmark, Germany, Greece, Spain, France, Ireland, Iceland, Italy, Luxembourg, the Netherlands, Norway, Austria, Portugal, Sweden, Switzerland, Finland and the United Kingdom.

bering of the Articles in each Convention correspond exactly.[21] Thus, the primary rule of jurisdiction is based on the defendant's domicile. The main differences from the Brussels Convention are as follows.

(a) Substantive jurisdictional rules

13.053 The Lugano Convention incorporates rulings of the ECJ under the 1971 Protocol on the interpretation of the Brussels Convention. However, the Brussels Convention was then itself amended by virtue of the Convention for the Accession of Spain and Portugal to the Brussels Convention signed in San Sebastian ("the San Sebastian Convention"). These amendments also incorporated much of the ECJ's jurisprudence on the Brussels Convention and thus harmony was re-established between the two texts. However, some substantive differences remain but which it is thought are not of concern to the intellectual property practitioner.[22]

For the purposes of the intellectual property practitioner, Article 2, 5(3), 16(4) and 19 are exactly the same.

(b) Interpretation of Lugano Convention

13.054 As mentioned avove, the constitution of many EFTA states did not permit them to recognise the binding authority of the ECJ. Accordingly, under the Lugano Convention, there is no interpretative body which gives binding judgments on the Lugano Convention. The authors of the Convention has sought to overcome this problem and the dangers of the development of diverging jurisprudence on the Lugano Convention in the Lugano states and between substantially similar provisions in the Brussels and Lugano Convention being interpreted differently by the ECJ and Lugano States by a series of Protocols and Declarations which form an integral part of the Convention[23] as follows:

(i) The courts of the Lugano states must pay "due account" of principles laid down by any relevant decision delivered by courts of the other Contracting States concerning provisions of the Lugano Convention.[24]

(ii) The EFTA states have declared that they consider it appropriate that the courts pay "due account" to the rulings contained in the ECJ and courts of the Member States in respect of provisions in the Brussels Convention which are substantially reproduced in the Lugano Convention.

[21] Even to the point that the Lugano Convention has a blank Art. 58 in order to maintain exact correspondence between the two Conventions.

[22] The principal differences are in Art. 5(1) (special jurisdiction based on place of performance of obligation in question in matters relating to a contract); Art. 16(1) (exclusive jurisdiction based on immovable property—difference in two texts pertains to jurisdiction in tenancy disputes).

[23] Art. 65.

[24] Protocol 2. For the fulfilment of this aim, the protocol sets up the Registrar of the ECJ as a clearing house of relevant judgments.

(iii) The E.C. states declared that they consider it appropriate that the ECJ when interpreting the Brussels Convention should pay "due account" to the rulings under the Lugano Convention.

(c) Jurisdictional overlap between Brussels and Lugano Convention

13.055 The Lugano Convention is expressed to be generally subject to the Brussels Convention.[25] In certain circumstances, it takes precedence over the Brussels Convention. These are where the defendant is domiciled in an EFTA state or the Lugano Convention confers exclusive jurisdiction in a dispute on an EFTA state; in relation to a *lis pendens* or to related actions as provided for in Article 21 and 22, when proceedings are instituted in an EFTA and in an E.C. State;[26] in matters of recognition and enforcement, where either the State or origin or addressed State is an EFTA State.[27] Furthermore, where one party seeks to enforce a judgment against another party who is domiciled in an EFTA state, the latter state's courts (but only the latter) may refuse to recognise such a judgment if the ground of jurisdiction on which the judgment was based differs from that under the Lugano Convention.[28] Otherwise, the Brussels Convention takes priority. Thus, where a defendant is not domiciled in an E.C. or EFTA state, the Brussels Convention applies and national jurisdictional rules under Article 4 apply.

For the purpose of the intellectual property litigator, it will rarely make any difference whether the Brussels or the Lugano Convention apply because of the identically-worded relevant provisions. The main difference will be that under the Lugano Convention an unsuccessful party could not seek an interpretative ruling from the ECJ.

(d) Jurisdictional overlap between Lugano and other Conventions

13.056 The Lugano Convention is expressed not to affect any conventions which the Contracting States are party to and which in relation to particular matters, govern jurisdiction or the recognition or enforcement of judgments.[29] This rule applies even if the defendant is domiciled in a Contracting State which is not party to the relevant convention.[30] Thus, like the Brussels Convention, the Lugano Convention does not affect the application of jurisdictional rules of the European Patent Convention, the Community Patent Convention or the Community Trade Mark Con-

[25] Lugano Convention, Art. 54B.
[26] This provision does not give any significance to the place where proceedings are first instituted.
[27] Art. 54B(2)(a)–(c).
[28] Art. 54B(3)—see also Art. 54(2)(c) which overrules the application of the Brussels Convention in such circumstances and Art. 28 which provides for additional grounds of non-recognition under Lugano Convention by referring to Art. 54B(3).
[29] Art. 57.
[30] Art. 57(2).

vention. Importantly, all Lugano states must recognise and enforce judgments given under a particular convention, regardless as to whether or not they are a member of the particular Convention.[31] Thus, in such a way, the particular convention forms part and takes precedence over the Lugano Convention.

4. European Patent Convention

13.057 The European Patent Convention takes precedence over the Brussels and Lugano Conventions in regard to jurisdictional matters.[32] Under the EPC, once a European patent has been granted, it becomes in effect a basket of national patents for the designated states. Thus questions of infringement and revocation proceedings for that state will be governed by the general rules of the Brussels Convention.

There was a doubt as to whether proceedings concerning European patents under Article 16(4) could be brought in the country where the patent was applied for or the relevant states to which it had been designated. Article VD of the Protocol to the Brussels Convention provides that where a European patent has been granted, proceedings concerning the registration or validity of any European patent granted for a state are a matter of exclusive jurisdiction for that State. Article VD is expressed to be without prejudice to the jurisdiction of the European Patent Office. Thus, the Brussels Convention does not alter the ability for a party to bring opposition proceedings at the EPO for the revocation of a European patent after grant.

It may well be the case that an infringement action is brought under a European patent after it has been granted but whilst opposition proceedings are under way in the Opposition Division.[33] In such circumstances, a court may consider staying the infringement action until determination of the opposition proceedings. This will mean that various factors like the likelihood of the patent being found invalid; the delay; the conduct of the parties and the relative prejudice to the parties will be taken into account.[34]

(a) The Protocol on Jurisdiction appended to the European Patent Convention

13.058 As stated above, once a European patent has been granted, revocation (other than opposition proceedings) and infringement are matters for the designated States. Generally, this will mean that there are few jurisdic-

[31] Art. 57(3).
[32] Art. 57 in both Conventions.
[33] Opposition proceedings to revoke the European patent at the E.P.O. in its entirety can be brought up to nine months after the publication of the grant of a European patent.
[34] An English court in *Amersham International plc v. Corning Limited and Corning Glass Works* [1987] RPC 53 refused to grant a stay of infringement proceedings in the High Court pending the outcome of the opposition proceedings in the EPO. A factor in the court's decision was that the defendant filed an opposition against the grant of the European patent on the last day of the opposition period.

tional problems. However, there may often be the question of who is entitled to the grant of a European patent. The EPC provides that the right to a European patent belongs to the inventor or his successor-in-title. It further provides that if the inventor is an employee the right to the European patent is to be determined according to the law of the state in which he is mainly employed. If that cannot be determined, then the applicable law is that of the state where the employer has his place of business to which the employee is attached.[35] The above provides for the applicable law in such disputes.[36]

The Protocol on Jurisdiction and the Recognition of Decisions in respect of the Right to the Grant of a European Patent provides for a jurisdictional framework where a person raises the question of who has the right to the grant of a European patent. It forms an integral part of the EPC.[37] It is only concerned with claims to the right to the grant of a European patent.[38] It takes priority over other jurisdictional provisions including the Brussels Convention.[39] Essentially, the Contracting State which is to have jurisdiction is determined according to the following list (in descending order of priority):

—that jurisdiction to which the parties agreed in writing.[40]
—if an employer-employee dispute, the state where the employee is mainly employed or if that cannot be determined, where the employer's place of business is.[41]
—if the applicant has his place of business or residence in one of the Contracting States, then in that state.[42]
—if the applicant has his place of business or residence outside the Contracting States, then the Contracting State where the party claiming the right to the grant of a European patent has his residence or principal place of business.[43]
—Federal Republic of Germany.[44]

The court[45] which is seised of the matter must decide of its own motion whether or not it has jurisdiction.[46] If an earlier application has been made to the court of another Contracting State, then the latterly seised

[35] Art. 60.
[36] For the procedure to be followed when a court has decided that someone other than the applicant is entitled to the grant of a European patent and the European application is still being prosecuted, see Art. 61.
[37] Art. 164.
[38] Art. 1.
[39] Art. 11, Protocol and Brussels Convention, Art. 57.
[40] Art. 5. If it is an employee-employer dispute, then this article only applies if the national law governing the contract of employment permits such an agreement—Art. 5(2).
[41] Art. 4.
[42] Art. 2.
[43] Art. 3.
[44] Art. 6.
[45] This is deemed to include authorities which have jurisdiction to decide such claims under national law (*i.e.* national patent offices)—Art. 1(2).
[46] Art. 7 Protocol.

court must decline jurisdiction or if the jurisdiction is challenged, stay the proceedings until determination of the issue.[47] It is not clear whether issues of residence, place of business and the phrase "mainly employed" are to be determined according to national law, private international law or whether there should be an independent Convention approach. It is thought likely that the approach to such matters in the Brussels Convention will provide considerable assistance to a court seised of a jurisdictional matter under this Protocol.

13.059 Challenges based on the entitlement to the grant of a European patent can be made after grant of the European patent. The Protocol will still apply and take priority over Article 16(4) or Article VD of the Brussels Convention. Courts of other Contracting States must recognise the decision of the appropriate court as to the entitlement to grant of a European patent.[48] Even if it appears to another court that the court who gave out the decision did not have jurisdiction, has applied the wrong law or was otherwise wrong, it cannot review the decision or not recognise its validity.[49] The two exceptions to this rule are that an applicant for a European patent can dispute the recognition of an adverse decision if he was not notified early and sufficiently enough for him to defend himself or if the decision is incompatible with another decision given in a Contracting State in proceedings between the same parties which were started before those in which the decision to be recognised was given.[50]

In England, the Court of Appeal, in construing section 82 of the Patents Act 1977 which gives effect to the Protocol under English law, held that the phrase "right to be granted a European patent" should not be interpreted narrowly and included the right to the patent or the fruits of the patent. Thus, where it was alleged that a party held a European patent application on constructive trust for another, the Court of Appeal held that was a matter which went to the right to the grant of a European patent and on the facts, declined jurisdiction.[51]

5. E.C. Intellectual Property Legislation, Brussels and Lugano Convention

13.060 Under the Brussels Convention, acts of the institutions of the European Community are not affected by the Convention.[52] Such an arrangement reflects the concern that the Brussels Convention would be deemed to limit the legislative competence of such institutions. Under the Lugano Convention, Protocol 3 confers the acts of such institutions with "particular Convention" status. Thus such acts take precedence over conflicting Lugano rules on jurisdiction. This Protocol is linked to a declaration

[47] Art. 7, 8.
[48] Art. 9.
[49] Art. 9(2).
[50] Art. 10.
[51] *Kakkar et al v. Szelke et al* [1989] FSR 225, C.A.
[52] Brussels Convention, Art. 57.

by the E.C. Member States that they will take all measures in their power to ensure respect for the principles of the Lugano Convention whenever Community Acts are drawn up. This is important to the intellectual property practitioner because of the existence of special jurisdictional rules in Community intellectual property legislation.[53]

[53] For instance, see Community Trade Mark discussed in Chap. 3 on Trade Marks in Europe; proposed Community Design discussed in Chap. 5 on Designs in Europe; proposed Community Patent Convention briefly discussed in Chap. 2 on Patents in Europe and Community Patent Variety Regulation at Chap. 6. It should be noted that these Regulations make detailed provisions on the interaction between the Brussels Convention and their own *sui generis* rules and jurisdictions.

INDEX

(Reference are to paragraph numbers)